Antique Trader™

Antiques & Collectibles

PRICE GUIDE 2004

D1008969

Edited by
Kyle Husfloen

Published by
Antique Trader, a division of

 **krause publications**
An F&W Publications Company

700 East State Street • Iola, WI 54990-0001
715-445-2214 • 888-457-2873
www.krause.com

Please call or write for our free catalog of publications.
Our toll-free number to place an order or obtain a free catalog is
800-258-0929
or please use our regular business telephone 715-445-2214.

ISBN: 0-87349-709-0

Printed in the United States of America

Table of Contents

A WORD TO THE READER

Greetings, fellow collectors! We're proud to introduce this new edition of the *Antique Trader Antiques & Collectibles Price Guide 2004*. This volume marks the 20th anniversary of our series of comprehensive annual pricing guides and carries on our tradition of offering the latest information on antiques and collectibles.

It was in late 1970 that the first *Antique Trader Price Guide* appeared as a quarterly magazine. Within a few years this evolved into a bimonthly price guide, followed in 1984 by our first annual compendium of prices. If you're looking for something interesting to collect, how about trying to complete a collection of all twenty of our annual price guides? Looking back over these guides can provide you with fascinating insights into the development and evolution of the collecting marketplace. Reading price listings from twenty or more years ago is also a wistful experience ... "If only I'd bought _____ back then!"

Since the very beginning of our price guide series we have taken special pride in covering the widest possible range of antiques and collectibles and including detailed, accurate listings for each entry. It is important to know as much as possible about an item in order to put the value in proper perspective. We strive to provide that extra information about objects and include details on the material, construction, color, pattern, maker, date of production and size whenever possible. Then, when you review the "price" given, you can appreciate exactly what it represents. We carefully select and edit our thousands of listings and draw them from numerous sources, including auction houses, dealers, collectors, and specialized experts. The prices in each of our categories represent a good overview of pieces you can find in today's market and generally represent a "retail replacement value." This is important to keep in mind since pricing of antiques and collectibles can be subjective, often reflecting local or regional demand as well as factors such as quality, rarity and visual appeal. We always stress that this volume should only be used as a guide to pricing. We want our readers to be well informed but also realistic about what a specific piece might sell for in a specific market. Pricing in this wide field can be fluid, so every collector needs to have a good understanding of what factors influence values in their special area of interest.

This all-new 2004 edition includes nearly 14,000 separate entries highlighted with more than 4,700 black and white photographs. In addition, we provide a brief introductory note for most of our categories and, in the Ceramics and Glass sections, a sketch of a factory or maker's mark wherever possible. For added excitement we also offer a special 16-page full-color supplement highlighting some of the rare and colorful pieces we are listing.

Large sections are included for the broad fields of Ceramics, Furniture and Glass, but we also have included a diverse range of other categories that reflect some of the latest collecting trends. New and interesting collecting possibilities are always evolving. As a market develops, we want to include it in our coverage. This year we are pleased to offer quite a number of new categories that include: Barwares; Cereal Promotional Collectibles; Cracker Jack Collectibles; Magic Collectibles; Mid-Century Modern Design; Motion Lamps (see Lighting Devices); Pedal Cars; Picture Cards (Non-Sports); Snowdomes and Tea Premiums & Figures. In addition, we have some greatly expanded listings in categories such as Art Deco, Compacts, Halloween Collectibles, Kitchenwares, and Movie Posters. A great deal of this new material has been provided by a dedicated group of special contributors. We list them and their fields of expertise on a separate page here. A big "thank you" is due them for their dedication and hard work in helping build this guide.

Again this year our editors and staff have worked long and hard to provide the most accurate and up-to-date information possible. To aid the reader we have also developed an extensive Index at the back of the book that includes numerous cross-references to help you locate that specific item you're tracking. Everything possible is done to give you the best, most comprehensive price guide on the market today. However, although our descriptions, prices, and illustrations have been double-checked and every effort has been made to ensure accuracy, neither the editors, publisher nor contributors can assume responsibility for any losses that might be incurred as a result of consulting this guide, or of typographical or other errors.

Antique Trader Antiques & Collectibles Price Guide categories follow an alphabetical format in most listings. However, we have separated all the categories under Ceramics, Furniture, and Glass and run them alphabetically within those sections. If you have any questions about where a specific category is found, just check through our detailed Index.

As noted earlier, a great variety of our listings and photographs are provided by our special contributors, but we also draw material from other sources, including photographers, dealers, auction houses, galleries, and private collectors. We thank them again for their cooperation and list them below in alphabetical order.

Photographers who have contributed to this issue include: Stanley L. Baker, Minneapolis, Minn.; Susan N. Cox, El Cajon, Calif.; Susan Eberman, Bedford, Ind.; Scott Green, Manchester, N.H.; Robert G. Jason-Ickes, Olympia, Wash.; and Pat McPherson, Ramona, Calif.

For other photographs, artwork, data or permission to photograph in their shops, we sincerely express appreciation to the following auctioneers, galleries, museums, individuals and shops: Alderfers, Hatfield, Pa.; American Social History and Social Movements, Pittsburgh, Pa.; Arman's, Portsmouth, R.I.; The Auction House-Paine Auction Service, Sacramento, Calif.; Auction Team Koln, Cologne, Germany; Autopia Advertising Auctions, Woodinville, Wash.; Jim and Dorothy Bernatz, Rochester, Minn.; Frank H. Boos Gallery, Bloomfield Hills, Mich.; Charlton Hall Galleries, Columbia, S.C.; Christie's, New York, N.Y.; Cincinnati Art Galleries, Cincinnati, Ohio; Collector's Auction Services, Oil City, Pa.; Copake

Country Auction, Copake, N.Y.; Daniel Auction Company, Sylvester, Ga.; DeFina Auctions, Austenburg, Ohio; William Doyle Galleries, New York, N.Y.; DuMouchelles, Detroit, Mich.; Early American History Auctions, Inc., La Jolla, Calif.; Fink's Off the Wall Auction, Lansdale, Pa.; John Fontaine Auction, Pittsfield, Mass.; Garth's Auctions, Inc., Delaware, Ohio; Glass-Works Auctions, East Greenville, Pa.; Green Valley Auctions, Mt. Crawford, Va.; and Guyette and Schmidt, West Farmington, Maine.

Also to Gene Harris Antique Auction Center, Marshalltown, Iowa; Hassinger & Courtney Auctioneers, Richfield, Pa.; Norman Heckler & Company, Woodstock Valley, Conn.; Jackson's Auctions, Cedar Falls, Iowa; Bev and Ray Jaeger, St. Louis, Mo.; James Julia, Fairfield, Maine; John Kruesel, Rochester, Minn.; Henry Kurtz, Ltd., New York, N.Y.; MastroNet, Inc., Oakbrook, Ill.; Russ McCall, Auctioneer, Onawa, Iowa; McMasters, Cambridge, Ohio; Dr. James Measell, Marietta, Ohio; Gary Metz's Muddy River Trading Company, Salem, Va.; Mom's Antique Mall, Oronoco, Minn.; Monsen & Baer Auctions, Vienna, Va.; New Orleans Auction Galleries, New Orleans, La.; Richard Opfer Auctioneering, Inc., Timonium, Md.; Pacific Glass Auctions, Sacramento, Calif.; Parker-Braden Auctions, Carlsbad, N.M.; Past Tyme Pleasures, Los Altos, Calif.; Rich Penn, Waterloo, Iowa; Dave Rago Arts & Crafts, Lambertville, N.J.; Skinner, Inc., Bolton, Mass.; Slawinski Auction Company, Felton, Calif.; Sloan's Miami, Miami, Fla.; Sotheby's, New York, N.Y.; George and Judy Swan, Dubuque, Iowa; Temples Antiques, Eden Prairie, Minn.; R. and K. Townsend, Rochester, Minn.; Tradewinds Antiques, Manchester-by-the-Sea, Mass.; Treadway Gallery, Cincinnati, Ohio; Vicki and Bruce Waasdorf, Clarence, N.Y.; C. Williams, Rochester, Minn.; York Town Auctions, York, Pa.

We hope that everyone who consults our *Antiques & Collectibles Price Guide* will find it the most thorough, accurate and informative guide on the ever-changing world of collecting.

The staff of *Antique Trader's Antiques & Collectibles Price Guide* welcomes all letters from readers, especially those of constructive critique, and we make every effort to respond personally.

–Kyle Husfloen, Editor

SPECIAL CONTRIBUTORS
Index by subject

ABC Plates: Joan George
Art Deco: Dana Cain, Beth Gottlieb, Mod Livin'
Barberiana - Razor Blade Banks: Deborah Gillham
Barware: Dana Cain, Beth Gottlieb
Cereal Collectibles: Jim Trautman
Character Collectibles: Kerra Davis
Children's Dishes
  Children's Feeding Dishes: Deborah Gillham
  Novelty & Whistle Cups: Deborah Gillham
Children's Figural Toothbrush Holders: Deborah Gillham
Clocks: Mark Moran, R.O. Schmitt, Clocksmith
Compacts and Vanity Cases: Roselyn Gerson
Cracker Jack Collectibles: Jim Trautman
Dolls (Composition Dolls): Kerra Davis
Farm-related Collectibles: Jim Trautman
Fire Fighting-related Collectibles: Jim Trautman
Furniture: Mark Moran
Halloween Collectibles: Dana Cain, Joe Fex, Ingrid Schultz, Margaret Carlblom
Jewelry
  American Painted Porcelain: Dorothy Kamm
  Costume: Marion Cohen
Kitchenwares
  Coffee Grinders: Mike White
  Egg Cups: Joan George
  Egg Timers: Ellen Bercovici
  Kitchen Utensils: Paul Smith
  Napkins Dolls: Bobbie Zucker Bryson
  Pie Birds: Ellen Bercovici
  Range Shaker Sets: Bobbie Zucker Bryson
  Reamers: Bobbie Zucker Bryson
  String Holders: Ellen Bercovici
Laundry Room Items
  Clothes Sprinkler Bottles: Bobbie Zucker Bryson
  Irons: Jimmy & Carol Walker
Lighting: Mark Moran, Dale and Lynn Newquist, Elden and Jenny Schroeder
  Fairy Lamps: Jim Sapp

Tiffany Lamps: Carl Heck
Magic Collectibles: Jim Trautman
Metals: Mark Moran
  Aluminum: Dannie Woodard
  Sterling Flatware: Rhona Nabi
Mid-century Modern Design: Dana Cain, Mod Livin'
Motion Lamps: Jim Trautman
Movie Memorabilia (Posters): Dana Cain, Joe Fex, Bruce Carteron
Paper
  Children's Greeting Cards: Kerra Davis
  Patriotic Sheet Music: Kerra Davis
Pedal Cars & Vehicles: Jim Trautman
Picture Cards (Non-sport): Jim Trautman
Plant Waterers: Bobbie Zucker Bryson
Political & Campaign Items: Bobbie Zucker Bryson
Pop Culture Collectibles (Recordings): Michael J. Goldberg
Railroadiana: Jim Trautman
Ribbon Dolls: Bobbie Zucker Bryson
Scottish Tartanwares: Ellen Bercovici
Sewing Adjuncts: Beth Pulsipher
Snowdomes: Jim Trautman
Tea Premiums & Figures: Jim Trautman
Teddy Bear Collectibles: Kerra Davis
Television Sets: Harry Poster
Toothpick Holders: Judy Knauer
Toys
  Model Kits: Joe Fex
  Squeeze Toys: Kerra Davis
Trade Catalogs: Jim Trautman
Trump Indicators: Ellen Bercovici

CERAMICS
  Abingdon: Elaine Westover
  Amphora-Teplitz: Les and Irene Cohen
  Belleek (American): Peggy Sebek
  Belleek (Irish): Del Domke
  Blue & White Pottery: Steve Stone
  Blue Ridge Dinnerwares: Pat McPherson
  Buffalo Pottery: Phillip Sullivan
  Ceramic Arts Studio of Madison: Tim Holthaus
  Cowan: Jim and Jamie Saloff
  Czechoslovakian Pottery: Cheryl Goyda
  Doulton/Royal Doulton - Bunnykins: Reg Morris

Florence Ceramics: David Miller
Flow Blue: Vivian Kromer
Franciscan Ware: James Elliot-Bishop
Geisha Girl Wares: Elyce Litts
Gonder: James Boshears
Hall China: Marty Kennedy
Haviland: Nora Travis
Hull: Joan Hull
Ironstone: Bev Dieringer
Jewel Tea Autumn Leaf: Jo Cunningham
Kitchen & Serving Accessories
  Butter Pats: Mary Dessoie
  Oyster Plates: Michael Strawser
Limoges: Debbie DuBay
Majolica: Michael Strawser
McCoy: Craig Nissen
Mettlach: Gary Kirsner
Minton: Michael Strawser
Old Ivory: Alma Hillman
Phoenix Bird Porcelain: Joan Collett Oates
Quimper: Sandra Bondhus
Rosenthal: Gary Kirsner
Royal Bayreuth: Mary McCaslin
Royal Copley: Tim Holthaus
Royal Worcester: Michael Strawser
R.S. Prussia: Mary McCaslin

Russel Wright Designs: Kathryn Wiese
Sascha Brastoff: Pat McPherson
Schafer & Vater: Gary Kirsner
Steins: Gary Kirsner
Torquay Pottery: Judy Wucherer
Uhl Pottery: Lloyd Martin
Vernon Kilns: Pam Green
Warwick: John Rader, Sr.
Wedgwood: Michael Strawser
Zeisel (Eva) Designs: Pat Moore
Zsolnay: Federico Santi

GLASS
Animals: Neila M. Bredehoft
Cambridge: Neila M. Bredehoft
Consolidated: Neila M. Bredehoft
Depression: Debbie and Randy Coe
Duncan & Miller: Neila M. Bredehoft
Fostoria: Neila M. Bredehoft
Heisey: Neila M. Bredehoft
Imperial: Neila M. Bredehoft
Milk Glass: Frank Chiarenza
Tiffin: Neila M. Bredehoft
Glass Wall Pockets: Bobbie Zucker Bryson

Contributor directory

Ellen Bercovici
5118 Hampden Lane
Bathesda, MD 20814
(301) 652-1140
bercovici@erols.com

Sandra Bondhus
P.O. Box 100
Unionville, CT 06085
nbondhus@pol.net

James R. Boshears
354 Whitewater Dr., Apt. 107
Bolingbrook, IL 60440-7911
jrbosh@uillinois.edu

Neila M. Bredehoft
10217 Stickle Rd.
St. Louisville, OH 43071-9753

Bobbie Zucker Bryson
1 St. Eleanoras Lane
Tuckahoe, NY 10707
(914) 779-1405
Napkindoll@aol.com

Dana Cain
5061 S. Stuart Ct.
Littleton, CO 80123
dana.cain@att.net

Margaret Carlblom
Littleton, CO

Bruce Carteron
Cinema Grafix Movie Posters
P.O. Box 1114
Hill City, SD 57745
(605) 574-2266
www.cinemagrafix.net

Frank Chiarenza
The Frank Chiarenza Museum of Glass
39 W. Main St.
Meriden, CT 06451-4110
(203) 639-9778
chiarenzaglassmuseum@snet.net

The Clocksmith
806 El Camino Real
San Carlos, CA 94070
http;//www.theclocksmith.com/

Debbie and Randy Coe
1240 S.E. 40th Ave.
Hillsboro, OR 97123

Les and Irene Cohen
P.O. Box 17001
Pittsburgh, PA 15235
(412) 795-3030
am4ah@yahoo.com

Marion Cohen
14 Croyden Ct.
Albertson, NY 11507
(516) 294-0055

Jo Cunningham
535 E. Normal
Springfield, MO 65807-1659
(417) 831-1320
hiresearcher@aol.com

Kerra Davis
925 Bud St.
Blackshear, GA 31516

Mary Dessoie
265 Eagle Bend Dr.
Bigfork, MT 59911-6235

Bev Dieringer
P.O. Box 536
Redding Ridge, CT 06876
dieringer1@aol.com

Del E. Domke
16142 N.E. 15th St.
Bellevue, WA 98008-2711
(425) 643-3359
delyicious@aol.com

Debbie DuBay
Limoges Antiques Shop
20 Post Office Ave.
Andover, MA 01810
(978) 470-8773

James Elliot-Bishop
500 S. Farrell Dr., S-114
Palm Springs, CA 92264
gmcb@ix.netcom.com

Joe Fex
5061 S. Stuart St.
Littleton, CO 80123
joefex@att.net

Joan M. George
67 Stevens Ave.
Old Bridge, NJ 08856
drjgeorge@nac.net

Roselyn Gerson
12 Alnwick Rd.
Malverne, NY 11565
(516) 593-8746

Deborah Gillham
47 Midline Ct.
Gaithersburg, MD 20878
dgillham@erols.com

Michael J. Goldberg
823 S.E. 25th Ave.
Portland, OR 97214
(503) 238-1977
emjaygee@inetarena.com

Beth Gottlieb
730 Poplar
Denver, CO 80220
(303) 399-7926

Cheryl Goyda
Box 137
Hopeland, PA 17533
Mzczech@aol.com

Pam Green
You Must Remember This
P.O. Box 822
Hollis, NH 03049
ymrt@aol.com
www.ymrt.com

Carl Heck
Box 8416
Aspen, CO 81612
(970) 925-8011
www.carlheck.com

Alma Hillman
362 E. Main St.
Searsport, ME 04974
oldivory@acadia.net

Tim Holthaus
CAS Collectors Association
P.O. Box 46
Madison, WI 53701-0046

Joan Hull
1376 Nevada S.W.
Huron, SD 57350
Hull Pottery Association
11023 Tunnel Hill N.E.
New Lexington, OH 43764

Dorothy Kamm
P.O. Box 7460
Port St. Lucie, FL 34985-7460
(772) 465-4008
dorothykamm@adelphia.let

Marty Kennedy
4711 S.W. Brentwood Rd.
Topeka, KS 66606
(785) 554-5837 or 273-4981

Gary Kirsner
Glentiques, Ltd.
1940 Augusta Terrace
P.O. Box 8807
Coral Springs, FL 33071
gkirsner@myacc.net

Judy Knauer
1223 Spring Valley Lane
West Chester, PA 19380
(610) 431-3477
winkjk@netaxs.com

Vivian Kromer
11 800 Shanklin St.
Bakersfield, CA 93312
(661) 588-7768

Elyce Litts
P.O. Box 394
Morris Plains, NJ 07950
(908) 964-5055
happymemories@worldnet.att.net

Lloyd Martin
1582 Gregory Lane
Jasper, IN 47546
lmartin@psci.net

Mary McCaslin
6887 Black Oak Ct. E.
Avon, IN 46123
(317) 272-7776
maryjack@indy.rr.com

Pat McPherson
Country Town Antiques
738 Main St.
Ramona, CA 92065

David G. Miller
1971 Blue Fox Dr.
Lansdale, PA 19446-5505
(610) 584-6127
Florence Ceramics Collectors Society
FlorenceCeramics@aol.com

Mod Livin'
5327 E. Colfax Ave.
Denver, CO 80220
(720) 941-9292
modlivin.com

Mark Moran
5887 Meadow Dr. S.E.

Rochester, MN 55904
(507) 288-8006

Pat Moore
695 Monterey Blvd., Apt. 203
San Francisco, CA 94124
ezcclub@pacbell.net

Reg G. Morris
7360 Martingale
Chesterland, OH 44026
min@modex.com

Rhona Nabi
The Silver Lady Antiques
P.O. Box 27
Foxboro, MA 02035
(781) 784-9184
silant@aol.com

Dale and Lynn Newquist
Rochester, MN

Craig Nissen
P.O. Box 223
Grafton, WI 53024-0223
(414) 377-7932
McCoyCN@aol.com

Joan Collett Oates
685 S. Washington
Constantine, MI 49042
(269) 435-8353
koates120@earthlink.net

Harry Poster
P.O. Box 1883
S. Hackensack, NJ 07606
(201) 794-9606
hposter@worldnet.att.net

Beth Pulsipher
Prairie Home Antiques
240 N. Grand
Schoolcraft, MI 49087
(616) 679-2062

John Rader, Sr.
Vice President, National Assn. of
Warwick China & Pottery Collectors
(Betty June Wymer, 28 Bachmann Dr.,
Wheeling, WV 26003, 304-232-3031);
editor, "The IOGA" Club Quarterly
Newsletter; author, *Warwick China*
(Schiffer Publishing, 2000)
780 S. Village Dr., Apt. 203
St. Petersburg, FL 33716
(727) 570-9906

Jim and Jamie Saloff
tgsaloff@erie.net
http://www.erie.net/~jlsaloff

Jim Sapp
Fairy Lamp Club & Newsletter
(703) 971-3229
sapp@erols.com
www.fairylampclub.com

Federico Santi
The Drawing Room Antiques
152 Spring St.
Newport, RI 02840
(401) 841-5060
www.drawrm.com

R.O. Schmitt Fine Arts
P.O. Box 1941
Salem, NH 03079
(603) 893-5915

Elden and Jenny Schroeder
Onalaska, WI

Ingrid Schultz
Englewood, CO

Peggy Sebek
3255 Glencairn Rd.
Shaker Heights, OH 44122
pegsebek@earthlink.net

Paul Smith
P.O. Box 487
Harlan, IA 51537

Steve Stone
12795 W. Alameda Pkwy.
Lakewood, CO 80225
Sylvanlvr@aol.com

Michael G. Strawser Auctions
P.O. Box 332
Wolcottville, IN 46795
(260) 854-2859
www.majolicaauctions.com

Phillip Sullivan
P.O. Box 69
South Orleans, MA 0266
(508) 255-8495

Nora Travis
13337 E. South St.
Cerritos, CA 90701
(714) 521-9283
Travishrs@aol.com

Jim Trautman
R.R. 1
Orton, Ontario, Canada LON 7N0
truatman@sentex.net

Jimmy and Carol Walker
P.O. Box 68
Waelder, TX 78959-0068
(830) 788-7166

jimmy@irontalk.com
http://www.irontalk.com

Elaine Westover
210 Knox Hwy. 5
Abingdon, IL 61410-9332

Mike White
P.O. Box 483
Fraser, CO 80442
(970) 726-0448
mwhite483@rkymtnhi.com
http://grinder.rkymtnhi.com

Kathryn Wiese
Retrospective Modern Design
P.O. Box 1138
Kamuela, HI 97643
retrodesign@earthlink.net

Dannie Woodard
1310 S. Bowie Dr.
Weatherford, TX 76080
al1310@aol.com

Judy Wucherer
Transitions of Wales, Ltd.
P.O. Box 1441
Brookfield, WI 53045
North American Torquay Society
214 N. Ronda Rd.
McHenry, IL 60050
(815) 385-2040

ABC PLATES

Ceramic

These children's plates were popular in the late 19th and early 20th centuries. An alphabet border was incorporated with nursery rhymes, maxims, scenes or figures in an apparent attempt to "spoon feed" a bit of knowledge at mealtime. An important reference book in this field is A Collector's Guide to ABC Plates, Mugs and Things by Mildred L. and Joseph P. Chalala (Pridemark Press, Lancaster, Pennsylvania, 1980)

Letter "A" ABC Plate

"A, Apple, Ape, Air," 6" d., black transfer w/color added to an apple and ape w/large "A" in center & words "Apple, Ape, Air" above picture, red line on rim, probably part of a series (ILLUS.) **$225**

"Baked Taters All Hot" ABC Plate

"Baked Taters All Hot," 7 1/8" d., blue transfer of man & woman dressed for the cold selling potatoes at a stove on the street (ILLUS.) **175**

"Band of Hope" ABC Plate

"Band of Hope - The Sabbath Keepers," 6" d., center illustration of congregation filing into church over "Rise early and thankfully put up your prayer - Be at school in good time and be diligent there," color has been added (ILLUS.) **250**

"Base Ball Caught on a Fly" Plate

"Base Ball Caught on a Fly," 6 3/16" d., from the "American Sports" series, black transfer of a baseball game in action showing a fielder catching the ball (ILLUS.) **600**

"The Beggar's Petition" ABC Plate

"Beggar's Petition (The)" 7 1/4" d., black transfer w/some color added of young girl giving something to a begging dog (ILLUS.) **225**

Letter "C" ABC Plate

"C, Cow, Cat, Clown," 5 1/4" d., black & white, large letter "C" surrounded by images of cow, cat & clown, part of alphabet series (ILLUS.) **275**

"Children and Chaise" ABC Plate

"Children and Chaise," 5" d., black transfer of boy & girl riding in a chaise pulled by a donkey, black line around rim (ILLUS.) **350**

"Christmas Day" ABC Plate

"Christmas Day," blue transfer of boy w/napkin tucked under chin, eating at a table, blue letters in border, blue trim at edge (ILLUS.) **375**

"Cinderella" ABC Plate

"Cinderella," 7 3/16" d., from "Nursery Tales" series, Brownhills Pottery Company, sepia transfer w/color added of Cinderella gazing into the kitchen fire (ILLUS.) **250**

Cricket ABC Plate

Cricket game, 7 1/4" d., brown transfer of cricket game in progress (ILLUS.) **175**

"Crusoe Finding the Foot Prints"

"Crusoe Finding the Foot Prints," 8" d., from "Robinson Crusoe" series, Brownhills Pottery Company, sepia transfer w/color added of Robinson Crusoe discovering Friday's footprints, letters printed in sepia around edge of plate (ILLUS.)...... **175**

"England's Hope" ABC Plate

"England's Hope. Prince of Wales," 7" d., black transfer of image of young prince astride pony, black lines around edge (ILLUS.) **450**

"The Favorite Rabbits" ABC Plate

"Favorite Rabbits (The)," 5" d., one of a series, black & white, "How joyous at each sunshine hour - I haunted ev'ry green retreat - of forest, garden, heath & bower - Their cell to store with clover sweet" surrounds center illustration of girl in period dress feeding pet rabbits, older plate (ILLUS.) **300**

Small "Franklin's Proverbs" Plate

"Franklin's Proverbs," 5" d., "Keep thy shop and thy shop will keep thee" over center illustration of merchant (ILLUS.) **175**

"Gathering Cotton" ABC Plate

"Gathering Cotton," 6" d., black transfer w/color added of two slaves picking cotton (ILLUS.) **275**

"The Guardian" ABC Plate

"Guardian (The)," 7 1/4" d., brown transfer w/color added of sleeping girl guarded by large dog (ILLUS.) **225**

Hens & Rooster ABC Plate

Hens & rooster, 6 1/2" d., colorful transfer of rooster & hens, pale blue embossed alphabet border, probably Germany (ILLUS.) **85**

"John Gilpin" ABC Plate

"John Gilpin Pursued as a Highwayman," 6 1/4" d., black print w/slightly painted details, one of a series showing the humorous anniversary adventures of a 19th c. draper, illustrations based on Cruikshank's published in 1828 (ILLUS.) **300**

"The Lion" ABC Plate

"Lion (The)," 7 5/16" d., from the "Wild Animals" series, Brownhills Pottery Company, sepia transfer w/color added (ILLUS.)...... **255**

"Little Red Riding Hood" ABC Plate

"Little Red Riding Hood," 8 3/16" d., from the "Nursery Tales" series, multicolor transfer in reserve of Little Red Riding Hood & the wolf, scattered alphabet to the side, Staffordshire (ILLUS.)...................... **250**

"Little Strokes Fell Great Oaks"

"Little strokes fell great Oaks," 8 1/4" d., black transfer w/red, yellow & green illustration of man w/ax standing by felled tree, Staffordshire (ILLUS.) **150**

Boys Playing Marbles ABC Plate

Marbles, 6 3/16" d., blue transfer of three boys in period clothes playing marbles, red lines around rim (ILLUS.) **250**

Boys Playing Music ABC Plate

Musicians, 6" d., mulberry transfer of two children playing stringed instruments, made for H.C. Edmeston, England (ILLUS.) **175**

"My Face is My Fortune" ABC Plate

"My Face is My Fortune," 6 3/4" d., blue & white transfer picture of a sitting bulldog (ILLUS.) **175**

Newspaper Seller ABC Plate

Newspaper seller, 8 1/4" d., black transfer w/color added of image of boy selling newspapers on a city street (ILLUS.) **260**

"Poor Richard's Maxims" ABC Plate

"Poor Richard's Maxims," 5 1/8" d., one of a series, black transfer of two boys chopping down a tree, the maxim "Handle your tools without mittens - remember the cat in gloves catches no mice - Constant chopping wears away stones & little strokes fell great Oaks," red luster edge (ILLUS.) **300**

"Rebekah at the Well" ABC Plate

"Rebekah at the Well," 7 1/4" d., from "Bible Pictures" series, Brownhills Pottery Company, brown letters & picture w/color highlights of women gathered at a well (ILLUS.) **250**

Owls Sign Language ABC Plate

Sign language, 6 1/2" d., black transfer illustration of schoolmaster owl at desk, little owls in attendance, circled by illustrations of hand signs & letters, blue line around rim (ILLUS.)... **300**

Sign Language ABC Plate

Sign language, 7" d., illustrations of hands forming letters of sign language in boxes in the middle of the plate, h.p. ("hand painted") flowers on rim, extremely rare (ILLUS.).. **600**

"Soldier Tired" ABC Plate

"Soldier Tired," 7 1/4" d., black transfer of sleeping boy in dress w/a sword & hat nearby guarded by a dog (ILLUS.) **300**

"Thames Tunnel" ABC Plate

"Thames Tunnel," 5 1/4" d., black transfer picture illustrating the opening of the Tunnel in London, 1843, w/people in period dress (ILLUS.)... **225**

"Union Troops" ABC Plate

"Union Troops in Virginia," 6 1/8" d., black transfer w/color highlights of a large number of soldiers in formation (ILLUS.)....... **400**

"Victoria Regina" ABC Plate

"Victoria Regina," 5 1/16" d., black transfer of portrait of Queen Victoria as a young woman over words "Born 25 of May 1818. Proclaimed 20 of June 1837" (ILLUS.).. **1,000**

"William Penn" ABC Plate

"William Penn," 7 1/2" d., pink transfer portrait, no mark (ILLUS.)..................................... **350**

ADVERTISING ITEMS

Thousands of objects made in various materials, some intended as gifts with purchases, others used for display or given away for publicity, are now being collected. Also see various other categories and Antique Trader Advertising Price Guide.

1956 Planters Peanuts Ashtray

Ashtray, "Planters Peanuts," chromed metal, a round dished base centered by a standing figure of Mr. Peanut, inscribed on disk below "Mr. Peanut Planters Peanuts 1906-1956," slight soiling, rust spotting, 5 3/4" d., 4 3/4" h. (ILLUS.) **$132**

Ashtray, "Schweppes Soda Water," porcelain, rectangular w/rounded corners w/cigarette holder slot at each corner, white ground w/red panels of advertising on each side flange, indented center w/a color scene of playing cards centered by the ace of clubs, early 20th c., 4 1/2 x 5 1/2" **161**

Bag holding rack, "7Up," color-printed metal, the large long rectangular front in white printed in red & black "You Like (7Up logo) Likes You - Take Some Home," the back wire frame w/slots for five different sized bags, ca. 1950s, some field & edge wear & soiling, 18 x 38 1/2", 4" deep (ILLUS. bottom of page) **105**

Arden Milk Plastic Truck Bank

Bank, "Arden Milk," plastic toy model of a delivery truck, white w/black tires, red & blue wording on sides reads "Arden Milk - Prize Winning - Flavor Fresh!," ca. 1950s, minor overall wear, 7" l. (ILLUS.)......... **66**

Bank, "National Shawmut Bank of Boston," cast metal w/bronzed finish, bust of a realistic American Indian brave w/a tall single feather at the back of his head, early 20th c., 3 x 4", 7" h. **165**

7Up Metal Bag Holding Rack

Banner, "Levi's Overalls," color-painted denim, long rectangular form w/a black background painted at the bottom w/the long figure of a reclining cowboy looking up at a large yellow full moon, printing in white, red & yellow reads "For solid comfort... Levi's - America's Finest Overall Since 1860," ca. 1950s, 72 1/4" l., 28" h. (slight paint wear, creases to center where folded)... **550**

Beverage heater, "Dr. Pepper," wire, ceramic & wood, a large looped wire at bottom joined at the center to an oval ceramic insulator above heating element & w/Dr. Pepper advertising in color on each side, wide wire top loop handle w/red wooden grip, ca. 1940s-50s, 7" h. (small chip on one ad) **83**

Bill spindle, "National Cash Register," round cast-iron base w/company name in outer ring & scrolls in inner ring, tall pointed center spike for bills, early 20th c., 3 1/2" d., 6" h. (slight overall soiling) **105**

Bottle carrier, "Pepsi-Cola," aluminum six-pack style, curved front & back bars centered by a long arched handle continuing to the bottom bar, front & sides printed in red w/"Pepsi-Cola" flanked by three short black bands at the sides, ca. 1940s-50s, 5 x 8 1/4", 7 3/4" h. (some wear & scratching) **55**

Bottle rack, "Pepsi-Cola," printed metal, three-tier style, each rectangular section w/dark blue sides printed outside w/a large Pepsi-Cola logo in red on white, each section joined by short metal bar legs, 1940s, each section 12 x 18", 14" h., overall 43" h. (professionally restored w/new hardware) **358**

Calendar, 1902, "The Good Store," die-cut color-lithographed cardboard, a tall rectangular form w/delicately scalloped edges, white background printed at the top in pink & green w/arching vases of flowers above advertising over a color scene of a young boy pushing a young girl in a wheelbarrow, colorful roses at the bottom flanking the small full calendar pad, 11 1/2 x 15 1/2" (few edge tears & soiling) **149**

Calendar, 1903, "Dupont," paper, a long rectangular form w/light orange printed advertising at the top of a long color print titled "Generations," depicting a scene in an autumn field w/an older man showing a youth how to fire a rifle, two hunting dogs in the foreground, small December only calendar page at the bottom, 14 x 28 1/4" (ILLUS. top of page) **1,430**

Calendar, 1904, "Peters Cartridge Co.," paper, a tall rectangular form, the upper three-quarters printed in sepia tones w/a scene of a large bull moose walking through a snowy woodland, full calendar pad at the bottom, 14 x 26 3/4" (minor holes bottom edges).................................... **1,265**

1903 Dupont Calendar

Calendar, 1905, "Metropolitan Life Insurance Co.," color-printed cardboard, tall narrow rectangular form, the black background printed w/a vertical row of four large colorful rose blossoms, each enclosing the face of a pretty child, tiny complete calendar blocks at the bottom, 7 1/2 x 25" (some creases, nail hole at top center)... **231**

Peters Cartridge 1915 Calendar

Calendar, 1915, "Peters Cartridge Company," paper w/metal edges, large color print at the top of two dogs on point in a field, overall creasing & some edge chipping, 15 x 20 1/2" (ILLUS.).............................. **715**

Calendar, 1926, "Calumet Baking Powder," paper, rectangular w/a rectangular top color print showing a sad-eyed young girl standing holding her baby doll w/a large collie standing behind her, tan border band, small full calendar pad at the bottom, 9 x 14" **77**

Calendar, 1927, "GE Mazda," paper, a tall rectangular form w/a tall upright color print of a pretty young woman wearing a one-piece swimsuit & long open red robe descending steps, a large electric wall light fixture in the background, titled "Twilight" & signed by Hayden Hayden small complete black & gold calendar pad at bottom, framed, calendar 8 1/2 x 20 1/4" (few creases on cover page) **281**

Winchester 1927 Calendar

Calendar, 1927, "Winchester," paper, a long rectangular form w/a tall rectangular color print at the top w/a snowy wilderness sunset scene of a hunter wearing snowshoes in the foreground spotting a large stag in the distance, artwork by Frank Stick, dealer advertising below, partial calendar pad w/Winchester advertising at the bottom, pinned to matte, 10 x 20 3/4" (ILLUS.)..................................... **880**

Calendar, 1929, "DeLaval Cream Separators," paper, very long rectangular form w/three-quarters of the page taken up w/a tall color print of a young blond-haired boy sitting on wooden steps & playing w/his puppy, an open door behind shows an interior w/an open window & a cream separator, small calendar pages at the bottom, in wooden frame, 13 1/4" w., 24 1/2" h. (crease across top center) **99**

Calendar, 1933, "Calotabs," paper, a long rectangular form w/wide border, a tall rectangular color print at the top showing a half-length portrait of a beautiful young woman wearing an off-the-shoulder gown & holding a large cluster of yellow mums, black calendar pages below w/white & red printing, reads "Your tongue tells you when you need Calotabs," in wooden frame, 14 1/2 x 30 1/2" (some very light creasing)... **39**

Calendar, 1934, "Wrigley's Spearmint Gum," paper, upper three-quarters w/a tall rectangular color photo of early radio stars

Myrt & Marge whose program was sponsored by Wrigley, advertising line below picture & above the small calendar page, only December 1934 page present, in wooden frame, 8 3/4 x 14 3/4" (several horizontal creases in picture)............................. **99**

Calendar, 1952, "Blue Ridge Lines," paper, a top rectangular color print of a large bus driving through the countryside w/an image of an early stagecoach in the sky above, advertising below image & above attached calendar pad, wood frame, 16 x 26" (slight soiling & wrinkling).................. **33**

1952 Trucking Company Calendar

Calendar, 1952, "Russell Crowther Trucking Company," desk-type w/metal easel back, die-cut color-printed tin, rectangular w/rounded end w/color image of a large red truck cab, the back of the truck enclosing the paper calendar pad w/partial pages, 3 3/4 x 5 1/2" (ILLUS.)................... **83**

Calendar, 1955, "Sun Crest Beverages," paper w/metal top edge, rectangular w/narrow orange border, upper half w/large rectangular color photo w/a half-length shot of a pretty 1950s girl holding a bottle of Sun Crest, small calendar blocks below, 15 x 21 3/4" (slight water staining at bottom edge).................................... **22**

Candy scoop, "B.P. Clark and Co.," clear pressed glass, rectangular flat-bottom w/arched tapering & scalloped low sides & back w/projecting back handle, late 19th - early 20th c., 7" l. (slight edge chipping)... **193**

Betsy Ross Bread Chalkboard

Chalkboard, "Betsy Ross Bread," one-sided painted tin, rectangular, narrow red top w/rectangular panel printed in white & yellow w/a loaf of bread & "Betsy Ross is good bread - Cakes and Pies," a large black square board below, mid-20th c., some scratching & wear, 20 x 28 1/4" (ILLUS.).. **39**

Chalkboard, "Dr. Pepper," self-framed tin over cardboard, rectangular w/rectangular upper panel w/yellow ground decorated at the left w/a small bottle of Dr. Pepper & company logo, red rectangle at right side printed in white "Drink Dr. Pepper - Good For Life," black chalkboard below, ca. 1940s, 17 1/4 x 23 1/4" (slight scratching & dent in bottom corner).............. **176**

Jersey Maid Chalkboard

Chalkboard, "Jersey Maid Dairy Products," self-framed tin over cardboard, rectangular, a dark grey panel at the top w/a white & pink cow head logo beside red & white advertising reading "We Serve Jersey Maid Dairy Products" above black chalkboard prints in white "Special To-day,"16 x 23 3/4" (ILLUS.)............................... **88**

Chalkboard, "Squirt," one-sided self-framed tin, rectangular w/narrow rectangular top panel w/red ground & large yellow oblong logo beside a small color picture of the bottle, reads "Enjoy Squirt - never an after-thirst," square black board below, ca. 1959, 19 3/4 x 28" (some scratching & denting) **88**

Clock, "Biltmore Dairy Products," electric, glass & metal, domed glass double-bubble light-up type, rounded domed glass front over white outer ring w/Roman numerals, center in white w/small logo figure above wording in yellow & black, sweep seconds hand, ca. 1940s-50s (light soiling, minor marks) **358**

Clock, "Bordens Fine Dairy Products," electric light-up wall model, metal & glass, round w/domed glass front, yellow border ring w/Arabic numbers centered by bold red wording above the Elsie the Cow & daisy logo, ca. 1950s, 15" d. (some paint loss on hands, overall soiling) **231**

Clock, "Carstar's White Seal Whiskey," figural, ceramic model of a white seal balancing a ProStaff golf ball on its nose, swirling waves molded at the front w/a round key-wind clock under the back of the seal, company name printed along the front edge of the oval base, 3 1/2 x 10", 14 3/4" h. (slight scratching)....... **132**

Clock, "Dr. Pepper," glass & aluminum, round w/background printed in black on the upper half & red the lower half, red & white company logo at the top, "Hot or Cold" printed in white in lower half, ca. 1960s, 12 1/4" d. (some soiling, rust spotting on back, surface tarnishing to sides) **121**

Clock, "Four Roses Whiskey," electric light-up counter top or hanging model, metal & plastic, a raised square frame enclosing a dial in white w/four Arabic numerals around the sides centered by a cluster of four red roses, sweep seconds hand, raised on a rectangular platform printed w/the brand name in white at the front, ca. 1960s, working, 12" w., 13" h. (overall wear & soiling) **44**

Rare Harley-Davidson Neon Clock

Clock, "Harley-Davidson Motor Cycles," round wall-mounted electric neon & aluminum, white dial w/four Roman numerals alternating w/small company logos around dial, large red, black & white company logo at the center, sweep seconds illusion wheel, neon border band, only available in the early 1990s, 20" d. (ILLUS.) **825**

Clock, "John Deere Quality Farm Equipment," electric light-up type, glass & metal w/fiberboard back, round frame w/large white dial w/Arabic numerals, centered by rectangular yellow & green John Deere advertising w/leaping deer logo, ca. 1950s, hour hand w/some wear, front glass w/scratch, 15" d................................ **413**

Clock, "NuGrape Soda," electric light-up wall model, metal & glass, rectangular metal frame enclosing glass front w/Arabic numerals around the sides on a white ground, a tall color picture of a bottle in the center w/a yellow oval w/brand name in black letters, ca. 1950s-60s, 13 1/4 x 16 1/4" (some soiling & surface rust, plug needs replacing)............................. **121**

1950s Pepsi-Cola Light-up Clock

Clock, "Pepsi-Cola," electric, glass & metal, domed glass double-bubble light-up type, rounded domed glass front over white outer ring w/Roman numerals, center w/yellow background & printed w/red, white & blue Pepsi bottle cap & black wording "say Pepsi, please," sweep seconds hand,1954, light soiling & wear, 15" d. (ILLUS.)................................. **578**

Clock, "Pepsi-Cola," electric, glass & metal, domed glass light-up type, rounded domed glass front over white outer ring w/Roman numerals, center w/red, white & blue Pepsi logo, sweep seconds hand, 1945, 15" d. (case soiling, outer metal band may be replaced)................................. **385**

Clock, "Polly Stamps," electric, glass & metal, domed glass double-bubble light-up type, rounded domed glass front over white outer ring w/Roman numerals, center in white w/large color image of colorful parrot perched at top w/red & white stamp, brand name in yellow, sweep seconds hand, ca. 1940s-50s (few light scratches) **770**

Clock, "Royal Crown Cola," metal & glass, round w/domed glass front, white ground printed w/a border band of four Arabic numerals spaced between small green crowns, logo & large circle & diamond w/red company name at the center, ca. 1960, 14 1/2" d. (minor paint loss, slight scratching) **209**

Clock, "Singer Sales & Service," light-up electric rectangular plastic wall-mounted model, long narrow rectangular shape w/a round clock dial w/Roman numerals at the left side & the round Singer Sewing Machine Company logo at the right end, wording in red in the center on the white & green ground, metal back, mid-20th c., working, 51" l., 14 3/4" h. (some soiling & scratching) **28**

Clock, "Vess Billion Bubble Beverages," round double-bubble style in glass w/metal body, domed glass printed w/green outer ring w/Arabic numerals, yellow background & white center circle printed in green & red "Drink Vess Billion Bubble Beverages," sweep seconds hand, mid-20th c., 15 1/2" d. (some body wear & rubbing from the seconds hand) **468**

Clock, "Weckerle Dairy Products," electric light-up wall-type, round glass & metal w/domed front, red on white ring in center w/advertising, working, ca. 1950s, 15" d. (some rust spotting on ring)............................. **61**

Counter display, "Card Seed Co., Fredonia, N.Y.," large narrow rectangular black metal frame w/four rows displaying 32 vegetable seed packs, original packs, early 20th c., 32 1/2" w., 24 1/4" h.................. **176**

Hills Bros. Coffee Counter Display

Counter display, "Hills Bros. Coffee," die-cut cardboard, the front of rectangular form w/cutout mesas above a color image of a cowboy riding his racing pony, a vintage 1 lb. coffee can sits directly behind front, front printed in black & red "Distinctive as the grandeur of the West - Hills Bros. Coffee - Roasting 'a few pounds at a time' is the secret of its flavor," ca. 1928, from the Hills Bros. museum, light crease at left, front 7 x 12 1/4" (ILLUS.)... **825**

Counter display, "Kellogg's Cereals," aluminum & plastic, a narrow rectangular raised plastic sign in white w/red advertising "Ask For Kellogg's Cereals" raised on a narrow flat upright metal support over two narrow rectangular aluminum open shelves, mid-20th c., 6 3/4 x 20 1/2", 16 1/2" h. (soiling, cracks in plastic at screw holes) **77**

Counter display, "Land o' Monts Gruyere - Swiss Cheese," self-framed tin, tall rectangular back panel w/arched & scalloped top in black w/orange & white printing above a shallow rectangular projecting box at the bottom w/further printing, reads "Delicious Genuine Imported 'Land o' Monts' Gruyere - Swiss Cheese - Mild, Mellow and Appetizing," bottom box reads "Made by Burgi & Co. Berne Switzerland," early 20th c., 8 1/2 x 13 1/4", 5 1/2" deep (slight soiling & scratching) **33**

Marquette Club Ginger Ale Display

Counter display, "Marquette Club Ginger Ale," die-cut color-printed cardboard, designed to resemble a large white early icebox w/a young woman squatting in front of an open door compartment checking a thermometer in her hand, compartment actually holds an empty original bottle of the product, light blue oblong panel at the bottom reads "Keep A Bottle On The Ice - Marquette Club Pale Dry Ginger Ale," ca. 1920s, minor spotting & water stains, minor field & edge wear, 21 3/4 x 26", 5 1/2" deep (ILLUS.)... **83**

Rare Rowntree's Gum Display

Counter display, "Rowntree's Gums," die-cut paper lithography on heavy cardboard, a flattened color figure of a young black boy standing wearing a large straw hat w/company name on it, wearing a white shirt & blue & white check pants, holding a long stick yoke across one shoulder, the ends suspending strings holding small shallow round cardboard

dishes w/yellow & red labels, a rectangular black-painted wood base printed "I sell Rowntree's Gums," early 20th c., some touch-ups, scruffs, tears, warping & soiling (ILLUS.).. **809**

Counter display, "Woodbury Face Powder," die-cut color-printed cardboard w/easel back, a taller rectangular central panel w/the company name above a half-length portrait of actress Laraine Day wearing a white hat & grey suit, the shorter upright side panels w/angle-cut edges feature two color bust portraits on each side, included are Veronica Lake, Paulette Goddard, Lana Turner & Dorothy Lamour, ca. 1940s, 19 1/2 x 21" (minor surface wear near top)..................... **330**

Counter display box, cov., "Wrigley's Juicy Fruit Chewing Gum," lithographed cardboard, low rectangular form, base & cover printed w/a green & white striped ground, the cover interior printed in blue w/early Wrigley arrow figure & name of gum printed in white & "Export Package" printed in blue above, blue & white band w/brand on front edge of box, ca. 1920s, 5 x 6 1/4", 5" h. (exterior w/some soiling & rough edges, interior excellent).................... **33**

Counter display box, "Ferry's Seeds," wood & metal, low rectangular wooden open box w/high upright wood back & two tiered black metal sleeves to hold seed packets, long yellow panel across front reads "Every Packet Dated - Ferry's - Flower Packets 5¢ 10¢ - Vegetable Packets 5¢," w/some old empty seed packets, early 20th c., 12 x 27", 17" h. (overall wear, some label edge damage) **231**

Rare Belding's Silk Spool Cabinet

Counter display cabinet, "Belding's Silk," mahogany & glass tall upright spool cabinet, a tall glass door at the top w/stenciled advertising & opening to a rotating spool carousel holding 396 spools, three narrow drawers at the bottom, flat narrow molded base, 1911, 16" sq., 32" h. (ILLUS.).. **2,365**

Counter display cabinet, "J.S. Fry and Sons Ltd. Chocolates," glass & wood, tall upright wooden framework w/glass sides, early 20th c., 13 3/4 x 17 1/2", 23 3/4" h. (shelves missing, some paint crazing).. **215**

Counter display case, "Cook's Leather Goods," glass & wood, a low rectangular case w/glass sides & top & mirrored bottom, slanted front pane w/etched advertising, wood-framed door at back, early 20th c., 12 1/2 x 18", 9 1/2" h. (slight wear).. **132**

Counter display case, "Humphreys Homeopathic Medicine," upright wooden box-like case angled at the front & enclosing a large black panel printed in gold w/the company name & list of medications, late 19th - early 20th c., 8 x 11", 11" h. (slight soiling)............................. **154**

Counter display case, "Tom's Toasted Peanuts," metal & glass, upright rectangular form w/red metal framing supporting a glass door & glass sides, four glass shelves, "Eat Tom's Toasted Peanuts" in white at top of door, ca. 1930s, repainted, 9 1/2 x 16", 23" h. (crease in upper back corner, some wear) **83**

Aracoma Textile Indian Bust

Counter display figure, "Aracoma Textile Company," cast metal w/gold wash, half-length realistic portrait of an American Indian chief wearing a feather headdress, arms crossed at the front, looking left, plinth base impressed "Aracoma," further impressed advertising down the flat back, ca. 1920s, 3 1/2" w., 6 1/2" h. (ILLUS. of front & back) **468**

Counter display figure, "Pahle Disc Records," large chalkware model of a strutting red rooster on round green disk base w/gold advertising, early 20th c., 12 1/2" w., 22 1/4" h. (damage to legs, chip to side of tail, light overall wear) **1,760**

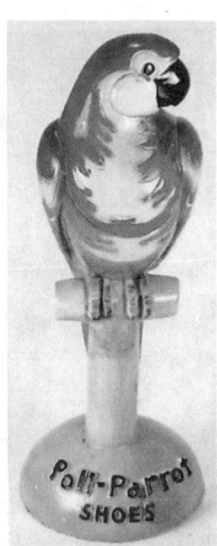

Poll Parrot Shoes Counter Display

Counter display figure, "Poll-Parrot Shoes," tall ceramic model of a colorful parrot in red, orange, green & blue on a yellow perch w/a domed base w/embossed company name, early 20th c., some paint touch-up, slight paint chips, 5 3/4" d., 15" h. (ILLUS.) **176**

Red Goose Shoes Counter Display

Counter display figure, "Red Goose Shoes," large plaster model of red goose on dark oblong base, embossed gold wording on breast, early 20th c., small paint flake & few base edge chips, 5 x 8 1/2", 11 1/2" h. (ILLUS.)........................ **303**

Gordon's Peanuts Display Jar

Counter display jar, cov., "Gordon's," clear cylindrical glass w/red fired-on pictures of Gorden delivery vans on sides, thin slightly domed red metal lid stamped w/company name inside, ca. 1940s, slight wear, some paint splatters & scratching on cover, 8 3/4" d., 10 1/2" h. (ILLUS.) **132**

Planters Hexagonal Display Jar

Counter display jar, cov., "Planters Peanuts," clear glass hexagonal jar and clear glass lid w/peanut handle, yellow lettering reads "Planters," yellow Mr. Peanut figure (ILLUS.) **125-150**

Counter display jar, cov., "Ramon's Co-Tabs," cylindrical glass printed around the sides in white w/a band of small walking doctor figures in top hats, the thin metal lid in yellow w/blue wording "Ramon's the Little Doctor," includes several boxes & tins of products, early 20th c., jar 7 1/4" d., 7 3/4" h., the group (soiling & minor scratching on lid & jar) **66**

Counter display jar, cov., "The Nut House," clear glass spherical form w/wide flattened rim, embossed wording at top front, ca. 1930s, 10 1/2" d., 9" h. (slight rim chipping) **94**

Tom's Toasted Peanuts Display Jar

Counter display jar, cov., "Tom's Toasted Peanuts," clear glass cylinder w/fitted flat cover w/knob handle, black wording on sides, ca. 1930s, small rim chip, 7" d., 8 1/2" h. (ILLUS.) **83**

Counter display sign, "Remington UMC Kleanbore Hi Speed 22's," die-cut cardboard w/easel back, printed in color w/a large picture of a shell on the left side & a parade of pest animals at the right, ca. 1930s, 11 1/2 x 19" (minor scuffs) **468**

Hills Bros. Coffee Cup & Saucer

Cup & saucer, "Hills Bros. Coffee," china, cappuccino-size cup w/tapering cylindrical sides, decorated w/a color decal image in a tapering rectangle w/a dark orange background & showing an Arab man in a long yellow robe drinking from a cup, black wording reads "Hills Bros. Tea and Coffee," made in Germany mark on base, ca. 1930s, saucer 5" d. (ILLUS.) **248**

Display case, floor model, "Nevin's Candy," metal & double-paned glass, upright eight-sided case w/a three-section glass door & individually revolving shelves, includes area to keep candy cool w/ice drains in bottom, decals on two sides reading "Ask for Nevin's Candy - Made in Denver," early 20th c., 25" w., 70 1/4" h. (some glass pieces broken or cracked) **770**

Display rack, floor-model, garden seeds, metal & wood, a revolving round metal top w/multiple slots to hold individual seed packs, raised on a wooden tripod base w/tapering flat legs joined by a small square shelf, no seed packs, early 20th c., 17" d., 72" h. (metal repainted, some dents & wear) **66**

Door handle, "Occident Flour," brass, long narrow vertical backplate w/slender arched bar handle, backplate vertically embossed "Occident Flour Costs More - Worth It," early 20th c., 3" w., 18 1/2" h. (small ding, slight tarnishing) **116**

Door handle, "Pepsi-Cola," printed tin, tall narrow rectangular form w/arched open integral handle, black ground w/red & white wording "Enjoy Pepsi-Cola - Bigger - Better," ca. 1940s, 12" l. (very minor spider web rust, light wear) **121**

Door handle, "Pepsi-Cola," printed tin, tall narrow rectangular form w/attached long Bakelite handle, black ground w/red & white wording at the top "Drink Pepsi-Cola - Bigger - Better," ca. 1940s, 12" l. (few minor paint nicks, some chips around top mounting holes, light edge wear) **143**

Door kick plate, "Pepsi-Cola," porcelain, long rectangular shape w/rounded corners, yellow ground printed at the right w/a large red, white & blue Pepsi bottle cap, long white panel at the left reads "Enjoy a Pepsi," ca. 1960s, 12 1/4 x 29 1/4" (minor edge chips & wear) **215**

Door palm press plate, "Canada Dry Spur," tall narrow rectangular embossed tin, white ground showing a large colored bottle of pop & wording in black, red & white, reads "Canada Dry - Spur - 5¢ - Zip In Every Sip!," ca. 1950s, 3 5/8 x 11 7/8" (minor edge & field wear) **94**

Butter-Nut Bread Door Push

Door push, "Butter-Nut Bread," heavy die-cut steel, large center color image of a loaf of bread in white w/red, white & blue brand name & advertising on it, narrow blue side mounting straps, ca. 1940s, some field scratches, paint worn on top edge, some wear & rust on back, 8 3/4 x 31 1/2" (ILLUS.) **281**

Door push, "Delaware Punch," embossed printed tin, tall narrow rectangular form, black ground w/color picture of small bottle at top above red & white wording "Drink Delicious Delaware Punch," ca. 1940s (light scratches, paint chip lower right)... **55**

Door push, "Hires Root Beer," printed tin, tall narrow rectangular form, Canadian version w/raised edge border, white ground w/a large color picture of the bottle below "Hires Root Beer - 'Hires To You' - 2 Glass Size - It's So Good," ca.

1940s, 4 x 14" (small dent in top mounting hole, light edge wear) **187**

Door push, "Old Style Bread," painted metal, narrow mounting bands flanking a large full-color loaf of bread, reverse reads "Thank You Call Again," adjustable, ca. 1950s, 27" l., 8 3/4" h. (some soiling & rust spotting, edge wear)...... **358**

Door push, "Orange Crush," printed tin, tall narrow rectangular form, in orange & black w/a large picture of the bottle below "Come In! Drink Orange Crush," ca. 1930s, 2 x 12" (mild dent, minor nicks) **198**

Sunbeam Bread Door Push

Door push, "Sunbeam Enriched Bread," heavy lithographed tin, a large die-cut loaf of the bread in white, blue, red & yellow featuring the Sunbeam girl, narrow dark blue end straps, ca. 1950s, minor scattered wear & scratches, no end caps, 8 3/4 x 26 5/8" (ILLUS.)..................................... **385**

Door push, "Texas Punch," printed tin, tall narrow rectangular form, yellow ground w/large bottle printed in red, green & yellow, reads "Hello! You'll Love It - Texas Punch," ca. 1940s, 4 x 10"................................. **88**

Bisque Buster Brown Figurine

Figurine, "Buster Brown Shoes," small bisque figure of Buster Brown wearing an orange outfit & blue tie, impressed on the back "Buster Brown Shoes - Japan," early 20th c., worn paint, 2 7/8" h. (ILLUS. of front & back).. **209**

Instruction book, "Indian Motorcycles," rectangular grey covers, much information & technical illustrations, cover reads "1916 - (logo) - Instruction Book - on - Operation Care - and Adjustment - of - Indian Motorcycles," 40 pp., 5 1/2 x 8 3/8" (soiling, cover wear, ink pen writing on back, some page soiling)................................ **187**

License plate attachment, "Cave of the Mounds," die-cut aluminum, arched form printed in red & white, reads "See - Cave of the Mounds - Blue Mounds, Wis. - On U.S. 18 & 151," new-old stock, ca. 1950s, 5 1/2 x 10"... **77**

License plate attachment, "Day's Banner Bread," celluloid-over-tin, oval w/red reflector background printed in white w/brand name, ca. 1930s-40s, 4 1/8 x 4 1/2".................. **44**

Pfister Hybrids License Attachment

License plate attachment, "Pfister Hybrids," die-cut embossed tin, a long narrow rectangular panel centered by a long angled ear of yellow & red corn, reddish orange background w/company name in large white letters, new-old stock, ca. 1930s-40s, 3 1/8 x 6" (ILLUS.) **72**

Saturday Evening Post Ad

Magazine ad, *Saturday Evening Post*, full-page ad for DeVilbiss spraying equipment, w/full-color illustration of gloved hand applying paint with sprayer under caption "Spray is the way to do it today!" & text under heading "Best labor-saver a painter ever had," May 2, 1953, 10 1/2 x 13 1/2" (ILLUS.) **30**

Match holder, "Juicy Fruit Gum," lithographed tin, hanging-type, rectangular w/rounded corners, printed in red, white, grey & black, an oval bust portrait of Wm. Wrigley at the top flanked by "The Man"

over "Juicy Fruit," bottom projecting holder printed "Made Famous," other advertising on the holder ends, early 20th c., 3 3/8 x 5", 1 3/8" deep (scratches & wear on holder, light wear on upper part) **149**

Sex-ine Pills Hanging Match Holder

Match holder, "Sex-ine Pills," lithographed tin, wall-hanging type, tall rectangular back w/the partially cutout profiles of facing young men at the top w/red & black wording between over the rectangular match holder w/red printing, further advertising at the bottom, early 20th c., slight soiling & wear, 5 1/4" w., 8 1/2" h. (ILLUS.)... **880**

Buffalo News Metal Match Striker

Match striker, "The Buffalo News," printed metal, wall-mounted, long narrow rectangular form w/fancy serpentine sides, printed at top in black & white "Tack Me Up - Read The Buffalo News - A Paper For All The People - For Sale Everywhere," rough striking panel in lower half, early 20th c., one slight crease, some wear, 1 3/4 x 4 3/4" (ILLUS.) **206**

Medallion, "Indian Motorcycles," cast brass, round w/hanging hole at top, front w/border band w/wording around profile bust of Native American, reads "Indian Motorcycle - 1901 - World's Finest - 1932," reverse w/commemoration of George Washington's 200th birthday, 1 1/4" d. (moderate wear)............................... 77

Menu board, "Barq's," embossed printed tin, rectangular w/a narrow red border band, dark blue rectangular top panel embossed & printed in red & white "Drink Barq's - 'It's Good'," black board below, ca. 1950s, 19 x 27 1/2" (slight scratching).......................... 55

Menu board, "Dad's Root Beer," embossed tin, upright rectangular form, white panel at the top printed w/blue & yellow bottle cap & red & blue advertising reading "Unbelievable - Dad's Root Beer," board below, ca. 1960s, 19 1/2 x 27 1/2" (scattered edge & field wear, few light bends)........ 83

Menu board, "Dad's Root Beer," rectangular embossed tin, thin white border & white panel at the top above the black board, shows a dark blue, yellow & red bottle cap beside the wording "The Original Draft Root Beer," new-old stock, ca. 1950s-60s, 20 x 28" 61

Kickapoo Joy Juice Menu Board

Menu board, "Kickapoo Joy Juice," self-embossed lithographed tin, tall rectangular shape w/rounded corners, yellow border band & bottom panel, top black board w/"Speshuls" (sic) in white, bottom panel w/Al Capp characters & wording "and don't forget - Kickapoo Joy Juice," dated 1965, edge wear w/some scattered denting, 19 1/2 x 30" (ILLUS.).............................. 330

Menu board, "Pepsi-Cola," self-framed color-printed tin, rectangular w/rounded corners printed to look like an early school handheld chalkboard w/Pepsi-Cola advertising in a panel at the top in red, white & blue, yellow & red border bands & black board, ca. 1940s, 19 1/2 x 30" (some edge wear w/bends, wear & soiling in board area)... 275

Buckeye Root Beer Mug

Mug, "Buckeye Root Beer," yellowware pottery, cylindrical w/hand applied handle, decorated w/double dark blue band, the bottom marked "100% Pure Buckeye," 4 3/4" h. (ILLUS.).............................. 20

Oiler can, "Indian Motorcycles," cylindrical metal w/sideways spout attachment on the screw-on metal lid, paper label w/black & red wording reads "Indian Chain Oil...," ca. 1930s, 4 1/2" h. (overall oil staining on label) 303

Oiler can, "Mohawk Gun & Reel Lubricant," upright oval can w/screw-on plastic cap & spout, wide white upper band w/printing in black & orange above a narrower black band w/an orange & black Indian head logo above narrow orange bottom band, ca. 1950s, full contents, 3 oz. (label soiled & stains).............................. 308

Casket Company Paperweight

Paperweight, "Boyertown Casket Company," figural silver plated cast metal, model of a casket on low platform base w/embossed advertising around the sides, ca. 1930s-40s, tarnished, scattered wear on base, 2 1/4 x 5 1/8", 2" h. (ILLUS.)................ 159

Porcelain Indian Bust Paperweight

Paperweight, "The Carborundum Co. - Trafford Park, Manchester," porcelain, figural bust of an American Indian chief in bronze-painted tones & wearing a white, brown & orange feather headdress, marked on the bottom "Royal Porcelain by Ridgways," English, early 20th c., 2 x 3", 5" h. (ILLUS.) **88**

Indian Motorcycle Enameled Pin

Pin, "Indian Motorcycles," cast enameled metal, round w/dark red enameled ground w/a slightly raised silver profile of an Indian Chief w/long headdress above silver word "Indian," w/two clevis-type mount studs, ca. 1930s, some wear, fasteners missing, 1 1/2" d. (ILLUS.) **413**
Pin, "Indian Motorcycles," stamped metal convention-type, profile of Native American warrior w/large upright red enameled feather at back of head, roll pin on back, ca. 1920s, 1 1/2 x 2" (may have been replated, feather new) **94**
Pin, "Indian Motorcycles," stamped metal, silver wings w/company name in red flanking an embossed gold-colored Indian Chief head, safety pin mount, ca. 1930s, 2" w. (small blemish on one wing) **270**

Comical Advertising Shriner Button

Pinback button, "International Shirt & Collar Co.," round celluloid, also a souvenir of a Shriner's convention, color scene of a blindfolded man in a nightshirt riding a large comical camel wearing a red fez & a collar suspending the Shriner logo, red wording reads "Oriental, Troy, N.Y. - Compliments of International Shirt & Collar Co.," early 20th c., minor edge foxing, 2 1/8" d. (ILLUS.) **44**
Pinback button, "Puritan Hosiery," round celluloid, a large color center scene of a sexy young Puritan woman w/her skirt pulled up adjusting her long black stock-

ing while resting her foot on a rock in a woodland, red border band w/yellow wording reads "Wear Puritan Hosiery - Burnham Hanna Munger D.G. Co., Kansas City, Mo.," early 20th c., 1 3/4" d. (minor surface scratches) **66**

Round Oak Stoves China Plate

Plate, "Round Oak Stoves," china, rounded w/scalloped rim & light molded fluting around rim, dark green border band enclosing a central color scene framed by a wreath of oak branches, the figure of a standing Native American in a landscape at the center, printed "Round Oak" above the figure & "Doe-Wah-Jack" below, back stamped w/Round Oak advertising, early 20th c., overall crazing & few small front chips, 9" d. (ILLUS.) **121**
Playing cards, "NuGrape," complete deck in original box, each card back w/a color half-length portrait of a 1930s girl holding a bottle of the product, blue box printed in gold "Compliments - NuGrape Co. of America. A Flavor You Can't Forget. Atlanta, Ga.," includes one joker & bridge points card, 2 3/8 x 3 7/8" (minor wear to cards & box) **33**
Postal envelope, "Winchester Model 1912 Light Weight Hammerless Repeating Shotgun," lithographed paper, the left half w/advertising in red & black above a color vignette of two hunters & two hunting dogs in the field, unused, 3 1/2 x 6 1/2" **187**

Indian Motorcycles Postcard

Postcard, "Indian Motorcycles," rectangular, printed in color w/image of a large red & silver motorcycle shown in a landscape, black & red wording reads "1941 Indian '45' - Featuring The New 'Double Action' Spring Frame," unused, 3 1/2 x 5 1/2" (ILLUS.) **105**

Radio, "Pepsi-Cola," transistor-type, plastic small model of a countertop dispenser supported in a leather carrying strap, Pepsi logo on side, front end panel reads "say 'Pepsi please'" above row of radio knobs, made in Japan, working, ca. 1960s, 3 1/2 x 6 1/4", 7" h. (some wear & soiling) **165**

Early Golden Sun Coffee Tin Scoop

Scoop, "Golden Sun Coffee," lithographed tin, spade-shaped w/rounded tab handle w/hanging hole, cream ground w/black wording reading "Use Navarre Steel Cut Golden Sun Coffee," early 20th c., unused, 1 3/4 x 4" (ILLUS.) **154**

Shirt, "Winchester," long-sleeved cotton hunting shirt in red w/black checks, each check printed w/the small image of a game animal, brass snaps marked "Winchester 30-30," made by Levi, size 16/33, ca. 1950 (minor fraying, small holes) **88**

Shop globe, "Beauty Shop," round black metal ring frame enclosing painted glass lenses, on a round foot, similar in design to gas pump globes, one side painted white on the interior & printed on the exterior w/"Beauty Shop" around the profile bust of a fashionable woman w/bobbed hair, other lens matching, ca. 1920s, 15" d. (one lens w/water staining to edge, small rust holes on body but paint removed & reprimed, slight soiling) **495**

Bottle-shaped Pepsi-Cola Radio

Radio, "Pepsi-Cola," tube-type, plastic upright bottle shape, looks like a full bottle w/two worn older Pepsi-Cola red, white & blue labels on the sides, set on deep plastic base, bottle cap is tuner, instructions on the bottom, ca. 1930s or 1940s, new cord, 8" d., 23 1/4" h. (ILLUS.) **303**

Recipe booklet, "Jell-O - America's Most Famous Dessert," paper, printed color cover of a fancily dressed woman entering the kitchen of a housewife pointing out her large Jell-O creation, factory scene on the back cover, early 1900s, 4 1/2 x 6" **66**

Beauty Shoppe Advertising Globe

Shop globe, "Hair Bobbing and Beauty Shoppe," round ring frame enclosing painted glass lenses, on a round foot, similar in design to gas pump globes, one side painted on the interior w/a large yellow circle within an orange ring, printed on the exterior w/"Hair Bobbing and Beauty Shoppe - Everything Sterilized," other lens w/similar interior color & printed in black "Ladies and Childrens Hair Cutting Shoppe," ca. 1920s, soiling, slight paint wear, 11 1/2" d., 5" deep, 12 1/2" h. (ILLUS.) **468**

Shop globe, "O'Sullivan's Shoe Repairing," milk glass, large bulbous globe raised on a round domed base, printed in red & green on one side "O'Sullivan's" & on the other side w/"O'Sullivan's Heels Attached - Expert Shoe Repairing," ca. 1920s or 1930s, 4 1/4 x 9 3/4", 12 1/2" h. (slight chipping around base cord hole, slight soiling, side w/name only repainted) **550**

Six-pack bottle holder, "Pepsi-Cola," unfolded cardboard printed in red, white & blue w/large early Pepsi-Cola logos, new-old stock, ca. 1930s-40s, flat 8 1/4 x 29 5/8" (very minor scattered wear) **33**

Rare Post Toasties String Dispenser

String dispenser, "Post Toasties," self-framed tin & metal, a large flat disk printed half in yellow & half in black, the upper yellow half w/a red rising sun & "Bully for Breakfast," lower black half w/"New Post Toasties," mount to support a spool of string behind disk & fitted w/metal strap handle, ca. 1916, overall rust spotting, ding to lower left, small dent at top center, 11 1/2" d. (ILLUS.) **710**

Thermometer, "7Up," tall narrow oval porcelain, white ground w/a large green pop bottle on the right side, red wording on the left side above & below the small thermometer reads "The 'fresh up' family drink - You like it...It likes you!," ca. 1950s, 6 x 15" (minor wear & chips) **176**

Thermometer, "B*1 Lemon-Lime," embossed tin, tall narrow rectangular form, background of blue & white horizontal stripes, printed in black at the top "More Zip in Every Sip," logo at bottom of thermometer, ca. 1950s, new-old stock, 4 5/8 x 16 3/8" **66**

CheerUp Round Thermometer

Thermometer, "CheerUp," glass & aluminum, round w/domed glass front over a white outer ring w/blue numbers enclosing a round reserve showing red & white wording in front of a bottle of the pop, wording reads "Drink CheerUp - A Sparkling Refresher," ca. 1950s, minor wear to case, slight soiling spots at center, 12" d. (ILLUS.) **138**

Thermometer, "Dad's Root Beer," embossed tin, tall rectangular form w/rounded corners, dark yellow ground printed at the left w/a very large color bottle of the pop beside the thermometer, black & red advertising at the top & bottom reads "Just Right...For Dad's - The Old Fashioned Root Beer," ca. 1940s, 9 3/4 x 25 5/8" (scattered nicks, flecks & scratches) **303**

Thermometer, "Doan's Pills," porcelain, long rectangular hanging-type, white ground printed at the top w/a half-length picture of a man above the thermometer beside advertising, further advertising in black at the bottom, early 20th c., 6 1/2 x 24" (chipping to edges)...................... **215**

Thermometer, "Dr. Pepper," glass & metal, round w/domed glass over border markings, yellow & white background w/oval red & white Dr. Pepper logo, reads "Hot or Cold Drink Dr. Pepper," 1960s, 12" d. (slight soiling) **358**

Thermometer, "Dr. Pepper," porcelain, long narrow rectangular form w/rounded ends & wider section near top, yellow round w/black clock dial logo at top above red rectangle w/Dr. Pepper logo over a large color image of the bottle enclosing the small thermometer, ca. 1930s, 5 x 17" (light wear, minor scratches, slightly darkened)... **341**

Thermometer, "Dr. Pepper," round metal & plastic, clear domed front over white dial w/blue & red Arabic numerals above red & blue wording & Dr. Pepper logo at bottom, reads "Hot or Cold," late 1950s - early 1960s, 12" d. **138**

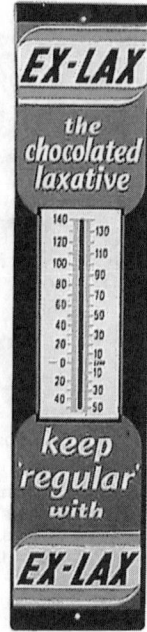

Tall Ex-Lax Thermometer

Thermometer, "EX-LAX," porcelain, long narrow rectangular form, large blue, black w/red & white bands at top & bottom, reads "EX-LAX - the chocolated laxative - keep 'regular' with EX-LAX," ca. 1920s, chips at top & bottom hole & edges, bulb cloudy, 8 1/4 x 36 1/4" (ILLUS.) **154**

Thermometer, "Five Roses Flour," porcelain, long narrow rectangular form w/rounded ends, dark red ground w/white wording "Buy Five Roses Flour - The All-purpose Flour," Canadian, ca. 1930s- 40s, 8 x 39" (small chip at mounting hole, light wear, minor marks, small edge chips) **242**

Thermometer, "Hires Root Beer," round tin & plastic, domed clear cover over a dark wood grained background w/white Arabic numerals around the top above the Hires logo in red, white & blue, ca. 1960s, 12" d. **88**

Thermometer, "International Ice Cream Co.," tall narrow rectangular porcelain w/rounded top, white ground w/black & red printing at top & bottom reading "International Ice Cream Co. - International Cream - Quality First/Always," ca. 1930s-40s, 7 x 27" (minor overall edge wear, chips & soiling, chip at top mount hole) **330**

Thermometer, "King Midas Flour," printed tin, tall narrow rectangular form w/rounded ends, black ground w/red & white wording & small image of girl in sunbonnet at the bottom, reads "King Midas Flour - King Midas Flour Mills - Minneapolis, Minnesota - The Highest Priced Flour in America and Worth All It Costs," ca. 1940s, few tiny sur-

face nicks, few small edge chips, 7 x 27" (ILLUS. below)... **825**

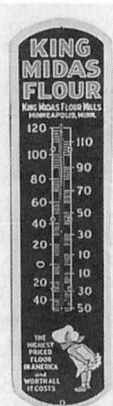

King Midas Flour Thermometer

Thermometer, "Lowney's Chocolate Bars and Cracker Jack," porcelain, tall flat rectangular shape, bright yellow ground w/black wording, ca. 1930s, 8 x 30 1/2" (slight soiling, water staining to sides) **259**

Thermometer, "Mason's Root Beer," round tin & plastic, domed clear front over dial w/narrow outer white band w/small black Arabic numerals, large center circle w/yellow ground & red & black advertising reading "Enjoy Mason's Root Beer - Bold refreshing flavor," ca. 1950s, 12" d. **132**

Nice Mission Orange Thermometer

Thermometer, "Mission Orange," embossed tin, tall rectangular form w/rounded corners, a large color bottle of the pop takes up all the center & encloses the thermometer, small blue panels at the top & bottom are printed in white "Mission Orange - Naturally Good," ca. 1950s, minor wear & edge bends, very minor scratches, 4 1/2 x 17" (ILLUS.) **550**

Thermometer, "Mower's Milk," celluloid, long oval form, printed at the top w/a sketch of a standing stork holding a baby in a diaper in its bill, company advertising & care tips printed in dark blue & red below, ca. 1930s or '40s, 2 x 6 1/2"................ **72**

Thermometer, "NuGrape Soda," round metal & plastic, domed clear front over white ground w/black Arabic numerals over black wording & color image of the bottle, reads "Have fun with (NuGrape) - Delicious Anytime!," ca. 1950s, 12" d. (paint wear, very minor scattered soiling & wear to case)................ **121**

Thermometer, "Orange Crush," painted metal, tall oval wall-mounted shape in black w/a large white & orange Orange Crush bottle cap at the top above the thermometer, ca. 1940s-50s, 5 3/4" w., 14 3/4" h. (overall surface rust) **99**

Thermometer, "Ox-Line Paints," round metal & glass, domed glass front over a white ground w/blue Arabic numerals above a large red center artist's palette w/orange & blue trim & wording, blue wording at bottom reads "Tomorrow's Paint Today," ca. 1950s, 12" d. **83**

Thermometer, "Pepsi-Cola," porcelain, long narrow rectangular form, black ground w/large color image of the bottle & white wording "Bigger - Better," ca. 1940s, 6 x 16" (minor wear at mounting holes, few tiny paint chips)................ **440**

Thermometer, "Pepsi-Cola," porcelain, long narrow rectangular form w/rounded ends, white center w/thermometer, black & white sections at top & bottom reading "Drink Pepsi-Cola - Big, Big Bottle - Pepsi-Cola...Hits the Spot Whether It's Cold or Whether It's Hot!," ca. 1940s, 7 x 27" (paint chip near top, other smaller chips & small scratches, light fading) **220**

Thermometer, "Royal Crown Cola," printed metal, long rectangular form w/rounded corners, red background, printed in white at the top "Drink Royal Crown Cola" above center tall yellow upward pointing arrow framing the thermometer, ca. 1953, 9 3/4 x 25 3/4" (slight surface rust, few dents) **105**

Thermometer, "Squirt," embossed tin, tall rectangular form w/rounded corners, white ground printed at the top w/a yellow lemon behind the red & white Squirt logo above a large green & yellow picture of a bottle on the right side & the head of the Squirt boy just at the top of the thermometer on the left, a small glass below the thermometer makes it appear the glass tube is forming a straw, ca. 1963, new-old stock, 5 7/8 x 13 1/2" **242**

Thermometer, "Sun Crest Beverages," round glass & metal, domed glass front over large face w/temperature gradients arched across the top in blue above advertising & large image of a bottle in dark blue & orange, reads "Get Tin-

gle*ated with Sun Crest ...all-weather refresher," mid-20th c., 12 1/4" d. (slight scratching & soiling)................ **88**

Thermometer, "Sun-Drop," round metal & plastic, domed plastic front, dark green ground centered by large yellow drop w/product name in large red letters, ca. 1960s, 12 1/4" d. (some soiling & scratching)................ **50**

Thermometer, "Whistle," glass & metal, round w/domed glass front over a white outer ring w/blue numbers enclosing a round reserve showing a large musical note & advertising in blue, orange & white, ca. 1962, 12" d. (very minor wear)...... **121**

Round Whistle Thermometer

Thermometer, "Whistle," glass & metal, round w/domed glass front over a white outer ring w/blue numbers enclosing a round reserve showing an elf pushing a cart w/a large bottle of the pop, wording in blue, white & red printed above & below image & reads "Thirsty? Just Whistle - Golden Orange Refreshment," ca. 1950s, minor field wear & tiny scratches, 12" d. (ILLUS.) **413**

Toy fountain dispenser, "Pepsi-Cola," plastic, rectangular model in white w/Pepsi-Cola bottle cap logo & name on sides & newer Pepsi logo & slogan at front, w/original cardboard & cellophane box, ca. 1960s, 4 3/4 x 10", 9 1/2" h. (some soiling, some wear to box w/tears in front panel) **71**

Toy kite, "Buster Brown Shoes," paper & wood, green paper printed in black w/"Buster Brown Shoes For Boys" above image of Buster & Tige, mid-20th c., 27 1/2" w., 34 1/4" h. (slight soiling & some overall wrinkling) **17**

Star-Kist Tuna Toy Truck

Toy truck, "Star-Kist Tuna," stamped steel, semi-style w/red cab & dark blue trailer w/red, white & black decal including image of can, black hard rubber tires, restored, ca. 1950s, 24" l. (ILLUS.) **220**

Indian Motorcycle Watch Fob

Watch fob, "Indian Motorcycles," stamped brass & enamel, relief-stamped bust of Indian Chief wearing colorful headdress, early 20th c., fob loop broken on one side, 1 3/4" h. (ILLUS.).................................. **380**

Watch fob, "Old Dutch Cleanser," porcelain & metal, small porcelain disk in yellow w/blue & white logo figure of Dutch girl chasing dirt, in metal frame suspended from a leather strap w/buckle, early 20th c., fob 1 1/2" d. (some chipping at edge, slight soiling)... **44**

Window display, "Chief Two Moon Bitter Oil," color-printed cardboard three-fold style, tall rectangular center panel w/arched top above the company name in large red letters above a moonlight scene of Niagara Falls w/ghost image of the Indian Chief in the sky, shorter curved-top side panels illustrate the product w/advertising & small color vignettes, ca. 1920s, 39 5/8 x 45 1/2" (minor soiling, paper loss in lower left)......... **259**

Window roller shade, "Winchester Rival Paper Shot Shells," h.p. vinyl, a large arched painted color center scene of hunting dogs in a field signed "Felicia Han," wording in red & black at the top & bottom edges, 20th c., 35 1/2 x 36" (few paint flakes) **1,320**

Grocery & Tavern Winterfront

Winterfront, "Strawhun's Grocery & Tavern - Coalfield, Wash.," waxed cardboard, shield-form w/a black ground printed at the top center w/a large red lion head above the advertising in white block letters, ca. 1940s, very minor soiling & wear, 17 3/4 x 19" (ILLUS.)............................ **110**

ARCHITECTURAL ITEMS

In recent years the growing interest in and support for historic preservation has spawned a greater appreciation of the fine architectural elements that were an integral part of early building, both public and private. Where, in decades past, structures might be razed and doors, fireplace mantels, windows, etc., hauled to the dump, today all interior and exterior details from unrestorable buildings are salvaged to be offered to home restorers, museums and even builders who want to include a bit of history in a new construction project.

Building finial, molded & painted sheet metal, a tall spiraling flame above four radiating Gothic-style scrolling foliate corbels at the base, weathered old silver paint, supported by wooden platform base, American, 19th c., 27" w., 69 1/2" h. (imperfections) **$546**

Building pediment, carved wood, a triangular panel mounted w/central masque & foliate carving, natural surface, America, late 19th c., 78" l., 19 1/2" h............................ **920**

Faux Marble Mantelpieces

Chimney top, terra-cotta, molded oval peaked cap w/three tiers of smoke vents above a spiraled oval column on a rectangular base, incised mark "Terra Cotta Co. 394 Federal St., Boston 1880," 11 1/2 x 14 1/2", 37 1/2" h. **1,265**

Lion's head ornament on fragment, copper w/old verdigris, w/mouth open as if roaring, soldered seams w/seven small holes drilled around edges for mounting & slightly larger hole in mouth, 13" h. **330**

Mantel, faux marble w/original grey-green paint w/white veining, the projecting shelf above molding & rectangular capitals on pilasters & plinths, probably Vermont, early 19th c., paint wear, 49 1/4" h. x 61" w., 6 1/2" d. (ILLUS. left, bottom previous page) **999**

Mantel, faux marble w/original white paint w/grey veining, rectangular shelf above cove molding & flanking rectangular capitals on pilasters & plinths, probably Vermont, early 19th c., surface wear, 48 1/4" h. x 60" w., 6 3/4" d. (ILLUS. right, bottom previous page) **705**

Mantel, painted pine w/old brown over tan graining, raised pilasters & facing above the opening, the shaped molded top w/rounded edges, square nail construction, 10 x 61 3/4", 51 3/4" h. (few small sections of molding missing) **193**

Model of a dove, cast iron, traces of white paint, New England, early 19th c., 8 1/4 x 12" (imperfections) **978**

ART DECO

Interest in Art Deco, a name given an art movement stemming from the Paris International Exhibition of 1925, continues to grow today. This style flowered in the 1930s and actually continued into the 1940s. A mood of flippancy is found in its varied characteristics - zigzag lines resembling the lightning bolt, sometimes steps, often the use of sharply contrasting colors such as black and white and others. Look for prices for the best examples of Art Deco design to continue to rise. Also see JEWELRY, MODERN.

Airbrush piece titled "The Hunt"

Artwork, airbrush piece, titled "The Hunt," unsigned stencil airbrush design, ca. 1930s, 36" (ILLUS.) **$350-400**

Ash stand, chrome, globe opens on blue square base, Chase Chrome, 3 x 4" (ILLUS. top of page) **75-95**

Chrome Globe Ash Stand

Art Deco Ashtray with Cigarette Box

Ashtray, brass w/silver, ashtray w/cigarette box, brass w/silver horse design, Silver Crest, 4 x 8" (ILLUS.) **75-100**

Figural Scottie Dog Ashtray

Ashtray, bronze-tone metal, figural Scottie dog, Frankart, ca. 1930s, 5 1/2" h. (ILLUS.) **100-150**

Woman with Headdress Ashtray

Ashtray, bronzed pot metal, model of woman w/headdress, 6" (ILLUS.) **90-120**

Ceramic Cat Ashtray

Ashtray, ceramic, black & white, black cat design, Kenwood, USA, ca. 1940s, 12" (ILLUS.)... **30-40**

Nuart Figural Nude Ashtray

Ashtray, pot metal, nude figure holding bowl, Nuart, ca. 1920s-30s, 6" l. (ILLUS.).. **195-250**

Jester with Mandolin Ashtray

Ashtray, pot metal, model of jester w/mandolin, 5 x 6" h. (ILLUS.)................................ **45-65**

Woman Holding Scales Book End

Book ends, brass, brass squares w/woman holding scales, PM Craftsman, 5 x 5 " h., pr. (ILLUS. of one).. **50-75**

Figural Kneeling Nudes Book Ends

Book ends, cast metal, figural kneeling nudes, Bronzart, ca. 1920s-30s., 7" h., pr., (ILLUS.).. **125-155**

Art Deco Chalkware Nudes on Rock

Book ends, chalkware, nudes on rock, 6 1/2" h., pr. (ILLUS.) **65-85**

Book ends, chrome, scroll design, curled chrome w/Bakelite end, ca. 1935, 4 1/2" h., pr. **20-30**

Book End with Chrome Scottie Dog

Book ends, chrome, rounded black book end w/chrome figural Scottie dog, Ronson, ca. 1930s, 4" h., pr. (ILLUS. of one) **40-50**

Art Deco "Scottie" Book End

Book ends, metal, Art Deco "Scottie" book ends, 5 1/2" h., pr. (ILLUS. of one) **100-150**

Rearing Horse Book End

Book ends, metal, figural horse rearing, angular design, 8" h., pr. (ILLUS. of one)....... **40-65**

Figural Metal Pheasant Book End

Book ends, metal, figural metal pheasants on marble bases, ca. 1920s, 7" h., pr. (ILLUS. of one).. **75-125**

Book End with White Horse

Book ends, metal, grey squared base w/white horse, 1920s-30s, 4 1/4 " h., pr. (ILLUS. of one).. **25-30**

Art Deco Camera with Box

Camera, camera w/box, geometric design by Walter Dorwin Teague for Kodak, ca. 1930 (ILLUS.)...................................... **1,800-2,400**

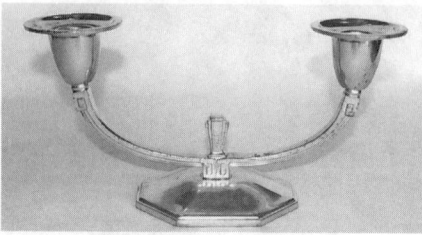

Farberware Chrome Candlestick

Candlestick, chrome, duet design, Farberware, 4 x 6" h. (ILLUS.) **30-50**

Art Deco Chrome Candlestick

Candlestick, chrome, flat chrome nude on round marble base, 9" h. (ILLUS.).......... **100-140**

Art Deco Black Wire Candlesticks

Candlesticks, black wire w/gold tops, ca. 1930s, 7" h., pr. (ILLUS.).............................. **8-12**

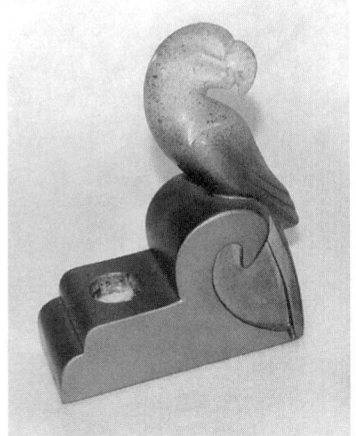

Chalkware Parrot Candlestick

Candlesticks, painted chalkware parrots, 6" h., pr. (ILLUS. of one)............................. **35-55**
Candlesticks, square tiered Manhattan style, Frederick Priess for Revere, ca. 1937, 3 1/2" h., pr. **75-90**

Chrome Candy dish

Candy dish, chrome w/Bakelite handle, 6" h. (ILLUS.)... **10-15**

Frankart Figural Nude Candy Dish

Candy dish, metal, black painted metal nude holds turquoise glass dish, Frankart, ca. 1930s (ILLUS.) **175-250**

Chiltery Jug Carafe

Carafe, Chiltery Jug, Acme Vacuum & Flask Co., 10 1/2" h. (ILLUS.) **40-50**

Cigarette Case with Native Design

Cigarette case, silver plate, cigarette case w/"native" design, ca. 1920s-1930s, 2 x 3" h. (ILLUS.)... **50-70**

General Electric Alarm Clock

Clock, electric alarm clock, peach colored mirror glass frame, General Electric, 5 x 5" h. (ILLUS.)... **75-95**

Electric Westclox Clock

Clock, electric, black w/gold feet, Westclox,
4 1/4" h. (ILLUS.) **30-40**

Marble Clock & Matching Book Ends

Clock, marble clock w/metal deer ornaments, matching book ends, France,
23 1/2" l., the set (ILLUS.) **750-950**

Chrome Coffee Service Set

Coffee service: cov. coffee urn, cov. sugar,
creamer, handled tray; chrome, Farber
Brothers, the set (ILLUS.)............................ **35-50**

"Coronet" Chrome Globe Coffeepot

Coffeepot, cov., chrome, "Coronet" globe
by Walter Von Nessen for Chase
(ILLUS.).. **350-400**

Labelle Silver Company Coffeepot

Coffeepot, cov., chrome globe w/black trim
handle, Labelle Silver Co., 15 1/2" h.
(ILLUS.) **70-90**

Coffeepot by Manning Bowman

Coffeepot, cov., chrome globe w/gold
Bakelite accents, Manning Bowman,
14 1/2" h. (ILLUS.)................................... **150-175**

Tricorne Pattern Console Set

Chase Chrome Creamer and Sugar Set

Console set: plate, cup & saucer; ceramic, Tricorne pattern in Mandarin Orange, Salem China, ca. 1930s (ILLUS.) **12-20**

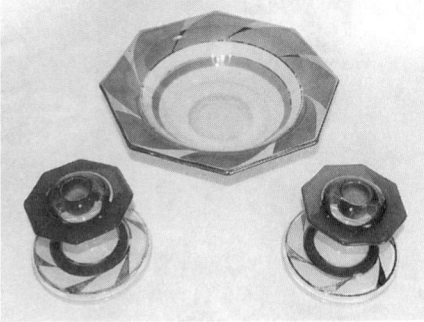

Painted Glass Console Set

Console set, wide bowl & pair of candlesticks, blue & white painted glass, 3 1/4" h., the set (ILLUS.) **65-85**

Chrome Creamer and Sugar Set

Creamer & open sugar bowl, chrome, Manning Bowman, 5" h., the set (ILLUS.).. **35-45**
Creamer, open sugar & tray, chrome, Chase Chrome, 11 1/2" l., the set (ILLUS. top of page) **75-115**

Ribbed Glass Dresser Jar

Dresser jar, cov., ribbed glass w/green top, 4" h. (ILLUS.) **20-35**

Combination Fan/Heater

Fan/Heater electric, combination-style, green-painted metal & chrome, Arvin, ca. 1940s-50s, 12 x 16" (ILLUS.) **40-60**

Chrome Nude on Black Base

Figure of a woman, chrome nude female on black base, by Ronson, 14" (ILLUS.) **300-350**

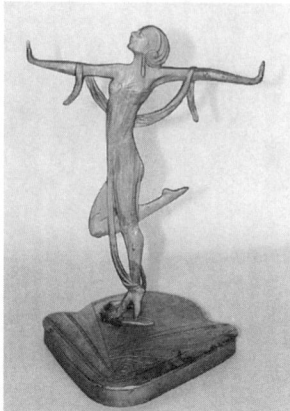

Dancing Woman by W.B. Mfg.

Figure of a woman, gold-washed metal dancing woman, W.B. Manufacturing, 10" h. (ILLUS.)... **150-200**

Frameless Glass Frame with Border

Frame, frameless glass style, black & gold flower border, 10 x 12" h. (ILLUS.)............ **40-50**

Black Ray Pattern Glass Frame

Frame, reverse-painted glass, black ray pattern on white, metal corners, 3 x 5" h. (ILLUS.)... **35-45**

Reverse-Painted Glass Frame

Frame, reverse-painted glass, black w/white inner border, 3 x 5" (ILLUS.) **35-45**

White Reverse-Painted Glass Frame

Frame, reverse-painted glass, white w/corner line decoration, 3 x 5" h. (ILLUS.) **35-45**

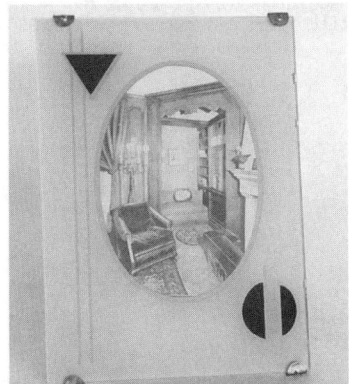

Geometric Design Glass Frame

Frame, reverse-painted glass, white w/gold & black geometric design, 3 x 5" h (ILLUS.) **35-45**

Jewelry Box with Glass Cover

Jewelry box, cov., wood base w/reverse-painted glass cover decorated w/image of a dancing nude, ca. 1920s-30s, 10 1/4" h. (ILLUS.) **65-85**

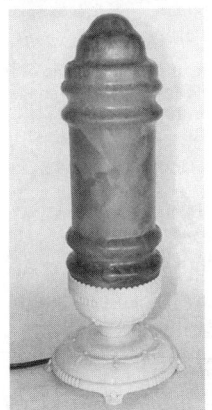

Blue Glass Boudoir Lamp

Lamp, boudoir-type, blue glass ringed cylinder shade on a white celluloid molded base on short feet, ca. 1930s, 12" h. (ILLUS.) **40-60**

Frosted Glass Boudoir Lamp

Lamp, boudoir-type, frosted glass paneled cylindrical shade w/finial, on a hexagonal tiered footed base, ca. 1920s-30s, 11 1/2" h. (ILLUS.) **100-150**

Aluminum & Glass Boudoir Lamp

Lamp, boudoir-type, white glass cylindrical ribbed shade w/aluminum base & domed stepped top, ca. 1920s-30s, 10 1/2" h. (ILLUS.) **35-50**

Figural Bronzed Cast-Iron Lamp

Lamp, bronzed cast iron, figural standing nude w/arched glass globe shade, ca. 1920s, 15 1/2" h., (ILLUS.)..................... **250-350**

Egyptian Deco Bronzed Metal Lamp

Lamp, bronzed metal, figural Egyptian design of a kneeling woman holding up spherical-shaped glass globe made up of quadrilateral forms, ca. 1920s, 16 1/2" h. (ILLUS.) **175-225**

Bronzed Metal Figural Nude Lamp

Lamp, bronzed metal, figural seated nude woman holding an amber glass globe shade, ca. 1930s, 7 1/2" x 8 1/2" h. (ILLUS.)... **350-400**

Gold Painted Chalkware Nude Lamp

Lamp, chalkware, gold painted chalkware nude w/stained glass backdrop, 14" h. (ILLUS.)... **235-275**

Figural Art Deco Lamp with Ashtray

Lamp, chrome, metal nude leans over ashtray, w/milk glass globe shade (not original), ca. 1920s, 14" h. (ILLUS.) **225-275**

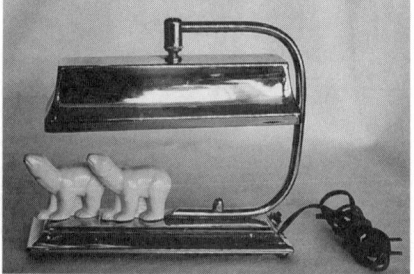

Chrome Desk Lamp with Polar Bears

Lamp, chrome, w/two ceramic polar bears on the rectangular base, C-form shaft holds light unit w/molded rectangular shade parallel to base, ca. 1930s, 8 x 9" h. (ILLUS.) **125-150**

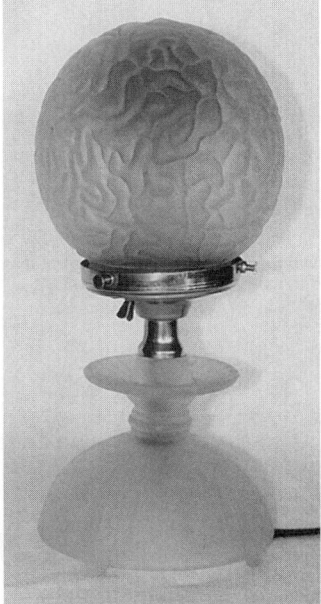

Frosted Glass Globe Lamp

Lamp, frosted glass globe shade w/abstract embossed design on frosted base, 11" h. (ILLUS. of lamp w/red bulb) **135-165**

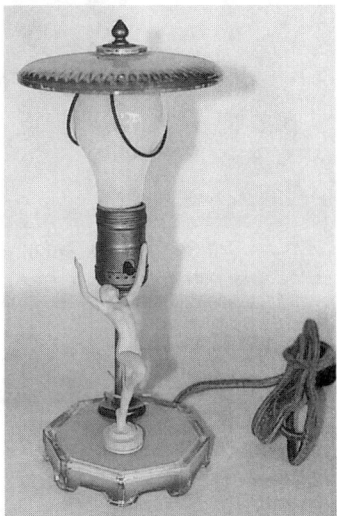

Art Deco Lamp with Figural Dancer

Lamp, green & white, w/nude dancer on octagonal base w/eight short feet, disk shade w/finial fits atop bulb, ca. 1930s, 11" (ILLUS.) **75-100**

Circular Iron "Rhythm" Lamp

Lamp, iron w/stained glass, titled "Rhythm," ring frame w/nude female figure in center, over stained glass backdrop, 8" h. (ILLUS.).. **150-200**

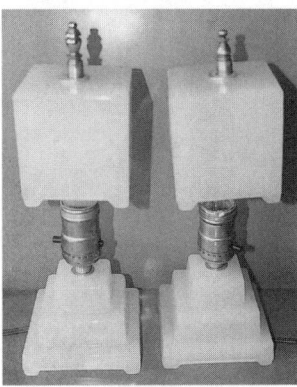

Milk Glass Boudoir Lamps

Lamps, boudoir-type, milk glass, cube-form shades, square stepped bases, 10" h., pr. (ILLUS.).. **80-120**
Mirror, geometric painted glass, square w/pyramid-shaped top, Atlas Glass, 26".. **75-100**

Swan Design on Round Mirror

Mirror, glass, round swan design w/cobalt glass insert, ca. 1930s, 29 1/2" (ILLUS.).. **300-350**

Makeup Mirror with Seal Silhouette

Mirror, makeup-type, Bakelite seal silhouette mounted on the round mirror, wood base, 8 x 11" (ILLUS.)................................. **68-80**

Brass Penguin

Model of a penguin, brass, 5 1/2" h. (ILLUS.) **15-20**

Chrome Figural Squirrel Nutcracker

Nutcracker, chrome, figural squirrel, 5 3/4" (ILLUS.) **20-25**

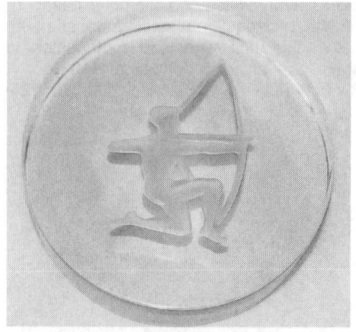

Intaglio-Etched Glass Paperweight

Paperweight, etched glass w/a design of an archer, marked "Intaglio," 4" (ILLUS.) **35-50**

Chrome Scottie Dog Pipe Caddy

Pipe caddy, black base w/chrome Scottie dog, 6" (ILLUS.) **50-75**

Figural Fish Design Pipe Caddy

Pipe caddy, silver plate, figural fish design, Seba, 3 1/2 x 4 1/2 " (ILLUS.)................. **100-120**

Art Deco Walnut Pipe Caddy

Pipe caddy, walnut rectangular base & square cov. caddy decorated on side w/nude silhouette, Craft Guild, ca. 1930s, 6 x 11 1/2 " (ILLUS.)........................ **40-60**

"HotaKold" Thermos Pitcher

Pitcher, cov., thermos-type, w/angled handle, pink "HotaKold" model by Manning Bowman, ca. 1930s, 10" h. (ILLUS.) **60-75**

Metal Angel Holding Torch Plaque

Plaque, metal, rectangular w/slightly domed top, figure of angel holding torch embossed on front, 4 1/2" x 8" (ILLUS.).......... **60-80**

Seafoam Green Glass Powder Dish

Powder dish, cov., round, seafoam green glass w/gold accents, ca. 1930s, 4 7/8" (ILLUS.).. **40-45**

Chrome Relish Dish Bakelite Handle

Relish dish, chrome, circular base w/Bakelite handle in center, 8" (ILLUS.).... **12-18**
Salt & pepper shakers, chrome, large & small spheres, Russel Wright for Chase Chrome, ca. 1937... **60-80**

"Martini" Design Smoking Set

Smoking set: ashtray, cigarette holder & lighter; chrome, "Martini" design widely flaring at top, disk base, Sollingen, Germany, ca. 1950s, the set (ILLUS.) **75-95**

Chrome and Black Glass Smoking Stand

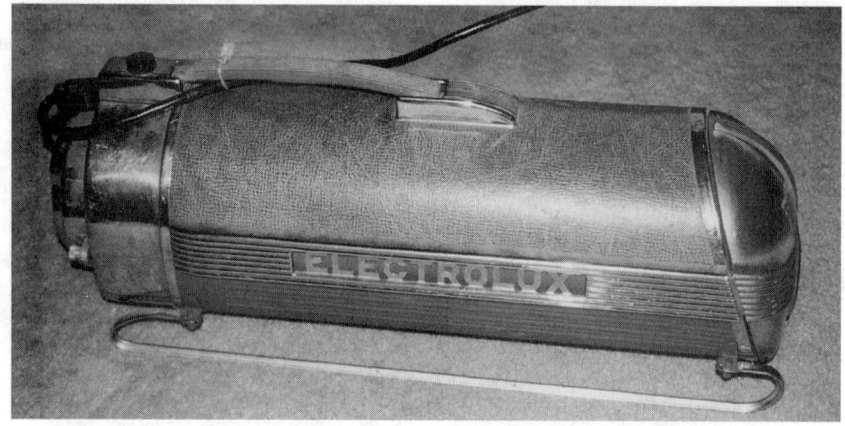

Electrolux Vacuum Cleaner

Smoking stand, electric, chrome & black glass, stepped base, w/accessories, Chaplick (ILLUS.) **300-450**

Tray, drinks-type, round metal w/square lattice background design & a square panel in center w/illustration of a woman dancing under a tree, 12 1/2" (ILLUS.) **25-35**

Vacuum cleaner, Electrolux, canister type, designed by Lurelle Guild, ca. 1937 (ILLUS., top of page) **75-100**

Green Glass Syrup Pitcher

Syrup pitcher, cov., green glass w/chrome top, Gemco, 6" h. (ILLUS.) **20-25**

Toaster, chrome & Bakelite, rounded top, Sunbeam Toaster T-9, ca. 1930s-40s **75-125**

Pink Ceramic Vase

Vase, ceramic, pink w/drip glaze, ca. 1930s-40s, 8 1/2" h. (ILLUS.) **5-10**

Manning Bowman Waffle Iron

Waffle iron, chrome w/Bakelite handles, circular form, Manning Bowman, 4 x 12" (ILLUS.) **50-75**

Art Deco Round Metal Drink Tray

Wall sconces, glass & bronze, a diamond-shaped frosted glass insert w/raised geometric design in a V-shaped nickled bronze mount, France, ca. 1930, 5 1/4" w., 14 1/4" h., pr. (minor wear to slip).. **863**

Watering can, chrome, half-round shape w/long spout, Revere, ca. 1937, 2 qt., 7 3/4" h. **75-95**

AUDUBON PRINTS

John James Audubon, American ornithologist and artist, is considered the finest nature artist in history. In about 1820 he conceived the idea of having a full color book published portraying every known species of American bird in its natural habitat. He spent years in the wilderness capturing their beauty in vivid color only to have great difficulty finding a publisher. In 1826 he visited England, received immediate acclaim, and selected Robert Havell as his engraver. "Birds of America," when completed, consisted of four volumes of 435 individual plates, double-elephant folio size, which are a combination of aquatint, etching and line engraving. W.H. Lizars of Edinburgh engraved the first ten plates of this four-volume series. These were later retouched by Havell, who produced the complete set between 1827 and early 1839. In the 1840s, another definitive work, "Viviparous Quadrupeds of North America," containing 150 plates, was published in America. Prices for Audubon's original double-elephant folio size prints are very high and beyond the means of the average collector. Subsequent editions of "Birds of America," especially the chromolithographs done by Julius Bien in New York (1859-60) and the smaller octavo (7 x 10 1/2") edition of prints done by J.T. Bowen of Philadelphia in the 1840s, are those that are most frequently offered for sale.

Anyone interested in Audubon prints needs to be aware that many photographically produced copies of the prints have been issued during this century for use on calendars or as decorative accessories, so it is best to check with a print expert before spending a large sum on an Audubon purported to be from an early edition.

American Redstart

American Redstart - Plate 40, hand-colored etching, engraving & aquatint by Robert Havell, Jr., London, 1827-38, few pale fox marks, minor soiling, 19 5/8 x 25 5/8" (ILLUS.)........................... **$2,233**

Baltimore Oriole - Plate 12, hand-colored etching, engraving & aquatint by Robert Havell, Jr., London, 1823-38, 25 3/4 x 38 3/4" (reinforced central horizontal fold, small margin edge repairs, minor soiling)... **15,275**

Bewick's Wren - Plate XVIII, hand-colored etching, engraving & aquatint by Robert Havell, Jr., London, 1827-38, 19 3/4 x 25 3/4" (minor soiling, one pale fox mark, few soft creases)........................ **1,116**

The Bird of Washington Print

Bird of Washington (The) - Plate 11, hand-colored etching, engraving & aquatint by Robert Havell, Jr., London, 1827-38, closely trimmed, reinforced central horizontal fold, minor soiling, two small repaired margin tears, 25 3/4 x 38 7/8" (ILLUS.).. **6,463**

Blue Winged Yellow Warbler - Plate 20, hand-colored etching, engraving & aquatint by Robert Havell, Jr., London, 1827-38, 19 3/4 x 25 3/4" (minor soiling, few soft creases)... **9,400**

Children's Warbler - Plate 35, hand-colored etching, engraving & aquatint by Robert Havell, Jr., London, 1827-38, 19 5/8 x 25 3/4" (few very pale fox marks, faint soiling) **1,116**

Cow Bunting - Plate 99, hand-colored etching, engraving & aquatint by Robert Havell, Jr., London, 1827-38, 19 7/8 x 25 5/8" (slightly rubbed along plate mark)... **1,116**

Great Carolina Wren - Plate 78, hand-colored etching, engraving & aquatint by Robert Havell, Jr., London, 1823-38, 19 1/2 x 25 3/4" (lettering below image slightly faded, few pale fox marks, few soft creases)... **1,880**

Green Black-Capt Flycatcher - Plate CXX-IV, hand-colored etching, engraving & aquatint by Robert Havell, Jr., London, 1827-38, 19 7/8 x 25 5/8" (minor surface soiling) **1,293**

Hooded Warbler - Plate CX, hand-colored etching, engraving & aquatint by Robert Havell, Jr., London, 1823-38, 19 7/8 x 25 5/8".. **1,880**

House Wren

House Wren - Plate 83, hand-colored etching, engraving & aquatint by Robert Havell, Jr., London, 1827-38, few pale fox marks, 20 1/4 x 25 5/8" (ILLUS.)................. **3,290**

Indigo-Bird - Plate 74, hand-colored etching, engraving & aquatint by Robert Havell, Jr., London, 1827-38, 19 3/4 x 25 5/8" (few pale fox marks, few soft creases, minor soiling) **5,288**

Kentucky Warbler

Kentucky Warbler - Plate 38, hand-colored etching, engraving & aquatint by Robert Havell, Jr., London, 1827-38, few pale fox marks, minor soiling, 19 5/8 x 25 3/4" (ILLUS.)... **3,055**

Le Petit Corporal - Plate 75, hand-colored etching, engraving & aquatint by Robert Havell, Jr., London, 1827-38, 19 5/8 x 25 3/4" (few pale fox marks, soft creases, minor soiling)................................ **2,233**

Marsh Wren - Plate 98, hand-colored etching, engraving & aquatint by Robert Havell, Jr., London, 1827-38, 19 7/8 x 25 5/8" (very minor surface soiling)......................... **1,410**

Maryland Yellow Throat - Plate 23, hand-colored etching, engraving & aquatint by Robert Havell, Jr., London, 1827-38, 19 3/4 x 25 3/4" (slight rubbing, minor margin soiling)..................................... **2,233**

Mississippi Kite - Plate CXVII, hand-colored etching, engraving & aquatint by Robert Havell, Jr., London, 1827-38, 25 5/8 x 39" (reinforced central horizontal fold, few pale fox marks, minor soiling).. **2,585**

Nashville Warbler - Plate 89, hand-colored etching, engraving & aquatint by Robert Havell, Jr., London, 1823-38, 19 7/8 x 25 5/8" (some rubbing at plate mark) **1,116**

Orchard Oriole - Plate 42, hand-colored etching, engraving & aquatint by Robert Havell, Jr., London, 1827-38, 25 5/8 x 38 3/8" (reinforced central horizontal fold, pale foxing, paper weak in left corner, minor soiling & soft creases)......... **2,820**

Painted Bunting

Painted Bunting - Plate 53, hand-colored etching, engraving & aquatint by Robert Havell, Jr., London, 1827-38, few pale fox marks, minor soiling, 19 11/16 x 25 3/4" (ILLUS.)............................. **7,050**

Pigeon Hawk - Plate 92, hand-colored etching, engraving & aquatint by Robert Havell, Jr., London, 1827-38, 25 5/8 x 38 3/4" (reinforced central horizontal fold, very pale offsetting, very pale fox marks)............ **2,233**

Yellow Bird or American Goldfinch

Prairie Warbler - Plate 14, hand-colored etching, engraving & aquatint by Robert Havell, Jr., London, 1827-38, 19 3/4 x 25 3/4" (some minor soiling, one small fox mark, some soft creases) **1,763**

Prothonotary Warbler - Plate III, hand-colored etching, engraving & aquatint by Robert Havell, Jr., London, 1827-38, 20 x 25 3/4" (scattered minor soiling, few tiny fox marks in margins) **1,528**

Purple Finch - Plate IV, hand-colored etching, engraving & aquatint by Robert Havell, Jr., London, 1827-38, 19 3/4 x 25 3/4" (very minor soiling, several soft creases) **1,998**

Rathbone's Warbler - Plate 65, hand-colored etching, engraving & aquatint by Robert Havell, Jr., London, 1827-38, 19 5/8 x 25 3/4" (small tear in lower edge, few pale fox marks, minor soiling) **5,640**

Red-Breasted Nuthatch - Plate CV, hand-colored etching, engraving & aquatint by Robert Havell, Jr., London, 1827-38, 19 7/8 x 25 5/8" (very minor surface soiling) **1,116**

Solitary Flycatcher - Plate 28, hand-colored etching, engraving & aquatint by Robert Havell, Jr., London, 1827-38, 19 13/16 x 25 3/4" (minor soiling, few pale margin fox marks).................................... **1,410**

Tyrant Flycatcher - Plate 79, hand-colored etching, engraving & aquatint by Robert Havell, Jr., London, 1827-38, 19 5/8 x 25 3/4" (pale foxing, two handling creases in corner, tiny tear at right edge, minor soiling).................................... **1,410**

Vigors Vireo - Plate 30, hand-colored etching, engraving & aquatint by Robert Havell, Jr., London, 1827-38, 19 13/16 x 25 3/4" (tiny center fox mark, very minor soiling, one corner creased)..... **2,233**

White Throated Sparrow - Plate VIII, hand-colored etching, engraving & aqua-

tint by R. Havell, Jr., 1823-38, 19 7/8 x 25 3/4" (minor soiling, several soft creases)................................. **2,820**

Yellow Billed Cuckoo - Plate II, hand-colored etching, engraving & aquatint by W.H. Lizars, 26 3/4 x 39" (minor soiling, reworked title, several tears w/some repairs).. **3,760**

Yellow Bird or American Goldfinch - Plate 33, hand-colored etching, engraving & aquatint by Robert Havell, Jr., London, 1827-38, minor soiling, small stain in bottom margin, few soft creases, 19 3/4 x 25 3/4" (ILLUS., top of previous column) **11,163**

AUTOGRAPHS

Beauregard, P.G.T. (1818-1893), Brigadier General of the Confederate Provisional Army, placed in command at Charleston, where he ordered the bombardment of Fort Sumter, ink signature, off-white slip, clipped from larger document 3 1/2 x 1", double matted with glossy photo of the general in uniform, fine condition, overall 9 x 15" **$253**

Bliss, Tasker (1853-1930), first commander of the U.S. War College, fountain pen signature, on an off-white card, fine condition, 2 x 3 .... **58**

Bradley, Omar (1893-1981), impressive matte-finish photo of Bradley in dress uniform, signed in blue ink in lower border, fine condition, 7 1/2 x 9 1/2" **215**

Custer, George A. (1836-1876), well-known general who lost his life at the Battle of The Little Bighorn, signed letter **6,958**

Doolittle, James (1896-1993), noted World War II Allied officer, matte-finish photo of Doolittle in full dress uniform, signed in blue ballpoint, fine condition, light wrinkling on top, 8 x 10" **70**

Groves, Leslie (1896-1970), Army officer who headed the Manhattan Project to develop the atomic bomb, matte-finish photo of Graves at desk, signed in black ink, fine condition, 4 x 6"... **144**

Hitler, Adolph (1889-1945), leader of the Third Reich, postcard photo of Hitler saluting from a reviewing stand w/Nazi emblem flying behind him, signed in fountain pen, fine condition **1,150**

Ley, Robert (1890-1945), head of the German Labor Front who plundered the pensions & unions & eventually committed suicide while awaiting trial in Nuremberg, vintage German postcard photo of Ley conferring with another officer, signed in fountain pen, fine condition, 3 1/2 x 5 1/4"... **1,945**

MacArthur, Douglas (1880-1964), fountain pen signature on an off-white card, dated 1950, fine condition w/light crease to tip of lower right corner, 3 x 5"........................... **170**

MacDonough, Thomas (1783-1825), naval officer who served in Tripolitan War, built and commanded small fleet on Lake Champlain during the War of 1812, ink signature on off-white slip clipped from a larger letter, scattered light toning & soiling, fine condition, 1 1/2 x 5".......................... **115**

AUTOMOTIVE COLLECTIBLES

Alarm clock, "Cadillac," metal & glass electric light-up table model, horizontal grey metal case w/clear glass over rectangular dial w/Arabic numerals, Cadillac emblem in center, working, ca. 1950s, 8 1/4 x 9 1/2" (some soiling) **$55**

Armband, "Standard Oil Products," oval cardboard, tan ground printed w/a large orange letter "O" behind a cartoon figure of a beaver w/a football representing the Orange State College football team, small blue Standard Oil logo below, part of a series for West Coast schools, ca. 1930s, 5 x 6 3/4" (minor wear at holes, tiny pin hole at top center).............................. **143**

Champion Spark Plugs Ashtray

Ashtray, "Champion Spark Plugs," white round dished base of Stillimanite insulator material centered by an upright spark plug, wording in blue around the outside base w/red Champion logo, ca. 1920s-30s, metal on spark plug rusty, minor wear on base, 4 1/4" d. (ILLUS.).................... **121**

Mobil Oil Company Figural Ashtray

Ashtray, "Mobil Oil Company," cast metal, oblong flat-bottomed form w/round deep ashtray at one end, the projecting opposite end mounted w/a copper-colored

model of the rearing Pegasus emblem, dark grey w/narrow copper-colored banding at the ends, ca. 1930s-40s, 3 3/4 x 5 1/2", 3 3/4" h. (ILLUS.) **259**

Early Texaco Marine Ashtray

Ashtray, "Texaco Marine," china, round dish w/flattened rim indented w/three cigarette rests, white w/green edge stripes, the center w/a tiny dark green flag decorated w/the Texaco star logo, ca. 1930s, 6" d. (ILLUS.)... **220**

Attendant's hat, "Sunset Oil Company," cloth garrison-style, dark yellow printed in dark blue w/"Sunset Ethyl Gasoline - Sunset Oil Company," size 6 7/8, ca. 1930s... **248**

Award piece, "Texaco," wood & pewter, desktop rectangular block of wood w/wide chamfered sides supporting a cast pewter model of an early Texaco gas station, 7 x 11", 6 1/2" h. (slight soiling) **308**

Badge, "Ford - Willow Run - Guard," silvered metal w/center round blue & white porcelain Ford logo, a spread-winged eagle at the top, a narrow scroll & rectangular panel at the bottom, ca. 1930s, 2 7/8" w., 3" h. (slight wear)............................. **50**

Bank, "Shell," figural plastic, model of the yellow Shell cockle logo shell w/red lettering, ca. 1950s, 2 x 4", 4" h. **94**

Bank, "Texaco," figural molded plastic, model of a standing fat man in green Texaco station attendant's uniform w/red star logo, plug in back, ca. 1950s, 5" h. (minor wear to decals)... **143**

Texaco Fire Chief Pump Bank

Bank, "Texaco Fire Chief," figural metal, realistic model of an early red gas pump w/milk glass globe on the top, complete w/realistic hose & nozzle at one side, Texaco & Fire Chief decals, w/original red, white & blue box w/comic gas station attendants, reads "Ideal's Replica of a Real Texaco Gas Pump - Bank," ca. 1930s, soiling to decals, wear to globe face, puncture in side of box, bank 9" h. (ILLUS.) **330**

Bank, "Texaco Fire Chief," figural plastic, dark grey model of a gas pump w/red, green, white & black Texaco Fire Chief decal, ca. 1950s, 4 5/8" h. (crazing & wear to decal, missing hose) **110**

Banner, "Dixcel Gasoline," rectangular cloth, one-sided, white ground printed in red, black & green, two robins perched on a branch at the left, orange, black & white company round logo at the lower right, wording in white & black reads "It's Spring... Time to Change to (Dixcel) - Warm Weather Lubricant," ca. 1950s, apparently unused, 33 3/4 x 57 1/4" **126**

Banner, "Super Pyro Anti-Freeze," rectangular cloth, printed w/a large red oval w/white wording being held at the left by a large white snowman, white band at bottom reads "Peace of Mind Protection at 25¢ Quart," appears to be new-old stock, ca. 1950s, 24 x 36" (stains at center) **33**

Hoppe Ambulance Bill Hook

Bill hook, "Private Ambulance - Hoppe," oval celluloid button on a long hooked wire w/a small hanging loop at the top, wide center band w/a sepia tone image of an early ambulance-hearse, black panels above & below w/white wording reading "Private Ambulance Hoppe - Progressive Funeral Service - 2742 Lincoln Ave....Phone Buckingham 6681," ca. 1920s, minor wear & scratches, 2 x 2 3/4" pin (ILLUS. of hook & close-up) **99**

Blotter, "Pan-Am Gasoline - Motor Oils," rectangular heavy paper, top printed in red, black & white on a grey ground w/an image of an early seaplane flying above waves, round red, black & white company logo at right, white wording below

plane reads "Keep Pace with Pan-Am Gasoline," 1920s, 3 x 6 1/4" (some soiling, corner crease) **72**

Blotter, "Texaco Motor Oil," printed paper, long rectangular form, printed in color w/a large 1920s roadster racing through the countryside, red & blue printing at top reads "Texaco Motor Oil - Will help you take the steepest hill on high," ca. 1920s, 3 x 6" (very minor corner wear) **154**

Early Texaco Motor Oil Blotter

Blotter, "Texaco Motor Oil," rectangular lithographed paperboard, printed in color w/a close-up scene of an early gas station mechanic checking under a hood w/the Texaco red star sign in the background, advertising on the right in black & red wording, ca. 1920s, 3 1/2 x 6" (ILLUS.) **121**

Texaco Bulletin Designs Booklet

Booklet, "Texaco Painted Bulletin Designs," paper covers, white cover w/narrow green border band around a small color Texaco logo over the title & above the date "1939" & further advertising, includes guidelines for sign painters, 16 pp., 8 1/2 x 11" (ILLUS.) **231**

Bottle, "Texaco Petroleum Products," cylindrical clear glass w/rounded shoulder to a short neck w/molded neck for cork closure, wide paper label in white, green & red, company name & star logo on left side of label, white panel w/writing at the right reading "Moth Exterminator," ca. 1920s, 10 1/2" h. (fair label color w/overall wear) **55**

Calendar, 1923 "Buick," rectangular paper w/metal edging, pale yellow background, top w/large rectangular photo of a 1923 Buick roadster, advertising for car dealer in Tower City, North Dakota, below image & above full calendar pad, 18 1/2 x 21" (two pages w/folded corners, slight crease & edge wear)...................... **66**

Calendar, 1939, "Enarco," die-cut cardboard, a standing boy wearing knickers standing behind & holding a large rectangular chalkboard-style sign w/black & white paper calendar pad, 5 x 7 3/4" (very minor bumps) **33**

Calendar, 1948, "Amoco," rectangular paper w/wood frame, grey ground w/a tall rectangular color picture at the top showing a period Amoco gas station w/cars below a ghost image of a huge oil refinery in the sky above, small dark green w/white numbers partial calendar pad below, 19 1/4 x 27 3/4"................ **99**

Calendar, 1952, "U.S. Royal Tires," long narrow rectangular paper, bluish green border & background w/a tall rectangular upper color print of a female water-skier wearing a red bikini & balancing on one leg, printed signed "Medcalf," advertising for tire dealer below picture & above black & white full calendar pad, printed by Brown & Bigelow, 16 x 33 1/4" (slight soiling & edge wear)... **66**

Mobil Captain's Hat

Captain's hat w/badge, "Mobil," tan hat w/wide brim band & visor mounted at the front w/an arched panel a raised gold thread, a spread-winged eagle above a wreath framing a red, white & blue enameled flag-shaped pin w/the red Pegasus logo, narrow leather strap across top of visor, ca. 1950s, minor soiling, wear & white paint drips on hat, size 6 7/8 (ILLUS.)... **468**

Texaco Glass Ceiling Fixture

Ceiling light fixture, "Texaco," glass & metal, milk glass Art Deco-style octagonal globe w/ribbed panels alternating w/plain panels decorated w/a red painted star, round black metal ceiling mount, ca. 1930s, base restored, 5 1/2" w., 8 1/2" h. (ILLUS.)...**435**

Chalkboard, "American Brakeblok," self-framed embossed tin, tall rectangular shape, narrow black border band, rectangular yellow top panel w/red & black wording "American Brakeblok - America's Safety Brake Lining - Our Specials," blackboard below, new-old stock, ca. 1954, 17 1/2 x 23 1/2" (some paper remnants on lettering, minor edge scratches)... **94**

Chart, "Gargoyle Mobiloil Chart," rectangular two-sheet cloth, red band at the top w/small gargoyle logo over white wording, printed in black & white w/recommendations on maintenance for various vehicles, dated 1923-26, 20 x 32" (overall soiling, metal edge strips coming loose at bottom).............................. **210**

Checker game, "Standard Oil," folding cardboard game board w/red & black squares, most printed w/a crown, some w/advertising, small box of black & red wooden checkers, complete, ca. 1930s-40s, the set (some mildew spotting on board) **61**

Richfield Race Car Cigarette Box

Cigarette box, "Richfield," figural molded chalkware race car, copper-colored finish, an oblong low platform supporting a low rectangular box impressed w/the word "Richfield," the lift-off figural cover in the shape of the vehicle, early 1920s, minor scattered flecks & flakes, slight copper loss & some tarnish, 4 x 9 1/2", 4 3/4" h. (ILLUS.)... **578**

Cigarette lighter, "Flying A Truck Stations," Zippo-style, silvered metal case w/etched red wording, new-old stock, 1950s, 2 1/4" h....................................... **94**

Cigarette lighter, metal & plastic, figural, plastic model of racing car based on the Blue-bird Racer, blue over black body w/white wheels, long metal lighter mechanism at top, Sarome, ca. 1940s, 3 1/8" l. (slight soiling) **44**

Mobil Slim-style Cigarette Lighter

Cigarette lighter, "Mobil," metal "slim-style" model, silvered ground centered by the Mobil logo in dark blue & red, thin blue border band, new-old stock in original box, ca. 1960s, 2 1/8" l. (ILLUS.) **77**

Cigarette lighter, "Richfield Oil Corporation," metal "slim-style" Japanese model, silvered ground w/dark blue & yellow top & bottom stripe & yellow & blue logo at center, probably new-old stock, ca. 1950s, 2 1/8" l. **77**

Cigarette lighter, "Texaco Marine Products," metal "slim-style" Japanese model, dark blue enameling on lower half w/worn red Texaco star logo & engraved image of small motor boat, Ideal Adliter mark, ca. 1950s, 2 1/8" l. **231**

Clipboard, "Shell," copper, long rectangular copper board w/clip at top decorated w/a large cast figural cockle shell w/"Shell" enameled in red, ca. 1920s-30s, 4 x 8 3/8" (some enamel damage, normal tarnish) **248**

Clock, "Exide Batteries," electric neon wall-hanging type, metal & glass, octagonal shape w/red border around the glass face over a wide white dial band w/Arabic numerals, large red center circle w/words in white & yellow, sweep seconds hand, ca. 1940s-50s, 18 1/4" w. (soiling, wear to edges) **528**

Mobil Pegasus Logo Clock

Clock, "Mobil," round plastic & metal electric light-up pam-type, metal frame enclosing clear face over dial w/red Arabic numerals centering a large red flying Pegasus logo, sweep seconds hand, ca. 1950s,

hands appear to be repainted, 15" d. (ILLUS.) **468**

Clock, "Pennzoil," wall-hanging round plastic electric light-up type, domed front over white face w/wide outer ring w/black Arabic numerals, a large yellow oval in center w/Pennzoil logo & wording "100% Pure Pennsylvania Pennzoil - Safe Lubrication," sweep seconds hand, ca. 1950s, works, 15" d. **495**

Clock, "Quaker State Oil," round plastic electric light-up Dualite brand, white plastic frame enclosing clear face over dial w/black Arabic numerals centering pale green advertising reading "Ask For Quaker State Motor Oil," sweep seconds hand, ca. 1950s, 16 1/2" d. (tiny crack at top edge of frame, missing electric plug, minor pitting to metal band on frame) **132**

Rare Texaco Lighted Wall Clock

Clock, "Texaco," wall-hanging plastic round electric light-up type, domed front over white face w/wide outer ring w/black Arabic numerals, a large red, black & green Texaco star logo in the center, sweep seconds hand, ca. 1950s, works, discolored & dingy face, slightly heat dimpled near 3, 14 3/4" d. (ILLUS.) **715**

Mobil Pegasus Clock-Award

Clock-award, "Mobil - General Petroleum," wood & cast-metal, the electric alarm clock set into an upright angular painted & stained wood block resting on one end of a nearly rectangular matching wooden platform w/an inscribed metal plaque commemorating 30 years of service, a silvered metal figural rearing Pegasus emblem at opposite end, ca. 1950s-60s, 5 1/4 x 9", 5 3/4" h. (ILLUS.) **149**

Cookie tin, cov., "Gilmore Oil Company," lithographed tin, round w/a pale yellow ground, the cover w/a center circle w/the large lion head company emblem in orange & black, a wide border band w/a green holly wreath w/red berries, station giveaway item, ca. 1930s, 10" d. (minor wear)....................... **61**

Counter display, "Bowes Seal-Fast Auto Lamps," upright shallow rectangular black metal box w/glass reverse-painted front, fitted w/two rows of inset bulbs for display, all-original, ca. 1930s, 4 1/2 x 7 3/4", 12" h. (scattered overall wear & corrosion, one bulb missing) **413**

Counter display box, "Monkey Link Tire Chains," cardboard, a shallow rectangular yellow box w/a high rectangular backboard w/advertising reading in part "Monkey Link Self Closing Repair Link - No Tool Required," complete w/20 cardboard boxes w/product, new-old stock, ca. 1948, 7 1/2 x 13", 7 1/2" h............. **33**

AC Spark Plugs Display Case

Counter display case, "AC Spark Plugs," painted tin upright cylindrical shape w/domed top, an opening in back gives access to rotating rack for plugs, two sides w/slots, two printed w/information on what plugs to use, black background w/narrow bands of white wording around the top & bottom, wide center band printed in white & orange "Ask For AC," mid-1920s, some rust spotting & surface scratching, 14 1/4" d., 18 1/4" h. (ILLUS.)..... **253**

Counter display figure, "AC Spark Plugs," figural, soft rubber figure of a comical man w/a spark plug body, in pink, brown, green & white, made in France, ca. 1950s-60s, 5 3/4" h. (light soiling & paint wear).................... **88**

Credit card application box, "DX," lithographed tin, an open narrow rectangular box w/a tall rectangular back w/a hanging hole, white ground w/blue & red, the back printed w/"Buy Modern! with a DX Credit Card - Honored Everywhere in North America," the box front reads "Credit Card Applications - Mail One Today," ca. 1960, appears to be new-old stock, 2 x 6 1/4", 9" h. (very minor scratches & wear)....................... **50**

Customer record box, cov., "Mobilubrication," rectangular metal 3 x 5" file card style w/flat hinged cover, red w/a white rectangular panel on the top printed w/small red flying Pegasus logo & reading "MobiLubrication Customer Record," ca. 1960s, 6 3/4 x 9 3/4", 8 1/2" h. (minor overall wear & light fading)....................... **33**

Desk accessory, "Mobil," bronzed cast metal, shield-shaped platform base w/an upright swiveling black plastic pen holder at one end & a shallow oval indentation for paper clips below a full-figure model of the flying Pegasus logo, ca. 1940s-50s, 4 x 4 1/4", 3 1/4" h. (slight soiling, no pen)....................... **240**

Fan, "Shell Petroleum Corp.," die-cut cardboard, cut in the shape of a large cockle shell & printed in color w/a 1920s beach scene, small white panel w/advertising below the Shell cockle shell logo in yellow & red, wooden stick handle, ca. 1920s, 7 3/4 x 13 3/4" (overall edge wear, scattered soiling & wear)....................... **44**

Texaco Fire Chief Helmet & Box

Fire chief helmet, "Texaco," life-sized molded plastic, red body w/green eagle head at front above a shield at front in white printed in red & green "Texaco Fire Chief," w/star logo, w/original green & red box, includes microphone & loudspeaker, ca. 1950s, box 11 x 14", 8" h., the group (ILLUS. of helmet & box)........ **99**

First Aid kit, "Mobil," shallow rectangular lithographed tin box, the top w/a dark blue ground centered by a large red flying Pegasus logo against a white circle, wording in white & blue reads "Flying Red Horse Mobilgas - Mobiloil First Aid Kit," w/Good Housekeeping seal, ca. late 1940s, 2 3/4 x 3 3/8", 3/4" h. (minor scattered scratches) **94**

Texaco First Aid Kit

First aid kit, "Texaco," lithographed metal, shallow wall-mounted rectangular box w/rounded corners & hinged cover, dark grey ground printed in white on the top w/the Texaco star logo & "First Aid," partial contents, ca. 1950s, minor overall wear, 5 1/4 x 8", 2 3/4" deep (ILLUS.).......... **149**

Mobil Cloth Flag

Flag, "Mobil," rectangular red cloth centered by a large white shield outlined in black & enclosing a large red Pegasus logo, used on tanker trucks, ca. 1950s, very minor wear, couple tiny holes, 17 x 25" (ILLUS.)... **210**

Flag, "Mobilgas Special," rectangular white cloth w/large dark green wording above & below the large red Pegasus logo, ca. 1950s-60s, 21 1/2 x 32 1/2" (some overall stains) **121**

Gas pump, Gulf Fry visible pump, glass & metal, dark blue metal base w/color decals below cylindrical glass top below a reproduction Capcolite milk glass globe dated 1982, globe printed in blue & red "That Good Gulf Gasoline," ca. 1920s, 25" w., 120" h. (ILLUS., top of page).......... **1,210**

Gas pump, Phillips 66 Fry Visible pump, metal & glass, cylindrical black body w/decal logos as pump signs, clear glass cylinder at top below a reproduction Capcolite milk glass globe w/red & black Phil-

lips shield logo, globe dated 1982, restored, ca. 1920s, 25" d., 120" h. **1,238**

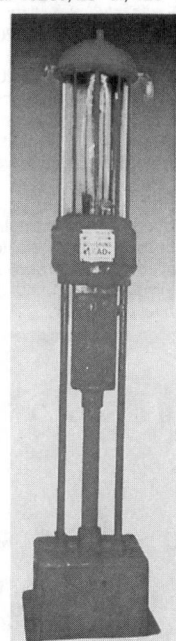

Early Gulf Fry Visible Gas Pump

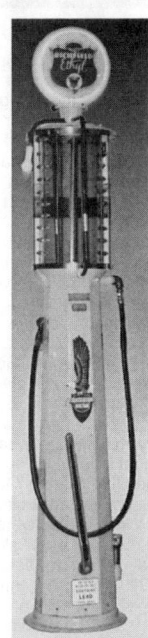

Richfield Fry Visible Gas Pump

Gas pump, Richfield Fry Visible pump, metal & glass, tall tapering octagonal metal base w/blue & yellow Richfield eagle decal, clear glass cylinder top below a reproduction Capcolite milk glass globe w/Richfield Eagle blue & yellow shield logo, globe dated 1982, ca. 1920s, restored, chrome & brass reworked, some paint scuffing, 25" w., 120" h. (ILLUS.) **1,458**

Gas pump, Starkey Visible coin-operated model, metal & glass, red repainted body w/glass cylinder in top, mechanism accepts quarters, half-dollars & silver dollars, one of 26 made in 1925, overall 120" h. (base crack rewelded) **4,015**

Gas pump globe, "Amoco," single milk glass Gill globe lens, no body, printed w/a large circle w/dark red bands above & below a wide black middle band printed w/brand in white, ca. 1930s **105**

Big West Gasoline Pump Globe

Gas pump globe, "Big West Gasoline," round complete globe w/two lenses, Art Deco design w/black outer band printed in white w/brand name, a center circle in orange w/a pointed & rayed black & white chevron design, ca. 1930s, back lens cracked & faded, display lens w/small flaw, 13 1/2" d. (ILLUS.)............................... **1,595**

Gas pump globe, "Buffalo Gasoline," single milk glass globe lens, no body, back narrow ring around brand name in large red letters centered by the black & white image of a running buffalo, ca. 1930s, 13 1/2" d. (very minor edge wear, red slightly spotty).. **1,815**

Gas pump globe, "Douglas Gasoline," round single globe lens, milk glass printed only w/red winged heart logo for a southern California company, ca. 1930s, 13 1/2" d. (very minor edge wear, sliver flake at left mount hole) **440**

Gas pump globe, "DX Marine Gasoline," round single globe lens, milk glass printed w/red & blue logo & blue wording, ca. 1930s, 13 1/2" d. (crack at left slot) **210**

Gas pump globe, "Flying A Diesel Fuel," round single Gill globe lens, milk glass printed w/large red circle w/white wording, ca. 1930s (very minor edge flecks & tiny scratches)................................. **990**

Gas pump globe, "Flying A Gasoline," round Gill globe w/two lenses, milk glass w/thin black circle around large red wording & logo, ca. 1930s... **660**

Rare Gilmore Gasoline Pump Globe

Gas pump globe, "Gilmore Gasoline," round single globe lens, black frame enclosing milk glass lens printed in red & green "Gilmore Blu-Green Gasoline," a large brown, black, red & white snarling lion head in the center, ca. 1920s, appears to be new-old stock, 15" d. (ILLUS.).. **6,600**

Kool Motor Gasolene Pump Globe

Gas pump globe, "High Test Anti Knock Kool Motor Gasolene," round complete globe w/two lenses, black frame w/milk glass lenses w/dark green border bands w/black & white lettering flanking the white center band w/the brand in large black letters, ca. 1930s, soiling & stains on both lenses, 15" d. (ILLUS.) **1,320**

Gas pump globe, "Marathon," two milk glass lenses in a low profile metal body, light green body, lens w/orange silhouetted figure of runner behind the brand name in large green letters, ca. 1930s, 15" d. (light facing & wear, small paint chip at bottom center)................................. **1,320**

Gas pump globe, "Mobilgas Aircraft," round single globe lens on wide glass body, milk glass printed w/red Pegasus logo above dark blue & red wording, ca. 1930s, 13 1/2" d. (crack on body back, minor surface scratches)............................. **1,788**

Rare & Early Texaco Pump Globe

Gas pump globe, "Mobilgas Special," round single globe lens, black frame enclosing milk glass lens printed in red & dark blue w/brand name below a large red flying Pegasus logo, ca. 1930s, 15" d. (minor edge wear & flecks, very minor wear & soiling on reverse)................... **187**

Gas pump globe, "Mobiloil - Gargoyle," horizontal milk glass debossed oval w/embossed lettering, black wording above & below a large red gargoyle logo, ca. 1930s, 17" l., 14" h. (some soiling & fading, chip out of base)................... **2,090**

Mohawk Gasoline Pump Globe

Gas pump globe, "Mohawk Gasoline," single milk glass globe lens & low profile reproduction metal body, the lens w/a wide dark orange outer band printed in white w/brand name, white center circle w/a large bust profile of a Native American warrior wearing a tall feather printed in orange & black, ca. 1930s (ILLUS.)............ **2,860**

Gas pump globe, "Royal Gasoline," two milk glass lenses in high profile metal body, wide pink frame, dark blue narrow border band around red words above & below a large dark blue map of Maine, ca. 1930s, 15" d. (light fading, small chip at bottom center, rust spotting & paint loss on body)................... **2,090**

Gas pump globe, "Sinclair Power-X," two milk glass lenses w/narrow glass body w/screw-on base, thin red ring encloses green & red wording "Sinclair Power-X - Over 100 Octane," ca. 1930s, 13 1/2" d. (slight background paint loss)........................ **440**

Texaco Ethyl Pump Globe

Gas pump globe, "Texaco Ethyl," round one-piece Gill-type milk glass, black wording surrounds the large red, black & green Texaco star logo in the center, all-original w/original box, ca. 1930s, very minor water damage to edge of star (ILLUS.) **226**

Gas pump globe, "Texaco," wide-bodied one-piece milk glass globe w/chimney, etched lettering & red & black Texaco star logo & outer ring, early & rare, small ding on chimney, minor paint loss, fading & scuffing, small chip on base, 7 1/2 x 15", 5 7/8" deep (ILLUS. of both sides, top of page)..................... **7,260**

Gas pump globe, "TP Ethyl Gasoline," complete globe w/milk glass lenses in original low profile metal body, printed in red w/a large Indian teepee flanked by "T-P," centered by a white circle w/black triangle w/yellow wording & "Ethyl," 1930s-40s (back lens cracks, slight haziness at bottom area of lens) **2,530**

Gas pump globe, "White Crown Gasoline," one-piece white milk glass crown-shaped globe w/no wording, screw neck base & collar, ca. 1930s, 16 1/2" h. **259**

Gas pump globe, "White Eagle Gasoline," figural, milk glass model of a perched blunt-nose all-white eagle, ca. 1924-32, 6 1/2 x 9", 21" h. (minor scratches)............. **1,980**

Gas pump globe, "Wildfire," two white milk glass Gill lenses in a blue metal rippled frame, brand name printed in large blue letters on lenses, ca. 1930s (minor scratches to lenses) **2,970**

Gas station display item, "Texaco," embossed porcelain, fully dimensional large red star, mounted on Texaco gas stations in the 1950s and 1960s, 15 1/4 x 16", 2" deep (minor tip chips) **231**

Gas station opening announcement, "Shell," pale blue paper, card-style opening to small colorful pop-up gas station opposite red-printed invitation information, ca. 1920s, open 4 1/4 x 6 1/4", 4 1/4" h. (very light soiling) **71**

Gas tank measuring stick, "Tydol - Veedol Forzol," painted wood, long narrow stick printed in red & dark blue "Tydol Economy Gasoline - Measure Your Savings From Veedol Forzol - the Economy Oil For Fords," ca. 1920s, appears unused, 17" l. **33**

Hand brush, "Indian Gas," long rectangular wooden top w/rounded ends, black background w/natural wood wording showing, reads in part "Brush Past 'Em With Indian Gas," appears to have original finish, ca. 1920s, 7 3/4" l. **176**

Handbook, "Shell Oil Company - Traffic Laws Governing Operation of Motor Vehicles in San Francisco...," paperback, dated July 1925, includes color ads & unusual illustrations, 64 pp., 3 x 5 1/2" (stain on outer upper corner, minor edge & corner wear)................................. **303**

Lapel pin, Buick fiftieth anniversary, round metal w/enameled trim, a gilt center circle w/a tiny image of an early Buick, panels of white, red & blue enamel ring the center & feature wording in gold "Buick - 1903-1953," single screw-post mount, 9/16" d. **44**

Lapel pin, Chevrolet Corvette Owner, round die-stamped metal w/crossed flags emblem trimmed w/red, black & white enamel, single clinch pin mount, late 1950s, 1/2" d. **149**

Early Bronzed Metal Letter Holder

Letter holder, bronzed cast metal, rectilinear pierced sides below an arched floral-pierced top, each side cast w/a scene of an early open auto & driver, flared corner block feet, early 20th c., slight tarnishing, 4 x 6 1/2", 4 1/2" h. (ILLUS.)........................... **198**

License plate, Maine, 1914, rectangular porcelain, black ground w/white letters & numbers, only one, 5 1/4 x 15 1/2" (edge chipping, some staining)................................. **61**

License plate, Virginia, 1912, rectangular porcelain in dark green w/white numbers & letters, touchup to outer edge, only one, 5 1/2 x 11" **330**

License plate attachment, "En-Ar-Co Motor Oil," die-cut tin, white ground w/black printing, a center rectangular dimpled reflector sign w/brand name being held from behind by a young boy, new-old stock, ca. 1930s, 3 7/8 x 6"................................ **66**

Ford License Plate Attachment

License plate attachment, "Ford Good Drivers League," die-cut tin, round top above rectangular panel, white ground printed in dark blue, reads "Ford Good Drivers League - 1940 - Member," minor scattered nicks & wear, 6 x 6 1/4" (ILLUS.)...... **330**

License plate attachment, "Harold's Club," die-cut tin, cutout & printed in color as an early covered wagon w/man leading team of oxen, red, white, blue & dark yellow, printed in red & white "Harold's Club or Bust! - Reno, Nevada," new old stock, ca. 1940s-50s, 8 1/4 x 14".................... **154**

License plate attachment, "Hi-Power Gasoline," die-cut tin, long narrow form arched in the center w/logo, orange w/black working reading "Hi-Power Gasoline - H. Earl Clark Co. - Helena," ca. 1930s, 5 1/4 x 10" (scattered wear & scratches, few paint chips)............................. **83**

License plate attachment, "Marathon," die-cut tin, round w/white border enclosing a round dimpled reflector printed w/a black & white racing figure & black wording "Marathon - Best in the Long Run," ca. 1930s, new old stock, 3 3/4 x 5" (very minor nicks & scratches) **154**

License plate attachment, "Mobil Gas," die-cut embossed tin, large red cutout figure of flying red Pegasus logo above a long narrow rectangular white panel printed in red "California World's Fair," 1939, new-old stock, 5 3/8 x 6 3/8" **204**

License plate attachment, "Pennzoil," die-cut tin & celluloid, squared form w/large & small brown & white owls perched at the left w/advertising & an oval red celluloid reflector panel at the right, yellow ground w/black wording reading "We Are For - Safety (on reflector) - Butch Logic Service - 3rd & Sprice St. - Shamokin - PA," ca. 1930s-40s, new-old stock, w/original envelope, 5 x 5 3/4" **413**

Rare License Plate Attachment

License plate attachment, "Remember Pearl Harbor," die-cut embossed tin, cut in the form of two waving American flags flanking a tapering V-shaped white center w/wording in red above a tall thin red "V" sign, World War II era, minor to moderate wear, 4 1/2 x 4 3/4" (ILLUS.) **853**

License plate attachment, "Woco Pep," die-cut embossed tin, a red scrolled banner w/white wording above a long rectangular black & white panel w/the company logo and red wording, reads "Pledge To Drive Safely," ca. 1930s-40s, new-old stock, 9 1/2" l., 5 3/4" h. **160**

License plates, Vermont, 1915, rectangular porcelain in white w/black letters & numbers, 6 x 15", pr. (overall scratching, heavy edge chipping on one, one grommet missing) **121**

Map display rack, "Amoco," upright rectangular openwork wire rack w/a long narrow horizontal painted metal sign in white, black & red across the top readings "Make It Amoco all the way," ca. 1950s, 17 3/4" l., 12 1/4" h. (overall surface rust) **132**

Mileage roll chart, "Texaco," board w/wood scroll posts & paper roll chart, shows mileage between California cities on reverse, w/original box, ca. 1920s-30s, 6 x 13 1/8" (box torn in a couple places & w/minor wear) **105**

Motor oil display rack, "Sunoco Motor Oil," porcelain & wood, deep rectangular wooden box frame w/arched aprons & stepped center platform holding a wire carrying rack w/two glass quart oil bottles w/metal pour spouts, yellow background w/red caduceus symbol & black wording "Mercury Made - Sunoco Motor Oil," letters in Sunoco word perforated & the interior fitted w/an electric light, ca. 1920s, new wiring, some edge chipping & water staining, 19 1/4 x 22", 22 3/4" h. (ILLUS., top next column) **1,100**

Sunoco Motor Oil Display Rack

Movie advertising slide, "Conoco," rectangular glass slide used for advertising between features in early movie houses, black & white photograph of a couple standing near early gas pump while attendant fills car, man stating "There's an extra day's vacation in that mileage," other red & black wording reads "Conoco Bronze Gasoline - Instant Starting - Lightning Pick Up - Vance Service Station," 1930s, 3 1/4 x 4" **27**

Oil bottle, "Essolube," clear cylindrical quart bottle w/stepped shoulder & tapering neck, embossed name on side, ca. 1920s-30s, 3 1/8" d., 15" h. (soiling) **55**

Oil bottle, "McColl-Frontenac Oil Co., Limited," clear cylindrical tapering embossed glass bottle, one full Imperial quart, metal lid w/tall tapering cylindrical pour spout, Canada, ca. 1930s, 3 1/4" d., overall 13 1/4" h. **291**

Mobiloil Gargoyle Filpruf Bottle

Oil bottle, "Mobiloil Gargoyle Filpruf," upright diamond-shaped clear glass bottle w/detailed embossing on sides & large tapering upright metal top pour spout, ca. 1920s-30s, slight interior soiling & exterior wear, 3 3/4 x 4 3/8", overall 14 1/4" h. (ILLUS.) **330**

Oil bottle, "Shell X-100 Motor Oil," clear cylindrical quart bottle w/fired-on black & yellow label, ca. 1930s, 3 1/8" d., 14" h. (slight base flaw & soiling) **61**

Sunoco Bottle Carrier & Bottles

Oil bottle carrier, "Sunoco," wire openwork rectangular basket w/compartments for eight quart bottles & center wire handle w/wire grip, complete w/eight clear bottles w/yellow & blue Sunoco labels & upright metal pour spouts, ca. 1920s, some rust on carrier, carrier 9 1/2 x 18", 14 3/4" h., the set (ILLUS.) **605**

Oil display rack & bottles, "Essolube Motor Oil," metal & glass, upright rectangular metal strap framework w/inner rack bars for eight clear glass one-quart bottles, Essolube name on bottom side frame, w/eight empty bottles, ca. 1930s-40s, rack 7 1/4 x 14 1/2", 16 1/2" h., the set (wear & corrosion on rack) **220**

Early Shell Motor Oil Pitcher

Oil pitcher, "Shell Motor Oil," lithographed tin, wide tapering cylindrical body w/a wide C-form strap handle & wide & long flaring rim spout, sides w/red ground & white & black wording & early shell logo, English, early 20th c., scattered nicks, scratches & dings, 5" h. (ILLUS.) **468**

Socony Oil Product Display Rack

Oil product display rack, "Socony Vacuum Specialties Upperlube Oil," embossed tin & wire, a tall rectangular sign flanked at each side of the lower half w/four wire display racks, raised on canted bar legs, sign w/white & red ground w/wording in red & black reading "Prevent Sticky Valves - Carbon - Noise - Wear With - Socony Upperlub Oil - Pour It Into Your Gasoline," ca. 1950s, overall paint splatter, soiling & wear, overall 17 3/4 x 40 1/4" (ILLUS.) **231**

Oil rack sign, "Shell Motor Oil," die-cut porcelain in the shape of a cockle shell, dark yellow & red w/red wording "Golden Shell Motor Oil," ca. 1930s-40s, 12 x 12 1/4" (minor edge & hole chips, some chips touched up) **853**

Oiler can, "Farmer's Price High Grade Oil," upright oval can w/screw-on cap w/spout, white ground w/wording in dark blue & light green, small color image of figures in center, empty, 4 oz. (minor nicks, scratches & soiling) **193**

Oiler can, "Marathon Handy Oiler," upright oval can w/screw-on plastic cap & lead spout, printed in red & white w/large racer logo on sides, 4 oz., no contents (minor nicks & scratches, small thumb dent) **50**

Paperweight, "Lion Oil Company," cast metal, figural, a large stalking male lion on a raised rectangular base w/embossed advertising across the front, early 20th c., 3 1/2" l. (small chip on tip of tail) **88**

Paperweight, "St. Louis Pumps," cast metal, model of a tall early visible-style gas pump w/top globe, repainted red body w/black lettering & details & black & white globe, ca. 1920s, 8" h. (minor paint chipping) **165**

Texaco Gas Pump Pencil Case

Pencil case, "Texaco Fire Chief," figural plastic, red model of a gas pump w/red, white, black & green Texaco logo decal & red & white Fire Chief decal, thin rubber hose down one side, ca. 1950s, small tear in paper label, 8" l. (ILLUS.) **198**

Photograph, "Texaco," early sepia-tone outdoor image of an early open-cabbed tanker truck parked by large Texaco storage tanks, wood frame, ca. 'teens or 1920s, overall 9 1/4 x 11 1/4" **88**

Pinback button, "Goodyear Tires," oval celluloid & metal, in the shape of narrow-rimmed tire centering the Goodyear logo in dark blue & yellow, German-made, ca. 1920s, 1 3/8" l., 5/8" h. (slight soiling) **66**

Pinback button, "Overland Cars," celluloid, round w/a black on white image of an early auto with wording above & below reading "Overland Cars - Sold by Oklahoma Motor Car Co. - Oklahoma City, Okla.," ca, 1910-20, 1" d. (minor surface wear & scratches) **61**

Pinback button, "Texaco Fire-Chief," round printed tin, white ground printed in dark blue & red "Did You Say Fill'er Up With Fire-Chief?," ca. 1930s, 4" d. (minor surface wear & scratches) **33**

Pinback button, "Try New [Flying A logo] Today," round celluloid, wide orange center band w/black & white logo, small white top & bottom bands w/black lettering, ca. 1950s, 2 1/4" d. (very minor wear & scratches) **121**

Platter, "Standard Oil Company - Indiana," fired china, oval, narrow dark blue leaf & blossom band on rim, script company logo on inner edge, by Shenango China, ca. 1920s-30s, 13 5/8" l. **193**

Playing cards, "Pontiac," paper & cardboard, two complete decks w/two jokers each, blue or red card backs each w/Pontiac Indian head logo & black advertising for Great Neck, New York, dealership,

dark red box w/black logos & wording on top, ca. 1930s, box 3 7/8 x 4 3/4" (slight box edge wear) **33**

Golden Shell Oil Watch & Fob

Pocket watch & fob, "Golden Shell Oil," open-faced watch w/a dial ring w/Roman numerals circling the visible works, a thin link chain connects it to the round enameled metal disk fob centered by the yellow Shell logo w/red lettering, watch runs, ca. 1920s-30s, minor wear & tarnish on fob, fob 1 1/4" d. (ILLUS.) **413**

1930s Exide Batteries Poster

Poster, "Exide Batteries," color print showing the figure of an elegant woman standing wearing a long red coat w/wide white fur collar & cuffs, a shaded column in the black & white background, reads "Let Exide See You Home," ca. 1930s, light wrinkles, 20 1/4 x 30" (ILLUS.) **72**

Promotional car, 1960 Mercury Comet, white plastic w/black & silver tires & silver trim, w/original shipping & inner box & promotional insert card, car 7 5/8" l. **66**

1960 Ford Promotional Toy Car & Box

Promotional toy car, 1960 Ford Galaxy, dark green plastic w/black & silver tires & silver trim, w/original box & insert informational card w/facsimile signature of Lee Iacocca, factory blemish on left front bumper, torn box end flaps, card 8 3/8" l., the group (ILLUS.) 121

Pump sign, "Atlantic," rectangular porcelain, red bands at top & bottom, center white band w/black company name, ca. 1950s-60s, 9 x 13" (few tiny nicks & flecks) 165

Pump sign, "Blue Sunoco 200," die-cut porcelain, tall narrow yellow diamond centered by blue-outlined yellow words & the red tail & tip of an arrow behind, ca. 1940s-50s, 15 x 20 3/4" (minor edge wear & chips)..................................... 198

Pump sign, "E-Z Serve Gasoline," rectangular porcelain, white border w/red peaked panel w/logo & wording in dark blue, red & white, narrow blue & yellow panel at bottom, ca. 1950s, 14 x 18" (light overall wear) 71

Pump sign, "Fighter Ethyl Gasoline," square porcelain, white ground w/orange, black & white wording & boxing glove logo, script printed across bottom reads "The Gas with the Punch," ca. 1930s, 10" sq. (soiling, wear, paint flecks & scattered scratches) 853

Husky Tri-Power Pump Sign

Pump sign, "Husky Tri-Power," square porcelain, dark orange ground w/blue & white standing figure of a husky dog above wording in orange & white, ca. 1950s, slight soiling, marks & scratches, 12" sq. (ILLUS.) 913

Pump sign, "Mobilgas Gasoline," die-cut porcelain, shield-shaped w/black border band, white ground w/large red Pegasus logo above the words in dark blue & red, ca. 1950s, 11 1/2 x 12" (minor chips at mounting holes, factory crazing at top corner)... 275

Pump sign, "Red Crown Gasoline," die-cut porcelain, a long rectangular sign in dark yellow w/red wording centered at the top by a large cutout red & yellow crown, ca. 1930s, 12 1/4 x 14" (professionally restored) 1,760

Pump sign, "Sinclair Gasoline," nearly square porcelain, white ground w/company logo w/small green dinosaur & red wording, ca. 1950s-60s, 12 x 13 1/2" (very minor chips & wear) 88

Pump sign, "Standard Red Crown," rectangular porcelain, white ground w/red wording at the top above the oval red, white & blue Standard torch logo, dated 1949, 12 x 15".................................... 94

Pump sign, "Texaco Diesel Chief (Diesel Fuel)," rectangular porcelain, white ground w/red & white fanned stripe design surrounding the Texaco star logo in the upper half, red ground in lower half w/black & white wording, dated 1940, perhaps rarest of Texaco pump signs, 12 x 18" (edge soiling, edge & mount hole chips, some tan rusted color)............. 1,980

Pump sign, "Texaco Fire-Chief Gasoline," curved rectangular porcelain, white ground w/red & black wording, red, black & green Texaco star logo & large red & white fire helmet, ca. 1940, 8 x 12" 154

Pump sign, "Utoco," die-cut porcelain, horizontal oval form w/red, white & blue bands w/company name in center white band, a torch logo behind the white band & over the other bands, ca. 1950s, touched-up large chip at bottom, small chip at top, 13 x 14" (ILLUS., top next page) 633

Utoco Porcelain Pump Sign

Radiator grille attachment, "Barnsdahl," round etched & enameled brass, a yellow center circle w/a large square enclosing a large black capital "B," dark red border band w/brass wording "Be Square To Your Motor," ca. 1920s, 3" d. (very minor scattered wear) **105**

Radiator grille attachment, "Oshkosh," die-cut etched & enameled brass, profile bust portrait of a Native American chief wearing headdress trimmed in orange above a narrow rectangle w/company name trimmed in orange, ca. 1930s-40s, 2 5/8 x 3 5/8" **270**

Radiator grille attachment, "The Milwaukee Journal Tour Club," die-cut etched & enameled aluminum, metal ground w/black enamel, downward pointing triangle w/comic head of goggled driver at the top above wording "1924 - The Milwaukee Journal Tour Club Wis.," 1924, 4 x 5 1/2" (minor surface wear & bends, extra hole at center) **50**

Radiator grille badge, "Insured Old Trails Indianapolis," die-cut metal w/cloisonne, arrowhead-shaped w/a thin border band of white enamel around a dimpled red ground w/small metal letters above & below the brand name in large white letters, ca. 1930s-40s, 3 x 5 3/4" (very minor wear)........................ **66**

Radiator water bag, "Minnequa Water Bag," rectangular flax canvas w/metal rims & hanging cord, printed in red w/a large Native American chief w/feathered bonnet, wording in blue & red reads "Minnequa Water Bag - Made From Imported Flax - Cools By Evaporation - For Best Results - Prefill - Mfd. by The Pueblo Tent & Awning Co. - Pueblo, Colorado," ca. 1920s, 10 x 15" (minor soiling, light rust on metal bar, cap missing)............... **55**

Restroom door sign, "Tidewater Associated," rectangular porcelain, white & red background w/grey & white wording reading "For your protection Please Obtain Key in Station Office," ca. 1960s, 3 x 5"......... **270**

Restroom door sign, "Women's Room," rectangular porcelain, light blue background w/dark blue center circle enclosing a white profile of a woman looking into her compact above the words "Women's Room" above a narrow black arrow, from Union Oil Company, dated 1939, 12 x 13" (very minor field wear) **413**

Restroom door signs, rectangular tin, each w/a white ground, one w/a black oval frame enclosing a silhouette figure of a Victorian woman in wide dress, the mate w/the oval enclosing the figure of a Victorian man wearing a top hat & long coat & w/a cane, ca. 1930s, new-old stock, each 9 x 11", pr. **413**

Road atlas, "Shell," notebook-style dark brown cover w/gold Shell cockle shell logo, opens to pages w/three punch holes each, maps of the U.S., Canada, Mexico & individual states & provinces as well as many cities, more than 90 maps, 1960, 13 3/4 x 18 1/2" (some cover wear).. **38**

Road map, "Conoco 1929 Road Map of Kansas," fold-out paper, three-fold back printed in color w/a continuous scene of cars arriving at an early gas station, title in center panel & blocks of advertising in the side panels, 9 x 12" (mild wear & soiling) **61**

Road map, "Gilmore," folded paper, front printed in deep red, black & white, large image of lion head, wording in white & black reads "Hi-way Map - California - Oregon - Washington - Ride with Gilmore," ca. 1940, closed 4 x 9" (some edge wear, few pencil marks & small cigarette burns)... **50**

Road map, "Gilmore Oil Company," fold-out paper, for California, Oregon & Washington, front cover in bright yellow & orange w/dark blue writing & a color photo of a lion head, the back cover w/advertising for Red Lion gasoline & Lion Head motor oil, ca. 1950s, 8 x 9" (appears misfolded, minor soiling & wear) **94**

Road map, "Hancock Oil Company," fold-out paper, for California, the cover w/a large cartoon image of a rooster driving a jumping open auto, printed in orange, dark blue & white, interior detailed image of the rooster & chipmunks, ca. 1948, closed 4 1/2 x 9 3/4" (some wear at folds & edges, some internal soiling & small tears) **33**

1940s Inland Empire Road Map

Road map, "Inland Empire Wasatch Refining," fold-out paper, dark orange background across three-fold back w/dark blue band across the top & a dark blue silhouetted image of an oil refinery across the bottom, reads across the top center "Map of the Western States," white panels on side panels w/advertising as well as an image of an older auto, company logos & pictures of oil cans, ca. late 1940s, very minor wear & soiling, 9 x 12" (ILLUS.).................................... **154**

Road map, "Linco," folded paper, front w/black ground printed w/red, white & pink w/a silhouette outline of the states included above a large round company logo, reads "Linco Highway Guide of Illinois, Indiana, Ohio, Kentucky - Linco Gasoline and Motor Oil - Distributed by The Ohio Oil Company, Incorporated - Findlay, Ohio," labeled First Edition, ca. 1940, folded 4 x 9" (very slight edge wear) **66**

Early Phillips 66 Road Map

Road map, "Phillips 66," fold-out paper, three-fold cover in white, brown, pale green & orange, panels form a continuous scene of an open roadster driving past a charming small gas station, Phillips 66 logos & advertising on outer panels, center panel reads "Phillips Highways of Oklahoma," 1931, minor soiling & scattered wear, 9 x 12" (ILLUS.) **121**

Road map, "Sinclair," folded paper, five-fold outer pages open to show a full color panorama of a Sinclair gas station w/a highway & hills in the background, late 1930s, folded 4 x 9" (slight edge wear) **17**

Salt & pepper shakers, "Atlantic," plastic, model of older gas pump, one in white w/red sides, other in all red, Atlantic stickers on sides & gas gauge stickers, ca. 1950s, 2 5/8" h., pr. (slight decal wear)........... **72**

Salt & pepper shakers, "Esso," plastic, figural gas pumps, one in red w/white front & back, other in blue w/white, Esso paper stickers & gauge faces, ca. 1950s, 2 3/4" h., pr. (wear to stickers) **22**

Salt & pepper shakers, "Mobil Gasoline," figural plastic, models of older gas pumps w/flying Pegasus logos, one shaker in red, the other in white, heat-stamped log-

os, one reads on the back "1955 Nebraska-Iowa 20 Yr. Club, Des Moines, Iowa," probably meeting giveaway, 2 3/4" h., pr. (ILLUS., below) **605**

Rare Mobil Gas Salt & Peppers

Mobilflame Salt & Pepper Shakers

Salt & pepper shakers, "Mobilflame Bottled Gas," plastic, models of grey gas cylinders printed in red "Raleigh Fuels Mobilflame Bottled Gas [Pegasus logo] Appliances - Phone 220-W - Brandon, VT," w/original cardboard box, new-old stock, ca. 1950s, 2 7/8" h., pr. (ILLUS.)......... **105**

Salt & pepper shakers, "Richfield," figural plastic, models of older gas pumps w/company logo decals, shakers in yellow, ca. 1950s, 2 3/4" h., pr. (heavy decal wear on one, other minor soiling & wear)... **83**

Salt & pepper shakers, "Shell Gasoline with TCP," figural plastic, models of older gas pumps w/flying Pegasus logos, one shaker in red, the other in yellow, Shell & TCP logo stencils, ca. 1950s, 2 3/4" h., pr....... **110**

Salt & pepper shakers, "Texaco," ceramic, model of an early gas pump w/globe on top, one in red & silver w/Texaco Fire Chief sticker on side & Texaco star logo on the globe, the other in silver w/a Texaco Sky Chief sticker & the Sky Chief logo on the globe, ca. 1930s, silver on one may be touched up, 1 x 1 3/8", 4" h., pr. (ILLUS., top next page)................................. **77**

Texaco Gas Pump Shakers

Texaco Service Station Uniform

Service station uniform, "Texaco," khaki, dark green & black cloth, a cloth & vinyl hat w/Texaco logo patch, size 7, a size medium short-sleeved shirt w/Texaco patch, size 40 short-sleeved overalls w/Texaco patch & 7/8" d. Texaco enameled metal button, ca. 1940s-50s, some soiling & wear, patch on overall leg, the group (ILLUS.)................................. **105**

Serving bowl, "Standard Oil Company - Indiana," fired china, oval, narrow dark blue leaf & blossom band on rim, script company logo on inner edge, by Shenango China, ca. 1920s-30s, 6" l. **231**

Serving bowl, "Sunoco," fired china, oval w/small Sunoco diamond & arrow logo printed in blue & yellow on one rim below thin yellow & blue border stripes, by Shenango China, ca. 1940s, 10" l. **121**

Serving bowl, "The A.R. Co. (Atlantic Refining)," fired china, oval w/small logo in light blue on one side, dark blue rim pinstripes, by O.P. Co. Syracuse China, ca. 1930s-40s, 10" l. (minor surface wear) **33**

Sign, "Buick Quick Service," porcelain, double-sided rectangle, wide red, white & blue bands each printed w/one of the words in white or blue, ca. 1930s-40s, 16 x 26" (edge & mount hole chips & wear, minor scratches & soiling) **578**

Soap dispenser, "Atlantic Refining Company," wall-mounted chromed metal, octagonal covered bowl form swiveling on a bracket mount, small rounded company logo on the top in red & blue, ca. 1930s, 6" w. (soiling, finish wear)................................. **55**

Station attendant's hat, "Amoco," khaki green canvas material w/an oval red, white & blue Amoco cloth tag on the front, black plastic visor, w/original Lee Co. cardboard box, ca. 1950s, size 7 1/2 .... **88**

Station attendant's hat, "Hancock," tan canvas material w/a long narrow black, white & orange Hancock cloth tag on the front complete w/rooster logo, black plastic visor, ca. 1950s (overall soiling & wear, inner sweat band worn away).............. **105**

Station attendant's hat, "Texaco," dark green cloth & black vinyl visor, round red, green, white & black Texaco logo patch on front, ca. 1950s, size 7 1/8 (very slight wear)... **44**

Sinclair Oil Company Sugar Bowl

Sugar bowl, open, "Sinclair Oil Company," fired china, round cup-form w/round side loop handles, white w/dark blue oil derrick logo on side flanked by dark blue gold-trimmed bands, gold rim band, by Walker China, Bedford, Ohio, ca. 1938, minor chip on inner rim, overall 6" w. (ILLUS.)......... **204**

Table lamp, "Bosch Spark Plugs," plastic & glass, round black base w/large upright plastic model of a silver & yellow spark plug printed in green "Bosch Germany," spherical open-topped frosted glass top shade, ca. 1960s, 10" d., 20" h. (slight soiling & wear, cord cut).................. **88**

Thermometer, "Atlas Wiper Blades," metal & glass, hanging-type, shallow rectangular horizontal metal case w/glass front over arched orange panel resembling windshield enclosing the orange & dark blue wording, orange & blue numbers above, w/hanging wire, ca. 1950s, 8 x 14 1/4" (case heavily pitted).................... **110**

Thermometer, "Ditzler Automotive Finishes," tin & glass, round w/domed glass front, arched white temperature gauge on a yellow ground w/blocks of blue & red w/white wording, center wording in black & red reads "Ditzler Automotive Finishes - Always Better - Whatever The Weather," ca. 1950s, 12" d. (wear, nicks & flecks, slight bends at bottom edge).......... **165**

Thermometer, "Fleet-Wing Petroleum Products," embossed tin, tall narrow rectangular form w/rounded top, pale yellow ground w/thin red wing logo above advertising in red & dark blue, w/original cardboard giveaway box, ca. 1930s, 2 x 6 3/8" (couple minor flaws)........................ **83**

Thermometer, "Fulmen Battery," long oblong painted metal, dark red ground w/a black & white image of a battery at the top, French wording at the bottom in black & white, France, ca. 1950s, 7 1/4 x 27 1/4" (some scratches) **39**

Rare Early Richfield Toy Tanker Truck

Thermometer, "Mobil," tall narrow rectangular self-framed metal w/rounded ends, white ground w/red flying Pegasus logo at the top, black wording reads "Socony Vacuum" at top, "Mobil Freezone - Mobil Permazone" at bottom, ca. 1930s-40s, 8 x 35 3/4" (some scratches & soiling) **275**

Thermometer, "Quaker State Oil," round aluminum & glass, domed glass front over white ground w/black Arabic numerals around ad reading "Use Quaker State Motor Oil," ca. 1950s-60s, 12" d. (minor metal pitting) **132**

Shellzone Anti-Freeze Thermometer

Thermometer, "Shellzone Anti-Freeze," tin, very tall narrow rectangular form w/round-

ed ends, dark red ground w/yellow wording at the top & Shell cockle shell logo at the bottom, ca. 1930s, scattered scratches & wear, 3 1/4 x 17" (ILLUS.) **413**

Thermometer, "Veedol Motor Oil," long & wide rectangular form, white ground w/large round Veedol logo in red, white & blue at the top, 1950s, 11 1/2 x 35 1/2" (slight soiling & small edge chips) **220**

Tire stand, "Goodyear Tires," self-framed tin, long upright trapezoidal shape, black ground w/an arched white banner w/Goodyear name & logo over yellow lettering reading "Truck - Bus - Farm Tires," ca. 1940s-50s, 20 1/2 x 21 1/2", 9 3/4" h. (scratches, some rubbing & a few dents) **55**

Tour guide & map booklet, "Red Indian," paper covers printed in black w/red image of a tall standing Native American chief wearing a headdress & holding a small model of a gas station above the wording "Let the Red Indian be your Guide," interior pages filled w/maps & information on sites as well as black & white photos, dated 1924, for Eastern Canada, 44 pp., closed 6 x 9" (very minor wear) **226**

Toy truck, "Richfield," pressed steel tanker truck, Mack-style cab, long tank on bed, yellow & black metal wheels, operable steering wheel, black w/red Richfield advertising along the sides of the tank, shield-shaped blue, yellow & white decals on front grille & end of tank reading "Richfield - The Gasoline of Power," only 200 made as executive giveaway, 1920s, heavy wear on tank, reproduction windshield frame, 28 1/2" l. (ILLUS., top of page) **7,150**

Toy truck, "Sinclair," pressed steel tanker truck, streamlined design w/teardrop fenders, dark green w/silver grille & headlights, original wooden wheels, Sinclair name in white along the sides of tank, red & white decals on cab doors read "Fuel Oil," 1930s, 17 3/4" l. (overall heavy play wear) **825**

Texaco Vinyl Wind Sock

Trophy, "Gulf Oil," mahogany & bronze, an upright wooden plaque set atop a wooden block base w/slanted front, the top mounted w/a large rectangular metal plaque arched at the center to show an embossed racing speedboat, copy below reads "Gulf Oil Gold Cup Awarded To (engraved inscription) - Marine Racing Hall of Fame's Outstanding Race Driver of the Year," the front of the lower block also mounted w/a metal rope & anchor medallion w/the company logo, dated 1963, 3 x 6 3/4", 8" h. (minor wear) **281**

Union pinback button, "Garage & Gas Station Employees," round celluloid, yellow ground printed in dark blue w/inscription "Garage & Gas Station Employees 18396 - A.F. of L. - Jun. 1936 - Green Bay Wis.," an early red gasoline pump shown in the center, 1 1/4" d. (very minor wear) **77**

Upholstery brush, "Dietrich Motor Car Co. - Allentown, PA.," flat round palm-sized top in celluloid w/metal rim band, white background w/black wording & large full-color Cadillac & LaSalle emblems, 1920s, 3 1/2" d. **154**

Watch fob, "California Oil Fields," enameled brass, round w/slightly scalloped edge & hanging loop at top, front side w/large central engraved scene of an early oil field surrounded by a narrow dark blue enameled border band w/brass lettering reading "California Oil Fields 1916," the reverse w/cast inscription "Christmas Souvenir from D&B Pump & Supply Co.," 1 3/8" d. (minor scratches & wear) **83**

Wind sock, "Texaco," long tapering red vinyl w/white, black, green & red star logo & company name in large white letters, large end clasps, ca. 1960s, few added holes, slight soiling, 142" l., tapers from 12" to 36" diameter (ILLUS., top of page) **396**

Windshield weather guard, "Triple 'X' Tydol," waxed cardboard, long rectangular form w/narrow flaps at bottom edge, dark blue ground printed in orange & white at the left w/the figure of a racing woman skater, wording at right in orange & white reads "Triple 'X' Tydol - 'It Lubricates as it Drives... Starts in 1/2

Second'," ca. 1930s, minor edge wear & bends, 12 x 19 1/2" (ILLUS., below) **413**

Triple X Tydol Windshield Guard

BARBERIANA

A wide variety of antiques related to the tonsorial arts have been highly collectible for many years, especially 19th- and early-20th-century shaving mugs and barber bottles and, more recently, razors. We are now combining these closely related categories under one heading for easier reference. A selection of other varied pieces relating to barbering will also be found below.

Barber Bottles

Amber, bulbous body tapering to a tall slender neck w/tooled mouth, Inverted Thumbprint patt., polished pontil, 7" h. **$231**

Art Nouveau design, bulbous base tapering to a lady's leg neck w/rolled lip & metal stopper, frosted lime green h.p. w/gold Art Nouveau bands & loops & a band of white & green blossoms, pontiled base, 8 1/4" h. **231**

Blue, dark shading to light blue, tall slender tapering form w/tooled lip, pontil scar, 12" h. **198**

Cased glass, bulbous body tapering to a ringed neck rolled lip, Hobnail patt., dark pink cased in clear, polished pontil, 6 3/4" h. (two chipped hobs) **413**

Cased glass, footed spherical body tapering to a tall slender neck w/tooled mouth, white cased in dark pink w/a satin finish, ornately enameled on the neck & shoulder w/stylized Mideastern designs in black & white, smooth base, 7 3/8" h. **253**

Cased Enameled Barber Bottle

Cased glass, wide ovoid body tapering to a ringed & gourd-form tall neck, white cased in frosted pinkish copper, enameled overall w/elaborate bands of spearpoint scrolls & four-petal floral designs, polished lip, smooth base, 8" h. (ILLUS.)... **165**

Cobalt blue, bulbous waisted body w/a tapering shoulder to the tall slender neck w/rolled lip, decorated w/large sprigs of green & white leaves & small yellow & white daisies, pontiled base, 7 5/8" h. **187**

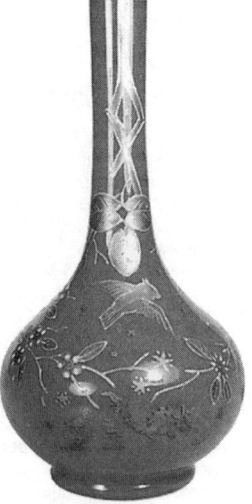

Cobalt Blue Enameled Barber Bottle

Cobalt blue, footed squatty bulbous body tapering to a tall slender neck, delicately enameled in white & gold w/leafy branch-

es & a bird in flight, polished lip, smooth base, 8 1/8" h. (ILLUS.)..................................... **220**

Fine Cut Glass Barber Bottle

Cut glass, spherical base cut overall w/a strawberry diamond design below cut shoulder bands & panels & a tall facet-cut neck w/polished lip & metal stopper, clear flashed w/light pinkish amethyst, polished base, 6 1/2" h. (ILLUS.) **440**

Purple Bell-shaped Barber Bottle

Deep purple, tall bell-shaped optic-ribbed body w/rounded shoulder to a tall slender neck w/rolled lip, enameled in white & touches of gold & orange w/delicate pointed arches alternating w/scrolls or small dot blossom clusters, pontiled base, 7 5/8" h. (ILLUS.)..................................... **330**

Frances Ware Hobnail Barber Bottle

Frances Ware, bulbous base tapering to ringed neck & rolled mouth, Hobnail patt. in frosted clear & amber stain, polished pontil, 7" h. (about 10 hobs chipped) (ILLUS.) **264**

Latticinio, slender stripes of red, green & blue alternating w/threaded white latticinio stripes, open pontil, porcelain stopper **176**

Mary Gregory, cobalt blue w/a white enamel scene of a girl playing tennis on one & a boy playing tennis on the other, bulbous base tapering to a tall lady's leg neck w/metal stopper, pontil scar, pr............ **413**

Green Mary Gregory Barber Bottle

Mary Gregory, ovoid body tapering to a lady's leg neck w/tooled mouth, dark grass green enameled in white w/a boy in a garden, pontiled base, 8 1/8" h. (ILLUS.) **275**

Mary Gregory, tapering cylindrical body w/tall slender neck & tooled lip, yellowish green decorated w/a white enamel boy in a garden, pontiled base, 7 7/8" h. **220**

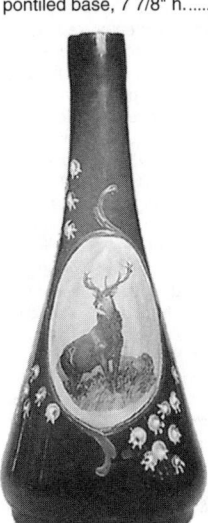

Stag-decorated Purple Barber Bottle

Medium purple, tapering conical form w/tooled mouth, optic ribbed interior, painted w/a large oval reserve featuring a color scene of a large brown stag, scattered white enameled small blossoms, pontiled base, 8" h. (ILLUS.)........................... **385**

Milk glass, cylindrical body w/rounded shoulder to tall cylindrical neck w/rolled lip, decorated w/a pale blue ground & a wide snowy winter landscape w/pond in foreground & cabin in background, words "Hair Oil" at the top, 9" h................................. **523**

Ornate Enameled Barber Bottle

Milk glass, footed spherical body tapering to a tall slender neck w/tooled mouth, beautifully enameled overall w/delicate floral scrolls in pink, green & white on a pale yellow ground, black enameled stylized leaf & point bands around the shoulder & mouth rim, smooth base, 8" h. (ILLUS.) **330**

Milk glass, gently tapering cylindrical body w/tall neck & rolled lip, decorated w/a large cluster of purple violets & green leaves crossed by a narrow white center band w/the words "Hair Tonic," pontil scar, 8 3/4" h. (slight paint wear) **121**

Milk glass, tapering cylindrical ringed body w/slender ringed neck & original pewter screw stopper, painted w/a large center shield-shaped reserve decorated w/a peacock perched on a crescent moon against a pale yellow ground, owner's name at top & "Tonic" at bottom, 8" h. **605**

Millefiori, bulbous base w/a tall slender neck & rolled rim w/original porcelain stopper, multicolored pastel shades in the cane design, 7 1/2" h. **330**

Opalescent glass, bulbous base tapering to a tall slender neck w/rolled lip, cranberry Stars & Stripes patt., smooth base, 7 1/4" h. **193**

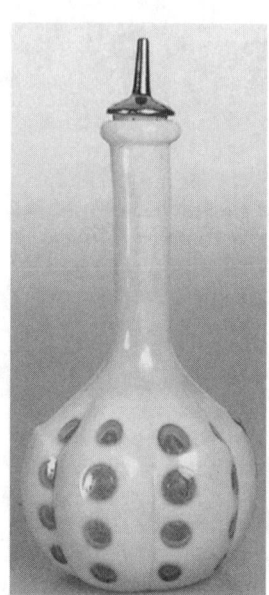

Opalescent Coinspot Barber Bottle

Opalescent glass, bulbous melon-lobed body tapering to a tall slender neck w/rolled lip, lime green Coinspot patt., smooth base, metal stopper, 7 1/8" h. (ILLUS.) **523**

Opalescent glass, squatty bulbous melon-lobed body w/wide shoulder tapering to a slender neck w/rolled lip, canary Daisy & Fern patt., smooth base, 7 1/4" h. **110**

White Stars & Stripes Barber Bottle

Opalescent glass, bulbous base tapering to a tall slender neck w/rolled lip, white Stars & Stripes patt., smooth base, 6 3/4" h. (ILLUS.) **242**

Rare Spanish Lace Barber Bottle

Opalescent glass, tall wasted body tapering to a tall slender neck w/rolled lip, blue Spanish Lace patt., smooth base, 7 5/8" h. (ILLUS.) **990**

Spatter, deep ruby to white spatter in clear, barrel-shaped body w/angled shoulder to tall cylindrical neck w/finished rim, 10" h. **209**

Spatter, tall squared body w/shoulder tapering to a tall slender neck w/tooled mouth, white, greenish yellow & maroon spatter cased in clear, polished pontil, 9" h. **110**

Striped, ovoid body tapering to tall slender neck w/sheared lip, composed of alternating slender red, white, blue & jade green stripes up the sides, pontil scar, 9" h. **303**

Mugs

Fraternal

Order of Redmen Shaving Mug

Order of Redmen, decorated w/a round gold ring enclosing a full-color profile bust of an Indian Chief, gilt trim bands & gold name at the bottom, 3 3/4" h. (ILLUS.) **$121**

General

Horseshoe & clover, decorated w/a wide band showing a large grey good luck horseshoe surrounded by pink & green clover, name in gold at bottom, T. & V. Limoges blank, 3 1/2" h. **44**

Patriotic Shaving Mug

Patriotic, crossed American flags centered by a large brown & yellow snare drum, base in gold & name in gold at top, 3 5/8" h. (ILLUS.) **605**

Sportsman, decorated w/a wide color scene of two hunting dogs among grass & bushes in brown, white, tan, black & green, peach top border band w/name in gold, gold base, T. & V. Limoges blank, 3 1/2" h. **231**

Sportsman, decorated w/the large head of a brown & white hunting dog holding a dead game bird in its mouth, head flanked by green grasses, gold trim bands & name in gold at the top, 4" h. **165**

Occupational

Barber Occupational Shaving Mug

Barber, decorated w/conjoined images of scissors, comb & straight razor among pink & green flowers, worn name in gold at bottom, 4" h. (ILLUS.) **285**

Butcher Occupational Shaving Mug

Butcher, decorated w/a colorful vignette of a butcher standing & working at a butcher block, sides of meat hanging in background, gold banding & name in gold at the top, 3 7/8" h. (ILLUS.) **990**

Cattleman, decorated w/a large head of a brown steer flanked by pink & green floral swags, gold rim band & name at top, 4" h. **220**

Cattleman Occupational Mug

Cattleman, decorated w/a large standing steer in dark brown & white, gold rim & name around top, 3 1/4" h. (ILLUS.).............. **176**

Delivery Wagon Driver Mug

Delivery wagon driver, decorated w/a large action scene of a horse-drawn canvas-topped delivery wagon in shades of brown, blue, white & black, gold base band & name in gold at top, T. & V. Limoges blank, 3 3/4" h. (ILLUS.)........................... **715**

Farmer Occupational Shaving Mug

Farmer, decorated w/a detailed scene of a farmer plowing w/two bright brown hors-

es, landscape & farmhouse in distant background, gold bands & gold name at bottom, 3 5/8" h. (ILLUS.) **440**

Farmer, decorated w/a large detailed color scene of a farmer behind a plow pulled by two horses, field, house & farm buildings in background, worn name in gold at the top, 4" h... **202**

Lathe worker, decorated w/a color scene of a large mechanical lather in grey & black on a pink ground, worn gold name above, 3 1/8" h... **231**

Oyster Dealer Occupational Mug

Oyster dealer, decorated w/a large oyster shell in grey, black, pink & white, gold band trim & gold name at top, 3 5/8" h. (ILLUS.)... **825**

Railroadman, decorated w/a large color scene of a brown box car, gold banding & gold name at the top, 3 3/4" h. **193**

Wagon Driver Occupational Mug

Wagon driver, decorated w/a large detailed color scene of a horse-drawn stake wagon & driver, large barrels in the back, full maroon wrap, name in gold at the top, T. & V. Limoges blank, 3 1/2" h. (ILLUS.) **660**

Razor Blade Banks

Blade Bank with Horse Decoration

Bell-shaped ceramics, w/horse head at top, image of trophy embossed on body in circles of rhinestones which also decorate horse head & spell out "BLADES" underneath, "Japan" sticker on bottom, 6 1/2" h. (ILLUS.) **$85-95**

"The Gay Blades" Bank

Gay Blades, ceramic, white w/black drawing of two Oriental-looking men in striped trousers, one w/Fu Manchu-type mustache, other w/goatee, the slot & "The Gay Blades" located between the two figures, hole in bottom for blade removal, marked "E. Murran, E.M. Pottery," 4 1/8" w., 4" h. (ILLUS.) **85-100**

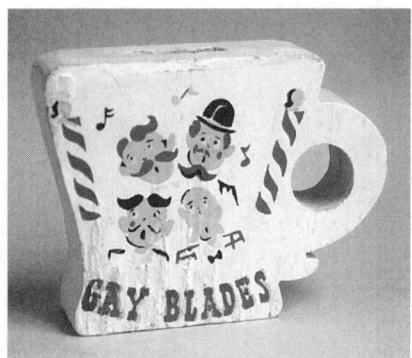

Mug-shaped Wooden Blade Bank

Gay Blades, wooden, cut out in the shape of a mug, front illustrated w/barbershop quartet flanked by barber poles, "Gay Blades" underneath, 3 1/2" version $35-45, 3" h. version (ILLUS.) **30-40**

Hedgehog Blade Bank

Hedgehog, ceramic, white w/blue highlights, reddish & black star decoration & "Razor Blades" on side, England (ILLUS.) **65-75**

Mustache Cup-form Blade Bank

Mustache cup form, metal, painted white w/polychrome decoration of bust of man over the words "Old Blades," ornate handle painted black, slot for blades in front, back holds soap or razor, removable bottom, 6" w., 3 3/4" h. (ILLUS.) **75-100**

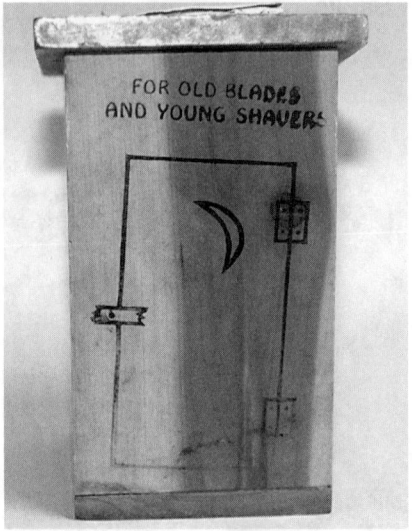

Outhouse Blade Bank

Outhouse, wooden, rustic-looking door w/crescent moon drawn on front under "For Old Blades and Young Shavers," 4 1/2" h. (ILLUS.) **45-65**

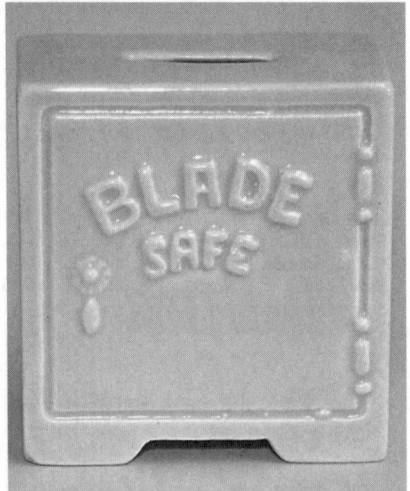

Blade Safe

Safe, ceramic, w/details of door & "Blade Safe" embossed on front, slot on top but no hole in bottom, can be hung or placed on surface, light green or blue, 2 1/2" h. (ILLUS.) **40-60**

Shaving mug form, ceramic, white w/line drawing of barbershop quartet above the words "Gay Old Blades," space for brush & blades, back flat for hanging, bottom marked "Goms of Ca., Pat. Pending," 4" h. (ILLUS., top next column) **65-75**

Shaving Mug-form Blade Holder

Floral Mug-form Blade Holder

Shaving mug form, ceramic, white w/poly-chrome floral decoration above the words "Gay Old Blades" in Gothic-style purple script, space for brush & blades, back flat for hanging, 4" h. (ILLUS.) **75-100**

Miscellaneous

Lighted Floor Model Barber Pole

Barber pole, floor-model, electric light-up type, porcelain w/glass cylinder & globe, a black cylindrical base below a red, white & blue spiral section below another cylindrical cream section, the top w/a glass cylinder enclosing the spiral red, white & blue upper sign below the large milk glass top globe, ca. 1920s-30s, 13" d., 87" h. (ILLUS.) **$3,300**

Wall-mounted Barber Pole

Barber pole, wall-mounted, glass & metal, hexagonal chromed mounts at the top &

base, glass red & white spiral pole, Emil J. Paidar Company, China, early 20th c., restored, rechromed, 22 1/4" h. (ILLUS.) **308**

Barber Pole

Barber poles, wooden, gilded acorn finials on red, white & blue painted poplar half-round poles, scattered paint loss, 79" h., pr. (ILLUS. of one).. **3,819**

Barbershop Face Tonic Bottle

Barbershop bottle, clear wide cylindrical body w/a wide shoulder tapering to a tall slender neck, decorated w/a large white pyro label printed in red & gold "Arista - Antiseptic Face Tonic," smooth base, faint tiny stress crack in side of neck, 7 1/4" h. (ILLUS.) 110

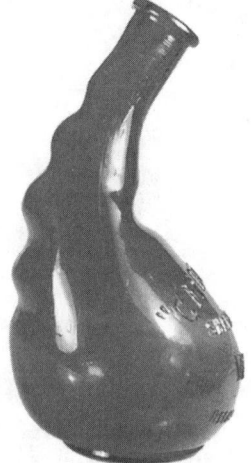

Barbershop Cremex Shampoo Bottle

Barbershop bottle, cobalt blue glass w/odd bulbous potato-shaped body tapering to a curved neck molded w/finger grip ridges, front w/molded lettering "Cremex - Shampooing - Vase - Registered Design," early 20th c., 8" h. (ILLUS.) 198

Brilliantine bottle, light turquoise blue, footed squatty spherical body tapering to a cylindrical neck w/polished lip, enameled overall w/orange & white interwoven dot bands & small five-petal white blossoms, smooth base, 3 7/8" h. 358

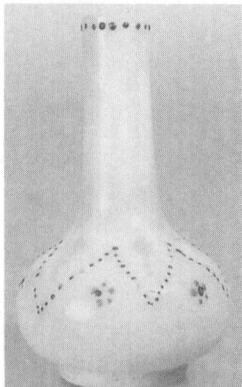

Milk Glass Brilliantine Bottle

Brilliantine bottle, milk glass, footed squatty rounded body tapering to a cylindrical neck w/polished lip, h.p. dot bands & blossoms in red & green w/pale shaded

green background, smooth base, 4 1/4" h. (ILLUS.) 220

Brilliantine bottle, short cylindrical body w/large thumbprint patt., deep ruby red, w/metal stopper, 5" h. 231

Giant Charlex Display Razor

Counter display piece, model of a giant straight razor, celluloid & metal, the flat brown celluloid blade case printed w/"Charlex Marque Deposé," blade engraved "Charlex Marque Deposé - Qualité Superieure - 60 Charlex," reverse of blade engraved "Forge Evide à Soligen," France, early 20th c., slight surface pitting, chrome wear on blade, closed 26 1/2" l. (ILLUS.) 715

Razor set, celluloid handles & Sheffield steel blades, a set of seven for use during the week, in original case, made by Joseph Allen & Sons, the set (some minor rust spotting on blades, wear on case & separated lid) 121

Shaving paper vase, cobalt blue, cylindrical w/optic ribbed design, h.p. w/clusters of small white lily-of-the-valley-like blossoms & gilt trim, smooth base, 7 1/4" h. 330

Green Enameled Paper Vase

Shaving paper vase, emerald green cylindrical w/optic ribbing, polished rim, h.p. w/large yellow blossoms on slender stems w/large green leaves, gilt trim, smooth base, 7 1/8" h. (ILLUS.) 550

Dolls

Red Haired Allan

Mary Gregory Shaving Paper Vase

Shaving paper vase, medium teal green, cylindrical w/optic ribbing, decorated w/Mary Gregory-style white enamel figure of girl standing amid a tall curved plant w/tiny dot blossoms, smooth base, 9 1/4" h. (ILLUS.) **440**

Allan, painted red hair, pink lips, bendable legs, wearing red jacket w/stripe trim & "A" decoration, blue swim trunks, near mint in box, clothing discolored w/age, box in poor condition (ILLUS.) **$125**

Allan, painted red hair, tan lips, straight legs, wearing striped jacket, blue shorts, wrist tag, in box w/cardboard arm insert, black wire stand, white cover booklet & cork sandals w/blue straps in cellophane bag, near mint in box (jacket age-discolored, wrist tag separated, box worn) **95**

Old Barber Shop Sign

Sign, porcelain, rectangular double-sized flange-hung type, wide red, white & blue chevron-design border band around narrow dark blue rectangle printed in white "Barber Shop," early 20th c., 12 x 24" (ILLUS.) **220**

BARBIE DOLLS & COLLECTIBLES

At the time of her introduction in 1959, no one could have guessed that this statuesque doll would become a national phenomenon and eventually the most famous girl's plaything produced.

Over the years, Barbie and her growing range of family and friends have evolved with the times, serving as an excellent mirror on the fashion and social changes taking place in American society. Today, after more than 40 years of continuous production, Barbie's popularity remains unabated among both young girls and older collectors. Early and rare Barbies can sell for remarkable prices, and it is every Barbie collector's hope to find mint condition "#1 Barbie."

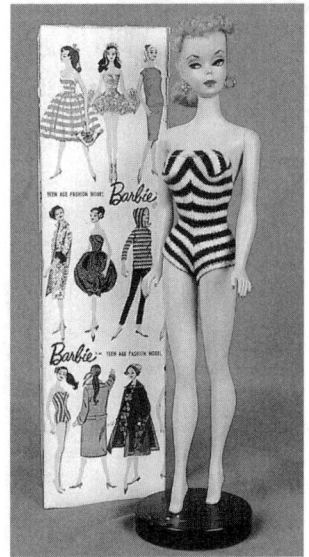

Blonde "#1 Ponytail Barbie" & Box

Barbie, "#1 Ponytail Barbie," blonde hair, red lips, blue eyeliner, eye shadow, finger

& toe paint, straight legs, wearing black & white striped one-piece swimsuit, hoop earrings, in box w/metal prongs, topknot has been retied, bottom of hair & bangs are fuzzy, ponytail seems shorter than usual, some body discoloration, lips are dull and faded on one side, metal rod is protruding from left foot, both feet have faint red stains from shoes, swimsuit is age-discolored, box is in poor condition (ILLUS.) **3,200**

Brunette "#1 Ponytail Barbie"

Barbie, "#1 Ponytail Barbie," brunette hair, red lips, finger & toe paint, straight legs, wearing green silk Pak sheath w/bow accent, brown #1 open-toe shoes, white nylon short gloves, hoop earrings, rubber band on top ponytail is replacement, bottom of hair & bangs are flat & slightly fuzzy, lips are faded, head is wobbly on neck knob, discoloration on feet (ILLUS.).. **2,200**

Barbie, "1988 Happy Holidays Barbie," #1703, never removed from box (box worn) **325**

"1992 'Cristalline' Barbie" in Box

Barbie, "1992 Happy Holidays 'Cristalline' Barbie" #1429, foreign issue, blonde Bar-

bie in gown, never removed from box, box is worn, two lower plastic seals split (ILLUS.) **55**

"#2 Ponytail Barbie"

Barbie, "#2 Ponytail Barbie," blonde hair, red lips, eye shadow & liner, finger & toe paint, straight legs, wearing black & white one-piece swimsuit, hoop earrings, black open-toe shoes, ponytail topknot has been retied, bottom of hair & bangs are fuzzy, some stains & discoloration, one eyebrow is higher than other (ILLUS.) **3,500**

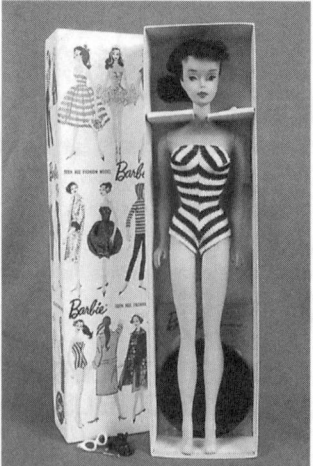

"#4 Ponytail Barbie" in Box

Barbie, "#4 Ponytail Barbie" in box, brunette hair in original set, red lips, finger & toe paint, straight legs, wearing black & white striped knit one-piece swimsuit, in box w/pedestal stand of black wire top & plastic base, pink cover booklet, cardboard neck insert, pearl earrings, white-rimmed sunglasses, black open-toe shoes, bottom ponytail rubber band is hard & broken, ends of ponytail are loose, green discoloration on ears, box w/"2.90" written in pencil is worn (ILLUS.)......................... **475**

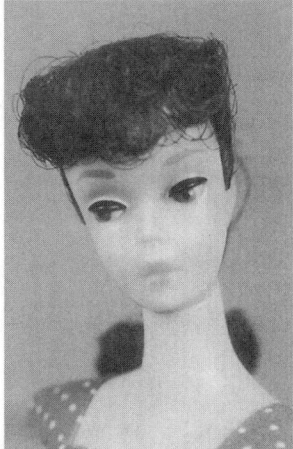

Brunette "#5 Ponytail Barbie"

Barbie, "#5 Ponytail Barbie," brunette hair w/original top ponytail knot, red lips, finger & toe paint, straight legs, wearing green Pak sheath w/polka dots & button accents, black open-toe shoes, bottom ponytail rubber band is replacement that has hardened, bottom of hair is flat & slightly fuzzy, face is oily & slightly darker tan color, sides of lips are faded (ILLUS.)..... **210**

Dark Blonde "#6 Ponytail Barbie"

Barbie, "#6 Ponytail Barbie," dark blonde hair, coral lips, finger & toe paint, straight legs, nude, ponytail rubber band is hard & melted, bottom hair slightly fuzzy & partly flat, faded dark color on bottom & sides of left foot from shoes (ILLUS.)............ **210**
Barbie, "American Girl Barbie," dark blonde hair, peach lips, finger paint, bendable

legs, wearing one-piece swimsuit w/striped top & aqua bottoms, gold wire stand (small dot above eye, indentations on left ankle).. **350**

Brunette "American Girl Barbie"

Barbie, "American Girl Barbie" in box, brunette hair, beige lips, finger paint, bendable legs, wearing original one-piece swimsuit w/striped top & aqua nylon bottoms, aqua open-toe shoes, in box w/gold wire stand, booklet, store price sticker reading "Twin Fair Dept. 5 $2.97," swimsuit faded, seam separated, box is in poor condition (ILLUS.) **550**
Barbie, "Benefit Ball Barbie," #1521, Classique Collection designed by Carol Spencer, first in series, box dated 1992, never removed from box (box is worn) **40**

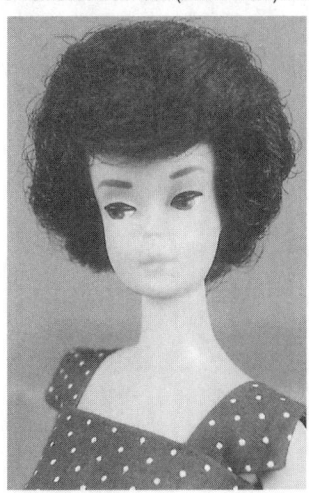

Brunette "Bubblecut Barbie"

Barbie, "Bubblecut Barbie," brunette hair, coral lips, finger & toe paint, straight legs, wearing blue Pak sheath w/polka dots & button accents, near-mint (ILLUS.).................. **85**

Barbie, "Bubblecut Barbie," dark blonde hair, coral lips, finger & toe paint, straight legs, wearing red nylon one-piece swimsuit, red open-toe shoes, blue cover booklet, near-mint (face appears darker than body, one ankle bends slightly inward, strap split on shoe, booklet worn w/age) **65**

Barbie with White Ginger Bubblecut

Barbie, "Bubblecut Barbie" in box, white ginger hair, pink lips, finger & toe paint, straight legs, wearing black & white striped knit one-piece swimsuit, in box w/black wire stand & cardboard neck & foot inserts, price sticker reading "G.E.T. Price 2.43," near mint, faint green discoloration on earring holes, box is worn, w/X marks in pencil (ILLUS.) **490**

Blonde "Bubblecut Barbie"

Barbie, "Bubblecut Barbie," light blonde hair, pale pink lips, finger & toe paint, straight legs, wearing pale pink Belle Pak dress w/bow accent, dress faded & worn (ILLUS.) **135**

Titian-haired "Bubblecut Barbie"

Barbie, "Bubblecut Barbie," titian hair, coral lips, finger & toe paint, wearing striped Knit Dress Pak item & gold cloth purse w/button closure, faded open-toe shoe strap lines on both feet (ILLUS.) **155**

Barbie, "Café Society Barbie," The Official Barbie Collector's Club Members' Choice Second Edition, #18892, box dated 1997, w/cardboard box sleeve & shipping box, never removed from box **55**

"Color Magic Barbie" in Plaid Outfit

Barbie, "Color Magic Barbie," lemon yellow hair w/blue metal barrette, pink lips, cheek blush, finger paint, bendable legs, wearing #4040 Designer Set green, yellow & blue plaid dress w/yellow waistband, near mint, dress is age-discolored & tag is frayed (ILLUS.) **500**

"Color Magic Barbie"

Barbie, "Color Magic Barbie," light red hair, coral lips, finger paint, bendable legs, nude, near-mint (ILLUS.)................................. **765**
Barbie, "Color Magic Barbie," yellow blonde hair, pink lips, finger paint, bendable legs, wearing one-piece diamond pattern swimsuit & matching headband (indentations on legs & feet)...................................... **300**
Barbie, "Eliza Doolittle," #15501, Hollywood Legends Collection, Barbie dressed in pink organza dress as character from My Fair Lady, box dated 1995, never removed from box (box is worn) **35**

"Fashion Queen Barbie"

Barbie, "Fashion Queen Barbie," painted brunette hair w/blue plastic headband, titian bubblecut wig, pink lips, finger & toe paint, painted straight legs, nude, some scratches in paint on upper legs & feet, paint worn on legs, lower back & bottom of feet (ILLUS.)................................. **65**
Barbie, "Gibson Girl Barbie," Great Eras Collection, #3702, box dated 1993, never removed from box (box worn)......................... **55**
Barbie, "Gold Barbie," First Limited Edition designed by Bob Mackie, 1990, mint in box (cardboard box & clear plastic case

insert missing, doll is displayed in plastic case w/boa).. **200**
Barbie, "Madame du Barbie," #17934, 10th in series designed by Bob Mackie, box dated 1997, mint in box (box is worn)........... **170**
Barbie, "Madame du Barbie," #17934, 10th Limited Edition designed by Bob Mackie, box dated 1997, never removed from box (some wear on box) **230**
Barbie, "Platinum Barbie," Third Limited Edition designed by Bob Mackie, #2703, near-mint in box (doll & accessories have been removed from original packaging, box is scuffed & creased)................................ **95**

"Side Part American Girl Barbie"

Barbie, "Side Part American Girl Barbie," brown hair, coral lips, finger paint, bendable legs, wearing Dressed-Up! Pak outfit of gold & beige brocade top w/attached belt & buckle & green satin skirt, replaced blue hair ribbon, eyebrows have been penciled in, pin indents near mouth & left ear, small amount of toe paint on left foot, outfit worn (ILLUS.) **1,025**

Brunette "American Girl Barbie"

Barbie, "Side Part American Girl Barbie," brunette hair w/replaced blue ribbon, full pink lips, finger & toe paint, bendable legs, wearing original one-piece swimsuit w/striped top & aqua bottoms, aqua open-toe shoes, lips repainted, faint blue stains on legs, clothing worn (ILLUS.)........ **1,025**

Barbie, "Snow Princess Barbie," #11875, Enchanted Seasons Collection limited edition, box dated 1994, never removed from box (box is worn) **65**

Barbie with Platinum Swirl Ponytail

Barbie, "Swirl Ponytail Barbie" in box, platinum hair in original set w/hairpin & yellow ribbon tie, clear plastic bag head wrap, white lips & nostril paint, finger & toe paint, straight legs, wearing red nylon one-piece swimsuit, pearl earrings, wrist tag, in box w/red open-toe shoes & booklet in cellophane bag, gold wire stand, cardboard box insert, price sticker reading "Montgomery Ward" w/"$1.87" & "$1.47" both crossed off & "$1.29," near mint, some green discoloration on left ear, wrist tag discolored & worn, box is worn, stapled & discolored (ILLUS.)........... **2,025**

"Swirl Ponytail Barbie" in Gown

Barbie, "Swirl Ponytail Barbie," platinum hair, light pink lips w/white outline, finger & toe paint, straight legs, wearing #983 "Enchanted Evening" pink satin gown w/flower accent, fur stole, long white nylon gloves, clear open-toe shoes marked "Japan" w/gold glitter, pearl drop earrings, three-strand pearl necklace, hair is reset w/loose topknot, bottom of hair is loose & flat, closure on necklace replaced w/wire, pearl drops are missing from discolored earrings, most of gold glitter missing from shoes, dress is faded & stained (ILLUS.).. **475**

Titian Hair "Swirl Ponytail Barbie"

Barbie, "Swirl Ponytail Barbie," titian hair, coral lips, finger & toe paint, straight legs, wearing red nylon one-piece swimsuit, hair redone, eyelashes & lips repainted, seam separations on swimsuit (ILLUS.)........ **250**

Barbie, "Talking Barbie," brunette hair in original set, pink lips, cheek blush, rooted eyelashes, bendable legs, wearing original two-piece nylon swimsuit w/metal accent on bottoms, lace cover-up, bright orange molded strap shoes, wrist tag, near-mint (wrist tag creased & torn, talker string is missing, metal accent is discolored) **175**

Barbie, "Twist 'n Turn Barbie," #3303, Beautiful Blues Gift Set, Sears Exclusive, medium brown hair w/bright orange bow accent, pink lips, faint cheek blush, rooted eyelashes, bendable legs, wearing blue lamé dress w/white & blue satin ribbon accents on bodice, blue satin coat w/fur trim, blue vinyl clutch purse w/button closure, blue pointed-toe pumps (finger paint on hands different shades, nose & chin light colored, ribbon trim & bow on dress slightly worn & soiled, coat is slightly faded & stained w/fur trim thinning & partially loose).. **600**

"Live Action Christie"

Christie, "Live Action Christie," black hair, beige lips, rooted eyelashes, bendable arms & legs, rotating wrists, wearing original nylon print pants w/attached orange plastic circle & purple fringe accent, matching top w/attached fringe on sleeves, w/clear plastic stand, near-mint, small faded area, clothing fraying (ILLUS.).. **145**

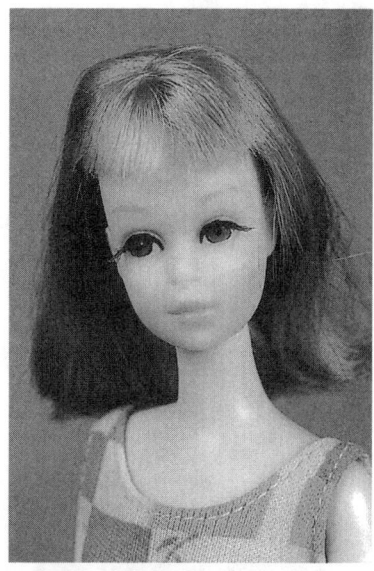

Blonde Francie with Bendable Legs

Francie, blonde hair, pink lips, rooted eyelashes, bendable legs, wearing one-piece nylon print swimsuit, w/white soft pumps, pink plastic eyelash brush, near-mint, one arm slightly lighter color than other, swimsuit & shoes age-discolored (ILLUS.).. **135**

"Black Francie"

Francie, "Black Francie," reddish brunette hair, pink lips, rooted eyelashes, bendable legs, nude, several earring holes on both ears, pin hole above right eyebrow (ILLUS.).. **500**

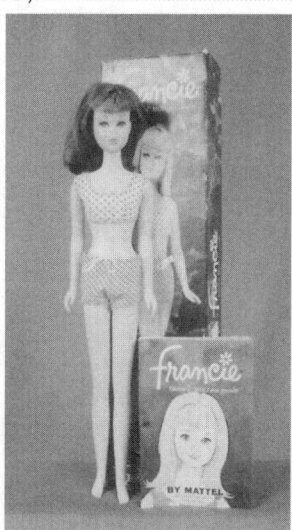

Brunette Francie in Box

Francie, brunette hair, pink lips, faint cheek blush, straight legs, wearing two-piece swimsuit of white midriff top w/red polka dots & red & white checked bottoms w/cord tie, in box w/booklet & black wire stand, discoloration to legs & swimsuit, box worn (ILLUS.).. **275**

Francie, "Busy Francie," blonde hair w/green ribbon hair bow & plastic head cover, peach lips, cheek blush, bendable arms & legs, rotating wrists, wearing original lime green sleeveless sweater, orange vinyl belt w/buckle, denim pants, lime green square-toe pumps, clear plastic stand, Living Barbie & Skipper booklet, brown plastic accessories include TV, record player & Ken record, telephone, travel bag, tray w/two inserts, near-mint **425**

Blonde "Twist 'n Turn Francie"

Francie, "Twist 'n Turn Francie," blonde hair, pink lips & cheeks, rooted eyelashes, bendable legs, nude (ILLUS.) **115**

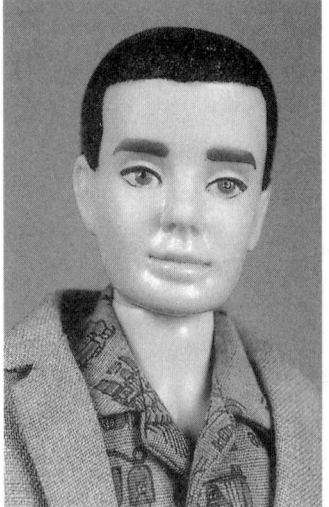

Brunette Flocked Hair Ken

Ken, brunette flocked hair, beige lips, straight legs, wearing #785 Dreamboat outfit of green jacket w/button accents, short-sleeve print shirt w/button accents, olive green pants w/zipper, yellow cotton socks, brown shoes, straw hat w/print hat

band & flower & feather accents, one leg longer than other, socks stained from shoes (ILLUS.)... **90**

Bendable Leg Ken in Box

Ken, brunette hair, beige lips, bendable legs, wearing blue jacket w/red trim & "K," red swim trunks, wrist tag, in box w/booklet & cork sandals w/red straps in cellophane bag, black wire stand, box worn (ILLUS.)... **245**

Ken, "Rhett Butler," #12741, Hollywood Legends Collection, Ken dressed as character from Gone with the Wind, box dated 1994, never removed from box (box is worn).. **35**

Straight-legged Midge

Midge, blonde hair, coral lips, finger & toe paint, straight legs, wearing two-piece nylon swimsuit, lower right leg bends slightly to the right (ILLUS.)............................... 70

Midge in Vacation Time Outfit

Midge, blonde hair, coral lips, finger & toe paint, straight legs, wearing #1623 Vacation Time pink knit sweater, pink & white checked shorts, near mint (ILLUS.).............. 165

Midge, molded head on straight-leg body, painted red hair missing headband, beige lips, finger & toe paint, wearing navy blue nylon one-piece swimsuit, three wigs including titian side ponytails w/rubberbands & ribbon ties, blonde swirl 'n curl, & brunette topknot pouf w/rubberband & black ribbon, near-mint (left leg slightly shorter than right).............................. 205

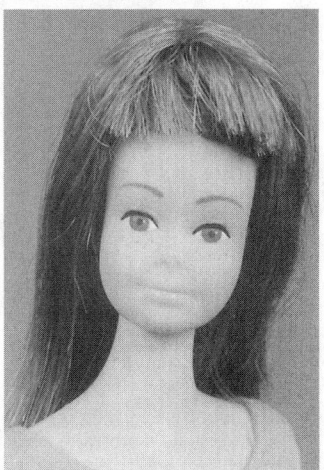

Molded Hair Midge

Midge, molded & painted titian hair w/orange plastic headband, titian double-ponytail wig, orange lips w/tint of beige, fin-

ger & toe paint, straight legs, wearing two-piece nylon pink & red swimsuit, ribbon ties on wig are missing, seam separation on back of swimsuit (ILLUS.).............. 100

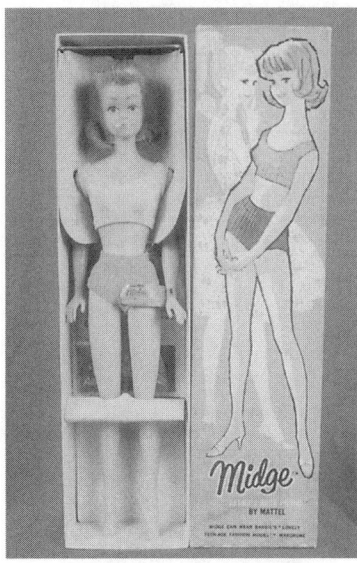

Titian-haired Midge in Box

Midge, titian hair, coral lips, finger & toe paint, straight legs, wearing two-piece nylon chartreuse & orange swimsuit, wrist tag, in box w/gold wire stand, white open-toe shoes, & booklet in cellophane bag, cardboard box insert, plastic head cover, near-mint, wrist tag & box worn (ILLUS.)... 220

Midge, titian hair, pink lips, finger paint, bendable legs, wearing gold & navy blue lamé sheath, gold clutch purse w/button closure, gold wire stand (earring holes, faint stain) 185

Titian-haired Midge

Midge, titian hair w/blue ribbon headband, pink lips, finger paint, bendable legs, wearing scoop-neck red play suit, faded green discoloration on back of left arm, headband & tag show wear (ILLUS.) **300**

Skipper, blonde hair, pink lips, straight legs, wearing #1934 "Junior Bridesmaid" outfit of pink gown w/lace tulle overdress w/lace trim & attached pink ribbon waist-band & back bow, long nylon slip w/lace trim, short white nylon gloves, white nylon ankle socks, flower headband w/attached net cap, pink flats, plastic flower basket w/flowers & ribbon bow accent, gold wire stand, near-mint (both shoes split) **275**

Near-mint Skooter in Box

Skooter, titian hair in original set w/ribbon ties, light pink lips, straight legs, wearing two-piece red & white swimsuit, wrist tag, in box w/plastic bag including booklet, red flats, white plastic comb & brush, w/gold wire stand, cardboard box insert, near-mint, some discoloration, plastic bag has been opened (ILLUS.)...................... **105**

Bicentennial "Malibu Skipper"

Skipper, "Malibu Skipper," blonde hair, beige lips, cheek blush, tan skin tone, "Twist 'n Turn" body, bendable legs, wearing Bicentennial Fashion outfit of long red skirt printed w/Revolutionary War soldiers & white top w/lace trim, blue suede vest w/cord tie, white pantaloons w/black bow accents & lace trim, white cap w/lace trim, red bag w/drawstring & flag decal (ILLUS.).. **55**

Skipper, titian hair w/metal headband & plastic bag covering, pink lips, straight legs, wearing red & white one-piece swimsuit, wrist tag, in box w/cellophane bag including booklet, red flats & white plastic comb & brush, gold wire stand, near-mint (headband discolored, swimsuit stretched & discolored, small tear & crease on wrist tag, worn box is marked for brunette hair color)...................................... **145**

Titian-haired Skooter in Box

Skooter, titian hair w/replaced rubber bands & hair ribbons, tan lips, cheek blush, straight legs, wearing two-piece swimsuit w/red & white striped top & red nylon bottoms w/metal accent, red flats, wrist tag, in box w/gold wire stand, yellow cover booklet, some light-discoloration, wrist tag is worn, torn & taped, box is faded & worn (ILLUS.) 95

Clothing & Accessories

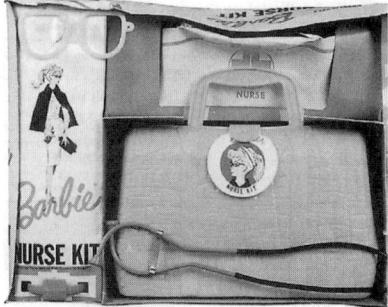

Barbie Nurse Kit

Accessory pak, Barbie Nurse Kit: pink plastic case w/handle, plastic closure & cardboard label, white paper nurse's cap w/red cross & "Nurse" on front, glasses w/yellow plastic frames, blue plastic watch, green & black plastic stethoscope, yellow plastic scissors, red plastic thermometer, red plastic hot water bottle w/yellow stopper, red plastic syringe, yellow plastic spoon, blue plastic reflex mallet; in box w/liners, Pressman Toy Corp., 1962, needle missing from syringe, some age discoloration & staining, box worn (ILLUS.) **$400**

"Dog 'n Duds" Accessory Pak

Accessory pak, "Dog 'n Duds," No. 1613, Barbie set, grey poodle w/felt features, red collar & red cord leash, red vinyl collar w/studs & gold chain leash, red w/gold trim & pink & black plaid coats, red & white ear muffs, pink tutu w/ribbon

tie, black plastic face mask w/elastic strap, yellow & black felt hat w/elastic chin strap, white plastic dog bone, dog food box, white plastic collar w/black ribbon tie, white wooden bowl w/dog food, booklet, paper label, never removed from box w/$3.00 paper label on cellophane, worn, dog food bowl is loose in package (ILLUS.) 265

Automobile, by Irwin, light blue w/pink interior, clear plastic windshield, black w/painted white wheels w/silver center caps, white plastic steering wheel, grey painted grill & headlights (scuffs & some discoloration on wheel areas, one plastic window loose from support screw) 170

Barbie Case

Case, oblong, black vinyl w/two images of Barbie in different fashions & "Barbie" on front, metal zipper, 1961, zipper discolored (ILLUS.) 100

Ken Case

Case, rectangular, gold vinyl w/picture of Ken standing in foreground & Ken lounging against convertible sports car w/date in background & "Ken," black plastic handle, metal clasp, metal clothing rack & two cardboard drawers inside, paper hang tag w/original price of $2.98, paper Barbie Fan Club membership application, 1962, near mint (ILLUS.) 40

Japanese Version of "After Five" Set

Clothing set, "After Five," #934, Japanese version, Barbie, white cotton dress w/red, orange & green polka dots & button accents, red open-toe shoes, orange clutch purse w/button closure, pearl necklace, near-mint (ILLUS. of Bubblecut Barbie not included) **1,900**

Clothing set, "Cheerleader," #0876, Barbie, white sweater w/red stitching & felt "M," red corduroy skirt, added white nylon ankle socks (originals were cotton), red tennis shoes w/white soles, red & white paper pompons, white plastic megaphone w/red trim & painted "M," near-mint (pompons creased, small melt areas & faint yellow stain on megaphone) **70**

Clothing set, "Cotton Casual," Barbie, navy & white striped dress w/bow accents, white #1 open-toe shoes, booklet, mint in box (shoes have holes, dress, shoes & booklet are loose in box, box is worn) **115**

Clothing set, "Country Club Dance," Barbie, white satin dress w/gold & white striped bodice & striped skirt trim, cardboard bodice insert, long white nylon gloves, white pointed-toe pumps, pearl necklace, gold clutch purse w/button closure, near-mint (bodice insert is age discolored & creased, one glove stained) **225**

Clothing set, "Country Picnic," #1933, Skipper, pink, green & blue dress w/appliqué butterflies, pink flats, red & white checked napkin & blanket w/fringe trim & flower print, pink glass w/fizz, blue plastic plate, plastic hamburger, wax watermelon, rubber ball, blue thermos w/Scottie dog decal, plastic hotdog, metal fork w/red plastic handle, butterfly net w/metal handle (cloth frayed & discolored, thermos top missing) **165**

Clothing set, "Drum Major," #0775, Ken, white jacket w/gold & red trim, red epaulettes w/gold fringe on shoulders & gold braid on left sleeve, red pants w/white stripe, white fur hat w/gold trim, accents & chin strap, white cotton socks, white shoes, gold baton w/gold cord, near-mint (some fading, discoloration) **45**

Clothing set, "Fun on Ice," #791, Barbie, plaid sweater, gold corduroy pants, gold knit scarf & gloves, black plastic skates w/metal blades, booklet, paper label, never removed from box (box worn) **75**

Clothing set, "Golden Elegance," #992, Barbie, red & gold brocade sheath, matching coat w/brown fur cuff trim, brown fur headband hat w/pearl trim, brown open-toe shoes, short white nylon gloves, pearl necklace & earrings, red velveteen clutch purse w/button closure, white hankie (discoloration on gloves, hankie & on metal of necklace & earrings) **145**

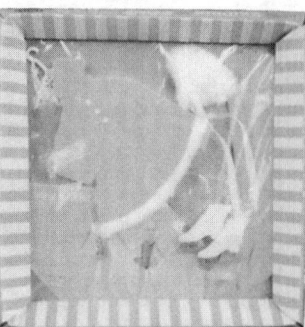

"Ice Skatin'" Clothing Set for Skipper

Clothing set, "Ice Skatin'," No. 3470, Skipper outfit, orange velour dress w/white fur trim & button accents, white fur hat w/ribbon ties, orange tights, white skates w/grey plastic blades, hanger, booklet, paper label, never removed from box w/"Winston, June 14, 77 - $1.99" written on back in blue ink & "Winston's Discount Centre $1.99" price tag on cellophane (ILLUS.) **85**

Clothing set, "In Training," #780, Ken, white cotton shirt, red & white polka dot shorts, white cotton briefs, black plastic dumbbells, "How to Build Muscles" book, pink cover booklet, paper label, never removed from box (box is worn) **45**

Clothing set, "Long on Looks," No. 1227, Francie outfit, white blouse w/lace trim, green stitching & button accents, long hot pink skirt w/white accents & yellow bow waist, pink nylon slip w/bow accent, hot pink fishnet stockings, pink soft bow shoes, hanger, booklet, w/paper label, in box marked "Francie and Casey," never removed from box, box worn (ILLUS., top next page) **130**

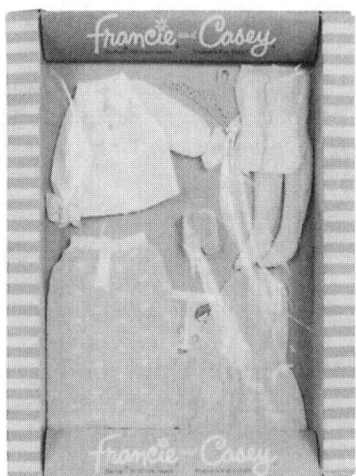

"Long on Looks" Clothing Set

Clothing set, "Midi Duet," #3451, Francie, white nylon dress w/pink, white & green floral pattern & attached pink bow at waist, long pink nylon vest, pink square-toe pumps, booklet, hanger, paper label, never removed from box (box is worn)......... **150**

Clothing set, "Polo Shirt," Ken Pak, red cotton w/button closure, cardboard backing w/attached black hanger, paper Ken label w/perforated price, booklet, never removed from box **25**

Clothing set, "Red Flare," Barbie, red velveteen coat w/bow accent, matching hat w/bow accent & clutch purse w/rhinestone closure, long white nylon gloves, red open-toe shoes, booklet, paper label, never removed from box (box worn, w/"3.00" written on back in pencil) **135**

"Satin 'n Rose" Clothing Set

Clothing set, "Satin 'n Rose," No. 1611, Barbie outfit, rose-colored satin bolero jacket, matching wrap skirt, blouse w/one shoulder & bow accent, pants, pale pink open-toe shoes w/silver glitter, clear rhinestone stud earrings in small cello-

phane bag, booklet, paper label, never removed from box w/$2.50 paper label on cellophane, worn (ILLUS.) **300**

Clothing set, "School Days," #1921, Skipper, red jacket w/button accents & crest on pocket, white sleeveless shirt w/red stitching & button accents, red & white pleated skirt, white nylon ankle socks, red flats, red felt hat w/red & white hat band & feather accent, wax apple, brown plastic glasses w/clear lenses, Arithmetic, English & Geography books, black plastic book strap, red & natural wooden pencils (some fraying & age discoloration, apple, red pencil & books are worn) **85**

Clothing set, "Senior Prom," #951, Barbie, green satin gown w/blue satin neckband & green & blue tulle panels, green open-toe shoes w/pearl accents, near-mint (tag on gown is frayed) **105**

Clothing set, "Sleeper Set," Ken, brown striped two-piece pajamas w/button accents, alarm clock, glass of milk, wax roll, booklet, paper label, never removed from box (box worn) **95**

Clothing set, "Student Teacher," #1622, Barbie, dress w/red & white skirt, red top & white insert w/button accents, red vinyl belt w/buckle, red pointed-toe pumps, plastic globe on white stand, painted wooden pointer, Geography book (discoloration on dress)... **155**

Clothing set, "Sweater Girl," #957, Barbie, pink knit sweater w/silver button closures, matching knit sleeveless shell, pink flannel skirt, pale pink open-toe shoes, metal scissors, wooden bowl w/green, pink & yellow yarn & two knitting needles, "How to Knit" book (yarn faded, small holes in sweater) **135**

"Sweet Dreams" Clothing Set

Clothing set, "Sweet Dreams," #973, Barbie outfit, yellow nightie w/flower embroidery & pale blue ribbon strap accent, matching panties w/ribbon bow accents, matching hair ribbon w/bow & attached metal ring, pale blue scuffs w/pompons, alarm clock, wax apple, booklet, "Dear Diary" book, paper label, near mint in box, box worn, some contents are loose in box or have been reattached to backing w/tape (ILLUS.) **115**

Clothing set, "Terry Togs," #784, Ken, blue terry robe w/embroidered "K," matching belt & scuffs, white cotton briefs, yellow terry towel marked "His," plastic soap, grey razor, black comb, partial grey sponge, booklet, paper label, never removed from box (sponge is deteriorated, booklet is loose, box is worn, w/cellophane torn or taped)... 55

Clothing set, "White Magic," #1607, Barbie, white satin coat w/rhinestone closure, matching hat w/bow accent, short white nylon gloves, silver clutch purse w/button closure, booklet, paper label, never removed from box (box w/"$2.00" on paper label) 275

Skipper Vinyl Coin Purse

Coin purse, rectangular, white vinyl w/metal clasp, front shows Skipper listening to records on record player & "Skipper - Barbie's Little Sister," yellow vinyl interior w/separate center section, 1964, metal discolored, two small seam separations (ILLUS.).............. 115

Comic book, "Barbie and Ken," No. 3, May-July 1963, Dell, 12¢ ("3 26" stamped on back corner in blue ink, general wear) 30

Diary, Barbie, black vinyl w/metal clasp, metal key encased in wax-type paper & taped to inside front cover, dated 1962 (pages age-discolored, clasp discolored, "Norma April 81450+" written inside upper front cover)............... 145

Barbie Dictionary

Dictionary, red vinyl, Webster's, w/picture of Barbie's head in profile on front surrounded by various grammatical terms & "Barbie Dictionary" at top, 1964, two faded ink dots on back vinyl, pages slightly discolored, small binding tears in first several pages (ILLUS.)..................... 125

Magazine, "Barbie Bazaar," The Barbie Collector's Magazine, 1988 Premiere Edition, never removed from package 50

Magazine, "The World of Barbie," The Barbie Magazine Annual, 1964 first issue (wear & discoloration)....................................... 50

Black Vinyl Barbie Pencil Case

Pencil case, rectangular, black vinyl showing two Barbie figures & Barbie head in profile & "Barbie Pencil Case," zipper closure w/attached bead chain, 1961, wear, discoloration to zipper & chain (ILLUS.) 45

"Perk Up" Case, oblong, red vinyl w/pictures of two Barbie figures & Barbie head in profile & "Barbie - Perk Up Case" on front, metal zipper, 1964, near-mint (ink stains, discoloration to zipper)........................ 100

Barbie Portable Record Player

Record player, black vinyl carrying case w/metal closure & black plastic handle, beige base, grey plastic working turntable & record arm, beige record size changer, white volume control knob, inside of lid shows figures dancing, Barbie changing records, and "Vanity Fair" & "Barbie," 1962, 33/45 r.p.m. adapter missing (ILLUS.) 450

Barbie Wallet

Wallet, rectangular, black vinyl w/three Barbie figures in various fashions & "Barbie" on front, metal clasp, red vinyl interior w/change purse w/zipper closure & attached gold chain, beige plastic change holder, clear plastic comb & cardboard fingernail file, four plastic photo holders, black & white paper photos of Rex Harrison & Maureen O'Hara, mirror, 1961, photos & mirror are discolored (ILLUS.) **90**

BARWARE

Man in the Moon Ashtray

Ashtray, black plastic round base w/two indentations for cigarettes flanking a flat standup chrome figure of a laughing man in the moon, 6" (ILLUS.) **$110-125**

Stork Club Ashtray

Ashtray, ceramic, black round form w/"STORK CLUB" in white block lettering on side, space for matchbook, Hall China, 5" (ILLUS.)... **80-100**

Novelty Ashtray

Ashtray, ceramic, the head of a top hatted man w/mustache & monocle, open mouth to put cigarettes in, base reads "Wanna See Smoke Come Out of my Ears?" in black just under man's bow tie, 6" (ILLUS.)... **40-50**

Flip-open Top Hat Ashtray

Ashtray, cov., enameled metal, in the form of a top hat, top flips open on hinge, red trim at "brim," Germany (ILLUS. open) **70-90**

"Century of Progress" Ashtray

Cigarette Box from Germany

Ashtray, metal, enamel, Chicago World's Fair "Century of Progress" souvenir, round, w/flat rim w/indentations for cigarettes, chrome center handle in the form of a gazelle w/horns curving back to meet tail, Ronson, ca. 1933, 4" (ILLUS.) **85-100**

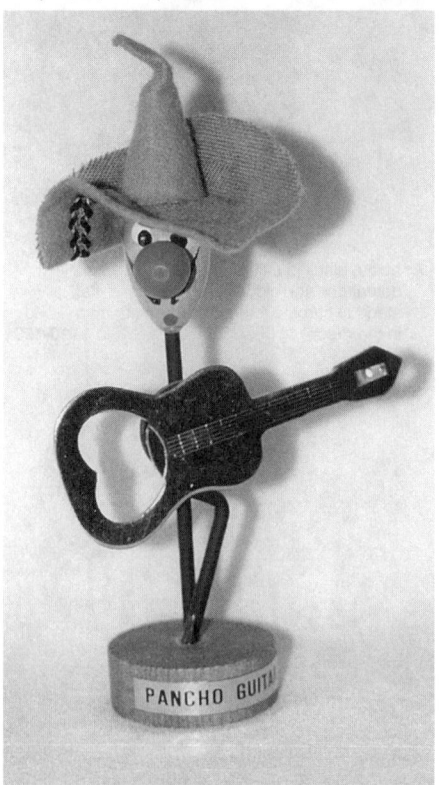

Copacabana Ashtray

Ashtray, plastic, from Copacabana nightclub in New York City, round black form w/"COPACABANA" in white block letters on side, "10 E. 60TH. ST. N.Y.C." on rim, rest of rim w/indentations for cigarettes & space for matchbook, Eagle USA, 4 1/2" (ILLUS.) **10-20**

Bottle opener, metal & wood, metal stick figure w/wooden head wearing felt sombrero-type hat holds metal bottle opener in the form of a guitar that sticks to magnetic torso of figure, on circular metal base that identifies it as "Pancho Guitar" (ILLUS., to the right) **6-10**

Cigarette box, cov., metal, black cube to set on tabletop or bar, hinged lid decorated w/diamond, holds insert w/holes for 25

cigarettes to stand upright, Germany, 3" (ILLUS., above) **85-100**

"Pancho Guitar" Bottle Opener

Roaring Twenties Cocktail Glasses

Cocktail glasses, clear glass tumblers tapering out slightly at top & at base, trimmed w/red line decoration at rim & base, sides feature color drawings of Roaring Twenties figures signed by John Held, Jr., 3 1/2" h., each (ILLUS. of three).. **15-20**

Morgantown Cocktail Glass

Cocktail glasses, glass, shallow bowls on short Rooster stems on disk bases, various colors w/clear stems, Morgantown, 1930s, each (ILLUS. of one)....................... **25-50**

Catalan Cocktail Glasses

Cocktail glasses, sea foam green Catalin plastic trumpet-form bowls & molded circular bases, ringed silvertone metal stems, NuDawn, 5" h., each (ILLUS. of two) **10-20**

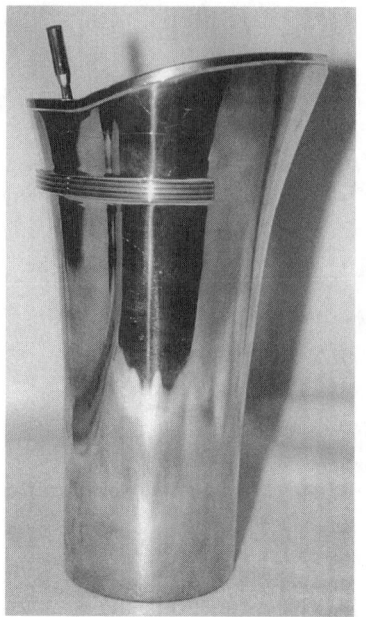

Cocktail Mixer with Spoon

Cocktail mixer, chrome, cylindrical shape tapering out at top to form spout, ringed decorative band near top, w/long-handled mixing spoon, Von Nessen for Chase Chrome, 8 3/4" h. (ILLUS.) **90-110**

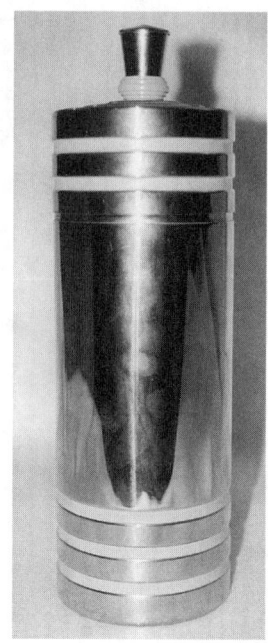

Chase Chrome "Gaiety" Shaker

Cocktail shaker, cov., chrome, "Gaiety" model, cylindrical form w/rare white horizontal striping at base & rim, Chase Chrome, 12" (ILLUS.) **90-110**

"Goldchester" Cocktail Shaker

Cocktail shaker, cov., aluminum, "Goldchester" model, simple cylindrical form, brass lid, Lurelle Guild, Kensington, England, 13" (ILLUS.) **125-150**

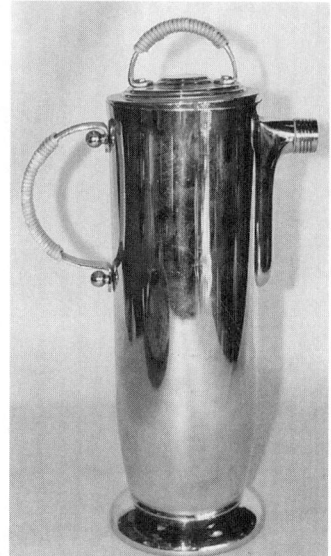

"Happy Days" Cocktail Shaker

Cocktail shaker, cov., chrome, "Happy Days" model, pitcher-type cylindrical form w/rounded disk base, short ringed spout, Cordex C-form side & lid handles, Manning-Bowman, 1941, 13" (ILLUS.) .. **125-150**

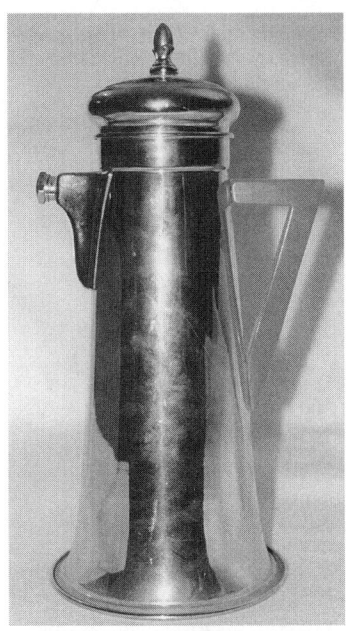

Chrome & Bakelite Cocktail Shaker

Cocktail shaker, cov., chrome, pitcher-type tapering cylindrical form on ringed base, molded lid w/finial, spout on side, angular red Bakelite side handle, recipes listed on bottom, Forman Brothers, ca. 1930s (ILLUS.) **175-200**

Chrome Cocktail Shaker Pitcher

Cocktail shaker, cov., chrome, pitcher-type, w/scroll handle & embossed trim, molded base & lid, short straight spout, 11 1/2" (ILLUS.) **25-35**

"Tally Ho" Cocktail Shaker

Cocktail shaker, cov., cobalt blue glass, "Tally Ho" model, tapering cylindrical form decorated w/silk-screened images of hunter on horseback & hounds,

Chrome Shaker with Green Handle

Cocktail shaker, cov., chrome, pitcher-type, w/green plastic handle, molded base, lid, & short straight spout, 12" (ILLUS.) **50-60**

chrome lid, Hazel-Atlas, ca. 1930s
(ILLUS.).. **95-125**

Cobalt Shaker with Drink Recipes

Cocktail shaker, cov., cobalt glass, cylindrical form w/silk-screen drink recipes listed along sides in white, metal molded lid w/short spout at side, 10" (ILLUS.).......... **85-100**

Hazel-Atlas Sportsman Series Shaker

Cocktail shaker, cov., cobalt glass, cylindrical form w/silk-screen Dutch-style deco-

ration of windmills & clouds in white, metal lid w/short spout at side, Hazel-Atlas Sportsman series, 1930s, 10" (ILLUS.) ... **75-100**

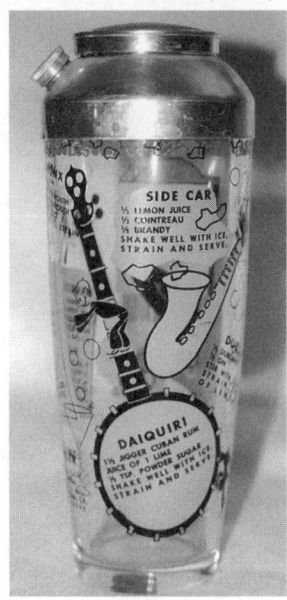

Cocktail Shaker with Musical Motif

Cocktail shaker, cov., glass, clear cylindrical form decorated w/images of musical instruments & drink recipes on side in black & white, narrow red decorative border at top, chrome lid w/side spout, 10" (ILLUS.).. **70-85**

Cocktail Shaker with Rooster Finial

Cocktail shaker, cov., glass, clear, cylindrical form w/short neck & flat rim, bell-shaped stopper w/rooster finial, three pieces, Paden City Glass Works, 13" (ILLUS.) **125-150**

Cocktail Shaker with Fighting Cocks

Cocktail shaker, cov., glass, clear sharply tapering form decorated w/applied sterling silver fighting cocks, metal lid & disk base, ca. 1920s, 9" (ILLUS.).................. **200-250**

Fighting Cocks Cocktail Shaker

Cocktail shaker, cov., glass, clear tapering cylindrical form w/rounded shoulders,

decorated w/fighting cocks painted in red, gold & black, coppertone metal lid tapering to pouring spout, 12" (ILLUS.) **175-200**

Hazel-Atlas Cocktail Shaker

Cocktail shaker, cov., glass, cobalt cylindrical form w/silk-screen decoration of sailboats & sea gulls in white, metal lid w/short spout at side, Hazel-Atlas, 1930s, 10" (ILLUS.)...................................... **65-85**

"Moondrops" Pattern Shaker

Cocktail shaker, cov., glass, "Moondrops" patt., ruby, stein form w/C-form handle, molded disk base, chrome lid, New Martinsville Glass, 10" (ILLUS.) **125-150**

Ruby Drink Recipe Cocktail Shaker

Cocktail shaker, cov., ruby glass, cylindrical form w/silk-screen drink recipes listed along sides in white, molded brass lid w/short spout at side, ca. 1930s, 11" (ILLUS.).. **95-125**

"The Hunt" Cocktail Shaker

Cocktail shaker, cov., ruby glass, "The Hunt" model, tapering cylindrical form

w/applied sterling silver design of hunter on horseback & hounds, metal lid, 11" (ILLUS.).. **250-275**

Barbell-shaped Cocktail Shaker

Cocktail shaker, cov., stainless chrome, barbell shape w/orbs on either end of cylindrical shaft, black Bakelite lid, 13" (ILLUS.) **150-175**

Frosty Polar Bear Shaker & Ice Bowl

Cocktail shaker & ice bowl, glass, clear slightly tapering cov. shaker w/chrome domed lid, short spout, cylindrical ice bowl, Frosty Polar Bear style, both decorated w/images of white polar bears & blue frost, ca. 1950s, 10", the set (ILLUS.) **75-100**

Cobalt Ribbed Glass Shaker Set

Cocktail shaker set: cov. shaker & five glasses; cobalt glass with vertical ribs, cylindrical shaker w/molded chrome lid & red Bakelite top, conical glasses on molded chrome conical bases, 1930s, 10 1/2", the set (ILLUS.) **250-275**

"Pig Orchestra" Cocktail Shaker Set

Cocktail shaker set: cov. shaker & four glasses; clear glass, tapering cylindrical shaker w/molded chrome lid & side spout, tapering glasses on heavy ring base, shaker & tumblers decorated w/silk-screened "Pig Orchestra" images in red of pigs playing musical instruments, 1940s-50s, 10", the set (ILLUS.) **150-165**

Silver Plate Cocktail Shaker Set

Cocktail shaker set: cov. shaker & five glasses; silver plate, modernistic angular design, conical glasses on short ringed stem, disk foot, Benedict, 11", the set (ILLUS.) **350-450**

Frosted Glass Shaker Set

Cocktail shaker set: cov. shaker & four glasses; frosted glass w/acid-etched design, tapering cylindrical shaker w/chrome lid, conical glasses on heavy cylindrical bases, 11", the set (ILLUS.) **100-140**

"Cocktail Rooster Goes to War" Set

Cocktail shaker set: cov. shaker & four small tumblers; clear glass, tapering cylindrical shaker w/molded chrome lid, shaker & tumblers decorated w/silk-screened "Cocktail Rooster Goes to War" images of roosters in military uniform w/weapons in red, white & blue, 1940s, 10", the set (ILLUS.)................................... **95-125**

Shaker Set with Camel Decoration

Cocktail shaker set: cov. shaker & two tall tumblers; clear glass, tapering cylindrical shaker w/molded chrome lid, shaker & tumblers decorated w/silk-screened images of camels & desert scene in white & green, 10", the set (ILLUS.) **95-125**

Cocktail Set with Greek Key Design

Cocktail shaker set: cov. shaker & two glasses; clear glass, cylindrical shaker w/chrome lid & side spout, cylindrical glasses, all decorated w/horizontal pink lines & black Greek key design, Anchor Hocking, 1950s, 9 1/2", the set (ILLUS.) **55-75**

Pink Elephant Drink Shaker Set

Cocktail shaker set: shaker w/metal cover & two small tumblers; glass, clear tapering cylindrical forms decorated w/whimsical pink elephants, 1940-1950s, 10", the set (ILLUS.) **90-120**

Cocktail shakers in holder, "The Foursome," four cov. silver plate shakers fit in holder w/wooden base & silver plate handle that clamps down to hold shakers in place so all can be shaken at once, Napier, 9", the set (ILLUS., top next page) **250-350**

"The Foursome" Shaker Set

Ribbed Decanter Set

Decanter set: cov. decanter & two tumblers; clear glass, cylinder-shaped w/deep horizontal ribbing & black bands around sides, the decanter w/black glass stopper on coppertone neck, the decanter & glasses w/black plastic bases, ca. 1930s, the set (ILLUS.) **150-175**

Artillery Shell Decanter

Decanter, metal, in the form of an artillery shell w/conical top, embossed on side "Jean Charlie" in script, bottom stores shot glasses, 1920s (ILLUS.) **350-400**

Painted Metal Man with Flask

Decorative figure, painted metal, man w/legs askew dressed in black tuxedo & wearing black top hat holds red flask in one hand, the other raised as if waving, 5 1/2" h. (ILLUS.).. **45-65**

"A Guide to Pink Elephants" Booklet

Drink recipe booklet, "A Guide to Pink Elephants - 200 most requested mixed drinks on alcohol resistant cards," pale pink cover w/stylized drawings of elephants, black plastic spiral binding, in box w/same design, 1950s, 4 1/2" (ILLUS.) **10-18**

Carved Box for Drink Recipes

Drink recipe box, wood, rectangular open box holds drink recipes, front decoration is carved painted figure of white-haired bartender in white jacket, black pants &

red tie, w/bar towel over one arm, holding drink, 1950s (ILLUS.) **30-40**

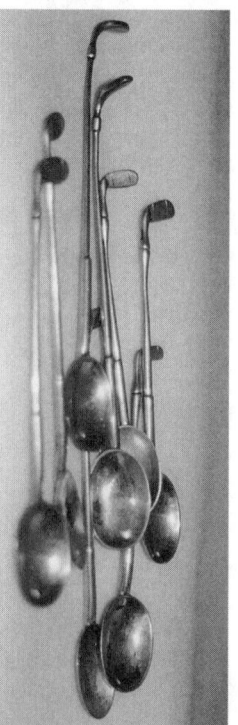

Golf Club Drink Stirrers

Drink stirrers, sterling silver, spoons w/handles in the form of golf clubs, 4", the set (ILLUS.) **75-100**

Silk-screened Glass Ice Bowl

Ice bowl, clear glass w/silk-screened "Cocktail Rooster Goes to War" design in red, white & blue of roosters in military uniforms in various poses w/various weapons, 1940s, 4 1/2" (ILLUS.) **75-90**

Pink Elephant Ice Bowl

Ice bowl, glass, clear cylindrical form w/whimsical pink elephants, stars & line decoration, 1940-1950s, 4 1/4" (ILLUS.) ... **70-90**

Russel Wright Ice Bowl for Chase

Ice bowl w/tongs, chrome, semicircular bowl shape w/ribbed strap handle curving over bowl, ending midway in curl that holds ribbed tongs, Russel Wright for Chase, 1934 (ILLUS.) **60-80**

Penguin Ice Bucket

Ice bucket, cov., chromed metal, penguin model hot/cold server, w/black Bakelite stubby wing-like side handles & knob lid handle, outlines of penguins in profile engraved around upper half of bowl, West Bend, 8" (ILLUS.) **20-30**

1940s Juice Tumbler

Juice tumbler, clear glass w/red, white & black stylized decoration of black saxophone player, 1940s (ILLUS.) **10-15**

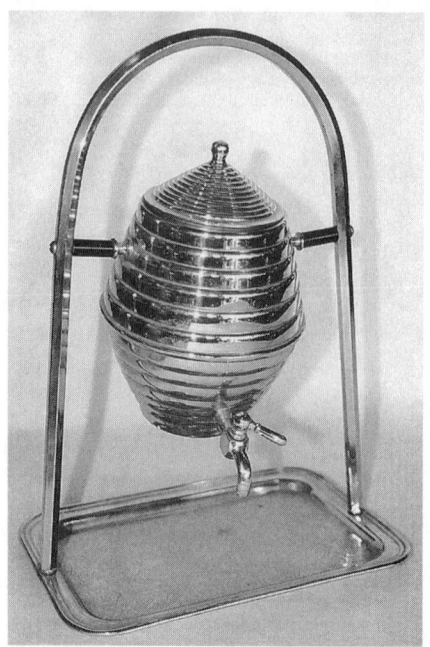

Chrome Beehive Liquor Dispenser

Liquor dispenser, cov., chrome, beehive-form dispenser w/tap hangs from arch attached at bottom to rectangular rimmed tray, 13" (ILLUS.) **55-75**

Nude Boy Liquor Dispenser

Liquor dispenser, plastic, in the form of a nude boy, on rectangular brown base w/"Master Piece" in label on front, all on tall black ceramic base w/pattern resembling bricks (ILLUS.)..................................... **12-20**

Martini Glasses

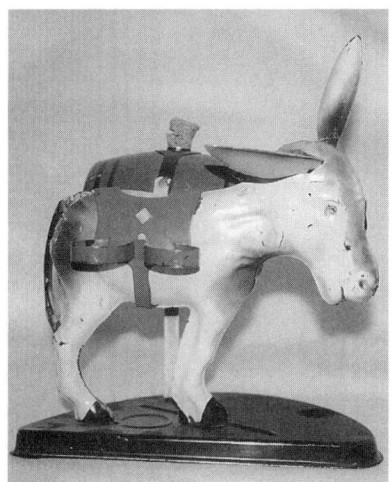

Donkey Liquor Dispenser

Liquor dispenser, tin, in the form of a donkey w/moveable tail & long ears, holds keg on one side & holders for bottles or glasses on other side of red harness, on black base, ca. 1920s, 9" (ILLUS.) **40-60**

Martini glasses, tapered bowls decorated w/red & silver horizontal stripes, molded bases, 4 1/2" h., each (ILLUS. of two, bottom previous page)................................. **10-20**

Bellhop Pitcher

Pitcher, glass, clear cylindrical form w/silk-screen decoration of black dachshunds & bellhop in red uniform carrying drink on tray, ca. 1940s, 7" (ILLUS.)...................... **75-100**

Foil-decorated Black Glass Tray

Serving tray, black glass, rectangular w/foil geometric design, chrome side handles, United States, ca. 1930s, 20" l. (ILLUS.) **95-125**

"Pig Shot" Shot Glass

Shot glass, clear glass, tapering form decorated w/green silk-screened images of pigs & "Pig Shot," 2 1/2" (ILLUS.) **10-12**

Musical Motif Shot Glasses

Shot glass, clear glass, tapering form on ringed base, decorated w/images of top hats & musical notes in black, 3", each (ILLUS. of four) **4-6**

"Bottoms Up" Shot Glass

Shot glass, clear glass tapering out at top, decorated w/gorillas & bananas in red & yellow & "Bottoms Up" in red, 2 1/2" (ILLUS.) **5-10**

Saint & Sinner Shot Glasses

Pink Elephant Shot Glasses

Shot glasses, glass, decorated w/whimsical pink elephants holding bottles & glasses & "SAY WHEN," 1940-1950s, 2 1/2", each (ILLUS. of two)........................ **10-12**

Shot glasses, silver plate, different size shot glasses connected by curved handle, one w/image of stylized winged figure w/halo & "SAINT" engraved on the side, the other w/stylized image of tailed & horned figure holding pitchfork & "SINNER" engraved on the side, 2 1/2" (ILLUS., bottom previous page)................ **30-40**

"Just Whistle" Swizzle Sticks

Swizzle sticks, plastic, "Just Whistle" clear stirrers w/glitter decoration, handles are working whistles in various colors, 1950s, the set (ILLUS.) **15-25**

Bakelite Tabletop Bar

Tabletop bar: holder & two cov. decanters, six glasses & four shot glasses; Bakelite Art Deco-style molded two-level holder w/wooden side handles & openings for clear glass decanters, cocktail glasses & shot glasses, 24" l. (ILLUS.) **80-120**

Tumblers with Rooster Decoration

Tumblers, black glass w/gilt decoration of stylized rooster on sides, signed, 1950s, 5 3/4" h., set of four (ILLUS.) **25-35**

Cooperstown, New York. A popular game from its inception, by 1869 it was able to support its first all-professional team, the Cincinnati Red Stockings. The National League was organized in 1876, and though the American League was first formed in 1900, it was not officially recognized until 1903. Today, the "national pastime" has millions of fans, and collecting baseball memorabilia has become a major hobby with enthusiastic collectors seeking out items associated with players such as Babe Ruth, Lou Gehrig, and others who became legends in their own lifetimes. Although baseball cards, issued as advertising premiums for bubble gum and other products, seem to dominate the field, there are numerous other items available.

Champagne Glass Wall Decoration

Wall decoration, ceramic, champagne glass & two bubbles in green, three pieces (ILLUS.) **20-30**

BASEBALL MEMORABILIA
Baseball was reputedly invented by Abner Doubleday as he laid out a diamond-shaped field with four bases at

1961 Signed World Series Banner

Banner, miniature colorful silk piece autographed by 1961 World Series players, long rectangular piece w/top hanger & gold bottom tassel, printed in dark blue & red "Souvenir of 1961 World Series - Cincinnati Reds - New York Yankees," w/large globe map in center & team logos below, signed in blue & black ink by Roger Maris (twice), Mickey Mantle, Yogi Berra & many others, one Maris signature smudged, few areas of light staining, 9 1/4 x 16" (ILLUS.) **$1,572**

Banquet program, 1906 National League Champion Chicago Cubs Banquet, cover printed w/cartoon scene of a Chicago bear w/banner printed in black, blue & yellow, autographed by 16 notables including Capt. Anson, John J. Evers & Frank Chance, 8 pp. (vertical pocket fold, some reverse soiling) **2,657**

Baseball, Babe Ruth & Lou Gehrig 1927 World Series ball, signed in black by several members of the team, some signatures faded or obscured, signed on the sweet spot by Ruth, moderately toned **4,767**

Baseball, Babe Ruth-signed official league ball, signed in black fountain pen on the sweet spot, slighted faded **7,216**

Baseball, Babe Ruth-signed, official league ball signed in black ink on the sweet spot, very lightly & evenly toned, near mint **27,435**

Baseball, Cy Young-signed unofficial Rawlings Official League ball, signed on the side panel, signed in June 1948, accompanied by posed original photo of Young taken on that occasion **6,412**

Baseball, Hack Wilson-signed official National League model w/red & blue stitching, some fading & dirt **3,289**

Baseball, Honus Wagner-signed official National League ball w/red stitching, signed in blue on the sweet spot, some fading & slight dirt **2,581**

Baseball, Jimmie Foxx-signed official American League ball w/red stitching, signed in green ballpoint ink on the sweet spot, lightly toned **24,032**

Baseball, New York Yankees-signed official American League ball w/red & blue stitching, signed by Babe Ruth on the sweet spot, Lou Gehrig & Tony Lazzeri, also two illegible signatures, 1927-34, some wear & fading **4,927**

Baseball, Satchel Paige-signed Official League ball w/red stitching, signed in blue ink at top of a side panel, medium toning **1,600**

Baseball, Tris Speaker-signed official International League ball, signed in black fountain pen on the sweet spot, some fading & overall light dirt **2,839**

Baseball cap, Lou Gehrig 1930s game-used New York Yankees cap, dark blue w/silver logo, size & name stitched in leather inner band, size 7 1/8 .... **32,816**

Baseball card, 1887 Four Base Hits sepia-toned card w/bust photo portrait of John Clarkson, Chicago White Sox pitcher, sharp image, clean on both sides, 2 1/4 x 3 7/8" (corners clipped) **7,760**

Rare 1887 Gypsy Queen Card

Baseball card, 1887 N175 "Gypsy Queen" card w/photograph of Dann Richerson posed holding a bat, strong & focused photo, rare size, 2 x 3 1/2" (ILLUS.) **13,753**

Baseball card, 1888 N43 Allen & Ginter color-printed card w/Wm. "Buck" Ewing, front w/color portrait of Ewing flanked by baseball vignettes, 1 3/4 x 2 3/4" **2,536**

Baseball cards, 1953 Topps uncut strip w/Mickey Mantle, 10-card color strip (heavy crease in center & another crease & edge water staining) **1,321**

Baseball cards, 1954 Bowman complete set, 224 color photo cards including the rare No. 66 of Ted Williams, all cards excellent, the set **16,002**

Bat, 1908 Spalding Ty Cobb game-used bat, 34 1/2" l. **19,861**

Bat, 1929 H&B Rogers Hornsby game-used bat, signature model, 34" l. **18,055**

Bat, 1934-36 H&B Hank Greenberg side-written game-used bat, 34 3/4" l. (9" l. H-crack in handle) **6,560**

Bat, 1950s Ted Williams autographed signature model game-used bat, signed in black marker on the barrel, number "9" written on base of the knob, 35" l. **19,364**

Bat, 1951-57 Adirondack Mickey Mantle game-used bat, stamped "Mantle Type," 35" l. **6,167**

Bat, 1961-64 H&B Willie Mays game-used bat, name-stamped model, 35" l. **18,725**

Bat, 1968-72 H&B Roberto Clemente game-used bat, signature model, 35 3/4" l. **8,536**

Book on The Cincinnati Reds

Book, "The Cincinnati Reds - an Informal History," by Lee Allen, autographed 1948 first edition, Putnam, excellent condition w/original dust jacket in dark red, black & white (ILLUS.).. **71**

Cincinnati 1949 Roster & Records

Booklet, "Cincinnati Reds Roster and Records - 1949," published by the Burger Brewing Co., cover in dark blue w/red Cincinnati skyline design & team logo, red, white & blue, excellent condition (ILLUS.).. **26**

Check, personal check signed by Christy Mathewson, drawn on the Adirondack National Bank & dated November 3, 1924, his name printed vertically along left edge, signed in black fountain pen ink.. **9,607**

Rare Joe Jackson-Boston Garter Card

Display card, window advertising-type, 1913 H813 Joe Jackson card, printed in color w/a drawing of Jackson batting above advertising for Boston Garter, very minor corner faults, small surface area restored, clean black-printed reverse, 3 7/8 x 8 1/4" (ILLUS.) **29,486**

1955 Brooklyn Dodgers Signed Doll

Doll, 1955 Brooklyn Dodgers-signed, tall stuffed vinyl figure of a happy Dodgers fan, white w/blue hands & feet & molded color face, signed by 27 team members in blue ballpoint pen, includes Jackie Robinson, Sandy Koufax, Roy Campanella, Gil Hodges, Pee Wee Reese &

more, few minor scratches on face, 12 1/2" h. (ILLUS.)...................................... **2,839**

Glove, Eddie Mathews game-used glove, early 1960s, w/letter of authenticity from Mathews.. **4,333**

Hat, Babe Ruth signed vintage straw boater-style, inscribed on inside leather band, near mint, size 7 1/8.................................... **2,415**

Jacket, 1957 Gene Conley Milwaukee Braves warm-up model, worn during 1957 World Series, black nylon w/woolen collar, shoulder split & cuffs, team name in red & white above outlined gold tomahawk, wool trim in red, black, white & gold bands, Wilson size 48, w/a signed 8 x 10" black & white photo of Conley **1,454**

Jersey, Don Mueller 1952 New York Giants road style, grey flannel w/red & dark blue name & number, MacGregor Goldsmith 40 model **2,346**

Fine Signed Ruth-Gehrig Photograph

Photograph, autographed black & white crisp image of Babe Ruth standing beside Lou Gehrig in a ball park, each leaning on his bat, boldly autographed by each player across his legs, original 1927-era shot, near mint, 4 x 5" (ILLUS.)...................................... **23,431**

Photograph, autographed by Jimmie Foxx, Eakin photo showing Foxx posed at the tail end of his swing, signed in black ink vertically beside the image, mint, 8 x 10" **2,346**

Photograph, autographed cabinet-size sepia-toned photograph of Rube Waddell, inscribed in upper right hand corner, also signed on the back, good quality photo, mount in fair condition, early 20th c., overall 4 1/4 x 6 3/8" (ILLUS., top of page)... **19,364**

Very Rare Signed Waddell Photo

Postal cover, 1945 Honus Wagner signed Franklin D. Roosevelt Memorial cover w/elaborate cachet, postmarked "September 18, 1945," signed in black fountain pen vertically up the center, the back displays two clippings picturing Wagner in uniform & after retirement, slight handling, 3 5/8 x 6 1/2".. **974**

Early Stein Postcard with Ty Cobb

Postcard, advertising-type, front w/Max Stein sepia tone photograph of Ty Cobb bunting, reverse w/black & white advertising for Stein's cards, early 20th c., 3 1/2 x 5 1/2" (ILLUS. of front & back)........ **1,572**

Program, 1895 Temple Cup Championship series, Baltimore vs Cleveland, covers in pale blue w/deep red printing, centerfold scorecard scored w/inning totals only, 14 pp., 5 3/8 x 6 3/4" (worn, cover separated, numerous tears, creases & some missing pieces) **2,221**

Program, 1923 Chicago White Sox game program for game against the New York Yankees in Chicago, white, orange & blue cover signed in pencil by Babe Ruth, dated May 22, 1923, unscored, very good condition.. **1,454**

1946 All-Star Game Program

Program, 1946 Fenway Park All-Star Game, cover in shaded pink w/large star & small scattered stars in black & grey w/wording in red, 16 pp., near mint, 6 1/2 x 9 3/4" (ILLUS.) **1,072**

Program, 1947 Cuban Minor League program printed in Spanish, game between the Havana Cubans & the Dodger's Minor League team, the Montreal Royals, includes full-page black & white photo of Jackie Robinson w/his biography in Spanish, cover in white printed in red, black & green, game dated March 8, 1947, 16 pp., 7 x 10"...................................... **830**

Salesman's booklet, 1950 Royal Pudding advertising piece, accordion-style w/21 baseball trading cards, white printed in black & red, includes Stan Musial, Pee Wee Reese, Warren Spahn & more, gently handled, folded 4 1/4 x 5"....................... **3,715**

Scorecard, 1883 St. Louis at Philadelphia, Charles Comisky in the lineup, pink-tinted paper, neatly scored in pencil **498**

Scorecard, 1884 Boston at New York Giants, included Ewing, Ward, Connor & Welch in lineups, front & back covers printed in color, the front w/a batter tossing away his bat & titled "Three Strikes and Out," back cover w/scene of a romantic couple in early 19th c. attire, neatly scored & dated in pencil......................... **1,180**

Scorecard, 1884 New York Mets at New York Giants, lineup includes Ewing, Ward & Connor, color-printed covers, the front w/a scene of a player falling backward but ready to throw a runner out, the back cover w/a scene of a romantic early 19th c. couple, neatly scored in pencil (minor chipping at fold)................................ **4,086**

Scorecard, 1887 World Championship, St. Louis vs Detroit, four-page fold-over style w/pictures of the team members on each cover, some pre-printed names erased, seven replaced w/names written in pencil, open 7 x 7"... **7,054**

Early Scorecard-Photograph

Scorecard-photograph, No. 1 Mort Rogers Base Ball Photographic Card, encloses sepia toned photograph of Harry Wright, printed under the inset photograph "Capt. & C.F., Boston Nine, 1871," finely scored, closed 3 1/2 x 5 1/4" (ILLUS.).................... **12,022**

Sign, 1945 World Series ticket sign from Wrigley Field, white background, large black wording at the top reads "Gate 2 - 1945 World Series," below are color images of the four different tickets, near mint, 10 x 14" **2,132**

Stadium seats, Yankee Stadium double seat, blue slatted backs & wood seat on iron frame, seat Nos. 10 & 11 (some paint touchup) **2,657**

Ticket, 1955 Brooklyn Dodgers World Series proof sheet, uncut four-ticket proof sheet w/tickets in white, red & dark blue, for three games held at Ebbets Field, near mint **1,180**

Ticket, Federal League Baltimore Federals vs All-Stars, June 20, 1914 at Victrix Base Ball Park, pink paper w/black printing on front including Rain Check, back w/pencil inscription, 1 1/2 x 3 1/2" (light soiling) **805**

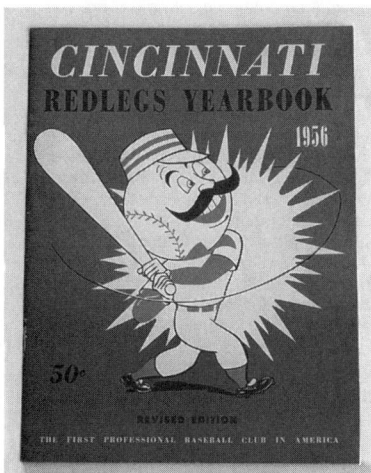

Cincinnati Redlegs 1956 Yearbook

Yearbook, 1956 Cincinnati Redlegs Yearbook, dark blue cover w/large red, white
& black team logo & white & black print-
ing (ILLUS.).. **67**

BASKETS

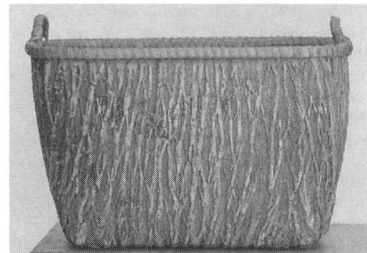

Large Bark Basket

Bark, rectangular, splint threading on
seams, rim & handles, 17 x 22 3/4",
14 1/4" h. (ILLUS.).. **$770**

"Buttocks" basket, woven splint, ribbed
basket painted green, w/red handle,
America, 19th c., 13 1/2" h. (minor break) .. **1,410**

"Buttocks" basket, woven splint, wooden
handle, old black paint, 13" d., 11 3/4" h. **165**

Gathering basket, woven splint, rectangular w/wooden sides, 19th c., 14 1/2 x 47",
3" h. (some breaks)..................................... **374**

Gathering basket, woven splint, round, two
wooden side handles, bottle bottom,
19" d., 14 3/4" h. **220**

"Melon" basket, finely woven splint, 22-rib
construction, brown & tan splints, arched
handle, 10" w., 8 1/4" h. (two minor splint
breaks).. **110**

"Melon" basket, woven splint, twenty-eight
ribs, multilayered "U"-shaped weaving on
either side of arched handle, nut brown
color w/old varnish.. **165**

Nantucket basket, oval, two-tone woven
splint, cutout walnut disk base, bentwood
rim, handles at either end w/brass tacks,
9 1/2" l., 3 3/4" h. (one glued handle)............ **413**

Nantucket basket, round, woven splint,
turned walnut foot, bentwood hickory rim
& swing handle, natural finish, 8 1/2" d.,
9" h. w/handle (minor split breaks) **413**

Nantucket basket, round, woven splint
w/band of darker splint around the middle, bentwood swivel handle, wooden
disk base, faint penciled inscription reads
"...Nantucket Basket Presented by
Capt..." (purportedly by Capt. Thomas
James of the first Nantucket lightship),
7 5/8" d., 5 1/8" h. w/handle......................... **2,530**

Nantucket basket, round, woven splint
w/bentwood swivel handle & turned disk
base, 9 1/2" d., 6" h. w/handle.................... **2,420**

Nantucket Basket

Nantucket basket, round, woven splint,
wooden base w/high sides, arched swing
handle, brown patina, 8 1/8" d., 10" h.
(ILLUS.)... **2,420**

Covered Splint Basket

Utility, cov., rectangular, woven splint,
some splints dyed, some stained designs
in fancy "X"s & dot flowers in dark brown
& light reddish-brown, 10 x 11", 8" h.
(ILLUS.)... **385**

Utility, rectangular, woven splint, decorated
w/original red, white & blue on exterior
splints, minor breaks, 12 x 20 1/4", 6" h. **825**

Utility, round, woven splint, wood handle,
decorated w/dyed green, light red & orange splints, 14" d., 12 1/2" h. (minor
damage)... **99**

Utility basket, miniature, round, finely woven sweetgrass, possibly Shaker, 19th
c., 2 1/2" d., 1 1/2" h..................................... **431**

Utility basket, woven splint, round,
w/carved wooden handles, probably New
England, 19th c., 29" d., 10 3/4" h. **881**

Wall basket, half buttocks basket of woven
splint w/bentwood handle & remnants of
old ivory paint, 6 x 8", 6 1/4" h. w/handle....... **193**

Wall Basket in Old Paint

Wall basket, woven splint, oblong shape w/a deep compartment & high crest, old blue green paint over an earlier red, 6 x 13 1/2", 14" h. (ILLUS.) **440**

BICYCLES

Early Wooden Boneshaker Bike

Boneshaker, wooden w/wooden-spoked wheels, wooden pedals & leather seat, restored, ca. 1860, rear wheel 35" d., front wheel 39" d. (ILLUS.) **$3,410**

Boneshaker tricycle, wrought-iron frame & wooden-spoked wheels, possibly black-smith-made, ca. 1860, rear wheels 30" d., front wheel 36" d. **3,740**

Cleveland Welding Co., "Roadmaster Su-preme" model, n.d. front brake, lobed horizontal sprung saddle, horn tank, illu-minated rear rack, Torrington jeweled pedals, US Royal "Super Master" centi-pede grip white wall tires, original creamy yellow w/maroon trim paint, original un-touched condition, ca. 1937 .... **8,800**

Near Mint Columbia Airrider

Columbia, boy's "Airrider" model, red & cream near mint original paint, perfect graphic decals on tank, front load head-light, rear bookrack, original saddle, fine

original chrome, original rims & pre-war tires, rear drop stand style kickstand, w/Geneva badge, near mint, 1940-41 (ILLUS.) **880**

Columbia, boy's "Superb" safety model, fine original untouched maroon & white paint, standard equipment including curved cross bar handlebars, front fender light, rear carrier & True Test Deluxe whitewall tires, all decals intact, some seat deterioration, ca. 1941 .... **578**

Columbia, girl's "3 Star Deluxe" Diamond Jubilee 75th Anniversary balloon-tire model, w/Tru-Sport head badge, original lime green & black paint pitted, 1952 (missing minor parts, rims w/surface rust) **110**

Girl's Columbia 5 Star Superb Model

Columbia, girl's "5 Star Superb" balloon-tire model, cream & blue paint, new-old stock, never ridden, original shipping tag, ca. 1951 (ILLUS.) **495**

Columbia, girl's "5 Star Superb" balloon-tire model, floating action spring fork & Good-year "Airwheel" whitewall all-weather 20 x 2.125 tires, very original paint, headlight missing, ca. 1950 .... **303**

Columbia, man's Model 200 chainless (shaft drive) double sprung pneumatic-tire safety model, very rare triple leaf spring front fork w/plunger rear suspen-sion, solar headlamp, period paint & pin-striping, Lobdel rims, early **2,090**

Columbia, man's Model 40 pneumatic-tire safety model, early style hammock seat, downswept handlebars, restored wood-en tire rims & replica chain grip tires, restored, ca. 1890s **715**

Columbia ordinary, "Expert" model, radial spoked wheel, restored nickel plate, open head badge, excellent leather seat, very good paint, last patent date Decem-ber 1881, older restoration, front wheel 52" d. **4,125**

Crescent, lady's pneumatic-type safety model, very original condition w/paint & plating, seat cover loose, American Cy-cle Mfg. Co., New York, ca. 1901 .... **248**

Elgin, girl's "Special" pneumatic-tire safety model, fine original condition, original co-balt blue paint & white pinstriping, original saddle & front load headlight, tank, rack & Art Deco-style skirt guards, painted drop-center rims & original Allstate tires, rear drop-stand style kickstand, 1939 .... **270**

Elliot Hickory, Model C, very rare & desirable, fine restored condition, ca. 1892 (no chain) **6,270**

Four-man model, Dayton rear wheel brake hub assembly, motorcycle grade wheels & fenders, unknown maker, possibly Dayton Mfg. Co., rare, ca. 1910-15 .... **6,270**

Scarce Early Gedron No. 7 Model

Gedron, man's Model No. 7 split-fame hard tire safety-type, unusual adjustable hanging crank gear assembly, by The Iron Wheel Co., Toledo, Ohio, ca. 1892, restored (ILLUS.) **2,750**

Hartford, lady's pneumatic-tire safety model, original spoon plunger brake & cork grips, wooden chain guard & rear fender, house painted, saddle early replacement, w/American Clock Co. cyclometer, ca. 1898 .... **330**

Higgins (J.C.), girl's spring fork balloon-tire type, green & cream paint w/gold pinstriping, amateur restoration, ca. 1950s (seat needs recovering) **165**

Huffy, racing bicycle, black frame w/Huffy decals, campagnolo stressed kevlar disc wheels & campagnolo crank set, ridden by Steve Heg to set 4000 meter individual pursuit world outdoor record in 1986, restored **1,760**

Indian, girl's pneumatic-tire safety model, original blue & red paint, New Departure truss mount, two-speed, messenger seat, chrome stepped fenders, cadmium-plated wooden rims, Indian profile logo, ca. 1920s (no front tire, rear tire inoperative) **715**

March Davis Cycle Co., man's "The March" pneumatic-tire safety model, downswept handlebars, excellent original green paint w/gold pinstriping, anatomical seat, excellent nickel plating, late 19th c. (needs tires & rims) **963**

Monarch, boy's "Silver King" M1 model, polished silver finish, very clean, ca. 1938 .... **687**

Norwood, man's Model 6 pneumatic-tire safety model w/white "display" tires, manufactured by Schlueter Cycle Mfg. Co., Cincinnati, restored, ca. 1890s **715**

Ordinary (high-wheel), open head & oval tube backbone, front molded forks, apparently original crank & pedals, w/seat & handlebars, ca. 1885, front wheel 52" d. (missing some brake hardware) **2,255**

Ordinary (high-wheel), tapered backbone, apparently original seat, bent handlebars, ca. 1890, front wheel 56" d. (no pedals or brake hardware) **2,420**

Ordinary (high-wheel), tapered backbone, possibly original seat & hardware, unusual non-original handlebars, painted red, ca. 1890, large tire 56" d. (missing brake hardware & pedals) **2,750**

Ordinary (high-wheel), unusual construction w/spoke wheels, twisted diamond stock iron framed & hand-forged cranks & pedals, very unusual wooden handlebars, possibly blacksmith-made, ca. 1870, front wheel 52" d. **2,860**

Pierce, lady's pneumatic-tire safety model, very original condition, ca. 1920 .... **220**

Schwinn, boy's "Aero-Cycle," red aluminum, original metal tank & glass "aero" headlamp lens, Delta gangway pancake horn, old restoration, ca. 1934 .... **4,070**

Schwinn, boy's "Challenger" deluxe model, key locking spring fork w/original key, complete horn tank w/horn unit, Delta ribbed front load headlight, deluxe "long wing" chain guard & nine-hole rack, thin & flaking leatherette seat, fair original paint, new red reproduction tires, BF Goodrich, 1940 .... **523**

Schwinn boy's "Mark IV Jaguar" safety middle weight model, original blue & chrome finish, front & rear carriers, headlight, whitewall Schwinn West Wind tires, ca. 1960s (headlight lens missing) **413**

Schwinn Boy's Motorbike Model

Schwinn, boy's "Motorbike" B107 model, black & silver, Delta silver ray headlight & tank w/tool box door, Wyeth Standard Hardware & Mfg. Co., St. Joseph, Missouri, head badge, old restoration, ca. 1936 (ILLUS.) **1,870**

Schwinn, boy's "Streamliner" safety B-6 model, original condition w/maroon & white paint, Streamliner tank, Schwinn knee action spring fork & BF Goodrich tires, ca. 1949 .... **523**

Schwinn, girl's "Debutant" balloon-tire model, maroon & black paint, amateur restoration, 1950s **110**

Schwinn, girl's "The Hollywood" safety BA307 model, black & white paint, hanging tank, locking fork w/key, Delta silver ray headlight, Arnold Schwinn Majestic head badge, old restoration, ca. 1936-37 (shipping dent on front fender) **495**

Shelby Flyer, boy's "Hiawatha Arrow" safety model, red & black paint, Shelby Flyer fender badge, reproduction taillight assembly w/no lens, horizontally sprung Lobdel recovered saddle, old restoration, ca. 1939 .... **2,850**

Sherrell Classic, type 1, Serial #41, red paint, restored, 1987 .... **715**

Standard, lady's pneumatic-tire safety model, original maroon paint w/gold pinstripes, fine nickel plating, seat cover loose, fine details, wooden tire rims & Universal Tire Co. rubber tires in fine condition, by National Sewing Machine Co., Bevidere, Illinois, ca. 1895 .... **743**

Star ordinary, safety-type w/nickel-plated front fork, unique lever & ratchet drive, very original, patented by Geo. Pressey, Hammonton, New Jersey, front wheel 52" d. (needs restoration) **11,000**

Starley Bros. Adult Tricycle

Starley Bros. adult tricycle, loop frame, original paint & pinstriping, possibly original 50" d. rubber rear wheels, white ribbed tread, 15" d. front wheel marked "John Bull North Pole patent 3/4 inch," chain guard w/original logo, left hand brake & elliptical leaf spring seat, very original, name plate missing, seat cover needs restoration, Coventry, England, ca. 1884 (ILLUS.) **14,645**

Swiss Army, balloon tires, rear wheel lock w/key, twin parcel bags, leather tool pouch w/tools, air pump, bell, generator & license plate, ca. 1941 .... **495**

Tricycle, wooden, very original w/dry red surface & worn wooden seat w/original pinstriping, front wheel 24" d., rear wheels 20" d., ca. 1875-85 (one rear wheel spoke missing) **1,210**

Victor, man's split-frame hard tire safety model, original seat w/partial tool kit, complete rear brake hardware, Overman Wheel Co., Chicopee Falls, Massachusetts, ca. 1891 (needs rear tire, seat cover, cleaning) **2,860**

Early Victor Ordinary

Victor ordinary, downswept handlebars w/pear grips, recovered seat, correct brake hardware, correct pedals, excellent grey rubber tires, black frames & wheels w/red pinstriping, older restoration, late 19th c., front wheel 54" d. (ILLUS.) **4,675**

Wards Hawthorn, boy's balloon-tire model, very complete including bright red & white paint, rear carrier w/side running lights, pre-1940, good condition **303**

Western Flyer Buzz Bike 2 + 1

Western Flyer, boy's "Buzz Bike 2 + 1" safety model, original blue & chrome finish w/rear wheelie bar, ca. 1960-70 (ILLUS.) **523**

White Sewing Machine Co., man's "The White" pneumatic-tire safety model, hammock seat, wind-up handlebar bell, handlebar mounted New Haven "Bulldog" watch, toe clip pedals, leather tool pouch, original plunger brake & hardware, rims good, late 19th c. (no tires) **935**

BLACK AMERICANA

Over the past decade or so, this field of collecting has rapidly grown. Today almost anything that relates to Black culture or illustrates Black Americana is considered a desirable collectible. Although many representations of African-Americans, especially on 19th- and early-20th-century advertising pieces and housewares, were cruel stereotypes, even these are collected as poignant reminders of how far American society has come since the dawning of the Civil Rights movement, and how far we still have to go. Other pieces related to this cate-

gory will be found from time to time in such categories as Advertising Items, Banks, Character Collectibles, Kitchenwares, Signs and Signboards, Toys and several others. For a complete overview of this subject see Antique Trader Books' Black Americana Price Guide *with a special introduction by Julian Bond.*

Rare Animated Alarm Clock

Alarm clock, windup metal animated-type, round metal case on slender legs & bell on top, paper lithographed face w/color scene of black woman rocking a black child in a cradle, foot & cradle are supposed to move, not working, probably German, early 20th c., 6" h. (ILLUS.) **$605**

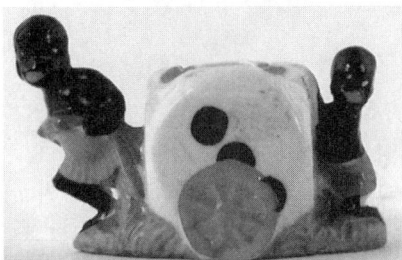

Ashtray with Black Natives

Ashtray, porcelain, figural, two black natives pulling & pushing a cart in the form of a large die, red wheels & skirts & green grass base, made in Japan, ca. 1930s, 2 x 4 1/2", 3" h. (ILLUS.) **28**

Autograph, Booker T. Washington, trimmed from letter, 2 1/4 x 5 1/4" **77**

Autograph, Cab Calloway, signed 8 x 10" professional glossy black & white photo, shows Calloway & his Cotton Club Orchestra, inscribed "To Mike - Sorry I didn't see you this trip. Lots of Luck. Hi-di Ho, Cab Calloway," bold clear signature (minor bends, writing on back) **75**

Book, "Anti-Slavery in America," by Mary Stoughton Locke, Boston, Ginn & Co., history of slavery in America, 1901, paper covers w/tan wraps, 22 pp. (cover worn, fragile & almost detached, missing back cover, some page browning) **55**

Salesman's Sample Book

Book, "Scott's American Negro in the World War," salesman's sample abbreviated edition, profusely illustrated, opens w/information on selling & promoting the book, red board covers, 1919 (ILLUS.) **198**

Book, "Story of the John Brown Bell," produced by the John A. Rawlins Post 43, Grand Army of the Republic, photos of sights in Harpers Ferry & the bell, w/the story of John Brown, 1910, hard covers, 20 pp., 6 x 8" **39**

Book, "The Fastest Bicycle Rider in the World...," autobiography of Marshall W. "Major" Taylor, personally inscribed & dated 1929, copyright 1928 (spine loose) **440**

Booklet, "John Brown's Expedition Reviewed - A Letter from Rev. Theodore Parker at Rome to Francis Jackson, Boston," published in Boston by The Fraternity, 1860, 20 pp., 4 5/8 x 7 1/2" **77**

Broadside, "Stop the Ku Klux Klan Propaganda in New York City," released by the NAACP urging the public to protest the showing of the movie "Birth of a Nation" in New York City, cream paper, ca. 1921, 9 x 13 1/2" (crudely repaired tear) **97**

Broadside, two-sided, a map of the South & promotional information printed in red & black, explains national fundraising efforts of the Freedman's Aid and Southern Educational Society of the Methodist Episcopal Church, ca. 1890, 26 x 30" (small tear in top margin, small splits at folds) **1,387**

Bust of a black man, carved & painted wood, mounted on a black-painted plinth, 19th c., 3" w., 8 1/8" h. (wear) **1,265**

Dish Towel with Black Girl

Dish towel, embroidered & painted cloth, color image of small black girl w/a large slice of watermelon, edge fringe, ca. 1940s-50s, 30" l. (ILLUS.)................................. **66**

Brayton Laguna Mammy Cookie Jar

Cookie jar, cov., figural Mammy, ceramic, light blue dress, polka dot kerchief, white apron, stamped mark of Brayton Laguna, small rim chip, light crazing, 12 1/2" h. (ILLUS.).. **358**

Doll, cloth, folk art style black boy w/stitched facial features, wearing red outfit w/white shirt, 12 1/2" h. (ILLUS. right, below) **165**

Doll, cloth, folk art style black girl w/stitched facial features, partially dressed, 12 1/2" h. (ILLUS. left, below)........................ **209**

Two Black Folk Art Dolls

Doll, cloth, black lady, handmade w/stocki-
nette head w/needle-sculpted nose, ears
& chin, painted eyes & mouth, wire earrings, yarn braids attached to head, black
cloth body w/no indication of fingers on
hands, feet shaped w/light wire &
stitched, wearing original red & white polka dot dress w/black shoe buttons on
front, white apron, original underclothing,
painted brown shoes, completely hand-
stitched, unmarked, 16" (three yarn
braids may have been added at a differ-
ent time as the yarn is heavier) **425**

Early Scottsboro Boys Flyer

Flyer, "Don't Let Them Burn! - Free the 9
Scottsboro Boys," six-panel paper, published by International Labor Defense,
cover photo of protesters, includes peti-
tions to fill out & photos of the defen-
dants, 4 x 9 1/2" (ILLUS.) **168**

Special Edition of "Liberation"

Magazine, "Liberation," December, 1956,
special issue released during the Montgomery bus boycott, early article by Martin Luther King as well as E.D. Nixon,
Eleanor Roosevelt, Ralph Bunche, Roy
Wilkins & others, yellow cover w/bus boycott drawing, 20 pp., cover soiling,
8 1/2 x 10 3/4" (ILLUS.) **281**

Mannequin, life-sized, chalkware & wood,
black man wearing a black derby hat,
dark blue & green checked shirt & dark
blue pants, jointed at shoulders, elbows,
wrists, neck & mid-body, jointed forefin-
gers & thumb, forehead scarred in a decorative fashion w/numerous bumps, late
19th - early 20th c., 19" w. at shoulders,
5' 9" h. (one finger missing, another par-
tially missing) **660**

Map, woodcut, map of the Southern slavery
states, titled "Moral Map of U.S. - Jan.
1837," proof copy by John Hall, Albany,
New York, mounted on album page,
6 x 6" (minor foxing, tear w/paper loss
not into image) **154**

Marionette, plastic head & hands w/wood-
en feet & body, oversized head wearing
primitive straw hat, a shirt in white w/tiny
blue flowers & orange & white check
pants, 14 1/2" h. (slight soiling & wear)........... **88**

Wire Black Man Matchbox Holder

Matchbox holder, wire, figural, model of a
wire figure of a black man riding a wire
bicycle w/front basket to hold a small box
of matches, zigzag wire base, man
w/wooden hat, red & white cloth shirt &
tan cloth pants, slight soiling,
3 1/4 x 5 1/2", 6" h. (ILLUS.) **61**

Meeting ticket, "Massachusetts Anti-Slavery Society - The Board of Managers
will meet on Wednesday Oct. 1st, 1851 at
10 1/2 o'clock a.m. at 21 Corhhill, R.F.
Wallcut, Rec. Sec.," card stock, 2 3/8 X
3 1/2" (very slightly browned) **69**

Military order, General Butler's General Order #88, New Orleans, H.Q. of the Gulf,
November 1, 1862, reads "No person will
be arrested as a slave...unless...owned
by a loyal citizen of the United States,"
disbound, one page... **83**

Newspaper, "Harper's Weekly," November
24, 1883, cover engraving of Frederick
Douglass, his biography included, complete issue (slight browning, margin pin
holes from earlier binding) **108**

Pinback button, celluloid w/photo of Bishop W.S. Brooks, 1865-1934, memorial-type, 1 1/4" d. **66**

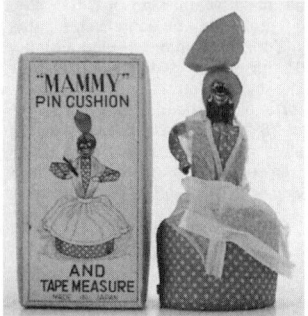

1963 March On Washington Button

Pinback button, "Emancipation March - August 28, 1963 On Washington," black & white celluloid, 1 3/4" d. (ILLUS.) **83**

Mammy Pincushion-Tape Measure

Pincushion-tape measure, cloth, figural, model of a black Mammy, red dress w/tiny white dots forms pincushion base w/tape measure, white apron & red kerchief, w/original cardboard box printed in black & red on white, made in Japan, ca. 1930s, mint in box, 5" h. (ILLUS.) **71**

Josephine Baker Postcard

Postcard, real photo of entertainer Josephine Baker posed w/a real leopard, Piaz Studio, Paris, ca. 1920s (ILLUS.).................. **121**

Print, titled "The Jackson Wagon Sun Flower Band - As they appeared at the Great Fairs of 1884," color lithographed outdoor scene of the all-male black band in a group in front of a Jackson wagon, inset photo of band leader in upper left, in early veneered frame, print 8 1/4 x 10 1/2" (small edge tear, minor veneer chips on frame) **231**

Program, "Announcing The Eastern Seaboard Conference of the Sojourners for Truth and Justice," cover art of Sojourner Truth by Charles White, call for meeting to work to free Mrs. Rosa Lee Ingram, produced by Charlotta Base, Vice Presidential candidate for the Progressive Party, March 1952, 4 pp. (foxing, edge wear).. **42**

Negro Youth Conference Program

Program, "Democracy - The Challenge of Victory - An Invitation to the Sixth All-Southern Negro Youth Conference - Atlanta, GA - Nov. 30 - Dec. 1-2-3, 1944," large photo of a young black couple on the cover, instructions on application & housing, tentative program, history of organization & officers, four-page flyer, some foxing, minor soil, 8 1/2 x 11" (ILLUS.) **99**

American Negro Exposition Program

Program with autograph, "American Negro Exposition - 1863 - 1940 - Chicago Coliseum - July 4 to Sept. 2 - Official Program and Guide Book," colorful cover art of black couple in foreground w/shadow of Lincoln's head behind, includes many photos w/autograph of Joe Louis over photo of someone else, celebrates 75 years of Emancipation, 64 pp. (ILLUS.)... **754**

Documentary Record Album

Record album, "Freedom In The Air - Albany, Georgia," 33 1/3 rpm, documentary on Albany, Georgia, in 1961-62, produced by Alan Lomax & Guy Carawan, manufactured by SNCC, extensive liner notes, cover split halfway along top edge, light edge foxing (ILLUS.).................................. **61**

Record album, "Negro Sinful Songs by Lead Belly," Musicraft Album 31, five 78 rpms, cover photo of black person picking cotton w/cabin in background, ca. 1940s (cover worn, spine split & soiled, records excellent) **435**

Salt & pepper shakers, molded plastic, figure of Mammy wearing dark yellow blouse, green & red striped dress, blue & white striped kerchief, holding tray w/coffeepot & cups & saucers, F&F Mold Co., embossed "Luzianne Mammy," from Luzianne Coffee, ca. 1950s, some paint flaking, 5" h., pr. (ILLUS. right) **121**

Plastic Mammy Salts & Peppers

Salt & pepper shakers, molded plastic, figure of Mammy wearing dark yellow blouse, red dress, blue & white striped kerchief, holding tray w/coffeepot & cups & saucers, F&F Mold Co., embossed "Langniappe of N.O.," ca. 1950s, some scratches, 5" h., pr. (ILLUS. left) **99**

Banjo-Pickaninnies
By
T. ROBIN MacLACHLAN

A DESCRIPTIVE PIANO PIECE

1920s Racial Sheet Music

Sheet music, "Banjo-Pickaninnies," by T. Robin MacLachlan, published by Harold Flammer, Inc., New York, 1928, six pages, minor soiling (ILLUS.)................................. **35**

Early Black Theme Sheet Music

Sheet music, "My Little Mule and I," by Fred Lyons, large caricature picture on cover w/seated black man playing banjo w/the mule beside him, cabin in the background, published by W.F. Shaw, 1884,

some overall soiling, 10 3/4 x 14"
(ILLUS.).. **110**

Rare Aunt Jemima Flour Hanger

Sign, "Aunt Jemina Pancake Flour," string-hung die-cut color-lithographed double-sided paper, large image of Aunt Jemima seated on a swing w/a plate of pancakes in her lap & packages of her flour beside her, early 20th c., foot creased, minor edge roughness, rare, 17 1/2" h.
(ILLUS.).. **4,747**

Sign, "Paul Jones Distiller," color lithographed on rectangular wood, large scene entitled "The Temptations of St. Anthony," comical outdoor scene w/a young black boy in the center & a black woman holding a huge slice of watermelon on the left & an elderly black man holding a bottle of whiskey on the right, cabin in the background, ca. 1901, 13 3/4 x 20" (slight wear)................................. **550**

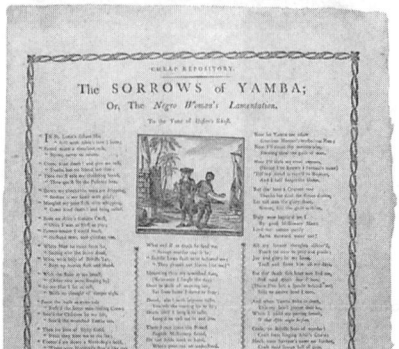

Early Songsheet-Broadside

Songsheet-broadside, "The Sorrows of Yamba - Or - The Negro Woman's Lamentation," published by Cheap Repository, England, w/woodcut of slave woman & white man on tropical dockside, ca. 1795, 10 3/4 x 17" (ILLUS. of part).. **1,265**

Weller Pottery Mammy Line Syrup

Syrup pitcher, cov., ceramic, figural Mammy, Weller Pottery Mammy Line, ca. 1930s, overall crazing, 6 1/2" h.
(ILLUS.).. **468**

Colorful Black Mammy Teapot

Teapot, cov., ceramic, figural, modeled as a black Mammy w/the base formed by her wide green skirt & apron, holding a long red wedge of watermelon at front, yellow blouse & white striped kerchief, bottom marked "USA," overall crazing, 8" l., 8" h.
(ILLUS.).. **94**

Rare Anti-Slavery Bazaar Ticket

Ticket, "1854-55 - Anti-Slavery Bazaar - 15 Winter Street - Season - No Transfer," card stock, slightly browned edge, 2 x 3 1/8" (ILLUS.) **220**

"Poor Pete" Windup Toy

Toy, windup celluloid & cloth, "Poor Pete," young black boy holding a slice of watermelon, a bulldog biting his posterior, Japan, ca. 1930s, paper label, working, 5 1/2" h. (ILLUS.) **358**

Toy, windup tin, "Poor Pete," young black boy holding a slice of watermelon, wearing red pants, white shirt & grey cap, a small dog biting his posterior, Germany, ca. 1930s, working, some scratches, 5 1/2" h. **495**

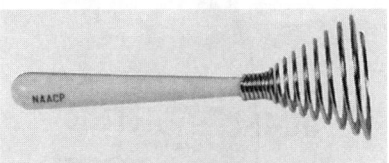

Early NAACP Potato Masher

Potato masher, plastic handle & wire loop masher, yellow & blue, handle printed "NAACP - Freedom Fund," 1950s (ILLUS.) **105**

BOTTLES

Bitters

(Numbers with some listings below refer to those used in Carlyn Ring's For Bitters Only.)

African Stomach Bitters, cylindrical w/applied top, smooth base, light amber, 9 5/8" h. **$77**

Light Amber Baker's Bitters Bottle

Baker's - Orange Grove - Bitters, square w/ropetwist corners, applied sloping collar mouth, smooth base, ca. 1865-75, light yellowish amber w/an olive tone, 9 1/2" h. (ILLUS.) **840**

Baker's - Orange Grove - Bitters, square w/ropetwist corners, applied sloping collar mouth, smooth base, ca. 1865-75, yellowish amber w/a shade of green, 9 5/8" h. **990**

Bennet's Celebrated Stomach Bitters - Jos. N. Souther & Co. Sole Proprietors, San Francisco, square w/applied mouth, amber, 9" h. (small polished chip off lip) **88**

Bourbon Whiskey Bitters, barrel-shaped, ten rings above & below center band, medium to deep plum, 9 1/4" h. **523**

Brown's Celebrated Indian Herb Bitters - Patented 1868, figural Indian Queen, rolled lip, bright yellowish amber w/a touch of green, 12 1/8" h. **935**

Brown's Celebrated Indian Herb Bitters - Patented 1868, figural Indian Queen, rolled lip, rare pure green, 12 1/8" h. **16,500**

Brown's Celebrated Indian Herb Bitters - Patented Feb. 11 1868, figural Indian Queen, ground lip, medium to light amber, 12 1/4" h. **605**

Professor Byrne Bitters Bottle

Byrne (Professor Geo. J.) New York - The Great Universal Compound Stomach Bitters Patented 1870, square w/fancy roped corners & arched panels, applied sloping collared mouth w/ring, smooth base, bright yellowish amber, hard to see small bruise on mouth, 10 1/4" h. (ILLUS.).. **1,344**

California Fig Bitters - California Extract of Fig Co. - San Francisco, Cal., square w/tooled lip, amber, 10" h. **44**

California Wine Bitters - Rennert, Prosch & Co. (on paper label), round w/lady's leg neck & applied lip, label 99% intact, amber, 12 5/8" h. **264**

Celebrated Nectar Stomach Bitters and Nerve Tonic - The Nectar Bitter Co. Toledo, O., square w/ropetwist neck & applied mouth, green, 9 3/4" h. (chip off side of mouth, tiny flake on other side) **358**

Clarke's Vegetable Sherry Wine Bitters Sharon Mass (below) Only 70 Cts, rectangular w/beveled corners & applied tapering top, open pontil, aqua, 11 3/8" h. **495**

Coleman's (Dr. A.W.) - Anti Dyspeptic and Tonic Bitters, rectangular w/arched shoulder & beveled corners, applied sloping collared mouth, smooth base, deep yellowish olive, 9 1/4" h. **2,352**

Curtis - Cordial - Calisaya - The Great - Stomach - Bitters - 1 - 8 - 6 - 6 -C - C - C -1- 9 - 0 - 0, cylindrical w/tall tapering paneled shoulder, cylindrical short neck w/applied mouth, ca. 1866-75, deep root beer amber, 11 1/2" h. **1,210**

Davis' (James L.) Sons Schiedam Bitters New York, square w/beveled corners, applied sloping collared mouth, smooth base, yellowish amber, 9 7/8" h. (some exterior highpoint wear & roughness on shoulder & corners) **420**

Dods (Dr. J. Bovee) - Imperial Wine Bitters - New York, rectangular w/beveled corners & paneled sides, applied double collared mouth, smooth base, aqua, ca. 1860-70, 9 7/8" h. (ILLUS., top next column) **420**

Doyle's - Hop - Bitters - 1872, semi-cabin, words around sides of sloping shoulder, square w/paneled sides w/raised clusters of hop berries & leaves, applied sloping double collar mouth, ca. 1872-80, amber, 9 3/8" h. **33**

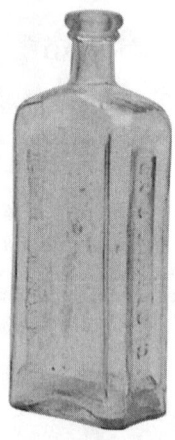

Dr. Dods Wine Bitters Bottle

Drake's (S T) - 1860 - Plantation - X - Bitters - Patented - 1862, cabin-shaped, six-log, applied sloping collared mouth, smooth base, crude, ca. 1862-70, medium reddish amber w/some cherry, 10" h. (D-106) **198**

Drake's (S T) - 1860 - Plantation - X - Bitters - Patented - 1862, cabin-shaped, six-log, applied sloping collared mouth, smooth base, ca. 1862-70, bright salmon, 10" h. (D-106) **770**

Drake's (S T) - 1860 - Plantation - X - Bitters - Patented - 1862, cabin-shaped, six-log, applied sloping collared mouth, smooth base, ca. 1862-70, brilliant puce, 10" h. (D-106) **1,064**

Fish (The) Bitters - W.H. Ware, Patented 1866, figural fish, crudely applied top, medium amber, 11 1/2" h. **264**

Fish (The) Bitters - W.H. Ware, Patented 1866, figural fish, "W.H. Ware Patent 1866" on bottom, applied small round collared mouth, smooth base, bright golden yellow, 11 1/2" h. **550**

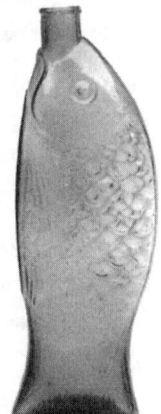

The Fish Bitters Figural Bottle

Fish (The) Bitters - W.H. Ware, Patented 1866, figural fish, "W.H. Ware Patent 1866" on bottom, applied small round collared mouth, smooth base, yellow w/amber tone, 11 1/2" h. (ILLUS.) **616**

Frisco Hop Bitters Company, square w/sloped shoulders & applied top, pale aqua, 9 1/4" h. (few scratches) **66**

German Balsam Bitters, W.M. Watson & Co., Sole Agents for U.S., square w/applied tapering collar, milk glass, 9" h. **605**

Grand Prize Bitters, square w/paneled sides, applied lip, ca. 1880-84, amber, 9 1/4" h. (flake off front edge) **165**

Great Tonic (The) - Caldwell's - Herb Bitters, triangular w/tall neck & applied sloping collar mouth, iron pontil, ca. 1870-80, medium amber, 12 3/4" h. (tiny radiated potstone) **198**

Greeley's Bourbon Bitters, barrel-shaped, ten rings above & below center band, applied square collared mouth, smooth base, medium to deep amber w/some puce, 9 3/8" h. (G-101) **413**

Greeley's Bourbon Bitters, barrel-shaped, ten rings above & below center band, applied square collared mouth, smooth base, 80% of original paper label, strawberry puce, 9 3/8", G-101 (tiny burst bubble near base) **1,456**

Greeley's Bourbon Bitters

Greeley's Bourbon Bitters, barrel-shaped, ten rings above & below center band, applied square collared mouth, smooth base, bright yellowish olive, 9 3/8" h., G-101 (ILLUS.) **1,792**

Greeley's Bourbon Bitters, barrel-shaped, ten rings above & below center band, smoky topaz green, 9 3/8" h. (G-101) **1,980**

Hall's Bitters - E.E. Hall New Haven - Established 1842, barrel-shaped, applied disk mouth, smooth base, reddish orange amber, 9 1/8" h. **275**

Hall's Bitters - E.E. Hall New Haven - Established 1842, barrel-shaped, applied square collared mouth, smooth base, golden amber, 9 1/4" h. **168**

Hartwig - Kantorowicz - (Star of David enclosing fish) - Posen - Berlin - Hamburg -Germany, tall lobed form w/tall slender neck & applied mouth, Germany, ca. 1880-95, bright grass green, 13" h. **242**

Harvey's Prairie Bitters - Patented (on shoulder), square w/roped corners & lattice shoulder panels, applied sloping mouth, dark amber, 9 1/2" h. (tiny cooling check in lip) **15,400**

Henley's (Dr.) Wild Grape Root - IXL (in oval) Bitters, cylindrical w/tall neck & applied mouth, smooth base, deep aqua, ca. 1870, 12 1/2" h. (hint of interior haze) **413**

Henley's (Dr.) Wild Grape Root - IXL (no oval) Bitters, cylindrical w/applied rim, deep aqua, 12 1/2" h. (tiny bit of interior stain) **88**

Herb (H.P.) Wild Cherry Bitters, Reading, Pa., cabin-shaped, square w/cherry tree motif & roped corners, tooled mouth, medium to light amber, 10 1/8" h. **413**

Holtzermann's Patent Stomach Bitters (on roof), cabin-shaped, four-roof, tooled mouth, original paper label, ca. 1880-1895, amber, 9 7/8" h. **330**

Hostetter's (Dr. J.) Stomach Bitters, square w/rounded shoulders & beveled corners, applied top, smooth base, medium amber w/olive tones, 9 1/2" h. **176**

Hostetter's (Dr. J.) Stomach Bitters, square w/rounded shoulders & beveled corners, applied top, smooth base, yellowish green, dug, 8 5/8" h. (touch of interior stain) **303**

Hostetter's (Dr. J.) Stomach Bitters - L & W (on base), square w/rounded shoulders & beveled corners, short neck w/applied sloping collar mouth, ca. 1860-70, bright yellow, dug, 8 7/8" h. (slight stain) **550**

Kelly's Old Cabin Bitters - Patented 1863 (on roof), cabin-shaped, applied mouth, smooth base, ca. 1863-70, amber, 9 1/8" h. **2,640**

Kreinbrook's (L.N.) Bitters, Mt. Pleasant, PA, flattened oval shape w/tooled collared mouth w/ring, smooth base, bright yellowish amber, pt., 7 1/2" h. (some minor highpoint wear) **1,008**

Langley's (Dr.) - Root & Herb - Bitters - 99 Union St. - Boston, cylindrical w/short neck & flattened applied mouth, ca. 1855-65, greenish aqua, 8 5/8" h. **121**

Lediard's Morning Call, round w/tall neck & applied sloping mouth, dark green, 8 1/4" h. **413**

Loew's (Dr.) Celebrated Stomach Bitters Nerve Tonic - The Loew & Sons Co Cleveland, rectangular w/paneled sides & spiral-twist neck w/probable ABM mouth, smooth base, 85% original paper label, green, ca. 1880, 9 1/4" h. **358**

Loew's (Dr.) Celebrated Stomach Bitters & Nerve Tonic - The Loew & Sons Co. Cleveland, O., sample size, square w/paneled sides, ribbed shoulder & spiral-twisted neck w/tooled mouth, pale yellowish green, 4" h. **209**

Mack's Sarsaparilla Bitters - Mack & Co. Prop'rs San Francisco, square w/beveled corners, applied top, ca. 1884-87, golden amber, 9 3/8" h. **413**

Mills' Bitters A.M. Gilman Sole Proprietor, cylindrical w/lady's leg neck & applied rim w/ring, bright honey amber, 11 1/4" h. (minor stain in neck, two flakes near top edge) **6,600**

Moffat (Jno.) - Phoenix Bitters - New York - Price 1$ rectangular w/wide beveled corners, rolled out lip, tubular pontil, dense amber approaching black, ca. 1835-55, 5 1/2" h. (minor shallow burst bubbles on lip) **2,800**

Moffat (John) & Cos Phoenix Bitters - New York - Price $1.00, rectangular w/tapering shoulders & applied top, deep aqua, 6 3/8" h. **187**

Moffat (John) - Phoenix Bitters - New York - Price $1.00, rectangular w/beveled corners & applied sloping collar mouth, base pontil, ca. 1835-50, crude, olive green, 5 1/2" h. **880**

National Bitters, figural ear of corn, "Patent 1867" on base, applied mouth w/ring, smooth base, tobacco amber, ca. 1870, 12 1/2" h. **385**

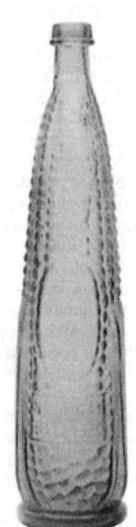

Rare Yellow National Bitters Bottle

National Bitters, figural ear of corn, "Patent 1867" on base, applied sloping collared mouth w/ring, smooth base, yellow w/hint of topaz, ca. 1870, 12 1/2" h. (ILLUS.) **6,160**

National Bitters Ear of Corn Bottle

National Bitters, figural ear of corn, "Patent 1867" on base, applied mouth w/ring, smooth base, golden amber, ca. 1870, 12 1/2" h. (ILLUS.) **392**

National Bitters, figural ear of corn, "Patent 1867" on base, applied mouth w/ring, smooth base, light to medium golden amber, ca. 1870, 12 1/2" h. **440**

National Bitters, figural ear of corn, "Patent 1867" on base, applied mouth w/ring, smooth base, bright yellowish amber w/slight olive tone, ca. 1870, 12 1/2" h. **560**

Rare National Tonic Bitters

National - Tonic - Bitters, square w/roped corners, arched shoulders, applied sloping collared mouth, smooth base, bright light yellowish amber, 9 1/4" h. (ILLUS.) **9,520**

Old Abe's Ague & Stomach Bitters, rectangular, tooled flared square collared mouth, smooth base, aqua, 7 1/4" h. **308**

Old Home Bitters Bottle

Old Home - Bitters - Laughlin Smith & Co. - Wheeling, W.Va., square semi-cabin, applied sloping collared mouth, smooth base, golden amber w/red tone, 9 3/4" h. (ILLUS.)... **2,800**

Old - Homestead - Wild Cherry - Bitters - Patent, cabin-shaped, scalloped shingles on four-sided roof, applied sloping collar mouth, ca. 1865-80, dark amber, 9 7/8" h. (tiny flakes on lip)............................ **413**

Old - Homestead - Wild Cherry - Bitters - Patent, cabin-shaped, scalloped shingles on four-sided roof, applied sloping collar mouth, ca. 1865-80, bright light amber, 9 1/2" h. **523**

Old Sachem - Bitters - and - Wigwam Tonic, barrel-shaped, ten-rib, applied mouth, apricot gold, 9 1/2" h....................... **1,320**

Old Sachem - Bitters - and - Wigwam Tonic, barrel-shaped, ten-rib, applied mouth, copper puce, 9 3/8" h.......................... **550**

Old Sachem - Bitters - and - Wigwam Tonic, barrel-shaped, ten-rib, applied mouth, dug, cleaned, light rose puce w/swirls of deeper puce, 9 3/8" h............... **4,400**

Panknin's - Hepatic Bitters New York, square w/beveled corners, applied sloping collar, amber, 8 5/8" h. (minor stain)....... **209**

Peruvian Bitters - "W&K" monogram in shield, square w/applied top, smooth base, amber, 9 1/4" h.................................. **121**

Peruvian Bitters - "W&K" monogram in shield, square w/applied top, smooth base, bright reddish amber, 9 7/8" h. **275**

Peychaud's American Aromatic Bitters (on paper label), round w/tall neck, original closure, 99% full label, amber, 10 1/2" h. **88**

Pineapple figural, embossed diamond-shaped panel, applied top, smooth base, reddish amber, 8 7/8" h. **220**

Pineapple figural - W. & Co. N.Y. (in small diamond), embossed diamond-shaped panel, applied double collar mouth, base pontil, medium amber, 8 7/8" h. **605**

Place's (Dr.) Cundurango Bitters (on label) - Cundurango - Cundurango (embossed on two sides), square w/label panel on one side, crude applied lip, light

to medium yellowish green, crude, 9 3/8" h. (label missing, minor interior stain)... **2,640**

Prickly Ash Bitters, square w/ABM, original paper label & box, w/contents, amber, bottle mint, box 75% intact, 9 3/8" h............. **176**

Reed's Bitters, round w/lady's leg neck w/applied top, light bright amber, 12 1/2" h. (minor interior stain)..................... **413**

Roback's (Dr. C.W.) - Stomach Bitters - Cincinnati, O., barrel-shaped, applied sloping collar mouth, smooth base, ca. 1860-70, bright amber, 9 1/2" h. **330**

Roback's Stomach Bitters Bottle

Roback's (Dr. C.W.) - Stomach Bitters - Cincinnati, O., barrel-shaped, applied sloping collared mouth, iron pontil, 60% of stained paper label present, ca. 1855-65, golden amber, 10" h. (ILLUS.)............. **728**

Sazerac Armotic Bitters (on base) - monogram in ring on shoulder, cylindrical w/tall lady's leg neck & applied rim ring, ca. 1870s, light amber, 10 1/4" h. **468**

Sazerac Armotic Bitters (on base) - monogram in ring on shoulder, cylindrical w/tall lady's leg neck & applied rim ring, smooth base, ca. 1870s, milk glass, 12 1/2" h... **420**

Simon's Centennial Bitters - Trade Mark, bust of George Washington on pedestal, applied double collar mouth, bright reddish amber, 10" h. **3,740**

Solomon's Strengthening & Invigorating Bitters - Savannah, Georgia, square w/paneled sides, applied sloping collar mouth, smooth base, cobalt blue, ca. 1880, 9 5/8" h... **1,210**

Soule (Dr.) - Hop - Bitters - 1872 (on shoulders), square semi-cabin w/embossed hop flowers & leaves design on one side, applied sloping double collar mouth, apricot, 9 1/4" h. **132**

Soule (Dr.) - Hop - Bitters - 1872 (on shoulders), square semi-cabin w/embossed hop flowers & leaves design on one side, applied sloping double collar mouth, yellowish green, 9 1/4" h.................... **231**

Soule (Dr.) - Hop - Bitters - 1872 (on shoulders), square semi-cabin w/embossed hop flowers & leaves design on one side, applied sloping double collar mouth, bright yellow w/some olive, 9 1/4" h. **303**

Suffolk Bitters - Philbrook & Tucker Boston, figural pig, applied double collar mouth, smooth base, medium amber, ca. 1870, 10 1/4" l. **990**

Suffolk Bitters - Philbrook & Tucker Boston, figural pig, applied square collar mouth, smooth base, bright gold to reddish amber, ca. 1870, 10 1/4" l. **2,090**

Taussig (Louis) & Co. - San Francisco, Cal., square w/applied sloping lip, dark amber, crude & bubbly, 9" h. **121**

Tippecanoe (birch bark & canoe design), H.H. Warner & Co., cylindrical, applied disc mouth, amber, 9" h. **110**

Warner's (Dr. C.D.) German Hop Bitters - 1880 - Reading, Mich., square, tooled top, amber, 8 7/8" h. **132**

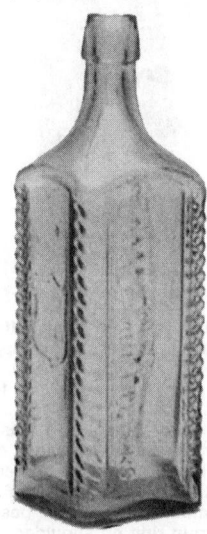

Dr. Wheeler's Bitters Bottle

Wheeler's (Dr.) Tonic Sherry Wine Bitters - Established 1848 (inside shield) - Boston, square w/roped corners, applied sloping collar mouth, smooth base, greenish aqua, shallow small chip near base, 9 1/2" h. (ILLUS.) **3,920**

Whitcomb's (Faith) Bitters - Boston, Mass. U.S.A. - Faith Whitcomb's Agency, rectangular w/paneled sides & tooled top, complete original paper label & box, w/contents, aqua, bottle mint, box 70% complete, 9 1/2" h. **132**

Wonser's (Dr.) U.S.A., Indian Root Bitters, cylindrical w/applied mouth, ringed neck, ribbed shoulder, golden amber, 11" h. **9,900**

Figurals

Automobile, miniature antique open auto w/driver, tooled mouth, embossed "Mirabel" across hood, deep bluish aqua, Europe, ca. 1900-20, 2 7/8" l. **308**

Figural Russian Bear Bottle

Bear, seated on haunches, applied face on head, cylindrical neck w/sheared mouth at top of head, thick shaped base, dense black glass, probably Russian, 1840-70, 11 3/4" h. (ILLUS.) **246**

Cat, miniature seated cat, rolled lip, smooth base, frosted clear, France, early 20th c., 1 3/4" h. **45**

Cherub faces, the wide oblong bulbous base molded in bold relief at each end w/a cherub face below "Aspaisa," the sides molded w/pairs of lovebirds on leafy vines that continue up the tall tapering neck, applied sloping collared mouth, smooth base embossed "Salve," opaque robin's egg blue, Europe, 1880-1900, 9 3/4" h. **224**

Christmas tree, tooled mouth, smooth base, embossed "Kyselak" on side of base, olive green, Europe, ca. 1900-20, 9 1/2" h. **67**

Rare Atterbury Duck Bottle

Duck, upright position w/neck extending from bird's beak, embossed oval label panel on breast, base embossed "Patd April 11th 1871," Atterbury Glass Co., milk glass decorated overall w/bright raspberry red looping, 11 1/2" h. (ILLUS.) **1,792**

Ear of corn, round foot & short pedestal supporting the upright ear w/a cylindrical neck & clear stopper, cobalt blue w/remnants of original gold paint trim, late 19th - early 20th c., 8 7/8" h. (small chip off lip) **330**

Grant's Tomb, ground lip, smooth base, milk glass model of the tomb fitted w/a pewter cap w/a bust of Grant finial, ca. 1893, 10" h. **784**

Lemon, rough sheared & ground lip, pale aqua, American, ca. 1890-1915, 4 1/4" l. **90**

Monkey sitting on barrel, shown pulling hat down over its ears, smooth base, tooled lip w/metal-over-cork stopper, milk glass, ca. 1890-1915, Europe, 9 3/8" h. **1,176**

Flasks

Flasks are listed according to the numbers provided in American Bottles & Flasks & Their Ancestry *by Helen McKearin and Kenneth M. Wilson.*

GI-2 - Washington bust below "General Washington" - American Eagle w/shield w/seven bars on breast, head turned to right, edges w/horizontal beading w/vertical medial rib, sheared lip, open pontil, deep greenish aqua, pt. **560**

GI-7 - Washington bust facing left below "Geo. Washington" - American eagle facing right, no shield on breast, below twelve small eight-point stars & above oval frame enclosing a band of small pearls around "F.L," sheared mouth, pontil scar, greenish aqua, pt. **2,240**

GI-11 - Washington bust below branches - American eagle w/head turned right & body curving, sunrays above eagle's head & 13 small stars, horizontal beading w/vertical medial rib, sheared mouth, pontil scar, bluish aqua, pt. **1,904**

GI-16 - Washington bust below "General Washington" - American eagle w/shield w/seven bars on breast, head turned to right, vertically ribbed edges, sheared mouth, pontil scar, pale aqua, pt. (some minor interior haze) **560**

GI-20 - Washington bust facing left w/"Fells" above & "Point" below - monument without statue above "Balto.," vertical medial rib, sheared mouth, pontil scar, topaz, pt. (tiny flake on top of mouth) **6,720**

GI-31 - "Washington" above bust - "Jackson" above bust, sheared mouth, pontil scar, greenish aqua, pt. **336**

GI-31 - "Washington" above bust - "Jackson" above bust, sheared mouth, pontil scar, bright yellow w/olive tone, pt. (some highpoint wear) **336**

GI-31 - "Washington" above bust - "Jackson" above bust, sheared mouth, pontil scar, golden amber, pt. **440**

GI-34 - Washington bust portrait obverse - Jackson bust portrait reverse, Coventry, Connecticut Glass Works, sheared mouth, pontil scar, light yellowish amber w/olive tone, 1/2 pt. (slightly weak impression) **416**

GI-36 - Washington bust not in oval panel, small classical bust facing left, large tree w/foliage, applied mouth, tubular pontil, aqua, qt. (some faint inside haze) **213**

Rare Washington - Taylor Flask

GI-37 - Washington bust below "The Father of His Country," - Taylor bust below "Gen Taylor Never Surrenders" below upper band w/"Dyottville Glass Works Philada," smooth edges, sheared mouth, smooth base, bright medium to deep cherry puce, qt. (ILLUS.) **7,840**

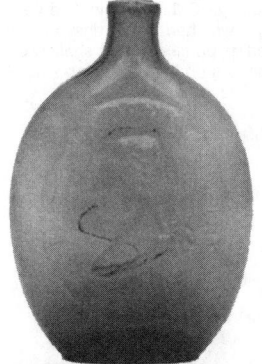

Very Rare Washington - Taylor Flask

GI-44 - Washington bust below "The Father of His Country" - Taylor bust below "I Have Endeavor'd To Do My Duty," smooth edges, sheared mouth, tubular pontil scar, bright cobalt blue, no exterior wear, strong embossing, pt. (ILLUS.) **13,440**

GI-44 - Washington bust below "The Father of His Country" - Taylor bust below "I Have Endeavor'd To Do My Duty," smooth edges, sheared mouth, pontil scar, medium yellowish green, pt. (small oval open bubble on medial rib) **392**

GI-79 - Grant bust in medallion - American eagle on shield & carrying ribbon in beak all above oval framed w/"Union," smooth edges, applied mouth, smooth base, aqua, pt. (exterior wear on head of Grant, minor highpoint wear) **213**

GI-81 - Lafayette bust facing right below "Lafayette" & above "S & C" - Clinton bust facing right below "Dewitt Clinton" & above "C-T," corrugated edges, sheared mouth, pontil scar, light yellowish amber w/olive tone, 1/2 pt. (small spider crack from bubble on the side) **672**

Lafayette - Liberty Cap Flask

GI-85 - "Lafayette" above bust & "Covetry [sic] - C-T" below - French liberty cap on pole & semicircle of eleven five-pointed stars above, "S & S" below, fine vertical ribbing, two horizontal ribs at base, sheared lip, pontil scar, two shallow chips on base ring on the liberty cap side, yellowish olive, pt. (ILLUS.) **896**

Lafayette - Liberty Cap Flask

GI-86 - "Lafayette" above bust & "Coventry - C-T" below - French liberty cap on pole & semicircle of eleven five-pointed stars above, "S & S" below, fine vertical ribbing, two horizontal ribs at base, sheared mouth, pontil scar, medium yellowish olive, 1/2 pt. (ILLUS.) **1,904**

GI-90 - Lafayette bust facing right below "General La Fayette," "Republican Grati-

tude" in border band - American eagle facing left w/shield below "E. Pluribus Unum" & above oval reserve w/twenty-one pearls & "T.W.D.," border band w/"Kensington Glass Works Philadelphia,"sheared lip, open pontil, nearly colorless pale aqua, pt.. **896**

GI-90 - Lafayette bust facing right below "General La Fayette," "Republican Gratitude" in border band - American eagle facing left w/shield below "E. Pluribus Unum" & above oval reserve w/twenty-one pearls & "T.W.D.," border band w/"Kensington Glass Works Philadelphia," sheared lip, open pontil, bright aqua, pt. **1,064**

GI-96 - Franklin bust below "Benjamin Franklin" - Dyott bust below "T.W. Dyott, M.D.," edges embossed "Eropuit Coelo Fulmen. Sceptrumque Tyrannis" and "Keningston Glass Works, Philadelphia," sheared mouth, pontil scar, aqua., qt. **532**

GI-98 - Franklin bust below "Benjamin Franklin" - "Wheeling Glassworks" in semicircle above bust of Thomas Dyott, vertically ribbed edges, sheared mouth, pontil scar, light green, pt..................... **3,920**

GI-99 - "Jenny Lind" above bust - view of glasshouse w/"Glass Works" above & "Huffsey" below, calabash, smooth sides, broad sloping shoulder, applied mouth, pontil scar, bright emerald green, qt. (tiny flake on mouth ring) **2,128**

GI-99 - "Jenny Lind" above bust - view of glasshouse w/"Glass Works" above & "Huffsey" below, calabash, smooth sides, broad sloping shoulder, applied mouth, pontil scar, rich bluish green, qt. **2,352**

GI-103 - "Jeny. Lind" (sic) above bust within wreath - view of glasshouse, no wording, vertically ribbed sides, calabash-form, applied sloping collar mouth, pontil scar, bright aqua w/numerous olive amber swirls, qt. **2,352**

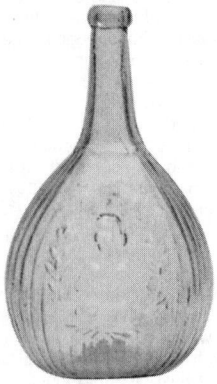

Jeny (sic) Lind Blue Calabash

GI-104 - "Jeny. Lind" (sic) above bust - view of glasshouse, calabash, vertically ribbed edges, rounded collar, pontil scar, cornflower blue, some interior stain especially near base, qt. (ILLUS.) **784**

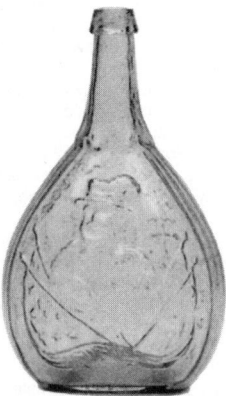

Louis Kossuth Bright Green Flask

GI-112 - "Louis Kossuth" above full-faced bust of Kossuth in uniform above crossed flags - frigate sailing left flying flags above "U.S. Steam Frigate Mississippi S. Huffsey," "Ph. Doflein Mould Maker Nth. 5t St 84" on base, calabash-form, applied sloping collar, tubular pontil, bright greenish aqua, qt. (ILLUS.) 336

GI-112 - "Louis Kossuth" above full-faced bust of Kossuth in uniform above crossed flags - frigate sailing left flying flags above "U.S. Steam Frigate Mississippi S. Huffsey," "Ph. Doflein Mould Maker Nth. 5t St 84" on base, calabash-form, crudely applied sloping collar mouth, iron pontil scar, deep aqua, qt. 364

GI-113 - "Kossuth" above bust - tall tree in foliage, calabash-style, smooth edges, applied collared mouth, pontil scar, yellow w/olive tone, qt. (burst bubble inside mouth) 560

GI-114 - Draped bust of Byron facing left - draped bust of Scott facing right, vertically ribbed edges, sheared mouth, pontil scar, medium olive amber, 1/2 pt. 476

Draped Byron Bust Flask

GI-114 - Draped bust of Byron facing left - draped bust of Scott facing right, vertical-

ly ribbed edges, sheared mouth, tubular pontil, bright light yellowish olive, 1/2 pt. (ILLUS.) **616**

GI-115 - Bust of man facing right below "Wheat, Price & Co. Wheeling, Va." w/the "n" in Wheeling reversed - view of glasshouse w/tall chimney surrounded by "Fair View Works," horizontally corrugated edges w/vertical medial rib, sheared mouth, pontil scar, medium bluish green, pt. **19,040**

GII-2 - American eagle on oval enclosing sixteen large pearls, head turned to the right & 10 stars in semicircle above - same design but w/nine stars, beaded edges w/narrow vertical medial rib, sheared mouth, pontil scar, deep aqua w/greenish tone, pt. **672**

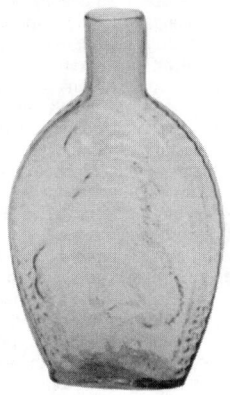

Extremely Rare Eagle Flask

GII-7 - American eagle w/shield & head turned left below six small stars - large circular sunburst w/32 rays, large round beading w/vertical medial rib on sides, sheared mouth, pontil scar, some minor exterior highpoint wear, dense amber, pt. (ILLUS.) **30,240**

GII-11 - American eagle facing left w/eleven stars above, standing on oval frame w/inner band of eighteen pearls - cornucopia with produce, horizontally beaded edges w/vertical medial rib, sheared mouth, pontil scar, bright aqua, 1/2 pt. **560**

American Eagle - Cornucopia Flask

GII-11 - American eagle facing left w/eleven stars above, standing on oval frame w/inner band of eighteen pearls - cornucopia with produce, horizontally beaded edges w/vertical medial rib, sheared mouth, pontil scar, bright medium citron, 1/2 pt. (ILLUS.) **3,920**

Rare American Eagle Flask

GII-13 - American eagle w/head turned to left & w/large beak & no shield above an oval frame cut off at the bottom & enclosing ten large pearls, a semicircle of eighteen stars above eagle - cornucopia inverted & coiled to left filled w/produce, horizontally beaded border w/medial rib, sheared mouth, pontil scar, bright medium bluish green, 1/2 pt. (ILLUS.) **10,008**

GII-18 - American eagle w/head turned to right above oval frame enclosing "Zanes - Ville" - cornucopia w/produce, vertically ribbed edges, sheared mouth, pontil scar, bright clear golden amber, 1/2 pt. (some mold impression weakness) **1,904**

GII-24 - American eagle facing left w/ribbon above head w/random ribbing, two arched rows of four-point stars at top, arrows & olive branch in talons above bottom oval frame enclosing an elongated eight-point star - large conventionalized floral medallion above an oval frame enclosing an elongated eight-point star, horizontally corrugated edges, sheared mouth, pontil scar, pale bluish green, pt. **532**

GII-26 - American eagle w/banner in beak above stellar motif obverse & reverse, horizontally corrugated edges, sheared mouth, pontil scar, bright medium bluish green, qt. (some exterior highpoint wear).. **1,792**

GII-26 - American eagle w/banner in beak above stellar motif obverse & reverse, horizontally corrugated edges, applied mouth w/rim, smooth base, bright olive yellow, qt. (small chip on top of mouth)...... **4,760**

GII-31 - American Eagle in large oval medallion obverse & reverse, overall heavy vertical ribbing except for medallions, pontil scar, applied double collar mouth, aqua, qt. (minor exterior highpoint wear) **364**

GII-31 - American eagle in large oval medallion obverse & reverse, overall heavy vertical ribbing except for medallions, sheared mouth, pontil scar, aqua, qt. **420**

GII-33 - American eagle below four stars in small oval panel on an overall vertically ribbed body - "Louisville Ky Glassworks" in oval panel on ribbed body, vertically ribbed edges, applied mouth, smooth base, deep golden amber, 1/2 pt. (some exterior highpoint wear, crudely formed mouth, body misshapen near base).......... **1,232**

GII-36 - eagle in oval panel above rectangular panel w/"Louisville Ky. Glass Works," entire flask except two panels on obverse covered w/angular vertical ribbing, applied lip, smooth base, aqua w/olive streak, pt. **253**

GII-43 - American eagle w/shield facing right, scattered sunrays around head, arrows & olive branch in talons resting on an oval frame w/band of small pearls around "T.W.D.," border w/"E Pluribus Unum One of Many" - cornucopia w/produce, border w/"Kensington Glass Works Philadelphia," sheared mouth, pontil scar, aqua, 1/2 pt. (exterior highpoint wear) **146**

GII-49 - American eagle on oval - stag w/antlers standing & facing left, surrounded by an oval ring of wording "Coffin & Hay - Hammonton," vertically ribbed edges w/heavy medial rib, sheared mouth, pontil scar, bright aqua, pt. (tiny mouth flake on interior of neck)..................... **364**

GII-52 - American eagle facing left w/large shield, stars above & crossed olive branches below - American flag furled above "For Our Country," sheared mouth, pontil scar, bright golden amber w/olive tone, pt. (some exterior highpoint wear, shallow partial bubble burst on mouth) **3,360**

GII-52 - American eagle facing left w/large shield, stars above & crossed olive branches below - American flag furled above "For Our Country," sheared mouth, pontil scar, pale yellowish amber w/olive tone, pt. (some exterior highpoint wear).. **4,760**

GII-53 - American eagle w/shield & furled flag - "For Our Country," wide bands of vertical edge ribbing, sheared mouth, pontil scar, pale aqua, pt. **308**

GII-54 - American eagle facing left on large shield, sunrays around head - U.S. flag furled on standard above "For Our Country," sheared mouth, tubular pontil, aqua, pt. (some interior haze spots)........................ **224**

GII-62 - American eagle below "Liberty" - inscription in five lines "Willington - Glass - Co - West, Willington - Conn.," smooth edges, sheared mouth, smooth base, bright yellowish olive, pt. (minor exterior highpoint wear) **308**

GII-63 - American eagle below "Liberty" - inscription in five lines "Willington - Glass - Co - West Willington - Conn.," smooth edges, applied double collared mouth, smooth base, deep yellowish olive, 1/2 pt. (in-the-making mouth roughness) **235**

GII-63 - American eagle below "Liberty" - inscription in five lines "Willington - Glass - Co - West Willington - Conn.," smooth edges, applied double collared mouth, smooth base, reddish amber, 1/2 pt. **420**

American Eagle - Liberty Flask

GII-63 - American eagle below "Liberty" - inscription in five lines "Willington - Glass - Co - West Willington - Conn.," smooth edges, applied double collared mouth, smooth base, bright light to medium yellowish olive, 1/2 pt. (ILLUS.) **1,680**

GII-65 - American eagle below "Liberty" - inscribed in five lines "Westford - Glass - Co - Westford - Conn.," smooth edges, applied collared mouth, smooth base, yellowish amber w/a reddish tone, 1/2 pt. **269**

GII-67 - American eagle below nine five-pointed stars standing on large laurel wreath - large anchor w/"New London" in a banner above & "Glass Works" in a banner below, smooth edges, applied double collar mouth, smooth base, aqua, 1/2 pt. **532**

GII-69 - American eagle w/head turned left w/thunderbolt in left talon & olive branch in right - inverted cornucopia filled w/produce, horizontally beaded w/vertical medial rib, inward rolled mouth, pontil scar, deep bluish green, 1/2 pt. (some light interior haze) **4,200**

GII-72 - American eagle w/head turned right & standing on rocks - cornucopia w/produce, vertically ribbed edges, sheared neck, pontil scar, light yellow w/olive tone, pt. **448**

GII-74 - American eagle w/head turned to the right & standing on rocks - cornucopia w/produce & "X" on left, smooth edges, sheared lip, pontil scar, medium green, pt. **330**

GII-76 - Eagle facing right in circle surrounded by thin concentric rings - same reverse, rounded shape w/tooled mouth, pontil scar, light yellowish green, small flat flake on second ring, qt. (ILLUS., top next column) **6,160**

GII-78 - American eagle, large spread-winged bird w/large shield at its breast below a wide arched banner w/flaring forked ends & above a large oval panel w/wide molding obverse & reverse, sheared lip, pontil scar, medium amber, qt. **605**

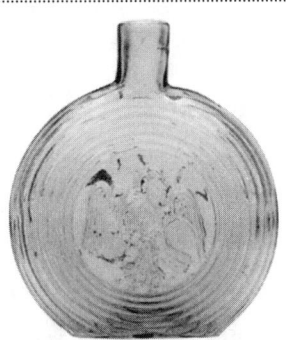

Rare Eagle in Circle Flask

GII-82 - American eagle above oval with no inscription - reverse the same except oval w/inscription in small letters "Stoddard - NH," faint periods after the "N" & "H," narrow vertical edge rib, sheared mouth, pontil scar, yellowish amber w/olive tone, pt. **202**

GII-92 - American eagle above oval, pronounced beak & eye, pennant in beak w/slender forked end obverse & reverse, smooth edges, lip w/applied band, smooth base, light cornflower blue, pt. **660**

GII-106 - American eagle w/shield facing left, holding banner, above oval panel w/"Pittsburgh PA" obverse - same on reverse w/plain panel, applied ring top, smooth base, ca. 1860, medium to dark olive green, pt. **468**

GII-107 - American eagle above oval obverse & reverse, w/"Pittsburgh, PA" in oval obverse, narrow vertical rib, crudely applied mouth w/ring, smooth base, dark olive green, pt. **616**

GII-135 - Eagle in medallion, small bird w/wings spread & raised upright - plain obverse, wide flat band down the edges, tooled collared mouth, smooth base, greenish aqua, qt. (some minor exterior wear) **146**

GII-139 - American eagle w/head turned to the left, plain reverse, applied collared mouth, smooth base, golden amber, 1/2 pt. **146**

GII-143 - American eagle w/plain shield in talons & pennants in beak, calabash-form, four-flute edges, applied collared mouth, iron pontil, bright yellowish green, qt. **308**

GIII-4 - Cornucopia w/produce - urn w/produce, vertically ribbed edges, sheared mouth, pontil scar, light olive yellow w/amber string of glass running around body, pt. (some highpoint wear) **269**

GIII-10 - Cornucopia w/produce - urn w/produce, vertically ribbed edges, heavy medial rib, sheared lip, pontil scar, dark to lighter green, 1/2 pt. **132**

GIII-15 - Cornucopia w/produce but no end curl on cornucopia - urn w/produce indistinctly molded, vertically ribbed edges, sheared mouth, pontil scar, bright bluish green, 1/2 pt. **448**

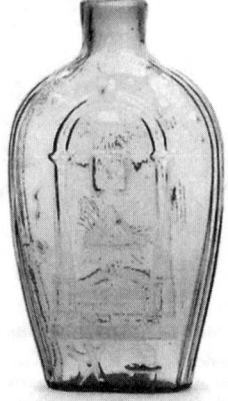

Masonic - American Eagle Flask

GIV-1 - Masonic emblems - American eagle w/ribbon reading "E Pluribus Unum" above & "I-P" (old-fashioned J) below in oval frame, sheared lip, open pontil, light bluish green, pt. (ILLUS.) **560**

GIV-1a - Masonic emblems - American eagle w/ribbon reading "E Pluribus Unum" above & initials "I P" (old-fashioned J) not joined by bar below in oval frame, inward rolled mouth, pontil scar, bluish green, pt. **728**

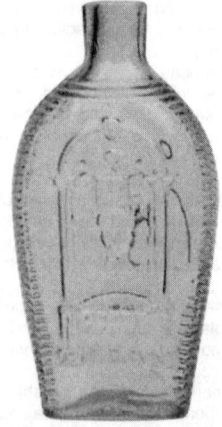

Masonic Arch & Eagle Flask

GIV-16 - Masonic arch, pillars & pavement w/Masonic emblems inside the arch - American eagle above plain oval frame, sheared mouth, pontil scar, some minor highpoint wear, clear aqua, pt. (ILLUS.) **2,688**

GIV-17 - Masonic arch, pillars & pavement w/Masonic emblems - American eagle w/oval frame enclosing "Keene" below, edges smooth w/single vertical rib, sheared mouth, pontil scar, medium yellowish olive, pt. (some minor highpoint wear)... **336**

GIV-19 - Masonic arch, pillars & pavement w/Masonic emblems - American eagle without shield on breast, plain oval frame below "KCCNE" inside, smooth edges w/single rib, sheared mouth, pontil scar, light to medium yellowish amber w/olive tone, pt. (needs cleaning)................................ **269**

GIV-20a - Masonic arch, pillars & pavement w/Masonic emblems - American eagle w/"KCCNC" in oval frame below, faint row of dots above eagle w/short rib between two dots, single vertical edge rib, sheared mouth, pontil scar, bright amber, pt. **440**

GIV-24 - Masonic arch, pillars & pavement w/Masonic emblems - American eagle grasping large balls in talons & without shield on breast, plain oval frame below, smooth edges w/single medial rib, sheared mouth, tubular pontil, medium yellowish olive, 1/2 pt. (some minor highpoint wear)... **448**

Very Rare Masonic Emblems Flask

GIV-29 - Masonic emblems w/pillars flanking a crescent moon surrounded by seven small stars above a large five-point star over an hourglass, obverse & reverse, sheared mouth, pontil scar, bright light yellowish olive w/deeper swirl of amber near base, 1/2 pt. (ILLUS.).................. **13,440**

GIV-32 - Masonic arch, pillars & pavement enclosing farmer's arms w/sheaf of rye & implements - American eagle & shield facing right below "Zanesville" & above oval frame enclosing "Ohio" above "J. Shepard (S reversed) & Co.," sheared mouth, pontil scar, pebbly surface, rich greenish aqua, pt.. **385**

GIV-32 - Masonic arch, pillars & pavement enclosing farmer's arms w/sheaf of rye & implements - American eagle & shield facing right below "Zanesville" & above oval frame enclosing "Ohio" above "J. Shepard (S reversed) & Co.," sheared mouth, pontil scar, pale bluish green, pt....... **616**

Masonic Arch - Eagle Flask

GIV-32 - Masonic arch, pillars & pavement enclosing farmer's arms w/sheaf of rye & implements - American eagle & shield facing right below "Zanesville" & above oval frame enclosing "Ohio" above "J. Shepard (S reversed) & Co.," inward rolled mouth, pontil scar, bright yellowish amber, pt. (ILLUS.) **3,080**

GIV-34 - Masonic arch w/"Farmer's Arms" & sheaf of rye & farm implements within arch & "Kensington Glass Works Philadelphia" around edge - sailing frigate above "Franklin" w/"Free Trade and Sailors Rights" around the edge, sheared mouth, pontil scar, aqua, pt. **672**

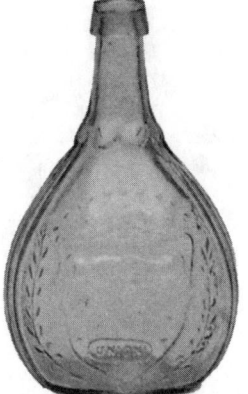

Clasped Hands - Eagle Citron Flask

GIV-42 - Clasped hands above square & compass above oval w/"Union" inside, all inside shield - American eagle above "A.R.S.," calabash form, fluted edges, applied collared mouth, pontil scar, strong embossing, light citron, qt. (ILLUS.) **952**

Rare Bluish Green Railroad Flask

GV-1 - "Success to the Railroad" around embossed locomotive - similar reverse, sheared lip, pontil scar, bright bluish green, one small spot of roughness on medial rib, one small spot of roughness on medial rib, pt. (ILLUS.) **5,600**

GV-3 - "Success to the Railroad" around embossed horse pulling cart - similar reverse, sheared mouth, pontil scar, bright yellowish olive, pt. (minor highpoint wear) **392**

GV-3a - "Success to the Railroad" around embossed horse w/no mane pulling cart - similar reverse, sheared mouth, pontil scar, bright light yellowish olive, pt. **1,344**

GV-9 - Horse pulling loaded cart & no inscription - large American eagle w/shield lengthwise, no stars, sheared mouth, pontil scar, deep olive amber, pt. **448**

GV-10 - "Railroad" above horse-drawn cart on rail & "Lowell" below - American eagle lengthwise & 13 five-point stars, vertically ribbed edges, sheared mouth, pontil scar, light to medium yellowish olive, 1/2 pt. (some minor mouth roughness) **308**

Lowell Railroad - Eagle Flask

GV-10 - "Railroad" above horse-drawn cart on rail & "Lowell" below - American eagle lengthwise & 13 five-point stars, vertically ribbed edges, crudely sheared mouth, pontil scar, bright clear yellowish green, 1/2 pt. (ILLUS.) **952**

GVI-1 - Baltimore Monument in oval panel obverse - "A Little More Grape Capt. Bragg" enclosed by oval grapevine on reverse, vertically ribbed sides, sheared mouth, pontil scar, light to medium strawberry puce w/an apricot tone, 1/2 pt. **8,400**

GVI-2 - Baltimore Monument above "Balto." - Sloop sailing to the right w/"Fells" above & "Point" below, vertically ribbed edges, sheared lip, pontil scar, colorless, 1/2 pt. (weak embossed lettering) **784**

GVI-2 - Baltimore Monument above "Balto." - Sloop sailing to the right w/"Fells" above & "Point" below, vertically ribbed edges, sheared lip, pontil scar, puce, 1/2 pt. (piece of slag stuck on base) **5,040**

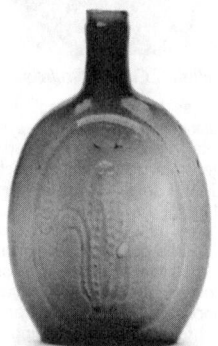

Baltimore Monument - Corn Flask

GVI-7 - "Baltimore" below monument - "Corn For The World" in semicircle above ear of corn, rounded collar, smooth edges, sheared mouth, tubular pontil, bright yellowish olive, 1/2 pt. (ILLUS.) **3,920**

GVIII-2 - Sunburst w/twenty-four triangular sectioned rays obverse & reverse, sheared mouth, pontil, potstone w/no radiation, some minor interior haze, colorless, pt. **1,120**

GVIII-2 - Sunburst w/twenty-four triangular sectioned rays obverse & reverse, sheared mouth, pontil scar, light to medium green, pt. **1,430**

Forest Green Sunburst Flask

GVIII-3 - Sunburst w/twenty-four rounded rays obverse & reverse, horizontal corru-

gated edges, sheared mouth, pontil scar, forest green, some minor exterior highpoint wear, pt. (ILLUS.) **1,350-1,450**

GVIII-8 - Sunburst w/twenty-eight triangular sectioned rays, obverse & reverse, center raised oval w/"KEEN" on obverse & w/"P & W" on reverse, sheared mouth, fat pontil, medium olive green, pt. **605**

Keene, NH Sunburst Flask

GVIII-9 - Sunburst w/twenty-nine triangular sectioned rays, obverse & reverse, center raised oval w/"KEEN" in reverse on obverse & w/"P & W" on reverse w/twenty-nine rays, sheared mouth, pontil scar, yellow olive, 1/2 pt. (ILLUS.) **616**

GVIII-9 - Sunburst w/twenty-nine triangular sectioned rays, obverse & reverse, center raised oval w/"KEEN" in reverse on obverse & w/"P & W" on reverse w/twenty-nine rays, sheared mouth, pontil scar, light yellowish amber w/olive tone, 1/2 pt. (very minor highpoint wear) **1,680**

Rare Green Sunburst Flask

GVIII-14 - Sunburst w/twenty-one triangular sectioned rays, obverse & reverse, sunburst centered by ring w/a dot in middle, sheared mouth, pontil scar, brilliant medium yellowish green, some minor exterior highpoint wear, 1/2 pt. (ILLUS.) **3,080**

GVIII-28 - Sunburst w/sixteen rays obverse & reverse, rays converging to a definite point at center & covering entire sides, horizontally corrugated edges, sheared mouth, pontil scar, aqua w/light yellowish green tone, 1/2 pt. 336

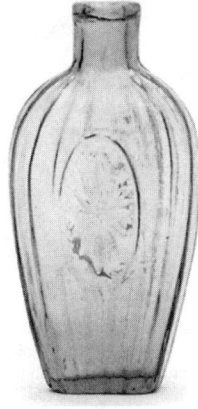

Bluish Green Sunburst Flask

GVIII-29 - Sunburst in small sunken oval w/twelve rays obverse & reverse, panel w/band of tiny ornaments around inner edge, sides around panels w/narrow spaced vertical ribbing, inward rolled mouth, pontil scar, bluish green, 3/4 pt. (ILLUS.).. 364

GIX-3 - Scroll w/two six-point stars, both medium-sized, obverse & reverse, vertical medial rib, crudely sheared lip, pontil scar, sapphire blue w/slight greyish cast, qt. (tiny in-the-making flake on side of mouth) 3,080

Rare Gasoline Topaz Scroll Flask

GIX-3 - Scroll w/two six-point stars, both medium-sized, obverse & reverse, vertical medial rib, applied mouth w/ring, huge red iron pontil scar, bright light to medium gasoline topaz, small chip on side of mouth, qt. (ILLUS.) 4,200

GIX-4 - Scroll w/two six-point stars, lower star larger than upper, obverse & reverse, vertical medial rib, applied mouth w/ring, pontil scar, deep yellowish olive, qt. (minor highpoint wear) 2,240

GIX-10 - Scroll w/six-point stars, a small one in upper space & medium sized one in lower space obverse & reverse, medial scrolls nearly touch, vertical medial rib, applied drippy mouth, iron pontil scar, medium green, pt. 1,430

GIX-14 - Scroll w/six-point star above seven-point star obverse & reverse, vertical medial rib on edge, rough sheared mouth, pontil scar, lime green, pt............... 1,120

GIX-33 - Scroll w/five-point star above fleur-de-lis obverse & reverse, vertical medial rib on edges, sheared lip, iron pontil scar, aqua, 1/2 pt. 110

GIX-34 - Scroll w/large eight-point star above a large pearl over a large fleur-de-lis obverse & reverse, vertical medial rib on edge, sheared mouth, pontil scar, some minor highpoint wear, bright deep strawberry puce, 1/2 pt. 6,160

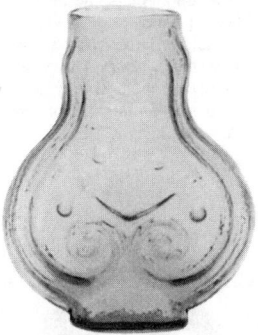

Rare Wide-mouthed Scroll Flask

GIX-41 - Scroll w/anchor w/large pearl above & below each fluke - fleur-de-lis w/large pearl below left & below right, vertical medial rib, wide tooled mouth, pontil scar, bright aqua, 1/2 pt. (ILLUS.).... 6,160

GX-1 - Stag standing above "Good Game" - weeping willow tree, vertically ribbed edges, sheared mouth, pontil scar, aqua, pt. 258

GX-6 - Cannon framed by "Genl Taylor Never Surrenders" in oval - grapevine frame around "A Little More Grape Capt Bragg," vertically ribbed sides, sheared lip, pontil scar, bright yellowish green, 1/2 pt. (potstone above cannon wheel, some mouth roughness, some rib wear) 3,080

GX-12 - Stout man wearing derby standing w/cane behind him & arguing w/a seated man wearing a derby & leaning on an umbrella - grotesque head w/large full face & elaborate headdress, smooth edges, sheared lip, pontil, bluish aqua, 1/2 pt. 358

GX-17 - Summer tree in oval panel obverse & reverse, sheared mouth, pontil scar, deep aqua, pt. 213

GX-27 - American flag (large) to right - "New Granite Glass Works" in arc over "Stoddard - N.H.," sheared mouth, pontil scar, yellowish olive (interior bubble burst, some minor exterior wear) **8,400**

GXI-34 - "For Pike's Peak" above prospector w/tools & cane standing on oblong frame - American eagle w/pennant above frame "Ceredo," applied mouth w/ring, smooth base, ice blue, qt. **308**

GXI-41 - "For Pike's Peak" above prospector w/tools & cane standing on oblong frame - American eagle w/pennant above frame, applied mouth, smooth base, medium aqua, pt.................. **110**

GXI-52 - Prospector w/small stocky body, thin arms & long large head wearing hat w/flat crown & narrow brim, short loose coat & full trousers, holding long staff w/two packets, cane in left hand below "For Pike's Peak" in semicircle & large letters - hunter at left shooting stag at right, small figure w/large head, no bottle hanging at his side, lip w/applied band, smooth base, bright bluish aqua, 1/2 pt....... **275**

GXII-29 - Clasped hands above oval, all inside large shield w/"Union" above - American eagle w/shield w/bars & long banner in beak, applied mouth w/ring, smooth base, dark brown amber, 1/2 pt. (minor highpoint wear)................................. **235**

Clasped Hands - Eagle Amber Flask

GXII-31 - Clasped hands above oval, all inside shield - American eagle above oval, applied collared mouth w/ring, smooth base, golden amber, 1/2 pt. (ILLUS.) **448**

GXII-33 - Clasped hands above oval all inside shield w/"Union" above shield - American eagle above shield-shaped frame, round applied collared mouth, bright golden amber, 1/2 pt. **364**

GXII-37 - Clasped hands above oval all inside shield w/"Union" above shield obverse & reverse, applied mouth, smooth base, light sapphire blue, qt. **5,320**

Union-Clasped Hands Flask

GXII-43 - Clasped hands above square & compass above oval w/"Union" all inside shield - American eagle, calabash, applied mouth, pontil scar, tiny flake on side of mouth, bright yellowish green, qt. (ILLUS.)... **840**

GXII-43 - Clasped hands above square & compass above oval w/"Union" all inside shield - American eagle, calabash, applied mouth, iron pontil scar, deep brownish amber, qt. (exterior haze w/some wear)... **1,232**

GXIII-3 - Girl wearing a full-length skirt & hat & riding a bicycle - American eagle w/head turned right above oval framed embossed "A & DH.C," applied mouth, smooth base, aqua, pt. **364**

GXIII-4 - Hunter facing left wearing flattop stovepipe hat, short coat & full trousers, game bag hanging at left side, firing gun at two birds flying upward at left, large puff of smoke from muzzle, two dogs running to left toward section of rail fence - fisherman standing on shore near large rock, wearing round-top stovepipe hat, V-neck jacket, full trousers, fishing rod held in left hand w/end resting on ground, right hand holding large fish, creel below left arm, mill w/bushes & tree in left background, calabash, edged w/wide flutes, applied collared mouth, iron pontil, puce amber, qt. (faint interior stain ring near base)... **420**

GXIII-8 - Sailor dancing a hornpipe on an eight-board hatch cover, above a long rectangular bar - banjo player sitting on a long bench, smooth edges, applied double collared mouth, smooth base, orangish amber, 1/2 pt...................... **1,568**

GXIII-16 - Horseman in full-dress uniform on high-stepping steed riding to right, saber held erect - large hound walking right, applied collar mouth, smooth base, bright light yellowish amber, qt. (some light exterior wear) **1,008**

GXIII-18 - Horseman wearing a short coat, hat blown off to the left, riding a horse w/tail flying back - hound running right, applied double collared mouth, smooth base, aqua w/pale green tone, 1/2 pt. (some light interior haze)................................. **246**

GXIII-18 - Horseman wearing a short coat, hat blown off to the left, riding a horse w/tail flying back - hound running right, sheared mouth, pontil scar, bright sapphire blue, 1/2 pt. (lightly professionally cleaned).. **12,320**

GXIII-23 - Flora Temple obverse, plain reverse, smooth edges w/beads at lower neck & shoulder, collared mouth, smooth base, teal blue green, pt. (minor exterior highpoint wear).. **448**

GXIII-23 - Flora Temple obverse, plain reverse, smooth edges w/beads at lower neck & shoulder, collared mouth, smooth base, shaded bluish green, pt. **550**

GXIII-29a - "Will You Take A Drink?" (w/small floral design) & "Will A [picture of duck] Swim?" - plain reverse, applied sloping collared mouth w/ring, smooth base, light bluish green, 1/2 pt. (small burst bubble between letters) **784**

Sheaf of Wheat - Star Flask

GXIII-38 - Sheaf of wheat w/rake & pitchfork crossed behind it - star on obverse, applied mouth w/ring, pontil scar, bright medium yellowish olive, interior bubble on top of shoulder w/some residue, qt. (ILLUS.)... **6,160**

GXIII-39 - Sheaf of grain above crossed rake & pitchfork - large five-pointed star, smooth edges, applied double collar mouth, tubular pontil, bright medium yellowish green, pt.. **4,200**

GXIII-40 - Sheaf of grain w/rake & pitchfork crossed behind sheaf - small five-point star, smooth edges, sheared mouth, pontil scar, bright aqua, 1/2 pt............................. **336**

Sheaf of Grain - Star Flask

GXIII-40 - Sheaf of grain w/rake & pitchfork crossed behind sheaf - small five-point star, smooth edges, applied double collared mouth, smooth base, medium golden amber, 1/2 pt. (ILLUS.) **1,904**

GXIII-43 - Sheaf of grain w/rake & pitchfork crossed behind sheaf obverse - eight-point star reverse, calabash, vertically ribbed edge, applied mouth, tubular pontil, light to medium yellowish green, qt. **364**

GXIII-46 - Sheaf of grain above crossed rake & pitchfork - tree & foliage, calabash, vertically ribbed, applied mouth, pontil scar, bright bluish green, qt. (some exterior highpoint scratches, flake on shoulder in making).. **672**

GXIII-53 - Anchor w/fork-ended pennants inscribed "Baltimore" & "Glass Works" on obverse - phoenix rising from flames on rectangular panel inscribed "Resurgam" on reverse, applied square collared mouth, smooth base, aqua, pt........................ **253**

GXIII-53 - Anchor w/fork-ended pennants inscribed "Baltimore" & "Glass Works" on obverse - phoenix rising from flames on rectangular panel inscribed "Resurgam" on reverse, applied square collared mouth, smooth base, deep strawberry puce, pt. **5,040**

GXIV-9 - "Traveler's Companion" arched above & vertical line below - "Railroad" in arc & "Guide" in vertical line below, metal cap on lip, pontil scar, medium teal blue, 1/2 pt... **660**

GXV- 7 - "Granite - Glass - Co." inscribed in three lines - "Stoddard - NH" inscribed in two lines, smooth edges, heavy collared mouth, smooth base, deep olive amber, pt. (small scratch below "Co.")...................... **336**

Grandfather flask, twenty-four vertical ribs, Midwest, early 19th c., sheared mouth, pontil scar, bright golden amber, 6 3/4" d., 8 3/4" h.. **2,016**

Grandmother pocket flask, sixteen vertical ribs, probably Mantua Glassworks, Mantua, Ohio, 1822-29, sheared mouth, pontil scar, medium to deep amethyst, 6 3/4" h.. **896**

Pitkin, sixteen ribs swirled to the right, Midwest, early 19th c., sheared mouth, pontil scar, bright yellowish green, 4 3/4" h. **672**

Yellowish Green Pitkin Flask

Pitkin, sixteen ribs swirled to the right, Midwest, early 19th c., sheared mouth, pontil scar, bright yellowish green, 6 7/8" h. (ILLUS.) **952**

Pitkin, sixteen vertical ribs & twenty-four ribs swirled to the right, Midwest, early 19th c., sheared mouth, pontil scar, bright yellowish green, 6 1/2" h. **616**

Pitkin, thirty ribs swirled to the left, Midwest, early 19th c., sheared mouth, pontil scar, bright medium sea green, 5 1/8" h. **448**

Pitkin, thirty-one ribs swirled to the left, Midwest, early 19th c., sheared mouth, pontil scar, bright forest green, 6" h. (some minor highpoint wear) **952**

Yellowish Olive Pitkin Flask

Pitkin, thirty-six ribs swirled to right, New England, early 19th c., sheared mouth, pontil scar, bright yellowish olive, 6 1/2" h. (ILLUS.) **616**

Pitkin, thirty-six ribs swirled to the left, Midwest, early 19th c., sheared mouth, partial tubular pontil, golden amber, 6" h. **1,232**

Pitkin, thirty-six ribs swirled to the left, New England, early 19th c., sheared mouth, pontil scar, medium yellowish olive, 7" h. (some minor exterior highpoint wear near base) **784**

Pitkin, thirty-six ribs swirled to the left, New England, early 19th c., sheared mouth, pontil scar, bright yellowish olive, 6 3/4" h. **896**

Pitkin, thirty-six ribs swirled to the right, New England, late 18th - early 19th c., sheared mouth, tubular pontil, yellowish olive, 5" h. **672**

Pitkin, thirty-six ribs swirled to the right, possibly Pitkin Glass Works, Connecticut, early 19th c., sheared mouth, pontil scar, yellowish olive, 5" h. **672**

Pitkin, thirty-two ribs swirled to the left, Midwest, early 19th c., sheared mouth, pontil scar, sea green, 6 1/2" h. **560**

Yellowish Green Pitkin Flask

Pitkin, thirty-two ribs swirled to the left, sheared mouth, pontil scar, Midwest, 1800-30, bright medium yellowish green, 6 1/2" h. (ILLUS.) **616**

Pitkin, thirty-two ribs swirled to the right, Midwest, early 19th c., sheared mouth, pontil scar, bright medium green, 6 3/4" h. (some minor exterior wear) **448**

Pitkin, thirty-two ribs swirled to the right, Midwest, early 19th c., sheared mouth, pontil scar, bright medium to deep sea green, 7 3/4" h. (two small areas of wear near base) **896**

Pitkin, twenty-four ribs swirled to the left, Midwest, early 19th c., sheared mouth, pontil scar, bright yellowish olive green, 7" h. **1,232**

Pocket flask, broken swirl 18 x 18 ribs, sheared lip, pontil scar, Pittsburgh district, 1800-30, rare deep blue lead glass, 5 3/4" h. **2,200**

Pocket flask, broken swirl diamond design, sheared lip, pontil scar, greenish aqua, Midwest, early 19th c., pt., 6 1/2" h. **358**

Pocket flask, flattened round free-blown form w/elongated neck w/crude sheared lip, ring pontil scar, American or Netherlands, early 19th c., medium to deep claret-amethyst, 6 1/2" h. **220**

Pocket flask, free-blown, Midwest, early 19th c., tooled flared mouth, pontil scar, bright medium golden amber, 6 1/2" h. **560**

Pocket flask, miniature, 20 ogival diamond mold, crude applied string ring on lip, pontil scar, Midwest or Mid-Atlantic re-

gion, late 18th - early 19th c., bluish
aqua, 3 1/2" h. **825**

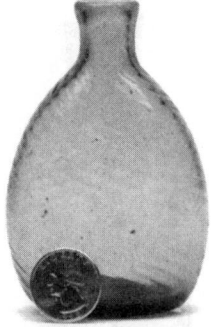

Miniature Pocket Flask

Pocket flask, miniature, fourteen ribs
swirled to the left, Midwest, early 19th c.,
sheared lip, pontil scar, bright yellowish
green, 4" h. (ILLUS.) **4,200**
Pocket flask, nineteen ribs swirled to the
left, Midwest, early 19th c., sheared
mouth, pontil scar, medium amethystine
w/profuse amethyst striations, 4 3/4" h. **1,792**
Pocket flask, pattern-molded, double-
dipped design w/eight vertical ribs molded
over an oval w/circles design draped below   shoulders,   attributed   to   the
Midwest, ca. 1820, medium green, shear
lip, pontil scar, 6 1/2" h. (some highpoint
wear) **220**
Pocket flask, ten-diamond mold-blown patt.,
Zanesville, Ohio, early 19th c., sheared
mouth, pontil scar, deep aqua w/teal over-
tone, 5" h. (some minor haze near base) **952**
Pocket flask, twenty vertical ribs, Midwest,
early 19th c., sheared mouth, pontil scar,
bright yellow w/slight olive tone, 6 1/2" h... **1,680**
Pocket flask, twenty vertical ribs, Midwest,
possibly Mantua, Ohio, early 19th c.,
sheared mouth, pontil scar, bright medi-
um amethyst, 6 1/2" h. **2,352**
Pocket flask, twenty-four ribs swirled to the
left, Midwest, early 19th c., sheared
mouth, pontil scar, deep amber, 4 3/4" h. **840**
Pocket flask, twenty-four vertical ribs, Midwest, early 19th c., sheared mouth, pontil
scar, bright olive yellow, 4 3/4" h. **1,456**

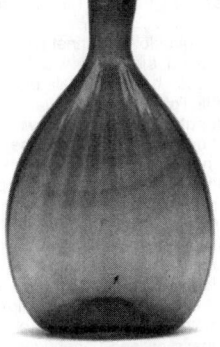

Rare Blue Pocket Flask

Pocket flask, twenty-four vertical ribs, Midwest, early 19th c., sheared mouth, pontil
scar, bright sapphire blue w/two faint
darker blue striations, small shallow chip
on side of mouth, 6 7/8" h. (ILLUS.) **4,480**
Pocket flask, vertically ribbed, sheared lip,
pontil scar, Midwest, early 19th c., citron
green, 4 3/4" h. **1,540**

Stiegel-type Pocket Flask

Stiegel-type pocket flask, Daisy & Diamond over flute molded patt., attributed
to American Flint Glass Works, Manheim, Pennsylvania, 1763-74, tooled
mouth, pontil scar, bright amethyst, several flat chips on side of mouth, 4 3/4" h.
(ILLUS.) **2,800**

Rare Amethyst Stiegel-type Flask

Stiegel-type pocket flask, Daisy & Diamond over flute molded patt., attributed
to American Flint Glass Works, Manheim, Pennsylvania, 1763-74, tooled
mouth, pontil scar, deep amethyst, good
impression, 5" h. (ILLUS.) **5,040**
Stiegel-type pocket flask, molded 28
ogival pattern, tooled mouth, pontil scar,
attributed to the American Flint Glass
Manufactory, Manheim, Pennsylvania,
1763-74, bright amethyst, 5 5/8" h. **2,420**

Inks

Rare Horizontal Barrel Ink

Barrel-shaped, horizontal ringed form w/central neck, colorless, inward tooled mouth, ground pontil scar, horizontal barrel embossed "Tippecanoe Extract - Hard Cider," associated w/1840 presidential campaign of William Henry Harrison, 2 1/4" l., 2" h. (ILLUS.) **1,568**

Barrel-shaped, upright ringed form, colorless, tooled disk mouth, pontil scar, ca. 1820-50, 2" d., 2" h. (some minor highpoint wear) **280**

Cathedral, master-size, six Gothic arch panels, cobalt blue, ABM lip, smooth base marked "Carter's," ca. 1920, 9 3/4" h. **110**

Cathedral, master-size, six Gothic arch panels w/three embossed at the bottom "CA - RT - ER," cobalt blue, ABM lip, smooth base marked "Carter's," original paper labels & closure, ca. 1920, 10 7/8" h. (minor contents)............................ **143**

Cathedral, master-size, six Gothic arch panels w/three embossed at the bottom "CA - RT - ER," cobalt blue, ABM lip, smooth base marked "Carter's," ca. 1920, 8" h. (slight exterior haze) **176**

Cathedral, master-size, six Gothic arch panels w/three embossed at the bottom "CA - RT - ER," cobalt blue, ABM lip, smooth base marked "Carter's," ca. 1920, 6 1/2" h. **303**

Cylindrical, blown-three-mold, dark olive green, Keene, New Hampshire, geometric design, tubular pontil, 2 1/4" d., 1 1/2" h. (GIII-29) **209**

Blown-Three-Mold Ink

Cylindrical, blown-three-mold, deep yellowish olive, disk mouth, pontil scar, Coventry Glass Works, Coventry, Connecticut, ca. 1820-40, GII-16, 2 1/4" d., 1 5/8" h. (ILLUS.) **168**

Cylindrical, blown-three-mold, dense yellowish olive, disk mouth, pontil scar, Coventry Glass Works, Coventry, Connecticut, ca. 1820-40, GII-18, 2 5/8" d., 1 3/4" h. **202**

S. Fine Amber Ink Bottle

Cylindrical, deep bubbly golden amber, inward rolled mouth, tubular pontil, embossed "S. Fine Blk. Ink," ca. 1845-55, 3 1/8" h. (ILLUS.) **1,568**

Cylindrical, master size, bright emerald green, drippy applied top, embossed down the side "Ward's Ink," 7 3/4" h. **187**

Cylindrical, master size, cobalt blue, cylindrical neck w/pour spout, embossed "Hyde 61 Fleet St. London," 5 3/4" h. (some interior stain, little ding on base)..................... **33**

Cylindrical, master size, cobalt blue, molded rings at shoulder & base, tooled lip w/pour spout, embossed side panels reading "S.S. Stafford's Inks - Made in U.S.A.," early 1900s, 9 1/2" h. **55**

Cylindrical, master size, cobalt blue, ringed neck ABM, original closure & paper label, label reads "Underwood's Everlasting Bank Ink...," label 90% intact, some content stain, early 20th c., 6 3/8" h. **88**

Cylindrical, master size, cobalt blue, ringed shoulder below tapering neck w/flared pouring lip, embossed "Underwood's Inks 8 oz.," dug, 9 1/2" h. (needs cleaning).. **55**

Cylindrical, master size, light amber, neck w/pour spout, early graphite pontil, unmarked, 7 1/2" h. **77**

Cylindrical, master size, pure green w/applied sloping collar, embossed down the side "Carter's Ink," 7 1/2" h. (some scratches) **121**

Cylindrical, mold-blown, funnel-type, embossed around the sides w/a band of seated bears holding oval placards, rough pontil, light greenish aqua, 2" h. **253**

Domical w/central neck, green w/amber streaks, burst top, smooth base embossed "Thacker London," 1 5/8" h. **88**

Eight-sided w/central neck, aqua, applied lip, pontil scar, embossed "Harrison's Columbian Ink," ca. 1845-55, 3 3/4" h. **143**

Eight-sided w/central neck, bright medium golden amber, sheared mouth, pontil scar, marked on panels "Farley's - Ink," probably Stoddard, New Hampshire, ca. 1846-60, 1 3/4" w., 1 3/4" h. (minor maker's roughness on one panel, weak embossing).. **560**

Rare Green Harrison's Columbian

Eight-sided w/central neck, bright medium
green, applied flared mouth, pontil scar,
marked in the panels "Harrison's - Colum-
bian - Ink," 2 1/8" w., 3 7/8" h. (ILLUS.) **5,040**

Harrison's Medium Green Ink

Eight-sided w/central neck, bright medium
green, inward rolled lip, jagged tubular
pontil, embossed "Harrison's Columbian
Ink," ca. 1845-55, 2 1/8" w., 2" h. (ILLUS.) **840**

Farley's Yellowish Amber Ink

Eight-sided w/central neck, bright yellowish amber, tooled flared mouth, pontil
scar, marked on panels "Farley's - Ink,"
probably Stoddard, New Hampshire, ca.
1846-60, small professional repair to
mouth, 2" w., 3 5/8" h. (ILLUS.) **1,064**
Eight-sided w/central neck, light aqua,
rolled lip, pontil scar, angled shoulder
panels, body embossed "Harrison's Co-
lumbian Ink," ca. 1845-55, 1 3/4" h. **121**
Figural, bell-shaped, aqua, roughly burst lip,
embossed "Arnold's London," 4 3/8" h.
(seed-shaped open bubble near base) **22**

Figural, blown-molded head of Ben Franklin
w/neck curving upward, aqua, sheared
lip, smooth base, 4 1/2" h................................ **358**

Ma & Pa Carter Ink Bottles

Figural, figures of Ma & Pa Carter, porcelain w/original paint, heads form stoppers
on cylindrical bodies, "Carter Inx" on the
reverse, "Made in Germany" on the
base, ca. 1910, 3 5/8" h., pr. (ILLUS.)........... **176**
Figural, model of a high-topped lady's boot,
clear, possibly French or American,
w/original cork closure, 3 1/4" l. **88**

Shoe-shaped Ink Bottle

Figural, model of a low-topped laced lady's
shoe, bright deep cobalt blue, sheared
mouth, smooth base, base marked "E.
Maurin," France, ca. 1830-60, 4 1/4" l.,
2 3/8" h. (ILLUS.)... **336**

Carter's Clover Pattern Ink Bottle

Hexagonal, deep cobalt blue, each panel w/a clover design, ABM lip, smooth base w/"Carter's," ca. 1930, 2 7/8" h. (ILLUS.)...... **165**

House-shaped w/central neck, aqua, tooled top, in-the-making neck crazing, very crude, 2 1/2" h. (slight interior stain) **132**

Unusual Teakettle Ink

Teakettle-type fountain inkwell w/neck extending out from base, free-blown, bright yellowish green, bulbous ovoid form w/applied bird finial, tooled mouth, smooth base, probably France, ca. 1830-60, 2 5/8" h. (ILLUS.) **728**

Barrel-shaped Ink Bottle

Teakettle-type fountain inkwell w/neck extending up at angle from base, barrel-shaped body, black w/gold trim on the staves & bands, ground mouth w/brass collar, smooth base, ca. 1830-60, no brass cap, 3 1/8" l., 2 1/8" h. (ILLUS.)........... **420**

Teakettle-type fountain inkwell w/neck extending up at angle from base, cobalt blue, eight-sided w/rough lip missing brass fitting, heavy & crude, possibly English, ca. 1830-60, 2 1/4" h. **242**

Teakettle-type fountain inkwell w/neck extending up at angle from base, cobalt blue, eight-sides divided by ribs, brass ring around lip, possibly English, ca. 1830-60, 2" h. **358**

Teakettle-type fountain inkwell w/neck extending up at angle from base, light amethyst, six-sided, brass ring on mouth, probably English, ca. 1830-60, 2 1/4" h. **385**

Teakettle-type fountain inkwell w/neck extending up at angle from base, light to medium blue, ten-sided, brass lid & fitting on mouth, probably English, ca. 1830-60, 2 1/4" h. **413**

Teakettle-type fountain inkwell w/neck extending up at angle from base, medium to deep cobalt blue, eight-sided w/small embossed blossom in center of top, probably English, mid-19th c., 2 1/2" h.. **385**

Teakettle-type fountain inkwell w/neck extending up at angle from base, medium to deep cobalt blue painted w/flowers & butterflies, a metal medallion in center of top reading "G. Riddle - London," original metal ring on mouth, 90% of paint intact, England, mid-19th c., 2 1/2" h... **385**

Teakettle-type fountain inkwell w/neck extending up at angle from base, opaque robin's egg blue, eight-sides divided by ribs trimmed in gold, brass ring around lip, possibly English, ca. 1830-60, 2" h.. **358**

Twelve-sided w/central neck, pure green, rolled lip, pontil scar, 2" d., 2" h..................... **253**

Aqua Umbrella Ink Bottle

Umbrella (8-panel cone shape), aqua, inward rolled mouth, crude pontil, panels embossed "Blake - N.Y.," ca. 1845-60, 2 3/4" w., 3" h. (ILLUS.).................................. **364**

Umbrella-type (8-panel cone shape), blue, very tall tapering sides w/tooled lip, quite crude, 4 3/8" h.. **413**

Umbrella-type (8-panel cone shape), bright cobalt blue, tooled top, 2 3/4" h. **303**

M & P New York Umbrella Ink

Umbrella-type (8-panel cone shape), bright emerald green, inward rolled mouth, tubular pontil, embossed in panels "M & P - New York," ca. 1840-60, some minor interior stain near base, 2 3/8" w., 2 1/2" h. (ILLUS.) **1,120**

Umbrella-type (8-panel cone shape), bright olive green, sheared lip, pontil scar, attributed to Stoddard, New Hampshire, ca. 1840-60, 2 1/2" h. 242

Umbrella-type (8-panel cone shape), bright olive lime green, rolled lip, tubular pontil, off-kilter neck & mouth, 2 1/2" h. 825

Umbrella-type (8-panel cone shape), bright orangish amber, rolled lip, tubular pontil, 2 1/4" h. 358

Umbrella-type (8-panel cone shape), bright sapphire blue, rolled lip, smooth base, very crude, 2 1/2" h. 880

Umbrella-type (8-panel cone shape), bright teal blue, rolled lip, pontil scar, very crude, 2 1/2" h. 825

Umbrella-type (8-panel cone shape), dark olive green, tooled top, 2 3/4" h. 1,320

Umbrella-type (8-panel cone shape), deep greenish aqua, rolled lip, sharp open pontil, 2 3/8" (needs slight cleaning) 66

Umbrella-type (8-panel cone shape), greenish blue w/touch of teal, rolled lip, pontil scar, whittled, 2 1/2" h. 176

Umbrella-type (8-panel cone shape), light greenish aqua, rolled lip, pontil scar, 2 1/2" h. 55

Umbrella-type (8-panel cone shape), light to medium yellowish olive, sheared lip, pontil scar, attributed to Stoddard, New Hampshire, ca. 1840-60, 2 1/2" h. 220

Umbrella-type (8-panel cone shape), medium amber, burst top, smooth base, 2 1/2" h. 176

Umbrella-type (8-panel cone shape), medium olive green, sheared mouth, pontil scar, probably New England, ca. 1840-60, 2 3/8" w., 2 3/8" h. 336

Umbrella-type (8-panel cone shape), puce to purplish amber, rolled lip, tubular pontil, 2 1/2" h. 825

Umbrella-type (8-panel cone shape), reddish amber, sheared lip, pontil scar, attributed to Stoddard, New Hampshire, 1840-60, 2 1/2" h. 275

Umbrella-type (8-panel cone shape), reddish amber, sheared & rolled lip, tubular pontil, very crude, 2 1/2" h. 303

Umbrella-type (8-panel cone shape), solid plum puce, rolled lip, smooth base, crude, 2 1/2" h. 1,430

Dark Amber Umbrella Ink

Umbrella-type (16-panel cone shape), golden amber, sheared mouth, pontil scar, 2 1/8" w., 2 1/8" h. (ILLUS.) 672

Medicines

Alexander's Silmaeau Bottle

Alexander's Silmaeau, flattened fiddle-shape w/tall bulbed neck w/applied collared mouth, tubular pontil, ca. 1845-55, lightly cleaned w/some minor interior stain, sapphire blue, 6 1/4" h. (ILLUS.) 476

Brant's Purifying Extract - M.T. Wallace & Co. Proprietors - Brooklyn, NY, rectangular w/paneled sides, applied double collar mouth, tubular pontil, ca. 1845-60, aqua, 10" h. (very minor interior haze) 308

Brinkerhoffs (C.) Health Restorative - Price $1.00 - New York, rectangular w/beveled corners, applied sloping collared mouth, pontil scar, deep yellowish olive, New England, ca. 1840-60, 7 1/4" h... 1,792

Carter's Spanish Mixture, cylindrical, applied sloping double collar mouth, iron pontil, ca. 1845-55, medium lime green, 8 1/4" h. 605

Curtis & Perkin's Cramp and Pain Killer, cylindrical w/rolled lip & open pontil, aqua, 4 7/8" h. 187

Duncan's (Dr.) Expectorant Remedy, rectangular w/beveled corners, outward rolled mouth, pontil scar, light green, probably Philadelphia factory, 1840-60, 6 1/8" h. 3,080

Feller's (Dr. S.) Eclectic Liniment, octagonal w/rounded shoulder & rolled lip on neck, pontil scar, aqua, 4 3/8" h. 99

Gargling Oil, Lockport, N.Y., rectangular w/ABM lip & smooth base, ca. 1910-15, teal blue, 7 1/2" h. 165

Guilmette's (Dr.) Extract of Juniper, Boston, square w/beveled corners, applied sloping collared mouth, smooth base, yellowish amber, ca. 1860-80, 9 3/8" h. (two potstones on side of plain panel) 224

Heimstreet (C.) & Co. - Troy, N.Y., tall octagonal shape w/applied double collar mouth, pontil scar, partial paper druggist label, ca. 1845-55, bright sapphire blue, 6 7/8" h. 420

Heimstreet (C.) & Co. - Troy, N.Y., tall octagonal shape w/applied double collar mouth, smooth base, full paper label, ca. 1860-80, deep sapphire blue, 7" h. 420

Henry's (Dr.) Botanic Preparations, rectangular w/applied top, aqua, 6 1/4" h........... **121**

Henshaw & Edmands Bottle

Henshaw & Edmands, Druggists, Boston, tall cylindrical form w/applied collared mouth w/matching stopper, tubular pontil, bright medium emerald green, ca. 1845-60, overall 11 3/8" h. (ILLUS.).......... **1,120**

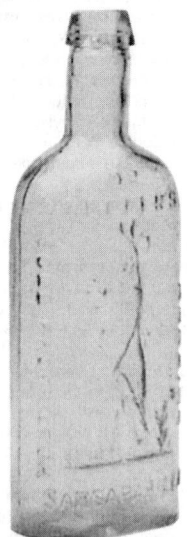

Dr. Keeler's Sarsaparilla Bottle

Keeler's (Dr.) - (full figure of Indian warrior) - Sole Proprietor, Sarsaparilla, Philada (reversed & backwards), tall oval w/applied sloping collared mouth, pontil scar, ca. 1840-60, aqua, small shallow flake on front base, 9 5/8" h. (ILLUS.)... **8,400**
Lepper's (Dr.) Oil of Gladness - Justin Gates - Sacramento, rectangular w/applied top, aqua, 5" h. **198**

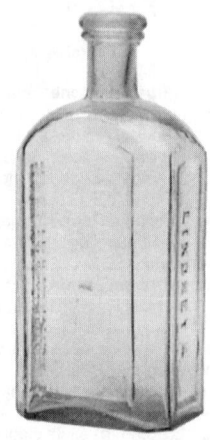

Lindsey's Blood + Searcher Bottle

Lindsey's - Blood + Searcher - Holli-daysburg, rectangular w/beveled corners & paneled sides, applied double collared mouth, smooth base, deep aqua bordering on pale bluish green, probably Pittsburgh, ca. 1860-70, 8 7/8" h. (ILLUS.)...... **336**
Louden & Co's Carminative Balsam, cylindrical w/cylindrical neck & flared lip, open pontil, aqua, 5 1/4" h. **77**

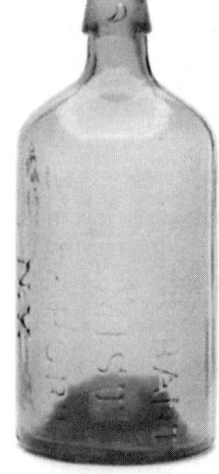

Merchant - Chemist Medicine

Merchant (G.W.) - Chemist, Lockport, N.Y., cylindrical w/applied sloping collared mouth, large iron pontil, Lockport green, probably Lockport Glass Works, Lockport, New York, ca. 1850-60, 7 1/8" h. (ILLUS.).. **364**
Merchant (G.W.) - From the Laboratory of - Chemist - Lockport, N.Y., rectangular w/paneled side, applied slopping collared mouth, iron pontil, Lockport green, Lockport Glass Works, Lockport, New York, 1850-60, 5 1/2" h. **336**

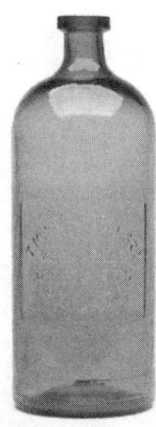

Morris Perot & Company Bottle

Morris (T). Perot & Co., Wholesale Druggists, Phildada., cylindrical w/embossed indented panel, applied collared mouth, smooth base, bright sapphire-steel blue, ca. 1860-80, 9 3/4" h. (ILLUS.) **1,344**

Morse's Celebrated Syrup - Prov. R.I., oval w/applied sloping collared mouth, iron pontil, aqua, ca. 1845-60, 9 1/4" h. **246**

Mosher (A.), oval w/applied sloping collared mouth, large iron pontil, bright deep teal green, ca. 1845-60, 8 3/4" h. **3,360**

Newell's - Pulmonary Syrup - Redington & Co., rectangular w/paneled sides, applied top, smooth base, aqua, 7 5/8" h. **55**

Old Dr. Dr. Townsend's Sarsaparilla

Old Dr. Townsend's Sarsaparilla - New York, square w/beveled corners, applied sloping collared mouth, iron pontil scar, bright ice blue, probably New England, ca. 1840-60, some minor light scratches, 9 5/8" h. (ILLUS.) **1,456**

Old Dr. Townsend's Sarsaparilla - New York, square w/beveled corners, applied sloping collared mouth, pontil scar, deep yellowish olive, probably New England, ca. 1840-60, 9 1/2" h. (some minor highpoint wear) **896**

Old Dr. Townsend's Sarsaparilla - New York, square w/beveled corners, tooled sloping collared mouth, smooth base, light yellowish green, ca. 1870-90, 10 1/8" h. **280**

Old Dr. Townsend's Sarsaparilla - New York - United States, rectangular w/beveled corners & paneled sides, applied sloping collared mouth, smooth base, deep greenish aqua, 1860-70, 8 1/8" h. (dug & cleaned w/some scratches) **1,344**

Olmstead & Company Medicine

Olmsted (W) & Company. - Constitutional Beverage - New York, rectangular w/beveled corners & paneled sides, heavy applied square collared mouth, smooth base, golden amber, ca. 1860-80, 10 1/8" h. (ILLUS.) **308**

Perry's (Dr.) Last Chance Liniment, rectangular w/applied top, aqua, 5 3/4" h **77**

Rare Dr. Poland Medicine Bottle

Poland (Dr. J.W.), tall oval w/arched embossed panel, applied square collared mouth, smooth base, olive amber, Stoddard, New Hampshire, ca. 1860-70, 7 3/4" h. (ILLUS.) **4,200**

Pratte (Lucien) - Le Renovateur de la Femme - Waterbury, Conn., rectangular w/beveled corners & three panels, applied square collared mouth, smooth base, cobalt blue, American, 1860-80, 9 1/4" h. (some minor mouth roughness) **280**

Preston's Veg. Purifying Catholicon, Portsm. NH, oval w/applied sloping collared mouth, tubular pontil, aqua, ca. 1840-60, 9 1/4" h. (pontil chip not extending out of base) **258**

Rheumatic (motif of tree) Trade Mark - Syrup 1882 - R.S. Co. Rochester. N.Y., square w/beveled corners & paneled sides, applied sloping collared mouth w/ring, smooth base, golden amber, ca. 1860-80, 10" h. **179**

David Scott Medicine Bottle

Scott (David) - Prepared By - Worcester, Mass, cylindrical w/applied sloping collared mouth w/ring, iron pontil, yellowish olive,   65% paper label reading "Cochrane's Horse Liniment, Administratix of William Coe," possibly Stoddard, New Hampshire, ca. 1850-60, 7 3/16" h. (ILLUS.) **4,200**

South Carolina Dispensary (over embossed palm tree), cylindrical w/tooled lip, clear, 9" h. **209**

Swaim's Panacea - Genuine - Philadelphia, rectangular w/applied sloping collar mouth, tubular pontil, ca. 1840-60, aqua, 7 3/4" h. (some minor exterior wear) **616**

Swaim's - Panacea - Philada, paneled cylinder, applied sloping collared mouth, pontil scar, bright medium yellowish olive, ca. 1840-60, 7 5/8" h. (ILLUS., top next column) **616**

Swaim's - Panacea - Philada, paneled cylinder, applied sloping collared mouth, pontil scar, aqua, ca. 1840-60, 8" h. (light interior stain) **728**

Swaim's - Panacea - Philada, paneled cylinder, applied sloping collared mouth w/ring, pontil scar, bright yellowish green, ca. 1840-60, 8" h. **896**

Townsend's (Dr.) Comp. Extract Sarsaparilla, square w/beveled corners, applied sloping collared mouth, iron pontil, bright aqua, 9 1/2" h. (very light interior stain in bottom) **2,240**

Swaim's Panacea Philada. Bottle

U.S.A.- Hosp. Dept., cylindrical w/rounded shoulder & applied double collar mouth, smooth base, ca. 1860-70, bright olive to lime green, 9 1/2" h. **770**

Wells' Genuine Liniment, Bloomington, Ill's, cylindrical w/rolled lip & pontil scar, aqua, 4" h. **330**

Wells' German Liniment, cylindrical w/rolled lip & pontil scar, aqua, 4" h. **413**

Wells' German Liniment - St. Louis MO, cylindrical w/applied sloping collar, pontil scar, deep aqua, 6" h. **440**

Wishart's (L.Q.C.) - Pine Tree Tar Cordial, Phila. - Patent (design of pine tree) 1859, square w/beveled corners, applied sloping collar, smooth base, ca. 1859-70, medium green, 8" h. **176**

Mineral Waters, Sodas & Sarsaparillas

Arcata Soda Works B.P., cylindrical w/tooled Hutchinson top, bubbles & overall crudity, aqua, 6 3/4" h. **231**

B&G Soda San Francisco Superior Mineral Water, cylindrical w/ten-sided base & applied blob top, pontil scar, medium cobalt blue, 1850s, near mint, 7" h. **468**

Bay City Soda Water Co SF - (star on reverse), cylindrical w/tapering shoulder & applied top, dark blue w/teal tone **143**

Billings (E.L.) Sacramento Cal, cylindrical gravitator-style w/applied Hutchinson top, dark greenish aqua, 7 1/8" h. **44**

Birmingham (P.) & Co. St. Louis (backward "N" in Birmingham), cylindrical w/applied sloping collared mouth, iron pontil w/kick-up, aqua, crude **55**

Burt (W.H.) San Francisco, cylindrical w/applied blob top, iron pontil, emerald green, ca. 1852 (open bubble on reverse) **121**

Burt (W.H.) San Francisco, cylindrical w/applied blob top, iron pontil, emerald green, ca. 1852, near mint, 7 1/4" h. **264**

C & K Eagle Works Sac. City, cylindrical w/applied top, smooth base, California,

1858-66, bright blue, probably cleaned, 7 1/8" h. **187**

C & K Eagle Works Sac. City, cylindrical w/applied top, smooth base, California, 1858-66, light cobalt blue (some wear & scratches) **77**

Caladonia Spring Amber Bottle

Caladonia Spring Wheelock VT, cylindrical w/applied sloping collared mouth w/ring, smooth base, golden yellow shading to golden amber, tiny shallow flake on underside of mouth ring, ca. 1860-80, qt. (ILLUS.)..................... **504**

California Natural Seltzer Water (walking bear motif over) H & C, cylindrical w/applied mouth, aqua............................. **110**

Carin (J.) & Co St. Louis, cylindrical w/applied sloping collared mouth, iron pontil w/kick-up, whittled, aqua **66**

Chase & Co Mineral Water San Francisco Cal., cylindrical w/tall neck & applied lip, iron pontil, emerald green, ca. 1850s, near mint, uncleaned, 7 1/2" h....................... **209**

Chase & Co Mineral Water San Francisco Cal., cylindrical w/tall neck & applied lip, iron pontil, light to dark emerald green, ca. 1850s (some wear)...................... **187**

Classen & Co. - design of crossed anchors - Sparkling, cylindrical w/applied mouth, sapphire blue, probably cleaned, 7 5/8" h. **303**

Congress & Empire Spring Co - C - Saratoga, N.Y. - Congress - Water, cylindrical w/applied sloping double collar mouth, smooth base, emerald green, ca. 1860-75, qt., 7 3/4" h............. **66**

Crawford (M.T.) - Hartford, Ct. - Union Glass Works Philad. - Superior Mineral Water, cylindrical w/paneled base, neck w/heavy collared mouth, iron pontil, sapphire blue, ca. 1845-60, 1/2 pt. **532**

Crawford (M.T.) - Springfield. - Union Glass Works Philad. - Superior Mineral Water, cylindrical w/paneled base, slender neck w/heavy applied collared mouth, iron pontil, cobalt blue, ca. 1845-60, 1/2 pt. (two small gouges on reverse done in the making).......................... **420**

Crump & Fox Bernardston Mass Superior Soda Water, cylindrical w/applied top, iron pontil, dark green, 7 1/8" h. **440**

Cudworth (A.W.) San Francisco Cal., cylindrical w/a tall neck & applied top, graphite pontil, emerald green, near mint, uncleaned, 7 1/8" h. **253**

Cudworth (A.W.) San Francisco Cal., cylindrical w/a tall neck & applied top, smooth base, deep aqua..................... **99**

Dearborn (J. & A.) New York Mineral Water, eight-paneled w/embossed star & applied top, graphite pontil, sapphire blue, near mint, 7 1/4" h. **440**

Eagle (embossed bird w/no wording), cylindrical w/ applied mouth, crude iron pontil, dark teal blue w/emerald tint............... **220**

Empire Soda Works San Francisco, cylindrical w/applied top, aqua **33**

Eureka Soda Works 723 Turk St. S.F., cylindrical w/Hutchinson applied top, aqua (few scratches)..................................... **66**

George at New York Medicine Bottle

George (over embossed eagle) - (Crystal Palace embossed over) At New York, cylindrical w/applied heavy collared mouth, iron pontil, pale bluish green, ca. 1845-60, in-the-making mouth roughness, 1/2 pt. (ILLUS.)......................... **3,080**

Gerdes (J.N.) SF Mineral Water, octagonal w/tapering neck & applied top, aqua............... **33**

Ghirardelli's Branch Oakland, cylindrical w/applied top, deep blue **303**

Goffe's Potash Water Birmim, cylindrical club-form w/applied top & rounded bottom, cobalt blue, England, 19th c., 9" l. **385**

H & M Eureka Cal, cylindrical w/tooled Hutchinson top, aqua, 7" h............................. **358**

Haas Bros - Natural - Mineral Water - Napa - Soda, cylindrical w/applied mouth, ca. 1860-70, deep sapphire blue w/some green streaks, 7 3/8" h. (tiny ding on lip)... **88**

Harris (J.W.) Soda New Haven, Conn., octagonal w/slender neck & heavy applied collared mouth, iron pontil, sapphire blue, ca. 1845-60, 1/2 pt. (one letter chipped) **504**

Harris (J.W.) Soda New Haven, Conn., octagonal w/slender neck & heavy applied mouth w/ring, iron pontil, cobalt blue, ca. 1845-60, 1/2 pt. 825

Hart (E.S. & H.) Superior Soda Water Union Glass Works, cylindrical w/applied mouth, cobalt blue, 7 1/4" h.................. 385

Harvey (J.) & Co. Providence RI ("H" reversed), short cylindrical form w/applied top, smooth base, crude, dark olive green..... 209

Hendersons (G.M.) Bonanza Mineral Water, cylindrical w/applied top, aqua 110

Highrock Congress Spring (design of a rock), C. & W. Saratoga N.Y., cylindrical w/applied sloping double collar, smooth base, ca. 1865-75, dark green, pt................. 253

Highrock Congress Spring (design of a rock), C. & W. Saratoga N.Y., cylindrical w/applied sloping double collar, smooth base, ca. 1865-75, deep teal blue, pt. (minor interior stain) 748

Holmes & Co 229 Graverie New Orleans Mineral Water, cylindrical w/fluted neck & applied top, iron pontil, dark aqua (slightly rough)..................................... 121

Hubbard (G.W.) Middletown, CT, cylindrical w/heavy collared mouth, iron pontil, deep aqua, ca. 1845-60, 1/2 pt. (minor exterior scratches) 560

Italian Soda Water Manufactory San Francisco, cylindrical w/applied blob top, iron pontil, dark green, late 1850s (little roughness, no embossing on reverse)..... 132

Jeenicke (Paul) San Jose, cylindrical w/applied top for Hutchinson stopper, rare amber variant, 6 3/4" h. 1,650

Klein & Hofneinz Rochester, N.Y., cylindrical w/applied top, "PAT 85" on base, sapphire blue, qt., 11 5/8" h. 1,320

Lomax (J.A.) 14 to 18 Charles Place Medicated Aerated Waters, cylindrical clubform w/rounded bottom & applied top, deep greenish aqua, 9" l. 198

Lynch & Clarke New York, cylindrical w/applied sloping double collar mouth, sand pontil, dark olive amber, ca. 1830-40, pt. 440

Lynde Putnam Mineral Water San Francisco Cal. A Union Glassworks Phillada, cylindrical w/applied top, iron pontil, cobalt blue 303

Missisquoi - A - Springs Mineral Water (embossed squaw & papoose), cylindrical w/applied top, yellowish green, ca. 1870-80, 9 1/2" h. (light cleaning, few scratches) 330

Napa Soda Phil Caduc Natural Mineral Water, cylindrical w/applied mouth, deep blue, 7" h. (couple of scratches)................... 154

Owen Casey Eagle Soda Works Sac City, cylindrical w/applied blob top & smooth base, bright green, overall crudity, probably cleaned, 7" h. 660

Owen Casey Eagle Soda Works Sac City, cylindrical w/applied blob top & smooth base, light to medium sapphire blue w/green streak, 7 1/4" h. 154

Owen Casey Eagle Soda Works Sac City, cylindrical w/applied blob top & smooth base, peacock blue, probably cleaned, 7 1/4" h.. 154

Owen Casey Eagle Soda Works Sac City, cylindrical w/applied blob top & smooth base, sapphire aqua, cleaned, 7 1/8" h. 66

Parker (J.C.) and Son New York, cylindrical w/applied top, electric blue (some scratches).. 88

Pioneer Soda Works - Trade (motif of shield) Mark, cylindrical w/applied top, deep aqua (slight wear)............................. 33

Knicker-Bocker Soda Water Bottle

Knicker (W.P.) - Bocker - Soda Water - 164. 18th St. N.Y. 1848, ten-sided w/applied heavy collared mouth, iron pontil, bright sapphire blue, ca. 1845-60, 1/2 pt. (ILLUS.) 728

Lancaster Glass Works N.Y., cylindrical w/applied sloping collar, iron pontil, light blue 88

Blue Plummer Boston Bottle

Plummer (J.P.) Boston. Bottle Not Sold, cylindrical w/heavy applied collared mouth, iron pontil, deep sapphire blue, ca. 1845-60, 1/2 pt. (ILLUS.) 672

Postens (E.) & Co. Providence R.I., cylindrical gravitator style w/tooled top, aqua, 7 1/4" h. 66

Reiners (C. A.) & Co 723 Turk St. SF Improved Mineral Water, cylindrical w/applied top, aqua.. 66
Reiners (C. A.) & Co Improved Mineral Water, cylindrical w/applied top, aqua......... 220
Ryan (John) Excelsior Mineral Water Savannah GA 1859 This Bottle Is Never Sold, cylindrical w/applied top, smooth base, whittled, dark blue (minor interior stain) 154
Sage's Pacific Congress Springs Saratoga, CA (arched around running deer motif), cylindrical w/tapering applied double collared top, bright green (couple of flakes around lower collar)...................... 660
Sammons Soda Works Sonora, Cal, cylindrical w/rounded shoulder & short neck w/thick tooled lip, aqua 99
San Luis Obispo Soda Water Works S. Ceribelli, cylindrical w/applied top, aqua, crude... 253
Scripture & Parker 31 Quart Square Boston, short cylindrical shaped w/applied double collared mouth, smooth base, teal blue (flake off lower collar) 66
Serwazi (Jos.) Manayunk (below) Return To, short cylindrical form w/applied top, smooth base, medium emerald green........... 121

St. Leon Bottle with Wicker

St. Leon Spring Water - J (in diamond) - Trademark - Early W. Johnson Boston, cylindrical w/applied slopping collared mouth w/ring, smooth base, in original woven wicker covering, teal green, ca. 1860-80, qt. (ILLUS.).................... 672
Swinley (R.) & Co. Patterson N.J., cylindrical w/rounded shoulder & short neck w/applied mouth for Hutchinson stopper, aqua, 9 1/2" h. 121
Taylor & Co. Soda Waters San Francisco, Eureka, cylindrical w/applied blob top & pontil scar, sapphire blue, probably cleaned, 1850s, 6 3/4" h.............................. 358
Vermont Spring - Saxe & Co. - Sheldon. Vt., cylindrical w/a tall tapering neck & applied sloping double collared mouth w/ring, smooth base, bright yellow w/slight olive tone, ca. 1870-80, qt. (ILLUS., top of next column) 616

Vermont Spring Soda Water Bottle

Weston (G.W.) & Co. Saratoga. N.Y., cylindrical w/applied sloping double collar mouth, pontil scar, yellowish olive, ca. 1860, pt. 224
Weston (G.W.) & Co. Saratoga. N.Y., cylindrical w/applied sloping double collar mouth, pontil scar, deep forest green, ca. 1860, pt. 448
Williams & Severance, cylindrical w/applied blob top, bright blue, ca. 1852-54, cleaned.. 165
Williams & Severance San Francisco, Cal. Soda and Mineral Waters, cylindrical w/applied blob top, iron pontil, dark green, ca. 1852-54 (some highpoint wear)... 143
Williams & Severance San Francisco, Cal. Soda and Mineral Waters, cylindrical w/applied blob top, pontil scar, dark green, ca. 1852-54, near mint, 7 1/4" h. 440
Winkle (Henry) Sac. City XX, cylindrical applied top, iron pontil, California, 1852-54, light greenish aqua 165

Peppersauces

Cylindrical Peppersauce Bottle

Aqua, cylindrical w/wide embossed banners swirling down the sides & enclosing wording "W.H. Clay's - Richmond - Sauce," applied sloping collar mouth, smooth base, ca. 1860-70, 10" h. (ILLUS.) **235**

Aqua, four-sided cathedral-type, elaborate Gothic arches on three sides, applied sloping collared mouth, tubular pontil, cleaned, ca. 1840-60, 11" h. **157**

Aqua Six-Sided Peppersauce

Aqua, six-sided cathedral-type, six Gothic arch sides tapering to tall cylindrical neck w/applied double collar mouth, pontil scar, 8 3/4" h. (ILLUS.) **78**

Light aqua, four-sided cathedral-type, four Gothic arch sides tapering to tall cylindrical neck w/applied top, big round pontil scar, 8 7/8" h. (couple tiny dings on base corners) **66**

Tall Light Green Peppersauce

Light emerald green, four-sided cathedral-type, four Gothic arch sides tapering to tall cylindrical neck w/applied double collar mouth, smooth base, 10 1/4" h. (ILLUS.) **101**

Pickle Bottles & Jars

Aqua, cylindrical w/molded petals on shoulder, applied top, unmarked, 9 7/8" h. (few scratches, light wear) **55**

Aqua, four-sided Cathedral-type, four Gothic arches, ringed wide neck w/applied lip, pontil scar, 11 5/8" h. **187**

Aqua, four-sided cathedral-type w/each panel composed of three arches, applied top, pontil scar, 8 1/4" h. (slight stain, pressure ding in one base corner) **209**

Aqua, lighthouse-shaped, tall tapering cylindrical form w/molded fences & three barrels on the front, embossed "Skilton Foote & Company - Bunker Hill Pickles - Trade Mark," modeled after the Cape May, New Jersey, lighthouse, 11 1/4" h. **385**

Bluish aqua, cylindrical w/five large full-body flutes below the tapering ringed shoulder, wide neck w/outward rolled mouth, tubular pontil, ca. 1860-80, 10 1/2" h. (some highpoint wear) **146**

Bright Aqua Cathedral Pickle

Bright bluish aqua, four-sided cathedral-type, a Gothic arch w/delicate arched ribbing on three sides, beveled corners, outward rolled mouth, smooth base, embossed on side "R. & F. Atmore," ca. 1860-80, 11 3/8" h. (ILLUS.) **308**

Bright green, four-sided cathedral-type, double-ringed molded outward-rolled mouth, smooth base, ca. 1860-70, 8 3/4" h. **523**

Bright green, four-sided cathedral-type, double-ringed molded outward-rolled mouth, smooth base, ca. 1860-70, 11 3/4" h. **896**

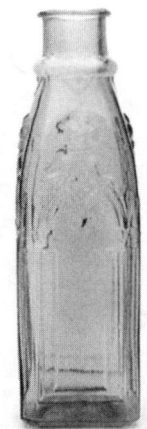

Deep Green Cathedral Pickle

Bright medium to deep green, four-sided cathedral-type w/Gothic windows, applied tooled collared mouth, iron pontil, ca. 1855-1865, 11 7/8' h. (ILLUS.).. **1,120**

Deep bluish aqua, square w/arched panels embossed on each side w/a central diamond device below a scroll, applied rim, graphite pontil, embossed "W.D. Smith, N.Y.," 8 5/8" h. **770**

Deep green, four-sided cathedral-type, plain pointed arch on each side, double-ring neck w/applied ring mouth, graphite pontil, 8 5/8" h. **1,045**

Deep greenish aqua, four-sided cathedral-type, plain pointed arch on each side molded at the point w/a leafy band design, double-ring neck w/applied ring mouth, some base, 14 1/4" h. **358**

Golden yellow, cylindrical w/tooled rim, embossed around the shoulder "J.M. Clark & Co. Louisville, K.Y.," 7" h. **88**

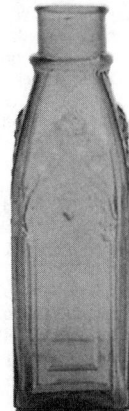

Large Green Cathedral Pickle

Medium bluish green, four-sided cathedral-type, double-ringed molded outward-rolled mouth, smooth base, ca. 1860-70, 11 3/4" h. (ILLUS.)........................... **784**

Olive green w/yellowish tone, cylindrical tapering milk bottle-form, ground mouth, smooth base, embossed large ring on front embossed "Sanborn, Park & Co. - Union (shield) Brand - Boston Pickles," ca. 1880-1900, 4 1/4" h. (in-the-making mouth roughness) **269**

Poisons

Rectangular Amber Poison Bottle

Amber, rectangular w/sawtooth corner bands, narrow sides embossed in large block letters "Poison," tooled lip, 7 7/8" h. (ILLUS.)... **413**

Bright grass green, six-sided w/inward rolled lip, smooth base marked "100," sides embossed "[skull & crossbones] - Gift [skull & crossbones] Flasche - [skull & crossbones] - Gift," Germany, ca. 1910-25, 5 1/8" h. (content stain, tiny flake on one corner)... **67**

Clear, cylindrical w/overall embossed diamond lattice design, tooled lip, smooth base, ca. 1890-1910, 3 7/8" h. (no stopper)... **55**

Very Rare Large Poison Bottle

Cobalt blue, cylindrical w/overall embossed diamond lattice design around shoulder & base, "Poison" embossed in large letters below shoulder on smooth label panel, tooled lip, smooth base, rectangular stopper w/points & "Poison," ca. 1890-1910, rare size, 9 3/8" h. (ILLUS.) **5,600**

Cobalt blue, cylindrical w/overall embossed diamond lattice design, tooled lip, smooth base, rectangular stopper w/points & "Poison," ca. 1890-1910, 4 3/4" h. **88**

Cobalt blue, cylindrical w/overall embossed diamond lattice design, tooled lip, smooth base marked "H.B. Co.," rectangular stopper w/points & "Poison," ca. 1890-1910, 3 3/4" h. **123**

Cobalt blue, cylindrical w/overall embossed diamond lattice design, tooled lip, smooth base marked "H.B. Co.," rectangular stopper w/points & "Poison," ca. 1890-1910, 5 5/8" h. **157**

Diamond Lattice Poison Bottle

Cobalt blue, cylindrical w/overall embossed diamond lattice design, tooled lip, smooth base marked "H.B. Co.," rectangular stopper w/points & "Poison," ca. 1890-1910, 4 3/4" h. (ILLUS.) **196**

Cobalt blue, cylindrical w/overall embossed diamond lattice design, tooled lip, smooth base marked "H.B. Co.," rectangular stopper w/points & "Poison," ca. 1890-1910, 7" h. **258**

Cobalt blue, irregular paneled shape w/tooled mouth & smooth base, a wide panel bordered w/small "Xs" around "Poison" running vertically next to a narrow plain panel marked "16 oz" at the top then another wide panel w/"Xs" around "Use With Caution," ca. 1890-1910, Canadian, 8 3/4" h. **224**

Cobalt blue, six-sided oblong form w/horizontal ribbing & four panels w/"Poison," tooled rim, smooth base marked "C.L.G. Co. - Patent Applied For," ca. 1890-1910, 5 5/8" h. **84**

Rare Canadian Poison with Heart

Cobalt blue, square w/rounded shoulder & tooled mouth, smooth base, one side w/"Contents 16 Fl. Oz." above a large embossed heart enclosing "The J.F. Hartz Co. Limited Toronto," overall design of small embossed hearts below, overall small embossed hearts on other sides, ca. 1890-1925, Canadian, tiny flake on label panel, 7 3/4" h. (ILLUS.) **896**

Cobalt blue, triangular w/rounded shoulder & ABM lip, smooth base, marked "Poison - (molded design of owl on mortar & pestle) - The Owl Drug Co.," ca. 1915-25, 5" h. **101**

Cobalt blue, triangular w/rounded shoulder & ABM lip, smooth base, marked "Poison - (molded design of owl on mortar & pestle) - The Owl Drug Co.," ca. 1915-25, 4" h. **101**

Cobalt blue, triangular w/rounded shoulder & ABM lip, smooth base, marked "Poison - (molded design of owl on mortar & pestle) - The Owl Drug Co.," ca. 1915-25, 6 1/2" h. **179**

Cobalt blue, triangular w/rounded shoulder & tooled mouth, marked "Poison - (molded design of owl on mortar & pestle) - The Owl Drug Co.," 7 3/4" h. **330**

Cobalt blue, triangular w/rounded shoulder & tooled mouth, marked "Poison - (molded design of owl on mortar & pestle) - The Owl Drug Co.," 9 3/4" h. **715**

Cobalt blue, triangular w/rounded shoulder & tooled mouth, smooth base, marked "Poison - (molded design of owl on mortar & pestle) - The Owl Drug Co.," ca. 1915-25, cleaned, 8 1/8" h. **224**

Medium grass green, six-sided w/tooled lip, smooth base marked "100," sides embossed "[skull & crossbones above three crosses] - [skull & crossbones above] Vorsicht Gift - [skull & crossbones above three crosses]," Germany, ca. 1910-25, 5" h. **90**

Rare Triangular Green Poison Bottle

Medium green, triangular w/ABM lip & smooth base marked "750," two sides embossed w/a skull & crossbones in a triangle above "De-Dro Giftflasche des Deutschen Drogisten Verbandes" above a "DDV" monogram, third side w/a skull & crossbones & the "DDV" monogram, Germany, ca. 1910-30, faint bruise on top of lip, 9 5/8" h. (ILLUS.) **672**

Medium yellowish green, six-sided w/ABM lip, smooth base marked "100," sides embossed "[skull & crossbones] - [skull & crossbones above] Giftflasche - [skull & crossbones] - Gift," Germany, ca. 1910-25, 4 7/8" h. **101**

Medium yellowish green, six-sided w/tooled lip, smooth base marked "100," sides embossed "[skull & crossbones] - Gift Flasche - [skull & crossbones] - Gift," Germany, ca. 1910-25, 5" h. **67**

Whiskey & Other Spirits

Beer, "Alabama Brewing Co. San Francisco (with monogram)," cylindrical w/applied top, amber, 1/2 pt. (trace of interior stain) **33**

Beer, "Breckenfelder & Jochem Oakland, Cal." (embossed) & "Valley Brew Lager" (on paper label), cylindrical w/tall neck & applied rim w/original porcelain & wire closure, label 90% intact, yellowish amber, pt., 9 1/4" h. **88**

Beer, "Buffalo Brewing Co. - Sacramento, Cal" in circle around a horseshoe, cylindrical w/applied top & original porcelain & wire closure, amber, pt., 9 3/8" h. **55**

Beer, "Buffalo Brewing Co. - Sacramento " in circle around a monogram, "This Bottle Not To Be Sold" on reverse, cylindrical w/applied top, amber, qt. **44**

Beer, "Buffalo Brewing Co. - Sacramento " in circle around a monogram, "This Bottle Not To Be Sold" on reverse, cylindrical w/applied top & original porcelain & wire closure, amber, 1/2 pt. **66**

Beer, "Buffalo Brewing Co. - SF Agency," cylindrical w/applied top, dark amber, qt. **44**

Beer, "Buffalo Brewing Co. - SF Agency (with monogram)," cylindrical w/applied top, amber, 1/2 pt., 7 1/2" h. (tiny bruise on mouth) **55**

Beer, "Buffalo Brewing Co. - SF Agency (with monogram)," cylindrical w/applied top & original porcelain & wire closure, clear, 1/2 pt., 7 3/4" h. **154**

Beer, "Buffalo Lager Beer (on paper label)," cylindrical w/tall neck & crown top, amber, label 95% intact, 9 3/8" h. (small chip in lip) **33**

Beer, "Cal Bottling Co. Export Beer," cylindrical w/applied top & original porcelain & wire closure, amber, 1/2 pt., 6 7/8" h. **33**

Beer, "Cervelli 1615 Francisco Street S.F.," cylindrical w/tall neck & tooled rim, amber, qt. **44**

Beer, "Cervelli 1615 Francisco Street S.F.," cylindrical w/tall neck & tooled rim, amber, 1/2 pt. **77**

Continental Brewing Beer Bottle

Beer, "Continental Brewing Co Philadelphia" in ring around large embossed revolutionary soldier, cylindrical w/applied top, dark aqua, very minor interior haze, pt. (ILLUS.) **66**

Beer, "Delaney & Young Eureka Cal," cylindrical tapering to an applied mouth, amber, qt. **33**

Beer, "Downing (Thos.) Hanford, Cal - Not To Be Sold," cylindrical w/tapering neck & crown top, amber, 1/2 pt., 7 3/4" h. **99**

Beer, "Enterprise Brewing Co. SF Cal" running vertically up the sides, cylindrical w/applied mouth w/original wire & porcelain stopper, clear, 1/2 pt., 7 7/8" h. (moon-shaped crack in shoulder) **22**

Beer, "Enterprise Brewing Co. SF Cal" running vertically up the sides, cylindrical w/applied mouth w/original wire & porcelain stopper, amber, qt. **33**

Beer, "Etna Brewery Etna Mills," cylindrical w/applied top, amber, 1/2 pt., 7 5/8" h. **22**

Beer, "Fondersmith's Beer," twelve-sided w/applied sloping collar mouth, smooth

base, ca. 1855-60, lightly cleaned, deep
root beer amber, 9 7/8" h. **672**

Rare Fondersmith's Beer Bottle

Beer, "Fondersmith's Beer," twelve-sided
w/applied sloping collar mouth, red iron
pontil, ca. 1850-60, dark root beer am-
ber, minor chips, 10" h. (ILLUS.).................... **952**

Beer, "Franks Bros San Francisco," cylindrical tapering to an applied mouth, amber,
qt. **44**

Beer, "Fredericksburg Bottling Co. S.F." in
ring w/shield & monogram above "This
Bottle Not To Be Sold," cylindrical w/tall
neck, amber, qt. (minor interior stain)............. **22**

Beer, "Fredericksburg Bottling Co. S.F." in
ring w/shield & monogram, cylindrical
w/tall neck/w/applied mouth, green, qt.,
11 1/2" h. (uncleaned)...................................... **33**

Beer, "Gambrinus San Francisco Cal. (in
circle around logo)," cylindrical tapering
to applied mouth w/original wire & porce-
lain stopper, amber, qt. **33**

Beer, "Grace Bros. Brewing Santa Rosa,
Cal. (with monogram)," cylindrical w/ap-
plied top, amber, 1/2 pt., 7 3/4" h..................... **33**

Beer, "Hansen & Kahler Oakland Ca," cylindrical w/blob top & original wire & porcelain stopper, amber, pt. (some interior
haze, flake off inside lip).................................. **143**

Beer, "K & M Oakland," cylindrical w/applied
top, California, amber, 1/2 pt. **33**

A.W. Kenison California Beer

Beer, "Kenison (A.W.) Co. Auburn, Cal.,"
cylindrical w/wide tall neck & tooled rim,
clear, qt. (ILLUS.) **22**

Rare Green Lutge Beer Bottle

Gold Edge Beer Bottle

Beer, "Gold Edge Bottling Works J F
Deninger Vallejo," cylindrical w/tooled
top, California, clear, 1/2 pt. (ILLUS.).............. **55**

Beer, "Lutge (Theodore) & Co San Jose Cal" in ring around "This Bottle Not To Be Sold," cylindrical w/blob top, light to dark green, small ding off back base, qt. (ILLUS.) **495**

Beer, "Mirrasoul Bros SF," cylindrical tapering to an applied top w/original wire & porcelain stopper, deep amber, qt. **22**

Beer, "National Bottling San Francisco Cal Adolph B. Lang (with embossed eagle)," cylindrical w/applied top, light to medium amber, qt., 11 5/8" h. **55**

Beer, "National Lager Beer H. Rohrbacher Agt. (w/monogram)," cylindrical w/tooled top & original porcelain & wire closure, golden amber, 1/2 pt., 7 7/8" h. **66**

Beer, "North Star S.F. Cal. (with embossed star)," cylindrical w/tooled top & original porcelain & wire closure, amber, 1/2 pt., 7 7/8" h. **55**

Beer, "Oakland Bottling Co Oakland Cal" in circle, cylindrical w/tooled top, amber, qt. **33**

Beer, "Palmtag & Co Eureka, Cal," cylindrical tapering to a tall neck w/tooled rim & original stopper, amber, qt. (tiny ding on one letter) **110**

Beer, "Rapp (John) & Son S.F. Cal.," cylindrical w/crown top, clear w/amethyst tint, 1/2 pt., 7 3/4" h. (slight dirt, few tiny top bruises) **33**

Beer, "Raspiller Brewing Co. West Berkeley," cylindrical w/applied mouth, California, amber, 1/2 pt., 7 5/8" h. **121**

Beer, "Ruhstaller Giltedge Lager," cylindrical w/tall neck & crown top, Sacramento, California, early 20th c., amber, pt. (minor interior stain) **22**

Beer, "Ruhstaller Giltedge Lager" (on paper label) pasted over embossed "Buffalo Brewing," cylindrical w/tall neck & original closure, amber, label 95% intact, qt., 11 1/2" h. **77**

Beer, "Salinas Valley Bottling Co., Salinas, Cal.," cylindrical w/applied top, light to medium amber, 1/2 pt., 7 5/8" h. **77**

Beer, "San Jose Bottling Co San Jose Cal," cylindrical w/tall neck & applied mouth, crude & whittled, 1/2 pt., 7 1/2" h. (small flake off top, some scratches, needs cleaning) **55**

Beer, "Sierra Bottling Co Wieland's Best Jamestown Cal.," cylindrical w/tooled top, reddish amber, 1/2 pt. **330**

Beer, "St. Helena Bottling and Cold Storage St. Helena Cal.," cylindrical tapering to a crown top, amber, 1/2 pt., 7 3/4" h. **44**

Beer, "Sunset Bottling Co. (over monogram) San Francisco, Cal.," cylindrical tapering to a tall neck w/tooled rim, amber, qt. **33**

Beer, "Sunset Bottling Co. (over monogram) San Francisco, Cal.," cylindrical tapering to a tall neck w/tooled rim & original porcelain & wire closure, amber, 1/2 pt., 7 1/2" h. **88**

Beer, "Union Brewing and Malting Co. S.F. Cal," cylindrical w/tooled top & original porcelain & wire closure, amber, 1/2 pt. **88**

Beer, "Wunder Bottling Co. San Francisco. Cal.," cylindrical w/applied top, amber, 1/2 pt. **22**

Brandy, "Lyons (L.) Pure Ohio Catawba Brandy Cini," cylindrical Hock wine form w/applied mouth w/ring, smooth base, some original foil seal on mouth, golden amber, ca. 1860-80, 13 3/4" h. (minor interior haze) **532**

Early Green Case Gin Bottle

Case gin, square tapering form, free-blown w/applied mouth & large tubular pontil, yellowish olive, Holland, 1770-1800, 17 3/4" h. (ILLUS.) **1,456**

Rare Blue Case Gin Bottle

Case gin, tall slender square tapering shape w/applied tooled mouth, smooth base, ca. 1880-95, deep cobalt blue, 10 1/8" h. (ILLUS.) **1,680**

Gin, "Booth & Sedgwick's London Cordial Gin," square w/beveled corners & applied sloping collar mouth, iron pontil, ca. 1855-65, medium bluish green, 8" h. **504**

London Jockey Club House Gin

Gin, "London (reversed "N"s) Jockey - Club House - Gin" w/design of jockey on horse, square w/rounded shoulder & short neck w/applied sloping collar w/original neck foil, smooth base, ca. 1865-75, deep yellowish green, 9 3/4" h. (ILLUS.) **532**

Udolpho Wolfe Schnapps Bottle

Schnapps, "Udolpho Wolfe's Aromatic Schnapps, Schiedam," rectangular w/beveled corners, applied sloping double collar mouth, iron pontil, light greenish aqua, ca. 1850-60, tiny very faint bruise on lip, 8" h. (ILLUS.) **179**

Spirits, free-blown onion-form w/tall neck & applied string lip, pontilled base, olive amber, England, 1700-1710, 5 5/8" h. (matte dullness, half of string lip gone) **336**

Early English Onion-form Bottle

Spirits, free-blown onion-form, wide "pancake" shape w/tall neck & applied string lip, pontilled base, deep olive amber, England, 1690-1700, found in Virginia river, heavily pitted, most of string lip gone, 5 3/8" h. (ILLUS.) **560**

Spirits, hexagonal w/applied seal embossed "F.J. Mampe - Stargard," applied sloping collar mouth, smooth base, bright medium yellowish olive, Europe, 1860-80, 9 1/4" h. **259**

Spirits, mold-blown club form w/tall neck & applied round collared mouth, tubular pontil, twenty-four ribs swirled to the right, Midwest, early 19th c., cornflower blue, 8 1/4" h. (small shallow bubbled blister below shoulder) **1,008**

Spirits, mold-blown globular form w/tall neck & rolled rim, twenty-four ribs swirled to the left, Midwest, early 19th c., bright golden amber, 8 1/4" h. (minor interior stain) **616**

Spirits, mold-blown globular form w/tall neck & rolled rim, twenty-four ribs swirled to the right, Midwest, early 19th c., yellowish green w/citron tone, 7 5/8" h. (several faint small spider cracks, some in-the-making crizzling) **1,344**

Globular Midwest Spirits Bottle

Spirits, mold-blown globular form w/tall neck & rolled rim, twenty-four vertical ribs, Midwest, early 19th c., bright golden amber, 7 5/8" h. (ILLUS.).............................. **3,080**

Midwest Citron Globular Bottle

Spirits, mold-blown globular form w/tall neck & rolled rim, twenty-four ribs swirled to the left, Midwest, early 19th c., citron, 8 1/4" h. (ILLUS.) **4,200**

Whiskey, "AAA Old Valley Whiskey," flask-shaped w/applied single-roll top, bright golden amber **1,760**

Whiskey, "Angeli (J.) & Co. San Francisco," flask-form w/single applied top, cleaned, amber, 1868-72, rare, 7 3/4" h. **12,100**

Balich & Hirsch Whiskey Bottles

Whiskey, "Balich (Andy) 170 Pacific Ave Santa Cruz Cal," pumpkin seed flask-form, sun-colored purple, pt. (ILLUS. right with Hirsch bottle) **550**

Whiskey, "Bininger (A.M.) & Co 338 Broadway N.Y. - Distilled in 1848 - Old Kentucky - 1849 Reserve Bourbon," ringed barrel shape w/applied double collar mouth, open pontil, ca. 1855-65, amber, 8 1/8" h. (tiny open bubble on one ring).. **258**

Bininger Old Kentucky Bourbon

Whiskey, "Bininger (A.M.) & Co 338 Broadway N.Y. - Distilled in 1848 - Old Kentucky - 1849 Reserve Bourbon," ringed barrel shape w/applied double collar mouth, open pontil, ca. 1855-65, medium amber, 8 1/8" h. (ILLUS.) **336**

Whiskey, "Bininger's (clock face) Regulator 19 Broad St. New York," round flat shape w/faint clock face, applied double collar mouth, open pontil, ca. 1855-65, medium amber, 6" h. **336**

Whiskey, "Bininger's Peep-o-Day No. 19 Broad St. N.Y.," oval flattened form w/short neck & applied double collared mouth, smooth base, ca. 1855-70, golden amber,7 5/8" h. (several pick marks on reverse & mouth) **784**

Whiskey, "Bischoff (B.) 193 Hamburg Ave. - Capacity 32 Ozs Brooklyn, N.Y." (in circle below) "Warrented Full Quart," flask-form w/tooled mouth, smooth base w/"DGC" in diamond, medium golden amber, 1900-1915, qt. **90**

Whiskey, "Brickwedel & Co. Wholesale Liquor Dealers 208 & 210 Front St. S.F. (in circle)," flask-shaped w/applied top, bright amber, ca. 1880-83, uncleaned, pt. (slight interior stain) **605**

Whiskey, "Chestnut Grove Whiskey, C.W." on applied seal, chestnut flask-shaped w/applied mouth w/ring & applied handle, tubular pontil, bright golden amber, 9" h........ **202**

Whiskey, "Christian (R.L.) & Co. Richmond Va." in ring below "Warranted Full 1/2 Pint," flask-shaped w/tooled mouth, smooth base marked "B.R.G. Co.," clear, ca. 1890-1910, 1/2 pt........................... **202**

Whiskey, "Cutter (J.F.) Extra Old Bourbon" centering a star in shield flanked by "Trade Mark," flask-shaped w/applied single-roll collar, light amber, 7 1/2" h........ **1,980**

R.B. Cutter's Pure Bourbon Bottle

Whiskey, "Cutter's (R.B.) Pure Bourbon," ovoid body w/applied mouth & handle, large iron pontil, ca. 1855-65, deep smoky pink puce, 8 3/4" h. (ILLUS.) **840**

Whiskey, "Hirsch (B.S.) Ukiah Cal," pumpkin seed flask-form, applied lip, clear, 1/2 pt. (ILLUS. previous pageleft with Balich bottle).. **935**

Whiskey, "Hoffman (A.W.) Claremont Hotel Bernardsville, N.J. - One Half Pint Full Measure," in circle, flask-shaped w/tooled mouth, smooth base marked "L. & MG 182 Fulton St. N.Y.," clear, ca. 1885-1900, 1/2 pt. **67**

Whiskey, "Hollingworth (F.S.) Wholesale Liquors, Winona, Minn.," flask-shaped w/applied ringed mouth, amber, 6 3/8" h. **77**

Whiskey, "Lilienthal & Co. S.F.," banded flask-form w/double roll applied collar, amber, 1878-82, 1/2 pt., 6 5/8" h. **1,430**

Louisville Liquor House Bottle

Whiskey, "Louisville Liquor House 306 Bennett Ave. Cripple Creek, Col.," coffin

flask-shaped w/tooled mouth, smooth base, clear, ca. 1890-1910, 6" h. (ILLUS.)... **840**

Rare Miller's Extra Bourbon Bottle

Whiskey, "Miller's Extra Trade Mark [above shield] - E. Martin & Co. Old Bourbon," flask-shaped w/applied mouth w/single roll collar & smooth base, ca. 1875-80, deep olive, 7 1/2" h. (ILLUS.) **1,430**

Whiskey, "Phoenix Old (motif of spreadwinged phoenix) Trade Mark (above) Bourbon Naber, Alfs & Brune San Francisco Sole Proprts," flask-form w/tooled mouth & smooth base, light to medium amber, ca. 1895, 1/2 pt. **330**

Barrel-shaped Ringed Whiskey

Whiskey, "That's The Stuff," barrel-shaped w/rings above & below center band, crudely applied flared mouth, tubular pontil, bright yellowish golden amber, ca. 1840-80, 10" h. (ILLUS.) **2,352**

Whiskey, "Wheelan's (after From) Sample Rooms C.B. 1878 X.X. Ukiah. Cal.," flask-shaped w/tall neck w/tooled top, clear, pt. **550**

Early English Wine Bottle

Wine, blown octagonal club-form w/tapering neck w/applied string lip, pontil scar, England, 1730-60, bright yellowish olive, one tiny flake on base edge, 3 3/8" w., 7 3/8" h. (ILLUS.) **952**

BOXES

Beaver-decorated Band Box

Band box, cov., oval, covered w/wallpaper in beaver pattern in black, brown & green on blue field, America, mid-19th c., 9 3/8 x 11 1/2", 6 1/4" h. (ILLUS.) **$764**

Band box, cov., oval, covered w/wallpaper in deer hunting scene pattern in green & brown on yellow field, America, ca. 1840, 12 3/4 x 16 3/4", 10 1/2" h. (wear, separations, fading) **881**

Band box, cov., oval, covered w/wallpaper w/fire brigade motifs in green, brown & tan on yellow ground, America, mid-19th c., 14 x 19 1/4", 12 1/4" h. (losses, wear, fading) **1,880**

Paint Decorated Bride's Box

Bride's box, cov., oval w/laced seams, old painted decoration of man wearing black coat, white pants & top hat walking arm in arm w/woman wearing green dress & hat, trees on either side on deep red ground, rosemaling around the sides of the base, glued splits in lid, edge chips, 13 x 19 3/4", 7 3/4" h. (ILLUS.) **1,265**

Hanging Candle Box

Candle box, cov., hanging type, walnut, square nail construction, base inset w/chamfered edges, slant lid has wire staple hinges, beveled edges & three panels decorated w/concentric circles, front has pinwheel design & inlaid mother-of-pearl diamond shapes, shaped crest w/triangle cutout, attributed to Pennsylvania, old refinishing, 6 x 11", 8" h. (ILLUS.) **550**

Candle box, cov., pine, sliding lid w/three finger notches, divided interior, T-head nails, old varnish, 6 3/4 x 17", 6 3/4" h. (age cracks, wear) **149**

Document box, cov., pine w/original black over red painted decoration, dovetailed construction, interior lined w/old block printed wallpaper in gold & grey on white, external iron hasp lock, 10 1/2 x 18", 7 1/2" h. **303**

Hanging box, cov., pine, dovetailed construction, scalloped crest w/two hanging holes, lift lid w/side pegs, one dovetailed drawer w/beaded edge & replaced ring pull, 7 1/4 x 12 1/4", 10 1/4" h. (late black paint covers minor damage at one hole) **495**

Hanging box, maple w/a trace of curl, dovetailed construction w/bottom attached by square nails, step-down sides, curved crest w/worn hanging hole, red stain in bottom & traces of green paint, old, mellow scrubbed surface, attributed to Pennsylvania, 5 1/2 x 12", 8 3/4" h. **468**

Inlaid box, cov., mahogany & exotic wood, rectangular w/carved chevron molding, the lid inlaid w/a variety of exotic woods arranged in stacked block pattern, interior of lid w/pen & ink chart depicting the inlay & identifying the woods used, box interior divided into four sections, America, 19th c., 9 3/4 x 13 3/4", 6" h. **411**

Ornately Carved Jewelry Box

Jewelry box, walnut & whalebone, ornately carved w/rosette, fan, lapped leaf, pendant & other designs, w/front & side drawers, hinged lid opening to mirror, which further opens to three oval frames w/rope trim, box interior fitted w/four compartments w/carved lids, handles of drawers & lids are carved whalebone, America, 19th c., 12 1/2 x 18 1/4", 10 3/8" h. (ILLUS.)...................................... **2,350**

Decorated Knife Box

Knife box, pine, canted sides & central divider w/delicate heart cutout handle, original mustard exterior w/faint stenciled scrolls, trees & grapes in red & brown, interior has remains of salmon paint w/stenciled gold flourishes around handle, mixture of old nails, mostly "T," wear & some red marker, 8 x 13 1/2", 6" h. (ILLUS.)............................. **2,090**

Money box, cov., pine, chamfered molding around base, interior fitted w/open till & lock, mixture of "T" & square-head nails, old blue paint, no key, 9 3/4 x 16 7/8", 7 1/4" h. **743**

Pantry box, cov., oval bentwood shape w/varnish finish, two fingers on base, one on the lid, all w/copper tacks, Shaker, 5 x 7 1/2", 3" h. (wear to lid).......................... **440**

Bentwood Pantry Box

Pantry box, cov., round, bentwood form decorated in original dark red ground decorated w/dark blue & yellow tulips w/green stems on lid & around body, faint pencil inscription on lid appears to read "April 5 1896...," 7 3/4" d., 3 1/2" h. (ILLUS.)... **2,090**

Pantry box, round, painted black, the top carved w/a central star within a medallion & a leafy border, crosshatch swags on the side, the interior lined w/partial advertising lithographs, New England, mid-19th c., 6 1/4" d., 2 1/4" h............................... **705**

Decorated Hanging Salt Box

Salt box, cov., painted wood, hanging type, dovetailed construction w/arched crest & lift lid w/beveled edge, old brown over dark mustard decoration, brick red painted interior, minor stains along bottom edge, chip, 6 3/4 x 10 1/2", 8" h. (ILLUS.)...... **660**

Seashell-decorated, cardboard, armoire shape decorated w/seashells, w/tortoiseshell print paper on sides, back & cornice, mirrored door & three interior shelves w/gold & pale blue paper interior, 4 x 7 1/2", 9 1/4" h. (some shells missing) **220**

Seashell-decorated, cov., cardboard box painted sky blue w/wide assortment of real glued seashells & red & gold composition shells, chromolithograph of Elizabethan woman in oval panel on center of lid & a lakeside log cabin on front panel, 7 1/2 x 10 1/2", 3 1/2" h. (some missing shells)... **220**

Sewing box, cov., pine & maple, oval Shaker-style, pine lid w/maple sides & lid rim, swing handle, five lapped fingers, the interior lined w/light blue padded silk, America, late-19 / - early-20th c., 11 1/4 x 15", 11" h. w/handle... **1,880**

Shaker, cov., oval, pine top & bottom, bentwood construction w/four swallow tails on base & one on lid, all w/copper tacks, golden refinishing, 13" **550**

Storage box, cov., basswood, dovetailed construction, dark brown graining on red ground w/gold stenciled decoration of leaves on front panel & an eagle on the lid w/a dog & hunter chasing two deer, iron hinges, copper ring handle, brass tab & wire lock, interior has leather strips tacked to lid, Maine, 6 x 10", 3 3/4" h. (wear) **715**

Storage box, cov., basswood & poplar w/original reddish brown over yellow vinegar grain decoration, dovetailed corners, square nails along base & lid, attributed to Maine, 13 3/4 x 28", 12 1/2" h. (minor areas of wear)...................................... **770**

Storage box, cov., cherry w/dark brown finish, dovetailed construction, raised panel, sliding lid, divided interior, 5 1/4 x 8 1/4", 2 5/8" h. (glued splits)............. **193**

Storage box, cov., mahogany case w/inlaid brass Art Deco geometric designs & flowers & corner supports, dovetailed construction, brass handles flush w/sides, lock w/key has flower escutcheon, interior lid w/vining leaf border, removable divided tray is heavily grained hardwood, tops of dividers are reeded, 10 x 15", 5" h. (paint splatters on lid) **193**

Storage box, cov., pine, dome-top, wire hinges, iron handles & latch, dovetailed joinery, America, 19th c., 11 x 19 3/4", 8 7/8" h. (minor cracks)................................... **999**

Polychrome Box with Sliding Lid

Storage box, cov., pine, dovetail constructed polychrome rectangular form w/sliding lid, the lid decorated w/red, white & blue diamond pattern basket filled w/strawberries, surrounded by grapes, leaves, flourishes & scrolls within a striped border, the box w/central shell design on three sides w/similar scrolling, leafy vines & geometric star devices in red, white, blue, gold & salmon colors on black ground, America, early 19th c., repair to lid, 4 x 8 x 12" (ILLUS.) **1,880**

Storage box, cov., pine, dovetailed construction & scalloped trim, red base w/dark slate blue on lid & dark red over alligatored black on trim, "E.J.C. Concord, Mass." in yellow on front & "CO" in nails on the lid, stained interior, 8 1/4 x 12 1/4", 5 1/4" h. (damage to one hinge)... **413**

Storage box, cov., pine, dovetailed corners, raised lid w/reeding, old decoration of red compote of tulips & other flowers on two sides, additional large flower & initials "A.P.S. Ar 1816" on the end, red, black & white decoration on blue/green ground, 9 x 17", 7 1/2" h. (small holes, some later screws added underneath)............................ **523**

Storage box, cov., poplar, dovetailed construction, step-down molding around base & cove molding around lid, square cut nails, original green paint, 10 x 16 1/2", 8" h. (wear to lid & edges) **523**

Storage box, dome-topped, painted & decorated wood, rectangular, the hinged top w/an iron latch, decorated w/the letters "ML" in an octagonal & linear border in red on a mustard yellow ground, red leather trim secured w/brass tacks around top edge, speckled pink floral wallpaper-lined interior, 19th c., 14" l., 5" h. (minor imperfections).......................... **2,300**

Storage box, dome-topped, wood, rectangular w/deep sides, dark green painted ground decorated w/a band of yellow leaves along front top edge, yellow banding around the sides, original paint, New England, 1830s, 16 1/2 x 28 3/4", 18 1/2" h. (minor surface imperfections)....... **978**

Storage box, oval, bentwood maple & pine single-lapped construction, painted grey, New England, early 19th c., 3 1/2 x 4 3/4", 1 3/4" h. (minor paint wear).. **705**

Tea chest, cov., camphor wood covered in leather, hinged lid w/small oval plate engraved "Jacob Tilton," brass handles, corners, banded edges & decorative studding, America, 19th c., 25" l., 10" h. (minor corrosion, dents) **353**

Wall box, chestnut stained red, rectangular shape divided into two compartments, w/extended backboard & round hanging loop, stamped w/initials "J.M." & several scribed circles, New England, mid-19th c., 6 3/4 x 11 1/2", 14" h. **235**

Wall Scrub Box

Wall scrub box, pine painted green, arched backboard, America, 19th c., 7 1/2" w., 11 3/4" h. (ILLUS.).. **705**

Wallpaper box, cov., round, several layers of paper w/pink, yellow & blue flowers on white & black ground being the topmost layer, bottom is wood w/piece of literary magazine print lining the inside, 6 1/2" d., 3 1/2" h. (edge wear) **358**

BREWERIANA

Beer is still popular in this country, but the number of breweries has greatly diminished. More than 1,900 breweries were in operation in the 1870s, but we find fewer than 40 major breweries supply the demands of the country a century later, although microbreweries have recently sprung up across the country.

Advertising items used to promote various breweries, especially those issued prior to Prohibition, now attract an ever growing number of collectors. The breweriana items listed are a sampling of the many items available. Also see Antique Trader Advertising Price Guide.

Backbar chalk w/bottle, Altes Beer, Altes Brewing, Detroit, Michigan, 1950s, 11 x 11 1/2" (some chips at corners & where bottle fits) **$95**

Rare Budweiser Millennium Bar Sign

Backbar light, plastic display-type, w/a fish about to bite lure, base may be brass, Schaefer Beer, Schaefer Brewing Co., New York, New York, 1950s **30**

Blatz Beer Backbar Statue

Backbar statue, Blatz Beer, banjo player & bottle, Pabst Brewing Co., Milwaukee, Wisconsin, 1950s, some scuffs to bottle labels (ILLUS.) **87**

Neuweiler Beer-Ale Backbar Statue

Backbar statue, plastic, Neuweiler Beer-Ale, Neuweiler Brewing Co., Allentown, Pennsylvania, 1950s, some worn & chipped paint, 8 1/2 x 12" (ILLUS.) **77**

Backbar statue w/bottle, chalk, Coopers Beer, bartender w/bottle, Liebert & Obert, Philadelphia, Pennsylvania, 1940s, 7 x 15" (lots of wear, chips, missing bottle labels) **150**

Backbar statue w/bottle, chalk, Old Reading Beer, Old Reading Brewing Co., Reading, Pennsylvania, 1940s (base broken in two & glued together, some chips) **150**

Bar sign, "Budweiser Millennium - Exported Since 1876," reverse-painted glass in ornate molded gilt plastic frame, rare, ca. 2000, 33 3/4 x 57" (ILLUS., top of page) **242**

Budweiser Bud Man Beer Stein

Beer stein, ceramic, figural Bud Man, red outfit, ca. 1980s, 8 1/4" h. (ILLUS.) **50**

Bottle display, cardboard, Hull's, Hull Brewing Co., New Haven, Connecticut, 1950s, 14 x 16" (small creases, label is on a Yeungling bottle) **46**

Bottle opener, die-cut metal, outlined flat figure of a baseball player about to make a pitch, stamped marking for M. Mortiz Bottlers, ca. 1940s, 3 1/4" h. (slight rust spotting) **50**

Cab light, reverse-painted glass, Schlitz Beer, Schlitz Brewing, Milwaukee, Wisconsin, 1930s, 13 x 7 1/2" (some oxidation on base, a few rust spots on rear cover) **406**

Calendar, 1950, cardboard, Royal Crown, no location listed, w/attached pad, 11 1/2 x 24" (overall yellowing, some creases & light wear).......................... **80**

Calendar, 1967, Horlacher Brewing Co., Allentown, Pennsylvania, w/attached pad, 16 x 33" (some wrinkles, light water stains, a few spots)........................... **46**

Cardboard display, Miller Brewing Co., Milwaukee, Wisconsin, 1955, 21 x 29" (missing back standup piece, some tears & staple holes) **36**

Unusual Faust Ceiling Light Globe

Ceiling light globe, "Faust On Draught," one-piece milk glass, etched & fire-painted in black & red w/wording & Anheuser Busch logo on both sides, ca. 1930s, some decal wear, slight soiling, 8" d. (ILLUS.)... **242**

Chalkboard, Kaiers Brewing Co., Mahonoy City, Pennsylvania, 1960s, 17 x 24" (spots, dings & scratches).............................. **27**

Large Falstaff Beer Charger

Charger, lithographed metal, round w/large colorful scene of the seated Falstaff being served by a pretty barmaid, a mountainous landscape in the background, his shield beside him w/the Falstaff Beer logo on it, ca. 1930s, slight scratches, 24" d. (ILLUS.)................................ **44**

Charger, tin, Falstaff Beer, Falstaff Brewing Co., St. Louis, Missouri, 1970s, 16" (some scratches & nicks to edges)................. **40**

Gibbons Beer Electric Wall Clock

Clock, "Gibbons Beer - Ale," round electric wall model, black Bakelite frame, domed glass front over white dial w/black Arabic numerals & red circle in the center, sweep seconds hand, by Telechron, ca. 1930s-40s, 15 1/2" d. (ILLUS.)......................... **99**

Rare Iroquois Beer Light-up Clock

Clock, "Iroquois Beer - Ale," round electric double-bubble light-up model, glass & metal, domed glass front over brown dial w/four white Arabic numerals in outer ring around large profile bust of American Indian chief in red, white, black & tan, red wording below, sweep seconds hand, ca. 1950s, small scratch on glass, some body wear, one light bulb cover missing, 15 1/2" d. (ILLUS.).. **523**

Narragansett Beer Clock

Clock, molded plastic, Narragansett Beer, Cranston, Rhode Island, 1960s, crack in upper left case w/small hole along crack, 15 x 21" (ILLUS.) **21**

Clock, plastic, Budweiser, Anheuser-Busch Brewing Co., St. Louis, Missouri, 1950s (cracks in plastic around clock face, minor wear) **25**

Cone sign, high profile-style, Neuweiler's Pilsener Beer, BCU 30-6, Neuweiler Brewing Co., Allentown, Pennsylvania, 1940s (minor nicks & tiny scratches) **1,000**

Cone sign, high profile-style, Schmidt's First Premium Lager Beer, BCU 34-15, K.G. Schmidt Brewing Co., Logansport, Indiana, 1940s (some small nicks & scratches) **187**

Cone sign, low profile-style, Piel's Special Light Beer, BCU 32-5, Piel Brothers, New York, New York, 1930s (a few small nicks in red, some minor canning dings) **427**

Hanley's Ale Counter Figure

Counter display figure, "Hanley's Ale," rubber, model of a reclining grey & black bulldog on rectangular black base w/red lettering, Rubber Products, Inc., Chicago, Illinois, ca. 1950, tear under head, some cracks & wear, slightly out of shape, 17 3/4" l., 9" h. (ILLUS.) **66**

Dart board, masonite, Pabst Blue Ribbon, w/drawings of Hitler & Tojo in the corners for playing poker & black jack w/darts, Pabst Brewing Co., Milwaukee, Wisconsin, 1940s (w/dart holes, some soiling & water stains, dinged corners) **58**

Hamm's Beer Bear Decanter

Decanter, ceramic bear, Hamm's Beer, 1972, Hamm Brewing Co., St. Paul, Minnesota (ILLUS.) **37**

Display, wood & plastic, Iroquois, International Brewing Co., Buffalo, New York, 1950s, 8 x 15" **6**

Unusual Composition Bartender Doll

Doll, bartender, composition head, shoes & hands, cloth body, wearing pink & blue striped shirt, dark red tie, white apron, black pants, ca. 1930s-40s, 24" h. (ILLUS.) **88**

Black Label Motorized Ferris Wheel

Ferris wheel, motorized, cardboard, Black Label, Carling Brewing Co., Cleveland, Ohio, 1960s, some damage to cardboard edges, some scuffs, 14 1/2 x 18 x 5 1/2" (ILLUS.) **51**

Light, glass & metal, Duquesne Beer, Duquesne Brewing Co., Pittsburgh, Pennsylvania, 1950s (some wear & scuffs)............ **42**
Light, hanging-type, plastic, 4-sided, Budweiser, Anheuser-Busch Brewing Co.,
St. Louis, Missouri, 1950s, 12 x 12" **41**

Budweiser Beer Duck Hunter Light

Light, metal, plastic & glass, depicting a
duck hunter, Budweiser Beer, Anheuser-
Busch Brewing Co., St. Louis, Missouri,
1950s, some rust on rear panel, 20 x 14"
(ILLUS.).. **60**

Miller High Life Beer Light

Light, metal & plastic, Miller High Life, Miller
Brewing Co., Milwaukee, Wisconsin,
1950s, overall wear & scuffs, bent plastic
accent piece, 20 x 18" (ILLUS.)....................... **12**
Light, plastic, Duquesne Brewing Co., Pittsburgh, Pennsylvania, 1950s, 18 x 20"
(minor scratches)... **26**
Light, pocket watch-shaped, Budweiser
Beer, Anheuser-Busch Brewing Co., St.
Louis, Missouri, 1950s, some wear &
scuffs in gold, 12 1/2 x 17" **82**

Schmidt Beer Wagon-shaped Light

Light, wood, metal & cloth, wagon-shaped,
Schmidt Beer, Jacob Schmidt Brewing
Co., St. Paul, Minnesota, 1950s, yel-
lowed & some stains on cloth cover
(ILLUS.)... **102**

The Little Duke Reverse Glass Mirror

Mirror, reverse-painted glass, in faux leath-
er cardboard frame, The Little Duke (Du-
quesne Pilsener), Duquesne Brewing
Co., Pittsburgh, Pennsylvania, 1940s,
some edge wear to frame, lifting silvering
along bottom edge, 11 1/4 x 6 1/4"
(ILLUS.).. **37**
Mirror, shows Indians on raft w/keg & case,
Anheuser-Busch Brewing Co., St. Louis,
Missouri, 1986, 18 x 24"................................... **38**

Old Dutch Beer Sign

Sign, composition, Old Dutch Beer, Eagle
Brewing Co., Catasauqua, Pennsylvania,
1950s, crackled & chipped yellow paint,
7 x 9" (ILLUS.)... **80**

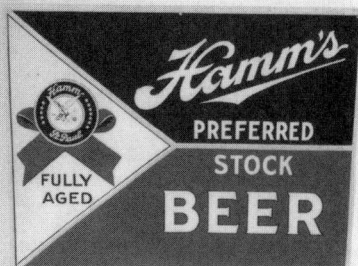

Hamm's Beer Sign

Sign, embossed tin, Hamm's Preferred
Stock Beer, Hamm Brewing Co., St.
Paul, Minnesota, 1930s, small rust spots
& light scuffs, 23 3/4 x 17 3/4" (ILLUS.)......... **435**
Sign, lithograph advertising Minnesota City
Brewery Bock Beer, Minnesota City
Brewing Co., Minnesota City,
Minnesota, ca. 1900, 25 x 37" framed
(light wear & stains, scratch across Bock

Beer at bottom, small spot to right of rider).. **622**

Sign, lithographed factory scene, w/die-cut printed matte, Bartel's Brewing Co., Edwardsville, Pennsylvania, original wood frame, 1900s (some wrinkling & water stains to both lithograph & matte, tear in upper left corner of matte)............................... **76**

Champagne Velvet Sign

Sign, plastic, Champagne Velvet w/3-D labeled bottle, Terre Haute Brewing Co., Terre Haute, Indiana, 1950s, some soiling, scuffs on bottle & label) 9 3/4 x 12 1/4" (ILLUS.) **105**

Sign, rectangular cardboard, Kingsbury Pale Beer, Kingsbury Brewery, Manitowoc, Wisconsin, 1950s, 17 x 20" (small creases & nicks)... **38**

Sign, rectangular lighted, Schoenling, shows riverboat scene in Cincinnati, Ohio, Schoenling Brewing Co., Cincinnati, Ohio, 1960s, 15 x 18"........................ **82**

Spinner shade, no light, Budweiser Beer, Anheuser-Busch Brewing Co., St. Louis, Missouri, 1950s (some crinkles & scuffs in plastic & foil) **33**

Ambassador Beer Knob

Tap knob, Bakelite & aluminum, w/enamel insert, Ambassador Beer, Krueger Brewing Co., Newark, New Jersey, 1950s, 1/4" chip on each side of knob (ILLUS.) **30**

Tap knob, Bakelite knob w/aluminum insert, Horlacher Beer, Horlacher Brewing Co., Allentown, Pennsylvania, 1950s (wear, scratches on insert)............................. **65**

Graupner's Beer Knob

Tap knob, Bakelite, w/copper insert, Graupner's Beer, R.H. Graupner, Harrisburg, Pennsylvania, 1940s, some minor scratches (ILLUS.)................................. **75**

Tap knob, Bakelite, w/enamel insert, Ballantine Ale, Ballantine Brewing Co., Newark, New Jersey, 1940s (nicks in enamel)........ **29**

Tap knob, Bakelite, w/enamel insert, Ballantine Beer, Ballantine Brewing Co., Newark, New Jersey, 1940s (overall light wear)... **23**

Tap knob, Bakelite w/enamel insert, Ballantine Beer, Ballantine Brewing Co., Newark, New Jersey, 1940s (wear) **29**

Tap knob, Bakelite w/enamel insert, Beverwyck Ale, Beverwyck Brewing Co., Albany, New York, 1950s (wear & dings to knob).. **29**

Budweiser Beer Knob

Tap knob, Bakelite, w/enamel insert, Budweiser Beer, Anheuser-Busch Brewing

Co., St. Louis, Missouri, 1940s, heavy wear & scuffs overall (ILLUS.) **50**

Tap knob, Bakelite, w/enamel insert, Budweiser Beer, Anheuser-Busch Brewing Co., St. Louis, Missouri, 1940s (a few small nicks & scuffs) **60**

Tap knob, Bakelite, w/enamel insert, Dab Beer, Dortmunder Brewing Co., Dortmund, Germany, 1950s (wear, small chip in knob) **45**

Tap knob, Bakelite w/enamel insert, F&S Beer, F&S Brewing Co., Shamokin, Pennsylvania, 1940s (overall light wear) **48**

Tap knob, Bakelite w/enamel insert, Falstaff Beer, Falstaff Brewing Co., St. Louis, Missouri, 1940s (chips in insert, overall heavy wear) **42**

Tap knob, Bakelite w/enamel insert, Gambrinus Beer, Wagner Brewing Co., Columbus, Ohio, 1940s (overall wear, peeling chrome plating on insert) **60**

Tap knob, Bakelite w/enamel insert, Genesee 12 Horse, Genesee Brewing Co., Rochester, New York, 1950s (heavy wear overall, oxidation on stem) **44**

Tap knob, Bakelite w/enamel insert, Genesee All Malt, Genesee Brewing Co., Rochester, New York, 1940s (wear to knob, scratches on stem) **99**

Genesee Beer Knob

Tap knob, Bakelite w/enamel insert, Genesee Beer, Genesee Brewing Co., Rochester, New York, 1950s, wear, oxidation on stem (ILLUS.) **33**

Tap knob, Bakelite w/enamel insert, Genesee Light Cream Ale, Genesee Brewing Co., Rochester, New York, 1940s (wear to knob) **47**

Tap knob, Bakelite w/enamel insert, Gibbons Beer, Lion Inc., Wilkes-Barre, Pennsylvania, 1940s (small scratches overall) **30**

Tap knob, Bakelite w/enamel insert, Pschorr Brau, brewery not listed, Munich, Germany, 1950s (wear, dings in base of knob) **30**

Tap knob, Bakelite w/enamel insert, Rams Head Ale, Adam Scheidt Brewing Co., Norristown, Pennsylvania, 1940s (a few scratches) **35**

Tap knob, Bakelite w/enamel insert, Rex Pilsner Beer, Burger Brewing Co., Cincinnati, Ohio, 1950s (stained & dinged knob) **100**

Tap knob, Bakelite w/enamel insert, Trommer's White Label, Trommer Brewing Co., Orange, New Jersey, 1940s (wear to knob) **30**

Tap knob, Bakelite w/enamel insert, Utica Club Beer, West End Brewing Co., Utica, New York, 1950s (small nicks in knob) **51**

Tap knob, Bakelite w/enamel insert, Utica Club Pilsener, West End Brewing Co., Utica, New York, 1940s (wear to knob) **49**

Tap knob, Bakelite w/enamel insert, Yuengling Beer, Yuengling Brewing Co., Pottsville, Pennsylvania, 1950s (light wear) **42**

Yonkers Beer Knob

Tap knob, Bakelite w/front & back enamel inserts, Yonkers Beer, Yonkers Colonial, Yonkers, New York, 1930s, overall wear, scuffs, missing half of enamel on rear insert (ILLUS.) **136**

Tap knob, Bakelite w/metal insert, Hohenadel Brewery, Hohenadel Brewing Co., Philadelphia, Pennsylvania, 1940s (wear, scratches to insert) **68**

Tax certificate, Internal Revenue Service, for brewers producing less than 500 barrels per year, from fiscal year 1875, punched w/triangle-shaped punch for cancellation, overall frame size 19 x 11 1/4" **35**

Toy train car, HO scale reefer, Ballantine Ale, Ballantine Brewing Co., Newark, New Jersey, 1970s (some grime, broken coupler) **20**

Toy train car, HO scale reefer, Budweiser Beer, Anheuser-Busch Brewing Co., St. Louis, Missouri, 1970s (applied weathering, some wear to print) **27**

Toy train car, HO scale reefer, Coors Beer, Coors Brewing Co., Golden, Colorado, 1970s **21**

Toy train car, HO scale reefer, Edelweiss Brew, Edelweiss Brewing Co., Chicago, Illinois, 1970s (missing brake wheel) **27**

CANES & WALKING STICKS

Carved ivory cane, large carved elephant ivory handle in the form of a jockey hugging the extended neck of a racing horse, finely carved, horse w/inset yellow glass eyes, full bark malacca shaft w/silver collar & metal & iron ferrule, probably American-made, ca. 1870, handle 5 1/2" l., 1 3/4" h., overall 33 7/8" l. **$5,040**

Carved ivory cane, the elephant ivory handle carved in the form of a lobster, gold gilt collar on stepped partridgewood shaft w/replaced brass ferrule, probably American-made, ca. 1880, handle 4 1/2" l., 2" h., overall 34 1/2" l. (old worn-down chip on one side of handle away from carving).. **896**

Carved ivory walking stick, erotic carved elephant ivory head in the form of a large devil head above a clinging nude maiden, tightly stepped partridgewood shaft, decorated silver collar & replaced brass ferrule, Europe, ca. 1860, handle 5 3/4" h., overall 36 1/4" l. **5,880**

Carved wood cane, carved Indian head handle w/metal ferule & cap, probably fraternity piece w/various names carved into it including "Dartmouth," "F.X. Heep" & "Tommy Rae" as well as an armorial shield w/"Delta Delta" & "1928," 36" l. (minor edge wear) **468**

Carved wood cane, carved snake twining around the cane & swallowing a person, dry, alligatored black paint w/black stripes on snake, 36" l. (minor wear)............. **468**

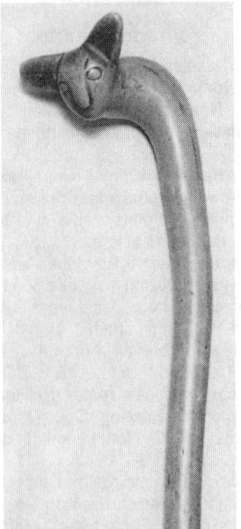

Animal Head Cane

Carved wood cane, knot handle carved in the likeness of a wide-eyed animal head w/big ears, possibly a stylized cat, 33 1/2" l. (ILLUS.) **413**

Carved wood cane, shaped handle w/carved free floating balls in boxes,

37 1/2" l. (dark red paint covers small glued break) **143**

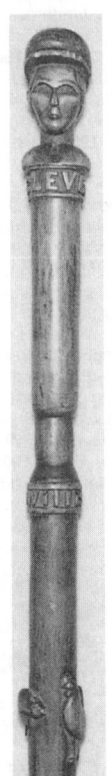

Folk Art Inscribed Cane

Carved wood cane, the knob carved in the form of the head of a man wearing a high billed cap, "To Lev from C.F.I., Williston, N.D." carved directly below knob, shaft decorated w/forms of an animal stalking a rooster, some edge damage, 37" l. (ILLUS.) **330**

Gadget cane, molded white metal handle in the shape of a stylized bird w/its head turned over its back & forming an ocarina w/pierced holes along the top back, head marked w/French maker's name "Mathieu" & "S.G.D.G.," hardwood shaft, brass & iron ferrule, ca. 1890, head 4" h., overall 34" l.. **1,456**

Inlaid silver-headed walking stick, silver handle w/faceted & engraved top above eight long oval panels, four engraved w/flowers, leaves & scrolls & the others w/an engraved inscription dated 1863, the top inset w/a faceted & polished piece of gold quartz w/lots of bright raw gold, heavy lignum vitae shaft & silver & iron ferrule, handle 2 1/4" h., overall 35 3/4" l.. **9,520**

Ivory & oak walking stick, elephant ivory knob handle inlaid at the top w/a small spherule of ebony, coin silver collar w/dated 1823 inscription, American-made, handle 1 3/4" h., overall 33" l............. **728**

Ivory & wood walking stick, presentation-type, ivory knop, w/silver band on shaft engraved "U.S. Frigate Constitution 1797. J.L.S.," brass & iron tip, America, 1797, 35" l. (age cracks on ivory)............... **1,293**

Pietra dura-inlaid cane, square tau handle of black hardstone inlaid w/Italian pietra dura designs of colored hardstones forming lily-of-the-valley & small blue flowers & green leaves, Art Deco-style design, ebony shaft, silver collar w/worn London hallmarks & replaced brass ferrule, ca. 1920s, head 4" h., overall 36 1/2" l............ **2,128**

Porcelain-head cane, the handle in tau-shape, KPM-Berlin porcelain w/molded scrolls & a full-figure molded head of an 18th c. lady at one end, painted w/realistic facial features & trimmed w/purple, yellow, blue & gold decoration, mounted on an ebony shaft w/gold collar, horn ferrule, ca. 1890, handle 4 1/4" l., 2" h., overall 38 1/2" l. **1,792**

Silver watch-head walking stick, French silver patented handle, round w/decorated sides & stem & flip-up lid over a white enamel-dialed working watch, snakewood shaft w/horn ferrule, ca. 1890, handle 1 1/4" h., overall 33 1/3" l. (several surface cracks in shaft)................................. **2,016**

Wood walking stick, Civil War commemorative, dog's head finial w/silver collar inscribed "Thos. Thompson Co. H. 106 Regt. Pa. Vols. Evacuation of York Town 1862," the natural branch carved w/a dog, squirrel, leafy vine & reeded & geometric devices, America, 1862, 36 1/4" l. **764**

Wooden Folk Art cane, presentation cane w/fist carved on cane top & carved snake spiraling up the shaft, silver plaque engraved "Made at camp A Hospital near South Mountain and Presented to H.C. Gray by J.C. Barlow & Th's Blasland of the 15th M.T. Feb. 1863," America, 36" l. **764**

CANS & CONTAINERS

Animal powder, "Bickmorine Bickmore Powder," shaker can, upright flattened oval shape w/short neck & cap, yellow background w/black wording & image of a horse, early 20th c., 2 1/2" w., 4 1/4" h. **$33**

Auto paste wax & cleaner, "Cities Service Auto Paste Cleaner & Wax," 8 oz. can, short cylindrical form w/pry-off lid, red & white background w/orange bands & white wording, full contents, ca. 1950s (minor nicks & scratches, minor wear & crazing on lid) **33**

Aviation oil, "Pureflight Aviation Oil," 1 qt. can, white & dark blue background w/blue wording & white logo at bottom, ca. 1950s (few nicks & dings) **99**

Early Buffalo Axle Oil Can

Axle oil, "Buffalo Axle Oil," 1 pt. can, upright rectangular form w/screw-on cap w/pouring spout, paper label in dark yellow w/black wording centering an image of a buffalo, early 20th c., some overall wear, no contents, cap missing (ILLUS.)................. **110**

Early Baby Formula Additive Can

Baby formula additive, "Peptonine - F. Coursol," cylindrical can w/paper label, gold lettering on pale blue ground, center round gold frame around color-tinted image of a cute baby, early 20th c., Montreal, Canada, 3" d., 4 1/2" h. (ILLUS.)................. **99**

Early Baking Powder Can

Baking powder, "Over The Top Baking Powder," 1/2 lb. can, cylindrical w/paper label, tan ground w/brown wording & large central reserve in white, tan & brown showing an early 20th c. woman holding the can, 2 1/2" d., 4" h. (ILLUS.)..... **413**

Bay State Bicycle Enamel Can

Bicycle paint, "Bay State Bicycle Colored Enamel," cylindrical can w/blue paper label w/dark blue wording & picture of early pneumatic tire safety bicycle, late 19th c., some rust, dirt & wear, 2 1/4" h. (ILLUS.)................. **61**

Biscuit, "Huntley & Palmers," bombe casket-form, each side w/a colorful panel depicting different sporting scenes including bicycling, skating, horseback riding, tennis & rowing, on outswept pierced tab feet, early 20th c., 5 1/2" h. (ILLUS. bottom, top next column) **385**

Huntley & Palmer Cabinet Tin

Biscuit, "Huntley & Palmers," china cabinet model, minor denting, some discoloration, 5 3/4" x 7 1/8" h. (ILLUS.)........... **500-1,100**

Biscuit, "Huntley & Palmers," triangular w/flat lid, decorated on each side & the lid w/a color sports vignette including runners & bicycle racers, w/lock but no key, early 20th c., 4 1/4" h. (ILLUS. center, top next column)...................................... **385**

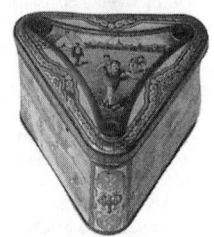

Three Huntley & Palmers Tins

Biscuit, "Huntley & Palmers," tall rectangular tin w/a flat lid, each side decorated w/a colored vignette of bicycling, rowing, tennis, horseback riding or skating, banded borders in blues, deep reds, green & yellow, early 20th c., 12 1/2" h. (ILLUS. top, above).. **330**

Views of Qckwork Brass Paste Can

Brass paste, "Hot Qckwork Brass Paste - Texaco," 1/4 lb. can, short cylindrical shape w/pry-off lid, green ground w/black & gold working & red, white, black & green Texaco star logos, no contents, scattered edge & field wear, 2 1/2" d. (ILLUS. of three views) **358**

Candy Tin with the Queen Mary

Candy, "Bensons Confectionary," short rectangular shape w/rounded corners, full-color scene of the Cunard Lines R.M.W. Queen Mary on the top, advertising around the sides, ca. 1930s, 5 1/2 x 7 1/2" (ILLUS.) **33**

Top of Whitman's Chocolates Can

Chocolates, "Whitman's Chocolates - Land, Sea and Air," cylindrical can, cover w/a dark yellow ground & black & pale blue skyline scene of Philadelphia w/pale blue panel & black wording, ca. 1930s, 5" d., 3 3/4" h. (ILLUS.) **48**

Early Bon Ami Powder Can

Cleansing powder, "Bon Ami Powder," upright rectangular shape w/rounded corners, small pry-off lid, paper label w/pale yellow background & dark red printing w/small scene of woman cleaning & the chick logo, early 20th c., 1 3/8 x 1 3/4", 2 1/2" h. (ILLUS.) **22**

Droste's Cocoa Upright Can

Cocoa, "Droste's Cocoa," upright square shape w/slightly domed lid, side panels w/red or pale blue background, lettering in gold w/royal crest logo in red, blue, gold & white, early 20th c., 2 3/4" w., 5" h. (ILLUS.) **58**

Cocoa, "Fargo Brand Pure Cocoa," upright tall flattened rectangular can, colorful paper label in red, white, blue & yellow, color image of a slice of cake & cup of cocoa, ca. 1930s-40s, 3 x 4 1/2", 9 1/2" h. **77**

Coffee, "Autocrat Pure Coffee - Brownell & Field Co.," 3 lb. can, large cylindrical shape w/white paper label w/a light tan rectangular panel w/red & black wording centered by a cup of coffee, early 20th c., 6 1/4" d., 8" h. **44**

Early Black Boy Coffee Can

Coffee, "Black Boy Pure Coffee," 1/2 lb. can, cylindrical w/fitted metal lid, paper label in dark orange w/black wording & image of a black boy wearing a turban, ca. 1920s-30s, 3 1/4" d., 4 1/4" h. (ILLUS. of front & back) **99**

Coffee, "Defiance Vacuum Packed Coffee,"
1 lb. can, printed w/narrow red, white &
dark blue bands w/wording in white &
black, a center oval w/a color picture of a
cup of coffee, ca. 1930s, 5" d., 3 1/2" h. **55**

Morning Joy Pure Coffee Can

Coffee, "Morning Joy Pure Coffee," 1 lb.
can, cylindrical w/keywind lid, black panel w/orange wording & black, white & orange oval panel w/bird singing at sunrise,
made by New Orleans Coffee Co., ca.
1930s, 5" d., 4 1/2" h. (ILLUS.)..................... **112**

Large Mount Cross Coffee Can

Coffee, "Mount Cross Brand Coffee," 3 lb.
can, tall cylindrical shape w/pry-off lid,
paper label in white w/red & white wording & dark blue & white view of a mountain peak, ca. 1930s, 5 1/2" d., 9 1/2" h.
(ILLUS.).. **198**

Colorful Peter Rabbit Pail-form can

Cookies, Peter Rabbit scenes, short oval
pail-form w/swing bail strap handle & flat
pry-off lid, full-color scenes around the
sides & on the lid w/Peter Rabbit & other
comic characters, ca. 1930s, 4 x 5",
2 1/2" h. (ILLUS.)... **135**

Early Crayel Crayon Can

Crayons, "Crayel Crayons - Made by the
Makers of Old Master - The Pressed
Crayon of Quality - Crayel- The School
Wax Crayon," long rectangular can w/fit-
ted flat lid, dark blue background, the lid
w/a large red diamond logo & white wording, white wording around the sides, ca.
1930s, 4 x 6", 3 1/4" h. (ILLUS.) **39**

Cup grease, "Polarine Cup Grease," 5 lb.
can, squat cylindrical shape w/fitted flat
plain tin lid & wire bail handle, sides
w/white background & red & blue logo &
wording, ca. 1930s, 6 1/2" d. (overall rust
spotting, scattered nicks, scratches &
wear)... **165**

Large Shell Cup Grease Pail

Cup grease, "Shell Cup Grease," 5 lb. pail,
yellow background w/red wording centered by the Shell logo, partial
contents, ca. 1930s, light to moderate
rust spots, dings & wear, heavy rust
spots on back (ILLUS.).................................... **127**

Engine grease, "Heccolene Grease," 1 lb.
can, short cylindrical shape w/fitted flat
lid, dark yellow background w/black
wording around the sides, the lid w/a
white circle w/black wording around a
white diamond logo, ca. 1930s (some
wear & scratches)... **33**

Engine grease, "Occident Elevator Premium Lubricant," 1 lb. can, cylindrical w/pry-
off lid, pale blue background w/shadow
image of a grain elevator above a black

band w/red & blue wording, ca. 1950s, 4 1/2" h. (tiny nicks & rim ding) **33**

Red Indian H.P. Grease Can

Engine grease, "Red Indian H.P. Grease - McColl-Frontenac Oil Company Limited," 1 lb. can, cylindrical w/pry-off lid, upper half in white w/red, black & white Indian Chief logo, lower half w/red & black ground & white & red wording, Canada, ca. 1930s, no contents, scattered nicks, dings & wear, 4 1/4" h. (ILLUS.) **385**

Firearm oil, "Howard's Perfection Oil," upright rectangular can w/rounded corners & screw-on cap, paper label in white, red & black w/small image of a rifle, ca. 1930s, 1 3/4 x 2 3/4", 3 1/2" h. **99**

Old Hartz Mountain Fish Food Can

Fish food, "Hartz Mountain Natural Gold Fish Food," rectangular can w/rounded corners, dark orange background w/black & white wording & color panel showing a yellow gold fish, full, ca. 1930s-40s, 1 x 2 1/4", 2" h. (ILLUS.) **14**

Early Atlas Food Coloring Can

Food coloring, "Atlas Colors For Food Products - Strawberine Red," 1 lb. can, square w/rounded corners, pry-off lid, yellow ground w/large center panels w/scrolled cartouche in pink, gold & yellow w/black & red wording, ca. 1930s (ILLUS.) **45**

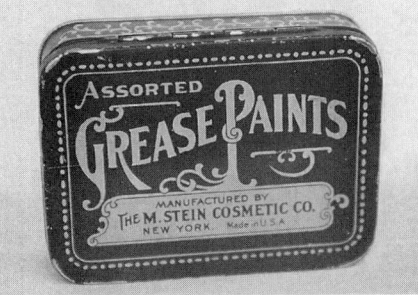

Early Grease Paints Can

Grease paint, "Assorted Grease Paints - Manufactured by The M. Stein Cosmetic Co. - New York," short rectangular shape w/rounded corners & fitted lid, dark green background w/white wording, full, ca. 1930s, 3 1/4 x 4 1/2", 1 1/4" h. (ILLUS.) **28**

Rare Early Gun Powder Can

Gun powder, "Dittmar's New Sporting Powder," upright rectangular form w/slightly domed top & small cap, dark red ground printed w/gold banding & a large black reserve w/pink & tan wording, ca. 1870s, 1 1/2 x 3 3/4", 5 1/2" h. (ILLUS.) **1,155**

Gun powder, "DuPont Indian Gun Powder," upright flattened rectangular shape, screw-on cap, dark red ground w/color oval paper label showing a Native American brave carrying a rifle, ca. 1908, 1 1/2 x 4", 6 1/4" h. **182**

Early DuPont Gun Powder Can

Gun powder, "E.I. DuPont de Nemours Powder Co. - Smokeless Powder," 1 lb. can, black cylindrical shape w/ribbed horizontal bands, round paper label on the top in black & white centering a scene of hunting dogs in the woods, early 20th c., 3 1/4" d., 3 3/4" h. (ILLUS.) **77**

Gun powder, "Schultze Gunpowder," upright flattened rectangular shape w/small screw-on cap, paper label in sepia & black, ca. 1900, 1 3/4 x 3 3/4", 5 1/2" h. **66**

Yardley's Old English Lavender Can

Hair dressing, "Yardley's Old English Lavender Solidified Brilliantine," flattened oval can, the lid w/a color scene of an 18th c. peasant woman w/two girls & a dog, wording in white, early 20th c., 2 1/8 x 3 1/4", 1" h. (ILLUS.) **49**

Early Texaco Harness Oil Can

Harness oil, "Texaco Harness Oil - The Texas Company," upright rectangular can w/metal top w/screw-cap, the sides in light green w/a black barred panel enclosing the Texaco star logo & wording in red, white, black & green, no contents, early 20th c., overall soiling & wear w/thin paint in spots, 2 3/4 x 4 1/4", 6" h. (ILLUS.) **99**

Early Caltex Home Lubricant Can

Home lubricant, "Caltex Home Lubricant," oiler can, upright narrow oval shape w/screw cap w/attached tall thin spout, red & black background w/a red, white, green & black scene of houses & red, white & black star logo & white wording, ca. 1930s, full contents, very minor scattered nicks & scratches, overall 3 3/4" h. (ILLUS.) **363**

Household oil, "Mohawk - Bush, Mize & Stillman Hardware Co. - Atchison, Kan.," cylindrical oiler can w/center cap & tall metal spout neck, yellow background w/large black ring w/wording in yellow enclosing bust portrait of Native American chief, no contents, early 20th c., overall 7" h. (paint wear & soiling) **88**

Hydraulic oil, "Husky Quality Controlled," 1 Imperial gal. can, upright rectangular form w/screw cap & small bail handle, orange ground w/large black & white husky logo over brand name in orange above white panel w/black wording, no contents, ca. 1950s, 12 1/2" h. (minor nicks & scratches) **33**

Milk-E Sugar Cones Can

Ice cream cones, "Milk-E Success Sugar Rolled Cones," upright cylindrical shape w/fitted flat cover, dark yellow ground w/red wording & sketch of an ice cream cone, ca. 1930s, soiling, rust spotting, 12 1/4" d., 15 1/4" h. (ILLUS.) **38**

Lighter fluid, "Junior Shell," dispenser can, narrow upright rectangular form w/rounded corners, dispenser cap on top beside thin strap handle, dark red ground w/large yellow shell overprinted w/black panel w/yellow & red lettering, black & yellow wording below reads "Specially Prepared for Cleaning and Automatic Lighters," ca. 1930s-40s, 2 x 4 1/2", 3 1/4" h. (minor scattered nicks & scratches, light rust spots) **44**

Lighter fluid, "Oronite Lighter Fluid," 1 pt. oiler can, cylindrical w/center cap w/plunger-style dispenser, dark blue background w/thin red bands at the top & bottom, white lettering & red & white flame logo, no contents, ca. 1930s (scattered scratches, rubs & wear) **121**

Lubricant, "General Petroleum Parabase Lubricant," 1 gal. can, upright rectangular form w/screw cap, strap handle & angled metal spout on top, plain metal w/dark blue side panels w/white wording, no contents, ca. 1920s, 11" h. (minor to moderate scratches, rubs & overall wear) **413**

Marine oil, "Gargoyle Marine Oils," 5 gal. can, large cylindrical shape w/lid fitted w/tab edges & screw cap, wire bail handle w/wood grip, white background w/reddish orange gargoyle logo w/black wording, narrow band around base, no contents, ca. 1930s (light rust & wear) **138**

Mineral oil, "Stanolind Liquid Paraffin Heavy White Mineral Oil," 1 gal. can, upright rectangular form w/screw cap & strap handle on top, yellow background w/black stripe at the top & bottom, black & red wording, no contents, ca. 1930s, 10 1/2" h. (scattered overall denting, scratches & wear) **77**

Kleen-O Oil Mop Can

Mop, "Kleen-O Oil Mop - A Mop of Quality - Cleans - Dusts - Polishes," upright cylindrical can, dark orange ground w/black & orange wording, ca. 1930s, 3 1/4" d., 7 1/4" h. (ILLUS.) **18**

Motor oil, "Capitan Parlube Motor Oil," 2 gal. can, upright rectangular shape w/top cap & strap handle, white background w/thin red bands at the top & bottom, wording in red & white above a red & white image of an auto racing on a hilly road, ca. 1930s, 5 3/4 x 8 1/2", 11" h. **198**

Motor oil, "Conoco Motor Oil," 1 gal. can, upright rectangular form w/top cap & strap handle, yellow ground w/large rectangular white panel w/a large central color image of a Colonial minuteman w/blue & yellow wording, no contents, ca. 1920s, 3 1/2 x 8", 11" h. (overall wear, rubs, scratches & paint loss) **880**

Very Rare Crozoil Motor Oil Can

Motor oil, "Crozoil Motor Oil," 1 qt. can, cylindrical, dark orange ground w/a large white full moon w/black crows flying in front of it, white & black wording below, full contents, minor rim ding, few tiny scratches (ILLUS.) **1,100**

Early Gargoyle Mobiloil Can

Motor oil, "Gargoyle Mobiloil 'BB' (Heavy)," 1 qt. can, cylindrical w/screw cap on short top spout, metal w/white label printed w/red gargoyle logo & black wording, no contents, ca. 1920s, minor wear & soiling, 7 5/8" H. (ILLUS.) **220**

Hi-Val-Ue Motor Oil Quart Can

Motor oil, "Hi-Val-Ue Motor Oil," 1 qt. can, cylindrical w/a silver background & red wording w/small black sketches of an airplane, oil derrick & truck, ca. 1950s, empty, bottom punched, minor scratches & wear, new top lid installed (ILLUS.) **182**

Motor oil, "Polarine 'F' for Fords - Winter," 1 gal. can, upright rectangular form w/screw cap & strap handle, paper labels form white panels w/red & black logo & wording, ca. 1920s, 11" h. (overall denting) **204**

Motor oil, "Racing Sta-Lube Premium Motor Oil," 1 qt. can, black background w/gold lettering & image of early racing car, full contents, ca. 1950 (scattered dings, dents, rubs & nicks) **110**

Colorful Rajah Motor Oil Can

Motor oil, "Rajah Motor Oil," 1 qt. can, cylindrical w/red ground & dark blue bands at top & base w/dark blue front panel below the head of a rajah & wording in red & white, empty, ca. 1930s, new top & bottom, seam resoldered, minor rust spots on back, scratch & rust on front (ILLUS.) **413**

Early Shell Motor Oil Gallon Can

Motor oil, "Shell Motor Oil," 1 gal. can, upright rectangular form, large yellow side panel w/wording in red flanking the large black & white Shell logo, ca. 1920s, no contents, scattered denting & minor scratches, 11" h. (ILLUS.) **550**

Motorcycle oil, "C.A.M. Castor Additive Motorcycle Oil," 1 qt. can, dark green background w/thin red bands at top & bottom, white lettering & image of a racing motorcycle on each side, ca. 1930s (top punched, tiny scattered dings, thumb dent on back) **176**

Kemp Salted Mixed Nuts Can

Nuts, "E.F. Kemp Golden Glow Salted Mixed Nuts," 1/4 lb. can, low rectangular form w/rounded corners, the top & sides printed w/pictures of mixed nuts, brown panels on the lid w/black & white wording, wear to top, ca. 1930s, 3 1/2 x 6", 1 3/4" h. (ILLUS.) **15**

Early Cuticura Ointment Can

Ointment, "Cuticura Ointment," short cylindrical can w/fitted top, metal w/black & orange round label on the top, ca. 1930s, 2 1/2" d., 1 1/8" h. (ILLUS.) **7**

Signal Outboard Motor Oil Can

Outboard motor oil, "Signal Outboard Motor Oil," 1 qt. can, cylindrical w/pinch lid, black over yellowish green background, image of older outboard motor & green, black & red wording, ca. 1950s, full contents, scattered dings & scratches (ILLUS.) **330**

Fi-Na-St Peanut Butter Pail

Peanut butter, "Fi-Na-St First National Peanut Butter," 1 lb. pail, cylindrical w/fitted flat lid & wire bail handle, dark red ground w/red, white & gold wording & center color image of a man in a white jacket, ca. 1930s, 3 1/2" d., 3 3/4" h. (ILLUS.) **110**

Tropical Peanut Butter Pail

Peanut butter, "Tropical Brand Peanut Butter," 1 lb. pail, cylindrical w/pry-off lid & wire bail handle, white ground w/dark blue wording & scattered tropical flowers, ca. 1930s, some wear, 3 3/4" d., 4" h. (ILLUS.) **69**

American Milko Powdered Milk Can

Powdered milk, "American Milko Powdered Whole Milk," 1 lb. can, cylindrical w/keywind lid, white background w/blue band at top & bottom & blue center panel w/name in white over picture of a pretty young girl, other wording in red & dark blue, ca. 1930s, slight scratching, 4 1/4" d., 4 1/4" h. (ILLUS.) **22**

Hurley's Boro-Iris Dry Shampoo Can

Shampoo, "Hurley's Boro-Iris Dry Shampoo," tall slender flattened oval shape w/shaker cap, tan ground & wording w/brown bands & brown & tan oval portrait of a cute baby, ca. 1930s, 1 1/2 x 2", 5 1/2" h. (ILLUS.) **121**

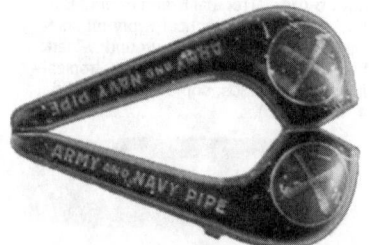

Army and Navy Pipe Tin

Smoking pipe, "Army and Navy Pipe," tin hinged figural pipe, black w/gold wording & logo, for a Manhattan size pipe, minor surface rust inside, 2 x 5 3/4" (ILLUS.) **99**

Spice, "Farmers Pride Whole Pickling Spices - Human & Co.," 3 oz. can, upright cylindrical shape, dark red ground w/gold bands forming panels w/advertising in white & gold & a central color oval showing a seated old farmer w/a young child, early 20th c., 2 1/2" d., 4 1/4" h. **71**

Great American Tea Spice Can

Spice, "Great American Tea Company - Cinnamon," small cylindrical can w/fitted copper-colored lid, paper label in pale blue w/black & white wording & a picture of a white cockatoo on the back, early 20th c., 1 7/8" d., 3 1/4" h. (ILLUS. of both sides) **44**

Jack Rose Cream Tartar Can

Spice, "Jack Rose Brand Pure Cream Tartar," 1/4 lb. can, flatted oval w/fitted lid, white background w/large red rose & green leaves flanked by red, green & black wording, ca. 1930s, 1 1/4 x 2", 3 1/2" h. (ILLUS.) **105**

Spice, "Juno Brand Tumeric," upright flattened rectangular shape w/fitted lid, red ground w/white & gold wording, black center band & oval reserve w/a white cameo-style profile of the goddess Juno, early 20th c., 1 x 2 1/4", 3 1/4" h. **55**

Spice, "Max-I-Mum - Chili Powder," 2 oz. can, upright flattened rectangular shape w/flat fitted top, red ground w/white wording & color central oval w/Arabs & pyramids scene, early 20th c., 2 1/4" w., 3 1/4" h. (slight wear) **66**

Early Karo Syrup Sample Can

Syrup, "Karo," sample size cylindrical can w/pry-off lid, dark blue label w/white & blue wording, full contents, ca. 1930s, 1 3/4" d., 2 1/2" h. **42**

Early Log Cabin Syrup Can

Syrup, "Towle's Log Cabin Syrup Absolutely Pure," rectangular cabin shape printed in color as a log cabin w/a large seated dog at one end below a window showing a boy, the side w/mother inside flipping a hot cake, a girl in winter dress standing at open door, banner above the front door, caption blocks by the figures, original tin cap, not made w/wheels, ca. 1930s, 5 7/8" h. (ILLUS.) **132**

Frontier Jail Log Cabin Syrup Can

Syrup, "Towle's Log Cabin Syrup," rectangular cabin shape printed in color as a log cabin w/cowboys inside & outside, sign over door reads "Frontier Jail," on metal spoked wheels, ca. 1930s-40s, wheels probably not original (ILLUS.) **154**

Family & Bear Log Cabin Syrup Can

Syrup, "Towle's Log Cabin Syrup," rectangular cabin shape printed in color as a log cabin w/boy carrying logs, mother cooking hot cakes inside w/a bear at the door, on red metal wheels, ca. 1930s-40s, 3 3/4" h. (ILLUS.) **165**

Log Cabin Tin with Family Scene

Syrup, "Towle's Log Cabin Syrup," rectangular cabin shape printed in color as a log cabin w/children playing inside & outside & woman cooking at open fireplace, on red metal wheels, sign at bottom edge reads "Log Cabin Express," ca. 1930s-40s, 4 3/4" h. (ILLUS.) **176**

Talcum powder, "Air Float Talcum Powder," upright flattened cylindrical can w/wide shoulder & small cap, white ground w/an oval panel w/a portrait of an early 20th c. woman framed by flowers & wording, 1 1/2 x 2 1/2", 4 3/4" h. **66**

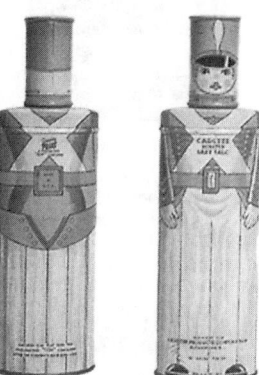

Cute Cadette Baby Talc Can

Talcum powder, "Cadette Baby Talc," 3 1/8 oz. can, tall slender flattened cylindrical form w/tall cylindrical cap, printed in color to look like a toy soldier, ca. 1930s, minor ding, 1 1/4 x 2 1/4", 71/4" h. (ILLUS.) **110**

Talcum powder, "Jergens Oriental Talcum," upright flattened cylindrical can w/wide shoulder & small cap, yellow ground w/colorful panels featuring a Japanese Geisha, early 20th c., 1 3/4 x 2 1/4", 4 1/2" h. **165**

Colorful American Ace Tea Can

Tea, "American Ace Tea," 4 oz. can, square w/pry-off lid, paper label w/light blue ground printed w/red & white wording & a color image of an early airplane pilot w/cup of tea who resembles Charles Lindbergh, ca. 1930, 3" w., 3 1/4" h. (ILLUS.) **72**

Monarch Green Tea Can

Tea, "Monarch Green Tea," upright square can w/fitted lid, colorful label w/name & lion head logo above color scene of tea fields, ca. 1930s, 3 1/4" w., 5 1/2" h. (ILLUS.)... **49**

Colorful Richelieu Midas Tea Can

Tea, "Richelieu Midas Brand Gunpowder Tea," 1/2 lb. can, square w/fitted lid, continuous color design of an Oriental landscape w/a woman on a bridge & flowering trees behind, wording in dark blue, gold, black, red & white, ca. 1930s, 3 1/8" w., 5 1/2" h. (ILLUS.) **35**

Early McCormick's Tea Bag Can

Tea bags, "Banquet McCormick's 100 Orange Pekoe Tea Bags," long rectangular can w/fitted flat lid, dark orange background w/black & white wording & trim, ca. 1930s, 4 1/2 x 7 1/2", 3 1/2" h. (ILLUS.)... **125**

Tennis balls, "Johnny Walker Tournament Tennis Balls," upright cylindrical can, red ground w/white rectangular upper panel w/image of tennis player, white panel w/brand below, England, ca. 1950s, 3" d., 8 1/4" h... **44**

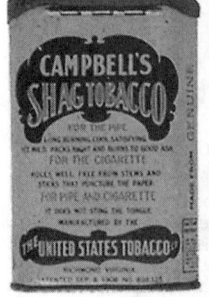

Unusual Campbell's Tobacco Tin

Tobacco, "Campbell's Shag Tobacco," pocket-size tin, flattened upright oval form w/pry-off lid, paper label in dark tan printed in black, the front w/a profile & shadow profile of a man smoking a pipe, the back w/advertising in tan, red & black, ca. 1920s, 1 x 3", 4 1/2" h. (ILLUS., of both sides) **440**

Scarce Niggerhair Tobacco Pail

Tobacco, "Niggerhair Tobacco," 1 lb. pail, cylindrical w/fitted lid & wire bail handle, dark orange background printed in black w/profile image of African native w/ring in nose & ear, ca. 1914, 5 1/2" d., 6 1/2" h. (ILLUS.)... **743**

English Cavendish Tobacco Can

Tobacco, "Pioneer Brand Golden Flake Cavendish - Richmond, Cavendish Co., Limited, Liverpool," short rectangular can w/hinged flat lid, exterior w/brown printed design & black wording, inside of lid w/original yellow, red & black paper print showing a bearded pioneer man seated near a log, England, early 20th c., 4 x 7", 1 7/8" h. (ILLUS.) **77**

Tobacco, "Repeater Fine Cut Mild Smoking Tobacco," short rectangular tin w/rounded corners, white w/red bands & color image on the top of a Royal Canadian Mounted Police officer on horseback, Montreal, Canada, early 20th c., 2 3/4 x 3 1/2" **55**

Diamond Brand Walnuts Can

Walnuts, "Diamond Brand Shelled Walnuts," 4 oz. can, cylindrical, dark blue ground w/yellow wording & pictures of nuts above large red & white diamond logo, ca. 1940s, 2 3/4" d., 4" h. (ILLUS.) **18**

CAROUSEL FIGURES

The ever popular amusement park merry-go-round or carousel has ancient antecedents but evolved into its most colorful and complex form in the decades from 1880 to 1930. In America a number of pioneering firms, begun by men such as Gustav Dentzel, Charles Looff and Allan Herschell, produced these wonderful rides with beautifully hand-carved animals, the horse being the most popular. Some of the noted carvers included M.C. Illusions, Charles Carmel, Solomon Stein and Harry Goldstein.

Today many of the grand old carousels are gone and remaining ones are often broken up and the animals sold separately as collectors search for choice examples. A fine reference to this field is Painted Ponies, American Carousel Art, *by William Mannas, Peggy Shank and Marianne Stevens (Zon International Publishing Company, Millwood, New York, 1986).*

Rare Dentzel Cat Figure

Cat, carved & painted leaping animal w/bird in its mouth, original realistic smoke grey body w/red & orange saddle & bird, Gustav Dentzel, Philadelphia, ca. 1905, park paint on polychrome trappings, rear piece of saddle missing, 52" l., 69 3/4" h. (ILLUS.) **$37,375**

Chicken, carved wood w/weathered surface, traces of paint, mounted on iron pole base, attributed to Herschell-Spillman, ca. 1915, 45" l., 53 3/4" h. (imperfections) **2,300**

Goat, carved & painted brown w/green glass eyes & horsehair chin, traces of white underpaint, mounted on a pole w/wooden base, probably American, 19th c., 35" l., 31" h. **1,610**

Horse, carved open mouth & side-swept mane, brown glass eyes, iron & leather bit, reins & stirrups, old surface w/wear, mounted on iron pole base, American, 19th c., 59" l., 43" h. **4,888**

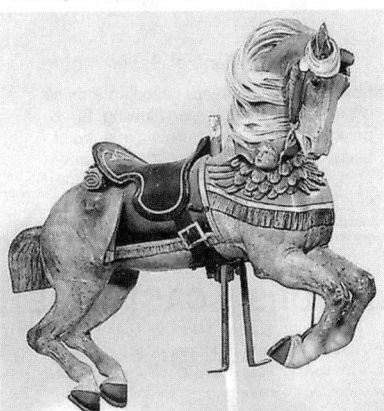

Fine Stein & Goldstein Horse

Horse, carved & painted jumper, dramatic carved mane & aggressive expression, chest carved w/a large buckle, fish scales & a cherub head, the body of Palomino coloring w/a brown saddle & gold trim, glass eyes, iron & brass attachments, Stein and Goldstein Carousel Co., Brooklyn, New York, ca. 1907-18, minor retouch to paint, carved tail partially missing, 64" l., 75 1/2" h. (ILLUS.) **21,850**

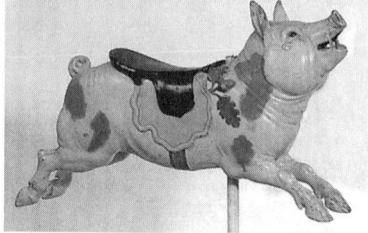

Dentzel Carousel Pig Figure

Pig, carved & painted, running animal w/head up & mouth open, colorful saddle & trappings including an acorn w/green leaves on one side, the body in peach w/brown spots, glass eyes, Gustav Dentzel Carousel Co., ca. 1905, some park paint, minor surface imperfections, pole & base missing, 50" l., 30" h. (ILLUS.)..... **11,500**

Very Rare Dentzel Rabbit Figure

Rabbit, carved & painted, galloping animal w/original fawn color w/billowing fur & polychrome trappings in original paint, glass eyes, Gustav Dentzel, Philadelphia, Pennsylvania, ca. 1905, minor crack in saddle seat, half of tail missing, narrow piece of ear missing, 50" l., 77 1/2" h. (ILLUS.)..................................... **63,000**

CASTORS & CASTOR SETS

Castor bottles were made to hold condiments for table use. Some were produced in sets of several bottles housed in silver plated frames. The word also is sometimes spelled "Caster."

Castor set, Simpson, Hall, Miller & Co. quadruple plated frame w/center loop handle

w/scroll decoration connecting the two-disc footed base, holds two amber pressed glass inserts w/plated lids w/ornate finials, fork hangs from center handle, 12" h.. **$475**

Pickle castor, amber, pressed glass, Heavy Panelled Finecut patt. cylindrical insert w/quadruple plated lid w/finial & frame w/arched handle w/ornate pierced decoration at top, simple round base, fork & tongs hanging at either side, 11 1/2" h....... **350**

Pickle castor, cranberry Inverted Thumbprint cylindrical glass insert w/bulging center panel, w/polychrome enamel floral decoration, Aurora quadruple plated domed lid w/ornate flame finial & frame w/arching handle & round ribbed footed base, 11 1/2" h.. **450**

Pickle castor, cranberry Inverted Thumbprint cylindrical glass insert w/polychrome enamel floral decoration & Rogers, Smith & Co. quadruple plate lid w/ringed finial, frame in elongated arch shape w/ornate decoration at sides, knob finial & saucer base, fork hanging at side, 8" h.. **350**

Pickle castor, cranberry Inverted Thumbprint cylindrical glass insert w/polychrome enamel floral decoration & Meriden quadruple plate round stepped lid w/ornate finial, arched frame, round base, tongs hanging at side, 9" h. (frame missing decoration from top of handle).......... **425**

Pickle castor, cranberry Inverted Thumbprint cylindrical glass insert w/quadruple plate domed & ringed lid w/finial & frame w/angled handle w/pierced decoration at top, round stepped base, tongs hanging at side, 13" h. **550**

Pickle castor, cranberry shaded ribbed optic cylindrical glass insert w/quadruple plated molded lid w/finial, frame w/angled handle w/ornate pierced decoration across top & bottom, round stepped base, tongs hanging at side, 12 1/2" h........... **550**

Pickle castor, Cupid & Venus patt. cylindrical pressed clear glass insert & original glass lid w/finial, Pairpoint gold plated frame w/arched handle w/pierced decoration at top, round footed base, applied decoration on sides, quadruple plate tongs hanging at side, 12 3/4" h. **250**

Pickle castor, ovoid Leaf Mold patt. translucent opal cased red spatter glass insert w/mica flakes, Empire quadruple plate oval frame w/wreath decoration, footed base, insert cover w/open finial & tongs, 9 1/4" h. **600**

Pickle castor, Pigeon Blood ribbed optic cylindrical glass insert w/bulbous base, Lexington quadruple plate lid w/finial & frame w/pierced decoration at base, fork hanging at side, 10" h.............. **375**

Pickle castor, pressed clear glass paneled cylindrical insert w/Derby quadruple plate lid w/butterfly finial & frame w/arched handle decorated w/owl & fan on crossbar near top & pierced decoration near round footed base, tongs hanging at side, 11 1/2" h.. **350**

Pickle castor, Royal Flemish glass satin finish bulbous insert decorated w/daisies & gilt highlights, w/Babcock quadruple plate gold-painted repoussé lid w/finial & frame w/reticulated feet, ornate angled handle, tongs hanging at side, 10" h. **2,100**

Pickle castor, Royal Flemish glass satin finish bulbous insert decorated w/pansies & gilt highlights, w/Tufts quadruple plate lid w/finial & footed frame w/arched ropetwist handle, tongs hanging at side, 10 1/2" h. **2,900**

Pickle castor, tapering ovoid cranberry insert w/white enamel floral decoration, Tufts quadruple plate lid w/ornate finial & frame w/arched handle, applied decoration & scalloped base on round stepped foot, tongs hanging at side, 14" h. **650**

CERAMICS

SEE ALSO Antique Trader Pottery & Porcelain Ceramics Price Guide, 4th Edition *(2003).*

Abingdon

From about 1934 until 1950, Abingdon Pottery Company, Abingdon, Illinois, manufactured decorative pottery, mainly cookie jars, flowerpots and vases. Decorated with various glazes, these items are becoming popular with collectors who are especially attracted to Abingdon's novelty cookie jars.

Abingdon Mark

Abingdon Leaf Ashtray

Ashtray, Leaf, in the shape of a maple leaf, white interior, black exterior, No. 660, 1948-50, 5 1/2" d. (ILLUS., top & bottom) **$20**

Abingdon Donkey & Elephant Ashtrays

Ashtray, round, black w/black donkey standing on top, No. 510, 1940-41, 5 1/2" d. (ILLUS. left, w/elephant ashtray) **150**

Ashtray, round, white w/black elephant standing on top w/trunk raised, No. 509, 1940-41, 5 1/2" d. (ILLUS. right, w/donkey ashtray) **150**

Abingdon Russian Dancer Book Ends

Book ends, figures of Russian dancers w/arms crossed at chest, fez-type hats, rectangular bases, white, No. 321, 1934-40, 6 1/2" h. (ILLUS.) **250-300**

Book ends, model of sea gull, spread wings, No. 305, ivory glaze, 1934-1942, 6" h., pr. (ILLUS. left w/model of sea gull) **150-165**

Book ends/planters, model of dolphin, No. 444D, blue glaze, 5 3/4" h., pr. **65**

Abingdon Chinese Bowl

Bowl, 9 x 11" oval, Chinese, gently flaring body on short rectangular feet, white floral decoration on white ground, No. 345, 1935-37 (ILLUS.) **90**

Abingdon Salad Bowl & Candleholders

Bowl, salad, 10" d., 5" h., Rope, scalloped rim, ropetwist foot, turquoise, No. 313, 1934-36 (ILLUS. center w/Quatrain candleholders) **75**

Candleholder, double, No. 479, Scroll patt., 4 1/2" h. **15**

Candleholders, Quatrain, quatrefoil shapes w/center hole for candle, turquoise, No. 360, 1935-36, pr. (ILLUS. w/Rope salad bowl) **50**

Console bowl, No. 532, Scroll patt., 14 1/2" l. **20**

Cookie jar, Baby, No. 561, 11" h. **750-1,000**

Abingdon Bo Peep Cookie Jar

Cookie jar, Bo Peep, No. 694D, 1950, 12" h. (ILLUS.) **375**

Cookie jar, Clock, No. 563, 9" h. **100**

Abingdon Daisy Cookie Jar

Cookie jar, Daisy, No. 677, 1949-50, 8" h. (ILLUS.).. 95
Cookie jar, Floral/Plaid, No. 697, 8 1/2" h. 350-550
Cookie jar, Humpty Dumpty, No. 663, 10 1/2" h. 208

Little Ol' Lady Cookie Jars

Cookie jar, Little Ol' Lady, No. 471, 9" h., various decorations, each (ILLUS.) 200-300

Mother Goose Cookie Jar

Cookie jar, Mother Goose, No. 695D, 1950, 12" h. (ILLUS.)................................ 425
Cookie jar, Pumpkin, No. 674D, 8" h. 550
Cookie jar, Windmill, No. 678, 10 1/2" h. 500

Wigwam Cookie Jar

Cookie jar, Wigwam, No. 665D, 11" h. (ILLUS.) 750-1,000

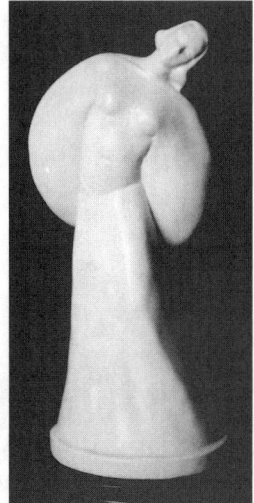

Scarf Dancer Figure

Figure, Scarf Dancer, No. 3902, 13" h. (ILLUS.)... 800 up

Various Flowerpots

Flowerpots, Nos. 149 to 152, floral decoration, 3 to 6" h., each (ILLUS. of three)........ 15-30

Abingdon Lamp Base

Lamp base, No. 254, draped shaft, 13" h. (ILLUS.)... 200

Abingdon Gull Figurine & Book Ends

Model of heron, No. 574, tan glaze, 5 1/4" h. **68**

Model of peacock, No. 416, turquoise glaze, 7" h. **96**

Model of sea gull, w/spread wings, No. 562, 1942, 5" h. (ILLUS. right w/book ends, top of page) **50-75**

Grecian Pitcher & Vase

Pitcher, 15" h., Grecian patt., No. 613 (ILLUS. right w/vase) **150**

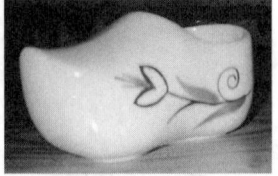

Abingdon Dutch Shoe Planter

Planter, Dutch shoe, stylized tulip decoration on white ground, No. 655D, 1948, 5" l. (ILLUS.) **95**

Planter, model of a puppy, No. 652D, 6 3/4" l. **50**

String holder, Chinese head, No. 702, 5 1/2" h. **500**

Vase, 3 1/2" h., No. A1, whatnot-type **100**

Vase, 5 1/2" h., No. 142, Classic line **40**

Abingdon Cattail Vase

Vase, 6 1/4" h., vertical ribs, three h.p. cattails, No. 152 (ILLUS.) **32**

Vase, 7" h., No. 171, Classic line **40**

Vase, 7 1/4" h., Fern Leaf, ribbed leaf-style sides flaring to bowl-style opening, green, No. 423, 1937-38 (ILLUS. right w/taller Fern Leaf vase, next page) **85**

Abingdon Delta Vase

Vase, 8" h., Delta, handles, ribbed base, rose, No. 108, 1938-39 (ILLUS.) **40**

Vase, 8" h., No. 132, Classic line **40**

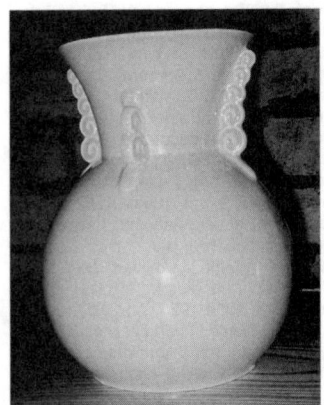

Abingdon Scroll Vase

Vase, 8" h., Scroll, bulbous body, neck w/four handles tapers out at top, green, No. 417, 1937-38 (ILLUS.) **80**

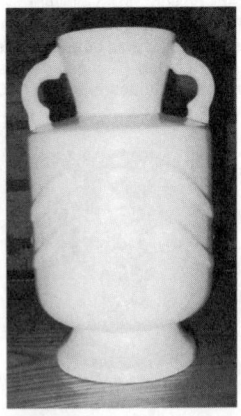

Abingdon Swedish Vase

Vase, 8 1/4" h., Swedish, handled, white, No. 314, 1934-36 (ILLUS.) **85**

Swirl Pattern Vase

Vase, 9" h., No. 513, Swirl patt., medium (ILLUS. of two) **20**

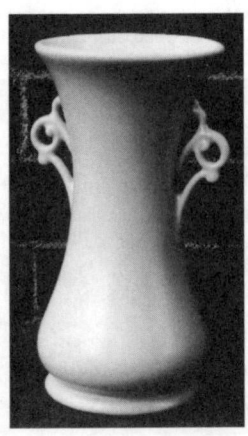

Boyne Pattern Vase

Vase, 9" h., No. 534, Boyne patt. (ILLUS.) **35**
Vase, 10" h., No. 114, Classic line **25**

Abingdon Fern Leaf Vases

Vase, 10 1/4" h., Fern Leaf, tall ribbed leaf-shape sides taper out to top opening, blue, No. 422, 1937-39 (ILLUS. left w/smaller Fern Leaf vase) **95**
Vase, 15" h., floor-type, Grecian patt., No. 603 (ILLUS. left w/pitcher, previous page) **150**
Wall pocket, figural butterfly, No. 601, 8 1/2" h. **150**
Wall pocket, figural Dutch boy, No. 489, 10" h. **150**

Abingdon Wall Pockets

Wall pocket, Leaf, overlapping pink veined leaves, No. 724, 1950, scarce, 10 x 5 1/2" (ILLUS. top w/Triad wall pocket)...................... **75**

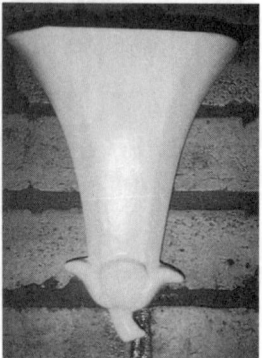

Morning Glory Wall Pocket

Wall pocket, Morning Glory, trumpet form, pink, No. 377, 1936-50, 7 1/2" h. (ILLUS.)....... **35**

Wall pocket, Triad, in the form of three pink connected flowerpots, No. 640, 1940, 5 1/2 x 8" (ILLUS. bottom w/Leaf wall pocket, previous page) **40-50**

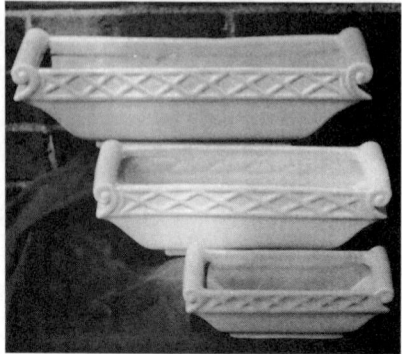

Various Size Window Boxes

Window boxes, No. 477, 13 1/2" l., No. 476, 10 1/2" l., No. 475, 7" l., each (ILLUS.)... **25-35**

American Painted Porcelain

During the late Victorian era American artisans produced thousands of hand-painted porcelain items, including tableware, dresser sets, desk sets, and bric-a-brac. These pieces of porcelain were imported and usually bear the marks of foreign factories and countries. To learn more about identification, evaluation, history and appraisal, the following books and newsletter by Dorothy Kamm are recommended: American Painted Porcelain: Collector's Identification & Value Guide, Comprehensive Guide to American Painted Porcelain, and Dorothy Kamm's Porcelain Collector's Companion.

Ashtray, decorated w/conventional butterflies in ochers, brown, yellow & apple green on ivory ground, signed "E.G.T." & marked "GDA, France," ca. 1900-1930, 6 1/4" d. **$35**

Berry set: 9 3/8" d. serving bowl & 5 1/2" d. individual saucers; decorated w/border design of clusters of pink roses, burnished gold rims & borders, signed "B. Bland, Feb. 1917" & marked "Haviland, France," the set.. **275**

Berry spoon holder, decorated w/two clusters of blackberries, light blue border, burnished gold rim & pierced handles, marked "Bavaria," ca. 1894-1914 .... **45**

Bonbon bowl, double-handled, decorated w/conventional-style dragonflies on an opal luster ground, burnished gold rim, ball feet, handles, signed "M. Sweum," ca. 1900-1925, 7 1/2" d. **50**

Cake plate, pierced handles, scalloped edge, decorated w/a four-panel design w/conventional-style flowers in each panel, burnished gold outlines, dotted grounds & rim, signed w/illegible cipher & marked "HR - Charlotte - Bavaria," ca. 1887+, 9 1/8" d. **75**

Celery set: 8 x 14" tray & twelve 6 1/4" d. coupe plates; decorated w/a conventional border design in yellow-browns, greens & purple on a ground of burnished gold dots, burnished gold rims & handles, signed "Ruth Lindorf" & marked w/various German manufacturers, ca. 1908-1920, the set... **275**

Chalice with Pomegranates & Grapes

Chalice, decorated w/conventional design of pomegranates & grapes on ivory ground, burnished gold rim, foot, borders & dotted background on the cup, marked w/a crown & two shields & "Vienna Austria," ca. 1890-1908, 9 3/4" h. (ILLUS.) **300**

Sugar & Creamer with Rose Design

Moth Decorated Creamer

Jam Jar with Plate

Creamer, decorated w/conventional-style border design at the top of yellow, yellow-brown, brown, banding blue & burnished gold moths on an opal luster ground, ivory ground below, burnished gold border, rim & handle, signed "Jennie - Katz. 1918" & marked "W.G. & Co., Limoges, France," 4 3/16" h. (ILLUS.) **45**

Creamer & cov. sugar, decorated in a conventional rose design medallion in polychrome enamels, burnished gold rim & handles, marked w/a palette & circle & "L," Belleek, 1906-1924, pr. (ILLUS., top of page) **125**

Creamer & open sugar, decorated w/geometric design in pale blue & yellow-brown, signed "C.B. Mook," ca. 1900-1920 .... **40**

Cup & saucer set, decorated w/flying swallows on opal luster ground, burnished gold rims & handles, marked "J & C, Bavaria," ca. 1902, set of 8 .... **250**

Hair receiver, cov., squatty round form on three gold curved legs, decorated w/conventional rose design in burnished gold, burnished gold rim & feet, signed "Ferver," ca. 1900-1910, 3 7/8" d., 3 1/4" h. **50**

Jam jar & plate set: 4 3/8" h. cov. jar & 6 1/4" d. plate (missing spoon); plate & jar lid decorated w/a border design of grapes & leaves in variegated blue enamels on a burnished gold ground, jar decorated w/same etched border design covered w/burnished gold, yellow luster border band & knob, signed "L. Vance-Phillips, 1917" (b. 1858, studio New York City), marked w/palette & circle & "L," Belleek (ILLUS.) **350**

Jardiniere, footed, w/attached gilded handles, decorated w/conventional-style peacock & flowers in pastel colors, burnished gold rim, signed "Mary Dobson" & marked "W.G. & Co., Limoges, France," ca. 1900-1932, 8 1/2" h. **400**

Lemonade set: 5 1/4" h. pitcher, 13 1/2" d. tray, six 3 3/4" h. handled cups; decorated w/conventional orange motif on an apple green border band, ivory ground, burnished gold rims & handles, marked w/various Limoges, France manufacturers, ca. 1900-1920, the set **500**

Mug, decorated w/border design of acorns on a burnished gold ground, black border band, celadon base, burnished gold handle, marked "Limoges, France," ca. 1891-1914, 4 1/2" h. **50**

Nut bowl, decorated in polychrome colors w/a squirrel, acorns & oak leaves on a branch, opal lustre interior, burnished gold feet & fluted rim, signed "Mrs. O.C. Oakes," 1900-20 .... **100**

Pitcher, 5 3/4" h., lemonade, bulbous body, decorated w/currants on a polychrome ground, ca. 1900-1920.................................... **225**

Pitcher, 6 3/4" h., cider, decorated on the top half w/conventional-style rural landscape w/shapes outlined in gold, burnished gold lip, handle, rim & border, signed "McCarty" & marked "D & Co., FRANCE," ca. 1905-1915 .... **225**

Plaque, decorated w/portrait of fashionable woman, signed "A.J. Riley" & marked "W.G & Co., France," ca. 1900-1910, 3 7/8 x 3 1/2" w. **200**

Plate, 6 5/8" d., coupe, decorated w/band of conventional roses & leaves on an ivory ground, pale green center, burnished gold rim, signed "P.M.T." & marked "BAVARIA," ca. 1892-1914 (ILLUS.)............... **20**

Plate, 7 1/4" d., coupe, decorated w/four Art Nouveau-style gilded water lilies on a pale blue border, ivory ground, marked "B & Co., France," ca. 1900-1915.................... **50**

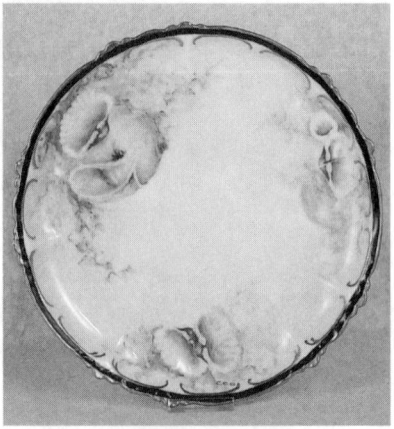

Plate with Sea Shells

Plate, 8 1/2" d., decorated w/sea shells & seaweed, black-green border band edged w/burnished gold scrolls & burnished gold rim, signed "C.C.O." & marked w/a crown, crossed swords & "R.C., Bavaria," ca. 1898-1906 (ILLUS.)........ **65**

Rose Decorated Plate

Crescent-shaped Salad Plate

Plate, 9" w., salad, crescent shape, decorated w/pink peonies & leaves, burnished gold stippled in spots on background, burnished gold rim, signed "JHK" & marked "T & V, Limoges," ca. 1890s (ILLUS. bottom, previous page) 50

Powder box, cov., round, lid decorated w/conventional floral design medallion & border band in pastels w/burnished gold leaves, baby blue ground, ca. 1900-1920, 4 1/2" d., 2 1/2" h. 40

Two-in-one Salt & Pepper Shaker

Salt & pepper shaker, two-in-one style, decorated w/a raised paste design of garlands of roses & forget-me-nots, covered w/burnished gold, forget-me-nots have turquoise enamel centers, ivory ground, burnished gold tops, handle & foot rim, base impressed w/mold number & "GERMANY," ca. 1891-1914, 4 3/4" w. x 2 1/2" h. (ILLUS.) 45

Soup tureen, cov., double-handled, decorated w/geometric border design in blue & burnished gold, burnished gold rims & handles, marked w/a crown & crossed swords & "Rosenthal, Selb, Bavaria, Donatello," ca. 1905-1920, 7 1/2 x 13", 5 1/2" h. 75

Stein, decorated w/Art Nouveau-style peacocks, black-green border, marked w/a palette & circle & "L," Belleek, ca. 1906-1924, 5 3/4" h. 150

Tobacco jar, cov., decorated w/conventional-style nighttime suburban scene, signed "Mangum," ca. 1910-1920, 5" h. 75

Toothpick holder, decorated w/double violets on a pastel ivory & green ground, burnished gold rim, signed "Wats" & "Pitkin & Brooks Studio" & marked "T & V, Limoges, France," 1903-1910, 2 3/4" h. 30

Vase, 4" h., decorated w/flying bat in front of an opal luster moon, wispy orange clouds, brown border band, ivory ground, marked w/a shield & crown & "Imperial, Austria," ca. 1892-1920 50

Vase, 6" h., decorated w/conventional-style parrots on grape vines, opal luster ground, lavender neck, opal luster interior, burnished gold rim & border, signed "Ella Resan" & marked w/a crown & shield & "PA, Arzberg, Bavaria," ca. 1910-1925 65

Amphora - Teplitz

In the late 19th and early 20th centuries numerous potteries operated in the vicinity of Teplitz in the Bohemian region of what was Austria but is now the Czech Republic. They included Amphora, RStK, Stellmacher, Ernst Wahliss, Paul Dachsel, Imperial and lesser-known potteries such as Johanne Maresh, Julius Dressler, Bernard Bloch and Heliosine.

The number of collectors in this category is growing while availability of better or rarer pieces is shrinking. Consequently, prices for all pieces are appreciating, while those for better and/or rarer pieces, including restored rare pieces, are soaring.

The price ranges presented here are retail. They presume mint or near mint condition or, in the case of very rare damaged pieces, proper restoration. They reflect such variables as rarity, design, quality of glaze, size and the intangible "in-vogue factor." They are the prices that knowledgeable sellers will charge and knowledgeable collectors will pay.

Amphora - Teplitz Marks

Bowl, 10 1/4" w., 5 1/4" h., consisting of two wonderfully detailed high-glazed fish swimming around the perimeter, each executed in the Art Nouveau style w/flowing fins & tails, tentacles drip from their mouths, high-relief w/gold & reddish highlights, rare theme, impressed in ovals "Amphora" & "Austria" w/a crown **$3,800-4,200**

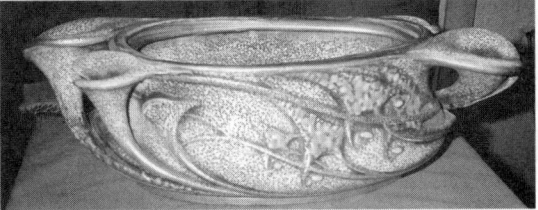

Exotic Paul Dachsel Bowl

Bowl, 14 1/2" w., 4 3/8" h., an exotic Paul Dachsel design of calla lilies growing out of stems which originate at the bottom & gracefully extend around the sides to fully developed calla lilies at each end, in the center on each side are several "jewels" w/abstract leaves of high-glazed green w/gold overtones, mottled texture w/"jeweled" greenish gold embellishments, stamped over glaze w/intertwined "PD - Turn-Teplitz," handwritten over glaze "0/45" (ILLUS., previous page) **5,000-5,500**

Bust of a Sultry Princess

Bust of a woman, perhaps Sarah Bernhardt in the role of a sultry princess, magnificently finished w/plentiful gold & bronze glazes without excessive fussiness, mounted on a base featuring a maiden on a horse in a forest setting, the bust seemingly supported by stag horns protruding from each side, impressed "Amphora" & "Austria" in a lozenge w/a crown, "1431" & "A" in blue, 13 1/2" w., 18 1/4" h. (ILLUS.) **3,000-4,000**

Bust of Richard Wagner

Bust of Richard Wagner, the somber looking composer mounted on a pedestal emblazoned "Wagner" on the front, the head w/a beautiful soft flesh-toned Amphora glaze, the pedestal w/a shriveled tan & white glaze w/shades of olive green highlights, one of a rare series of composers, impressed "Amphora" & "Austria" in ovals w/a crown, a circle w/"Imperial Amphora" & "250 -1," 19 3/4" h. (ILLUS.) **2,000-2,500**

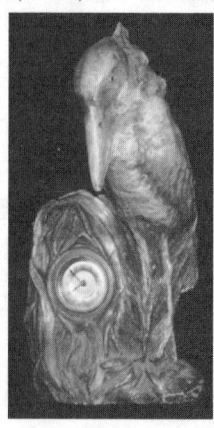

Rare Amphora Candlestick

Candlestick, rare Amphora piece w/many of its special characteristics including jewels, spider webs, butterflies & wonderful soft muted Amphora glazes w/reds, blues & gold, a large handle extends from near the top of the socket, four smaller handles extend up & outward from the base, eleven jewels of various sizes & colors, impressed "Amphora" in an oval & a crown & "28," 14" h. (ILLUS.) **4,000-4,500**

Centerpiece, an expansive bowl w/a "jeweled" effect along the rim, supported by two seated male lions w/fine details, a round base w/a "jeweled" effect, the underside of the bowl suggests a tropical jungle, a better example of a design featuring animals supporting a bowl, multicolored "jewels," lion in a natural brownish glaze, stamped "Amphora - Made in Czecho-slovakia" in an oval, "734 - 261" in black ink, 12" w., 9 5/8" h. **1,000-1,500**

Fantasy Stork Clock

Clock, table model, a fantasy stork, similar to Martin Bros. birds, stands next to a clock dial framed by Art Nouveau-style leaves, fine detailing, soft brownish tan glaze, rare, raised rectangle w/factory logo & "AK-Turn," impressed "319," 13" h. (ILLUS.).................................. **4,000-4,500**

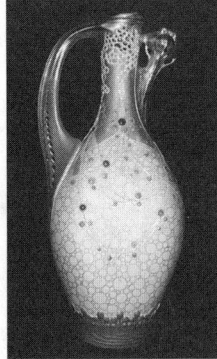

Amphora Teplitz Ewer

Ewer, an Art Nouveau design w/extraordinary detail combining a reticulated handle suggesting Paul Dachsel & varied circles on the body suggesting Gustav Klimt, a reticulated top, many "jewels" of different colors & sizes randomly located over the body suggesting a spectrum of stars in the Milky Way, unusual gold bud spout, high-glazed blue garlands randomly draped about the body, heavy gold trim on the upper part of the handle, top & spout, a subdued gold trim extends down the handle to & around the bottom where there is an abstract tree design, very difficult to produce, rare, impressed "Amphora" in a circle & "40 -537," 14" h. (ILLUS.)... **6,000-6,500**

Figure group, a small fine scenic figural group w/a rooster & hen perched side by side overlooking a pond, a small gold frog climbing into the pond, gives a barnyard feeling, soft muted shades of tan w/highlights of gold, a realistic theme & valuable because of the small size, impressed "Amphora" in an oval & illegible numbers, 6 1/2" w., 7 3/4" h. **850-1,100**

Unique Figural Humidor

Humidor, cov., figural, a fantasy piece featuring a large globe representing the world being shot from a tiny cannon & caught by a jester lying on his back, the jester reputedly represents a prime minister of the time, a hat at the top of the globe forms the handles, soft muted grey Amphora glaze, rare, impressed "Amphora" in an oval & "4216," 14" w., 9" h. (ILLUS.)...................................... **3,500-4,500**

Oil lamp-vase, a massive tiered form w/a swelled shoulder & wide flat-topped lower section decorated w/a variety of multicolored "jewels" w/a removable lamp font insert, rare, impressed "Amphora" & "Austria" in ovals & "8796/52," 12 1/2" h. .... **4,500+**

Plaque, a large oval shape centered by an Art Nouveau woman in high relief attired in a luminescent pink dress blowing a double-horned musical instrument and seated on a rocky ledge, the border of the plaque consisting of garlands of flowers & leaves in high relief, especially the buds, basic color of seafoam green, the surrounding florals in greens & tans, impressed "Ernst Wahliss," 17 x 19 1/2"...................................... **1,600-2,000**

Plaque with Art Nouveau Woman

Plaque, terra cotta rectangular form depicting a very stylized beautifully coifed Art Nouveau woman in profile in high relief, her unique elegance suggesting a woman of high social stature, the borders garlanded leaves & buds in high relief, organic mossy shades of green, soft purples, tans & warm browns, impressed marks "Ernst Wahliss - Made in Austria - Turn - Wien - 157," 11 3/4 x 17" (ILLUS.) **1,400-1,700**

Vase, 5 3/4" h., figural, elegantly executed Paul Dachsel creation w/a greenish cast & numerous vertical ribs extending up from the base, four intertwined gold-bodied dragonflies form a reticulated top, immediately below a series of smaller dragonflies encircle the vase, two multilayered handles within handles complete the design, stamped over glaze w/intertwined "PD - Turn - Teplitz," impressed "104".................................... **2,000-2,500**

Vase, 8 3/4" h., four-paneled high-shouldered squared form w/a front-faced Mucha-style Art Nouveau princess portrait, elaborate gold enameling against a landscape decorated w/blue & purple trees w/gold highlights above a base decorated w/Paul Dachsel-style abstract red flowers in a green base, impressed "Amphora" in oval & "579-40," red "RStK Austria" overglaze mark, artist mark "Fr" in gold overglaze **3,500-4,000**

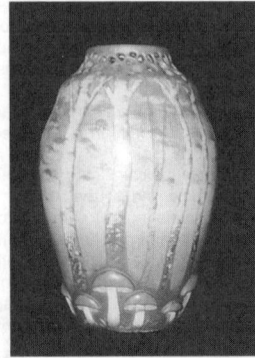

Paul Dachsel Forest Scene Vase

Vase, 9" h., a bulbous Paul Dachsel forest scene w/reticulated gold top & varied reddish mushrooms in high relief encircling the bottom, a production mold but h.p. to produce a uniquely different forest scene, stamped over the glaze w/intertwined "PD - Turn - Teplitz," impressed "1106 -2," blue overglaze "094" (ILLUS.) **3,500-4,000**

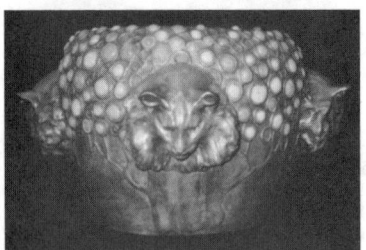

Rare Amphora Cat Head Vase

Vase, 9" h., wide bulbous tapering form, rare form suggesting an inverted Tiffany lamp shade, four large Persian cat heads molded in full relief & projecting from the sides w/a forest of abstract trees w/160-170 opal-like translucent "jewels" symbolizing fruits, the jewels in various sizes & shades of opal blue mounted in gold surrounds, heavy gold rim, the tree branches extending to the jewels on a background of Klimt-like subtle gold circles, holes behind the jewels permit candlelight or an electric bulb to illuminate the jewels, cat heads finished in a soft pinkish gold w/traces of green & gold highlights on the ears, impressed "Am-

phora - Austria" in a lozenge, a crown & "8183 - 28" (ILLUS.) **14,000-16,000**

Vase, 10 5/8" h., figural, in the form of a prancing male lion, snarling open mouth, standing on a broad base narrowing at the top, numerous concentric circles form bands around the top & bottom, lion reflects an iridescent gold, green & rose combination of color, body of base in metallic green w/undertones of blues & splotches of reds, impressed "Amphora" & "Austria" in oval, a crown & "500-52," handwritten in black ink over glaze "CB - 613417," estimated value without jewels, $1,500-2,000, value w/jewels **2,500-3,500**

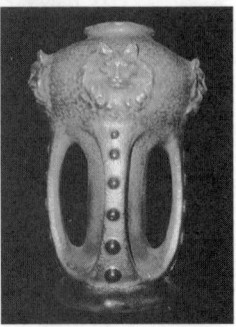

Vase with Persian Cat Heads

Vase, 11" h., four gold Persian cat heads adorn a center-pillared body w/four surrounding gold "jeweled" arms extending from each cat head to the base, metallic blue w/a gold wash, cobalt blue "jewels," rare design, more common versions have cabochons instead of animal heads, marked "Amphora" & "Austria" in ovals, a crown & impressed "Imperial" circle mark & "11677 - 51" (ILLUS.) **2,500-3,000**

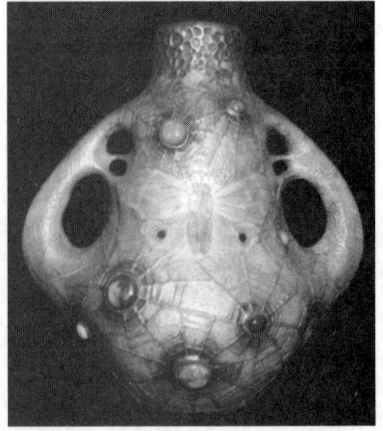

Ornate Jeweled Art Nouveau Vase

Vase, 11 1/4" h., tapering lobed ovoid form of exceptional Art Nouveau design w/numerous "jewels," spider webs & two butterflies w/heavy pierced extended handles suggesting a larger butterfly, 17 "jewels" in varying sizes & colors, red abstract circles drape from the gold-edged top, soft muted tan, red, blue & green glazes w/gold iridescence, impressed "Amphora" & "Austria" in ovals, a crown & "8551-42," red "RStK Austria" overglaze mark (ILLUS.) **4,500-5,000**

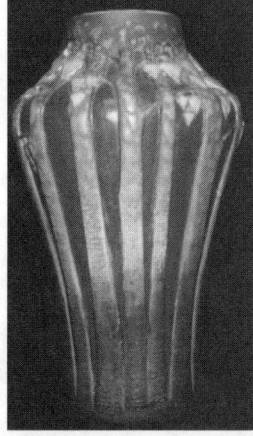

Dachsel "Enchanted Forest" Vase

Vase, 13" h., wide-shouldered tapering cylindrical body, a fantasy design by Paul Dachsel worthy of the description "enchanted forest," the design consists of slender molded abstract trees extending from the narrow base to the bulbous top, lovely heart-shaped leaves extend in clusters from the various branches, trees in muted green, the leaves in pearlized off-white w/gold framing, the symbolic sky in rich red extending between the trees from the bottom to the top, rare, intertwined "PD" mark rubbed off (ILLUS.) **6,000-6,500**

Vase, 14" h., figural, a fantasy dragon featuring two flaring wings, one extending practically from the top to the bottom of the body, the other well above & beyond the rim, creature w/a convoluted tail, spine & teeth, the head w/open mouth positioned at top of the vase, bluish green gold iridescence, glazes vary from a flat tan to a variety of very iridescent colors, made in 14" & 17" size, impressed "Amphora" in oval, illegible numbers, large size w/better glazes, $6,500, 14" size w/drab glazes **4,500**

Vase, 16 1/2" h., fine Paul Dachsel creation in an undulating freeform design consisting of several abstract trees extending from the bottom to the top where a branch wraps around the top & then down dividing into other branches w/a series of red-glazed leaves, numerous white "jewels" suggesting seeds & seed pods attached to the branches & trunks, red leaves w/gold-tinged ends, very rare form, stamped over the glaze w/intertwined "PD - Turn - Teplitz," impressed "1115" **4,500-5,500**

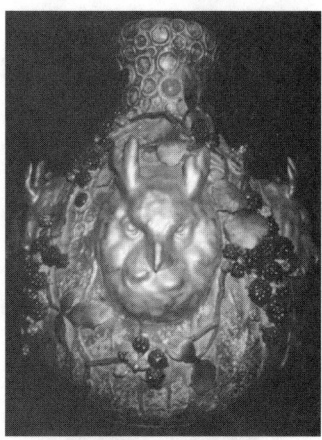

Rare Owl Head Vase

Vase, 17" h., massive bulbous bottle-form w/four finely detailed gold-finished owl heads projecting from the sides surrounded by brambles, leaves & many clusters of berries & numerous "jewels" of various sizes & colors interspersed among the brambles, unusual & complicated design, some similar pieces w/other animal heads exist but few survive intact, rare, impressed "Amphora" in oval, a crown & "8160" (ILLUS.) **8,500-9,500**

Vase, 17 1/8" h., tall Art Nouveau form gradually tapering to a narrower top, the bottom w/seven delicate female heads w/long flowing hair emerging from a swirling ocean, tan w/highlights of gold & green, a similar example found in a Berlin museum, marks include a raised Art Nouveau girl's head & "Amphora" in a raised rectangle, red "RStK Austria" mark over the glaze, impressed illegible numbers, handwritten "1081 - L - 372" over the glaze **2,000-3,000**

Rare Reticulated Amphora Vase

Vase, 17 1/2" h., an important reticulated piece composed of a basket-like vase within a vase elaborately entwined w/swooping gold handles joined in the middle, numerous varied colored "jewels" around the sides, viewed through the reticulation a high-glazed blue swirly design w/gold highlights is seen, the exterior w/a metallic bluish green w/gold wash & gold highlights, high-glazed gold rim, only one known so far, impressed "Amphora" & "Austria" in ovals, a crown & "3791-45" (ILLUS.)...................... **12,000-14,000**

Tall Vase with Pine Cones

Vase, 20" h., tall slightly tapering cylindrical form w/a widely flared base, boldly molded pine cones hang around the top section from symbolic green trees divided by red indented vertical panels, a Paul Dachsel Secessionist design, rare, stamped over the glaze w/intertwined "PD - Turn - Teplitz" & impressed "2038 - 6" (ILLUS.) **9,000-10,000**

Massive Amphora Mermaid Vase

Vase, 21" h., 18" w., figural, a wide squatty bulbous base centered by a tall neck, Art Nouveau style w/a mermaid clinging to

the top rim, her well-defined body extends down along the side, applied berries, vines & leaves complete the decoration, finished in a matte tan w/gold wash & highlights, bluish berries, red stems, greenish red leaves & a high-glazed gold rim, important & very rare, would be rare even without the applied foliage, impressed "Amphora" in oval & "07 - 7 - 3" (ILLUS.)... **8,000-10,000**

Vases, 10 1/2" h., footed bulbous ovoid body tapering to a slender cylindrical neck w/a flattened disk rim, painted in shades of purple, pink, green, blue, black & gilt w/the bust of a young maiden wearing a voluminous hood surmounted by a Byzantine crown surrounded by a gilt aura, a lower border of roses, the crown & roses w/applied bosses, one printed w/mark "Turn - Teplitz - Bohemia - R.St. - Made in Austria," the other impressed "Amphora," each impressed "2014 -28," pr. **6,900**

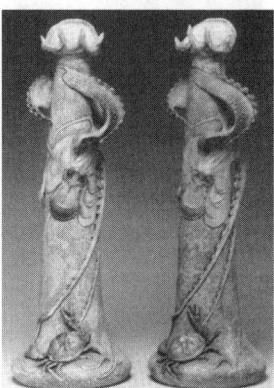

Amphora Sea Life Vases

Vases, 19 1/2" h., tapering cylindrical form w/cushion foot & spiky rim, applied w/a realistically modeled octopus capturing a crab, covered in a sponged blue, white & yellow glaze, the creatures in beige & burnt orange, printed in blue "AMPHORA - Made in Czecho-Slovakia" & impressed numbers, pr. (ILLUS.) **5,500-6,500**

Belleek

American Belleek

Marks:

American Art China Works - R&E, 1891-95

AAC (superimposed), 1891-95

American Belleek Company - Company name, banner & globe

Ceramic Art Company - CAC palette, 1889-1906

Colombian Art Pottery - CAP, 1893-1902

Cook Pottery - Three feathers w/"CHC," 1894-1904

Coxon Belleek Pottery - "Coxon Belleek" in a shield, 1926-1930

Gordon Belleek - "Gordon Belleek," 1920-28

Knowles, Taylor & Knowles - "Lotusware" in a circle w/a crown, 1891-96

Lenox China - Palette mark, 1906-1924

Ott & Brewer - crown & shield, 1883-1893

Perlee - "P" in a wreath, 1925-1930

Willets Manufacturing Company - Serpent mark, 1880-1909

Cook Pottery - Three feathers w/"CHC

Baskets and Bowls
Lenox, bowl, 10 1/2" d., 3" h., h.p. Art Deco cameos of tulips accented w/heavy gold, artist-signed "Clara May," dated "22," palette mark **$350**

Ott and Brewer, basket, applied floral & leaf decoration, crown & sword mark, 6 x 8", 3" h. **600**

Ott and Brewer, bowl, h.p. flowers on a cream ground w/gilded thistle handles, crown & sword mark **500**

Handpainted Bowl with Gilt Trim

Willets, bowl, ovoid form w/small h.p. sprays of flowers over entire outside, gilding on ruffled rim, foot & handles, serpent mark (ILLUS.) **600**

Willets, bowl, 6 1/2" d., 3" h., handled, h.p. delicate floral sprays, ruffled top trimmed w/gold, gilt shaped handles, serpent mark **425**

Willets, bowl, fruit, 10" d., 4" h., deep scalloped rim, h.p. inside & out w/images of grapes & foliage, highlighted w/heavy gold **700**

Candlesticks and Lamps
Lenox, candlestick lamps, hexagonal inverted tulip shaped shades, h.p. roses joined by green swags & gilding, artist-signed "Trezisc," palette mark, shades 6" d., overall 18" h., pr. **560**

Cups and Saucers
Ceramic Art Company, cabinet cup, on square footed base, enameled pink & gold saucer, 3 3/4" h. **175**

Ceramic Art Company, cup & saucer, "Tridacna" body shape, cream-colored exterior, blue lustre interior w/gold handle & trim, CAC palette mark, saucer 5 1/4" d. **350**

Coxon Belleek, demitasse cup & saucer, h.p. "Boulevard" patt. gold

around the rim of the cup & saucer, saucer 5" d. **125**

Cup with Sterling Holder & Saucer

Lenox, demitasse cup & saucer, colored porcelain w/double gold rim & pink border w/enameled flowers, hammered sterling holder & saucer, palette mark, 2 1/2" d. saucer (ILLUS.) **125**

Demitasse Cup & Saucer with Holder

Lenox, demitasse cup & saucer, cream-colored porcelain w/double gold bands, flared rim, sterling saucer & reticulated holder w/angled handle, palette mark, 2" h. cup, 2 3/4" d. saucer (ILLUS.) **125**

Morgan, cup & saucer, h.p. in the "Orient" patt., urn mark, saucer 5 1/4" d. **250**

Ott and Brewer, cup & saucer, "Tridacna" body shape, cream-colored exterior, blue lustre interior w/gold handle & rim, crown & sword mark, saucer 5 1/4" d. **300**

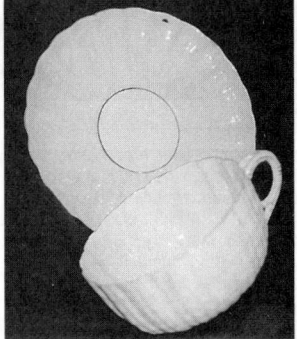

"Tridacna" Bouillon Cup and Saucer

Willets, bouillon cup & saucer, "Tridacna" body patt., pearlized pale blue exterior & white interior, serpent mark, 6 1/2" d. saucer (ILLUS.)... **225**

Willets, cup & saucer, coffee-size, cream-colored fluted body w/gold handle & trim, serpent mark, saucer 5 1/2" d. **175**

Jars and Boxes

Ceramic Art Company, box, cov., lid w/ruffled edge, h.p. w/violets & foliage, accented w/gold, CAC palette mark, 1 3/4" h., 3 7/8" w. **295**

Lidded Dresser Jar

Ceramic Art Company, dresser jar, cov., hand-decorated w/gold paste roses & stripes, CAC palette mark, 3 1/2" d., 5" h. (ILLUS.)... **220**

Knowles, Taylor & Knowles Lotus Ware, rose jar, cov., "Orleans," body & lid w/ornately patterned & pierced overall design.. **3,200**

Morgan Covered Mustard

Morgan, mustard, cov., h.p. cobalt band w/Deco-style enameled basket of fruit on front, gold-colored finial on lid w/opening for spoon, 5" h., 4" d. (ILLUS.)........................ **175**

Ott and Brewer, cracker jar & cover, hand-decorated w/gold paste flowers & gold handles, sword & crown mark, 5" d., 7" h. **475**

Willets, humidor, cov., h.p. college crest on one side & painting of cigarettes & matches on other, serpent mark, 5 1/2" h., 4 1/4" w. **375**

Mugs

Ceramic Art Company, Art Deco design w/heavy gold accents, CAC palette mark, 7" h... **295**

Baluster-form Mug

Ceramic Art Company, baluster-form, h.p. overall w/flowers & foliage on green ground, artist signed, CAC palette mark, 6" h. (ILLUS.)... **245**

Ceramic Art Company, h.p. peasant women in the Delft style of monochromatic blue on white, CAC palette mark, 5 1/2" h... **275**

Ceramic Art Company, h.p. scene of children flying kites, artist-signed "CHT," CAC palette mark, 4 3/4" h., 5 1/4" d. **325**

Ceramic Art Company, portrait-type, h.p. portrait of a Native American Chief, CAC palette mark, 6" h. **1,100**

Stein-type Mug with Grape Design

Ceramic Art Company, stein-type, h.p. all over w/images of grapes & foliage on blue & purple ground, CAC palette mark, 7 1/2" h. (ILLUS.)... **375**

Lenox, h.p. bird decoration, palette mark, 4 1/4" h... **110**

Lenox, h.p. off-white & multicolored poppies on a soft cream matte ground accented

w/gold & a gold curved handle, palette
mark, 7" h.. **200**

Mug with Plum Decoration

Lenox, ovoid shape, w/h.p. Deco-style blue
plums & foliage in cream panel around
top, lower mug solid green, palette mark,
4 1/2" h. (ILLUS.) **120**
Willets,   goblet,   toasting-type,
"Aforetone," h.p.,   artist-signed   "E.S.
Wright," dated "1903," serpent mark,
5" d., 11" h. **350**

Willets Belleek Mug with Monk

Willets, h.p. scene of a monk w/a wine
cask, deep maroon base & handle, ser-
pent mark, 6" h. (ILLUS.)................................. **325**

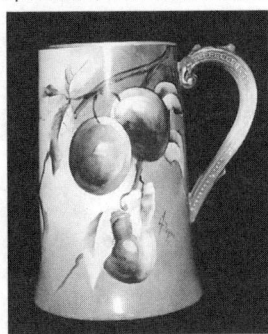

Art Nouveau-style Mug

Willets, ovoid form w/Art Nouveau-
style h.p. hearts & whiplash decoration in
pale lilac, serpent mark, 4" h. (ILLUS.) **85**
Willets, small h.p. bunches of grapes & foliage all around, heavy gilded handle &
rim, serpent mark, 4 1/2" h............................... **275**

Mug with Design of Ripe Plums

Willets, tall cylindrical form w/slightly flaring
base, applied handle, h.p. all over w/imag-
es of ripe plums & foliage, artist-signed,
additional "Darcy's Hand Painted, #6007,"
serpent mark, 5 1/2" h. (ILLUS.)...................... **270**

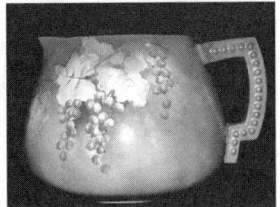

Artist-signed Mug

Willets, tapering cylindrical form w/gilt
handle, h.p. w/grape foliage on lilac band
on paler ground, artist signed "M. Schaf-
fer '10," serpent mark, 6" h. (ILLUS.) **145**

Pitchers, Creamers and Ewers
Ceramic Art Company, cider pitcher, h.p.
all around w/large pink roses & leaves,
accented w/gold, beaded gold handle,
CAC palette mark, 8" h., 6" d., ... **600**

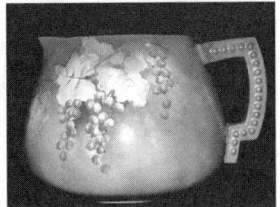

Cider Pitcher with Currants

Ceramic Art Company, cider pitcher, h.p.
orange & currants & pale green leaves,
8" h., 6" d., CAC palette mark (ILLUS.)......... **450**
Ceramic Art Company, pitcher, 6 1/2" h.,
tankard-type, h.p. grapes, leaves & vines
on rust ground, heavy gold accents, CAC
palette mark.. **800**

Lenox Silver Overlay Creamer

Lenox, creamer, cream-colored body
w/swags of silver overlay, 5 1/4" h., pal-
ette mark (ILLUS.) **110**
Lenox, lemonade pitcher, w/h.p. lemons &
foliage over entire body, artist-signed,
10 1/2" h., palette mark.................................. **750**
Lenox, pitcher, 9" h., jug-type, handled, h.p.
w/an overall floral design, trimmed in
gold, palette mark.. **600**
Ott and Brewer, creamer, cream-colored,
hand-decorated w/gold paste foliage &
an applied gilded thistle handle, crown &
sword mark, 3 1/2" h. **450**
Willets, apple cider pitcher, decorated
w/h.p. apples & foliage on purple to pale
ground, 6" h. **600**

Willets Jug with Cavalier

Willets, pitcher, 8" h., jug-type, handled wide
ovoid form w/short neck, h.p. scene of a
bearded cavalier seated at a table w/a
wine jug & goblet, serpent mark, (ILLUS.) **600**
Willets, pitcher, 11 1/4" h., tankard-type,
dragon-handled, h.p. w/wisteria, artist-
signed ....
.... **900**
Willets, pitcher, 15" h., tankard-type, h.p.
blackberries, leaves & vines on light
green matte ground, artist-signed "Fish-
er," serpent mark **825**

Plates and Platters
Gordon Belleek, plate, 8" d., decorated
w/birds, heavy enameling & gold trim **75**
Lenox, plate, 7 1/2" d., h.p. medallions surrounded & connected by heavy silver
overlay by the Rockwell Silver Company,
palette mark.. **65**
Lenox, platter, 16 1/2" l., Art Deco design
w/h.p. border & solid handles w/gold trim,
palette mark.. **130**
Morgan, plate, 10 1/2" d., decorated w/intri-
cate enameled design of fruit, flowers &
birds **225**

Salt Dips

Scalloped-rim Salt Dip

Ceramic Art Pottery, h.p. violets & leaves,
scalloped gold rim, CAC palette mark,
1 1/2" d. (ILLUS.)... **96**
Lenox, h.p. w/a soft pink ground & small
purple blossoms & green leaves w/gold
trim, palette mark, 1 1/4" d., set of 12 .... **500**

Footed Lenox Salt Dip

Lenox, three-footed, lustre body, gold-
trimmed feet & scalloped rim, palette
mark, 1 1/4" d. (ILLUS.).................................... **56**

Footed Willets Salt Dip

Willets, three-footed, lustre exterior w/gold
rim & feet, serpent mark, 3" d. (ILLUS.)........... **35**

Sets
Lenox, cider set: pitcher & six cups; h.p. red
apples, leaves & stems in an overall design, palette mark, cups 5" h., pitcher
6" h., the set **950**

Lenox Creamer & Sugar Bowl

Lenox, creamer & cov. sugar bowl, pedestal base, urn-form bodies, cream ground w/hand-decorated Art Deco design of enameled beading & gold paste, palette mark, 7" h., pr. (ILLUS.) **600**

Silver Overlay Creamer & Sugar

Lenox, creamer & open sugar, cream color w/silver overlay of flying geese, trees & foliage, palette mark, 3" h., pr. (ILLUS.) **325**

Lenox Rose-decorated Tea Set

Lenox, tea set: cov. teapot, cov. sugar bowl & creamer; each w/a pedestal base & square foot, boat-shaped body w/angled handle, h.p. w/pink roses & blue blossoms w/green leaves, gold handles & finial, palette mark, teapot 11" l., the set (ILLUS.) **1,050**

Vases

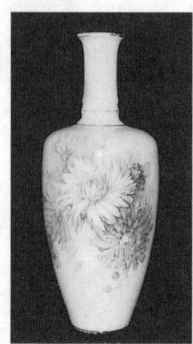

Vase with Chrysanthemums

Ceramic Art Company, 7 1/2" h., ovoid body w/short neck & flared rim, h.p. chrysanthemums on a light green matte ground w/gold trim & gold on neck & neck rim, artist-signed "DeLan," CAC palette mark (ILLUS.) **625**

Ceramic Art Company, 10" h., w/h.p. roses & gold embellishments, CAC palette mark **700**

Ceramic Art Company, 10 1/2" h., pearshaped body w/short neck opening w/slightly flaring rim, h.p. w/large pink roses on a green ground, high glaze, CAC palette mark **800**

Ceramic Art Company, 16" h., 7" d., portrait-type, cylindrical, h.p. Art Nouveaustyle standing woman w/flowing hair, CAC palette mark **1,600**

Knowles, Taylor and Knowles Lotus Ware, 8" h., 5" d., front h.p. w/a scene of a Victorian woman standing by a beehive looking up at two flying cherubs, the back w/a bouquet of flowers, applied "fishnet" work on body **1,400**

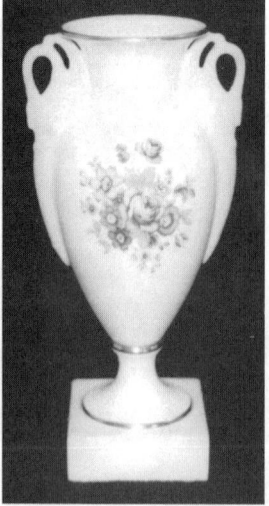

Early Lenox Urn-shaped Vase

Lenox, 8" h., urn-shaped on a flaring pedestal & square foot, swan's-neck handles, white ground h.p. w/a central floral medallion on the front & back, early wreath mark (ILLUS.) **300**

Lenox, 8" h., 3" d., h.p. flowers w/fine gilding, signed "Valborg, 1905," fluted top w/attached handle to side of tilted bowl, palette mark **650**

Lenox, 9 1/2" h., 3" d., cylindrical, h.p. bird on branch w/flowers, palette mark **450**

Lenox, 10 1/4" h., 3" d., cylindrical, decorated w/a stylized bird highlighted in gold, artist-signed "E.R. Martin," palette mark **300**

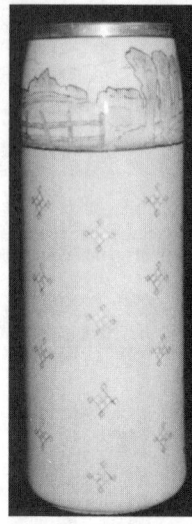

Lenox Vase with Landscape Band

Lenox, 13" h., cylindrical w/slightly incurved rim, a wide rim band h.p. w/a stylized country landscape & gold border, the lower body w/a pale ground h.p. overall w/diamond devices, palette mark (ILLUS.) **675**

Lenox, 18 1/2" h., decorated w/h.p. roses accented w/gold, heavily gilded shaped handles, palette mark **3,200**

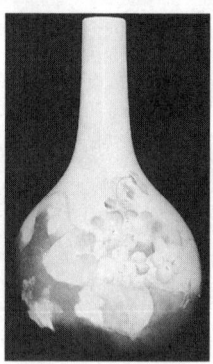

Willets Gourd-style Vase

Willets, 7" h., gourd-type, w/h.p. flowers & foliage on white ground, serpent mark (ILLUS.)... 325

Willets, 10" h., bulbous form w/all over floral decoration, artist-signed, dated 1905, serpent mark.. 1,200

Willets, 10" h., 8" d., bulbous body w/a short pinched neck & fluted rim, h.p. overall w/large pastel roses & foliage, serpent mark.. 500

Willets, 10 1/2" h., 6" d., h.p. Pickard decoration of a full-length Art Nouveau woman w/flowing hair & gown on a pink lustre ground, serpent mark.............................. 1,600

Willets, 11" h., 6 1/2" d., bulbous shape w/a short, small neck w/fluted rim, h.p. w/flowers & heavy gold paste accents, serpent mark.. 900

Willets, 12" h., tapering from a small top to a flared bottom, h.p. clusters of roses, artist-signed "M.A. Minor - 1902," serpent mark 1,400

Willets, 13" h., 9" d., bulbous shape w/a short pinched neck w/fluted rim, h.p. overall w/pink, red & white roses, serpent mark 1,850

Willets, 15 1/2" h., waisted cylindrical form, h.p. overall w/hyacinths w/gold accents, artist-signed "E. Miler," serpent mark 1,050

Willets, 15 1/2" h., 4" d., cylindrical w/flared bottom & flared scalloped top, h.p. completely w/pink & red roses on a soft pastel pink ground, serpent mark 1,200

Miscellaneous

Ceramic Art Company, loving cup, h.p. images of grapes & foliage, gilded rim, base & handles, topped w/figural children's heads, serpent mark, 8 1/4" h., 6 1/4" d.. 2,000

Knowles, Taylor & Knowles Lotus Ware rose bowl, 7" d., 7 1/2" h., cov., h.p. ornately patterned pierced cover & handles, applied gilded roses & "jewels"........ 2,500

Lenox Teapot with Roses Decoration

Lenox, teapot, cov., pedestal base on square foot, boat-shaped body w/angled handle, h.p. sprays of pink & white roses w/green leaves, gold band trim, palette mark, 10" l., 8" h. (ILLUS.) 450

Willets Sherbet in Holder

Willets, sherbet, porcelain insert in sterling silver reticulated holder w/pedestal base, serpent mark, 3 1/2" d., 3 3/4" h. (ILLUS.)...... 125

Irish Belleek

Belleek china has been made in Ireland's County Fermanagh for many years. It is exceedingly thin porcelain. Several marks were used, including a hound and harp (1865-1880), and a hound, harp and castle (1863-1891). A printed hound, harp and castle with the words "Co. Fermanagh Ireland" constitutes the mark from 1891. The earliest marks were printed in black followed by those printed in green. In recent years the marks appear in gold.

The item identification for the following listing follows that used in Richard K. Degenhardt's reference "Belleek - The Complete Collector's Guide and Illustrated Reference," first and second editions. The Degenhardt illustration number (D...) appears at the end of each listing. This number will be followed in most cases by a Roman numeral "I" to indicate a first period black mark while the Roman numeral "II" will indicate a second period black mark. In the "Baskets" section an Arabic number "1" indicates an impressed ribbon mark with "Belleek" while the numeral "2" indicates the impressed ribbon with the words "Belleek - Co. Fermanagh." Both these marks were used in the first period, 1865-1891. Unless otherwise noted, all pieces here will carry the black mark. A thorough discussion of the early Belleek marks is found in this book as well as at the Web site: http://members.aol.com/delyicious/index.html.

Prices for items currently in production may also be located at this site, especially via the 1983 Suggested Retail Price List. Prices given here are for pieces in excellent or mint condition with no chips, cracks, crazing or repairs, although, on flowered items, minimal chips to the flowers is acceptable to the extent of the purchaser's tolerance. Earthenware pieces often exhibit varying degrees of crazing due to the primitive bottle kilns originally used at the pottery.

Basket Ware

Basket, cov., oval, small size (D114-I)........... **6,000**

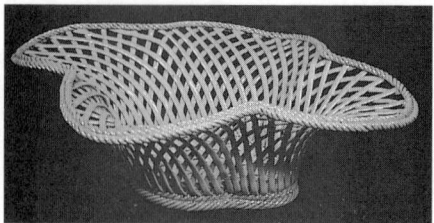

Lobed Belleek Basket

Basket, four-lobed form w/widely flared rims, D1693-1 (ILLUS.).............................. **3,000**

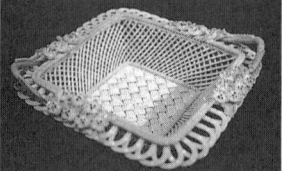

Belleek Melvin Basket

Basket, Melvin Basket, painted blossoms, D1690-5 (ILLUS.)... **800**

Two Belleek Shamrock Baskets

Basket, Shamrock basket, three different flowers around the rim, small size, D109-1, each (ILLUS. of two)................................... **520**

Box, cov., Forget-Me-Not trinket box, flower blossoms on the cover (D111-III)................. **600**

Belleek Flower Bouquet in Frame

Flower bouquet, hand-formed in green ware, features samples of all flower styles used on Belleek wares, mounted in a shadowbox frame, marked with two ribbons & "Belleek (R) Co. Fermanagh," ca. 1955-79 (ILLUS.) **2,200**

Unique Belleek Woven Mirror Frame

Frame, woven mirror frame, oval, unique, Second Period Mark II (ILLUS.)................. **4,000**

Menu holder, decorated w/applied flowers, various designs, D275-II, each....................... **600**

Comports & Centerpieces

Cherub Candelabra

Candelabra, Cherub Candelabra, w/drip cups, D341-II (ILLUS.)................................ **6,000**

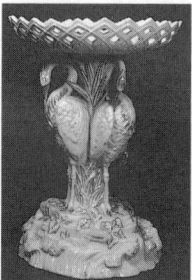

Rare Belleek Bittern Comport

Comport, Bittern Comport, figural tall birds form pedestal, gilt trim, D6-II (ILLUS.) **10,000**

Earthenware

Earthenware Bowl with Inscription

Bowl, deep sides, Celtic inscription that translates "Friendship is Better than Gold," D857-II (ILLUS.).................................. **400**

Jelly mold, deep slightly flaring rounded sides, design on the interior (D880-I) **460**

Pottery Scene on Earthenware Plate

Plate, 10" d., black transfer-printed pottery scene in the center, a crest on the flanged rim, D887-I (ILLUS.)........................... **400**

Toothbrush tray, cov., found w/various transfer-printed designs (D932-I) **440**

Floral-decorated Earthenware Tray

Tray, oval, brown transfer-printed floral design, D900-I (ILLUS.) **400**

Figurines

Belgian Hawkers Figurines

Belgian Hawker, female, fully-decorated, D15-II (ILLUS. right) **3,000**

Belgian Hawker, male, fully-decorated, D21-II (ILLUS. left)....................................... **3,000**

Bust and Figure of Lesbie

Bust of Lesbie, trimmed w/flowers & highlighted w/colors, D1651-I (ILLUS. right)..... **3,600**

Boy & Girl Figural Candlesticks

Candlestick, boy w/basket on shoulder, fully decorated & pierced, D1126-I (ILLUS. left).. **3,200**

Candlestick, girl w/basket on her shoulder, fully-decorated & pierced, D1137-I (ILLUS. right with Boy candlestick) **3,200**

Belleek Figure of a Cavalier

Figure of Cavalier, standing, D22-II (ILLUS.) **3,400**

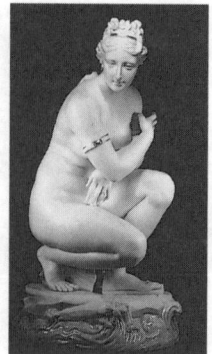

Rare Belleek Crouching Venus

Figure of Crouching Venus, gilt highlights, D16-I (ILLUS.) **10,000**

Figure of Lesbie, standing, highlighted w/colors, D1656-I (ILLUS. left with bust of Lesbie, previous page) **3,600**

Very Rare Horse & Snake Figurine

Model of Horse & Snake, D1139-III (ILLUS.) **12,000**

Museum Display Patterns (Artichoke, Chinese, Finner, Five O'Clock, Lace, Ring Handle Ivory, Set #36 & Victoria)
Chinese creamer w/dragon head spout & open sugar bowl, decorated (D485-I & D486-I), pr **880**

Chinese Pattern Teacup & Saucer

Chinese teacup & saucer, decorated, D483-I (ILLUS.) **520**

Chinese teapot, cov., small size, decorated (D484-I) **2,000**
Lace tray, round, decorated (D803-I) **6,000**

Religious Items & Lithophanes
Figure of the Blessed Virgin Mary, large size (D1106-II) **1,800**

Sacred Heart Font #4

Holy water font, Sacred Heart font, #4, D1115-III (ILLUS.) **260**
Lithophane, Madonna, Child & Angel (D1544-III) **3,200**

Child Looking in Mirror Lithophane

Lithophane, round, child looking in mirror, D1539-VII (ILLUS.) **480**

Tea Ware - Common Patterns (Harp Shamrock, Limpet, Hexagon, Neptune, Shamrock & Tridacna)

Harp Shamrock Plate for Butter

Harp Shamrock butter plate, D1356-VI (ILLUS.) **100**

Harp Shamrock Teakettle

Shamrock Marmalades & Mustard

Harp Shamrock teakettle, cov., overhead handle, large size, gilt trim, D1359-III (ILLUS.) **660**

Hexagon Pattern Teapot

Hexagon teapot, cov., large size, D407-II (ILLUS.) **600**

Neptune biscuit jar, cov. (D531-II) **460**

Neptune marmalade jar, cov., barrel-shaped, D1561-IV (ILLUS. right, top of page) **100**

Neptune marmalade jar, cov., cup marmalade, D1323-III (ILLUS. center, top of page) **100**

Neptune mustard jar, cov., D298-III (ILLUS. left with marmalades, top of page) **100**

Neptune teapot, cov., medium size, green tint (D415-II) **480**

Shamrock bread plate, round w/loop handles (D379-III) **180**

Shamrock Large & Name Mugs

Shamrock mug, large size, D216-II (ILLUS. right) **120**

Shamrock mug, Name Mug, impressed reserve for name, small size, D216-II (ILLUS. left) **140**

Shamrock Low-Shape Cup & Saucer

Shamrock teacup & saucer, low shape, D366-III (ILLUS.) **160**

Tridacna Boat-shaped Creamer

Tridacna creamer, boat-shaped, D247-VI (ILLUS.) **60**

Tea Ware - Desirable Patterns (Echinus, Limpet (footed), Grass, Hexagon, Holly, Mask, New Shell & Shell)

Echinus creamer & open sugar bowl, decorated (D647-I & D648-I), pr. **1,000**

Echinus egg cup, footed (D666-I) **400**

Grass coffeepot, cov., large size (D1402-I).. **1,600**

Grass Egg Cup with Crest

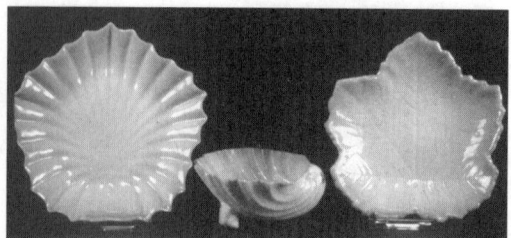

Cardium on Shell Dish & Sycamore & Worcester Plates

Grass egg cup, footed, crested decoration,
D754-I (ILLUS.).. **420**
Grass honey pot, cover & stand, model of
a beehive on a low table-form base, the
set (D755-I)... **1,000**

Small Mask Pattern Powder Bowl

Mask powder bowl, small size, D1548-III
(ILLUS.)... **160**

Tea Ware - Rare Patterns (Aberdeen, Blarney, Celtic (low & tall), Cone, Erne, Fan, Institute, Ivy, Lily (high & low), Scroll, Sydney, Thistle & Thorn)

Aberdeen Pattern Breakfast Set

Aberdeen breakfast set: cov. teapot,
creamer, open sugar & cups & saucers;
no tray, D494-II (ILLUS.) **2,200**
Cone teacup & saucer, pink tint (D432-II) **440**

Fan Pattern Teacup & Saucer

Fan teacup & saucer, decorated, D694-II
(ILLUS.) **600**

Thorn Brush Tray & Scent Bottles

Thorn brush tray & scent bottles, turquoise & gilt decoration, D333-I & D335-I
(ILLUS.)... **2,200**
Thorn teapot, cov., small size, decorated
(D759-I) **800**

Tea Ware - Miscellaneous
Items produced, but with NO matching tea set pieces.

Cardium on Shell dish, Size 2, pink tint,
D261-I (ILLUS. center, top of page) **180**

Greek Dessert Plate with Scene

Greek dessert plate, tinted & gilt-trimmed, h.p. center scene titled "Eel Fishery on the Erne," by E. Sheerin, D29-I (ILLUS.)... **3,200**

Armorial Souvenir Loving Cup

Loving cup, three-handled, armorial souvenir, D1503-I (ILLUS.) **400**

Shell-shaped Nautilus Creamer

Nautilus creamer, shell-shaped, pink tint, D279-I (ILLUS.) **600**

Shell creamer, large size (D601-I) **720**

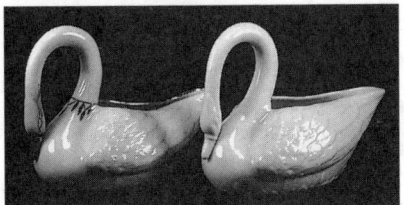

Two Large Swan Creamers

Swan creamer, figural, large size, D254-III (ILLUS. left) **320**

Swan creamer, figural, large size, D254-VI (ILLUS. right) **120**

Sycamore plate, leaf-shaped, Size 2, pink tint, D642-II (ILLUS. right with Cardium on Shell dish, previous page) **120**

Toy creamer & open sugar bowl, Ivy patt., small size (D241-I), pr. **240**

Worcester plate, Size 2, D682-II (ILLUS. left with Cardium on Shell dish, previous page) **120**

Vases & Spills

Belleek Coral and Shell Vase

Coral and Shell Vase, D133-II (ILLUS.) **880**

Belleek Flowered Spill

Flowered Spill, raised on twig feet, large size, D45-III (ILLUS.) **380**

Belleek Marine Jug Vase

Marine Jug Vase, coral designs, ruffled foot, D134-II (ILLUS.) **800**

Belleek Ram's Head Flower Holder

Ram's Head Flower Holder, figural, D1180-I (ILLUS.) **1,400**

Belleek Ribbon Vase

Ribbon Vase, flowered, D1220-III (ILLUS.)...... **340**
Triple Fish Vase, painted (D1231-I) **4,600**

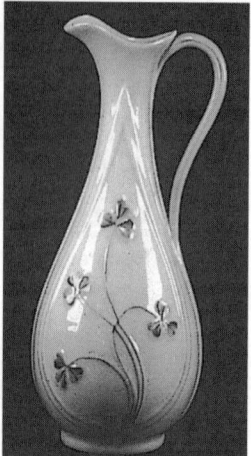

Belleek Typha Jug Spill

Typha Jug Spill, decorated w/shamrocks,
D1790-VI (ILLUS.) **120**

Blue & White Pottery

The category of blue and white or blue and grey pottery includes a wide variety of pottery, earthenware and stoneware items widely produced in this country in the late 19th century right through the 1930s. Originally marketed as inexpensive wares, most pieces featured a white or grey body molded with a fruit, flower or geometric design and then trimmed with bands or splashes of blue to highlight the molded pattern. Pitchers, butter crocks and salt boxes are among the numerous items produced, but other kitchenwares and chamber sets are also found. Values vary depending on the rarity of the embossed pattern and the depth of color of the blue trim; the darker the blue, the better. Some entries refer to several different books on Blue and White Pottery. These books are: Blue & White Stoneware, Pottery & Crockery *by Edith Harbin (1977, Collector Books, Paducah, KY);* Stoneware in the Blue and White *by M.H. Alexander (1993 reprint, Image Graphics, Inc., Paducah, KY); and* Blue & White Stoneware *by Kathryn McNerney (1995, Collector Books, Paducah, KY).*

Embossed Peacock Baking Dish

Baking dish, embossed Peacock patt., round w/heavy egg-and-dart-molded rim over gently curved sides, Brush-McCoy Pottery Co., 9" d. (ILLUS.)............................ **$800**

Miniature Uhl Pottery Barrel

Barrel, cov., miniature, Uhl Pottery Co., 2" d., 4 1/4" h. (ILLUS.)...................................... **80**
Basin, embossed Apple Blossom patt., Burley-Winter Pottery Co., 7" d. **165**
Basin, embossed Bow Tie patt. w/rose decal, Brush-McCoy Pottery Co., basin 15" d. **150**
Bean pot, cov., marked "Boston Bean Pot," 10" d., 9" h. **450**
Bowl, 3 1/2" d., miniature, w/bail handle, heavy dark blue rim band.............................. **50**
Bowl, 7" d., embossed Beaded Rose patt., A.E. Hull Pottery Co. **150**
Bowl, 9" d., nesting-type, embossed Pyramid patt., ... **130**
Brush vase, embossed Apple Blossom patt., Burley-Winter Pottery Co., 5 3/4" h. **500**
Butter crock, cov., embossed Apple Blossom patt., Burley-Winter Pottery Co., 7" d., 5" h. **500**

Cows & Columns Butter Crock

Butter crock, cov., embossed Cows and Columns patt., found in five sizes from 2 lbs. to 10 lbs., Brush-McCoy Pottery Co., ranges (ILLUS.) .... **425-650+**
Butter crock, cov., embossed Daisy and Waffle patt., 7" d., 6 3/4" h. **235**
Butter crock, cov., embossed Indian & Deer patt., Brush-McCoy Pottery Co., 2 lb. **800**
Butter crock, cov., embossed Indian & Deer patt., Brush-McCoy Pottery Co., 3 lb. **900**

Lovebird Butter Crock & Flying Bird Salt Box

Butter crock, cov., embossed Lovebird patt., A.E. Hull Pottery Co., 6" d., 5" h. (ILLUS. right with Flying Bird salt crock)....... **750**

Willow Pattern Butter Crock

Butter crock, cov., embossed Willow (Basketweave & Morning Glory) patt., bail handle, Brush-McCoy Pottery Co., 3 lb. (ILLUS.).. **285**

Butter crock, cov., stenciled Cows patt., 6 1/2" d., 5" h... **150**

Butter crock, cov., stenciled Wildflower patt., Brush-McCoy Pottery Co., four sizes available, each...................................... **150**

Three Diffused Blue Canisters

Canister, cov., Diffused Blue patt., "Raisins," "Salt" or "Tea," A.E. Hull Pottery Co., 5 3/4" d., 6 1/2" h. each (ILLUS.)............ **175**

Row of Stenciled Vines Canisters

Canister, cov., stenciled Vines patt., "Coffee," "Rice" & "Sugar," A.E. Hull Pottery Co., 5 1/2 to 6" h., each (ILLUS. center) **250**

Canister, cov., stenciled Vines patt., "Prunes" & "Oat Meal," A.E. Hull Pottery Co., 7 1/4" h., each (ILLUS. far left & right) **400**

Chamber pot, cov., embossed Beaded Rose patt., A.E. Hull Pottery Co., large 9 1/2" d., 6" h. **250**

Chamber pot, cov., embossed Beaded Rose patt., A.E. Hull Pottery Co., small **225**

Chamber pot, open, embossed Beaded Rose patt., A.E. Hull Pottery Co., large, 9 1/2" d., 6" h. (ILLUS., to the right) **250**

Chamber pot, open, embossed Beaded Rose patt., A.E. Hull Pottery Co., small **200**

Open Beaded Rose Chamber Pot

Swirl Pattern Coffeepot & Teapot

Coffeepot, cov., Swirl patt., tapering ovoid body w/a pointed rim spout, heavy C-form handle w/thumb rest, inset lid w/acorn finial, tin base, w/bottom plate, 11" h. (ILLUS. right, no bottom plate) .. **1,225**

Cookie jar, cov., Brickers patt., 8" d., 8" h. **750**

Butterflies Cuspidor

Cuspidor, embossed Butterflies patt., 6" h. (ILLUS.) **210**

Cuspidor, embossed Peacock patt., Brush-McCoy Pottery Co., 10" d., 9" h. **425**

Miniature Blue Swirl Cuspidor

Cuspidor, miniature, souvenir-type, dark blue & white swirl design (ILLUS.) **224**

Ewer, embossed Beaded Rose patt., small, A.E. Hull Pottery Co., 7" h. **300**

Bow Tie/Bluebird Mouth Ewer

Ewer, embossed Bow Tie (Our Lucile) patt., mouth ewer, Bluebird decal, Brush-Mc-Coy Pottery Co., 8" h. (ILLUS.) **275**

Small Willow Pattern Ewer

Ewer, embossed Willow (Basketweave & Morning Glory) patt., Brush-McCoy Pottery Co., small, 7 1/2" h. (ILLUS.) **365**

Small Wildflower Ewer

Ewer, stenciled Wildflower patt., small w/angled handle, Brush-McCoy Pottery Co., 7 1/4" h. (ILLUS.) **295**

Ewer & basin set, embossed Feather and Swirl patt., ewer 8 1/2" d., 12" h., basin 14" d., 5" h., pr. **550**

Embossed Lily Ewer & Basin Set

Spear Point & Flower Panels Measuring Cup & Two Pitchers

Ewer & basin set, embossed Lily patt., Red Wing Pottery Co., pr. (ILLUS.)..................... **1,750**

Grease jar, embossed Flying Bird patt., A.E. Hull Pottery Co., 4" h........................... **1,100**

Iced tea cooler, cov., w/spigot, Maxwell House, 13" d., 15" h. **325**

Apple Blossom Jardiniere

Jardiniere, embossed Apple Blossom patt., Burley-Winter Pottery Co., 6" h. (ILLUS., at left).. **425**

Measuring cup, embossed Spearpoint and Flower Panels patt., A.E. Hull Pottery Co., 6 3/4" d., 6" h. (ILLUS. top of page, center) **450**

Milk bowl, embossed Daisy & Lattice patt., Burley-Winter Pottery Co., three sizes, depending on size **200-275**

Mixing bowl, nesting-type, flaring sides, molded rim, embossed Peacock patt., Brush-McCoy Pottery Co., 6" d. (ILLUS. right, below).. **300**

Mixing bowl, nesting-type, flaring sides, molded rim, embossed Peacock patt., Brush-McCoy Pottery Co., 7" d. (ILLUS. center, below)... **325**

Mixing bowl, nesting-type, flaring sides, molded rim, embossed Peacock patt., Brush-McCoy Pottery Co., 8" d. (ILLUS. left, below) **375**

Graduated Peacock Mixing Bowls

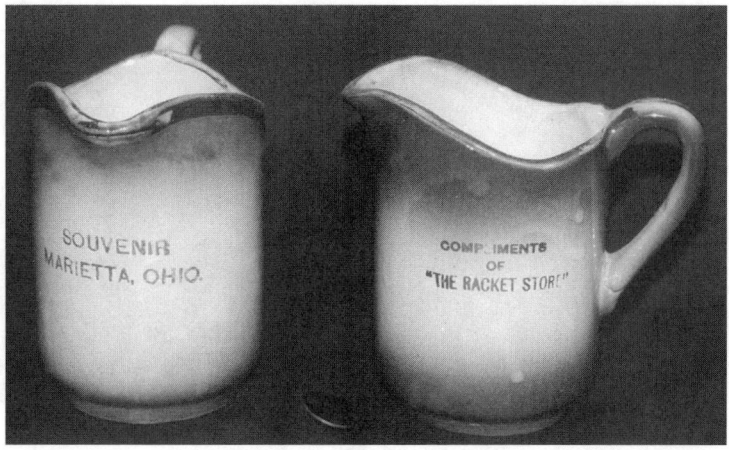

Miniature Advertising Pitchers

Mug, embossed Beaded Rose patt., A.E. Hull Pottery Co., 7" d. **500**

Mug, embossed Flying Bird patt., A.E. Hull Pottery Co., 3" d., 5" h. **200**

Mug, embossed Willow (Basketweave & Morning Glory) patt., Brush-McCoy Pottery Co., 3" d., 5" h. (ILLUS. left with pitcher, page 220) **175**

Mug, stenciled Wildflower patt., Brush-McCoy Pottery Co., 4 1/2" h. (ILLUS., to the right) **250**

Pitcher, Diffused Blues, miniature w/souvenir markings in gold lettering, each (ILLUS., top of page) **325**

Pitcher, 10" h., 7" d., embossed American Beauty Rose patt., Burley-Winter Pottery Co. (ILLUS. right, below) **475**

Stenciled Wildflower Mug

American Beauty Rose & Cosmos Pitchers

Apricot & Swan & Deer Pitchers

Pitcher, 8" h., embossed Apricot patt., A.E. Hull Pottery Co., 5 pt. (ILLUS. right, above)..... **235**

Embossed Butterfly Large Pitcher

Pitcher, 9" h., embossed Butterfly patt., Nelson McCoy Sanitary Stoneware Co. (ILLUS.).. **450**

Pitcher, 9" h., 6 1/2" d., embossed Cosmos patt., w/advertising, Nelson McCoy Sanitary Stoneware Co... **2,500**

Pitcher, 9" h., 6 1/2" d., embossed Cosmos (Wild Rose) patt., Nelson McCoy Sanitary Stoneware Co. (ILLUS. left with American Beauty Rose pitcher, bottom previous page) **415**

Bulbous Daisy Cluster Pitcher

Pitcher, 8" h., 8" d., embossed Daisy Cluster patt., Burley-Winter Pottery Co. (ILLUS.)... **700**

Rare Girl with Dog & Stag Pitchers

Indian Good Luck Sign & Indian in War Bonnet Pitchers

Pitcher, 8 3/4" h., embossed Girl with Dog patt., Logan Pottery Co. (ILLUS. left, previous page) **1,500**

Pitcher, embossed Grape Cluster in Shield patt., Nelson McCoy Sanitary Stoneware Co., 4 pt. **450**

Pitcher, embossed Grape Cluster in Shield patt., Nelson McCoy Sanitary Stoneware Co., 5 pt. **475**

Pitcher, embossed Grape Cluster in Shield patt., Nelson McCoy Sanitary Stoneware Co., 2 pt. **400**

Pitcher, embossed Grape Cluster in Shield patt., Nelson McCoy Sanitary Stoneware Co., 3 pt. **425**

Pitcher, 9" h., 7" d., embossed Indian Good Luck Sign (Swastika) patt., made by Nelson McCoy Sanitary Stoneware Co., Robinson-Ransbottom Pottery Co. & The Crooksville Pottery Co. (ILLUS. left, top of page) **225**

Pitcher, 9" h., 6 1/2" d., embossed Indian in War Bonnet patt., Nelson McCoy Sanitary Stoneware Co. (ILLUS. right with Indian Good Luck Sign pitcher, top of page) **375**

Pitcher, 9" h., 5 1/2" d., embossed Iris patt., J.W. McCoy Pottery Co. & Brush-McCoy Pottery Co. (ILLUS. bottom right w/Spear Point & Flower Panels measuring cup, on page 216) **400**

Leaping Deer & Standing Deer Pitchers

Pitcher, 8 1/2" h., 6" d., embossed Leaping Deer patt., Burley-Winter Pottery Co. (ILLUS. left, bottom previous page) **400**

Pitcher, 8 1/2" h., 7 3/4" d., embossed Poinsettia with Square Woven Cane patt., spherical shape **350**

Embossed Stag Pattern Pitcher

Pitcher, 9" h., 6 1/2" d., embossed Stag patt., Robinson-Ransbottom Pottery Co. (ILLUS. above and on right with Girl with Dog pitcher, bottom on page 218) **1,000**

Pitcher, 8 1/2" h., 6" d., embossed Standing Deer with Fawn patt., Brush-McCoy Pottery Co. (ILLUS. right with Leaping Deer pitcher, previous page) **275**

Pitcher, 8 1/2" h., 6" d., embossed Swan patt. on one side, Leaping Deer on reverse, Burley-Winter Pottery Co. (ILLUS. left with Apricot pitcher, on page 218 top).. **1,500**

Pitcher, 8" h., 4" d., embossed Tulip patt., J.W. McCoy Pottery Co. & Brush-McCoy Pottery Co. (ILLUS. bottom left with Spear Point & Flower Panels measuring cup, top on page 216) **350**

Pitcher, 7" h., embossed Windmill & Bush patt., J.W. McCoy Pottery Co. & Brush-McCoy Pottery Co. **250**

Pitcher, stenciled Cattail patt., straight-sided, Western Stoneware Co. **195**

Pitcher, stenciled Cattail patt., Western Stoneware Co., 1/4 gal. **195**

Pitcher, stenciled Cattail patt., Western Stoneware Co., 1/2 gal. **250**

Pitcher, stenciled Cattail patt., Western Stoneware Co., 5/8 gal. **325**

Pitcher, stenciled Cattail patt., Western Stoneware Co., 1 gal. **450**

Pitcher, 9" h., 8" d., stenciled Dutch Farm patt., J.W. McCoy Pottery Co. & Brush-McCoy Pottery Co. **250**

Stenciled Snowflake Pattern Pitcher

Pitcher, 8 3/4" h., stenciled Snowflake patt., A.E. Hull Pottery Co. (ILLUS.) **250**

Tall Waisted Wilderflower Pitcher

Pitcher, 8" h., stenciled Wildflower patt., tall waisted body w/long spout, five stencils per side, Brush-McCoy Pottery Co., also found in 8 1/2" h. size (ILLUS.) **800**

Willow Pitcher and Mug

Pitcher, 9" h., 6 1/2" d., embossed Willow (Basketweave & Morning Glory) patt., tankard-type, Brush-McCoy Pottery Co. (ILLUS. right) **255**

Roaster, cov., embossed Daisy, Burley-
Winter Pottery Co., 9" d., 4" h......................... **250**
Salt box, cov., Diffused Blue patt., 6" d.,
4" h.. **130**
Salt box, cov., embossed Apricot patt., A.E.
Hull Pottery Co., 5 3/4" d., 5" h...................... **250**
Salt box, cov., embossed Blocks patt.,
6 1/2" d., 6 3/4" h. **175**
Salt box, cov., embossed Daisy patt., 6" d.,
6 1/2" h. **250**
Salt box, cov., embossed Flying Bird patt.,
A.E. Hull Pottery Co., 6 1/2" d., 6" h.
(ILLUS. left w/Lovebird butter crock, top
page 213)... **625**
Salt box, cov., embossed Grape and Lattice
patt., Brush-McCoy Pottery Co.,
6 3/4" d., 6 1/2" h. **400**
Salt box, cov., embossed Waffleweave
patt. **230**

Stenciled Nautilus Hanging Salt Box

Salt box, cov., hanging-type, stenciled Nautilus patt., A.E. Hull Pottery Co. (ILLUS.) **275**

Vines Hanging Salt Box

Salt box, cov., hanging-type, stenciled
Vines patt., hinged wooden lid, A.E. Hull
Pottery Co., lid missing (ILLUS. with no
lid).. **200**
Sand jar, embossed Standing Stag patt.,
A.E. Hull Pottery Co., 14" h............................ **825**

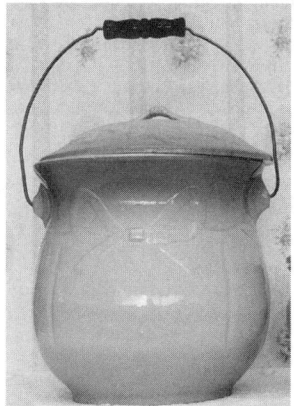

Embossed Bow Tie Pattern Slop Jar

Slop jar, cov., embossed Bow Tie patt., bail
handle w/wooden grip, Brush-McCoy
Pottery Co., 9 1/2" h. (ILLUS.)........................ **200**
Soap dish, embossed Beaded Rose patt.,
slab-type, A.E. Hull Pottery Co., 4 3/4" d....... **125**

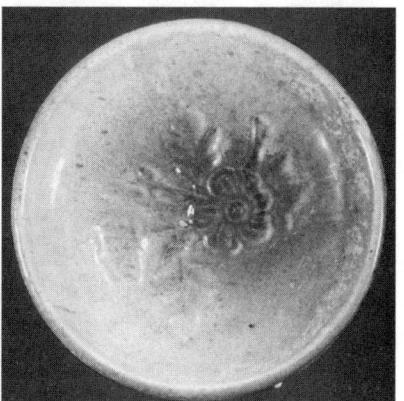

Embossed Flower Cluster Soap Dish

Soap dish, embossed Flower Cluster
w/Fishscale patt., small round form,
4 1/2" d., 3/4" h. (ILLUS.) **135**
Soap dish, cover & drainer, embossed
Bow Tie patt., Brush-McCoy Pottery Co.,
5 1/4" d., 2 1/8" h., the set.............................. **225**

Wildflower Soap Dish

Soap dish, cover & drainer, stenciled Wildflower patt., knob finial on cover, Brush-McCoy Pottery Co., 5 1/4" d., 2" h., the set (ILLUS.)...................................... **600**

Spice jar, cov., embossed GrapeWare patt., "Pepper," "Allspice," "Cinnamon," "Nutmeg," "Ginger" & "Cloves," Brush-McCoy Pottery Co., 3 3/8" h., each **400-800**

Stenciled Snowflake All-Spice Jar

Spice jar, cov., stenciled Snowflake patt., various spices, A.E. Hull Pottery Co., each (ILLUS. of All-Spice)...................... **150-225**

Stein, embossed Grape with Leaf Band patt., 5" h.. **125**

White Hall "Lunch Hour" Stein

Stein, embossed grapevine design, "lunch hour" type, dated "1/31/41," White Hall Sewer Pipe & Stoneware Co., Illinois (ILLUS.).. **775**

Stewer, cov., stenciled Wildflower patt., Brush-McCoy Pottery Co., 2 qt...................... **345**

Teapot, cov., Swirl patt., spherical body w/row of relief-molded knobs around the shoulder, inset cover w/knob finial, swan's-neck spout, shoulder loop brack-

ets for wire bail handle w/turned wood grip, blue 6" d., 6" h. ((ILLUS. left with Swirl coffeepot, bottom of page 214) **800**

Stenciled Nautilus Pattern Vase

Vase, 6" h., stenciled Nautilus patt., bulbous form, A.E. Hull Pottery Co. (ILLUS.).............. **325**

Water cooler, cov., embossed Elk and Polar Bear patt., w/spigot, A.E. Hull Pottery Co., 9 1/2" d., 14" h.. **825**

Water cooler, cov., embossed Standing Stag patt., w/spigot, A.E. Hull Pottery Co., several sizes known **825**

Blue & White Polar Jug

Water jug, Polar jug, footed flat-sided moon-shape w/short cylindrical top spout, Uhl Pottery Co., 9 3/4" d., 10" h. (ILLUS.)... **650**

Blue Ridge Dinnerwares

The small town of Erwin, Tennessee, was the home of the Southern Potteries, Inc., originally founded by E.J. Owen in 1917 and first called the Clinchfield Pottery.

In the early 1920s Charles W. Foreman purchased the plant and revolutionized the company's output, developing the popular line of handpainted wares sold as "Blue Ridge" dinnerwares. Freehand painted by women from the surrounding hills, these colorful dishes in many patterns continued in production until the plant's closing in 1957.

Blue Ridge
Hand Painted
Underglaze
Southern Potteries Inc.
MADE IN U.S.A.

Blue Ridge
CHINA

Blue Ridge Dinnerwares Mark

Ashtray, individual, Tralee Rose patt. $18

Shell-shaped Blue Ridge Bowl

Bowl, 9" d., deep shell shape, in shades of blues & pinks (ILLUS.) 75
Butter pat/coaster, Lyonnaise patt., 4" d. 48

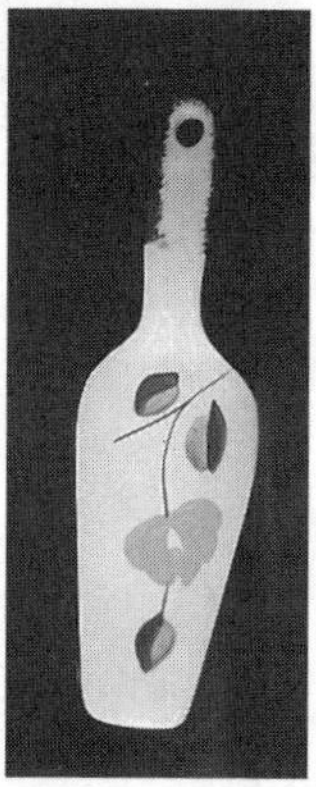

Pomona Pattern Cake Lifter

Cake lifter, Pomona patt., 9" l. (ILLUS.).............. 32
Cake tray, maple leaf shape, French Peasant patt. 145

Fruit Fantasy Pattern Celery

Celery, leaf-shaped, Fruit Fantasy patt., 10 1/2" l. (ILLUS.).. 75
Coffeepot, cov., ovoid, various floral patterns, 10 1/2" h., each..................................... 150
Creamer, Mardi Gras patt..................................... 15

Garden Lane Creamer & Sugar

Creamer & cov. sugar bowl, Colonial shape, Garden Lane patt., the set (ILLUS.).. 55
Pie plate, Cassandra patt., wine-colored border.. 35
Pitcher, 5" h., china, Annett's Wild Rose patt., Antique shape 85
Pitcher, china, decorated w/grapes, Helen shape... 95
Plate, 6" d., Bluebell Bouquet patt......................... 8
Plate, 6" sq., "Milkmaid," Provincial Farm Scene, Candlewick shape................................ 65
Salt & pepper shakers, Dogtooth Violet patt., pr. 75

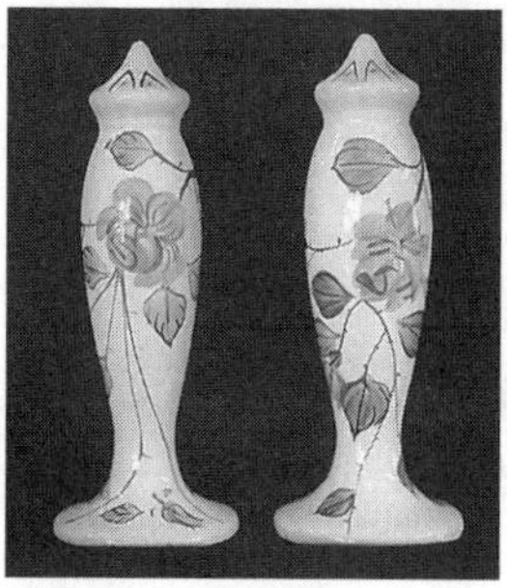

Blue Ridge Salt & Pepper Shakers

Salt & pepper shakers, tall, footed, various floral decorations, 5 1/2" h. pr. (ILLUS.) 89
Teapot, cov., Ball shape, Bluebelle Bouquet patt. 225

Cherry Pattern Teapot

Teapot, cov., Colonial shape, Cherry patt., 8 3/4" h. (ILLUS.)... 150
Vase, 5 1/2" h., china, Hampton patt., Hibiscus shape 100

Vegetable bowl, open, round, Ridge Daisy
patt. 29

Buffalo Pottery

Incorporated in 1901 as a wholly-owned subsidiary of the Larkin Soap Company, founded by John D. Larkin of Buffalo, New York, in 1875, the Buffalo Pottery was a manufactory built to produce premium wares to be included with purchases of Larkin's chief product, soap.

In October 1903, the first kiln was fired and Buffalo Pottery became the only pottery in the world run entirely by electricity. In 1904 Larkin offered its first premium produced by the pottery. This concept of using premiums caused sales to skyrocket and, in 1905, the first Blue Willow pattern pottery made in the United States was introduced as a premium.

The Buffalo Pottery administrative building, built in 1904 to house 1,800 clerical workers, was the creation of a 32-year-old architect, Frank Lloyd Wright. The building was demolished in 1953, but many critics considered it to be Wright's masterpiece.

By 1910 annual soap production peaked and the number of premiums offered in the catalogs exceeded 600. By 1915 this number had grown to 1,500. The first catalog of premiums was issued in 1893 and continued to appear through the late 1930s.

John D. Larkin died in 1926, and during the Great Depression the firm suffered severe losses, going into bankruptcy in 1940. After World War II the pottery resumed production under new management, but its vitreous wares were generally limited to mass-produced china for the institutional market.

Among the pottery lines produced during Buffalo's heyday were Gaudy Willow, Deldare, Abino Ware, historical and commemorative plates and unique handpainted jugs and pitchers. In the 1920s and 1930s the firm concentrated on personalized wares for commercial clients including hotels, clubs, railroads and restaurants.

In 1983 Oneida Silversmiths bought the pottery, an ironic twist since, years before, Oneida silver had been featured in Larkin catalogs. The pottery has now ceased all domestic production of ceramics. - Phillip M. Sullivan.

Buffalo Pottery Mark

Abino Ware (1911-1913)
Candlestick, Nautical, 9" h............................ $1,000
Pitcher, 7" h., jug-form, octagonal, Portland
Head Light.. 2,300+
Vase, 8" h., seascape decoration 2,200

Blue Willow Pattern (1905-1916)
Match safe, 2 3/4 x 6" 200

Blue Willow Wash Pitcher

Pitcher, wash, Blue Willow patt. (ILLUS.).......... 750
Pitcher, cov., jug-type, 3 1/2 pts...................... 400
Salad bowl, square, 9 1/4" w............................. 275
Teapot, cov., square, 2 pts., 5 1/2 oz. 350
Vegetable dish, cov., square, 7 1/2 x 9 1/2"...... 300

Deldare Ware (1908-1909, 1923-1925)
Note: "Fallowfield Hunt" and "Ye Olden Days" scenes are similarly priced for the equivalent pieces in this line.

Calendar plate, 1910, 9 1/2" d. .... 2,500+

Buffalo Deldare Ware Card Tray

Calling card tray, round w/tab handles, "Ye
Olden Days" scene, 7 3/4" d. (ILLUS.)........ 450+

Deldare Candlestick & Pitcher

Deldare "Fallow Field Hunt" Plates

Candlestick, "Ye Olden Days" scene, 9 1/2" h. (ILLUS. right) **750**
Fruit bowl, 9" d., 3 3/4" h..................................... **600**

Buffalo Deldare 8" Octagonal Pitcher

Pitcher, 8" h., octagonal, "Ye Olden Days" scene (ILLUS.) **850**
Pitcher, 12 1/2" h. tankard-type, "Ye Olden Days" scene (ILLUS. left with candlestick, previous page) .... **1,000+**
Plates, 9 1/4" d., "The Fallow Field Hunt - The Start," artist-signed, set of 4, each (ILLUS., top of page) **225**
Punch bowl, footed, 14 3/4" d., 9 1/4" h. ...... **7,000+**
Vase, 8 1/2" h., 6" d., footed tapering ovoid body w/a flaring rim, "Ye Olden Days" scene, black ink mark .... **1,200+**
Wall plaque, 12" d. **850**

Emerald Deldare (1911)
Candlestick, Bayberry decoration, 9" h. **1,000**

Emerald Deldare Chocolate Pot

Coffee/chocolate pot, cov., tall tapering hexagonal form w/pinched spout & angled D-form handle, inset lid w/blossom

finial, stylized symmetrical designs highlighted w/white flowers on body & lid, band just under spout w/stylized moths & large butterfly, decorated by L. Newman, ca. 1911, artist's name in green slip, ink stamp logo & "7," 10 1/2" h. (ILLUS.)..................................... **3,000**
Plaque, round, "Lost," scene of herd of sheep in blizzard, 13 1/2" d. .... **2,000+**

"Dr. Syntax" Emerald Deldare Plate

Plate, 7 1/4" d., h.p. floral border & center scene, "Dr. Syntax Soliloquizing," by E. Missel, marked w/Emerald Deldare logo, "1911" & "4" (ILLUS.) **1,400**

Emerald Deldare Vase

Vase, 8" h., 6 1/2" d., ovoid w/a wide shoulder tapering to a short flaring neck, olive green ground decorated in shades of green & white w/a kingfisher & iris, signed by J. Gerhardt, 1911 (ILLUS.) **1,800**

Large Display of Gaudy Willow Pottery

Gaudy Willow (1905-1916)

Note: Pieces dated 1905 and marked "First Old Willow Ware Manufactured in America" are worth double the prices shown here. This line is generally priced five times higher than the Blue Willow line.

Bone dish, 3 1/4 x 7 1/4" 225
Butter dish, cover & insert, the set,
    7 1/4" d. 750
Creamer, round, 1 pt., 2 oz. 500
Pickle dish, square, 4 1/2 x 8 1/4" 350
Platter, 18" l., oval... 1,000
Sugar bowl, cov., round, 24 1/4 oz................... 500

Jugs and Pitchers (1906-1909)
Jug, "George Washington," blue & white,
    1907, 7 1/2" h. 650
Pitcher, "Art Nouveau," gold & blue, 1908,
    9 1/2" h. .... 1,200+

"Buffalo Hunt" Pitcher

Pitcher, "Buffalo Hunt," jug-form, Indian on
    horseback hunting buffalo, dark bluish
    green ground, 6" h. (ILLUS.)........................... 350

"Holland" & "Gloriana" Pitchers

Pitcher, "Gloriana," blue on white, ca. 1908, 9" h. (ILLUS. right, previous page)................ 900

Pitcher, "Holland," decorated w/three colorful h.p. scenes of Dutch children on the body w/band near the rim decorated w/a rural landscape, ca. 1906, marked w/Buffalo transfer logo & date, "Holland" & "9," overall consistent staining, 5 3/4" h. (ILLUS. left with Gloriana Pitcher, previous page) 750

Pitcher, "Marine Pitcher, Lighthouse," blue & white, 1907, 9 1/4" h............................. 1,000

Pitcher, "Pilgrim," brightly colored, 1908, 9" h. 1,000

Pitcher, "Roosevelt Bears," beige, 1906, 8 1/4" h. 3,200

Pitcher, "Whirl of the Town," brightly colored, 1906, 7" h. 675

Plates - Commemorative (1906-1912)

Great Falls, Montana Plate

B. & M. Smelter, and the largest smoke-stack in the world. Great Falls, Montana, deep green, ca. 1909, 7 1/2" d. (ILLUS.) 125

George Washington & Martha Washington, deep bluish green, 7 1/2" d., each........ 250

Locks (The), Lockport, New York, deep bluish green, 7 1/2" d. 125

Buffalo Pottery Niagara Falls Plate

Niagara Falls, dark blue w/Bonrea pattern border, ca. 1907, 7 1/2" d. (ILLUS.)............... 150

State Capitol, Helena, Montana, deep bluish green, 7 1/2" d. 150

Plates - Historical - Blue or Green (1905-1910)

Faneuil Hall, Boston, 10" d................................. 75

Mount Vernon, 10" d. 75

White House, Washington, 10" d. 75

Miscellaneous Pieces

Bluebird Pattern Pieces

Cup & saucer, Bluebird patt, china mark (ILLUS. right)... 125

Dutch Children Feeding Dish

Feeding dish, child's, alphabet border, Dutch children at play in center, ca. 1916, Buffalo China, 7 3/4" d. (ILLUS.).................... 125

Pitcher, 8 3/4" h., bone china, melon-shaped, white, 1909.................................... 1,000

Large & Small Geranium Pitchers

Rare Buffalo China Turkey Platter

Pitcher, Geranium patt., blue & white, small size (ILLUS. front row, right with other Geranium pitchers, previous page).............. 275

Pitcher, Geranium patt., pale green & brown on white, small size, 1906-1909 (ILLUS. front row, left with other Geranium pitchers, previous page)......................... 175

Pitchers, Geranium patt., large sizes, multi-colored design or dark blue & white, 1906-1909, each (ILLUS. in back row, previous page) 400

Plate, 6 1/2" d., Bluebird patt., china mark (ILLUS. left with cup & saucer, previous page).. 75

Plate, 9" d., dinner, Hotel Robert Fulton service, Buffalo China.. 250

Plate, 9 1/2" d., Bing Crosby portrait, Buffalo China 500

Plate, 10" d., New York World's Fair, 1939 500

Plate, 10 1/4" d., dinner, Japan patt., multi-colored, 1906... 250

Plate, 10 3/4" d., Jack Dempsey photograph, Buffalo China 500

Plate, 11" d., Breakfast at the Three Pigeons, Fallowfield Hunt line, on Colorido Ware 750

Platter, 13 1/4 x 18 1/2", Turkey patt., large colorful turkey in landscape in center, fall landscape border scenes, Colorido Ware, 1937, Buffalo China (ILLUS., top of page) 3,000

Teapot, cov., tea ball-type w/built-in tea ball, Argyle patt., blue & white, 1914.................... 300

Ceramic Arts Studio of Madison

During its 15 years of operation, Ceramic Arts Studio of Madison, Wisconsin, was one of the nation's largest producers of figurines, shakers and other decorative wares. Its originality and high production standards make its wares highly collectible works of art. In 1940, the artistic talent of Lawrence Rabbitt merged with the business acumen of Reuben Sand to start Ceramic Arts Studio. Their partnership was successful. Rabbitt remained artist in residence and the Studio produced hand-thrown bowls, pots and vases exploring the potential of Wisconsin clay. After Rabbitt's departure in 1942, a serendipitous meeting between Sand and Betty Harrington brought her artistic talents to the Studio. Under her artistic direction, the focus was changed to finely sculpted decorative wares, including figurines of people, animals and fantasy figures.

Metal Art accessories to complement the ceramic pieces were assembled at the Studio under the direction of Zona Liberace (stepmother to the famous pianist), who also functioned as the Studio's decorating director.

From 1942 to 1948, the Studio's business flourished while imports from Europe and the Far East were suspended as a result of World War II. Annual production of 500,000 pieces and employment of 100 people were typical for these years. Harrington, although not the only designer on staff, is credited with the creation of the vast majority of the 800+ pieces put into production. This level of output and quality helped to solidify the Studio's reputation as one of the most original and enduring ceramic producers in America.

The popularity of the Studio's work drew many poor quality imitations and outright copies. After World War II, lower-priced decorative imports began to flood the market, forcing the Studio's eventual close in 1955. Attempts to continue the enterprise in Japan resulted in products bearing the name Ceramic Arts Studio - Japan and/or Mahana Imports. Some of the original molds were taken there and many of the models were produced with little or no design change, but with wide variations in quality. The ink stamp on these Japanese Studio wares is in red or blue and the clay color is bright white. In contrast, the semicircle mark, Ceramic Arts Studio, Madison, WI is always in black and the clay is ivory and heavier. But since only one out of four Madison Ceramic Arts Studio works were ink-stamped, other clues to authenticity are the decoration and clarity of the glaze.

Ceramic Arts Studio Marks

Hamlet & Ophelia Wall Plaques

Accordion Lady, 8 1/2" h. **$500-600**
Adonis, 9" h. 250-350
African Man wall pocket, 7 3/4" h............ 150-175
African Woman wall pocket, 7 3/4" h. 150-175
Ancient Kitten, 2 1/2" h. 70-90
Autumn Andy, Four Seasons group,
    5" h. 160-190
Baby Mermaid, sitting, 3" h........................ 175-200
Bedtime Boy, 4 3/4" h.................................... 75-95
Billy Boxer, 2" l. 60-80

Hear No Evil Candleholder

Hear No Evil candleholder, 5" h. (ILLUS.). **80-100**
Honey Pot with bee, 4" h............................ 150-175
Hunter, Al, 7 1/2" h. **125-200**

Realistic Bear Cub & Mother

Black Bear Cub Realistic, 2 1/4" h. (IL-
    LUS. left) 140-160
Boy Doll, 12" h. 1,200-1,400
Boy with Towel, 5" h................................... 300-350
Cellist Man, 6 1/2" h. 500-600
Cowboy, shelf-sitter, 4 1/2" h..................... 125-150
Cowgirl, shelf-sitter, 4 1/2" h...................... 125-150
Drum Girl, 4 1/2" h....................................... 160-180
Dutch Dance Boy, 7 1/2" h......................... 200-250
Dutch Dance Girl, 7 1/2" h......................... 200-250
English Setter, Kirby, 2" l. 150-175
Fire Woman, 11 1/4" h. 200-250
Flute Lady, 8 1/2" h. 500-600
Girl with Kitten, shelf-sitter, 4 1/4" h. 75-100
Gremlin, standing, 4" h. 250-300
Hamlet wall plaque, 8" h. (ILLUS. right, top
    of page) 180-220
Harem Girl, kneeling, 4 1/2" h. 100-125
Harlequin Boy with mask, 8 3/4" h........... 900-950

Jack in Beanstalk Wall Plaque

Mermaid, Neptune & Sprites

Jack in Beanstalk wall plaque, 6 1/2" h.
 (ILLUS.)... **360-400**
King's Jester Flutist Man, 11 1/2" h........ **100-200**
Lightning Stallion, 5 3/4" h. **150-175**
Lion King, 4" h. **350-400**
Lorelei on Shell planter, 6" h.................... **250-300**

Mother Black Bear Realistic, 3 1/4" h.
 (ILLUS. right with cub, previous page)... **180-220**
Mouse, Hickory Dickory Dock, 3" l.............. **90-110**

Mrs. Blankety Blank Bank

Mrs. Blankety Blank bank, 4 1/2" h.
 (ILLUS.)... **120-140**
Neptune wall plaque, 6" h. (ILLUS. bottom
 left with Mermaid) **350-400**
Ophelia wall plaque, 8" h. (ILLUS. left with
 Hamlet wall plaque, previous page) **180-220**
Panda with hat, 2 3/4" h............................. **200-225**

Madonna with Halo Figure

Madonna with Halo, 9 1/2" h. (ILLUS.)..... **300-700**
Mermaid wall plaque, 6" h. (ILLUS. top
 left, top of page)....................................... **350-400**

Promenade Man & Woman

Promenade Man, 7 3/4" h. (ILLUS. right) . **100-150**
Promenade Woman, 7 3/4" h. (ILLUS. left
with Promenade Man)............................ **100-150**
Saucy Squirrel, 2 1/4" h. **175-350**
Seal Pup on rock, 5" l.................................. **450-500**
Skunky bank, 4" h. **260-280**
Space bowl, 5 1/4" h. **100-125**
Spring Sue, Four Seasons group, 5" h. **140-170**
Sprite wall plaque, fish down, 4 1/4" h.
(ILLUS. bottom right with Mermaid, previ-
ous page) **300-350**
Sprite wall plaque, fish up, 4 1/4" h.
(ILLUS. top right with Mermaid, previous
page).. **300-350**
Squeaky Squirrel, 3 1/4" h. **50-70**
Sultan on Pillow, 4 1/2" h. **120-145**
Sultan only, 4" h. **130-155**
Swan Lake Woman, 7" h........................... **900-950**
Temple Dance Man, 7" h........................... **450-500**
Temple Dance Woman, 6 3/4" h. **450-500**
Tony the Barber bank, bust of man,
4 3/4" h. **75-100**
Triad Girl center, 5" h.................................. **90-120**
Triad Girl left, 7" h...................................... **80-110**
Triad Girl right, 7" h..................................... **80-110**

Water Man & Water Woman

Water Man, chartreuse, 11 1/2" h. (ILLUS.
right).. **175-200**
Water Woman, chartreuse, 11 1/2" h.
(ILLUS. left) **175-200**
Winter Willie, Four Seasons group, 4" h. ... **90-120**
Zebra, 5" h.. **350-450**

Cowan

*R. Guy Cowan opened his first pottery studio in 1912
in Lakewood, Ohio. The pottery operated almost continu-
ously, with the exception of a break during the First World
War, at various locations in the Cleveland area until it
was forced to close in 1931 due to financial difficulties.*

*Many of this century's finest artists began with Cowan
and its associate, the Cleveland School of Art. This fine
art pottery, particularly the designer pieces, are highly
sought after by collectors.*

*Many people are unaware that it was due to R. Guy
Cowan's perseverance and tireless work that art pottery is
today considered an art form and found in many art museums.*

Cowan Marks

Ashtray, model of a ram, green, designed
by Edris Eckhardt, 5 1/4" l., 3 1/2" h.
(ILLUS. lower left with chick ashtray/nut
dish, top left, next page)............................... **$200**
Ashtray/nut dish, ivory glaze, Shape No.
769, 1" h... **25**

Cowan Clown Ashtrays & Vases

Ashtray/nut dish, figural clown Periot, blue
or ivory glaze, designed by Elizabeth
Anderson, Shape No. 788, 2 1/2 x 3",
each (ILLUS. lower center) **150**

Cowan Ashtrays, Flower Frog & Vase

Ashtray/nut dish, model of a chick, green glaze, Shape No. 768, 3 1/2" h. (ILLUS. bottom center) **75**

Book ends, figural Art Deco-style elephant, push & pull, tan glaze, designed by Thelma F. Winter, one Shape No. 840 & one Shape No. 841, 4 3/4" h., pr. **1,600**

Cowan Book Ends & Model of Horse

Book ends, figural, model of a seated polar bear, front paws near face, ivory glaze, designed by Margaret Postgate, 6" h., pr. (ILLUS. left) **1,600**

Book ends, figural, a little girl standing wearing a large sunbonnet & full ruffled dress, verde green, designed by Kat. Barnes Jenkins, Shape No. 521, 7" h., pr. **700**

Variety of Cowan Animal Pieces

Book ends, figural, model of a unicorn, front legs raised on relief-molded foliage base, orange glaze, designed by Waylande Gregory, Shape No. 961, mark No. 8, 7" h., pr. (ILLUS. left) **1,000**

Book ends, "Pierette," stylized figure of young woman wearing a short flaring skirt & holding a scarf behind her, russet & salmon glaze, designed by Elizabeth Anderson, Shape No. 792, 8 1/4" h. (ILLUS. center with polar bear book ends) **2,300**

Bowl, 7 1/2" w., octagonal, the alternating side panels hand-decorated w/floral design, brown & yellow glaze, Shape No. B-5-B **375**

Bowl, w/drip, 3 x 9 1/2", blue lustre finish, Shape No. 701-A.. **80**

Bowl, 3 x 11 1/4", designed to imitate hand molding, two-tone blue glaze, Shape No. B-827.. **300**

Bowl, 3 x 6 x 12 1/2" oblong, caramel w/light green glaze, Shape No. 683 .... **50**

Bowl, 3 x 8 1/2 x 16 1/4", footed shallow form, flaring scalloped sides & rim, down-curved side handles, ivory exterior w/blue interior glaze, Shape No. 743-B **120**

Buttons, decorated w/various zodiac designs, by Paul Bogatay, 50 pcs..................... **500**

Candleholder, figural, model of a Viking ship prow, green glaze, Shape No. 777, 5 1/4" h... **35**

Candleholders, ivory glaze, Shape No. 692, 2 1/4" h., pr. **30**

Various Cowan Pieces

Candlestick, flared base below twisted column, blossom-form cup, green & orange drip glaze, Shape No. 625-A, 7 3/4" h. (ILLUS. far right) **90**

Candlestick, figural, Byzantine figure flanked by angels, golden yellow glaze, designed by R.G. Cowan, 9 1/4" h. (ILLUS. left) **300**

Byzantine Angel Candlesticks

Candlestick, figural, Byzantine figure flanked by angels, salmon glaze, designed by R.G. Cowan, 9 1/4" h. (ILLUS. right) 350

Candlestick/bud vase, tapering cylindrical shape w/flared foot & rim, blue lustre, Shape 530-A, 7 1/2" h. 80

Candlesticks, figural grape handles, ivory glaze, 4" h., pr. 80

Candlesticks, "The Girl Reserve," designed by R.G. Cowan, medium blue, Shape No. 671, 5 1/2" h., pr. 275

Centerpiece set, 6 1/4" h. trumpet-form vase centered on 8" sq. base w/candle socket in each corner, Princess line, vase Shape No. V-1, Mark No. 8, candelabra Shape No. S-2, Mark No. 8, black matte, 2 pcs., together w/four nut dishes/open compotes, green glaze, Shape No. C-1, Mark No. 8, the set 900

Charger, wall plaque, yellow, 11 1/4" d. 150

Cigarette/match holder, sea horse decoration, pink, No. 726, 3 1/2 x 4" 65

Clip dish, green, 3 1/4" d. (part of desk set, Shape PB-1) 20

Console bowl, octagonal, stand-up-type, verde green, Shape No. 689, 3 x 8 x 8 1/2" 95

Console bowl, April green, Shape No. B-1, 11 1/2" l., 2 1/4" h. 95

Console bowl, ivory & pink glaze, Shape No. 763, 3 1/4 x 9 x 16 1/2" 80

Console bowls, 3 3/4 x 4 1/2 x 11", two-handled, footed, widely flaring fluted sides, verde green, Shape No. 538, pr. 280

Cowan Decanters & Wine Cups

Decanter w/stopper, figural King of Clubs, a seated robed & bearded man w/a large crown on his head & holding a scepter, black glaze w/gold, designed by Waylande Gregory, Shape E-4, 10" h. (ILLUS. left) 1,100

Figurine, kneeling female nude, almond glaze, 9" h. 350

"Persephone" Figurine

Figurine, "Persephone," standing female nude holding a long scarf out to one side and near her shoulder, ivory glaze, designed by Waylande Gregory, Shape No. D-6, 15" h. (ILLUS.) 3,500

Figurine, "Nautch Dancer," female w/a flaring pleated skirt on rectangular base, semi-matte ivory glaze w/silver accents, incised "Waylande Gregory," impressed mark, 6 3/4 x 9 1/4", 17 3/4" h. 8,500

Finger bowl, Egyptian blue, Shape No. B-19, 3" 80

Flower frog, figure of a nude female, one leg kneeling on thick round base, head bent to one side & looking upward, one arm resting on knee of bent leg w/the other hand near her foot, ivory glaze, designed by Walter Sinz, 6" h. (ILLUS. left with Diver flower frog, next page) 450

Various Cowan Flower Frogs

Flower frog, figural, "Repose," Art Deco style, a seminude sinewy woman standing & slightly curved backward, her arms away from her sides holding trailing drapery, in a cupped blossom-form base, ivory glaze, designed by R.G. Cowan,

Shape No. 712, 6 1/2" h. (ILLUS. lower center) **450**

Flower frog, figural, "Scarf Dancer," Art Deco-style nude dancing woman in a curved pose standing on one leg & holding the ends of a long scarf in her outstretched hands, ivory glaze, designed by R.G. Cowan, Shape No. 686, 7" h. (ILLUS. top with "Repose" flower frog).......... **350**

Flower frog, figural, Art Deco style, two nude females partially draped in flowing scarves, each bending backward away from the other w/one hand holding the scarf behind each figure & their other hand joined, on an oval base w/flower holes, ivory glaze, designed by R.G. Cowan, Shape No. 685, 7 1/2" h. (ILLUS. lower right with "Repose" flower frog)............ **850**

Cowan Female Form Flower Frogs

Flower frog, "Diver," waveform base w/tall wave supporting nude female figure, back arched & arms raised over head, ivory glaze, designed by R.G. Cowan, Shape No. 683, 8" h. (ILLUS. right) **1,200**

Flower frog, figural "Marching Girl," Art Deco style, a nude female partially draped w/a flowing scarf standing & leaning backward w/one hand on her hip & the other raising the scarf above her head, on an oblong serpentine-molded wave base w/flower holes, ivory glaze, designed by R.G. Cowan, Shape No. 680, 8" h. (ILLUS. lower left with "Repose" flower frog) **450**

Flower frog, figural "Wreath Girl," figure of a woman standing on a blossom-form base & holding up the long tails of her flowing skirt, ivory glaze, designed by R.G. Cowan, Shape No. 721, 10" h. (ILLUS. center with Diver flower frog) **1,000**

Flower frog, model of a deer, designed by Waylande Gregory, ivory glaze, Shape No. F-905, 8 1/4" h. (ILLUS. right with unicorn book ends, bottom left on page 232).. **550**

Flower frog, figural Pan sitting on large toadstool, ivory glaze, designed by W. Gregory, Shape No. F-9, 9" h. (ILLUS. with ram & chick ashtrays, top of page 232).. **1,000**

Flower frog, a standing seminude Art Deco woman, posed w/one leg kicked to the back, her torso bent back w/one arm raised & curved overhead, the other arm curved around her waist holding a long feather fan, a long drapery hangs down the front from her waist, on a rounded incurved broad leaf cluster base, overall Original Ivory glaze, designed by R.G. Cowan, Shape No. 806, stamped mark, 4" w., 9 1/2" h. **1,700**

Flower frog, model of a reindeer, designed by Waylande Gregory, polychrome finish, Shape No. 903, 11" h. (ILLUS. center with unicorn book ends, bottom left on page 232).. **1,600**

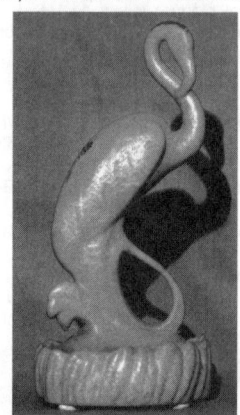

Cowan Flamingo Flower Frog

Flower frog, model of a flamingo, orange glaze, designed by Waylande Gregory, Shape No. D2-F, 11 3/4" h. (ILLUS.).......... **1,000**

Ginger jar, cov., blue lustre, Shape No. 513, 6 3/4" h. **300**

Lamp, foliage decoration, 9" h. **375**

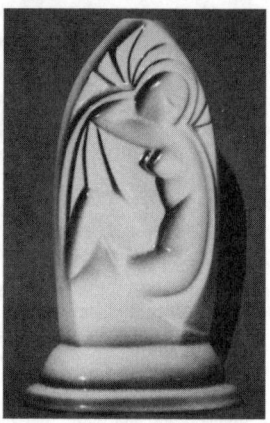

Cowan Lamp Base

Lamp base, round domed base below modernist teardrop-shaped body decorated w/nude female figure, ivory & brown glaze, designed by Waylande Gregory, 11" h. (ILLUS.)... **1,500**

Model of elephant, standing on square plinth, head & trunk down, rich mottled Oriental Red glaze, designed by Margaret Postgate, ca. 1930, faint impressed mark on plinth & paper label reading "X869 Elephant designed by M....et P....," 10 1/2" h.. **5,500**

Model of horse, standing animal on an oblong base, Egyptian blue glaze, designed by Viktor Schreckengost, 7 3/4" h. (ILLUS. right with polar bear book ends, on page 232) **3,900**

Pen base, maroon, Shape No. PB-2, 3 3/4"....... **80**

Plaque, hand-decorated by Arthur E. Baggs, Egyptian blue, artist-signed "AEB," 2 1/2 x 12 1/2" **2,500**

Strawberry jar w/saucer, light green, designed by R.G. Cowan, Shape No. SJ-6, 6" h., 2 pcs. **200**

Cowan Lakeware Urn & Vases

Urn, Lakeware, blue, Shape V-102, 5 1/2" h. (ILLUS. left).. **90**

Cowan Urn w/Figural Grape Handles

Urn, cov., black w/gold trim & figural grape cluster handles, Shape No. V-95, 10 1/4" h. (ILLUS.).. **450**

Vase, 4" h., bulbous ovoid tapering to cylindrical neck, Jet Black glaze, Shape No. V-5 (ILLUS. center w/urn).............................. **300**

Vase, 4" h., waisted cylindrical body w/bulbous top & wide flaring rim, mottled or-

ange glaze, Shape No. 630 (ILLUS. second from left w/No. 625-A candlestick, on page 232).. **80**

Vase, 4 3/4" h., bulbous body w/horizontal ribbing, wide cylindrical neck, green glaze, Shape No. V-30 (ILLUS. lower left with clown ashtrays, on page 231) **90**

Vase, 4 3/4" h., wide tapering cylindrical body, mottled orange, brown & rust, Shape No. V-34 (ILLUS. second from right w/No. 625-A candlestick, on page 232).. **80**

Vase, 5 1/2" h., Lakeware, bulbous base w/wide shoulder tapering to wide cylindrical neck, blue glaze, Shape No. V-72............. **90**

Vase, 6 1/4" h., experimental, polychrome, designed by Arthur E. Baggs, Shape No. 15-A, artist signed "AEB"............................. **1,500**

Vase, bud, 6 1/4" h., flaring domed foot below ovoid body tapering to cylindrical neck w/flaring rim, plum glaze, Shape No. 916... **80**

Cowan Decorated Vases

Vase, 6 1/2" h., bulbous body w/short molded rim, black w/Egyptian blue bands & center decoration, designed by Whitney Atchley, Shape No. V-38 (ILLUS. right) **2,000**

Vase, 6 1/2" h., footed, squatty bulbous base w/trumpet-form neck, flattened sides w/notched corners, green glaze, Shape No. V-649-A (ILLUS. right w/urn) **150**

Vase, 6 1/2" h., wide bulbous body, yellow glaze, Shape V-91.. **250**

Vase, 6 5/8" h., bright yellow glaze, Shape No. 797.. **80**

Vase, 7" h., fan-shaped w/scalloped foot & domed base decorated w/relief-molded sea horse decoration, pink glaze, Shape No. 715-A.. **60**

Vase, 7" h., Lakeware, bulbous base w/trumpet-form neck, Oriental Red glaze, Shape No. V-75... **90**

Vase, 7 1/4" h., footed slender ovoid body w/flaring rim, Oriental Red glaze, Shape No. V-12.. **175**

Vase, 7 1/2" h., flared foot below paneled ovoid body, orange lustre glaze, Shape No. 691-A, mark No. 6.. **75**

Vase, 7 1/2" h., footed, tapering cylindrical body, green drip over yellow glaze, Shape No. 591, 8" h. (ILLUS. far right with clown ashtrays, on page 231) **275**

Vase, 7 1/2" h., tall slender ovoid body w/short cylindrical neck, orange lustre, Shape No. 552 (ILLUS. lower right with chick & ram ashtrays, on page 232)................ **90**

Vase, 8" h., blue lustre, Shape No. 615............. **100**

Vase, 8" h., bulbous body tapering to cylindrical neck w/flaring rim, gold, Shape No. V-932 (ILLUS. far left w/No. 625-A candlestick, on page 232).................................... **250**

Vase, 8" h., bulbous body tapering to cylindrical neck w/flaring rim, black drip over Feu Rouge (red) glaze Shape No. V-932 (ILLUS. top with clown ashtrays, oon page 231)... **550**

Vase, 8" h., cylindrical body, black w/overall turquoise blue decoration, triple-signed (ILLUS. left with bulbous vase, on previous page).. **880**

Vase, 8" h., footed bulbous body w/trumpet-form neck, yellow shading to green drip glaze, Shape No. 627 (ILLUS. top center w/No. 625-A candlestick, on page 232) **250**

Vase, 8 1/4" h., "Logan," footed, compressed bulbous base w/trumpet-form neck, flattened sides w/notched corners, decorative side handles, designed by R.G. Cowan, verde green glaze, Shape No. 649-B **225**

Vase, 8 1/2" h., matte greenish blue, Shape No. V-897... **160**

Vase, 8 3/4" h., Lakeware, green, Shape No. V-71 .... **100**

Vase, 9" h., 6 1/2" d., footed trumpet-form, the sides w/horizontal ribbing, overall Russet Brown glaze, stamped mark............. **138**

Vase, 11 1/4" h., Chinese Bird patt., footed urn shape w/relief-molded birds at base, green glaze, designed by R.G. Cowan, Shape No. V-747 (ILLUS.)............................. **950**

Vase, 11 3/4" h., two-handled, flared foot below tall slender fluted ovoid body w/cylindrical neck, orange lustre, Shape No. 652-B, mark No. 8 .... **300**

Vase, 12" h., footed ovoid body, mother-of-pearl finish, Shape No. 847 .... **300**

Wall plate, flat, blue, 11 1/4" d............................ **150**

Wine cups, Oriental Red glaze, Shape No. X-17, 2 1/2" h., each (ILLUS. of two, front left with decanters, on page 233)...................... **45**

Czechoslovakian

Czechoslovakia did not exist until the end of World War I in 1918. The country was put together with parts of Austria, Bohemia and Hungary as a reward for the help of the Czechs and the Slovaks in winning the war. In 1993 Czechoslovakia split and became two countries: the Czech Republic and the Slovak Republic. Items are highly collectible because the country was in existence only 75 years. For a more thorough study of the subject, refer to the following books: Made in Czechoslovakia Books 1 and 2 by Ruth A. Forsythe; Czechoslovakian Glass & Collectibles Books I and II by Dale & Dian Barta and Helen M. Rose and Czechoslovakian Perfume Bottles and Boudoir Accessories by Jacquelyne Y. Jones North.

Ashtray Topped with Figure of Dog

Ashtray, rectangular yellow tray topped w/figure of white dog w/nose to ground, ears flapping & tail erect, black & red detailing, 5" h. (ILLUS.) **$175**

Cowan Chinese Bird Vase

Various Czechoslovakian Pieces

Hand-painted Beverage Set

Basket, orange & green h.p. floral decoration on cream ground, low orange handle, 4 1/2" h. (ILLUS. front row, left w/various Czechoslovakian pieces, previous page) 85

Beverage set: cov. pitcher & four tumblers; tapering cylindrical shapes, pitcher w/applied black C-scroll handle & knobbed lid, h.p. floral decoration in red, blue, green & yellow on white ground w/black trim, the set (ILLUS., top of page)................. 275

Book ends, in the form of a boy & girl, Erphila, 6" h., pr. 125

Bowl, 14" l., shallow shape, green & yellow, Eichwald.. 65

Various Peasant Art Pieces

Box, cov., round, floral decoration on yellow sponge ground, J. Mzarek, Peasant Art Industries, 6" d., 6" h. (ILLUS. front row, second from left w/various Peasant Art pieces).. 225

Canister set, green background w/floral decoration, 15-piece set 600

Crab ramekin, cov. 25

Creamer, floral decor on blue sponge ground, J. Mrazek, Peasant Art Industries, 3" h. (ILLUS. front row, second from right, w/various Peasant Art pieces)............... 65

Cup & saucer, "Highlander" patt. 25

Slip Decorated Covered Jar

Jar, cov., cylindrical shape, slip decorated overall in orange, blue, green & black, w/stylized fan on front, 7" h. (ILLUS.)............. 475

Models of horse heads, white high glaze, 9" h., pr.. 175

Mug with Bird Handle

Mug, cylindrical form w/figure of bird forming handle, cream w/red & black accents, Erphila (ILLUS.) 175

Mug, slightly tapering cylindrical form w/floral medallion on orange sponge ground, Peasant Art Industries, 5" h. (ILLUS.

front row far right, w/various Peasant Art
pieces).. **65**
Mustard w/underplate, cov., floral decor on
green sponge ground, J. Mrazek, Peasant Art Industries, 4" d., 4" h. (ILLUS.
middle row, second from right, w/various
Peasant Art pieces, on previous page)......... **145**
Pitcher, 1-liter, white stencil design on cobalt blue ground, Ditmar-Urbach (ILLUS.
back row, left w/various Czechoslovakian
pieces, on page 236) **125**

Airbrushed "Himalaja" Pitcher

Pitcher, 1 1/2-liter, footed bulbous form
w/tapering neck & flared rim, black C-
scroll handle dividing into two sections at
base, "Himalaja" patt., airbrushed purple,
white, yellow & green, CORA, Ditmar-Ur-
bach (ILLUS.) **275**
Pitcher, 4 1/2" h., in the form of a standing
cow, w/blue, yellow & orange spots................ **95**
Pitcher, 6 1/2" h., w/stencil of man & wom-
an w/heart in red & green **45**
Pitcher, 7" h., simple form w/overall h.p. floral decoration on white ground, angled
handle, BERN (ILLUS. front row, right
w/various Czechoslovakian pieces, on
page 236) **85**
Pitcher, 8" h., straight-sided, in the form of
blown-out fruit... **150**
Pitcher, 9" h., "Monte Carlo" patt., red,
black & white striped **195**

Plate, 8 1/2" d., white, each decorated in
center w/different fruit: one w/pear, one
w/grapes, one w/apple, one w/orange,
one w/strawberries, one w/plums, each.......... **25**
Plate, 10" d., "Highlander" patt., red, blue &
black plaid.. **25**
Plate, 12" d., floral center on yellow sponge
ground, J. Mrazek, Peasant Art Industries (ILLUS. back row, w/various Peas-
ant Art pieces, previous page)......................... **85**
Punch bowl w/underplate, "Highlander"
patt., 15" d., the set...................................... **175**

Airbrushed Salt & Pepper Shakers

Salt & pepper shakers, ovoid form, airbrushed decoration of stagecoach
w/horses & attendants in black silhouette
against white ground w/blue, gold &
green, 4 1/2" h., pr. (ILLUS.) **35**
Vase, 5" h., bulbous form w/two small side
handles at shoulder, decorated w/orange
flowers & green leaves (ILLUS. front row,
center w/various Czechoslovakian piec-
es, page 236) **75**
Vase, 5 1/2" h., squatty shape, h.p. multi-
color floral decoration (ILLUS. second
from left w/other Czechoslovakian vases,
bottom of page)... **110**
Vase, 6" h., ovoid w/flaring rim & tapering
out at base, overall floral design, Peasant
Art Industries (ILLUS. front row, far left,
w/various Peasant Art pieces, previous
page) **125**
Vase, 6" h., slightly ovoid cylindrical form
w/floral band on black ground, Peasant
Art Industries (ILLUS. middle row, second from left w/various Peasant Art piec-
es, previous page)... **115**

Czechoslovakian Vases

Vase, 7" h., bulbous form w/flaring neck & short circular base, decorated w/red flowers w/black trim on cream ground, Ditmar-Urbach (ILLUS. second from right w/other Czechoslovakian vases, previous page) **175**

Vase, 8" h., flaring neck & short stepped base, airbrushed w/crosshatching & dots in lavender, red, brown & pink (ILLUS. far right w/other Czechoslovakian vases, previous page) **125**

Vase, 8" h., flaring rim, short circular base, slip decorated w/orange circles w/green centers outlined in blue w/black spider webbing on white ground, trimmed in yellow & black (ILLUS. far left w/other Czechoslovakian vases, previous page) **250**

Vase, 8" h., octagonal form w/flaring rim & base, h.p. floral decoration on white ground (ILLUS. back row, right w/various Czechoslovakian pieces, on page 236) **125**

Vase, 9" h., bulbous body w/cylindrical neck flaring slightly at rim, wide floral band on yellow sponge ground, Peasant Art Industries (ILLUS. middle row far right, w/various Peasant Art pieces, on page 237) **250**

Slip-decorated Czechoslovakian Vase

Vase, 12" h., tall, slightly ovoid cylindrical shape, slip decoration, cream & dark green swirls on ground of large purple & orange circles, cobalt trim (ILLUS.) **450**

Vase, 12 1/2" h., short bulbous base w/long cylindrical neck flaring out slightly at rim, blue sponge ground w/floral medallions, Peasant Art Industries (ILLUS. middle row, far left w/various Peasant Art pieces, on page 237) **350**

Doulton & Royal Doulton

Doulton & Co., Ltd., was founded in Lambeth, London, in about 1858. It was operated there until 1956 and often incorporated the words "Doulton" and "Lambeth" in its marks. Pinder, Bourne & Co., Burslem was purchased by the Doultons in 1878 and in 1882 became Doulton & Co., Ltd. It added porcelain to its earthenware production in 1884. The "Royal Doulton" mark has been used since 1902 by this factory, which is still in operation. Character jugs and figurines are commanding great attention from collectors at the present time.

ROYAL DOULTON

Royal Doulton Marks

Bunnykins Figurines

60th Anniversary, DB 137, yellow & white, 1994 .... **$70**

Aerobic, DB 40, yellow, blue, 1985-88 .... **225**

American Firefighter, DB 268, yellow pants, red hat, 2002, colorway limited edition of 2001 (part of proceeds donated to New York Firefighters 9/11 Disaster Relief Fund) **80**

Artist (The), DB 13, burgundy, yellow & blue, 1975-82 .... **375**

Bunnykins Astro Music Box

Astro, Music Box, DB 35, white, red, blue, 1984-89 (ILLUS.) **300**

Aussie Surfer, DB 133, gold & green outfit, white & blue base, 1994 .... **115**

Ballerina, DB 176, pink dress, yellow footstool, 1998 to present **45**

Basket Ball Bunnykin, DB 262, yellow w/blue trim, limited edition of 2,000, 2002 ...... **150**

Bath Night Bunnykins

Bath Night, DB 141,tableau RDICC exclusive, limited edition of 5,000, 2001 (ILLUS.)... **160**

Batsman, DB 144, white, beige & black, 1994, limited edition of 1,000......................... **265**

Fourth Variation of Bedtime

Bedtime, DB 103, fourth variation, yellow & green striped pajamas, brown Teddy bear, 1991 (ILLUS.)....................................... **265**

Bedtime, DB 63, second variation, red & white striped pajamas, 1987, limited edition **425**

Beefeater, DB 163, red, gold, black & white livery, black hat w/red, blue & white band, 1996, limited edition of 1,500......................... **525**

Billie and Buntie Bunnykins Sleigh Ride, DB 81, green, yellow & red, 1989................. **155**

Bogey, DB 32, green, brown & yellow, 1984-92.. **150**

Boy Skater, DB 152, blue coat, brown pants, yellow hat, green boots & black skates, 1995-98 .... **45**

Bunnykins Bride

Bride, DB 101, cream dress, grey, blue & white train, 1991 to 2001 (ILLUS.) **45**

Britannia, DB 219, blue, 2000, limited edition of 2,500.. **100**

Buntie Bunnykins Helping Mother, DB 2, rose-pink & yellow, 1972-93......................... **65**

Busy Needles, DB 10, white, green & maroon, 1973-88... **75**

Carol Singer, DB 104, dark green, red, yellow & white, 1991, UK backstamp, limited edition of 700.. **250**

Carol Singer, Music Box, DB 53, red, yellow & green, 1986-89... **325**

Cheerleader, DB 142, red, 1994, limited edition of 1,000 .... **300**

Choir Singer, DB 223, white cassock, red robe, 2001, RDICC exclusive **45**

Cinderella, DB 231, pink & yellow, RDICC exclusive, 2001 .... **70**

Clown, DB 128, white costume w/black stars & pompons, red square on trousers & red ruff at neck, 1992, limited edition of 750 .... **750**

Collector Bunnykins

Collector, DB 54, brown, blue & grey, 1987, RDICC (ILLUS.) **550**

Cooling Off, DB 3, maroon coat, 1972-87........ **185**

Cymbals, DB 107, dark green, red & yellow, from the Oompah Band series, 1991, limited edition of 250 .... **525**

Cymbals, DB 25, red, blue & yellow, from the Oompah Band series, 1984-90................. **115**

Daisie Bunnykins Spring Time, DB 7, blue, white & yellow, 1972-83...................... **325**

Detective, DB 193, 1999, limited edition of 2,500.. **165**

Dodgem Car Bunnykins, DB 249, red car, 2001, limited edition of 2,500......................... **175**

Dollie Bunnykins Playtime, DB 80, white & yellow, 1988, by Higbee, limited edition of 250 .... **225**

Dollie Bunnykins Playtime, DB 80, white & yellow, 1988, by Hornes, limited edition of 250... **225**

Double Bass Player, DB 185, green & yellow striped jacket, green trousers, yellow straw hat, 1999, limited edition of 2,500........ **150**

Downhill, DB 31, yellow, green, maroon & grey, 1985-88.. **195**

Drum-Major, DB 27, red, blue & yellow, Oompah Band series, 1984-90 .... **110**

Limited Edition Drummer

Drummer, DB 108, dark green & red, white drum, Oompah Band series, 1991, limited edition of 200 (ILLUS.) **525**

Drummer, DB 26A, blue, yellow, red & cream, 50th anniversary edition, Oompah Band series, 1984 .... **150**

Drummer, DB 89, blue trousers & sleeves, yellow vest, cream & red drum, Royal Doulton Collectors Band series, 1990, limited edition of 250 .... **525**

Easter Surprise, DB 225, yellow, pink & mauve, 2000, limited edition of 2,500 .... **75**

Eskimo, DB 275, yellow coat & boots, orange trim, Figure of the Year, 2003 .... **65**

Family Photograph, DB 67, pink, black & white, 1988 .... **165**

Father Bunnykins, DB 227, red braces, red-striped tie, 2001, limited edition of 2,000, pr. (sold only as a pair w/Mother & Baby) **150**

Father, Mother and Victoria, DB 68, blue, grey, maroon & yellow, 1988-96 .... **65**

Federation, DB 224, green, Australian flag, 2000, limited edition of 2,500 .... **125**

Fireman Bunnykins

Fireman, DB 75, dark blue & yellow, 1989 to present (ILLUS.) **45**

Bunnykins Fisherman

Fisherman, DB 84, maroon, yellow & grey, 1990-93 (ILLUS.) **125**

Footballer, DB 117, green & white, 1991, limited edition of 250 .... **650**

Footballer, DB 121, blue shirt & white shorts, 1991, limited edition of 250 .... **650**

Fortune Teller, DB 218, red, black & yellow, white ball, 2000 .... **65**

Freefall, DB 41, grey, yellow & white, 1986-89 .... **325**

Gardener, DB 156, brown jacket, white shirt, grey trousers, light green wheelbarrow, 1996-98 .... **50**

Goalkeeper, DB 116, green & black, 1991, limited edition of 250 .... **650**

Goalkeeper, DB 120, yellow & black, 1991, limited edition of 250 .... **650**

Golfer, DB 255, maroon & yellow, 2002............ **80**

Grandpa's Story, DB 14, burgundy, grey, yellow, blue & green, 1975-83........................ **350**

Guardsman, DB 127, scarlet jacket, black trousers & bearskin hat, 1992, limited edition of 1,000 .... **775**

Halloween, DB 132, orange & yellow pumpkin, 1993-97................................... **80**

Happy Birthday, Music Box, DB 36, 1984-93 .... **175**

Harry the Herald, DB 115, yellow & dark green, 1991, Royal Family series, limited edition of 300...................................... **1,000**

Harry the Herald, DB 95, blue, red & yellow, 1990, Royal Family series, limited edition of 250....................................... **575**

Hornpiper, DB 261, brown, 2003 Special Event **43**

Indian, DB 202, yellow buckskin, red trim, 1999, limited edition of 2,500........................ **125**

Jack & Jill, DB 222, tableau, brown pants, yellow & white dress, 2000 .... **125**

Jockey, DB 169, green, white & yellow jockey suit, black shoes, 1997, limited edition of 2,000 .... **240**

Jogging, Music Box, DB 37, yellow & blue, 1987-89 .... **275**

Bunnykins Limited Edition Joker

Joker, DB 171, yellow jacket, orange & white trousers, black hat, 1997, limited edition of 2,500 (ILLUS.) **225**

Judy, DB 235, blue & yellow, 2001, limited edition of 2,500 .... **180**

Juliet, DB 283, RDICC 2003 membership renewal figure................................... **50**

King John, DB 91, purple, yellow & white, Royal Family series, 1990, limited edition of 250................................... **550**

Knockout, DB 30, yellow, green & white,
1984-88 .... **225**
Liberty Bell, DB 257, green & black, 2001,
limited edition of 2,001 .... **125**
Little Boy Blue, DB 239, blue, white & yel-
low, 2002 .... **60**
Little John, DB 243, brown cloak, 2001 .... **60**
Lollipop Man, DB 65, white & yellow, 1988-
91 .... **125**

Limited Edition Magician

Magician, DB 159, black suit, yellow shirt,
yellow table cloth w/red border, 1998,
limited edition of 1,000 (ILLUS.) **695**
Mandarin, DB 252, yellow & black, 2001,
limited edition of 2,500 .... **185**
Master Potter, DB 131, blue, white, green &
brown, 1992-93, RDICC Special **250**
Merry Christmas, DB 194, tableau, 1999,
limited edition 2000 .... **525**
Minstrel, DB 211, 1999, limited edition of
2,500 .... **105**
Mother, DB 189, blue, white & red, 1999,
Figure of the Year series **45**
Mother and Baby, DB 226, blue, white
apron, 2001, limited edition of 2,000, pr.
(sold only w/Father) **150**
Mountie, DB 135, red jacket, dark blue trou-
sers, brown hat, 1993, limited edition of
750 .... **800**
Mr. Bunnybeat Strumming, DB 16, pink &
yellow coat, blue & white striped trousers,
white w/blue polka dot neck bow, 1982-
88 .... **200**
Mr. Bunnykins at the Easter Parade, DB
18, red, yellow & brown, 1982-93 .... **85**
Mr. Bunnykins Autumn Days, DB 5, ma-
roon, yellow & blue, 1972-82 .... **300**
Mrs. Bunnykins at the Easter Parade, DB
19, pale blue & maroon, 1982-96 .... **75**
**Mrs. Bunnykins at the Easter Parade, Mu-
sic Box,** DB 39, blue, yellow & maroon,
1987-91 .... **295**
Mystic, DB 197, green, yellow & mauve,
1999 (ILLUS., top of next column) **55**
Nurse, DB 74A, dark & light blue & white,
red cross, 1989-94 .... **250**
Old Balloon Seller, DB 217, multicolored,
1999, limited edition of 2,000 .... **195**
Olympic, DB 28B, gold & green, 1984 .... **600**

Bunnykins Mystic

Oompah Band, DB 105, 106, 107, 108,
109, green, 1991, limited edition of 250,
the set **2,750**
Oompah Band, DB 86, 87, 88, 89, blue,
1990, limited edition of 250, the set **2,750**
Out for a Duck, DB 160, white, beige &
green, 1995, limited edition of 1,250 .... **315**

Partners in Collecting by Bunnykins

Partners in Collecting, DB 151, red, white
& blue, 1995, RDICC (ILLUS.) **125**
Piper, DB 191, green, brown & black, 1999,
limited edition of 3,000 .... **150**

Bunnykins Polly

Polly, DB 71, pink, 1988-93 (ILLUS.)................ **125**
Prince Frederick, DB 48, green, white &
red, Royal Family series, 1986-90 .... **125**
Prince John, DB 266, orange & green
cloak, 2002 .... **60**
Princess Beatrice, DB 93, yellow & gold,
Royal Family series, 1990, limited edition
of 250.. **465**
Queen Sophie, DB 92, pink & purple, Royal
Family series, 1990, limited edition of 250..... **465**
Ringmaster, DB 165, black hat & trousers,
red jacket, white waistcoat & shirt, black
bow tie, 1996, limited edition of 1,500........... **500**
Robin Hood, DB 244, green, 2001................. **60**
Rock and Roll, DB 124, white, blue & red,
1991, limited edition of 1,000......................... **395**
Sailor, DB 166, white & blue, 1997, Bun-
nykins of the Year series **45**

Sands of Time Bunnykins

Sands of Time, DB 229, yellow, 2000, limited order period of three months (ILLUS.)....... **60**

Santa Christmas Tree Ornament

Santa, DB 62, Christmas tree ornament, red
& white, edition limited to 1987 (ILLUS.).... **1,500**
Santa's Helper, DB 192, red, green & yel-
low, 1999, limited edition of 2,500.................. **65**
School Days, DB 57, dark green, white &
yellow, 1987-94... **125**
Schoolmaster, DB 60, black, green &
white, 1987-96... **60**

Seaside, DB 177, blue bathing costume,
white & blue bathing cap, yellow sandy
base, Bunnykins of the Year, 1998.................. **55**
Shopper, DB 233, green, pink, brown, Bun-
nykins of the Year, 2002.................................. **50**
Sleepytime, DB 15, brown, white, yellow,
blue & red, 1975-93... **75**

Bunnykins Sleighride

Sleighride, DB 81, green, yellow, red, 1989
(ILLUS.).. **155**
Soccer Players, DB 209, 1999, limited edi-
tion of 2,500, the set (sold only in set of 5)...... **625**
Sousaphone, DB 23, red, blue & yellow,
Oompah Band series, 1984-90 .... **115**
Statue of Liberty, DB 198, red, white &
blue, 1999, limited edition of 3,000................ **140**
Storytime, DB 59, dress w/green polka dots
on white, yellow shoes & yellow dress
w/green shoes, 1987 .... **345**
Strawberries, DB 278, tableau, issued in a
pair w/Tennis, 2003, limited edition of
3,000, pr.. **150**
Susan, DB 70, white, blue & yellow, 1988-
93 .... **125**
Sweet Dreams Baby Bunnykins, DB 276,
2002.. **60**

Bunnykins Sweetheart

Sweetheart, DB 174, white & blue, pink
heart, 1997, limited edition of 2,500
(ILLUS.).. **205**

Sydney, DB 195, blue, white, black & brown, 1999, limited edition of 2,500............ **175**

Tally Ho Bunnykins

Tally Ho!, DB 78, light blue coat & white rocking horse, yellow sweater, 1988 (ILLUS.).. **205**

Tally Ho!, Music Box, DB 33B, "William," red coat, maroon tie, 1988-91 .... **300**

Tom, DB 72, brown, white & blue, 1988-93 .... **90**

Touchdown, DB 29A, blue & white, 1985-88 .... **165**

Touchdown, DB 96 (Ohio State University), grey & orange, 1990, limited edition of 200 .... **625**

Touchdown, DB 98 (Cincinnati Bengals), orange & black, 1990, limited edition of 200 .... **625**

Tourist, DB 190, blue & yellow, ICC on hat, 1999, limited order period of three months... **85**

Trick or Treat, DB 162, red dress, black hat, shoes & cloak, white moon & stars, 1995, limited edition of 1,500........................ **850**

Trumpeter, DB 106, dark green, red & yellow, Oompah Band series, 1991, limited edition of 250.. **500**

Trumpeter, DB 87, blue uniform & yellow trumpet, Oompah Band series, 1990, limited edition of 250 .... **500**

Uncle Sam, DB 175, red jacket, yellow shirt, blue & white striped trousers, red, white & blue hat, platinum bow tie, 1997, limited edition of 1,500.. **205**

Vicar, DB 254, 2002, limited to renewing members of RDICC **45**

Wee Willie Winkie, DB 270, blue w/yellow tinges to nightgown, 2002 .... **55**

Wicket Keeper, DB 150, white, beige & black, 1995, limited edition of 1,000 .... **265**

William, DB 69, red & white, 1988-93................. **85**

Wizard, DB 168, brown rabbit, purple robes & hat, 1997, limited edition of 2,000 .... **400**

Florence Ceramics

Some of the finest figurines and artwares were produced between 1940 and 1962 by the Florence Ceramics Company of Pasadena, California. Florence Ward began

working with ceramics following the death of her son, Jack, in 1939.

Mrs. Ward had not worked with clay before her involvement with classes at the Pasadena Hobby School. After study and firsthand experience, she began production in her garage, using a kiln located outside the garage to conform with city regulations. The years 1942-44 were considered her "garage" period.

In 1944 Florence Ceramics moved to a small plant in Pasadena, employing fifty-four employees and receiving orders of $250,000 per year. In 1948 it was again necessary to move to a larger facility in the area with the most up-to-date equipment. The number of employees increased to more than 100. Within five years Florence Ceramics was considered one of the finest producers of semi-porcelain figurines and artwares.

Florence created a wide range of items including figurines, lamps, picture frames, planters and models of animals and birds. It was her extensive line of women in beautiful gowns and gentlemen in fine clothes that gave her the most pleasure and was the foundation of her business. Two of her most popular lines of figurines were inspired by the famous 1860 Godey's Ladies' Book and by famous artists from the Old Master group. In the mid-1950s two bird lines were produced for several years. One of the bird lines was designed by Don Winton and the other was a line of contemporary sculpted bird and animal figures designed by the well-known sculptor Betty Davenport Ford.

There were several unsuccessful contemporary artware lines produced for a short time. The Driftware line consisted of modern freeform bowls and accessories. The Floraline is a rococo line with overglazed decoration. The Gourmet Pottery, a division of Florence Ceramics Company, produced accessory serving pieces under the name of Scandia and Sierra.

Florence products were manufactured in the traditional porcelain process with a second firing at a higher temperature after the glaze had been applied. Many pieces had overglaze paint decoration and clay ruffles, roses and lace dipped in slip prior to the third firing.

Florence Marks

Figures

"Abigail," Godey lady, beige full-skirted dress, cape & bonnet w/green bow tied under chin, 8" h. **$100-150**

"Adeline" Figure

"Adeline," brown hair w/applied roses in both sides of hair, green off-the-shoulder full pleated dress, holding a pink shawl wrapped around her lower arms, 9" h. (ILLUS.) **275-325**

"Amelia," Godey lady, brocade fabric dress, 12" h. **1,500-2,000**

Rare Version of Florence "Angel"

"Angel," rare late version w/spread wings, 7 3/4" h. (ILLUS.) **100-125**

"Ann," pink dress & white hat, 6" h. **50-75**

"Annabel," Godey lady, standing w/right arm bent & holding a card in hand, left arm in outward position, long full jacket w/gold trim, large hat, articulated fingers, 8 " h. **375-400**

"Ava," dirndl-type dress w/brown skirt & tan peasant blouse, left hand on hip & right arm raised & holding a large green basket on her head, 10 1/2" h. **175-225**

"Barbara," Colonial era woman standing in a full gown w/slipper toe showing under front, applied decor in her tall hairdo, 8 1/2" h. **550-600**

"Bea," teal dress w/white hat, 6" h. **100-125**

"Blossom Girl," Chinese girl standing wearing a round cap and long side-button coat flaring at the hem above a floor-length dress, 8 1/4" h. **100-125**

Florence "Blueboy" Figure

"Blueboy," figure of man standing on base, blue pants & coat w/white trim, white stockings, holding plumed hat in right hand, 12" h. (ILLUS.) **350-400**

"Bride," lace veil, 8 1/2" h. **1,250-1,500**

Florence "Bryan" Figure

"Choir Boys" Florence Figures

"Bryan," young man in dress suit standing next to pedestal, gray suit, 11" h. (ILLUS.) **2,000-2,500**

"Camille," figure of standing woman wearing white dress trimmed in gold, shawl over both arms made entirely of hand-dipped lace, brown hair, white triangular hat w/applied pink rose, ribbon tied to right side of neck, 8 1/2" h. **175-225**

"Camille," figure of standing woman wearing white dress trimmed in gold, shawl over both arms made entirely of hand-dipped lace, brown hair, white triangular hat w/applied pink rose, ribbon tied to right side of neck, one hand, 8 1/2" h. .. **250-275**

"Carmen," woman dancer w/head slightly turned & tilted to left, right arm bent w/fingers touching black hair, left arm across body at waist, ruffled lace short-sleeved white dress w/red & gold trim, 14" h. **1,200-1,500**

"Carol," woman standing wearing a wide gown, one hand holding up the front hem exposing her foot, the other arm away from her body, 10" h **550-600**

"Catherine," seated on an open-backed settee, holding a hat, 7 3/4" l., 6 3/4" h. **500-600**

"Cecile," woman standing wearing a long full gown & a lace shawl, aqua gown, 8 1/2" h. (ILLUS., next column) ...... **1,200-1,250.**

"Charmaine," woman holding a parasol, ruffled long dress, large hat w/flowers, 8 1/2" h. **175-200**

"Chinese boy," standing wearing flaring jacket & long flaring pants, holding a vase under one arm, 7 3/4" h.......................... **100-125**

"Choir Boys," royal red robes, 6 " h., set of 3 (ILLUS., top of page) **150-225**

Florence "Cecile" Figure

"Cinderella and Prince Charming" Figure Group

"Cinderella & Prince Charming," dancing couple on raised base, both in white Renaissance period costume, white w/gold trim & gold tiara on her blonde hair, he holds a silver slipper behind her back in his right hand, 11 3/4" h. (ILLUS.).... **1,750-2,000**

"Clarissa," woman in full-sleeved jacket & long swirled & pleated skirt, bonnet & holding a muff in right hand, left hand on her shoulder, 7 3/4" h.............................. **125-150**

"Claudia," ruffled dress w/lace trim, lace shawl on shoulders, large hat, bouquet in left hand, no hands showing, 8 1/4" h. . **175-200**

"Claudia," ruffled dress w/lace trim, no lace shawl, large hat, articulated hands, 8 1/4" h. **200-225**

"Colleen" with Articulated Hands

"Colleen," woman standing w/head slightly turned to left, both arms at the front w/articulated hands, long wind-blown dress w/white collar, bonnet w/ribbon tied under chin, 8" h. (ILLUS.) **225-250**

Florence "Cynthia" Figure

"Cynthia," standing w/left arm extended slightly backward, head turned slightly to left, right hand holding large white hat trimmed w/flowers, aquamarine overdress w/white underskirt, lacy jabot at neck & lace cuffs, articulated fingers, 9 1/4" h. (ILLUS.)..................................... **450-500**

"Dear Ruth," 9" h. **800-1,000**

Florence "Deborah" Figurine

"Deborah," woman in a long flaring & swirling gown w/lace at collar & shoulder cuffs, moss green gown, 10" h. (ILLUS.)........... **650-725**

"Grandmother and I" Figure Group

"Diane," woman in Victorian costume wearing a high rounded bonnet w/feather & a high-collared long coat opening over a ruffled dress, one arm down at side holding a muff, 8" h. **200-225**

"Don," man standing in 1950s era tuxedo, 9" h. **225-275**

"Douglas," man standing in front of square column wearing Victorian outfit w/top hat, dress coat & vest, one arm behind his back, one hand on lapel, 8 1/4" h. **125-150**

Florence "Elaine" Figure

"Elaine," woman wearing a long, flaring Victorian coat w/wide sleeves, a small bonnet tied on w/a large ribbon under her chin, her hands in a muff at the front, 6" h. (ILLUS.) **50-75**

"Elizabeth," woman in 18th c. costume w/a wide flaring aqua gown w/half-sleeves & a lace-trimmed bodice, long curls down her neck, seated on a grey settee, 7" w., 8 1/4" h. **250-300**

"Fair Lady," woman in Gay Nineties gown standing on scrolled base decorated w/roses & gold trim, rose dress w/ornate white lace trim panel in front of dress, rose trim at bodice, upswept brown hair w/roses, right hand raised, articulated fingers, 11 1/2" h. **1,750-2,000**

Florence Figure of "Geoff"

"Geoff," boy wearing 18th c. costume standing beside a seated dog, 6" h. (ILLUS.) **375-400**

"Grandmother & I," two women sitting at a round table covered w/a white tablecloth w/a teapot on it, the older woman sitting on a white chair holding a teacup in her right hand, wearing a violet dress w/lace trimmed cuffs & collar, the young woman dressed in a pink dress w/lace trim at

the neck & a bow tied in the back, holding a teacup in her left hand, 6 3/4" h.
(ILLUS., top of previous page) **2,000-2,500**
"Irene," Godey lady in long dress w/gold
trim, flower in upswept hair, right hand
holding muff near face, 6" h. **50-75**
"Jeannette," Godey lady, rose colored full-
skirted dress w/peplum, white collar,
flower at neck, left hand holding hat
w/bow, right hand holding parasol, articu-
lated hands, 7 3/4" h. **175-200**
"Josephine," woman in Gay Nineties cos-
tume wearing a large feathered hat &
long gown w/leg-o-mutton sleeves, one
hand on her hip, the other holding up
hem of gown, 9" h.................................. **250-275**
"Joyce," woman wearing full off-the-shoul-
der gown w/shoulder ruffles, a wide-
brimmed picture hat, arms away at the
front, 9" h... **400-475**
"Karla," ballerina, standing "en pointe"
w/head tilted & one arm stretched out,
the other curved close to her face, deeply
ruffled tutu, 9 3/4" h. **200-225**
"Lantern Boy," 8 1/4" h............................. **100-125**
"Lillian Russell," woman in Gay Nineties
gown, her hair piled high & her arms
away from her body, the off-the-shoulder
gown w/floral trim around the collar &
bands down around the widely flaring
skirt w/wide overlapping ruffled panel,
13 1/2" h... **1,750-2,000**

Florence "Little Don" Figure

"Little Don," boy standing w/a grey cat at
right side w/both arms extended outward,
red pants & shirt w/ruffled lace trim, white
cummerbund & shoes, from the Old Master group, Francisco Goya's "Don Manuel
Osorio," 7 3/4" h. (ILLUS.) **1,000-1,250**
"Lorry," youth wearing late Victorian outfit
w/cap & short jacket, books under one
arm, 8" h. **400-450**

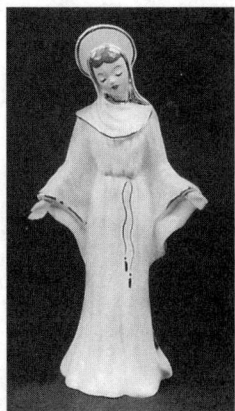

Florence "Madonna" Figure

"Madonna," woman standing wearing
white hood and long-sleeved long white
gown w/gold trim, halo around head,
10" h. (ILLUS.).. **100-125**
"Marcella," girl ballerina standing w/right
foot pointed in front of left leg, arms w/el-
bows slightly bent & pointed downward,
pink tutu, applied roses in brown hair,
7" h. **125-150**
"Marie Antoinette," woman in ornate 18th
c. gown, her hair piled high & trimmed
w/flowers, high lace collar & wide rounded gown w/center flower-trimmed drapes
opening over tiered lace panels, arms in
front, one holding a closed fan, large skirt
style, 10" h. **300-350**

"Marlene" Figure in Brocade Gown

"Marlene," woman standing w/her hair up
w/curl down the back, arms away in front,
wearing a mint green brocade gown,
10" h. (ILLUS.) **1,500-2,000**
"Mary," woman seated in balloon-back
armchair, wearing a small feathered hat,

gown w/lace jabot & long sleeves, her hands in lap & on chair arm, 7 1/2" h. .. **500-550**

"Memories" Figure

"Memories," elderly woman sitting in a white wing chair w/gold trim, reading a book, white dress w/gold trim, white lace shawl around shoulders, 5 3/4" w., 6 1/2" h. (ILLUS.) **650-700**

"Musette," Godey lady, standing & slightly leaning forward, wearing a picture hat & off-the-shoulder gown w/lace collar & cuffs, front gathers expose slips, 8 3/4" h. **300-325**

"Pamela," girl standing but not wearing a bonnet, long swirling short-sleeved dress, a basket of flowers in one hand, 7 1/2" h. **400-450**

"Peter," boy standing w/legs apart & holding a package in his right hand, white jacket, shirt & shoes, pale blue pants & hat, brown hair, 5 1/2" h. **100-125**

Florence "Pinkie" Figure

"Pinkie," figure of woman standing on base, wearing white dress w/rose trim & hat w/loose ribbon, right arm behind back, left arm held in front of body, 12" h. (ILLUS.) **350-400**

"Princess," woman in simple 18th c. costume, the gown w/flower trim at neck, large bow tied to right side of waist w/ruffle extending down the dress front, left hand holding fan, roses in hair, articulated fingers, 10 1/4" h. **500-550**

"Rhett," man standing in front of low stone wall, right hand on vest, left hand in pocket, white ruffled shirt trimmed in color, flaring frock coat, 9" h. **150-175**

"Rosalie" Figure by Florence

"Rosalie," woman wearing long dress w/lace ruffle at the off-the-shoulder neckline, brown hair w/roses, holding skirt out at each side, articulated fingers, 9 1/2" h. (ILLUS.)... **550-600**

Florence "Scarlett" Figure

"Scarlett," Godey lady, wearing royal red dress & bonnet, right hand holding a muff near face, left hand holding handbag, no hands showing, 8 3/4" h. (ILLUS.)......... **100-125**

"Spring Reverie," maiden standing in long simple dress, arms away from body at front w/bird on one hand, 12 1/2" h. . **1,000-1,250**

"Story Hour" Figure with Boy

"Story Hour," seated mother & girl, woman reading book held in left hand, rose dress w/lace at neck, roses in her hair, girl w/blonde hair w/right arm on bench, ruffled lace short-sleeved white dress w/blue & pink trim, small boy dressed in blue shirt & pants & standing near girl 8" l., 6 3/4" h. (ILLUS.) **900-1,000**

"Suzanna," woman in Gay Nineties outfit, standing w/one hand up to rim of large tilted picture hat, the long fur-trimmed jacket w/leg-o-mutton sleeves, other hand holding back coat to expose lace-tiered long gown, 9 1/4" h........................ **350-400**

"Tess," woman standing wearing long dress w/no lace ruffle at neckline, large picture hat, arms away w/one hand holding edge of skirt up over shoe, 7 1/4" h. **200-250**

"Virginia" Figure with Lace Collar

"Virginia," woman standing wearing a wide picture hat & off-the-shoulder gown w/lace-trimmed collar & short sleeves, long flaring & tiered moss green gown, 9" h. (ILLUS.)...................................... **1,500-1,750**

Florence Figure of "Victoria"

"Victoria," woman in Victorian dress seated on serpentine-back tufted Victorian settee, wearing a small bonnet tied w/a bow, rose red gown w/ruffle-trimmed panels at waist, ruffled hem trim, arms away, 8 1/4" l., 7" h. (ILLUS.).................. **250-300**

"Wood Nymph" Ballerina Figure

"Wood Nymph," girl ballerina standing on domed base w/flower-trimmed tree stump at back, one arm outstretched behind, one bent in front, 7 3/4" h. (ILLUS.)... **225-275**

"Yvonne" Florence Figure

"Yvonne," woman standing wearing Victorian outfit, small ribbon-trimmed bonnet, long-sleeved jacket w/peplum over long wide dress, arms at side, one holding a small ribbon-trimmed box, 8 3/4" h. (ILLUS.)... **200-225**

Other Items

Ford Dog Advertising Bank

Bank, "Ford," model of dog standing w/left paw across body w/"Ford" advertising under left paw & right paw on top of head, head turned slightly to left, glossy grey w/black highlights, in-mold mark "Florence Ceramics Pasadena, California" & copyright symbol, 6 3/4" h. (ILLUS.).......... **25-30**
Bust, "David," young boy w/crewcut, 9 1/2" h. **100-125**
Bust, "Modern Boy," 9 1/2" h. **100-125**
Bust, "Pamela," girl w/ponytail, 9 1/2" h. ... **100-125**

Flower holder, "Belle," Gay Nineties woman w/a large hat & long flaring gown, holder at the back, 7 1/2" h. **50-75**
Flower holder, "Blossom Girl," Chinese woman standing wearing a round cap and long side-button coat flaring at the hem above a floor-length dress, w/flower vase, 8 1/4" h. **50-75**
Flower holder, "Chinese Child/Boy," bamboo-form holder at side, 7" h. **100-125**
Flower holder, "Chinese Girl," holder at the back, 7 3/4 .... **40-50**
Flower holder, "Lantern Boy," 8 1/4" h. **50-75**
Flower holder, "Rene," standing woman in European peasant costume w/lobed upright headpiece on head, dirndl outfit w/long sleeves & a wide apron w/peasant decoration over long dress, a basket in each hand at sides, 8 1/2" h. **150-175**
Flower holder, "June," girl in front of pleated-edge block, 6" h. **35-40**
Powder box, "Ballet," 6" h. **300-325**

Flow Blue

Flow Blue ironstone and semi-porcelain was manufactured mainly in England during the second half of the 19th century. The early ironstone was produced by many of the well known English potters and was either transferprinted or hand-painted (brush stroke). The bulk of the ware was exported to the United States or Canada.

The "flow" or running quality of the cobalt blue designs was the result of introducing certain chemicals into the kiln during the final firing. Some patterns are so "flown" that it is difficult to ascertain the design. The transfers were of several types: Asian, Scenic, Marble or Floral.

The earliest Flow Blue ironstone patterns were produced during the period between about 1840 and 1860. After the Civil War Flow Blue went out of style for some years but was again manufactured and exported to the United States beginning about the 1880s and continuing through the turn of the century. These later Flow Blue designs are on a semi-porcelain body rather than heavier ironstone and the designs are mainly florals. Also see Antique Trader Pottery & Porcelain Ceramics Price Guide, 4th Edition.

ABBEY (George Jones & Sons, ca. 1900)
Beeker, 3 1/2" d., 4" h. **$100**
Bowl, 8" d., 4 1/2" h. **550**
Bowl, 9" d., 4 1/2" h. **600**
Hot water pot, 6" h. **125**

Abbey Punch Bowl

Punch bowl, 10 1/2" d., 6" h. (ILLUS.)............... **750**
Shredded wheat dish, 6 1/4" l., 5" w. **150**

ABBEY (Petrus Regout Co., Maastricht, Holland, date unknown)

Abbey Cup & Saucer

Farmer's cup & saucer, oversized, cup
 5" d., 4" h. & saucer, 8" d. (ILLUS.) 165

ABERDEEN (Bourne & Leigh), ca. 1900, Floral, goes with path name
Butter pat, 3 1/2" d. 40

ACME (Sampson Hancock & Sons, ca. 1900)
Plate, 9" d., five-sided 150

Acme Plate

Plate, 9" d., scalloped (ILLUS.) 125

ADDERLEY (Doulton & Company, ca. 1886), Floral
Vegetable bowl, open, round, 8 1/2" d.,
 2 3/4" h. 195

ALASKA (W.H. Grindley & Company, ca. 1891)
Bowl, berry, 5" d. 40
Creamer, 5 1/4 h. 200
Plate, 10" d., scalloped 115
Platter, 14" l. 300
Soup plate w/flanged rim, 9" d. 90

ALBANY (Johnson Bros., ca. 1900)
Plate, 8" d. 65
Tea cup & saucer, cup, 2 1/2" h., 3 1/2" d,
 saucer, 6" d. 115

ALBANY (W.H. Grindley & Company, ca. 1899)
Butter pat, 3 1/2" d. 45
Plate, 6 1/2 d. 50

Albany Platter

Platter, 14 1/2" l. (ILLUS.) 275

ALTHEA (Podmore, Walker & Company, ca. 1834-1859)

Althea Coffeepot

Coffeepot, cov., 11" d. (ILLUS.) **1,200**
Creamer, 6" h. **300**
Sugar, cov., footed, two-handled, 7" h. **475**
Tea cup & saucer, cup, 4" d., 2 1/2" h.,
 saucer, 5 3/4" d. 165

ALTON (W.H. Grindley & Company, ca. 1891)

Alton Platter

Platter, 18" l. (ILLUS.) 550

AMOUR (Societé Céramique, Dutch, ca. 1865)

Amour Footed Compote

Compote, footed, two-handled, 10" d.
 (ILLUS.).. 575

ANDORRA (Johnson Bros., ca. 1901)

Andorra Vegetable Bowl

Vegetable bowl, open, round, 9 1/2" d.
 (ILLUS.).. 165

ANEMONE (Lockhart & Arthur, ca. 1855)
Plate, 10 1/4" d.. 135
Platter, 16" l... 525

ARGYLE (W.H. Grindley & Company, ca. 1896)

Argyle Platter

Platter, 16" l. (ILLUS.)... 450
Platter, 18" l... 575

ASHBURTON (W.H. Grindley & Company, ca. 1891)
Plate, 8" d.. 75

Plate, 9" d.. 90
Platter, 12" l... 175
Platter, 14" l... 295

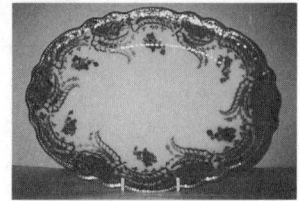

Ashburton Platter

Platter, 16" l. (ILLUS.)... 425
Platter, 18" l... 550

Ashburton Sauce Ladle

Sauce ladle, 7" l. (ILLUS.) 295
Plate, 10" d.. 115

ATALANTA (Wedgwood & Company, ca. 1900)

Atalanta Platter

Platter, 14" l. (ILLUS.)... 295

BALTIC (W.H. Grindley & Company, ca. 1891)
Gravy boat, 7" l. 125
Plate, 10" d.. 100

BEAUFORT (W.H. Grindley & Company, ca. 1903)

Beaufort Underplate

Underplate, for cov. butter, two-handled, 9" d. (ILLUS.) 125

BELMONT (J.H. Weatherby & Sons, ca. 1892)
Plate, 9" d. 75
Plate, 10" d. 95

BLUE DANUBE, THE (Johnson Bros., ca. 1900)
Creamer, 4" h. 200
Plate, 10" d. 95
Soup bowl, open, 9" d. 80
Sugar, cov., 5" h. 275
Tea cup & saucer 100

BLUEBELL (Dillwyn-Swansea, Welch, ca. 1840)

Bluebell Syrup Pitcher

Syrup pitcher w/pewter lid, 8 1/2" h (IL-LUS.) 800

BOUQUET (Henry Alcock, ca. 1895)

Bouquet Vegetable Dish

Vegetable dish, cov., footed, 12" l. (ILLUS.)...... 300

BRAZIL (W.H. Grindley & Company, ca. 1891)

Brazil Sugar Bowl

Sugar bowl, cov., 5" h. (ILLUS.) 250

BRITISH SCENERY (Davenport & Company, ca. 1856)
Charger, 13" d. 350

British Scenery Platter

Platter, 19" l. (ILLUS.) 750
Vegetable bowl, oval, 10" l., 3 1/2" h 400

BURMESE (Thomas Rathbone & Company, ca. 1912)
Serving dish, rectangular, pierced, two-handled, 13 1/2 l., 9" w. 375

CALICO (Warwick China Company, American, ca. 1900, aka Daisy Chain)

Calico Tankard-type Pitcher

Pitcher, 7 1/2" h., 9" w. (ILLUS.) 275

CAMBRIDGE (Alfred Meakin, ca. 1891)
Platter, 14" l. 325
Relish dish, oval, 8 1/2" l. 145

CANISTER (Unknown, marked "Germany," ca. 1891)

Sugar Canister

Canister, cov., marked "Sugar," 6" d., 8" h. (ILLUS.) 225
Spice jar, cov., 5" h. 75

CASHMERE (Francis Morley, ca. 1850)

Cashmere Soup Plate

Plate, 10 1/2" d. **250**
Soup plate, 10" d. (ILLUS.).................................. **225**

CECIL (F. Till & Son, ca. 1891)
Bone dish, crescent-shaped.................................. **65**
Plate, 6" d.. **50**

CHINESE (Dimmock, ca. 1845)

Chinese Pattern Teapot

Tea set: cov. teapot, oversized cov. sugar & creamer; Primary body shape, teapot 9" h., the set (ILLUS. of teapot) **2,800**

CHRYSANTHEMUM (Myott, Son & Co., ca. 1907)

Chrysanthemum Platter

Platter, 14" l. (ILLUS.)... **400**

CLARENCE (W.H. Grindley & Co., ca. 1900)

Clarence Platter

Platter, 16" l. (ILLUS.).. **450**

CLAYTON (Johnson Bros., ca. 1902)

Part of Clayton Chamber Set

Chamber set: pitcher & bowl, chamber pot, shaving mug & small water pitcher; the set (ILLUS. of part) **2,500**
Chamber set: pitcher & bowl, chamber pot, toothbrush holder & shaving mug; the set .. **2,000**
Platter, 16" l.. **450**

Clayton Soup Plate

Soup plate w/flanged rim, 9" d. (ILLUS.)........... **95**
Vegetable dish, open, oval, 9" l. **165**

CLYTIE (Wedgwood & Co., Ltd., ca. 1908)
Plate, 10" d., w/turkey design **175**
Platter, 19" l., w/turkey design.......................... **1,000**

COLONIAL (J. & G. Meakin, ca. 1891)
Butter pat, 3 1/2" d. **45**
Vegetable bowl, open, oval, 9" l........................ **125**

CONWAY (New Wharf Pottery, ca. 1891)

Conway Vegetable Bowl

Vegetable bowl, open, 9 1/2" d. (ILLUS.) **195**

DAISY (Burgess & Leigh, ca. 1897)

Daisy Soup Plate

Soup plate w/flanged rim, 9" d. (ILLUS.) 95

DELFT (Minton, ca. 1893)

Delft Oyster Plate

Oyster plate, 10" d. (ILLUS.) 300

Delft Platter

Platter, 14" l. (ILLUS.) 325

DERBY (W.H. Grindley, ca. 1891)

Plate, 9" d. 85

Derby Platter

Platter, 14" l. (ILLUS.) 295
Soup plate w/flanged rim, 9" d. 85
Vegetable dish, cov., 12" l., 7" h. 275

DOT FLOWER (Unknown, ca. 1840)

Dot Flower Creamer

Creamer, 5" h. (ILLUS.) 275

EGERTON (Doulton & Co., Ltd., ca. 1905)

Cheese dome w/underplate, half-Stilton, very unusual, dome 8" w., 6" h., underplate, 10" d. 325
Plate, 8 1/2" d. 65
Plate, 9 1/2" d. 90
Plate, 10 1/2" d. 100
Platter, 12" l. 165
Platter, 16" l. 400
Platter, 18" l. 500
Soup plate w/flanged rim, 10 1/2" d. 100

Egerton Covered Vegetable

Vegetable dish, cov., 13" w., 6 1/2" h.
(ILLUS.)... 375

ENGLISH ROSE (Unknown, ca. 1891)

English Rose Soup Plate

Soup plate w/flanged rim, 9" d. (ILLUS.) 90

FAIRY VILLAS III (W. Adams & Sons, ca. 1891)

Plate, 8" d... 75
Plate, 10 1/4" d.. 125
Platter, 16" l... 450

FLORA (Thomas Walker, ca. 1845)

Flora Plate

Plate, 10 1/2" d. (ILLUS.).................................... 200

FLORIDA (Ford & Sons, ca. 1891)

Plate, 10 1/4" d... 100

Florida Platter

Platter, 17" l. (ILLUS.)... 500

Vegetable dish, cov., 12" w., 7" h. 300

GAINSBOROUGH (Ridgways, ca. 1905)

Creamer, 4" h.. 200
Sugar, cov., 5" h. 275

GERANIUM (Doulton & Co., ca. 1890s)

Bowl, heavily gilded, scalloped, footed,
10" l. 400

GIRONDE (W.H. Grindley, ca. 1891)

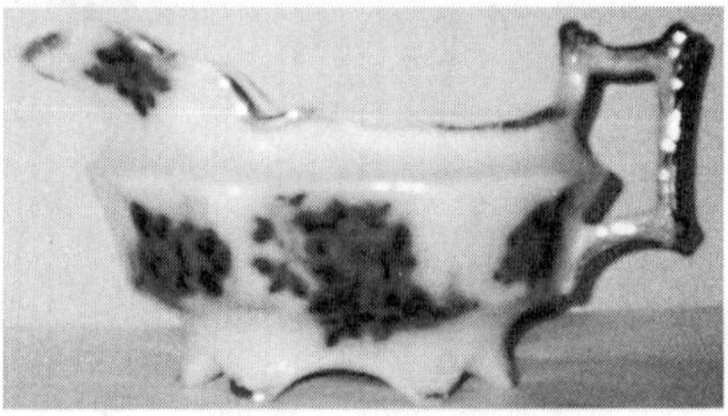

Gironde Gravy Boat

Gravy boat, 6 1/2" l. (ILLUS.)............................. 125
Plate, 10 1/4" d., 14-sided................................... 100

GLOIRE DE DIJON (Doulton & Co., ca. 1895)

Gloire de Dijon Pitcher

Pitcher, belonging to pitcher/bowl wash set
(ILLUS.) 275

GRACE (W.H. Grindley, ca. 1897)

Butter pat, 3 1/2" d. 45
Platter, 16" l.. 375

GRECIAN SCROLL (T.J. and J. Mayer, ca. 1850)

Grecian Scroll Teapot

Teapot, 10" h. (ILLUS.) 695

HADDON (Libertas, ca. 1891, Prussian)
Butter pat, 3 1/2" d. 45
Butter w/insert, cov. 325
Plate, 9" d. 90
Plate, 10" d. 100
Platter, 12" l. 175
Vegetable bowl, cov., round, 11" d.,
  6 1/2" h. 300
Vegetable bowl, open, oval, 9" d. 165

HEATH'S FLOWER (Thomas Heath, ca. 1830)

Heath's Flower Plate
Plate, 9 1/2" d., 12-sided (ILLUS.) 165

HOLLAND (Johnson Bros., ca. 1891)
Gravy boat, 6 1/2" l. 125

HOLLAND (Johnson Bros., ca. 1891)oll
Soup bowl, open, 8" d. 85
Vegetable dish, cov., footed, 12" l.,
  6 1/2" h. 275

HONC (Petrus Regout, ca. 1858)

Honc Bedpan
Bedpan (ILLUS.) 1,000

IVANHOE (Wedgwood & Co., ca. 1900)
Plate, 9 1/2" d. 125

Ivanhoe Plate
Plate, 10 1/2" d. (ILLUS.) 150

IVY (Davenport Potteries, ca. 1820-60)

Ivy Platter
Platter, 22" l., w/meat well (ILLUS.) 875

JENNY LIND (Arthur Wilkinson Ltd., Royal Staffordshire Pottery, ca. 1895)
Cup & saucer, cup 3 1/2" d., saucer
  5 3/4" d. 100
Plate, 6" d. 55

KENWORTH (Johnson Bros., ca. 1900)
Berry bowl, 5" d. 45

Kenworth Plate
Plate, 10" d. (ILLUS.) 100
Soup bowl, open, 9" d. 80

KNOX (New Wharf Potteries, ca. 1891)
Plate, 7" d.. 48
Tea cup & saucer, cup 4" h., 3 1/2" d., saucer 6" d.. 125

KYBER (W. Adams & Co., ca. 1891)
Plate, 9" d.. 85

LABELLE (Wheeling Pottery, ca. 1900)
Charger, 13" d.. 450

Labelle Portrait Plate

Portrait plate, 13" d., Lovely Ladies (ILLUS.) 495

LaBelle Ring-handled Dish

Ring-handled dish, 11" l., 10 1/2" w.
(ILLUS.).. 325

LAKEWOOD (Wood & Sons, ca. 1900)
Butter pat, 3 1/2" d.. 60
Tea cup & saucer, cup 4" h., 3 1/2" d., saucer 6" d.. 110

LORNE (W.H. Grindley, ca. 1900)
Bowl, berry, 5" d... 45
Platter, 12" l.. 165

MANHATTAN (Henry Alcock, ca. 1900)
Bowl, berry, 5" d... 45
Butter dish w/insert, cov. 325
Cake plate, two-handled....................................... 175

Plate, 8" d.. 55
Plate, 9" d.. 95
Platter, 14" l... 275
Platter, 16" l... 400
Soup plate w/flanged rim, 9" d..................... 90-95
Tea cup & saucer 100

Manhattan Covered Sugar

Tea set: teapot, sugar & creamer; the set
(ILLUS. of sugar)... 1,100
Vegetable dish, cov., footed 300

MARIE (W.H. Grindley, ca. 1891)

Marie Pitcher

Pitcher, 7" h. (ILLUS.) 275
Plate, 10 1/4" d.. 100

MARLBOROUGH (W.H. Grindley, ca. 1891)
Butter pat, 3 1/2" d... 45

Marlborough Graduated Pitchers

Pitcher, 6" h. (ILLUS. right)................................ 225
Pitcher, 8" d. (ILLUS. middle)............................ 325
Pitcher, 10" h. (ILLUS. left)................................ 400

Marlborough Open Vegetable Bowl

Vegetable bowl, open, oval, 9" l. (ILLUS.)........ **165**

MARTHA WASHINGTON (Unknown, English, ca. 1900, aka Chain of States)

Martha Washington States Plate

Plate, 9" d. (ILLUS.).. **150**

MEISSEN (F. Mehlem, ca. 1891)

Meissen Vegetable Bowl

Vegetable bowl, open, 10" d. (ILLUS.).............. **165**

MELBOURNE (W.H. Grindley, ca. 1891)
Bowl, berry, 5" d. **45**
Butter pat, 3 1/2" d. **45**
Cake plate, 12" d., two-handled **165**
Plate, 6" d.. **50**
Plate, 8" d.. **70**
Plate, 9" d... **90-95**

Melbourne Dinner Plate

Plate, 10" d. (ILLUS.) **125**
Platter, 14" l.. **275**
Platter, 16" l... **200-375**
Platter, 18" l.. **495**

Melbourne Soup Tureen

Soup tureen, cov., oval, footed, 14" l.,
  7 1/2" h. (ILLUS.) **650**
Vegetable bowl, cov., oval **300**
Vegetable bowl, open, round............................. **200**

MELROSE (Doulton & Co., ca. 1891)
Plate, 10 1/4" d... **90**
Platter, 20" l.. **600**

MIKADO (A.J. Wilkinson, ca. 1896)

Mikado Dinner Plate

Plate, 10 1/2" d. (ILLUS.)..................................... **100**
Platter, 18" l.. **600**
Soup plate w/flanged rim, 10 1/2" d. **100**

MILTON (Poutney & Bristol, ca. 1890s)

Milton Luncheon Plate

Plate, 9" d. (ILLUS.) **90**
Plate, 10" d. **115**
Platter, 18" l.. **575**
Sauce boat w/ladle & underplate, cov.,
  oval, footed.. **425**

Mongolian Gravy Boat

MONGOLIAN (F. & W., Unidentified Manufacturer, mid-to-late Victorian)
Charger, 14" d... **400**
Gravy boat, footed (ILLUS., top of page)......... **195**

MONTANA (Johnson Bros., ca. 1900)

Montana Luncheon Plate

Plate, 9" d. (ILLUS.).. **85**

MORNING GLORY (Elsmore/Forster, ca. 1853-71)

Morning Glory Cup & Saucer

Cup & saucer, no handle (ILLUS.)..................... **195**

MURIEL (Upper Hanley Potteries, ca. 1895)

Muriel Platter

Platter, 14"l. (ILLUS.).. **325**

NANKIN (Mellor, Venables & Co. or Thomas Walker, ca. 1845)

Plate from Nankin Tea Set

Tea set: teapot, oversized cov. sugar, creamer, 6 cups w/no handles & 6 saucers, 6 9" d. plates; Primary body style, the set (ILLUS.) **3,200**

NON PAREIL (Middleport Potteries, ca. 1891)
Butter pat **50**
Platter, 16" l.. **475**
Soup plate w/flanged rim, 9" d............................ **95**

NORMANDY (Johnson Bros., ca. 1900)
Bowl, berry, 5" d. 45
Butter pat, 3 1/2" d. 45
Plate, 9" d. 95-120

Normandy Soup Plate

Soup plate w/flanged rim, 10" d. (ILLUS.) 115

OLD CURIOSITY SHOP (Ridgways, ca. 1910)

Old Curiosity Shop Platter

Platter, 16" l. (ILLUS.) 450
Vegetable bowl, open, oval, 10" l. 195

ORCHID (John Maddock & Sons, Ltd., ca. 1896)
Platter, 16" l. 375
Platter, 18" l. 475

ORIENTAL (Samuel Alcock, ca. 1840)
Plate, 9 1/2" d. 150
Plate, 10 1/2" d. 200
Platter, 16" l. 600

Oriental Underplate

Underplate, two-handled w/reticulated tab
  handles, 13" d. (ILLUS.) 450

ORMONDE (Alfred Meakin, ca. 1891)
Plate, 8" d. 65

Plate, 10 1/4" d. 100

PAISLEY (Mercer, ca. 1890)

Paisley Platters, Bone Dishes, Gravy

Bone dish, crescent-shaped (ILLUS. lower
  left) 60
Gravy boat (ILLUS. lower right) 125
Platter, 20" l. (ILLUS. upper right) 650
Relish dish, 9" l. 125
Soup tureen, cov., round 675

PEKIN (Johnson Bros., ca. 1891)

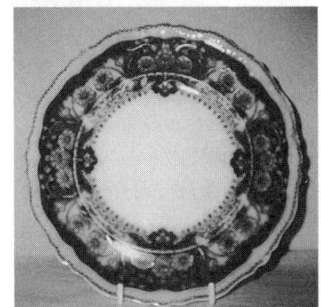

Pekin Dinner Plate

Plate, 10" d. (ILLUS.) 90

PLYMOUTH (New Wharf Pottery, ca. 1891)
Plate, 8" d. 85

Plymouth Dinner Plate

Plate, 10" d. (ILLUS.) 100
Tea cup & saucer 100

POPPY (Doulton & Co., ca. 1902)
Jardiniere, 10" h. 650

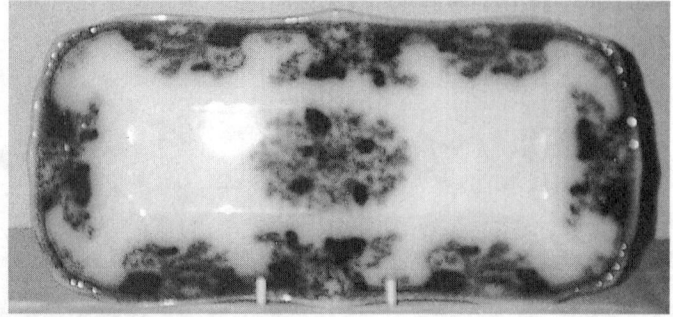

Roseville Celery Dish

PORTMAN (W.H. Grindley, ca. 1891)

Portman Platter

Platter, 14" l. (ILLUS.) **225**

QUEBEC (Paul Utzchneider, ca. 1891)

Quebec Plate

Plate, 10" d. (ILLUS.) **85**

RALEIGH (Burgess & Leigh, ca. 1906)

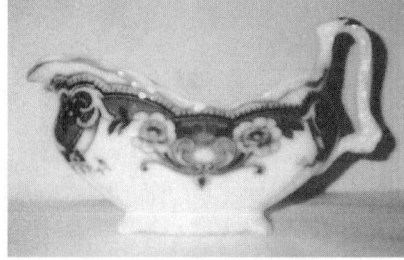

Raleigh Gravy Boat

Gravy boat, 6 1/2" l. (ILLUS.) **125**

REBECCA (George Jones, ca. 1900)

Rebecca Luncheon Plate

Plate, 9" d. (ILLUS.) **125**

REEDS & FLOWERS (Unknown, ca. 1855)

Reeds & Flowers Soup Plate

Soup plate w/flanged rim, 10 1/2" d.
(ILLUS.) **200**

REGENT (Johnson Bros., ca. 1910)
Plate, 8" d. **65**
Plate, 9" d. **90**
Plate, 10" d. **100**
Platter, 18" l. **575**
Tea cup & saucer **100**
Tea set: cov. teapot, sugar & creamer; the
set **1,000**

ROSEVILLE (John Maddock & Sons, ca. 1891)
Celery dish, 11" l. (ILLUS., top of page) **175**

SCINDE (J&G Alcock, 1840)

Scinde Jam Jar

Jam jar w/attached tray, w/lion's head handles, only one of its kind (ILLUS.) **6,000**

Scinde Platter

Platter, 18" l. (ILLUS.) **750**

Scinde Teapot

Teapot, primary body style, 9" h. (ILLUS.) **900**

SEVILLE (New Wharf Pottery, ca. 1891)

Seville Dinner Plate

Plate, 10" d. (ILLUS.) **115**

SHANGHAI (W.E. Corn, ca. 1900)

Shanghai Dinner Plate

Plate, 10" d. (ILLUS.) **100**

SHUSAN (F. & R. Pratt & Co., ca. 1855)

Shusan Dinner Plate

Plate, 10 1/2" d. (ILLUS.) **195**

SLOE BLOSSOM (Wm. Ridgway & Co., ca. 1830)

Sloe Blossom Waste Jar

Waste jar, part of dresser set (ILLUS.) **1,500**

Sloe Blossom Water Pitcher

Water pitcher, 7 1/2" h. (ILLUS.) **475**

SPINACH (Brushstroke, maker unknown)

Spinach Waste Bowl

Waste bowl, 5" d. (ILLUS.) **125**

SYRIAN (W.H. Grindley, ca. 1892)

Syrian Chamber Pot

Chamber pot, cov., 11" w., 7" h. (ILLUS.).......... **325**

TOKIO (Johnson Bros., ca. 1900)

Tokio Luncheon Plate

Plate, 9" d. (ILLUS.) **95**

TULIP (Copeland & Garrett, ca. 1845)

Tulip Fruit Compote

Fruit compote, footed, 10" d., 6" h. (ILLUS.)...... **875**

TURKEY (Cauldon, Ltd., ca. 1905)

Turkey Dinner Plate

Plate, 10 1/2" d. (ILLUS.)..................................... **200**

TURKEY (Ridgways, ca. 1900)

Turkey Set

Turkey set: platter, 22" l., & 12 dinner
plates, 10" d.; the set (ILLUS. of platter) **3,200**

VERMONT (Burgess & Leigh, ca. 1895)

Vermont Sauceboat with Underplate

Sauceboat w/underplate, 9" l., 5" h.
(ILLUS.)... **275**

VIRGINIA (John Maddock & Sons, ca. 1891)

Virginia Platter

Platter, 16" l. (ILLUS.) 450

WATER NYMPH (Josiah Wedgwood, ca. 1872)
Bowl, footed, 8" d., 5" h. 295

WATTEAU (Doulton & Co., ca. 1900)
Oil lamp, converted to electric, 26" h. 2,200

Watteau Dinner Plate

Plate, 10 1/2" D. (ILLUS.) 150

WAVERLY (John Maddock & Son, ca. 1891)

Waverly Platter

Platter, 16" l. (ILLUS.) 425

WENTWORTH (J. & G. Meakin, ca. 1907)
Butter pat, 3 1/2" d. 40

Wentworth Dinner Plate

Plate, 10" d. (ILLUS.) 90
Vegetable bowl, cov., 12" l., 6 1/2" h. 250

Franciscan Ware

A product of Gladding, McBean & Company of Lincoln, California, Franciscan Ware was one of a number of lines produced by that firm over its long history. Products made at the Lincoln Plant were Architectural Terra Cotta, Terra Cotta Tiles, and Garden Ware. In 1923, Gladding, McBean purchased the Tropico Pottery in Glendale, California. At this location Gladding, McBean began producing dinnerware. Franciscan Ware was introduced in 1934 beginning with the colorful dinnerware pattern of El Patio. Coronado, a swirled pattern offered in satin and gloss glazes, was introduced in 1935. Gladding, McBean also introduced Art Ware in 1934 as Tropico Art Ware; later, after the acquisition of the Catalina Clay Products company on Catalina Island in 1937, the line was marketed as Catalina Art Ware as well as Franciscan Art Ware. In 1940, Gladding, McBean introduced the handpainted dinnerware line Apple and in 1941 Desert Rose. Desert Rose has the distinction of being one of the most popular patterns ever produced in dinnerware history. In 1942, Gladding, McBean introduced the first of many lines of fine china. Art Ware was discontinued in 1942. In the 1950s, Franciscan introduced three very popular patterns on the Eclipse shape designed by George James: Starburst, Oasis, and Duet. In 1962, Gladding, McBean merged with the International Lock Pipe and Joint Co. to form the company Interpace. Fine china was discontinued in 1977. In 1979, Interpace's Glendale Franciscan Ware Division was purchased by Wedgwood, Ltd. Finally, in October of 1984, the Glendale Franciscan Ware Plant was closed and all dinnerware operations were moved to England. All Franciscan dinnerware patterns produced prior to 1984, except for Apple, Desert Rose and Fresh Fruit, were discontinued. Fresh Fruit was discontinued in 1989. Wedgwood continues to manufacture Desert Rose and Apple, adding new pieces each year. In 2001, Wedgwood, Ltd. reintroduced Franciscan Ivy.

For Oasis and Duet, use prices for Starburst, less 20 percent. For Strawberry Fair and Fresh Fruit, use prices for Desert Rose. Café Royal and Meadow Rose prices are about 20 percent less than Desert Rose. Bountiful and Strawberry Time are 20 percent higher than Desert Rose. For Small Fruit, use prices for Poppy. For Fine China patterns, use prices for Arden except for Mariposa, which is 20 percent more. The prices for Desert Rose, Ivy, Fresh Fruit, and Apple are for pre-1984 "Made in USA" items. Desert Rose, Ivy and Apple that are marked "Made in England" are 70 percent less than "Made in USA" items. "Made in England" Fresh Fruit is 20 percent lower than "Made in USA" Fresh Fruit.

Ashtray, El Patio tableware, coral satin
glaze $8
Ashtray, individual, Wildflower patt., Mariposa Lily shape, 3 1/2" d. 95
Ashtray, individual, Apple patt., apple-shaped, 4" w., 4 1/2" l. 28
Ashtray, Apple patt., 4 3/4" sq. 150
Ashtray, Desert Rose patt., 4 3/4 x 9" oval 85
Baker, half-apple-shaped, Apple patt.,
4 3/4" w., 5 1/4" l., 1 3/4" h. 225
Baking dish, Cafe Royal patt.,
8 3/4 x 9 1/2", 1 qt. 160
Baking dish, October patt., 1 qt. 100
Baking dish, Desert Rose patt., 9 x 14",
2 1/4" h., 1 1/12 qt. 225
Bank, figural pig, Desert Rose patt. 160
Bell, Desert Rose patt., Danbury Mint,
4 1/4" h. 75
Bell, dinner, Franciscan 95
Bowl, fruit, 4 1/2" d., California Poppy patt. 33
Bowl, fruit, 5 1/4" d., Desert Rose patt. 12
Bowl, fruit, 5 1/2" d., Wildflower patt. 95
Bowl, soup, footed, 5 1/2" d., Desert Rose
patt. 32

Various El Patio Plates & Tumblers

Bowl, cereal, 6" d., Desert Rose patt. 18
Bowl, cereal or soup, 6" d., Fresh Fruit patt......... 18
Bowl, cereal or soup, 6" d., Meadow Rose
patt.. 12
Bowl, 7" d., Picnic patt. 8
Bowl, salad, 10" d., Apple patt. 95
Bowl, salad, 10" d., Wildflower patt. 450
Bowl, salad, 11 1/4" d., Ivy patt., green rim
band 145
Box, cov., Desert Rose patt., heart-shaped,
4 1/2" l., 2 1/2" h. 150
Box, cov., Apple patt., round, 4 3/4" d.,
1 1/2" h.. 245
Box, cov., Twilight Rose patt., heart-shaped...... 225
Butter dish, cov., California Poppy patt............. 175
Butter dish, cov., Ivy patt................................... 75
Butter dish, cov., Twilight Rose patt................. 125
Candleholders, Desert Rose patt., pr................. 75
Casserole, cov., Apple patt., in metal holder.. 1,500
Casserole, cov., Apple patt., 1 1/2 qt. 90
Casserole, cov., Wildflower patt., 1 1/2 qt........ 850
Celery dish, Apple patt., 7 3/4 x 15 1/2".............. 28
Cigarette box, cov., Desert Rose patt.,
3 1/2 x 4 1/2", 2" h. 150
Coffeepot, individual, cov., Desert Rose
patt.. 425
Coffeepot, cov., Desert Rose patt.,
7 1/2" h. 140
Coffeepot, cov., 10" h., Daisy patt....................... 65
Compote, open, Desert Rose patt., 8" d.,
4" h. 65
Condiment set: oil & vinegar cruets w/orig-
inal stoppers, cov. mustard jar & three-
part tray; Starburst patt., the set 275
Cookie jar, cov., Desert Rose patt. 200
Creamer, Bountiful patt.. 35
Creamer, October patt. 24
Creamer, Ivy patt., 4" h. 30
Creamer & cov. sugar bowl, Daisy patt.,
pr.. 45
Creamer & cov. sugar bowl, El Patio table-
ware, Mexican blue glossy glaze, pr. 35
Creamer & cov. sugar bowl, individual,
Apple patt., pr. 53
Creamer & cov. sugar bowl, Meadow
Rose patt., pr. 45

Creamer & open sugar bowl, individual,
Desert Rose patt., pr. 140

Apple Pattern Plate, Cup & Saucer

Cup & saucer, Apple patt. (ILLUS. w/bread
& butter plate) 9
Cup & saucer, Arden patt. 15
Cup & saucer, Coronado Table Ware, coral
satin glaze 10
Cup & saucer, demitasse, Apple patt. 55
Cup & saucer, demitasse, El Patio table-
ware, golden glow glossy glaze........................ 18
Cup & saucer, demitasse, El Patio table-
ware, turquoise glossy glaze............................ 18
Cup & saucer, Desert Rose patt., jumbo
size 60
Cup & saucer, Ivy patt. 22
Cup & saucer, Starburst patt. 16
Cup & saucer, tea, Desert Rose patt. 5
Dish, Desert Rose patt., heart-shaped,
5 3/4" l. 95
Egg cup, Apple patt., double................................. 32
Egg cup, Meadow Rose patt., 2 3/4 d.,
3 3/4" h. 36
Ginger jar, cov., Desert Rose patt...................... 295
Goblet, Meadow Rose patt., 6 1/2" h. 85
Gravy boat, Arden patt... 65
Gravy boat, Desert Rose patt. 45
Gravy boat w/attached undertray, Apple
patt. 42

Gravy boat w/attached undertray, Ivy patt........ 62
Jam jar, cov., Apple patt., redesigned style 275
Microwave dish, oblong, Desert Rose patt.,
1 1/2 qt. 275
Mixing bowl, Desert Rose patt., 6" d. 75
Mixing bowl, Desert Rose patt., 7 1/2" d. 95
Mixing bowl, Desert Rose patt., 9" d. 125
Mixing bowl set, Desert Rose patt., 3 pcs........ 350
Mug, Meadow Rose patt................................... 25
Mug, Cafe Royal patt., 7 oz.............................. 16
Mug, Desert Rose patt., 7 oz............................ 18
Mug, Desert Rose patt., 12 oz............................ 65
Pepper mill, Duet patt.. 75
Pickle dish, Desert Rose patt., 4 1/2 x 11" 42
Pitcher, water, Coronado Table Ware, bur-
gundy glaze.. 75
Pitcher, 4" h., Desert Rose patt. 395
Pitcher, milk, 6 1/2" h., Desert Rose patt., 1
qt. 85
Pitcher w/ice lip, El Patio tableware, tur-
quoise glossy glaze, 2 1/2 qt............................. 85
Plate, dinner, Arden patt. 15
Plate, salad, Arden patt. 8
Plate, bread & butter, 6 1/4" d., Ivy patt. 10
Plate, bread & butter, 6 1/2" d., Apple patt.
(ILLUS. w/cup & saucer, previous page).......... 6
Plate, bread & butter, 6 1/2" d., El Patio, ap-
ple green (ILLUS. w/various El Patio
plates & tumblers, top of previous page).......... 6
Plate, bread & butter, 6 1/2" d., Wildflower
patt.. 45
Plate, coupe dessert, 7 1/2" d., Apple patt. 65
Plate, dessert, 7 1/2" d., El Patio, Mexican
blue (ILLUS. w/various El Patio plates &
tumblers).. 12
Plate, snack, 8" sq., Apple patt......................... 145
Plate, side salad, 4 1/2 x 8", Apple patt.,
crescent-shaped.. 38
Plate, side salad, 4 1/2 x 8", Ivy patt., cres-
cent-shaped.. 49
Plate, salad, 8 1/2" d., Apple patt. 16
Plate, salad, 8 1/2" d., El Patio, bright yel-
low (ILLUS. w/various El Patio plates &
tumblers).. 14
Plate, salad, 8 1/2" d., Meadow Rose patt.......... 15
Plate, salad, 8 1/2" d., Picnic patt...................... 8
Plate, child's, 7 x 9" oval, divided, Desert
Rose patt., ... 125
Plate, luncheon, 9 1/4" d., ivy patt...................... 28
Plate, luncheon, 8 1/2" d., El Patio, coral
satin (ILLUS. w/various El Patio plates &
tumblers).. 14
Plate, luncheon, 9 1/2" d., Coronado Table
Ware, glossy coral glaze.................................. 10
Plate, luncheon, 9 1/2" d., Wildflower patt......... 125
Plate, small dinner, 9 1/2" d., El Patio, ma-
roon (ILLUS. w/various El Patio plates &
tumblers).. 14
Plate, dinner, 10 1/2" d., Apple patt. 15
Plate, dinner, 10 1/2" d., California Poppy
patt.. 32
Plate, dinner, 10 1/2" d., Coronado Table
Ware, ivory matte glaze 16
Plate, dinner, 10 1/2" d., October patt. 28
Plate, dinner, 10 1/2" d., Picnic patt..................... 10
Plate, large dinner, 10 1/2" d., grey (ILLUS.
w/various El Patio plates & tumblers) 26
Plate, coupe, steak, 11" l., Desert Rose
patt.. 125
Plate, grill, 11" d., Apple patt.............................. 95
Plate, chop, 12" d., Apple patt. 65
Plate, chop, 12" d., Wildflower patt. 325

Plate, chop, 14" d., Desert Rose patt. 125
Plate, chop, 14" d., Wildflower patt.................... 350
Plate, chop, 14" d., Willow tableware (1937-
40)... 145
Plate, T.V. w/cup well, 8 1/4 x 14", Starburst
patt.. 75
Platter, 13" l., California Poppy patt. 150
Platter, 11 1/4" l., Ivy patt.................................. 65
Platter, 12 3/4" l., Apple patt.............................. 38
Platter, 13" l., oval, Ivy patt............................... 67
Platter, 14" l., Desert Rose patt. 65
Platter, 14" l., October patt. 65
Platter, 15" l., Starburst patt. 75
Platter, 19" l., oval, Ivy patt., green rim band 300
Platter, 19" l., turkey-size, Meadow Rose
patt.. 195
Relish dish, three-part, Apple patt.,
11 3/4" l. 70
Relish/pickle dish, Wildflower patt., interior
design, 4 1/4 x 12" oval.................................... 245
Salt & pepper shakers, figural rose bud,
Desert Rose patt., pr. 22
Salt & pepper shakers, Apple patt.,
2 1/4" h., pr. 23
Salt & pepper shakers, Ivy patt., 2 3/4" h.,
pr... 45
Salt & pepper shakers, Apple patt.,
6 1/4" h., pr.. 95
Salt & pepper shakers, Meadow Rose
patt., 6 1/4" h., pr.. 35
Salt shaker & pepper mill, Desert Rose
patt., 6" h., pr. 225
Serving bowl, Cafe Royal patt., aka Long &
Narrow, 7 3/4 x 15 1/2", 2 1/4" h. 225
Sherbet, Apple patt., footed, 4" d., 2 1/2" h. 24
Sherbet, Ivy patt., footed, 4" d., 2 1/2" h. 32
Soup bowl, footed, Desert Rose patt. 28
Soup plate w/flanged rim, Arden patt. 15
Soup plate w/flanged rim, Ivy patt.,
8 1/2" d. 45
Sugar bowl, cov., Bountiful patt........................... 45
Sugar bowl, cov., Desert Rose patt. 38
Sugar bowl, cov., October patt. 25
Sugar bowl, cov., Apple patt., 3" h...................... 25
Syrup pitcher, Desert Rose patt., 1 pt.,
6 1/2" h. 85
Syrup pitcher, Starburst patt., 5 3/4" h. 65
Tea set: cov. teapot, creamer & sugar bowl;
Coronado Table Ware, white, the set............. 85
Teapot, cov., Arden patt. 95
Teapot, cov., Desert Rose patt., 6 1/2" h. 95
Teapot, cov., individual, Desert Rose patt.,
6 1/4" h. 295
Tidbit tray, two-tier, center handle, Ivy patt. 145
Tile, Desert Rose patt., 6" sq............................. 45
Trivet, tile, Desert Rose patt............................... 145
Tumbler, El Patio tableware, apple green
(ILLUS. w/various El Patio plates & tum-
blers) 28
Tumbler, El Patio tableware, flame orange
(ILLUS. w/various El Patio plates & tum-
blers) 28
Tumbler, El Patio tableware, glacial blue
glossy glaze (ILLUS. w/various El Patio
plates & tumblers)... 28
Tumbler, El Patio tableware, golden glow
(ILLUS. w/various El Patio plates & tum-
blers) 28
Tumbler, El Patio tableware, Mexican blue
glossy glaze 28
Tumbler, Desert Rose patt., juice, 6 oz.,
3 1/4" h. 35
Tumbler, Apple patt., 10 oz., 5 1/4" h. 38

Tumbler, Desert Rose patt., 10 oz.,
5 1/4" h... 38
Tureen, cov., footed, Apple patt., 8 3/4" d.,
5 3/4" h... 450
Vase, bud, 6" h., Meadow Rose patt. 65
Vegetable bowl, divided, Ivy patt.,
8 x 12 1/4" 95
Vegetable bowl, open, oval, Desert Rose
patt., 9" l... 35
Vegetable bowl, open, round, Apple patt.,
8 1/4" d.. 45
Vegetable bowl, open, round, Apple patt.,
9" d.. 50
Vegetable bowl, open, round, Desert Rose
patt., 8" d... 24
Vegetable bowl, open, round, Ivy patt.,
7 1/4" d.. 45
Vegetable bowl, open, round, Wildflower
patt., 9" d... 225

Geisha Girl Wares

Geisha Girl Porcelain features scenes of Japanese women in colorful kimonos along with the flora and architecture of old Japan. Although bearing an Oriental motif, the wares were produced for sale in the West and are primarily found in Occidental dinnerware and decorative forms. Geisha Girl Porcelain was an offshoot of the fine Kutani hand-painted porcelains. Less expensive production methods, e.g. stenciling as a foundation for hand painting, enabled the company to sell to a larger target market. Geisha ware was sold in five-and-dime stores and used as marketing premiums in addition to being sold through distributors and in high-end department stores. Among the hundreds of patterns and producers, quality can vary greatly. Advanced collectors favor those examples that are well executed, with detailed and careful painting and gilding. Beware, however, of overly ornate and gilded items, which are often indicative of modern day reproductions that combine Kutani and Satsuma styling on ware with fake Nippon marks.

Collectors tips: Geisha Girl Porcelain is found in a variety of border colors, the most common being shades of red-orange. Other border colors include shades of blue and green as well as multi-colors and patterns. Geisha ware was sold in sets as well as open stock; actual sets will share the same pattern, border color and border embellishments. Cocoa sets were not sold with sugars and creamers. Teacups and saucers, 7" lunch plates, powder jars and hair receivers are among the most common forms found. Despite being destined for the Western market, where an even number of accessory items is considered standard, many Japanese sets were produced with five accessory pieces, e.g. individual nut bowls, cups and saucers. Therefore, sets may be found with either five or six accessory pieces. Due to the proliferation of Geisha ware manufacturers, Geisha ware can bear a wide variety of makers' marks. Many examples, however, are unmarked. With perhaps the exception of Nippon collectors, Geisha collectors do not currently place much focus or value on particular marks. Reference: Litts, E. The Collector's Encyclopedia of Geisha Girl Porcelain, Collector Books, 1988 (out of print).

Bowl, Garden Bench C patt., tri-footed,
rose, cobalt blue border w/gold embel-
lishments.. $45
Bowl, 8 1/2" d., Drum D patt., pale cobalt
blue border, signed "Kutani" 55
Box, manicure, Lady in Kaga patt., red bor-
der, 2 1/2" d.. 15

Geisha Girl Candlesticks

Candlesticks, Temple A patt., multicolor
border, Noritake's green M-in-wreath
Nippon mark, 5 3/4" h., pr. (ILLUS.).............. 250

Geisha Girl Chocolate Pot

Chocolate pot, cov., Parasol F patt., cobalt
blue border w/gold lacing, unusual spout,
8 1/2" h. (ILLUS.) 125
Cup & saucer, child's, bouillon w/lid, Point-
ing D patt., black border, signed in Japa-
nese "Tashiro" 45
Cup & saucer, cocoa, Bamboo Trellis patt.,
wavy red border w/gold lacing 18
Cup & saucer, tea, Parasol C patt., red bor-
der, marked "Japan" 10
Dish, Garden Bench F patt., figural leaf
shape, ornate multicolor border & highly
gilded decoration.. 25
Egg cup, double, Playing Catch patt., red
border.. 18
Mustard jar w/lid & spoon, Lunchtime
patt., blue-green border, marked "Made
in Japan".. 25

Geisha Girl Perfume Bottle

Perfume bottle, Temple A patt., multicolor
border, R K Nippon mark, 4 1/2" h.
(ILLUS.) **95**

Geisha Girl Plate with Enamel Detail

Plate, 7 1/4" d., Parasol patt. variant, dark
green border w/unusual raised white
enamel detailing (ILLUS.) **15**
Platter, 10" l., Duck Watching A patt., gold
border, marked "Made in Japan" **35**
Salt & pepper shakers, Lantern Boy patt.,
pine green border, 2 3/4" h., pr. **15**

Geisha Girl Sauce Dishes

Sauce dish, Fan A patt., refined, detailed &
unusual underglaze blue, signed in Japa-
nese, 2 5/8" d., 1" h. (ILLUS. of two) **30**

Geisha Girl Tea Caddy

Tea caddy, cov., Parasol B patt., cobalt
blue, scalloped border w/gold, missing
interior lid, 4" h. (ILLUS.).................................. **28**
Teapot, cov., Bow B patt. in reserve on flo-
ral backdrop, cobalt blue border w/gold
striping, gold upper edge & spout rim **45**
Toothpick holder, Carp A patt., three-sid-
ed, red border w/interior gold lacing................ **25**

Geisha Girl Vase

Vase, 6 3/4" h., Gardening patt., red border
w/interior band of gold lacing (ILLUS.) **28**

Gonder

*Lawton Gonder founded Gonder Ceramic Arts in
Zanesville, Ohio, in 1941 and it continued in operation
until 1957.*

*The firm produced a higher priced and better quality
of commercial art potteries than many firms of the time
and employed Jamie Matchet and Chester Kirk, both of
whom were outstanding ceramic designers. Several special glazes were developed during the company's history
and Gonder even duplicated some museum pieces of
Chinese ceramic. In 1955 the firm converted to the production of tile due to increased foreign competition. By
1957 its years of finest production were over.*

*Increase price ranges as indicated for the following
glaze colors: red flambé - 50 percent, antique gold
crackle - 70 percent, turquoise Chinese crackle - 40 per
cent, white Chinese crackle - 30 per cent.*

Ashtray, boomerang shape, Mold No. 223,
6 1/4 x 10 1/2" l. **$25-40**

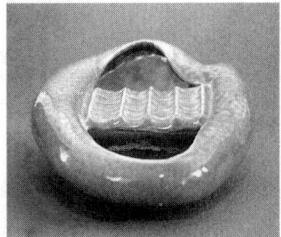

Center Rest Cigar Ashtray

Ashtray, Center Rest Cigar, marked
"Gonder Original 219" in script, Red
Flambe glaze, 2 1/4 x 7 1/2" (ILLUS.)........ **50-75**
Ashtray, form of a bird, Mold No. 224,
8 7/8" l.. **25-40**
Ashtray, form of a fish, Mold No. 113,
4 x 9" l. **75-100**
Ashtray, round, piecrust rim, Mold No. 807,
9" d... **20-40**
Ashtray, "S" Swirl, Mold No. 626,
6 1/2 x 9 1/8" l.. **20-30**
Ashtray, Sovereign Fluted Rectangular,
Mold No. 807, 1 7/8 x 3 1/4" l...................... **20-30**
Ashtray, Sovereign Fluted Round, Mold No.
808, 2 3/4" d.. **20-30**

Ashtray, spiked fish, Mold No. 224, 4 x 7 3/8" l... **40-60**

Ashtray, square, Mold No. 1800A, 10 11/16" sq.. **50-75**

Ashtray, square, w/inside concentric ridges, Mold No. 815, 10" sq..................... **25-50**

Ashtray, square w/rounded corners, Mold No. 814, 8" sq................................... **20-40**

Ashtray set: ashtray, cigarette holder; Mold No. 406, 3 7/8" sq. **50-75**

Ashtrays, Mold No. 808, set of 3, each **20-30**

Base for ginger jar, Mold No. 530-B **100-125**

Book ends, in the form of horses, Mold No. 211, 10" h. **100-125**

Bowl, 4 3/8" d., fruit, La Gonda, Mold No. 905... **15-20**

Bowl, 5 11/16" d., 1 3/8" h., w/small leaves, Mold No. B-17................................. **40-60**

Bowl, 6 7/8 x 11 7/8", 2 1/2" h., S-shaped, Mold No. 592.................................. **20-40**

Bowl, 8 1/2" w., 5 1/8" h., hexagonal, w/Chinese figures, Mold No. 742.............. **25-40**

Bowl, 8" d., 2 3/8" h., Mold No. 715.............. **15-25**

Bowl, 8" d., 2 7/8" h., fluted, Mold No. 629 or H-29 .... **20-30**

Candleholder, cubic, Mold No. 726, 3 x 3", 2 1/4" h. **20-30**

Candleholder, fluted, Mold No. 314, 414, E-14, 4 5/8" w., 1 7/8" h. **10-15**

Candleholder, single shell, Mold No. 506, 2 3/4" w., 4 5/8" h. **10-20**

Casserole, cov., handled lid, La Gonda, Mold No. 954, 6 1/2 x 10 1/8", 5 1/4" h...... **30-40**

Casserole, cov., tab handled lid, La Gonda, Mold No. 955, 6 3/4 x 11", 5 3/8" h.......... **75-100**

Chop plate, oblong, Mold No. 912, 8 7/8 x 12 1/4"... **100-125**

Cigarette box, cov., Mold. No. 806, 3 1/2 x 4 3/8", 2 5/8" h. **60-80**

Cigarette cup, Sovereign, Mold No. 804, 2 5/8" h... **40-60**

Cigarette holder, Mold No. 804, 2 5/8" h..... **40-60**

Console bowl, rectangular base, body w/relief-molded center fan shape flanked by cornucopia forms, Mold K-14, 7 1/2 x 12 1/2" **150-200**

Console bowl, seashell design, Mold No. 505, 7 1/4 x 17 1/2"...................... **50-65**

Cookie jar, cov., bulbous shape w/sleeping dog finial, Mold No. 924, 8 1/2" h. **75-100**

Cookie jar, cov., Pirate, Mold No. 951, 10 1/2" or 12" h................................ **1,500-1,800**

Cookie jar, cov., "Ye Olde Oaken Bucket," brown w/tan & yellow glaze, marked "Gonder Original 974" in script, only two known to exist, 7" h. .... RARE

Cornucopia-vase, held by figural hand, oval base, Mold No. 675, 7 1/2 x 8" **75-100**

Cornucopia-vase, shell form, Mold No. H-84, 8" h.. **25-40**

Cornucopia-vase, square base, Mold No. H-14, 9" h. **20-35**

Cream soup dish, handled, La Gonda, Mold No. 908, 5 1/2 x 5 3/4", 3 3/8" h........ **20-25**

Creamer, La Gonda, Mold No. 907, 7" w., 4" h... **15-20**

Creamer, La Gonda, Mold No. P-33, 3 1/2" h... **15-25**

Creamer, squashed shape, Mold No. 404, 7" h... **25-40**

Creamer, squashed shape, Mold No. 904........ **8-10**

Custard, cov., handled, La Gonda, Mold No. 952, 3 1/4" h. **15-25**

Ewer, shell-shaped, Mold No. 508, 14" h. (no starfish) **75-100**

Ewer, shell-shaped w/starfish on base, Mold No. 508, 14" h. **40-60**

Figure of bearded Oriental man, Mold No. 775, 8 5/8" h.................................. **50-60**

Figure of Fatima, w/rosary, Mold No. 772, 9 1/2" h. **75-100**

Figure of madonna, standing, Mold No. 549, 9 1/4" h....................................... **50-75**

Figure of Oriental man, Mold No. 551, 7" h. .. **40-60**

Figure of Oriental woman, holding ginger jar, Mold No. 573, 4 7/8" h...................... **40-60**

Figure of Oriental woman, w/hands together, Mold No. 570, 6 1/4" h............... **40-60**

Figure of Oriental woman, w/right hand to head, Mold No. 776, 9" h. **60-80**

Figure of turbaned woman w/baskets, Mold No. 762, 14 1/2" h. **50-75**

Flower frog, three-tier flower, Mold No. 250, 5 7/8" w., 2 5/8" h. **100-125**

Jar, cov., in the form of an Oriental plum, Mold No. 529, 9 3/16" h. **125-150**

Lamp, Aladdin oil style, no number **75-100**

Lamp, bullet-shaped, Mold No. 2228, 11" h... **75-100**

Lamp, Double Swirl, Mold No. 2020, 30" h. .. **40-60**

Lamp, Driftwood, Mold No. 2017, 30" h...... **75-100**

Lamp, Mill TV, Mold No. 1905, 12" w., 8 1/4" h. **75-100**

Dogwood Globe Lamp Base

Lamp base, Dogwood Globe, Catalog #5507, no mark, Italian Pink Crackle glaze, scarce, 15 1/4" h. (ILLUS.) **175-200**

Lamps, Double Link, Mold No. 4039, 24 1/2" h., pr. **45-65**

Lazy Susan, medium, Mold No. 8, 11 1/2" d.. **80-110**

Model of elephant, Mold No. 207, 11 1/2" l., 8 7/8" h.............................. **75-100**

Model of elephant, Mold No. 209, 8" l, 6 1/8" h. **40-50**

Model of frog, standing, pistachio w/black trim glaze, experimental, no mold number or mark, rare, 10 1/2" h. .... RARE

Model of gamecock, w/flowers, Mold No. 525, hard to find, 7 1/8" w., 10 3/4" h. ... **150-175**

Indian Porters Bearing Planter Bowl

Model of gamecock, w/plain tail feathers, Mold No. 525, hard to find, 7 1/8" w., 10 3/4" h. **150-175**

Model of head of Chinese coolie, Mold No. 541, 11 1/2" w., 11" h. **400-500**

Model of head of racing horse, Mold 874, 9 1/4" h. **165-185**

Model of hen w/worms, Mold No. 525, hard to find, 9" l., 6 3/4" h. **125-150**

Model of horse head, Mold No. 872, 15" l, 7" h. **150-175**

Model of penguin, Mold No. A-9, 3 1/4" w., 4 7/8" h. **25-50**

Model of racing horse head, Mold No. 576, 13 1/2" l., 5 3/4" h. **150-175**

Model of rooster, Mold No. 212, scarce, 4" w., 10 1/2" h. **150-175**

Model of two running deer, Mold No. 690, 9 1/4" l., 6" h. **75-100**

Pitcher, lizard handle, slotted, Mold No. J-54, 8 1/2" l., 10 5/8" h. **100-125**

Pitcher, pistol grip, Mold No. 102, 9 1/8" h. **125-150**

Pitcher, twisted twig handle, Mold No. 301, 7 1/2" l., 7 7/8" h. **100-125**

Pitcher, 8 1/8" h., LaGonda patt., Mold No. 917 .... **40-50**

Gonder Pitcher in Coral Lustre Glaze

Pitcher, 9 1/4" h., Classical style, "606 Gonder USA" mark in script, Coral Lustre glaze, Mold No. 606 (ILLUS.) **75-100**

Planter, African Violet two-piece w/flared top, Mold No. 792, 5 1/4" sq., 5 1/8" h. **20-40**

Planter, cov., rectangular w/ridges & leaves, Mold No. 1004, 5 1/2 x 9 1/2", 4 1/2" h. **35-50**

Planter, figure of Gay 90s woman w/basket, no mold number, 13 1/4" h. **150-175**

Planter, figures of Basque dancers, Mold No. 766, 12" h. **125-150**

Planter, four-footed flared square pedestal, Mold No. 753, 7 x 7 1/4", 7 1/4" h. **25-40**

Planter, four-footed small flared square, Mold No. 748, 5 x 5 1/4", 3 7/8" h. **15-30**

Planter, gondola or lamp, no mold number, 5 3/4" h., 14" l. **60-80**

Planter, Indian Porters Bearing Planter Bowl, marked "© 1950 Gonder Ceramic Arts" in block print, Victorian Wine glaze, Mold No. 764, very hard to find w/bowl, 12 1/4" h., the set (ILLUS., top of page) **100-150**

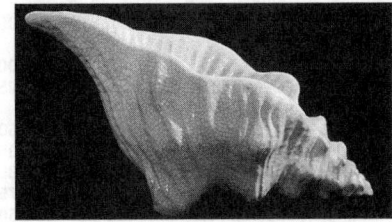

Large Conch Shell Planter

Planter, Large Conch Shell, no mark, Chinese White Crackle glaze, Mold No. 793, very hard to find, 5 3/4 x 17 1/4", 8" h. (ILLUS.) **200-250**

Planter, large rectangle w/round corners, Mold No. 752, 4 1/2 x 9 1/4", 3 1/8" h. **10-20**

Planter, large swan, Mold No. L-14, 8 1/4" h. **50-75**

Planter, reclining panther, Mold No. 237, 5 1/2" h., 14 7/8" l **125-150**

Planter, rectangular pagoda, Mold No. 727, 5 x 12 1/2", 2 3/4" h. **25-35**

Planter, shell cornucopia, Mold No. 692, 5 1/4 x 9", 4 3/4" h. **50-75**

Planter, square ridges & leaves, Mold No. 1001, 5 1/8" sq., 3 3/4" h. **15-25**

Planter, square w/ridge & leaves, Mold No. 1002, 5 1/4 x 5 1/2", 5 3/16" h. **15-25**

Planter, twist shoe strap, Mold No. 585,
4 5/8 x 10 5/8", 4" h.................................. **40-60**

Planter, Zig Zag, Mold No. 737, 11 3/4 l.,
2 1/2" h... **15-30**

Planter bottom, Mold No. 724, for African
Violet planter No. 738, 4 x 5"........................ **5-10**

Planter set, figurine of doe w/turned head,
side planters, Mold No. 213, 3 x 4 1/2",
10 5/8" h., the set **75-100**

Planter set: Oriental man & woman water
bearers w/baskets; Mold No. 777, man
10 1/2" w., 14 1/8" h., woman 10 1/4" w.,
14 1/4" h., each **50-75**

Planter set: top & bottom; Mold No. 738, African Violet, 2 3/4" h., 4 1/4" w., the set..... **15-25**

Planter top, No. 1000, for African Violet
planter No. 738, 4 x 4", 5 1/4" h................. **25-40**

Planters, for doe or rooster figurine, Mold
No. 218, 3 3/4 x 3, 2 3/4" h., pr. **25-50**

Plaque, African mask, Mold No. 231,
5 1/8 x 8 1/4" **75-100**

Plaque, African mask, Mold No. 232,
5 x 7 3/4"... **75-100**

Salt & pepper shakers, La Gonda, Mold
No. 913, 7 3/4" d., 3" h. **15-20**

Saucer, La Gonda, Mold No. 904, 5 3/8" d...... **8-10**

Server, La Gonda, Mold No. 916,
5 7/8 x 9 5/8" **20-30**

Stack set: sugar & creamer; La Gonda,
Mold No. 923, 3 7/8 x 4", 2 7/8" h.............. **30-40**

Sugar bowl, Mold No. P-33, 4 5/8" h. **15-25**

Tankard, Mold No. M-9, 14" h. **60-80**

Tankard, shell, Mold No. 400, 9 1/2" h....... **150-175**

Tea cup, La Gonda, Mold No. 903,
2 1/2 x 3 1/4" **8-10**

Teapot, cov., coiled beehive, Mold No. 662,
5 3/4" h.. **75-100**

Teapot, cov., rectangular, La Gonda, Mold
No. 396, 6 1/4" h. **50-75**

Teapot, cov., vertical ridges, Mold No. P-
424, 6 7/16" h.. **75-100**

Tray, 8-section, Mold No. 100, 10
15/16 x 19 1/4"... **150-200**

Tray, shell, Mold No. 865, 12 x 14"............. **175-225**

Urn, Sovereign cigarette footed, Mold No.
801, 3 1/2" h... **40-60**

Vase, applied leaf, Mold No. 370, E-70......... **20-35**

Vase, large cylindrical, Mold No. 712............. **25-35**

Vase, modeled pillow, Mold No. 506.............. **50-75**

Vase, pigtail handles, Mold No. H-608 .... **100-150**

Vase, 2 1/2" h., square mini, Mold No. 407 ... **15-20**

Vase, 3 1/2" h., footed Chinese rectangle,
Mold No. 707.. **15-25**

Vase, 6" h., waisted twisted form, Mold E-64.. **10-20**

Vase, 6 1/16" h., "Z"-handled ewer, Mold
No. 365, E-65, E-365................................. **15-25**

Vase, 6 1/8" h., small V horn, Mold No. E-5 .. **30-50**

Vase, 5 x 6 1/4", rectangular, Mold No. 709.. **10-25**

Vase, 6 1/4" h., applied leaf, Mold No. E368.. **20-25**

Vase, 6 1/4" h., square banded, Mold No.
369, 703, E-69, E-369 .... **20-30**

Vase, 6 1/2" h., bulbous base w/scalloped
trumpet-form neck, Mold E-49.................... **10-25**

Vase, 6 1/2" h., large flat rectangular, Mold
No. 708 .... **15-25**

Vase, 6 1/2" h., metallic-look pitcher form,
Mold No. 382.. **30-45**

Vase, 6 1/2" h., ribbon handle ewer, Mold
No. 373, E-73, E-373.................................. **25-35**

Vase, 6 5/8" h., shell & seaweed, Mold No.
402, H-401 .... **75-100**

Vase, 6 3/4" h., opposite leaf handle, Mold
No. H-602 .... **75-100**

Vase, 8" h., medium ewer form, Mold No.
673, H-73... **15-25**

Vase, 8" h., raised circular ewer, Mold No.
410... **25-40**

Vase, 8" h., rectangular footed maze, Mold
No. 401 .... **35-50**

Vase, 8 5/16" h., butterfly w/flowers, Mold
No. H-88 .... **50-75**

Vase, 8 1/16" h., berries & leaves, Mold No.
H-55.. **75-100**

Vase, 8 1/4" h., pine cone, Mold No. 507 ...... **65-85**

Vase, 8 3/8" h., medium cylindrical, Mold
No. 711 .... **15-75**

Vase, 5 x 8 1/2, rectangular, Mold No.
H-74.. **15-25**

Vase, 6 x 8 1/2", modified rectangle
w/raised flowers, Mold No. 687.................... **50-75**

Vase, 7 x 8 1/2", flaring body w/one angled
handle at rim, the other at base, Mold No.
H-56.. **15-30**

Vase, 8 1/2" h., bottle form, Mold No.
1204 .... **40-60**

Vase, 8 1/2" h., bottle form, Mold No.
1211 .... **50-75**

Vase, 6 x 9", tulip form, Mold No. H-68.......... **15-30**

Vase, 9 1/8" h., 4 x 6 3/16", tapering cylindrical form w/relief-molded pea pod dec-
oration, Mold No. 487 H-87 .... **30-40**

Gonder Sunfish Vase

Vase, 9" h., 10 1/4" w., Scarla Sunfish,
marked "Gonder 522," Sea Swirl glaze
(ILLUS.) **100-125**

Vase, 9" h., double open handles, Mold No.
604.. **75-100**

Vase, 9" h., footed, square double bulb
form, Mold No. 607 & H-607 .... **125-150**

Vase, 9" h., footed, two-handled, bulbous
base, squared top, Mold No. H-7 .... **20-30**

Vase, 9" h., gazelle, Mold No. 215................. **50-75**

Vase, 9 3/4" h., Art Deco cactus, Mold No.
686.. **60-80**

Vase, 9 3/4" h., bottle form w/ridges, Mold
No. 383 .... **50-75**

Vase, 9 x 10", model of angel fish on waves,
Mold No. 522 .... **75-125**

Vase, 10 1/4" h., bent tube, Mold No.
595.. **75-100**

Vase, 10 1/4" h., flared flower, Mold No.
876.. **150-175**

Vase, 10 1/4" h., swirled "S" handle, w/four
lips, Mold No. 872.......................................**50-75**

Vase, 4 1/2 x 10 1/2, square form w/round
top, Mold No. 534...................................... **50-75**

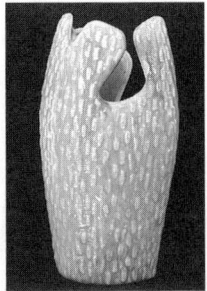

Gonder Freeform Vase

Vase, 10 3/4" h., Nubby Freeform shape, marked "869 Gonder Original" in script, Dijon glaze, hard to find (ILLUS.) **150-200**

Vase, 10 3/4" h., round leaf-in-leaf, Mold No. J-59 .... **60-80**

Vase, 10 7/8" h., off-center double handle, Mold No. J-35... **75-100**

Vase, 11" h., ewer form, J-25 .... **50-75**

Vase, 11" h., flat form, model of swan, Mold No. 530 .... **100-125**

Vase, 8 1/2 x 11", flame design, Mold No. 510 .... **60-75**

Vase, 8 x 11", figural leaf design, Mold No. 504 .... **25-35**

Vase, 11 1/2" h., fan shape, relief-molded shell decoration, Mold No. J-60 .... **40-55**

Vase, 7 x 11 1/2", triple "S" design, Mold No. 594 .... **50-75**

Vase, 14 1/2" h., tall tapered, Mold No. 598 .... **75-100**

Vase, 18 3/8" h., large bottle form, Mold No. 531 .... **175-200**

Hall China

Founded in 1903 in East Liverpool, Ohio, this still-operating company at first produced mostly utilitarian wares. It was in 1911 that Robert T. Hall, son of the company founder, developed a special single-fire, lead-free glaze that proved to be strong, hard and nonporous. In the 1920s the firm became well known for its extensive line of teapots (still a major product), and in 1932 it

introduced kitchenwares, followed by dinnerwares in 1936 and refrigerator wares in 1938.

The imaginative designs and wide range of glaze colors and decal decorations have led to the growing appeal of Hall wares with collectors, especially people who like Art Deco and Art Moderne design. One of the firm's most famous patterns was the "Autumn Leaf" line, produced as premiums for the Jewel Tea Company. For listings of this ware see "Jewel Tea Autumn Leaf."

Helpful books on Hall include, The Collector's Guide to Hall China *by Margaret & Kenn Whitmyer, and* Superior Quality Hall China - A Guide for Collectors *by Harvey Duke (An ELO Book, 1977).*

Hall Marks

Ashtray, triangular, deep, No. 683, turquoise **$15**

Baker, French Fluted shape, Blue Bouquet patt. **25**

Baker, French Fluted shape, Yellow Rose patt. **25**

Batter jug, Sundial shape, Blue Garden patt. **250**

Bean pot, cov., New England shape, No. 2 & No. 4, each (ILLUS., bottom of page)... **120-140**

Bean pot, cov., New England shape, No. 4, Crocus patt.. **325**

Bean pot, cov., New England shape, No. 4, Wild Poppy patt. **250**

Bean pot, cov., one handle, orange **55**

Bean pot, cov., tab-handled, Pert shape, Rose Parade patt.. **135**

Bowl, 6" d., Radiance shape, No. 4, Crocus patt. **25**

Bowl, 6" d., Thick Rim shape, Blue Blossom patt. **40**

New England Shape Bean Pots

Bowl, 7" d., Radiance shape, Crocus patt. 40
Bowl, 8 1/2" d.,Thick Rim shape, Tulip patt. 30
Bowl, 9" d., Radiance shape, Crocus patt. 45
Bowl, 9" d., salad, Serenade patt. 20

Medallion Shape Bowl

Bowl, 10" d., Medallion shape (ILLUS.) 45

Primrose Cake Plate

Cake plate, Primrose patt. (ILLUS.) 20
Casserole, cov., Five Band shape, Flamingo patt. 75
Casserole, cov., Radiance shape, Blue Bouquet patt. 60
Casserole, cov., Ribbed line, russet 45
Casserole, cov., Sundial shape, No. 4, Chinese Red 55
Casserole, cov., tab-handled, Rose White patt. 35
Coffeelator, cov., cobalt blue 125
Coffeepot, cov., Drip-O-Later, Sash shape, red 70
Coffeepot, cov., Drip-O-Lator, Scoop shape, Wildflower patt. 40
Coffeepot, cov., Drip-O-Lator, Waverly shape 35

Crocus Pattern Coffeepot

Coffeepot, cov., drip-type, all-china, Kadota shape, Crocus patt. (ILLUS.) 350
Coffeepot, cov., drip-type, all-china, Medallion line, lettuce green 175
Coffeepot, cov., melt-down w/basket, Crocus patt. 90

Ansel Shape Tricolator Coffeepot

Coffeepot, cov., Tricolator, Ansel shape, yellow art glaze (ILLUS.) 75

Coffee Queen Tricolator Coffeepot

Coffeepot, cov., Tricolator, Coffee Queen, yellow (ILLUS.) 35
Coffeepot, cov., Waverly shape, Minuet patt. 65

Five Band Cookie Jar

Cookie jar, cov., Five Band shape, Chinese Red (ILLUS.) 125
Cookie jar, cov., Flareware, Gold Lace design 75
Cookie jar, cov., Grape design, yellow, gold band 60
Cookie jar, cov., Red Poppy patt. 500

Sundial Cookie Jar

Cookie jar, cov., Sundial shape, Chinese
Red (ILLUS.) **235**
Creamer, Art Deco, Crocus patt. **25**
Creamer, Modern, Red Poppy patt. **35**
Creamer, individual, Sundial shape, Chi-
nese Red, 2 oz. **65**
Creamer & cov. sugar bowl, Blue Bouquet
patt., pr. **70**
Custard cup, Medallion line, lettuce green **12**
Custard cup, straight-sided, Rose White
patt. **25**

Radiance Shape Drip Jar

Drip jar, cov., Radiance shape, Chinese
Red (ILLUS.) **60**
Drip jar, open, No. 1188, Mums patt. **35**
Gravy boat, Springtime patt. **35**
Leftover, cov., loop handle, Blue Blossom
patt. **150**

Leftover with Loop Handle

Leftover, cov., loop handle, Chinese Red
(ILLUS.) **95**
Leftover, cov., square, Crocus patt. **125**

Fantasy Leftover

Leftover, cov., Zephyr shape, Fantasy patt.
(ILLUS.) **225**
Mug, beverage, Silhouette patt. **60**

Irish Coffee Mug

Mug, Irish coffee, footed, 6" h. (ILLUS.) **15**

Commemorative Irish Coffee Mug

Mug, Irish coffee, footed, commemorative
United States Bicentennial "Era of
Space" Series (ILLUS.) **35**

Orange Poppy Pie Plate

Pie plate, Orange Poppy patt. (ILLUS.) **45**
Pitcher, ball shape, No. 3, Chinese Red **55**

Hall Ball-type Pitcher

Pitcher, ball shape, No. 3, orchid (ILLUS.)......... 85
Pitcher, cov., jug-type, Radiance shape,
No. 4, No. 488 patt.. 195

Doughnut-shape Jug-type Pitcher

Pitcher, jug-type, large, Doughnut shape,
Chinese Red (ILLUS.) 135
Pitcher, jug-type, Loop-handle, emerald
green 65
Pitcher, jug-type, No. 628, maroon..................... 50
Pitcher, jug-type, Pert shape, Rose Parade
patt.. 30-40
Pitcher, jug-type, Streamline shape, canary
yellow 55

Tankard-type Pitcher

Pitcher, tankard-type, black (ILLUS.).................. 65

Plate, salad, 8 1/4" d., No. 488 patt..................... 15
Plate, dinner, 10" d., Wildfire patt. 20
Platter, 13 1/4" l., oval, Mums patt. 50
Pretzel jar, cov., Pastel Morning Glory patt. 125

Canister-style Salt & Pepper Shakers

Salt & pepper shakers, canister style, red,
pr. (ILLUS.)... 90
Salt & pepper shakers, handled, range-
type, Blue Blossom patt., pr. 80
Salt & pepper shakers, Medallion line, let-
tuce green, pr. 85
Salt & pepper shakers, Teardrop shape,
Blue Bouquet patt., pr. 35
Soup tureen, Thick Rim shape, Blue Bou-
quet patt.. 300
Stack set, Radiance shape, Carrot patt. 125
Sugar bowl, cov., Medallion line, Silhouette
patt. 35
Syrup pitcher, cov., Five Band shape, Blue
Blossom patt... 165
Tea tile, round, Chinese Red............................... 50
Teapot, cov., Airflow shape, Chinese Red 130
Teapot, cov., Aladdin shape, cobalt blue
w/gold trim, 6-cup 125
Teapot, cov., Aladdin shape, oval opening,
w/infuser, cobalt blue w/gold trim 110

Serenade Teapot

Teapot, cov., Aladdin shape, w/infuser, Serenade patt. (ILLUS.) 350
Teapot, cov., Albany shape, emerald green
w/"Gold Special" decoration 60

Automobile Shape Teapot

Teapot, cov., Automobile shape, Chinese Red (ILLUS.) 800
Teapot, cov., Baltimore shape, Gold Label line, ivory 125

Basket Shape Teapot

Teapot, cov., Basket shape, Chinese Red (ILLUS.) 300
Teapot, cov., Basketball shape, cobalt blue 600
Teapot, cov., Birdcage shape, maroon 350
Teapot, cov., Boston shape, cobalt blue w/gold Trailing Aster design, 6-cup 150

Bowling Ball Teapot

Teapot, cov., Bowling Ball shape, turquoise (ILLUS.) 500
Teapot, cov., Cleveland shape, warm yellow 60
Teapot, cov., Cube shape, emerald green 100
Teapot, cov., Doughnut shape, Chinese Red 500
Teapot, cov., Flareware line, Gold Lace design 60
Teapot, cov., Football shape, maroon 600
Teapot, cov., French shape, maroon w/gold decoration, 6-cup 45
Teapot, cov., Illinois shape, maroon w/gold decoration 225
Teapot, cov., Illinois shape, yellow 200
Teapot, cov., Kansas shape, ivory w/gold decoration 400

Warm Yellow Lipton Shape Teapot

Teapot, cov., Lipton shape, warm yellow (ILLUS.) 40
Teapot, cov., Pert shape, Chinese Red, 6-cup 75
Teapot, cov., Philadelphia shape, blue w/hearth scene patt. 150
Teapot, cov., Plume shape, pink 40
Teapot, cov., Rhythm shape, Chinese Red 350
Teapot, cov., Rhythm shape, yellow w/gold decoration, 6-cup 150
Teapot, cov., Star shape, cobalt blue 145

Star Shape Teapot

Teapot, cov., Star shape, cobalt blue w/gold decoration (ILLUS.) 125
Teapot, cov., Thorley series, Starlight shape, pink w/gold & rhinestone decoration 125
Teapot, cov., Thorley series, Windcrest shape, lemon yellow w/gold decoration 95

Birch Teapot

Teapot, cov., Victorian series, Birch shape, blue w/gold decoration (ILLUS.) 175
Teapot, cov., Victorian series, Connie shape, celadon green, 6-cup 45
Teapot, cov., Windshield shape, Gold Label line, white w/gold dots 50
Twin-Tea set: cov. teapot, cov. hot water pot & matching divided tray; art glaze green 125
Vase, Edgewater, No. 630, cobalt blue 25
Vase, bud, No. 631 1/2, maroon 15

Blue Garden Water Bottle

Water bottle, cov., refrigerator ware line, Zephyr shape, Blue Garden patt. (ILLUS.).. **650**

Water server, cov., Montgomery Ward refrigerator ware, Delphinium blue..................... **55**

Water server w/cork stopper, Hotpoint refrigerator ware, Dresden blue........................... **85**

Haviland

Haviland porcelain was originated by Americans in Limoges, France, shortly before the mid-19th century and continues in production. Some Haviland was made by Theodore Haviland in the United States during the last World War. Numerous other factories also made china in Limoges. Also see LIMOGES.

Haviland Marks

Ashtray, rectangular, white w/gold Embassy eagle, 3 x 5"... **$45**

Basket, mixed floral decoration w/blue trim, Blank No. 1130, 5 x 7 1/2"........................... **154**

Bonbon plate, w/three dividers, h.p., H & Co, 9 1/2" d.. **175**

Bone dishes, No. 146 patt., Blank No. 133, set of 4... **100**

Bouillon cup & saucer, Ranson blank, Schleiger 42A, flared shape decorated w/pink roses.. **45**

Bouillon w/saucer, cov., Marseilles blank, decorated w/blue flowers, H & Co................... **75**

Bowl, 10" d., 3" h., salad, Schleiger 19, Silver Anniversary.. **225**

Broth bowl & underplate, No. 448, 2 pcs....... **110**

Butter dish, cov., No. 271A patt., Blank No. 213... **187**

Cake plate, square, CFH/GDM, decorated w/spray of yellow wildflowers, 9" sq................ **95**

Cake plate, handled, No. 1 Ranson blank, patt. No. 228, 10 3/4" d..................................... **95**

Cake plate, handled, Ranson blank No. 1......... **125**

Candlesticks, Marseille blank, h.p. floral decoration, 6 3/4" h., pr...................................... **250**

Celery tray, Baltimore Rose patt., Blank No. 207, 5 5/8 x 12".. **225**

Cereal, Schleiger 57A, Ranson blank, decorated w/pink roses & blue scrolls, 6 x 2"....... **32**

Chocolate cup & saucer, No. 72A................. **45**

Chocolate pot, cov., scallop & scroll mold w/floral decoration & gold trim, marked "Haviland Limoges, France," 9" h................. **275**

Chocolate set: cov. pot & eight cups & saucers; Schleiger 235B, decorated w/pink & green flowers & gold trim.............................. **750**

Coffeepot, cov., demitasse, Osier, Blank No. 211, impressed "Haviland & Co. - Limoges - France" & English mark.................. **187**

Coffeepot, cov., Paradise, blue edge w/decoration of birds, Theodore Haviland, 8" h.. **225**

Coffeepot, cov., Sylvia patt., 1950s.................. **225**

Footed Comport with Reticulated Rim

Comport, pedestal on three feet w/ornate gold shell design, top w/reticulated edge, peach & gold design around base & top, 9" d. (ILLUS.)... **425**

Compote, Meadow Visitors patt., smooth blank, 5 1/8" h., 9 7/8" d............................... **165**

Cracker jar, cov., Marseille blank...................... **350**

Creamer, Schleiger 146, commonly known as Apple Blossom, Theodore Haviland, 4"... **60**

Creamer & open sugar, dessert, Cloverleaf patt., Schleiger 98, pr....................................... **145**

Creamer & sugar, Schleiger 223A, Blank 1, decorated w/pink flowers, pr............................ **125**

Cup & saucer, coffee, Schleiger 39D, decorated w/pink roses & gold trim....................... **55**

Cup & saucer, tea, Schleiger 19, white w/gold trim... **45**

Cup & saucer, Rosalinde patt........................... **45**

Cuspidor, smooth blank, bands of roses decorating rim & body, 6 1/2" h..................... **193**

Dessert set: 8 1/2 x 15" tray & four 7 1/4" dishes; Osier Blank No. 637, fruit & floral decoration, the set.. **250**

Fish set: 23" l. platter & six 9" d. plates; each w/different fish scene, dark orange & gold borders, Blank No. 1009, 7 pcs....... **1,250**

Fish set: 23 1/4" l. platter & twelve 7 3/8" plates; Empress Eugenie patt., No. 453, Blank No. 7, 13 pcs...................................... **2,500**

Gravy boat w/attached underplate, No. 98 patt., Blank No. 24.. **145**

Haviland Hair Receiver

Hair receiver, cov., squatty round body on three gold feet, h.p. overall w/small flowers in blues & greens w/gold trim, mark of Charles Field Haviland (ILLUS.)..................... **150**

Ice cream set: tray & 6 individual plates; Old Pansy patt. on Torse blank, 7 pcs.......... **303**

Jam jar w/underplate, cov., No. 577 patt., smooth blank.. 225

Mustard pot, cov., No. 266 patt. on Blank No. 9.. 220

Nut dish, footed, No. 1070A patt. 55

Oyster plate, Ranson blank, Schleiger 42A, decorated w/pink roses 175

Oyster plate, The Princess patt., Schleiger 57C, 9 1/2" d. 175

Oyster plates, five-well, 72C patt., Blank No. 24??, center indent for sauce, 9" d., pr. 350

Oyster tureen, Henri II Blank, decorated by Dammouse 1,050

Pickle dish, shell-shaped w/gold trim, leaf mold, 8 3/4" l. 65

Pin tray, rectangular, open handles, decorated w/pink roses, Blank 1, Schleiger 251, 3 x 5" 125

Pitcher, 7" h., milk, Schleiger 98, Blank 12, Cloverleaf patt. 125

Pitcher, 8 3/8" h., Ivy patt. w/gold trim 175

Pitcher, 8 5/8" h., Ranson blank No. 1 225

Haviland Lemonade Pitcher

Pitcher, 9" h., lemonade-type, Schleiger 1026B variation, Blank 117, decorated w/lavender flowers & brushed gold trim, Theodore Haviland (ILLUS.) 225

Place setting: dinner, salad, bread & butter plates, cup & saucer; w/scalloped double gold edge, Schleiger 91A 135

Plate, dinner, No. 9 patt., set of 10 300

Plate, Partridge in a Pear Tree from 12 Days of Christmas series, 1970 75

Paisley Pattern Plate

Plate, bread & butter, 6 1/2" d., Paisley patt., smooth blanks w/gold edge, brownish red ground w/flowers in yellow, bright blue, green & white border design w/yellow flowers & bright blue leaves, turquoise scroll trim, Haviland & Co. mark (ILLUS.) 26

Plate, coupe salad, 7 1/2" d., Baltimore Rose patt, Blank No. 207, set of 8 520

Plate, dinner, 10" d., Schleiger 150, known as Harrison Rose, decorated w/small pink & yellow roses 30

Plate, chop, 11 1/4" d., 33A patt., Blank No. 19 125

Plates, luncheon, 8 3/8" d., Club Ware, Meadow Visitors patt. & various fruits, set of 8 242

Platter, 12 1/4 x 18" oval, Moss Rose patt. w/blue trim, smooth blank 150

Pudding set, Schleiger 24, white w/gold trim, complete w/unglazed insert & undertray 475

Punch cup, tapering scalloped pedestal foot supporting wide shallow cup bowl, decorated w/flowers in shades of green w/some pink flowers & green leaves, variation of Schleiger No. 249B on Blank 17, Haviland & Co. mark, 4" h. 75

Relish, oval, Schleiger 570, two-tone green flowers, gold edge, 8" l. 45

Salt, CFH/GDM, h.p. flowers, 1 1/2 x 3/4" 45

Sauce tureen w/attached underplate, cov., No. 146 patt., Blank No. 133, 7" d. underplate, bowl 5 1/4" d. 145

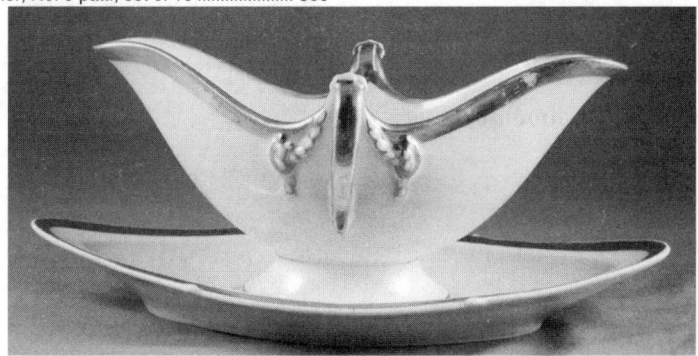

Double-spouted Sauceboat & Tray

Sauceboat & undertray, footed double-spouted boat-shaped sauceboat w/looped side handles w/molded rope trim, matching dished undertray, heavy gold trim on white, old Haviland & Co. mark, 2 pcs. (ILLUS.)...................................... 150

Soup bowls, No. 271A patt., Blank No. 213, set of 8... 280

Soup tureen, cov., pink Drop Rose patt., on Blank No. 22... 695

Haviland Covered Sugar Bowl

Sugar bowl, cov., large cylindrical form w/small loop side handles & inset flat cover w/arched handle, white ground decorated w/sprays of pink daisies touched w/yellow & greyish brown leaves, variation of Schleiger No. 1311, 1 lb. size, Charles Field Haviland, marked "CFH/GDM" (ILLUS.) 75

Tea set: cov. teapot, creamer & sugar bowl; floral & leaf mold w/gold trim, 3 pcs. 400

Tea & toast set: scalloped plate & cup; Marseilles blank, decorated w/pink roses, H & Co.. 175

Tea tray, round, Schleiger 29A, decorated w/pink flowers, unglazed bottom, 16" d. 275

Teapot, cov., 4-cup, CFG/GDM, white w/gold, ribbon handle 225

Toothbrush box, cov., Moss Rose patt. w/gold trim, smooth blank, ca. 1860s-70s, 8" l. 225

Vegetable dish, oval, Schleiger 142A, decorated w/pink daisy-like flowers, blue fences & scrolls, gold trim, Theodore Haviland, 8 x 10" 85

Vegetable dish, cov., decorated w/small orange roses, Blank No. 24, 10" d. 145

Waste bowl, Schleiger 233A, The Norma, decorated w/tiny pink & yellow flowers & gold daubs, 5 x 3"... 47

Historical & Commemorative Wares

Numerous potteries, especially in England and the United States, made various porcelain and earthenware pieces to commemorate people, places and events. Scarce English historical wares with American views command highest prices. Objects are listed here alphabetically by title of the view.

Most pieces listed here will date between about 1820 and 1850. The maker's name is noted at the end of the entry.

Almshouse, New York platter, flowers within medallions border, Beauties of America series, dark blue, Ridgway, 12 3/4 x 16 1/2" (scratches, scattered minor staining)...................................... **$1,265**

Arms of Delaware Platter

Arms of Delaware platter, trumpet flower & vine border, dark blue, Thomas Mayer, ca. 1830, 17 1/8" l. (ILLUS.)............ **5,600**

Arms of Rhode Island Plate

Arms of Rhode Island plate, flowers & vines border, dark blue, T. Mayer, minor glaze scratches, 8 1/2" d. (ILLUS.) 748

Baltimore & Ohio Railroad, level (The) plate, shell border, dark blue, E. Wood, 10 1/8" d. (stains, minor roughness on table ring).. 990

Battle of Bunker Hill platter, vine border, dark blue, R. Stevenson, 10 1/4 x 13"....... **8,625**

Boston State House basket & undertray, flowers & leaves border, basket w/reticulated sides & scalloped flaring rim, dark blue, J. Rogers, basket 6 1/2 x 9 1/4", the set (hairline cracks)....................................... **2,760**

Boston State House dish, flowers & leaves on flanged rim, deep sides, dark blue, J. Rogers, 12 3/4" d. (minor glaze scratches)... **2,070**

Boston State House pitcher, Rose Border series, fully opened roses w/leaves border, dark blue, Stubbs, 6" h. (small chip on handle) 978

Boston State House sauce tureen, cover & undertray, flowers & leaves border, pedestal base w/upward looped handles, high domed cover, dark blue, J. Rogers, tureen 7 1/4 x 8 1/4", the set........................ **3,738**

Cadmus (so-called) plate, shell border, irregular center, dark blue, Wood, 10" d. (light scratches) **500-600**

Capitol, Washington (The) serving bowl, vine border, embossed white rim, dark blue, Stevenson, 11" d. (glaze imperfections) **2,645**

Esplanade & Castle Garden Platter

Christianburg Danish Settlement on the Gold Coast, Africa platter, shell border, well-and-tree center, dark blue, E. Wood, 18 3/4" l. (minor glaze imperfections) **3,220**

City Hotel, New York plate, oak leaf border, double portrait reserves at border of Washington & Lafayette, inset view of the Entrance to the Erie Canal, dark blue, R. Stevenson, 8 1/2" d. (minor scratching) **4,600**

Columbia College, New York plate, acorn & oak leaves border, portrait medallion at rim of "President Washington," inset of "View of the Aqueduct Bridge at Rochester," dark blue, R. Stevenson, 7 1/2" d. (minor scratches)...................................... **8,625**

Commodore MacDonnough's Victory tea set, shell border, dark blue, cov. teapot, cov. sugar bowl & creamer, E. Wood, teapot 7 1/2 x 11", the set......................... **1,293**

Court House, Baltimore plate, fruit & flowers border, dark blue, Henshall, Williamson & Co., 8 1/2" d. (light wear, hairline) **470**

Dam & Water Works (The), Philadelphia (Sidewheel Steamboat) plate, fruit & flowers border, dark blue, Henshall, Williamson & Co., 9 7/8" d. **646**

port, minor wear, scratches & small area of professional repair on back rim, 18 3/4" d. (ILLUS.)...................................... **3,025**

Doctor Syntax Amused with Pat in the Pond platter, flowers & scrolls border, dark blue, E. Wood, 14 1/4 x 19" (glaze scratches, scattered minor staining).......... **1,840**

Entrance of the Erie Canal into the Hudson at Albany - View of the Aqueduct Bridge at Little Falls pitcher, floral border, dark blue, E. Wood, excellent condition, 6" h. **1,500-1,725**

Esplanade and Castle Garden, New York - Almshouse, Boston pitcher, vine border, dark blue, R. Stevenson, 10" h........... **2,300**

Esplanade and Castle Garden, New York platter, vine border, dark blue, R. Stevenson, minor glaze scratches, 14 1/2 x 18 1/2" (ILLUS., top of page)........ **5,750**

Fulton's Steamboat soup plate, floral border, dark blue, unknown maker, 10 1/4" d. (minor scratches & rim chips) **881**

Highland, Hudson River Platter

Highlands, Hudson River platter, shell border, dark blue, E. Wood, minor roughness on interior rim, 10 x 12 3/4" (ILLUS.) **3,335**

Lake George, State of New York platter, shell border, dark blue, E. Wood, 16 1/2" l. (very minor glaze scratches) **2,585**

Detroit Platter from Cities Series

Detroit platter, Cities series, groups of flowers & scrolls border, dark blue, Daven-

Landing of Lafayette Plate

Landing of General Lafayette at Castle Garden, New York, 16 August 1824 plate, primrose & dogwood border, dark blue, Clews, minor wear & scratches, 8 7/8" d. (ILLUS.).. 303

Mount Vernon, The Seat of the Late Gen'l. Washington tea set: cov. teapot, cov. sugar bowl, creamer, waste bowl & handleless cup & saucer; large flowers border, dark blue, unknown maker, teapot, 10" l., 5" h., the set (minor imperfections).. 3,819

Park Theatre, New York bowl, oak leaf border, dark blue, R. Stevenson, 8 3/4" d. (minute scratches) 2,530

Park Theatre Plate with Medallions

Park Theatre, New York plate, oak leaf border, four portrait medallions at the border of Jefferson, Washington, Lafayette & Clinton, inset of the Aqueduct Bridge at Little Falls, dark blue, R. Stevenson, 10" d. (ILLUS.).......................... **3,738**

Pennsylvania Hospital, Philadelphia platter, flowers within medallions border, Beauties of America series, dark blue, Ridgway, few minor scratches, 14 1/8 x 18 3/8" (ILLUS., bottom of page)... **1,880**

State House, Boston platter, spread-eagle border, dark blue, Stubbs, 14 3/4" l. (minor scratches & crazing) **1,265**

States series pitcher, building, two wings, water in foreground, border w/names of fifteen states in festoons separated by five-point stars border, dark blue, Clews, 6 3/4" h. (minor interior staining) **978**

States series plate, two-story building w/curved drive, border w/names of fifteen states in festoons separated by five-point stars border, dark blue, Clews, 7 3/4" d. (small rim bruise) **330**

States series plate, building, sheep on lawn, border w/names of fifteen states in festoons separated by five-point stars border, dark blue, Clews, 8 3/4" d. (rim w/area of glaze flakes, stain)......................... **289**

States series platter, mansion, foreground a lake w/swans, names of states in festoons separated by five-point stars border, dark blue, Clews, ca. 1830, 16 3/4" l., ... **2,280**

Table Rock, Niagara plate, shell border - circular center, dark blue, E. Wood, 10 1/8" d. (a few scratches)........................... **499**

Upper Ferry Bridge over the River Schuylkill platter, spread-eagle border, dark blue, Stubbs, 15 1/2 x 18 3/4" (hairline) **705**

Wadsworth Tower tea service: cov. teapot, two large tea cups, one saucer, five regular tea cups, six saucers; shell border, dark blue, E. Wood, 15 pcs. (imperfections)... **2,645**

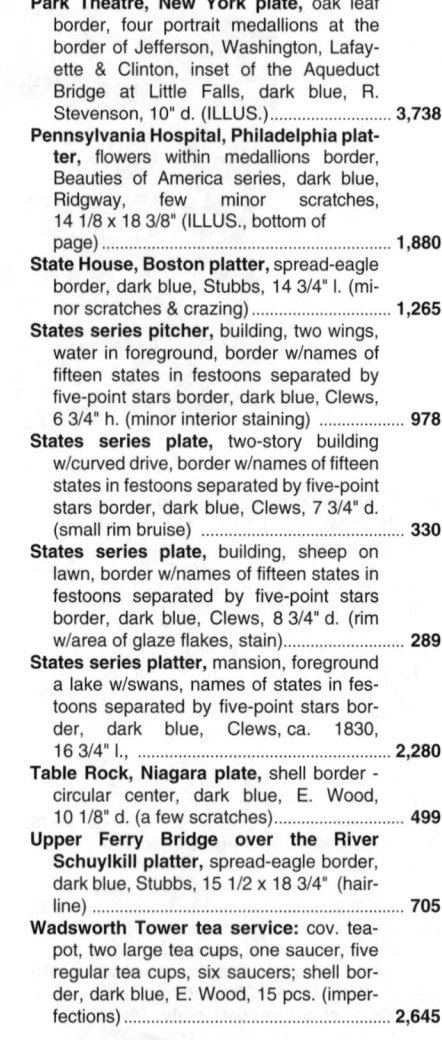

Pennsylvania Hospital Platter

Washington Standing at Tomb, scroll in hand waste bowl, floral border, dark blue, E. Wood, 6 1/4" d., 3 1/4" h. (minor imperfections) **748**

West Point Military Academy platter, shell border, dark blue, E. Wood, 9 1/4 x 11 3/4" (minor glaze scratches) **2,760**

Winter View of Pittsfield Platter

Winter View of Pittsfield, Massachusetts platter, vignette views & flowers border, dark blue, Clews, glaze scratches, 14 x 16 1/2" (ILLUS.) **3,450**

Hull

In 1905 Addis E. Hull purchased the Acme Pottery Company in Crooksville, Ohio. In 1917 the A.E. Hull Pottery Company began to make a line of art pottery for florists and gift shops. The company also made novelties, kitchenware and stoneware.

Hull's Little Red Riding Hood kitchenware was manufactured between 1943 and 1957 and is a favorite of collectors, as are the beautiful matte glaze vases it produced.

In 1950 the factory was destroyed by a flood and fire, but by 1952 it was back in production. Hull added its newer glossy glazed pottery plus pieces sold in flower shops under the names Regal and Floraline. Hull's brown dinnerware lines achieved great popularity and were the main lines being produced prior to the plant's closing in 1986.

References on Hull Pottery include: Hull, The Heavenly Pottery, 7th Edition, 2001 and Hull, The Heavenly Pottery Shirt Pocket Price Guide, 4th Edition, 1999, by Joan Hull. Also The Dinnerwares Lines by Barbara Loveless Click-Burke (Collector Books 1993) and Robert's Ultimate Encyclopedia of Hull Pottery by Brenda Roberts (Walsworth Publishing Co., 1992). -- Joan Hull, Advisor.

Hull Marks

Hull Advertising Piece

Advertising piece, "The A.E. Hull Co. Pottery" in raised lettering within scroll border, very rare, 11 x 5" (ILLUS.) **$6,000**

Ashtray, Butterfly patt., B3, 7" l. **55**

Ashtray, Serenade patt., No. S23, 10 1/2 x 13" **95**

Little Red Riding Hood Pieces

Bank, Little Red Riding Hood patt., standing-type (ILLUS. bottom left) **795**

Basket, hanging-type, Sun Glow patt., No. 99, 6" h. **65**

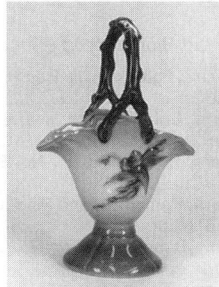

Hull Woodland Basket

Basket, Woodland patt., fan shape, twig-form handle, glossy pink, green & beige, 8 3/4" h., 9" w. (ILLUS.) **110**

Basket, Parchment & Pine patt., No. S-3, 6" h. **95**

Basket, Open Rose (Camellia) patt., No.142, 6 1/4" h. **350**

Tokay Pattern Basket

Basket, Tokay patt., No. 6, overhead branch handle, white ground, 8" h. (ILLUS.) 95
Basket, Royal Woodland patt., No. W9, 8 3/4" h. 50
Basket, Woodland Matte patt., fan-shaped w/center handle, yellow & green, W9-8 3/4", 8 3/4" h. 245
Basket, Ebb Tide patt., E5, 9 1/8" h. 150
Basket, Butterfly patt., three-handled, No. B17, 10 1/2" h. 350
Basket, Wildflower patt., No. W-16-10 1/2", 10 1/2" h. 375
Basket, Serenade patt., pink ground, ruffled sides, No. S14, 12" h. 350
Bonbon, Butterfly patt., No. B4, 6" d. 45
Bowl, cereal, 6" d., Floral patt., No. 50 10
Bowl, 7" d., Orchid patt., No. 312 150
Bowl, 8" d., Calla Lily patt., No. 500-32 135
Bowl, salad, 10" d., No. 49 50

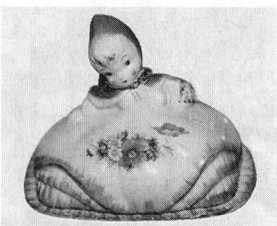

Little Red Riding Hood Butter Dish

Butter dish, cov., figure of Little Red Riding Hood (ILLUS.) 475
Candleholders, Ebb Tide patt., No. E-13, 2 3/4" h., pr. 75
Candleholders, Bow-Knot patt., No. B17, 4" h., pr. 225
Candleholders, Parchment and Pine patt., No. S-10, 5" h., pr. 50
Candy dish, Butterfly patt., No. B6, 4 3/4 x 5 1/2" 45
Candy dish, cov., Serenade patt., No. S3C, 8 1/4" h. 95
Canister, cov., Little Red Riding Hood patt., "Cereal" 1,250
Casserole, cov., French handle-type & warmer, House 'N Garden line, No. 979, Mirror Brown, 3 pt., 3 pcs. 125
Casserole, cov., Floral patt., No. 42, 7 1/2" d. 60
Casserole, cov., Serenade patt., No.S20, 9" d. 125

Compote, Tokay patt., No. 9 65
Console bowl, Iris patt., No. 409-12", 12" l. 250
Console bowl, Orchid patt., No. 314, 13" l. 375
Consolette, Tokay patt., footed oblong form w/end branch handles, No. 14, 15 3/4" l. 165
Cookie jar, cov., figural Duck 125
Cookie jar, cov., Floral patt., No. 48, 8 1/4" h. 65
Cookie jar, cov., Gingerbread Man, sand, 12" h. 550
Cookie jar, cov., Little Red Riding Hood, open basket, gold stars on apron 395
Cookie jar, cov., Little Red Riding Hood patt., closed-basket style, band of orange blossoms around skirt (ILLUS. top with bank, previous page) 300-1,000
Cornucopia-vase, Butterfly patt., No. B2, 6 1/2" h. 40
Cornucopia-vase, Ebb Tide patt., No. E3, 7 1/2" h. 225

Hull Bow-Knot Cornucopia-Vase

Cornucopia-vase, Bow-Knot patt., blue & pink, No. B-5-7 1/2, 7 1/2" h. (ILLUS.) 250
Cornucopia-vase, Tokay patt., No. 10, white ground, 11" l. 65
Cornucopia-vase, Parchment & Pine patt., No. S-6, 12" 125
Cracker jar, cov., Little Red Riding Hood patt. 800
Creamer, Water Lily patt., No. L-19-5", 5" h. 75
Creamer, Ebb Tide patt., No. E15 60
Creamer & cov. sugar bowl, Little Red Riding Hood patt., side-pour creamer, pr. 1,000
Dish, leaf-shaped, Tokay patt., No. 19, 14" l. 95

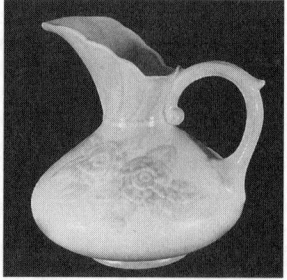

Hull Open Rose Pattern Ewer

Ewer, Open Rose patt., No. 105, 7" h. (ILLUS.) 225
Ewer, Magnolia Gloss patt., No. H-3, 5 1/2" h. 55
Ewer, Royal Woodland patt., No. W6, 6 1/2" h. 45
Ewer, Iris patt., No. 401-8", cream & rose, 8" h. 275

Little Red Riding Hood Advertising Plaque

Ewer, Ebb Tide patt., No. E-10, figural fish
handle, 14" h. 275
Flowerpot, Sun Glow patt., No. 98, 7 1/2" h. 45
Flowerpot w/attached saucer, Sueno Tu-
lip patt., No. 116-33-4 3/4", 4 3/4" h. 135
Flowerpot w/attached saucer, Woodland
patt., No. W11, 5 1/2" h. 150-175
Grease jar, cov., Sun Glow patt., No. 53,
5 1/4" h. 60
Jardiniere, Woodland patt., dark green &
blue, No. W7-5 1/2", 5 1/2" h. 125
Jardiniere, Calla Lily patt., No. 591, 7" h. 300
Jardiniere, Bow-Knot patt., wide bulbous
body w/short & wide molded neck
w/small bows at each side, B-19-9 3/8",
9 3/8" d. 950
Lamp base, Sueno Tulip patt., 6 1/2" h. 600
Lamp base, Iris patt., No. 414, 16" h. 750
Mug, Serenade patt., No. S22, 8 oz. 55

Early Art Stoneware Pitcher

Pitcher, 3 3/4" h., Early Art stoneware
w/embossed flowers & scrolls, cobalt,
maroon & turquoise splotching over
cream ground (ILLUS.) 85

House 'N Garden Pitcher

Pitcher, 7" h., House 'N Garden Rainbow
serving ware, Tangerine glaze, two-quart
capacity, No. 925 (ILLUS.) 30
Pitcher, 8" h., Sueno Tulip patt., No. 109-
33-8" 235

Dogwood/Wild Rose Pitcher

Pitcher, 13 1/2" h., Dogwood/Wild Rose
patt., No. 519-13 1/2 (ILLUS.) 800
Planter, baby w/pillow, pink w/gold trim, No.
92, 5 1/2" h. 35
Planter, model of lovebirds, pink & brown,
Novelty line, No. 93, 6" h. 40
Planter, model of a Dachshund dog, 14" l.,
6" h. 110
Planter, model of Bandanna Duck, Novelty
line, No. 74, 9" h. 50
Plaque, advertising "Little Red Riding
Hood," very rare, only 6 known to exist,
11 3/4" l., 6 1/2" h. (ILLUS., top of
page) 20,000
Salt & pepper shakers, Sun Glow patt., No.
54, 2 3/4" h., pr. 20
Sandwich tray, Gingerbread Man patt. 150
String holder, Little Red Riding Hood patt.
(ILLUS. bottom right w/bank, on page
285) 1,600
Sugar bowl, cov., Rosella patt., No. R-4,
5 1/2" h. 60
Tea set: cov. teapot, creamer & cov. sugar
bowl; Butterfly patt., Nos. B18, B19 &
B20, 3 pcs. 325
Tea set: cov. teapot W26, cov. sugar bowl
W28 & creamer W27; Woodland Gloss
patt., teapot 6 1/2" h., 3 pcs. 275
Teapot, cov., Dogwood patt., No. 507,
5 1/2" h. 350

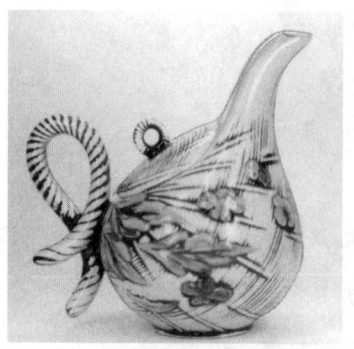

Blossom Flite Pattern Teapot

Teapot, cov., Blossom Flite patt., No. T14, 8" h. (ILLUS.) **100**

Teapot, cov., Royal Woodland patt., No. W26, 8-cup **95**

Vase, 4 3/4" h., Magnolia Matte patt., No. 13-4 3/4" **75**

Hull Early Art Ware Vase

Vase, 5 1/2" h., 4 1/2" d., Early Art ware, 1920s, unmarked, cobalt & rose brushstroke pattern over pale blue w/a hint of green at rim, fake handles from shoulder to rim on each side (ILLUS.) **85**

Vase, 6" h., Sueno Tulip patt., No. 110-33-6" **150**

Bow-Knot Pattern Vase

Vase, 6 1/2" h., Bow-Knot patt., blue & cream, No. B-3-6 1/2" (ILLUS.) **250**

Vase, 6 1/2" h., Royal Woodland patt., No. W4 .... **35**

Vase, bud, 7" h., Open Rose (Camellia) patt., No. 129 .... **155**

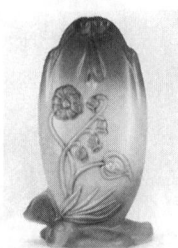

Hull Bow-Knot Vase

Vase, 8 1/2" h., Bow-Knot patt., No. B-9-8 1/2" (ILLUS.) **325**

Vase, 8 1/2" h., Magnolia Gloss patt., gold trim, No. H-8 .... **75**

Vase, 8 1/2" h., Magnolia Matte patt., the baluster-form body w/slender scroll handles from the mid-body to the foot, pink & blue, No. 2-8 1/2" **125**

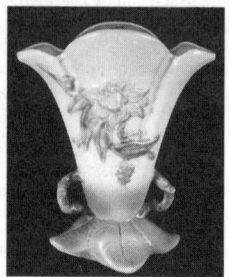

Hull Woodland Pattern Vase

Vase, 8 1/2" h., Woodland patt., Dawn Rose pastel, No. W16-8 1/2 (ILLUS.) **185**

Vase, 9" h., Mardi Gras/Granada patt., pink & blue, No. 47-9" **55**

Vase, 9 1/4" h., Ebb Tide, pink w/gold, No. E-6 .... **175**

Vase, 10" h., Orchid patt., No. 302 .... **350**

Vase, 10 1/2" h., Magnolia Matte patt., No. 8-10 1/2" **200**

Hull Poppy Vase

Vase, 10 1/2" h., Poppy patt., No. 607-10 1/2, two-handled, blue bottom, matte finish, original label (ILLUS.) **450**

Vase, 10 1/2" h., Wildflower patt., yellow & rose, No. 59-10 1/2" **350**

Vase, 12" h., Open Rose (Camellia) patt., No. 124-12" **450**

Vase, 12 1/2" h., Water Lily patt., No. L-16-12 1/2" **395**

Wall pocket, model of a flying goose, Novelty line, No. 67, 6" h............................... 45
Wall pocket, model of a cup & saucer, Sun Glow patt., No. 80, 6 1/4" h. 75
Wall pocket, Royal Woodland patt., shell-shaped, No. W13, 7 1/2" l. 50
Wall pocket, Woodland Matte patt., No. W13-7 12", 7 1/2" l. 190
Wall pocket, Open Rose (Camellia) patt., fan-shaped, No. 125-8 1/2", 8 1/2" l. 325
Window box, Dogwood patt., No. 508, 10 1/2" l. 195
Window box, Serenade patt., pink, No. S-9, 12 1/2" l. 100

Hummel Figurines & Collectibles

The Goebel Company of Oeslau, Germany, first produced these porcelain figurines in 1934, having obtained the rights to adapt the beautiful pastel sketches of children by Sister Maria Innocentia (Berta) Hummel. Every design by the Goebel artisans was approved by the nun until her death in 1946. Although not antique, these figurines with the "M.I. Hummel" signature, especially those bearing the Goebel Company factory mark used from 1934 and into the early 1940s, are being sought by collectors, although interest may have peaked some years ago. A good reference is Luckey's Hummel Figurines & Plates, Identification and Value Guide *by Carl F. Luckey (Krause Publications).Trademarks:TMK 1 - Crown - 1934-1950TMK 2 - Full Bee - 1940-1959TMK 3 - Stylized Bee - 1958-1972TMK 4 - Three Line Mark - 1964-1972TMK 5 - Last Bee - 1970-1980TMK 6 - Missing Bee - 1979-1991TMK 7 - Hummel Mark - 1991-1999TMK 8 - Goebel Bee - 2000-*

Hummel Marks

A Gentle Glow candleholder, #439, 5 1/4" h., Trademark 6................................. $200
A Stitch in Time, #255, 6 3/4" h., Trademark 4 375-425
Accompanist (The), #453, 3" h., Trademark 6 100
Adoration, #23/I, 6 1/4" h., Trademark 1 1,000-1,300
Adoration, #23/III, 9" h., Trademark 1 1,600-2,100
Angel Cloud font, #206, 2 1/4 x 4 3/4", Trademark 3.. 200-250
Angel Duet candleholder, #193, 5" h., Trademark 2.. 600-700
Angel Serenade, #214/N (angel standing), color decoration, part of Nativity set, 5 1/2" h., Trademark 3........................... 250-285
Angel with Accordion, #238B, 2 1/4" h., Trademark 5 55
Angelic Sleep candleholder, #25, 3 3/4" h., Trademark 6................................... 185
Apple Tree Boy, #142/3/0, 4 1/4" h., Trademark 6 150
Apple Tree Girl, #141/3/0, 4" h., Trademark 2 300-350
Apple Tree Girl, #141, 6" h., Trademark 2 600-700

Auf Wiedersehen, #153/0, 5 1/2" h., Trademark 2 .... **425-525**
Auf Wiedersehen, #153/I, 7" h., Trademark 3 .... **475-525**
Ba-Bee Ring plaque, #30/0/B, boy, 5" d., Trademark 5..................................... **250-260**
Baking Day (Die Backerin), #330, 5 1/4" h., Trademark 6................................. 315
Band Leader, #129, 5 1/4" h., Trademark 5 .... **245-270**
Bashful, #377, 4 3/4" h., Trademark 4 .... **1,000-1,500**
Be Patient, #197/I, 6 1/4" h., Trademark 3 .... **425-475**
Bird Duet, #169, 4" h., Trademark 1 .... **425-550**
Birthday Candle candleholder, #440, 5 1/2" h., 1963, Exclusive Special Edition No. 10 for Members of the Goebel Collectors' Club 375
Birthday Serenade, #218/2/0, 4 1/4" h., Trademark 2.................................... **610-650**
Book Worm, #8, 4" h., Trademark 1 .... **700-850**

Book Worm

Book Worm, #8, 4" h., Trademark 2 (ILLUS.) 475
Boots, #143/0, 5" h., Trademark 2 300
Boy with Bird ashtray, #166, 6 1/4" l., Trademark 3.................................... **195-210**
Busy Student, #367, 4 1/4" h., Trademark 6.. 175
Candlelight candleholder (Engel mit Kerze, Leuchter), #192, 7" h., Trademark 6 265
Celestial Musician, #188/0, 5" h., Trademark 6 245
Celestial Musician ornament, #646, 3" h., first issue 1993, original box.................. 105
Chef, Hello, #124, 6 1/2" h., Trademark 1 .... **800-1,000**

Chick Girl

Chick Girl, #57/I, 4 1/4" h., Trademark 5 (ILLUS.)... **345-355**
Chicken-Licken (Kukenliesl), #385, 4 3/4" h., Trademark 6.................................. **325**
Christ Child, #18, 2 x 3 1/4", Trademark 6 ...... **150**
Cinderella, #337,4 1/2" h., Trademark 6- **320**
Close Harmony, #336, 5 1/2" h., Trademark 6 .... **335**
Confidentially, #314, 5 1/2" h., Trademark 2 .... **4,000-5,000**
Coquettes, #179, 5 1/4" h., Trademark 2 .. **500-650**

Culprits

Culprits, #56A, 6 1/4" h., Trademark 6 (ILLUS.)... **335**
Daisies Don't Tell, #380, 5" h., 1981, exclusive special edition No. 5 for members of the Goebel Collectors' Club **275**
Doctor, #127, 5" h., Trademark 6 .... **165**
Doll Bath, #319, 5 1/4" h., Trademark 5 .... **350-375**
Easter Time, #384, 4" h., Trademark 4 .... **1,000-1,500**
Eventide, #99, 4 3/4", Trademark 2............ **600-750**
Farm Boy, #66, 5 1/4" h., Trademark 6 .... **260**
Feathered Friends, #344, 4 1/2" h., Trademark 6 .... **325**
Feeding Time, #199/0, 4 1/4" h., Trademark 6 .... **220**
Festival Harmony, #173/4/0, 3" h., first issue 1995.. **100**

Festival Harmony

Festival Harmony, Adventsengel mid Mandolin, #172/0, 8", original box, Trademark 6 (ILLUS.)..................................... **355**
Flower Girl, #548, 4 1/2" h., 1989, exclusive edition M.I. Hummel Club, 5 year membership, original box................................ **120**

Flower Madonna, #10/I, color, 9 1/2" h., Trademark 2.. **800-950**
Follow the Leader, #369, 7" h., Trademark 3.. **4,000-5,000**
For Father, #87, 5 1/2" h., Trademark 6........... **240**
Forest Shrine, #183, 9" h., Trademark 1 .... **1,500-1,900**
Friends, #136/1, 5 3/8" h., Trademark 1.... **800-950**
Friends, #136, 10 3/4" h., Trademark 2.. **2,000-3,000**
Girl with Trumpet, #389, 2 1/2" h., Trademark 4 .... **175-225**
Goebel Hummel Figurines Dealer Display Plaque #187A, 4 x 5 1/2" h., Trademark 5.. **200**
Going to Grandma's, #52/0, 4 3/4" h., Trademark 2.. **450-600**
Goose Girl, #47/0, 4 3/4" h., Trademark 2.. **300-400**
Happy Birthday, #176/0, 5 1/2" h., Trademark 3.. **325-375**
Happy Traveler, #109/II, 8" h., Trademark 1.. **1,200-1,500**
Heavenly Protection, #88/I, 6 3/4" h., Trademark 4.. **575-660**
Homeward Bound, #334, 5" h., Trademark 4 .... **475**
It's Cold, #421, 5 1/4" h., 1981, exclusive special edition No. 6 for members of the Goebel Collectors' Club **375**
Joyful, #53, 4" h., Trademark 5 .... **150**
Just Resting, #112/3/0, 3 3/4" h., Trademark 2.. **275-350**
Kindergartner (The) (Schulmachen), #467, 5 1/4" h., Trademark 6 .... **220**
Knitting Lesson, #256, 7 1/2" h., Trademark 3.. **875-1,150**
Let's Sing, #110/0 , 3 1/4" h., Trademark 5..... **140**
Little Cellist, #89/1, 6" h., Trademark 3 .... **350**

Little Drummer

Little Drummer, #240, 4 1/4" h., Trademark 5 (ILLUS.).. **170**
Little Fiddler, #2/II, 11" h., Trademark 2... **1,800-2,300**
Little Hiker, #16/I, 5 1/2" h., Trademark 2... **400-500**
Little Pair (The), #449, 5 1/4" h., 1990-2000, exclusive edition Ten Year Membership, M.I. Hummel Club, original box **200**
Little Shopper, #96, 4 3/4" h., Trademark 1.. **430-550**
Little Tailor, #308, 5 1/2" h., Trademark 5....... **275**
Mail Is Here (The), #226, 4 1/4 x 6 1/4", Trademark 4.. **700-800**

March Winds, #43, 5" h., Trademark 5............. **175**

Meditation

Meditation, #13/2/0, 4 1/2" h., Trademark 6
(ILLUS.)... **165**
Merry Wanderer, #7/II, 9 1/2" h., Trade-
mark 1 .... **3,000-3,500**
Mother's Darling, #175, 5 1/2" h., Trade-
mark 4 .... **300**
Not for You, #317, 5 1/2" h., Trademark 4........ **410**
On Secret Path, #386, 5 1/2" h., Trademark
5 .... **310**
Photographer (The), #178, 4 3/4" h.,
Trademark 1... **750-1,000**

The Photographer

Photographer (The), #178, 5" h., Trade-
mark 6 (ILLUS.) **320**
Playmates, #58/0, 4" h., Trademark 6 .... **185**

Postman

Postman, #119, 5 1/4" h., Trademark 2
(ILLUS.).. **350-450**
Retreat to Safety, #201/I, 5 1/2" h., Trade-
mark 3 .... **475-525**

Rare Ring Around the Rosie

Ring Around the Rosie, #348, 6 3/4" h.,
Trademark 2 (ILLUS.)................... **10,000-15,000**
School Boys, #170/I, 7 1/2" h., Trademark
3.. **1,650-1,750**
Searching Angel plaque, #310, 4" h.,
Trademark 6... **115**
Serenade, #85/0, 4 3/4" h., Trademark
1 .... **400-500**

Serenade

Serenade, #85/II, 7 1/2" h., Trademark 3
(ILLUS.).. **650-700**
Shepherd's Boy, #64, 5 1/2" h., Trademark
6.. **260**
Silent Night candleholder, #54,
3 1/2 x 4 3/4", Trademark 6........................... **400**
Singing Lesson, #63, 2 3/4" h., Trademark
5 .... **135**
Skier, #59, 5 1/4" h., Trademark 6...................... **220**

Soldier Boy

Soldier Boy, #332, 5 3/4" h., Trademark 5
(ILLUS.).. **255**
Song of Praise, #454, 3" h., Trademark 6 .... **110**
Sounds of the Mandolin, #438, 3 1/2" h.,
Trademark 6.. **135**
Stormy Weather, #71/2/0, 4 3/4" h., Trade-
mark 6 .... **335**
Street Singer, #131, 5" h., Trademark 1 ... **550-700**
Strolling Along, #5, 4 3/4" h., Trademark 5...... **275**
Surprise, #94/3/0, 4 1/4" h., Trademark 6......... **165**
Sweet Music, #186, 5 1/4 " h.,
Trademark 3... **300**
Thoughtful, #415, 4 1/2" h., Trademark 6......... **255**
To Market, #49/3/0, 4" h., Trademark 5..... **200-210**
Trumpet Boy, #97, 4 3/4" h.,
Trademark 1.. **400-425**
Tuneful Angel, #359, 2 3/4" h., Trademark
5 .... **85**

Umbrella Boy

Umbrella Boy, #152/0/A, 4 3/4" h., Trade-
mark 6, (ILLUS.) **700**

Umbrella Girl

Umbrella Girl, #152/0/B, 4 3/4" h., Trade-
mark 6 (ILLUS.) **700**
Vacation Time plaque, #125, 4 x 4 1/4",
Trademark 6.. **220**
Valentine Joy, #399, 5 3/4" h., 1979, exclu-
sive special edition for members of the
Goebel Collectors' Club **275**
Village Boy, #51/0, 6" h., Trademark 1...... **700-900**
Volunteers, #50/2/0, 5" h., Trademark 5 ... **275-305**
Waiter, #154/0, 6" h., Trademark 6.................... **235**
Wash Day, #321/4/0, 3" h., Trademark 6........... **115**

Wayside Devotion

Wayside Devotion, #28/2, 7 1/2" h., Trade-
mark 4 (ILLUS.)... **575**
Wayside Harmony lamp, #224/II, 9 1/2" h.,
Trademark 2.. **650-800**

Weary Wanderer

Weary Wanderer, #204, 6" h., Trademark 6
(ILLUS.) **275**
Which Hand?, #258, 5 1/4" h.,
Trademark 3.. **625-825**
With Loving Greetings, #309, 3 1/2" h.,
Trademark 6.. **275**
Worship, #84/0, 5 " h., Trademark 2................. **350**

Ironstone

*The first successful ironstone was patented in 1813
by C.J. Mason in England. The body contains iron slag
incorporated with the clay. Other potters imitated
Mason's ware, and today much hard, thick ware is
lumped under the term ironstone. Earlier it was called
by various names, including graniteware. Both plain
white and decorated wares were made throughout the
19th century. Tea Leaf Lustre ironstone was made by
several firms.*

General

Cabinet plates, each w/a scalloped rim,
"Japan" patt., floral border & center,
painted in the Imari palette, Hick &
Meigh, England, ca. 1830, 10 3/8" d., pr.
(one w/hairline)... **$235**

Various Red Cliff Pieces

Cups & saucers, handleless, "gaudy" Blackberry patt. in underglaze-blue trimmed w/yellow & orange enamel & lustre, E. Walley mark, ca. 1850, some variation, set of 10 .... **1,375**

Gravy boat, Long Octagon shape, all-white, ca. 1847, T.J. & J. Mayer **125-140**

Mayer Table-type Pitcher

Pitcher, 9" h., table-type, Full-Panelled Gothic shape, all-white, ca. 1847, T.J. & J. Mayer (ILLUS.) **190-210**

Pitcher, 9 3/4" h., table-type, Grape Octagon shape, all-white, Pearson & Hancock **150-180**

Plate, 8 3/8" w., paneled shape, "gaudy" freehand Strawberry patt., underglaze-blue w/green & two shades of red enamel & copper lustre trim, mid-19th c. **385**

Plate, 8 1/2" d., "gaudy" style, center w/urn in flow blue w/pink & red flowers & copper lustre highlights (stains) **110**

Plate, 9 1/4" w., paneled shape, "gaudy" freehand Morning Glory patt., underglaze-blue trimmed w/two shades of green, red & black enamel, mid-19th c. **303**

Plate, 9 1/2" w., paneled sides, "gaudy" Floral Urn freehand patt., underglaze-blue & green & trimmed w/two shades of red enamel & copper lustre, mid-19th c. (light stains, tiny enamel flake) **330**

Plate, 10 1/4" d., New York shape, all-white, ca. 1858, J. Clementson.................. **50-65**

Plate, 10 1/2" d., Fig shape, all-white, ca. 1856, Davenport/Wedgwood..................... **60-75**

Plates, 9 5/8" d., paneled edge, central transfer-printed garden landscape w/urn of flowers, flower & scroll border, Florilla patt., purple highlighted w/yellow, green, blue & red enamel, mid-19th c., set of 6 (stains) **138**

Platter, oval, 10" l., President shape, all-white, John Edwards **30-40**

Platter, 13 1/2" l., rectangular w/cut corners, "gaudy" freehand Morning Glory patt., underglaze-blue trimmed w/two shades of green, red & black, mid-19th c. (old red flaking, minor stains) **385**

Platter, 14 3/4" oval, "gaudy," blue transfer-printed War Bonnet patt. trimmed in red, orange & yellow, marked "Ironstone China," mid-19th c. (wear, scratches)................ **165**

Platter, oval, 16" l., Corn & Oats shape, all-white, Davenport/Wedgwood..................... **65-75**

Platter, 16 1/4" l., oval w/lightly scalloped rim, "gaudy" freehand Strawberry patt., underglaze black, mid-19th c. (small chips on one corner)...................................... **413**

Platter, 16 x 21", well-and-tree-type, oval, Rural Scenery patt., broad floral border surrounding a meadow landscape w/figures & animals, Davewell & Goodfellow, England (chips on foot, hairline)................... **440**

Platter, 22" l., oval, polychrome floral decoration w/gilt trim, Stokes Works mark on base, mid-19th c. **863**

Punch bowl, footed deep rounded bowl, floral embellishments around the rim & base, twig urn w/flowers & bird at center & sides, in shades of cobalt blue, yellow, pink, orange & green w/gilt highlights, mid-19th c., 14 1/4" d., 6 1/2" h. **1,035**

Relish dish, Berlin Swirl, all-white, ca. 1856, Mayer & Elliot **65-75**

Salt & pepper shakers, Boote's 1851 shape, all-white, ca. 1960s, Red Cliff, 4" h., pr. (ILLUS. far right & far left, top of page).. **50-60**

Soap box, cover & liner, plain oval, all-white, ca. 1872-87, Thomas Elsmore & Son, 3 pcs. **40-45**

Soap dish, open, plain hollow rectangular body w/drain holes in well & one on side for cleaning, all-white, various potters **20-30**

Soup plate, Sharon Arch shape, all-white, Davenport, 9 1/2" d..................................... **50-60**

Soup tureen, undertray, cover & ladle,
Vista England patt., footed deep tureen,
grape leaf & vine border, cranberry, tray
14 3/4" l., tureen 10 1/2" h., the set **605**

Teapot, cov., Memnon shape, six panels
w/branch handle & bud finial, all-
white, ca. 1850s, John Meir & Son,
8 3/4" h. **175-200**

Vegetable dish, cov., Scotia (Poppy)
shape, oval, all-white, ca. 1870, F. Jones
& Co., 9" l. **100-120**

Wash bowl & pitcher, miniature, Classic
Gothic shape, all-white, Red Cliff, ca.
1960s, overall 4 1/2" h. (ILLUS. second
from right w/salt & pepper shakers, previ-
ous page) **50-75**

Wash bowl & pitcher, miniature, Fig (registered Union shape), all-white, Red
Cliff, ca. 1960s, overall 3 1/2" h. (ILLUS.
second from left w/salt & pepper shakers,
previous page) **30-45**

Wash bowl & pitcher, miniature, Syden-
ham shape, all-white, Red Cliff, ca. 1960s,
overall 4 1/2" h. (ILLUS. center w/salt &
pepper shakers, previous page) **60-90**

Tea Leaf Ironstone

Apple bowl, fluted sides, Anthony Shaw
(some utensil marks) **325**

Tea Leaf Scalloped Bone Dish

Bone dish, crescent-shaped w/scalloped
rim, Alfred Meakin (ILLUS.) **30**

Brush box, cov., Cable patt., Anthony
Shaw **800**

Brush vase, footed, Anthony Shaw **425**

Brush vase, Simple Square patt., Wedg-
wood & Co. **200**

Butter dish, cover & insert, Fleur-de-Lis
patt., Wedgwood & Co. **450**

Cake plate, Bamboo patt., Alfred Meakin **65**

Cake plate, Brocade patt., Alfred Meakin **155**

Cake plate, Daisy patt., Anthony Shaw **55**

Cake plate, Polonaise patt., Edge, Malkin **200**

Cake plate, Sunburst patt., Wilkinson **130**

Chamber pot, cov., Daisy 'n Chain patt.,
Wilkinson **175**

Chamber pot, cov., Maidenhair Fern patt.,
Wilkinson (mild lustre & glaze wear) **450**

Compote, open, Hexagon patt., pedestal
base, Anthony Shaw **375**

Compote, open, square, Red Cliff, ca.
1960s **190**

Creamer, Bordered Fuchsia patt., Anthony
Shaw **1,000**

Creamer, gold Tea Leaf, Cartwright Bros.,
6 3/4" h. **55**

Creamer, Lily of the Valley patt., Anthony
Shaw, 5 1/4" h. **375**

Creamer, Lily of the Valley patt., high-lip
variation, Anthony Shaw **375**

Cylindrical Tea Leaf Cup & Saucer

Cup & saucer, handled, cylindrical squatty
cup, Wilkinson (ILLUS.) **50**

Doughnut stand, footed, square, Red
Cliff, ca. 1960s, 8" w. **135**

Egg cup, unmarked (bottom edge repaired) **275**

Gravy boat, bathtub-shaped, J. & E. Mayer **180**

Gravy boat, Chinese patt., Anthony Shaw
(two pit marks) **210**

Gravy boat, Square Ridged patt., Wedg-
wood & Co. **80**

Ladle, soup-type, Wedgwood & Co. **475**

Pitcher, 6" h., Maidenhair Fern patt., Wilkin-
son **225**

Pitcher, 6 5/8" h., jug-form, Pagoda patt., T.
Burgess **170**

Pitcher, 7 1/2" h., Square Ridged patt., Mel-
lor, Taylor & Co. **200**

Pitcher, 8" h., Bamboo patt., Alfred Meakin **190**

Pitcher, 8" h., Peerless patt., Edwards **400**

Pitcher, 8 1/2" h., Maidenhair Fern patt.,
Wilkinson **425**

Pitcher, 8 3/4" h., Rondeau patt., Daven-
port (flake on base rim) **300**

Pitcher, milk, Bordered Fuchsia patt., An-
thony Shaw **725**

Platter, 10 1/4 x 14 1/4", Chelsea patt., Al-
fred Meakin **50**

Posset cup, Chinese shape, Anthony Shaw **325**

Relish dish, mitten-shaped, Chinese patt.,
Anthony Shaw (some discoloration) **220**

Relish dish, mitten-shaped, Lily of the Val-
ley patt., Anthony Shaw **250**

Salt & pepper shakers, Empress patt., Mi-
cratex by Adams, ca. 1960s, pr. **310**

Sauce ladle, Anthony Shaw **250**

Sauce tureen, cover, ladle & underplate,
Daisy 'n Chain patt., Wilkinson (slight dis-
coloration) **350**

Shaving mug, Cable patt., Anthony Shaw **170**

Shaving mug, Little Cable patt., Thomas
Furnival **275**

Shaving mug, Ridged patt., Mellor, Taylor
& Co. **600**

Slop jar, Daisy 'n Chain patt., Wilkinson, no
cover **800**

Slop jar & silencer, Alfred Meakin (crazing
on base & silencer, slight discoloration) **2,000**

Soap dish, cover & drainer, Simple
Square patt., Wedgwood & Co. (lid
w/edge roughness) **180**

Soap dish, cover & insert, Ruth Sayers
decoration, ca. 1980s **110**

Soup tureen, cover, ladle & undertray,
Simple Square patt., Wedgwood & Co.,
the set **200**

Sugar bowl, cov., Bordered Fuchsia patt., Anthony Shaw (slight cracks & small chip).. 600

Sugar bowl, cov., Niagara Fan patt., Anthony Shaw (under rim base chip) 500

Tea set: Daisy 'n Chain patt., Wilkinson 120

Teapot, cov., child's, East End Pottery (tiny nick on spout lip) 200

Vegetable dish, cov., Cable patt., oval, footed, Anthony Shaw, 10" l. 110

Vegetable dish, cov., Daisy 'n Tulip patt., Wedgwood & Co. 80

Vegetable dish, cov., Square Ridged patt., Wedgwood & Co. 110

Wash bowl & pitcher, Bamboo patt., Alfred Meakin, pr.. 225

Wash bowl & pitcher set, Square Ridged patt., Mellor, Taylor & Co. 325

Waste bowl, Chinese patt., Anthony Shaw (one pit mark)... 140

Water pitcher, Maidenhair Fern patt., Wilkinson (repaired base chip)...................... 250

Tea Leaf Variants

Brush box, cov., Reverse Teaberry patt., Portland shape, Elsmore & Forster (two small chips) 2,500

Cake plate, Berry Cluster & lustre band, Jacob Furnival... 325

Cake plate, Teaberry patt., Augusta shape, J. Clementson (one handle flake, some rim roughness).. 400

Coffeepot, cov., Reverse Teaberry patt., Portland shape, Elsmore & Forster 500

Creamer, lustre band decor, Prairie shape, J. Clementson, 6" h.. 300

Creamer, lustre trim, Ceres shape, Elsmore & Forster (light crazing)............................... 210

Creamer, Teaberry patt., Elegance shape, Clementson Bros. (slight discoloration, roughness on base) 600

Cup, handleless, Morning Glory patt., Ceres shape, Elsmore & Forster (tiny rim potting flaw) 85

Cup & saucer, handled, Reverse Teaberry patt., Portland shape, Elsmore & Forster (two small chips on saucer) 190

Cup & saucer, handleless, Teaberry patt., Balanced Vine shape, J. Clementson............. 55

Cup & saucer, handleless, Tobacco Leaf patt., Fanfare shape, Elsmore & Forster 95

Gravy boat, copper lustre bands & cobalt blue trim, Tulip shape, Elsmore & Forster (foot flake, medium hairline) 275

Gravy boat, lustre trim, Ceres shape, Elsmore & Forster 450

Mug, lustre Chelsea Grape Sprig patt., paneled sides, unmarked 225

Pitcher, milk, Pinwheel patt., attributed to Jacob Furnival (minor wear).......................... 500

Plate, 9" w., Thistle & Berry patt., ten-sided shape, unmarked... 110

Platter, 19" oval, Morning Glory patt., Portland shape, Elsmore & Forster (mild crazing) 200

Relish dish, mitten-shaped, copper lustre & cobalt blue trim, Tulip shape, Elsmore & Forster (slight edge roughness)..................... 425

Soup plate, Teaberry patt., New York shape, Clementson Bros................................... 60

Sugar bowl, cov., copper lustre & cobalt blue trim, Arched Wheat shape, Cochran (lustre wear) 425

Sugar bowl, cov., Reverse Teaberry patt., Portland shape, Elsmore & Forster (mild lid crazing, small hairline in body) 450

Sugar bowl, cov., Teaberry patt., Heavy Square shape, Clementson Bros. (teapot lid, mild crazing & inside rim chips).............. 450

Teapot, cov., Teaberry patt., Prairie shape, J. Clementson (one hairline in handle, three in base).. 400

Vegetable dish, cov. lustre band, pinstripe & blue leaves, Gothic shape, Elsmore & Forster... 450

Vegetable dish, open, oval, Pre-Tea Leaf patt., Niagara shape, E. Walley, 9" l. (minor crazing)... 400

Wash pitcher, Teaberry patt., Beaded Band shape, Clementson Bros. 475

Waste bowl, Morning Glory patt., Portland shape, Elsmore & Forster.............................. 260

Waste bowl, Pinwheel patt., 14-paneled sides, attributed to Jacob Furnival (minor wear) 140

Jewel Tea Autumn Leaf

Although not antique, this ware has a devoted following. The Hall China Company of East Liverpool, Ohio, made the first pieces of Autumn Leaf pattern ware to be given as premiums by the Jewel Tea Company in 1933. The premiums were an immediate success and thousands of new customers, all eager to acquire a piece of the durable Autumn Leaf pattern ware, began purchasing Jewel Tea products. Although the pattern was eventually used to decorate linens, glasswares and tinware, we include only the Hall China Company items in our listing.

Autumn Leaf Bean Pot

Bean pot, one-handled, 2 1/4 qt. (ILLUS.) **$800**

Autumn Leaf Cereal Bowl

Bowl, cereal, 6 1/2" d. (ILLUS.)............................ 15

Jewel Tea Flat Soup Bowl

Bowl, flat soup, 8 1/2" (ILLUS.) **15**

Jewel Tea Salad Bowl

Bowl, salad, 9" d. (ILLUS.).................................... **25**

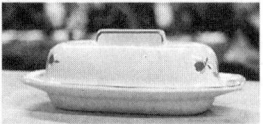

Jewel Tea Butter Dish

Butter dish, cov., square top w/straight finial, 1/4 lb. (ILLUS.) **1,200**

Butter Dish with Butterfly Handle

Butter dish, cov., w/butterfly-type handle (ILLUS.)... **1,500**

Drip-type Coffee maker

Coffee maker, cov., all china, drip type (ILLUS.) **350**

Autumn Leaf Electric Percolator

Coffeepot, cov., electric, percolator (ILLUS.) **350**
Cup & saucer **10**

Soufflé-style French Baker

French baker, swirled soufflé-style, 2-pt. (ILLUS.) **19**

Gravy Boat with Undertray

Gravy boat (ILLUS.) **30**

Mixing Bowl

Mixing bowl, 7" d., part of set (ILLUS.) **15**
Pickle dish (gravy undertray)................................ **25**

Jewel Tea Pie Baker

Pie baker, 10" d. (ILLUS.) **22**

Jewel Tea Dinner Plate

Plate, 10" d., dinner (ILLUS.) **12**

Jewel Tea Salt & Pepper Shakers

Salt & pepper shakers, small, bell-shaped
     (ILLUS.)... **35**

Aladdin Shape Teapot

Teapot, cov., Aladdin shape (ILLUS.) **60**
Teapot, cov., Newport shape w/gold trim,
     1978 version.. **125**

Autumn Leaf Teapot

Teapot, cov., Newport shape w/gold trim
     (ILLUS.).. **150**

Oval Vegetable Bowl

Vegetable bowl, 10 1/2" oval (ILLUS.) **20**

Kitchen & Serving Accessories

Butter Pats

Butter pats (sometimes referred to as "butter chips") became an important part of everyday dining beginning in the second half of the 19th century. Victorians placed this little dish by each diner's plate so it could hold a single pat of butter. Thousands of designs were used to decorate ceramic examples, with many sturdy ironstone examples featuring transfer-printed decoration while many finer porcelain ones were hand-painted. Prices here are based on pieces in excellent condition without chips, cracks or crazing.

Noted author and authority Mary Dessoie provided the following broad listing of collectible butter pats. She founded the Butter Pat Patter Association in 1997. It is listed in our Appendix of Collectors Clubs.

Household

Limoges porcelain, decorated w/a garland
     of green vines w/tiny pink flowers
     trimmed w/gold, double stamped marks
     of   Charles   Field   Haviland/GDA
     Limoges, ca. 1900-1941 .... **$17**
Limoges porcelain, decorated w/apple
     blossoms on a white ground w/a scal-
     loped rim, Theodore Haviland mark & im-
     pressed initials "TH," 1904 - mid-1920s **28**

Tressemann & Vogt Limoges Pat

Limoges porcelain, decorated w/large florals in pinks, pale yellow & blue, scalloped & fluted borders, backstamp for Tressemann & Vogt, Limoges, ca. 1891 (ILLUS.)... **50**

Limoges porcelain, five-sided form w/a scalloped gold rim, three h.p. sprays of pink & white dogwood surrounded by pale green leaves, double-stamped Haviland marks, ca. 1880s-1900 .... **30**

Latrille Brothers Floral Butter Pat

Limoges porcelain, gently scalloped side, large pink blossom & green leaf sprigs, backstamp of Latrille Brothers, Limoges, ca. 1900 (ILLUS.)............................ **22**

Limoges porcelain, green floral decoration w/delicately embossed rim, carries the mark of the Alluaud Company of Limoges, France, also a potter's mark of a red rooster standing on one foot, author Mary Gaston notes this mark is rarely found in this country, 1891+... **30**

Limoges porcelain, green & white h.p. decoration w/tiny green flowers on a shiny white ground, a garland of leaves surrounds the rich gold trim, mark of Charles Field Haviland/GDM France, 1891-1900 .... **25**

Limoges porcelain, overall floral design in mint green, amber & traces of pink surrounded by a ruffled rim, double Haviland & Co. marks & the pattern name "The Countess," 1893-1930...................................... **30**

Elite - Limoges Floral Butter Pat

Limoges porcelain, pink & green floral ring & cluster surrounded by a dark blue border band w/ornate gold trim, backstamp for the Elite Works, Limoges, ca. 1900 (ILLUS.)........... **42**

Limoges porcelain, round, blue cornflowers, daisies & blue bachelor's buttons on a shiny white ground, mark of Latrille Brothers, Limoges & the pattern name "Old Abbey," ca. 1908-13................................. **22**

Limoges porcelain, round w/a delicate thin sea foam design on the border & gold rim band, double Wm. Guérin stamped mark, 3" d. **15**

Limoges porcelain, round w/slightly ruffled rim, decorated overall w/autumnal flowers, mark of A. Lanternier, ca. 1891-1914, 3 1/8" d. **22**

Early Theodore Haviland Butter Pat

Limoges porcelain, round w/slightly scalloped rim, pink floral sprigs & green leaves, backstamp for Theodore Haviland, 1903-1925 (ILLUS.) **25**

Early Haviland & Co. Butter Pat

Limoges porcelain, square w/cut corners, blue & yellow bird perched on a flowering branch, scattered blue & pink blossoms, backstamp of Haviland & Co., 1879-1889 (ILLUS.) **34**

Limoges porcelain, squared form molded to resemble a linen napkin w/folded over corners, one corner w/a h.p. flower, Haviland mark "H & Co" over "L," ca. 1880s.......... **35**

Limoges porcelain, squared form w/rounded corners, color scene of a fairy seated on a branch w/pink blossoms, gold trim, Charles Field Haviland mark, 1882-1890 (ILLUS. bottom left with novelty pats, next page) **55**

Novelty, majolica, molded fan-shaped design trimmed in blue, pink, red, green & gold, unmarked, late 19th c. (ILLUS. bottom right, with novelty pats).................... **110-125**

Novelty, majolica molded fan-shaped design trimmed in blue, pink, yellow, green & gold, unmarked, late 19th c. (ILLUS. top right, with novelty pats)..................... **110-125**

Group of Novelty Butter Pats

Novelty, round w/tiny scallops on rim, embossed standing Kate Greenaway-like child wearing a pink bonnet, blue & white cloak & yellow dress, pink blossom & green leaves on green & brown ground, unmarked, late 19th c. (ILLUS. top left, with novelty pats) **40**

Staffordshire, blue Tower patt., piecrust rim, Copeland - Spode, England **40**

Staffordshire, Blue Willow patt., Allerton's, England **30**

Staffordshire, Blue Willow patt., Grimwades Ltd., England, ca. 1930+ **25**

Staffordshire, Chinese patt., ironstone china decorated w/an Aesthetic Movement design in bluish green featuring an Oriental landscape w/pagodas, a temple, bridge & lush trees & flowers, impressed mark of Wedgwood & Co., England & pattern name, late 19th c. **50**

Staffordshire, h.p. bold green ivy design w/large leaves joined by a brown vine surrounded by a green pinstripe, marked by hand on the reverse "Napoleon Ivy as used by Napoleon at St. Helena in 1815 - Wedgwood of Etruria & Barlaston - Made in England - Pattern No. A.L. 4751," 1940+ **45**

Staffordshire, ironstone china decorated w/green flowers, Alfred Meakin, England, early 1900s **15**

Staffordshire, ironstone china w/a dynamic Art Nouveau design in bold colors of black, orange, blue & gold, mark of J. & G. Meakin, England & registration number for 1902 .... **18**

Staffordshire, Jewel Billingsley Rose patt., h.p. rose in full bloom surrounded by green leaves & a smaller rosebud, Copeland - Spode, England pink mark, England registration number & U.S. Patent number dated to June 15, 1926, pattern name & Staffordshire marks also on back **45**

Staffordshire, Melbourne patt., flow blue china, W.H. Grindley & Co., England **75**

Staffordshire, Roma patt., flow blue china, scrolled gold trim, Wedgwood & Co., England, ca. 1905, 3 1/4" d. **80**

Copeland-Spode Rosebud Chintz Pat

Staffordshire, Rosebud Chintz patt., bright rosebuds, green vines & a sprinkling of tiny yellow flowers, Copeland - Spode, England mark & pattern name on back, 3" d. (ILLUS.) **45**

Staffordshire, round ironstone decorated overall w/big, bold colorful flowers, bright red pinstripe on the rim, Alfred Meakin, England, ca. 1907 .... **16**

Round Tea Leaf Pattern Butter Pat

Staffordshire, round ironstone decorated w/the copper lustre Tea Leaf patt., mark of Henry Alcock & Co., England, late 19th c. (ILLUS.) **38**

Ironstone China Floral Pat

Staffordshire, square ironstone printed w/an overall black flowering branch design, British registry number 51,058 for 1886 (ILLUS.)... **28**

Staffordshire, square ironstone w/a piecrust rim, decorated w/the copper lustre Tea Leaf patt., mark of Wedgwood & C., England, late 19th c.............................. **42**

Staffordshire, square ironstone w/copper lustre Tea Leaf patt. & lustre band border, mark of W.H. Grindley, England, late 19th c. **18**

Restaurant Ware

Hospital, decorated w/the hospital's logo in rust & "City Hospital 1871, Worcester, Massachusetts, Science Trimming the Lamp of Life," early, 3" d................................. **52**

Hospital, "Research Hospital" in ornate script framed by a highly stylized border of roses & swags of leaves, heavy duty china, 3 3/4" d.. **50**

Hotel, decorated w/a leafy branch w/two berries, from the Mandarin Oriental - Hong Kong, the city's most exclusive hotel, fine porcelain, marked on the back "Mandarin Oriental Hong Kong, Royal Doulton Bone China, England" & the hotel's fan logo, 3" d................................ **95**

Hotel, decorated w/the hotel logo & name "Hotel San Diego," 3" d. **58**

Hotel, decorated w/the words "Raffles Hotel, Singapore" & the hotel logo, two green pinstripes on the rim, landmark hotel built in the 19th c., bone china, backstamped w/the Royal Doulton mark & "Specially for Raffles Hotel," 2 7/8" d............. **95**

Restaurant, three green pinstripes surrounding "Barbeque Inn Waikiki," heavy duty china, mid-20th c. **55**

Transportation - Airlines

Aerolineas Argentinas (Argentine Airlines), airline name on the front, maker's mark Verbano on the back **19**

Air France First Class Butter Pat

Air France, white ground w/a blue & brown hippocampus & blue teardrop band around the rim, "Première Class" (First Class) presentation-type, made by Bernardaud, Limoges, France, full factory & airline backmarks, 1970s-90s, 3" d. (ILLUS.) **90**

Air New Zealand Butter Pat

Air New Zealand, turquoise ground w/a Maori tribal design in brown, marked on the back "Air New Zealand - Crown Lynn Pottery," 3" d. (ILLUS.).................................... **30**

Alitalia (Italian Airlines), decorated w/a Leonardo DaVinci design of a winged flying machine, marked on the back "Alitalia - Richard Ginori," 3 1/2" d. **15**

Alitalia (Italian Airlines), decorated w/a scene of a vintage airplane, marked on the back "Alitalia - Richard Ginori," 3 1/2" d. **15**

Transportation-related Butter Pats

Alitalia (Italian Airlines), squared form, decorated w/an early hot air balloon in blue, gold & white (ILLUS. top left, above)........ **15**

American Airlines, white w/cobalt blue & silver trim, used in first class for international travel, airline & Jackson China backmarks, ca. 1980s, 3 7/8" d...................... **18**

BOAC (British Overseas Airways), blue speckled band trimmed in silver, designed exclusively for use in the first class cabins by Royal Doulton in 1989, marked on the back w/the airline & Royal Doulton marks, 3" d. **30**

BOAC (British Overseas Airways), Coat-of-Arms patt. in gold on white, airline & Royal Doulton backstamps, used from 1972-1989, 3" d................................. **32**

BOAC (British Overseas Airways), Golden Net patt., Copeland - Spode & airline marks on the back, 1960s, 2 13/16" d. **32**

Canadian Pacific, white ground w/a mustard yellow airline logo & pinstripe border, used 1968-1988, backmark reads "Made exclusively for C.P. Air," 3" d............................ **20**

Civil Aviation Administration (China), porcelain w/stylized Oriental floral design in blue, the organization was formed in 1949 after the establishment of the People's Republic of China (ILLUS. bottom left, above)...................... **85**

Delta Airlines, Blue-Gold Rope patt., a cobalt blue band w/the rope & pinstripes in gold, airline backmark................................... **15**

Delta Airlines, top marked w/airline name in script... **18**

Finnair, butter ramekin decorated in grey & silver, presented to First Class passengers in a special box marked "Finnair," back-stamped "Arabia".................................. **70**

Gulf Air, octagonal, the top w/the airline logo in gold & a gold rim band, airline & Wedgwood & Co., England back marks.......... **90**

Iberia (Spanish Airline), white w/a yellow pinstripe border & the Iberia logo in red & yellow w/a crown, manufacturer's & airline name & logo on the back, 3 11/16" d........ **50**

PanAm, all-white, marked on the back "Bauscher Weiden, Bavaria, Germany - PanAm," 3 1/8" d. **30**

SwissAir, all-white, back-stamped in green "SwissAir - Suisse, Langenthal," 2 3/4" d. **25**

Thai Airlines, floral design in light & delicate pink & green tones w/"Thai" in gold, Noritake back stamp, 3 3/4" d...................... **55**

Transportation - Ocean Liners

Clipper Line (Sweden), white w/a blue & gold logo w/line name & gold pinstripe border, Rorstrand factory mark on reverse, 3 3/8" d. **40**

Cunard White Star Line, white shell-shaped form w/a gold fleur-de-lis & gold trim, used on the Queen Mary & Queen Elizabeth, Minton backstamp........................... **45**

Greek Line, heavy ceramic in white w/the company logo in cobalt blue, used on trans-Atlantic liners between 1939 and 1975, backstamp for A.J. Wilkinson, England, 2 7/8" d. **32**

Transportation - Railroads

Atchison, Topeka & Santa Fe, Adobe patt., heavy ceramic w/tan design, distinctive Econo-Rim form on this stock pattern used from 1941 to 1969, no railroad logo, marked on the back "Syracuse China 92-E USA," 3" d. **15**

Baltimore & Ohio, Centenary patt., dark blue on white, introduced in 1927 to celebrate the railroad's centennial, full railroad & Shenango China backstamps, 3 7/16" d. (ILLUS. top right, above) **98**

British Rail, heavy white body decorated w/a leaf design surrounded by a gold pinstripe, back marked "BTH" for "British Transport Hotel," as well as a decorator's mark & Ridgways Potteries, Ltd. mark, used in railroad-owned hotels, 4" d................. **28**

Chicago, Burlington & Quincy, Violets and Daisies patt., Buffalo China backstamp **78**

Chicago, Milwaukee, St. Paul & Pacific Railroad, Traveler patt., dark pink decoration w/a flying goose in the center, made by Syracuse China (ILLUS. top right with animal design pats, next page)........ **70**

Early steam engine, square ironstone china w/a scene of an early steam engine &

passenger car printed in black within a black border band, novelty piece not used on a railroad, England, late 19th c. (ILLUS. bottom right, previous page) **14**

Erie Railroad, Starucca patt. **325**

Kansas City Southern Railroad, Roxbury patt., flower on the top surrounded by the distinctive Syracuse China Econo-Rim, Syracuse backstamp, stock pattern, 3" d........ **35**

Advertising

Don (Edward) & Co., printed on the top "Compliments of Edward Don & Co., Chicago National Restaurant Exposition, October, 1940 - Made by Jackson China Company of Falls Creek, Pa.," backstamped "Ed Don & Co. Chicago - Jackson - Made in USA," 3 3/4" d............................. **50**

Royal Copenhagen, white w/the Royal Copenhagen logo in blue, intricately embossed trim, probably designed as an advertising piece or corporate gift, Royal Copenhagen backstamps & logo, 2 3/4" d... **90**

Syracuse China, printed on the top "Syracuse China - 1871-1971 - A century of fine services," 100th Anniversary commemorative, Syracuse China backstamp, 3 3/4" d... **38**

Warsaw Restaurant, printed on the top "Warsaw Restaurant   820 N. Ashland Ave. Chicago," backstamp logo of the Jackson Vitrified China Company, 1917-1930s, 3 5/8" d... **55**

Fraternal Organizations

Benevolent & Protective Order of Elks, round ironstone china decorated in green "BPOE Lodge 374," 3 3/8" d................. **30**

Fraternal Order of Eagles, round top decorated w/an eagle w/a banner reading "F.O.E. 1090," Aerie No. 1090 was located in Clifton Forge, Virginia, instituted on June 1, 1905, charter surrendered January 2, 1920 .... **35**

International Order of Odd Fellows, square ironstone china printed on top "IOOF 1081," backstamp for Greenwood China, late 19th - early 20th c. **30**

Masons, top printed in blue w/a picture of a Victorian-era Temple & "Harrisburg Association Masonic Temple" in ornate script lettering, marked on the back "O.P. Co. Syracuse China" which dates this piece to 1911 .... **58**

Masons, top printed w/the Masonic logo in green on a pale yellow ground w/a gold pinstripe border, 3 7/8" d................................. **32**

Military

Grand Army of the Republic (GAR), top printed in gold "Amasa B. Watson, W.R.C. 171," gold trim, Major Watson was a Civil War veteran & The Amasa B. Watson Post No. 395 of the Department of Michigan Grand Army of the Republic was established in his memory in 1888, back impressed w/"91" in a circle, the Syracuse China date code for 1911, 3 1/8" d... **75**

Hill Military Academy, Portland, Oregon, printed on the top w/the school logo & name in green, pre-1948 Shenango China Co. backstamp, 3 1/2" d............................. **65**

United States Army Military Academy, West Point, round heavy duty type, top printed w/the West Point logo & "Duty - Honor - Country - West Point - MDCCCII - USMA," backstamped "Made by Carr China Co. for James M. Shaw & Co. expressly for The Cadet Mess, West Point, New York," early to mid-20th c., 3" d.............. **65**

Miscellaneous

Animal design, ironstone china, squared w/napkin-style folded corners, Aesthetic Movement-style transfer-printed design in brown & black showing birds & plants, England, late 19th c. (ILLUS. bottom right, below) **22**

Animal design, porcelain w/lightly scalloped rim, decorated w/brown & black crab in blue water, unmarked (ILLUS. bottom left, below)... **12**

Butter Pats with Various Animals

Animal design, porcelain w/lightly scalloped rim, decorated w/brown & black fish in blue water, unmarked (ILLUS. top left, above) **12**

Buffalo China Singapore Pattern Pat

Buffalo Pottery, Singapore patt., stylized flower sprigs in red, dark gold, dark blue, green & brown w/a red border band, ca. 1930 (ILLUS.) **25**

German Porcelain Butter Pat

Oscar & Edward Gutherz, Altrohau, Germany, round porcelain w/a gold band of stamped shamrocks within a green rim band, 1899-1918 (ILLUS.) 50

Portrait design, asymmetrical porcelain shape decorated w/a bust portrait of a peasant girl wearing a straw hat & white & blue dress, unmarked, late 19th c. (ILLUS. top right, below) 50-90

Portrait design, porcelain shell-form w/small tab handle, portrait of a Victorian boy wearing a large straw hat w/feather & lace-collared blue suit on a gold ground, unmarked, late 19th c. (ILLUS. bottom left, below) 50-90

Portrait design, porcelain shell-form w/small tab handle, portrait of a Victorian girl wearing a blue bonnet w/white fur trim & pink ribbon, pink dress w/wide white collar, unmarked, late 19th c. (ILLUS. bottom right, below) 50-90

Fine Porcelain Portrait Butter Pats

Portrait design, porcelain w/h.p. bust portrait of a Renaissance woman w/large hat & high-collared gown in reddish brown, black & white on a gold ground, unmarked, late 19th c. (ILLUS. top left, above) 50-90

Oyster Plates

Oyster plates intrigue a growing number of collectors. Oysters were shucked and the meat served in wells of these attractive plates specifically designed to serve oysters. During the late 19th century they were made of fine china and majolica. Some plates were decorated in

the realistic "trompe l'oeil" technique while others simply matched the pattern of a dinner service. Also see HAVILAND and LIMOGES.

Majolica, eight-well, shell-form wells in turquoise blue divided by molded green seaweed, a white shell well at the center, George Jones, England, late 19th c. (minor rim nick) **$2,750**

Majolica, six-well, alternating dark pink & white shell-form wells each separated by a band w/a small long shell & a small white shell at the rim, a central ring of small white shells around the dark green center well, 9 1/4" d. 385

Majolica, six-well, miniature, five pink-trimmed cockle shell wells & one white well centered by a round scalloped green-trimmed well, Wedgwood, late 19th c., 7" d. 1,210

Majolica, six-well, shell-shaped wells in turquoise blue divided by brown molded seaweed, white shell well at the center, George Jones, England, late 19th c., 10" d. 1,870

Very Rare G. Jones Oyster Plate

Majolica, six-well, six cobalt blue shell-form wells separated by brown coral branches & green leaves, white shell-form center well, George Jones, England, late 19th c., 10" d. (ILLUS.) **4,950**

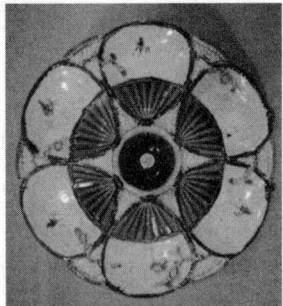

Fan Pattern Majolica Oyster Plate

Majolica, six-well, six fan-shaped wells in cream & brown decorated w/colorful bugs, cobalt blue round center well, minor glaze rub on rim, S. Fielding & Co., England, late 19th c., 9 1/2" d. (ILLUS.)..... 2,310

Majolica, six-well, six grey shaded to pink cockle shell wells divided by white & cen-

tered by a pink central well, Sarreguem-
ines, France, ca. 1920, 9 1/2" d..................... **110**

Majolica, six-well, six rounded oyster shell-
form cobalt blue wells & a long cobalt
blue cracker well each separated by a
pink fan device & centered by a pink ring
around the round cobalt blue center well,
Minton, England, late 19th c., 9" d. **4,400**

Majolica, six-well, six rounded oyster shell-
form turquoise blue wells & a long turquoise blue cracker well each separated
by a cobalt blue fan device & centered by
a cobalt blue ring around the round turquoise blue center well, Minton, England,
late 19th c., 9" d.. **990**

Minton Majolica Oyster Plate

Majolica, six-well, six shell-shaped wells in
mottled dark green & brown separated by
narrow white shells on brownish green
w/small white shells at the rim, inner
white shell band around the dark green
center well, shape No. 1323, date code
for 1870, Minton, England, 9" d. (ILLUS.).. **1,430**

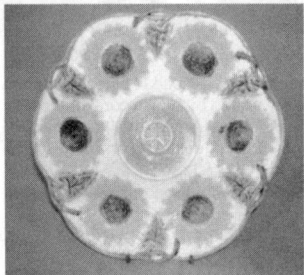

Sunflower Majolica Oyster Plate

Majolica, six-well, six sunflower-shaped
wells in yellow & brown separated by
green leaves on a white ground, pale
blue center well, brown vine border band,
Samuel Lear, England, late 19th c., minor
hairline, 9 3/4" d. (ILLUS.)........................... **2,090**

Majolica, six-well, turquoise blue ribbed
scallop shell wells separated by slender
light green shells & dark green seaweed,
white round scalloped center shell,
George Jones, England, late 19th c.,
8 1/2" d... **1,100**

Majolica, six-well, white ribbed scallop shell
wells separated by thin yellow shells &
green seaweed, round white center well
w/pink border, George Jones, England,
late 19th c., 8 1/2" d. **1,760**

Majolica, six-well, wide tapering turquoise
blue shell wells divided by wide bands
w/a slender pink shell on green grass & a
small white shell at the rim, a central ring
of small white shells around the dark
green round center well, Minton, En-
gland, late 19th c., 9" d. **770**

Majolica, six-well, yellow ground w/six
shell-form wells painted w/dark green &
blue stylized scrolls, dots & florals around
a pale blue center well, Henriot Quimper,
France, ca. 1960, 8 1/2" d. **165**

Majolica, six-well, yellow spiraled arms centered by a brown-banded turquoise blue
center well, the arms dividing the dark
green fish head-shaped wells w/a large
fish-shaped cracker well at one side,
9 3/4" d. (minor rim glaze wear)..................... **660**

Limoges

*Limoges is the generic name for hard paste porcelain
that was produced in one of the Limoges factories in the
Limoges Region of France during the 19th and 20th centuries. There are more than 400 different factory identification marks, the Haviland factory marks being some of the
most familiar. Dinnerware was commonly decorated by
the transfer method and then exported to the United States.*

*Decorative pieces were hand painted by a factory art-
ist or were imported to the United States as blank pieces
of porcelain. At the turn of the 20th century, thousands of
undecorated Limoges blanks poured into the United
States, where any of the more than 25,000 American porcelain painters decorated them. Today hand-painted decorative pieces are considered fine art. Limoges is not to be
confused with American Limoges. (The series on collecting Limoges by Debby DeBay, Living With Limoges,
Antique Limoges at Home and Collecting Limoges Boxes
to Vases are excellent reference books.)*

Limoges Cache Pot

Cache pot, underglaze factory mark in
green "W.G.&Co." (William Guerin),
12" h. (ILLUS.)... **$1,500**

Limoges Cake Plate on Pedestal

Cake plate on pedestal, h.p., underglaze factory mark in green "T&V Limoges France Depose" (Tressemann & Vogt), 4 x 12" (ILLUS.) **395**

Limoges Candlesticks

Candlesticks, h.p. roses, heavy gold, underglaze factory mark in green "T&V," 16" h., pr. (ILLUS.) **600**

Limoges Charger with Gold Rim

Charger, dramatic h.p. roses on dark ground, gold scroll on rim, underglaze factory mark in green "AK [over] D France" (A. Klingenberg), 15" d. (ILLUS.) **1,000**

Four-piece Limoges Chocolate Set

Chocolate set: 12" pot, two cups, 12" tray; h.p., underglaze factory mark in green "J.P.L. France" (Jean Ponyat, Limoges) the set (ILLUS.) **1,500**

Limoges Cracker Jar

Cracker jar, cov., h.p., underglaze mark in green "T&V Limoges France," 7 1/2" h. (ILLUS.) **325**

Limoges Dresser Set

Dresser set: tray, cov. jar & hair receiver; h.p. by amateur artist, underglaze factory mark in green "W.G.&Co., France" (William Guérin), the set (ILLUS.) **500**

Jardiniere on Fluted Pedestal

Jardiniere, fluted pedestal base, fluted handles, underglaze factory mark in green "J.P.L. France" w/anchor, 12 x 14" (ILLUS.) **2,500**

Jardiniere with Lion Head Handles

Limoges Planter with Mums

Jardiniere, on original base, lion head handles, h.p. roses & detail, underglaze factory mark in green "D&Co." (R. Delin-iéres) 12 x 14" (ILLUS.)............................... **4,500**

Limoges Cider Pitcher

Pitcher, cider, 10 1/2" h., h.p. & signed by factory artist "Roby," underglaze factory mark in green "T&V France," "T&V" decorating mark in purple (ILLUS.) **800**

Planter, h.p. w/vibrant chrysanthemums, gilt handles & four feet, underglaze factory mark in green "D&Co.," 8 x 12 1/2" (ILLUS., top of page) **2,000**

Plate, 10 1/2" d., heavy gold rim & h.p. roses, underglaze factory mark in green "J.P.L. France," overglaze factory decorating mark w/pink & green wreath (ILLUS., next column)...................................... **225**

Platter, game, 18" l., h.p. & signed by factory artist "Dubois," "Limoges France" & star, Flambeau studio decorating mark (ILLUS., bottom of page)............................. **2,000**

Limoges Plate

Limoges Punch Bowl

Punch bowl, rare mammoth blank w/three gold feet, h.p. w/dramatic roses by unknown artist, underglaze factory mark in green "J.P.L. France," 13 x 26" (ILLUS.) **5,500**

Limoges Game Platter

Painting on Porcelain

Tile, h.p. porcelain of woman & cherub, underglaze factory mark in green "T&V France," 11 x 14" (ILLUS.) **3,000**

Limoges Tureen

Tureen, h.p. w/berries, artist signed "Andrew," underglaze factory mark in green "P&P" (Paroutaud Frères), 8 x 9" (ILLUS.) **1,500**

Unusual Limoges Vase

Vase, 8" h., 13 1/2" d., underglaze factory mark in green "T&V Limoges France" & artist signed "Vera Gray," unusual shape & size (ILLUS.) **3,000**

Limoges Vase

Vase, 14" h., factory h.p. & artist signed "Rouncon," underglaze mark in green "PBM DE M Limoges, France" (Malaleix) overglaze decorating mark in green "Coronet" in crown (ILLUS.) **3,000**

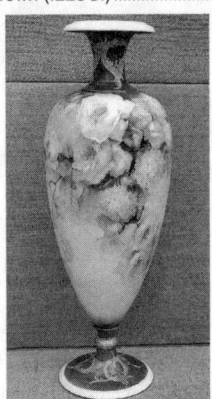

One of a Pair of Limoges Vases

Vase, 22" h., one of a pair, h.p. w/roses & enameled w/raised gilt, underglaze factory mark in green "W.G.&Co.," each (ILLUS.) **3,000**

Liverpool

Liverpool is most often used as a generic term for fine earthenware products, usually of creamware or pearlware, produced at numerous potteries in this English city during the late 18th and early 19th centuries. Many examples, especially pitchers, were decorated with transfer-printed patriotic designs aimed specifically at the American buying public.

Bowl, 10 1/2" d., creamware, deep rounded sides, the interior transfer-printed in black w/polychrome trim w/a figure of Hope w/a three-masted sailing ship flying two American flags surrounded by six figural reserves around the sides, three transfer-printed country scenes on the exterior, red enamel rim, England, early 19th c. (repaired) **$805**

Pitcher, 7 1/4" h., creamware, jug-form, decorated on one side w/a black transfer-printed design of a large round compass & verse, on the other side w/"The Sailors Adieu," early 19th c. (minor imperfections) **748**

Pitcher, 8 1/4" h., creamware, jug-form, transfer-printed in black on one side w/an American eagle & shield & on the other w/a figure of Independence & a poem, early 19th c., imperfections (ILLUS. right with other two pitchers, next page) **1,150**

Pitcher, 8 5/8" h., creamware, jug-form, transfer-printed & enamel-trimmed w/a scene titled "Tom Truelove Going to Sea" on one side & a three-masted sailing ship w/"Success to Trade" on the other, an oval reserve of three figures by a lake w/"Peace to All Nations" under the spout, worn gilt lettering for "John Frank," early 19th c. (imperfections) **1,093**

Three Early Liverpool Pitchers

Pitcher, 8 3/4" h., creamware, jug-form, transfer-printed in black on one side w/"Commodore Prebles Squadron Attacking the City of Tripoli Aug 3, 1804," the other side w/a scene of the Salem Shipyard & a verse, an American eagle & shield below the spout, early 19th c. (imperfections).. **2,300**

Pitcher, 9" h., creamware, jug-form, transfer-printed in black w/a large oval reserve showing Washington, Liberty & Franklin examining a large world map, the other side w/a three-masted sailing ship, an American eagle & shield & figure of Hope below the spout, polychrome trim, early 19th c. (imperfections)..................................... **978**

Pitcher, 9 1/8" h., creamware, jug-form, black transfer-printed portrait medallion of Commodore Preble on one side, scene of "Commodore Prebles Squadron Attacking the City of Tripoli Aug 3, 1804" on the other, imperfections (ILLUS. left with two other pitchers, top of page)......... **2,815**

Pitcher, 9 1/4" h., creamware, jug-form, one side transfer-printed in black w/polychrome trim w/a figure of Hope, a three-masted sailing ship flying the American flag on the other, American eagle below the spout w/a Jefferson quote, dated 1804 (imperfections).................................... **3,738**

Pitcher, 9 1/2" h., creamware, jug-form, one side transfer-printed in black w/polychrome trim w/the figure of a Boston Fusilier within an oval reserve, the other side w/"United We Stand - Divided We Fall," American eagle & shield below the spout, early 19th c. (imperfections)......... **17,250**

Pitcher, 10" h., creamware, jug-form, black transfer-printed design of "Peace, Plenty and Independence" w/Classical figures & American eagle on one side, a three-masted sailing ship on the other side, a shield below the spout, England, early 19th c. (imperfections)..................................... **920**

Pitcher, 10" h., creamware, jug-form, one side transfer-printed in black & trimmed in color w/an oval scenic reserve & "Pro-

scribed Patriots," the other side w/an oval reserve w/a militiaman in uniform & "Success to America whose Militia...," American eagle, shield & Jefferson quote under the spout, dated 1802 (repaired)......... **3,220**

Pitcher, 10 1/4" h., creamware, jug-form, transfer-printed in black on one side w/a scene titled "Salem Shipyard" & on the other w/a large sailing ship titled "Boston Frigate," polychrome highlights, a cartouche w/monogram above an eagle & shield under the spout, early 19th c., imperfections (ILLUS. center with two other pitchers)... **4,888**

Pitcher, 11 3/4" h., creamware, jug-form, one side transfer-printed w/the ship "Massachusetts," the other side w/a map of Newburyport Harbor w/"Success to the Commerce of Newburyport," circular reserve of Columbia under the spout, gilt trim, early 19th c. (minor imperfections) **14,950**

Pitcher, 14 1/4" h., creamware, jug-form, one side transfer-printed in black trimmed w/color w/vignette showing a seated figure of Hope beside a scene of a sailing ship, a quote "her lefs'ning boat unwilling rows to land," on the other side a three-masted sailing ship flying an American flag below the spout, small transfer scenes scattered around the rim & mast, a reserve w/motto "From Rocks & Sands And every ill May god preserve The Sailor still" below the handle, gilt trim, early 19th c. (imperfections)............... **6,325**

Lustre Wares

Lustred wares in imitation of copper, gold, silver and other colors were produced in England in the early 19th century and onward. Gold, copper or platinum oxides were painted on glazed objects that were then fired, giving them a lustred effect. Various forms of lustre wares include plain lustre, with the entire object coated to obtain a metallic effect, bands of lustre decoration and painted lustre designs. Particularly appealing is the pink or purple "splash lustre" sometimes referred to as "Sun-

derland" lustre in the mistaken belief it was confined to the production of Sunderland-area potteries. Objects decorated in silver lustre by the "resist" process, wherein parts of the objects to be left free from lustre decoration were treated with wax, are referred to as "silver resist."

Wares formerly called "Canary Yellow Lustre" are now referred to as "Yellow-Glazed Earthenwares."

Sunderland Pink & Others

Pitcher, 7" h., jug-form, black transfer-printed w/two oval reserves, one "Captain Hull of the Constitution" & the other "Pike - be always ready to die for your country," pink lustre trim, early 19th c. (imperfections)... **$5,750**

Pitcher, 8 3/4" h., jug-form, black transfer-printed design of the farmer's arms flanked by a farmer & wife surrounded by various symbols in a landscape, the other side w/an inspirational verse, oval reserve below the spout signed "Mary Hayward Farmer Sandhurft Kent," polychrome trim, highlighted w/pink lustre trim & florals, early 19th c. (imperfections)... **1,150**

Pitcher, 9 3/8" h., jug-form, bulbous cream-colored body decorated w/vignettes on each side, one side w/a polychrome-trimmed black transfer-printed scene of a British sailing ship & a verse in a cartouche reading "May Peace and Plenty On Our Nation Smile and Trade with Commerce Bless the British Isle," the other side w/a verse in a floral wreath, under the spout is "The Sailor's Tear" beneath a printed Mariner's Compass flanked by British ships, red, green & yellow trim, pink lustre squiggles around the sides, early 19th c., imperfections (ILLUS. center w/other pitchers).. **646**

Pitcher, 9 3/8" h., jug-form, the bulbous body decorated on the sides w/large banded reserves, one w/a black transfer-printed figural scene titled "The Sailor's Farewell," the other one w/a sailor's verse, a large panel under the spout inscribed "George Henry Page - Born Sept. 7th 1800 - Charlotte Page - Born Feb. 7th 1802," w/a whimsical puzzle verse, wide Sunderland pink lustre bands around the top & base, polychrome trim in yellow & green, early 19th c., imperfections (ILLUS. left, bottom of page)....................... **3,290**

Pitcher, 10 1/8" h., jug-form, wide bulbous body decorated w/large black transfer-printed reserves on the sides, one titled "A West View of the Iron Bridge over the Wear under the Patronage of R. Burdon Esq. M.P.," the reverse w/an inspirational verse in a floral wreath, a pouring handle under the spout centering a black transfer-printed sailing ship & an inscription "Arther Rutter 1840," overall spattered pink lustre decoration, minor imperfections (ILLUS. right, bottom of page)............ **1,645**

Unusual Lustre-trimmed Pitcher

Pitchers, 7 3/8" h., jug-type, bulbous body tapering to a short neck w/large rim spout, angled handle, pink lustre band trim, each transfer-printed in puce w/figural designs, one side w/a standing American Indian & large eagle flanking an American flag above a banner reading "Success to the United States of America," the reverse w/"Peace, Plenty and Independence" & depicting a star & ribbon wreath w/the names of New York & ten other states all surmounted by a large eagle & American flag & flanked by allegorical figures of Peace & Plenty, a foliate geometric design beneath the spout, early 19th c., imperfections, pr. (ILLUS. of one)... **2,233**

Three Early Pink Lustre Pitchers

Majolica

Majolica, a tin-enameled glazed pottery, has been produced for centuries. It originally took its name from the island of Majorca, a source of figuline (potter's clay). Subsequently it was widely produced in England, Europe and the United States. Etruscan majolica, now avidly sought, was made by Griffen, Smith & Hill, Phoenixville, Pa., in the last quarter of the 19th century. Most majolica advertised today is 19th or 20th century. Once scorned by most collectors, interest in this colorful ware so popular during the Victorian era has now revived and prices have risen dramatically in the past few years. Also see MINTON, OYSTER PLATES, ROYAL WORCESTER, and WEDGWOOD.

Etruscan

Majolica Etruscan Mark

Bowl, 8" d., Shell & Seaweed patt., green & pink exterior, pink interior............................ **$275**
Butter pat, Geranium patt. **55**
Cake stand, conventional design w/brown sunburst w/yellow middle in center surrounded by a band of yellow & an order band of green leaves, 10" d.......................... **385**
Cake stand, Maple Leaves patt., pink ground... **193**
Cake stand, Morning Glory patt., rare burgundy ground, 8" d., 4" h. **358**
Cake stand, Morning Glory patt., white ground, 8" d., 4" h. **193**

Shell and Seaweed Cake Stand

Cake stand, Shell & Seaweed patt., very minor rim nicks (ILLUS.).................................. **715**

Swan & Water Lily Cheese Dish

Cheese dish, cov., Swan & Water Lily patt., tall cylindrical cover w/flat top centered by a figural swan finial, water lilies, leaves & butterflies around the sides & base, fine color (ILLUS.) **1,430**
Humidor, cov., Shell & Seaweed patt., natural colors (one shell on cover replaced) ... **1,100**
Mug, Pineapple patt. **121**
Pickle dish, footed oval, Daisy patt., 8 1/2" l. (rim nick) **330**

Shell & Seaweed Plates & Platter

Plate, 8" d., Shell & Seaweed patt., great color (ILLUS. bottom left)................................. **248**
Plate, 9" d., Maple Leaf on Basket patt............. **220**
Plate, 9" d., Overlapping Begonia Leaves patt. **165**
Plate, 9 1/4" d., Shell & Seaweed patt., great color (ILLUS. front right, with shell & seaweed dishes) **330**
Platter, Geranium patt., large leaf w/twig handles, light pink ground, fine color **275**
Platter, 14" l., oval w/scalloped rim, Shell & Seaweed patt. (ILLUS. top with Shell & Seaweed plates) **413**
Syrup pitcher w/hinged pewter cap, Bamboo patt., 7 1/2" h. **495**
Syrup pitcher w/hinged pewter cap, Sunflower patt., cobalt blue ground...................... **605**
Tray, Oak Leaf patt., pink edge, 12" l. **220**

General

Bank, figural, model of a cat w/a ball, French, 5 1/4" h... **385**
Bowl, 11" l., large shell-shaped bowl w/pink interior & pale green exterior, on three brown shell feet, Joseph Holdcroft, England, late 19th c...................................... **275**
Box w/hinged cover, deep square form w/flat top, cobalt blue ground molded w/birds & mice in color & small figural owl feet at the corners, Joseph Holdcroft, England, 6" w., 6" h. **3,300**
Bread tray, oblong, Wheat & Basket patt., cobalt blue border band embossed w/"Give Us This Day Our Daily Bread," 14" l. **358**
Bread tray, oval, Fish patt., low-relief fish in the center, brown w/green seaweed border trim, border embossed "And Jesus Broke And Gave Thanks And They Did Eat," 13 1/2" l. **330**
Bread tray, oval, Pineapple patt., probably Wardle & Co., England, 13" l. **275**
Butter dish, cover & drainer, domed cover, Shell, Seaweed & Waves patt., in pale blues, browns & yellow, 19th c. **330**

Cake stand, pedestal base, Pond Lily patt. in green w/white blossom, pedestal composed of three standing figural storks, 10 1/2" d, 9 1/2" h... **385**

Candlestick, figural, model of a nude seated putto beside a tall baluster-form pale blue candlestick draped w/a pink swag, a shell at the foot of the figure, on a brown rockwork base, George Jones, England, late 19th c., 10 3/4" h..................................... **660**

Chambersticks, footed shell-form triangular bowl center w/a large ribbed brown socket, a molded classical woman's head at the base of the C-form upright rim handle, Joseph Holdcroft, England, 6" l., 1/2" h., pr.. **605**

Fine George Jones Cheese Dish

Cheese dish, cov., Apple Blossom patt., tall domed cover w/a brown branch handle above a turquoise blue dome decorated w/branches of apple blossoms above a wide band of brown basketweave, basketweave design on flanged base, George Jones, England, late 19th c., 12" h. (ILLUS.)... **2,860**

Very Rare G. Jones Cheese Dish

Cheese dish, cov., Water Lily - King Fisher with Dragonfly patt., tall cylindrical cover w/large water lily leaves in green w/white blossoms & green & brown cattails on a cobalt blue ground, slight domed top w/leaves & a large figural kingfisher finial, brown wicker molded design on base, George Jones, England, minor profes-

sional repair to beak, hairline in base, rare, 13 1/2" h. (ILLUS.)........................... **13,750**

Cheese dish, cov., wide cylindrical cover w/slightly domed top & twig handle, Picket Fence & Floral patt., pink & green blossoms on pale blue ground, George Jones, England, late 19th c., 7 1/2" h........ **2,200**

Compote, open, 10 1/2" d., deep bowl, low pedestal, Tobacco Leaf & Floral Rosette patt. **209**

Creamer & cov. sugar bowl, Bird & Fan patt., blue, brown & pink on a pale yellow ground, S. Fielding & Co., England, late 19th c., pr. **198**

Cup & saucer, rounded cup & squared saucer, each molded w/white blossoms & green leaves, bud handle, all on cobalt blue ground, part of the Monkey tea service, George Jones, England.......... **1,550-1,950**

Rare George Jones Game Dish

Game dish, cov., deep oval form w/brown branch & leaf end handle, the sides molded in relief w/rabbits among green ferns & leaves on a cobalt blue ground, low domed cover molded w/green ferns centered by a large model of a brown quail, George Jones, England, late 19th c., professional repair to bird beak, 11" l. (ILLUS.) **9,350**

Humidor, cov., figural, model of a small, long-haired begging dog, 9" h....................... **440**

Jardiniere, a large slightly tapering cylindrical container in cobalt blue w/a molded rim band of green leaves, an oval reserve on the side w/a large pale blue bow at the top & framing a bird perched on a branch, supported around the bottom by three figural caryatids resting on a brown tripartite platform on hoof feet, Joseph Holdcroft, England, late 19th c., 13 1/2" d., 16 1/2" h. (professional repair to one foot & wing tip).. **1,925**

Jardiniere & underplate, bell-form pot molded w/Neoclassical designs with Gothic arch panels all in pale brown, pale blue, cream w/a cobalt blue rim band, Brownfield & Son, England, late 19th c., 10 1/2" d., 10" h., 2 pcs.................................. **880**

Mug, Picket Fence & Floral patt. **121**

Pitcher, 5 1/2" h., Pineapple patt. **99**

Pitcher, 6 1/2" h., figural, Double Pelican patt., one pelican forms the handle, the other forms the front of the body against green leaves **825**

Pitcher, 7" h., Corn patt. **187**

Pitcher, 7 1/4" h., figural, model of a brown bear w/a drum, great color, Joseph Holdcroft, England, mint **1,100**

Pitcher, 8" h., Fish patt., flattened round disk sides molded w/pairs of realistic fish on a cobalt blue ground, oval pale blue foot & short neck, angled branch handle, Joseph Holdcroft, England **1,210**

Pitcher, 8 1/2" h., Sunflower patt., yellow ground **143**

Pitcher, 9" h., figural, model of a rooster w/shield on the side reading "Chante Clair Pour La France," Frie Onnaing, France, late 19th c. **660**

Pitcher, 9" h., triangular shape, Owl & Fan patt., yellow ground **330**

Pitcher, 10" h., tapering ovoid body, Lily of the Valley, Fern & Rope patt., green & pink on cream ground, lavender rim, Samuel Lear, England, late 19th c. **523**

Pitcher, 11" h., figural, model of a seated dog, St. Clement, France, marked "CYPP" on collar, late 19th c. **1,100**

Pitcher, 12 3/4" h., figural, tall model of fish standing on its tail **275**

Plate, 7 1/4" d., Strawberry & Vine patt., looped vine border, cobalt blue ground **176**

Plate, 8 1/2" d., Fish & Daisy patt., cobalt blue ground, brown rim band, Joseph Holdcroft, England, late 19th c. **440**

Plate, 8 3/4" d., lightly scalloped rim, Floral & Butterfly patt., leafy vines on a brown ground **154**

Plate, 9" d., Pond Lily patt., overlapping leaves & floral center, George Jones, England, late 19th c. **495**

Plate, 9" l., model of a wide flattened fish, natural colors **176**

Plate, 10" d., large bright pink flowers on green leafy stems against a cobalt blue ground, great color **220**

Platter, 11" d., round, molded in the center w/a small cluster of overlapping pink shells on a white ground, orange border band & pink coral edge handles **413**

Platter, 12 3/4" l., rectangular w/rounded corners, Tobacco Leaf & Rosette patt., Joseph Holdcroft, England, late 19th c. **275**

Platter, 13 1/2" l., oval, Bamboo & Fern patt., cobalt blue center, Wardle & Co., England, late 19th c. (scratches in center) **303**

George Jones Sardine Dish

Sardine dish, cov., a rectangular upswept basketweave raft base in mottled green & brown, the rectangular basketweave box w/the cover molded in full relief w/large

grey & white fish on green & pink shells & grass, George Jones, England, late 19th c., 9 1/4" l. (ILLUS.) **2,090**

Spooner, Fan & Scroll patt., footed, S. Fielding & Co., England, 6" h. **220**

Strawberry server, round dish w/attached small round cream & sugar wells, embossed strawberry leaves & blossoms, turquoise ground trimmed in yellow, green, brown & pink, England, 19th c., 10" d. **358**

Strawberry spoon, green w/pink blossom in pierced bowl, George Jones, England, 4" l. (professional repair to handle) **715**

Syrup pitcher w/hinged pewter cover, Blackberry patt., Edwin Bennett Pottery, Baltimore, Maryland, late 19th c. **165**

Syrup pitcher w/hinged pewter cover, Heron patt., Edwin Bennett Pottery, Baltimore, Maryland, late 19th c. **165**

Syrup pitcher w/hinged pewter cover, Sunflower patt., Edwin Bennett Pottery, Baltimore, Maryland, late 19th c. **165**

Teapot, cov., Blackberry patt., upright square shape, blackberries & leaves embossed in side panels on a pale green ground, figural blackberry finial, 6 1/2" h. **358**

Tureen, cov., figural, long, narrow, oval brown basket-form base molded on the top w/a large realistic mackerel on a bed of green leaves & ferns, George Jones, England, late 19th c., 19" l. **2,420**

Extremely Rare Umbrella Stand

Umbrella stand, figural, unique design of a standing dark-skinned bearded man wearing an Eskimo outfit & holding a baby seal, on an oblong white & grey iceberg base, in shades of black, brown, grey & white, extremely rare, T.C. Brown, Westhead, Moore & Co., England, late 19th c., near mint, 39" h. (ILLUS.) **22,000**

European Figural Majolica Vases

Vases, 12 1/2" h., figural, Art Nouveau style, a large cylindrical vase in shaded grey, blue & pink topped by a ring of pink blossoms w/green vines looping down the sides, one w/a young girl in peasant costume reaching up w/large poppy blossoms beside her, the other w/a young boy in peasant costume holding a basket & standing near a large pink daisy-like blossom, Europe, late 19th c., very minor nick, pr. (ILLUS.) **440**

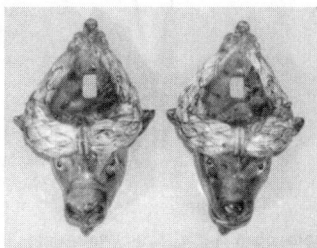

Unusual Bull's Head Wall Pockets

Wall pockets, figural, each modeled as a brown bull's head w/woven green leaf wreath looping up to form the pointed top, browns & greens w/cobalt blue accents, Thomas Sergent, late 19th c., 5 3/4" l., pr. (ILLUS.) **1,375**

McCoy

Collectors are now seeking the art wares of two McCoy potteries. One was founded in Roseville, Ohio, in the late 19th century as the J.W. McCoy Pottery, subsequently becoming Brush-McCoy Pottery Co., later Brush Pottery. The other was also founded in Roseville in 1910 as Nelson McCoy Sanitary Stoneware Co., later becoming Nelson McCoy Pottery. In 1967 the pottery was sold to D.T. Chase of the Mount Clemens Pottery Co., who sold his interest to the Lancaster Colony Corp. in 1974. The pottery shop closed in 1985. Cookie jars are especially collectible today.

A helpful reference book is The Collector's Encyclopedia of McCoy Pottery, *by the Huxfords (Collector Books), and* McCoy Cookie Jars From the First to the Latest, *by Harold Nichols (Nichols Publishing, 1987).*

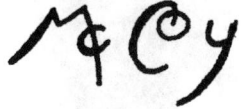

McCoy Mark

Freddie the Gleep Cookie Jar

Cookie jar, Freddie the Gleep, 1974 (ILLUS.) **$475**

Indian Head Cookie Jar

Cookie jar, Indian Head, ca. 1954 (ILLUS.) **325-425**

Leaves & Berries Jardiniere & Pedestal

Jardiniere & pedestal base, Leaves & Berries design, ca. 1930s, overall 21" h., 2 pcs. (ILLUS.) **250-350**

Sand Butterfly Jardiniere & Pedestal

Jardiniere & pedestal base, sand butterfly decoration, shaded brown & green ground, overall 21" h., 2 pc. (ILLUS.)..... **250-350**

Large Oil Jar

Oil jar, bulbous ovoid body w/slightly flaring rim, angled shoulder handles, red sponged glaze, 18" h. (ILLUS.).............. **300-400**

Figural Bear Planter

Planter, model of bear w/ball, yellow w/black trim, red ball, 5 1/2 x 7" (ILLUS.)...................................... **100-125**
Planter, model of Cope monkey head, 5 1/2" h...................................... **100-200**

Fish Planter

Planter, model of fish, green, ca. 1955, 7 x 12" (ILLUS.)................................ **1,000-1,200**
TV lamp, model of fireplace, ca. 1950s, 6 x 9" **75-100**
Vase, 8 1/2" h., figural wide lily-form, white, brown & green, ca. 1956...................... **350-400**

Meissen

The secret of true hard paste porcelain, known long before to the Chinese, was "discovered" accidentally in Meissen, Germany by J.F. Bottger, an alchemist working with E.W. Tschirnhausen. The first European true porcelain was made in the Meissen Porcelain Works, organized about 1709. Meissen marks have been widely copied by other factories. Some pieces listed here are recent.

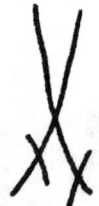

Meissen Mark

Compote, open, 12" h., figural, the figures of two nude youths encircle the stump stem set upon an applied-floral rocky base, supporting a double-handled bowl decorated w/colored applied florals around the exterior & painted decoration on the interior, 19th c. **$1,100**
Figure group, two young children dressed in 18th c. attire, on a base, enameled decoration & incised marks, late 19th c., 6 1/2" h. **690**
Figure group, Monkey Band, composed of a conductor, oboe player, flute player, trumpet player, piano player on monkey-back, cello player, French horn player & violin player, late 19th - early 20th c., tallest 7" h., the set (various chips & small damages) **6,038**
Figure group, allegorical, "North America," modeled as a Native American wearing a feathered headdress & riding his horse while spearing a charging buffalo, underglaze-blue crossed swords mark, modeled in 1903 by Erich Hoesel, 14" l., 14" h. **3,500-4,500**

Figure of a woman, allegorical, modeled holding a stringed instrument & seated on a scrolled freeform base, polychrome & gilt trim, incised "#369 - 6," late 19th - early 20th c., 16 1/2" h. **3,000-3,200**

Pair of Meissen Figurines

Figurines, man & woman in 18th-c. floral dress, each carrying flowers in hand, the man w/his coat flaring over a tree stump, each mounted on raised base w/applied flowers, marked w/crossed swords, 17" h, pr. (ILLUS.) **3,024**
Model of a monkey, seated animal holding an apple, 2 3/4" h. **2,000-2,200**
Pitcher, cov., 10 1/4" h., ovoid body w/heavy leaf design, scrolling handle, wreath finial, late 19th c. **448**
Plate, 9" d., flower-encrusted, round form piled high in the center w/a profusion of colorful flowers & fruit within a pierced gilt-edged border, the underside printed & painted w/forget-me-not sprigs & insects, underglaze-blue crossed swords mark, ca. 1830 (some damage & restoration).............. **1,955**
Plates, 9 3/4" d., Blue Onion patt., crossed swords mark, late 19th - early 20th c., set of 6... **385**

Fine Meissen tête-à-tête Tea Set

Tea set, tête-à-tête size: cov. teapot, cov. sugar bowl, creamer, two cups & saucers & an oblong tray; each decorated w/colorful encrusted flowers w/painted flowers on the tray, cups w/six feet, underglaze-blue crossed swords mark, 19th c., tray 16" l., the set (ILLUS.) **3,500-4,000**
Teapot, cov., figural, model of a rooster, enamel decoration, late 19th - early 20th c., 6" l... **575-600**
Tray, squared form w/ornately molded dished edges w/rocaille shells & blue floral decoration, polychrome floral decoration at center & gilt enamel trim, scrolled loop side handles, late 19th c., 16 1/4" w... **1,093**
Vases, 19" h., baluster form w/entwined snake handles, cobalt blue ground, the mouth, collar & foot molded & trimmed

w/gilt, late 19th - early 20th c., blue crossed swords marks & incised & impressed numbers, mounted as lamps, pr. ... **2,990**

Mettlach

Ceramics with the name Mettlach were produced by Villeroy & Boch and other potteries in the Mettlach area of Germany. Villeroy and Boch's finest years of production are thought to be from about 1890 to 1910. Also see STEINS.

Mettlach Mark

Mettlach Cracker Jar

Cracker jar, cov., silver plate rim, bail handle & flat cover w/knob finial, cylindrical w/molded base & rim bands in dark brown, a wide tan middle band w/a mosaic design of a white-dotted zigzag band forming triangles w/three-petal flowers in brown & white, No. 1306, 4" h. (ILLUS.) **$230**

Mettlach Ewer with Figural Handle

Ewer, stoneware, domed-footed ovoid body w/a tall cylindrical neck & wide mask spout, green ground applied w/brown pointed leaves above the foot below a wide relief-molded band of classical figures in the woods hunting w/dogs against a dark brown ground, a neck band w/brown woven design, full-figure Cupid handle in cream w/brown trim, No. 2356, 4 2/3 liter (ILLUS.) **805**

Jardiniere, Art Nouveau design, a deep bowl-form container w/gently ruffled rim, glossy mossy green sides molded w/an upright cluster of berries & long leaves, supported on curved & stepped-out short end legs in dark green w/moss green bands, pale yellow interior, No. 2735, 13" l., 5 1/4" h.. **805**

Jardiniere, cameo-style, low long narrow rectangular form w/low bracket end feet, flat rim w/stepped ends, the long sides each w/two oblong dark green panels w/reclining classical women in white relief, tan border bands w/white stripping, No. 3041, 11 2/3" l., 4 1/4" h. **311**

Girl & Swans Mettlach Plaque

Plaque, pierced for hanging, charming printed-under-glaze color scene of a little Victorian girl wearing a feather hat & purple gown & holding a small basket, standing on the shore of a large lake feeding white swans w/a village in the background, gold trim w/slight wear, No. 1044/1122, 17" d. (ILLUS.) **920**

Plaque, pierced to hang, etched w/a surrealistic seascape w/a large black raven flying over stormy dark blue waves between dark brown craggy cliffs, the shaded dark blue sky w/pale blue moon highlighted w/stripes of pink clouds, slight gold wear, No. 2551, 18" d... **1,668**

Plaques, pierced to hang, each w/an overall etched scene, one w/a gnome seated on leafy blossoming branches drinking from a mug, various beetles flying & perched, all against a shaded medium to light blue ground, the other w/a gnome seated in a nest on a leafy vine w/butterflies flying about, against a shaded medium to light blue ground, No. 2112 & 2113, 16" d., facing pr. **2,128**

Plaques, pierced to hang, rectangular dark green ground, each decorated w/a narrow white relief border around a scene of a classical woman & cupids, No. 7067 & 7068, 4 x 6", facing pair **806**

Vase, 4 1/4" h., bulbous ovoid body w/short flared neck, on three knob feet, mosaic design w/wide upper & lower grey bands decorated w/brown & blue double circles, narrow brown middle band w/small brown & white roundels, No. 1640 .... **345**

Vase, 7" h., footed ovoid body w/short, wide flaring neck, dark blue ground decorated w/an overall mosaic design of almond-form panels composed of brown leaves & stylized four-petal blossoms in rust red & pale blue, small scattered dot blossoms on the shoulder & neck, No. 1573.................. **230**

Vase, 7 3/4" h., wide ovoid body w/a short, flared neck, a mosaic decoration of dark brown horizontal bands decorated w/opposing bands of serrated lappets in dark blue, green & deep rose, rounded smaller bands of lappets around the base & neck, No. 1596... **374**

Vase, 10 1/2" h., classical-style, a pedestal base in dark brown w/rust red lappet band supporting the bulbous body decorated w/two large heart-shaped reserves w/pink ground & white relief figures of putti under leafy branches, dark brown & rust red border bands continuing up & forming stripes on the tall trumpet neck flanked by long brown S-scroll handles, No. 2432... **240**

Very Fine Mettlach Vase with Fairy

Vase, 26" h., tall baluster-form body, beautifully decorated in relief w/a lovely winged fairy dressed in deep rose, blue & white, perched on slender contorted leafy vine w/pink blossoms, all against a subtly shaded dark to medium blue ground, gold highlights, No. 1610 (ILLUS.) **5,635**

Minton

The Minton factory in England was established by Thomas Minton in 1793. The factory made earthenware, especially the blue-printed variety, and Thomas Minton is sometimes credited with the invention of the blue "Willow" pattern. For a time majolica and tiles were also an important part of production, but bone china soon became the principal ware. Mintons, Ltd., continues in operation today. Also see MAJOLICA.

Minton Marks

Bowl, 4" d., 2 1/2" h., majolica, modeled as a round bird's nest in dark brown supported by molded oak leaves & acorns **$330**

Centerpiece, majolica, figural, a large, wide & shallow deep yellow shell w/pink interior supported atop a figural merman on an oval foot, shape No. 865, date code for 1870, 12" w., 14" h. **1,650**

Fancy Minton Game Dish

Game dish, cov., majolica, oval, the tapering brown basketweave base w/green relief oak leaves & acorns, the cover molded in full relief w/dead game & a branch handle, professional handle repair on base, chip on wing of bird, hairline & rim repair on insert, late 19th c., 13" l. (ILLUS.) **1,210**

Garden seat, majolica, Oriental-style, round turquoise top centered by a circle of molded scrolls, the curved shoulder molded w/oblong panels of pink & green scrolls within yellow borders, S-scroll tapering legs curve down to join at an open center ring, scroll feet, date code for 1863, 19" h. **4,400**

Large Minton Jardiniere

Jardiniere, Majolica, footed oval urn form w/rolled rim, turquoise blue ground w/white & brown molded snake handles, a green rope band around the foot & shoulder of the body, chain-molded rim band in ochre, green & brown, pink interior, shape No. 532, date code for 1869, professional repair to rim, 24" l., 12" h. (ILLUS.) **3,575**

Plate, 9 3/4" d., majolica, a dark green center w/the wide border molded w/three large green & yellow sunflower heads separated by deep rose reticulated panels **413**

Salt dip, master size, majolica, oblong four-lobed form in a marbleized malachite & gold glaze, 5" l., 2 1/2" h. **165**

Spill vases, majolica, figural, a large standing seminude putto beside an upright trumpet-form basketweave basket w/turquoise blue interior & the exterior trimmed w/leafy vines, all on a round leaf-trimmed base, shape No. 405 & 406, date code for 1867, 10 3/4" h., pr. (professional repair to rims of baskets) **3,850**

Tray, majolica, round, cobalt blue inner rim band around the mottled green & brown center, wide border band molded in brown, yellow & green w/putti, birds & leafy scrolls, yellow floral rosette border band, 10 3/4" d. **440**

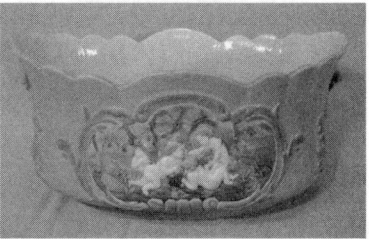

Unusual Minton Wine Cooler

Wine cooler, majolica, oval, deep, slightly flared sides w/a scalloped rim, turquoise ground w/scroll-trimmed side panels molded w/scenes of putti in the forest, large green leaves form end handles, late 19th c., 14 x 23", 11" h. (ILLUS.) **3,300**

Mocha

Mocha decoration is found on basically utilitarian creamware or yellowware articles and is achieved by a simple chemical reaction. A color pigment of brown, blue, green or black is given an acid nature by infusion of tobacco or hops. When this acid nature colorant is applied in blobs to an alkaline ground color, it reacts by spreading in feathery seaweed designs. This type of decoration is usually accompanied by horizontal bands of light color slip. Produced in numerous Staffordshire potteries from the late 18th until the late 19th centuries, its name is derived from the similar markings found on mocha quartz. In addition to the seaweed decoration, mocha wares are also seen with Earthworm and Cat's Eye patterns or a marbleized effect.

Mocha Bowl and Mugs

Bowl, 7" d., footed deep rounded form, marbleized slip in dark blue, medium brown & dark brown on a white ground below a green reeded rim band, early 19th c., base & rim chips, hairline in base, glaze wear, pitting (ILLUS. right with mugs)......... **$881**

Mug, cylindrical, w/extruded handle w/foliate terminals, banded at the top & base in dark brown & ochre w/dark brown, medium brown & white scroddled dot slip on a rust field, early 19th c., circular crack, two vertical cracks in body, discoloration, 5 3/4" h. (ILLUS. center with bowl & mug) **1,175**

Mug with Two Earthworm Bands

Mug, cylindrical, w/extruded handle w/foliate terminals, banded in dark brown & rust w/two rows of blue, dark brown, rust & white Earthworm patt. flanked by upper & lower white rouletted bands, early 19th c., circular & spider cracks in base, three rim chips, 6" h. (ILLUS.) **1,175**

Mocha Mug with Earthworm Bands

Mug, cylindrical, w/molded base & extruded handle, narrow bands of rust at the top & base, wide grey center band decorated in the Earthworm patt. in blue, rust & black, early 19th c., chips, 5 3/4" h. (ILLUS.)........ **2,350**

Mug, pearlware, cylindrical, w/extruded handle w/foliate terminals, a pale green rim band over dark brown bands w/Cat's Eye decoration flanking a central grey band w/dark brown, tan, grey & white Earthworm patt., early 19th c., small hairline in base (ILLUS. left with bowl & mug) **5,288**

Early Mocha Mustard Pot

Mustard pot, cov., low cylindrical body w/D-form handle & inset cover w/knob finial, blue banded cover & blue reeded band above a wide blue band decorated w/the Earthworm patt. in white, black & brown, England, chips to lid, small crack in body, discoloration, early 19th c., 2 1/2" h. (ILLUS.) **1,293**

Small Mocha Pitcher with Seaweed

Pitcher, 6 1/2" h., baluster-form, banded in dark brown & rust w/a green-glazed rouletted upper band, black mocha Seaweed patt. in the wide rust band, extruded handle w/green-glazed foliate terminals, England, early 19th c. (ILLUS.) **2,585**

Unusual Banded Mocha Pitcher

Pitcher, 8" h., barrel-shaped, pearlware, banded in rust & black w/rouletted green glazed upper & lower bands, decorated w/blue, dark brown & white Earthworm patt., white & black trailing slip "branches," extruded handle w/green-glazed foliate terminals, England, early 19th c., rim & spout chips, long crack at rim, crack across lower handle terminal, glaze hairlines on base (ILLUS.)................................. **3,525**

Moorcroft

William Moorcroft became a designer for James Macintyre & Co. in 1897 and was put in charge of the art pottery production there. Moorcroft developed a number of popular designs, including Florian Ware, while with Macintyre and continued with that firm until 1913, when it discontinued the production of art pottery.

After leaving Macintyre in 1913, Moorcroft set up his own pottery in Burslem, where he continued producing the art wares he had designed earlier, introducing new patterns as well. After William's death in 1945, the pottery was operated by his son, Walter.

MOORCROFT

Moorcroft Marks

Bowl, 7 1/4" d., 1 1/2" h., Clematis patt., signed **$200-225**
Pitcher, 5" h., 6" d., footed, bulbous, nearly spherical body w/a wide short cylindrical neck w/pinched spout, C-form strap handle, decorated w/yellow & pink irises on a shaded dark blue to light green ground, impressed "MOORCROFT - MADE IN ENGLAND" & script signature **375-400**
Potpourri jar, cov., footed, bulbous, ovoid, shouldered body w/a fitted flat-topped cover pierced w/small holes, the sides of the body w/incised roundels enclosing a cluster of three small heart-shaped leaves, overall cinnabar red glossy glaze, ink script signature, impressed "W225,"

3 1/2" d., 3 1/4" h. (chip to threaded inside rim of cover & base) **440-460**
Vase, 4" h., deep blue ground decorated w/purple plums, grapes & green leaves .. **225-250**
Vase, 7 1/2" h., 4 1/2" d., disc foot below the simple ovoid body flaring to a wide, flat mouth, decorated w/purple grapes & yellow leaves on a shaded green to dark blue ground, die-stamped "Moorcroft - MADE IN ENGLAND" & w/ink signature **650-700**

Tall Moorcroft Vase

Vase, 16" h., tall slender ovoid body, Wisteria patt. w/flambé glaze, impressed marks, ca. 1930, drilled (ILLUS.)......... **975-1,000**

Nippon

"Nippon" is a term used to describe a wide range of porcelain wares produced in Japan from the late 19th century until about 1921. It was in 1891 that the United States implemented the McKinley Tariff Act, which required that all wares exported to the United States carry a marking indicating the country of origin. The Japanese chose to use "Nippon," their name for Japan. In 1921 the import laws were revised and the words "Made in" had to be added to the markings. Japan was also required to replace the "Nippon" with the English name "Japan" on all wares sent to the United States.

Many Japanese factories produced Nippon porcelain, much of it hand-painted with ornate floral or landscape decoration and heavy gold decoration, applied beading and slip-trailed designs referred to as "moriage." We indicate the specific marking used on a piece, when known, at the end of each listing. Be aware that a number of Nippon markings have been reproduced and used on new porcelain wares.

Important reference books on Nippon include: The Collector's Encyclopedia of Nippon Porcelain, Series One through Three, *by Joan F. Van Patten (Collector Books, Paducah, Kentucky) and* The Wonderful World of Nippon Porcelain, 1891-1921 *by Kathy Wojciechowski (Schiffer Publishing, Ltd., Atglen, Pennsylvania).*

Basket, on three feet, finely painted in stylized flowers & gilt w/"coralene" trim, "US Patent" mark, 4 3/4" h. **$202**

Nippon Floral-decorated Bowl

Bowl, 7 1/2" d., 3 3/4" h., wide shallow bowl w/lightly scalloped rim, raised on three gilt-trimmed scroll feet, gold & cobalt blue rim band, pink & white apple blossoms & green leaves on the interior & exterior, green "M" in wreath mark (ILLUS.)................. 135

Cigar receiver, heart-shaped, h.p. in raised enamel w/a playing card motif, 4 3/4" l......... 448

Condensed milk container, cover & underplate, cylindrical handled container, h.p. w/a floral band outlined in gold, magenta "M" in wreath mark, overall 6" h., 3 pcs. 101

Humidor, cov., decorated w/a tree-lined shore scene, green "M" in wreath mark, 5 1/2" h... 224

Mug, decorated w/a h.p. scene of an Oriental landscape w/a pagoda & garden in raised enamel, green "M" in wreath mark, 5" h. 67

Plaque, pierced to hang, decorated w/a h.p. scene of a horse race, geometric border in raised enamel, green "M" in Wreath mark, 9" d. 392

Blossom-decorated Relish Dish

Relish dish, oval w/pierced end handles, cobalt blue & gold rim band, the interior h.p. w/pink & white apple blossoms & green leaves on a creamy pale green ground, green "M" in wreath mark, 5 x 8 1/2" (ILLUS.)... 65

Tazza, miniature, footed, decorated w/roses on a stippled gold ground, "Kinran" crown mark, 5" l... 34

Vase, 9" h., molded basketweave body painted w/red & white roses, blue "M" in wreath mark 748

Vase, 11" h., two-handled, rare "sharkskin" glaze, h.p. flowers & grapes, marked "Patent No. 1705 Feb. 26, 1910 - Royal Kinjo Japan".. 489

Wall plaque, pierced to hang, relief-molded w/a squirrel eating peanuts, green "M" in wreath mark, ca. 1915, 10 3/4" d. 575

Wall Plaque with Lions

Wall plaque, pierced to hang, round, molded in relief w/a lion & lioness in a rocky landscape, natural coloration, green "M" in wreath mark, 10 3/4" d. (ILLUS.)............... 575

Old Ivory

Old Ivory china was produced in Silesia, Germany, in the late 1800s and takes its name from the soft white background coloring. A wide range of table pieces was made with the various patterns, usually identified by a number rather than a name.

The following prices are averages for Old Ivory at this time. Rare patterns will command higher prices, and there is some variance in prices geographically. These prices are also based on the item being perfect. Cups are measured across the top opening.

Berry set: 10 1/2" master bowl & six small berries; No. 7 Clairon blank, the set............ $300

Bowl, 5 1/2" d., waste, No. 11 Clairon blank 285

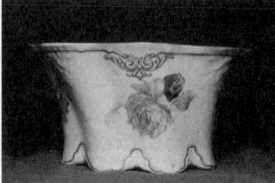

No. 84 Worchester Bowl

Bowl, 5 1/2" d., waste, No. 84 Worchester blank (ILLUS.)... 300

No. 28 Alice Bowl

Bowl, 7" d., whipped cream, No. 28 Alice blank (ILLUS.)... 300

Bowl, 10" d., No. 5 Elysee blank....................... 350

Bowl, 10" d., No. 73 Empire blank.................... 250

Pieces from No. 12 Clairon Cake Set

Cake set: 11" d. serving plate & 5 individual plates; No. 12 Clairon blank, the set (ILLUS. of two pieces)..................................... 450

Celery dish, No. 22 Clairon blank, 11 1/4" l....... **300**

No. 90 Clairon Charger

Charger, No. 90 Clairon blank, 13 1/2" d.
(ILLUS.).. **500**
Chocolate set, No. 22 Clairon blank, rare,
7-pc. set.. **2,500**
Cracker jar, No. 11 Clairon blank, 8 1/2" h. **500**

No. 75 Deco Variant Creamer

Creamer, No. 75 Deco blank variant, ser-
vice, 5 1/2" h. (ILLUS.) **195**
Creamer & cov. sugar bowl, No. 10
Clairon blank, 4" h., pr.................................... **175**

No. 53 Empire Sugar & Creamer

Creamer & cov. sugar bowl, No. 53 Em-
pire blank, 4" h., pr. (ILLUS.).......................... **450**
Cup & saucer, demi, No. 10 Clairon blank,
2 1/2" d... **135**
Cup & saucer, No. 22 Clairon blank, very
rare, 3 3/4" d. **500**
Cup & saucer, No. 99 Empire blank, rare,
3 1/2" d... **450**
Cup & saucer, No. 204 Deco blank, scarce,
3 3/4" d... **175**
Demitasse pot, No. 97 Clairon blank, very
rare, 7 1/2" h. **2,000**
Demitasse set: 7 1/2" pot & 4 cups & sau-
cers; No. U22 Eglantine blank.................... **1,800**

No. 200 Deco Jam Jar

Jam jar, cov., No. 200 Deco blank, 3 1/2" h.
(ILLUS.) **400**
Mustard pot, cov., No. 12 Clairon blank,
3 3/4" h. **425**
Nappy, No. 65 Clairon blank, rare, 6" l. **550**
Olive dish, No. 75 Empire blank, 6 1/2" l. **75**
Plate, 6 1/2" d., No. 121 Alice blank.................... **50**
Plate, 7 1/2" d., No. 119 Clairon blank, rare..... **300**
Plate, 9 3/4" d., dinner, No. 16 Clairon blank **200**
Plate, 6 1/2" d., No. U4 Deco blank..................... **40**
Plate, 7 1/2" d., No. 107 Empire blank, rare...... **250**
Plate, 9 3/4" d., dinner, No. 34 Empire blank **300**

No. U26 Mignon Dinner Plate

Plate, 9 3/4" d., dinner, No. U26 Mignon
blank (ILLUS.).. **385**

No. 34 Alice Platter

Platter, 21" l., No. 34 Alice blank (ILLUS.) **800**
Powder jar, No. 84 Deco blank variant,
scarce **400**
Tea tile, No. 11 Alice blank, 6" d....................... **250**
Toothpick holder, No. 73 Clairon blank,
2 1/4" h. **340**
Vase, 9" h., No. U12 blank............................. **1,700**

Old Ivory Covered Vegetable Dish

Vegetable dish, No. 28 blank, 10 1/2" l.
(ILLUS.).. **1,500**
Vegetable dish, cov., No. 84 Carmen
blank, 10 1/2" l. **1,300**

Phoenix Bird & Flying Turkey Porcelain

The phoenix bird, a symbol of immortality and spiritual rebirth, has been handed down through Egyptian mythology as a bird that consumed itself by fire after 500 years and then rose again, renewed, from its ashes. This bird has been used to decorate Japanese porcelain designed for export for more than 100 years. The pattern incorporates a blue design of the bird, variously known as the "Flying Phoenix," the "Flying Turkey" or the "Ho-o," stamped on a white ground. It became popular with collectors because of the abundant supply resulting from the long period of time the ware was produced. Pieces can be found marked with Japanese characters, with a "Nippon" mark, a "Made in Japan" mark or an "Occupied Japan" mark. Although there are several variations to the pattern and border, we have grouped them together since values seem to be quite comparable. A word of caution to collectors: Phoenix Bird pattern is still being produced. The standard reference for this category is Phoenix Bird Chinaware *by Joan Collett Oates.*

Berry server, style "B," w/seven drain
holes, 6" d.. **$238**
Bouillon cup & saucer, cov. **61**
Butter pat **14**
Cann, w/handle, straight sides........................... **26**
Casserole, style #1, oval..................................... **305**
Celery, style #1, 13 1/2" l................................... **180**
Cheese & cracker plate, tiered **280**

Style #1 Chocolate Pot

Chocolate pot, style #1, 8 3/4" h., 5 1/4" d.
(ILLUS.)... **144**
Chocolate pot, style #2, scalloped body &
base... **341**
Chocolate set: style #1 pot w/five demi
cups & saucers; the set................................ **149**
Coffeepot, style #1 .... **72**
Coffeepot, style #6.. **95**
Condensed milk jar, cov., style #1 .... **110**
Cracker jar, style #3... **145**

Phoenix Bird Cup & Saucer

Cup & saucer (ILLUS.)... **15**
Espresso cup & saucer **21**
Gravy boat, style #6 .... **36**
Gravy boat, style #6, w/underplate **75**
Hot water pot **45**
Ice cream dish, w/inverted scallops, 7" l.......... **129**
Lemonade glass, w/flared top **56**
Lemonade pitcher **130**
Mustard jar, style #9, w/attached plate **52**
Pancake, cov., w/two steam holes **184**

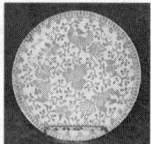

Phoenix Bird Plate

Plate, 7 1/4" d. (ILLUS.).. **6**
Plate, 8 1/2" d., luncheon **13**
Platter, 12" l., oval, scalloped edge.................... **78**
Platter, 16 1/8" l., scalloped rim **192**
Ramekin, style "A".. **23**
Ramekin, style "B".. **21**
Reamer, two-piece **255-330**
Relish, style #10, 9 5/8" l. **39**
Rice tureen, style #3... **65**
Salt dip, style #3, three round feet **15**
Sauce boat, style #2, w/handle, spout & un-
derplate... **78-83**
Syrup, cov., style #1 .... **35**
Syrup, cov., style #2 .... **86**

Quimper

This French earthenware pottery has been made in France since the end of the 17th century and is still in production today. Because the colorful decoration on this ware, predominantly of Breton peasant figures, is all hand-painted and each piece is unique, it has become increasingly popular with collectors in recent years. Most pieces offered today date from about the mid-19th century to the present. Modern potteries continue to operate today, with contemporary examples available in gift shops.

The standard reference in this field is Quimper Pottery A French Folk Art Faience *by Sandra V. Bondhus (privately printed, 1981).*

Quimper Marks

Baby's feeding pitcher, 4 1/2" h., tiny
spout, decorated w/only a flower garland
band, unsigned, 19th c., excellent............... **$150**
Bell, bagpipe shape w/original unglazed
clapper, "Ivoire Corbeille" patt., bust portrait of man on front, half sunburst
w/sponged circlets design on reverse,
"HenRiot Quimper 73," 3 1/4" h., mint **75**

Doll's Dish Set

Quimper Card Tray

Card tray, rococo amorphous form, "decor riche" patt., center decorated w/pair of Breton musicians surrounded by flower sprays of wild gorse & broom, "HenRiot Quimper 148," 13 x 10 1/2", mint (ILLUS.)............ 350

Cigarette box, cov., image of woman w/flower branches on lid, geometric patt. on base, "HenRiot Quimper 116," 4 1/2" l., 3 1/4" w., mint...................... 95

Cup & saucer, "croisille" style, the 4" lip-to-handle cup decorated w/image of seated woman in trefoil cartouche w/"tennis ball" latticework trim, 5" d. saucer, "HR Quimper," mint, pr. 50

Dish, fish shape, center w/design of woman wearing the costume of La Rochelle & surrounded by flower branches, "La Rochelle HenRiot Quimper 137," pierced for hanging, 10" l., 4 1/2" w., mint.................... 85

Doll dish set: 4" d. cov. tureen, 4" d. charger, 3" l. gravy boat, two 2 3/4" d. plates & two 1 3/4" d. plates; each w/decoration of sailboat on waves, creamy buff glaze & rose pink sponged border, unsigned, attributable to HenRiot, excellent, set of eight (ILLUS., top of page) 100

Doll plate, Modern Movement colors w/geometric stylized flower patt. in brown, yellow, blue & rose red, "HenRiot Quimper 106," 2 3/4" d., mint 30

Figure group, Modern Movement bride & groom by artist Fanch, from "Noce Bigoudenne" group, the bride wears white dress & loaf coif painted w/yellow "embroidery" work, the groom a dark navy suit & red tie, "HB Quimper," mint 150

Figure of "Fanch," wearing pantaloons & playing flute, Modern Movement colors, "HenRiot Quimper France 597," 3 1/2" h., mint... 75

Figure of St. Yves, the patron saint of lawyers wears legal garb of the period, "HenRiot Quimper," 4 3/4" h., mint........................ 100

Holy water font, base w/figure of the Christ Child holding a cross in relief, the top adorned w/image of eye of God enclosed within radiant sun & two stars, Modern Movement colors, "HB Quimper 119," 5 1/2" l., mint 110

Inkwell, cov., square w/cut corners, design of peasant man w/flowers & red S-link chain border, w/original inset & lid, "HB Quimper 497," 3 1/2" sq., excellent............... 180

Quimper Inkwell & Pen Tray

Quimper Crown-shaped Jardinier

Handled "Decor Riche" Jardiniere

Inkwell w/pen tray, cov., oblong, w/four feet & center apron, "demi-fantasie" patt., scene on front of Bretonne woman balancing milk pail on her head surrounded by flowering branches & lattice work, original inset & knobbed lid, "HenRiot Quimper France 99," excellent (ILLUS., bottom, previous page)..................................... 275

Jardiniere, crown shape, "decor riche" patt. w/seated couple facing each other on front, back w/Crest of Brittany held by lions, "HenRiot Quimper 23," 11 1/2" l., one handle professionally restored (ILLUS., top of page) 650

Jardiniere, oval shape w/cutout rim, short oval outcurved base, dainty scroll handles, "decor riche" patt., main cartouche shows seated woman holding a jug, reverse features crowned Crest of Brittany, "HB Quimper," 12 1/2" l., 7" h., mint (ILLUS., second from top of page) 500

Knife rest, figural, Modern Movement-style form of reclining woman w/her head on her hands & her elbows extended, "HenRiot Quimper" and mark of artist C. Maillard, 4" l., mint... 100

"Ivoire Corbeille" Liqueur Set

Liqueur set: barrel keg w/original wooden spigot, wooden stand & six original small handled cups; "Ivoire Corbeille" patt. w/bust portrait of woman in profile on side of keg, "HenRiot Quimper," mint, the set (ILLUS.) 150

Match holder, wall-mounted type, pocket features image of peasant woman w/flowers, back panel has lattice & dot geometric design, "HR Quimper," 3 x 2 1/2", mint... 175

Artist-signed Flower Holder

Pique fleurs (flower holder), figural, Modern Movement-style image of a kneeling Bigoudenne lifting a basket of flowers, the basket w/holes for flower stems, "HenRiot Quimper" and signature of artist C.H. Maillard on base, 8" h., 9" l., mint (ILLUS.) 750

"Decor Riche" Pattern Plates

Odetta Gresware Pitchers

Pitcher, 3" h., Odetta gresware w/concentric double diamond patt. in white & rich brown on navy blue/cobalt ground, "HB Quimper Odetta 494," mint (ILLUS. top right, w/other Odetta pitchers) **150**

Pitcher, 3 3/4" h., Odetta gresware w/concentric double diamond patt. in white & rich brown on navy blue/cobalt ground, "HB Quimper Odetta 424," mint (ILLUS. bottom right, w/other Odetta pitchers) **150**

Pitcher, 9 1/2" h., Odetta gresware w/a rich deep chocolate brown glaze over a light tan matte glaze "biscuit," bold geometric patt., "HB Quimper Odetta 423-1081+," mint (ILLUS. left, w/other Odetta pitchers) **300**

Plate, 8 3/4" d., "decor riche" patt. w/unusual scene of a Breton knight, Bertrand Du-

guesclin, "HR Quimper," mint (ILLUS. right, w/peasant plate, top of page) **525**

Plate, 9 1/2" d., "decor riche" patt. w/scalloped border & pair of nicely detailed peasant folk, "HR Quimper," mint (ILLUS. left, w/Breton knight plate, top of page) **350**

First Period Porquier Beau Plate

Plate, 9 1/2" d., First Period Porquier Beau, entitled "Ramasseur de goemon-Guisseny," scene of fisherman on shoreline holding a pike, w/Crest of Brittany above him in acanthus border, signed w/intersecting "PB" and name of scene, mint (ILLUS.) **1,250**

Plate, 9 3/4" d., "Broderie Bretonne" geometric patt., ten-pointed star on metallic gold background glaze, intricate raised-to-the-touch heart-shaped patterns in border, "HB Quimper P.F. 163 D 708," mint **100**

Set of Five Peasant Plates

"Ivoire Corbeille" Fish Platter

Plates, 8 1/2" d., "demi-fantasie" patt., w/different Breton peasant on each, marked w/"HenRiot Quimper France" and various two-digit numbers, mint, set of 5, each (ILLUS., bottom previous page)........................ 50

Platter, 13" l., 10" w., rectangular w/cut corners, decorated w/image of open basket w/bouquet of flowers, corners w/black ermine tails, "HenRiot Quimper France," excellent.. 150

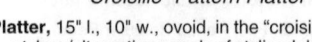

"Croisille" Pattern Platter

Platter, 15" l., 10" w., ovoid, in the "croisille" style w/alternating panels of stylized dogwood blossom, finely detailed couple posed in conversation in the center, "HenRiot Quimper France 162," mint (ILLUS.).. 450

Platter, 20 3/4" l., 10" w., oval fish platter, "Ivoire Corbeille" patt. w/portrait busts of young Breton couple framed w/Celtic motifs, "HenRiot Quimper," pierced for hanging, mint (ILLUS., top of page) 275

Salt, open oval w/yellow glaze & flower sprig patt. on sides, "HenRiot Quimper," 2" l., mint...................... 25

Tea set: 7" h. cov. teapot, creamer, five cups & six saucers; traditional peasant patt., decorative scalloped borders, "HR Quimper," excellent (ILLUS., bottom of page).. 750

Tray, pyrographic wooden tray by Paul Fouillen, w/scene depicting interior of cottage where woman serves meal from Quimper cov. tureen, "Fouillen" signature on front & his trademark logo on back, excellent painting w/vibrant colors, 7 1/4 x 14 3/4".................................... 325

Tumbler/beaker, w/traditional design of Breton woman & flowers, "HenRiot Quimper France 124," 4 1/2" h., mint 65

Vase, 3 1/2" h., 5 1/2" w., fan shape, front decorated w/image of peasant man flanked by flower branches, back w/flower sprig & four blue dots, feet are molded butterflies sponged in blue, "HenRiot Quimper," mint................................. 150

"Broderie Bretonne" Vase

Scalloped Tea Set

Vase, 8 1/2" h., cylindrical form tapering in at top & in to short base, "Broderie Bretonne" patt., w/scene of standing peasants, a woman knitting, a man smoking a pipe, raised-to-the-touch Breton embroidery work on the sides, "HB Quimper," mint (ILLUS., previous page).......................... **450**

Quimper "Demi-fantasie" Vase

Vase, 15" h., slightly ovoid cylindrical body, flaring to narrow neck w/outcurved rim, side loop handles, "demi-fantasie" patt., portly man smokes pipe on front panel, reverse shows bold double daisy w/wheat flower spray, "HenRiot Quimper France 73," mint (ILLUS.) **350**

Wall pocket, bagpipe shape w/double blue bows, decorated w/image of peasant man holding walking stick & posed in an open field, "HB Quimper" beneath figure, 5 1/2" l., mint **100**

Rookwood

Considered America's foremost art pottery, the Rookwood Pottery Company was established in Cincinnati, Ohio, in 1880 by Mrs. Maria Nichols Longworth Storer. To accurately record its development, each piece carried the Rookwood insignia or mark, was dated, and, if individually decorated, was usually signed by the artist. The pottery remained in Cincinnati until 1959, when it was sold to Herschede Hall Clock Company and moved to Starkville, Mississippi, where it continued in operation until 1967.

A private company is now producing a limited variety of pieces using original Rookwood molds.

Rookwood Mark

Plaque, rectangular, landscape w/slender trees in the immediate foreground w/a large lake beyond, Vellum glaze, titled on back "Penacook Lake, Concord, NY," 1916, Ed Diers, framed, 8 3/4 x 14 1/4" .. **$8,625**

Vase, 9 1/2" h., 3 1/2" d., slender very slightly swelled cylindrical form w/a tapering shoulder & short cylindrical neck, decorated w/tall stems of white, grey & green Queen Anne's Lace on a shaded dark blue to white ground, Iris glaze, No. 941G, 1906, Sara Sax **2,700**

Vase, 9 1/2" h., 3 3/4" d., short wide ovoid body w/wide flat rim, decorated around the rim & down the sides w/three large cicada on twigs in blue, cream & tan on a pale blue ground, Carved Vellum glaze, No. 942D, 1905, Ed Diers...................... **4,781**

Vase, 9 3/4" h., 3 3/4" d., tall slightly swelled cylindrical body tapering slightly to a short rolled rim, decorated w/large orange poppies & green leaves against a dark brown shaded to tan ground, Standard glaze, No. 904CC, 1903, Mary Nourse **1,125**

Vase, 10" h., 3 3/4" d., tall slender swelled cylindrical form tapering to a short cylindrical neck, decorated w/a pastel hillside landscape w/water & trees in background, in shades of light & dark green, dark blue, light blue & cream, No. 932D, 1917, Sallie Coyne (very small flat base nick)... **1,575**

Vase, 10" h., 4 1/2" d., tall slightly swelled cylindrical form w/a short flared rim, continuous Venetian harbor scene in dark blue, pale green & lavender against a shaded blue to cream to blue ground, Vellum glaze, No. 1121C, 1925, Carl Schmidt... **7,313**

Vase, 10" h., 4 3/4" d., tall ovoid form tapering to a short cylindrical neck w/flat rim, decorated w/a continuous landscape of large trees & bushes around a pond, in shades of dark & light blue, green, pale yellow & cream, Vellum glaze, No. 940D, 1921, E.T. Hurley... **3,375**

Vase, 10" h., 9" d., large bulbous ovoid body w/a wide rounded shoulder centered by a short neck w/a widely flaring, flattened rim, decorated around the upper half w/large leafy branches of peaches on a shaded tan to dark green ground, Standard glaze, No. 488F, 1890, Matt Daly **1,800**

Vase, 10 1/2" h., 4 1/2" d., baluster-form, decorated w/a continuous lakeside landscape w/trees at sunset, in shades of dark blue, violet, green, pale yellow & cream, No. 1667, 1909, E.T. Hurley (small restoration at rim) **900**

Vase, 10 1/2" h., 5" d., simple ovoid form, decorated w/large stylized mushrooms in shades of blue, grey & tan against a shaded white to grey ground, Vellum glaze, No. 939B, 1905, Carl Schmidt....... **12,375**

Vase, 10 3/4" h., 5" d., tall ovoid body tapering to a short rolled neck, decorated w/large stylized pink water lilies w/yellow centers & pale green stems & leaves on a butter yellow & blue butterfat ground, Wax Matte glaze, No. 614D, 1930, Sallie Coyne... **2,250**

Vase, 12" h., 12" d., large bulbous ovoid body w/a short, wide cylindrical neck, decorated w/large clusters of hydrangea on a shaded gold to dark green ground, Standard glaze, No. 531D, 1891, A.R. Valentien (lightly crazed, restored drill hole in base)... **3,150**

Vase, 12 1/4" h., 5" d., tall slightly tapering cylindrical form w/flat rim, dark violet ground decorated around the top w/a wide pale orange band painted w/ochre dogwood blossoms on violet stems, Matte glaze, No. 950B, 1906, H. Wilcox.... **4,219**

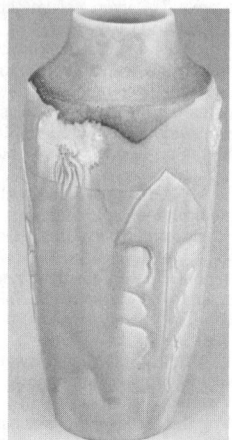

Rookwood Matte Dandelion Vase

Vase, 12 1/4" h., 5" d., gently flaring cylindrical form w/a shoulder & short tapering cylindrical neck, lightly carved decoration of upright dandelion leaves alternating w/white blossom heads, streaky dark grey to light green Matte glaze, No. 946, 1905, Rose Fescheimer (ILLUS.).............. **1,495**

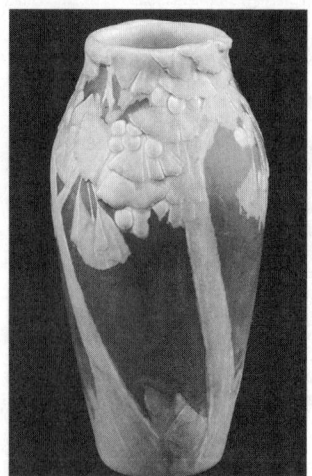

Rare Rookwood Carved Matte Vase

Vase, 12 1/2" h., 6" d., ovoid body tapering to a flat molded mouth, decorated

w/crisply tooled gingko leaves & nuts in green on a brown ground, Matte glaze, No. 925B, 1901, tight 4" firing line in body, Kataro Shirayamadani (ILLUS.)..... **25,875**

Vase, 13" h., 3" d., tall slender footed baluster-form w/a very slender trumpet neck, decorated w/a scene of a mother & young child playing amid waves on a beach, bisque finish w/Aerial Blue glaze, No. 242D, 1895, William McDonald........ **12,375**

Vase, 13" h., 5" d., tall slender ovoid body tapering to a small trumpet neck, decorated w/a large cluster of blue irises on green leafy stems against a dark brown to amber ground, Standard glaze, No. 702A, 1898, A.R. Valentien (fine overall crazing) **1,463**

Unusual Standard Glaze Vase

Vase, 14" h., a low stepped round foot supporting a tall slender trumpet body w/two long loop handles down one side, decorated w/yellow dogwood blossoms on branches down the sides against a shaded yellow, green, umber & orange ground, Standard glaze, 1889, K. Shirayamadani (ILLUS.)............................... **2,185**

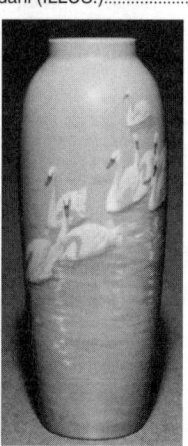

Rookwood Vase with Swans

Vase, 14" h., tall slender gently swelled cylindrical form tapering to a short cylindrical neck, decorated w/a scene of a flock of white swans swimming on shaded blue water, Vellum glaze, 1915, Carl Schmidt (ILLUS.).. **22,000**

Vase, 14" h., 5" d., tall slender very slightly swelled cylindrical form tapering to a short cylindrical neck, decorated around the shoulder w/large orange poppies on pale green leafy stems against a dark brown to green to light orange ground, Standard glaze, No. 907C, 1900, Mary Nourse.. **2,588**

Vase, 14" h., 5 1/2" d., tall slightly tapering swelled cylindrical form w/a flat rim, large abstract blue blossoms & green leaves on a mottled turquoise ground, Wax Matte glaze., No. 2441, 1925, Katherine Jones.. **1,688**

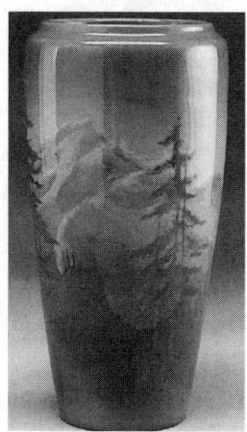

Large Iris Glaze Vase with Mountains

Vase, 14 3/4" h., 7 1/2" d., slightly tapering cylindrical form w/a slightly indented wide flat rim, decorated w/a bold mountainous landscape w/ice-blue mountains & light & dark green fir trees in the foreground, shaded moss green to dark gold sky, Iris glaze, No. 1369B, 1911, Ed Diers, light overall crazing (ILLUS.)............................. **18,400**

Rosenthal

The Rosenthal porcelain manufactory has been in operation since 1880, when it was established by P. Rosenthal in Selb, Bavaria. Tablewares and figure groups are among its specialties.

Figure group, "Expectation," a woman in late 18th c. costume w/a tall grey hairdo trimmed w/blue & pink blossoms, seated on a bench wearing a deep mustard yellow gown w/pale green & white underskirt, one arm resting on the thick bench arm, looking up at the figure of a kneeling cupid atop a short column in white trimmed w/floral swags & a blue bow, oblong white base, No. K476, signed by A. Opel, ca. 1920, 6 3/4" h. **$633**

Figure group, "Storming Bacchus," a figure of Bacchus in white, nude except for brown drapery across his thighs, leaning forwarding & striding w/each arm outstretched behind a young Bacchante in white w/brown hair, each seminude w/long dark blue drapery billowing around her legs, oblong white base, No. K190, signed by A. Caasmann, ca. 1922, 8" h. **748**

Figure group, "Venus & Parrot," a nude woman w/a high blonde pompadour hairdo seated on a bench w/a dark blue drapery & turned toward a white bird perched on the rim of a dark blue urn-bowl w/gold scroll handles resting on short columns w/a molded satyr mask, white oblong base, No. K288, signed by A. Opel, ca. 1920, 6 7/8" h. **546**

Figure group, young girl & fawn, a blonde toddler wearing a blue play suit & dark red blouse holding up a head of lettuce above the head of a light brown fawn, oval white base, No. 1665, by Friedrich Gronau, ca. 1937, 6 2/3" h. **230**

Figure group, modeled as a nude female riding the back of an ostrich, rectangular base, glazed all-white, 18" h. **920**

Figure of dancer, young woman in 18th c. peasant costume, wearing a long-sleeved white blouse w/dirndl & full ankle-length rust red dress & large white apron decorated w/scattered rust red blossoms, small cap on her head, posed w/one foot pointed to the side & holding up the corners of her apron, small rounded white base, by Opel, No. 1518/1, 1950s, 8 1/8" h. **288**

Figure of Harlequin, standing w/legs together & head raised, playing an accordion, white w/blue trim & gold highlights, white mound base, signed by A. Caasmann, No. K436, ca. 1918, 7 1/2" h. (slight gold wear)..................................... **374**

Model of dog, Borzoi, long slender reclining animal w/head erect, white & dark charcoal, no base, No. K200/0, signed by M. Valentin, ca. 1929, 9 1/4" l., 4" h. **345**

Model of dog, Dachshund puppy, seated, shades of dark brown, signed by Kuspert, No. 1909, 1950s, 3 1/2" h.............................. **150**

Model of dog, German Shepherd, seated animal w/open legs, black w/tan face & chest, No. K260/2, by Diller, ca. 1923, 11 3/8" h. **322**

Model of dog, Whippet, seated w/one paw raised, white w/black spots, oval base, signed by K. Himmelstoss, No. 511, 2 1/8" h. **196**

Model of fish, Angelfish, large graceful fish w/dark & light brown stripes, supported on slender tendrils of sea grass above an oval base, signed by F. Heidenreich, No. 1637, 1950s, 7 3/4" h. **242**

Model of horse, large brown animal in prancing pose, black mane & tail & white chest, on narrow oblong white base, by Zugel, No. N958, ca. 1935, 7 3/4" h............. **299**

Plaque, rectangular, color transfer-printed copy of the Mona Lisa, framed, 1930s, without frame 10 x 12 1/2" 265

Plaque, rectangular, painted w/a scene of the snow-covered Matterhorn w/a lake in the foreground & dark blue sky & white clouds behind, original giltwood shadow-box frame, 10 x 12" 770

Plates, 8 1/2" d., "Rosenthal Ivory" patt., six different colorful fruit designs w/h.p. accents & gilt trim, late 19th - early 20th c., set of 16 440

Royal Bayreuth

Good china in numerous patterns and designs has been made at the Royal Bayreuth factory in Tettau, Germany since 1794. Listings below are by the company's lines, plus miscellaneous pieces. Interest in this china remains at a peak and prices continue to rise. Pieces listed carry the company's blue mark except where noted otherwise.

Among the important reference books in this field are Royal Bayreuth - A Collectors' Guide *and* Royal Bayreuth - A Collectors' Guide - Book II *by Mary McCaslin (see Special Contributors list).*

Royal Bayreuth Mark

Corinthian

Cake plate, classical figures on black ground, 10" d. $150

Creamer & cov. sugar bowl, classical figures on black ground, pr. 120

Corinthian Pitcher

Pitcher, tankard, 6 7/8" h., 3 3/4" d., orange inside top, classical figures on black satin ground, gold bands w/black & white geometric design around neck & base (ILLUS.) 150

Planter, classical figures on red ground 120

Devil & Cards

Ashtray 125-150

Ashtray w/match holder 250-275

Salt dip, master size 275-325

Stamp box, cov., 3 1/2" l. 550-600

Sugar bowl, open, short............................... 300-350

Mother-of-Pearl

Ashtray, Murex Shell patt. 75-100

Creamer, grape cluster mold, pearlized white, 3 3/4" h. 150-175

Creamer & cov. sugar bowl, grape cluster mold, pearlized yellow, colorful foliage, pr. 300-375

Cup & saucer, demitasse, Oyster & Pearl mold.. 300-350

Hatpin holder, white pearlized finish 150-175

Sugar bowl, cov., footed, figural Spiky Shell patt., pearlized finish, 3 1/2" h................. 250-300

Toothpick holder, Murex Shell patt., pearlized finish 150-175

Rose Tapestry

Rose Tapestry Basket

Basket, rope handle, base & outer rim, three color roses, 4 1/4" w., 4" h. (ILLUS.) 250-350

Bowl, 10 1/2" d., shell- & scroll-molded rim, three-color roses 950-1,050

Rose Tapestry Chocolate Pot

Chocolate pot, cov., apricot, white, pink & yellow roses, leaf finial, gold trim, 8 1/2" h. (ILLUS.) 1,800-2,000

Creamer & cov. sugar bowl, pink & white roses, pr... 550-650

Dessert set: large cake plate & six matching small serving plates; three-color roses, 7 pcs...................................... 1,000-1,200

Nappy, tri-lobed leaf shape, decorated w/orange roses, 4 1/2" l................................ 150-200

Rose Tapestry Pitcher

Pitcher, 5 3/4" h., waisted shape, C-scroll handle angled at bottom, three-color roses (ILLUS.).. **350-500**

Rose Tapestry Vase

Vase, 4 1/2" h., ovoid body decorated w/clusters of small red roses at top & base, large yellow roses in center, short neck flaring slightly at rim (ILLUS.)......... **200-300**

Sunbonnet Babies

Ashtray, babies cleaning............................. **250-275**
Candlestick, babies washing, 5" d., 1 3/4" h.. **275-300**
Creamer, babies ironing, 3" h..................... **250-300**
Cup & saucer, babies washing.................. **250-350**
Tea set, child's... **750-900**

Miscellaneous

Ashtray, figural elk **250-275**
Ashtray, figural shell, 4 1/2 x 4 1/2".............. **50-75**
Ashtray, stork decoration, artist-signed, 4 1/2" l.. **75-100**
Basket, "tapestry," footed, bulbous body w/a ruffled rim & ornate gold-trimmed overhead handle, portrait of woman w/horse, 5" h. **550-600**
Bell, scene of musicians, men playing a cello & mandolin **300-350**

Royal Bayreuth Bowl

Bowl, 9 1/2" l., 3 3/4" h., raised enameled white roses & foliage on creamy ivory ground, flared, gently ruffled rim, four

gold-trimmed reticulated reserves, four short gold feet (ILLUS.)........................... **225-350**
Bowl, 6 7/8" d., 2 1/2" h., footed, shallow slightly scalloped sides, Cavalier Musicians decoration, gold trim on feet........ **100-125**
Cracker jar, cov., figural poppy, 6" h. **800-1,000**
Creamer, figural clown, red suit **400-450**

Eagle Creamer

Creamer, figural eagle, grey (ILLUS.)....... **300-400**
Creamer, figural girl w/pitcher, red **800-900**
Creamer, figural leopard...................... **6,000-6,500**
Creamer, figural oak leaf............................ **200-250**
Creamer, figural Santa Claus, attached handle, red, 4 1/4" h. **3,000-3,200**

Standing Trout Creamer

Creamer, figural trout, standing on tail, shaded brown to white w/reddish dots (ILLUS.) **4,500**
Creamer, flow blue, Babes in Woods decoration **250-300**
Creamer, scene of girl w/basket, salmon color.. **600-800**
Creamer, figural seashell, boot-shaped, 3 3/4" h. **150-195**
Creamer & cov. sugar bowl, figural poppy, pr... **300-350**
Creamer & cov. sugar bowl, figural strawberry, unmarked, pr. **450-500**
Ewer, cobalt blue, Babes in Woods decoration, 6" h. **600-650**
Hair receiver, cov., "tapestry," scene of farmer w/turkeys...................................... **250-300**

Penguin Hatpin Holder

Hatpin holder, model of a penguin, in red, white & grey, signed (ILLUS.) **800-900**
Model of a man's high top slipper **250-300**

Cavalier Pitcher

Pitcher, 3 1/4" h., 2" d., decorated w/Cavalier scene, two Cavaliers drinking at a table, grey & cream ground, unmarked (ILLUS.).. **65**
Pitcher, miniature, 4 1/2" h., scene of a skiff w/sail **100-125**
Pitcher, 5" h., figural crow **175**

Royal Bayreuth Santa Pitcher

Pitcher, 5 1/4" h., figural, Santa Claus, pack on back serves as handle (ILLUS.)... **3,500-4,000**
Pitcher, lemonade, 7 1/2 " h., figural apple.. **1,000-1,200**
Pitcher, milk, figural red & white parrot handle... **550-600**
Pitcher, milk, musicians decoration............ **150-175**
Pitcher, water, tankard, 9 1/2" h., h.p. pastoral cow scene....................................... **250-300**
Pitcher, water, 6" h., figural Santa Claus, red.. **6,000-9,000**
Pitcher, water, 7 1/4" h., pinched spout, scenic decoration of cows in pasture **250-300**
Plate, 5 1/4" d., leaf-shaped, decorated w/small yellow flowers on green ground, green curved handle... **40**
Plate, 8 1/2" d., scene of man hunting................ **135**

Hanging Rooster Head String Holder

String holder, hanging-type, figural rooster head (ILLUS.) **400-550**
Toothpick holder, figural bell ringer, 3 1/2" h. **200-250**
Toothpick holder, three-handled, scene of horse & wagon.. **150-175**
Vase, 3" h., scene of children w/St. Bernard dog... **75-125**
Vase, 3 5/8" h., footed conical body tapering to a swelled neck flanked by four loop handles, decorated w/hunting scene, man & woman on horses, unmarked........ **50-75**
Vase, 4" h., two-handled, decorated w/long-tailed Bird of Paradise............................ **300-350**
Vase, 5" h., "tapestry," bulbous ovoid body tapering to a short slender flaring neck, "Castle by the Lake" landscape scene **300-350**
Vase, 5 1/4" h., ovoid body w/short cylindrical neck, medallion portrait framed w/gold band in incised leaf design w/enamel trim **200-250**
Vase, 7 3/4" h., mercury & floral finish, ca. 1919, artist-signed & signed "Kgl. Priv. Tettau"... **250**

Royal Bayreuth Waterfall Vase

Vase, 8" h., bulbous body on short quatrefoil foot, side C-scroll handles w/decorative ends, short reticulated neck w/flaring rim, decorated w/waterfall scene (ILLUS.) **200-250**
Vase, 8" h., decorated w/scene of hunter & dogs... **200-250**

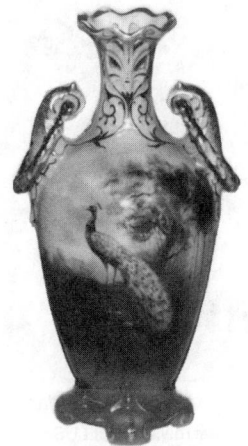

Vase with Peacock

Vase, 9 1/2" h., peacock decoration, openwork on neck & at base, ornate scroll
handles, lavish gold trim (ILLUS.).......... **700-750**
Vase, double-bud, ovoid body w/two angled
short flaring necks joined by a small han-
dle, scene of Dutch children **100-150**

Small Royal Bayreuth Vases

Vases, 3 1/8" h., 2 5/8" d., squatty bulbous
lower body below the tall tapering sides
ending in a ringed neck & flanked by
loop handles, one w/scene of Dutch boy
& girl playing w/brown dog & the other
w/scene of Dutch boy & girl playing
w/white & brown dog, green mark, pr.
(ILLUS.) **75-125**

Royal Copley

*Royal Copley was a trade name used by the Spauld-
ing China Company of Sebring, Ohio, during the 1940s
and 1950s for a variety of ceramic figurines, planters
and other decorative pieces. Similar pieces were also
produced under the trade name "Royal Windsor" as
well as the Spaulding China mark.*

*The Spaulding China Company stopped producing in
1957, but for the next two years other potteries finished
production of its outstanding orders. Today these originally inexpensive wares are developing a dedicated collector following.*

Figurines

Airedale Figurine

Airedale, seated, brown & white, 6 1/2" h.
(ILLUS.) **$35-40**
Cockatoos, 7 1/4" h. **40-50**
Deer & Fawn, 8 1/2" h. **50-60**
Dog, 8" h. **35-40**
Hen & Rooster, Royal Windsor mark, 6 1/2"
& 7" h., pr. **100-120**
Kingfishers, 5" h. **35-45**

Oriental Boy & Girl Figurines

Oriental Boy & Oriental Girl, standing,
7 1/2" h., pr. (ILLUS.) **30-50**
Sea Gulls, 8" h. **30-50**
Swallow with extended wings, 7" h. **90-110**
Thrushes, 6 1/2" h. **15-20**
Wrens, 6 1/4" h. **15-20**

Planters

Angel on Star Planter

Angel on Star, white relief figure on creamy
yellow ground, 6 3/4" h. (ILLUS.)............... **25-35**
Balinese Girl, 8 1/2" h. **40-50**
Big Hat Chinese Boy & Girl, 7 1/2" h., pr. ... **40-50**
Cinderella's Coach, 6" h., 3 1/4" h. **20-25**
Cocker Spaniel, 8" h. **25-30**

Doe & Fawn Head Planter

Doe & Fawn Head, rectangular log-form
planter, 5 1/4" h. (ILLUS.) **40-50**

Dog with Raised Paw Planter

Dog with Raised Paw, 7 1/2" h. (ILLUS.) **60-70**
Dogwood, oval, 3 1/2" h................................... **25-30**
Duck with Mailbox, 6 3/4" h............................ **60-70**
Dutch Boy & Girl with Buckets, 6 1/4" h.,
pr.. **50-75**

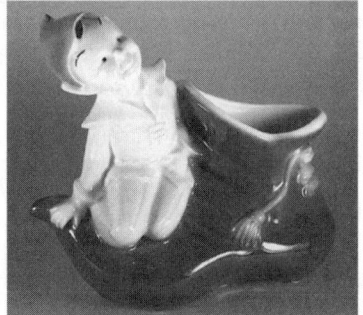

Elf and Shoe Planter

Elf and Shoe, 6" h. (ILLUS.) **50-60**
Fighting Cock, 6 1/2" h.................................... **50-60**

Girl on Wheelbarrow Planter

Girl on Wheelbarrow, 7" h. (ILLUS.)............. **40-45**
High Tail Rooster, 7 3/4" h. **50-60**

Kitten and Book Planter

Kitten and Book, 6 1/2" h. (ILLUS.)............... **40-50**
Mallard Duck, standing, 8" h.......................... **15-20**
Mature Wood Duck, 7 1/4" h. **30-40**
**Oriental Boy with Basket on Back & Ori-
ental Girl with Basket on Back,** 8" h.,
pr... **120-130**
Peter Rabbit, 6 1/2" h. **80-90**

Reclining Poodle Planter

Poodle, reclining, white w/black nose &
eyes, 8" l. (ILLUS.)...................................... **70-80**

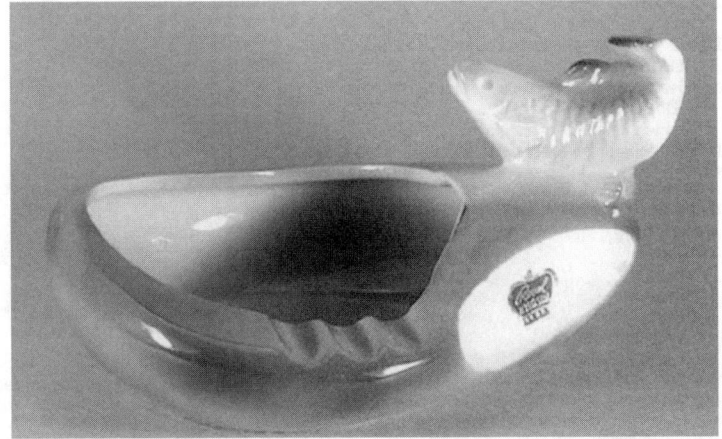

Leaping Salmon Ashtray

Ribbed Star Royal Windsor Planter

Ribbed Star, all-white, "Royal Windsor" sticker, 4 3/4" h. (ILLUS.)............................ **30-35**

Rare Teddy Bear with Concertina

Teddy Bear with Concertina, rare, 7 1/4" h. (ILLUS.) **100-125**

Stuffed Animal Elephant Planter

Stuffed Animal Elephant, pale green & white, 6 1/2" h. (ILLUS.) **80-90**
Tanagers, 6 1/4" h.. **25-35**
Teddy Bear, white, 8" h.................................... **75-90**

Tony Head Planter

Tony Head, man wearing large blue hat, 8 1/4" h. (ILLUS.) **50-75**
Woodpeckers, 6 1/4" h. **25-35**

Miscellaneous

Ashtray, Leaping Salmon, oblong boat-
shaped bowl w/figural salmon on rim,
5 x 6 1/4" (ILLUS., top of page) **30-40**
Bank, Teddy Bear, 7 1/2" h. **100-120**
Pitcher, Floral Beauty, 8" h. **70-85**
Vase, 5 3/4" h., Fish, open center **45-60**
Vase, 6 1/4" h., footed pillow-shape, ivy
decoration **20-25**
Vase, 7 1/4" h., Deer, open center **35-40**
Vase, 8 1/4" h., Dogwood **30-40**
Wall plaque-planters, Hen & Rooster,
6 3/4" h., pr. **120-150**

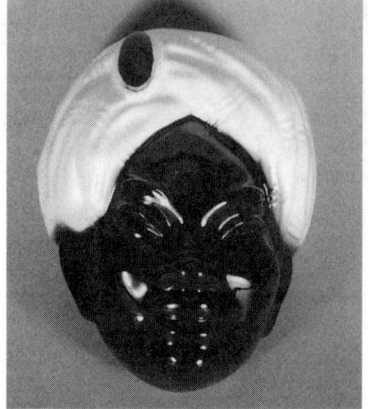

Island Man Wall Pocket

Wall pocket, Island Man, black head wear-
ing white turban, 8" h. (ILLUS.) **130-150**
Wall pocket, Spice Box, 5 1/2" h. **80-90**

Royal Worcester

*This porcelain has been made by the Royal Worcester
Porcelain Co. at Worcester, England, from 1862 to the
present. Royal Worcester is distinguished from wares
made at Worcester between 1751 and 1862, which are
referred to only as Worcester by collectors.*

Royal Worcester Marks

Game plates, each naturalistically painted
w/a curing game bird against a yellow
ground & within a faux textile-patterned
brown border, brown printed crowned
globe mark, date code for 1883, 9 1/8" d.,
set of 11 .... **$353**
Vase, 6 1/2" h., majolica, figural, a trumpet-
form green vase w/large green leaves
behind the figure of a large brown & grey

bird (professional repair to vase rim & tail
& wing of bird) **413**

Royal Worcester Majolica Vases

Vases, 8 1/2" h., majolica, modeled as large
white & tan nautilus shells raised on red
coral stems & green seaweed on an oval
shell-molded foot, late 19th c., pr.
(ILLUS.) **4,400**
Wall pockets, majolica, molded as a long,
pointed bird's nest in greens & brown, a
tall pointed leaf-form top w/a large
spread-winged bird swooping down, professional repair to points, late 19th c.,
12" l., pr. **825**

R.S. Prussia & Related Wares

*Ornately decorated china marked "R.S. Prussia" and
"R.S. Germany" continues to grow in popularity.
According to the Third Series of Mary Frank Gaston's
Encyclopedia of R.S. Prussia (Collector Books, Pad-
ucah, Kentucky), these marks were used by the Reinhold
Schlegelmilch porcelain factories located in Suhl in the
Germanic regions known as "Prussia" prior to World
War I, and in Tillowitz, Silesia, which became part of
Poland after World War II. Other marks sought by col-
lectors include "R.S. Suhl," "R.S." steeple or church
marks, and "R.S. Poland."*

*The Suhl factory was founded by Reinhold
Schlegelmilch in 1869 and closed in 1917. The Tillowitz
factory was established in 1895 by Erhard Schlegelmilch, Reinhold's son. This china customarily bears the
phrase "R.S. Germany" and "R.S. Tillowitz." The
Tillowitz factory closed in 1945, but it was re-opened for
a few years under Polish administration.*

*Prices are high and collectors should beware of the
forgeries that sometimes find their way onto the market.
Mold names and numbers are taken from Mary Frank
Gaston's books on R.S. Prussia.*

*The "Prussia" and "R.S. Suhl" marks have been
reproduced, so buy with care. Later copies of these
marks are well done, but quality of porcelain is inferior
to the production in the 1890-1920 era.*

*Collectors are also interested in the porcelain prod-
ucts made by the Erdmann Schlegelmilch factory. This
factory was founded by three brothers in Suhl in 1861.
They named the factory in honor of their father, Erdmann Schlegelmilch. A variety of marks incorporating
the "E.S." initials were used. The factory closed circa
1935. The Erdmann Schlegelmilch factory was an earlier and entirely separate business from the Reinhold
Schlegelmilch factory. The two were not related to each
other.*

R.S. Prussia & Related Marks

R.S. Germany

Berry set: 9" master bowl & six matching 5 1/2" sauce dishes, Iris mold, decorated w/large red roses, 7 pcs....................... **$500-550**

Bowl, 10" d., decorated w/wild roses, raspberries & blueberries, glossy glaze **125-175**

Bowl, large, Lettuce mold, floral decoration. lustre finish **300-350**

R.S. Germany Cake Plate

Cake plate, double-pierced small gold side handles, decorated w/a scene of a maid-en near a cottage at the edge of a dark forest, 10" d. (ILLUS.)............................. **275-325**

Creamer, Mold 640, decorated w/roses, gold trim on ruffled rim & ornate handle **35-50**

Cup & saucer, demitasse, ornate handle, eight-footed **75-100**

Mustard jar, cov., calla lily decoration **65-100**

Plate, 7 1/4" d., poppy decoration.................. **30-50**

Salad set, 10 1/2" d. lettuce bowl & six 8" d. matching plates, Mold 12, Iris decoration on pearl lustre finish, 7 pcs..................... **300-350**

Tray, handled, decorated w/large white & green poppies, 15 1/4" l. **275-300**

R.S. Prussia

Bell, tall trumpet-form ruffled body w/twig handle, decorated w/small purple flowers & green leaves on white ground, unmarked, 3 1/2" l. **300-350**

Berry set: master bowl & six sauce dishes; five-lobed, floral relief rim w/forget-me-nots & water lilies decoration, artist-signed, 7 pcs... **400-450**

Berry set: master bowl & six sauce dishes; Ribbon & Jewel mold (Mold 18) w/Melon Eaters decoration, 7 pcs. (ILLUS., bottom of page)..................................... **3,500-3,800**

Bowl, 9 3/4" d., Iris variant mold, rosette center & pale green floral decoration... **250-300**

Bowl, 10" d., Icicle mold (Mold 7), red & gold border around the creamy satin interior decorated w/large gold roses **450-525**

Bowl, 10" d., Mold 202, gold beaded rim, double swans center scene in shades of beige & white, unmarked **200-225**

Bowl, 10 1/4" d., center decoration of pink roses w/pearlized finish, border in shades of lavender & blue w/satin finish, lavish gold trim (unlisted mold) **400-450**

Bowl, 10 1/2" d., Countess Potocka portrait decoration, heavy gold trim **4,000-4,300**

Bowl, 10 1/2" d., decorated w/scene of Dice Throwers, red trim................................. **900-1,200**

Bowl, 10 1/2" d., Iris mold, poppy decoration... **350-400**

Ribbon & Jewel Melon Eaters Berry Set

Ornate Mold 211 Bowl with Roses

Bowl, 10 1/2" d., Mold 211, deeply fluted scalloped border, decorated w/large roses in pink, white & yellow, shadow flowers & blue trim around border (ILLUS.)... **250-300**

Bowl, 10 1/2" d., Point & Clover mold (Mold 82), decorated w/pink roses & green leaves w/shadow flowers & a Tiffany finish **250-300**

Bowl, 11" d., 3" h., Sunflower mold, satin finish **450-500**

Bowl, 11" d., Mold 22, four large jewels, satin finish... **250-300**

Bowl, 11" d., 3" h., Fishscale mold, decorated w/white lilies on purple & orange lustre ground, artist-signed................................ **325-375**

Rare Icicle Bowl & Chocolate Pot

Bowl, 15" d., Icicle mold (Mold 7), Snow Bird decoration, scenic reserves around the rim, very rare (ILLUS. right with chocolate pot)... **12,000-14,000**

Butter dish, cover & insert, Mold 51, floral decoration, unmarked.............................. **200-250**

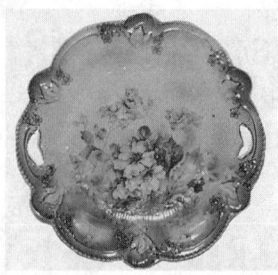

Floral Decorated Cake Plate

Cake plate, open handled, decorated w/pink & white flowers, green leaves, pink & yellow ground, gold trim, 9 3/4" d. (ILLUS.) **225**

Cake plate, open-handled, Mold 155, hanging basket decoration, 10" d.................... **325-350**

Cake plate, open-handled, Fleur-de-Lis mold, decorated w/a castle scene in rust, gold, lavender & yellow, 10 1/4" d... **1,000-1,300**

Cake plate, Iris mold, yellow poppy decoration, 11" d. **250-300**

Cake plate, open-handled, modified Fleur-de-Lis mold, floral decoration, beaded, satin finish, artist-signed, 11" d.............. **175-225**

Cake plate, open handles, Mold 256, satin ground decorated w/flowers in blue, pink & white w/gold trim, 11 1/2" d. **120-150**

Cake plate, open-handled, Mold 343, Winter figural portrait in keyhole medallion, cobalt blue inner border, gold outer border, 12 1/2" d. **400-450**

Cake plate, open-handled, Carnation mold, decorated w/multicolored roses............. **300-350**

Celery dish, Hidden Image mold, colored hair, 5 x 12".. **400-450**

Celery tray, Mold 254, decorated w/green & pink roses, lavish gold tracery, artist-signed, 12" l. **275-325**

Celery tray, Mold 255, decorated w/Surreal Dogwood decoration, pearlized lustre finish, artist-signed, 12 1/4" l. **200-225**

Celery tray, Carnation mold, decorated w/pink & yellow flowers on lavender satin finish, 6 1/2 x 13 1/4" **300-350**

Lebrun-decorated Chocolate Set

R.S. Prussia Tankard Pitchers

Chocolate cup & saucer, decorated w/castle scene **125-150**

Chocolate pot, cov., Icicle mold (Mold 641), rosebush decoration, 10" h. (ILLUS. left with 15" bowl, previous page) **300-400**

Chocolate pot, cov., peacock & pine trees decoration.. **650-750**

Chocolate set: cov. pot & four cups & saucers; sunflower decoration, the set......... **700-750**

Chocolate set: 10" h. cov. chocolate pot & four cups & saucers; Ribbon and Jewel mold, scene of Dice Throwers decoration on pot & single Melon Eater scene on cups, the set..................................... **4,500-5,000**

Chocolate set: 10" h. cov. chocolate pot & six cups & saucers; Mold 517, Madame Lebrun portrait decoration, the set (ILLUS., previous page) **7,500-8,200**

Cracker jar, cov., Mold 540a, beige satin ground w/floral decoration in orchid, yellow & gold, 9 1/2" w. handle to handle, overall 5 1/2" h. **300-350**

Cracker jar, cov., Mold 704, grape leaf decoration, 7" h.. **450-500**

Cracker jar, cov., Hidden Image mold, image on both sides, green mum decoration **900-1,000**

Creamer & cov. sugar bowl, floral decoration, green highlights, pr.......................... **125-150**

Melon Eaters Creamer & Sugar

Creamer & cov. sugar bowl, Ribbon & Jewel mold, single Melon Eaters decoration, pr. (ILLUS.) **1,500-1,800**

Cup & saucer, decorated w/pink roses, peg feet & scalloped rim, cup 1 3/4" h., saucer 4 1/4" d., pr. **125-175**

Dessert set: pedestal cup & saucer, oversized creamer & sugar bowl, two 9 3/4" d., handled plates, eleven 7 1/4" d.

plates, nine cups & saucers; plain mold, decoration w/pink poppies w/tints of aqua, yellow & purple, all pieces are matching, the set................................ **2,200-2,500**

Dresser tray, Icicle mold, scenic decoration, Man in the Mountain, 7 x 11 1/2".. **600-700**

Hair receiver, cov., Mold 814, Surreal Dogwood decoration **150-175**

Model of a lady's slipper, embossed scrolling on instep & heel & embossed feather on one side of slipper, a dotted medallion w/roses & lily-of-the-valley on the other, shaded turquoise blue w/fancy rim trimmed w/gold, 8" l. **250-300**

Mug, rose decoration on pink satin finish .. **125-175**

Mustard pot, cov., Mold 509a, decorated w/white flowers, glossy light green ground... **150-175**

Nut bowl, footed, Point & Clover mold, decorated w/ten roses in shades of salmon, yellow & rose against a pink, green & gold lustre-finished ground, 6 1/2" d. **150-200**

Pin dish, cov., Hidden Image mold, floral decoration, 2 3/4 x 4 3/4"........................ **350-450**

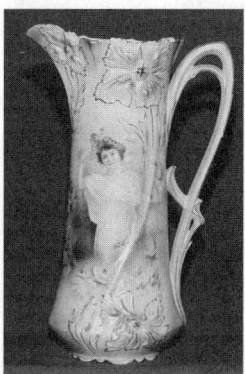

Carnation - Summer Season Pitcher

Pitcher, tankard, 12 1/2" h., Carnation mold (Mold 526), Summer Season decoration, pink border trim (ILLUS.) **7,000-8,000**

Pitcher, cider, 7" h., iris decoration w/green & gold background.................................... **250-300**

Pitcher, tankard, 10" h., Mold 584, decorated w/hanging basket of pink & white roses.. **700-750**

Pitcher, tankard, 12" h., Mold 538, decorated w/Melon Eaters scene (ILLUS. left, top of previous page)........................ **3,500-4,000**

Pitcher, tankard, 13" h., decorated w/scene of Old Man in Mountain & swans on lake (ILLUS. right w/other tankard pitcher, top of previous page)............................. **4,000-4,500**

Pitcher, tankard, 13 1/2" h., Carnation Mold, pink poppy decoration, green ground.. **750-850**

Plaque, decorated w/scene of woman w/dog, 9 1/4 x 13"............................. **2,000-2,500**

Plate, 7 1/2" d., Carnation mold, decorated w/pink roses, lavender ground, satin finish.. **200-250**

Plate, 8 1/2" d., Gibson Girl portrait decoration, maroon bonnet................................. **500-550**

Plate, 8 1/2" d., Mold 263, pink & white roses decoration..................................... **175-200**

Plate, 8 3/4" d., Mold 278, center decoration of pink poppies on white ground, green border.. **150-175**

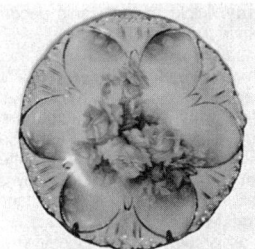

Mold 91 Rose-decorated Plate

Plate, 8 3/4" d., Mold 91, yellow roses decoration on pink ground, shiny yellow border (ILLUS.)... **150-200**

Plate, 9 3/4" d., Icicle mold, swan decoration.. **800-900**

Plate, 11" d., Point & Clover mold, Melon Eater decoration................................... **900-1,100**

Plate, dessert, Mold 506, branches of pink roses & green leaves against a shaded bluish green to white ground w/shadow flowers & satin finish.............................. **100-125**

Relish Dish with Spring Season

Relish dish, Iris mold (Mold 25), oval w/scalloped sides & end loop handles, Spring Season portrait surrounded by dark border w/iris, 4 1/2 x 9 1/2" (ILLUS.)... **1,200-1,400**

Relish dish, scene of masted ship, 4 1/2 x 9 1/2"... **250-300**

Relish dish, Mold 82, decorated w/forget-me-nots & multicolored carnations, six jeweled domes... **125-175**

Spooner/vase, Mold 502, three-handled, decorated w/delicate roses & gold trim, unsigned, 4 1/4" h...................................... **75-100**

Syrup pitcher & underplate, Mold 507, white & pink roses on a shaded brown to pale yellow ground, 2 pcs...................... **200-250**

Tea set: cov. teapot, creamer & cov. sugar bowl; floral decoration, the set............... **300-350**

Tea set: cov. teapot, creamer & cov. sugar bowl; pedestal base, scene of Colonial children, 3 pcs. **600-700**

Toothpick holder, ribbed hexagonal shape w/two handles, decorated w/colorful roses **265-300**

Toothpick holder, three-handled, decorated w/white daisies on blue ground, gold handles & trim on top **150-175**

Tray, pierced handles, Mold 82, decorated w/full blossom red & pink roses, gold Royal Vienna mark, 8 x 11 1/8" **250-300**

Vase, 4" h., salesman's sample, handled, Mold 914, decorated w/large lilies & green foliage, raised beading around shoulder, gold handles, shaded green ground, artist-signed................................ **150-175**

Vase, 5 1/2" h., cottage & mill scene decoration, cobalt trim...................................... **550-650**

Vase, 6 1/4" h., decorated w/brown & cream shadow flowers.. **75-100**

Vase, 8" h., cylindrical body w/incurved angled shoulder handles, decorated w/parrots on white satin ground, unmarked **2,200-2,600**

R.S. Prussia Vases with Animals

Vase, 8" h., ovoid body w/wide shoulder tapering to cylindrical neck w/flared rim, decorated w/scene of black swans (ILLUS. left).. **1,200-1,500**

Vase, 10" h., ovoid body decorated w/scene of two tigers, pastel satin finish (ILLUS. right) **5,500-7,000**

Other Marks

Bowl, 10" d., Cabbage mold w/center rose decoration (R.S. Tillowitz)........................ **250-300**

Chocolate pot, cov., Art Nouveau decoration, glossy finish (R.S. Tillowitz - Silesia)....... **55**

Coffee set: 6 5/8" l., 3 1/4" d., cov. ovoid coffeepot & two cups & saucers; each piece decorated w/a color oval reserve w/a different romantic scene within a thin gilt border & a deep burgundy panel against a creamy white ground trimmed w/gilt scrolls, a wide red & narrow dark green border band on each, saucers 2 3/4" d., cups 2 1/4" h., blue beehive & R.S. Suhl marks, the set **650**

Match holder, hanging-type on attached backplate decorated w/a scene of a man w/mug of beer & pipe (E.S. Prov. Saxe) **175-200**

Plate, 7 3/4" d., Sunflower mold, rose pink & yellow roses w/Tiffany finish (Wheelock Prussia).. **125-150**

Plate, 10 1/2" d., lovely center portrait of Madame DuBarry, four cameos in different poses on a deep burgundy lustre border band (E.W. Prov. Saxe).................... **500-600**

E. Schlegelmilch Handled Server

Server, center-handled, decorated w/orange, white & pink poppies on a shaded bluish grey ground, w/a narrow gilt border band, 8 1/2" d., 3 3/4" h., E. Schlegelmilch - Thuringia (ILLUS.) **100-150**

Tray, rectangular, open-handled, bright colored bird decoration, 5 x 14" (R.S. Tillowitz) **75-100**

Melon Eaters Vase

Vase, 6 3/8" h., 3" d., wide, ovoid, shouldered body tapering to slender, flaring cylindrical neck, Melon Eaters decoration surrounded by gold border w/reverse decorated w/heart-shaped area w/dainty pink roses on pastel ground, two-thirds of vase covered in purplish lustre w/fine gold leaves & flowers overall, neck in off white w/fine gold floral decoration, artist-signed in gold, Red Crown "Viersa" mark, Suhl or Tillowitz (ILLUS.) **350-400**

Vase, 7 1/2" h., wide, squatty, bulbous base tapering sharply to a tall, slender, cylindrical neck w/an upturned four-lobed rim, long slender gold handles from rim to shoulder, decorated w/a center reserve of a standing Art Nouveau maiden w/her hands behind her head & a peacock behind her framed by delicate gold scrolls & beading & floral bouquets, all on a pearl lustre ground (Prov. Saxe - E.W. Germany)... **375-425**

Vase, 9 1/4" h., gently tapering cylindrical body w/a wide, cupped, scalloped gilt rim, pierced gold serpentine handles from rim to center of sides, decorated around the body w/large blossoms in purple, pink, yellow & green on a shaded brownish green ground (Prove. Saxe)... **125-150**

Vase, 10" h., gold Rococo handles, scene of sleeping maiden w/cherub decoration (E.S. Royal Saxe) **350-400**

Vase, 13 1/2" h., twisted gold handles, portrait of "Goddess of Fire," iridescent burgundy & opalescent colors w/lavish gold trim (Prov. Saxe, E.S. Germany)........... **650-700**

Russel Wright Designs

The innovative dinnerwares designed by Russel Wright and produced by various companies beginning in the late 1930s were an immediate success with a society that was turning to a more casual and informal lifestyle. His designs, with their flowing lines and unconventional shapes, were produced in many different colors, which allowed a hostess to arrange creative tables.

Although not antique, these designs, which we list below by line and manufacturer, are highly collectible. In addition to dinnerwares, Wright was also known as a trendsetter in the design of furniture, glassware, lamps, fabric and a multitude of other household goods.

IROQUOIS
CASUAL CHINA
Russel Wright

*Russel
Wright*
**MFG. BY
STEUBENVILLE**

Russel Wright Marks

American Modern (Steubenville Pottery Co.)

Baker, glacier blue, small $55
Bowl, child's, black chutney 100
Bowl, fruit, lug handle, cedar green 30

Group of American Modern Pieces

Bowl, fruit, lug handle, chartreuse (ILLUS. left) 20
Bowl, salad, cedar green 100
Bowl, soup, lug handle, bean brown 35
Butter dish, cov., white 365
Carafe w/stopper, bean brown 500
Coaster, granite grey 20
Coffee cup cover, black chutney 175
Coffeepot, cov., black chutney 250
Coffeepot, cov., seafoam blue 275
Coffeepot, cov., demitasse, coral 120
Creamer, cedar green 20
Cup & saucer, coffee, cantaloupe 40
Cup & saucer, demitasse, cantaloupe 60
Gravy boat, chartreuse 20
Hostess plate & cup, cedar green, pr. 100
Ice box jar, cov., black chutney 225
Mug (tumbler), black chutney 90
Pickle dish, seafoam blue 25
Pitcher, cov., water, cedar green .... 400+
Pitcher, water, 12" h., bean brown 150
Pitcher, water, 12" h., seafoam blue 125
Plate, salad, 8" d., seafoam blue 18
Plate, dinner, 10" d., cantaloupe 40
Plate, chop, 13" sq., chartreuse 30
Plate, child's, coral 60
Platter, 13 3/4" l., oblong, granite grey 35
Ramekin, cov., individual, bean brown 250
Relish dish, divided, raffia handle, coral 175
Relish rosette, seafoam blue 250
Salad fork & spoon, white, pr. 300
Sauceboat, coral 40
Shaker, single, glacier blue 20
Stack server, cov., cedar green (ILLUS. back, with fruit bowl) 270
Stack server, cov., granite grey 250
Sugar bowl, cov., granite grey 15
Teapot, cov., seafoam blue............................... 135
Tumbler, child's, granite grey 125
Vegetable bowl, cov., coral, 12" l. 45
Vegetable dish, open, divided, cedar green (ILLUS. right front, with fruit bowl) 130
Vegetable dish, open, oval, granite grey, 10" l. 25

Casual China (Iroquois China Co.)

Bowl, 5" d., cereal, ripe apricot 15
Bowl, 5 3/4" d., fruit, oyster grey 20
Butter dish, cov., brick red, 1/4 lb. .... 1,000+
Butter dish, cov., pink sherbet 95

Carafe, cov., oyster grey .... 500+
Casserole, deep tureen, lemon yellow 250
Coffeepot, cov., nutmeg brown.......................... 140
Coffeepot, cov., sugar white 200
Coffeepot, cov., demitasse, lemon yellow 125
Cover for cereal/soup bowl 30
Cover for water pitcher 60
Creamer, family-style, pink sherbet...................... 40
Cup & saucer, avocado yellow 20
Cup & saucer, coffee, oyster grey (ILLUS. front center w/other cups & saucers).............. 30
Cup & saucer, tea, lemon yellow (ILLUS. front left w/other cups & saucers)................... 25

Casual Cups & Saucers & Shakers

Cup & saucer, demitasse, avocado yellow (ILLUS. front right w/other cups & saucers) 150-175
Cup & saucer, demitasse, sugar white 225
Gravy, redesigned w/cover which becomes stand, sugar white.. 250
Gravy stand, ice blue 40
Gravy w/attached stand, avocado yellow 100
Gumbo soup bowl, cantaloupe, 21 oz.............. 60
Gumbo soup bowl, ice blue, 21 oz. 40
Mug, pink sherbet, 13 oz. 100
Mug, restyled, ice blue....................................... 100
Pepper mill, lemon yellow .... 300+
Pitcher, cov., ice blue, 1 1/2 qt......................... 150
Plate, bread & butter, 6 1/2" d., lettuce green.. 10
Plate, luncheon, 9 1/2" d., pink sherbet 17
Plate, chop, 13 7/8" d., ice blue.......................... 50
Platter, 10 1/4" oval, individual, lettuce green.. 50
Platter, 12 3/4" oval, parsley green 40
Salt & pepper shakers, stacking-type, ice blue, pr. 25
Salt & pepper shakers, stacking-type, oyster grey, pr. (ILLUS. left rear, with cups & saucers)... 60
Salt shaker & pepper mill, redesigned, lemon yellow, pr. (ILLUS. right rear, with cups & saucers).. 500+
Soup, cov., redesigned, 18 oz............................. 30
Sugar, redesigned, brick red .... 275+
Sugar, stacking-type, sugar white, family size 40
Tumbler, iced tea, Pinch patt., seafoam blue, Imperial Glass Co., 14 oz. 50
Vegetable dish, open, cantaloupe, 10" d........... 85
Vegetable dish, open, nutmeg brown, 8 1/8", 36 oz.. 35

Iroquois Casual Cookware

Casserole, 3 qt. .... 225+
Dutch oven .... 500+
Fry pan, cov. .... 500+

Sauce pan, cov. .... **500+**
Serving tray, electric, 12 3/4 x 17 1/2"......... **2,000+**

Sascha Brastoff

Sascha Brastoff dedicated his life to creating works with a flair all his own. He was a costume designer for major movie studios, a dancer, a window dresser and a talented painter. The creator in Sascha put him on the path to ceramics early in life, when he was awarded a scholarship to the Cleveland Art School; however, he also worked with watercolors, charcoals, pastels, resin, fabrics, ceramics, metal sculptures, and enamels. Nelson Rockefeller, Brastoff's friend, understood the uniqueness of his talents and, in 1953, he built a complex in Los Angeles, California, to house the many creations Sascha was able to produce.

A full line of handpainted china with names such as Allegro, La Jolla, Roman Coin and Night Song was created. Surf Ballet was a popular dinnerware line with a look achieved by dipping pieces of blue, pink or yellow into real gold or platinum. Also highly popular was Sascha's line of enamels on copper. Many collectors do not know that Sascha dabbled in textiles. A yard of cloth in good condition might command several hundred dollars on today's market. His artware items included patterns such as Star Steed, a leaping-fantasy horse, and Rooftops, a series of houses where the roofs were the prominent feature. These pieces were - and continue to be - two of the most highly collectible Sascha artware patterns.

Sascha Brastoff also created a line of Alaskan-motif items. Many collectors confuse Matthew Adams pieces with those of Sascha. Even though Adams worked for Brastoff for a period of time, his pieces are not nearly as sought after as those that Sascha created.

Brastoff's crystal ball served him well during his lifetime. In the late 1940s and early 1950s he created a series of Western-motif cache pots that excite any collector when found today. Almost a decade before the poodle craze in the 1950s, Sascha created a line of poodle products. In the 1950s, cigarette smoking was at an all-time high and Sascha was there with smoking accessories.

From 1947 to 1952 pieces were signed "Sascha B." or with the full signature, "Sascha Brastoff." After 1953 and before 1962, during the years of his factory-studio, pieces done by his employees showed "Sascha B." and, more often than not, also included the Chanticleer back stamp. Caution should be taken to understand that the Chanticleer with the full name "Sascha Brastoff" below it is not the "full signature" mark that elevates pieces to substantial prices. The Chanticleer mark is usually in gold and will incorporate Sascha's work name in the same color. Sascha's personal full signature is the one commanding the high prices.

Health problems forced Sascha to leave his company in 1963. After 1962 pieces were marked "Sascha B." and also included the "R" in a circle trademark. Ten years later the business closed.

Sascha Brastoff died on February 4, 1993. The passing of this flamboyant artist, whose special character was well reflected in his work, means that similar creations will probably never be achieved again.

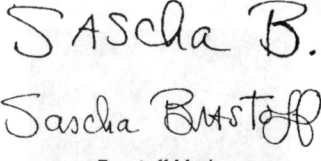

Brastoff Marks

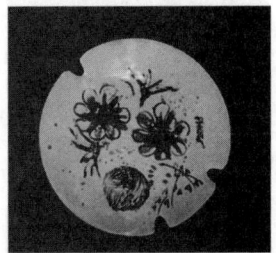

Sascha Brastoff Enamel Ashtray

Ashtray, enamel, floral design on white, 5 1/2" d. (ILLUS.) **$25**
Ashtray, Western scene w/covered wagon, rare promotional piece, 14" w. **210**
Bowl, 8" d., footed, abstract design..................... **45**
Candleholder, resin, green or blue, 6" h., each.. **65**
Cigarette box, cov., "Star Steed" decoration.. **100**
Dish, horse decoration on green ground, 6 1/2" sq. **45**

Sascha Brastoff Gravy Boat

Gravy boat, w/attached undertray, scalloped rim, pink w/silver accents (ILLUS.) **65**

Model of polar bear, blue resin, 10" h............... **550**
Model of Victorian shoe, Surf Ballet glaze,
10" h. **255**

Sascha Brastoff Pipe

Pipe, sinuous shape, abstract design w/gold
accents, 4" l. (ILLUS.)....................................... **75**

Sascha Brastoff Fish Plate

Plate, 6 1/2" d., fish shape & design
(ILLUS.)... **75**
Plate, 9" d., Merbaby patt. **145**

Sascha Brastoff Enamel Plate

Plate, 11 1/2" d., enamel, orange & gold ab-
stract design, factory hanger on back
(ILLUS.)... **85**
Vase, 5" h., Provincial Rooster patt., No.
F20... **515**

Schafer & Vater

*Founded in Rudolstadt, Thuringia, Germany in 1890,
the Schafer and Vater Porcelain Factory specialized in
decorative pieces of porcelain usually in white or colored bisque. It produced many novelty figural items such
as creamers, toothpick holders, boxes and hatpin holders, and also a line of jasper ware with white relief decoration in imitation of the famous Wedgwood jasper
wares. The firm also decorated whiteware blanks.*

*The company ceased production in 1962, and collec-
tors now seek out its charming pieces, which may be
marked with a crown over a starburst containing the
script letter "R."*

Schafer & Vater Mark

Bottle, figural, a figure of a male golfer in
color & wearing a white outfit w/knickers
& a cap leaning over a large brown flat-
sided round flask w/a short neck projecting at an angle, the flask inscribed "Golf
and Good Spirits Make a Good Highball,"
4 1/2" h. (missing stopper)............................ **$322**
Bottle, figural, a skeleton standing envel-
oped in a sheet marked on the front
"Gift!" (Poison), white w/brown trim, No.
6109, 9 1/2" h. **334**
Bottle, figural, large rounded head of a
young man w/wild hair wearing an inverted funnel for a hat, the funnel inscribed
"Nurnberger Trichter," overall glossy
washed blue glaze, No. 6218, 8" h. **403**
Bottle, tall cylindrical form w/rounded shoulder to small cylindrical neck & small
shoulder handle, brown, the front molded
w/a naughty maiden in color seated in the
bowl of a large white champagne glass &
holding a single red rose, inscribed below
"Prosit Blume," 7" h. (stopper missing)......... **138**
Bottle set: figural bottle, one shot glass &
oblong tray; the bottle in the form of a
standing stocky man in clown outfit holding up a small pig & w/grapevines below,
a small cylindrical short glass molded as
a comical face, overall glossy washed
dark blue glaze, bottle 7 3/4" h., the set
(small chip on bottom of man's foot, stop-
per missing) **184**
Bottle set: figural bottle, six cups & tray;
bottle in the form of a comical short, fat
doctor w/curled wig standing beside a
large upright syringe, six small cylindrical
cups w/names of medicines around the
base resting on a round tray, pointed tip
of syringe forms bottle stopper, overall
glossy washed blue glaze, bottle
9 3/4" h., the set **575**

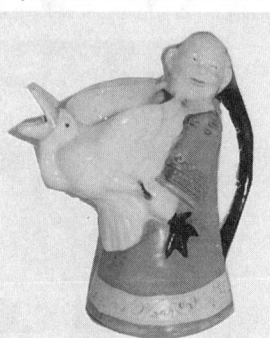

Figural Chinese Man Creamer

Creamer, figural, in the form of a Chinese man wearing a long orange robe, holding a large white goose by the feet while it tries to fly away, thus forming the spout w/the open beak for pouring, the man's long black pigtail forming the handle, unmarked, 2 1/4" w., 4" h. (ILLUS.) **125**

Figurines, Sun Ladies & Moon Men, two w/a smiling cream-colored sun head on the body of a seated late-Victorian woman, one w/her arms away from her body, wearing a black jacket, white dress & red slippers w/a red handbag in her lap, the other w/a matching outfit but playing a banjo; the three men w/a cream crescent moon head, one head smoking a pipe & attached to the body of a reclining late-Victorian man wearing a short white coat w/black collar & white knee breeches, a second man wearing a similar outfit but kneeling & holding out a bouquet w/one hand & a pink hat in the other, the third man reclining on his stomach w/his lower legs in the air, No. 3150 through 3155, 3 1/2 to 4 1/2" l., the set of 5 (two women w/minor chip repairs) **1,380**

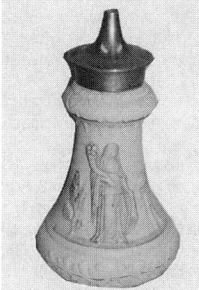

Schafer & Vater Sugar Shaker

Sugar shaker w/original metal top, bisque, a slender waisted cylindrical white form w/a band of embossed scrolls around the wide bottom & a molded lappet band at the top, the body molded in relief w/figures of Grecian women tinted grey w/an altar in pink & foliage in green, 3 1/4" d., 6 1/8" h. (ILLUS.)............................. **135**

Tea set: cov. teapot, cov. sugar bowl, creamer & two cups & saucers; figural, all in pink bisque w/grey-green trim, the teapot body formed by the wide deep skirt of a woman, a slender ribbed spout at the front, the cover formed by the torso of the woman wearing a ruffled collar & balloon sleeves, a tall ribbon on her head, the handle formed by a slender, elongated figure of a bent-over gentleman wearing a tall top hat, the figural sugar bowl in the form of a similar lady but w/small scroll handles at the sides, the open creamer in the form of a wide skirt w/the handle in the form of the bent-over gentleman, each cup w/a gentleman handle & on a ruffled saucer, all pieces w/molded ornate scrolls & swags, No. 3861, 3862 &

3863, 4" to 7" h., the set (few small chips, repaired lines)................................. **834**

Staffordshire Figures

Small figures and groups made of pottery were produced by the majority of the Staffordshire, England potters in the 19th century and were used as mantel decorations or "chimney ornaments," as they were sometimes called. Pairs of dogs were favorites and were turned out by the carload, and 19th-century pieces are still available. Well-painted reproductions also abound, and collectors are urged to exercise caution before investing.

Benjamin Franklin, standing on oblong base w/incorrect inscription "Washington," first half 19th c., 15 1/2" h. (cracks, very minor chips) **$900-950**

Dog, Spaniel, seated position, white w/tan head, ears & portion of back, lock & chain collar, glass eyes, worn gold trim, 13 1/2" h. **250-275**

Dogs, full-bodied w/four separate feet, white, tan & black w/glass eyes, gold collars, 14" l., pr. (one foot chipped) **468**

Figure group, seated mother poodle & two puppies, all in white w/sanded fur trim, painted facial details, deep blue oblong base, 19th c., 4" h. **375-400**

Figure group, Dick Turpin on horseback, ca. 1840, England, 12 1/4" h. **350-400**

Figure group, man & woman sitting under a woven vine, ca. 1860, 13 1/2" h. **168**

Staffordshire Hen on Nest

Hen on nest, white hen trimmed w/black & brown w/red wattle on light brown basketweave base, bisque finish, 5 3/8 x 7", 7" h. (ILLUS.) **650-700**

Horse, yellowware, the standing animal wearing reins, head lowered, on a molded oval base, body heavily splashed w/dark brown, attributed to The Don Pottery, England, ca. 1800-22, 6 1/4" h. (tail & both ears restored) **1,000-1,200**

Rabbits, each recumbent animal w/long ears decorated in polychrome & shown nibbling on lettuce leaves, 19th c., 10 1/4" l., pr. **4,000-4,200**

Staffordshire Transfer Wares

The process of transfer-printing designs on earthenwares developed in England in the late 18th century, and by the mid-19th century most common ceramic wares were decorated in this manner, most often with romantic European or Oriental landscape scenes, animals or flowers. The earliest such wares were printed in dark blue, but a little later light blue, pink, purple, red, black, green and brown were used. A majority of these wares were produced at various English potteries right up until the turn of the 20th century, but French and other European firms also made similar pieces and all are quite collectible. The best reference on this area is Petra Williams' book Staffordshire Romantic Transfer Patterns - Cup Plates and Early Victorian China *(Fountain House East, 1978).*

Rural Scenery Footed Bowl

Bowl, 11" d., 4 1/2" h., footed, deep sides w/lightly scalloped rim, Rural Scenery patt. w/sheep, cow & horse, light blue, Adams, unseen foot rim chip, chip on extreme rim edge (ILLUS.) **$300-350**

Brush box, cov., long oblong form, Wild Rose patt., lakeside landscape on cover, medium blue, 7 1/4" l. (very small unseen base flake) **275-300**

Coffeepot, cov., tall baluster-form body w/bulbous tapering neck w/rolled rim & high domed cover w/acorn finial, swan's-neck spout & angled & pointed handle, dark blue scene of two men talking beside a horse near a stable, ca. 1830, 11 1/2" h. (chip on edge of spout) **1,000-1,200**

Cup & saucer, handleless, Horse patt., dark blue, Stubbs & Kent (small unseen table ring flake on saucer, cup w/mellowing) **375-400**

Pitcher, jug-type, 8 1/2" h., wide ovoid body tapering to a short, rolled neck w/long rim spout & C-scroll handle, scene of a large manor house w/covered walkway, a stream w/sailboat in foreground, large leaves around rim, ochre line around mouth rim, dark blue, ca. 1830s, unknown maker (small spout tip chip, traces of two small spiders in base) **375-400**

Plate, toddy, 5 1/8" d., Running Setter patt., Quadrupeds series, dark blue, Hall, ca. 1830s **275-300**

Plate, 7 1/4" d., Mastiff (Guard Dog) patt., Quadrupeds series, dark blue, Hall, ca. 1830s (stacking wear) **165-185**

Plate, 8 3/4" d., Christmas Eve patt., central scene of family in interior, floral border, Wilkie Series by Clews, ca. 1830s **300-350**

Plate, 10 1/2" d., Canova patt., brown................. **75**

Platter, pearlware blue decorated, chinoiserie motif, England, mid 19th c., 20 1/2" l. (rim ships, knife marks) **600-625**

Platter, 12 1/4" l., oval, Fountain Scenery patt., medium blue, Adams **175-200**

Platter, 13 1/4" l., oval, lightly scalloped rim, Palestine patt., light blue, Adams, ca. 1840 .... **250-275**

Platter, 15 1/2" l., oval, Oriental patt., purple, ca. 1840 (slight edge wear) **330-350**

Fine Palestine Pattern Platter

Platter, 17" l., oval, lightly scalloped rim, Palestine patt., light blue, Adams (ILLUS.) **325-350**

Platter, 19" l., oval, lightly scalloped rim, Tyrolean patt., light blue, Wm. Ridgway, ca. 1840 .... **350-375**

Platter, 19 5/8" l., oval, lightly scalloped rim, Delhi patt., brown, ca. 1840 .... **475-500**

Early Staffordshire Platter

Platter, 20 3/4" l., oval well-and-tree style, Ruins with Horseman in Foreground patt., dark blue, ca. 1830s, unseen foot chip (ILLUS.) **1,200-1,300**

Platter, 21" l., The Italian Pattern, attributed to Spode, blue, early 19th c. (glaze wear, scratches)... **575**

Sauce tureen, cover & undertray, Hare & Pointer patt. on base, Rooster & Fox patt. on undertray, tureen w/footed bulbous body w/rolled rim & domed cover w/berry finial, loop shoulder handles, Quadrupeds series, dark blue, Hall, the set **1,425-1,475**

Soup plate, Common Wolf Trap patt., Oriental Sports series, dark blue, Edward Challinor, ca. 1830s, 8 3/8" d. **300-325**

Soup plate, Llama patt., Quadrupeds series, dark blue, Hall, 10" d. **325-350**

Rare Caledonia Soup Tureen

Soup tureen, cov., bulbous oval tapering deep ribbed body on four peg feet, upturned loop end handles, high domed cover w/squared ropetwist handle, Caledonia patt., purple, Adams, ca. 1840, in-the-making separations in base & ladle hole, 14" l., 9 3/4" h. (ILLUS.) **650-700**

Vegetable dish, open, oval, Shell patt., dark blue, Stubbs & Kent, early 19th c., 12 1/4" l., 2 1/2" h. (scratches, wear)......... **1,150**

Waste bowl, wide flat flaring sides, scene of a woman w/child talking to a man w/a bundle on his stick, dark blue, ca. 1830s, 5 3/4" d., 3" h. **125-150**

Stoneware

Stoneware is essentially a vitreous pottery, impervious to water even in its unglazed state, that has been produced by potteries all over the world for centuries. Utilitarian wares such as crocks, jugs, churns and the like were the most common productions in the numerous potteries that sprang into existence in the United States during the 19th century. These items were often enhanced by the application of a cobalt blue oxide decoration. In addition to the coarse, primarily salt-glazed stonewares, there are other categories of stoneware known by such special names as basalt, jasper and others.

Butter churn, tall, slender, slightly tapering cylindrical form w/short flared neck & eared handles, large cobalt blue slip-quilled sunflower-style blossom on stem w/four leaves below an "8," impressed label "J. Burger, Rochester, N.Y.," late 19th c., 8 gal., 22 3/4" h. (minor lime deposits) **$900-1,100**

Crock, two-handled, slip-quilled cobalt blue bird on branch, impressed "F.A. Plaisted, Gardiner, Maine," 11 1/2" h. **400-450**

Stoneware Crock with Codfish Decoration

Crock, ovoid w/flared mouth & eared handles, incised w/horizontal lines & two codfish on front, "Boston" & "JF" on reverse, Jonathan Fenton, Boston, ca. 1794-97, minor chips, 13" h. (ILLUS.)... **6,000-6,500**

Jar, cov., eared handles, brushed cobalt blue double flower design, "W.A. Mac-Quoid & Co., NY, Little West 12th St.," ca. 1870, 1 1/2 gal., 10" h. (minor staining, lid has some damage)..................... **440**

Jar, ovoid body w/thick molded rim, brushed cobalt blue wide band of leafy scrolls & blossoms around the sides, 12 1/4" h. (hairlines) **325-350**

Jar, tall, swelled, cylindrical body w/short cylindrical neck & eared handles, large upright cobalt blue stenciled flower & leaf wreath flanking a central scroll band above a large "4," late 19th c., 4 gal., 15 1/4" h. **440-460**

Jug, ovoid, decorated w/cobalt blue swags, impressed "C. Croleus Stonemaker New York".. **1,750-1,850**

Jug, ovoid, w/ochre decorated flower, impressed "Lyman and Clark, Gardiner," 12 1/2" h. **1,900-2,100**

Jug, ovoid, w/handles, impressed "Lyman and Clark, Gardiner, #3," w/a freehand "3" in ochre in center, 3 gal., 15" h. **450-500**

Iowa Stoneware Preserving Jar

Preserving jar, cylindrical, w/applied eared handles & rolled rim, brushed cobalt blue floral motif & "2," impressed "Tolman, Eldora, IA," 2 gal. (ILLUS.).................. **3,250-3,500**

Preserving jar, cylindrical, w/heavy molded flat rim, vertical stripes of cobalt blue stenciled stars, 19th c., 9" h. **650-700**

Preserving jar, slightly ovoid w/molded rim, cobalt blue stenciled & freehand decoration, printed "Excelsior Works, Isaac Hewitt, Jr. Rices Landing, PA," 9 1/2" h. **325-350**

Teco Pottery

Teco Pottery was actually the line of art pottery introduced by the American Terra Cotta and Ceramic Company of Terra Cotta (Crystal Lake), Illinois, in 1902. Founded by William D. Gates in 1881, American Terra Cotta originally produced only bricks and drain tile. Because of superior facilities for experimentation, including a chemical laboratory, the company was able to develop an art pottery line, favoring a matte green glaze in the earlier years but eventually achieving a wide range of colors including a metallic lustre glaze and a crystalline glaze. Although some hand-thrown pottery was made, Gates favored a molded ware because it was less expensive to produce. By 1923, Teco Pottery was no longer being made, and in 1930 American Terra Cotta and Ceramic Company was sold. A book on the topic is Teco: Art Pottery of the Prairie School*, by Sharon S. Darling (Erie Art Museum, 1990).*

Teco Mark

Jardiniere, round bulbous body w/heavily molded wide shoulder band around the wide flat mouth supported on four buttressed legs, smooth matte green glaze, stamped "TECO," 11" d., 7" h. **$6,750**

Pitcher, 9" h., 3 1/2" d., corseted form w/an organic wishbone handle & an undulating rim, smooth matte green glaze, stamped "TECO" (small firing flaw to handle) **1,125**

Vase, 3 3/4" h., 3 1/4" d., footed ovoid body w/dimpled sides, wide molded rim, dark speckled matte green & charcoal glaze, incised "Teco/519" (ILLUS. front row, second from right with group of Teco vases)... **619**

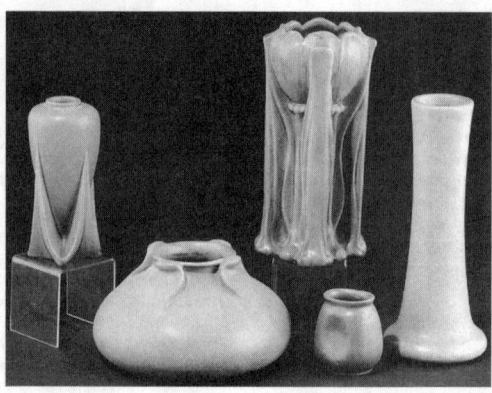

Group of Teco Vase

Vase, 6" h., 9 1/2" d., squatty bulbous body, the wide shoulder tapering to a slightly flared rim w/four curled leaves, smooth matte green glaze, restoration to two rim chips, stamped "Teco/272" (ILLUS. front row, left with group of Teco vases)............. **2,700**

Vase, 8 3/4" h., quatrefoil long ovoid bulbs around the upper half over a gently flaring cylindrical lower half, matte greyish green glaze, two impressed marks............. **1,725**

Vase, 8 3/4" h., 4" d., a tall bullet-shaped body w/a rounded shoulder & small molded mouth, supported by four tall V-form buttresses around the base, smooth medium matte green glaze, stamped mark (ILLUS. back row, left with group of vases, top of page).. **4,219**

Vase, 9" h., 4" d., "rocket ship" style, long tapering ovoid body w/a small molded mouth, wide molded V-shaped fins at the base, unusual mauve matte glaze, stamped "Teco" **7,875**

Vase, 12 1/4" h., 5" d., a large cupped tulip blossom framed by four heavy buttress leaf-molded supports forming the squared body, matte green glaze, stamped "Teco" (ILLUS. back row, right with group of Teco vases)............................ **5,063**

Vase, 13 1/4" h., 5 1/4" d., tall slender tapering cylindrical body w/cushion foot, smooth matte grey glaze, stamped "Teco" (ILLUS. far right with group of Teco vases).. **1,688**

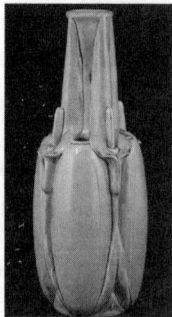

Rare Teco Vase

Vase, 17 1/2" h., 6 1/2" d., tall lobed body w/tapering cylindrical neck & molded rim, embossed calla lily between each lobe & extending to rim, light green matte glaze, restoration to small drill hole on side at base, small nick on leaf point (one of two known), stamped "TECO" (ILLUS.).......... **28,125**

Torquay Pottery

In the second half of the 19th century several art potteries were established in the South Devon region of England to take advantage of a belt of fine red clay there. The coastal town of Torquay gives its name to this range of wares, which often featured incised sgraffito decoration or colorful country-style decoration with mottos.

The most notable potteries operating in the Torquay area were the Watcombe Pottery, The Torquay Terra-cotta Company and the Aller Vale Art Pottery, which merged with Watcombe Pottery in 1901 and continued production until 1962. Other firms whose wares are collectible include Longpark Pottery and The Devonmoor Art Pottery.

Early wares feature unglazed terra cotta items in the Victorian taste including classical busts, statuary and vases and some painted and glazed wares including examples with a celeste blue interior or highlights. In addition to sgraffito designs, other decorations included flowers, Barbotine glazes, Devon pixies framed in leafy scrolls and grotesque figures of cats, dogs and other fanciful animals, produced in the 1890s.

The dozen or so potteries flourishing in the region at the turn of the 20th century introduced their most popular product, Motto Wares, which became the bread and butter line of the local industry. The most popular patterns in this line included Cottage, Black and Colored Cockerels and Scandy, based on Scandinavian rosemaling designs. Most of the mottoes were written in English, with a few in Welsh. On early examples the sayings were often in Devonian dialect. These Motto Wares were sold for years at area seaside resorts and other tourist areas, with some pieces exported to Australia, Canada and, to a lesser extent, the United States. In addition to standard size teawares and novelties, some miniatures and even oversized pieces were offered.

Production at the potteries stopped during World War II, and some of the plants were destroyed in enemy raids. The Watcombe Pottery became Royal Watcombe after the war, and Longpark also started up again but produced simpler patterns. The Dartmouth Pottery, started in 1947, produced cottages similar to those made at Watcombe and also developed a line of figural animals, banks and novelty jugs. The Babbacombe Pottery (1950-59) and St. Marychurch Pottery (ca. 1962-69) were the last two firms to turn out Motto Wares, but these later designs were painted on and the pieces were lighter in color, with less detailing.

Many books on the various potteries are available, and information can be obtained from the products manager of the North American Torquay Society.

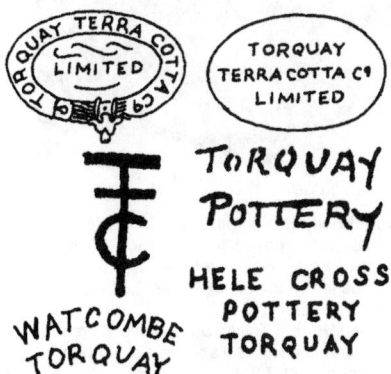

Torquay Pottery Marks

Cockerel Pattern
Cup & saucer, Black Cockerel patt., Motto Ware, "Du 'ee 'ave a cup a Tay," Watcombe Torquay impressed mark, ca. 1910-27, saucer 4 1/2" d., cup 2 1/2" h. **$50**
Dairy jug, Black Cockerel patt., Motto Ware, "Good Morning - Straight from the Dairy," no mark, Watcombe, ca. 1910-20, 3 1/2" h. 50
Inkwell, Colored Cockeral patt., round, Motto Ware, "Us be always glad tu yer frum 'ee," Aller Vale impressed mark, ca. 1891-1910, 2 1/2" h. 80
Pitcher, 6" h., Colored Cockerel patt., Motto Ware, "Good Morning - A man may travel thro' the world and sow it thick with friendships," Aller Vale, Devon, England mark, early, ca. 1891-1902 165
Wall pocket, Colored Cockerel patt., Motto Ware, "See a pin pick it up - And all day have good Luck," no mark, H.M. Exeter Pottery, rare, ca. 1920, 6 5/8" l. **225**

Cottage Pattern
Cheese dish, cov., round, Motto Ware, "Masters two will never do," Dartmouth Pottery, ca. 1960, 6 1/2" d., 3 3/4" h. 99
Coffeepot, cov., ribbed "beak" spout, Motto Ware, "Say not always what you know - but Always know what you say," Watcombe Torquay mark, ca. 1930, 6 5/8" h. 165
Creamer, Motto Ware, "Tak a little Craim," early Aller Vale mark, ca. 1902-24, 2 3/4" h. 41
Cup & saucer, Motto Ware, "Where friends there riches," "Made in England" black

stamp, Watcombe Torquay mark, ca. 1930s **52**
Honey pot, cov., Watcombe Torquay, ca. 1920s, overall 4 3/8" h. 80
Inkwell, cov., round, Motto Ware, "Us be always glad tu hear from 'ee," Watcombe Torquay, England mark, ca. 1925-35, scarce w/cover, overall 2 1/2" h. 125
Pitcher, 5 1/2" h., Motto Ware, "Be like the Sun Dial - Count only Sunny hours," Watcombe Torquay, "Made in England" mark, ca. 1930s 86
Plate, 8" d., Motto Ware, "Talk little, Hear much, Learn more," Made in DMW England, Watcombe mark, ca. 1918-27 80
Tea set: cov. teapot, cov. sugar & creamer; Motto Ware, "Du' ee zit down an' 'ave a cup a Tay," each also says "Isles of Scilly," Watcombe Torquay incised mark, ca. 1901-20, teapot 3 1/2" h., the set 125
Teapot, cov., Motto Ware, "Yu'll 'ave a Cup a Tay now, wa'ant 'ee - Princetown," Watcombe Torquay mark, ca. 1925-35, overall 6 1/2" l., 3 5/8" h. 80

Scandy Pattern
Chamberstick, Motto Ware, "I slept and dreamt that life was beauty; I woke and found that life was duty," Aller Vale mark, ca. 1902-24, 5 3/8" h. **99**
Hatpin holder, Motto Ware, "I'll take care of the Hat Pins," Watcombe, ca. 1930, 4 1/2" h. 106
Hot water-coffeepot, cov., Motto Ware, "Success comes not by wishing - But hard Work bravely done," Aller Vale mark, ca. 1891-1910, overall 6 3/4" h. 140
Jardiniere, ruffled rim, Motto Ware, "It's a long lane that has no turnin'," Watcombe, 5" h. 152
Mug, child's, Motto Ware, "He soars not high who fears to fall," Aller Vale, ca. 1910, 2 1/2" h. 50
Pitcher, 6 1/2" h., pierced rim, Motto Ware, "Be always as merry as ever you can - For few will Delight in a sorrowful man," H.M. Exeter Pottery, ca. 1910-20 146
Plate, 7 3/4" d., Motto Ware, "Work on, Hope on - Self help is noble schooling. You do your best and leave the rest to God Almighty's ruling," early Aller Vale mark, ca. 1891-1901 149

Large Scandy Pattern Tankard

Aller Vale Jardiniere & Pitcher

Tankard, large, slightly tapering cylindrical form, Motto Ware, long motto in Devon dialect, impressed Aller Vale mark, ca. 1891-1910, small sealed hairline, 8 1/4" h. (ILLUS.)................................ **220**

Vase, miniature, 1 3/4" h., two handles at back, Motto Ware, "Niver zay die - Up man an' try," unmarked **70**

Other Patterns

Large Daisy-decorated Basket

Basket, Daisy patt., large h.p. colorful daisy flowers, Royal Torquay, ca. 1930, overall 8 5/8" h. (ILLUS.)................................ **198**

Candlesticks, Cherries patt., Motto Ware, one w/"Good - Night," the other "Pleasant Dreams," no mark, Torquay Pottery Co., ca. 1930s, 8" h., pr. **142**

Chocolates bowl, cov., commemorative, "Rotary International" on white raised slip wheel against a blue ground, "Service not Self - 1924 Torquay Conference," Hele Cross Pottery, overall 6" h. **125**

Dog bowl, B1 Scroll patt., Motto Ware, "Love Me - Love My Dog," fancy calligraphy, white clay, early Aller Vale impressed mark, ca. 1891-1902, 4 7/8" d., 2" h. **170**

Inkwell, Purple Thistle patt., Motto Ware in Devon dialect, "Gie's a scrae o' yer pen," Longpark, 1 7/8" h. **58**

Jardiniere, Kerswell Daisy patt., commemorative, two handles, "Horton Bucks - 1837 - VR - 1897," made for Queen Victoria's Diamond Jubilee, rare, Aller Vale, 4 1/8" h. (ILLUS. right, top of page) **257**

Mug, two handles, Floral patt., Art Nouveau flower on blue ground, Crown Dorset, ca. 1910, 2 7/8" h. **74**

Pitcher, 4 1/8" h., Q1 Pattern, Motto Ware, two mottoes, "All is not gold that Glitters" & "Adventures are to the Adventurous," no mark, Aller Vale, ca. 1890s...................... **106**

Pitcher, 5 3/4" h., Q1 Pattern, Motto Ware, "Have courage boys to do the right - Be bold, be brave, be strong. By doing right you earn the might - To overcome the wrong," early Aller Vale, repaired base chip, ca. 1890s (ILLUS. left with jardiniere) **76**

Scent bottle, Jazz patt., blue ground w/Art Deco design in color band at top, advertising on base "Boots The Chemist," no stopper, unmarked, ca. 1930s, 2 3/4" h. **68**

Scent bottle, Rose patt., inscribed "Toogoods Devon Rose Perfume London England," rose on cream ground, gold crown-form stopper, "Made in England" mark, Watcombe, ca. 1925, 2 1/2" h. **77**

Scent bottle, Violets patt., inscribed "Ye Olde Devon Violets," impressed "B" mark for Bovey Tracey Pottery, England, no stopper, ca. 1930, 2 7/8" h. **35**

Toby jug, inscribed "Bill Brewer from Widecombe Fair," Royal Torquay, ca. 1924-30, 3 3/4" h. **102**

Toby jug, large, inscribed "An Auld Uncle Tom Cobleigh An' All," Bovey Tracey Pottery impressed mark, ca. 1920, 6" h. **165**

Small Tintern Abbey Vase

Vase, 4 5/8" h., Tintern Abbey patt., slightly tapering cylindrical body w/flared rim flanked by three twisted loop handles, scene of the abbey ruins, Longpark Tormohun Ware Torquay mark, very slight rim chip, ca. 1903-14 (ILLUS.) **86**

Fine Fish Pattern Art Vase

Vase, 7 5/8" h., Fish patt., art piece, ovoid body tapering to a short neck w/ruffled rim, colorful fish swimming among scrolling water plants, impressed H.M. Exeter mark, ca. 1910-20 (ILLUS.) **265**

Uhl Pottery

Original production of utilitarian wares began at Evansville, Indiana, in the 1850s and consisted mostly of jugs, jars, crocks and pieces for food preparation and preservation. In 1909, production was moved to Huntingburg, Indiana, where a more extensive variety of items was eventually produced including many novelty and advertising items that have become highly collectible. Following labor difficulties, the Uhl Pottery closed in 1944.

Unless it is marked or stamped, Uhl is difficult to identify except by someone with considerable experi-

ence. Marked pieces can have several styles of ink stamps and/or an incised number under glaze on the bottom. These numbers are die-cut and impressed in the glazed bottom. Some original molds were acquired by other potteries. Some production exists and should not be considered as Uhl. These may have numbers inscribed by hand with a stylus and are usually not glazed on the bottom.

Many examples have no mark or stamp and may not be bottom-glazed. This is especially true of many of the miniature pieces. If a piece has a "Meier's Wine" paper label, it was probably made by Uhl.

While many color variations exist, there are about nine basic colors: blue, white, black, rose or pink, yellow, teal, purple, pumpkin and browns/tans. Blue, pink, teal and purple are currently the most sought after colors. Animal planters, vases, liquor/wine containers, pitchers, mugs, banks, kitchenware, bakeware, gardenware and custom-made advertising pieces exist.

Similar pieces by other manufacturers do exist. When placed side by side, a seasoned collector can recognize an authentic example of Uhl Pottery.

A Variety of Uhl Marks

Ashtray, #199, in the form of a dog lifting its leg at a hydrant, marked (ILLUS. top row, left w/Uhl Pottery pieces, bottom next page) **$525**

Ashtray, green, hand-turned mark, 3" d. **145**

Bank, figural, large grinning pig, yellow, unmarked **375**

Bean pot, brown/blue, marked "Boston Bean Pot" **175**

Bowl, basketweave, blue, unmarked **88**

Bowl, 5" d., shouldered mixing bowl, unmarked **140**

Bowl, 8" d., luncheon, blue, marked **70**

Canteen, commemorative of Uhl Collectors Society, 1988 .... **260**

Casserole, cov., blue, #528 & marked **50**

Churn, 4-gal., cov., white, acorn mark, solid lid **185**

Creamer, light tan, hand-turned square mark, 5 1/2" h. **150**

Flowerpot, ribbed, yellow, no attached saucer, unmarked, 6" **33**

Jar, 1-gal., white, acorn mark **45**

Various Uhl Pottery Items

Jar, 3-gal., tan, Evansville, Ind., mark 360
Jar, 6-gal., white, acorn mark................................. 38
Jar, cov., cottage cheese, white, metal lid
embossed "UHL" 500
Jug, 3-gal., light tan, Evansville, Ind., mark...... 200
Jug, 5-gal., blue/white, marked "Dillsboro
Sanitarium, Dillsboro, Ind." 575
Jug, 6-gal., light tan, Evansville, Ind., oval
mark... 90
Jug, blue & white, "Colonial Mineral
Springs, Martinsville, Indiana" (ILLUS.
top left w/various Uhl Pottery items, top of
page) 1,200
Jug, brown/white, miniature shoulder, front
acorn mark 550

Jug, form of football, large, 5" l., rarer than
smaller version (ILLUS. middle row, left
w/Uhl Pottery pieces).. 250

Jug, form of softball, Meier's label, 3 3/8" d.
(ILLUS. middle row, right w/Uhl Pottery
pieces) 250
Jug, miniature acorn, marked "Acorn
Wares"... 60
Jug, miniature, marked, 1" h............................... 110
Jug, red/green, "1940 Merry Christmas,"
marked "Uhl Pottery Company," 2 3/8" h. 255
Lamp, Liberty Bell... 128
Model of cat, potter's name engraved, un-
marked... 1,000
Model of cowboy boot, marked (ILLUS.
bottom row, right w/Uhl Pottery pieces)......... 150
Model of dog & hydrant, similar to ashtray
#199, two separate pieces, no marks
(ILLUS. top row, center & right w/Uhl Pot-
tery pieces)... 350
Model of military boot, marked (ILLUS.
bottom row, center w/Uhl Pottery pieces) 95
Model of shoe, miniature woman's slipper,
marked (ILLUS. of two bottom row, left
w/Uhl Pottery pieces) 120
Model of shoes, white, marked #2, pr.............. 110
Mug, "Chicco Beverage Co." 90
Mug, "Chicco Beverage, Norristown" 90
Mug, coffee, blue, marked.................................... 55
Mug, coffee, pink, marked................................... 55
Mug, "Homestead Hotel, No. 7 Water"
(ILLUS. bottom right w/various Uhl Pot-
tery items).. 125
Mug, "West Baden Springs Hotel" (ILLUS.
bottom left w/various Uhl Pottery items) 110
Pepper shaker, dark blue, unmarked................. 25
Pitcher, barrel-shaped, blue, marked.................. 55
Pitcher, barrel-shaped, brown, unmarked.......... 35
Pitcher, bulbous grape, pumpkin, #183.............. 55
Pitcher, Hall Boy, blue & white, unmarked........ 150
Pitcher, miniature, blue, marked "Norris-
town, Tenn."... 180
Pitcher, squat grape, blue, unmarked............... 175

Uhl Pottery Pieces

Rare Uhl Plate

Plate, 6 3/4" d., stamped "Santa Claus, Indiana," very rare, only three known to exist (ILLUS.)... **500+**

Stein, 3-oz., miniature, brown, marked **70**

Stein, miniature, w/box, commemorative of Uhl Collectors Society, 1987 .... **500**

Teapot, 2-cup, blue, marked #131 .... **200**

Tulip bowl, yellow, marked #119 .... **80**

Vase, blue, hand-turned mark........................... **600**

Vase, dark blue, marked #154 .... **90**

Vase, waisted form, "Merrill Park Florist, Battle Creek, Mich.," extremely rare (ILLUS. top right w/various Uhl Pottery items, previous page) .... **price unknown**

Vase, 4 3/4" h., bud vase, #107, hard to find, price depends on color, w/blue & especially purple being most popular (ILLUS. center w/various Uhl vases).......... **45-75**

Various Uhl Vases

Vase, 5" h., handled, #152, very hard to find, marked, price depends on color, w/blue & especially purple being most popular (ILLUS. bottom left w/various Uhl vases)... **45-75**

Vase, 5 1/4" h., fan-shaped w/scalloped rim, #157, hard to find, price depends on color, w/blue & especially purple being most popular (ILLUS. bottom right w/various Uhl vases) **45-75**

Vase, 5 1/4" h., flaring ribbed neck, #158, incised, hard to find, price depends on color, w/blue & especially purple being most popular (ILLUS. top left w/various Uhl vases) **45-75**

Vase, 5 1/4" h., side handles, #156, incised, hard to find, price depends on color, w/blue & especially purple being most popular (ILLUS. top right w/various Uhl vases) **45-75**

Water cooler, 5-gal., cov., white, acorn mark **200**

Vernon Kilns

The story of Vernon Kilns Pottery begins with the purchase by Mr. Faye Bennison of the Poxon China Company (Vernon Potteries) in July 1931. The Poxon family had run the pottery for a number of years in Vernon, California, but with the founding of Vernon Kilns, the product lines were greatly expanded.

Many innovative dinnerware lines and patterns were introduced during the 1930s, including designs by such noted American artists as Rockwell Kent and Don Blanding. In the early 1940s items were designed to tie in with Walt Disney's animated features "Fantasia" and "Dumbo." Various commemorative plates, including the popular "Bits" series, were also produced over a long period of time. Vernon Kilns was taken over by Metlox Potteries in 1958 and completely ceased production in 1960.

Vernon Kilns Mark

"Bits" Series

Plate, 8 1/2" d., Bits of Old New England Series, The Cove **$30**

Plate, 8 1/2" d., Bits of the Old South Series, Cotton Patch **40**

Plate, chop, 14" d., Bits of the Old Southwest Series, Pueblo.. **75**

Dinnerwares

Bowl, chowder, tab handle, Gingham patt. **15-18**

Bowl, soup, Coronado patt. **15-20**

Bowl, 13" d., salad, Homespun patt.................... **85**

Butter dish, cov., Casual California patt. **25-30**

Butter dish, cov., Tickled Pink patt. **30-40**

Candleholders, teacup form w/metal fittings, Tam O'Shanter patt., pr............... **100-125**

Casserole, cov., Heavenly Days patt............ **35-45**

Casserole, cov., Tam O'Shanter patt. **45-55**

Coaster, Gingham patt. **25-30**

Coffeepot, cov., Heavenly Days patt., 8-cup **65**

Creamer, Modern California patt. **10-15**

Early California Egg Cup & After Dinner Cups & Saucers

Cup & saucer, after-dinner size, Early California patt., red or cobalt blue, each (ILLUS. front) **25-30**
Egg cup, Early California patt., turquoise (ILLUS. with Early California cups & saucers).. 20
Gravy boat, Gingham patt. **20-25**
Mixing bowls, nesting set, Gingham patt., 5" to 9" d., five pcs. **150-175**
Mug, Barkwood patt., 9 oz.................... 25
Pepper mill, Homespun patt.................... 175

Hawaiian Coral Streamline Pitcher

Pitcher, Streamline shape, Hawaiian Coral patt., 1 qt. (ILLUS.)....................................... **45-55**
Pitcher, 5" h., Streamline shape, Barkwood patt., 1/2 pt. 30
Plate, 7 1/2" d., Frontier Days patt. **35-45**
Plate, 9 1/2" d., luncheon, Organdie patt... **10-12**
Plate, 9 1/2" d., Trader Vic patt.................. **100-125**
Plate, 10 1/2" d., dinner, Calico patt. 25
Plate, chop, 12" d., Frontier Days patt........ **150-175**
Plate, chop, 14" d., Gingham patt. **35-40**
Platter, 12" d., round, Organdie patt............. **20-25**
Relish dish, leaf-shaped, four-part, Native California patt... **40-60**
Salt & pepper shakers, large size, Tam O'Shanter patt., pr....................................... **45-65**
Salt & pepper shakers, regular size, Gingham patt., pr... 20
Spoon rest, Organdie patt. **75-85**

Tweed Pattern Sugar Bowl

Sugar bowl, cov., Tweed patt. (ILLUS.) **30-35**
Teacup & saucer, jumbo size, Homespun patt. **45-55**
Teacup & saucer, Winchester '73 patt......... **30-35**
Teapot, cov., Tam O'Shanter patt. **45-55**
Tumbler, Bel Air patt... 20
Tumbler, Tickled Pink patt. 20

Disney "Fantasia" & Other Items
Bowl, 8" d., soup, Flower Ballet patt. 50
Figure of Baby Weems, No. 37, 6" h. **150-175**
Tray, hors d'oeuvre, May & Vieve Hamilton design, 16" d.. **400-600**
Vase, 12" h., carved handles, May & Vieve Hamilton design... **1,500+**

Don Blanding Dinnerwares
Cup & saucer, Coral Reef patt., blue................. 50
Sugar bowl, cov., Coral Reef patt., blue **85-95**
Tumbler, Hilo patt., #4, 5 1/2" h................ **125-150**

Rockwell Kent Designs
Bowl, chowder, "Our America" series, coconut tree, blue... **45-50**
Cup & saucer, Moby Dick patt., maroon....... **30-45**
Plate, 6 1/2" d., "Our America" series, steamship, blue **45-50**
Plate, 9 1/2" d., Moby Dick patt., blue **110-145**
Sugar bowl, cov., Moby Dick patt., blue...... **85-105**

States Map Series - 10 1/2" d.
Plate, Texas... **40-45**

States Picture Series - 10 1/2" d.
Plate, North Dakota, multicolored 25
Plate, Virginia, maroon **18-20**

Miscellaneous Commemoratives
Cup & saucer, after-dinner size, Niagara
Falls **25**

Christmas Tree Pattern Pieces

Plate, 10 1/2" d., Christmas Tree patt.
(ILLUS. w/Christmas Tree teacup & sau-
cer) **65-75**
Plate, 10 1/2" d., Hollywood Stars, blue **70-80**
Plate, 10 1/2" d., Notre Dame University,
brown **25**
Plate, Statue of Liberty, multicolor **50-75**
Teacup & saucer, Christmas Tree (ILLUS.
with Christmas Tree plate) **30-35**

Warwick

*Numerous collectors have turned their attention to
the productions of the Warwick China Manufacturing
Company that operated in Wheeling, West Virginia, from
1887 until 1951. Prime interest seems to lie in items produced before 1914 that were decorated with decal portraits of beautiful women, monks and Native Americans.
Fraternal Order items, as well as floral and fruit decorated items, are also popular with collectors.*

Warwick Mark

Salesman's Sample Ashtray

Ashtray, salesman's sample, white
trimmed in gold w/"Warwick China" in
script & knight's helmet in black, no mark
on back, ca. 1940s, 4 3/4" l., 3 1/2" w.
(ILLUS.) **$75**

"Tudor Rose" Sugar & Creamer

Creamer & cov. sugar, white w/red "Tudor
Rose" decor patt. (rare), marked w/War-
wick knight's helmet in green, ca. 1940s,
creamer 4 1/2" h., sugar 5" d., pr.
(ILLUS.) **95**

Warwick Ewer

Ewer, matte brown & tan w/hazelnuts, gold
trim, marked w/IOGA knight's helmet in
green, decor code M2, ca. 1908, 11" h.
(ILLUS.) **175**

Humidor with B.P.O.E. Elk Logo

Humidor, cov., brown & tan w/elk's head &
clock, "Cigars" on back, marked w/IOGA
knight's helmet in grey & "Warwick China" in black, decor code A-13 in red,
scarce, ca. 1903, 6 1/2" h., 4 1/2" d.
(ILLUS.) **295**

Platter in "June Bride" Pattern

Mug, cylindrical, decorated w/the head of an elk & the "BPOE" emblem.................................. **45**

Pitcher, 6 1/2" h., Tokio #3, brown shaded to brown ground, decorated w/color portrait of Native American, A-12 .... **300**

Pitcher, 7 3/4" h., Tokio #1 shape, overall red ground w/color portrait of fisherman in yellow slicker, No. E-3................................ **185**

Lemonade Pitcher with Woman

Pitcher, 9 3/4" h., lemonade shape, overall pink ground w/color "Gibson Girl" type bust portrait of a young woman w/dark hair in a bouffant style & holding purple flowers, No. H-1 (ILLUS.)................................. **265**

Platter, 22" l., white w/small pink flowers & gold rim in "June Bride" decor patt., marked w/Warwick knight's helmet in maroon, decor code #B2062, ca. 1940s (ILLUS., top of page) **25**

Portrait Spirits Jug

Spirits jug, matte tan & brown w/woman in low-cut gown & flowing hair, marked w/IOGA knight's helmet in green, decor code M-1 in red, scarce, ca. 1908, 6 1/4" h. (ILLUS.) **225**

VP Style Stein with Bulldog

Stein, VP style, brown & cream w/photographic transfer of bulldog, "Ch. l'Almassadeur," marked w/IOGA knight's helmet, decor code A-32, ca. 1906, 2 2/4" d., 4 1/2" h. (ILLUS.).. **70**

Warwick Portrait Teapot

Teapot, cov., h.p. portrait, "Gibson Girl" decor, turquoise & pink, matte finish, signed "H. Richard Boehm," marked w/IOGA knight's helmet in green, decor code M5, rare in this color, ca. 1910, 7 1/2" h. (ILLUS.) **425**

Vase, 4" h., Pansy shape, yellow shading to green ground, color portrait of Anna Potaka, K-1 .... **200**

Violet Vase with Beechnut

Vase, 4" h., Violet shape, brown shading to
tan ground, color beechnut decoration,
matte finish, M-2 (ILLUS.)............................... **110**
Vase, 4 1/2" h., Dainty shape, brown shad-
ed to brown ground, colored floral deco-
ration, No. A-27 .... **145**
Vase, 6 1/2" h., Clytie shape, overall red
ground w/poinsettia decoration, No. E-2 .... **210**

Clytie Portrait Vase in Red Glaze

Vase, 6 1/2" h., Clytie style portrait vase,
portrait of Madame Lebrun, red glaze,
marked w/IOGA knight's helmet in grey,
decor code I14 in red, rare, ca. 1908
(ILLUS.)... **325**
Vase, 6 3/4" h., Narcis #2 shape, overall red
ground, color portrait of Princess Potaka,
No. E-1 .... **220**
Vase, 7 1/4" h., Cuba shape, brown shading
to brown ground, color pine cone decora-
tion, A-64 .... **260**
Vase, 8" h., Carol shape, green shaded to
green ground, red rose decoration, No.
F-2 .... **255**
Vase, 9" h., Flower shape, green shaded to
green ground, portrait of a young woman
w/flowing red hair, No. M-1 .... **200**

Warwick Verbena Style Vase

Vase, 9" h., Verbena #1 style, grey w/pink
poppies & pink & white daisies, rim
trimmed in gold, marked w/IOGA knight's
helmet, decor code C-6 in red, ca. 1906
(ILLUS.) **160**
Vase, 9 1/4" h., Windsor shape, brown
shaded to brown ground, acorn decora-
tion, No. A-67... **290**
Vase, 9 1/2" h., Penn shape, overall green
color w/no decoration, matte finish, No.
M-6 .... **270**
Vase, 9 1/2" h., Verbenia #1 shape, brown
shaded to brown ground, color floral dec-
oration, No. A-6 .... **165**

Warwick Vase with Pink Roses

Vase, 10" h., baluster form w/scroll handles,
brown w/pink roses, marked w/IOGA
knight's helmet, decor code A-12 in red,
scarce, ca. 1904 (ILLUS.)................................. **205**
Vase, 10" h., Henrietta shape, brown shad-
ed to brown ground, color portrait of a
seminude young woman, No. A-30................... **275**
Vase, 10" h., Roberta shape, brown shaded
to brown ground, portrait of a monk, No.
A-36... **260**
Vase, 10" h., Virginia shape, overall pink
ground, "Gibson Girl" type decoration
w/portrait of a young woman w/a flower in
her hair, No. H-1... **300**

Portrait Vase with Gypsy Girl

Vase, 10 1/4" h., Bouquet #2 portrait style in tan & brown, bust portrait of Gypsy girl in red dress & headscarf, marked w/IOGA knight's helmet in green, decor code M-1 in red, ca. 1908 (ILLUS.)................................. 240

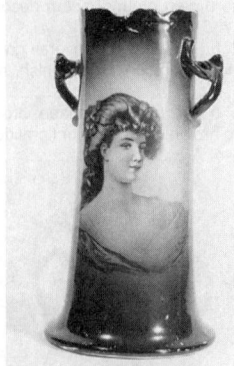

Vase with Woman with Hibiscus

Vase, 10 1/4" h., Bouquet #2 style, brown & tan w/decal portrait of young Victorian woman w/hibiscus flower in hair, marked w/ IOGA knight's helmet in green, decor code A-17 in red, scarce, ca. 1907 (ILLUS.).. 295

Vase with "Gibson Girl" Decor

Vase, 10 1/4" h., Bouquet #2 style, tan & brown matte w/"Gibson Girl" decor of hatted woman holding rose, marked w/IOGA knight's helmet in green, decor code M1 in red, scarce, ca. 1909 (ILLUS.).................. 305
Vase, 10 1/2" h., Monroe shape, overall pink ground, "Gibson Girl" type decoration w/portrait of a young woman wearing a large hat, No. H-1 275
Vase, 11" h., Oriental shape, brown shading to brown ground, color floral decoration, A-21.. 240
Vase, 11 1/2" h., Bouquet #1 shape, brown shaded to brown ground, portrait of young woman wearing a pearl necklace, No. A-17 215

Warwick Vase with Hibiscus Flower

Vase, 11 1/2" h., footed ovoid base angling to long narrow neck & flaring rim, slender graceful handles from base to top of neck, brown w/hibiscus flower, marked w/IOGA knight's helmet, decor code A27 in red, scarce, ca. 1904 (ILLUS.).................. 200
Vase, 11 1/2" h., President shape, tan shaded to tan ground, acorn decoration, matte finish, No. M-4 220
Vase, 11 1/2" h., Roman shape, overall white ground, color bird decoration, D-1 220
Vase, 12" h., Gem shape, brown shading to brown ground, color floral decoration, A-16.. 190
Vase, 12" h., Queen shape, overall charcoal ground, color floral decoration, No. C-6 290

Warwick Vase with Poppies

Warwick Restaurant Soup Bowls

Vase, 12 1/2" h., baluster form, brown w/pink poppies, marked w/IOGA knight's helmet in green, decor code A40, scarce, ca. 1904 (ILLUS., bottom previous page) **200**

Vase, 13 1/2" h., Chrysanthemum #2 shape, overall charcoal ground decorated w/colored florals, No. C-6 .... **145**

Vase, 15" h., A Beauty shape, brown shaded to brown ground w/red rose (American Beauty) decoration, No. A-20 .... **300**

Vase, 15" h., Princess shape, brown shading to brown ground, color floral decoration, A-27 .... **350**

Vase, 15 1/2" h., Chrysanthemum #1 shape, overall red ground w/a Madame Lebrun child portrait, No. E-1 .... **180**

Commercial China

Bowl, 3 3/4" d., soup, double-handled, white w/black & orange decorative band below rim & on handles, marked w/Warwick knight's helmet in green, ca. 1940s, each (ILLUS. of six, top of page) **6**

Butter pat, white w/"The Brass Rail" logo, 3" **20**

Various Warwick Restaurant Mugs

Mug, various decorations, marked w/Warwick knight's helmet in green, ca. 1940s, 3" d., 3 1/4" h., each (ILLUS. of five) **9**

Warwick "Sumter Hospital" Creamer

Creamer, white w/two green bands & "Sumter Hospital" logo, 2 1/2" h. (ILLUS.) **22**

Cup & saucer, brown wave decoration, Santone finish **25**

Cup & saucer, white w/"Liggett's" logo **20**

Cup & saucer, white w/Crestwood pattern **25**

Warwick "Duckwall's" Mustard Jar

Mustard jar, cov., white w/"Duckwall's" logo (ILLUS.) **28**

Plate, 9" d., white w/"Hotel Anthony" logo **18**

Plate, 10" d., white w/"compliments of Dine Furniture Company" **40**

Plate, 10 1/4" d., white w/"The Washington Duke" logo **35**

Warwick B&O Railroad Platter

Platter, 8 1/4" l., white w/22k gold decorative band on rim & B&O Railroad symbol, marked w/Warwick knight's helmet in green, ca. 1938 (ILLUS.).................................. **125**

Warwick "Sumter Hospital" Sugar Bowl

Sugar bowl, cov., white w/two green bands, "Sumter Hospital" logo, 3 3/4" h. (ILLUS.)........ **25**
Tray, oval, white w/"The Washington" logo, 3 1/2 x 9 3/4".. **30**

Dinnerwares

Bowl, oval, Pattern No. 2000............................... **25**
Cup & saucer, Pattern No. 9903, Grey Blossom decoration **18**

Warwick Demitasse Cup & Saucer

Demitasse cup & saucer, Gray Blossom decor patt. w/platinum rim, saucer only marked w/Warwick knight's helmet in gold w/patt. name "Gray Blossom - Pat. #9903," ca. 1940, 2 1/4" h. cup, 5" d. saucer, cup & saucer (ILLUS.)......................... **26**

Pitcher, 8" h., buttermilk-type, white ground w/floral decoration of small pink flowers......... **45**
Plate, 6 1/2" d., bread & butter, Pattern No. 9437-M, Windsor Maroon decoration **5**
Plate, 6 1/2" d., bread & butter, Pattern No. E-9450 .... **15**
Plate, 9" d., Pattern No. B-9059......................... **15**
Plate, 10" d., dinner, Pattern No. 9584, Bird of Paradise decoration w/single bird............... **10**
Platter, 13" l., Pattern No. B-9272, coin gold trim.. **40**
Vegetable bowl, handled, Pattern No. 2062 .... **30**

Wedgwood

Reference here is to the famous pottery established by Josiah Wedgwood in 1759 in England. Numerous types of wares have been produced through the years to the present.

WEDGWOOD
Early Wedgwood Mark

Jasper Ware
Bowl, 8 1/4" d., 4 1/4" h., low wide pedestal foot below the deep upright sides in black decorated w/white relief classical figures, 20th c. **$125**
Cache pot & underplate, deep bell-shaped cache pot set into a shallow round underplate, light blue ground decorated w/white relief classical figures, ca. 1900, 8 1/2" d., 8 1/4" h. (small rim chip on underplate) **315**
Vase, 8" h., flaring foot tapering to a tall slightly ovoid body w/a wide flared mouth, black ground decorated w/white relief classical figures, 20th c. **180**

Miscellaneous
Butter pat, majolica, Oriental Floral patt., turquoise ground **193**
Butter pat, majolica, Shell & Coral patt., yellow, green & pink (minor hairline).................. **165**
Cake stand, majolica, Overlapping Leaf patt., green & yellow leaves on round top, raised on a brown trunk base, 8 3/4" d., 5 1/4" h. **165**
Center bowl, majolica, oval, upright yellow reticulated basketweave sides above green leafy garland w/pink trim raised on a low cobalt blue base, 15" l. **1,150**
Compote, open, 11" d., majolica, Cauliflower patt., brown, pink & green leaves on a turquoise ground **248**
Ewer, majolica, footed spherical body w/tall flaring cylindrical neck, Cattail patt., horizontal green bands of cattails around the middle w/alternating dark brown & yellow bands above & below, 6 1/4" h. **275**
Pitcher, 7" h., "Argenta Ware," Ocean patt., molded seashells & coral on a cream ground, shell finial on handle, great color **550**
Pitcher, 7 1/2" h., "Argenta Ware," Bird & Fan patt., pinks & mottled browns & greens on a cream ground **440**

Very Rare Wedgwood Punch Bowl

Pitcher, 7 3/4" h., majolica, Overlapping Grapes & Leaves patt., dark greens & browns... 550

Pitcher, 9" h., "Argenta Ware," Bird & Fan patt., pinks & mottled browns & greens on a cream ground... 990

Plate, 7 3/4" d., "Argenta Ware," Strawberry patt., pink berries & green & brown leaves on a pale yellow ground..................... 220

Plate, 8 3/4" d., "Argenta Ware," Triple Fish patt., three lifelike fish on a cream ground...... 385

Plate, 8 3/4" d., majolica, Strawberry patt., yellow ground.. 303

Plate, 9" d., majolica, Angel & Putti patt., four slender standing angels in blue divide the rim into four panels, each molded w/putti & swags on a cream ground, deep rose border band.................................. 495

Plate, 9" d., majolica, green center w/classical putti & drapery, reticulated brown border band.. 330

Plate, 9" d., majolica, Ocean patt., pink & brown coral spring on yellow shell in center, mottled brown & green shell border........ 248

Plate, 9" d., majolica, Shell & Coral patt., turquoise basketweave ground..................... 660

Plate, 9" d., majolica, Stork in Marsh patt., reticulated border 880

Plate, 9" d., majolica, Strawberry & Leaf patt., yellow ground... 440

Plate, 9 1/4" d., majolica, Botanical Bird & Floral patt., reticulated border 275

Punch bowl, majolica, "Punch & Judy" model, deep sides molded w/a wide rim band of yellow "coins" on a turquoise blue band, four large full-relief heads of Punch around the sides, cobalt blue lower body raised on four seated brown dog legs, each dog wearing a clown hat & ruffled collar, professional repair to dogs' feet & bowl rim, ca. 1878, extremely rare (ILLUS., top of page) 33,000

Relish tray, majolica, oblong, Onion & Pickle patt., the center w/a large group of molded white onions, green pickles, beans & red cabbage on a cobalt blue ground, yellow wheat head end handles, 9" l... 385

Wedgwood Majolica Salad Set

Salad bowl, fork & spoon, majolica, deep round sides molded w/large alternating yellow & deep rose scallop shells & green coral on a cobalt blue ground, silver rim band, silver plate utensils w/matching majolica handles, late 19th c., bowl 9 1/2" d., the set (ILLUS.) 1,540

Sardine box, cov., majolica, Oriental Floral patt., domed cover divided into four panels, two w/small pink blossoms...................... 385

Extremely Rare Majolica Tea Set

Tea set: cov. teapot, cov. sugar bowl & creamer; majolica, Punch & Judy patt., squatty bulbous turquoise blue bodies w/flared rims, figural Punch head handles w/cobalt blue & pink hats curving up to rims, low domed covers w/reclining brown dog finials, professional repair to collar of one dog, extremely rare, late 19th c., teapot 7 3/4" l., the set (ILLUS.) **37,400**

Teapot, cov., majolica, Chrysanthemum patt., colored blossoms on a turquoise ground, 6 1/2" h. (very slight hairline) **770**

Umbrella stand, "Argenta Ware," cylindrical, molded in the Japanese taste w/open vertical fans entwined w/blossoming prunus branches, insects in flight & birds, above a key-pattern band, edged in yellow, date code for 1881, 21 3/4" h............. **2,820**

Vase, 8 1/4" h., majolica, Narcissus patt., tapering ovoid body w/flaring rim, raised on three knob feet, yellow blossoms & long green leaves on a dark brown ground **660**

Weller

This pottery was made from 1872 to 1945 at a pottery established originally by Samuel A. Weller at Fultonham, Ohio, and moved in 1882 to Zanesville. Numerous lines were produced, and listings below are by pattern or line.

Reference books on Weller include The Collectors Encyclopedia of Weller Pottery *by Sharon & Bob Huxford (Collector Books, 1979) and* All About Weller *by Ann Gilbert McDonald (Antique Publications, 1989).*

WELLER **Weller Pottery**

Weller Marks

Ardsley (1928)
Various shapes molded as cattails among rushes with water lilies at the bottom. Matte glaze.

Bulb bowl, lobed blossom form base w/leaf-form openwork top, half kiln ink stamp logo, 4 7/8" h............................... **$100-125**

Candleholders, lily pad & blossom disc base centered by a flaring blossom-form socket, half kiln ink stamp logo & old sales tag, one w/original "Weller Ardsley Ware" paper label, 2 3/4" h., pr. (minor glaze inconsistencies) **125-150**

Vase, 19" h., floor-type, compressed domed base w/lotus blossom & tall trumpet-form body embossed w/cattails & leaves, marked w/full circle kiln ink stamp logo **1,200-1,300**

Aurelian (1898-1910)
Similar to Louwelsa line but with brighter colors and a glossy glaze. Features bright yellow/orange brush-applied background along with brown and yellow transparent glaze.

Lamp, oil, bell-shaped body on small knob feet, decorated w/two medallions of ivory roses, by C. Mitchell, complete w/oil font,

artist-signed & stamped "K116," 10 1/2 x 11"... **600-650**

Mug, tapering cylindrical body w/C-form handle, cherry decoration by Charles Chilcote, ca. 1900, impressed w/circular "Aurelian Weller" logo & incised shape number "435" w/"Chil" painted on side near bottom of handle, 6 1/8" h. **275-300**

Aurelian Umbrella Stand

Umbrella stand, decorated w/bright yellow irises, late 19th c., unmarked, removable galvanized sheet metal insert, 23 7/8" h. (ILLUS.) **1,650-1,750**

Baldin (about 1915-20)
Rustic designs with relief-molded apples and leaves on branches wrapped around each piece.

Baldin Vase

Vase, 5 1/2" h., spherical body tapering to slightly flared rim, impressed "Weller" in large block letters (ILLUS.)..................... **275-325**

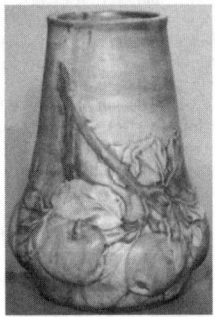

Unmarked Baldin Vase

Vase, 10 5/8" h., bulbous base w/slightly tapering wide cylindrical neck & flat rim, unmarked (ILLUS.) **300-350**

Blue & Decorated Hudson (1919)
Handpainted lifelike sprays of fruit blossoms and flowers in shades of pink and blue on a rich dark blue ground.

Vase, 9 1/8" h., ovoid body w/rolled rim, decorated near top w/bright orange & yellow flowers painted by Hester Pillsbury, unmarked, artist-initialed among flowers (4" crack descending from rim).. **175-200**

Vase, 10" h., slender cylindrical body flaring at base & tapering to small flat rim, center of body decorated w/a band of brightly colored flowers & impressed "Weller" in large block letters **250-275**

Blue Louwelsa (ca. 1905)
A high-gloss line shading from medium blue to cobalt blue with underglaze slip decorations of fruits & florals and sometimes portraits. Decorated in shades of white, cobalt and light blue slip. Since few pieces were made, they are rare and sought after today.

Vase, 5 3/8" h., pillow form w/nasturtium decoration, unmarked (1/4" chip off left edge of rim) **525-550**

Chase (late 1920s)
White relief fox hunt scenes, usually on a deep blue ground.

Vase, 7 5/8" h., footed baluster form w/rolled rim, dark blue ground w/white hunt scene, incised "Weller Pottery" on bottom **250-275**

Chase Vase with Silver Overlay

Vase, 8 7/8" h., ovoid form w/flat rim, mottled blue matte ground decorated w/applied silver overlay hunt scene, marked "Sterling" & impressed "Weller Pottery" in script (ILLUS.) **350-400**

Claywood (ca. 1910)
Etched designs against a light tan ground divided by dark brown bands. Matte glaze.

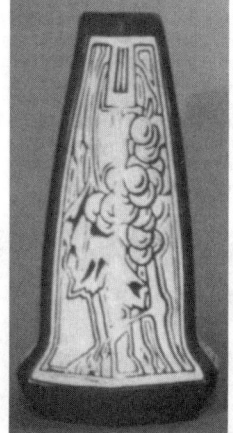

Claywood Vase

Vase, 8" h., tapering cylindrical body w/compressed base, the sides divided into tall panels by dark brown bands, each panel etched w/a grape cluster on leafy vines in creamy white outlined in brown (ILLUS.) **50-75**

Coppertone (late 1920s)
Various shapes with an overall mottled bright green glaze on a "copper" glaze base. Some pieces with figural frog or fish handles. Models of frogs also included.

Flower frog, model of lily pad bloom w/seated frog, 3 7/8" h. (small chip inside edge of one petal).. **175-200**

Rare Weller Coppertone Fish Pitcher

Pitcher, 7 5/8" h., bulbous ovoid body w/arched spout, figural fish handle, marked w/half kiln ink stamp logo, couple of burst bubbles inside mouth (ILLUS.) **1,750-1,800**

Vase, 5 3/4" h., wide tapering cylindrical body w/rolled rim, marked in script "Weller Hand Made" **350-375**

Vase, 8" h., bulbous ovoid body w/molded rim, figural frog shoulder handles, ink kiln mark (short tight line to rim)............. **1,525-1,550**

Vase, 8 3/8" h., bulbous base w/trumpet-form neck, scrolled handles from base to below rim, incised "Weller Hand Made" on bottom (three small burst bubbles on back side of vase) **225-250**

Eocean and Eocean Rose (1898-1925)
Early art line with various handpainted flowers on shaded grounds, usually with a clear glossy glaze. Quality of artwork varies greatly.

Eocean Mug

Mug, tapering cylindrical body w/C-form handle, wild rose decoration on shaded green ground, 4 7/8" h. (ILLUS.)............ **125-150**

Vase, 4 7/8" h., pillow form, wild rose decoration on shaded green ground, unmarked (glaze on four stubby feet a bit gritty in the making)................................. **200-225**

Vase, 5 3/4" h., corseted form w/pink nasturtium on shaded grey ground, decorated by Mary Pierce, incised "Eocean-Weller 890 6" & artist-signed "MP"........ **300-325**

Vase, 6" h., 5" d., swelled cylindrical body w/a wide flat shoulder to the short cylindrical neck, decorated w/wild roses in ivory & red on shaded grey ground, incised "Eocean-Rose Weller 9061"........ **350-400**

Vase, bud, 6 5/8" h., decorated w/daisies, impressed "Weller" in large block letters **200-225**

Vase, 8 1/2" h., slender ovoid body decorated w/Virginia creeper against a shaded dark green to cream ground, by William Stemm, incised "Eocean Weller," artist-initialed "F." on side below leaves **650-700**

Vase, 10 1/2" h., squared shape w/pink thistle decoration on dark green shaded to cream ground, incised "Eocean Rose Weller" & "S" on bottom & impressed "447" & "4" (pinhead glaze nick on top of rim).. **425-450**

Vase, bulbous ovoid tapering to rolled rim, decorated a/portrait of a spaniel w/brown eyes, shaded grey ground, incised "Eocean Weller S" & impressed "2".. **1,550-1,575**

Forest (mid-teens to 1928)
Realistically molded and painted forest scene.

Cylindrical Weller Forest Vase

Vase, 8" h., cylindrical w/slightly flared rim (ILLUS.) **124**

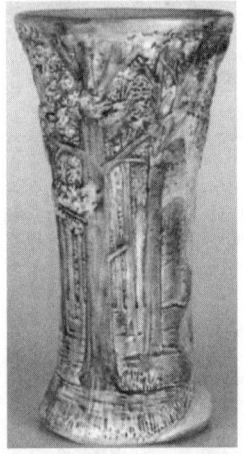

Tall Flaring Weller Forest Vase

Vase, 12" h., tall footed expanding cylindrical body w/flaring rim (ILLUS.)............... **250-350**

Hudson (1917-34)
Underglaze slip-painted decoration, "parchment-vellum" transparent glaze.

Vase, 6 7/8" h., ovoid body w/wide flat rim, blue pansy decoration by Edith Hood, pink shaded to green ground, marked w/full kiln "Weller Pottery" ink stamp logo (tight line at rim)..................................... **225-250**

Vase, 7 1/2" h., octagonal ovoid body w/flat rim, pastel orange & yellow wild rose decoration around top, grey shading to light green ground, faintly impressed "Weller" in small block letters (some dirty crazing especially on interior) **300-325**

Vase, 8 1/4" h., baluster form w/flaring rim, decorated w/blue flowers & green leaves on green shaded to pink ground, by

Naomi Walch, marked w/half kiln ink stamp logo & artist-signed **725-750**

Vase, 8 1/4" h., 3" d., cylindrical, decorated w/large blue & yellow iris on a pale yellow to pale sage green ground, matte glaze, artist-signed.. **500-525**

Vase, 8 5/8" h., ovoid body, top decorated w/wild roses & green leaves on green shaded to pink ground, by Sarah Timberlake, impressed "Weller" in large block letters, artist-initialed................................ **425-450**

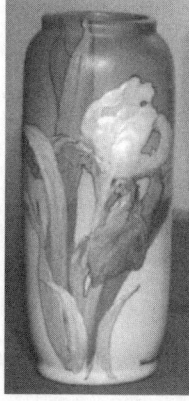

Hudson Vase with Iris Decoration

Vase, 9 3/8" h., footed cylindrical body w/flat rim, decorated w/blue & yellow irises in very heavy slip by Mae Timberlake, shaded green to yellow ground, professional repair of two cracks at rim, artist-signed (ILLUS.).. **600-650**

Vase, 10 1/4" h., footed bulbous base tapering to cylindrical neck w/flat rim, white dogwood decoration by Hester Pillsbury, grey shading to pink ground, impressed "Weller" in script & artist-initialed **775-800**

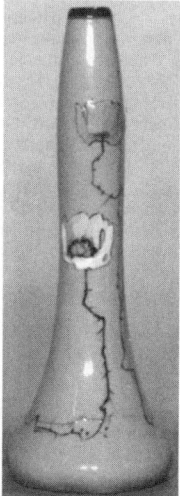

Unusual Hudson Bud Vase

Vase, bud, 10 1/4" h., slender waisted cylinder w/flaring base, decorated w/pink & white poppies on trailing stems in stylish Art Nouveau manner, glossy tan ground w/dark band at rim, impressed "Weller" in large block letters (ILLUS.) **775-800**

Vase, 10 5/8" h., cylindrical body w/short, slightly flared rim, blackberry decoration in pastel colors on light grey shading to yellow ground, impressed "Weller" in small block letters **425-450**

L'Art Nouveau (1903-04)

Various figural and floral-embossed Art Nouveau designs.

L'Art Nouveau Powder Box

Powder jar, cov., footed round body w/cabochons, restored, 4 1/2" d. (ILLUS.) **275**

Vase, bud, 7 1/4" h., flaring base w/two figural birds holding a lily bud (short tight line to body, touchup to nick at rim) **495**

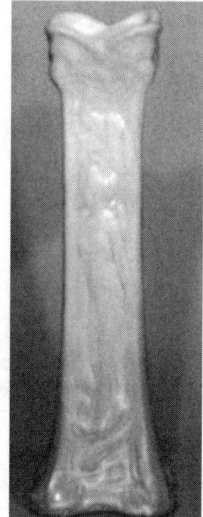

Unusual L'Art Nouveau Vase

Vase, 8" h., slender four-sided body w/molded florals at the top, decorated on one side w/embossed figure of young woman & floral decoration on the other side, semi-gloss glaze of rose to blue to cream, marked "Weller" in small block letters, unobtrusive stilt pulls on bottom (ILLUS.) **248**

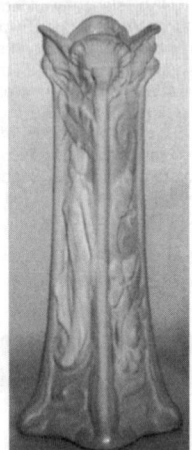

L'Art Nouveau Four-sided Vase

Vase, 10 1/4" h., slender four-sided body w/embossed panels of flowers & Art Nouveau woman, impressed "Weller" in small block letters (ILLUS.) **350-375**

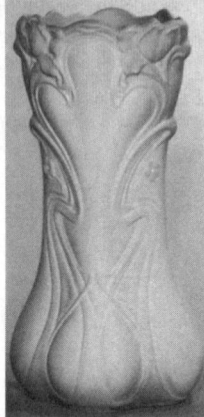

Large L'Art Nouveau Vase

Vase, 11 1/4" h., waisted cylindrical body w/four-lobed base & molded florals at top, very minor glaze rubs on one side at bottom, impressed "Weller" in small block letters (ILLUS.) **450-500**

Louwelsa (1896-1924)
Handpainted underglaze slip decoration on dark brown shading to yellow ground; glossy yellow glaze.

Clock, curvilinear stylized five-point star-shaped case decorated w/chrysanthemum blossoms in orange & yellow on standard glaze brown ground, artist-initialed "ER" on side, round white enamel clock face w/black Roman numerals, impressed "Louwelsa Weller," early 20th c., 10" h. (minor foot chip) **850-900**

Clock, mantel-type, scalloped case w/orange nasturtiums, Gilbert clock works,

stamped "Louwelsa Weller 706," 4 x 10 1/2 x 12 1/2" (colored-in chip to side & a few glaze flakes & chip to base) **525-550**

Cruet, bulbous body decorated w/palm fronds, by Mary Gillie, impressed "Louwelsa Weller," artist-initialed, 4 3/8" h. **75-100**

Ewer, squatty bulbous body decorated w/cherry blossoms, impressed "Louwelsa Weller," 6 1/2" h. **175-200**

Jardiniere, wide flaring waisted cylindrical body w/a wide molded rim, decorated w/a large yellow iris among green leaves on a shaded brown & ochre ground, glossy glaze, impressed mark, 9" h. (glaze scratches) **275-300**

Planter, cylindrical tree trunk form w/three small foxes peeking out at side, 4 1/2" h. **325-350**

Unusual Louwelsa Pillow Vase

Vase, 7" h., pillow form, decorated w/scene of a small house at end of a dirt path w/scruffy plants in foreground & cloudy sky in background, impressed "Louwelsa Weller 41 0" (ILLUS.) **1,000-1,200**

Vase, 9" h., tapering cylindrical form w/wild rose decoration, unmarked (very minor scratches & glaze inconsistencies) **200-225**

Vase, 10 1/2" h., wide cylindrical body decorated w/bright red wild roses, possibly by Albert Haubich, impressed on bottom "Louwelsa Weller 602 5" & artist initialed "A.H." on side (glaze scratches) **350-400**

Vase, 18 1/2" h., slightly tapering cylindrical shouldered body w/small flaring neck, decorated w/lifelike red & purple grapes hanging from finely detailed vine, by Frank Ferrell, impressed "Louwelsa Weller" logo & "200" & "55" (professional repair of small base chip) **1,550-1,575**

Muskota (1915 - late 1920s)
Figural pieces with human figures, birds, animals or frogs. Matte glaze.

Centerpiece, disc base w/two figural baby chicks on grassy mound, unmarked, 5" h. (repair to beaks of both birds) **150-175**

Flower frog, Fishing Boy, boy seated on rockwork w/original "Weller Muskota Ware" paper label, 6 7/8" h. **325-350**

Muskota Figural Garden Ornament

Garden ornament, Fishing Boy, boy standing on round base, brown pants w/one leg rolled up to knee, light blue shirt & black hat, marked w/half-kiln ink stamp logo, two unobtrusive glazed over chips on base, 20 5/8" h. (ILLUS.) **6,225-6,500**

Roma (1912-late '20s)
Cream-colored ground decorated with embossed floral swags, bands or fruit clusters.

Vase, 6 7/8" h., footed tapering cylinder w/molded ring rim, floral decoration, impressed "Weller" in large block letters **50-75**

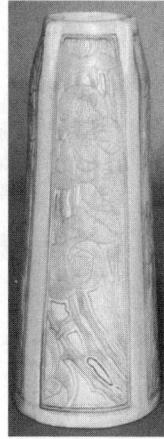

Roma Vase

Vase, 12 3/8" h., tapering cylindrical body w/four panels of stylized roses, unmarked (ILLUS.) **250-275**
Wall pocket, conical, incised vertical lines & decorated w/roses & grape cluster near top, green leaves w/yellow center at base, cream ground, marked "28" in blue slip on back, 8 1/4" h. (very minor staining from use & small bruise on one horizontal band at mid body)......................... **150-175**

Sicardo (1902-07)
Various shapes with iridescent glaze of metallic shadings in greens, blues, crimson, purple or coppertone decorated with vines, flowers, stars or freeform geometric lines.

Vase, 5 1/2" h., waisted cylindrical body w/swelled shoulder tapering to small, flat rim, cloud-like decoration, iridescent blue, green & burgundy glaze, unmarked **600-650**
Vase, 9 1/4" h., expanding cylinder w/rounded shoulders & rolled rim, decorated w/wild violets, iridescent gold, burgundy & green glaze, signed "Weller Sicard" & impressed "6" **925-950**

Monumental Weller Sicardo Vase

Vase, 26 1/2" h., floor-type, large ovoid body tapering to a widely flaring trumpet neck, overall swirling floral design (ILLUS.) **11,550**

Silvertone (1928)
Various flowers, fruits or butterflies molded on a pale purple-blue matte pebbled ground.

Silvertone Vase

Vase, 6" h., footed squatty, bulbous body w/wide flaring rim, decorated w/embossed pink roses & green leaves against a purple ground, ink mark (ILLUS.).. **325-350**

Woodcraft (1917)

Rustic designs simulating the appearance of stumps, logs and tree trunks. Some pieces are adorned with owls, squirrels, dogs and other animals. Matte finish.

Bowl, 4 1/2" h., shallow bulbous form w/oak leaves & acorns around the rim & figural squirrel seated on rim eating a nut, unmarked (repair to oak leaves on rim opposite squirrel) **175-200**
Bowl, 5 7/8" d., 2 7/8" h., footed round body w/flared sides & scalloped rim, decorated w/embossed squirrels & trees, unmarked.. **200-225**

Woodcraft Jardiniere

Jardiniere, log form w/woodpecker on side, impressed "Weller" in large block letters on bottom, short tight line at rim, 6" h. (ILLUS.).. **350-400**
Planter, log form w/three embossed foxes on front, crossed branch handles across top, impressed "Weller" in large block letters, 5 3/4" h. **225-250**
Vase, bud, 10 1/4" h., cylindrical tree trunk form, hollow branch opening in front, flared base & molded apples, branches & leaves, impressed "Weller" in large block letters.. **125-150**
Wall pocket, relief-molded log w/flowers & berries, marked "Weller" in large block letters on back, 9" h. (minor glaze flakes)... **200-225**

Zeisel (Eva) Designs

One of the most influential ceramic artists and designers of the 20th century, Eva Zeisel began her career in Europe as a young woman, eventually immigrating to the United States, where her unique, streamlined designs met with great success. Since the 1940s her work has been at the forefront of commercial ceramic design, and in recent decades she has designed in other media. Now in her ninth decade, she continues to be active and involved in the world of art and design.

Castleton - Museum Ware
Bowl, 11" d., salad, White **$160**

Castleton - Museum Ware Coffee Set

Coffeepot, cov., tall, slender form w/C-scroll handle (ILLUS. second from left w/coffee set).. **500**
Creamer, handleless (ILLUS. second from right w/coffee set)...................................... **300**
Cup & saucer, flat, Mandalay **20**
Cup & saucer (ILLUS. far left w/coffee set).. **150-200**
Plate, 8 1/4" sq., salad, White.............. **135**
Plate, 10 1/2" d., dinner, White............... **50**
Sugar, cov., handleless (ILLUS. far right w/coffee set)...................................... **250**

Hall China Company - Kitchenware

Golden Clover Cookie Jar

Cookie jar, cov., Golden Clover (ILLUS.)............ **65**
Marmite, Casual Living... **30**

Tri-tone Nested Mixing Bowls

Mixing bowls, nested, Tri-tone, set of 5 (ILLUS.) **250**
Refrigerator jug, cov., Tri-tone........................... **150**
Sugar, Tri-tone... **45**

Tri-tone Teapot

White Vegetable Bowl

Teapot, cov., 6-cup, Tri-tone (ILLUS.)................. 85

Hallcraft - Century Dinnerware
Creamer, Fern... 30
Gravy boat & ladle, Fern..................................... 95
Plate, 10" d., dinner, Sunglow............................. 22
Relish, divided, White.. 90
Vegetable bowl, 10 1/2" d., White (ILLUS.,
  top of page)... 18

Hallcraft - Tomorrow's Classic Dinnerware

Bouquet Cup & Saucer

AD cup & saucer, Bouquet (ILLUS.)................... 25
Bowl, 9" d., coupe soup, Spring........................... 15

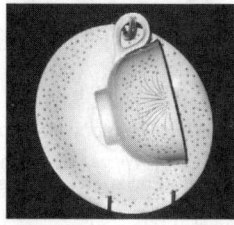

Dawn Cup & Saucer

Cup & saucer, Dawn (ILLUS.)............................. 20
Cup & saucer, White.. 25
Gravy boat & ladle, Lyric.................................... 80

Bouquet Dinner Plate

Plate, 11" d., dinner, Bouquet (ILLUS.)............... 15
Plate, 11" d., dinner, White.................................. 18

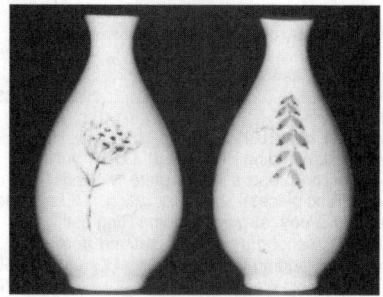

Bouquet Shakers

Shakers, Bouquet, 4" h. (ILLUS.)........................ 15

Hollydale

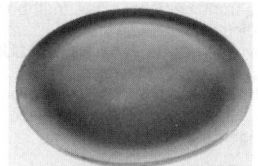

Hollydale Chop Plate

Chop plate, 14" l., brown (ILLUS.)...................... 60
Gravy bowl, bird-shape.. 85
Sauce dish, bird-shape, yellow/turquoise......... 200
Tureen & ladle, bird design, the set.................. 300

Hyalyn "Z Ware"
Bowl, cereal, oxblood, commercial
  grade/restaurant ware....................................... 40

Satin Black "Z Ware" Coffee Server

Wedding Ring Pieces

Coffee server, cov., satin black w/white lid (ILLUS.)... **125**
Creamer, handleless, autumn gold, 4 3/4" h. **85**

Johann Haviland

Bowl, fruit, Wedding Ring patt. (ILLUS. front center, on bread & butter plate, w/Wedding Ring pieces)... **12**
Creamer & cov. sugar, Wedding Ring patt. (ILLUS. second from left & second from right w/Wedding Ring pieces) **60**
Cup & saucer, Wedding Ring................................ **20**
Dinnerware set, Wedding Ring, 20-pc. service for 4 (ILLUS. of dinner plate, far right, & cup & saucer, center, w/Wedding Ring pieces, top of page) **200-250**
Plate, bread & butter, Wedding Ring patt. (ILLUS. front center, under fruit bowl, w/Wedding Ring pieces) **10**
Platter, oval, Wedding Ring patt. (ILLUS. rear, w/Wedding Ring pieces) **60**
Serving bowl, round, Wedding Ring patt. (ILLUS. far left w/Wedding Ring pieces) **40**
Tureen/vegetable bowl, cov., White.................... **80**

Monmouth Dinnerware

Butter pat, Pals, 4" **16**
Creamer, Lacy Wings... **50**

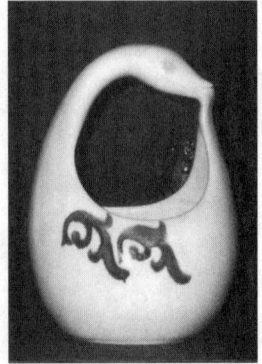

Goose-shaped Gravy Boat

Gravy boat, goose shape, Lacey Wings (ILLUS.)... **175**
Sugar, cov., bird lid, Blueberry **25**

Monmouth Bird-shaped Sugar

Sugar, cov., bird lid, Lacey Wings (ILLUS.) **50**

Lacey Wings Teapot with Rooster

Teapot, cov., Lacey Wings, wire handle w/ceramic grip, Prairie Hen, w/rooster decoration (ILLUS.)... **150**
Vegetable bowl, 9 1/2" d. **65**

Norleans Dinnerware by Meito

(pieces marked "Made in Occupied Japan" are worth 25% more)

Fairfield Cup & Saucer

Cup & saucer, Fairfield (ILLUS.) **8**

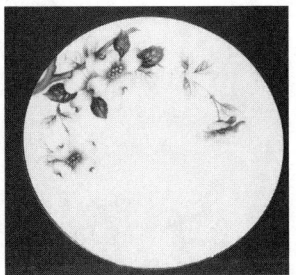

Livonia Dinner Plate

Plate, dinner, Livonia (ILLUS.)............................... **12**
Service for six, Livonia, 36-piece set **200**

Riverside

Riverside Bowl

Bowl, 8 1/2" d., celadon & moss yellow
  (ILLUS.).. **600**
Plate, dinner, yellow & olive green....................... **60**

Schmid Dinnerware

Casserole, cov., bird lid, 9 1/2 x 8" **80**

Schmid Dinnerware Coffeepot

Coffeepot, cov., Lacey Wings/Rosette
  (ILLUS.)... **35**

Schmid Dinnerware Pitcher

Pitcher, 10" h., Lacey Wings & Sunburst
  (ILLUS.) **28**

Schmid Bird-shaped Teapot

Teapot, cov., bird shape, rattan handle,
  Lacey Wings (ILLUS.) **50**

Schramberg

Schramberg Triangular Ashtray

Ashtray, triangular, Gobelin 13 (ILLUS.)........... **160**
Cup & saucer, Gobelin 13 .... **75**

Mondrian Covered Jar

Jar, cov., terraced, Mondrian, 5" (ILLUS.) **1,000**
Pitcher, 4 1/2" h., Mondrian **225**
Plate, 7 1/2" d., dessert, Gobelin 13.................... **60**

Gobelin 13 Teapot

Town and Country Mustard Jar

Teapot, cov., Gobelin 13 (ILLUS.) **900**

Gobelin 8 Vase

Vase, 6" h., offset oval, Gobelin 8 (ILLUS.) **200**

Stratoware

Stratoware Candlestick

Candlestick, brown trim (ILLUS.) **120**

Stratoware Cup & Saucer

Cup & saucer, gold interior (ILLUS.) **50**

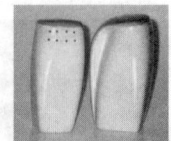

Stratoware Shakers

Shakers, green trim, pr. (ILLUS.)......................... **80**

Town and Country Dinnerware - for Red Wing Potteries

Bowl, 5 3/4" d., chili or cereal............................... **60**

Town and Country "Yawn" Creamer

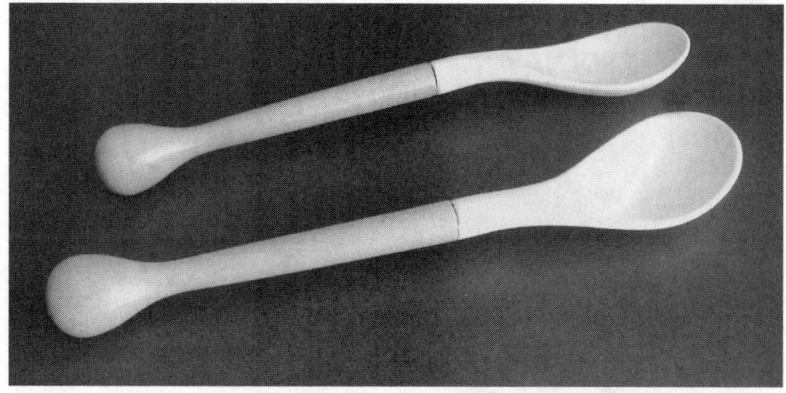

Salad Serving Spoons

Creamer, "yawn," bronze (ILLUS.)...................... **70**

Lazy Susan Relish Set

Lazy Susan relish set w/mustard jar
(ILLUS.)... **500**
Mustard jar, cover & ladle, dusk blue, the
set (ILLUS., previous page)............................. **250**
Plate, 6 1/4" d., bread & butter............................. **15**
Plate, 10 1/2" d., dinner, bronze **50**

Large & Small "Schmoo" Shakers

Shaker, large "schmoo," Ming green
(ILLUS. right w/small "schmoo" shaker) **75**
Shaker, small "schmoo," rust (ILLUS. left
w/large "schmoo" shaker) **35**
Spoons, salad servers, white, the set
(ILLUS., top of page) **1,600**

Covered Soup Tureen

Tureen, cov., soup, sand (ILLUS.)...................... **650**

Watt Pottery

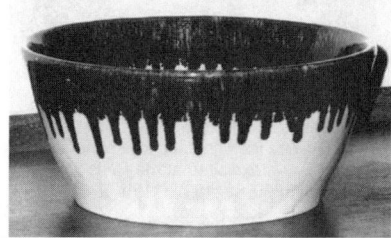

Watt Pottery Drip Glaze Bowl

Bowl, 8 1/4" d., blue drip glaze (ILLUS.)............. **25**
Chop tray, Mountain Road, 14 1/2".................... **210**
Teapot, cov., rattan handle, Animal Farm **600**

Zsolnay

*This pottery was made in Pecs, Hungary, in a factory
founded in 1862 by Vilmos Zsolnay. Utilitarian earthenware was originally produced, but by the turn of the 20th
century ornamental Art Nouveau-style wares with bright
colors and lustre decoration were produced; these wares
are especially sought today. Currently Zsolnay pieces
are being made in a new factory.*

ZSOLNAY
PÉCS

Zsolnay Marks

Zsolnay Domed Box

Box, cov., rectangular, w/domed lid, Ivory Ware medieval design w/later metallic eosin glaze, incised Zsolnay factory mark, unknown form number, ca. 1900, 3 1/4" h. (ILLUS.)................................... **$400-600**

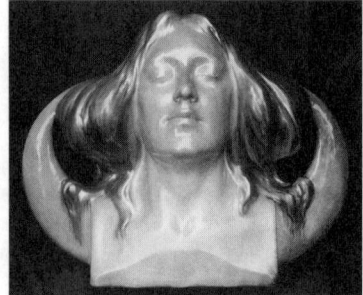

"Luna" Portrait Bust by Zsolnay

Bust, "Luna" by Sandor Apati Abt, realistic portrait of woman w/long hair & closed eyes, various metallic eosin glazes, incised Zsolnay factory mark, incised form number 5494, exhibited at the Paris Exposition in 1900, ca. 1899, 11" h. (ILLUS.)... **25,000-30,000**

Zsolnay Armin Klein Charger

Charger, painted w/scene of peasants in folkloric costumes pressing grapes in a vineyard, design by Armin Klein, printed

Zsolnay factory mark, incised form number 470, ca. 1880, 15" d. (ILLUS.)... **1,500-2,000**

Zsolnay Tadé Sikorsky Jug

Jug, form designed by Tadé Sikorsky, shriveled glaze w/applied pierced decorations, incised Zsolnay factory mark & form number 1379, ca. 1885, 8" h. (ILLUS.) **350-550**

Zsolnay Lamp by Lajos Mack

Lamp, figural, Art Nouveau model of a woman in the style of Loïe Fuller, w/arms upraised & flowing hair, designed by Lajos Mack, mostly gold/green eosin glazes, round raised Zsolnay factory mark, incised form number 6324, ca. 1900, 22 1/2" h. (ILLUS.) **20,000-25,000**

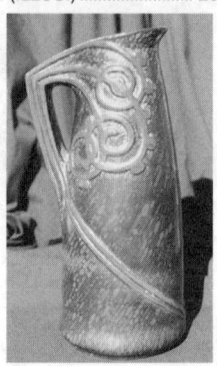

Zsolnay Pitcher with Metallic Glaze

Zsolnay Plaque-like Tile

Pitcher, 9 1/2" h., slightly bulbous tankard shape w/angular handle, metallic eosin glazed decoration in the style of Loetz Bohemian glass, round raised Zsolnay factory mark, incised form number 8925, ca. 1918 (ILLUS.) **2,500-3,500**

Zsolnay Dragon Motif Pitcher

Pitcher, 13" h., cov., decorative Ivory Ware lid, dragon form handle & spout, cream ground w/gilt trim, incised & applied decoration of dragon & gargoyle copying 18th-c. designs, printed Zsolnay factory mark, incised form number 2994, ca. 1889 (ILLUS.) **600-800**

Zsolnay Cock-form Pitcher

Pitcher, 18" h., in the form of a crowing cock w/stylized feathers on oval base, open beak forms spout, pale green eosin glaze, incised Zsolnay factory mark, incised form number 1132, ca. 1903 (ILLUS.) **4,000-5,000**

Tile, rectangular plaque form w/oval cartouche w/relief decoration of idyllic setting w/Art Nouveau-style female dancer & Pan-like figures playing musical instruments, multicolored eosin glazes, designed by Lajos Mack, incised Zsolnay factory mark, incised form number 7892, ca. 1906, 8 1/4 x 10 3/4" (ILLUS., top of page) **7,500-9,500**

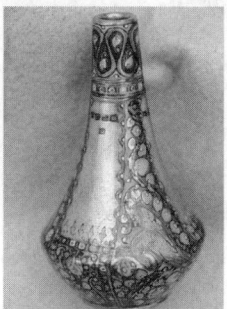

Miniature Zsolnay Vase

Vase, miniature, 4" h., wide base tapering to ring foot & long neck, richly decorated w/Hungarian folkloric designs in gold & blue/green eosin glazes, incised Zsolnay factory mark, ca. 1912 (ILLUS.) **1,000-1,250**

Egyptian Decor Zsolnay Vase

Vase, 5" h., cylindrical, tapering out toward top, then in toward short neck w/small opening, Art Deco Egyptian decor, designed by Teréz Mattyasovszky-Zsolnay, printed Zsolnay factory mark, ca. 1915 (ILLUS.)... **1,250-1,500**

Zsolnay Vase with Landscape Scene

Vase, 9 3/4" h., cylindrical body tapering to short, flared neck, painted w/landscape scene of trees, sunset, clouds & flowers, brilliant eosin glazes, round raised Zsolnay factory mark, incised form number 8196, ca. 1909 (ILLUS.)............... **12,500-15,000**

Zsolnay Vase by Sándor Pillo-Hidasy

Vase, 10 3/4" h., ovoid body tapering in at neck, which tapers further to short molded rim, decorated w/three spotted leopards around body, silver metallic leaves w/red early Deco decorations, signed by Sándor Pillo-Hidasy, round raised Zsolnay factory mark, incised form number 8589, ca. 1912 (ILLUS.)............... **20,000-25,000**

Hungarian Millennium Vase

Vase, 11 3/4" h., bulbous waisted form w/short bulbous applied feet, Hungarian Millennium decoration of painted stylized birds & flowers, round printed Zsolnay factory mark, incised form number 933, ca. 1882 (ILLUS.).................... **2,500-3,500**

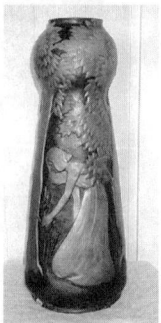

Lajos Mack Vase with Relief Design

Vase, 28" h., tapering cylindrical form w/squat ovoid neck, decorated w/relief design of figures in forest setting including Pan-like form, various eosin metallic glazes, designed by Lajos Mack, incised Zsolnay factory mark, incised form number 5902, ca. 1900 (ILLUS.)......... **25,000-30,000**

CEREAL PROMOTIONAL COLLECTIBLES

For close to 100 years the manufacturers of cereal have offered giveaways - from toy soldiers in the box to mail-away offers for secret decoder rings - to promote their products. For many decades the material could be purchased for as little as 5-10 cents. In addition to the give-away items, advertising connected to the products and even the packaging itself have become valuable to collectors. Eventually, many of the giveaways were tied in to radio or television shows sponsored by the cereal companies.

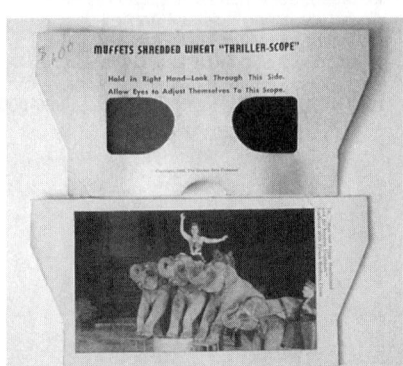

3D Glasses & Views

3D views & viewer, cardboard 3D glasses w/"Muffets Shredded Wheat 'Thriller-scope'" on front, w/set of 16 cards of scenes from Polack Circus, Quaker Muffets Shredded Wheat giveaway, 1953, 2 3/4 x 5 3/4", each (ILLUS.).......................... **$10**

Comic Book Ad for Wheaties

Advertisement, for Kellogg's Pep Cereal comic character button giveaways, "Free - one in every package of Kellogg's Pep" & "Save 'em, trade 'em" w/illustrations of characters available, 1947 .... **85**

Advertisement, from Superman #24 comic book, double-page spread for Wheaties, w/color illustrations & headline "Are You 'Pre-Flight' Material?" w/text promoting the benefits of eating Wheaties & tag line "Breakfast of Champions," September-October 1943 (ILLUS., top of page) **50**

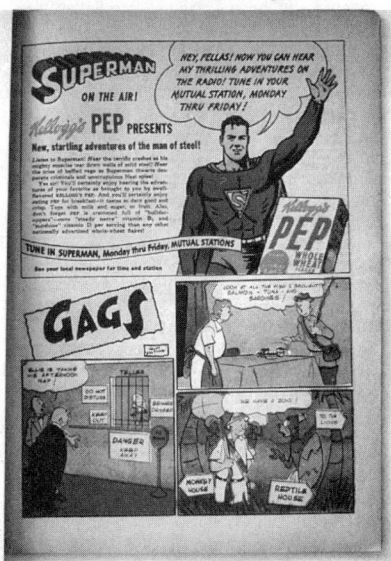

Comic Book Ad for Radio Show

Advertisement, half-page ad from Superman comic #24, full-color illustrations & text promoting Superman radio show, of

which Kellogg's Pep Cereal was a sponsor, 1943 (ILLUS.) **80**

Advertisement, promoting Post Raisin Bran's set of rings w/likenesses of comic strip characters, offered free in boxes of the cereal, 1948, 15 1/4 x 20" **400**

Book, "Dick Daring's Bag of Tricks" book of magic tricks, offered as premium by Quaker Oats, 1933 .... **50**

Cardboard aircraft, to be cut from boxes of Kellogg's Rice Krispies & assembled, 1955 .... **15**

Cardboard military air base set, to be cut from boxes of Cheerios & assembled, included fighter planes, hangar, missile defense station w/small spring-fired missiles & radar station, 1958, the set **175**

Catalog, issued by Ralston Purina for Tom Mix promotional material **55**

Ralston Cereal Bowl

Cereal bowl, ceramic, from Ralston Cereal, decorated w/color images of Tom Mix inside & out & "Ralston Hot Cereal - Since 1895," 1980 (ILLUS.) **35**

Froot Loops Cereal Bowl

Cereal bowl, plastic, w/full-color image of Toucan Sam in bottom of bowl, "Kellogg's Froot Loops" & "Toucan Sam" in red & blue around rim, 1992 (ILLUS.).......... **10**

Cereal bowl, silver plate, inside features impressed likeness of one of the Dionne Quints & her name, Quaker Oats promotion, 1935 .... **55**

Kellogg's Decoder

Decoder, plastic, green, w/"Dig 'ems Secret Decoder" embossed on front, Kellogg's giveaway, 1983 (ILLUS.) **5**

Diving figures, plastic figures of U.S. Navy frogmen, three poses & various colors, would dive & resurface when filled w/baking powder, Kellogg's Corn Flakes promotion, 1954, 2" h., each **25**

Diving figures, plastic figures of U.S. Navy frogmen, three poses & various colors, would dive & resurface when filled w/baking powder, Kellogg's Corn Flakes offered three divers for a box top & 25 cents, 1955, 3 1/2" h., each **25**

Doll, Cream of Wheat promotion, cloth, in the image of the Cream of Wheat black chef w/red bow tie & white apron, one version holds a steaming bowl of cereal, the other holds box of cereal, meant to be sewn & filled w/cereal, 1930-1940s, each **100**

Kellogg's Rice Krispies Doll

Doll, Kellogg's Rice Krispies, vinyl, color figures of Snap, Crackle or Pop, each w/its name on front of its cap, 1975, 8" h., set of three, each (ILLUS. of one)........................ **45**

Doll patterns, Goldilocks & the Three Bears, six-color muslin patterns were meant to be sewn & filled w/corn flakes, Kellogg's promotional item, Papa Bear holds box of Kellogg's Corn Flakes, Baby Bear an empty bowl, etc., 1925, rare, each **500**

Doll patterns, Kellogg's Fairyland Series, six-color muslin patterns of nursery rhyme figures were meant to be sewn & filled w/corn flakes, came w/cloth nursery rhyme book, could be ordered for one box top & 30 cents, 15" h., 1928, set of four, each **100**

Figures of football players, plastic, red or white, football players in various poses, Kellogg's giveaway, 1960, 2 1/2" h., each **10**

Figures of hockey players, plastic, red or blue, hockey players in various poses, Kellogg's giveaway, 1960, 2 1/2" h., each **10**

Figures of skaters, plastic, Ice Capades skaters, came w/solution that allowed figures to "skate" on water for hours, Kellogg's Corn Flakes promotion, set of 18 was offered for 25 cents & two box tops, 1956, each.. **5**

Lone Ranger Deputy Kit, Cheerios tie-in to last Lone Ranger movie, included badge, certificate, punch-out black mask, story folder of movie & 17 x 22" color poster of Lone Ranger & Tonto, 1980 .... **45**

Marbles, each w/the face of Montreal Canadiens or Toronto Maple Leaf hockey player, Post Cereal giveaway, 1960s, each **35**

Mask, paper, artwork by Vernon Grant, masks of Kellogg's Rice Krispies' Snap, Crackle & Pop, to introduce public to new Rice Krispies cereal, 1933, each **95**

Model of U.S.S. Nautilus Atomic Sub

Model of submarine, Kellogg's giveaway, plastic model of U.S.S. Nautilus atomic submarine could be "powered" by baking powder, hard to find w/metal cap for baking powder reservoir, 1950s, 4 1/2" l., sub alone $50, w/instruction sheet (ILLUS.)... **100**

Models of animals, plastic, grey, various wild animals, Kellogg's Sugar Corn Pops giveaway, "Big Game Hunter's Favorite - Wild Animals - One Free in Each Package," 1956, 1 to 2 1/2", each **10**

Models of characters from Lady & the Tramp, plastic, tie-in to Walt Disney movie, Kellogg's Rice Krispies promotion, 1955, 2" h., set of 12, each................................ **25**

Mug, plastic, in the form of Roy Rogers, w/the spout in his hat, Quaker Oats promotion, "Boys, Girls, Mothers, get your autographed Roy Rogers Souvenir mug,"offered for 35 cents & a brand label, 1950, 4" h. **25**

"Ore detector," black battery-operated toy w/compass & meter to detect ore, Quaker Puffed Rice & Puffed Wheat promotion tied in to Sergeant Preston of the Yukon radio show, 3", 1952, detector alone $150, in red version $250, w/instructions & mailer **225**

Packaging, Kellogg's Corn Flakes box w/figural Superman offer, "Not a bird, Not a plane, It's Flying Superman -Get Yours First! Only 10 cents and one box top," 1955.. **300**

Packaging, Kellogg's Corn Flakes cereal box promoting offer of Ice Capades set of miniature skaters, 1956..................................... **80**

Packaging, Kellogg's Sugar Corn Pops cereal box that contained wild animal giveaways, 1956.. **135**

Kellogg's Pencil Sharpener

Pencil sharpener, plastic, yellow w/"Rice Krispies ®" on front, Kellogg's giveaway tied in w/start of school year, one of a number of school supplies offered, 1960s (ILLUS.)... **8**

Movie Star Pinback Buttons

Pinback button, Quaker Puffed Wheat & Rice, each w/picture of movie star's face, w/the name of the star in red above & the studio in red below, on back "Quaker Puffed Wheat and Rice Shot from Cannons," 1948, set of 20, each (ILLUS. of six) **25**

Post Giveaway Railroad Sign

Railroad sign, metal, Post Cereals giveaway, from series on railroads, each brightly colored w/logo of railroad line, 1954, 4" (ILLUS. of Southern Pacific Lines) **25**

Ring, brass, Lone Ranger ring mounted w/plastic model of atomic bomb, Kix Cereal promotion, 1947...................................... **200**

Ring/viewer, Lone Ranger movie tie-in, brass bands w/aluminum viewing tube w/25-frame 8mm color filmstrip of the U.S. Marines, Cheerios promotion, ring only $125, filmstrip only $100, both **225**

Rings, w/likenesses of comic strip characters, offered free in boxes of Nabisco Raisin Bran, 1948, value depends on popularity of character depicted, each **65-130**

Kellogg's Robin Hood Giveaways

Robin Hood figures, plastic, green figures of Robin Hood & his Merry Men in various poses w/bows, swords, or staffs, Kellogg's giveaway tied in w/TV show, 1950s, 1 3/4 to 2" h., each (ILLUS. of three) **5**

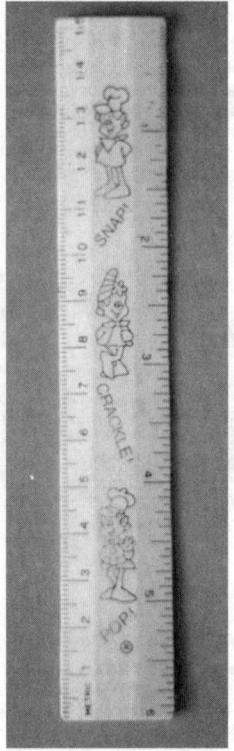

Snap, Crackle, Pop Ruler

Ruler, plastic, w/images of Snap, Crackle & Pop on front, measures in inches & metric units, Kellogg's giveaway tied in w/start of school year, one of a number of school supplies offered, 1960s, 6" l. (ILLUS.).. **8**

"Secret Whistling Ring," brass, decorated w/Egyptian symbols, Wheaties Cereal promotion tied in to Jack Armstrong, All-American Boy, 1937, code instruction sheet $90, ring alone **150**

"Space Patrol Cosmic Smoke Gun," red, issued by Ralston Purina Rice Chex & Wheat Chex, 1952-55, 4 1/2" l........................ **275**

Space Patrol view cards, w/characters & scenes from the TV show, promotion by sponsor Ralston Purina Rice Chex & Wheat Chex, 1953, 4", set of 24, each............ **10**

Space Patrol view cards viewer, plastic, green, w/Space Patrol logo & rocket, promoted w/set of view cards of the TV show, promotion by sponsor Ralston Purina Rice Chex & Wheat Chex, 1953, 5" **160**

Kellogg's "Spooner"

Spoon holder, plastic, figures in the form of various characters from the Disney movie The Black Hole, meant to keep one's spoon from slipping into cereal bowl, various colors, Kellogg's giveaway, 1979, 4" h., each (ILLUS. of robot)............................. **12**

Kellogg's Jiminy Cricket "Spooner"

Kellogg's Eskimo Figures

Spoon holder, plastic, figures in the form of various Walt Disney characters, meant to keep one's spoon from slipping into cereal bowl, red, yellow, or blue, Kellogg's giveaway, 1960, 2" (ILLUS. of Jiminy Cricket).. **10**

Wheaties Giveaway Airline Sticker

Sticker, of the type to be stuck on a piece of luggage, Wheaties giveaway in boxes of cereal, full color picture of airplane & its name underneath, 1954-55, 3 x 3 3/4", set of 15, each (ILLUS. of one)......................... **10**

Store display, cardboard, standup image of Straight Arrow holding box of Nabisco Shredded Wheat & "Listen to Straight Arrow," w/section listing local Mutual Radio stations that aired the show, 1949, 66" h... **1,600**

Superman figure, plastic, in flying pose, blue w/colored cape, Kellogg's Corn Flakes offer for one box top & 10 cents, 1955, 6 1/2".. **150**

"Superman Flying Rocket & Pump Launcher," plastic, advertised on box as "real jet-propelled missile," Kellogg's Sugar Corn Pops offered both for box top & 50 cents, made by Park Plastic of Linden, New Jersey, 1956.................................... **100**

"Superman Flying Rocket & Pump Launcher" cereal box, Kellogg's Sugar Corn Pops, front shows rocket at bottom under picture of Wild Bill Hickok from TV show sponsored by Kellogg's, 1956, 9 1/2" h. **300**

Telegraph key, plastic, Nabisco Cereal giveaway tied in to Rin Tin Tin TV show, dark brown base w/bright yellow key, 1956, 1 3/4" l.. **40**

Tom Mix secret writing kit, included manual w/code information, cardboard decoder, two glass vials of ink, developer material, Ralston Purina promotion, 1940 ..... **425**

Lucky Charms Leprechaun

Toy, plush Lucky Charms leprechaun, 1996, 5 1/4" h. (ILLUS.) **5**

Kellogg's Stuffed Tony the Tiger

Toy Soldiers Promotional Figures

Toy, plush Tony the Tiger, sold in stores in connection w/45th anniversary of Kellogg's Sugar Frosted Flakes, 1997 (ILLUS.)... **30**

Toy figures, plastic, Eskimo figures in various poses, tie-in to TV show & International Geophysical Year of 1957, Kellogg's giveaway, made by Marx Toys of New York City, 1 3/4 to 2" h., rare, each (ILLUS. of five, top of page)..................... **10**

Toy soldiers, Kellogg's Sugar Pops promotion, plastic, khaki-colored figures of soldiers in various poses, entire set of 12 could be ordered w/box top & 25 cents, 1 1/2 to 2 1/4" h., each (ILLUS. of three, top of page) **6**

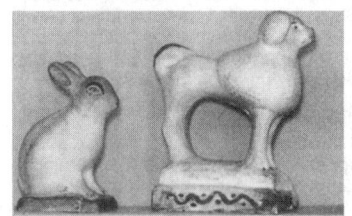

Kellogg's Toy Soldier Giveaway

Toy soldiers, silvered metal figures of Soldiers of the World (included Scotsman, African warrior, Native American, etc.), Kellogg's giveaway, 1960s, 2 1/4" h., each (ILLUS. of French Foreign Legion figure) **3**

Toy submarine, plastic, Cheerios promotion, "atomic" submarine fires "torpedoes," 1958, 12" l. **60**

"Wheel of Knowledge," Kellogg's cereals pictured along edge w/questions, 1921, 6 1/2" d.. **45**

Whistle, plastic, in the form of a glow-in-the-dark crocodile w/three holes in the top to get different tones, 1940, rare Wheaties test market item (only three known to exist) **4,600**

CHALKWARE

So-called chalkware available today is actually made of plaster-of-Paris, much of it decorated in color and primarily in the form of busts, figurines and ornaments.

It was produced through most of the 19th century, and the majority of pieces were quite inexpensive when made. Today even 20th century "carnival" pieces are collectible.

Basket of fruit, mantel ornament, trimmed in color, 19th c., 7" w., 8 1/2" h. (imperfections) **$748**

Cat, nodder-type, crouching animal in grey & tan w/touches of red on the ears, mouth & collar, indistinctly inscribed "Boston 1883" on base, 3 1/2 x 7", 3 3/4" h. (wear) **1,035**

Cat, w/curled tail w/brown spots, red collar & ears, yellow eyes, seated on dark green base w/brown daubs, 5 1/2" h., small patch, touch-ups **550**

Dog, seated, looks like cross between poodle & dachshund, pinkish brown paint & black ears, mouth, collar & base, 6 1/2" l. (minor wear).. **330**

Garniture, on stand, w/fruit & foliage decoration, reddish brown & yellow polychrome w/worn white base, 10 3/4" h. (edge wear) **1,705**

Garniture, urn in natural white w/design of fruit & kissing birds in original yellow, red & brown polychrome, 12" h. (minor wear) .. **4,290**

Pigeon, red & green wings & base, black beak & feet, on molded perch w/incised design, wear, 6" h. **265**

Poodle, w/long legs, molded fur on shoulders & ears, greenish blue base w/black design, black tail & details, minor wear, 6 7/8" h. (ILLUS. right)................................... **275**

Chalkware Rabbit & Poodle

Rabbit, big yellow eyes, orange ears & mouth, seated on green base, original sizing left on head has darkened, one eye is worn, 5 1/4" h. (ILLUS. left)................. **468**

CHARACTER COLLECTIBLES

Numerous objects made in the likeness of or named after comic strip and comic book personalities or characters abounded from the 1920s to the present. Scores of these are now being eagerly collected and prices still vary widely. Also see DISNEY COLLECTIBLES and TOYS and "ANTIQUE TRADER TOY PRICE GUIDE."

Archie & friends coloring book, The Archies, Whitman, No. 1135......................... **$12 -20**
Archie & friends lunch box & thermos, The Archies, steel box & plastic thermos, Aladdin, 1969.. **75-125**
Baby Huey puppet, hand-type, cloth body, vinyl head, Gund **15-35**
Barnacle Bill toy, windup tin walker, J. Chein, very good, 6" h. **395**
Batman trading cards, 1966 Topps TV Batman cards w/color shots from the program, "Riddler Back" design type, top condition, complete set of 38...................... **2,581**

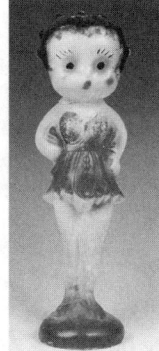

Early Betty Boop Chalk Figure

Betty Boop figure, chalkware, early Carnival-type, ca. 1930-40, repaired, some paint wear,15" h. (ILLUS.)........................ **200-250**
Bugs Bunny alarm clock, battery-operated, Janex, 1974 .... **40-80**
Bugs Bunny bank, metal, Bugs w/barrel on base, 1940s, 5 1/2" h................................. **75-150**
Bugs Bunny bank, plastic, Bugs on carrot box, Dakin, 1971 .... **30-50**

Bugs Bunny Soaky Container

Bugs Bunny bubble bath bottle, figural plastic Bugs, Soaky, Colgate-Palmolive, 1960s, 10" h. (ILLUS.)............................... **15-40**

Bugs Bunny Clothes Rack

Bugs Bunny clothes rack, painted wood, flat figure of Bugs w/pegs, reads "Hang It Up, Doc!," on base, Brachs, 1991, 54" h. (ILLUS.) **35-55**
Bugs Bunny comic book, Bugs Bunny No. 46, Dell, 1956.. **2-5**
Bugs Bunny comic book, Looney Tunes No. 157, Bugs paints Elmer on cover, Dell, 1954 .... **2-8**

Talking Bugs Bunny Doll

Bugs Bunny doll, talking-type, plush w/rubber mask face & hands, Mattel, 1971, 22" h. (ILLUS.)... **35-65**

Rare Captain Marvel Figure & Box

Bugs Bunny Vinyl Figure

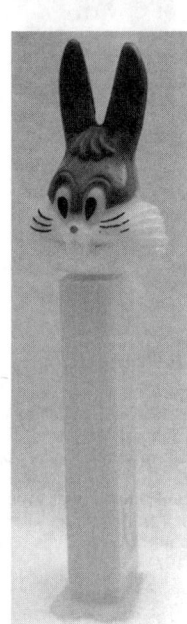

Bugs Bunny Pez Dispenser

Bugs Bunny figure, articulated vinyl, Dakin, 1971, 10 1/2" h. (ILLUS.)................ 15-30

Bugs Bunny figure, bendable, Applause, 1980s, 4" l.. 5-12

Bugs Bunny figure, talking-type, plastic w/pull string, "Chatter Chum," Mattel, 1982.. 20-40

Bugs Bunny game, "Bugs Bunny Bagatelle Game," Ideal, 1975 12-25

Bugs Bunny game, "Bugs Bunny Under the Cawit Game," Whitman, 1972 15-30

Bugs Bunny Pez dispenser, plastic, no feet 15-20

Bugs Bunny Pez dispenser, plastic, yellow body w/feet, 1978, 5" h. (ILLUS.) 1-4

Bugs Bunny puppet, hand-type, cloth w/rubber head, Zany, 1940s 50-100

Bugs Bunny puppet, plush w/pull string, Talking Bugs Bunny, Mattel, 1962, 13" h.. 35-75

Bugs Bunny ring, plastic flicker-type, Arby's premium, 1987 20-35

Bugs Bunny toy, Magic Slate, Golden, 1987 5-9

Bugs Bunny wristwatch, Lafayette, 1978 ... 30-60

Caption Action Toy & Box

Captain Action toy, Silver Streak Amphibian vehicle, dark blue plastic on black rubber tires, shoots red rubber-tipped rockets, Ideal Toy Company, 1967, small repair on vehicle, near mint box w/instruction sheet, vehicle 12 x 22", 7 1/2" h. (ILLUS.)............................. **991**

Captain Marvel figure, plastic, molded standing figure w/hands on hips, wearing bright red & yellow outfit, on oblong tan base w/name, R.W. Kerr Co., 1946, mint condition in excellent full color box (ILLUS., top of previous page) **2,195**

Captain Marvel toy, windup tin, Captain Marvel Lightning Race Car, Automatic Toy Co., 1947, 4" l. **100-200**

Casper the Friendly Ghost bubble bath bottle, plastic, figural Casper, Soaky, Colgate-Palmolive, 1960s.......................... **35-50**

Casper the Friendly Ghost costume, Casper, Collegeville, 1960s........................ **25-50**

Casper the Friendly Ghost doll, cloth body, Mattel, 1960s, 15" h. **50-85**

Casper the Ghost Talking Doll

Casper the Friendly Ghost doll, talking-type, terry cloth w/plastic face, pull string, Mattel, 1961, 15" h. (ILLUS.).................... **45-125**

Casper the Friendly Ghost lamp, figural Casper, Archlamp, 1950, 17" h.................. **75-95**

Casper the Friendly Ghost puppet, Casper, cloth body, plastic head, Gund, 1960s, 8" h. **25-50**

Casper the Friendly Ghost squeak toy, rubber Casper w/logo, Sutton & Sons, 1972 .... **25-50**

Casper the Friendly Ghost toy, Casper jack-in-the-box, metal box, plays theme song, Mattel, 1960 .... **40-70**

Creature from the Black Lagoon, windup plastic walking toy w/red winder, Hong Kong, 3" h.. **15-25**

Creature from the Black Lagoon Toy

Creature from the Black Lagoon toy, windup tin, Robot House, 1992, 9" h. (ILLUS.).. **85-115**

Creature from the Black Lagoon game, "Creature from the Black Lagoon Mystery Game," Hasbro, 1963.............................. **225-295**

Creature from the Black Lagoon button, black & white photo on colored background, 1960s, 7/8" d. **12-20**

Creature from the Black Lagoon figure, bendee, made in China, 1991, 4" l........... **10-15**

Creature from the Black Lagoon figure, Figure No. 2, AHI, 1973, 8" h................ **350-900**

Creature from the Black Lagoon figure, plastic, unarticulated, Marx, 1963, 6" h. **15-20**

Creature from the Black Lagoon Halloween costume, Ben Cooper, 1973............. **40-60**

Creature from the Black Lagoon Pez dispenser, pearl green, 1965..................... **150-200**

Dick Tracy Board Game

Dick Tracy Police Station Toy

Dick Tracy game, board-type, "Dick Tracy - The Master Detective Game," SeeRight - Selchow & Righter, 1961 (ILLUS.) **35-75**
Dick Tracy game, target-type, lithographed tin target, Marx, 1941, 10" w/target **100-200**
Dick Tracy toy, windup tin Dick Tracy Police Station w/car, Marx, 1950s, 3 1/2 x 8" (ILLUS., top of page) **300-600**
Dick Tracy Ford pedal car, metal, chromed hubcaps, Dick Tracy decal on both sides, Garton, 35" l. **413**

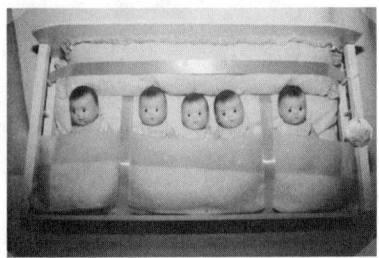

Alexander Dionne Quintuplets Dolls

Dionne Quintuplets dolls, composition baby dolls, all-original w/clothing, blanket, bedding & bed, original hang tag, Madame Alexander, 1930s, small size, the set (ILLUS.) **2,200**
Dracula button, black & white photo on colored background, 1960s, 7/8" d. **12-20**
Dracula figure, mini-monster, glow version, Remco, 1980s, 3 3/4" h. **15-30**
Dracula figure, plastic, unarticulated, Marx, 1960s, 6" h. **12-20**
Dracula game, "Dracula Mystery Game," Hasbro, 1963 .... **175-225**
Dracula Halloween costume, Ben Cooper, 1963... **50-100**
Dracula paint-by-number set, Hasbro, 1963.. **165-300**
Dracula wallet, Hasbro, 1963..................... **100-150**
Elsie the Cow magazine ad, Life magazine, full-page ad for Borden's Hemo instant drink mix, w/full-color illustration of Elsie the Cow standing at soda counter w/sign listing various vitamins & minerals & saying to man, girl & boy drinking at counter "CAPTURED! All these neces-

sary vitamins & minerals in one delicious drink!" above caption "Here's HEMO - Borden's new way to drink your vitamins and like 'em!" over text & inset illustrations of how to mix product, Nov. 11, 1940 (ILLUS., below).. **35**

Ad for HEMO with Elsie the Cow

Foghorn Leghorn Pez dispenser, plastic, no feet **65-95**
Foghorn Leghorn Pez dispenser, w/feet, brown head, yellow beak, red wattle.......... **50-75**
Foghorn Leghorn puppet, hand-type, cloth w/rubber head, Zany, 1940s............ **50-100**
Frankenstein book, flip-type, Monster Flip Movies, Topps Gum, 1963, 2 1/2", each... **10-15**
Frankenstein bubble bath bottle, Soaky, 1960s **75-150**
Frankenstein bucket, for Halloween candy, figural Frankenstein head, Clinton, 1963 .... **75-150**
Frankenstein Halloween costume, Ben Cooper, 1963... **60-100**
Frankenstein mask, Don Post, 1967 .... **200-250**
Frankenstein pencil topper, rubber, yellow Frankenstein head, 1960s, 1" **15-20**

Giant Frankenstein Poster

Frankenstein poster, mail-order offer (w/small toys in tube), 1960s, 6' h. (ILLUS.)... **150-200**

Frankenstein ring, flicker-type, blue base, 1960s.. **35-50**

Godzilla action figure, blue or brown vinyl, small scale, Bullmark, 1975, each............ **50-100**

Godzilla coloring book, "Godzilla - King of the Monsters," Resource Publications No. 630, 1977 .... **35-45**

Godzilla game, Ideal, 1963 .... **200-400**

Godzilla toy, battery-operated, radio-controlled, walks, moves head & tail, roars, Tokyo Marui, 21" h. **750-900**

James Bond Movie Figures & Box

James Bond figures, molded plastic, includes characters from the first three James Bond movies, decorated in color, Gilbert, 1965, loose figures w/mint unassembled cardboard box, each figure 3 1/2" h., the set (ILLUS. of figures & box) **307**

James Bond Board Game

James Bond game, board-type, "James Bond - Secret Agent 007 Game," Sean Connery cover art, Milton Bradley, 1964 (ILLUS.).. **30-70**

King Kong costume, DeLaurentis version, Ben Cooper, 1976...................................... **45-65**

King Kong Bendee Figure

King Kong figure, bendee, based on cartoon series, mid-1960s, 5 1/2" h. (ILLUS.) **20-35**

King Kong figure, chalkware, 1940s carnival prize, 14" h.. **50-100**

King Kong figure, plastic, red, Palmer Plastics, 1963, 3" h. **20-35**

King Kong game, board-type, Ideal, 1963, 10 x 20" box.. **40-65**

Ideal King Kong Game

King Kong game, board-type, Ideal, 1976 (ILLUS.).. **18-25**

Li'l Audrey squeak toy, soft hollow vinyl, late 1950s - early 1960s, 13 1/2" h............. **25-50**

Mary Marvel figure, plastic, molded standing figure dressed in red & yellow outfit, on a tan rectangular base w/her name, R.W. Kerr Company, 1946, new mint in original colorful box..................... **2,195**

Mummy (The) book, flip-type, "Monster Flip Movies," Topps Gum, 1963, 2 1/2", each .. **10-15**

Mummy (The) bubble bath bottle, Soaky, figural, 1963 .... **65-100**

Mummy (The) button, black & white photo on colored background, 1960s, 7/8" d. **12-20**

Mummy (The) figure, plastic, MPC, mid-1960s, 2 1/2" h.. **15-25**

Mummy (The) Halloween costume, Ben Cooper, 1973... **15-30**

Mummy (The) ring, flicker-type, round, 1960s... **20-30**

Rare Odd Job Action Figure

Odd Job (James Bond) action figure, Gilbert, 1965, sealed mint in box (ILLUS.)..... **1,761**

Rare Operator 5 Club Ring

Operator 5 Club ring, silvered metal w/black enamel trim, flat top w/image of a skull w/a "5" on the forehead, premium from 1930s Pulp hero series, made by

Popular, some light dings on band, couple small flakes on face, resized, 1934 (ILLUS.) **2,717**

Rare 1948 Orphan Annie Watch

Orphan Annie wristwatch, New Haven Clock and Watch Company, color standing image of Annie on the dial, mint in original green back w/color image of Annie & Sandy on the top & inside, 1948 (ILLUS. of box & watch).............................. **1,572**

Rare Aurora Penguin Model Kit

Penguin (Batman comics) model kit, Aurora, 1967, sealed mint in box (ILLUS.)......... **731**

Phantom of the Opera toy, windup nodder, Japan, 1963 .... **75-100**

Phantom of the Opera game, "Phantom of the Opera Mystery Game," Hasbro, 1963.. **175-225**

Pink Panther toy, windup plastic walker, 3" h. **12-20**

Planet of the Apes bank, plastic, figural Dr. Zaius, Play Pal, 1974, 11" h. **30-50**

Rare Popeye NOMA Light Set

Popeye Christmas tree light set, eight lights on a continuous wire, matching plastic color bell-shaped shades w/color decals of popular Popeye characters, NOMA, 1930s, first version, mint in box (ILLUS.)... **498**

Popeye coloring book, Lowe, 1958 .... **25-45**

Articulated Vinyl Popeye Figure

Popeye figure, articulated vinyl, squeak head, Cameo, 1950s, 13 1/2" h. (ILLUS. without pipe)... **80-160**

Popeye game, board-type, "Adventures of Popeye," Transogram, 1957...................... **50-100**

Popeye lunch box & thermos, metal box & bottle, Popeye & boat, King Seeley Thermos, 1964.. **100-150**

Popeye Pez dispenser, plastic, no feet, painted hat... **75-125**

Popeye Pez dispenser, plastic, no feet, removable hat.. **50-75**

Popeye Pez dispenser, plastic, no feet, removable hat & pipe...................................... **50-75**

Popeye Gund Hand Puppet

Popeye puppet, hand-type, cloth w/soft vinyl head, Gund, 1957, 10" l. (ILLUS.)........ **20-45**

Popeye toy, Colorforms, Popeye TV Kit, 1966, the set... **35-70**

Popeye toy, pull-type, "Popeye Spinach Eater," Fisher-Price #488, Popeye eats can of spinach, 1939 .... **475**

Popeye toy, pull-type, "Popeye the Sailor," Fisher-Price #703, Popeye as ship captain, 1936.. **700**

Rare Premium Ring for The Spider

Spider (The) ring, silvered metal w/squared black flat top centered by a large red spider, premium from 1930s Pulp series, 1934 (ILLUS.) **2,717**

Super Heroes Trading Card Set

Super Heroes trading cards, complete colorful display box w/24 unopened card packets, yellow background printed in red, blue, black & white w/various Super Heroes, Marvel Comics, produced by Donruss, 1966, near mint box, mint packets, the group (ILLUS.) **2,346**

Superman bubble bath bottle, plastic, figural Superman, Soaky, Colgate-Palmolive, 1965, 10" h.. **40-75**

Superman lunch box & thermos, metal box & thermos, King Seeley Thermos, 1967 .... **150-300**

Superman lunch box & thermos, steel, Universal, 1954 .... **350-500**

Very Rare Superman Patch

Superman patch, rectangular fabric w/white ground & gold circle in center w/color image of Superman, red arched banners above & below stitched in white "Superman of America - Strength - Courage - Justice," 1942, near mint, 2 x 2 7/16" (ILLUS.) **3,618**

Australian Superman Button

Superman pinback button, celluloid, promotional premium for the Australian Sunday Mail Comics Club, white w/red & blue image of Superman & the wording "Superman - The Sunday Mail Comics Club," early 1940s, 1" d. (ILLUS. actual size) **338**

Superman puppet, hand-type, soft vinyl head, cloth or plastic body, Ideal, mid-1960s, 12" h. **30-60**

Superman toy, windup tin Superman Roll-over Airplane, bronze tone, Marx, 1940s, 6 1/2" l. **750-1,500**

Superman toy, windup tin, Superman Roll-over Airplane, red or blue, Marx, 1940s, 6 1/2" l., each **1,200-2,000**

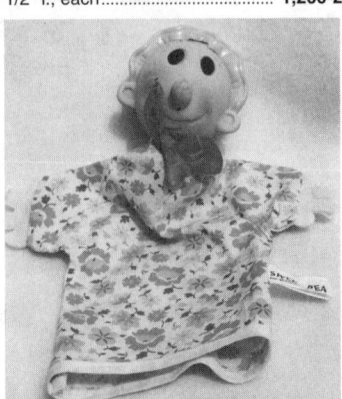

Swee' Pea Gund Hand Puppet

Swee' Pea puppet, hand-type, cloth w/soft vinyl head, Gund, 1957, 10" l. (ILLUS.) **20-45**

Three Stooges trading cards, 1959 Fleer complete set, color photo images, set of 96 .... **2,984**

Wolfman bubble bath bottle, Soaky, figural, 1963 .... **85-140**

Wolfman candy & toy, Phoenix Candy Co., 1963, 3 1/2" h. box...................................... **25-40**

Wolfman figure, plastic, Palmer Plastics, 1963, 3" h. **20-35**

Wolfman game, "Wolfman Mystery Game," Hasbro, 1963 .... **300-325**

Wolfman paint-by-number set, Hasbro, 1963 .... **165-300**

Wolfman pencil topper, Wolfman head, no mark, 1960s **10-20**

Wolfman ring, silver base, 1960s **35-50**

Woody Woodpecker alarm clock, plastic, Woody's Cafe, Columbia Time, 1959 .... **100-150**

Woody Woodpecker Soaky Bottle

Bear Dish with Spoon Snout (shown with spoon out & put away)

Woody Woodpecker bubble bath bottle,
plastic, figural Woody, Soaky, Colgate-
Palmolive, 1960s, 9" h. (ILLUS.)................ **15-35**
Woody Woodpecker coloring book, Whit-
man, 1950s... **30-50**
Woody Woodpecker figure, plastic nod-
der-type, 1950s.. **75-150**
Woody Woodpecker game, board-type,
Milton Bradley, 1959................................. **60-100**

Woody Woodpecker Hand Puppet

Woody Woodpecker puppet, talking hand-
type, cloth w/vinyl head, pull string, Mat-
tel, 1962, 12" l. (ILLUS.)............................. **40-80**
Woody Woodpecker toy, jack-in-the-box,
Mattel, 1960s **50-100**
Woody Woodpecker View-Master reels,
three-reel packet, No. B522, the set.......... **10-18**
Woody Woodpecker puzzle, jigsaw-type,
frame tray-type, Whitman, No. 4428-29,
1956.. **8-15**

Early Yellow Kid Cloth Doll

Yellow Kid doll, stuffed cloth, based on
R.F. Outcault comic character, white
w/color trim & scattered black print
quotes, 1899 copyright date, excellent
condition w/only two tiny holes & light
soiling, 8" h.
(ILLUS. of three views).................................... **886**

CHILDREN'S DISHES

Children's Feeding Dishes

Getting toddlers to eat has always been a struggle for many mothers. In 1948 E. Nudelman received a patent for an amusement device designed to help moms. This was a pig that hung on the side of a bowl; the mouth was hinged, creating the effect of feeding the pig while also feeding the baby. The food actually traveled through the pig's mouth and back into the bowl. Produced by Topic Toys in 1949, it was marketed as Hungry Piggy. This opened the door for other designs and other dishes. Some were designed so a separate feeder sat on the side of the dish and others so the feeder was actually attached to the dish, usually in the form of a head.

Bear, ceramic, brown, bear appears to lie on its back, w/paws embossed on rim of bowl, snout is handle of spoon that's hidden in head when not in use, 4" d. (ILLUS., top of previous page) **$65-85**

Royal Winton Feeding Dish

Bird, ceramic, bottom of dish illustrated w/image of baby robins in nest, "ONE FOR THE BIRDIE - ONE FOR BABY" printed on rim, bottom marked "Royal Winton, Grimwades, Made in England," rare, 6 3/4" d. (ILLUS.) **150-200**

Smiling Clown Face Feeder

Clown, blue-green bowl w/hands & feet painted on rim in white & black, widely smiling face on rim in pink, white & brown, 6" d. (ILLUS.) **50-60**

Clown Feeding Dish

Clown, bowl features drawing of clown in bottom, feeder is clown perched on rim w/mouth wide open, both in red, white, yellow & blue, w/box that reads "One For You, One For Me" & spoon, late 1940s-50s, bowl 6" d., clown feeder 4" h., bowl only $40-50, feeder only $80-100, the set - add $20-25 for original box - (ILLUS. of bowl & feeder) **125-150**

Clown Feeder Made in Taiwan

Clown, bowl w/clown head w/yellow hair & undersize hat for feeder, hands & feet are embossed & painted on sides of bowl, sticker on bottom reads "Made in Taiwan," 5" d. (ILLUS.) **50-60**

Similar Clown Feeders

Clown, bowl w/overhanging clown face feeder, bowl w/pale yellow, blue & green drawing inside of cavorting clown & the words "One for Baby - One for the Clown," Japan, 6" d. (ILLUS. left w/Cleminson feeder) **100-125**

Clown Head Feeding Dish

Clown, bowl w/pale blue rim & drawing of clown head in bottom, open-mouthed clown head feeder on rim, both in red, yellow, white & pale blue, found in several color variations, some marked "Italy," bowl 6 1/4" d., clown feeder 2 1/2 x 4", feeder only $50-60, bowl only $40-50, the set (ILLUS.) **90-125**

Clown, by California Cleminsons, ca. 1955, rare (ILLUS. right w/Japanese-made clown feeder, top of page) **150-200**

Duck feeding set: bowl, feeder, cup; cartoon of large-billed duck in bottom of bowl in pale blue & yellow surrounded by words "One for the Baby - One for the Duck," feeder in the form of a duck that resembles Disney's Donald Duck, also in pale blue & yellow, sits on edge of bowl w/head back & mouth open, handled cup has image on front similar to that of the one in the bottom of the bowl, bowl 6" d., feeder, 5" h., bowl only $40-50, feeder only $75-95, the set (ILLUS., next column) **120-150**

Duck Feeder Set

Feeder Dish from Set

Feeding set: bowl, feeder, cup, towel & bib; bottom of feeder decorated w/illustration of bird on branch & "One for the Baby - One for the Bird," feeder bird perches on rim w/head back & mouth wide open, sticker on bottom of bowl & cup reads "Wales" & "Made in Japan" w/crown, sticker on box reads "Bouquet Linens," bowl 5" d., feeder 3 1/2" h., bowl only $40-50, feeder only $75-95, the set (ILLUS. of bowl & feeder) **150-200**

Cat Whistle Cups

Novelty & Whistle Cups

In the early 1950s ceramic cups from Japan were a popular import item sold in the local five and dime stores. Many of these had figural handles or attached whistles, the intent being to make mealtime fun and encourage children to drink their milk or juice. All cups listed are approximately 3 1/2" unless otherwise noted. Many of these cups are found in both pink and blue colors.

Cat whistle cup, ceramic, mug decorated w/black & white cat w/oversize head, wearing dotted bow around neck, blue wiggly eyes, "Whistle for your milk," black & white kitten crouches on stem-form handle, whistle is attached to handle, stamped "Made in Japan" (ILLUS. left, top of page) **45-55**

Cat whistle cup, ceramic, mug decorated w/head of ginger cat w/black wiggly eyes, "Whistle for your milk," pale blue bird perches on branch-form handle, whistle is attached to handle, stamped "Made in Japan" (ILLUS. right, top of page) **45-55**

Cow Whistle Cup

Cow whistle cup, ceramic, decorated w/head of black & white cow w/wiggly eyes, musical notes, and "Whistle for Your Milk," pale blue bird perches on green handle w/white mouthpiece (ILLUS.) **45-55**

Lion Whistle Mugs

Lion whistle cup, ceramic, decorated w/face of lion w/painted eyes & "Whistle for your milk," yellow bird sits on branch-form handle that serves as whistle, Japan (ILLUS. left) **45-55**

Mystery Mug

Lion whistle cup, ceramic, decorated w/face of lion w/wiggly eyes & "Whistle for your milk," yellow bird sits on branch-form handle that serves as whistle, Japan (ILLUS. right, previous page) **45-55**

Mystery mug, ceramic, decorated w/draw-ings of cat, dog, fish & "What's at the bot-tom of the well?" & interior w/creature ly-ing at the bottom, Nasco, New York & Los Angeles, 3" h. (ILLUS., two views, top of page) **25-30**

Pixie cup, ceramic, front decorated w/face of pixie above "Always Drink Milk," pixie-form handle (ILLUS., to the right of col-umn) **35-45**

Sip n' Whistle, ceramic, decorated w/deer on front looking back at butterfly on its tail & "Sip n' Whistle milk mug - for a little dear," back reads "Whistle Whistle in my cup, when I blow Mom fills it up," blue bird whistle sits on branch-form handle that doubles as a drinking straw (ILLUS. left, below).. **45-55**

Pixie Cup

"Sip n' Whistle" Milk Mugs

Sip n' Whistle, ceramic, decorated w/squirrel on front looking at butterfly on its tail & "Sip n' Whistle milk mug - for a little dear," back reads "Whistle Whistle in my cup, when I blow Mom fills it up," green bird whistle sits on branch-form handle that doubles as a drinking straw (ILLUS. right on bottom of previous page).............. **45-55**

New York Souvenir Whistle Mug

Souvenir whistle cup, ceramic, decorated w/New York scene of Statue of Liberty & Empire State Building, "Souvenir Whistle Milk Mug" & "New York City" on front, bird whistle on handle (ILLUS.)......................... **40-50**

New Jersey Turnpike Whistle Cup

Souvenir whistle cup, ceramic, decorated w/scene of New Jersey Turnpike, "New Jersey Turnpike" & "Make the Birdie Whistle for Milk" on front, yellow bird sits on green handle w/white mouthpiece, very rare (ILLUS.).. **50-60**

Teddy Bear Whistle Cup

Teddy bear whistle cup, ceramic, decorated w/sitting & waving Teddy bear w/oversize head & big blue eyes, "Whistle for your milk," small white bear sits on branch-form handle (ILLUS.)...................... **45-55**

Children's Toothbrush Holders

Convincing children to brush their teeth is always a challenge. Figural toothbrush holders made this chore a bit easier because children had something fun and cute that held their toothbrush and oftentimes toothpaste. Toothbrushes have been found in the ancient pyramids, but the cute and comical devices to hold them have only been found as early as the late 1920s or early 1930s, and most are from the 1940s and 1950s. Nursery rhyme characters, children, cartoon characters, cowboys, soldiers and animals were popular themes. Whimsical holders are still produced, but the pieces today tend towards cartoon characters and are much larger in size than the older models. Some of the early toothbrush holders were tin lithographs, wooden, or bisque, while later ones were produced in ceramic and chalkware. Many early pieces were made in the United States, and later pieces came from both Japan and Germany; those made in Germany command higher prices.

—D. Gillham

Toothbrush Accessory Set

Bird, tail holds toothbrush, part of set that includes tumbler decorated w/chirping bird by words "Good Morning" & sleeping bird by words "Good Night," & tray, Japan, the set (ILLUS.) **85-95**

Boy & Girl Toothbrush Holders

Frog Toothbrush Holders

Boy, one of a series in this shape, dressed in short red double-breasted jacket, flare-legged yellow trousers w/black buttons on lower leg, red hat w/strap, carrying bouquet of flowers, on polka-dotted base, two holes for toothbrushes in back, 5 1/4" h. (ILLUS. right w/girl, previous page) **150-175**

Man with Bee Toothbrush Holder

Dismal Desmond Toothbrush Holder

Dismal Desmond, model of seated dog based on early cartoon character, hole for one toothbrush, Japan, 5" h. (ILLUS.).. **95-125**

Figure of man, oversize head w/toothy smile & bee on nose, hole in top of head for toothbrush, hands hold tray for toothpaste, Japan, 3" h. (ILLUS.) **125-150**

Frog, standing w/head back, open mouth forms toothbrush holder, stands on edge of tray meant for toothpaste, Germany, 3" h. (ILLUS. right w/other frog, top of page) **150-175**

Toothbrush/Tooth Powder Holder

Frog, wearing red shorts & big white bow tie w/black polka dots, sits on lily pad, joined arms form toothbrush holder, similar to cartoon character Flip the Frog, Germany, 3" h. (ILLUS. left w/other frog, top of previous page) **150-175**

Girl, bisque, wearing short dress, w/short hair, one hand to mouth, compartment for toothbrush in back, top of head features holes to dispense tooth powder, Irice Products, 7" h. (ILLUS., two views, top of page) **150-175**

Girl, one of a series in this shape, wearing old-fashioned dress w/full pink skirt & green bodice, pink bonnet, holding doll, on polka-dotted base, two holes for toothbrushes in back, Germany, 5 1/4" h. (ILLUS. left w/boy, on page 596) **150-175**

Girl & dog, on three-sided base (to fit in corner) holding trumpet-form holder for toothbrush & figure of girl standing next to yellow stool & brushing the teeth of a spotted dog sitting atop it, Japan, 5" h. (ILLUS., to the right) **75-100**

Corner Toothbrush Holder

Kissing Couple Toothbrush Holders

Kissing couple, on square base, figures of boy & girl in Dutch costumes, short boy stands on raised platform to kiss taller girl, two holes for toothbrushes, found in many color combinations, Japan, 6" h. (ILLUS. of two variations, above) **75-95**

Model of bird, lustre ware, black toucan-type bird w/yellow wings & red beak, on high decorative base, w/two holes in base for toothbrushes, Japan, 6" h. (ILLUS. right w/other bird)........................ **95-125**

Bird Toothbrush Holders

Model of bird, lustre ware, grey & gold penquin-type, on high decorative base, w/two holes in base for toothbrushes, Japan, 6" h. (ILLUS. left w/other bird).......... **95-125**

Cat Toothbrush/Toothpaste Holder

Model of cat, cat appears to be howling, hole in top of head holds toothbrush, curve of seated body holds toothpaste, Germany, 3 1/2" h. (ILLUS.).................... **125-150**

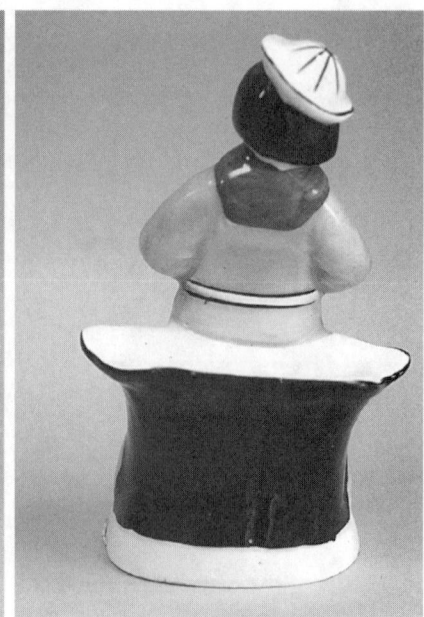

Sailor Boy Toothbrush Holder

Seated Pierrot Toothbrush Holder

Pierrot clown, lustre ware, sitting figure wearing pale green outfit w/white ruff, holding bouquet of red, yellow & white flowers, two holes in ruff for toothbrushes, Germany, 4 1/2" h. (ILLUS.).............. **175-200**

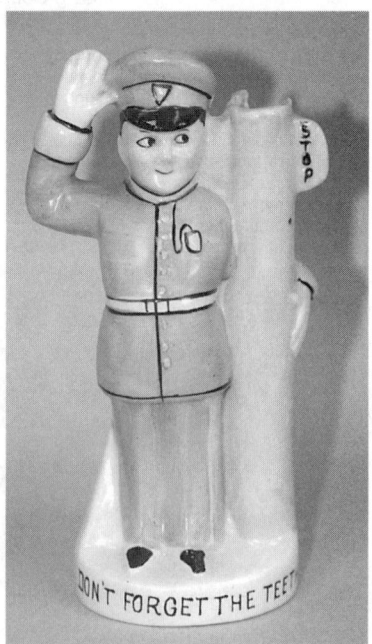

Policeman Toothbrush Holder

Policeman, smiling figure stands w/arm around cylindrical toothbrush holder w/stop sign on it, other arm held up in gesture to stop, on base that reads "Don't forget the teeth," Germany, 5 1/2" h. (ILLUS.) **125-150**

German & Japanese Swami Holders

Sailor boy, figure of boy dressed in blue sailor uniform w/red neckerchief & white cap, stands w/feet apart, hands on hips, arms form two holes for toothbrushes, tray on back for toothpaste, Germany, 5 1/4" h. (ILLUS., two views, top of previous page)... **150-175**

Swami, sitting, wearing pale green shirt, red trousers, white turban w/black polka dots, two holes in turban for toothbrushes, on white oval base w/yellow stripe, Germany, 3 1/2" h. (ILLUS. left w/Japanese-made swami, top of page) **125-150**

Swami, sitting, wearing pink shirt & turban, green trousers, two holes in turban for toothbrushes, on white oval base w/red stripe, Japan, 3 1/2" h. (ILLUS. right w/German-made swami, top of page)...... **75-100**

Clocks

ALSO SEE "Antique Trader Clocks Price Guide," 2003.

Plush-covered Terry Alarm Clock

Alarm clock, Terry Clock Co., Pittsfield, Massachusetts, upright narrow oval case covered w/worn purple plush, angled metal top handle, nickel plated bezel around the dial w/Roman numerals & sweep seconds hand, original glass over dial, alarm rings loudly, 30-hour movement, ca. 1883, 8 1/4" h. (ILLUS.)........ **134**

Small Ansonia Alarm Clock

Alarm clock, Ansonia Clock Co., Ansonia, Connecticut, tin case w/peg feet, round, dial w/Roman numerals & sweep seconds hand, ring handle at top, beveled glass in face, late 19th - early 20th c., 2 1/2" h. (ILLUS.)....................................... **$60-70**

Westclox "Baby Ben" Alarm Clock

Alarm clock, Westclox, LaSalle, Illinois, "Baby Ben" model, nickel-plated brass, round case w/Arabic numerals & seconds dial, small peg feet, ca. 1920s, 2 3/4 x 4" (ILLUS.).. **40-50**

Ingraham 1920s Banjo Wall Clock

Banjo clock, Ingraham (E.) Co., Bristol, Connecticut, "Nyanza" model revival-style banjo wall clock, walnut case w/pointed ball finial atop the round dial w/Arabic numerals above the slender tapering neck w/a reverse-painted glass panel over the bottom pendulum box reverse-painted in black w/a narrow gold-bordered window to show the pendulum bob, tapering concave bottom drop, copy of an early 19th c. model, ca. 1920, 4 1/2 x 10 1/8", 39" h. (ILLUS.) **450**

Late New Haven Banjo Wall Clock

Banjo clock, New Haven Clock Co., New Haven, Connecticut, "Welton" model revival-style banjo wall clock, ebonized wood case, brass eagle finial above the steel dial w/Arabic numerals, the tall waisted neck w/long edge scrolls & a glass panel above the rectangular pendulum box w/black reverse-painted glass panel w/small gold oval showing the pendulum bob, tapering concave base drop, time only, ca. 1940s, 3 1/2 x 8 1/2", 25" h. (ILLUS.).. **150**

Banjo clock, New Haven Clock Co., New Haven, Connecticut, "Whitney" model, mahogany-finished softwood case, a small gilt-metal eagle finial above the round brass bezel enclosing the silvered metal dial w/black Arabic Art Deco-style numerals, the tall slightly tapering throat w/a reverse-painted looping vine panel, the rectangular base frame enclosing a glass pane reverse-painted w/a garden scene, tapering pointed base drop, hour & half-hour rod strike movement, ca. 1930-35, 9 1/2" w., 30 1/2" h. **600-700**

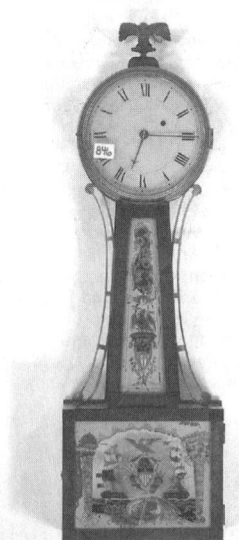

John Sawin Banjo Clock

Banjo clock, Sawin (John), Boston, Massachusetts, a gilt-metal eagle finial above the round bezel enclosing the signed metal dial w/Roman numerals, the tall slender slightly tapering waist section fitted w/a reverse-painted pane of glass decorated w/patriotic designs, long pierced brass C-scrolls at the sides, the rectangular bottom section w/a reverse-painted glass pane decorated w/a warship scene, eight-day time-only movement, early 19th c., bottom pane damaged, 31" h. (ILLUS.)................................... **2,588**

Boudoir clock, Gallet & Co. Swiss eight-day movement in a small rectangular Gorham Mfg. Co. sterling silver case, porcelain dial w/Arabic numerals, early 20th c., lines in the dial, 3 1/4" w.................... **158**

Hermlie Music Box Bracket Clock

Bracket clock, Hermlie (Franz), Germany, music box clock, stained fruit wood case w/a domed, stepped top w/bail handle, square front door opening to a brass & enamel dial w/Roman numerals, pairs of knob-turned spindles on each side, platform base w/flat feet, eight-day time & strike movement, 8 1/4 x 11 1/2", 11" h. (ILLUS.).. **300-350**

Thomas Double-dial Calendar Clock

Calendar shelf or mantel clock, Thomas (Seth) Clock Co., Plymouth, double-dial, walnut case w/arched coved crest fitted w/three urn finials above an arched glazed door flanked by slender turned colonettes, on a deep flaring molded base, the upper black dial w/Roman numerals, the lower black perpetual calendar dial w/Arabic numerals, time & strike movement, late 19th c. (ILLUS.) **2,400**

Waterbury No. 43 Calendar Clock

Calendar shelf or mantel clock, Waterbury Clock Co., Waterbury, Connecticut, No. 43 model, ornate pressed oak case, the high paneled & scroll-carved & impressed pediment w/long central block above a flat cornice w/matching long blocks above corner fan design over the tall round-topped glazed door w/a reverse-painted black ground & gilt band trim opening to an upper clock dial w/Roman numerals & a lower calendar dial, reeded side columns w/scroll capitals & blocked bases, stepped flaring wide base, original finish, eight-day movement, time & strike, ca. 1910, 5 1/2 x 16 1/4", 29 1/8" h. (ILLUS.) **800-900**

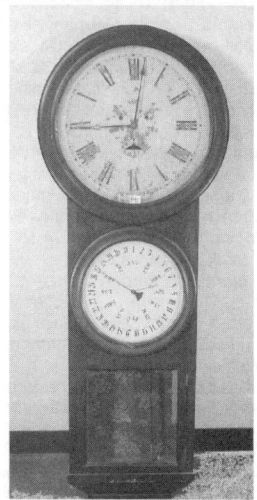

Welch, Spring & Co. Calendar Clock

Calendar wall clock, Welch, Spring & Co., Forestville, Connecticut, rosewood grained case, the large round molded top enclosing the brass bezel & large time dial w/Roman numerals, the long rectangular drop case w/a round molding enclosing the repainted calendar dial w/Arabic numerals, a square glass pane at the base, eight-day time-only movement, late 19th c., time dial flaking, 56 1/2" h. (ILLUS., previous page) **1,913**

Carriage clock, Ansonia Clock Co., Ansonia, Connecticut, "Extra" model, nickel-finished case w/glass front & sides, fancy pierced swivel handle, one-day movement, half-hour strike & alarm, 6 1/2" h. **169**

Carriage clock, Jennings Brothers, Model 699, ornately scroll-cast upright brass-plated spelter case w/scroll swing handle on top, round glass over the dial w/Arabic numerals & subsidiary seconds dial **124**

1950s German Carriage Clock

Carriage clock, Schmitt, Germany, brass case w/tall beveled glass front & sides framed by colonettes enclosing a steel dial w/Roman numerals suspending a brass lyre-form pendulum, ca. 1950s, 3 1/2 x 6 3/4", 10 1/2" h. (ILLUS.) **180-200**

Carriage clock, upright brass frame enclosing glass sides & front, top angled swing handle, dial w/Roman numerals, made in Paris, France for Sir John Bennett Ltd., England, eight-day movement, 4 1/4" h. (corner crack in side glass) **169**

Carriage clock, Waterbury Clock Co., Waterbury, Connecticut, "Conductor" model, brass upright case w/glass sides & front, porcelain dial w/Arabic numerals, in original velvet-covered case, 4" h. **84**

Cartel wall clock, ornately carved oak case composed of a large pierced leafy wreath enclosing a round molding around the dial w/enamel cartouches w/black Roman numerals, eight-day time & strike movement, France, ca. 1880-90, 18" w., 25" h. **1,500-1,750**

Fine Ansonia Crystal Regulator

Crystal regulator, Ansonia Clock Co., Ansonia, Connecticut, & New York, New York, gold-painted cast-spelter case w/a large urn finial, pierced cast scrolls at the top & base corners, beveled glass front, back & sides, large brass bezel enclosing the enameled dial w/Roman numerals, open escapement, faux mercury pendulum, late 19th - early 20th c., 6 1/2 x 7 1/2", 15 1/4" h. (ILLUS.) **700-800**

German Black Forest Cuckoo Clock

Cuckoo wall clock, Black Forest-style, carved hardwood, a large figural stag head w/antlers at the top of the oak leaf-carved crest w/crossed rifles above carved dead game flanking the cuckoo door & round dial w/white Roman numerals, a pair of carved small birds, game bag & leaves at the base, chain & weight mechanism, dial marked "Germany," probably post-World War II, 13 1/2 x 15", 23" h. plus chains (ILLUS.) **200-250**

Fine French Mantel Garniture Set

Early English Gallery Clock

Gallery clock, Cochran (Samuel), London, England, round mahogany wall-mounted case enclosing a large signed silvered metal dial w/Roman numerals, fusée w/eight-day crown wheel movement, 15" d. (ILLUS.) **2,925**

Lantern clock, Colver (John), Woodbridge, England, upright brass case w/a domed bell at the top above an arched & pierced brass gallery over the signed & engraved round brass dial w/Roman numerals, on small brass ball feet, 1739-47, 30-hour movement, missing brass cross arms over bell, no pendulum, 11" h. **1,800**

Mantel garniture set: clock & a pair of porcelain urns; the large round porcelain dial w/Arabic numerals & the works framed by delicate ornate openwork ormolu scrolls, wreath & flower basket finial & suspending a flower basket pendulum between four marble-topped columns w/ormolu pineapple & urn & flower finials, the columns in dark blue-glazed porcelain w/gilt wreath decoration & all set on an oblong white marble base w/small brass feet, the matching porcelain tall urns w/domed covers & ormolu finials, handles & a pedestal foot on a white marble platform w/small brass feet, France, ca. 1880, eight-day movement, time & strike, clock 5 1/2 x 9", 15 1/2" h., the set (ILLUS., top of page) **1,400-1,500**

Unusual Figural Folk Art Clock

Novelty shelf or mantel clock, carved & stained maple, a hand-carved folk art figure of a standing woman w/wavy hair & a long draped gown, her arms over her head holding the round frame for the clock w/a brass bezel & Arabic numerals, on a dished round base, original surface, American, early 20th c., 8" d. base, overall 29" h. (ILLUS.) **3,450**

Two Mastercrafter Motion Clocks

Novelty shelf or mantel clock, figural, upright china model of a windmill w/moveable blades, a small round dial in the base, blue Delft-style decoration, Kienzle, Germany movement, 8 1/4" h. **146**

Novelty shelf or mantel clock, Gilbert Mfg. Co., Winsted, Connecticut, figural gilt cast spelter case in the form of two horses leaning over a water trough w/cast leaf decoration, a small round dial w/Arabic numerals inset at the left end of the trough, 6" h. (slight wear) **135**

Novelty shelf or mantel clock, Mastercrafter electric motion clock, a brown plastic model of a fireplace w/fender, fireplace shimmers when plugged in, large round frame & dial at the top, white dial w/Arabic numerals, ca. 1950s, 4 3/4 x 7 1/4", 10 1/2" (ILLUS. right, top of page) **85**

Novelty shelf or mantel clock, Mastercrafter electric motion clock, white plastic case in the form of a stylized church, a bell ringer standing in the door pulls a string to ring the bell in the steeple, large steel dial w/Roman numerals & sweep seconds hand, ca. 1950s, 2 3/4 x 7 1/4", 12" h. (ILLUS. left, top of page) **125**

Plato calendar clock, Junghans, Germany, upright brass & glass cylindrical case showing two stacks of digital white turning pages w/numbers to indicate the date, swivel handle **101**

Plato calendar clock, upright brass French-style case w/glass front showing two stacked digital numbered white turning pages to indicate the date, swivel handle **84**

Plato calendar clock, upright brass & glass French-style case w/swing handle on top, two stacks of digital white pages w/numbers to indicate the date, 4 3/4" h. **180**

Shelf or mantel clock, a tall upright ornate French porcelain case w/elaborate scrolls across the top & down the sides ending in high arched scroll front legs, a wide brass bezel around the upper round dial w/Roman numerals, a lower front scroll reserve painted w/a scene of florals & cherubs w/a harp, floral decoration down the sides, eight-day time & strike movement, late 19th c., 16" h. (lines in dial) **563**

American Clock Co. Gothic Clock

Shelf or mantel clock, American Clock Co., New York, New York, Gothic-style iron-front case w/bronze finish, the Gothic arch facade cast w/flowering vines, round brass bezel around the white dial w/Roman numerals above a center panel of repainted red, white & green flowers over a small round pendulum window, block-molded base, 30-hour movement, time only, ca. 1855, 12" h. (ILLUS.) **280**

Ansonia Bank-Clock with Scene

Shelf or mantel clock, Ansonia Clock Co., Ansonia, Connecticut, bank-clock, pointed arch gilt cast-spelter case, the front cast in relief w/a wild boar hunt in a forest, dial w/Arabic numerals, flat molded base, two slots for coins in the back, ca. 1920s, 2 3/4 x 4 3/4", 5 3/4" h. (ILLUS.)........ **100**

Ansonia Iron Clock with Large Dial

Shelf or mantel clock, Ansonia Clock Co., Ansonia, Connecticut, black-finished iron temple-style case, the flat rectangular top above a wide ornate brass bezel w/beveled glass around the dial w/Arabic numerals & a raised central gilt-

brass center ring, gilt-trimmed incised sprigs flank the dial, the thick platform base w/further gilt sprigs, eight-day movement, time & strike, ca. 1900, 6 x 9", 10 1/2" h. (ILLUS.)...................... **300-350**

Atkins "London" Shelf Clock

Shelf or mantel clock, Atkins Clock Co., Bristol, Connecticut, "London" model, upright rosewood case w/molded pediment over gilt three-quarter round ring-turned columns flanking glazed two-panel door, the upper pane over the white dial w/gilt spandrels, brass bezel & black Roman numerals, the lower pane w/gilt leaf decoration, on a high base w/molding & bracket feet, eight-day time & strike movement, some dial restoration, ca. 1865, 16 3/4" h. (ILLUS.)............................... **476**

Atkins Rounded Double-Ring Clock

Shelf or mantel clock, Atkins Clock Co., Bristol, Connecticut, walnut round-topped model, a half-round molding around the top & continuing to slender columns flanking the face w/double large wooden rings, the upper ring enclosing the dial w/Roman numerals, the lower ring decorated w/a reverse-painted scene of a robin on a branch of cherries w/paint loss, molded base, eight-day movement, strike & alarm, missing minute hand, ca. 1880, 4 1/4 x 9", 15 1/4" h. (ILLUS.) **400**

Attleboro Clock Company Clock

Shelf or mantel clock, Attleboro Clock Co., Attleboro, Massachusetts, late Victorian Neo-Gothic oak case, the wide pointed & scallop-notched crest w/incised line decor above a tall paneled arch door w/beaded molding, gilt stencil decoration of geometrics & birds & cattails, large brass bezel & dial w/Roman numerals, angular side cutouts flank the door, deep arched & stepped base, ca. 1890 (note that no clocks were actually made in Attleboro but were supplied by other makers), 4 1/2 x 15", 22" h. (ILLUS.) **300-350**

Nice Gustav Becker Mahogany Clock

Shelf or mantel clock, Becker (Gustav), Germany, mahogany round-topped case w/a wide glazed door opening to a large silver plated dial w/Arabic numerals, molded base, eight-day movement, time & strike, ca. 1890, 5 3/4 x 8", 10 3/4" h. (ILLUS.) **300-350**

Rare Early Triple-deck Clock

Shelf or mantel clock, Birge, Mallory & Co., Bristol, Connecticut, triple-deck Classical style, gilt-trimmed mahogany veneer, a high gilded leaf-carved crest flanked by corner blocks w/incised rings above a pair of half-round columns w/gilt capitals & bases flanking the top glazed door opening to a painted wooden dial w/Roman numerals & gilt spandrels above a rectangular center reverse-painted glass panel featuring a colorful landscape w/a large classical home flanked by gilded half-round columns, the lowest section also w/a long rectangular door w/a reverse-painted colorful landscape flanked by another pair of short half-round columns, flat blocked base on gilt knob feet, eight-day movement, time & strike, open escapement, 5 x 17 1/2", 38 3/4" h. (ILLUS.) **1,500-1,700**

Shelf or mantel clock, Blakesly (M.), Plymouth, Connecticut, upright mahogany ogee case w/gessoed relief detail, the tall two-pane glazed door opening to a painted wooden dial w/Roman numerals & open escapement, the lower pane reverse-painted w/a landscape scene, 30-hour movement, flaking on scene, veneer damage, crack in glass, partial label inside, ca. 1840-50, 26" h. **197**

Early Bloomer & Sperry Clock

Shelf or mantel clock, Bloomer & Sperry, New York, New York, Empire-style mahogany and/or rosewood case, the wide stepped flat top & frieze supported by four slender turned colonettes flanking a two-pane glazed door, the upper pane over the large painted metal dial w/Roman numerals & floral-painted spandrels, the narrow lower pane reverse-painted w/leaves & floral wreaths, deep molded base, eight-day movement, time & strike, open escapement, ca. 1840, 4 3/4 x 16", 25 3/4" h. (ILLUS.) **350-400**

Gilbert Art Nouveau Shelf Clock

Shelf or mantel clock, Gilbert (Wm. L.) Clock Co., Winsted, Connecticut, Art Nouveau "Standard X," oak case, the rounded upper case composed of entwined looping bands centering the brass dial w/Arabic numerals & copper hands, flat leaf-carved open lower case w/center

leaf drop in front of the pendulum, some repairs to case, ca. 1910, 4 x 10", 16 1/4" h. (ILLUS.) **400**

Fancy Gilbert Scroll-cut Clock

Shelf or mantel clock, Gilbert (Wm. L.) Clock Co., Winsted, Connecticut, "Lake No. 5" model, walnut case w/a high ornate scroll-cut & line-incised crest centered by a roundel above a slender half-round turned rail over the tall rectangular glazed door w/a beaded edging, the glass stenciled in silver w/leafy vines & birds, the large dial w/Roman numerals, the brass pendulum decorated w/grape leaves, the lower case trimmed w/further cut scrolls on the deep flaring platform base, eight-day movement, time & strike, ca. 1890, 4 3/4 x 14", 22" h. (ILLUS.) **200-250**

Miniature Gilbert Steeple Clock

Shelf or mantel clock, Gilbert (Wm. L.) Clock Co., Winsted, Connecticut, miniature walnut steeple case, a Gothic arch frame flanked by simple columns w/small metal spires, a round dial w/Roman numerals above a square molding around a glass pane over a print of Victorian women, back of case w/paper label reading "No. 52T English Lancet," original finish, time only, 19th c., 2 1/4 x 4 3/4", 7" h. (ILLUS.) **70**

Ornate Gilbert "Lebanon" Clock

Shelf or mantel clock, Gilbert (Wm. L.) Clock Co., Winsted, Connecticut, Victorian Renaissance Revival walnut "Lebanon" model, the tall pointed fanned pediment w/roundel above a row of short turned spindles above stepped sides ending in curled-down ears w/roundels over the paneled arched tall door w/reeded molding, decorated w/a fancy silver stencil spider web & grass design below the brass bezel & large dial w/Roman numerals, brass pendulum w/embossed flowers & leaves, rectangular deep platform base w/sawtooth band, eight-day movement, time & strike, ca. 1890, 4 1/2 x 13 1/8", 20 1/2" h. (ILLUS.) **400-450**

Late Steeple-type Electric Clock

Shelf or mantel clock, Hamilton-Sangamo Corp., Springfield, Illinois, electric steeple clock, pointed mahogany case w/pointed finials flanking the two-pane pointed door, the upper pane over the dial w/Roman numerals & h.p. floral spandrels, the lower pane w/a reverse-

painted landscape, flat molded base, revival of a 19th c. style clock, ca. 1940, 4 7/8 x 9 1/2", 14 3/4" h. (ILLUS.)............ **150-175**

Rare Admiral Dewey Shelf Clock

Shelf or mantel clock, Ingraham (E.) Co., Bristol, Connecticut, ornate pressed oak commemorative clock, scenes from the Spanish-American War, the wide three-lobed crest centered by a large profile portrait of Admiral Dewey in a wreath flanked by vignettes of crossed flags & cannon balls above the arched paneled tall door ornately decorated w/gilt stenciling showing the Battleship Maine & crossed American flags, the round dial w/brass bezel & Roman numerals, lower shaped side scroll panels w/flags & cannons, the wide molded base decorated w/a repeating design of stars & anchors, original finish, 1898, eight-day movement, time & strike, 4 1/4 x 14 1/4", 23" h. (ILLUS.) **2,000-2,500**

Handsome Ingraham Eastlake Clock

Shelf or mantel clock, Ingraham (E.) & Co., Bristol, Connecticut, Victorian Eastlake style stained maple case w/applied black trim, the stepped cornice topped by a starflower & leaf sprig, a tall paneled arched glazed door w/delicate stenciled gilt scrolling, brass bezel around dial w/Roman numerals, scroll-cut side panels w/applied black trim, flaring platform base w/applied black panels & a central starflower, eight-day movement, time, strike & alarm, some black trim missing, ca. 1880, 5 x 13", 20" h. (ILLUS.)... **350-400**

Ingraham "Doric" Model Clock

Shelf or mantel clock, Ingraham (E.) & Co., Bristol, Connecticut, walnut "Doric"

model figure-eight case, the pointed top above tall molded sides flanking two stacked round molded glazed openings & two roundels, the upper opening over the dial w/Roman numerals, the lower opening decorated w/a colorful floral bouquet on white, molded base, original varnish finish, eight-day movement, time & strike, ca. 1870, 4 1/4 x 9", 16 1/4" h. (ILLUS.) **400**

Shelf or mantel clock, New Haven Clock Co., New Haven, Connecticut, Rococo-style gilt-spelter case, an ornate scroll crest above the round dial w/Arabic numerals supported by ornate openwork scrolls flanked by standing putti, on an oblong base decorated w/scrolls & on scroll feet, 30-hour movement, time & alarm, ca. 1900, 3 x 6 1/4", 10" h. (ILLUS. left, below) **250-300**

Shelf or mantel clock, New Haven Clock Co., New Haven, Connecticut, Rococo-style gilt-spelter case, an ornate scroll crest above the round dial w/Arabic numerals supported by ornate openwork scrolls on a small platform enclosing a h.p. porcelain plaque all flanked by figures of standing putti, pierced scroll apron & scroll feet, 30-hour movement, time & alarm, ca. 1900, 3 3/4 x 5", 11 1/4" h. (ILLUS. center, below) **400-500**

Shelf or mantel clock, New Haven Clock Co., New Haven, Connecticut, Rococo-style gilt-spelter case, an ornate scroll crest above the round dial w/Arabic numerals enclosed by cast flowers & raised on a ribbed stem-form support issuing leaf-form feet, a large standing Cupid at one side, 30-hour movement, time & alarm, ca. 1900, 2 1/4 x 3 1/4", 6 1/2" h. (ILLUS. right, below)............................... **180-250**

Three Gilded Ansonia Clocks

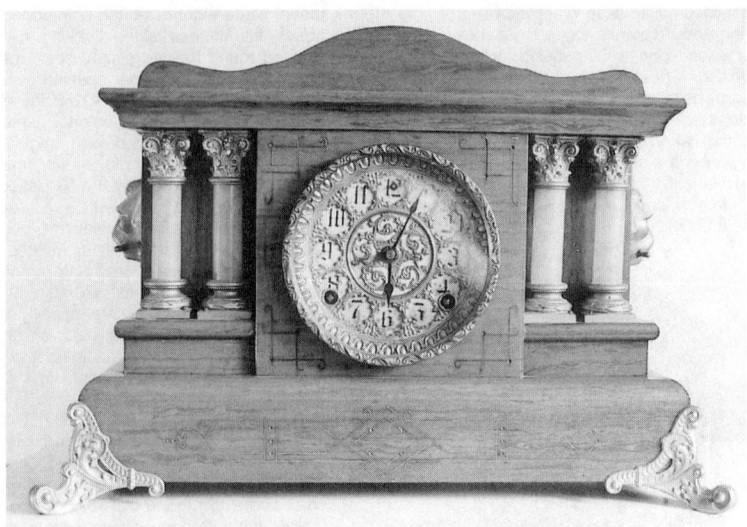

Sessions Temple-style Mantel Clock

Ornate French Clock with Figures

Shelf or mantel clock, Rococo-style, gilt cast-metal upright case, a small pierced urn finial & tall leafy scrolls on the pediment above the brass bezel enclosing the porcelain dial w/Arabic numerals above a lower inset h.p. porcelain plaque decoration w/an 18th c. courting scene, fitted at each side w/a large cast figure of a seated putto, one holding a bird's nest, the other a bird, the high blocked base centered by a cartouche & scrolls, France, late 19th c., 6 x 11 1/2", 18 1/4" h. (ILLUS.) **1,000-1,200**

Shelf or mantel clock, Sessions Clock Co., Bristol, Connecticut, temple-style, hardwood case w/honey-colored varnish, serpentine top above the deep brass bezel & glass door opening to an ornate brass dial w/Arabic numerals flanked by pairs of celluloid half-columns w/brass capitals & bases, deep molded base w/gilt-metal scroll feet, lion head & ring end handles, incised line decoration on case, eight-day time & strike movement, ca. 1900, 7 1/4 x 18 3/4", 12 1/2" h. (ILLUS., top of page) **200**

Telechron Ship's Wheel Clock

Shelf or mantel clock, Telechron Clock Co., electric, the stained wood case center w/a large ship's wheel w/brass pegs enclosing the dial w/Arabic numerals, tapering sides & flat base w/metal ropetwist trim, 1950s, 4 1/4 x 16", 8 1/4" h. (ILLUS.) **125**

Shelf or mantel clock, Terry (E.) & Son, Plymouth, Connecticut, upright rectangular Classical mahogany veneer case, the flat serpentine crest rail stenciled w/a fruit basket flanked by corner blocks above the case w/slender colonettes flanking the tall two-pane glazed door, the large upper pane over the painted wood dial w/Arabic numerals, the lower smaller pane reverse-painted w/a repainted landscape w/building, on carved paw front feet, partial label inside, 30-hour wood time & strike movement, minor veneer damage, ca. 1830-40, 28 1/2" h. **478**

Fine Classical Eli Terry Clock

Shelf or mantel clock, Terry (Eli) & Co., Plymouth, Connecticut, Classical style mahogany veneer stenciled case, the flat scalloped pediment stenciled w/a fruit-filled compote & leaves flanked by corner blocks above half-round columns flanking the tall two-pane door, the top glazed pane over a wooden painted dial w/Arabic numerals & gilt spandrels, the lower pane w/a mirror, flat base w/stenciled corner blocks, ivory keyhole escutcheon, eight-day movement, time & strike, ca. 1845, 5 3/8 x 16 1/2", 35" h. (ILLUS.)............ **900-1,000**

Shelf or mantel clock, Thomas (Seth) Clock Co., Plymouth, Connecticut, "beehive" style, the upright peaked walnut case w/a glass door opening to a steel dial w/Arabic numerals & small speed & chime adjustment dials all backed by ornately scroll-incised gilt brass, molded base, eight-day movement w/Westminster chimes, ca. 1920, 7 3/4 x 10 1/2", 14 3/4" h. (ILLUS.) **600-700**

Thomas Classical Revival Clock

Shelf or mantel clock, Thomas (Seth) Clock Co., Plymouth, Connecticut, Classical Revival mahogany veneer case, the deep blocked ogee cornice above a long door w/a large pane over a short rectangular mirrored pane, the large repainted dial w/Roman numerals, door flanked by colonettes w/gilt capitals & bases, ogee blocks at the base flanking a setback panel w/a round pendulum window, eight-day movement, strike & alarm, ca. 1900, 4 7/8 x 10 3/4", 16" h. (ILLUS.)............ **175**

Nice Seth Thomas Cottage Clock

Shelf or mantel clock, Thomas (Seth) Clock Company, Plymouth, Connecticut, arched & angled rosewood veneer case, the front door w/an octagonal frame en-

Fine Thomas Late Beehive Clock

closing the worn painted dial w/Roman numerals above a narrow panel enclosing a mirror, deep molded flat base, 30-hour movement, time & strike, ca. 1840-60, 3 3/4 x 7", 9 1/2" h. (ILLUS.) **200-250**

Fine Enamel & Onyx Clock

Shelf or mantel clock, Tiffany & Company, New York, New York, an upright rectangular case w/a stepped green onyx top mounted w/a gilt metal spread-winged eagle, the base also of green onyx, the sides of the case w/h.p. enamel-painted romantic scenes, dial w/Roman numerals & the Tiffany name, artist-signed panels, late 19th c. (ILLUS.)............................... **2,100**

Waterbury Wooden Temple Clock

Shelf or mantel clock, Waterbury Clock Co., Waterbury, Connecticut, black-painted wood temple-style case, flat rectangular top above the projecting central section w/an ornate brass bezel enclosing the dial w/Roman numerals, small creamy celluloid column w/gilt-metal capitals & bases at each side, deep stepped base w/rounded corners, raised on

scrolling gilt-metal feet, eight-day movement, time & strike, ca. 1900, 7 1/4 x 15 1/2", 10 5/8" h. (ILLUS.) **200-250**

Pretty Waterbury China Case Clock

Shelf or mantel clock, Waterbury Clock Co., Waterbury, Connecticut, china case, upright form w/flared shell-form crest & serpentine scroll sides & case, purple trim on white w/a transfer-printed panel of yellow & purple flowers below the round brass bezel & floral-decorated porcelain dial w/Arabic numerals, eight-day time & strike movement, late 19th - early 20th c., 4 3/4 x 9", 11 1/4" h. (ILLUS.) **500-600**

Waterbury Classical Revival Clock

Shelf or mantel clock, Waterbury Clock Co., Waterbury, Connecticut, mahogany veneer Classical Revival case, the deep ogee cornice above a pair of large grain-painted columns flanking the two-pane door, the large upper pane over the worn painted metal dial w/Roman numerals, the lower pane decorated w/a decoupaged color print of white doves in a basket of pink roses, deep ogee base, eight-day movement, time & strike w/alarm, ca. 1880, 4 1/4 x 12 1/4", 16 1/4" h. (ILLUS.) **350**

Classical Revival Rosewood Clock

Shelf or mantel clock, Welch (E.N.) Mfg. Co., Bristol, Connecticut (attributed), Classical Revival rosewood veneer case, the arched paneled top above a conforming glazed door opening to a dial w/Roman numerals centered by an embossed brass disc, brass pendulum w/pierced scroll trim, rectangular base w/ogee border, eight-day movement, time, strike & alarm, ca. 1880, 4 3/4 x 10 1/2", 16" h. (ILLUS.).. **250-300**

Welch Clock with Unique Vignettes

Shelf or mantel clock, Welch (E.N.) Mfg. Co., Bristol, Connecticut, oak kitchen-style clock, the wide flat cornice w/an elaborate pierced & scroll-cut crest above a tall glazed door flanked by similar scroll cutting, the glass ornately stenciled w/various figural vignettes including black minstrel figures, a woman playing a harp, a violinist & trumpeter, brass pendulum w/a black weight w/the raised letter "W," original finish w/ebonized trim,

eight-day movement, time & strike, ca. 1890, 5 1/4 x 14 1/2", 22" h. (ILLUS.).... **600-700**

Welch Walnut Eastlake Clock

Shelf or mantel clock, Welch (E.N.) Mfg. Co., Bristol, Connecticut, Victorian Eastlake style walnut case, the high two-tier pediment w/a palmette top over a turned roundel flanked by reeded blocks & pierced designs, similar lower tier above the tall molded glazed door decorated w/ornate gilt stenciling over the dial w/Roman numerals, cutout & line-incised side panels, wide reeded rectangular flat base, eight-day movement, time, strike & alarm, ca. 1890, 4 3/4 x 15 1/4", 24 1/2" h. (ILLUS.) **350-400**

Ansonia Swinging Arm Clock

Swinging arm clock, Ansonia Clock Co., Ansonia, Connecticut, patinated cast metal, a figure of an Art Nouveau maiden standing on rockwork & holding the swinging clock up w/one arm, late 19th c., 24" h. (ILLUS.)... **3,250**

Japanese Copy of Swinging Arm Clock

Swinging arm clock, Fuji, Japan, brass & spelter, a tall brass figure of a classical woman holding up the dial & swinging pendulum in one arm, on a black plastic base, a copy of a late Victorian design, ca. 1960s, 13 3/4" h. (ILLUS.)........... **200**

Swinging arm clock, Junghans, Germany, "Diana" model, tall bronze-finished cast spelter classical figure w/one arm holding the round clock movement & dial continuing to the long pierced pendulum w/bob, on a round wood base, late 19th c. **900**

Swinging arm clock, Junghans, Germany, figural, round movement & dial w/long pendulum held aloft on the raised trunk of a later cast metal walking elephant on an oval base **591**

Vienna Regulator wall clock, post office model, tall oak case w/an arched molded cornice above raised blocks above the tall arched molding enclosing the glass front, brass bezel around the white porcelain dial w/Roman numerals, a long brass weight & pendulum w/large brass bob, molded base w/tapering, stepped drop, eight-day single weight movement, Austria, ca. 1900, 13" w., 41" h. **2,000-2,250**

Vienna Regulator wall clock, tall walnut-veneered case w/a broken-arch pediment centered by a large urn finial over a paneled block over tall reeded columns w/carved capitals & turned bases flanking the tall arched glass front, brass bezel enclosing the enameled dial w/Roman numerals, three plain brass weights & large brass bob on pendulum, blocked & molded base over turned corner drop finials & a rounded drop section w/finial, eight-day time & strike movement, Austria, ca. 1880-90, 50" h. **3,800-4,200**

Early Dutch Friesland Wag-on-Wall

Wag-on-wall clock, early "stoelklok," the carved & painted case w/a pointed & pierced painted arch crest above a wide painted backboard w/scalloped sides h.p. w/large mermaids flanking the clock works w/a high arched & pierced metal crest over the dial plate w/painted angels above the painted metal dial w/a white chapter ring w/Roman numerals, a wooden platform shelf above the long free-hanging weights & pendulum, time & strike movement w/turned angle posts, Dutch Friesland, damage to mounts, case 27" h. (ILLUS.) **844**

Ansonia "Eclipse" Model Wall Clock

Wall clock, Ansonia Clock Co., Ansonia, Connecticut, "Eclipse" model, oak Victorian Eastlake style case, the high pierce-carved pediment w/a palmette finial over a roundel & reeded blocks & corner ears above a lower rail w/cutout spear points & corner ears above long notch-cut & line-incised side brackets flanking the tall glass door w/delicate gilt stencil decoration, brass bezel & dial w/Roman numerals, the base w/a deep scallop-cut & line-incised apron, eight-day movement, time, strike & alarm, ca. 1885-90, 5 x 15", 27 1/2" h. (ILLUS.) **350-450**

Wall clock, Art Deco box-type, rectangular walnut veneer case w/step-carved bands & geometric designs along the outer edges flanking an upper octagonal opening over the silvered metal dial w/Arabic numerals & a lower octagonal opening w/vertical bands of leaded glass over the pendulum w/octagonal chrome bob, eight-day time & strike movement w/Westminster chimes, France, ca. 1930s, 14" w., 29" h. **1,000-1,200**

Alden Atkins Early Ogee Clock

Wall clock, Atkins (Alden A.), Bristol, Connecticut, rectangular upright ogee case w/mahogany veneer, two-pane glass door, the upper pane over the painted dial w/Roman numerals & floral-painted spandrels, the lower pane reverse-painted w/a color landscape scene of a large white classical home w/a large tree in the foreground, some flaking, original dark, dirty finish w/some veneer chips, pendulum bob an old replacement, 30-hour movement, time & strike, ca. 1845, 26 1/2" h. (ILLUS.) **280**

Black Forest Clock with Eagle Finial

Wall clock, Black Forest-type, ornately carved walnut case w/a large spread-winged eagle at the top above spreading leafy branches & acorns across the top & around the sides centering the wood dial w/Roman numerals, a stag & hunting dog carved at the bottom, eight-day movement, some damage to case, Germany, late 19th - early 20th c., 37" h. (ILLUS.)..... **1,181**

Wall clock, hooded "staartklok" model, the arched pediment centered by a cast-metal figure of Atlas holding a globe & w/figural metal angel finials at each corner, an arched glazed frame around the arched dial plate w/painted scene in the top above the painted metal dial w/Roman numerals framed by embossed metal spandrels all within a brass bezel, scroll-cut tapering brackets flank the long flat drop board w/a three-lobed end, large decorative pierced brass pendulum bob, time & strike one-bell movement, Dutch, 19th c., 44" h. **1,575**

Unusual Ingraham Oak Wall Clock

Wall clock, Ingraham (E.) Co., Bristol, Connecticut, ornate oak kitchen-style, the peaked scroll crest w/an applied pressed shell & scrolls above applied trefoils & scallop-cut side panels w/an overall small block design flanking the angled arched tall glass door w/egg-and-dart trim & ornate gilt stenciling w/a courtyard scene of ferns, palms & pillars, the dial w/badly worn numbers, shelf-style base w/scallop-cut apron w/further block design above the pointed scroll-cut back drop, eight-day movement, time, strike & alarm, late 19th c., 4 1/8 x 14 1/8", 25 1/2" h. (ILLUS.) **350-450**

Wall clock, Junghans, Germany, box-style, walnut veneer case w/a thick flat top w/beveled front corners above a conforming case & a long door w/an upper wood panel cut to show the round silvered metal dial w/Arabic numerals, the lower door divided into three vertical panes of glass showing the pendulum & brass bob, molded base, eight-day time & strike movement, ca. 1910-20, 10" w., 19" h. **700-800**

Wall clock, Junghans, Germany, box-type, solid & veneered walnut case w/an arched top w/a floral-carved frieze & floral-carved swag below the face, silvered metal dial w/Arabic numerals, the lower door w/beveled glass w/an oval center, eight-day time & strike movement w/Westminster chime, ca. 1920-30, 12 1/2" w., 32" h. **1,500-1,750**

Wall clock, Mauthe (F.), Schwenningen, Germany, box-type, tall oak-veneered case w/a simple arched crest above a case w/a thin beaded band at each side flanking the tall door, the upper wood door panel w/a round opening for the silvered metal dial w/Arabic numerals, the lower door glazed w/clear beveled glass segments showing the pendulum & large brass bob, eight-day spring-wound time & strike movement, ca. 1910-20, 12 1/2" w., 30" h. **800-1,000**

Herman Miller Brand Wall Clock

Wall clock, Miller (Howard) Clock Co., Zeeland, Michigan, Herman Miller brand ceramic wall clock, white hexagonal shape printed in blue on four sides w/Dutch scenes, hexagonal dial w/Arabic numerals, eight-day movement, time-only, ca. 1950s, 9" w. (ILLUS.) **70-80**

Large New Haven Oak Wall Clock

Wall clock, New Haven Clock Co., New Haven, Connecticut, oak long-case type, the arched crest decorated w/a pressed design of lappets & scrolls above the tall two-pane door w/egg-and-dart molding, the upper pane over a large dial w/Roman numerals, the lower pane over the large brass pendulum bob & printed in gold "Standard Time," flat base, original finish, ca. 1910, 5 1/4 x 15 1/2", 37 1/2" h. (ILLUS.) **600-700**

New Haven "Saxon" Figure-eight

Wall clock, New Haven Clock Co., New Haven, Connecticut, "Saxon" model w/figure-eight case, rosewood w/a large brass ring around the upper dial w/Arabic numerals, brass roundels at the center above another large brass ring around a glass pane w/a stenciled lacy silver ring framing the pendulum, eight-day movement, time & strike, late 19th c., 4 x 11", 19" h. (ILLUS.) **300-400**

Sessions Oak Wall Clock

Wall clock, Sessions Clock Co., Bristol, Connecticut, oak case w/a flat top & deep cornice above a large square reeded glazed door w/black reverse-painted ground & gold ring over the large dial w/Arabic numerals, angled side brackets flank a backboard at the bottom, eight-day movement, time only, ca. 1900, 4 3/4 x 18", 24 1/2" h. (ILLUS.) **200-300**

Sessions Octagonal Drop Wall Clock

Wall clock, Sessions Clock Co., Bristol, Connecticut, octagonal short-drop model, golden oak case, the octagonal top w/a large brass bezel over the dial w/Roman numerals, the drop case w/a pointed base & small glazed pointed door w/gilt banding, original finish, replaced eight-

day time-only movement, ca. 1900, 5 1/4 x 17", 28" h. (ILLUS.) **300-400**

Seth Thomas Box Wall Clock

Wall clock, Thomas (Seth) Clock Co., Plymouth, Connecticut, box-type, mahogany-stained hardwood case, flat top w/narrow cornice over a simple square frame w/a glass door reverse-painted in black w/a gold band around the large old replaced dial w/Roman numerals, flat molded base, eight-day movement, time only, ca. 1900, 4 1/4 x 15 1/4", 15 1/4" h. (ILLUS.) **250-300**

Seth Thomas "Eclipse" Wall Clock

Wall clock, Thomas (Seth) Clock Co., Plymouth, Connecticut, "Eclipse" model, Victorian Eastlake style walnut case, the high pierce-carved pediment w/a half-round wheel molding w/top knobs over a sunburst device on a blocked molding w/cutout spear points & corner arches over a molded cornice & angular line-incised brackets flanking the tall glass door w/elaborate gilt stencil leaf & lacy net decoration, the dial w/Roman numerals, stamped brass pendulum bob w/a sunflower design, the lower molding w/scroll-cut brackets flanking the lower case & w/a deep double-arch cut apron w/a central sunflower device above spear point & block drops, eight-day movement, time, strike & alarm, ca. 1880s, 4 3/8 x 14 1/2", 26" h. (ILLUS.) **400-500**

Wall clock, Thomas (Seth) Clock Co., Plymouth, Connecticut, oak short drop schoolhouse-style case, wide octagonal top framing the heavy brass bezel & painted dial w/Arabic numerals, the short pointed drop w/a small conforming glass window showing the brass pendulum bob, eight-day time-only movement, ca. 1920s, 15" w., 22" h. **500-600**

Fine Classical Revival Wall Clock

Wall clock, Waterbury Clock Co., Waterbury, Connecticut, Classical Revival style rosewood veneer case, the flat stepped cornice over an ogee panel flanked by end blocks above half-round maple columns w/gilt capitals & bases flanking the two-pane door, the large upper pane over the painted tin face w/Roman numerals & green-stenciled leaves, the lower door pane reverse-painted w/a bluebird in a gilt ring surrounded by flowers on a tan ground, deep blocked ogee base, open escapement, paper label inside, ca. 1890, 4 3/8 x 14 3/4", 24 3/4" h. (ILLUS.) **600-700**

Waterbury "Galesburg" Model Clock

Wall clock, Waterbury Clock Co., Waterbury, Connecticut, "Galesburg" model, long oak case, the molded arched crest centered by a block w/turned urn finial flanked by turned corner finials, short reeded columns & turned drops flank the top sides above the tall arched & glazed door, a wood molding encloses the brass bezel & original paper dial w/Roman numerals, the long lower pane shows the pendulum & large brass bob, short reeded columns & finials flank the bottom of the door, a long stepped & tapering base drop w/a turned finial, two drop finials at the bottom case corners, original finish, late 19th - early 20th c., eight-day time & strike movement w/half-hour gong strike, 52" h. (ILLUS.) **1,069**

Elaborate Oak Hanging Clock

Wall clock, Welch (E.N.) Mfg. Co., Bristol, Connecticut (attributed), hanging oak kitchen-style, the high arched crest w/a carved shell above scrolls & blocked corners above carved scrolls & notch-cut sides flanking the angled arched door w/beaded edging & ornate gilt stencil decoration, dial w/Roman numerals, flat built-in shelf above a scroll-stamped apron centered by an inset level above the pointed scallop-cut drop, eight-day movement, strike & alarm, old case refinish, late 19th c., 4 1/2 x 14 3/8", 27 3/4" h. (ILLUS.) **350-400**

E.N. Welch Octagonal Wall Clock

Wall clock, Welch (E.N.) Mfg. Co., Bristol, Connecticut, octagonal drop model, oak case, the octagonal upper section w/a stamped star band around the brass bezel over the dial w/Roman numerals & an outer calendar date band & sweep seconds hand, the pointed drop base w/matching glass door w/stamped star band trim, large stamped brass pendulum bob, original finish, eight-day movement, time only, ca. 1880, 4 x 17 1/2", 33" h. (ILLUS.) **400-500**

Wall regulator clock, Ansonia Clock Co., Ansonia, Connecticut, "Regulator A" model, ash case, the large octagonal top w/a molded black band around the brass bezel & paper dial w/Roman numerals, the pointed drop case w/a molded & pointed glazed door w/"Regulator A" over the pendulum & large brass bob, eight-day time & strike movement, ca. 1905-10, 17" w., 32" h. **1,000-1,250**

English Wall Drop Regulator

Wall regulator clock, drop-style hardwood case, the large round molded top centering the dial w/Roman numerals & an out-

er month calendar ring, the lower case w/a small glazed door printed in gold "Regulator," scroll cutouts at the sides, the deep ogee scroll base drop w/horizontal rods & finials at the top & base, England, late 19th - early 20th c., 4 1/2 x 12 1/4", 22" h. (ILLUS.) **200-250**

Fine Gilbert "Regulator No. 11"

Wall regulator clock, Gilbert (Wm. L.) Clock Co., Winsted, Connecticut, "Regulator No. 11" model, Victorian Eastlake style walnut case, the high pediment w/a sawtooth-carved crest rail rail over a cornice above a frieze band of small knobs & a sawtooth band, the long case w/reeded panels above the round-topped glass front flanked by reeded pilasters, a molded base above a narrow sawtooth apron supported by angular cut support brackets flanked by lower back panel, eight-inch dial w/Roman numerals & small seconds dial, wooden pendulum w/large brass bob, eight-day movement, time & strike, ca. 1885, 7 1/2 x 17 14", 50" h. (ILLUS.) **2,000-2,200**

Wall regulator clock, Thomas (Seth) Clock Co., Plymouth, Connecticut, "Regulator No. 1 Extra" model, rosewood-veneered case, the large twelve-sided top section centered by a round molding enclosing the brass bezel & painted dial w/Roman numerals & sweep seconds hand, the long rectangular drop case w/long glass door showing the pendulum w/a very large ornately scroll-pierced teardrop-form brass bob, eight-day single-weight movement w/original label on panel in front of weight, ca. 1875, 20" w., 40" h. **3,000-3,800**

S. Thomas "Regulator No. 2"

Wall regulator clock, Thomas (Seth) Clock Co., Plymouth, Connecticut, "Regulator No. 2" model, long oak case w/wide round molding around the large replaced dial w/Roman numerals & sweep seconds hand, the long case w/a glass front showing the heavy cylindrical weight & pendulum, refinished, ca. 1884, 5 1/2 x 15 1/2", 36" h. (ILLUS.) **1,000-1,200**

Waterbury Octagonal Regulator

Wall regulator clock, Waterbury Clock Co., Waterbury, Connecticut, octagonal long-drop oak case, large octagonal top w/beaded band decoration around the large dial w/Roman numerals & Arabic calendar numbers around the border, long pointed drop base w/beaded molding around the glass door printed in gold "Regulator," eight-day movement, time & calendar, ca. 1900, 4 1/2 x 16 3/4", 31 3/4" h. (ILLUS.) **500-600**

Waterbury Advertising Regulator

Wall regulator clock, Waterbury Clock Co., Waterbury, Connecticut, octagonal long-drop regulator, large octagonal top w/beaded molding around the dial w/Roman numerals, the long pointed drop case w/beaded molding, the glass door printed w/advertising reading "Fine Clothes - Made To Order - H.M. Marks & Co. - Chicago - Established 1872," eight-day movement, time-only, original case finish, stained dial, ca. 1900, 4 1/2 x 17", 32" h. (ILLUS.).. **800-900**

"Sembrich" Model Wall Regulator

Wall regulator clock, Welch, Spring & Co., Forestville, Connecticut, "Sembrich" model, walnut Victorian Renaissance Revival style case, a large plume crest & scroll ears on the flaring flat cornice over a line-incised frieze above the long rounded glass front over the dial w/Roman numerals, pendulum w/large brass bob, molded base w/slender tapering side brackets above the pointed & scroll-cut, line-incised front apron, eight-day movement, time & strike, refinished case, ca. 1880, 5 1/2 x 14", 39" h. (ILLUS.) **700-800**

COCA-COLA ITEMS

Coca-Cola promotion has been achieved through the issuance of scores of small objects through the years. These, together with trays, signs and other articles bearing the name of this soft drink, are now sought by many collectors. The major reference in this field is Petretti's Coca-Cola Collectibles Price Guide, 11th Edition, *by Allan Petretti (Antique Trader Books). An asterisk (*) indicates a piece which has been reproduced.*

Ashtray, porcelain, low rectangular form w/narrow angled edges, upright cigarette rest at the center, black w/red band along one edge w/"Coca-Cola" spelled out in various languages, unused, 12 1/2" l......... **$105**

Calendar, 1926, tall rectangular style, the top three-quarters w/a color image of a pretty seated girl tennis player wearing white w/a red scarf & holding a glass of Coca-Cola, black background, short rectangular full calendar pad at the bottom, framed, image 10 x 18 1/2" (very minor creases) **1,073**

Calendar, 1940, "Fishing Girl," horizontal rectangular form, 10 1/2 x 13 1/4" **550**

Calendar, 1941, tall rectangular form, white background printed in black across the top "Boy Scouts of America" above a tall color print of a Scout rescuing a baby from a flood, based on a Norman Rockwell painting, Coca-Cola distributor advertising below w/small full calendar pad, 22 x 46" (very minor wear & tiny stains).... **3,960**

1946 Sprite Boy Coca-Cola Calendar

Calendar, 1946, tall rectangular cover in blue w/the date in large yellow numbers at the top above the color image of the Sprite Boy head, six interior pages w/different images, only very light edge soiling & wear, cover 13 x 21" (ILLUS.) **660**

Round 1950s Coca-Cola Wall Clock

Clock, electric wall-type, glass, metal & plastic, round, white rounded edges w/a thin green band around a narrow red circle w/white wording around white dial ring w/black Arabic numerals, center red circle w/wording in white, ca. 1950s, slight scratching, bottom back attachment missing, 4 1/4" deep, 16 1/2" d. (ILLUS.)............... **385**

Clock, neon, octagonal, black over green & red outer band over neon tube, Arabic numbers & red center w/"Ice Cold Coca-Cola" above silhouette of woman drinking from bottle, 1941, neon replaced, light crazing on face, light case wear & soiling **2,860**

Rare Coca-Cola Round Neon Clock

Clock, neon spinner-type, round, metal, wide white border around dial w/dark green pierced band over the neon band, center w/red Arabic numerals around a red circle w/white wording & small red silhouette of a girl drinking from a bottle, ca. 1940, slight wear, bit of rusting & light paint chipping, 6" deep, 22" d. (ILLUS.) **4,400**

Rare Coca-Cola Door Kick Plate

Rare Early "Baird" Coca-Cola Clock

Clock, wall-type, "Baird" advertising model, wood & papier-mâché, figure-8 style case, large round top border molded w/wording "Coca-Cola - The Ideal Brain Tonic," lower round section w/pendulum window molded w/"Delightful Beverage - Specific For Headache - Relieves Exhaustion," round white dial w/Roman numerals, some stain on dial, ca. 1891-95 (ILLUS.)... **12,100**

Door kick plate, porcelain, long narrow rectangular form, narrow green border band, red center ground w/large white wording reading "Drink Coca-Cola," dated 1931, overall edge wear, chip at top edge, slight rust stain, 10 x 30" (ILLUS., top of page).. **633**

Festoon, die-cut cardboard, band of colorful maple leaves, girl holding bottle at center, 1927, 5 pcs. (minor wear & marks)...... **3,080**

Festoon, die-cut cardboard, colorful design of red & pink orchids & green leaves, two sections feature two glasses of Coca-Cola above a white rectangular sign w/red wording, made for Canadian market, unused, 1936, 5 pcs., overall 13' l. (ILLUS., bottom of page) **3,630**

Mirror, hanging, glass in metal sleeve, tall rectangular frame w/a hanging hole at the top, a red & white Coca-Cola button logo above a tiny picture of a bottle at the top above the mirror, late 1930s, 3 1/2 x 12" (light foxing, partial silver & frame ware)... **330**

Rare Coca-Cola Radio-Clock

Radio-clock, red plastic, model of a cooler w/"Drink Coca-Cola" in white above a small round clock dial at the bottom front, very minor wear, working, ca. 1950 (ILLUS.) **3,630**

Rare 1936 Coca-Cola Orchid Festoon

Unusual Coke Radio-Music Box

Radio-music box, conversion-type, plastic, red figural cooler marked "Drink Coca-Cola - Ice Cold," the top fitted w/a small music box & a small standing doll dressed as a Southern Belle that rotates above radio, 1950s, some paint chips on case, light wear & soiling, overall 18" h. (ILLUS.).. **1,705**

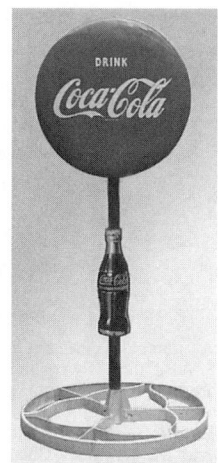

Coca-Cola Curb Sign

Sign, curb-type, two-sided, metal, large red button top w/wording in white, raised on a black pole fitted w/embossed tin Coca-Cola bottles, painted round lattice base, ca. 1950s, reverse w/some water staining & some touchup, base 29" d., overall 63" h. (ILLUS.).................................... **605**
Sign, die-cut 3D cardboard, hanging-type, tall rectangular form, green background w/cutout 3D image of a red & white rectangular Coca-Cola sign above a large bottle w/a large hotdog behind it, "Great Together" in black at the bottom, ca. 1932, 10 x 20" (very minor wear) **2,750**

Rare Coca-Cola Sixty Year Pin

Service pin, 10k gold w/12 diamond chips & enamel trim, round scalloped sixty year service pin w/embossed bottle at center, mint in original presentation box, 9/16" d. (ILLUS.).. **1,980**

Rare Early Coca-Cola Bell Cutout

Sign, die-cut cardboard, colorful design of a large red Christmas bell w/an orange bow & draped w/green holly, white wording reads "Drink Coca-Cola - 5¢," ca. 1905-10, minor soiling, 12 x 12" (ILLUS.) .. **3,850**
Sign, die-cut cardboard, the head of the Sprite Boy peaking around a 6-pack of Coca-Cola that he is holding, printed in color w/"King Size" above the pack & "Take Along 2" along the bottom, ca. 1950s-60s, 17 x 19" (few very faint edge stains, light edge wear) **1,760**

Coca-Cola Fountain Service Sign

Sign, die-cut porcelain, double-sided, "Fountain Service" in yellow against narrow dark green panel at bottom, sides formed by cutout silver fountain spigots framing a large red panel printed in yellow & white "Drink Coca-Cola," ca. 1939, some overall scratches, 14 x 27" (ILLUS., top of page)................................... **1,705**

Coca-Cola Die-cut Six-pack Sign

Sign, die-cut tin depicting 6-pack of bottles, 1954, few minor chips & nicks near edge, 11 x13" (ILLUS.)... **990**

Unique Coca-Cola Neon Spinner Sign

Sign, neon, countertop spinner-type, aluminum & metal, octagonal w/rounded corners, silver border around large red sign w/an outer band of small pierced holes, large Coca-Cola bottle in color in center w/"Have a Coke" in a yellow banner & "Coca-Cola - Ice Cold" in white, ca. 1950, only minor wear, 18" w. (ILLUS.)................ **8,470**

Rare Coca-Cola Neon Sign

Sign, neon, countertop type, "Coca-Cola" in large cutout letters at the top w/red neon resting on a narrow rectangular base w/red neon band outlining a black rectangle w/"In Bottles" in white, ca. 1939, some spot repair to neon, light wear & soiling, 12 x 24 (ILLUS.).............................. **6,820**

Plastic Neon Coca-Cola Sign

Sign, neon, plastic button-type, round w/neon border band, red plastic button printed in white "Drink Coca-Cola," ca. 1960s, some discoloring at edging, slight scratches, 4 3/4" deep, 16" d. (ILLUS.) **550**

Porcelain Two-Sided Coke Sign

Sign, porcelain, double-sided, rectangular w/rounded corners, color image of a large red Coca-Cola counter dispenser against a yellow background, ca. 1941, some chipping around grommet holes & edges, one small chip in right center, few rub mark & some scratching, 25 1/4 x 26 1/4" (ILLUS.)............................ **1,100**

Rare Policeman School Crossing Sign

Sign, school crossing-type, metal, two-sided figure of a policeman holding a shield w/"SLOW School Zone," on a round cast-iron base marked "Drink Coca-Cola," new-old stock, 1950s (ILLUS.).................... **6,820**

Sign, self-framed tin, long horizontal rectangular form, silver border frame, large color bottle of Coca-Cola at the left end, large red rectangle w/"Drink Coca-Cola" in white over narrow green band at bottom reading "Delicious - Refreshing," ca. 1937, dents, creases, some paint loss, 32 3/4 x 57" **385**

Rare 1920s Coca-Cola Sign

Sign, self-framed tin, oval, horizontal form w/narrow gold border around dark green band enclosing a large red oval w/"Coca-Cola" in white behind a pretty 1920s girl holding out a glass, ca. 1926, only a few light smudges & minor marks, 13 x 19" (ILLUS.) **3,520**

Sign, self-framed tin, rectangular w/narrow gold border band, white background w/"Refreshment Area" in blue letters above a bolt-on gold arrow, a small rectangular red Coca-Cola sign in the bottom left corners, probably new-old stock, 17 3/4 x 23 3/4" **242**

Sign, self-framed tin, referred to as the "New Betty" sign, long horizontal rectangular style, red background w/"Drink Coca-Cola" at the left w/a color bust image of a brown-haired girl holding a bottle at the right, 1941, 11 x 35" (few factory flaws, light scattered surface rust spots, minor edge wear) **908**

Sign, self-framed tin, tall rectangular form, red background w/"Take home a carton" at the top above a yellow circle w/a large color image of a Coca-Cola six-pack, "Drink Coca-Cola" at the bottom, dated 1937, scattered edge wear w/overall rust, scattered field scratches & wear, 18 x 54" **1,320**

Sign, silk-screened glass, rectangular, red background w/white wording & white glass at right end w/a five cent sign in black, reads "Drink Coca-Cola - Serve Yourself a Fresh Drink," modern frame, ca. 1930s-40s, 5 x 15 1/2" (small chip in corner under frame, light wear)......... **990**

Unusual Coca-Cola Sign

Sign, wood & metal, squared shield-shaped w/notched corners & pierced metal stylized leaves & blossoms at the top, gold beveled edges, dark yellow ground w/color image of two glasses of Coca-Cola above a red reserve w/white wording, Kay Displays, probably new-old-stock, 9 x 11 1/2" (ILLUS., previous page) 853

Thermometer, glass & aluminum, round, domed glass over dark red background w/narrow white temperature band at rim, "Drink Coca-Cola" in large white letters in the center, ca. 1950s, 12" d. (minor wear & pitting to metal) 385

1926 Golfers Coca-Cola Tray

Tray, 1926, serving, man & woman golfers, tiny marks & hairline scratches, average rim chips & light soiling (ILLUS.) **688**

Extremely Rare "Topless Tray"

Tray, 1908, "Topless Tray," round tin w/color center scene of seated half-nude young woman holding a bottle of Coca-Cola, wide green inner band printed in gold "Wherever Ginger Ale, Seltzer or Soda is Good - Coca-Cola is Better - Try It," outer flanged border w/bold gold scrolls alternating w/color floral reserves & three dark blue reserves printed in white w/different phrases reading "Drink Coca-Cola High Balls," "Drink Coca-Cola Gin Rickies," or "Drink Coca-Cola," Western Coca-Cola Bottling Co., Chicago, very light surface scratch, one light metal crease, slight paint chipping on edge & outer band, 12 1/4" d. (ILLUS.) **7,150**

Tray, 1909, change, oval, girl at St. Louis Fair (very small dent, light surface wear, few minor chips & marks) **440**

Tray, 1910, change, rectangular, Hamilton King Girl above "Drink Delicious Coca-Cola" lower right corner & "The Coca-Cola Girl" in left corner (few minor marks, one tiny burn, small nicks & chips) **413**

Tray, 1913, change, Hamilton King Girl in a picture hat holding a glass (light crazing, some shallow tiny dents, light wear & minor marks) **248**

Coca-Cola 1931 Serving Tray

Tray, 1931, serving, rectangular, smiling young barefoot boy wearing blue shirt, brown trousers, suspenders & straw hat, relaxing under a tree, eating a sandwich w/a bottle of Coca-Cola, his small black & white dog watching, Norman Rockwell artwork, 10 1/2 x 13 1/4" (ILLUS.) **1,595**

1934 "Tarzan & Jane" Serving Tray

Tray, 1934, serving, rectangular, Johnny Weismuller & Maureen O'Sullivan (Tarzan & Jane), 10 1/2 x 13 1/4" (ILLUS.).......... **853**

1937 Running Girl Serving Tray

Tray, 1937, serving, Running Girl, blonde woman in swimwear running on beach w/a Coca-Cola in each hand and a white cape flowing off her back, American Art Works, Inc., Coshocton, Ohio (ILLUS.)........... **369**

Tray, 1938, serving, Girl in the Afternoon in yellow dress & large flaring hat sitting w/bottle of Coca-Cola in hand, American Art Works, Inc., Coshocton, Ohio, very minor scratches & rim wear, 10 1/2 x 13 1/4" **220**

Tray, 1939, serving, Springboard girl, artwork by Haddon Sundblom, American Art Works, Inc. (minor rim wear, very minor surface wear & scratches, couple of small rust spots) **358**

Tray, 1941, serving, girl ice skater seated on log... **440**

Uniform, cloth coverall-style, tan w/metal buttons & Coca-Cola patch on left breast pocket, large patch on back, size 40-L, w/size 6 3/4" hat, appears never worn, ca. 1950s **149**

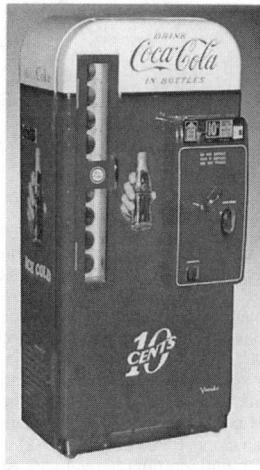

Vendo Model 81 Vending Machine

Vending machine, Model 81 Vendo machine, tall upright form w/rounded top, white top section w/red wording, red lower case w/long narrow dispensing door on the left side, dime operation, slot mechanism on the right, professionally restored, works, 27" w., 59" h. (ILLUS.)..... **3,905**

COMPACTS & VANITY CASES

A lady's powder compact is a small portable cosmetic make-up box that contains powder, a mirror and puff. Eventually, the more elaborate compact, the "vanity case," evolved, containing a mirror, puffs and compartments for powder, rouge and/or lipstick. Compacts made prior to the 1960s when women opted for the "au natural" look are considered vintage. These vintage compacts were made in a variety of shapes, sizes, combinations, styles and in every conceivable natural or man-made material. Figural, enamel, premium, commemorative, patriotic, Art Deco and souvenir compacts were designed as a reflection of the times and are very desirable. The vintage compacts that are multipurpose, combined with another accessory—the compact/watch, compact/music box, compact/fan, compact/purse, compact/perfumer, compact/lighter, compact/cane, compact/hatpin—are but a few of the combination compacts that are not only sought after by the compact collector but also appeal to collectors of the secondary accessory.

Today vintage compacts and vanity cases are very desirable collectibles. There are compacts and vanities to suit every taste and purse. The "old" compacts are the "new" collectibles. Compacts have come into their own as collectibles. They are listed as a separate category in price guides, sold in prestigious auction houses, displayed in museums, and several books and many articles on the collectible compact have been written. There is also a newsletter, Powder Puff, written by and for compact collectors. The beauty and intricate workmanship of the vintage compacts make them works of fantasy and art in miniature.

For additional information on the history and values of compacts and vanity cases, readers should consult Vintage and Vogue Ladies' Compacts *by Roselyn Gerson, Collector Books, KY.*

Bakelite Compact/Lipstick/Perfume

Bakelite Necessaire

Bakelite compact/lipstick/perfume, circular, black, the lid w/rhinestone lily-of-the-valley decoration, the interior containing mirror & powder well, a carrying cord & three tassels hang from the compact at 12:00, 3:00, 6:00 & 9:00 positions, two tassels conceal lipsticks marked "Paris" & one tassel hides a Bakelite tube holding perfume bottle (ILLUS., previous page) **$700**

Bakelite necessaire, black & ivorene, tube shape w/rhinestone decoration opens lengthwise to reveal mirror & compartments for rouge & powder on one side & fabric pocket on other side for miscellaneous items, large tassel hangs from bottom of tube, carrying cord is attached to top, 1 3/4 x 4" (ILLUS. closed & open, top of page) **450**

Brushed goldtone compact, round, "Pepsi-Cola" engraved on the lid, upper rim decorated w/polished goldtone design, Stratton, England, 3 1/4" d............................. **125**

Brushed goldtone compact, round, "Victory," decorated w/three raised stars & red, white & blue ribbons, made for 1996 Olympics in Atlanta, Georgia, Estee Lauder **75**

Composition compact/lipstick, black "Plate Trio-ette," front & back outer rims decorated w/clear crystals, one side opens to reveal powder well, the other rouge well, handle conceals lipstick **350**

Damascene vanity case, gold & silver view of Mt. Fuji capped in silver on black matte lid, contains compartments for powder, lipstick & rouge, w/carrying chain **150**

Enamel carryall, "Oval Sophisticate," black faille case w/black enameled lid decorated w/silver, center band slides to open compartments for powder & utilities, tassel pulls to reveal lipstick, Volupte **150**

Enamel & Crystal Compact/Perfume

Enamel & cut crystal compact/perfume, 12-sided disk-shaped crystal bottle w/etched floral decoration w/center round compact of cobalt blue enamel w/goldtone bezel, cobalt blue enamel cap (ILLUS.).. **600**

Enameled goldtone compact, round, "Boutique," light blue & cobalt enamel centered on the lid by a turquoise blue cabochon stone, Estee Lauder, 1 1/2" d......... **45**

Enameled metal compact, oval, an Art Deco design in green & blue enamel, w/tango-chain matching lipstick, interior reveals beveled mirror, powder & rouge compartments w/puffs, compact 1 1/2 x 2 3/4", lipstick 2 1/4" **325**

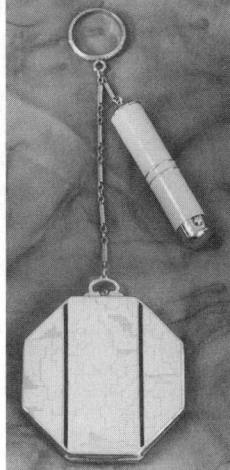

Art Deco Enameled Compact/Lipstick

Enameled silvertone compact, octagonal, an Art Deco design in yellow & black enamel, w/tango chain matching lipstick connected from finger ring by yellow enameled chain, compact 2 1/8" w., lipstick 2 1/8" (ILLUS.) **275**

Fabric-covered compact, round, designed to resemble picture hat, lid covered w/fabric resembling beads & decorated w/colorful beads & mother-of-pearl petals, trimmed in pink velvet, reverse side of black silk **350**

Hatbox-style Compact

Faux leather compact, designed to resemble hatbox, red, circular shape w/faux zipper around perimeter, strap handle, lid snaps open to reveal interior w/mirror, puff & powder well (ILLUS.) **125**

Goldtone & blue enamel compact, roll-top style, Germany, ca. 1940 .... **175**

Goldtone compact, circular, the lid decorated w/fish & centered w/a green cabochon, Max Factor, 2" d. **75**

Beveled Glass & Goldtone Compact

Goldtone compact, round w/beveled glass bottom & lid that shows image of female flamenco dancer wearing applied lace skirt, 2 3/4" d. (ILLUS.) **125**

"Prinzess" Goldtone Compact

Goldtone compact, designed to resemble purse, overall engraved design, the lid w/center design of colored stones & raised enamel flowers, push-back handle reveals powder compartment, "Prinzess," Czechoslovakia, 3 1/2 x 3" (ILLUS.) **225**

English Goldtone Compact/Bracelet

Goldtone compact/bracelet, designed to resemble wristwatch, bubble link chain holds center round compact set w/clear & green "jewels" for numbers, hour & minute movable hands, interior of compact contains mirror, puff & powder well, Le Rage, England, 1 1/2" d., 7" l. (ILLUS.) **550**

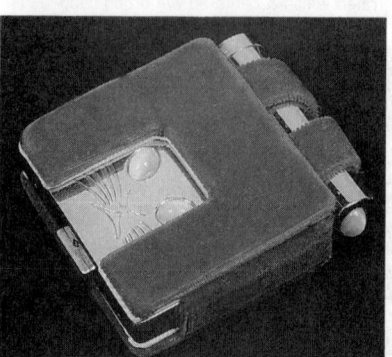

Cat Motif Compact/Lipstick

Goldtone compact/lipstick, square, covered in maroon velvet, w/lipstick sleeve at hinged end, cover cutout on lid shows mirror underneath w/decoration of stylized cat's face w/green cabochon eyes, Flato (ILLUS.)..................................... **400**

Goldtone compact/lipstick, square, the lid decorated w/enamel & colored crystal coat-of-arms, the top of lipstick tube decorated w/crown & clear crystals, comes w/faille carrying case, Ciner............................. **350**

"Dial-a-Date" Compact

Goldtone "Dial-a-Date" compact, circular, the lid decorated w/two dials w/movable hands, the smaller one to indicate the time of day, the larger center dial w/one hand that points to any of the various labeled activities illustrated around the dials ("Tennis," "Hairdresser," "Cocktail," "Lunch," "Cinema," "Rendezvous," "Dressmaker," "Milliner," "Bridge," "Dinner," "Theatre"), La Rage, England (ILLUS.) **350**

Dresser Compact in Form of a Chair

Goldtone dresser compact, armchair shape w/legs, arms & back heavily engraved, filigree on back & skirt of chair elaborately decorated w/floral decoration of pink stones & rhinestones, seat of chair is a mirror that opens to reveal puff & compartment for powder, label affixed to inside of lid reads "Original by Robert" (ILLUS.) **525**

Lancome "Le Cherubin" Compact

Goldtone & enamel compact, square, "Le Cherubin" limited edition, black enamel lid decorated w/a goldtone angel head, Lancome, 2 1/4" w. (ILLUS.) **55**

Goldtone & enamel compact, square, w/red, white & blue enamel lid decorated w/service emblem, souvenir of Camp Croft, Henriette **45**

"Merry-Go-Round" Compact

Goldtone "Merry-Go-Round" compact, circular, w/colorful red, white & blue carousel horses decorating sides, the lid w/alternating panels in goldtone & white fanning out from center (ILLUS.) **350**

Compact with Terrier Decoration

Goldtone & plastic compact, circular, the pearlized plastic lid holding image of terrier whose head moves right & left in 3D effect, Great Britain (ILLUS.) **125**

Gunmetal mini carryall, designed to resemble book, lid decorated w/four faux amethysts, contains compartments for powder & rouge, bills, writing slate & slim metal pencil, w/carrying chain **225**

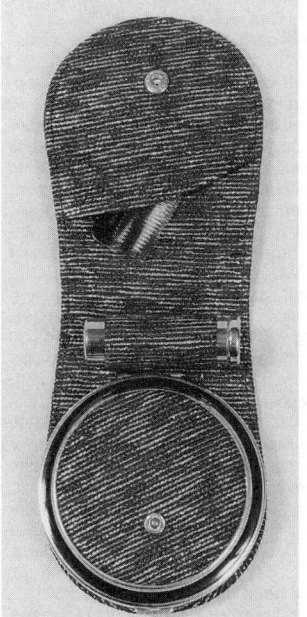

Lamé Saddlebag-style Vanity Case

Lamé vanity case, purple & black saddlebag-shaped case opens to reveal attached compact, sleeve for lipstick, pocket for comb, folds over to snap shut (ILLUS.) **125**

Starburst-decorated Lucite Compact

Lucite compact, square clear hinged Lucite frame, a sunburst medallion w/mask center molded & painted separately & hand-applied to lid, interior holds mirror & powder compartment, Roger & Gallet, 4 x 4" (ILLUS.) **225**

Onyx & Goldtone Compact/Bracelet

Onyx & goldtone compact/bracelet, wide cuff w/cutout five-pointed stars on either side of round onyx center compact decorated w/more goldtone stars & framed w/goldtone braid & beading, signed by Claudine Cereola, Flamand-Fladium, France (ILLUS.) **475**

Plastic compact, round, blue "Love Pat" composition compact, the lid decorated w/white daisies & a girl w/a blonde bouffant hairdo, Revlon, 4 1/4" d **85**

Polished metal compact/lipstick, "Lucky Purse," w/metal tango chain, flap on lid decorated w/multicolored stones, tango chain lipstick **225**

Silver Compact/Parasol

Baseball Card Replica Set

Silver compact/parasol, black silk ruffled parasol w/braided wrist cord, black wooden shaft, metal ferrule & collared knob-shaped silver handle decorated w/elaborate engraving & repoussé work, holds compact w/gilded interior containing framed mirror, puff & powder well, parasol replaced (ILLUS.).............................. **650**

Silvertone compact, round, the lid designed to resemble the shell of a turtle, Polly Bergen, 1 1/2" d.. **55**

Silvertone compact, square, "Triple Compact," complete w/two lipsticks, one for daytime & one for the evening, either one can be snapped tandem to the compact, lid centered w/a family picture, interior metal mirror separates rouge from powder compartment, in presentation box, Yardley, compact 1 7/8" sq., w/tandem lipstick 2 1/4".. **150**

Sterling silver compact, square, lid decorated w/raised swirls w/vase & flowers in center, interior contains mirror, puff & powder well, Volupte.. **125**

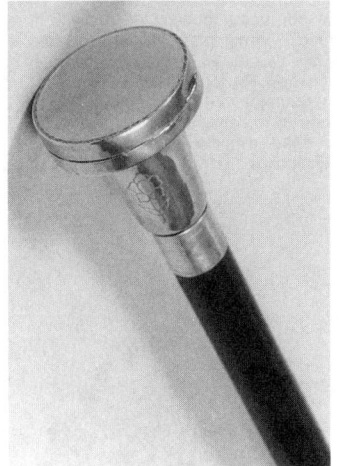

Sterling Silver Compact/Cane

Sterling silver compact/cane, cane w/black wood shaft, metal ferrule, & circular handle of hallmarked sterling silver & blue cloisonné w/collar decorated w/incised flower, the handle a compact w/gilded interior containing framed mirror & powder compartment, 1 7/8" d. (ILLUS.) **550**

CRACKER JACK COLLECTIBLES

Advertising, paper image of Cracker Jack's horse-pulled wagon delivering the product, 1910.. **$225**

Air Corps wings, pot metal, 1930s.................. **100**

American flag, tin, standup item, 1936-46 .... **40**

Badge, silvered metal, Cracker Jack Junior Detective badge associated w/radio show, 1931, 1 1/4" d.. **45**

Badge, tin, featuring image of Sailor Jack & Bingo the dog, 1930s, very rare **450**

Baseball card, #12 from 1914 series, featuring Connie Mack, 2 1/4 x 3"................ **160-700**

Baseball card, #133 from 1914 series, featuring Branch Rickey, 2 1/4 x 3" **140-300**

Baseball card, #68 from 1914 series, featuring Honus Wagner, 2 1/4 x 3" **700-3,000**

Baseball cards, 100th Anniversary set containing mini replicas of 1915 baseball cards, "Cracker Jack Ball Players" is printed at top of each card, under player's picture is his name & team, 1994, 1 1/4 x 1 3/4", set of 24 (ILLUS. of Maranville, Jackson & Bush cards, top of page).. **12**

Baseball cards, featuring players from American, National & Federal Leagues, 2 1/4 x 3", 1914, set of 144 .... **14,500-65,000**

Baseball cards, reissued & expanded version of 1914 set featuring players from American, National & Federal Leagues, 2 1/4 x 3", 1915, set of 176 .... **16,500-56,000**

Bear wheel toy, plastic, orange figure of bear cub that moves along on wheel, one of several wheel toys made, 1960s.................. **15**

Blowspinners, tin litho, w/slogans like "Keep 'em Flying" & "Let's Go US," made by Cosmo Manufacturing Company, 1940s, 1 3/4" raised propellers, each **90**

Bobbin' head doll, Bingo the dog, 2001............ **60**

Booklet, from Chicago Century of Progress World's Fair, contains miniature photos of 10 sites at the Fair, 1933............................ **270**

Bookmark, die-cut lithographed image of brown bulldog, from series of dog-related items, 1930s.. **60**

Box of Cracker Jack, unopened, 1896, very rare **600**

Button, black & white, w/"I'm A Cracker Jack Prize," 1950s.. 55

Cracker Jack Commemorative Tin

Canister, rectangular, "Cracker Jack 100th Anniversary Commemorative Canister" in red banner at top of front, unbroken red banner winds around sides at bottom, w/"1893" in banner on front under picture of 1893 Chicago Columbian Exposition, "1922" on one side under picture of family sitting listening to the radio, "1945" on one side under picture of sailor home from World War II, and "1993" on other side under picture of fans & Cracker Jack vendor at baseball game, 1993, 5 x 5", 8" h. (ILLUS.) 20

3D Card Picturing Fish

Card, color picture of fish, from 3D set issued in early 1970s, each (ILLUS.)................... 1

Supermarine Walrus Airplane Card

Card set, 50-card set of airplanes of World War II, each card w/color depiction of plane on front w/its name, the reverse w/description of the plane, card number & "Cracker Jack," manufactured & distributed in Canada under license agreement w/Walter M. Lowney Candy Company, Montreal, Canada, 2 1/2 x 3", 1940s, each (ILLUS. of one) 10

Catalog, 116 pages listing items to be sent for using coupons from boxes of Cracker Jack, dates from before actual prizes were placed in boxes, 1912, very rare.......... 400

Circus wagons, tin, each marked "Cracker Jack Shows," set of 5 different wagons, 1947, each 175

Clicker beetle, comes in many different colors, made from 1930s through 1960............... 12

John Quincy Adams Mystery Coin

Coins, Cracker Jack Mystery Coins, silvered metal, front w/embossed profile of a U.S. president w/his name & dates of office, reverse w/"Join the Cracker Jack Mystery Club - Save This Coin" (coins were found in boxes of Cracker Jack & could be saved & sent in to become a member of the "Mystery Club"), 1933-1936, 1" d., set of 31 (ILLUS. of one) 20

Cracker Jack Mystery Club Certificate of Membership, w/picture of Sailor Jack & Bingo the dog & text "Jack the Sailor Boy, Grand Magician," 2 3/4 x 5 1/2" 50

Diesel train, engine & three different cars, each a different color, blue, red, green or yellow, each marked "Cracker Jack," 1950s, each 10-15

Doll, Vogue, 1979.. 200

Drawing books, 8 pages to paint or apply transfers to, 1930s, 1 1/2 x 2 1/2", rare in unused form... 80

Figure of baseball player, plastic, standup model of player swinging bat, various colors, made by S.P. Eisner and Company, 1950-52, 2" h. 10

Figures of cartoon characters, standup figures of Little Orphan Annie, Moon Mullins, et. al., 1930s, set of 10, each.................. 105

Figures of spacemen, series of 9 plastic spacemen, including Sailor Jack & Bingo the dog, made by NOSCO Plastics Company, 1958-9, 1 11/16" h., each....................... 15

Cracker Jack Prize

Game, tic-tac-toe type, w/tiny metal ball, early 1970s (ILLUS.) **1**

Halloween masks, paper, set of 4, 1950s, each **30**

Harmonica, offered through catalog, full range for playing, 1912, 5 1/8" l **600**

Indian headdress, paper, 1950s, very rare **350**

Instant Win Game Piece

Instant win game piece, for plush Bingo the dog, in conjunction w/FAO Schwartz Toy Company of New York City, 1990 (ILLUS.) **1**

Magazine ad, American Boy magazine for Akro Agate marbles giveaway, shows boy shooting marble into pile of other marbles, w/coupon, late 1920s **50**

Magazine ad, Youth's Companion magazine, shows boy doing homework & text "A cold winter's night; ten math problems to do, three pages of history to study and on the table a box of Cracker Jack to make your brain clear. How you wiz through those problems! How you memorize those history dates! Those crisp, delicious kernels of popcorn and roasted peanuts all covered with old fashioned molasses can actually make it fun to study at home," November 1920 .... **60**

Magnifying Glass in Mini Box

Magnifying glass, in miniature replica of Cracker Jack Box, when a yellow button on front of box is pushed, Bingo the dog pops out holding the magnifying glass, Subway Sandwich Shop giveaway, 1999, 1 1/2 x 3 1/2" (ILLUS.) **1-2**

Key Chain Magnifying Glass

Magnifying glass, in shape of key (could be put on key chain), 1960s (ILLUS.) **3**

Marbles, Akro Agate marbles, coupons in box could be mailed in to receive marbles, late 1920s, rare, set of 12 in box $2,500, each **150**

Model of grandfather clock, metal, 1947 .... **50**

Model of motor boat, w/man driving, tin, 1930s **35**

Model of radio, tin, w/"Tune in with Cracker Jack" (advertising item for the Cracker Jack radio show) **300**

Model of schoolhouse, tin, 1930s **350**

Model of truck, tin, die-cut lithographed model of Cracker Jack delivery truck, yellow w/green roof, 1930s **125**

Mystery Picture cards, cards featured likenesses of John Paul Jones, Teddy Roosevelt, Abe Lincoln, et. al., w/instructions to "Stare at the dots in the center of the picture. Count to 45. Look toward sky or a light wall for 15 seconds and then see the photo likeness appear and reappear," made by Gensburg Manufacturing Company, 1934, 2" sq., each **75**

Cracker Jack Notepad

Notepad, cover featured bubbles of various sizes & "Bubble Book for Notes," early 1970s (ILLUS.) **2**

"Old Timers Baseball Classic" set, two uncut sheets of baseball cards, cards 1-8 feature former American League players, cards 9-16 former National League players, front has picture of Sailor Jack & Bingo the dog in the corner, back has "Cracker Jack" & mail-in offer, complete

sheet measures 7 1/2 x 10 1/2", 1982, each uncut sheet **12**
Packing crate, wooden, used for shipping Cracker Jack, 1940s **275**

Miniature Pinball Game

Pinball game, plastic transparent case reveals World War I-era biplanes in battle, metal ball, 1950s, 2 1/4 x 3 1/4" (ILLUS.)........ **12**

Unopened Cracker Jack Prize Packet

Prize packet, unopened prize packet from Cracker Jack box, two text boxes on packet read "You are about to miss a boat" & "Opportunity is going to knock. Be home," 1960s, price depends on condition & whether the bulk of the package indicates a plastic toy or just a paper item inside (ILLUS.) **3-15**

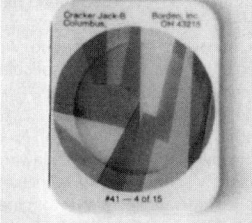

Cracker Jack "Rainbow Viewer"

"Rainbow Viewer," white rectangular paper frame w/circle in middle containing cellophane of various colors, produced rainbow effect when placed near light source, "Have Fun Looking Through This Rainbow of Colors!" on front, "Cracker Jack-B - Borden Inc. - Columbus, OH 43215" & "#41 - 4 of 15" on back, 1970s (ILLUS.) **1**
Replica of Model T Ford, tin, 1916, very rare **850**

Toy Roulette Wheel

Roulette wheel, plastic, pink frame w/transparent plastic over paper insert w/roulette numbers & tiny metal ball, 1960s, 1 1/2" d. (ILLUS.) **1**
Score counter, for baseball, paper, early 1900s **150**
Spinner, Cracker Jack Rainbow Spinner, paper, panels w/red, blue & yellow design, one identifying it as a Cracker Jack item, activated by string inserted through two holes, 1920s **130**

Baseball Glove Spy Glass

Spy glass, shaped like baseball glove, "Cracker Jack" in white on brown glove, 1 3/4 x 2" (ILLUS.) **2**
Steam train, engine & three different cars, yellow, plus pieces of track, each marked "Cracker Jack," 1950s, each **10-15**
Top, Cracker Jack Aerial Top, die-cut yellow lithographed tin propeller lettered in red & mounted on thin red wooden dowel, 1920s **125**
Toy mustache, two cardboard punch-out pieces joined by single grommet, 1950s **60**
Toy soldiers, tin, standup figures, 1930s........... **20**

Train engine, marked on bottom "#512,"
1930s.. 125
Vendor's hat, paper, worn by Cracker Jack
vendors at baseball parks, "Cracker
Jack" on both sides, 1930s.............................. 35
Writing tablet, store giveaway, school note-
book has "Cracker Jack" on it, late 1920s,
8 x 10" 210

CURRIER & IVES PRINTS

*This lithographic firm was founded in 1835 by
Nathaniel Currier, with James M. Ives becoming a partner in 1857. Current events of the day were portrayed in
the early days, and the prints were hand-colored. Landscapes, vessels, sport and hunting scenes of the West all
became popular subjects. The firm was in existence until
1906. All prints listed are hand-colored unless otherwise
noted. Numbers at the end of the listings refer to those
used in* Currier & Ives Prints - An Illustrated Checklist,
by Frederick A. Conningham (Crown Publishers).

American Fireman (The) - Always Ready,
medium folio, 1858, framed, 152 (overall
darkening, few stains, repaired tear,
glued down)..................................... $660
Celebrated Mare Flora Temple - "The
Queen of the Turf," large folio, undated,
framed, 891 (restoration) 1,650
Celebrated Stallions - "George Wilkes"
and "Commodore Vanderbilt" (The),
large folio, 1866, later frame, 897 (resto-
rations to sky).. 1,650
Celebrated Trotting Team Edward and
Swiveller - Owned by Frank Work,
Esq., N.Y., large folio, 1882, framed, 940
(faint stain in lower margin) 3,245
Clipper Ship "Three Brothers," large folio,
1875, framed, 1169 (overall toning, mar-
gin stains) 978
Fiend of the Road (The), large folio, 1881,
framed, 1945 (glued-down, minor stains
& edge damage)....................................... 990
Great West (The), small folio, 1870,
framed, 2658 (repaired margin tear, few
scattered stains & fox marks, toning)......... 1,035
Home On The Mississippi (A), small folio,
1871, framed, 2876 (margin tears, two
small holes in margin, stains)..................... 220
Life in the Woods - Returning to Camp,
large folio, 1860, framed, 3513 (some
stains, surface wear w/a few repairs,
margins trimmed) 1,650
Life of a Fireman (The): The Metropolitan
System, large folio, 1866, 3516 2,400
Life of a Fireman (The): The Night Alarm
- "Start Her Lively Boys," large folio,
1854, matted & framed, 3518 (minor light
staining across the image, old tape stain
on upper sheet edge, small hole extreme
right margin).. 1,920
Life of a Fireman (The): The Race -
"Jump Her Boys, Jump Her!" large folio, 1854, matted & framed, 3519 (overall
discoloration & scattered stains throughout, stained on verso from former wood
backing) 1,680

Steamship Bothnia of the Cunard Line
(The), small folio, undated, framed,
5750 275-300
Summer Ramble (A), medium folio, undat-
ed, framed, 5874 (trimmed margins, mi-
nor foxing, a few repairs) 550

DECOYS

*Decoys have been used for years to lure flying water
fowl into target range. They have been made of carved
and turned wood, papier-mâché, canvas and metal.
Some are in the category of outstanding folk art and
command high prices.*

Black bellied plover, feeding position, with
head down, original paint, South Shore of
Long Island, New York, rare, last quarter,
19th c. (age split, shot marks, touchup on
bill) $2,310
Black bellied plover, Obediah Verity,
Seaford, Long Island, New York, plump
body style w/"beetle" head & relief wing
carving, much original feather painting,
1870s 11,825
Black bellied plover, Obediah Verity,
Seaford, Long Island, New York, very
plump body style, relief wing carving,
carved eyes, two coats of paint by Verity
worn to the original 5,225

Black Bellied Plover by Bowman

Black bellied plover, William Bowman,
Lawrence, Long Island, New York, relief
wing & shoulder carving w/raised wing
tips, shoe button eyes, branded "R.L." for
Robert Lawrence, whose family established Lawrence, Long Island, profes-
sional repair to part of bill (ILLUS.)............. 9,350
Black duck, Elmer Crowell, East Harwich,
Massachusetts, Crowell's oval brand on
underside, old in-use paint appears to be
by Norman Hudson, ca. 1905 (head has
been reglued on) 1,045
Black duck, Ira Hudson, Chincoteague, Vir-
ginia, "football" form w/stylized specula,
original paint, first quarter 20th c. (two
cracks part way through head) 2,640
Black duck, Paul Green, Yardville, New
Jersey, hollow body, classic Delaware
River raised "V" carved wings w/incised
primary feather delineation, original
paint, retains maker's original brass
name tag, second quarter 20th c................ 1,155

Canvasback Hen & Black Duck

Black duck, Ward Brothers, Crisfield, Maryland, 1932 model, cedar body, original paint (ILLUS. right, top of page)................. **3,575**

Black duck hen, sleeping position, old black paint w/tan feather detail, lines of green, black & white on wings, eyes & bill w/later paint, 11 1/2" l. (age splits on base) **165**

Bluebill, Robert Elliston, Bureau, Illinois, original paint, some old overpaint on lower half, last quarter 19th c. **2,200**

Bluebill drake, August Guhl, Oshkosh, Wisconsin, branded "A O G" on underside, original paint, mid-20th c. **825**

Bluebill drake, Billy Ellis, Whitby, Ontario, Canada, original paint, second quarter 20th c. **550**

Bluebill drake, Hormidas Thibert, Valleyfield, Quebec, Canada, relief carving, thin coat of overpaint partially removed to reveal original pattern, second quarter 20th c. (drying splits in breast) **495**

Bluebill drake, Ira Hudson, Chincoteague, Virginia, flat-bottom style, turned head, fluted tail, original paint, second quarter 20th c. **2,640**

Bluebill drake, Mason Decoy Factory, Detroit, Michigan, Premier grade w/traces of premier stamp on underside, original paint (moderate discoloration & wear, several small cracks & dents) **1,760**

Bluebill drake, Morris Boat Works, Hamilton, Ontario, Canada, hollow body, original scratch paint, thin coat of black overpaint has been removed from the white on the speculum, repair to thin chip on underside of bill, first quarter 20th c. (ILLUS. left, bottom of page) **5,500**

Bluebill drake, Thomas Gelston, Quogue, New York, original paint w/old overpaint on white area, glass eyes, ca. 1890........... **3,025**

Matched Bluebills & J. Tax Mallard

Bluebill drake & hen, Paul Lipke, Whiting, Indiana, hollow bodies, original paint of black on white & brown on white, second quarter 20th c., matched pr. (ILLUS. top) **4,345**

Hollow Bluebill & Redhead Drakes

Rare Bluebill Hen

Bluebill drake & hen, Ridgeway Marter, Burlington, New Jersey, hollow bodies, both w/maker's original brass tag, later repaint by Ridgeway Marter, second quarter 20th c., pr... **1,210**

Bluebill hen, Bill Cooper, Verdun, Quebec, Canada, finely detailed feather carving w/slightly turned head & combing on back, original paint, rare, second quarter 20th c., shot marks, short crack at knot in back (ILLUS., top of page).......................... **2,310**

Bluebill hen, Davy Nichol, Smith Falls, Ontario, Canada, strong comb painting on back, original paint.. **715**

Bluebill hen, Mason Decoy Factory, Detroit, Michigan, Premier grade, Mason's "Premier" stamp on underside, original paint w/good detail (several small dents, hairline crack in one side)............................ **4,070**

Bluebills, Chauncey Wheeler, Alexandria Bay, New York, signed on underside, two coats of paint by Wheeler, second quarter 20th c., pr... **1,870**

Matched Pair of Bluebills

Bluebills, Joel Barber, Long Island, New York, bodies w/laminated construction & inlet heads, each branded "BARBER DECOYS," first to second quarters, 20th c., matched pr. (ILLUS.) **7,260**

"Bobtail" Canvasback Drake & Hen

Bluewing teal hen, Clovis Vizier, Galliano, Louisiana, relief wing carving, turned head, original paint (shot scar on head) **1,320**

Bluewing teal hen, George Warin, Toronto, Ontario, Canada, hollow body, original paint, last quarter 19th c. **3,410**

Bluewing teal hen, Judge Glen Cameron, Chillicothe, Illinois, original paint under old coat of varnish, branded "A.L.A." for Andy Anderson, first quarter 20th c. **2,750**

"Bobtail" canvasback drake & hen, Mason Decoy Factory, Detroit, Michigan, Premier grade, special order, both w/original paint, rare, each has roughness to end of bill, hen lightly hit by shot, pr. (ILLUS., top of page) **2,750**

Rare Chauncey Wheeler Brant

Brant, Chauncey Wheeler, Alexandria Bay, New York, detailed feather carving, original paint, rare, small chip reattached (ILLUS.) **3,080**

Eider Drake & Two Brants

Rare "Highhead" Canvasbacks

Brant, stickup type, old repaint, Malpeque Bay, Prince Edward Island, Canada, first quarter 20th c., age split, filler added to neck seam (ILLUS. right w/eider drake & roothead brant, bottom previous page) **550**

Rare Balsa Canada Goose

Canada goose, attributed to Tony Bianco or John McLoughlin, Bordentown, New Jersey, balsa body, two-piece vertically laminated construction, two-piece head & neck, original paint, "TONY BIANACHI, 1938, BORDENTOWN" written in pen on body near tail, rare, early second quarter 20th c. (ILLUS.) **1,760**

Canada goose, Ed Phillips, Cambridge, Maryland, dry original paint, early second quarter 20th c... **5,775**

Canada goose, extended neck, tack eyes, old grey, black & white paint w/areas of earlier green paint underneath, 30 1/4" l., 7" h. (age splits, pieced restoration where neck meets body)................................ **605**

Canada goose, Harry V. Shourds, Tuckerton, New Jersey, paint restored by john

Hillman, hollow body, neck extended in aggressive pose, last quarter, 19th c......... **1,925**

Canada Goose Stamped "BJ"

Canada goose, realistic paint, brown glass eyes, stamped signature "BJ," 24 1/2" l., 13" h. (ILLUS.)... **275**

Canvasbacks, Scott Peters, Potowattimi Indian, Walpole Island, Ontario, Canada, "highhead" style, original paint, only 2-3 pairs known to exist, last quarter 19th c., pr. (ILLUS., top of page) **4,015**

Coot, Ben Schmidt, Detroit, Michigan, head turned approx. 45 degrees, original paint, second quarter 20th c. **770**

Coot, Mason Decoy Factory, Detroit, Michigan, Challenge grade, w/original "Challenge" stamp, original paint w/detailed feathering, first quarter 20th c. (one minor shot scar)... **7,975**

Crow, carved & painted wood, black w/white speckles, late 19th - early 20th c., 12" l. (wear) **374**

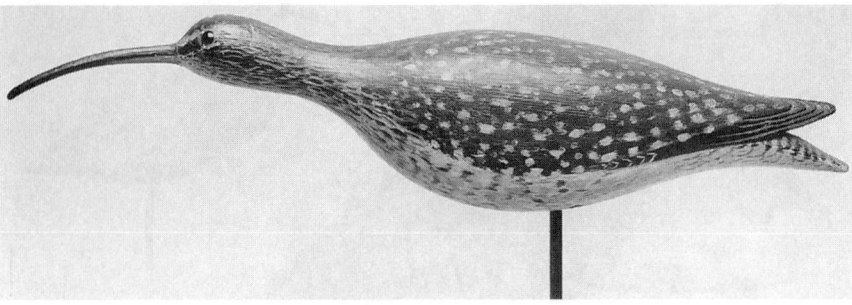

Rare Running Curlew by Crowell

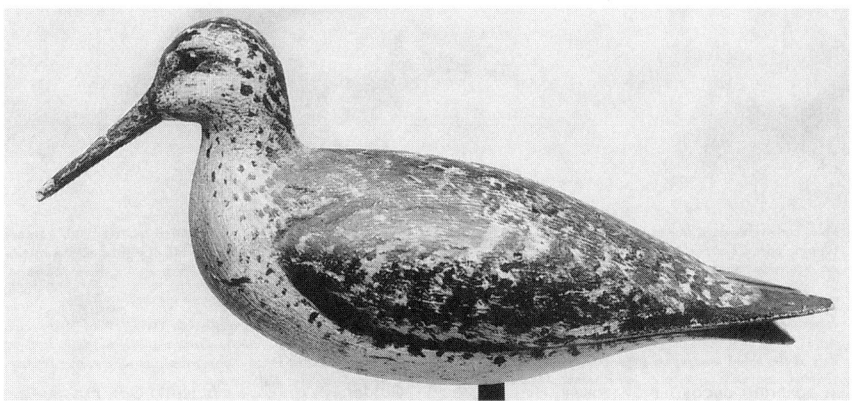

Rare Dowitcher in Fall Plumage

Curlew, Elmer Crowell, East Harwich, Massachusetts, running position, finely detailed early paint pattern w/carved wing tips, glass eyes, original paint, extremely rare, ca. 1900, two small holes in underside where wire legs were added at one time, professional repair to end of bill (ILLUS., bottom previous page) **70,000**

Curlew, H.E. Herrick, Lawrence, Long Island, New York, relief wing carving, glass eyes, original paint, first quarter 20th c. (reglued crack in neck) **1,320**

Dove, Herters Company, Waseca, Minnesota, early "Model Perfect" style, detailed relief carving on wings & tail, second quarter 20th c. (one glass eye is cracked, the other missing) **1,815**

Dowitcher, William Bowman, Lawrence, Long Island, New York, relief wing carving, extended wing tips, original paint in black & white colors of fall plumage, rare, last quarter 19th c., chips in wings & bill, reglued crack in bill (ILLUS., top of page) **20,350**

Duck drake, old black, burgundy & white paint w/dark green detail, glass eyes, 16 1/4" l., 7 1/4" h. (age split at breast) **605**

Egret or heron, flat-sided confidence decoy, old repaint flaked to original, Pacific Coast, mid-20th c. (cracks, chip missing from a wing) **605**

Eider drake, attributed to William Rawlings, Musquodobit Harbor, Nova Scotia, original paint, ca. 1920s, crack in head strengthened by two nails (ILLUS. left w/two Brants on page 441) **1,980**

Very Rare Preening Eider Hen

Eider hen, inlet head w/bill set into the back of the body in preening position, head attached to body w/wooden dowel, worn old paint may be original, rare, Tancook Island, Nova Scotia, first half 20th c., significant crack in neck (ILLUS.) **5,500**

Fish, original mustard paint w/black stripes, tin fins & red faceted bead eyes, 13 1/4" l. (some wear, mostly to underside) **358**

Fish spearing decoy, Leroy Howell, Hinkley, Minnesota, brown w/burned scales & wooden tail, first to second quarter 20th c., 4 1/4" l. (ILLUS. left w/other spearing decoys, bottom of page) **825**

Fish spearing decoy, Leroy Howell, Hinkley, Minnesota, gold w/paint dots & brown face, first to second quarter 20th c., 6 1/2" l. **1,870**

Fish spearing decoy, Leroy Howell, Hinkley, Minnesota, metal, sunfish, one of only two known to exist, first to second quarter 20th c., 4 1/4" l. (ILLUS. center w/other spearing decoys) **2,200**

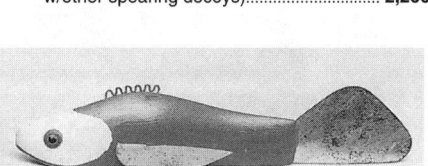

Fish Spearing Decoys

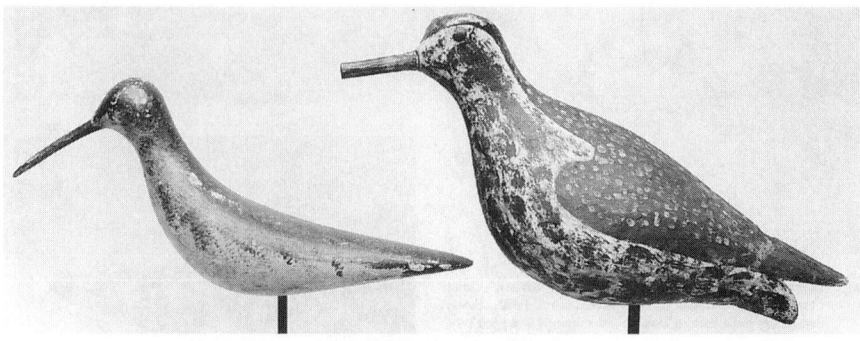

Lesser Yellowlegs & Golden Plover

Fish spearing decoy, Leroy Howell, Hinkley, Minnesota, metallic green & silver, wooden tail, first to second quarter 20th c., 9 1/4" l. **1,595**

Fish spearing decoy, Leroy Howell, Hinkley, Minnesota, orange w/white face & belly, first to second quarter 20th c., 9 1/2" l. (ILLUS. right w/other spearing decoys, previous page) **1,760**

Golden plover, flattie type, maker unknown, iron bill, original paint, possibly Nantucket or South Shore Massachusetts, last quarter, 19th c. (canvas or tape wrapped around bill where it meets the head) **770**

Golden plover, Frank Adams, West Tisbury, Martha's Vineyard, Massachusetts, original blue paint w/white breast, rare, ca. 1910... **3,575**

Golden plover, maker unknown, tack eyes, characteristic split tail carving, dry original paint, flat-tip bill appears to have been made that way, South Shore Massachusetts, last quarter, 19th c. (ILLUS. right, top of page) **5,225**

Goldeneye drake, attributed to C.R. Foss, slightly turned inlet head, carved eyes, old repaint, branded "LP GILES" twice on underside, ca. 1900 .... **770**

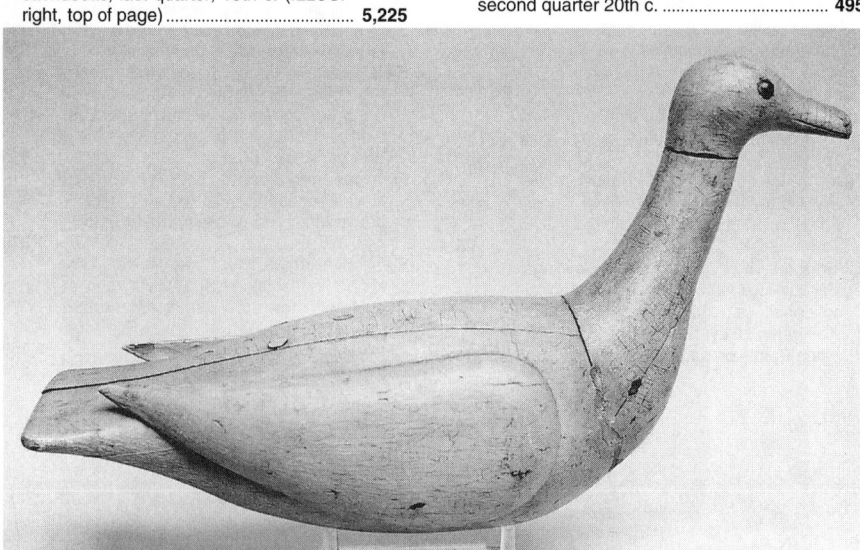

Goldeneye Drake

Goldeneye drake, Ken Anger, Dunnville, Ontario, Canada, original paint (ILLUS.) **2,090**

Goldeneye hen, Ray Andress, Gananaque, Ontario, Canada, original paint, rare, second quarter 20th c. **495**

Nineteenth-century Gull Confidence Decoy

Gull, confidence decoy, applied wings w/extended tips & square nail construction, tack eyes, four small pegs in back, original paint, Long Island, New York, 19th c., neck seam separation w/small amount of filler added a long time ago, crack in back extends through tail (ILLUS., bottom previous page) **25,850**

"Indian Blanket" Fish Decoy

"Indian Blanket" fish, metal fins, original red, yellow & green paint on white ground, red tail & fins, western New York state, ca. 1940s, approx. 5" l. (ILLUS.) **1,320**

Mallard, oversize, cork body w/wooden head slightly turned, inserted wooden tail & wooden bottom board, original paint, Wisconsin **330**

Mallard drake, Elmer Crowell, East Harwich, Massachusetts, Crowell's rectangular stamp on underside, original paint, ca. 1930 (green on head is old touchup) **1,980**

Mallard drake, grey, brown, black & white paint, raised carved feathers on the back, green head w/glass eyes & yellow bill, attributed to Frank Schmidt, 16" l. **1,210**

Mallard hen, John Tax, Osakis, Minnesota, hollow body, slightly turned head, original natural color paint w/blue, black & white on wing tips, rare (ILLUS. bottom, w/matched pair of bluebills) **6,050**

Rare Balsa Horned Owl

Horned owl, balsa, Leonard Doren, Pekin, Illinois, original paint, glass eyes, rare, second quarter, 20th c. (ILLUS.) **11,550**

Mallard Hen with Original Paint

Mallard hen, slightly turned head, light brown glass eyes, original paint, minor wear, keel replaced, 21 1/2" l., 9" h. (ILLUS.) **413**

Rare Mason Factory Mallards

Red-breasted Merganser Drake

Mallards, Mason Decoy Factory, Detroit, Michigan, special order hollow Challenge grade decoys, both w/initials "TL" & "FDW" painted on, original paint, rare, first quarter, 20th c., pr. (ILLUS., bottom previous page) **7,150**

Merganser, maker unknown, believed to be from Long Island, paint completely worn away, leaving mellowed natural surface, third to fourth quarter, 19th c. **550**

Merganser drake, George Huey, Friendship, Maine, large red-breasted body w/slightly turned inlet head attached to body w/small wooden dowel, carved eyes, "G R HUEY" carved in underside, original paint, second quarter, 20th c., professional repair to bill (ILLUS., top of page) **11,275**

Merganser drake, Mason Decoy Factory, Detroit, Michigan, Challenge grade, re-painted by Elmer Crowell (filled crack in underside, small chip missing from neck filler) **4,840**

Merganser hen, attributed to Eugene Cuffee, Shinnecock Reservation, Eastern Long Island, New York, cork & wood, initials "EN" carved on underside, original paint, rare **880**

Merganser hen, Marcel Dufour, Verdun, Quebec, Canada, swimming position, relief wing carving, original paint **715**

Mergansers, Harry V. Shourds, Tuckerton, New Jersey, first quarter, 20th c. (paint & bill restoration to both), pr. **1,100**

Old squaw, Gus Wilson, South Portland, Maine, w/characteristic carved eyes & raised shoulder & wings, dry original paint, swivel heads, rare, second quarter, 20th c., pr. (ILLUS., below) **5,500**

Pair of Old Squaw by Gus Wilson

Pair of Benjamin Schmidt Pintails

Early Hollow Pintail Drake

Pintail drake, attributed to O.H. Payne, "O.H. Payne" written on bottom in ink & initials "OHP" branded into bottom, hollow body, thin shell, thin bottom board, original comb paint, first quarter 20th c. (ILLUS.).. **3,850**

Pintail drake, Benjamin Schmidt, Detroit, Michigan, metal inserted tail, highly carved feathering on back, original paint, first to second quarter 20th c., wooden keel has been removed (ILLUS. left, top of page)... **4,620**

Pintail drake, Clark Madera, Pitman, New Jersey, rare hollow body w/exceptional combed vermiculation, original paint, first-second quarter 20th c. **4,400**

Pintail drake, John Reeves, Toronto, Ontario, Canada, hollow body, "H.H."

carved into bottom for Horatio Hathaway, member of Long Point Shooting Company, last quarter 19th c. (bill is professional replacement)... **1,430**

Pintail hen, Benjamin Schmidt, Detroit, Michigan, original paint, first to second quarter 20th c., wooden keel has been removed (ILLUS. right w/Schmidt pintail drake)... **5,225**

Pintail hen, Charles Perdew, Henry, Illinois, carved wing tips, original paint, retains Perdew weight, some old varnish, second quarter 20th c. **3,080**

Redhead drake, George Warin, Toronto, Ontario, Canada, solid body, original comb paint, branded "A.H. BUHL" & "MILLS" for St. Clair Shooting Company members Arthur H. Buhl & Francis H. Mills, last quarter 19th c. **5,390**

Redhead drake, John R. Wells, Toronto, Ontario, Canada, hollow body w/extremely thin shell, dry original paint, last quarter, 19th c. - first quarter 20th c. (ILLUS. right w/Bluebill drake, on page 439).. **2,750**

Redhead drake, Phineas or John Reeves, Toronto, Ontario, Canada, hollow body, original paint, initials "H.H." painted on bottom for Horatio Hathaway, member of the Long Point Shooting Company, mid-last quarter 19th c. **1,705**

Rare Redhead Drake & Hen Pair

Rare Small Mouth Bass Fish Decoy

Redhead drake & hen, Edward Keller, Bartonville, Illinois, both w/"EK" painted on undersides, original paint, rare, mid-20th c., hen has small crack in back of neck, pr. (ILLUS., bottom previous page) **5,225**

Roothead brant, John Brooks, Freeland, Prince Edward Island, Canada, stickup type, original paint, age split (ILLUS. center w/Eider drake & other Brant, on page 441) **1,045**

Ruddy turnstones, tin, folding type, attributed to Straiter & Sohier, Boston Massachusetts, "October 1874" patent stamped inside, original paint, rare, set of 11 .... **3,025**

Sickle bill curlew, Mason Decoy Factory, Detroit, Michigan, original paint w/fine detail, rare, ca. 1910, age split & small crack in one side, 17 1/2" l. (ILLUS. of head) **16,500**

Small mouth bass, Hans Janner, Lake St. Clair, Michigan, original natural wood sides, curved wooden tail, metal fins, glass eyes, some paint on head & underside, traces of paint on fins, rare, ca. 1940s, approx. 12" l. (ILLUS., top of page) **14,300**

Trout Decoy with Leather Tail

Trout, metal fins, leather tail, Lake Chautauqua, New York, approx. 7 1/2" l. (ILLUS.) .. **2,090**

Trout, metal fins, leather tail, original paint, Lake Chautauqua, New York, approx. 7" l. **3,465**

Trout, metal fins, western New York state, 7 3/4" l. (ILLUS., below) **3,960**

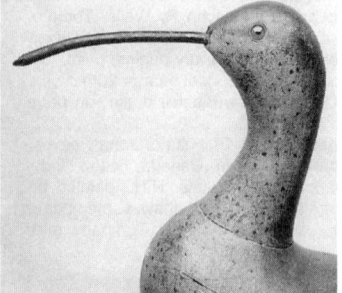

Detail of Rare Sickle Bill Curlew

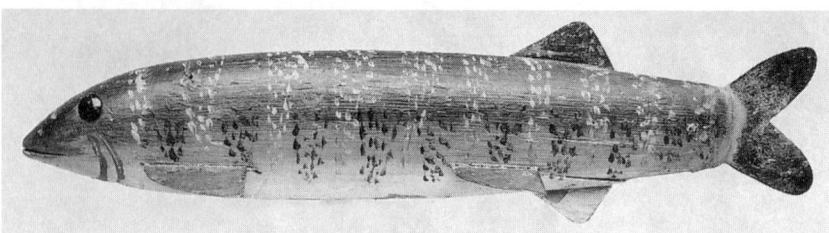

Trout Decoy

Two Yellowlegs

Rare Whitewing Scoter Drake

Whitewing scoter drake, Elmer Crowell, East Harwich, Massachusetts, carved cross wing tips w/good detail & fluted tail, head turned approx. 30 degrees, original paint, Crowell's oval brand on underside, extremely rare, first quarter 20th c., professional repair to bill chip (ILLUS.) **14,300**

Widgeon hen, original brown & tan paint w/olive bill, orange glass eyes, includes sinker weights & cord, New Jersey, ca. 1890, 15" l. (wear, putty-filled splits) **495**

Wood duck, dark ruddy head, olive body w/black wings, yellow eyes, original paint, signed "W.H. Finch," 10" l., 4" h. (age hairline in bill, some paint wear) **303**

Yellowlegs, "Lumberyard" type, pronounced cheek carving, glass eyes, relief wing carving w/extended wing tips, original paint, New Hampshire or Connecticut, ca. 1900 (ILLUS. right top of page w/another Yellowlegs) **3,355**

Yellowlegs, of the type attributed by some to Joseph Lincoln, relief wing carving, glass eyes, small dowel through top of head into neck, original paint, Hingham, Massachusetts, area, lightly hit by shot, small crack in bill (ILLUS. left, top of page) **2,640**

Yellowlegs, original paint, similar to decoys from "Lumberyard Rig," ca. 1900 .... **495**

Yellowlegs, silhouette decoy in running position, original paint, New Jersey, ca. 1900 ...... **495**

DISNEY COLLECTIBLES

Scores of objects ranging from watches to dolls have been created showing Walt Disney's copyrighted animated cartoon characters, and an increasing number of collectors now are seeking these, made primarily by licensed manufacturers.

ALSO SEE Antique Trader Toy Price Guide.

Alice In Wonderland Cookie Jar

Alice in Wonderland cookie jar, ceramic, figural w/Alice standing w/arms up, marked "Walt Disney Productions," Regal China, 1950s, 13 1/2" h. (ILLUS.) **$1,760**

Annette Moonstone Bay Mystery

Annette Funicello book, "Annette and the Mystery at Moonstone Bay," Whitman, 1962, hard covers (ILLUS.) **10**

1950s Disney Characters Tea Set

Annette Mystery at Smugglers' Cove

Annette Funicello book, "Annette and the Mystery at Smugglers' Cove," Whitman, 1963, hard covers (ILLUS.) **10**

Annette Mystery at Medicine Wheel

Annette Funicello book, "Annette - Mystery at Medicine Wheel," Whitman, 1964, hard covers (ILLUS.) **10**

Cinderella Railcar Windup Toy

Cinderella toy, windup tin "Cinderella Railcar," a handcar driven by the composition figures of Gus & Jaq, complete w/track, Well-Brimtoy, England, in original box (ILLUS.) **1,870**

Davy Crockett coonskin cap, "Official Davy Crockett Indian Fighter Hat," Walt Disney Productions, 1955, mint in box **543**

Disney characters tea set, porcelain, color transfers on each piece of various Disney characters, Louis Marx & Co., 1950s, complete w/original worn box w/seven punch-out stand-up figures, box 11 1/2 x 15 3/4", 23 pcs. (ILLUS., top of page) **385**

Disney characters Christmas tree lights, string w/eight figural Disney character bulbs including Mickey Mouse, Minnie Mouse & Donald Duck, by Diamond Brite, w/original colorful cardboard box w/cellophane window, 1950s, box 5 3/4 x 11" (slight box edge wear & tea in cellophane) **75-100**

Disneyland toy, windup tin, roller coaster, featuring a three-tiered course colorfully lithographed w/a host of Disney characters, when wound the two cars glide along the track & are pulled up the large hill by a treadmill mechanism while bell rings, Chein, w/original box, 9 1/2" h. **495**

Donald Duck camera, Walt Disney Enterprises, Herbert George Co., w/plastic strap, 1947, mint in box **250**

Donald Duck cereal bowl, "Post Bran Flakes" advertising, Walt Disney Enterprises **60**

Donald Duck figure, bisque, long-billed Donald, w/horn, made in Japan, ca. 1930, 3" h. **110**

Donald Duck figure, ceramic, Donald dressed as sailor, cold painted, 12" h. **265**

Donald Duck figure, chalkware, early Carnival-type, ca. 1934, 13" h. **83**

Donald Duck figure, composition, long-billed Donald w/socket head, black-painted side-glancing eyes, molded & painted blue sailor hat, accented nostrils, one-piece body w/sailor shirt, wearing original felt sombrero & red felt vest, marked "Walt Disney Knickerbocker Toy Co." on back, 9" h. (few cracks in finish on neck, left arm & side, piece of finish flaked off on right side of neck & left upper arm) **975**

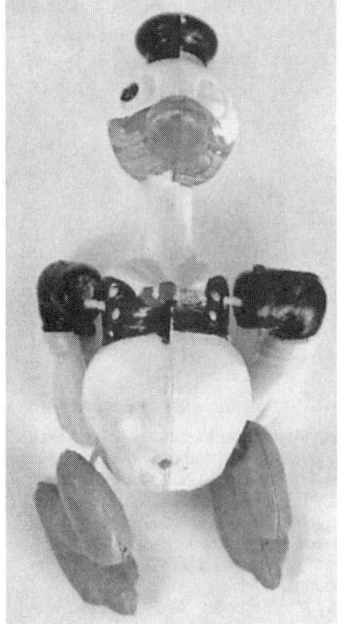

Early Celluloid Donald Duck Figure

Donald Duck figure, jointed celluloid, long-billed Donald wearing sailor suit, made in Japan, movable arms & legs, small paint chip on hat, ca. 1930s, 3 1/2" h. (ILLUS.) **99**

Donald Duck ink blotter, Sunoco premium **26**

Early Donald Duck Pencil Sharpener

Donald Duck pencil sharpener, celluloid, figure w/sharpener inside, made in Japan, ca. 1930s, 2 1/2" h. (ILLUS.) **185**

Donald Duck projector, plastic, modeled as Donald seated in a train engine, w/original box (box worn) **85**

Donald Duck salt & pepper shakers, ceramic, Walt Disney Enterprises, pr. **35**

Donald Duck sand pail, tin, Disneyland candy container-type, color scenes of Donald & his nephews on the beach around the sides, blue, yellow, red, white & orange, w/small red metal shovel, 1950s, pail 3 1/4" d., 3" h. **125**

Double Donald Toothbrush Holder

Donald Duck toothbrush holder, bisque, modeled as two long-billed Donalds standing side to side, Japan, ca. 1935, 4" h. (ILLUS.) **400**

Donald Duck toy, Delivery Wagon, Line Mar/WDP, colorful celluloid & tin litho, moving legs, cart lithoed w/Disney characters & marked "Mickey's Delivery," mint in box, 6" long **550**

Donald Duck toy, push-type, "Struttin' Donald Duck," Fisher-Price No. 900N, rubber feet & moving arms, 1940 .... **400**

Donald Duck toy, windup tin & celluloid, celluloid Donald drives his tricycle in circles as a revolving bell rings, in original lithographed box, Line Mar, 4" h. **1,000**

Donald Duck toy, windup tin & celluloid, "Donald Duck Whirlygig," Donald sits on a four-wheeled cart w/an umbrella w/attached dangling balls balanced on his head, the cart & umbrella both move in circular movements, 1958, Whirlybird.............. **45**

Donald Duck Viewmaster reels & booklet, 1957, set of 4 .... **30**

Donald Duck Toy Watering Can

Donald Duck watering can, lithographed tin, cylindrical w/strap handle & slender angled spout, pink & red background w/scenes of Donald in white, blue & orange around the sides, blue top & spout, ca. 1940, slight surface rust, overall 5 3/4" l., 3" h. (ILLUS.)............................... **193**

Dumbo creamer & sugar bowl, ceramic, figural, W. Disney U.S.A., 1940s, pr. **245**

Doc & Dopey Toothbrush Holder

Dwarfs Doc & Dopey toothbrush holder, bisque, colorful figures standing in front of large green rectangular holder, Walt Disney copyright, late 1930s, minor paint loss, 3 1/2" w., 4 1/4" h. (ILLUS.).................. **248**

Ferdinand the Bull book, "Ferdinand the Bull," ca. 1938..................................... **29**

Ferdinand the Bull Toy

Ferdinand the Bull toy, windup tin, preproduction w/original Louis Marx & Co. sample tag from 5/21/38, black & white, some paint wear, Marx (ILLUS.).................... **175**

Jiminy Cricket (from Pinocchio) doll, stuffed cloth, 14" h. **300**

Mary Poppins teaspoon, silver plate, figural handle, sugar shell **60**

Mickey Mouse alarm clock, animated "Wagging head" Mickey, Bayard Co., France, 1930s to 1969, original box....... **300-425**

Mickey Mouse alarm clock, shaped like oversized pocket watch, Bradley, 1979........ **195**

Mickey Mouse baby cup, silver plate, 1 3/4" h. **60**

Composition Mickey Mouse Bank

Mickey Mouse bank, composition, Mickey w/movable head standing beside chest, Crown Toy Co., 1940, mint condition, 6 1/4" h. (ILLUS.) **600**

Mickey Mouse bank, silver plate, figural Mickey w/large black nose, made in England & authorized by Walt Disney Productions, 6" h.. **95**

Mickey Mouse book, "Mickey Mouse Has A Busy Day," 1937, paperback........................ **55**

"Mickey Mouse in Giantland" Book

Mickey Mouse book, "Mickey Mouse in Giantland," color illustrations, David McKay Company, hardbound, 1931-34 (ILLUS.) **180**

Mickey Mouse book, "Mickey Mouse Presents Walt Disney's 'The Golden Touch'," hardbound, 1937, 212 pp. (no dust jacket) **90**

Mickey Mouse book, "Mickey Mouse Stories No. 2," hard cover, 1930s......... **90**

Rare "Mickey Mouse Story Book"

Mickey Mouse book, "Mickey Mouse Story Book," David McKay Company, hard cover, 1931, near mint (ILLUS.)...... **850**

Mickey Mouse book, "Mickey Mouse the Miracle Maker," 1948......... **38**

Mickey Mouse book, "Mickey Mouse Waddle Book," published by Blue Ribbon Book, Inc., New York, 1934, pictorial boards w/dust jacket band, runway & waddle characters intact, unused & complete........ **9,350**

Mickey Mouse book, "Mickey Mouse's Friends Wait for The County Fair," 1937........ **88**

Mickey Mouse book, "Mickey Mouse's Picnic," Little Golden Book, No. D15, first edition, 1950 .... **35**

Mickey Mouse book, "Mickey Wins the Race," 1934, Whitman **60**

Mickey Mouse book, "The Adventures of Mickey Mouse Book No. 1," published by David McKay Co., Philadelphia, ca. 1931, mint condition **600**

Mickey Mouse candy container jar, cov., pottery, cylindrical, raised figures of Mickey around the sides w/brightly colored trim, marked "Copyright 1961 Walt Disney Productions" **100**

Early Porcelain Mickey Candy Dish

Mickey Mouse candy dish, porcelain, round shallow dish w/lavender lustre border band & color center image of Mickey the waiter serving Minnie seated at a table, wicker bail handle, Japan, 1930s, 6" d. (ILLUS.) **125-150**

Mickey Mouse coloring book, 1931, large, not used........ **160**

Mickey Mouse coloring book, "Mickey Mouse Goes To Frontierland," Dell Books, 1957........ **90**

Mickey Mouse & Drum Cookie Jar

Mickey Mouse cookie jar, cov., pottery, Mickey & drum, marked "Walt Disney Productions - #864," California Originals, 1977 (ILLUS.).. **200-250**

Early Mickey Mouse China Creamer

Mickey Mouse creamer, china, figural Mickey w/mouth forming spout, black & white w/gold & blue lustre finish, Japan, 1930s, 4 3/8" h. (ILLUS.)................................. **125**

Mickey Mouse Warmer Feeding Dish

Mickey Mouse feeding dish, china & metal, warming-type, white china interior w/large center color image of pie-eyed Mickey playing a tambourine, small color images of other characters around the rim, fitted in a metal warming dish w/side filling spout, ca. 1930s, slight wear on interior & exterior, 6 1/2" d., 2 1/4" h. (ILLUS.) **253**

Mickey Mouse figure, bisque, Mickey playing saxophone, marked "Walt Disney," 3" w. base, 5 1/2" h.. **600**

Early Large Mickey Mouse Doll

Mickey Mouse doll, cloth, dressed in two-button shorts & yellow gloves, manufactured by Charlotte Slark, first licensed Mickey Mouse doll, early 1930s, 19" (ILLUS.).. **3,100**

Mickey Mouse doll, "Talking Mickey," Mattel, 1976, 7" h... **45**

Mickey Mouse dollhouse w/battery powered lights, plastic furniture including a Mickey crib & a Donald playpen, also Mickey's car w/wooden wheels, Louis Marx & Co. **300**

Early 5" Bisque Mickey Figure

Mickey Mouse figure, bisque, standing w/hands on hips, red shots, marked "Mickey Mouse" on chest & "Made in Japan" on back, 5" h. (ILLUS.)................... **350-450**

Mickey Mouse figure, bisque, "The Hunter," Disney Productions, 4" h. **145**

Mickey Mouse figure, celluloid, jointed head & arms, 5" l. tail, Japan, 1930s............. **600**

Early Cloth Mickey Mouse Figure

Mickey Mouse figure, cloth & pipe cleaners, black & white sewn head w/cloth hands & feet joined by pipe cleaners, Muscho, made in Germany, ca. 1932, in original Marshall Fields & Co. cardboard box, figure 4 1/2" h. (ILLUS.) **605**

Mickey Mouse figure, hard rubber, Seiberling, Akron, Ohio, 3 1/2" h., ... **300**

Mickey Mouse figure, jointed wood, painted red, black, white & yellow, w/original pie-cut eyes & flexible tail, 9 1/2" h. **1,200**

Small Mickey Fun-E-Flex Figure

Mickey Mouse figure, jointed wood & string, Fun-E-Flex, painted wooden head w/wood knob hands & shaped wood feet, string joints, cardboard ears, paper label on chest marked "Mickey Mouse Reg. US Pat. Off. Copr. Walt E. Disney," ca. 1930s, 3 3/4" h. (ILLUS.) **138**

Mickey Mouse figure, plastic, standing Mickey w/movable head, hands on hips, feet apart, black & white w/red shorts, ca. 1950s, 5 1/2" h. (slight wear) **99**

Mickey Mouse lamp, table model, metal base & rod w/bobbin-head Mickey mounted on base, parchment-type paper shade, three-way light switch, ca. 1950, overall 19 1/2" h. **375**

Mickey Mouse pencil holder, composition, figure of standing Mickey in black & white, facing sideways w/one hand extended w/opening for pencil, made by Dixon, U.S.A., Walt Disney Enterprises, 1930s, 5" h. (some cracking & edge wear) **138**

Mickey Mouse pinback button, celluloid, "Mickey Mouse Club," pictures MIckey w/one hand raised & the other on his hip, marked "Copy. 1928-1930 by W.E. Disney" **125-175**

Early Mickey Mouse Radio

Mickey Mouse radio, upright rectangular pressed wood-colored composition case, the top featuring Mickey playing the piano, the right side Mickey playing the clarinet, the left side Mickey on the tuba & the front, Mickey playing the string bass, w/"Selections" & "Volume" knobs, the back w/a plate w/a serial number & "Designed to operate on AC & DC current," a small rectangular tag on the front bottom reads "Emerson - Mickey Mouse," fitted   w/cords, ca.   1933-40, 5 1/4 x 7 1/4 x 7 1/4" (ILLUS.) **2,800**

Mickey Mouse ring, sterling silver, shows Mickey standing, small size **325**

Mickey Mouse rug, pictures Mickey launching a space rocket & a bunny rabbit looking on, ca. 1950s, 21 x 37" **225**

Early Mickey Sand Pail & Shovel

Mickey's Mousekemovers Toy Truck

Mickey Mouse sand pail & shovel, lithographed tin, tapering cylindrical pail w/swing strap handle, exterior w/colorful continuous design of Mickey leading a marching band, red shovel, Ohio Art, Walt Disney Enterprises, 1930s, some surface rust, edge wear & dents, top 6" d., 5 3/4" h., pr. (ILLUS., previous page) **187**

Mickey Mouse scissors, child-size, metal, slender red loop handles fitted w/colorful metal cutout of a running Mickey Mouse, Walt Disney Enterprises, 1930s, 3 1/4" l. (some rust spotting on blades, slight paint wear on handles & Mickey) **160**

Mickey Mouse Choo-Choo

Mickey Mouse toy, pull-type, "Mickey Mouse Choo-Choo," Fisher-Price No. 485, Mickey driving train engine, this is a new version of No. 432, 1949 (ILLUS.) **120**

Mickey Mouse Safety Patrol

Mickey Mouse toy, pull-type, "Mickey Mouse Safety Patrol," Fisher-Price No. 733, Mickey driving motorcycle, pulling cart, siren sounds, 1956 (ILLUS.) **250**

Mickey Mouse watering can, lithographed tin, cylindrical w/metal strap handle & long angled spout, sides in dark blue w/black & white images of Mickey & Minnie Mouse, red top & yellow spout, Ohio Art, Walt Disney Enterprises, 1930s, minor soiling, 5 3/4" l., 3" h. **176**

Mickey Mouse & Clarabelle Cow bowl, tin, colorfully lithographed, featuring Mickey presenting an apple to Clarabelle in the center, surrounded by Pluto, Minnie & the letters of the alphabet encircling the rim, stamped on the back "Bavaria Schumann Mickey Mouse," ca. 1930s, 8" d. **600**

Early Mickey Toothbrush Holder

Mickey Mouse toothbrush holder, bisque, standing Mickey w/right arm movable & left arm curved to form loop, black & white w/red mouth & shorts & yellow shoes, cloth tail, Japan, Walt E. Disney copyright, early 1930s, some soiling & edge paint loss, 5" h. (ILLUS.) **198**

Mickey Mouse toy, "Mickey's Mousekemovers" moving tractor trailer w/images of Mickey, Minnie & Donald on trailer, Louis Marx, some wear (ILLUS., top of page) **250**

Mickey Mouse & Donald Duck card, "Greetings From Kay Kaymen, Commemorating The Coronation of King George VI" on front, two British flags on front, Mickey & Donald holding rope w/left hands, from Waldorf Astoria **200**

Mickey Mouse & Donald Duck toy, rubber, Mickey & Donald riding fire truck, Sun Rubber Co., 1940s, 6 1/2" l. **125**

Early Unique Mickey & Donald Toy

Mickey Mouse & Donald Duck toy, celluloid, rowboat w/seated Mickey facing long-billed Donald holding an oar in his movable arms, made in Japan, Walt E. Disney copyright, original inspection stamp on bottom, early 1930s, near mint condition, 6" l. (ILLUS.) **1,953**

Rare Mickey & Minnie Figures

Mickey & Minnie figurine set, bisque, Mickey w/toothy smile & whiskers, both wearing black & white with red shoes marked on bottom "Germany," made 1929, Mickey 1 3/4" h., Minnie 1 7/8" h. pr. (ILLUS.) **1,200**

Mickey & Minnie Mouse & Pluto tooth-brush holder, bisque, 1930s **325**

Mickey Mouse Club Mousekartooner set, 1950s, w/original box **68**

Mickey Mouse Club TV Bulb

Mickey Mouse Club TV bulb & nite lite, glass & metal, oblong milk glass light bulb w/transfer-printed color image of Mickey on the side, Solar Electric Corp., 1950s, w/original colorful cardboard box w/cellophane window, creases & wear to box, box 6 1/2" h., bulb 6" h. (ILLUS.) **88**

Open Minnie Mouse Pop-up Book

Minnie Mouse book, "pop-up" type, "The Pop-up Minnie Mouse," Blue Ribbon Books, hard cover, 1933 (ILLUS. open, bottom previous page)..................................... 250

Minnie Mouse lapel pin, enameled metal, 1930s.. 155

Early Celluloid Minnie Mouse Figure

Minnie Mouse figure, celluloid, flat die-cut design of pie-eyed Minnie wearing a red dress & yellow shoes, standing on a small black oval base, made in Japan, early 1930s, slight paint loss, 2" h. (ILLUS.)... 176

Minnie Mouse toothbrush holder, bisque, standing Minnie wearing red & white polka dot dress, yellow shoes, movable right arm, Japan, 1930s, 5" h. 450

101 Dalmatians Movie Poster

101 Dalmatians movie poster, yellow background w/Pongo & Perdita in the center w/other characters above & below, wording in red, white & green, one-sheet, 1961, matted & framed, poster 28 x 40" (ILLUS.)... 805

Peter Pan wristwatch, on original card w/several Peter Pan characters illustrated, Germany 145

Pinocchio on Whale Ceramic Bank

Pinocchio bank, ceramics, figural, Pinocchio on the back of a giant grey whale, coin slot in top of whale, Schmid, Germany, ca. 1980s (ILLUS.) **50-75**

Pinocchio clock, Bayard, France, 1964, original box.. 350

Pinocchio cutout circus, 1939 bread company promotion, 18 x 20", uncut................... 125

Unique Mechanical Pinocchio Figure

Pinocchio display figure, mechanical, large jointed standing figure of Pinocchio w/composition head, hands & feet, wood arms & legs on a thin wood base, a tiny plastic Jiminy Cricket in one hand, arms move & head turns, made by Mechanical Man, Inc., New York City, ca. 1940, 38 1/2" h. (ILLUS.) **2,200**

Pinocchio figure, bisque, Walt Disney Enterprises, 4 1/2" h... 125

Pinocchio hand puppet, Gund, 1950s............... 40

Early Pinocchio Lunch Pail

Pinocchio lunch pail, tin, cylindrical w/swing handle, red background w/various characters in black & white marching around the sides, dated 1940, mint condition, 5" d., 6 1/4" h. (ILLUS. of two sides) **375**

Pinocchio playing cards, full deck...................... **35**

Pinocchio toy, windup tin, figure of a walking Pinocchio carrying buckets, marked "Walt Disney Ent. copyright 1939, Marx," 8 1/2" h...................... **525**

Pluto child's seat, die-cut & painted wood, steel pipe non-moving legs & handle bars, marked "W.D.P.," 33" l., 18" h............... **150**

Pluto figure, lead, 2 1/2" h.................................. **58**

Pluto toy, windup tin, "Pluto the Unicyclist," Pluto on a unicycle, Line Mar, w/original colorful box, 5 1/2" h....................................... **625**

Pluto Windup Walker

Pluto toy, windup tin walker, head bobs & tail rotates, Line Mar, 1950s, original box (ILLUS.).............. **463**

Snow White figure, bisque, 1930s, 6 1/2" h................. **200**

Snow White stove, tin, Wolverine, 6 1/2 x 11", 11 1/2" h. **45**

Snow White & the Seven Dwarfs figures, bisque, colorfully decorated, each Dwarf w/a different musical instrument, made in Japan, Walt E. Disney copyright, distributed by George Borgfeldt, in original colorfully printed cardboard box, 1930s, slight paint wear on figures & box, figures range from 2 1/2" to 3 5/8" h., set of 8 .... **605**

Snow White & the Seven Dwarfs figures, bisque, each painted, produced for George Borgfeldt Corporation of New York, 1938, 5" h. Dwarfs, 7" h. Snow White, set of 8... **725**

Snow White & the Seven Dwarfs figures, bisque, trimmed in color, made in Japan, 1938 Walt Disney Enterprises copyright,

distributed by George Borgfeldt, 1930s, complete set w/original box, Dwarfs 4" h., Snow White 5 1/4" h., the set (slight paint wear, wear & repair to box) **413**

Snow White & the Seven Dwarfs radio, plastic, embossed scene of Snow White & the Seven Dwarfs, white background w/colorfully painted figures, Emerson Radio and Photograph Corporation, Model No. 411, 1938.. **3,000**

Three Little Pigs China Ashtray

Three Little Pigs ashtray, china w/lustre finish, figures of the three pigs on the back edge of the triangular ashtray, Japan, 1930s, 4 1/2" w., 3" h. (ILLUS.) **140**

Early Three Pigs Bisque Figures

Three Little Pigs figures, bisque, standing, each playing an instrument, made in Japan, stamped on back w/No. 570, 571 or 572, ca. 1930s, slight paint wear, each 4 1/2" h., the set (ILLUS.) **235**

Three Little Pigs Toothbrush Holder

Three Little Pigs toothbrush holder, bisque, the Three Pigs standing in a row w/holder behind them, on a green base, color trim, made in Japan, slight soiling & paint wear, 1930s, 4 1/2" h. (ILLUS.) **100-150**

Three Little Pigs Windup Pig Toy

Three Little Pigs toy, windup tin, pig in blue overalls & cap hops when wound, Line Mar, Japan, w/original house-shaped cardboard box w/cellophane window intact, only slight wear on box, box 8" h., toy 4 1/4" h. (ILLUS.) **715**

Walt Disney World world globe, lithographed tin, colorful world globe above domed gold metal base w/color images of Disney characters, ca. 1970s, 9" d., 10" h. (dent in Pacific Ocean, some soiling) **132**

DOLLS
Also see: STEIFF TOYS & DOLLS.

A.B.G. Bisque Shoulder Head Girl

A.B.G. (Alt, Beck & Gottschalck) bisque shoulder head girl, marked "974 #6" on bottom of shoulder plate, w/painted blue eyes w/red accent line, single-stroke brows, closed pouty mouth w/accent line between lips, molded & painted blonde hair to shoulders, cloth body, bisque lower arms, rivet joints at hips & knees, wearing white dotted Swiss blouse, blue print skirt, underclothing, new socks & shoes, 19" (ILLUS.) **$625**

A.B.G. bisque shoulder head lady, marked "1123 1/2 #4" on shoulder plate, turned head w/set brown eyes, feathered brows, open mouth w/six upper teeth, h.h. (human hair) wig, kid body w/cloth torso, bisque lower arms, gussets at hips & knees, wearing green silk dress trimmed w/lace, antique underclothing, new socks & shoes, 14" (two tucks taken in cloth torso) **300**

A.B.G. Bisque Queen Louise

A.B.G. bisque shoulder head Queen Louise, unmarked, pale blue threaded paperweight eyes, multi-stroke brows, closed mouth w/accent line between lips, molded & painted blonde curly hair cascading to shoulders, w/molded blue scarf draped over head & front of shoulder plate, no body, but old bisque arms & legs marked "8" are included, 5" (ILLUS.) **975**

A.B.G. bisque socket head baby, marked "ABG [entwined] - 1361 - 62 - Made in Germany - 18," brown flirty sleep eyes w/tin lids & real lashes, feathered brows, open mouth w/accented lips, two upper teeth & wobble tongue, h.h. wig, bentlimb composition baby body w/working crier, wearing antique baby dress w/embroidery trim, antique baby bonnet, antique baby diaper cover, new socks, 25" (white adhesive residue on head, body color uneven, probably repainted, arms repainted a different color, right little finger repaired & not painted)............................. **450**

A.B.G. china shoulder head girl, marked "890 #9" along bottom of shoulder plate, "Cork Stuffed" stamped on front of torso, painted blue eyes w/red accent line, single-stroke brows, closed mouth w/heavy accent line between lips, molded black curly hair, pink kid body w/bisque lower arms, pin joints at elbows, hips & knees, wearing antique white dress trimmed w/lace & tucks, antique underclothing, new socks & white boots, 20".......................... **280**

Armand Marseille Socket Head Girl

A.M. (Armand Marseille) bisque socket head girl, marked "Germany - A. 10/0 M," brown sleep eyes, open mouth w/four upper teeth, original blonde mohair wig, five-piece composition body w/painted socks & shoes, wearing factory original dress trimmed w/red ribbon, matching bonnet, original underclothing, 8" (ILLUS.).. **310**

A.M. Bisque Socket Head "Googlie"

A.M. bisque socket head "googlie" baby, marked "G. 253 B. - Germany - A. 11/0M.," large side-glancing blue sleep eyes, single-stroke brows, closed smiling mouth, dark mohair wig, crude composition five-piece toddler body, wearing lace-trimmed organdy baby dress, matching bonnet, slip, diaper, stockings & crocheted booties, body repainted, 6 1/2" (ILLUS.)... **675**

Armand Marseille Bisque "Googlie"

A.M. "googlie" bisque socket head girl, marked "Germany - 323 - A11/0 M," brown sleep eyes to side, single-stroke brows, closed smiling mouth, original brown mohair wig, five-piece composition body w/molded & painted socks & shoes, wearing original blue & red print dress w/lace collar & cuffs, original panties & white cap, 7" (ILLUS.) **750**

Alexander (Madame) American Girl in box, marked "Alex" on back of doll, "'American Girl' - by Madame Alexander" on dress tag & on small gold wrist tag, "388 American Girl" stamped on Alexander label on box, hard plastic head attached to walking mechanism, blue sleep eyes w/molded lashes, single-stroke brows, closed mouth, original synthetic wig, hard plastic body jointed at shoulders, hips & knees, walking mechanism turns head when legs move, wearing original red & white gingham dress, white eyelet pinafore, straw hat w/flowers, original white underclothing, white cotton socks, black suede shoes w/two gold dots, contained in original box, 8" **285**

Alexander (Madame) Amy, marked "Alex." on head, "Louisa M. Alcott's - 'Little Women' - 'Amy' - By Madame Alexander, N.Y. U.S.A. - All Rights Reserved" on dress tag, hard plastic head w/blue sleep eyes w/real lashes, single-stroke brows, closed mouth, original blonde floss hair in loop curls, five-piece hard plastic body, wearing original flowered dress w/white pique bodice & sleeves, original slip & pantaloons w/eyelet trim, original socks & black side-snap shoes w/bows, 14".......... **550**

Madame Alexander "Bride" Walker

Alexander (Madame) "Bride" walker, marked "Alexander," "Madame Alexander - All Rights Reserved - New York, U.S.A." on dress tag, hard plastic head attached to walking mechanism, blue sleep eyes w/real lashes, single-stroke brows, closed mouth, original wig, five-piece hard plastic body, wearing original bride dress, flower-trimmed hat, original panties, stockings & shoes, 17" (ILLUS.)...... **375**

Cissy as Queen Elizabeth II

Alexander (Madame) Cissy as Queen Elizabeth II, marked "Alexander" on

head, "'Cissy' - by Madame Alexander" on dress tag, hard plastic head w/blue sleep eyes w/real lashes, feathered brows, closed mouth, pierced ears, original synthetic wig, hard plastic body jointed at hips & knees, vinyl arms jointed at elbows, wearing original tagged brocade gown w/pale blue sash, original panties, crinoline slip, shoes, jeweled tiara, earrings, long gloves & bracelets, small tear at top of right glove, 21" (ILLUS.).................. **600**

Alexander (Madame) Coco Lissy portrait doll, marked "Alexander - 19©66" on head, "Madame Alexander - All Rights Reserved - New York U.S.A." on dress tag, vinyl head w/brown sleep eyes w/real lashes, feathered brows, closed mouth in slight smile, pierced ears, rooted hair, vinyl body jointed at shoulders & waist, bent right leg, wearing original pale pink dress w/lace overlay, pleated tulle skirt, original underclothing, stockings & shoes, "diamond" tiara, earrings & ring, in replacement box, 21" (hair has been re-pinned in place).. **600**

Alexander "Princess Margaret Rose"

Alexander (Madame) Princess Margaret Rose, marked "Alexander" on head, "'Margaret Rose' - Madame Alexander - New York, U.S.A. - All Rights Reserved" on dress tag, hard plastic head w/blue sleep eyes w/real lashes, single-stroke brows, closed mouth, brown mohair wig, five-piece hard plastic body, wearing original yellow nylon dress w/lace & ribbon trim, original panties, long rayon stockings, black snap shoes, straw bonnet, flowers on dress & hat probably replaced, 17" (ILLUS.).. **375**

Alexander (Madame) Queen, marked "Alexander - 19©61" on head, "Madame Alexander - All Rights Reserved" on dress tag, vinyl head w/blue sleep eyes w/real lashes, feathered brows, closed mouth, pierced ears, rooted synthetic hair, hard plastic body jointed at shoulders, hips & knees, vinyl arms, high heel feet, wearing original white brocade gown, red sash of the Order of the Bath, original underclothing, stockings, satin shoes, tiara, earrings, bracelets & gloves, "diamond" ring, 21" (some holes in clothing) **225**

Madame Alexander Sonja Henie

Alexander (Madame) Sonja Henie, marked "Genuine - 'Sonja Henie' - Madame Alexander, N.Y. U.S.A. - All Rights Reserved" on dress tag, "Madame Alexander - Sonja Henie - Style #3400J" on box label, composition head w/brown sleep eyes w/real lashes, single-stroke brows, open mouth w/six upper teeth, molded dimples, original blonde h.h. wig in original set, five-piece composition body, wearing original pink rayon skating dress w/matching panties, original gold skates, only bottom of box remains, 17" (ILLUS.)... **750**

Madame Alexander Sweet Violet

Alexander (Madame) Sweet Violet, marked "Alexander" on head, "Madame Alexander - All Rights Reserved - New York, U.S.A." on tag on dress, hard plastic head w/walking mechanism, blue sleep eyes w/real lashes, feathered brows, closed mouth, original synthetic wig, hard plastic body jointed at shoulders, elbows, wrists, hips & knees, wearing original blue cotton dress, underclothing, flowered bonnet, white gloves, black side-snap shoes, carrying original pink Alexander hat box, comb & curler missing from hat box, socks probably replaced, 18" (ILLUS.) **1,700**

Alexander (Madame) Wendy Bride, marked "Alexander" on head, "Madame Alexander - All Rights Reserved - New York, U.S.A." on dress tag, "Fashion Academy Award" wrist tag, hard plastic head w/blue sleep eyes w/real lashes, single-stroke brows, closed mouth, original wig in original set, five-piece hard plastic body jointed at shoulders & hips, wearing white satin wedding gown w/rhinestones, original underclothing, stockings & shoes, veil w/flower headpiece, contained in original box w/small handled box marked "Comb and Curlers - for your - Madame Alexander - Doll," 17" **550**

Amberg Bottle Babe Twins, marked "A.M. - Germany - 341/3" on heads, "Amberg's - Bottle Babe - Pat. Pending - Amberg Dolls - The World Standard" on one dress tag, solid dome bisque heads w/light blue sleep eyes, softly blushed brows, open mouths w/molded tongues, lightly molded & painted hair, cloth bodies w/non-working criers, composition arms, right arms molded to hold celluloid bottles, wearing original white lace-trimmed baby dresses, slips, crocheted bonnets, diapers, socks, both dolls come w/bottle & blue & white celluloid rattle, 12 1/2", pair (bottles missing rubber nipples, rattles dented, one has reglued split)........................ 500

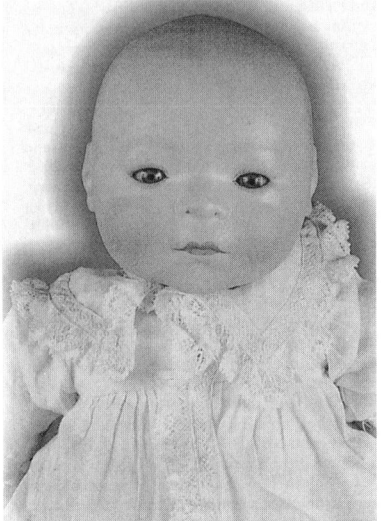

Amberg New Born Baby

Amberg solid dome bisque head new born baby, marked "© L.A. & S. 1914 - #G' 45520 - Germany #4," blue sleep eyes, softly blushed brows, closed mouth, lightly molded & painted hair, cloth body w/composition hands, wearing white lace-trimmed antique baby dress, slip & diaper, left side seam split near bottom of torso, 15" (ILLUS.).......................... 305

American Character Betsy McCall, marked "McCall - 19©58" on head, "Betsy - McCall - American Character Doll Corp. - etc." on box, "Betsy McCall" in star design on outside of trunk, original cardboard insert marked "...this trunk and clothing are made exclusively for your 14" Betsy McCall Doll," vinyl head, blue sleep eyes w/real lashes, feathered brows, rooted hair, vinyl body w/jointed waist tied in bottom of original box, wearing black body suit, rayon socks, one black strap shoe, comes w/trunk containing Princess-style blue felt jumper outfit w/straw bonnet, slip & attached panties, socks & white snap shoes, pink taffeta pajamas, quilted robe, Birthday Party dress, half slip, panties, socks & white snap shoes, red velvet coat & matching hat made for Betsy, 14" (box missing lid, crayon marks on label, one corner of trunk damaged) 400

American Character Toni, marked "American - © - Character" in circle on back, "The - Toni - Doll - With Rooted Hair" on wrist tag, "The Toni Doll - with play wave kit - 2006" on box label, vinyl head w/blue sleep eyes w/real lashes, feathered brows, closed mouth, pierced ears, rooted hair in original set, vinyl lady body jointed at shoulders, hips & waist, high heel feet, wearing original wedding gown, underclothing, nylon stockings, high heel shoes & veil, contained in original box w/wrist tag & booklet, 20"................. 395

Arranbee Nancy Lee, marked "R & B," composition head w/brown sleep eyes w/real lashes, single-stroke brows, closed mouth, original h.h. wig in original set, five-piece composition body, wearing original brown flannel belted dress w/white ruffle trim, original underwear combination, original socks & brown suede shoes w/fringe tongue, 17"............ 300

Arranbee Nanette, marked "R & B" on head, "Nanette - An R & B Quality Doll - R & B Doll Company * New York City" on wrist tag, hard plastic head w/walking mechanism, blue sleep eyes w/real lashes, single-stroke brows, closed mouth, saran wig, five-piece hard plastic walking body, wearing original red & white striped dress w/red organdy sleeves & apron, wide blue vinyl belt w/charms attached, includes wrist tag, curlers on card, comb, w/box, 21" (box lid damaged & repaired) 700

Arranbee solid dome bisque flange head infant, marked "Germany - Arranbee - 3," blue sleep eyes, soft single-stroke brows, closed mouth, lightly molded & painted hair, cloth body w/crier, rubber hands, wearing probably original pink organdy dress, underclothing, socks, matching pink silk coat & bonnet, 14" (crier not working, hands hardened, small holes near neck on cloth body, silk of bonnet deteriorating).. 130

China Head Man & Walking Lady

Autoperipatetikos, marked "Patented July 15th, 1862; also in Europe 20 Dec. 1862" on label on wooden base, bisque shoulder head lady w/molded & painted blonde hair, painted blue eyes w/red accent line, single-stroke brows, closed heart-shaped mouth, carton body w/working clockwork walking mechanism w/metal feet, leather arms, wearing off-white organdy dress, two slips, key for winding mechanism included, kid hands worn & split, mechanism housing covered w/cellophane & taped, 10" (ILLUS. right w/china head man, previous page) **800**

Averill (Georgene) Bonnie Babe, marked "Copr. by - Georgene Averill - 1005/3652/3 - Germany," solid dome bisque flange head w/blue sleep eyes, softly blushed brows, open laughing mouth w/two lower teeth, molded tongue, deeply molded dimples, lightly molded & painted curly hair, cloth mama-doll body w/crier, composition arms & lower legs, wearing possibly original white lace-trimmed baby dress, slip, underwear, socks & knit booties, silk & lace bonnet, 17" (crier not working, most paint flakes off arms) **600**

B. J. & Co. "My Sweetheart" Doll

B. J. & Co. "My Sweetheart," marked "101 - 11 - My Sweetheart - B. J. & Co.," "58" stamped in red on bottom of both feet, bisque socket head girl w/blue sleep eyes, feathered brows, open mouth w/accented lips & four upper teeth, antique mohair wig, jointed wood & composition body wearing antique silk doll dress w/lace collar & cuffs, underclothing, new socks, antique shoes, crack in finish around socket, 22 1/2" (ILLUS.) **210**

Belton-type Indian

Bahr & Proschild Belton-type Indian, marked "244 - 7," bisque socket head w/flat top, three stringing holes, set brown frowning eyes, feathered brows, closed mouth, pierced ears, original mohair wig, five-piece composition body jointed at shoulders & hips, molded & painted shoes, wearing original brown Native American costume w/yarn fringe trim, feather headdress, missing belt, minor repairs on upper arms & legs at stringing holes, 16 1/2" (ILLUS.) **1,300**

Barrois bisque shoulder head girl, marked "E 4 B" on shoulder plate, pale cup-and-saucer swivel head w/set blue eyes, fine multi-stroke brows, closed mouth w/accented lips & accent line between lips, original blonde mohair wig w/original tortoiseshell comb, kid body w/kid-over-wood upper arms & mortise-and-tenon type joints, bisque lower arms, gussets at hips, mortise-and-tenon type knee joints, wearing white dotted Swiss dress, possibly original underclothing, socks & shoes, 17 1/2" (lower bisque arms replaced) **1,200**

Belton-type bisque socket head girl, marked "1," blue threaded paperweight eyes, feathered brows, closed mouth w/accented lips, pierced ears, white skin wig, jointed wood & composition body w/straight wrists, wooden upper arms & upper legs, wearing French-style dress & matching bonnet of antique fabric, underclothing, socks & handmade leather boots, right lower arm old replacement, repainted left upper leg & under side of left lower arm, comes w/lap dog, 10" **960**

Bergmann (C.M.) bisque socket head Eleanore, marked "C.M.B. - Simon & Halbig - Eleanore," blue sleep eyes, molded & feathered brows, open mouth w/accented lips & four upper teeth, pierced ears, mohair wig, jointed wood & composition body, wearing antique child dress, pale pink pinafore, antique underclothing, new stockings & shoes, 25" **550**

Bergmann (C.M.) bisque socket head girl, marked "S & H - C.M.B. - 9," blue sleep eyes w/real lashes, feathered brows, open mouth w/accented lips & four upper teeth, pierced ears, antique h.h. wig, jointed wood & composition body, wearing antique striped dress, red wool cape lined w/silk, new underclothing, socks & new boots, 22" **300**

Bisque shoulder head boy, unmarked, turned head w/painted blue eyes w/red accent lines & molded lids, single-stroke brows, closed mouth, molded & painted blond hair, cloth body w/bisque lower arms & lower legs, wearing original-looking outfit w/white shirt that buttons in front, black velvet pants trimmed w/blue silk taffeta, blue silk taffeta jacket trimmed w/black velvet ribbon, 13 1/2" (left hand & foot repaired) **300**

lids, multi-stroke brows, closed mouth w/accent line between lips, molded earrings, molded & painted blonde hair w/copper tiara, two black ribbons across top of head & lying against left side of neck, molded bun w/"waterfall" effect, cloth body w/leather lower arms, red leather boots as part of lower legs, wearing antique ecru wool dress w/lace trim, antique underclothing, 18" (dress has small holes)....................................... **1,650**

Bisque socket shoulder head child, marked "0," pale blue set eyes, multi-stroke brows, closed mouth w/accented lips, pierced ears, original mohair wig, cloth body w/kid arms, jointed at shoulders & gusseted at elbows, fingers indicated w/stitching, wearing original traditional folk-type costume w/white shirt trimmed w/blue ribbon at cuffs, black velvet pants & vest trimmed w/red, buttoned leather suspenders, lace stockings, black leather boots, black velvet cap, olive green silk bow at neck, 12" (hairline in middle of forehead splits in two, right earring hole chipped & pulled through) **800**

George Borgfeldt Bisque Head Girl

Bisque Shoulder Head Lady

Bisque shoulder head lady, unmarked, turned head w/painted blue eyes w/red accent lines, single-stroke brows, closed mouth w/dark accent line, pierced ears, molded & painted blonde hair w/braided coronet, kid body w/bisque lower arms, pin-jointed at hips, gussets at knees, cloth lower legs, redressed in aqua taffeta two-piece outfit, underclothing, new stockings & boots, 16" (ILLUS.) **450**

Bisque shoulder head Miss Liberty, unmarked, painted blue eyes w/molded

Borgfeldt (George) bisque socket head girl, marked "Germany - G.B.," brown sleep eyes, real lashes, feathered brows, open mouth w/accented lips & four upper teeth, original brown mohair wig, jointed wood & composition body, wearing antique dropped-waist dress, underclothing, replaced socks & old shoes, hairline, some chips & flaking, 24" (ILLUS.) **265**

Bru Socket Head Girl

Bru bisque socket head girl, marked "Bru Jne - 9," "No. 10" on right shoulder, "Bru Jne" on left shoulder, brown paperweight eyes, heavy feathered brows, closed mouth w/accented lips, molded tongue, pierced ears, brown wig, kid body w/bisque lower arms, wooden lower legs, wearing new French-style plum & black outfit, underclothing, new socks & shoes, black fur cape, hat & muff, head broken & repaired, wig replaced, kid body deteriorating, upper arms are old kid replacements w/elbow gussets, bisque hands probably reproductions, 24" (ILLUS.)......... **4,000**

Bru Bisque Socket Head Lady

Bru bisque socket head lady, marked "Bru Jne - 6" on head, "Bru Jne" on left shoulder, "No. 6" on right shoulder, "6 - Bru Jne - Paris" on sole of one shoe, blue paperweight eyes, two-tone feathered brows, closed mouth w/tip of tongue showing, accented lips, pierced ears, replaced mohair wig, bisque shoulder plate w/molded breasts, kid body w/bisque lower arms, wooden lower legs, wearing outfit of antique fabric & trim, ribbon & plume matching decoration in hair, underclothing, socks, one marked shoe & one antique shoe resembling marked original, partial paper label on chest, 19" (ILLUS.).......... **12,700**

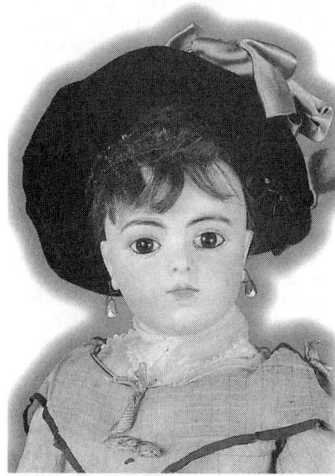

Bru Lady Walker

Bru bisque socket head lady walker, marked "Bru Jne - 9," head mounted on base for mechanism, brown paperweight eyes w/blush above, feathered brows, closed mouth w/accent lines & shading, pierced ears, original brown h.h. wig over cork pate, wood & composition body w/unjointed legs, leather shoes w/metal soles & rollers for walking, wearing possibly original clothing & underclothing, turns head, swings arms, rolls on rollers on bottom of feet, opening in front torso missing crier, mechanism works slowly, 23" (ILLUS.) **7,100**

Buddy Lee, marked "Buddy Lee" on back, "Union Made - Lee - Sanforized" on label on back of pants, "Phillips - 66" on label on front of shirt, hard plastic head w/stiff neck, painted eyes to side, single-stroke brows, closed mouth, molded & painted hair, hard plastic body jointed at shoulders only, molded & painted black boots, wearing original Phillips 66 suit w/shirt & pants, black imitation leather belt, 12" (belt has split in back)..................................... **285**

Bye-Lo Baby, marked "Bye-Lo Baby - © - Germany - G.S. Putnam" on round label on chest, "20-10" on back & arms, "16-10" on legs, bisque head w/stiff neck, painted blue eyes, softly blushed brows, closed mouth, lightly blushed hair, all-bisque baby body jointed at shoulders & hips, wearing diaper only, comes w/wicker cradle & celluloid rattle, 4" **350**

Bye-Lo Baby, marked "Copr. by - Grace S. Putnam - Made in Germany" on head, illegible faint stamp on body, solid dome bisque head w/brown sleep eyes, softly blushed brows, closed mouth, lightly molded & painted hair, cloth body w/celluloid hands & "frog" legs, redressed in white lace-trimmed baby dress, old baby sweater, slip, diaper, socks, 11" **425**

Bye-Lo Baby, marked "Copr. by - Grace S. Putnam - Made in Germany," turtle mark on wrists, solid dome bisque head w/blue sleep eyes, softly blushed brows, closed mouth, lightly molded & painted hair, cloth body w/"frog" legs, celluloid hands, wearing original white Bye-Lo dress, slip, flannel diaper, 21" (tag cut off front of dress) **600**

Chase Stockinette baby, marked "Chase - Stockinet Doll - Trade Mark" in round stamp on left hip, "Feb. 20 - 1912 - 'Polly'" handwritten on front of torso, oil painted stockinette head, painted brown eyes, single-stroke brows, closed mouth, applied ears, oil painted hair, cloth body w/sateen covered torso, wearing antique white baby dress, slip & diaper, 13" **325**

Chase Stockinette baby, unmarked, oil painted stockinette head w/painted blue eyes, multi-stroke brows, closed mouth, applied ears, oil painted hair w/texture, cloth body w/sateen-covered torso, oil painted arms & legs, jointed at shoulders, elbows, hips & knees, wearing old embroidered baby dress & matching slip, old sweater & cap, socks & baby shoes, 27" (touchup on left ankle) **385**

Chase Hospital Mannequin

Chase Stockinette hospital mannequin, marked "Chase - Hospital Doll - Trade Mark - Pawtucket, R.I. - Made in U.S.A." under left arm, oil painted stockinette head w/painted blue eyes, single-stroke brows, pierced nostrils painted red, closed red mouth, applied ears, painted hair, oil painted cloth body tab-jointed at shoulders & hips, stitch-jointed at elbows & knees, wearing smocked dotted Swiss baby dress, matching bonnet, underclothing, booties, repair on right hip joint, bandage on back, finish cracked w/holes from "shots" on rear torso, 25" (ILLUS.) **475**

"Covered Wagon" Lady

China shoulder head "covered wagon" lady, "TP/25" handwritten on front of torso, painted blue eyes slightly to right w/red accent line, single-stroke brows, closed mouth, molded & painted black center-parted hair, original cloth body w/china lower arms & lower legs, painted flat black shoes, wearing old simple white blouse, black & red gathered skirt, black silk fringed cape, some scratches in hair, right foot missing, 8 1/2" (ILLUS.) **205**

Large "Covered Wagon" Lady

China shoulder head "covered wagon" lady, unmarked, painted blue eyes w/red accent lines, single-stroke brows, closed mouth, molded & painted black hair w/vertical curls, cloth body w/china lower arms & lower legs, wearing red taffeta dress trimmed w/black velvet & lace, underclothing, cloth body is new w/old limbs, right china lower leg has been broken & reglued, 22" (ILLUS.)............................ 500

China shoulder head man, unmarked, dark painted & molded hair, painted blue eyes w/red accent line, single-stroke brows, closed smiling mouth, kid body w/tiny waist, gussets at hips, upper cloth arms, kid hands, wearing white wool jacket w/gold buttons, black wool pants, black socks & shoes, upper arms replaced or recovered w/cloth, each w/wire but no sawdust, both ankles mended, right leg shorter than left, 12" (ILLUS. left w/lady autoperipatatikos walker, on page 464) 650

China shoulder head man, attributed to Dornheim, Koch & Fischer, marked "0" on shoulder plate, painted blue eyes w/red accent lines, single-stroke brows, closed mouth w/accent line between lips, molded & painted curled black hair w/brush strokes around face, molded dress shirt w/blue plaid bow, gold accent paint, homemade cloth body w/wooden lower arms & lower legs, wearing black suit, blue brocade vest, antique red crocheted socks, original brown leather shoes, 21".. 1,700

"Adolph Menjou" Doll

Composition shoulder head "Adolph Menjou," unmarked, painted brown eyes w/accent lines, molded monocle on right eye, feathered brows, molded & painted mustache, open-closed mouth w/seven upper teeth, molded white shirt collar w/hole (presumably for tie), molded & painted hair, excelsior-stuffed cloth body w/long limbs, composition white hands as gloves, composition lower legs as

socks & shoes, wearing original black two-piece suit w/satin lapels, surface cracks & lifting of composition at seam behind ears & back of head, repaint on areas w/cracks, may be missing shirt, 32" (ILLUS.) 725

Connie Lynn baby, marked w/"Terri Lee Nursery Registration" form & three "Admission Cards to Terri Lee Hospital, Connie Lynn" tag on clothing, hard plastic head w/blue sleep eyes w/real lashes, single-stroke brows, closed mouth, original skin wig, hard plastic baby body, wearing original two-piece pink baby outfit, plastic panties, original socks & white baby shoes, in original box, 18".................... 625

Demalcol "Googlie" Girl

Demalcol bisque socket head "googlie" girl, marked "Demalcol - 5/0 - Germany," blue eyes set to side, single-stroke brows, closed smiling mouth, h.h. wig, jointed composition body, wearing blue & white flowered dress w/matching bonnet, new underclothing, socks & shoes, new body, 9 1/2" (ILLUS.)...................................... 525

"Dolley Madison" China Shoulder Head

"Dolley Madison" china shoulder head lady, marked "10" on back of shoulder plate, light pink tint, painted blue eyes w/red accent lines, single-stroke brows, closed mouth w/accent line between lips, molded & painted black hair w/molded bow & ribbon in back, cloth body w/china lower arms & lower legs, wearing antique ecru velvet dress trimmed w/fringe, sequins & chenille, antique underclothing, lower legs replaced, 21" (ILLUS.).................. **350**

Dressel (Cuno & Otto) bisque socket head girl, marked "Cuno & Otto Dressel - Germany," painted head w/blue sleep eyes w/real lashes, feathered brows, open mouth w/four upper teeth, original h.h. wig, jointed wood & composition teenage body w/high knee joints, wearing original clothing of short dress, slip, teddy, socks & leather shoes, 15 1/2".. **450**

E.D. Bisque Socket Head Girl

E.D. bisque socket head girl, marked "E. 10.D - Depose," brown paperweight eyes, feathered brows, open mouth w/accented lips & four upper teeth, pierced ears, replaced brown h.h. wig, jointed wood & composition French body, wearing old off-white dress w/lace trim, underclothing, socks & shoes, left earring hold pulled through, 21" (ILLUS.) **1,500**

Eden bisque socket head girl, marked "Eden Bebe - Paris - 7 - Depose" on back of neck, "7" on front of neck, blue paperweight eyes, feathered brows, open mouth w/six upper teeth, pierced ears, replaced mohair wig, jointed wood & composition French body, redressed in pale blue & ecru outfit w/blue & beige jacket, antique underclothing, new stockings, old shoes, 16 1/2" **1,200**

Eden Bisque Socket Head Girl

Eden bisque socket head girl, marked "Eden Bebe - Paris - 11 - Depose" on head, "11" on front of neck, blue paperweight eyes, multi-stroke brows, open mouth w/accented lips & six upper teeth, pierced ears, brown h.h. wig, jointed wood & composition body w/jointed wrists, wearing red silk dress w/white lace bodice & cuffs, red wool bonnet, underclothing, black socks & leather shoes, touchups/minor repairs at neck socket, shoulders, elbows, hips & feet, 23" (ILLUS.) **1,200**

Effanbee "American Child" boy, unmarked, composition head w/painted blue eyes, multi-stroke brows, closed smiling mouth, original h.h. wig, five-piece composition child body, wearing original blue wool two-piece suit w/jacket & shorts, white shirt, multicolored tie, original socks & black leatherette shoes, 17" **1,050**

Effanbee "American Child" girl, marked "Effanbee - American - Children" on head, "Effanbee Anne-Shirley" on back, composition head w/blue sleep eyes w/real lashes, multi-stroke brows, closed mouth, original h.h. wig, five-piece composition child body, wearing original blue & white striped zippered dress, matching romper, original socks & black shoes w/fringe trim, 19" (right eye cracked) **650**

Effanbee "American Child" girl, marked "Effanbee - American - Children" on head, "Effanbee Anne-Shirley" on back, composition head w/blue sleep eyes w/real lashes, multi-stroke brows, closed mouth, original h.h. wig w/original curlers, five-piece composition child body, wearing original blue & white striped zippered dress, nylon panties, original white socks w/blue trim & blue leatherette tie shoes, 19 1/2"... **1,500**

Effanbee "Baby Tinyette," marked "Effanbee" on head, "Effanbee - Baby Tinyette" on back, composition head w/painted blue eyes to side, single-stroke brows, closed mouth, molded & painted hair, composition baby body, wearing original pale blue organdy baby dress, matching underclothing, bonnet, socks w/ribbon trim, 7" **335**

Effanbee "Candy Kid"

Effanbee "Candy Kid," marked "Effanbee" on head & back, "An / Effanbee - Durable Doll - The Doll With - Satin-Smooth - Skin" in heart on label on end of original box, composition head w/blue sleep eyes w/real lashes, single-stroke brows, closed mouth, molded & painted hair, five-piece composition toddler body, wearing original red & white gingham sun suit & bonnet, original socks & red leatherette tie shoes, 12" (ILLUS.) **375**

Effanbee "Patsy" & "Skippy"

Effanbee "Patsy," marked "Effanbee - Patsy" on head, "Effanbee - Patsy - Doll" on back, composition head w/brown sleep eyes w/real lashes, single-stroke brows, closed "rosebud" mouth, molded & painted bobbed hair, five-piece composition child body w/bent right arm, wearing original light green silk dress w/evidence of

tag on back seam, matching underclothing & bonnet, original socks & brown leather tie shoes, right little finger missing, finish chipped off left thumb, flaking, 14" (ILLUS. left w/Skippy) **200**

Effanbee "Patsy Ann," marked "Effanbee - 'Patsy-Ann' - © - Pat. #1283558" on back, "Effanbee - Durable - Dolls" on dress tag, composition head w/brown sleep eyes w/real lashes, closed mouth, molded & painted hair, five-piece composition body w/bent right arm, wearing original pink organdy dress & bonnet, original two-piece pink cotton underclothing, replaced socks & shoes, 19" (eyebrows missing, touchup on arms & hands) **370**

Effanbee "Patsy Mae," marked "Effanbee - Patsy Mae" on head, "Effanbee - Lovums - © - Pat. No. 1283658" on should plate, "Effanbee - Durable Dolls" on metal heart bracelet, composition shoulder head, brown sleep eyes w/real lashes, feathered brows, closed "rosebud" mouth, h.h. wig, cloth body w/composition arms & legs, wearing original blue-grey dress w/red print, faded tag on back, original blue-grey romper & matching slip, rayon socks, replaced red leather shoes, 30" (eyes cloudy, three short lines around left eye) **900**

Effanbee "Skippy," marked "Effanbee - Skippy - © - P.L. Crosby" on head, "Effanbee Dolls - I Am Skippy - Trade Mark - The Real American Boy" on original button, composition head on wooden neck plug, painted blue eyes to side, peaked brows, closed mouth, molded & painted hair, cloth torso w/composition arms & legs, wearing original blue & white plaid flannel suit of shorts & jacket, matching hat, original white shirt, blue tie, original socks & black tie shoes, some flaking, minor crack in finish of left palm, 14" (ILLUS. right w/Patsy) **625**

Effanbee "Skippy" Policeman

Effanbee "Skippy" Policeman, marked "Effanbee - Skippy - © - P.L. Crosby" on head, "Effanbee - Durable - Dolls - Made in U.S.A." on tag on pants, composition head w/painted blue eyes to side, peaked brows, closed mouth, molded & painted hair, cloth body w/composition arms & legs w/molded & painted black socks & shoes, wearing very rare policeman outfit w/dark blue pants, light blue shirt, black ribbon tie, black belt w/holster containing original gun, dark blue cap w/black oil-cloth bill, original button, 14" (ILLUS.)........ **1,950**

Frozen Charlie, unmarked, china doll w/pink tint, painted blue eyes w/blue accent lines, single-stroke brows, closed mouth w/accent line between lips, painted blonde hair w/brush strokes around face, unjointed body w/arms extended, hands held w/fingers curled, fingernails & toenails outlined, 11 1/2"................................. **450**

nal blue & white two-piece outfit w/train, antique underclothing, replaced shoes, one left finger missing, 10 1/2" (ILLUS.) **1,250**

Francois Gaultier Girl

Gaultier (Francois) bisque socket head girl, marked "F.G. [in scroll] - 8 [possibly 3]," large blue paperweight eyes, feathered brows, full closed mouth w/molded tongue, pierced ears, replaced blonde mohair wig, jointed wood & composition body w/straight wrists, wearing new blue silk dress w/matching bonnet, new underclothing, socks & lace-up boots, fingers touched up, minor repair to front of ankles & hip sockets, 21" (ILLUS.)............. **2,200**

German bisque socket head "Princess," marked "295 - Princess - 2 - Germany" on head, "Germany - 4" stamped in red on right hip, brown sleep eyes, molded & feathered brows, open mouth w/accented lips & four upper teeth, replaced synthetic wig, jointed wood & composition Kestner body, wearing antique organdy dress w/lace trim, antique underclothing, socks & old shoes, 23" (index finger on right hand reglued).. **325**

German solid dome bisque socket head character boy, marked "11" on head, "Germany 1 1/2" on back, painted brown eyes, single-stroke brows, open-closed mouth w/accented lips, lightly molded & brush-stroked hair, jointed wood & composition Kestner body, wearing antique black two-piece outfit, lace-trimmed shirt, black silk tie, cotton socks, antique shoes, 17" **450**

Francois Gaultier Lady

Gaultier (Francois) bisque shoulder head lady, marked "2/0" on head, "F.G." on right shoulder, illegible mark on left shoulder, socket head w/light blue paperweight eyes, feathered brows, closed mouth, pierced ears, original mohair wig, cloth body w/kid arms, individually stitched fingers, wearing probably origi-

"Godey's Little Lady" Doll in Box

Gibbs (Ruth) china shoulder head "Godey's Little Lady," marked "Ruth Gibbs" on shoulder plate, painted blue eyes, single-stroke brows, closed mouth, molded & painted brown hair, cloth body w/china lower arms & lower legs, wearing original organdy camisole & long panties, doll contained in original box w/paper lace edge, box marked "Ruth Gibbs - Godey's - Lady Book - Dolls" on cover & "Mrs. Mary Ruth - in Camisole and Long Panties" on end label, 12" (ILLUS.) **200**

Handwerck (Heinrich) bisque socket head black girl, marked "119 - 10 1/4x - Handwerck - Germany - Halbig - 2," deep brown face w/brown sleep eyes, molded & feathered brows, open mouth w/four upper teeth, pierced ears, original mohair wig, jointed wood & composition brown body, wearing antique white dress w/embroidery, straw hat, antique undercloth- ing, black cotton socks, leather shoes colored red, 19" (repair around neck socket, left shoulder & arm socket, miss- ing tip of left thumb & little finger, missing right middle & little fingers) **900**

Heinrich Handwerck 17 1/2" Girl

Handwerck (Heinrich) bisque socket head girl, marked "109 - 7 1/2 - Germany - Handwerck" on head, "Heinrich Hand- werck - Germany" stamped on back, brown sleep eyes, feathered brows, open mouth w/accented lips, pierced ears, original platinum mohair wig, jointed wood & composition body, wearing an- tique white dress, new underclothing, new socks & leather shoes, 17 1/2" (ILLUS.) **675**

Handwerck (Heinrich) bisque socket head girl, marked "109-15 - DEP - Ger- many - Handwerck - 6" on head, "Hein- rich Handwerck - Germany - 6" stamped in red on back, brown sleep eyes, molded & feathered brows, open mouth w/ac- cented lips & four upper teeth, pierced ears, h.h. wig, jointed wood & composi- tion Handwerck body, wearing ecru & melon French-style dress, new under- clothing, old socks & shoes, 30" (chips around neck socket, finish dented w/cracks on lower torso) **500**

Heinrich Handwerck Bisque Girl

Handwerck (Heinrich) bisque socket head girl, marked "16 - 99 - DEP - Ger- many - Handwerck - 7" on head, "Heinrich Handwerck - Germany" stamped on left hip, "HH" in heart on shoes, blue sleep eyes, molded & feathered brows, open mouth w/accented lips & four upper teeth, pierced ears, original blonde h.h. wig, jointed wood & composition Handwerck body, wearing beige polka dot dress w/rib- bon & lace trim, antique underclothing, lace socks made from lace gloves, original rose satin shoes, 32" (ILLUS.) **1,275**

Handwerck (Heinrich) bisque socket head girl, marked "Germany - Heinrich - Handwerck - Halbig -8" on head, "Heinrich Handwerck - Germany - 8" stamped in red on back, brown sleep eyes, molded & feathered brows, open mouth w/accented lips & four upper teeth, pierced ears, replaced h.h. wig, jointed composition body, wearing new white lace dress, purple velvet coat & bonnet trimmed w/satin & lace, new underclothing, socks & shoes, 36" **1,750**

Hertel, Schwab & Co. bisque socket head baby, marked "Made in Germany - 152 - 13," blue-grey sleep eyes, feathered flyaway brows, open mouth w/accented lips & molded tongue, original mohair wig, composition baby body, wearing antique long baby dress w/lace trim, crocheted bonnet, newer underclothing, booties, 22" (repair on right thumb & first finger) **525**

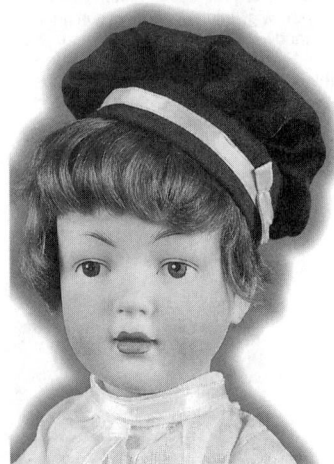

Hertel, Schwab & Co. Character Child

Hertel, Schwab & Co. bisque socket head character child, marked "140 - 4," painted brown eyes w/red accent lines, feathered brows, closed mouth w/accented lips, mohair wig, jointed wood & composition body w/straight wrists, wearing white factory chemise as shirt, dark green pants w/matching cap, cotton socks, new leather shoes, minor repair at neck socket, 15" (ILLUS.) **4,200**

Heubach (Ernst) bisque socket head baby, marked "Heubach * Koppelsdorf - 300 * 6 - Germany," set brown eyes, feathered brows, open mouth w/accented lips, four upper teeth, replaced wig, composition bent-limb baby body, wearing antique long white baby dress, lace-trimmed antique baby bonnet, underclothing, diaper, booties, 21" (arms and legs repainted, neck socket touched up, repair on right arm joint & right wrist) **275**

Heubach (Ernst) bisque socket head girl, marked "Heubach Koppelsdorf - 300 * 1 * - Germany," blue sleep eyes, feathered brows, open mouth w/accented lips & four upper teeth, old mohair wig, jointed composition body w/separate balls at shoulders & elbows, wearing faded blue antique dress w/blue ribbon trim, antique

underclothing, old socks, replaced shoes, straw bonnet, 20" (left ring finger missing) **500**

Heubach (Ernst) solid dome painted bisque socket head black baby, marked "Heubach * Koppelsdorf - 399 * 9/0 - Germany," brown sleep eyes, single-stroke brows, closed mouth, lightly molded & painted hair, composition bent-limb baby body, wearing original multicolored "grass" skirt pinned to torso, 12 1/2" **350**

Heubach (Gebruder) bisque shoulder head character boy, marked "0 - Germany - 29 [green stamp] - [illegible number]" on head, "0" on shoes, blue intaglio eyes, single-stroke brows, open-closed mouth w/two lower teeth, molded & painted hair, pink cloth body w/composition arms & lower legs, redressed in aqua wool two-piece suit w/short pants, old socks, antique shoes, 10 1/2" (excelsior stuffing of body showing at top of torso, arms repainted, elastic in body loose) **330**

Heubach (Gebruder) bisque socket head coquette, marked "2 - 77 Heubach [in square] 63 - Germany" on head, "10. 3/4" embossed on back, blue intaglio eyes, open-closed mouth w/four tiny painted teeth, molded & painted blonde hair w/aqua molded ribbon, jointed wood & composition body w/wooden upper arms & stick upper legs, wearing white lace-trimmed dress, underclothing, new socks, blue leatherette shoes, 12 1/2" (repair on left foot) **1,000**

Mary Hoyer Hard Plastic Girl

Hoyer (Mary) hard plastic girl, marked "Original - Mary Hoyer - Doll" in circle on back, blue sleep eyes w/real lashes, single-stroke brows, closed mouth, original wig, five-piece plastic body wearing mauve knit outfit made from Mary Hoyer pattern, rayon socks, white leatherette center-snap shoes, w/red First Place ribbon from 1953 show for Best Dressed Doll, clothing looks newly made, cheeks possibly reblushed, 14" (ILLUS.) **335**

Ideal "Deanna Durbin" Doll

Ideal "Deanna Durbin," marked "Deanna Durbin - Ideal Doll" on head, "Ideal Doll - 25" on back, composition socket head w/hazel sleep eyes w/remnants of real lashes, single-stroke brows, open mouth w/six upper teeth, original brown h.h. wig, five-piece composition body, wearing original flower print full-length dress, original underclothing, replaced socks & shoes, surface crack & repaint on right side seam of head, eyes cloudy, small repair on right hip joint, 25" (ILLUS.) **400**

Ideal "Lori Martin" Doll

Ideal "Lori Martin," marked "© Metro Goldwyn Mayer Inc - Mfg by - Ideal Toy Corp - 80" on head, "© Ideal Toy Corp. - 6-30-5" on back, "National Velvet's - Lori Martin - © Metro Goldwyn Mayer, Inc. - All Rights Reserved" on tag on shirt, vinyl socket head w/blue sleep eyes w/real lashes, feathered brows, closed smiling

mouth, rooted hair, vinyl body jointed at waist, shoulders, hips & ankles, wearing original clothing of tagged plaid shirt, jeans, vinyl Western-style boots decorated w/images of horses, 28" (ILLUS.) **550**

Ideal "Mary Hartline"

Ideal "Mary Hartline," marked "P-91 - Ideal Doll - Made in U.S.A." on head, "Ideal Doll - P-91" on back, "Mary" in heart on bodice of dress, "Mary Hartline" in script on skirt, hard plastic head w/blue sleep eyes w/real lashes, feathered brows, closed mouth, original wig, five-piece hard plastic body, wearing original red dress w/name & musical notes around hem, attached slip & matching panties, majorette boots, missing baton, new hair ribbon, 15" (ILLUS.) **300**

Ideal "Snow White"

Ideal "Snow White," marked "Shirley Temple - 13" on back, "Rayon - An Ideal Doll" on dress tag, composition head w/green sleep eyes w/real lashes, single-stroke brows, open mouth w/six upper teeth, chin dimple, original black mohair wig, five-piece composition body, wearing original dress w/red velvet bodice, rayon skirt w/red figures of Seven Dwarfs, red velvet cape, original underclothing, socks & shoes, crazing, 13" (ILLUS.)........................ **300**

Ideal 14" "Toni"

Ideal "Toni," marked "P-90 - Ideal Doll - Made in U.S.A." on head, "Ideal Doll - P-90" on back, hard plastic head w/blue sleep eyes & real lashes, single-stroke brows, closed mouth, original wig, five-piece hard plastic body, wearing original dress w/yellow dotted Swiss bodice & sleeves, red skirt, both trimmed w/embroidery, attached slip w/matching panties, replaced rayon socks, center-snap shoes, shoes worn, tiny chin scratch, 14" (ILLUS.)... **200**

Ideal "Toni" walker, marked "90W -Ideal Doll" on head, "Ideal Doll - 90W" on back, "Ideal Toy Corp. - 14" on shoes, "Ideal's New - Toni - Walker Doll" on original box & wrist tag, hard plastic head w/walker mechanism, blue sleep eyes w/real lashes, closed mouth, original nylon wig in original set, five-piece hard plastic walking body jointed at shoulders & hips, wearing original dotted organdy dress, panties, socks & vinyl shoes, w/permanent wave set in "Toni Play Wave" box including Directions, Lotion, Curlers, Shampoo, End Tissues & comb, doll & set contained in original box, 14 1/2" (box aged, dented & torn) **625**

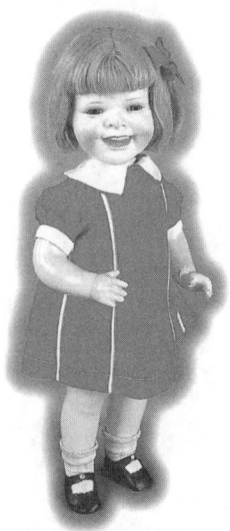

"Gladdie" Character Girl

Jensen (Helen W.) "Gladdie" character girl, marked "Gladdie - Copyright by - Helen W. Jensen - Germany - 1005/1421-4," Biscaloid flange head w/set blue eyes, feathered brows, open-closed laughing mouth w/molded tongue & teeth, molded & painted hair under original h.h. wig, cloth body w/composition arms & legs, wearing red dress w/white pique collar & cuffs, underclothing, socks & black center-snap shoes, small repair under left eye, torso w/tuck pinned around waist, flaking, cracks in finish, 21" (ILLUS.) **415**

Terri Lee's Jerri Lee Doll

Jerri Lee, marked "Terri Lee - Pat. Pending" on back, "Terri Lee" on tag on shirt, hard plastic head w/painted brown eyes, single-stroke brows, closed mouth, original skin wig, five-piece hard plastic body, wearing blue & white checked Western-style shirt, blue pants, original socks & shoes, includes extra Roundup Costume #4550 from 1954, missing hat, no gun, 16" (ILLUS.).. **650**

Jumeau Bisque Socket Head Girl

Jumeau (Emile) bisque socket head girl, marked "1907 - 7," blue paperweight eyes, open mouth w/accented lips & six upper teeth, pierced ears, replaced mohair wig, jointed wood & composition late French body, redressed in peach silk French-style dress, white silk bonnet, antique underclothing, old socks & white leather shoes, hands repainted, repairs & wear at knees touched up, 18" (ILLUS.).... **1,700**

Jumeau (Emile) bisque socket head girl, marked "DEP - 9" incised & "Tete Jumeau" stamped in red on head, "Bebe Jumeau - Diplome d'Honneur" on oval label on back, "Bebe Jumeau" on remnants of original ribbon label on dress, "9 - Paris [bee] - Depose" on soles of shoes, set blue eyes w/real lashes, molded & painted brows, open mouth w/accented lips, four upper teeth, pierced ears, replaced h.h. wig, jointed wood & composition Jumeau body w/jointed wrists, wearing completely original red silk & lace dress w/red grosgrain ribbon, underclothing, socks, shoes, elaborate red velvet hat trimmed w/ribbon & feathers, 20" (eyes broken off rocker & set, touchup or repaint on arms, hands, upper legs & feet, dress is fragile, w/repairs & extra lining to reinforce it)... **1,500**

Jumeau Bisque Socket Head Lady

Jumeau (Emile) bisque socket head lady, marked "Depose / Tete Jumeau / Bte S.G.D.G. - 7" on head, "7" on neck, "Bebe Jumeau / Diplome d'Honneur" on oval label on torso, "9 Paris - [bee] - Depose" on soles of shoes, large blue paperweight eyes, heavy feathered brows, closed mouth w/accented lips, pierced ears, replaced h.h. wig, jointed wood & composition Jumeau lady body w/adult figure, wearing antique ecru & blue dress w/lace overlay, new underclothing, black stockings, original Jumeau shoes, hole in bottom of left foot appears to accommodate a stand, 20" (ILLUS.) **3,100**

Painted Bisque "Just Me"

"Just Me" painted bisque socket head girl, marked "Just Me - Registered - Germany - A.310/6/0M.," blue side-glancing sleep eyes, single-stroke brows, closed mouth, original mohair wig, five-piece composition body jointed at shoulders & hips, wearing original white dress w/orange & green felt trim, original gauze-type underclothing, original white cotton socks & white paper shoes w/buckles, needs to be restrung, 10" (ILLUS.)................. **900**

K & K Bisque Should Head "Mama"

K & K bisque shoulder head "Mama," marked "42" on head, "K & K - 56 - Made in Germany" on shoulder plate, blue sleep eyes, feathered brows, open mouth w/two upper teeth, brown wig, cloth body w/non-working crier, composition lower arms, oilcloth legs, wearing old blue & white dress w/smocked bodice, white romper underwear, replaced socks & leather shoes, blue straw bonnet, wig replaced, lower arms repainted, 18" (ILLUS.).. **345**

K [star] R (Kammer & Reinhardt) bisque socket head baby, marked "I - K [star] R - Simon & Halbig - 115/A - 30," blue sleep eyes, feathered brows, closed mouth, original mohair wig, five-piece composition baby body, wearing antique-style white baby dress, lace-trimmed panties, eyelet bonnet, 10" (arms mostly repainted).. **1,300**

K [star] R (Kammer & Reinhardt) bisque socket head baby, marked "K [star] R - 28" on back of head, "W" at crown in front, brown sleep eyes, feathered brows, open mouth w/two upper teeth & spring tongue, original mohair wig, bent-limb composition baby body, wearing antique white baby dress, underclothing, 11" (arms repainted)... **345**

K [star] R Bisque Socket Head Baby

K [star] R (Kammer & Reinhardt) bisque socket head baby, marked "K [star] R - 28" on head, "W" on forehead at crown, blue sleep eyes w/remnants of real lashes, feathered brows, open mouth w/two upper teeth & spring tongue, original mohair wig, bent-limb composition baby body, wearing old baby dress, knit sweater, flannel diaper, newer booties, 11" (ILLUS.) **435**

K [star] R (Kammer & Reinhardt) bisque socket head black girl, marked "S&H - K [star] R - 50," dark brown head w/brown sleep eyes, feathered brows, open mouth w/four upper teeth, pierced ears, antique h.h. wig, jointed wood & composition brown body, wearing antique white dress, antique underclothing, socks & oilcloth shoes, missing sole of left foot, hands repainted, right little finger repaired, 18" **1,150**

K [star] R Character Girl

K [star] R (Kammer & Reinhardt) bisque
socket head character girl, marked "K
[star] R - Simon & Halbig - 117/A - 39,"
brown sleep eyes, feathered brows,
closed pouty mouth, mohair wig, K [star]
R jointed wood & composition body,
wearing antique blue dress w/white embroidery, antique underclothing, replaced
socks & shoes, 2 1/2" firing line with 1/4"
hairline traveling from crown in rear along
left side to center front just below rim, 15"
(ILLUS.)... **1,850**
K [star] R (Kammer & Reinhardt) bisque
socket head toddler, marked "K [star] R
- Simon & Halbig - 126 - 42," blue sleep
eyes, feathered brows, open mouth
w/two upper teeth & wobble tongue, old
mohair wig, jointed wood & composition
body w/diagonal hip joints, wearing white
dress w/pink & white striped bodice, underclothing, replaced socks & shoes,
18 1/2" (arms repainted & possibly re-
placed) **575**

Kestner All Bisque Girl

Kestner (J.D.) all bisque girl, marked "184
- 9" on head, "184.9" on arms, "9" visible
on legs (joints covered w/kid), stiff neck,
brown sleep eyes, heavy feathered
brows, closed mouth, original mohair
wig, body jointed at shoulders & hips,
molded & painted white socks w/blue
garters, yellow boots w/black side gussets, toes & heels, wearing probably original ecru wool dress w/blue ribbon trim,
wool slip, no pants, 6 1/2" (ILLUS.).............. **435**

Kamkins Cloth Head Girl

Kamkins cloth head girl, marked "Kamkins
- A Dolly Made ... - Patented By... - Atlantic City, N.J." (part of mark missing)
stamped on head, faint heart on upper
left torso, oil painted head w/painted blue
eyes, single-stroke brows, closed mouth,
original mohair wig, cloth body tab-jointed at shoulders, stitch-jointed at hips,
wearing pink ruffled organdy dress, pink
organdy bonnet, white lace-trimmed teddy, pink socks, white shoes, soiled &
darkened w/age, hole on seam of right
foot, 18" (ILLUS.)... **475**

Kestner Bisque Head Toddler

Kestner (J.D.) bisque head toddler, marked "150.5" on head, "150/5" inside upper arms, brown sleep eyes, feathered brows, open mouth w/four upper teeth, original blond mohair wig, stiff neck, all-bisque body jointed at shoulders & hips, molded & painted blue shirred socks & black one-strap shoes, wearing antique white dress w/ribbon shoulder ties, panties, wig is sparse, 10" (ILLUS.)...................... **575**

Kestner (J.D.) bisque shoulder head Gibson Girl-style lady, no marks visible, brown sleep eyes w/real lashes, single-stroke brows, closed mouth, original mohair wig upswept to top of head, kid body w/bisque lower arms, pin joints at elbows, hips & knees, redressed in white linen dress w/lace bodice & trim, matching underclothing, new socks & shoes, old pale pink straw hat w/lace & flower trim, 20".... **1,700**

Kestner "Bessy"

Kestner (J.D.) bisque socket head "Bessy," marked "9" on head, "Bessy" on label on chest, brown sleep eyes, feathered brows, closed well-modeled mouth w/accent line between lips, blonde mohair wig, kidette body w/pin joints at hips & knees, kid upper arms & bisque lower arms, wearing rose dress trimmed w/ribbon, matching bonnet, new underclothing, socks & shoes, body aged & not original to head, replaced arms each w/repair on kid, 18 1/2" (ILLUS.) **1,300**

Kestner Bisque Shoulder Head Girl

Kestner (J.D.) bisque shoulder head girl, marked "C" at bottom edge of shoulder plate, set brown eyes, feathered brows, closed mouth w/accent line between lips, h.h. wig, kid body w/cloth torso, bisque lower arms, cloth feet, gussets at elbows, hips & knees, wearing blue flower print dress, white apron, underclothing, socks & new shoes, right elbow gusset & both knee gussets patched, 18" (ILLUS.)... **550**

Kestner (J.D.) bisque shoulder head girl, marked "9 154. Dep. - E. made in Germany," blue sleep eyes w/remnants of real lashes, molded & feathered brows, open mouth w/accented lips & four upper teeth, replaced synthetic wig, kid body w/jointed wood & composition arms, rivet-jointed hips & knees, wearing antique white dress w/insert lace, antique underclothing, socks & pink cloth shoes, 21".......... **275**

Kestner Bisque Socket Head Boy

*Harley Davidson neon
advertising clock, $825.*

Courtesy Autopia

*Hills Brothers Tea and
Coffee china cup and
saucer, $248.*

Courtesy Autopia

*Poll Parrot Shoe ceramic
display, $176.*

Courtesy Collectors Auction
Services

*One of a pair of Art Deco
Scottie book ends,
$100-150.*

Courtesy Dana Cain

*Bronzed metal Art Deco
globe lamp with nude
figure, $350-400.*

Courtesy Dana Cain

*Salem China
"Tricorne"
pattern plate,
cup and saucer
in Mandarin
orange,
$12-20.*

Courtesy Dana Cain

Kodak camera and box with Art Deco design by Walter Dorwin Teague, 1930, $1,800-2,400.
Courtesy Dana Cain

Art Deco console set of bowl and candlesticks in blue and white painted glass, $65-85.
Courtesy Dana Cain

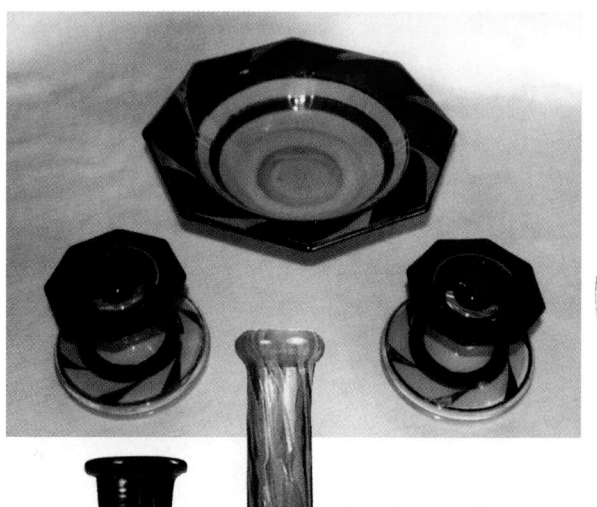

Opalescent blue glass barber bottle Spanish Lace pattern, 1890-1925, $990.
Courtesy Glass Works Auctions

Big West Gasoline globe, $1,595.
Courtesy Autopia

Grass green barber bottle with Mary Gregory-style decoration, 1890-1925, $275.
Courtesy Glass Works Auctions

Ceramic salt and pepper shaker set in the form of Texaco gas pumps, $77.
Courtesy Collectors Auction Services

Patriotic shaving mug for "A. Sutterlin," 1885-1925, $605.
Courtesy Glass Works Auctions

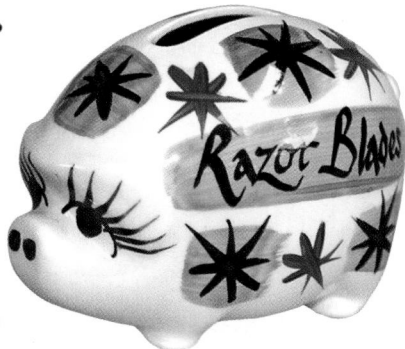

Ceramic hedgehog razor blade bank, $65-75.
Courtesy Deborah Gillham

Cobalt glass cocktail shaker with silkscreen decoration, from Hazel Atlas Sportsman series, 1930s, $75-100.
Courtesy Dana Cain

Swirl Ponytail Barbie in box, $2,095.
Courtesy McMasters Harris

Cobalt glass cocktail shaker with chrome lid and matching glasses with chrome bases, 1930s, $250-275 the set.
Courtesy Dana Cain

Boston Garter Joe Jackson window display card, 1913, $39,486.

Courtesy MastroNet

Droste's Cocoa can, $58.

Courtesy C. Williams

Richelieu Midas Gunpowder Tea tin, $35.

Courtesy Mark Moran

Animated alarm clock with paper litho face, featuring Mammy figure rocking cradle with foot, $605.

Courtesy Richard Opfer

"Poor Pete" wind-up toys, celluloid and fabric from Japan, $358 (left), and lithographed tin, Germany, $495.

Courtesy Richard Opfer

Aunt Jemima lithographed paper string hanger display, $4,747.

Courtesy Richard Opfer

Wheaties cereal promotional giveaway airline sticker, 1954-55, $10.

Courtesy Jim Trautman

"Superman of America Club" fabric patch, 1942, $3,618.

Courtesy MastroNet

Wheaties cereal promotional giveaway metal railroad sign, 4" diameter, 1954, $25.

Courtesy Jim Trautman

Betty Boop 15" figurine, $248.

Courtesy Jackson's Auctioneers

Carousel figures of a cat, Gustav A. Dentzel Carousel Co., ca. 1905, $37,375 (above), and carousel jumper, Stein and Goldstein Carousel Co., 1907-18, $21,850 (right).

Both courtesy Skinner, Inc.

Coleman Model No. 611 fuel iron in turquoise porcelain, $175.
Courtesy Jimmy and Carol Walker

Reliable Mfg. Co. egg scale, $60.
Courtesy Paul Smith

Scene in Action forest fire motion lamp, 1931, $250.
Courtesy Jim Trautman

Regal Ware aluminum pitcher, 1950s, $15-25 (left), and Sculptura model telephone by Western Electric (right), 1970s, $40-60.
Courtesy Dana Cain

Kreskin's ESP "magic" game, 1966, $40.
Courtesy Jim Trautman

Nautical items (from left): cast bronze ship's bell, $1,175, one of a pair of wooden billet heads, $4,944 the pair, and another wooden billet head, $705.

Courtesy Skinner, Inc.

Universal's Creature from the Black Lagoon movie poster, 1954, $2,500-4,000.(below)

Courtesy Dana Cain

Cardboard plaque commemorating the 200th anniversary of George Washington's birth, 1932, $25-30.

Courtesy Bobbie Zucker Bryson

Album for German Orders and Decorations picture cards (German cigarette giveaway), 1930s, $75.

Courtesy Jim Trautman

American wool hooked rug, ca. 1880, $4,113.

Courtesy Skinner, Inc.

*Maple Shaker sewing basket with
silk-covered padding inside,
$1,100.*

Courtesy Garth's Auctions, Inc.

*Civil War cotton quilt,
$21,150.*

Courtesy Skinner, Inc.

*Needlework
family
record, 1836,
$3,819.*
Courtesy
Skinner, Inc.

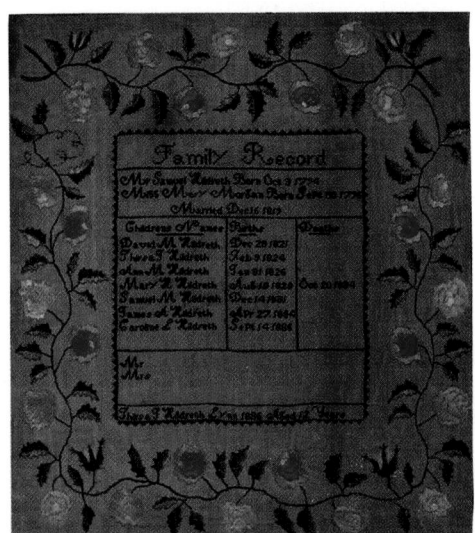

*Painted copper weathervane,
late 19th century, $15,275.*

Courtesy Skinner, Inc.

Rococo sofa by Meeks in Stanton Hall pattern, ca. 1855, $5,500.

Courtesy Mark Moran

Victorian Baroque plant stand in mahogany, ca. 1890, $2,600.

Courtesy Mark Moran

Walnut Victorian Renaissance Revival bed, ca. 1875, $3,500.

Courtesy Mark Moran

Mahogany Victorian Rococo marble-top washstand, ca. 1865, $1,100.

Courtesy Mark Moran

Victorian Golden Oak armoire, ca. 1895, $4,000.
Courtesy Mark Moran

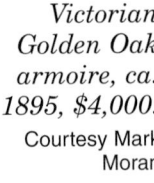

Victorian Golden Oak rocker, ca. 1895, $350.
Courtesy Mark Moran

Rosewood marble-top center table by Meeks, ca. 1850s, $18,000.
Courtesy Mark Moran

Eastlake gentleman's chest in cherry, ca. 1885, $750.
Courtesy Mark Moran

Rococo rosewood etagere by Meeks, ca. 1860, $20,000.

Courtesy Mark Moran

Victorian Murphy bed in Golden Oak, patent dated 1886, $1,250.

Courtesy Mark Moran

Victorian Baroque partner's table in mahogany by Horner, $5,500.

Courtesy Mark Moran

Victorian Rococo walnut marble-top server, ca. 1860, $2,400.

Courtesy Mark Moran

Oak bookcase with leaded-glass doors, ca. 1900, $1,800.

Courtesy Mark Moran

Transitional Victorian Eastlake writing desk, in walnut, ca. 1880, $4,800.

Courtesy Mark Moran

Golden Oak sideboard, ca. 1895, $1,800.

Courtesy Mark Moran

Kestner (J.D.) bisque socket head boy, marked "M1/2 made in Germany 16 1/2 - 164" on head, "Excelsior - Germany - 7" stamped in red on lower back, blue sleep eyes, molded & feathered brows, open mouth w/accented lips & four upper teeth, skin wig, jointed wood & composition Kestner body, wearing faded dark blue velvet sailor suit, white shirt w/red star, old socks & shoes, right little finger repaired, 32" (ILLUS.)................................ **1,200**

Kestner 20" Bisque Socket Head Girl

Kestner (J.D.) bisque socket head girl, marked "J. made in Germany. 13. - 143," blue sleep eyes, feathered brows, open mouth w/accented lips & two upper teeth, replaced h.h. wig, jointed wood & composition Kestner body, wearing antique light blue organdy dress w/embroidered roses, lace trim, new underclothing, socks & shoes, body repainted, 20" (ILLUS.) **1,500**

Kestner (J.D.) bisque socket head toddler, marked "C made in Germany 7 - 211, 211" incised on pate, "Germany" stamped in red on back, brown sleep eyes, feathered brows, open-closed mouth w/accented lips & molded tongue, original mohair wig over plaster pate, jointed composition body w/stubby toddler proportions, redressed in beige wool jacket, brown tweed pants, underclothing, new socks & shoes, 13" (tiny eye flake repair, light touchup on body) **675**

Kley & Hahn bisque socket head girl walker, marked "250 - K. H. - Walkure - 3 1/4 - Germany," brown sleep eyes, molded & feathered brows, open mouth w/accented lips & four upper teeth, h.h. wig, jointed wood & composition body, wearing red & white polka dot dress w/antique white bodice, antique under-

clothing, socks, old shoes, 23 1/2" (body repainted, three fingers repaired on left hand).. **200**

Kley & Hahn solid dome bisque socket head baby, marked "4 - Germany - K & H [in banner] - 525," blue sleep eyes, feathered brows, open-closed mouth, lightly molded & brush-stroked hair, composition baby body, wearing antique-style baby dress, slip, diaper, knit booties & sweater, 11 1/2" (body repainted) **275**

Kling china shoulder head girl, marked "Germany - 189 14" on shoulder plate, overall pink tint, painted blue eyes w/red accent lines, single-stroke brows, closed mouth w/accent line between lips, molded & painted black wavy hair w/partially exposed ears, deeply molded shoulder plate w/shoulder creases, three sew holes front & back, no body, 8" **240**

Konig & Wernicke bisque socket head toddler, marked "K & W - W [in circle] - 179.9," brown sleep eyes w/real lashes, feathered brows, open mouth w/accented lips & two upper teeth, h.h. wig, jointed wood & composition toddler body w/diagonal hip joints, wearing antique white clothing w/blue & white gingham trim, antique underclothing, new socks & shoes, 19" (left hand old replacement, crack in wood on upper left arm) **450**

Kathe Kruse Cloth Girl

Kruse (Kathe) girl, marked "Kathe Kruse - 1687" on left foot, "Made in Germany U.S. Zone" on right foot, "Kathe Kruse - Made in Germany - US Zone - Original gekleidet - Kathe Kruse - Rose X - Original gekleidet" on paper tag around neck, "Kathe Kruse - Germany - Art Dolls - Unique" on paper wrist tag, oil painted swivel cloth head w/single seam in back, painted brown eyes w/highlights, single-stroke brows, closed mouth, painted hair, cloth body w/stitched fingers, jointed hips, wearing original pink linen dress & kerchief, blue print jacket, nylon teddy, original socks & shoes, 14" (ILLUS.).......... **1,050**

Gebruder Kuhnlenz Belton-type Girl

Kuhnlenz (Gebruder) Belton-type bisque socket head girl, marked "G.K. - 13.27," head w/flat top & two small stringing holes, blue paperweight eyes, heavy feathered brows, closed mouth w/outlined lips & white space between lips, pierced ears, antique h.h. wig, jointed wood & composition body w/separate balls at shoulders, elbows, hips & knees, wearing blue & white factory chemise, antique underclothing, antique beige socks, brown shoes, numerous scratches on torso, some wear & chips, 15" (ILLUS.)................ **1,800**

Lenci Girl

Lenci girl, marked "2" on bottom of right foot, "Lenci - Made in Italy" on cloth label inside coat, pressed-felt swivel head w/painted brown eyes to side, molded single-stroke brows, closed mouth w/two-tone lips, accent dots on lower lip, original mohair wig, cloth torso w/felt arms & legs, wearing original pink felt dress w/blue trim, blue felt coat w/matching hat, original underclothing, socks & blue felt shoes, spot of moth damage at hairline on right side w/foundation showing, 12" (ILLUS.).. **400**

Lenci Ethnic Girl

Lenci girl, unmarked, pressed-felt swivel head w/painted brown eyes to side, single-stroke brows, closed two-tone mouth w/accents, applied felt ears, original mohair wig in long braids, felt torso & arms, long cloth legs stitch-jointed at knees, wearing original elaborate felt ethnic costume, original organdy underclothing, original socks, black felt shoes, some moth damage, stains, hole in right foot, 26" (ILLUS.) **700**

Limbach bisque socket head character doll, marked "W - [crown] - 17 72 [in shamrock] - Limbach," blue sleep eyes w/real lashes, knitted feathered brows, open mouth w/accented lips & six upper teeth, h.h. wig, jointed wood & composition body, wearing new white lacy dress, underclothing, new socks & shoes, 23" (two right fingers & three left fingers repaired)... **625**

Low Brow China Shoulder Head Lady

Low brow china shoulder head lady, unmarked, turned head w/painted blue
eyes w/red accent lines, single-stroke
brows, open mouth w/molded teeth,
molded & painted wavy black hair, cloth
body w/china lower arms & lower legs,
wearing possibly original beige print
dress, underclothing, several small repairs, small holes in left china lower arm
have been filled, 18" (ILLUS.) **850**

"Mary Todd" China Shoulder Head

"Mary Todd" china shoulder head lady,
unmarked, painted blue eyes w/red accent lines, single-stroke brows, closed
mouth w/white space between lips, molded & painted black hair w/snood, molded
bows on sides, brush strokes at temples,
cloth body w/leather lower arms, wearing
antique maroon top, black skirt, antique
underclothing, socks, no shoes, new lower legs & upper arms, gold lustre missing
from bows, 23" (ILLUS.) **675**

Nippon Character Doll

**Nippon bisque socket head character
doll,** marked "FY - Nippon - 304," brown
glass eyes, feathered brows, closed
pouty mouth, h.h. wig, jointed wood &
composition body, wearing old peach &
ecru dress, panties, socks & shoes, body
repainted, eyes on rockers but not set,
some joints stuck together w/paint,
18 1/2" (ILLUS.) **875**

P.M. Bisque Socket Head Toddler

P.M. bisque socket head toddler, marked "P.M. - 914 - Germany - 5," blue sleep eyes w/real lashes, feathered brows, open mouth w/molded tongue & two upper teeth, original mohair wig, five-piece composition toddler body, wearing original white shirt, black felt liederhosen w/appliqué flowers, original socks & shoes, green felt cap, torso repaired on back, finger tips chipped, new stringing hooks set in arms, 15" (ILLUS.) **305**

Pansy Bisque Socket Head Girl

Pansy bisque socket head girl, marked "Pansy - II - Germany," blue sleep eyes w/real lashes, feathered brows, open mouth w/four upper teeth, h.h. wig, jointed wood & composition body, redressed in peach taffeta, w/antique white pinafore, new underclothing, socks & shoes, replacement wig, repairs to neck socket of body & right foot, repainted lower arms & hands, 24" (ILLUS.) **525**

Papier-mâché shoulder head lady, unmarked, painted blue eyes, single-stroke brows, closed mouth, molded & painted hair in "covered wagon" style, kid body w/wooden lower arms & lower legs, painted dark blue shoes, wearing original dress w/blue ribbon trim, original underclothing, 9 3/4" (some soiling) **255**

Papier-mâché shoulder head lady, unmarked, painted brown eyes, single-stroke brows, closed mouth, molded & painted black hair w/long curls to shoulders, kid body w/wooden lower arms & lower legs, painted red shoes, wearing original pink polished cotton dress w/net overlay & ribbon trim, original underclothing, 11" **375**

Papier-mâché Milliner's Model

Papier-mâché shoulder head milliner's model, unmarked, painted blue eyes, single-stroke brows, closed mouth, molded & painted black hair w/high beehive & side curl clusters, kid body w/wooden lower arms & lower legs, painted red shoes, wearing probably original off-white dress w/pongee skirt, matching leggings for pants, ecru satin apron trimmed w/brown ribbon & brown ribbon at waist, end of nose worn & flat, clothing soiled & deteriorated, 11" (ILLUS.) **500**

Parian lady, unmarked, untinted bisque shoulder head w/painted light blue eyes w/red accent lines, single-stroke brows, closed mouth, pierced ears, molded & painted cafe au lait hair w/curls & waves around face, molded curls in back, elaborately decorated shoulder plate w/glazed pink ribbon around neck, blue & white ruffle w/gold trim, cloth body w/kid lower arms, striped lower legs w/brown cloth boots for feet, wearing pinstriped dress of antique silk, underclothing, 15" (small chip on left earlobe, arms replaced, cloth boots worn) **620**

Parian Shoulder Head Lady

Parian shoulder head lady, unmarked, painted blue eyes w/red accent lines, single-stroke brows, closed mouth, molded & painted cafe au lait hair w/curls on back, gold beads, pink & white flowers & white leaves decorating hair, molded blue & gold necklace, cloth body w/untinted bisque lower arms, red & white striped lower legs w/red leather boots as feet, wearing antique white dotted Swiss dress, antique underclothing, 20" (ILLUS.)................ 875

Parian Swivel Head Lady

Parian swivel-head lady, unmarked, untinted bisque socket head on bisque shoulder plate, set blue eyes, multi-stroke brows, closed mouth, pierced ears, molded cafe au lait hair w/waves pulled back to removable cluster of curls on back of head, kid body w/gussets at elbows, hips & knees, fingers indicated by stitching, wearing white blouse made w/antique fabric, antique blue print skirt, underclothing, no socks or shoes, two long shallow chips at opening for curls on back of head, body is small for head & shoulder plate, 14 1/2" (ILLUS.) **3,600**

Norwegian Boy & Girl

Petterssen (Ronnaug) Norwegian boy & girl, marked "Ronnaug Petterssen" on round label on girl's dress, pressed felt swivel heads, painted brown eyes, single-stroke brows, closed mouths, original mohair wigs, cloth bodies jointed at shoulders & hips, wearing original elaborate embroidered Norwegian folk costumes by Ronnaug Petterssen of Oslo, original socks & shoes, age discoloration, small hole in girl's skirt, 14", the pair (ILLUS.) 815

Poupee Peau bisque shoulder head girl, marked "E 5 S" on shoulder plate, set cobalt blue eyes, fine multi-stroke brows, closed mouth w/accent lines on lips & between lips, mohair wig, kid body w/gussets at elbows, hips & knees, individually stitched fingers, wearing purple two-piece outfit w/gold threads, antique underclothing, socks & shoes, black velvet hat, comes in unmarked white box w/extra clothing, including green & white dress, white nightgown, white guimpe, beige wool short coat, green & white apron, two newer skirts, imitation straw hat, 19 1/2" (body has settled to squatty position due to sawdust settling at gussets, several minor repairs on body, two left hand fingers have wire protruding)..................... **1,800**

Poupee Peau Lady

Poupee Peau bisque shoulder head lady, unmarked, socket head w/set blue eyes, multi-stroke brows, closed mouth w/accented lips, pierced ears, replaced mohair wig, kid fashion body w/gussets at elbows, hips & knees, redressed in dark brown & peach French-style outfit, antique underclothing, black socks, handmade shoes, feather-trimmed hat, 16" (ILLUS.).. **2,700**

Poupee Peau bisque shoulder head lady, marked "5," socket head w/pale blue paperweight eyes, multi-stroke brows, closed mouth w/accented lips & accent line between lips, pierced ears, original h.h. wig, kid body w/gussets at hips & knees, wearing grey & navy fashion ensemble, antique underclothing, socks & brown high button boots, 20" (hands appear small, w/stubby fingers)..... **1,950**

Poured Wax Shoulder Head Lady

Poured wax shoulder head lady, unmarked, blue glass eyes w/inserted lashes, painted brows w/hair inserted, closed mouth, original blonde mohair wig inserted into wax, cloth body w/poured wax lower arms & lower legs, wearing original blue silk blouse, ecru silk skirt w/blue silk trim, original underclothing, socks & leather shoes w/heels, in wooden box, shape of face has been somewhat altered by heat, clothing fragile, 20" (ILLUS.)............................ **350**

Queen Louise bisque socket head girl, marked "28,5 - Germany - Queen Louise -6," brown sleep eyes w/red mohair lashes, feathered brows, open mouth w/accented lips & four upper teeth, antique mohair wig, jointed wood & composition body, wearing possibly original red gingham dress w/eyelet trim, antique underclothing, new socks & shoes, antique beige & blue wool coat & hat, 21 1/2" **400**

Raynal Poupee Girl

Raynal Poupee girl, "Paris" typed on piece of paper pinned to back, pressed-felt swivel head w/painted blue eyes, single-stroke brows, closed mouth w/three-tone lips, original mohair wig in original set, five-piece cloth body w/stitched fingers, wearing original light blue organdy dress w/pink flower appliqués, matching floppy-brimmed hat, original teddy, blue organdy slip, socks, white leather shoes, 19" (ILLUS.) **725**

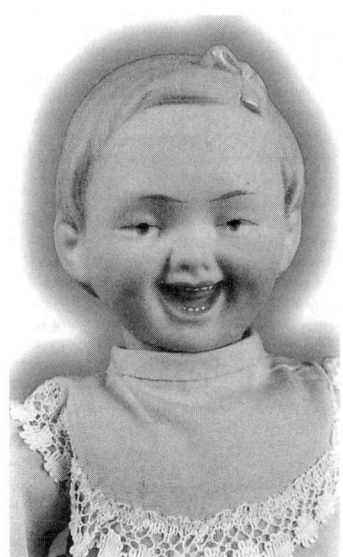

Recknagel Character Girl

Recknagel bisque socket head character girl, marked "R 57 A - 8/0," tiny painted blue eyes squinting from laughter, single-stroke brows, open-closed laughing mouth w/five painted upper teeth & four lower teeth, molded tongue, molded & painted short hair w/molded pink bow, five-piece chubby composition body of the type normally found on googlies, crude unpainted torso, molded & painted socks & shoes, redressed in pink lace-trimmed dress, lace panties, 9" (ILLUS.)....... **675**

Recknagel solid dome socket head girl, marked "RA - 22-7/0," painted blue eyes, single-stroke brows, open-closed mouth w/two upper teeth, molded white bonnet w/blue ribbons & shading, blonde hair peeking out from bonnet, jointed wood & composition body w/straight wrists, wooden upper arms & upper legs, wearing antique pink dress, antique under-clothing, new socks & leather shoes, 12"...... **425**

Reinforced poured wax shoulder head lady, unmarked, set blue glass eyes, multi-stroke brows, closed smiling mouth, pierced ears, original mohair wig, cloth body w/wax over composition lower arms & lower legs, wearing antique red & white gingham full-length dress, original under-clothing, socks & leather shoes, some cracks & fading, body repaired in places, 18" (ILLUS., top of next column).................... **475**

S.F.B.J. (Société Francaise de Fabrica-tion de Bebes et Jouets) bisque sock-et head girl, marked "SFBJ - 301 - Paris - 1" on head, "2" incised between shoul-ders, "2" on bottoms of feet, blue sleep eyes w/real lashes, feathered brows, open mouth w/four upper teeth, pierced ears, h.h. wig, jointed wood & composi-tion body w/jointed wrists, wearing an-

tique white lace dress, bonnet, under-clothing, socks & shoes, 11" (repair on left knee joint) **600**

Reinforced Poured Wax Lady

S.F.B.J. (Société Francaise de Fabrica-tion de Bebes et Jouets) bisque sock-et head girl, marked "D - SFBJ - 60 - Par-is - 8/0" on head, "Fabrication Francaise - SFBJ - Paris" in colorful round label on back, "2" impressed between shoulders, "1" impressed on bottoms of feet, blue sleep eyes w/real lashes, feathered brows, open mouth w/four upper teeth, replaced h.h. wig, jointed wood & compo-sition body w/jointed wrists, wearing pale green silk dress, oversize light green straw hat, underclothing, new socks & shoes, 11 1/2" (minor touchup at neck socket) **1,025**

S.F.B.J. (Société Francaise de Fabrica-tion de Bebes et Jouets) Jumeau bisque socket head girl, marked "Tete Jumeau" stamped in red & "S.F.B.J. - Paris - 11" incised on head, "Bebe Jumeau - Diplome d'Honneur" on oval la-bel on back, blue paperweight eyes, feathered brows, open mouth w/accent-ed lips & six upper teeth, pierced ears, replaced h.h. wig, jointed wood & compo-sition Jumeau body, wearing First Com-munion or Confirmation outfit of long white lawn dress trimmed w/lace, ribbon & tucks, matching veil w/flowers, under-clothing, new white socks, brown leather shoes, crucifix on ribbon around neck, 24" (repair on back of right hand, touchup at hips & knees)... **1,550**

S & Q bisque socket head baby, marked "+ - 201 - SQ [superimposed] - Germany - 14," set brown eyes, feathered brows, open mouth w/two upper teeth & molded tongue, mohair wig, composition baby body, wearing navy blue velvet boy's shorts, jacket & matching hat, white shirt, stockings, white baby shoes, 28"................... **700**

Sasha Limited Edition Princess

Sasha Princess, marked "Limited Edition - 1986 - 297" on head, "Sasha - Serie - Made in England" on round wrist tag, "186A - Princess Sasha - Real Hair" on label on end of box, vinyl socket head w/painted brown eyes, single-stroke brows, closed mouth, original blonde h.h. wig, five-piece vinyl child body, wearing original pink cotton ruffled dress, velvet coat lined w/matching pink fabric, original underclothing, socks & shoes, comes w/certificate, 16" (ILLUS.) **495**

Bruno Schmidt Bisque Head Boy

Schmidt (Bruno) solid dome bisque socket head boy, marked "5 - B. S. W. [in heart] - 2042" on head, "Handwerck" stamped in red on back, painted brown eyes, two-tone single-stroke brows, open-closed mouth w/accented lips, brush-stroked hair, jointed composition body, re-dressed in maroon velour two-piece suit, ecru satin shirt w/lace trim, black cotton socks, new black shoes, right big toe damaged, finish chipped around neck edge of body, 22" (ILLUS.) **1,500**

Schmidt (Franz) & Co. bisque socket head girl, marked "1295 - F.S.&C. - 34," brown sleep eyes w/real lashes, open mouth w/two upper teeth & wobble tongue, replaced h.h. wig, jointed wood & composition toddler body w/diagonal hip joints, jointed elbows, wrists & knees, wearing white antique eyelet dress, underclothing, rayon socks, antique shoes & bonnet, 15" (arms & lower legs repainted) **675**

Schmitt & Fils bisque socket head girl, marked "Bte. S.G.D.G. - 0" on head, Schmitt shield on flat bottom of torso, "40" written in ink on all body pieces, light blue threaded paperweight eyes, feathered brows, closed mouth w/accented lips & accent line between lips, pierced ears, replaced mohair wig, jointed composition Schmitt body w/straight wrists, separate balls at shoulders, elbows, hips & knees, wearing possibly original antique white embroidered & lace-trimmed dress, antique slip, no pants, antique socks, antique leather shoes, 14" (soles of shoes missing, finish cracked & lifted on lower right arm).. **3,900**

Schoenau & Hoffmeister Baby

Schoenau & Hoffmeister bisque socket head baby, marked "SPB [in star] H - 8/0 - Germany," blue sleep eyes w/real lashes, single-stroke brows, open mouth w/two upper teeth, original blonde mohair wig, bent-limb composition baby body, wearing original ecru baby dress, factory chemise, replaced diaper, 8" (ILLUS.).......... **340**

Schoenau & Hoffmeister 8 1/2" Girl

Schoenau & Hoffmeister bisque socket head girl, marked "SPB [in star] H - 1909 - 11/0 - Germany," blue sleep eyes w/real lashes, single-stroke lightly molded brows, open mouth w/five upper teeth, original brown mohair wig in original set, jointed wood & composition body w/original finish, wearing factory-original slate blue dress w/brown floss feather stitching, original unwashed factory underclothing, original socks, shoes & hair ribbon, upper left arm split & glued, 8 1/2" (ILLUS.) **350**

Schoenau & Hoffmeister Girl

Schoenau & Hoffmeister bisque socket head girl, marked "SPB [in star] H - 4000-10," brown sleep eyes, heavy feathered brows, open mouth w/accented lips & four upper teeth, original brown mohair wig, jointed composition body, wearing pale

green silk dress w/pink flowers, new underclothing, socks & shoes, right ring finger repaired, 25" (ILLUS.)................................ **550**

Schoenau & Hoffmeister bisque socket head "Hanna," marked "Germany - S P B [in star] H - Hanna - 0," brown sleep eyes w/real lashes, feathered brows, open mouth w/two upper teeth, original mohair wig, composition baby body, wearing deep pink embroidered baby dress & bonnet, undershirt & diaper, 13 1/2"... **355**

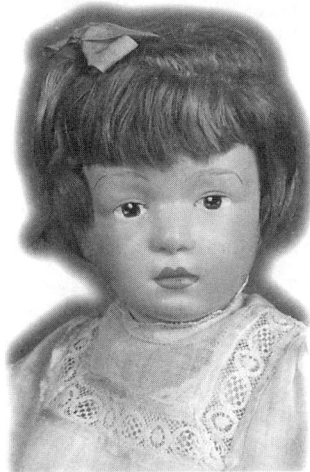

Schoenhut Wooden Character Girl

Schoenhut wooden socket head character girl, marked "Schoenhut Doll - Pat. Jan. 17th 1911 - U.S.A." on oval label on back, blue intaglio eyes w/white highlights, feathered brows, closed pouty mouth, original brown mohair wig, wooden body spring-jointed at shoulders, elbows, wrists, hips, knees & ankles, wearing white lace- & ribbon-trimmed dress, antique underclothing, black cotton socks, brown leather sandals, 16" (ILLUS.) **1,900**

Schoenhut Girl

Schoenhut wooden socket head girl, "Schoenhut Doll - Pat. Jan. 17, '11, U.S.A. - & Foreign Countries" impressed on back, blue intaglio eyes, feathered brows, closed mouth, carved & painted hair w/blue hair band, spring-jointed wooden body jointed at shoulders, elbows, wrists, hips, knees & ankles, wearing antique white dress, slip, knit union suit, cotton socks, antique white shoes, repair on part of face & blue ribbon, right hand partially repainted, 14" (ILLUS.)............ **625**

Shirley Temple, marked "Ideal Doll - ST-12" on head, "Shirley Temple - made by Ideal Toy Corp." on tags on slip & dress, "Shirley Temple Doll - Made in USA by Ideal Toy Corporation, Hollis, N.Y." on end of box, vinyl head w/hazel sleep eyes w/molded lashes, single-stroke brows, open-closed mouth w/six upper teeth, rooted hair in original set w/net & plastic clips, five-piece vinyl child body, wearing orange & white dress w/lace trim, original white panties, black vinyl shoes, white vinyl purse & pin w/"Shirley Temple" in script, includes tagged pink taffeta slip & panties, extra knit panties, in box, 12" **350**

Ideal Shirley Temple Doll

Shirley Temple, Ideal, marked "13 - Shirley Temple" on head, "Shirley Temple - 13" on back, composition head w/hazel sleep eyes w/real lashes, feathered brows, open mouth w/six upper teeth, original mohair wig in original set, five-piece composition body, wearing original plaid "Bright Eyes" dress, underwear combination, replaced socks, original shoes, tag cut off back of dress, 13" (ILLUS.)................. **700**

Shirley Temple, marked "Ideal Doll - ST-15-N" on head, "Shirley Temple" script

pin, vinyl head w/hazel sleep eyes w/real lashes, feathered brows, open-closed mouth w/six upper teeth, rooted hair in original set, five-piece vinyl body, wearing original blue sailor dress w/white pique collar, attached half slip, original panties, socks & marked Ideal vinyl shoes, white pique sailor cap, 15"................. **180**

Shirley Temple vinyl head doll, marked "Ideal Doll - ST-12" on head, "Shirley Temple - made by Ideal Toy Co." on tag on slip, hazel sleep eyes w/molded lashes, single-stroke brows, open/closed mouth w/six upper teeth, molded dimples, rooted hair in original set, five-piece vinyl child body, wearing original blue velvet & white dotted Swiss dress, pink nylon slip w/matching panties, original black vinyl shoes, white signature purse & plastic pin both w/"Shirley Temple" in script, comes w/original marked box, 12"...... **230**

Simon & Halbig bisque shoulder head ethnic lady, marked "SH 2/0," dark brown set eyes w/no pupils, single-stroke brows, closed mouth, original mohair wig, cloth body w/bisque lower arms, wearing original ethnic-type black clothing, underclothing & paper shoes, 8" (black velvet vest worn in back, w/left back shoulder worn away)............................... **250**

Simon & Halbig Character Girl

Simon & Halbig bisque socket head character girl, marked "S H 16 - 949" on head, "Heinrich Handwerck - Germany - 7" stamped on body, blue paperweight eyes, feathered brows, closed pouty mouth w/accented lips, pierced ears, replaced h.h. wig, jointed wood & composition body, wearing white lace dress, antique underclothing, white crocheted socks, leather shoes, replaced organdy bonnet, repainted body, repair around neck socket of body, 32" (ILLUS.).............. **2,800**

Simon & Halbig bisque socket head ethnic girl, marked "1078 - Simon & Halbig - S&H - 2," blue sleep eyes, feathered brows, open mouth w/four upper teeth, original mohair wig, jointed wood & composition body, wearing original ethnic outfit, original underclothing, replaced socks & shoes, 10 1/2" (may be missing a hat) **315**

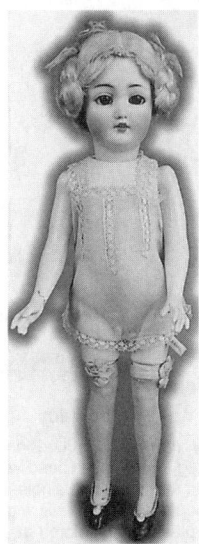

Simon & Halbig Flapper-style Lady

Simon & Halbig bisque socket head flapper, marked "1159 - Simon & Halbig - S&H - 5" on head, "Made in Germany" on paper tag on bottom edge of left leg opening, blue sleep eyes, feathered brows, open mouth w/four upper teeth, original blonde mohair wig in coiled braids in blue silk ribbon, composition flapper body w/high knee joints, wearing factory silk crepe lace-trimmed teddy, silk stockings, ribbon garters, original black high heel shoes w/silk-covered buttons, right wrist broken & glued, 13" (ILLUS.) **1,600**

Simon & Halbig bisque socket head girl, marked "1078 - Simon & Halbig - S & H - 10" on head, "Germany" on partially illegible stamp on body, blue sleep eyes, feathered brows, open mouth w/four upper teeth, pierced ears, h.h. wig, jointed wood & composition body, wearing antique white embroidered dress, antique underclothing, socks, red center-snap shoes, 22" (finish cracked & piece missing on outside of right foot) **365**

Simon & Halbig bisque socket head lady, marked w/incised "S&H - DEP - 1159 - Germany - 9 1/2" & "Wimpern/Gesetzel Schutz" in oval red stamp, blue sleep eyes, heavy feathered brows, open mouth w/accented lips & four upper teeth, pierced ears, h.h. wig, jointed composition body w/straight wrists, lady body w/adult figure, wearing antique white

dress, black & green velvet jacket & matching hat, antique underclothing, socks & shoes, 24" (missing real lashes, eyes have been reset & right eye is out of alignment, knee balls replaced, repair on bottom of torso at seam) **900**

Steiner (Jules) bisque socket head girl, marked "Figure B No 2 - Steiner Bte S.G.D.G. - Paris" on head, "Bebe Steiner - Le Petit Parisien" in purple stamp on left hip, blue eyes made to sleep w/lever left back of head, feathered brows, open smiling mouth w/seven upper & seven lower teeth, pierced ears, h.h. wig, jointed composition Steiner body w/jointed wrists, torso cut for crier, wearing pale blue silk dress w/lace trim, matching hat, underclothing, socks & old shoes, 18" (crier not working) **2,900**

Steiner (Jules) "gigoteur" bisque head girl, unmarked, blue threaded paperweight eyes, delicate feathered brows, open mouth w/accented lips & four upper & three lower teeth, original blonde mohair wig, papier-mâché torso w/walking & crying mechanism (when wound, head turns & cries), kid coverings on lower torso, composition arms, kid-covered upper legs, wax-over-composition lower legs, wearing possibly original white openwork & lace dress, antique underclothing, socks & white leather shoes, 17 1/2" (replaced arms, torso seams taped w/adhesive tape, kid covering torso deteriorating, very limited movement in legs)............. **1,050**

Jules Steiner Girl "Gigoteur"

Steiner (Jules) "gigoteur" solid dome bisque head girl, marked "Le Petit Parisien - Bebe Steiner - Medaille d'Or - Paris 1889" stamped in blue on back, straight neck, blue paperweight eyes, feathered brows, open mouth w/five upper & six lower teeth, replaced wig, carton torso housing working mechanism, composition one-piece arms w/white nails, metal upper legs covered w/kid, composition lower legs w/white toenails, wearing rose dress w/lace overlay, antique underclothing, socks & shoes, when wound, doll turns head, moves arms up & down & kicks feet, left first finger repaired, doesn't cry, 16" (ILLUS.) **1,900**

Steiner "Le Parisien" Girl

Steiner (Jules) "Le Parisien" bisque socket head girl, "A. 13" incised & "Le Parisien - Bte S.G.D.G./A. 13" stamped on head, "Le Petit Parisien - Bebe Steiner - Medaille d'Or/Paris 1889" on front of left hip, "France" stamped in red on upper back, blue paperweight eyes, heavy feathered brows, closed mouth, pierced ears, brown h.h. wig, jointed composition Steiner body w/straight wrists & slender hands, wearing new blue silk lace-trimmed dress, new underclothing, old socks & shoes, shallow sliver of bisque off inside corner of upper right eyelid, 20" (ILLUS.).................................... **2,700**

Terri Lee, marked "Terri Lee" on head, back & dress tag, hard plastic head w/painted brown eyes, single-stroke brows, closed mouth, saran wig, five-piece hard plastic body, wearing yellow organdy dress, original nylon slip & panties, socks & shoes, 16".. **425**

Terri Lee Garden Party girl, marked "Terri Lee" on back, hard plastic head w/painted brown eyes, single-stroke brows, closed mouth, synthetic wig, five-piece hard plastic body jointed at shoulders & hips, wearing original Garden Party outfit from 1952, 16" (panties replaced) **395**

Terri Lee Lady

Terri Lee lady, marked "Terri Lee" on back & on coat tag, hard plastic head w/oversize painted brown eyes, single-stroke brows, closed mouth, synthetic wig, five-piece hard plastic body jointed at shoulders & hips, wearing original yellow Evening Formal #3570D from 1954 w/matching panties, gold shoes & purse & Long White Coat #3690A w/matching hat, 16" (ILLUS.)... **475**

Verlingue (J.) "Gibson Girl" Doll

Verlingue (J.) "Gibson Girl"-style doll, marked "Lutin - France - J [anchor] V - 3/0," bisque shoulder head w/painted brown eyes, single-stroke brows, closed mouth, original blonde mohair wig in Gibson Girl style, kid body w/bisque lower arms, gussets at hips & knees, wearing rose silk dress w/leg-o'-mutton sleeves, matching hat w/ostrich-type feather, possibly original underclothing, replaced socks & shoes, 11" (ILLUS.)............................ **400**

Vogue "Ginny" Doll

Vogue "Ginny," marked "Vogue Doll" on back, "Original - Vogue - Dolls, Inc." on rayon tag on dress, hard plastic head w/blue sleep eyes, single-stroke brows, closed mouth, original blonde wig, five-piece strung child body, wearing original clothing as Christine (1952) from Frolicking Fables series or Gretel (1953) #53 from Twin series, w/extra outfit June (1953) #41 Tiny Miss series, w/tagged dress, red straw hat, pink & white vinyl marked Ginny shoes, in original unmarked box w/pink & white Ginny print design, purple stain on torso from clothing, 7 1/2" (ILLUS.)............................ **365**

Vogue "Ginny" Coronation Queen, marked "Vogue Doll" on back, "Vogue" rayon tag on cape, hard plastic head w/blue sleep eyes, single-stroke brows, closed mouth, original wig, five-piece strung hard plastic body, wearing rare 1953 outfit to commemorate coronation of Queen Elizabeth w/brocade dress trimmed w/beads, sequins & pearls, blue ribbon sash w/star decoration, taffeta slip & panties, purple velvet long cape w/fur trim, replica of St. Edward's crown, includes gold scepter, 7 1/2" **725**

Wax over papier-mâché shoulder head lady, unmarked, dark eyes w/no pupils, single-stroke brows, closed mouth, mold-ed & painted green bonnet w/painted flowers, original mohair curls & bun w/net, cloth body w/wooden lower arms & lower legs w/ribbon trim, original slip, no pants, 16" (several areas of lifted wax & papier-mâché on forehead & shoulder plate, spot of wax missing from bonnet)... **250**

Adolph Wislizenus Girl

Wislizenus (Adolph) bisque socket head girl, marked "8 - A.W. - Germany - 6" on head, "46" stamped in red on bottoms of feet, "8" on shoes, brown sleep eyes, feathered brows, open mouth w/accented lips, pierced ears, replaced h.h. wig, jointed composition body, wearing probably original clothing w/white low-waisted dress, antique underclothing, socks & shoes, blue velvet coat & matching hat w/ribbon trim, 18" (ILLUS.) **550**

Wooden head lady, unmarked, carved, painted blue eyes w/red accent lines & outlined irises, single-stroke brows, closed mouth w/accent line between lips, carved & painted brown hair appears brushed back into pointed bun w/long curls hanging below, coarse cloth body probably filled w/grain or something similar, carved wooden lower arms & lower legs, painted orange shoes, wearing probably original brown print dress, slip & pants w/tucks & blue embroidery, 20" (doll in slouched position from filling in body settling) **800**

Composition Dolls

AM Doll Co., clown, molded hair, painted features, decal eyes, composition shoulder, head & full arms, straw stuffed body & legs, 1920s, 28"... **100**

Amberg (Lewis) Company, "Charlie Chaplin," composition portrait head, molded hair, painted eyes to side, molded mustache, straw-filled cloth body w/composition hands, original clothing, 1915, 14".......... **600**

Amberg (Lewis) Company, "Dolly Drake," resembles Campbell Soup Kid, cloth body, 8"... **75**

Amberg (Lewis) Company, "Vanta Baby," composition head w/molded, painted hair, sleep eyes, open mouth w/two teeth, muslin body, jointed at hips & shoulders, a tie-in with Vanta Baby Garments, 20".. **325**

Amburg (Lewis) Company, "Body Twist," molded hair, composition body w/unusual joint in torso to allow twisting from side to side, painted black shoes and socks, 8".. **150**

American Character, "Campbell Kid," all composition w/swivel-head, jointed shoulders & hips, molded & painted hair, eyes to side, watermelon mouth, original clothes, designed by Grace Drayton, 12"...... **600**

American Character, "Sally," all composition w/painted eyes, molded hair, original clothes, 1930, 16"................................ **250**

American Character Mama Doll, composition head, arms & legs, cloth torso, closed or open mouth, mohair or h.h. wig, 1923-on, 16"....................................... **225**

Composition Baby Doll

Baby daoll, unmarked, molded hair, painted features, large composition head, swing arms & legs with cloth body, 1918, 24" (ILLUS.)... **95**

Composition Boudoir Doll

Boudoir doll, unmarked, mohair wig, painted features, composition shoulders, head & half arms, cloth top arms, body &

legs, dressed in satin & lace, 1920s, 28" (ILLUS.).. **75**

Bucherer Doll, composition character head w/molded hat, metal ball-jointed body w/large composition hands, molded shoes, Switzerland, 1921, 8"........................ **175**

Buddy Lee, no mark, all composition w/jointed arms only, dressed in Lee overalls & cap, 1940s, 12".................................... **255**

Cameo Doll Company, "Kewpie," molded hair, starfish hands, painted features, jointed at shoulders only, body and blue wings made of composition, "Rose O'Neill" printed on heart seal in middle of chest, 1930-late 1940s, 11"................... **60**

Cameo Doll Company, "Margie," composition head on wood segmented body, designed by Joseph Kallus, label with name, 1929, 10"................................... **225**

Dionne-type Toddler

Dionne-type toddler, unmarked, all composition, molded painted hair, sleep eyes, open mouth w/teeth, appropriate clothes, 16" (ILLUS.) **75**

Effanbee, "Anne Shirley," all composition, h.h. or mohair wig, sleep eyes, jointed at neck, original clothes, 1935-1940, 18"... **300**

Effanbee "Baby Dainty"

Effanbee, "Baby Dainty," composition shoulder head, full arms, swing legs on cloth body, original clothes, Effanbee heart necklace, 1922, 16" (ILLUS.)............... **225**

Effanbee "Bubbles"

Effanbee, "Bubbles," composition shoulder head, arms & legs, finger molded to fit into mouth, 1924, 24" (ILLUS.) **500**

Effanbee "Nancy"

Effanbee, "Nancy," all composition, jointed at neck, shoulders & hips, original clothes, 1930, 16" (ILLUS.) **300**

Three-Head Famlee Doll

Famlee doll, three interchangeable heads that could be screwed in like a light bulb, sets had up to 16 interchangeable heads with outfits, some bodies had composition legs, others had cloth, mint in box three head set with clothes, 1918-1922 (ILLUS.) **495**
Fly-Lo baby, composition head, cloth body, 10" **800**

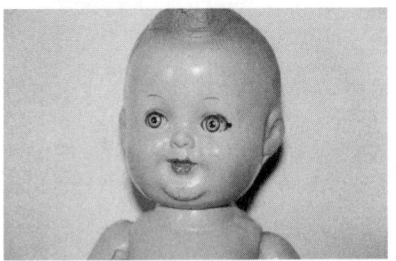

"Baby Sandy"

Freundlich Company, "Baby Sandy," molded head with brown painted hair, tin sleep eyes, open mouth, fully jointed composition body, early 1940s, 16" (ILLUS.) **250**
Freundlich Company, "Douglas Mac-Arthur," portrait doll of general, all composition, 18" **250**

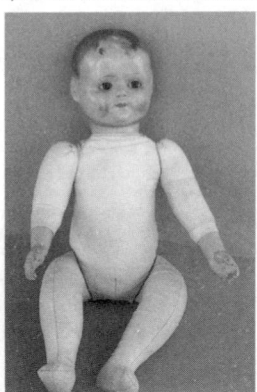

German Character Baby

German character baby, composition head & hands, molded hair, glass eyes, hard-stuffed kid body, 26" (ILLUS.) **500**
Goo-Goo Eye Doll Jolly Jumps, large painted eyes, composition head attached to cloth body, voice box in body, 1912, 20" **85**

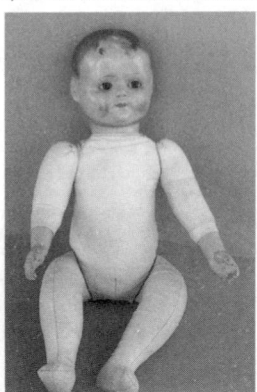

"Alice in Wonderland" Marionette

Hazelle marionette, "Alice in Wonderland," all composition, 1940s (ILLUS.) **85**
Horsman, "Baby Bumps," composition flange head, cloth body, Horsman label attached, 1910-1912, 14" **145**
Horsman, "Gene Carr Character Blink," composition head, molded & painted hair, eyes painted closed, wide smiling mouth w/teeth, cloth body, composition hands, 1916, 8" **200**

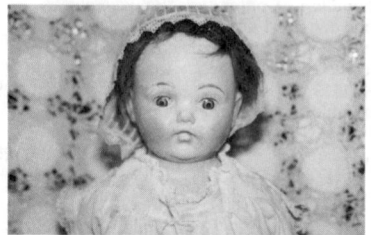

Horsman Mama Doll

Horsman, Mama doll, composition head, shoulder plate, arms & swing legs, mohair wig, sleep tin eyes, original clothes, 1920s, 16" (ILLUS.) **165**

Ideal Dwarf Dopey

Ideal Toy Company, Dwarf "Dopey," composition flange head w/hinged mouth on a drawstring, molded tongue, cloth body, arms & legs, composition hands, long trailing coat, cotton pants & felt shoes, 1937, 20" (ILLUS.) **750**

Ideal Toy Company, "Judy Garland as Dorothy" from "The Wizard of Oz," all composition, jointed at neck, shoulders & hips, all original, 1939, 16" **1,350**

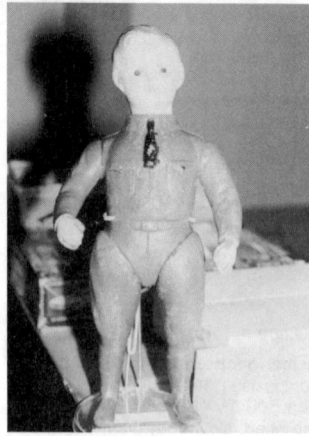

Ideal "Liberty Boy"

Ideal Toy Company, "Liberty Boy," very heavy composition, all molded body w/clothes molded on to body, jointed at head, shoulders & hips, spring strung,

missing removable doughboy hat, 1917, 12" (ILLUS.) **145**

Ideal Mama Doll

Ideal Toy Company, Mama doll, composition head, arms & legs on cloth body, all original, 1920s, 16" (ILLUS.) **225**

Ideal Toy Company, "Pinocchio," painted molded composition head w/smiling mouth attached to wood segmented body, 1940, 10" **350**

Ideal "Princess Beatrix"

Ideal Toy Company, "Princess Beatrix," composition head, arms & swing legs on cloth body, original clothes included a bonnet & leather boots, 1939, 16" (ILLUS.).......... **100**

Ideal "Shirley Temple"

Ideal Toy Company, "Shirley Temple," flirty eyes, all composition, jointed at neck, arms & legs, 1930s, 27" (ILLUS.)............... **1,800**

Ideal Toy Company, "Snoozie Smiles," two-faced doll, one smiling, the other crying, composition head & hands, cloth body & limbs, dressed in checked rompers & matching hat, 1923, 15"......................... **400**

Loop doll, painted features, composition loop formed on top of molded hair where ribbon could be tied, composition shoulders, head & arms attached to cloth body, 1920s, 14"... **50**

Madame Alexander, "Dionne Quintuplet," all-composition w/swivel head, jointed hips & shoulders, original tagged clothing, 14".. **375**

Madame Alexander, "Dionne Quintuplets," matching set of all five, all original, 1935, 8"... **1,500**

Alexander "Fairy Princess"

Madame Alexander, "Fairy Princess," all composition, jointed at neck, shoulders & hips, all original, 1942, 18" (ILLUS.).............. **600**

Madame Alexander, "Miss Scarlet," black hair w/blue or green eyes, all composition, jointed at neck, shoulders & hips, 1937, 21".. **1,200**

Alexander "Princess Elizabeth"

Madame Alexander, "Princess Elizabeth," blonde mohair wig, sleep eyes, all-composition, jointed at neck, arms & legs, 1937, 16" (ILLUS.) **450**

Madame Alexander, "Sonja Henie," all-composition, jointed at neck, shoulders & hips, dressed in ice skating outfit, 1939, 21" **900**

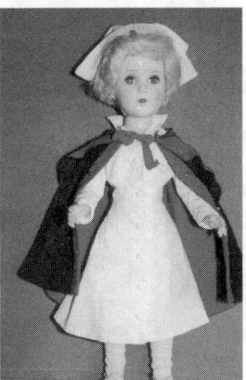

Mama Doll

Mama doll, unmarked, composition head, arms & swing legs, mohair wig, sleep glassine eyes, appropriate clothing, late 1940s, 16" (ILLUS.) **50**

Mama Dolls

Mama dolls, molded hair w/sleep eyes, teeth and tongue, swing arms and legs, cloth bodies have cry box, in appropriate old clothing, 16", each (ILLUS.) **75**

Minerva Doll Company, "Darling Baby," all original, drink & wet baby complete w/layette in original box, early 1940s, 8"................. **85**

Miss Curity Nurse Doll

Miss Curity Nurse doll, all-composition, jointed at neck, shoulders & hips, original nurse uniform & cape, 1940s, 18" (ILLUS.)... **600**

Monica doll, all-composition, hair implanted in head, painted eyes, blue eye shadow, jointed at neck, shoulders & hips, 1941-1951, 18".. **550**

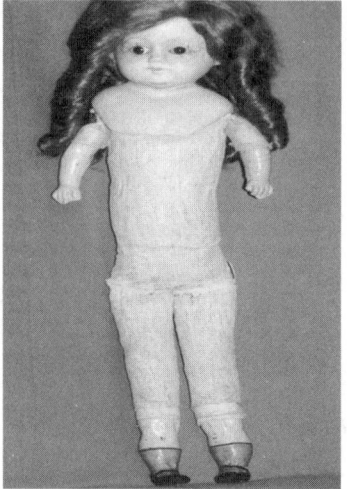

Patent Washable Doll

Patent Washable, composition shoulder & head w/mohair wig, glass eyes, closed mouth, cloth body with lower composition arms & legs, molded & painted stockings & shoes, appropriately dressed, 1890s, 22" (ILLUS.).. **350**

Patsy-type girl, all-composition w/molded bobbed hair, jointed at neck, shoulders & hips, 1930s, 20".................................. **275**

Quaker Quality Doll, composition shoulder head & hands on cloth body w/disk jointed legs, 1915-1918, 23"............................... **375**

Skookum Indian doll, painted features, molded composition head, black mohair wig, body stuffed with straw, wooden legs covered with soft leather boots, Indian clothing, 1916, 10".. **80**

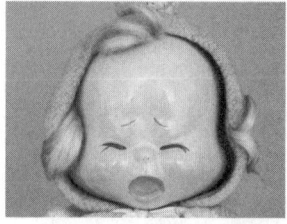

Three-face "Trudy"

Three-In-One Doll Corporation, "Trudy," head has three faces turned by a knob on the top of the head in sleeping, smiling & crying mien, wispy mohair curls around face attached to flannel hat, composition head on cloth body, matching flannel outfit, 15" (ILLUS.)...................................... **160**

Uneeda, "Rita Hayworth," red mohair wig, all-composition, totally jointed, 1940s, 14".. **400**

Vogue, "Toodles," all-composition, jointed at neck, shoulders & hips, mohair wig, painted eyes looking to side, original clothes, 1937-1948, 8".......................... **200**

FARM-RELATED COLLECTIBLES

Advertising trade card, Krebs Company, promoting "Empire Riders, Reapers, & Mowers Sunrise," 1884.. **$7**

Taco Annual Report

Farm Equipment Dealer Calendar

Annual report of TACO plant, one of the largest manufacturers of farm wagons, wheels, barbed wire & farm implements in North America, double-page spread features black & white drawing of plant surrounded by black & white photos of members of management team, 1930s (ILLUS., previous page) 100

Apple peeler, manufactured by Hudson Parer Company, Leominster, Massachusetts, patented 1883 75

Asparagus buncher, iron, handle painted red, 1920s, 9 1/2 x 12" 80

Bean slicer, cast iron, painted blue, crank w/wooden handle, suction cups hold slicer on table or other surface, Spong, 1940s, 6 1/2" h 15

Blueberry picker, tin, leather strap handle, homemade, 1920s, 14" l. 80

Booklet, "Better Hay, How to Make It and Market It," put out by John Deere of Moline, Illinois, 36 pp., black & white photos, cover shows farmer standing on hay wagon pulled by two horses, 1916, 7 3/4 x 8 1/4" 20

Brochure, issued by Celotex Insulation Corporation, "80 Pages of Farm Experiences," 35 pp., 1936 7

Bucket, blue w/white interior, bail handle w/wooden grip, 1920s 50

Bucket, cov., grey w/white interior, tin lids, 1920s, 4" h., 6" d. 30

Bucket, cov., grey w/white interior, tin lids, 1920s, 5 1/4" h., 8 1/2" d 40

Butter churn, box-type, cast iron w/wooden handles, made by "G. Jones Excelsior Churn Company," patent date of April 26, 1870, late 1800s, 16" square, 28" h 500

Butter churn, wood, barrel-type, w/iron hoops & original red paint, 1800s, 22 1/2" h. 300

Calendar, 1910, Capewell Horsenail Company, picture of horse sticking head in the door & being fed by family at dinner w/caption "One of the Family," 19 x 25" 225

Calendar, 1914, New England Fertilizer Company, 15 x 23" 85

Calendar, 1929, DeLaval Separators, w/picture of girl & collie, by Minnesota Binders, 12 x 23" 40

Calendar, 1953, giveaway by "Harry Hurren Authorized George White Dealer," tearaway pages for each month in middle, back panel features dealer's name & lists equipment offered ("Tractors - Threshers - Forage Harvesters - Implements") w/line art illustrations of equipment in top corners, all months up to November torn off (ILLUS., top of page) 25

Catalog, Fairbanks, Morse & Company, offered scales & windmills, color, 1880s, 9 x 12" 60

Catalog, for Murray Company, manufacturers of horse-drawn vehicles, 160 pp., 1912 70

Catalog, Stanley Mills & Company, offering "Corn Planter 'King of the Field' the best hand corn planter ever made," 75 cents, late 19th to early 20th c 80

Catalog, The Boggs Manufacturing Company, advertising Standard Potato Graders, Onion Graders & General Warehouse Equipment, 24 pp., 1928 30

Clock, promoting Wayne Feeds, made by Pam Clock Company, 1950s, 14 1/2" 285

Corn planter, pressed steel, red or black wooden handles, 1900, 32" l 55

Marx Farm Play Set

Cowbell, wrought iron, by Stanley Company, 1900, various sizes, 5 1/2 to 7 1/2".... **35-45**

Wooden Crate for Butter

Crate, wooden, top reads "Canadian Butter Co-op Saskatchewan - Always Good," "CH. NO.," "DATE" (w/space for date to be stamped) & "56 LBS. NET," 1910-20 (ILLUS.)... **50**

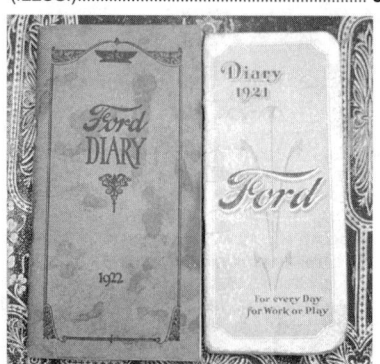

Ford Giveaway Diaries

Diary, Ford giveaway to purchasers of tractors & other equipment manufactured by Ford, w/space to record oil changes, mileage, operating costs, etc., 1920s, each (ILLUS. of 1922 & 1921) **25**

Farm play set, includes barn, people, animals & farm paraphernalia, Louis Marx, 1950s (ILLUS. of part, top of page).............. **250**

Farm Gas Pump

Gas pump, small red farm model w/Texaco logos & meter, manufactured by Gilbarco, late 1940s (ILLUS.) **1,000**

Grain cradle, steel bladed scythe w/wooden pronged cradle, 1875-1900 .... **150**
Instructions parts list, for John Deere Model A tractor, 1936 .... **30**

Ad with Rockwell Illustration

Magazine ad, Life magazine, full-page ad for General Motors Instalment Plan, w/full-color illustration by Norman Rockwell of farmer in straw hat & overalls reading booklet titled "GMC figuring chart" w/caption "Makes Good Sense to Me ... to figure the financing yourself," w/cutout coupon, Nov. 11, 1940 (ILLUS.)........ **40**

Life Magazine Ad for Green Giant

Magazine ad, Life magazine, full-page ad for Green Giant Niblets Corn, w/full-color illustration of corn field w/farmstead in background under caption "Looks like a good stand of corn in the Land of the Green Giant," text at bottom of page w/Green Giant holding giant ear of corn next to open can of Niblets, 1930s (ILLUS.) **40**

Ad for International Trucks

Magazine ad, Life magazine, full-page ad for International Trucks, w/full-color illustration of green truck w/"The Lumber and Building Supply Company" on its side being loaded w/wooden planks under the caption "You can buy INTERNATIONAL TRUCKS on Convenient Terms," April 25, 1938 (ILLUS.)...................................... **50**
Milk can, cov., metal, 10-gal.................................. **30**
Milk can, cov., metal, grey w/white interior, bail handle w/wooden grip, several styles, 1920s.. **40-55**
Miller's scale, used to measure moisture content of grain, 1/16 bushel brass pail w/12" beam, issued by government, 1900 .... **225**
Pitchfork, three metal tines, wooden handle painted red, 1920s-style.................................... **15**
Poster, printed in red, white, blue & black showing farm implements, meadow mower, rake & plow, advertising Gregg & Company Implements, Trumansburg, New York, 1870, 18 x 24" **400**
Sap pail, cast iron, w/handle, 1850s, 21" d....... **150**
Sap pail, wooden w/steel bands at bottom & top, wire bail handle, 1890s, 11" h................ **125**
Scale, wood & metal wheels & frame, portable wheelbarrow-type used to weigh grain sacks, milk cans, livestock, Renfrew Company, 1911-1932, excellent, restored condition **700**
Seed bag, cloth, for Monument Field Seeds **15**
Seed catalog, Minneapolis Harvester Works, Minneapolis, Minnesota, w/pictures of women picking fruit, late 19th c........... **2**

Ford Tractor, 1950

Sign, Fairbanks, Morse & Company, color, advertising windmills & scales, 1880s, 9 x 12" **60**

Spring scale, cast iron w/embossed decoration of wheat, oats, barley, peas & flax, 1890s, 12" l. **40**

Tobacco-drying basket, woven wood painted red, 19th c., 38" square **225**

Toy tractor, green & yellow colors of John Deere, Britains, England, 1950s (ILLUS., to the right) **50**

Tractor, Ford, w/red paint, few working parts, 1950 (ILLUS., top of page) **300**

Tractor owner's manual, for Fordson tractor, 1948 .... **45**

Tractor pull, for use w/horse, wooden w/metal hooks, 36" (ILLUS., below) **40**

Vegetable cutter/corer, tin box w/hinged lid, 1870, 6 1/2" h. **70**

Wagon wheel, wooden, w/original black & red paint, 1900 .... **95**

Britains Toy Tractor

Washboard, "Economy," glass scrubbing surface, 1900, 12 x 24" **30**

Water pump, red or black, manufactured by Smart-Brookville, 1920s, 15 1/2" h **45**

Tractor Pull

Farm Water Pumps

Water pump, various makers (Smart & Company, R. McDougall & Company Ltd., & Brockville, Ontario), turn of the 20th century, each (ILLUS. of various models) **75**

Weed cutter, wooden frame, metal blade, "Patented Lively Ladd Weed Cutter, August 10, 1926," 38" l. **35**

FIRE FIGHTING-RELATED COLLECTIBLES

American fire fighting "antiques" are considered those items over 100 years old that were directly related to fire fighting, whereas fire fighting "collectibles" are items less than a century old. Pieces from both eras are very sought-after today.

Foreign-made fire fighting antiques and collectibles have a marketplace of their own and, for the most part, are not as expensive and in demand as similar American pieces.

Alarm box, cast iron, red, manufactured by Ostrander, w/hammer attached w/chain to break glass in order to pull handle of alarm or hit a button inside, side of box lists penalties for turning in false alarm, 1940s... **$56**

Alarm box, iron, stand-alone model (unlike later smaller models mounted on telephone poles), manufactured by Star Electric Company of Milwaukee, 1916, 7' h. **1,600**

Alarm trumpet, silver, to be blown from fire wagon on way to fire to warn people to get out of the way, 1890s, 14 1/2" l. **600**

Fire Fighting Apparel

Apparel, includes leather belt ($40), helmet w/goggles, 1960s ($75), metal nut turner ($50), heavy rubber coat (ILLUS. on mannequin) **80**

Ashtray, clip-on type, w/"Smokey says, 'Use Your Ashtray,'" 1950s.............................. **45**

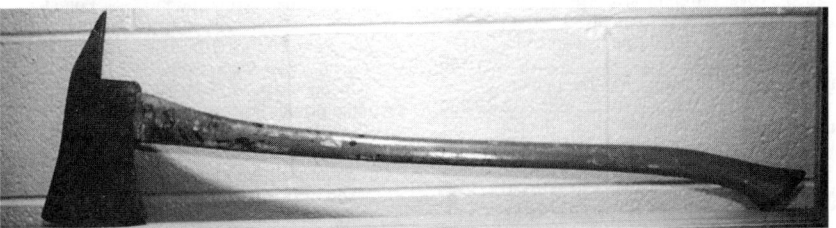

Fire Ax

"Emergency" Board Game

Ax, metal head w/special implement to lift & pry, red handle, 1940s, 35" l. (ILLUS., bottom previous page)................................... **175**

Badge, from Iowa State Fireman's Association Annual Meeting, 1928............................... **25**

Board game, "Emergency," tie-in to TV show of the same name, box lid features full-color illustration of fire fighters in action, Milton Bradley, 1974 (ILLUS., top of page) **25**

Book, "Our Firemen - History of New York Firemen" by A.E. Costello, first edition, 1887................. **260**

Broadside, "Hydropult - the Most Efficient Fire Engine in the World," w/scene of fire engine at the Palace Garden fire during the American Institute Fair in 1860................. **200**

Brochure, for American Fire Extinguisher Company of Boston, cover features illustration of horse-drawn fire engine, 60 pp. of material & equipment, 1867 .... **60**

Bucket, galvanized metal, painted red w/"Fire" on front, 19th c. **25**

Bucket, leather, black lettering reading "WARREN FIRE CLUB J. SHOVE DANVERS 1929" in oval cartouche surrounded by foliate scrolls & drapery in shades of red, mustard & brown paint on a mustard ground, 12" h. (leather handle broken, scattered paint loss)............................ **4,406**

Bucket, leather, green w/gilt stencil reading "C.H. REED," America, 19th c., 12 1/2" h. (replaced handle, wear, crack)...................... **147**

Bucket, leather, "Jesse Smith active (?), 1806" in oval surrounding a depiction of a winged goddess w/trumpet, 9 1/4" d., 11" h. (handle unattached, damaged, paint loss) **1,880**

Bucket, leather, w/swing handle, marked "W.F.C.," 1847, 13" h................................. **2,200**

Bucket, metal, w/handle, front pocket w/"Drink Coca-Cola in bottles," for use in kitchen of eating establishment, 1920s **275**

Calendar, features Smokey the Bear & different fire safety tip for each month, 1950s... **15**

Fire Boat Card

Card, #187 from "Rails & Sails" set by Topps, Brooklyn, New York, front features full-color illustration of fire boat, the back contains U.S. Navy signal flag, sea lore, & information on the boat pictured on front, 1955, 2 3/4 x 3 3/4" (ILLUS.)............. **7**

Card set w/fire fighting theme, fronts feature illustration of piece of fire equipment, backs contain fire safety slogan/information, by Bowman Gum Company, developed w/the "cooperation of Uniformed Firemen's & Uniformed Fire Officers Association of the City of New York," 1953, 2 1/2 x 3 3/4", set of 64, wrapper $50, each card.......................... **7**

Catalog, for Dayton Fire Equipment Company of Dayton, Ohio, features various products for fighting fires, 28 pp., 1940s........ **25**

Coloring book, "A Smokey Bear Read & Color Book," issued by the U.S. Forest Service, cover w/illustration of Smokey the Bear operating bulldozer fighting a raging forest fire while birds & animals flee, printed by Western Publishing, 1962 ...... **25**

Comic book, Smokey the Bear, by Dell Publishing, issued from October 1955 to August 1961, issue #1.................................... **100**

Commemorative medal, scene of angels flying over Great Chicago Fire, made by U.S. Mint from metal of Chicago Court House bell, 1871 .... **85**

Doll, Smokey the Bear, cloth, in full uniform w/either yellow or tan hat, Ideal, 1960, 12" h. **30**

1940s Fire Extinguisher

Fire extinguisher, metal canister painted bright red w/"DO NOT USE ON LIVE EQUIPMENT" stamped in black on front, pump handle at top, rubber hose, 1940s, 30" h. (ILLUS.) **40**

Fire extinguisher, Phoenix Compound Metal Canister Fire Extinguisher, 1899, 21 7/8" h. **500**

Fire extinguisher bottle, amber, Magic Fire-Extinguisher, 1870-1890......................... **100**

Fire extinguisher bottle, aqua, Little Giant Automatic Fire-Extinguisher, 1870-1890........ **95**

Fire extinguisher bottle, cobalt, Hardin's Improved Hand Grenade, 1870-1890............ **200**

Hero Fire Extinguisher in a Can

Fire extinguisher in a can, "Hero Fire Extinguisher," in red can w/illustration of helmeted figure running w/hose under the word "pressurized," meant to "...be employed to fight a fire in the kitchen, bedroom," manufactured in Bridgeport, Connecticut, unused, 1940s-50s (ILLUS.).............. **35**

Cloth Fire Hose

Fire hose, cloth w/brass 6 1/2" nozzle & handles, 1900, 31 1/2" l. (ILLUS.)................................. **200**

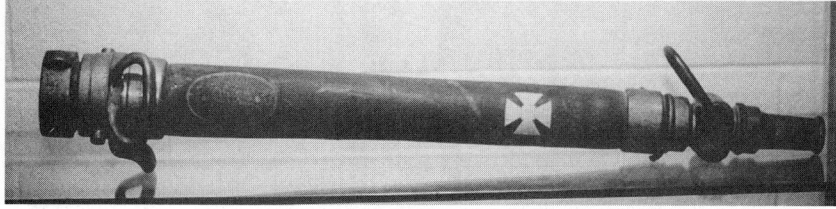

Rubber Fire Hose

Fire hose, rubber w/cross formée decoration, brass nozzle & handles, 1920s, 34 1/2" l. (ILLUS.) **100**

Lieutenant's Fire Helmet

Helmet, hard black plastic shell w/black leather section riveted to front on which is printed "LIEUTENANT" & "G.F.D.," manufactured in Pittsburgh, Pennsylvania, 1940s (ILLUS.).. **150**

Captain's Fire Helmet

Helmet, hard black plastic shell w/light leather section riveted to front on which is printed "CAPTAIN" in red & "G.F.D." in cutout section, manufactured in Pittsburgh, Pennsylvania, 1940s (ILLUS.)............ **200**

Canadian Fire Helmet

Helmet, hard red shell w/white section riveted to front on which is printed "OTTAWA," "1" & "P D," leather inside, Canada, 1940s (ILLUS.).. **500**
Horse collar, for use w/horse-drawn fire wagons, bright red, some w/name of city and/or fire company painted on them **200**
Jigsaw puzzle, depicts horse-drawn fire engine racing to a fire, w/fireman in driver's

seat & one on back, w/flaming boiler in middle of wagon, paper litho box cover, 67 pieces, made by McLoughlin Brothers of New York City, 1890 .... **90**

Fire Fighting Breathing Mask

Mask, early version of fireman's respirator kit, based on type used in mines, Bureau of Mines approved No. 1405, made by Mine Safety Appliance Company, Pittsburgh, Pennsylvania, in carrying case w/instructions, 1940s-50s (ILLUS.)............... **125**
Movie poster, for "Fireman, Save My Child" w/Joe E. Brown, Guy Kibbee, First National, one-sheet, 1932, 27 x 41"................... **300**
Movie poster, for "Fireman, Save My Child" w/Spike Jones & the City Slickers, Universal, remake of 1932 movie, one-sheet, 1954, 27 x 41".................................... **100**
Movie poster, for "The Fireman" w/Charles Chaplin & Edna Purviance, Mutual, one-sheet, 1916, 27 x 41"................................. **14,000**

Volunteer Fire Department Mug

Mug, ceramic, white w/red circular design comprising fire fighting paraphernalia & "Port Blandford Volunteer Fire Dept - 1974" (ILLUS.).. **5**

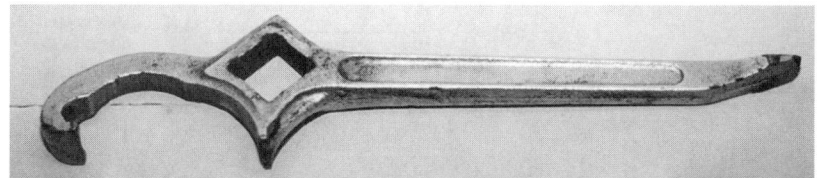

Nut Turner/Pry Bar

Scale Model Fire Truck Award

Name plates, for fire engines, manufactured by various companies including LaFrance, Mack Trucks, Ahren-Fox (Mack Trucks w/bulldog brings higher prices) **15-30**

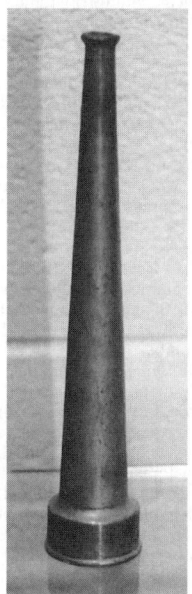

Brass Fire Hose Nozzle

Nozzle, brass, for fire hose, by Elkhart Brass Company, 1900, 10" l. (ILLUS.) **200**
Nut turner, metal, for opening fire hydrant or adjusting various equipment, hook on end can also be used as pry bar, 1920s-40s, 15" l. (ILLUS., top of page) **50**
Pin, tin lithograph, "I'm Helping Smokey Prevent Forest Fires," 1950s **50**
Pin, tin lithograph, "Join Smokey's Campaign - Prevent Forest Fires" & image of Smokey the Bear, 1950s **45**

Pinback button, w/illustration of fireman rescuing baby from burning building, white rim w/blue lettering, 1898, 1 3/4" d. **45**
Postcard, Sweetwater's Fire Department, w/picture of fire fighters & pumper, 1912 .... **40**
Promotional item, given out by salesmen in various cities, front features name of company, back lists locations of fire boxes in a particular city, early 1900s **25**
Ruler, wooden, w/"A Rule to Prevent Forest Fires," 1950s-60s **12**
Scale model of LaFrance fire truck, w/aluminum aerial ladder, lights & Goodyear rubber tires, made by Doepke, given as award during Fire Prevention Week, 1950, 33 1/2" l. (ILLUS., second from top) **500**
Sheet music, "The Midnight Fire Alarm," cover illustration of horse-drawn fire wagon racing through the streets w/black smoke pouring from its boiler, published by E.T. Paull Music Company, 1907, 10 1/2 x 13 1/4" **15**
Sign, cardboard, from Phoenix Insurance Company of Brooklyn, New York, multicolored illustration of elderly couple & skyline of raging fire, 1890 .... **225**

Smokey the Bear Hat Giveaway

Smokey the Bear hat, plastic, yellow model of the hat seen on Smokey the Bear promoting fire safety, "Smokey" printed in black on front, 1950s (ILLUS.) **15**

Toy Fire Truck

Smokey the Bear Junior Forest Ranger kit, included letter from Smokey, bookmark w/image of Smokey & fire safety slogans, membership card, blotter, four postage stamps, a Junior Ranger certificate, illustrated material, & sometimes a metal lithograph badge (rare), 1950s-60s, complete kit **110**

Spike, for probing on roofs & other areas during & after a fire, wooden handle w/metal spike at end, 1940s, 62 1/2" l. **150**

Stereo views, featuring fires in various U.S. cities (Portland fire of 1866, Chicago fire of 1871, Boston fire of 1872, etc.), late 1800s, each **10**

Tool box, to carry on fire engine, w/compartments for various fire fighting tools, w/"Engine Company #1 - Newark, New Jersey," patent date of 1914, 4 x 9 x 16" **300**

Toy fire truck, metal, painted red, w/two 10 3/4" aluminum ladders, "Bay-Ridge" painted on side, Buddy L or Keystone, 4 1/2 x 18" (ILLUS., top of page) **600**

Toy fire wagon, cast iron, "Fire Patrol Wagon," w/two horses & driver, six firemen, Ives, rare, 1880-1890, 20 1/2" l. **2,300**

Fire Fighting Training Manual

Training manual, paper, "Guelph Fire Service Training" on front in panels sur-rounding triangle printed w/"Heat," "Fuel," & "Oxygen," Guelph, Ontario, Canada, 1960s (ILLUS.) **20**

Watch fob, celluloid, w/"Lawson Hose Company #5 - Highland Falls, New York," 1911 .... **45**

FIREARMS

Carbine, Burnside percussion fourth model, .54 cal., faint signatures on frame & lock, walnut forearm & refinished butt stock, 21" l. round barrel, 39" l. (missing rear sight) **$770**

Carbine, Model 1884 "Springfield" trapdoor model, .45-70 cal., walnut stock, 22" l. round barrel, 41 1/4" l. (stock shows heavy wear) **385**

Carbine, Richmond Armory Type III model, walnut stock w/faint carving & worn name & numbers, brass & steel hardware, stamped "C.S. - 1863" w/address, 25" l. round barrel, 40 3/4" l. **6,270**

Carbine, Sharp's New Model 1859 percussion model, stamped signatures on lock & barrel, walnut stock w/inspector marks & brass hardware, 22" l. round barrel, 39" l. (minor stock damage) **4,620**

Long rifle, Bedford flintlock model, relief-carved curly maple stock w/brass hardware including an engraved patch box, silver cheek piece inlay, illegible signature, 39" l. swamped octagonal barrel, 54 1/2" l. (restoration) **6,875**

Long rifle, Bedford percussion model, curly maple stock w/brass hardware including an engraved patch box, eagle cheek piece inlay, signed "G. Honaker," 36 3/4" l. octagonal barrel, 52" l. **1,430**

Long rifle, Maryland flintlock model, curly maple stock w/relief-carving & brass hardware w/engraved patch box, 13 nickel silver inlays including an eagle cheek piece, initials of John Armstrong, 40" l. octagonal barrel, 56 1/2" l. (restoration) **3,300**

Long rifle, Maryland flintlock model, relief-carved curly maple stock w/brass hardware including an engraved patch box, silver thumb piece & man-in-the-moon inlay, signed "Geo. Rizer," 45 3/4" l. octagonal to round barrel, 62" l. **10,450**

Long rifle, Ohio percussion full-stock model, walnut fish belly stock w/brass hardware & side slapper lock, attributed to Wellsville, Ohio, 36" l. octagonal barrel, 51 1/2" l. **550**

Long rifle, Ohio percussion half-stock model, curly maple stock w/brass hardware including a pierced & engraved patch box & additional cap box, signed "A. Ager," 38" l. octagonal barrel, 54 1/2" l. (powder drum missing) **1,705**

Long rifle, Ohio percussion half-stock model, curly maple stocks w/brass hardware including engraved patch box, signed "W. Johnson," 38" l. octagonal barrel, 53 1/2" l. (pitting, restored split at wrist) **440**

Long rifle, Pennsylvania flintlock model, curly maple stock w/incised carving & brass hardware including pierced patch box, 23 silver inlays, initialed "G.A.," 39 1/4" l. octagonal barrel, 55" l. (pieced restoration around lock) **2,970**

Long rifle, Pennsylvania flintlock model, relief-carved curly maple stock w/engraved brass hardware including patch box, attributed to John Shuler, 44" l. octagonal barrel, 59 1/4" l. (minor restorations along barrel channel) **29,700**

Long rifle, Pennsylvania percussion model, curly maple stock w/brass hardware & pierced patch box, 13 German silver inlays, unusual scrolled overlay w/repair at wrist, atypical lock, initialed "G.S.K." for George King, 36" l. octagonal barrel, 52" l. **660**

Long rifle, percussion full-stock model, curly maple stock w/brass hardware & engraved patch box, 21 silver & brass inlays, signed "J. Stapleton," 38 1/2" l. octagonal barrel, 53 1/2" l. (stock chips, one inlay missing, lock restoration) **990**

Long rifle, Virginia flintlock model, curly maple stock w/incised carving & brass hardware including engraved patch box, three silver inlays, attributed to Frederick Sheetz, 46" l. octagonal barrel, 61 1/2" l. ... **5,500**

Musket, Committee of Safety flintlock model, curly maple stock w/an old finish & relief carving, brass hardware, lock signed "I. Hughes," 38 1/2" l. round barrel, 54" l. ... **4,950**

Musket, flintlock model, walnut stock w/an engraved silver thumb piece inlay & iron hardware, lock stamped "Middletown" w/eagle, 42" l. round barrel, 58" l. **2,090**

Musket, Harpers Ferry flintlock model, walnut stock w/old alterations, steel hardware, lock is signed w/"1816" & eagle, 42" l. round barrel stamped "Ohio," 57 1/4" l. **908**

Musket, Model 1841 percussion model, walnut stock w/steel hardware, made without a patchbox, lock signed "Tryon, Philada. Pa. 1846," 29 1/2" l. round barrel, 44 1/2" l. **1,320**

Musket, Richmond Armory percussion model, walnut stock w/steel hardware including cap box, lock signed "Richmond, Va. 1861," 40" l. round barrel, 56" l. **6,160**

Musket, "Springfield" percussion model, walnut stock w/steel hardware, lock signed "US 1852" w/eagle, 40" l. round barrel, 55" l. (small chips around barrel tang) **1,155**

Pistol, 1805 flintlock model, .54 cal., walnut stock w/brass hardware, lock signed "Harpers Ferry 1807 - US" w/eagle, 10" l. round barrel, 16" l. (pieced restoration) **2,255**

Pistol, English flintlock Tower model, European walnut stock w/brass hardware including engraved side plate w/"W. Edc. 1818," relief-carving around the barrel tang, lock signed "GR" w/crown, 12" l. round barrel, 19" l. (replaced lock bolts & ramrod pipes) **770**

Pistol, French "Charleville" flintlock model, walnut stock w/brass hardware, steel belt clip, 7 3/8" l. round barrel, 13 1/2" l. (frizzen spring broken, some replaced screws) **715**

Pistol, Manhattan percussion model, .36 cal., series 5, six-shot cylinder w/faint engraving, overall varnished finish, end of barrel threaded, 4" l. octagonal barrel, 9 1/2" l. **330**

Pistol, Model 1816 flintlock model, walnut stock w/clear inspector markings & iron hardware, w/brass pan, 9" l. round barrel, 15" l. (overall pitting) **1,045**

Pistol, Model 1836 flintlock model, walnut stock w/iron hardware, lock signed "R. Johnson, 1838," 8 1/2" l. round barrel, 13 1/2" l. (minor old splits around the lock & side plate) **495**

Pistol, North (S.) flintlock Model 1819, partially signed on the lock w/eagle, address & "1822," iron hardware w/good inspector mark, 10 1/8" l. round barrel, 16" l. **1,430**

Pistol, "Springfield" 1855 percussion model, walnut stock w/brass hardware, Maynard primer system on the lock, 12" l. round barrel, 18" l. (minor hairline near lock bolt) **2,420**

Pistol, U.S. Model 1842 percussion model, lock signed "H. Aston US 1850," faint inspector's mark, 8 1/2" l. round barrel, 14" l. **715**

Pistol, Waters Model 1836 percussion model, flintlock conversion, walnut stock w/inspector marks & iron hardware, lock signed "A. Waters, 1837," 8 1/2" l. round barrel, 13 1/2" l. **495**

Revolver, Colt 1849 pocket model, .31 cal., w/barrel signatures & cylinder scene w/good silver plating on trigger guard, 5 7/8" l. octagonal barrel, 11" l. **935**

Revolver, Colt 1849 pocket model, octagonal barrel w/attached loading lever, brass, metal & wood grip, five-shot cylinder, address in two lines on barrel, barrel 4" l. (overall wear) **358**

Revolver, Colt 1851 Navy model, .36 cal., grips w/carved initials, all signatures & cylinder scene remain, matching serial numbers, 7 1/2" l. octagonal barrel, 13 1/4" l. (areas of pitting) **1,320**

Colt Model 1851 Navy Revolver

Revolver, Colt 1851 Navy model, octagonal barrel w/attached loading lever, six-shot cylinder, wood grips, address in one line on top of barrel, tight action, w/wooden box, some overall wear, barrel 7 1/2" l. (ILLUS.).. **1,650**

Revolver, Colt 1860 Army model, .44 cal., good cylinder scene & inspector markings, matching serial numbers, 8" l. round barrel, 14" l.. **1,760**

Revolver, Colt Model 1855 sidehammer pocket model, octagonal barrel, metal & wood grip, address on two lines on top of barrel, barrel 3 1/2" l. (overall wear).............. **495**

Revolver, Colt Python .357 Magnum model, royal blue finish, engraved & inlaid w/gold by Floyd E. Warren of Ohio, horse inlaid on left side, mountain lion on right, full-shouldered ejector rod, adjustable rear sight, plain walnut & ivory grips, signed "Engraved by F.E. Warren 1962. Colts PTFA Mag. Co., Hartford, CT U.S.A." on right side of barrel & "Python .357 - .357 Magnum CTG" on left side, w/velvet-lined wooden box, barrel 5" l., overall 12" l. **1,980**

Revolver, Smith & Wesson .22 cal. model, six-shot, stainless steel, early engraving by Rex Peterson, marked "Smith and Wesson" on left side of barrel, ".22 Long Rifle Ctg." on left side, also marked "Made in U.S.A. - Marcas Registradas - Smith and Wesson, Springfield, Mass.," signed "Rex" just above trigger, w/velvet-lined wooden box, barrel 3 1/2" l., overall 9" l... **825**

Rifle, 1819 "Hall" flintlock model, walnut stock, lock signed "H. Ferry US 1838," 33" l. round barrel, 53" l. (minor hairline beneath hammer)... **3,685**

Rifle, "Deringer" flintlock military model, walnut stock w/brass hardware & patch box, faint signatures on barrel & lock w/Philadelphia addresses, 36" l. octagonal to round barrel, 51" l.............................. **2,750**

Rifle, Harpers Ferry Model 1803 flintlock model, later production w/signature, ea-gle & "1815," walnut stock w/inspector markings & brass hardware, 33 1/4" l. octagonal to round barrel w/seven-groove rifling, 49 1/2" l. (pieced restoration around the lock)... **8,690**

Rifle, Model 1873 "Springfield" trapdoor model, walnut stock w/carved initials & stamped numbers, 30" l. round barrel, lock w/eagle stamp & "1884," w/original sling, 49" l.. **303**

Rifle, Remington percussion Zouave model, lock signed w/eagle & "1863," walnut stock w/brass hardware, 32" l. round barrel, 48" l.. **880**

Rifle, US 1817 flintlock model, walnut stock w/steel hardware including an oval patch box, boldly signed on lock "R. & J.D. Johnson - 1826" w/eagle, 36" l. round barrel w/inspector markings, 51" l. (pieced restoration to fore-end, missing band spring).. **1,870**

Shotgun, "Browning" over-and-under model, .12 gauge, checkered walnut stock, 30" l. barrels w/vent rib, Belgian-made, 46 1/4" l... **633**

Shotgun, "Winchester" pump-action Model 1200, .12 gauge, checkered walnut stock, worn bluing, 30" l. barrel, 50 1/2" l. **330**

Sidearm, Colt .45 cal. Model CF Army Issue, wood grips w/diamond pattern checkering, ring attached at end of handle for chain, small brass inserts on handle w/rearing horse & word "Colt," rearing horse stamped on back end of barrel, patent dates from 1897 through 1911, various markings on sides of barrel, original bluing, 8 1/4" l., 5 1/4" h. **770**

FIREPLACE & HEARTH ITEMS

Andirons, brass, cast in sections w/solid, scrolled legs & ball feet, held together w/iron rods, 19 1/4" h. (one iron rod replaced & held w/square nut)........................ **$358**

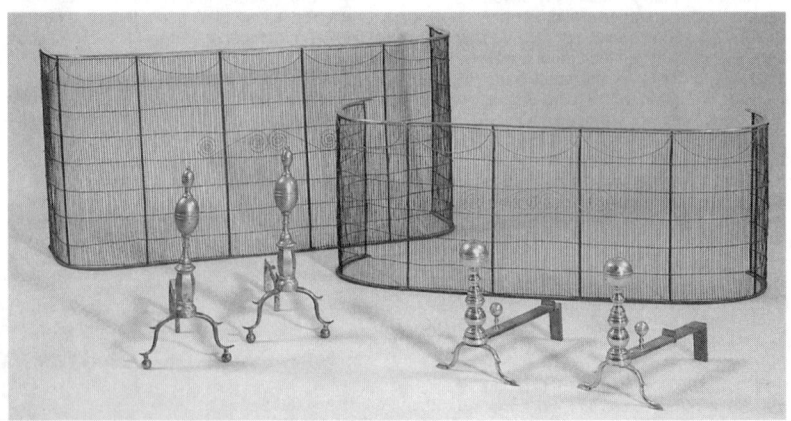

Andirons & Fireplace Fenders

Andirons, brass & iron belted ball-top style, ring-turned baluster shaft w/conforming log stops, spurred knees, probably Boston, ca. 1800, repair to logs, dent in one ball finial, 9 1/4 x 15", 12 3/4" h., pr. (ILLUS. right front w/other andirons & fenders, previous page) **529**

Andirons, brass & iron belted lemon-top style, columnar shafts over square plinths w/engraved meandering vine motifs, cabriole legs on ball & claw feet, late 18th/early 19th c., pr. **1,116**

Andirons, brass & iron, double lemon-top style, baluster form shaft on spurred cabriole legs & ball feet, America, early 19th c., 9 3/4 x 16 1/2", 21" h., pr. (minor pitting) **382**

Andirons, brass & iron, double lemon-top style, baluster-form shaft on spurred cabriole legs & ball feet, America, 19th c., 9 x 17 1/4", 19 1/8" h., pr. (minor pitting) **881**

Andirons, brass & iron double lemon-top style, beaded belting on finials, ring-turned & swollen hexagonal plinths on spurred cabriole legs w/ball feet, America, first quarter 19th c., dents & pitting, small crack on shaft, 9 x 18", 19" h., pr. (ILLUS. left front w/other andirons & fenders, previous page) **558**

Andirons, brass urn-top & iron knife blade style, w/arched legs & penny feet, America, late 18th c., 11 x 20", 19 3/4" h., pr. (minor rust) **588**

Art Deco-style Peacock Andiron

Andirons, cast bronze Art Deco-style peacocks w/mixture of old verdigris & areas of later silver & blue paint, on molded octagonal bases w/paneled columns & ball-shaped perch on each, iron log rests, combs are later, 32" h., pr. (ILLUS. of one) **5,610**

Bellows, turtle back type, original burnt umber ground w/mustard edge & gold stenciled conch shell on bed of leaves, brass nozzle, releathered w/brass tacks, 18" l. (wear) **248**

Fireboard, wide central raised panel w/paint-decorated depiction of seaside village w/ships & houses, the surround painted to resemble tiles w/numerous ships, houses & trees, America, early 19th c., 36 x 44 3/8" (wear, fading) **7,638**

Fireplace fender, brass & wire, brass rim over entwined wirework, America or England, late 18th/early 19th c., 49 5/8" l., 11 3/8" h. (minor pitting) **558**

Fireplace fender, brass & wire, brass top rail over conforming wirework screen w/swag & scrollwork, America or England, late 18th/early 19th c., 14 x 49", 24" h. (ILLUS. left rear w/andirons & other fender, previous page) **2,350**

Fireplace fender, brass & wire, D-shaped w/brass rim above vertical wirework decorated w/brass swag & scrollwork, America or England, late 18th - early 19th c., 45 1/2" l., 18" h. (ILLUS. right rear w/andirons & other fender, previous page) **2,233**

Fireplace tool set: shovel & tongs; brass & iron, ball finial on belted ball-top shovel & tongs, America, early 19th c., 30 7/8 & 31 3/8" l. (minor dents, scattered pitting), the set **411**

Hearth broom, smoke decorated in original black over yellow, turned handle, 27" l. (some bristles missing) **110**

FRAKTUR

Fraktur paintings are decorative birth and marriage certificates of the 18th and 19th centuries and also include family registers and similar documents. Illuminated family documents, birth and baptismal certificates, religious texts and rewards of merit, in a particular style, are known as "fraktur" because of the similarity to the 16th century typeface of that name. Gay watercolor borders, frequently incorporating stylized birds, often frame the hand-lettered documents, which were executed by local ministers, schoolmasters or itinerant penmen. Most are of Pennsylvania Dutch origin.

Flying Angel Fraktur

Birth & baptismal fraktur, h.p. & written record done in red, yellow & brown on laid paper, w/images of flowers, birds & signature flying angels in the corners, the central medallion noting the birth of Magdalena Miller, November 13, 1803 in Linn Township, Northampton, Pennsylvania, additional notes in German on the front dated 1826 and in pencil on the back dated 1876 (possibly dates for marriage & death), modern frame cut & stained to resemble curly maple, surface wear & stains, holes from ink, old taped edge tears, 16 x 19" (ILLUS.) **$4,950**

Birth certificate, for Amenda Gilbert, Berks County, Pennsylvania, 1851, freehand ink & watercolor in red, blue & yellow, handwritten "Published by Benneville Weidner in Rockland, 1852," decorated frame, 9 1/2 x 11 1/2" (stains, fading) **330**

Birth record, printed detail w/eagle, angels, cherub & birds, hand colored, dated "1823," from Adams County, printed at Hanover, Pennsylvania, by D.P. Lange, 1822, in 19th c. frame, 11 5/8 x 15" without frame (margin damage & stains) **440**

"Certificate of Birth & Baptism," recording the birth of Charles Henry, October 9th, 1844 in Warren Township, Trumbull County, Ohio, hand-colored, printed by "Lutz & Scheffer, Harrisburg, Pa," matted & framed, 12 1/2 x 16 1/2" **99**

"Reading, By Gebbrudt und zu haben ben Ritter und Comp," decorated w/hand-colored images of angels, birds, a cherub & bible w/bright blue, red, yellow & green detail, dated "1839," in cherry frame, Pennsylvania, 13 x 16" without frame (taped margin tears) **193**

"Reading" by "Johann Ritter," decorated w/two angels, birds & a cherub colored in blue, red & yellow, dated "1816," w/line added in pencil below "Died Jan. 9, 1884," painted & hand-colored, cherry frame, Pennsylvania, 13 x 16" without frame (tear at top & bottom) **248**

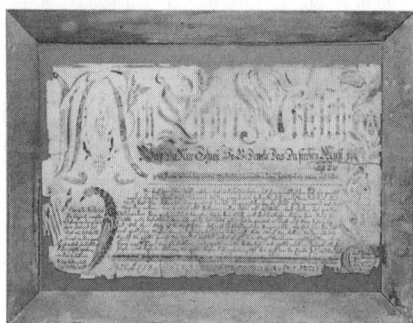

Vorshrift Fraktur

Vorshrift fraktur, watercolor & ink on laid paper, delicately drawn vining tulips & calligraphic text w/more flowers & birds emerging from the letters, a thin bird off to the left, in shades of light blue, pinkish red & faint brown, faint date of 1788 at the bottom, beveled frame w/traces of red graining, stains & damage, 12 x 16" w/frame (ILLUS.) **330**

FRUIT JARS

"A. Stone and Company - Phila Fruit Jar"

A. Stone &, Co - Phila, cylindrical, deep aquamarine, applied wax sealer mouth, iron pontil mark, ca. 1845-1860, an unearthed jar with some exterior and interior stain, 7" h., approx. 1 qt. (ILLUS.) **$472**

Atherholt, Fisher & Co., Philada. cylindrical, aquamarine, applied collared mouth w/blown glass "Kline" stopple, smooth base, ca. 1863-1880, qt. (stopple is incorrect size, stained, small fake at the base) **476**

BBGM Co., (monogram) cylindrical, aquamarine, ground mouth w/glass lid & zinc band, smooth base, ca. 1880-1890, midget pt. (some light interior haze) **672**

Bester Tafel Senf Compound Dusseldorf, on label only, simplex glass lid, unmarked, original lid, pt. **358**

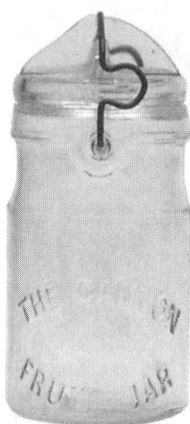

Canton Domestic Fruit Jar

Canton Domestic, cylindrical, colorless, ground mouth w/glass lid & wire bail, smooth base, ca. 1889-1900, pt. (ILLUS.) **224**

Cohansey Glass Mfg Co Patd Mar 20 77, w/original tin lid, barrel-shaped, qt. **132**

Eagle Fruit Jar

Eagle, cylindrical, aquamarine, ground
mouth w/glass lid & iron yoke clamp,
smooth base, ca. 1860-1870, qt.
(ILLUS.).. **269**
Flacus Bros Steers head, embossed cow,
yellow, original clear screw top, pt................. **468**
Gem (The), cylindrical, aquamarine, ground
mouth w/glass lid & metal screw band,
smooth base, ca. 1860-1880, gal. (3/8"
by 1/4" chip on the top of the ground
mouth, covered by glass lid).................... **1,792**
Globe, cylindrical, deep greenish aquamarine, machined mouth w/glass lid & wire
bail, smooth base, ca. 1886-1900, pt........... **336**
Globe, deep aqua, original lid, rarer wide
mouth size **110**
Globe, w/original closure, 1/2 gal...................... **143**
Globe, w/"65" on base, original closure, bril-
liant amber.. **110**
Griffen's Patent Oct. 7 1862, on lid **121**

Air Tight Cover Lid Fruit Jar

**Hartell's Glass Air Tight Cover Lid Em-
bossed fruit jar, Patented Oct 19 1858,**
cylindrical, apple green, ground mouth
w/glass lid, smooth base, ca. 1860-1870,
pt. (ILLUS.).. **840**
Howe Jar Scranton, PA, cylindrical, color-
less, ground mouth w/glass lid & wire
bail, smooth base, ca. 1888-1900, pt............. **560**

Huyett and Fridley/Carisle, PA., cylindrical, aquamarine, ground mouth, smooth
base, ca. 1860-1870, qt. (no closure,
small manufacturer's chips on the top of
the mouth) **1,064**
J.D. Willoughby, Patent Jan 4, 1859, on
wingnut, unmarked jar, iron pontil, aqua,
original closure, qt... **198**

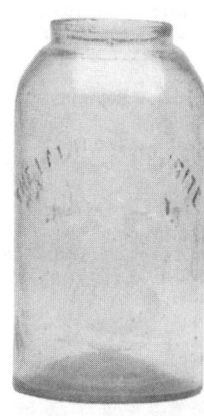

Ladies Favorite, Wm L. Haller Fruit Jar

Ladies Favorite (The), Wm. L. Haller Car-
isle, PA, cylindrical, aquamarine, ground
mouth, smooth base, ca. 1860-1870, no
closure, some exterior stain & scratches,
qt. (ILLUS.).. **6,160**
Mason Jar, cylindrical, colorless w/a 3" ol-
ive streak on the reverse, ground mouth
w/zinc lid, smooth base, ca. 1880-1900,
rare midget pt. (small pieces of slag in the
glass without damage) **258**

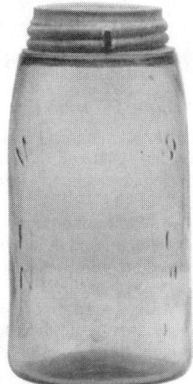

1858 Mason's CFJ Co., Fruit Jar

Mason's CFJ Co., Patent Nov 30 1858, cylindrical, light yellow green, ground
mouth w/zinc lid, smooth base, ca. 1870-
1890, qt. (ILLUS.)... **168**
**Mason's (maltese cross) Patent Nov. 30,
1858,** cylindrical, yellow amber, ground
mouth w/zinc lid, smooth base, ca. 1870-
1890, 1/2 gal. (tiny pick mark to the left of
"P" in "Patent").. **179**

Mason's Patd Nov 30 1858, "H328" on base, ground top, w/original porcelain & metal cap, medium amber (some interior stain) 715

Mason's Patent Nov. 30, 1858, cylindrical, aquamarine, ground mouth w/zinc lid, smooth base, ca. 1865-1880, qt. (some minor deterioration of the metal lid) 532

Mason's Patent Nov. 30th 1858, cylindrical, aquamarine, ground mouth w/zinc lid, smooth base, ca. 1870-1890, midget pt. 364

Mason's Patent Nov 30th 1858, "HGW" (monogram), cylindrical, aquamarine, ground mouth w/zinc lid, smooth base, ca. 1860-1890, midget pt. (mouth roughness) 672

MGM Co., (monogram), cylindrical, colorless w/a very pale grey amethystine tone, ground mouth w/zinc lid, smooth base, ca. 1880-1900, midget pt. 420

Patent June 27 1865 Fruit Jar

Patent June 27 1865, cylindrical, cornflower blue w/colorless lid, ground mouth w/glass lid & iron clamp, smooth base, ca. 1865, qt. (ILLUS.) 2,128

Porcelain BBGM Co., (monogram), cylindrical, aquamarine, ground mouth w/zinc lid, smooth base, ca. 1880-1900, midget pt. 840

Porcelain BBGM Co. Lined, (monogram), cylindrical, colorless, ground mouth w/zinc lid, smooth base, ca. 1880-1990, midget pt. 2,688

Porcelain Lined, cylindrical, aquamarine, ground mouth w/unusual zinc lid, unusual smooth base, ca. 1870-1890, midget pt. 269

Potter and Bodine Philladelphia, w/original closure (minor area of exterior haze) 99

Puritan (The), cylindrical, aquamarine, ground mouth w/glass lid & ramped iron ring w/wire clamp, smooth base, ca. 1870-1890, pt. (wire clamp rusty) 364

Reservoir (The), cylindrical, aquamarine, applied collared mouth w/blown stopper, smooth base,ca. 1870-1890, qt. 364

Rose (The), cylindrical, colorless, machined mouth w/glass lid & zinc band, smooth base, ca. 1880-1900, midget pt. 246

Schaffer Jar, Rochester, NY (The), cylindrical, aquamarine, ground mouth w/glass lid & wire coil clamp, smooth base, ca. 1879-1890, qt. (some minor mouth roughness) 280

The Smalley Jar

Smalley Jar (The), cylindrical, aquamarine, ground mouth w/glass lid & wire bail, smooth base, ca. 1890-1900, qt. (ILLUS.) 560

Star-[star], cylindrical, aquamarine, ground mouth w/metal band & zinc lid, smooth base, closure insert stamped "Haller's Patent Feb 5 67" with a star in the center, ca. 1867-1880, qt. (some minor interior haze & exterior scratches) 336

Sun, "Trademark JP Barstow" on base, original closure, qt. 143

Sun, "Trademark JP Barstow" on the base, original closure, pt. ....

Trade Mark Lightning, cylindrical, yellow amber, almost a true yellow, ground mouth w/glass lid & wire bail, smooth base, ca. 1880-1890, pt. 336

Trademark - Lightning, cylindrical, citron, ground mouth w/matching glass lid, smooth base, ca. 1870-1890, wire neck ring old, wire bail appears new, qt. 532

Trademark - Lightning, cylindrical, yellow w/a slight olive tone, ground mouth w/glass lid & wire bail, smooth base, 1870-1890, qt. 280

Van Vliet Improved Patd May 3-81, w/original closure, qt. 990

Van Vliet Jar of 1881, w/original closure, 1/2 gal. (few minor scratches) 825

FURNITURE

Furniture made in the United States during the 18th and 19th centuries is coveted by collectors. American antique furniture has a European background, primarily English, since the influence of the Continent usually found its way to America by way of England. If the style did not originate in England, it came to America by way of England. For this reason, some American furniture styles carry the name of an English monarch or an English designer. However, we must realize that, until recently, little research has been conducted and even less published on the Spanish and French influences in the area of the California missions and New Orleans.

After the American revolution, cabinetmakers in the United States shunned the prevailing styles in England and chose to bring the French styles of Napoleon's Empire to the United States and we have the uniquely named "American Empire" (Classical) style of furniture in a country that never had an emperor.

During the Victorian period, quality furniture began to be mass-produced in this country with its rapidly growing population. So much walnut furniture was manufactured, the vast supply of walnut was virtually depleted and it was of necessity that oak furniture became fashionable as the 19th century drew to a close.

For our purposes, the general guidelines for dating will be: Pilgrim Century - 1620-85 William & Mary - 1685-1720 Queen Anne - 1720-50 Chippendale - 1750-85 Federal - 1785-1820 Hepplewhite - 1785-1820 Sheraton - 1800-20 American Empire (Classical) - 1815-40 Victorian - 1840-1900 Early Victorian - 1840-50 Gothic Revival - 1840-90 Rococo (Louis XV) - 1845-70 Renaissance - 1860-85 Louis XVI - 1865-75 Eastlake - 1870-95 Jacobean & Turkish Revival - 1870-95 Aesthetic Movement - 1880-1900 Art Nouveau - 1890-1918 Turn-of-the-Century - 1895-1910 Mission (Arts & Crafts movement) - 1900-15 Art Deco - 1925-40

All furniture included in this listing is American unless otherwise noted.

Bedroom Suites

Victorian Aesthetic Movement substyle: double tester bed, wardrobe & washstand; walnut & burl walnut, the high-backed headboard supporting a half-tester w/a ornate stepped crown-form crest rail w/a pierced lattice band & quarter-round cut corner ears, the headboard w/a matching crestrail over an arched rectangular burl panel over lower burl panels, the low footboard w/a flat crestrail over a row of sunbursts; the wardrobe w/a matching crest rail above a pair of tall burl panel doors over a pair of base drawers; the washstand w/a matching crest rail above a square mirror swiveling between tall uprights above a white marble backsplash & rectangular top over a case w/a single long drawer over two small drawers beside a small paneled door, refinished, ca. 1880, bed overall 10' 5" h. (ILLUS., bottom of page)..........................$7,000

Victorian Aesthetic Movement Bedroom Suite

Top-quality Aesthetic Design Pieces

Victorian Aesthetic Movement substyle:
half-tester double bed, chest of drawers, washstand & knockdown wardrobe; walnut & burl walnut, the high-back bed w/a large half-tester w/a gently arched crestrail centered by a narrow rectangular panel of leaf carving over a long frieze of leaf carving, the headboard w/a matching carved crestrail above large burl veneer panels & twist-carved colonette, low foot-

board w/flat crestrail over matching carved panels, the other pieces w/matching crestrails, the chest of drawers & washstand w/carved uprights flanking large square beveled swiveling mirrors over rectangular pink marble tops, the chest case w/a row of three drawers over two long drawers, the washstand w/two long drawers over a pair of paneled doors, the wardrobe w/tall doors w/beveled mirrors, original hardware & finish, ca. 880, bed 64 x 85", 10' h. (ILLUS. of bed, chest & washstand) **35,000**

Aesthetic Movement Bed from Suite

Victorian Aesthetic Movement substyle:
high-backed double bed, chest of drawers & washstand, oak, each piece w/a flat-topped crestrail w/dentil carving over a band of leafy scrolls centered by a small shield & flanked by rounded scroll-carved corner ears, the headboard w/a further bands of dentil carving over a narrow rectangular leaf-carved panel flanked by square panels w/carved rosettes, a matching low footboard, the chest of washstand w/swiveling mirrors, original hardware, refinished, ca. 1890, bed 58 x 78", 6' 6" h. (ILLUS. of bed) **2,800**

Aesthetic Movement Suite with Grapevine Carving

Aesthetic Suite with Fancy Crests

Victorian Aesthetic Movement substyle: high-backed double bed, chest of drawers & washstand; quarter-sawn oak, the bed & chest w/a flat flaring crestrail over a thin beaded band over a grapevine-carved band flanked by knob finials, the bed w/carved side pilasters flanking a large rectangular raised panel, the low footboard w/around fan-carved corners over a rectangular panel over a band of grapevine carving; the chest crest rail raised on narrow uprights w/pilasters flanking the large rectangular beveled mirror above the rectangular top over a case w/two small & one long raised panel drawers over a single long drawer over a shorter drawer beside a small square cupboard door all flanked by pilasters; the washstand w/a rectangular grey marble top above a case w/a single long drawer over two drawers & a square door, original hardware, original finish, ca. 1890, bed 60 x 78", 7' h. (ILLUS., bottom previous page) **4,000**

Victorian Aesthetic Movement substyle: high-backed double bed, chest of drawers & washstand; walnut & burl walnut veneer, the bed & chest w/high ornate crestrails w/a pierced sunburst center crest above a wide panel centered by a pierced lattice panel centered by a carved florette flanked by triangular raised burl & leaf-carved panels, the bed w/long rectangular burl veneer panels, the chest w/flat uprights w/candleshelves flanking the large square swiveling square mirror above the rectangular white marble top on the case w/a row of three burl veneer drawers over two long burl veneer drawers, flat apron, washstand w/white marble tall splashback on a case w/a long narrow burl panel drawer over two burled drawers & small door, flat apron, original fancy brass hardware, refinished, ca. 1880, chest overall 7' 8" h. (ILLUS., top of page) **3,500**

Victorian Eastlake Bedroom Suite

Four-piece Golden Oak Suite

Victorian Eastlake substyle: double bed, chest of drawers & washstand; walnut & burl walnut, the bed & chest w/high backs topped w/a wide molded crestrail w/a carved central roundel & pointed carved corner ears above a scallop-cut frieze band, the bed headboard w/stepped narrow panels of burl & a matching low footboard, the chest w/a large swiveling square mirror flanked by small quarter-round shelves at the base of the side supports above the rectangular top over a case w/a row of three drawers over two long drawers; the washstand w/a marble splashback over a case w/a long narrow drawer over two small drawers beside a small raised-panel door, original narrow rectangular brass pulls, ca. 1880, chest 21 x 42", 6' 8" h. (ILLUS., bottom previous page).. **6,500**

Victorian Golden Oak style: double bed, chest of drawers, chiffonier & washstand; oak & oak veneer, the high-backed bed w/a double-arch crestrail centered by a carved shell over large C-scrolls & smaller leafy scrolls, a plain low footboard; the chest w/a serpentine crestrail w/small shell & scroll carving curves down to form an oblong tall frame around a large beveled mirror swiveling between S-scroll uprights w/scroll-carved trim over the rectangular top w/serpentine edges over a conforming serpentine case w/a pair of drawers over two long drawers over a serpentine apron & short legs w/paw feet; the tall chiffonier w/a matching rectangular serpentine frame around a long rectangular beveled mirror of S-scroll uprights above a serpentine top over a case w/a pair of drawers over a stack of four long drawers, serpentine apron & paw feet; the washstand w/a towel bar supported by S-scroll scroll-carved uprights over the serpentine top & case w/a long drawer over two small drawers beside a small door, on paw feet, refinished, ca. 1900, bed 6' h. (ILLUS., top of page)......... **4,000**

Golden Oak Bed & Chest with Simple Details

Heavy Golden Oak Bedroom Suite

Victorian Golden Oak style: high-backed double bed & chest of drawers; oak, the headboard w/a central shell-and-scroll-carved low crest on a slightly serpentine crestrail above a scroll-carved cluster on the wide plain backboard, the low footboard w/a rod crestrail over a scroll-carved cluster; the chest of drawers w/a large rectangular beveled mirror in a molded frame w/matching crestrail, swiveling between S-scroll supports w/scroll-carved trim above the rectangular top w/a double-serpentine front over the conforming case w/a pair of drawers over two long lower drawers, serpentine apron & simple curved legs, original brass hardware, original dark finish, ca. 1900, bed 58 x 78", 6' h. (ILLUS., bottom previous page)........... **1,400**

Victorian Golden Oak style: high-backed double bed, chest of drawers & washstand; each piece w/a serpentine cre-strail centered by a shell carved over leafy scrolls on a wide half-round rail; the bed headboard w/half-round columns flanking a rectangular molding panel w/a scroll-and-cartouche crest, the low footboard w/a matching raised panel; the chest w/columnar uprights flanking an arched rectangular beveled swiveling mirror over a rectangular top over a case w/a pair of projecting drawers over two long graduated bow-front drawers flanked by half-round columns over heavy paw feet; the washstand also w/columnar uprights flanking a narrow rectangular oblong beveled mirror over a towel bar, the rectangular top over a pair of projecting drawers over a single long bow-front drawer over a pair of bow-front doors all on heavy paw feet, original dark finish, ca. 1895, bed 58 x 78", 7' 7" h. (ILLUS., top of page) **8,500**

Simple Golden Oak Bedroom Suite

Golden Oak Pieces with Delicate Carving

Victorian Golden Oak style: high-backed double bed, chest of drawers & washstand; oak, the headboard w/a slightly serpentine crestrail over delicate leafy scroll carving above plain panels, the chest w/a matching crestrail over flat uprights flanking a large rectangular swiveling mirror above the rectangular top over a case w/three long drawers, flat apron; the washstand w/a towel bar on uprights above the rectangular top & case w/a long drawer over two small drawers & a small door, refinished, ca. 1910, chest of drawer overall 6' 6" h. (ILLUS., bottom previous page) **1,600**

Victorian Golden Oak style: high-backed double bed & chests of drawers; quarter-sawn oak, each piece w/a flat molded crestrail centered by an arched scroll-carved crest, the headboard w/a large flat panel decorated w/delicate leafy scroll carving w/matching carving on the low footboard, the chest of drawers crest above a large oblong beveled mirror swiveling between S-scroll scroll-carved supports over a rectangular top w/serpentine edges over a double-serpentine case w/a pair of drawers over two long drawers over simple curved feet, refinished, ca. 1900, bed 58 x 78", 6' 6" h. (ILLUS., top of page) **2,750**

Simple Renaissance Revival Bedroom Suite

Victorian Renaissance Revival substyle: double bed, chest of drawers & washstand; walnut, the high-backed bed & chest w/tall broken-scroll arched crests centered by carved fruit finials above shaped raised burl panels, the bed w/a low arched footboard w/raised fruit & scroll carving, the chest w/an arched molding below the crest over a tall arched mirror flanked by shaped sides w/small candle shelves & raised burl panels above the drop-well white marble top w/stacks of four small drawers flanking two longer center drawers; the washstand w/an arched white marble splashback over a long narrow single drawer over a pair of arched-panel doors, original black pear-shaped drawer pulls, ca. 1875, refinished, chest overall 8' h. (ILLUS., bottom previous page) **3,500**

Renaissance Bed & Chest of Drawers

Victorian Renaissance Revival substyle: high-backed double bed & chest of drawers; walnut & burl walnut, each piece w/a high crestrail centered by a large pointed palmette-and-scroll-carved crest flanked by pierced leafy scrolls over an angled pediment w/burls panels, the headboard w/further shaped burl panels flanking a large roundel flanked by urn-form finials all above three tall narrow molded panels, the lower footboard w/a peeked top over matching burl panels & angled paneled legs, the chest w/scroll-cut sides flanking the tall rectangular mirror above the drop-well white marble top over a case w/pairs of small drawers over two long drawers all w/raised burn panels, original black pear-shaped drops, 1870s, bed 58 x 78", 8' h. (ILLUS.) **5,800**

Victorian Renaissance Revival substyle: high-backed double bed & chest of drawers; walnut & burl walnut, each w/a matching crestrail w/peaked leafy scroll center bracket crest w/burl panel above an arched molding over further burl & molded panels flanked by brackets, the

headboard w/block-and-roundel corner finials above block-molded sides flanking long narrow panels, the low arched footboard w/a central diamond-shaped burl panel flanked by shaped panels over long rectangular panels & heavy square blocked legs; the crest on the chest above a tall arched rectangular mirror flanked by paneled sides w/small candle shelves & scroll-carved lower sides above the drop-well top w/white marble tops, two small drawers at each side above two long lower drawer drawers w/raised burl panels & original pulls, refinished, ca. 1875, bed 58 x 78", overall 7' 10" h. (ILLUS. of chest of drawers, below) **6,500**

Fine Renaissance Revival Bed

Victorian Renaissance Revival substyle: high-backed double bed & chest of drawers, walnut & burl walnut, each w/a tall ornately carved broken-scroll crestrail centered by a large palmette & fruit-carved finial over further carved scrolls & a blocked crestrail, the headboard w/half-round columns below the blocked rail flanking a very tall raised burl panel flanked by shorter side panels below urn-form finials palmette-carved drops, the low footboard w/a flat crestrail over an arrangement of raised burl panels, the chest of drawers w/a similar design of columns & scroll-carved sides flanking a tall beveled mirror w/a paneled top above the white marble drop-well top, the side sections w/outset beveled corners above a conforming section w/two small burl paneled drawers above two long burl paneled drawers flanked by slender side columns, original T-form pulls, refinished, ca. 1875, bed 58 x 78", 8' 6" h., pr. **7,500**

Fine Mitchell & Rammelsberg Chest

Victorian Rococo substyle: high-backed double bed & chest of drawers; carved mahogany, the chest of drawers w/a very high superstructure topped by a Prince-of-Wales plumes carved finial over a broken-arched pediment w/scroll-pierced panels above wide pierced scroll-carved sections supporting two half-round shelves on each side & flanking a tall arched swiveling mirror, the rectangular white marble top w/a serpentine front & outset chamfered corners above a conforming case w/four long bow-front drawers w/ornate scroll-carved panels & pulls, molded bow-front apron; the bed headboard w/a pierced & scroll-carved finial on the wide arched & molded crest rail above a wide arched flame veneer panel flanked by heavy side posts w/large urn-form finials, low footboard w/raised scroll-carved corners & arched center crest above a cartouche-carved roundel, deep side rails, by Mitchell & Rammelsburg Co., Cincinnati, Ohio, ca. 1850-60, bed 62 x 80", overall 9' h., pr. (ILLUS. of chest).......................... **10,000**

Victorian Rococo substyle: high-backed double bed & chest of drawers; carved rosewood, the bed headboard w/a high pierced arched crest elaborately carved w/scrolling leafy vines w/an exotic bird perched at each side over the arched & stepped crestrail above the three-panel backboard w/further scroll carving flanked by block-and-column-carved stiles w/urn-form finials, the lower arched footboard w/ornate scroll carving centered by a large oval knob above two arched panels, curved low corner boards; the chest w/a tall superstructure w/ornately pierced-carved twining branches w/an exotic bird on each side & resting on tall square plinths w/round candle shelves all enclosing a tall oblong swiveling mirror, the rectangular white marble top w/a serpentine front above a conforming case w/ three long drawers w/scroll-carved pulls flanked by canted front corners w/further carved scrolls, low serpentine apron, Mitchell & Rammelsberg Co., Cincinnati, Ohio, ca. 1855, original finish, bed 64 x 82", 8' 6" h., pr. (ILLUS., below)...................................... **20,000**

Ornate Rosewood Bed & Chest

Extraordinary Rococo Bedroom Suite

Feather-grained Rococo Bed

Victorian Rococo substyle: high-backed double bed & chest of drawers; feather-grained walnut; the high bed headboard w/an arched crest w/ornately carved scrolls on an open C-scroll above the arched crest rail w/further scrolls above a large oval grained panel flanked by narrow arched rectangular panels between the serpentine stiles w/further scroll carving, the low footboard w/a raised, arched center w/fruit-and-flower carving & curved low corner posts; the chest w/a tall superstructure w/a high pierced scroll-carved crest & upturned corners over a tall rectangular mirror w/serpentine top swiveling between ornate shaped & scroll-carved uprights above the rectangular white marble top over a case w/two long, deep drawers decorated w/raised banded panels w/scroll carving, serpentine apron w/scroll carving between bun feet, labeled "O. P. Merriman, Baltimore," original finish, ca. 1860, bed 64 x 82", 6' 6" h., pr. (ILLUS. of bed) **8,500**

Victorian Rococo substyle: high-backed double bed, chest of drawers & washstand; carved rosewood, the bed headboard w/a large arched & peaked pierce-carved crest composed of ornate scrolls centered by a Prince of Wales plumes finials above the arched & molded crestrail above raised burl panels over three small pierced-carved panels above three tall arch-topped veneer panels all flanked by block-and-scroll-carved stiles, the low arched footboard w/three arched veneer panels centered w/a scroll-carved cluster, curved & paneled corner boards; the chest w/a tall superstructure w/a pierced crest matching the bed above pierced & scroll carved uprights w/small half-round shelves flanking a tall, swiveling arched-topped rectangular mirror, the rectangular white marbled top w/projecting canted corners above columns flanking a conforming case w/three long drawers decorated w/raised oval banding & fruit-carved pulls, the washstand w/a rectangular white marble top over a case of three long drawers, Mitchell & Rammelsberg Co., Cincinnati, Ohio, ca. 1860, original finish, bed 64 x 84", overall 9' 6" h., the set (ILLUS. of bed, top of previous page) **35,000**

Beds

Art Nouveau-influenced Oak Bed

Art Nouveau style bed, quarter-swan oak, the high oval headboard w/molded edges topped by a cartouche-carved crest, a flat-topped matching lower footboard w/scroll-carved trim & short outswept legs w/paw feet, refinished, ca. 1900, 58 x 78", 6' 2" h. (ILLUS.) **800**

Classical Mahogany Low-poster Bed

Classical low-poster bed, mahogany, matching head- and footboards w/curved

tops w/scrolled ends above pairs of rectangular burl veneer panels, ropetwist posts w/large knob finials above blocked sections on heavy tapering ovoid legs, brass bolt covers, refinished, ca. 1830s, 58 x 76", 45" h. (ILLUS.) **1,200**

Fine Classical Bed with Bronze Trim

Classical low-poster bed, mahogany, the flat-topped headboard w/a knob-ended bar over delicate applied bronze cupids flanking swags, acanthus leaf & ribbed knob carved side posts w/small bronze pineapple finials & heavy acanthus-carved turned legs, matching foot posts joined by a rail, original finish, ca. 1840, 60 x 80", 5' h. (ILLUS.) **2,400**

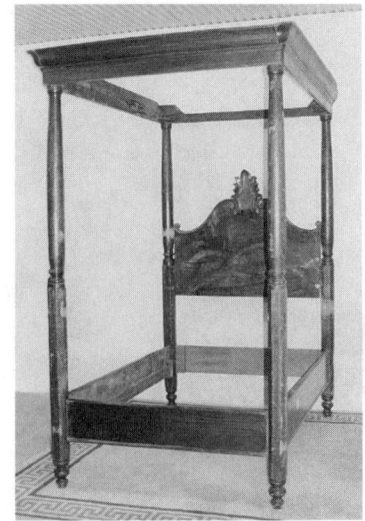

Classical Full-tester Bed

Classical tall-poster tester bed, mahogany, a wide cove-molded rectangular tester frame raised on columnar posts, an arched headboard w/a cartouche-and-scroll-carved finial, wide side & foot rails, short ring-turned feet, original finish, ca. 1840, 60 x 78", 9' h. (ILLUS.) **2,500**

Nicely Carved Classical Revival Bed

Classical Revival tall-poster bed, mahogany, high flame veneer headboard w/flat crestrail w/knob ends above cutout scrolls flanked by leaf-carved spiraling posts w/ring-turned & pineapple finials, matching foot posts joined by a turned leaf-carved upper rail & a flat lower rail, short heavy tapering turned legs w/bun feet, original finish, ca. 1890-1910, 56 x 76", 6' h. (ILLUS.) **1,500**

Classical Revival Reeded Post Bed

Classical Revival tall-poster bed, mahogany, the high flat-topped headboard w/scroll trim over a leaf-carved band w/roundel above a rectangular panel w/beaded molding, flanked by posts w/baluster- and ring-turned leaf-carved sections below tall tapering reeded sections w/carved knob finials, matching shorter footrails joined by a wide rail, tapering reeded short legs, late 19th c., 60 x 78", 6' h. (ILLUS.) **1,500**

Classical Revival Paneled Post Bed

Classical Revival tall-poster bed, mahogany, the wide arched headboard centered by a pair of large delicate cutout scrolls, heavy paneled tapering side posts w/flattened knob finials, matching foot posts joined by a paneled narrow upper rail & gently arched lower rail, heavy C-scroll feet, original finish, ca. 1890-1910, 60 x 80", 5' 6" h. (ILLUS.) **1,000**

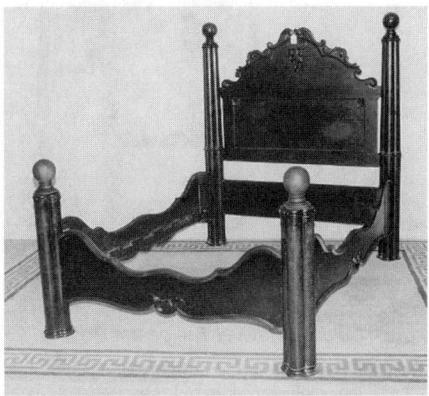

Classical-Rococo Transitional Bed

Classical-Rococo transitional tall-poster bed, mahogany, the high arched headboard w/ornate carved scrolls flanked by tall posts formed by a cluster of four columns topped w/a ball finial, shorter matching foot posts, serpentine scroll-trimmed side- and foot rails, possibly original finish, ca. 1845, 66 x 84", 6' h. (ILLUS.) **4,500**

Simple Federal Revival Twin Beds

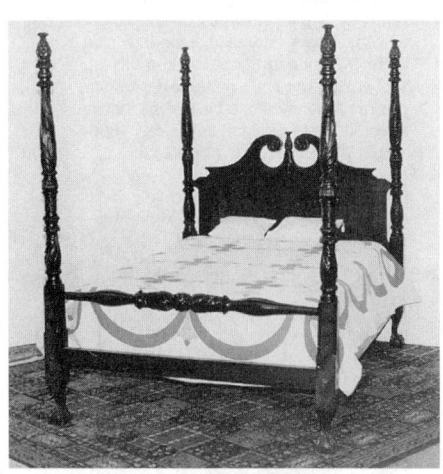

Colonial Revival Tall-poster Bed

Colonial Revival tall-poster bed, mahogany, the high broken-scroll headboard w/turned center finial flanked by slender leaf-carved baluster- and ring-turned posts w/carved pineapple finials, matching foot posts joined by a turned & leaf-carved upper rail & flat lower rail, short legs w/claw-and-ball feet, original finish, full-sized, early 20th c., 58 x 78", 6' h. (ILLUS.).. **2,400**

Fine Federal Tall-Poster Bed

Federal tall-poster bed, mahogany, the headboard w/an arched crestrail over two rectangular panels flanked by tall slender ropetwist columns w/carved pineapple finials, matching foot posts joined by a rail, ropetwist legs on original brass feet, original bolt covers, original finish, ca. 1820s, 60 x 80", 7' 8" h. (ILLUS.) **7,500**

Rare Early New Orleans Bed

Federal tall-poster bed, mahogany, the high shaped headboard topped by a baluster- and ringed-turned bar w/acorn terminals, slender baluster- and ring-turned posts w/baluster-turned finials, matching foot posts joined by a lower rail, bulbous turned & tapering legs, original finish, made in New Orleans, ca. 1825-35, 60 x 80", 7' 6" h. (ILLUS.)............................ **10,500**

Federal Revival tall-poster twin-sized beds, mahogany, the wide flat headboard w/a narrow flat crestrail w/scrolled ends flanked by slender tapering reeded posts topped by stylized plume finials, matching foot posts joined by a knob-turned reeded upper rail & a flat bottom rail, early 20th c., 42 x 74", 5' 6" h., pr. (ILLUS., top previous page) **1,800**

Fine Victorian Spool-turned Bed

Victorian cottage-style tall-poster bed, walnut, a flat-topped headboard w/scroll-carved sides over a row of short spool-turned spindles above a spool-turned rail, flanked by tall spool-turned posts, matching foot posts joined by a spool-turned upper rail & flat lower rail, tall spool-turned legs, original finish, mid-19th c., 58 x 76", 6' h. (ILLUS.).................... **1,200**

Interesting Country-style Carved Bed

Victorian country-style double bed,
carved butternut, high matching head-
and footboards w/stepped crestrails over
three wide panels flanked by flattened
posts carved at the top w/a cornucopia
above raised leaf-carved panels centered by a roundel, wide side rails
w/scroll-carved top brackets & long
raised panels carved w/leafy vines & centered by a carved roundel, heavy block
feet, original finish, ca. 1870s, 56 x 76",
4' h. (ILLUS., bottom of previous page)........ **750**

Golden Oak Child's Bed

Victorian Golden Oak child's bed, demountable, the high headboard w/a serpentine top w/carved scroll trim above a
raised oval scroll band, side stiles
w/scroll-carved ears, matching lower
footboard, deep slatted side rails, original
finish, ca. 1900 24 x 48", 40" h. (ILLUS.) **500**

Compact Victorian "Murphy" Bed

Victorian Golden Oak "Murphy" bed, a
high scalloped & scroll-carved crestrail
above the rectangular top of the conform-

ing case, the wide flat paneled & scroll-
carved front folds out to expose the bed
springs & mattress, original finish, ca.
1900, closed 20 x 50", overall 5' 4" h.
(ILLUS.)............. **650**

Early Wardrobe-style "Murphy" Bed

Victorian Golden Oak "Murphy" bed,
wardrobe-style, the tall case w/a serpentine crestrail delicate leafy scroll carving
on the door-like panel enclosing an
arched beveled mirror, the tall side panels w/rod cornices above tall slightly serpentine panels over flat panels, paneled
& shaped side panels, full front folds
down to expose the bed mattress &
springs, patent-dated 1886, refinished,
22 x 60", 7' h. (ILLUS.)................................ **1,250**

Rare Gothic Revival Half-tester Bed

Victorian Gothic Revival half-tester bed,
mahogany, the rectangular bow-fronted
tester frame cut w/repeating low Gothic
arches & cutout trefoils, raised on tall baluster-turned & paneled posts w/Gothic
arch brackets, the tall headboard w/a
gently arched scroll-carved crestrail over

three tall Gothic arch flame veneer panels, the low footboard w/a serpentine crestrail over three arched panels between heavy paneled legs w/urn-form finials & raised on knob feet, refinished, ca. 1840, 60 x 80", 9' 9" h. (ILLUS.)............................ **5,500**

tened block finial over further raised burl panels, heavy square legs w/matching finials & carved drops, heavy square block feet, refinished, ca. 1875, 60 x 80", 8' 6" h. (ILLUS.).. **3,500**

Quality Renaissance Revival Bed

Simple Child's Tall-poster Bed

Victorian Renaissance Revival bed, walnut & & burl walnut veneer, the tall arched headboard w/a fan- and scroll-carved crest centered by a raised burl shield above narrow curved burl panels over small burned panels flanking a roundel over two large arched burl panels, flat side stiles carved drop decoration, the low arched footboard w/a central flat-

Victorian Renaissance Revival tall-poster child's bed, walnut, the arched & scallop-cut headboard over a row of short turned spindles between rod-and-baluster-turned tall posts w/ball finials, matching foot posts joined by a low gently arched footboard, heavy baluster- and ring-turned legs, brass bolt covers, old refinish, ca. 1870s, 42 x 76", 5' 4" h. (ILLUS.).. **600**

Rosewood Bed with Bold Carving

Victorian Rococo bed, carved rosewood, the arched headboard w/a high arched crestrail pierced & carved w/heavy scrolls centered by an oval button, heavy rounded columnar legs w/flattened urn-form finials, the side- and foot rails w/scroll-carved corner brackets & cartouche-carved aprons, shorter columnar footboard legs w/matching finials, refinished, ca. 1860, 68 x 80", 5' h. (ILLUS., bottom previous page) **6,500**

Elaborately Carved Rococo Bed

Victorian Rococo bed, carved rosewood, the very tall headboard w/an extremely ornate crest, a wide arched & pierced & scroll-carved crest centered by a full-figure seated putti above an arched molding over further elaborate leafy scroll & flower-carving above three tall rectangular panels w/arched & serpentine tops flanked by heavy paneled side posts w/disk-turned finials, the low arched footboard w/further ornate scroll carving flanked by heavy panel legs w/disk finials, heavy disk-turned feet, ca. 1850s, 64 x 82", 8' 10" h. (ILLUS. of complete bed)........................... **10,000**

Victorian Country-style Rococo Bed

Victorian Rococo country-style bed, cherry & mahogany, the high arched headboard w/an ornate scroll-carved crestrail over the tall panels flanked by rod-turned posts w/ring-turned finials, low foot posts joined by narrow rails, original finish, ca. 1850s, 56 x 76", 6' h. (ILLUS.)... **1,000**

Fine Full-Tester Rococo Bed

Victorian Rococo full-tester bed, mahogany, the deep cove-molded tester frame raised on slender paneled tapering posts above heavy tapering columnar posts above large columnar lower legs, the high headboard w/a pierced & scroll-carved crestrail over a wide veneer panel, the wide side- and foot rails w/scroll-carved corner brackets & serpentine aprons, refinished, ca. 1845, 68 x 84", overall 10' 6" h. (ILLUS.)........................... **15,000**

Wonderful Rococo Half-tester Bed

Victorian Rococo half-tester bed, carved rosewood, the rectangular half-tester w/a deep frame w/a coved cornice over a band of delicate scroll carving w/rounded projecting corners w/further detailed carving, supported by ornate scroll brackets above heavy columnar posts flanking the high arched headboard w/a scroll-carved central cartouche & scroll trim over a raised burl panel, the low footboard w/a serpentine top & a lower vine-carved panels flanked by short heavy paneled legs w/knob finials, refinished, Philadelphia, ca. 1855, 66 x 84", overall 10' h. (ILLUS., previous page) **18,000**

Benches

Bucket bench, poplar, shaped ends w/beveled edges, top shelf & crest also beveled, center shelf is covered w/zinc, black & red over mustard decoration & initials "SB" within decoration on either end, New England, 19th c. (small unexplained oval cutouts beneath two lower shelves) ... **3,410**

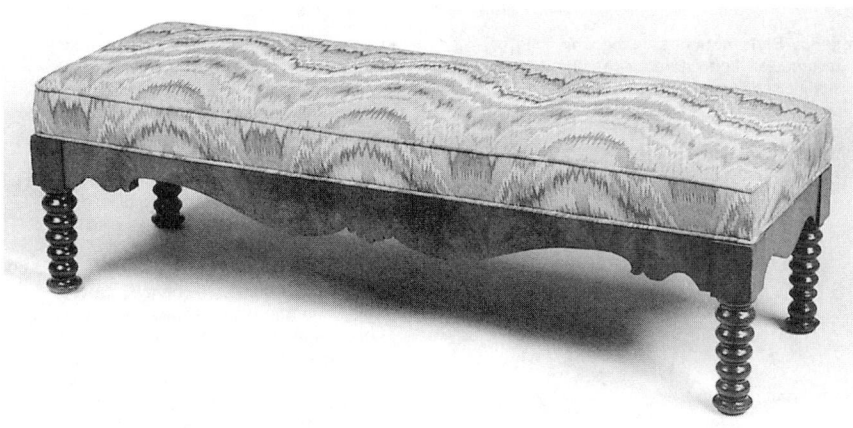

American Classical Bench

Classical bench, mahogany, long narrow upholstery seat on a mahogany-veneered scalloped apron, raised on bobbin-turned legs, American, ca. 1840, 48" l., 15" h. (ILLUS.) **1,265**

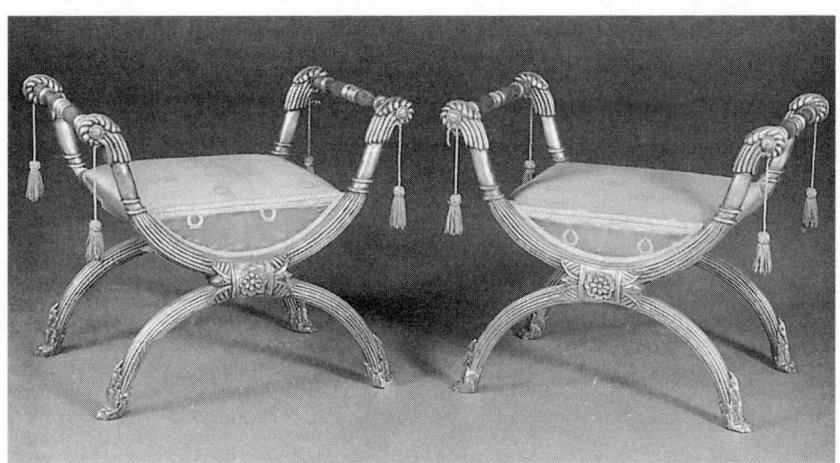

Fine Neoclassical Giltwood Benches

Neoclassical benches, giltwood, delicate X-form reeded frame w/rolled top ends joined a ring-turned rail, a central florette-carved block below the rectangular upholstered seat, stylized animal carved feet, Europe, 19th c., 17 x 29", 20" h., pr. (ILLUS.) **863**

Nice Regency-Style Benches

Regency-Style benches, mahogany, long rectangular upholstered seat above a line-incised flat apron raised on turned tapering reeded legs on brass casters, England, 19th c., 25 1/2 x 47 1/2", 21 1/2" h., pr. (ILLUS.)................................... **2,300**

Ornately Carved Bench with Figures

Victorian Baroque-style bench, carved fruit wood, the high arched back ornately carved w/a figural lion head at the top center over scrolls above wide border band w/concave sides centering bold carving of military trophies & cornucopias & flanked by figural seated putti playing horns, the wide serpentine-sided seat above an ornately carved front panel centering a panel w/a carved grotesque face & the sides w/carved profile grotesque crouching figures above scroll-carved feet, original finish, ca. 1870s, Europe, 20 x 36", 42" h. (ILLUS.)................ **1,000**

Victorian Baroque-style bench, carved fruit wood, the high stepped back composed of three panels, the largest center rectangular panel topped by a high crest carved w/facing griffins & the panel carved w/a pair of scrolling griffins flanking a center round reserve w/a Cupid, the small side panels w/scrolled griffin crests & each carved w/scrolling designs, heavy end arms each carved w/a reclining lion flanking the long lift-top seat above a three-panel front further carved w/ornate scrolls & scrolling beasts, raised on two central short legs carved w/winged masks & large figural griffin corner legs, original finish, Europe, last quarter 19th c., 26 x 70", 44" h. (ILLUS., below)............ **5,000**

Very Ornate Victorian Bench

Baroque-style Paneled Hall Bench

Victorian Baroque-style bench, carved walnut, the high rectangular back w/a large panel carved overall w/ornate leafy scrolls centering a fruit-filled urn, heavy scroll end arms on block supports flank the rectangular leather-covered hinged seat above the front w/two scroll-carved panels, deep paneled apron w/front kick board missing, original finish, Europe, ca. 1870s, 18 x 50", 40" h. (ILLUS.) **1,000**

Victorian Zebra-covered Ottoman

Victorian ottoman, upholstered mahogany, deep rectangular form, the hinged top opening to storage, narrow wood base molding on bun feet, covered in zebra skin, third quarter 19th c., 18 1/2 x 49", 19" h. (ILLUS.) **3,910**

Bookcases

Arts & Crafts Leaded Glass Bookcase

Arts & Crafts bookcase, mahogany & mahogany veneer, rectangular top w/narrow cornice above a pair of tall finely leaded glass doors, flat molded base, divided interior w/adjustable shelves, original dark finish & brass hardware, ca. 1900, 16 x 44", 5' h. (ILLUS.) **1,400**

Fancy Classical Revival Bookcase

Classical Revival bookcase, mahogany & mahogany veneer, an arched & ornately pierced scroll-carved crest board flanked by small urn finials above the rectangular back above a pair of tall glazed doors opening to adjustable wooden shelves w/a mirror behind the top shelves, all flanked by acanthus leaf-carved baluster-turned side columns, flat base on heavy paw feet, original finish, ca. 1890, 18 x 40", 5' 8" h. (ILLUS.) **1,800**

Rare Roycroft Oak Bookcase

Arts & Crafts bookcase, oak, the rectangular top above tall paneled sides w/corner corbels & a tall wide door w/ornate geometric glazing, flat base, Roycroft mark, early 20th c. (ILLUS.) **11,600**

Simple Classical Revival Bookcase

Classical Revival bookcase, mahogany & mahogany veneer, the rectangular top above a pair of tall bow-front glazed doors flanked by long serpentine pilasters above a rounded bowed apron, rolled front feet, refinished, ca. 1910, 18 x 48", 5' 4" h. (ILLUS.) **1,400**

Fine Colonial Revival Bookcase

Early Classical Revival Bookcase

Classical Revival bookcase, mahogany & mahogany veneer, the rectangular top w/blocked front corners over a conforming case w/two tall glazed doors opening to three wooden shelves flanked by acanthus leaf & pineapple-carved side columns above a pair of bow-front base drawers, raised on front paw feet, original finial, ca. 1900, 18 x 42", 5' 4" h. (ILLUS.).. **1,500**

Colonial Revival bookcase, mahogany, the long rectangular top w/a high backboard w/a flat crestrail centered by ribbon carving & flanked by turned finials above a narrow shelf raised on short carved balusters in front of a long narrow raised panel all flanked by incurved end brackets, the top w/a coved molding over a thin beaded band over a long leaf-carved central band all above a case of four tall glass doors w/beveled glass opening to adjustable wooden shelves in the maple interior, raised on eight tapering blocked & carved legs joined by simple stretchers, original finish, late 19th c., 20 x 84", 6' h. (ILLUS., top of page)........................... **4,000**

Nice Colonial Revival Bookcase

Colonial Revival bookcase, mahogany & mahogany veneer, the rectangular arched top centered by a shell-carved crest above a pair of tall arched glazed doors w/applied geometric grillwork, glass side panels, serpentine apron raised on cabriole legs ending in claw-and-ball feet, original casters, refinished, ca. 1920s, 18 x 48", 6' h. (ILLUS.) **1,800**

Leaded Glass Stacking Bookcase

Early 20th century bookcase, oak, four-section stacking lawyer's-type, the rectangular top w/rounded crestrail above four lift-front geometrically-leaded doors, narrow base drawer, Macy Stacking Bookcase Co., ca. 1900, 12 x 34", 4' 8" h. (ILLUS.) **1,800**

Quality Globe-Wernicke Bookcase

Late Victorian bookcase, mahogany & mahogany veneer, four-section stacking lawyer's-type, the rectangular top w/carved

projecting front corners flanking a dentil-carved band above a stack of four long lift-front beveled glass doors each flanked by reeded half-columns, the projecting base w/a long drawers w/brass bail pulls flanked by leaf-carved brackets, the Ideal Model by Globe-Wernicke, original dark finish, ca. 1890, 16 x 38", 5' h. (ILLUS.)....... **2,000**

Rare Harvey Ellis-designed Bookcase

Mission-style (Arts & Crafts movement) bookcase, oak, a thin rectangular top overhanging a tall case w/a single door w/a row of three small four-pane glazed panels over three long glass panes, arched front & side aprons, designed by Harvey Ellis for Gustav Stickley, early 20th c. (ILLUS.) **19,550**

Charles Limbert Mission Bookcase

Large Neoclassical Bookshelves

Mission-style (Arts & Crafts movement) bookcase, oak, the rectangular top w/a low back rail above a pair of tall two-pane glazed doors opening to three adjustable shelves, side stiles continue down to form tapering front legs flanking the slightly arched apron, round copper pulls, medium brown finish, branded mark of Charles Limbert Co., Grand Rapids, Michigan, early 20th c., 14 x 40 1/2", 4' 9" h. (ILLUS.) **2,760**

Early Oak Revolving Bookcase

Mission-style (Arts & Crafts movement) bookshelf, quarter-sawn oak, revolving-type, a square top above two sides composed of narrow slats flanking three shelves, a wide adjustable book shelf at the side, rotating on a cross-form base on casters, refinished, ca. 1910, 22" w., 44" h. (ILLUS.) **750**

Neoclassical Revival bookcases, mahogany, a rectangular top w/one end angled out above a tall corner alcove w/a tall raised panel over a paneled lower door carved w/a classical urn & swags, the main case w/a pair of tall & wide glass doors

opening to three adjustable wooden shelves, deep molded base, original finish, ca. 1900, 18 x 70", 5' h., pr. (ILLUS., top of page).. **2,800**

Aesthetic Movement Bookcase

Victorian Aesthetic Movement bookcase, walnut, the high superstructure w/a tall square central panel w/flat crestrail & finials above a recessed panel boldly carved w/leaves, half-round carved crests & corner blocks w/finials top the top side sections each w/a narrow shelf raised on short knob-turned spindles, the rectangular top w/a flaring cornice above a pair of tall beveled glass doors opening to fixed shelves all flanked by slender reeded side columns, the projecting base w/a pair of drawers each centered by a raised half-round panel, original cast-brass bail pulls, deep molded base, refinished, ca. 1885, 18 x 38", 6' 4" h. (ILLUS.) **2,400**

Fine Victorian Aesthetic Bookcase

Victorian Aesthetic Movement 'break-front' bookcase, walnut, the superstructure w/a high projecting central section w/an arched crest carved w/leaves & acorns above a scalloped apron raised on reeded baluster-turned supports backed by a rectangular mirror, the backboard sides w/a flat crest over a band of blocks over dentil carving & a rectangular panel also carved w/acorns & leaves all flanked by blocked ends w/acorn finials, the rectangular top w/projecting center section above the conforming case, the projecting center section w/a narrow leaf & acorn-carved panel over the tall glazed door opening to adjustable wooden shelves, the setback side sections w/a tall glazed door opening to four adjustable wooden shelves, each section w/drawers w/brass butterfly pulls on the molded base band, original hardware & finish, ca. 1885, 20 x 72", 7' h. (ILLUS.)..... **4,500**

Victorian Baroque Revival bookcase, beech, demountable, the rectangular top w/four blocked sections above a conforming case w/a wide frieze band cased in the projecting blocks carved w/turbaned heads flanking bands of large carved shells all above the tall glazed arched doors each separated by tall ornately carved panels featuring caryatids, grotesque masks & leafy scrolls, the base w/three deep scroll-carved drawers separated by blocks carved w/grotesque masks, on flattened bun feet, Europe, late 19th c., sold refinished, 22 x 84", 7' h. (ILLUS., below) **5,000**

Ornate Baroque Revival Bookcase

Ornately Carved Horner Bookcase

Victorian Baroque Revival bookcase, mahogany, a long rectangular top w/a deep curved & ornately carved cornice raised on two inner turned columns & two figural seated winged lion end supports all backed by a long beveled mirror over a rectangular top w/a convex center section above a conforming base, a wide bowed glass central door opening to shelves & flanked by scroll-and-button carved columns flanked by tall flat glazed doors also flanked by matching side columns, the molded base on compressed paw feet, original finish, made by Horner of New York City, ca. 1880s, 18 x 84", 6' h. (ILLUS.) **8,000**

peaked scroll-and-leaf-carved crest, the case w/a single tall & wide glazed door opening to two shelves flanked by chamfered front corners carved w/thin reeded quarter-columns, a long deep base drawers w/brass bin pulls, flat base, original finish, may have had a base at one time, ca. 1880, 18 x 36", 6' 8" h. (ILLUS.) **700**

Finely Detailed Eastlake Bookcase

Victorian Eastlake bookcase, walnut, a low stick-and-ball gallery rail w/carved palmettes above a case w/two tall side cabinets flanking a shorter center cabinet, the center section w/a narrow band of carved spearpoints above a glazed door topped by a narrow band of carved crosses, the tall side sections w/tall glazed doors also carved w/a band of crosses, each section w/adjustable wooden shelves, the slightly stepped-out

Victorian Country-style Bookcase

Victorian country-style bookcase, walnut, the arched crestrail centered by a high

base w/a carved band of spearpoints above three burl-paneled drawers w/original brass ring pulls, refinished, ca. 1880, 22 x 60", 6' h. (ILLUS.) **5,000**

Oak Bookcase with Pierced Gallery

Victorian Golden Oak bookcase, oak, a high arched & delicate scroll-pierced top back rail & low cutout sides on the rectangular top w/a deep flaring molding over a pair of tall glazed cupboard doors w/pierced scroll-cut bands at the top of each & narrow scroll-cut panels at the base, on a narrow scroll-incised apron w/scroll feet on casters, refinished, ca. 1900, 16 x 40", 5' 8" h. (ILLUS.) **2,000**

Open Oak Bookcase with Spindles

Victorian Golden Oak bookcase, oak, the high three-quarters gallery top w/a back rail topped w/a low raised crestrail over tiny spindles over a carved thin block band flanked by scrolled corner brackets & knob-turned finials above curved solid ends over a rectangular top shelf above a three-part serpentine apron supported by two turned tall spindles flanked by low

spindle rails all flanked by large round end cutouts, three open lower shelves over a scroll-cut short apron, original finish, ca. 1895, 15 x 42", 5' 4" h. (ILLUS.) **950**

Golden Oak Bookcase with Gallery

Victorian Golden Oak bookcase, oak, the superstructure w/a low top gallery w/a knob rail over a narrow shelf raised on baluster-turned front supports & a back panel divided into three beveled mirrors, the top over a case w/a pair of tall glazed doors w/downswept tops highlighted by tapering panels of carved scrolls, the bottom of each door w/matching carved panels, simple block feet on casters, adjustable wooden shelves, original finish, ca. 1900, 16 x 42", 6' h. (ILLUS.) **1,500**

Fine Oak Renaissance Bookcase

Victorian Renaissance Revival bookcase, oak, three-section, the rectangular top w/a wide cornice centered by a broken-scroll pediment w/large urn finial above the carved face of a classical woman flanked by wide leafy scrolls, all above a tall recessed center section backed by a tall beveled mirror & w/pierced scroll upper corner brackets flanked by slender colonettes, tall glazed doors at the sides flanked by larger reeded & knob-turned freestanding side columns above the stepped-out lower cabinet, the lower section w/a rectangular top w/a bowed center section over a stack of three paneled drawers w/pierced brass pulls flanked by narrow leaf-carved pilasters & large paneled side cupboard doors & wide leaf-carved pilasters topped by lion heads at the sides, refinished, ca. 1890, 24 x 72", 8' 4" h. (ILLUS.) **5,500**

One-door Renaissance Bookcase

Victorian Renaissance Revival bookcase, walnut, an arched & stepped cornice w/carved leaves, blocks & center roundel above a deep flaring blocked cornice over a single tall glazed door flanked by plain raised pilasters & raised side panels, the stepped-out base w/two small drawers over the deep flat molded base, adjustable wooden shelves, refinished, original pulls, ca. 1875, 18 x 32", 7' h. (ILLUS.) **1,800**

Handsome Renaissance Bookcase

Victorian Renaissance Revival bookcase, walnut & burl walnut, the top section w/a high broken-scroll pediment centered a platform w/an urn-form finial over triangular raised burl panels, a deep coved cornice above a pair of tall glazed doors w/rounded top corners flanked by slender quarter-round corner columns, the stepped-out lower section w/a pair of cupboard doors w/raised burl panels, deep molded base w/rounded corners, refinished, ca. 1875, 24 x 48", 8' 6" h. (ILLUS.) **3,000**

Large 'Breakfront" Walnut Bookcase

Victorian Renaissance Revival 'breakfront' bookcase, figured circassian walnut, the high stepped-out center section w/an arched crestrail centered by a carved cartouche above a frieze band of roundels over blocked corners above the tall rectangular glazed arched door above a narrow base drawer, the shorter side cabinets w/crestrails carved w/upright pierced leaf bands over a flaring cornice, each side w/a band of roundels above shorter matching glazed doors above a narrow base shelf, adjustable wooden shelves, deep molded base, ebonized wood pulls, refinished, ca. 1875, 20 x 88", 6' 6" h. (ILLUS., bottom previous page).. **5,500**

Extraordinary Rococo Bookcase

Victorian Rococo bookcase, carved rosewood, the top front w/a high pointed pierced leafy-scroll-carved crest over a wide arched molding above a fan-carving above a tall glazed door opening to four shelves, the angled top side moldings topped by four pointed finials over angled tall side panels each flanked by slender spiral-twist colonettes & framing a tall slender arched mirror below a scroll-carved top panel, deep stepped conforming base, possibly by J. & J. Meeks, New York, New York, ca. 1850s, 20 x 57", 8' 9 1/2" h. (ILLUS.) **20,125**

Simple Victorian Rococo Bookcase

Victorian Rococo bookcase, walnut, the rectangular top w/a low arched & ornately scroll-carved crestrail above a flared cornice over a pair of tall glazed arched doors separated by three tall slender incised oval bands, opening to adjustable wooden shelves, the stepped-out lower section w/a molded edge above a group of four drawers w/carved wooden fruit pulls, deep molded base, ca. 1865, refinished, 18 x 54", 7' 10" h. (ILLUS.) **2,500**

Bureaux Plat

Louis XV-Style Bureau Plat

Simple Louis XVI-Style Bureau Plat

Louis XV-Style bureau plat, mahogany, kingwood & parquetry, the shaped rectangular top w/an inset leather writing surface & ormolu banding above an apron w/three drawers each inset w/diamond pattern parquetry panels & fitted w/scrolling ormolu mounts, on cabriole legs headed by ormolu mounts & ending w/ormolu foot mounts, France, third quarter 19th c., 31 1/4 x 57 1/2", 32 3/4" h. (ILLUS., bottom previous page) **575**

Louis XVI-Style bureau plat, mahogany, the rectangular top w/a floral-carved edge above an apron fitted w/a central foliate-carved drawer flanked by plain drawers w/bail pulls, simple square fluted tapering legs, France, ca. 1900, 32 x 68", 30" h. (ILLUS., top of page) **2,185**

Napoleon III bureau plat, brass-inlaid ebonized wood, the serpentine rectangular top centered by elaborate brass inlay & brass edge banding above an apron fitted w/one end drawer & brass banding on the serpentine edges, on cabriole legs headed by large ormolu shields & scrolls & ending in feet w/ormolu mounts, France, third-quarter 19th c., 31 1/2 x 51 1/2", 30" h. (ILLUS., bottom of page) **2,530**

Brass-inlaid Napoleon III Bureau Plat

Cabinets

Delicate Art Nouveau Cabinet

China cabinet, Art Nouveau-influenced, mahogany & mahogany veneer, the narrow rectangular top w/an upright short superstructure w/narrow shelf flanked by pierced scroll-carved ears & raised on a slender center leg backed by a narrow beveled mirror, the top above a central tall curved glass door opening to a mirrored compartment above a lower open compartment w/delicate curved legs, the center cabinet flanked by two open shelves backed w/narrow vertical mirrors & supported by delicate incurved corner supports, the base supported on slender cabriole legs, original dark finish, ca. 1890s, 17 x 34", 5' h. (ILLUS.) **1,500**

Small Mirrored Art Nouveau Cabinet

China cabinet, Art Nouveau-influenced, mahogany, the superstructure w/an

arched crestrail w/scroll-carved crest over an arch-topped beveled mirror flanked by small shelf on slender serpentine supports backed by pierced scroll-brackets over a half-round top above a pair of curved glass doors opening to mirror-backed compartment raised on an S-scroll support over a lower half-round open shelf backed by a mirror, flat outswept base, refinished, ca. 1900, 16 x 22", 4' 10" h. (ILLUS.) **800**

Early Classical Rosewood Cabinet

China cabinet, Classical style, rosewood, two-part construction: the upper section w/a rectangular top w/a deep flaring coved cornice w/a beaded band above a pair of wide glazed doors flanked by freestanding columns & opening to wooded shelves; the stepped-out lower section w/a pair of deep drawers projecting over a pair of cupboard doors flanked by bold S-scrolls ending in paw feet on platforms, original hardware, refinished, ca. 1850s, 24 x 42", 6' 10" h. (ILLUS.) **1,500**

Nice Colonial Revival China Cabinet

China cabinet, Colonial Revival, mahogany & mahogany veneer, rectangular top above a veneered frieze band over a pair of wide glazed doors overlaid w/decorative scroll-cut fretwork, a medial band over the lower section w/a very long single drawer w/decorative veneer & butterfly brass pulls, serpentine scroll-carved apron raised on cabriole legs w/scrolled returns & claw-and-ball feet, original finish, ca. 1920s, 21 x 42", 6' h. (ILLUS.) **750**

Ebonized Colonial Revival Cabinet

China cabinet, Colonial Revival, mahogany w/ebonized finish, two-part construction: the upper section w/a rectangular top & pierced broken-scroll pediment over a frieze band carved w/lunettes over a pair of glazed doors w/applied geometric grillwork; the stepped-out lower section w/a rectangular top over two long serpentine-fronted florette-carved drawers all raised on slender square tapering legs joined by a curved cross-stretcher, original hardware, late 19th c., 20 x 38", 7' 4" h. (ILLUS.) **1,600**

French Provincial China Cabinet

China cabinet, French Provincial, mahogany & hardwood, the rectangular top above a narrow rectangular light wood inlaid band above the tall glass door w/an asymmetrical pane of glass over an asymmetrical light wood panel above two narrow base drawers w/shell-carved pulls flanked by light wood panels, serpentine apron on short scroll front legs, paneled sides, adjustable interior shelves, France, mid-19th c., original finish, 18 x 26", 6' h. (ILLUS.) **1,200**

Unusual Oriental China Cabinet

China cabinet, Oriental-style, inlaid mahogany, an ornate superstructure composed on one side w/a large upper cupboard w/a stepped pagoda-style top over a mother-of-pearl inlaid band above a glass cupboard door raised on slender spindles, the other side w/a smaller open compartment w/a pierced scroll crest & front spindles over a narrow inlaid drawer; the rectangular lower section top w/one end curled up & the other curled down, above an ornate arrangement of mother-of-pearl inlaid doors beside a stack of small carved drawers over a stepped small shelf & long bottom shelf all trimmed w/pierced scrolls, the narrow serpentine apron carved w/Oriental scrolls above short paw-footed legs, probably China, ca. 1880, original finish, 20 x 36", 6' h. (ILLUS.) **2,000**

Fine French Rococo China Cabinet

China cabinet, Rococo Revival style, bleached figured walnut veneer, the arched serpentine top w/a bold scroll-carved center crest over a conforming frieze band above a very wide serpentine-topped glazed door w/applied ornate scrollwork flanked by wide rounded corners, a lower gadrooned band over a wide bombe base band w/a wide drawer, ornate scroll-carved serpentine apron raised on scrolled cabriole legs, original finish, France, early 20th c., 20 x 36", 6' h. (ILLUS.) **3,600**

Ornately Carved Baroque Cabinet

China cabinet, Victorian Baroque Revival, carved oak, two-part construction: the upper section w/a rectangular top w/a high arched scroll-carved crest centered by a large cartouche over the flaring cornice above a frieze band of carved fruit & scrolls above the tall glazed door opening

to shelves & flanked by fruit-carved side drops; the stepped-out lower section w/a long fruit-carved drawer over a wide rectangular door boldly carved w/dead game & flanked by fruit-carved side bands, flaring carved base on compressed bun feet, original dark finish, probably Europe, late quarter 19th c., 20 x 36", 8' 8" h. (ILLUS.) .. **2,800**

Smaller Baroque Revival Cabinet

China cabinet, Victorian Baroque Revival, mahogany, a rectangular top w/a narrow cornice over a pair of tall paneled doors flanked by rounded & carved front corners raised on heavy incurved carved supports on blocks backed by a valanced backboard over a rectangular top above a pair of wide paneled cupboard doors, heavy front bun feet, replaced hardware, probably Europe, refinished, ca. 1900, 20 x 34", 5' h. (ILLUS.) **900**

Fancy Classical Revival Cabinet

China cabinet, Victorian Classical Revival style, quarter-sawn oak, the large half-round top w/blocked projecting front corners over carved lion heads, scrolls &

cartouche above tall columns flanking a tall curved glass door top by an ornately scroll-carved band, curved glass sides, mirrored interior back, molded base w/blocks over large paw feet, original dark finish, ca. 1895, 20 x 48" h., 6' h. (ILLUS.)... **4,800**

Large Colonial Revival Cabinet

China cabinet, Victorian Colonial Revival, mahogany, the half-round top w/a projecting center section w/an arched palmette & scroll-carved crest over a band scrolls above the wide arched glass door flanked by slender turned & reeded columns, curved glass sides, flaring molded base on short cabriole legs w/paw feet, original dark finish, ca. 1890, 19 x 56", 6' 3" h. (ILLUS.) **3,000**

Unusual Eastlake China Cabinet

China cabinet, Victorian Eastlake substyle, carved mahogany, the tall superstructure w/sawtooth crestrail over a short spindle band forming a canopy supported by turned spindles, the interior of the recess w/three carved panels over a rectangular mirror flanked by triangular pierced leaf-carved side brackets over small triangular shelves, the wide center section & side shelves w/short spindle rails, the flat center cabinet w/a large glazed cupboard door over a narrow drawer projecting over a low shelf w/a front spindle rail, the curved sides w/fan-carved top corner brackets above three open quarter-round shelves each w/a low spindle or lattice front rail, simple short curved legs, ca. 1880, 12 x 44", 6' 6" h. (ILLUS.) **2,300**

Ornate Eastlake China Cabinet

China cabinet, Victorian Eastlake substyle, walnut & burl walnut, the tall crestrail w/a flat dentil-carved center section above a narrow rectangular scroll-carved panel flanked by angled sides over a long narrow rectangular shelf over an arrangement of two stepped open shelves backed by a tall rectangular & narrow rectangular beveled mirrors, one side w/a tall door w/a row of three small square beveled glass panes over a tall beveled glass pane opening to adjustable shelves, the other side w/a shorter door w/a beveled glass pane, trimmed w/turned spindles & narrow burl panels, stepped & molded base on tiny bun feet, refinished, ca. 1880, 18 x 40", 6' h. (ILLUS.) **4,800**

Oak Cabinet with Fancy Top Shelf

China cabinet, Victorian Golden Oak style,
a high superstructure w/a low arched gadrooned crest on a top shelf raised on flat
S-scroll supports in front of a wide backboard w/scroll & leaf carving & rounded
reeded ends, the half-round top over a tall
flat glazed door above a long bow-fronted
base drawer flanked by curved glass
sides over plain lower panels, four wood-
en shelves, original hardware, carved paw
feet on casters, refinished, ca. 1900,
19 x 58", 6' 4" h. (ILLUS.)............................. **3,000**

High-crested Oak China Cabinet

China cabinet, Victorian Golden Oak style,
quarter-sawn oak, a high top back crest
w/an arched broken-scroll center a large
feather finial over delicate leafy scrolls,
the D-form top w/projecting blocks over
carved lion heads & scrolls atop columns

flanking the wide curved glass door,
curved glass sides, three wooden
shelves, molded base on two short cabriole legs w/paw feet & plain square back
legs, refinished, ca. 1900, 18 x 48", 6' h.
(ILLUS.) **2,800**

Large China Cabinet with Lions

China cabinet, Victorian Golden Oak style,
quarter-sawn own, the half-round case
w/a deep flaring cornice w/a central serpentine projection above a tall curved
glass door flanked by columns topped
by lion heads above paw feet, curved
glass sides, four wooden shelves, conforming shaped molded apron on heavy
paw feet, refinished, ca. 1900, 20 x 48",
6' h. (ILLUS.) **3,500**

European Rococo China Cabinet

China cabinet, Victorian Rococo substyle, carved beechwood, two-part construction: the upper section w/a high arched & scroll-carved pediment centered by a large carved cartouche above a flaring cornice over a wide scroll-carved frieze band above a pair of tall glazed doors w/arched serpentine tops flanked carved corner bands; the stepped-out lower section w/a rectangular molded edge overhanging a pair of leafy band-carved drawers over a pair of paneled cupboard doors boldly carved w/large clusters of fruits & vegetables, carved corner bands, paneled projecting front feet & molded flat base, original dark finish, Europe, ca. 1870, 22 x 45", 8' 6" h. (ILLUS.) **3,200**

Nice Rosewood Rococo Cabinet

China cabinet, Victorian Rococo substyle, carved rosewood, two-part construction: the upper section w/an arched broken-scroll pediment centered by an ornate pierced scroll crest above an arched beaded frieze band over a pair of tall glazed doors w/ornate scrolling grillwork opening to shelves; the projecting lower section w/a narrow white marble shelf over a pair of narrow long drawers w/leaf-carved pulls over a pair of paneled cupboard doors w/carved leaf sprigs in each corner & a central carved cartouche, deep scalloped & scroll-carved apron on short cabriole legs w/scroll feet on casters, New York City, ca. 1855, refinished, 22 x 42", 7' 6" h. (ILLUS.)............................ **4,800**

Pair of Colonial Revival Cabinets

China cabinets, Colonial Revival style, mahogany & mahogany veneer, each w/a rectangular top above a cornice w/dentil carving & carved spearpoints over a single tall glass door w/geometric applied grillwork opening to adjustable wooden shelves, a medial band over the bow-fronted base top & conforming case w/a single bowed door w/a panel of raised banding, molded base over a serpentine apron ending in French feet, original finish, ca. 1920s, 18 x 22", 6' 6" h., pr. (ILLUS.) **1,000**

Fine Irish Chippendale Cabinet

China corner cabinet, Chippendale, mahogany, the top w/a pierced broken-scroll pediment over a carved cornice above a pair of tall geometrically-glazed cupboard doors opening to shelves & surrounded by blind-fretwork carving & scroll-carved side panels, a medial rail above a pair of short geometrically-glazed doors also surrounded by carving, molded base on bracket feet, George III period, Ireland, last quarter 18th c., 21 x 43", 8' 1/2" h. (ILLUS.).. **11,500**

Unusual Rococo Corner Cabinet

China corner cabinet, Victorian Rococo substyle, rosewood, the superstructure composed of two wide quarter-round open shelve topped by a delicate pierced scroll-carved crest, each backed by low pierced-carved back rails & supported on pierced S-scroll front brackets & slender ring-turned spindles, the quarter-round top w/molded edge above a case small center drawer flanked by recessed panels over a pair of curved glass doors bordered w/ornate scroll carving & slender side colonettes, molded curved apron, lower interior in maple, original finish, ca. 1855, 20 x 36", 6' h. (ILLUS.).................................. **3,000**

Simple Oak Corner China Cupboard

China corner cupboard, Victorian Golden Oak style, a low scalloped crest on the flat top above a wide flat glass door opening to a mirrored interior w/three glass shelves, slightly shaped apron on simple cabriole front legs, refinished, ca. 1900, 18 x 28", 5' h. (ILLUS.).................................... **900**

Ornate Oak Corner China Cupboard

China corner cupboard, Victorian Golden Oak style, quarter-sawn oak, the high superstructure w/a pointed center scroll-carved crest flanked by low flat side crests over a narrow curved shelf supported by slender spindles, a central square mirror flanked by shaped beveled side mirrors & S-shaped scroll corners, the oblong top over a tall central flat door w/an upper panel enclosing an oval center surrounded by angled corners all in beveled glass above a plain tall glass panel, curved glass side panels, original finish, ca. 1900, 24 x 44", 6' h. (ILLUS.)..... **3,400**

Nice Victorian Dental Cabinet

Dental cabinet, Victorian Eastlake sub-style, mahogany, a low slightly arched & paneled top crest board on the rectangular top w/molded edges over a stack of three drawers beside a small square beveled glass door above a pair of tall beveled glass lower doors opening to two shelves, deep scalloped apron encloses base drawer, on blocked curved legs, paneled sides, original brass hardware, refinished, 14 x 22", 40" h. (ILLUS.) **1,400**

Rare Painted Dyer's Cabinet

Dyer's cabinet, painted & decorated wood, rectangular top above a case fitted w/four rows of four drawers each over a bottom row of three drawers, each drawer w/block letter stenciled dye color names, flat molded base, Pennsylvania, late 19th c., 16 1/2 x 44 1/2", 40 1/2" h. (ILLUS.) **6,463**

Very Large Oak Filing Cabinet

File cabinet, oak, a tall case w/a rectangular top above a top section composed of 15 narrow & small drawers over a section of 24 card file drawers over two sections each w/seven vertical wide file drawers

above a pair of long base drawers, original brass hardware, molded base, refinished, ca. 1900, 15 x 48", 6' h. (ILLUS.) **1,600**

Fancy Louis XV-Style Music Cabinet

Music cabinet, Louis XV-Style 'Vernis Martin' style, a rectangular top w/serpentine sides above the bombé cabinet w/a single wide door w/gilt-brass border band & center reserve enclosing a colorful romantic landscape scene, gilt-brass scroll front corner mounts above slender outswept legs, dark gold painted background, open to shelves, ca. 1910, 18 x 22", 34" h. (ILLUS.) **750**

Rococo Revival Music Cabinet

Music cabinet, Rococo Revival style, mahogany-finished wood, a serpentine low three-quarters gallery on the rectangular top above a pair of tall flat doors decorated w/gilt-metal borders & centered by a two-part h.p. romantic courting scene, base corner brackets above the simple tapering & slightly shaped legs, original finish, ca. 1900, 14 x 22', 38" h. (ILLUS.)...... **450**

Music cabinet, Victorian Golden Oak style, rectangular top w/narrow carved cornice above a pair of tall paneled doors centered by wreath-and-ribbon-carved decoration, side panels w/matching carving, wide curved apron raised on simple squared cabriole legs, interior w/shelves for records & cylinders, original finish, ca. 1900, 16 x 26", 36" h. (ILLUS.)...................... **600**

Country-style Pantry Cabinet

Fine Eastlake Music Cabinet

Music cabinet, Victorian Eastlake substyle, mahogany, a superstructure w/a low three-quarters gallery w/knob finials on the rectangular shelf supported by slender spiral-twist spindles & cutout sides above a rectangular beveled mirror over a rectangular top w/knob front finials over a single door w/line-incised bands & centered by a large round bronze plaque showing children playing musical instruments, ornate brass hinges, flat apron, small turned front legs, original finish, ca. 1880, 16 x 20", 4' h. (ILLUS.) **650**

Pantry cabinet, country-style, pine, a rectangular top above a square paneled door beside an arrangement of five drawers over a wide cylindrical-roll bin cover w/iron bin handle, narrow long drawer at the bottom w/small wood pulls, scalloped apron, refinished, second half 19th c., 18 x 24", 4' 6" h. (ILLUS.) **1,000**

Nice Golden Oak Music Cabinet

Golden Oak Sewing Cabinet

Sewing cabinet, Victorian Golden Oak style, a low spindled three-quarters gallery w/shaped crest on the rectangular top w/molded edges above a cast w/a pair of scroll-carved drawers over a pair of scroll-carved doors flanked by ropetwist side columns, machines often removed & case used for storage today, refinished, ca. 1900, 16 x 30", 35" h. (ILLUS.)........................ **550**

Louis XV-Style Inlaid Side Cabinet

Side cabinet, Louis XV-Style, inlaid mahogany, the rectangular red marble top w/tapering serpentine sides above a bombé case w/two long drawers inlaid w/a continuous design of leafy flowering vines, serpentine apron w/a gilt-brass scroll mount, gilt-brass corner mounts above the simple cabriole legs w/gilt-brass foot mounts, scrolled gilt-brass pulls, probably France, ca. 1920, original finish, 18 x 30", 30" h. (ILLUS.) **1,600**

Fancy Marble-top Inlaid Cabinet

Side cabinet, Victorian Renaissance Revival substyle, inlaid walnut & burl walnut, a rectangular top inset w/white marble above a raised section w/a single long drawer w/raised burl panels centered by a flower-inlaid center oval & flanked by raised corner blocks, all raised on four tapering turned & leaf-carved columns above the lower rectangular top over a long rectangular door w/a raised burl panel centered by a flower-inlaid cartouche panel & flanked by raised veneer side panels, flaring molded base on compressed ring-turned feet, original hardware, possibly by Herter, ca. 1875, 16 x 20", 30" h. (ILLUS.) **2,000**

Elaborate Renaissance Side Cabinet

Side cabinet, Victorian Renaissance Revival substyle, mahogany & marquetry inlay, the top w/a raised, stepped center rectangular platform on the top w/wide incurved sides above a conforming case, the flat front section w/a leaf-inlaid frieze above a large paneled door centered by an elaborate marquetry panel centered by a bow supporting a leafy swag w/trophies all framed by a wide band w/scrolls, the door flanked by carved & gilt-trimmed blocked pilasters, the concave side panels w/similar marquetry panels, the apron band w/incised geometric gilt bands, original finish, ca. 1875, 24 x 60", 4' h. (ILLUS., bottom previous page) **3,500**

Unique Folk Art Spice Cabinet

Spice cabinet, Victorian folk art-style, walnut & maple, the tall arched three-quarters gallery composed of ornately pierce-carved scrolls centered at the top by an oval maple inside w/pyrography initials, the rectangular top over a case w/a central scroll-pierced band over a tall pierced-carved rectangular door centered by a round maple plaque w/a pyrography scene of a young maiden & flowers above a narrow pierce-fronted drawer, each side w/a stack of four tin-lined drawers w/scroll-pierced fronts, each inset w/a narrow maple rectangular incised w/the name of a different spice, scalloped cutout bands down the front sides, all above a wide arched & ornately pierce-carved apron, original finish, ca. 1890, 5 x 21",. 27" h. (ILLUS.) **1,200**

Mission Oak Vice Cabinet

Vice cabinet, Mission-style (Arts & Crafts movement), oak, a rectangular top overhanging a case w/a thin pullout bar shelf inset w/hammered glass above a long narrow drawer over a pair of flat cupboard doors, square brass pulls, cleaned finish & hardware, branded mark of the Limbert Furniture Co., early 20th c., 19 x 31", 36" h. (ILLUS.) **2,300**

Inlaid Vitrine with Lower Shelf

Vitrine cabinet, Louis XV-Style, inlaid mahogany, the rectangular top w/serpentine edges above a conforming case w/floral-inlaid frieze bands, the wide curved glass door w/gilt-brass edging flanked by glass sides, curved apron w/floral inlay flanked by gilt-brass scroll mounts above the simple tall cabriole front legs joined by an open lower shelf to the square tapering rear legs, brass mounts on front feet, original finish, France, ca. 1900, 18 x 26", 5' 4" h. (ILLUS.)............................ **1,800**

Louis XV-Style Vitrine Cabinet

Vitrine cabinet, Louis XV-Style, mahogany, the half-round top w/a low gilt-brass gallery over a gilt-brass scroll band above a tall curved glass door w/gilt-brass edge trim, curved glass sides w/gilt-brass trim, serpentine front apron, simple cabriole legs w/gilt-brass mounts, two adjustable shelves, original shelves, France, ca. 1910, 18 x 24", 5' h. (ILLUS.) **950**

Wall cabinet, early American country-style, walnut & tiger stripe maple, a high arched & scroll-cut crest board pierced w/a hanging hole above a rectangular top over a roll-up tambour front w/two small brass knobs opening to a shelved interior above a single cockbeaded drawer w/small ring pulls & brass keyhole escutcheon, ca. 1820, 9 x 14", 22" h. (ILLUS., top next column) **1,200**

Early American Hanging Cupboard

Unusual Golden Oak Wall Cabinet

Wall cabinet, Victorian Golden Oak style, a rectangular top w/dentil- carved cornice & scalloped apron overhanging an open shelf w/a scroll-carved back panel above a pair of short rectangular glass doors opening to a mirror-backed compartment, a narrow recessed base shelf backed by a narrow scroll-carved panel above a serpentine, scroll-carved apron, deep shaped sides, refinished, ca. 1900, 12 x 30", 36" h. (ILLUS.) **1,000**

Chairs

Fine Baroque Revival Armchairs

Baroque Revival armchairs, oak, the square upholstered back w/arched crest above open S-scroll molded arms raised on baluster-and-block-turned supports flanking the wide upholstered seat, block-and-baluster-turned front legs w/disk feet joined by a high knob-turned stretcher, turned H-stretchers join all the legs, original finish, Europe, ca. 1900, 38" h., pr. (ILLUS.) **2,000**

scrolling legs on knob-carved rockers, Europe, late 19th c. (ILLUS.)...................... **4,500**

Italian Baroque Revival Side Chair

Ornately Carved Baroque Rocker

Baroque Revival rocking chair w/arms, oak, the tall back w/arched crest over ornately scrolling pierce-carved back flanked by square stiles w/knob finials, open arms resting on boldly carved winged sphinx arm supports on ornate

Baroque Revival side chairs, carved fruit wood, a rectangular upholstered back below scroll-carved finials, rectangular upholstered seat above a deep front seat rail carved w/ornate scrolls around a center cartouche, plain square legs, remnants of original upholstery, Italy, late 19th c., 36" h., pr. (ILLUS. of one)................. **400**

Stone-inlaid Chinese Side Chair

Chinese side chair, carved hardwood, the low rounded crestrail carved w/scrolls above a wide pierced scroll-carved lower rail centered by a round red soapstone insert above the rectangular seat inset w/soapstone, narrow pierce-carved apron between plain square legs joined by box stretchers, China, late 19th c., original finish, 36" h. (ILLUS.) **650**

Chippendale Revival corner chair, mahogany, the low U-form crestrail continues to flat arms over ornately pierce-carved sea serpent supports flanking a curved center upholstered back panel, upholstered seat on carved seat rail raised on three cabriole legs w/leaf-carved knees & bold paw feet, refinished, new upholstery, late 19th c., 34" h. (ILLUS., top next column) **850**

Chippendale Revival corner chair, mahogany, the low U-form crestrail curves to rounded hand grips, three columnar spindles alternating w/loop-pierced back splats, spring-upholstered seat, cabriole front leg ending in paw foot, square back

legs joined by two ring-turned & two plain stretchers, late 19th c., old needlepoint upholstery, refinished, 34" h. (ILLUS., bottom this column) **850**

Nicely Carved Corner Chair

Chippendale Revival Corner Chair

Finely Carved Chippendale Revival Dining Chairs

Chippendale Revival dining chairs, mahogany, a serpentine crestrail centered by a shell carving over a rounded hand grip over the vasiform splat centered by a large carved rayed diamond & a small pierced lower diamond, wide overupholstered spring seat on a serpentine gadroon-carved seat rail centered by a carved shell, cabriole legs w/a carved knee & claw-and-ball feet, original finish, late upholstery, late 19th c., 42" h., set of 6 (ILLUS., bottom previous page)............. **3,500**

Chippendale Revival Side Chair

Chippendale Revival side chair, mahogany, the oxyoke crest centered by a carved shell above the pierced vasiform splat, wide upholstered seat over a seat rail w/a small center drop, cabriole front legs ending in claw-and-ball feet, turned H-stretcher, ca. 1900, 38" h. (ILLUS.)............ **300**

Pair of Chippendale Revival Chairs

Chippendale Revival side chairs, walnut, an oxyoke crest rail centered by a carved shell above a solid scroll-cut back splat, wide upholstered seat on a seat rail w/a carved shell, cabriole front legs ending in claw-and-ball feet, refinished, ca. 1900, 40" h., pr. (ILLUS.).. **600**

Chippendale Revival Wing Chair

Chippendale Revival wing-back armchair, mahogany, the high upholstered back w/a serpentine crest flanked by serpentine upholstered wings over rolled upholstered arms, cushion seat over upholstered seat rail, cabriole front legs w/leaf-carved knees & claw-and-ball feet, probably original finish & upholstery, ca. 1930s, 4' h. (ILLUS.).. **400**

One of a Pair of Classical Armchairs

Classical armchairs, mahogany, a flat slightly curved crestrail raised on fanning leaf-carved brackets continuing to form a lower rail over long scrolled open arms, original horse hair-upholstered seat, on sabre legs, old refinish, ca. 1830, 30" h., pr. (ILLUS. of one) **1,000**

Classical Country Side Chair & Rocker

Classical country-style rocking chair w/arms, painted pine & maple, the tall back w/a wide flat crestrail w/rounded corners & traces of original stenciled decoration above a thin rail & wider rail over a rail of arrow slats, S-scroll arms over two arrow slats & canted turned arm support, wide rounded plank seat, canted turned front legs joined by a simple stretcher, carpet-cutter rockers, overall traces of original painted & stenciled decoration, ca. 1840s, 46" h. (ILLUS. right above with side chair)............................. **300**

stenciled fruit basket & scrolls above the wide shaped splat decorated w/gold stenciled leaf scrolls, caned seat, sabre front legs joined by a flattened arrow-style front stretcher, original caned seat, ca. 1830s, 34" h. (ILLUS.)..................... **350**

Classical country-style side chair, tiger stripe maple, the wide curved & rolled crestrail above a vasiform splat over a caned seat, front sabre legs joined by a flat curved stretcher, ca. 1840, 32" h. (ILLUS. left, top of page)................................. **200**

Nicely Decorated Classical Chair

Classical country-style side chair, painted & stenciled, the long curved crestrail w/rounded ends decorated w/original

Classical Dining Chair from a Set

Classical dining chairs, mahogany & mahogany veneer, a low rolled crest on the wide rounded crestrail continuing down to form shaped stiles flanking the vasiform splat, upholstered slip seat, sabre front legs, refinish, reupholstered, ca. 1840, 32" h., set of 8 (ILLUS. of one) **1,600**

Rare Classical Highchair

Classical highchair, mahogany & mahogany veneer, a serpentine crestrail w/rounded corners above a vasiform splat flanked by open scrolled arms joined by a protection bar, upholstered slip seat, raised on tall front sabre legs joined by a rounded footrest, refinished, new upholstery, ca. 1840, 40" h. (ILLUS.)...... **800**

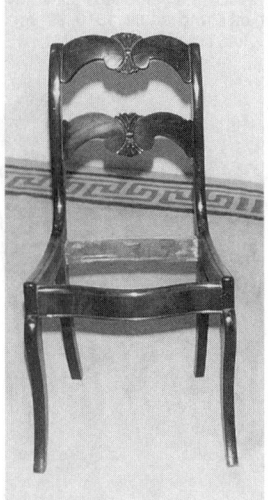

Classical Mahogany Side Chair

Classical side chairs, mahogany, two double-arched back rails centered by fan-carving above slip seats (not shown), front sabre legs between serpentine front

seat rail, original finish, ca. 1840s, 34" h., pr. (ILLUS. of one) **500**

Classical Revival Armchair

Classical Revival armchair, hardwood, wide squared back w/upholstered panel flanked by serpentine open arms on stylized carved dolphin arm supports, upholstered seat, square slightly curved front sabre legs, probably Europe, ca. 1910, 35" h. (ILLUS.)... **259**

Mahogany Transitional Side Chair

Classical-Victorian transitional side chairs, mahogany, an open balloon back w/triple-arch crestrail over incurved sides joined by a pierced double scroll splat, overupholstered seat on a serpentine seat rail on simple sabre front legs w/scroll feet, refinished, ca. 1845, 37" h., pr. (ILLUS. of one) **500**

Colonial Revival Chair from a Set

Colonial Revival dining chairs, oak, a wide serpentine crestrail carved leafy floral scrolls centered by a cartouche & w/carved lion head corner ears, zipper-carved stiles flanking the square upholstered back panel w/a scroll-carved lower rail, the wide upholstered spring seat on heavy cabriole front legs w/leafy scroll-carved knees & returns & ending in paw feet, simple H-stretcher, labeled by the Phoenix Furniture Co., Grand Rapids, Michigan, ca., original finish, ca. 1890s, 42" h., set of 12 (ILLUS. of one) **12,000**

Early American Maple Highchair

Early American country-style highchair, maple, the back w/three graduated flat slats between square stiles, simple rod

arms on baluster-turned arm supports continuing into the front legs, original woven rush seat, simple double stretchers on three sides, original finish, early 19th c., 40" h. (ILLUS.).. **300**

Decorated Country-style Rocker

Early American country-style rocking chair w/arms, painted & decorated, the wide flat crestrail w/rounded corners decorated w/fruit & floral stencil decor on black, five slender slightly curved spindles between straight tapering stiles, flattened S-scroll arms over an arrow slat & a canted baluster-turned arm supports, wide plank seat on ring-turned front legs joined by a stretcher, on rockers, original dark finish & decoration, ca. 1840s, 42" h. (ILLUS.)... **350**

Child's Decorated Federal Side Chair

Rare Set of Decorated Federal Side Chairs

Federal country-style side chair, child's, painted & decorated, a flat gently curved crestrail above a flat lower rail over the woven rush seat, ring-turned & tapering front legs w/button feet joined by a flat curved front stretcher, black ground decorated w/gold banding & gold floral stenciling on the lower rail, ca. 1830, 26" h. (ILLUS.).. **200**

Federal country-style side chairs, painted & decorated, a wide flat crestrail painted w/a stylized leaf & diamond design in green & red, backswept tapering stiles flanking three curved arrow slats above the rounded plank seat, canted & lightly turned front legs joined by an arrow front stretcher, creamy yellow ground w/further green sprig & band trim, New England, early 19th c., 32 1/2" h., set of 6 (ILLUS., top of page) **16,450**

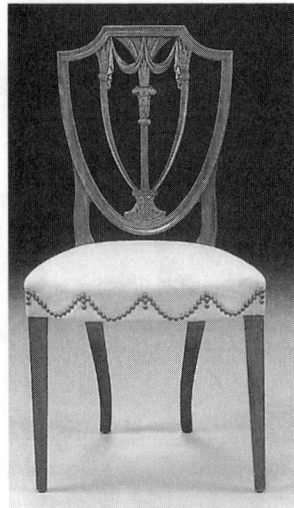

Rare Federal Side Chair

Federal side chair, carved mahogany, the shield back centered by carved swags over three slender slats, wide over-upholstered seat, squared tapering front legs, attributed to Samuel McIntire, Salem, Massachusetts, 1790-1810, 38" h. (ILLUS.) **10,575**

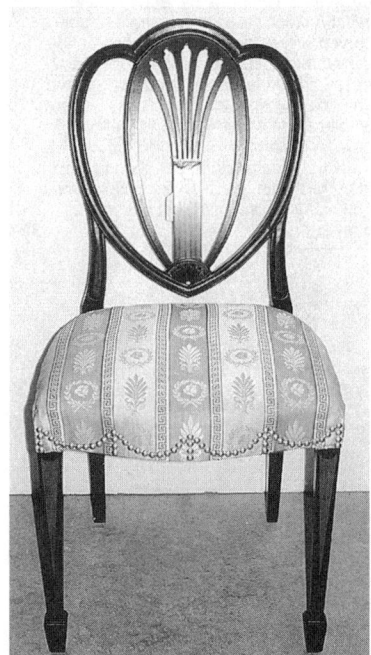

Nice Federal Revival Side Chair

Federal Revival side chair, inlaid mahogany, rounded shield-back w/fanned & pierced center slat inlaid w/light bands, wide over-upholstered seat on square tapering front legs ending in spade feet & inlaid w/long triangular panels, refinished, early 20th c., 36" h. (ILLUS.).............. **275**

Federal Revival Wing Chair

Federal Revival wingchair, mahogany, the tall upholstered back w/a curved crest above flaring rounded & tapering upholstered side wings continuing to closed upholstered arms ending in scroll-carved hand holds on tapering reeded arm supports, cushion seat above a curved reeded seatrail, round tapering reeded front legs, refinished, new upholstery, ca. 1920s, 45" h. (ILLUS.) **350**

Fine Karpen Jacobean Revival Chair

Jacobean Revival armchair, carved oak, the tall ornately carved back w/a wide pierce-carved crestrail featuring a pair of putti flanking an eagle surrounded by scrolls, the barley-twist stiles topped by knob finials, long scroll-ended padded open arms raised on barley-twist arm supports over the wide upholstered seat, narrow diamond-carved seatrail on barley-twist front legs joined by a w/pierce-carved stretcher matching the crest rail,

knob feet, barley-twist stretchers & rear legs, original label of the Karpen Furniture co., Chicago, ca. 1890s, 4' h. (ILLUS.) **800**

Figural-carved Jacobean-type Chair

Jacobean Revival armchair, carved oak, the wide arched & pierce-carved crestrail composed of a pair of mermaids flanking a center shield above turned columnar stiles flanking the arched wide center splat centered by an upholstered panel surrounded by ornate scroll carving, shaped open arms on tall S-scroll carved arm supports above the upholstered seat, heavily carved angled front legs w/carved nude figures over scrolls joined by a wide pierce-carved front stretcher w/scrolls flanking a pair of putti flanking a basket of flowers, original dark finish, old but not original upholstery, ca. 1890s, 4' 2" h. (ILLUS.) **700**

Fancy Carved Late Victorian Chair

Louis XV Revival Giltwood Side Chairs

Late Victorian armchair, oak, the wide arched & rounded crestrail carved to resemble a large shell w/scroll trim above a short vasiform splat w/carved scrolls & a pierced center opening, shaped arms on three canted slender ropetwist spindles & a matching larger arm support, wide shaped seat on canted ropetwist legs on ball feet & joined by double ropetwist stretchers, ca. 1890, 34" h. (ILLUS.)............. **350**

Louis XV Revival side chairs, giltwood, the caned balloon back w/a pierced scroll-carved crest & a pierced scroll-carved lower rail, wide over-upholstered seat w/a serpentine scroll-carved seat rail continuing to cabriole front legs w/carved knees & scroll feet w/pegs, France, early 20th c., 36" h., pr. (ILLUS., top of page) **450**

Louis XV Revival wing chair, mahogany, the high tufted upholstered back w/an arched crestrail w/a pierced scroll crest flanked by serpentine flaring side wings separated from the back by narrow pierce-carved wood panels, slightly rolled upholstered arms flank the cushion seat, serpentine scroll-carved seatrail centered by a carved shell, cabriole front legs w/carved knees & ending in scroll feet on pegs, original upholstery & finish, ca. 1920s, 4' h. (ILLUS.)...................... **600**

Mission-style (Arts & Crafts movement) armchair & rocking chair w/arms, oak, curved crestrail over six vertical back slats, shaped open arms, corbel supports, offset front, back & side stretchers, spring cushion seats, mortise & tenon joinery, medium brown finish, unsigned, early 20th c., armchair 35 1/4" h., pr............. **489**

Carved Louis XV Revival Chair

Rare Gustav Stickley 'Morris' Chair

Mission-style (Arts & Crafts movement) 'Morris' armchair, oak, the tall adjustable back composed of horizontal slats between wide flat & slight angled arms over multiple small square spindles, cushion seat w/missing back cushion, Gustav Stickley, early 20th c. (ILLUS.).... **37,375**

Rare L. & J.G. Stickley 'Morris' Chair

Mission-style (Arts & Crafts movement) 'Morris' armchair, oak, the tall adjustable back composed of horizontal slats, wide gently arched flat arms above four slats on each side over a deep apron, front arms w/corbels, slightly arched front seatrail, Model No. 406, L. & J. G. Stickley, early 20th c. (ILLUS.) **23,000**

L. & J. G. Stickley Rocking Chair

Mission-style (Arts & Crafts movement) rocking chair w/arms, oak, the high back composed of horizontal slats above wide flat & slightly arched arms over four wide slats on each side, corbels under the front arms, gently arched front seat rail, leather-covered back & seat pads, Model No. 427, L. & J. G. Stickley, early 20th c. (ILLUS.) **5,750**

Modern Bertoia "Diamond" Chair

Modern style armchair, upholstered steel "Diamond" chair, elongated diamond-shaped upholstered seat raised on a slender steel framework, designed by Harry Bertoia, Model No. 422 LU, manufactured by Knoll Associates, original blue upholstery & paper label, ca. 1955, 44 3/4" w., 28" h. (ILLUS.) **460**

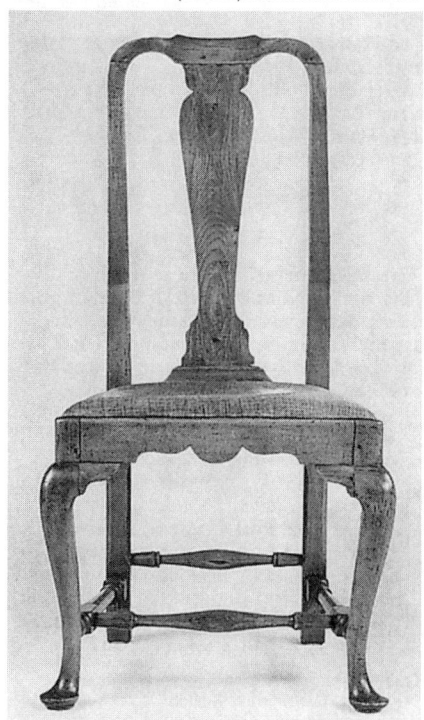

Queen Anne Maple Side Chair

Queen Anne side chair, maple, the yoked crest over a vasiform solid splat & molded shoe flanked by raked & chamfered stiles & a trapezoidal slip seat, scalloped front apron above cabriole front legs ending in pad feet, swelled & block-turned stretchers, old refinish, Massachusetts, ca. 1740-60, 41" h. (ILLUS.) **4,313**

Queen Anne Revival Dining Chairs

Fine Queen Anne Walnut Side Chair

Queen Anne side chair, walnut, shaped crestrail over a solid vasiform splat over an upholstered balloon-shaped seat above a shaped seatrail, cabriole front legs ending in padded disk front legs, blocked-and turned stretchers, Massachusetts or Rhode Island, 1740-60, 40 1/2" h. (ILLUS.) **9,400**

Queen Anne Revival dining chairs, quarter-sawn oak, shaped & rounded crestrail above a solid wide vasiform splat, trapezoidal slip seat above cabriole front legs ending in paw feet, square H-stretchers, refinished, ca. 1910, nine side chairs &

one armchair, 40" h., set of 10 (ILLUS., top of page)... **2,750**

Golden Oak Fancy Platform Rocker

Victorian Golden Oak platform rocking chair w/arms, oak, the wide arched crestrail carved w/leafy scrolls above a fanned cluster of bobbin-turned spindles above a pierced looping scroll lower rail, ring-and-block-turned stiles w/oval finials, shaped arms on incurved arm supports over the original needlepoint seat, platform rocker base, refinished, ca. 1895, 42" h. (ILLUS.).. **350**

Pair of Gothic Revival Side Chairs

Victorian Gothic Revival side chairs, walnut, a high pierced & scroll-carved Gothic arch crestrail topped by a spire-form finial flanked by tall molded stiles w/spire finials flanking the arched upholstered back panel, short scroll-carved skirt guards on the wide rounded seat w/a line-incised seatrail raised on ring-and-rod-turned front legs, third quarter 19th c., 45" h., pr. (ILLUS., above) **748**

Spiral-twist Victorian Novelty Chairs

Victorian novelty chairs, mahogany, two armchairs, one w/two horizontal bamboo-turned back rails forming two sections, the top section w/four spiral-twist spindles & the lower section w/six spiral-twist spindles, tall spiral-twist stiles topped w/brass ball finials, spiral twist open arms w/knob ends on spiral-twist arm supports above the wide squared seat w/a spiral-twist border, on canted spiral-twist legs joined by a spiral-twist H-stretcher; the other of similar construction but w/an angled & flat bamboo-turned rail from the top of the back stiles to shorter stiles w/brass ball finials, two small spiral-twist spindles between these rails, the front legs w/brass claw feet holding glass balls, original dark finish, ca. 1885, 38" h., the pair (ILLUS.) **1,000**

Rosewood Renaissance Armchair

Victorian Renaissance Revival armchair,
carved rosewood, an arched crestrail
carved w/a scroll-carved cartouche crest
flanked by columnar stiles w/disk finials
flanking the tall arched upholstered back
panel, padded open arms on ring-turned
arm supports over the deep spring-cush-
ion seat, curved seat rail w/scroll-carved
drop, turned inverted trumpet-form front
legs on casters, old refinish, newer
upholstery, ca. 1870, 44" h. (ILLUS.)......... **1,000**

**Victorian Renaissance Revival child's
highchair-stroller,** oak, the rounded
crestrail w/applied carved scrolls above
the caned back flanked by a hinged lift-up
feeding tray & low shaped arms over the
seat w/board replacing original caning, a
curved front footrest & turned spindles
above the four hinged outswept legs on
metal wheels w/lower to form a
stroller, ca. 1880, overall 42" h., as is
(ILLUS., top, next column)............................. **350**

**Victorian Renaissance Revival corner
chair,** mahogany, U-form crestrail w/a
raised center section carved w/scrolls,
rail continues to form rounded, molded

arms raised on three ring-and-knob-
turned spindles alternating w/scalloped
leaf-and-scroll-carved splats, rounded
seat w/original leather insert, on four ring-
and-knob-turned tapering legs, original
finish, ca. 1880s, 32" h. (ILLUS., bottom,
this column)... **450**

Renaissance Highchair-Stroller

Renaissance Revival Corner Chair

Ornate European Renaissance Revival Dining Chairs

Renaissance Revival Dining Chairs with Padded Crests

Victorian Renaissance Revival dining chairs, fruitwood, an arched & scroll-carved crest on the crestrail molding above a large ornate scroll-cut splat centered by a carved medallion, the carved stiles decorated at the outside edge w/the head & leg of a beast, trapezoidal possibly original leather seats, seatrail w/incised carving above the turned tapering trumpet-form front legs, original finish, Europe, ca. 1875, 38" h., set of 12 (ILLUS. of part, bottom, previous page) **3,600**

Victorian Renaissance Revival dining chairs, walnut, a short ring-and-block-turned crestrail rail above the squared back w/an upholstered crest w/a curved lower rail joined to a lower rail by a carved roundel splat, straight burl-paneled stiles w/carved detail, over-upholstered seat on a burled seatrail w/two small knob drops, block-and-ring-turned front legs on casters joined by a ring-turned front stretcher, ca. 1870s, original finish, later upholstery, 34" h., set of 4 (ILLUS., top of page) **1,000**

Quality Renaissance Side Chair
1855, original finish, new upholstery,

Victorian Renaissance Revival side chair, walnut, the gently arched & molded crestrail w/scroll-carved corners above a pierced back composed of large loops centered by a large palmette design, the incised stiles flanked by long S-form skirt guards flanking the rounded over-upholstered seat on a molded seatrail, tapering ring-and-rod-turned front legs on casters, old upholstery, refinished, ca. 1875, 36" h. (ILLUS.)............. **350**

Meeks Hartford Pattern Armchair

Victorian Rococo substyle armchair, carved & laminated rosewood, the large balloon-back w/a wide arched pierce-carved frame w/an arched crest centering a carved leaf cluster flanked by ornate scrolling continuing down to frame the arched upholstered back panel, serpentine padded open arms on incurved molded arm supports above the wide upholstered seat on a scroll-and-leaf-carved serpentine seatrail continuing to demi-cabriole front legs, Hartford patt. by J. & J. Meeks, New York, New York, ca. 44" h. (ILLUS.).. **4,800**

A Rose Pattern Rosewood Armchair

Belter Rosalie Pattern Armchair

Victorian Rococo substyle armchair, carved & laminated rosewood, the oval upholstered back within a molded frame w/a high pierced scroll-carved crest centered by a rose blossom, open padded arms on incurved molded arm supports over the wide rounded upholstered seat w/a serpentine seatrail above demi-cabriole front legs on casters, A Rose patt., possibly by George Henkels, Philadelphia, refinished, ca. 1855, 44" h. (ILLUS.) **3,500**

Victorian Rococo substyle armchair, carved & laminated rosewood, the tall balloon-form back w/a floral-carved arched crestrail continuing down to form the frame enclosing the upholstered back panel, serpentine open arms on incurved arm supports above the wide upholstered seat w/a serpentine seatrail continuing to demi-cabriole front legs on caster, Rosalie patt. by John H. Belter, New York, New York, ca. 1855, 40" h. (ILLUS.) **3,000**

Nice Mahogany Rococo Armchairs

Victorian Rococo substyle armchairs, carved mahogany, the tall tapering balloon-form back w/a pierced scroll-carved crest on the molded back rail enclosing the tufted upholstered back panels, serpentine padded open arms on heavy scrolled arm supports above the wide upholstered seat w/a serpentine seatrail carved w/scrolls & continuing into scroll-carved demi-cabriole front legs on casters, original finish, old upholstery, ca. 1860, 46" h., pr. (ILLUS., bottom previous page).. **1,700**

Partial Set of Rococo Dining Chairs

Victorian Rococo substyle dining chairs, chestnut, balloon-back w/molded rail enclosing a pierced splat composed of rings & scrolls above curved skirt guards flanking the seats w/original horsehair upholstery & serpentine seatrails continuing to cabriole front legs on casters, original finish, ca. 1865, one arm & seven side chairs, 36" h., set of 8 (ILLUS. of part) **3,600**

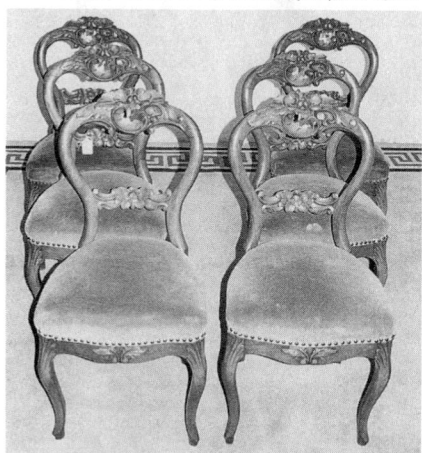

Victorian Rococo Dining Chairs

Victorian Rococo substyle dining chairs, walnut, the balloon-back w/a pierced scroll-carved crestrail above a scroll-carved lower rail, over-upholstered seat w/serpentine leaf-carved seatrail on simple cabriole front legs, old refinish, later upholstery, ca. 1860, 32" h., set of 6 (ILLUS.)... **1,500**

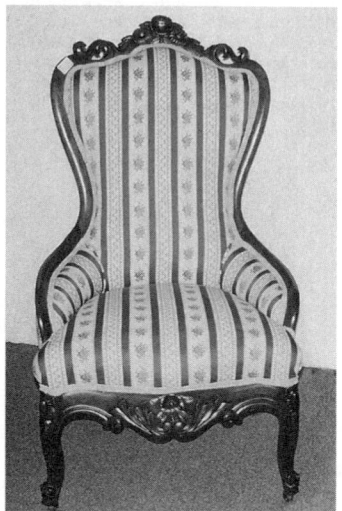

Nice Rococo Lady's Parlor Chair

Victorian Rococo substyle lady's parlor chair, walnut, tall back w/a pierced serpentine crestrail centered by carved flowers, incurved sides continuing to low arms flanking the upholstered back, wide upholstered seat w/serpentine seatrail w/carved scrolls, demi-cabriole front legs on casters, ca. 1860, refinished, new upholstery, 42" h. (ILLUS.).................................. **500**

Unique Early Rococo Recliner

Victorian Rococo substyle reclining armchair, carved walnut, the tall balloon-back w/a pierced scroll-carved crest w/the rail continuing to scroll-carved projections above the padded shaped arms w/eagle head-carved hand grips over incurved supports, wide seat w/serpentine seatrail w/a unique scroll-carved pullout foot rest on short turned legs, short turned front legs on main frame w/carved knees, the tall back jointed to tilt backward, original wooden casters, new leather upholstery, attributed to George Henkels of Philadelphia, ca. 1860, 46" h. (ILLUS.).. **1,800**

of scrolls centered by a carved grape cluster, round needlepoint seat w/a scroll-carved apron above simple molded cabriole front legs, original finish, ca. 1855, attributed to J. & J. Meeks, New York City, 36" h. (ILLUS.) **1,800**

William & Mary Revival Wing Chair

William & Mary Revival wing chair, mahogany & pine, the tall arched upholstered back flanked by shaped upholstered wings above the rolled upholstered arms flanking the cushion seat over a serpentine upholstered seatrail, on cabriole front legs ending in hoof feet & joined by an arched pierced scroll-carved stretcher, late 19th - early 20th c., 4' 3" h. (ILLUS.).............................. **2,500**

Grape & Scroll-carved Side Chair

Victorian Rococo substyle side chair, carved & laminated rosewood, the tall serpentine pierced & carved balloon back w/a floral-carved crest over bands

Two early Windsor Child's Chairs

Early Grain-painted Blanket Chest

Windsor child's "continuous-arm" rocker, painted hardwood, the slender bowed crestrail continues down to flat arms, nine bamboo-turned back spindles & two spindles & a canted arm support under arms, wide shaped seat on heavy bamboo-turned canted legs joined by a swelled H-stretcher, inset carpet-cutter rockers, original black paint, early 19th c., 32" h. (ILLUS. right, bottom previoius page) 500

Windsor child's "step-down" side chair, painted hardwood, the narrow stepped crestrail above six slender curved spindles flanked by curved stiles above the wide shaped seat, canted turned legs joined by box stretchers, old refinish, early 19th c., 24" h. (ILLUS. left with rocker, previous page) 300

Early Windsor "Low-back" Armchair

Windsor "low-back" armchair, painted hardwood, the U-form crestrail w/a thick center crest continuing to form flat arms w/carved hand grips above numerous simple spindles & canted baluster- and ring-turned arm supports, wide shaped saddle seat on canted baluster- and ring-

turned legs joined by a swelled H-stretcher, old repaint, early 19th c., 32" h. (ILLUS.) 500

Chests & Chests of Drawers

Blanket chest, country-style, painted & decorated pine, rectangular hinged top w/molded edges opening to a deep well, molded base on turned double-knob bun feet, original grain-painted surface, brass keyhole escutcheon & original lock, ca. 1840, 18 x 38", 22" h. (ILLUS., top of page) 400

Blanket chest, poplar, applied molding around the top, dovetailed bracket base w/scalloping across the front & semi-curved cutouts on end aprons, w/interior till & lock w/diamond-shaped escutcheon inlay, original black on red decoration w/old alligatored coat of overvarnish, 18 1/4 x 37 1/2", 20" h. (wear, some chips, areas of touch up) 935

Blanket chest, poplar, dovetailed construction, two drawers at bottom, till w/lid, turned feet, w/original red & brown flame graining w/black striping & gold stenciled initials "L [heart] W - 1861," backboards are stenciled "PJS," Ohio (old overvarnish, minor surface damage) 15,400

Mahogany Chippendale Chest

Chippendale chest of drawers, mahogany, the rectangular top w/molded edges above a case w/four long graduated cock-beaded drawers w/simple bail handles & oval brass keyhole escutcheons, molded base on short cabriole legs w/claw-and-ball feet & scroll-cut returns, Massachusetts, ca. 1770-1800, 19 1/2 x 37 1/4", 35 1/2" h. (ILLUS.) **4,700**

Chippendale chest of drawers, walnut, two-board top w/applied trim molding, five dovetailed drawers (two small side-by-side drawers over three full-length drawers) w/molded trim & figured fronts w/full dust shelves & replaced brasses, scalloped ogee feet w/molded base, internal locks present on three bottom drawers, Pennsylvania, 19 3/4 x 40", 38 7/8" h. (internal locks for top two drawers missing, pieced restorations) **3,025**

Chippendale Country-style Chest

Chippendale tall chest of drawers, maple, dovetailed case w/cove molded cornice, five dovetailed drawers w/replaced batwing brasses & beaded edges, the top drawer w/carved fan at center & three false fronts, second drawer w/two false fronts, molded base w/shaped returns & bracket feet, 21 1/8 x 39 3/4", 58 1/2" h. (restorations to drawer lips & runners, feet replaced)... **7,700**

Chippendale Chest-on-Chest

Chippendale chest-on-chest, mahogany & mahogany veneer, two-part construction: the top section w/a rectangular top & flaring cornice above a border of crotch-grained mahogany veneer around a pair of drawers over three long graduated drawers; the lower section w/a mid-molding over a crotch-grain veneer band above three long graduated drawers, molded base on ogee bracket feet, old but no original brasses, refinished, ca. 1780, 20 x 38", 6' 4" h. (ILLUS.) **2,400**

Chippendale country-style chest of drawers, figured maple, rectangular top w/molded edges overhanging a case w/four long graduated thumb-molded drawers w/replaced butterfly brasses & keyhole escutcheons, molded base on scroll-cut bracket feet, refinished, second half 18th c., 22 x 38", 34" h. (ILLUS., top of next column) **1,800**

Fine Classical Butler's Chest

Classical butler's chest of drawers, mahogany & mahogany veneer, the rectangular top over florette-carved corner blocks flanking two long narrow round-fronted drawers projecting over a case w/a long central false drawer folding down to form a writing surface & small interior drawers above a pair of tall paneled doors, a stack of three small tall drawers down each side flanked by heavy turned side columns, flat apron on heavy acanthus leaf-carved paw feet on casters, refinished, ca. 1830s, 20 x 40", 44" h. (ILLUS.) **1,800**

Ornately Carved Classical Chest

Classical chest of drawers, mahogany & mahogany veneer, a long narrow rectangular mirror raised & swiveling between ornately carved scrolling uprights composed of a large scrolling dolphin above a boldly scrolling cornucopia all raised on a row of three small handkerchief drawers across the rectangular top over a long round-fronted drawer projecting above three long drawers flanked by boldly carved baluster-form acanthus leaf-carved columns, flat apron raised on scroll-carved paw front feet, original finish, replaced brass hardware, ca. 1840, 22 x 44", 5' 10" h. (ILLUS.) **2,400**

Classical Chest with Large Mirror

Classical chest of drawers, mahogany & mahogany veneer, the superstructure w/a two rectangular mirror in a wide ogee frame topped by a pointed scroll crestrail & swiveling between S-scroll uprights on short columns above a pair of handkerchief drawers on the rectangular top above double-tier apron w/a long narrow drawer in the lower tier projecting over the case w/three long graduated drawers all w/crotch-grain veneering, rounded front corners, flat base on tapering ring-turned front feet, wooden pulls, refinished, ca. 1840, 21 x 44", overall 7' 4" h. (ILLUS.) **1,000**

Grain-painted Butler's Chest

Classical country-style butler's chest of drawers, grain-painted pine, rectangular top over a wide band divided into an arrangement of false drawers & a small door flanked by carved scrolls all folding down to expose a pullout writing surface & interior storage, the lower case w/three long drawers, scroll-carved brackets at the top corners of the front, decorated overall w/bold grain painting simulating crotch-grain rosewood, simple bracket feet, original hardware & ivory pulls on interior, ca. 1850, 16 x 38", 42" h. (ILLUS.) **1,000**

Country Classical Cherry Chest

Classical country-style chest of drawers, cherry, a rectangular top above a long drawer slightly projecting over a case of three long graduated drawers flanked by rope-twist-turned columns, flat base on tapering knob-turned front legs, replaced glass pulls, old refinish, ca. 1840s, 20 x 42", 40" h. (ILLUS.) **650**

Unusual Grained Classical Chest

Classical country-style chest of drawers, grain-painted pine, a high ornate scroll-carved crestrail centered by silhouetted lovebirds above a small chest w/a rectangular top over two long round-fronted drawers flanked by knob-turned columns & on knob feet atop the rectangular chest top over a projecting long narrow drawer above three long drawers flanked by heavy columns each w/a spiral-turned knob over a plain knob on blocks flanking the flat apron, raised on turned tapering bulbous front legs, overall original grain painting, brass bail pulls, ca. 1850, 20 x 42", 5' 4" h. (ILLUS.) **1,200**

Mahogany & Cherry Classical Chest

Classical country-style chest of drawers, mahogany & cherry, the rectangular top over a long deep projecting drawer above three long graduated drawers flanked by ring-and-spiral-turned tapering columns, flat apron on tapering bulbous knob feet, simple wooden pulls, paneled sides, original finish, ca. 1845, 18 x 40", 4' h. (ILLUS.) **750**

Classical Country Mahogany Chest

Classical country-style chest of drawers, mahogany & mahogany veneer, the rectangular top over an upper projecting section w/a pair of narrow drawers over a deep long drawer above a lower stack of three long graduated drawers flanked by ring-and-knob-turned columns, flat apron on ring-and-knob-turned legs, old pressed glass pulls, original dark finish, ca. 1840s, 20 x 40", 4' h. (ILLUS.) **750**

Striped Maple & Mahogany Chest

Classical country-style chest of drawers, tiger stripe maple & mahogany, a rectangular top over a deep long projecting drawer w/tiger stripe maple framed by mahogany veneer banding, the lower case w/three long graduated tiger stripe maple drawers flanked by spiraling acanthus leaf-carved columns, flat apron on leaf-carved paw front feet, replaced hardware, refinished, ca. 1840, 22 x 44", 4' h. (ILLUS.)... **900**

Walnut Country Classical Chest

Classical country-style chest of drawers, walnut, a wide peaked crestrail on the rectangular top over a projecting arrangement of two small drawers over a single long drawer all above three long graduated drawers flanked by ring-turned & leaf-carved columns, flat apron on turned tapering bulbous front feet on casters, old refinish, replaced hardware, ca. 1850, 20 x 40", 4' 4" h. (ILLUS.).............................. **750**

Tall Country Pine Chest of Drawers

Country-style chest of drawers, pine, rectangular top on a tall case w/a long deep drawer over four shorter drawers above the long bottom drawer, scalloped apron w/bracket feet, dovetailed & square nail construction, original cast-iron pulls, second half 19th c., 18 x 34", 46" h. (ILLUS.)................................. **500**

Federal 'Bow-front' Chest of Drawers

Federal 'bow-front' chest of drawers, birch, figured maple & mahogany veneer, the scroll-cut crestrail above the rectangular top w/ovolo front corners over baluster-and-ring-turned reeded columns flanking the case w/four long bow-front drawers w/crotch-grain mahogany veneer, baluster-and-ring-turned legs w/knob feet, refinished, replaced hardware, ca. 1830, 22 x 42", 4' h. (ILLUS.).................................. **1,200**

Quality Federal Mahogany Chest

Federal chest of drawers, inlaid mahogany, the rectangular top above four long graduated drawers, the top one w/two oval inlays & leaf spring corner inlays & banding, an inlaid shield-shaped keyhole escutcheon, the three lower drawers w/leaf-sprig & banded inlay, quarter-round reeded corner columns, molded base on scroll-cut bracket feet w/some damage, original dark finish & oval brass pulls, early 19th c., 21 x 44", 36" h. (ILLUS.).................. **3,500**

Federal Chest with Carved Basket

Federal chest of drawers, mahogany & mahogany veneer, the scroll-cut crestrail decorated w/a relief-carved basket of fruit above the rectangular top w/ovolo front corners over ring-and-spiral-turned front corner columns flanking four long graduated drawers w/crotch-grain veneering, scalloped apron, baluster-and-ring-turned legs on peg feet, original brass pulls, original finish, ca. 1815-20, Boston or Salem, Massachusetts, 22 x 46", 4' h. (ILLUS.) **2,500**

Mahogany Federal Chest of Drawers

Federal chest of drawers, mahogany, rectangular top w/four ovolo corners over reeded corner columns, the case w/four long graduated drawers w/probably original oval brass pulls & keyhole escutcheons, baluster-and-ring-turned legs w/peg feet, refinished, ca. 1820s, 20 x 42", 40" h. (ILLUS.) **1,200**

Federal Bucks County Walnut Chest

Federal chest of drawers, walnut, rectangular top w/molded edges above a case w/four long graduated cock-beaded drawers w/simple bail pulls & brass keyhole escutcheons flanked by chamfered front corners, serpentine apron on tall French feet, Bucks County, Pennsylvania, original finish & hardware, early 19th c., 20 x 36", 40" h. (ILLUS.)............. **1,800-2,000**

Federal tall chest of drawers, walnut, six dovetailed drawers situated two over four, graduated, w/applied beading & turned walnut knobs, angled bracket feet w/inlaid fan drop on lower front, a band of inlay around base & top, attributed to Ohio, 20 1/2 x 38 3/4", 55 1/4" h. (some beaded trim replaced, some rodent damage, minor restorations)................................ **1,980**

Louis XV-Style Bombé Chest

Louis XV-Style chest of drawers, banded rosewood & oyster-shell veneer, the rectangular top w/serpentine edges above a bombé case w/three long drawers fitted w/scroll-cast ormolu mounts, the serpentine sides w/ormolu mounts, the serpentine front apron w/a long scrolling ormolu mount, flared legs w/ormolu mounts on the feet, original finish, France, second half 19th c., 16 x 28", 30" h. (ILLUS.)......... **2,500**

Rare Gustav Stickley Chest

Mission-style (Arts & Crafts movement) chest of drawers, a low slightly peaked crestrail on the rectangular top w/through-tenon front stiles flanking a pair of small drawers over four long graduated drawers, paneled sides, original copper plate & bail pulls, signed by Gustav Stickley, early 20th c. (ILLUS.).... **36,800**

Rare Herter Aesthetic Chest

Victorian Aesthetic Movement chest of drawers, inlaid mahogany, a tall rectangular upright beveled mirror w/a sunflower-and-leaf-carved crest on the reeded framework w/knob finials flanked by short

square beveled mirrors on the rectangular top w/reeded edges & front stiles, the case w/four long graduated drawers, the top & bottom drawers w/delicate sunflower inlay, simple brass bail pulls, flat molded apron, attributed to Herter Brothers, New York City, ca. 1880s, 22 x 48 1/2", 6' 2" h. (ILLUS.)... **11,163**

Short Aesthetic Movement Chest

Victorian Aesthetic Movement chest of drawers, mahogany, the rectangular top w/flaring molded edges above two small drawers beside a large square scroll-carved door all slightly projecting over three long reverse-graduated drawers, the bottom drawer carved w/a lappet band, reeded lower side stiles, molded base, paneled sides, original dark finish, ca. 1885, 18 x 40", 44" h. (ILLUS.) **650**

Tall Aesthetic Chest with Mirror

Victorian Aesthetic Movement chest of drawers, mahogany, the tall superstructure w/a rectangular crest panel carved w/floral vines & flanked by fan-carved & blocked corners above a narrow plain panel flanked by pierced spindled bands above reeded stiles flanking the large beveled rectangular swiveling mirror, the rectangular white marble top above a case w/a pair of drawers over two long drawers all flanked by blocked & reeded stiles, original cast-brass pulls, refinished, ca. 1890, 20 x 40", overall 6' 8" h. (ILLUS.) **650**

Chest with Scandinavian Decoration

Victorian cottage-style chest of drawers, painted & decorated oak, a large oblong beveled mirror swivels within a scroll-carved frame supported between tall S-form scroll-carved uprights on the rectangular top w/a serpentine front over a pair of serpentine drawers above two long flat drawers, gently shaped apron & bracket feet, unique folk decoration painted in the Scandinavian tradition w/a dark blue background highlighted by green, red & gold scrolls & colorful blossoms, the top w/a painted landscape w/mountains & a lake, inscribed & dated "1898" on one end, 18 x 38", overall 6' 2" h. (ILLUS.) **2,000**

Victorian cottage-style chest of drawers, painted & decorated pine, the superstructure w/a tall scroll-carved crestrail centered by a cartouche continuing to molded posts on C-scroll bases enclosing a tall arched swiveling mirror, the rectangular white marble top w/a serpentine front above a conforming case w/three long drawers flanked by ring-and-rod-turned columns on rounded base corners, painted & decorated in shades of dark brown, cream & black,

each drawer front w/a grained panel decorated w/a long cluster of fruits & leaves, original finish, ca. 1875, 22 x 44", overall 7' 4" h. (ILLUS., below) **800**

Unique Cottage-style Painted Chest

Miniature Victorian Country Chest

Victorian country-style chest of drawers, miniature, walnut, an oval-framed mirror swiveling between scrolled upright on small handkerchief drawers on the rectangular top, the case w/a pair of small drawers over three long graduated drawers, a finely-cut sawtooth band under the top edge & above the serpentine apron w/bracket feet, turned wood pulls, original dark finish, ca. 1860, 9 x 15", 24" h. (ILLUS.) **650**

Walnut Chest with Wishbone Mirror

Victorian country-style chest of drawers, walnut, an oval mirror w/a pierced scroll-carved crest swiveling between a wishbone-form bracket on a narrow rectangular top over two narrow drawers on the rectangular top over four long drawers w/fruit-and-leaf-carved pulls, quarter-round brackets at the front corners, scalloped short apron on bracket feet, original finish, ca. 1865, 19 x 40", overall 5' 10" h. (ILLUS.) **650**

Tall Eastlake Cherry Chest

Victorian Eastlake tall chest of drawers, cherry, the high crestrail w/a flat top & band of incised cross-form leaves between small roundels over line-incised bands flanked by shaped brackets on the rectangular top w/molded cornice over a tall case w/two short drawers beside a

square doors w/a raised panel carved w/stylized sunflowers above three long lower drawers, serpentine apron & bracket feet, paneled sides, original stamped brass pulls, paneled sides, ca. 1885, refinished, 20 x 32", 4' 10" h. (ILLUS.) **750**

Tall Eastlake Side-lock Chest

Victorian Eastlake tall side-lock chest of drawers, walnut & burl walnut, the rectangular top w/molded edges & blocked corners above projecting corner blocks over tall reeded corner columns flanking the long drawers w/scroll-incised burl panels & pairs of black teardrop pulls, large corner blocks at the base flanking the flat apron, paneled sides, a single locking mechanism accessed through a side keyhole, refinished, ca. 1880, 20 x 36", 4' 10" h. (ILLUS.) **2,500**

Golden Oak Serpentine-front Chest

Victorian Golden Oak style chest of drawers, quarter-sawn oak, the large serpentine-framed rectangular beveled mirror w/an arched scroll-and-bar-carved crestrail swiveling between C-scroll side brackets continuing to an serpentine scroll-carved crestrail above the rectangular top w/serpentine edges above a double-serpentine case w/a pair of drawers over two long drawers, short slightly shaped legs on casters, original brass bail pulls, refinished, ca. 1900, 18 x 36", overall 6' 2" h. (ILLUS.) **700**

Figured Oak Tall Chest of Drawers

Victorian Golden Oak style tall chest of drawers, figured quarter-sawn oak, an oval horizontal beveled mirror swiveling between S-scroll uprights on the rectangular top w/a serpentine front above a pair of serpentine-front drawers over four long flat drawers, simple serpentine apron & square tapering feet, simple bail pulls, original dark finish, ca. 1895, 20 x 28", 5' 8" h. (ILLUS.)............................... **500**

Victorian Golden Oak style tall chest of drawers, oak, a horizontal oblong beveled mirror in a frame w/a shell-and-scroll-carved crest swivels between simple S-scroll uprights on the rectangular top w/molded edges, the case w/five long graduated drawers w/simple bail pulls, serpentine apron & square stile legs on casters, paneled sides, refinished, ca. 1900, 20 x 34", 5' 6" h. (ILLUS., top next column) **550**

Tall Flat-front Golden Oak Chest

Tall Chest with a Serpentine Drawer

Victorian Golden Oak style tall chest of drawers, oak, a long rectangular horizontal beveled mirror w/rounded corners in a frame w/a scroll-carved crest & swiveling between simple S-scroll uprights on the rectangular top w/a serpentine edge above one long serpentine drawer above four long flat drawers, carved keyhole escutcheons & stamped brass pulls, flat apron & square stile legs on casters, paneled sides, refinished, ca. 1900, 18 x 34", 6' h. (ILLUS.).. **550**

Tall Bow-front Golden Oak Chest

Victorian Golden Oak style tall chest of drawers, quarter-sawn oak, a long oval beveled mirror swiveling between simple S-scroll uprights on the rectangular bow-fronted top above a conforming case w/five long bow-fronted drawers w/simple bail pulls, serpentine apron on tapering shaped legs on casters, refinished, ca. 1900, 18 x 32", 5' 6" h. (ILLUS.)....................... **600**

Tall Serpentine Golden Oak Chest

Victorian Golden Oak style tall chest of drawers, quarter-sawn oak, a rectangular beveled mirror w/rounded corners in a framed w/a small carved crest swiveling between slender S-scroll upright above the rectangular top w/serpentine edges, case w/a long double-serpentine drawer over a conforming arrangement of two short drawers beside a cupboard door over two long bottom drawers, short front cabriole legs on casters, original bail pulls, original finish, ca. 1900, 19 x 30", 5' 10" h. (ILLUS.)... **700**

Victorian Chest with Inner Drawers

Victorian Renaissance Revival chest of drawers, rosewood, the tall superstructure w/an arched & pierced scroll-carved crest raised above an arched crestrail centered by a round medallion carved in relief w/a lady's face flanked by shaped narrow raised burl panels above carved uprights supported by carved scrolling dolphins, the tall arched mirror mounted on accordion brackets so it can be pulled forward, the rectangular white marble top w/serpentine sides & projecting front corners above a conforming case w/a single long drawer decorated w/raised oval molding flanking a carved oval medallion above a pair of large cabinet doors w/rectangular raised molding around a central oval medallion, the doors opening to reveal four long interior drawers w/figured maple fronts, the case w/chamfered front corners carved w/leafy scrolls, the wide serpentine scroll-carved apron hides along long drawer, original dark finish, ca. 1865, 24 x 46", overall 6' 8" h. (ILLUS.) **4,500**

Drop-well Walnut Renaissance Chest

Victorian Renaissance Revival chest of drawers, walnut & burl walnut, the tall superstructure w/a tall peaked leaf-and-scroll-carved pediment over an arched crestrail w/scroll-carved rounded corners above small raised burl panels over a tall rectangular mirror flanked by burl-paneled sides w/a square candleshelf on each side above the white marble drop-well top, a small raised burl panel drawer on each side above two long drawers w/small rectangular raised burl panels, flat molded base, brass ring pulls, refinished, ca. 1870s, 20 x 40", overall 7' h. (ILLUS.) **750**

Marble-top Renaissance Chest Base

Victorian Renaissance Revival chest of drawers base, mahogany & mahogany veneer, a rectangular white marble top w/rounded corners above a long slightly projecting top drawer w/raised oval banding & a central fruit-and-scroll-carved pull, two matching long lower drawers over a plain narrow base drawer, rounded front corners on the case, original dark finish, mirror missing from the top, ca. 1865, 20 x 44", 31" h., as is (ILLUS.) **500**

Tall Renaissance Revival Chest

Victorian Renaissance Revival tall chest of drawers, walnut & burl walnut, a rectangular top w/molded edges above a case w/six long drawers w/long raised burl panels w/pointed ends, chamfered front corners, flat molded base on flat block feet, refinished, ca. 1870s, 20 x 38", 4' 6" h. (ILLUS.) **900**

'Bow-front' Rococo Rosewood Chest

Victorian Rococo 'bow-front' chest of drawers, carved rosewood, a large egg-shaped mirror in a molded frame topped by an ornate pierced & scroll-carved crest & swiveling between tall slender pierced uprights carved as large serpents, the rectangular white marble top a/wide rounded front corners & a bowed front above a conforming case w/four long drawers leaf-carved pulls, rounded bracket w/feet, original dark finish, ca. 1855, probably made in Philadelphia, 20 x 42", overall 7' h. (ILLUS.) **3,000**

Bow-fronted Rococo Mahogany Chest

Victorian Rococo 'bow-front' chest of drawers, mahogany & mahogany veneer, a tall oblong serpentine-framed mirror swiveling below a high arched & scroll-carved crestrail continuing to serpentine uprights w/scroll trim, the rectangular top w/a bowed center section above a long bowed & ogee-fronted crotch-grain veneered drawer above three long bowed drawers w/further veneering & centered by large scroll-carved pulls, bowed apron w/bracket feet, original finish, ca. 1850, 22 x 38", overall 6' 8" h. (ILLUS.) **1,200**

Rare Rococo Carved Rosewood Chest

Victorian Rococo chest of drawers, carved rosewood, a tall oblong mirror within a molded serpentine frame below a tall ornately pierce-carved crest featuring allegorical figures flanked by foliage, grapes & a bird, the tall scrolled uprights continuing down to bold scrolling resting atop the rectangular white marble top w/serpentine sides above a conforming case w/three long graduated drawers centered by bolding carved clusters of fruit & foliage, molded base on flattened bun feet, ca. 1855, 27 x 56 1/2", 8' 8" h. (ILLUS.) **10,350**

Fine Carved Rosewood Rococo Chest

Victorian Rococo chest of drawers, carved rosewood, the superstructure w/a tall arched frame w/a high fruit-and-scroll-carved crest continuing to scroll-carved sides flanking large arched mirror, rectangular white marble top w/projecting front corners above a conforming case w/three long graduated drawers w/raised oval banding w/scroll-carved ends & carved keyhole escutcheons, the flat apron hides another long drawer, the chamfered front corners carved w/scrolls above the bottom blocked corners, original dark finish, ca. 1855, 20 x 45", overall 7' 6" h. (ILLUS.) **2,800**

Chest with Swan-head Brackets

Victorian Rococo chest of drawers, mahogany & mahogany veneer, a large oval beveled mirror w/a scroll-carved crest swiveling between an ornately scroll-carved wishbone bracket terminating in carved swans' heads, between two small handkerchief drawers on the rectangular top w/rounded front corners above a case w/a pair of large plain drawers w/beaded edge molding slightly projecting above three long drawers w/scroll-carved ends, beaded band above the scroll-carved apron w/bracket feet, turned wood pulls, old refinish, ca. 1860, 21 x 38", overall 6' h. (ILLUS.) **850**

Unique Rococo Chest with Shelves

Victorian Rococo chest of drawers, walnut & feather-grained walnut veneer, the superstructure w/a high arched molded frame w/floral- and scroll-carved crest enclosing a large arched mirror flanked by small arched side panels below small half-round candleshelves & resting on very thin handkerchief drawers on the half-round top w/a wide flat central section, the flat center over three long paneled feather-grained drawers w/scroll-carved pulls flanked by scroll-carved pilasters, quarter-round side sections w/a curved veneer panel above two open rounded shelves w/pierced scroll-cut back brackets, deep conforming molded base, Philadelphia, ca. 1855, refinished, 18 x 44", overall 7' 2" h. (ILLUS.) **3,500**

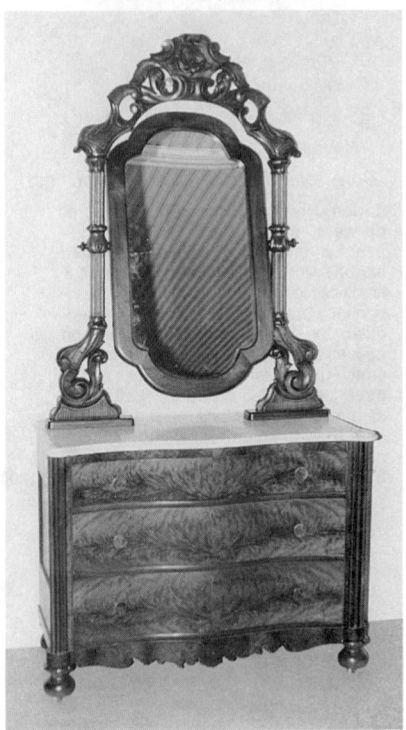

Rococo Walnut Serpentine Chest

Victorian Rococo chest of drawers, walnut & feather-grained walnut veneer, the tall oblong mirror in a shaped frame swiveling below a high arched & pierced scroll-carved crest centered by a cartouche supported on reeded columnar uprights raised on large scroll-carved brackets, the rectangular white marble top w/molded edges & a serpentine front above a conforming case w/three long feather-grained veneered serpentine drawers above the serpentine scroll-cut apron above bun feet on casters, refinished, ca. 1860, 22 x 44", overall 7' 2" h. (ILLUS.) **1,800**

New Orleans-made Rococo Chest

Victorian Rococo chest of drawers, walnut & feather-grained walnut veneer, the tall oblong mirror in a molded serpentine-edges frame w/pierced shell-and-scroll-carved crest swiveling between scroll-carved uprights, the rectangular white marble top w/molded edges above a long feather-grained drawer w/central scroll-carved bands & scroll-carved corner blocks all slightly projecting above three more long matching feather-grained drawers flanked by slender spiral-twist corner columns, deep flat apron w/hidden drawer, thin block front feet, made in New Orleans, ca. 1850s, old refinish, 20 x 40", overall 6' h. (ILLUS.) **2,800**

Rococo Serpentine-front Chest Base

Victorian Rococo chest of drawers base, walnut, rectangular white marble top w/serpentine sides above a conforming base w/four long graduated drawers centered by shell & fan carving & flanked by angled front corners w/scroll-tipped columns, deep scroll-carved serpentine apron, possibly by Mitchell & Rammelsberg, Cincinnati, Ohio, ca. 1860, original dark finish, missing mirrored superstructure, 22 x 42", 36" h., base only (ILLUS.)...... **850**

Cupboards

Chimney cupboard, country-style, painted pine, cove molding, three interior shelves, single door w/raised panel & cast-iron latch, cut bracket feet, old orange over mustard paint & polka dot designs, 19th c., 15 1/2 x 30 1/4", 75 1/2" h. (minor wear at base)..................................... **4,070**

Fine Chippendale Corner Cupboard

Corner cupboard, Chippendale, mahogany, two-part construction: the upper section w/a broken pitched pediment w/dentil-molded cornice containing a field of latticework flanking a fluted plinth topped by a carved cartouche crest above a foliate & geometric blind-fret carved frieze above a pair of tall geometrically-glazed cupboard doors opening to four shaped shelves & flanked by fluted canted corners; the lower section w/a mid-molding over a pair of paneled cupboard doors opening to two shelves & flanked by fluted canted corners, molded base on ogee bracket feet, Philadelphia, 1760-80, 24 x 54 1/2"., 8' 10 1/2" h. (ILLUS.)......... **28,200**

Corner cupboard, Chippendale, poplar, cove-molded cornice w/a broken-arch top, arched door in the top w/15 panes of glass, butterfly shelves, interior of top painted white, worn wallpaper inside the bottom, w/two paneled doors in base & beaded openings, ogee feet, applied molding around the case, pegged construction, old black over red painted decoration, attributed to Pennsylvania, 23 1/2 x 49 1/2", 90 1/2" h. (restorations, finials are late) **5,280**

Chippendale Revival Cupboard

Corner cupboard, Chippendale Revival, mahogany, two-part construction: the upper section w/a broken-scroll pediment w/rosettes flanking an urn-and-flame-carved finial & flanked by matching corner finials above two tall geometrically-glazed cupboard doors opening to two shelves & flanked by canted front corners; the lower section w/a gadrooned mid-molding above a pair of paneled cupboard doors over another gadrooned molding over the shallow scalloped apron & claw-and-ball front feet, by Feldenkreis, ca. 1920s, 29" w., 7' h. (ILLUS.)..................................... **1,540**

Corner cupboard, country-style, cherry, cove-molded cornice curved at ends, one door on top w/twelve panes of old wavy glass w/molded mullions, two paneled doors in base, beaded edging around all doors, corners of case rounded & have reeded top to bottom, deeply scalloped apron, bracket feet, 17 x 41 1/2", 84 1/4" h. (two hinges replaced, repair at corner).. **6,875**

Fine 'Turkey-breast' Corner Cupboard

Corner cupboard, country-style 'turkey-breast' form, pine & poplar, one-piece construction, a flat top w/a pointed projecting central section above the wide stepped- and cove-molded cornice over a conforming case w/a pair of tall two-panel cupboard doors w/brass thumb latch above a double mid-molding over a pair of shorter paneled doors, flat pilasters down the front sides, molded base w/scalloped apron, old finish, original brasses, first half 19th c., 55 1/2" w. top, overall 88" h. (ILLUS.).................................. **4,400**

European Walnut Corner Cupboard

Corner cupboard, country-style, walnut, one-piece construction, the flat cornice above a tall narrow door w/two raised panels & an ornate scrolling metal keyhole escutcheon, raised molding around the sides, flat base, opens to shelves, Europe, 19th c., 21" w., 4' 2" h. (ILLUS.)....... **748**

Early Walnut Corner Cupboard

Corner cupboard, country-style, walnut, two-part construction: the upper section w/a narrow flat & flaring cornice above canted corners flanking a pair of two-panel cupboard doors opening to shelves; the lower section w/a mid-molding over chamfered corners flanking a pair of paneled cupboard doors, 19th c., restoration, repairs, back replaced, 21 x 50", 7' 4" h. (ILLUS.)... **1,840**

Early Southern Corner Cupboard

Corner cupboard, Federal country-style, walnut, one-piece construction, the thin cornice molding above canted sides flanking an open front w/two shelves above a small two-paneled cupboard door, flat apron on small bracket feet, Southern United States, ca. 1790, 22 x 39", 7' 4" h. (ILLUS.) **2,800**

English Edwardian Corner Cupboard

Corner cupboard, Georgian Revival style, inlaid mahogany, one-piece construction, a small broken-scroll cornice centering an urn-form finial above a narrow molded cornice above reeded canted corners flanking a tall geometrically-glazed cupboard door opening to shelves above a lower door w/a satin-wood-inlaid door w/a round center design, deeply scalloped apron & bracket feet, England, Edwardian era, early 20th c., 35" w., 7' 5" h. (ILLUS.) **805**

German Baroque-Style Cupboard

Early Queen Anne Corner Cupboard

Corner hanging cupboard, Queen Anne, lacquered & decorated, a high arched & stepped back crest w/a small quarter-round shelf above the bowed cornice above a bow-fronted case w/a pair of tall cupboard doors, decorated w/elaborate polychrome Oriental landscapes in red &

gold, molded base, England, early 18th c., 15 x 23", 43" h. (ILLUS.)......................... **1,380**

Hutch cupboard, Baroque-Style, oak, two-part construction: the upper section w/a rectangular top w/a widely flaring stepped cornice above a pierced scroll-carved frieze band above two shallow shelves w/knob-form cup hooks all flanked by barley-turned side columns; the stepped-out lower section w/a flaring molded edge above three two-paneled cupboard doors each w/a recessed cross-form panel & each separated by chevron-carved panels, flat apron on projecting scroll feet, composed of earlier elements, Germany, 19th c., 24 x 81", 7' 3" h. (ILLUS., top of page)......................... **923**

Hutch cupboard, French Provincial, oak, two-part construction: the upper section w/a rectangular top w/an arched center crest above a frieze band w/small rectangular side panels flanking the arched central shell-carved panel above a central open compartment fitted w/three narrow plate rack shelves flanked by tall narrow cupboard doors w/two shaped raised panels; the stepped-out lower section w/a pair of paneled small drawers flanking a long paneled center drawer above a long rectangular center cupboard door flanked by smaller cupboard doors, each door w/shaped raised panels, scroll-carved serpentine apron on short cabriole front legs w/scroll feet, France, ca. 1890, 22 x 67", 7' 6" h. (ILLUS., top next page) **2,688**

French Provincial Hutch Cupboard

French Provincial Hutch Cupboard

Hutch cupboard, Louis XV Provincial style, oak, two-part construction: the upper section w/a rectangular top w/a flaring molded cornice above a scalloped leafy scroll-carved frieze band above four open spindle-galleried shelves, the bottom shelf centered by an ecclesiastical-carved door; the stepped-out lower section w/a long narrow drawers mounted w/a long ornately pierced brass mounted above a pair of paneled cupboard doors w/leafy scroll-carved bands above the door panels, deep scalloped apron on short scrolled legs, France, first quarter 19th c., 24 x 53 1/2", 7' 6" h. (ILLUS.) **3,680**

Jelly cupboard, country-style, poplar, stepped cornice, chamfered corners, two doors w/inset panels, cut side aprons, semi-curved front bracket feet, old red paint, 19th c. (some touch-ups, brass pull on one door missing interior lock) **3,080**

American Chippendale Linen Press

Linen press, Chippendale, walnut, two-part construction: the upper section w/a rectangular top w/a widely flaring stepped cornice above a pair of arched-panel tall cupboard doors opening to linen slides & flanked by wide reeded side panels; the lower section w/a mid-molding above a case w/three long graduated drawers w/butterfly pulls & oval keyhole escutcheons, molded base on ogee bracket feet, probably New Jersey, 1780-1800, feet replaced, 22 x 50 1/2", 6' 2" h. (ILLUS.) **3,760**

English Georgian Linen Press

Linen press, Georgian, mahogany, two-part construction: the upper section w/a rectangular top w/a flaring stepped cornice over a pair of tall paneled cupboard doors opening to a compartmented interior; the lower section w/a mid-molding over a pair of drawers over two long drawers all w/oval brasses, scalloped apron on tall French feet, England, George III era, late 18th - early 19th c., 22 1/2 x 50", 7' 4" h. (ILLUS.)...................... **2,185**

Country Pine Punched Tin Pie Safe

Pie safe, country-style, pine, a rectangular top w/molded edges above a pair of drawers w/fruit-and-leaf-carved pulls over a pair of tall three-panel cupboard doors fitted w/three diamond-and-circle-design punched tin panels, three punched panels on each side, flat base raised on heavy flat stile legs, refinished, ca. 1870-80, 16 x 42", 5' h. (ILLUS.) **750**

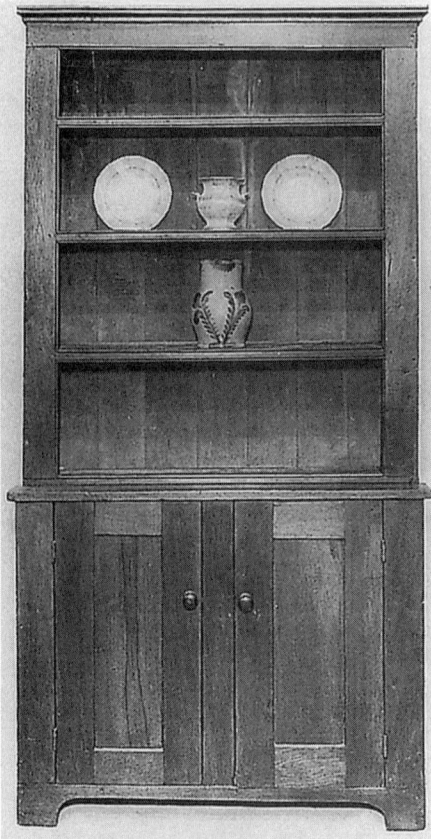

Country-style Pewter Cupboard

Pewter cupboard, country-style, walnut & poplar, two-part construction: the upper section w/a rectangular top w/narrow molded cornice above a large beaded-edge open compartment w/three open shelves; the stepped-out lower section w/a pair of tall paneled cupboard doors w/wooden knobs, gently arched apron w/bracket feet, square nail construction, 19th c., pieced restorations & putty repair on base, refinished, 14 1/2 x 41 1/2", 6' 6 3/4" h. (ILLUS.)... **1,760**

Grain-painted Step-back Cupboard

Large Step-back Wall Cupboard

Step-back wall cupboard, country-style, painted & decorated, two-part construction: the upper section w/a rectangular top w/flaring cornice over a reeded frieze band above a pair of tall cupboard doors each w/two small raised panels above to long raised panels, all flanked by side pilasters; the slightly stepped-out lower section w/a pair of drawers w/glass pulls over a pair of doors w/two raised panels each, molded base w/a scalloped apron & bracket feet, overall original grain-painted finish, 19th c., 18 x 49 1/2", 7' 1" h. (ILLUS.)..................... **1,093**

Early Painted Ohio Cupboard

Step-back wall cupboard, country-style, painted oak, pegged construction, two-part construction: the upper section w/a long rectangular top w/a wide flaring & stepped peaked cornice fitted w/a low arched-pierced crestrail centered by a rectangular panel w/a pierced heart design, small blocks at the canted front corner each fitted w/a small knob finial, the upper case w/canted end corners flanking a pair of long rectangular cupboard doors w/angled tops over six panes of glass opening to two shelves above an open pie shelf w/shaped bracket ends; the stepped-out lower section w/a molded edge & molded band above the canted corners flanking a pair of large square paneled cupboard doors centered by raised diamonds, narrow molded base w/shaped bracket feet, areas of repaint on the exterior, sections of molding replaced, attributed to New Bremen Ohio, 19th c., 17 x 61", 7' 1" h. (ILLUS.).............. **7,425**

Step-back wall cupboard, country-style, painted wood, two-part construction: the upper section w/a long rectangular top w/a flaring cornice over a row of five tall paneled cupboard doors; the stepped-out lower section w/a pullout cutting board above a row of three paneled cupboard doors flanked at one end by a stack of four small drawers & at the other end by a pullout potato bin, original creamy white paint, early 20th c., 20 x 110", 7' h. (ILLUS., top of page)............ **800**

Step-back wall cupboard, country-style, walnut, molded cornice, two paneled doors in top w/scalloped supports on either side of pie shelf, w/two dovetailed drawers beneath, unusual sliding work surface between drawers & base, base w/two paneled doors & scalloped supports to match those above, shaped bracket feet & arched cutout ends, old refinish, 19th c., 19 x 40 1/2", 85" h. (minor molding chip on bottom door & some damage to backboards) **3,300**

Step-back wall cupboard, country-style, walnut, two-part construction: the upper section w/a cove-molded stepped cornice over two doors, each w/six panes of old glass & beveled mullions, over pie shelf w/two small candle drawers on either side & three dovetailed drawers beneath; the lower section w/two over base paneled mortised doors w/cast-iron latches, turned tapered legs end in ball feet below molded base, Ohio, 19th c., 19 1/2 x 48 1/2", 82" h. (old applied molding on one end only & brass pulls replaced) **5,775**

Wall cupboard, country-style, cherry & pine, door w/a molded surround w/two raised panels, each w/diamond & block designs, original pewter lock escutcheon, over dovetailed drawer w/a raised diamond design & chamfered edges, brass pull, applied molding around base, sides & cornice, finely turned feet, mortised construction w/square nails, Zoar, Ohio, 19th c., 14 x 26 1/4", 39 7/8" h. (minor chip on lower drawer lip, cut in back corner of cornice) **13,200**

Wall cupboard, country-style, pine, one board & batten door, two interior shelves, molded base & bracket feet, square nail construction, original blue paint, 19th c., 13 1/4 x 27 1/8", 41 1/2" h. (base is replacement, pieced corner repair) **2,090**

One of Two Chippendale Cupboards

Wall cupboards, Chippendale, painted pine, a pitched pediment w/dentil molding above fluted pilasters headed by rectangular molded cornice w/similar dentil molding centering a molded & arched frame headed & flanked by keystones enclosing a recessed interior w/a demilune

upper section fitted w/slats arranged in a fan over a blind fret-carved frieze centering a carved rosette above four shaped shelves, overall matching dentil molding above a rectangular lower case fitted w/two raised panel doors, all painted green w/red interior, affixed to a panel surround, Kutztown, Pennsylvania, ca. 1790, 23 7/8 x 66 3/4", 10' 4" h., pr. (ILLUS. of one) **19,975**

Desks

Mahogany Chippendale Desk

Chippendale slant-front desk, mahogany, narrow rectangular top above a wide hinged slant front opening to an interior fitted w/a prospect door flanked by document drawers further flanked by three pigeonholes & two short drawers over a long drawer; all above a long narrow drawer flanked by pullouts over three long graduated drawers all w/butterfly brasses & keyhole escutcheons, molded base w/center carved sunburst drop, raised on ogee bracket feet, New England, 1760-80, 21 3/4 x 43 1/2", 42 1/2" h. (ILLUS.) **5,875**

Chippendale "Serpentine" Desk

Quality Colonial Revival Desk

Chippendale slant-front "serpentine-front" desk, mahogany, a narrow rectangular top above the wide hinged slant front opening to a fitted interior above a long double-serpentine drawer flanked by pullout supports over three long graduated double-serpentine drawers all w/butterfly brasses & keyhole escutcheons, serpentine base molding on claw-and-ball feet, old refinish, replaced brasses, late 18th c., 20 x 38", 40" h. (ILLUS.) **3,200**

Fancy Chippendale Revival Desk

Chippendale Revival slant-front desk, quarter-sawn oak, a narrow top w/a low brass spindled gallery above the wide hinged slant front centered by a large paneled carved w/large leafy scrolls enclosing an urn, the case w/a long blocked drawer centered by a carved shell above the arched scroll-carved kneehole opening flanked by two small blocked drawers, pierced brass butterfly pulls & keyhole escutcheon, molded apron on cabriole legs w/leaf-carved knees & ending in claw-and-ball feet, refinished, ca. 1890s, 18 x 30", 38" h. (ILLUS.) **2,500**

Colonial Revival partner's desk, mahogany, a wide rectangular top w/rounded corners above a case fitted on each side w/a row of three narrow ornate scroll-carved drawers over two deeper scroll-carved drawers flanking the serpentine kneehole opening, each corner carved w/a large grotesque lion head above heavy cabriole legs w/leaf-carved knees & ending in paw feet, attributed to Horner of New York City, original dark finish, ca. 1890, 28 x 56", 30" h. (ILLUS., top of page) **3,500**

Colonial Revival partner's desk, mahogany, the rectangular hourglass-shaped top above a conforming case w/a stack of two rounded drawers on the right side & a long drawer at the top of each end, short cabriole legs w/claw-and-ball feet, brass bail pulls, carved scrolls at the top of each corner, refinished, ca. 1900, 30 x 54", 30" h. (ILLUS., top next page) **1,200**

Colonial Revival Hourglass-shaped Partner's Desk

Colonial Revival Carved Partner's Desk

Colonial Revival partner's desk, mahogany, the wide rectangular top w/molded edges above a case fitted on each side w/a scroll-carved central drawer over the arched kneehole opening flanked on one side by a large square cupboard door carved w/ornate scrolls centering a cartouche & on the other side by two scroll-carved small drawers, large carved lion heads carved at each corner above large wing-form brackets over the cabriole legs w/leaf-carved knees & large paw feet, uncarved plain side panels, attributed to Horner of New York City, original dark finish, ca. 1880s, 30 x 60", 30" h. (ILLUS.)... **5,500**

Ornate Colonial Revival Partner's Desk

Colonial Revival partner's desk, mahogany, the wide rectangular top w/molded edges above a case fitted on each side w/a scroll-carved central drawer over the arched kneehole opening flanked on one side by a large square cupboard door carved w/ornate scrolls centering a cartouche & on the other side by two scroll-carved small drawers, large carved lion heads carved at each corner above large wing-form brackets over the cabriole legs w/leaf-carved knees & large paw feet, ornately scroll-carved side panels, attributed to Horner of New York City, original dark finish, ca. 1880s, 30 x 60", 30" h. (ILLUS.) **7,500**

Unusual Colonial Revival Desk

Colonial Revival slant-front 'bombé' desk, mahogany veneer, a narrow rectangular top above the wide hinged slant front opening to a fitted interior above a pair of small square pullouts over the wide bombé case fitted w/three long drawers, serpentine apron & short curved legs w/claw-and-ball feet, original finish, ca. 1900, 20 x 42", 40" h. (ILLUS.) **1,800**

Carved Colonial Revival Slant-front

Colonial Revival slant-front desk, mahogany, an arched & scroll-carved crest rail flanked by brass rail ends on the narrow rectangular top over the wide hinged slant front boldly carved w/rounded panels of leafy scrolls above a case w/three long graduated drawers w/ornate stamped brass pulls, narrow rounded apron above leaf-carved ogee bracket feet, old refinish, ca. 1890s, 22 x 38", 42" h. (ILLUS.) **1,000**

Nice Paneled Oak Writing Desk

Colonial Revival Bombé Desk

kneehole opening flanked on each side w/a pullout writing surface over a stack of four drawers w/long carved pulls, paneled ends & deep molded base, refinished, ca. 1900, 30 x 54", 45" h. **2,500**

Early 20th century writing desk, quartersawn oak, the wide rectangular top w/molded edges over a center long drawer w/serpentine edge above the kneehole opening w/paneled interior sides flanked on each side by a stack of four drawers w/simple wood pulls, a pullout writing surface above one set of drawers, six-paneled ends, deep molded base, refinished, ca. 1900, 30 x 60", 30" h. (ILLUS., top of page)........................ **1,200**

Colonial Revival slant-front desk, mahogany veneer, a narrow rectangular top above a wide hinged slant front opening to a fitted interior over the bombé case w/a long drawer w/a center shell carving over the kneehole opening flanked by small drawers, butterfly brasses, simple cabriole legs w/front paw feet, original finish & hardware, ca. 1910, 16 x 32", 40" h. (ILLUS.)... **700**

Early 20th century "roll-top" desk, quarter-sawn oak, a narrow rectangular top over the S-scroll tambour roll opening to a fitted interior, the case w/a long center drawer w/arched apron over the paneled

Very Fine Federal Revival Desk

Mid-Century Modern Curved Desk

Federal Revival writing desk, inlaid mahogany, a narrow rectangular top w/a low three-quarter gallery & a concave center section above a cabinet w/three small banded inlay drawers flanked the concave central section w/vertical letter slots, the wide rectangular desk top w/bowed center section above a conforming apron w/a long line-inlaid bowed center drawer flanked by two small line-inlaid drawers flanked by inlaid paterae at each corner, on tapering square line-inlaid legs ending in spade feet, original round brasses & finish, early 20th c., 20 x 32", 40" h. (ILLUS., previous page) **650**

Delicate Louis XV Revival Desk

Louis XV Revival slant-front desk, giltwood, a narrow top shelf w/a low pierced brass gallery above the wide hinged slant front opening to an interior w/three small decorated drawers, the apron w/a single

long drawer w/applied brass scroll banding, on simple tall cabriole legs, original finish, probably French, early 20th c., closed 16 x 30", 38" h. (ILLUS. open) **850**

Modern style desk, walnut veneer, a leather-covered semicircular top over a narrow center drawer over the kneehole opening flanked by three hinged swingout drawers w/round brass pulls, the front w/a triple-shelf bookcase, marked "Dunbar," Linn Grove, Illinois, mid-20th c., wear, 19 x 57 1/2", 29 1/8" h. (ILLUS., top of page)..................................... **230**

Oriental desk, carved mahogany, two-part construction: the superstructure w/a high crestrail carved as a mountain & clouds above stepped compartments w/dragon-carved doors flanking central slots & further carving, the wide rectangular top w/a bead-carved edge above an apron w/two small carved drawers flanking an ornate pierce-carved panel & apron, raised on cabriole legs w/boldly carved knees & ending in scroll feet, China, late 19th c., probably refinished, 23 x 36", 4' 4" h. ... **1,500**

Victorian Aesthetic Movement 'cylinder-front' desk, walnut & burl walnut, the high superstructure w/a narrow rectangular shelf w/a Chinese Chippendale-style pierced gallery w/corner blocks & knob finials supported on slender turned columns & backed by a high curved burl panel above another rectangular shelf above the paneled burl-veneered cylinder-front opening to a fitted interior, flanked on each side w/galleried side sections over the case w/a long central burl veneer drawer w/three brass pulls over the kneehole opening w/fret brackets & a concave lower shelf, the kneehole flanked by a small veneered drawer over a tall door w/a raised veneered panel, a spindled band at the bottom of each side, short tapering square legs, refinished, ca. 1880s, 22 x 46", 5' 6" h. **2,500**

Elaborate Baroque Revival Partner's Desk

Unique Aesthetic Fall-front Desk

Victorian Aesthetic Movement fall-front desk, walnut & burl walnut, a rectangular top w/a sawtooth crestrail & plain side rails flanking a large round projecting ears mounted w/large brass disks w/Oriental designs, the case w/a long narrow shelf over a hinged fall-front door decorated w/lattice-incised border panels & a central burl panels & opening to a fitted interior, each side of the case mounted w/a quarter-round projecting shelf w/a pierced gallery & lattice braces, the stepped-out lower section w/a long drawer overhanging a pair of line-incised cupboard doors each centered w/a pair of small square floral-carved recessed panels, a long round-fronted veneered drawer at the very base above the flat line-incised apron, original hardware, original finish, ca. 1880s, 22 x 44", 5' 6" h. (ILLUS.) **2,500**

Victorian Baroque Revival partner's desk, oak, rectangular top w/a plain center & wide scroll-carved border band & gadroon-carved edges above aprons each fitted w/a pair of long scroll-carved drawers centered by a lion head, raised on full-figure carved sphinx legs atop animal legs & large paw feet, a wide medial shelf w/gadrooned edges, attributed to Horner of New York City, ca. 1880s, refinished, 28 x 52", 30" h. (ILLUS., top of page) **9,800**

Baroque Revival Fall-front Desk

Victorian Baroque Revival slant-front desk, oak, narrow rectangular top w/a gadroon-carved edge above the wide hinged slant front carved w/a pair of large leafy scrolls centering a relief-carved lion head above a pair of drawers w/scroll-carved panels over the narrow scroll-carved apron, raised on front legs carved in full-relief w/winged sphinxes above legs w/large paw feet on casters, square tapering back legs, a lower medial shelf w/a gadroon-carved border, attributed to Horner, New York City, ca. 1880s, refinished, 18 x 36", 42" h. (ILLUS.).................. **4,600**

Norwegian-American Country Desk

Victorian country-style fall-front desk, butternut, a rectangular top w/ovolo front corners above a tall case w/columns down the front sides carved in the middle w/a bold ropetwist design, the case w/a long drawer w/carved fruit & leaf pulls above a wide flat fall front opening to an arrangement of five small drawers flanking a center section w/a narrow drawer above & below two pigeonholes centered by a prospect door, the lower case w/two long deep drawers w/carved pulls, low apron w/small center carved knobs, Norwegian-American influence, central Midwest, ca. 1870, 22 x 44", 5' h. (ILLUS.) **2,500**

Victorian Country Slant-front Desk

Victorian country-style slant-front desk, walnut, a narrow rectangular top above two narrow drawers over the wide hinged slant front w/two long recessed

octagonal panels opening to a fitted interior, the lower case w/three long graduated drawers w/wooden knobs, serpentine apron & square stile feet, dovetailed construction, refinished, ca. 1875, 22 x 38", 44" h. (ILLUS.)..................... **500**

Victorian Eastlake Captain's Desk

Victorian Eastlake captain's desk, walnut, the superstructure w/a crown-form crestrail w/center sunburst & incised scrolls above a narrow rectangular shelf raised on incurved pierced brackets flanking a large rectangular burl panel over the hinged angled felt-lined writing surface over a burl front panel, raised on angular cutout line-incised side supports joined by two wide open shelves, original dark finish, ca. 1880s, 22 x 30", 4' 10" h. (ILLUS.)... **800**

Country Eastlake Oak Desk

Victorian Eastlake country-style fall-front desk, oak, a high line-incised crestrail w/small carved fan devices above a narrow shelf above the narrow rectangular top above the line-incised flat fall front opening to a fitted interior, the lower case fitted w/three open shelves, narrow scalloped aprons, refinished, ca. 1890, 16 x 30", 5' h. (ILLUS.) **650**

pet-form legs joined by U-form end stretchers joined by a turned center stretcher w/an urn finial, original finish, ca. 1885, 28 x 40", 4' 5" h. (ILLUS.) **4,800**

Nice Eastlake Fall-front Desk

Very Elaborate Eastlake Desk

Victorian Eastlake desk, walnut & burl walnut, an ornate superstructure w/a high stepped, paneled, blocked & bobbin-trimmed crest above a narrow rectangular shelf over a pair of ring-and-urn-turned spindles flanking a cupboard w/a scroll-carved paneled door beside an open compartment w/a bobbin rail over a tiny drawer, all flanked by open shelves w/back bobbin rails & raised over a pair of burl paneled drawers centered by a recess on the wide rectangular desk top w/molded edges, the apron w/a long drawer w/a long brass escutcheon raised on turned trum-

Victorian Eastlake fall-front desk, walnut, a superstructure w/a gallery top w/a raised rectangular center leaf-carved panel flanked by pierced sides on the rectangular shelf supported on incurved pierced brackets above the rectangular top backed by a long narrow leaf-carved panel over the wide flat fall front w/a recessed panel carved in the center w/a monogram & opening to a fitted interior, the lower cabinet w/a long drawer projecting over three long drawers flanked by carved brackets & each w/brass plate & bail pulls, deep molded base, paneled sides, original finish, ca. 1880, 20 x 30", 5' 4" h. (ILLUS.) **1,800**

Eastlake Walnut Writing Desk

Victorian Eastlake writing desk, oak, rectangular top w/molded edges above a long center drawer w/a central panel over the paneled kneehole opening blanked on each side by a projecting drawer w/small panel & simple carved wood pulls above three additional matching drawers, molded base, paneled ends, refinished, ca. 1880s, 30 x 54", 30" h. (ILLUS.).. **1,000**

Simple Golden Oak Slant-front Desk

Victorian Golden Oak slant-front desk, oak, a narrow top w/a low scroll-carved crestrail over the wide flat hinged slant front centered w/a scroll-carved band & opening to a fitted interior, a long drawer w/slightly shaped apron above the simple cabriole legs, refinished, ca. 1900, 16 x 30", 44" h. (ILLUS.) **650**

Oak Slant-front Desk with Ornate Top

Victorian Golden Oak slant-front desk, quarter-sawn oak, the ornate superstructure w/a large serpentine-sided beveled center mirror w/a scroll-carved frame flanked by scroll-carved crests & small shaped shelves supported on baluster-turned spindles above a small narrow drawer flanked by smaller rounded square beveled mirrors, all atop the wide hinged slant front w/a small scroll-carved panel at the top & opening to a fitted interior, above a case w/a pair of glazed cupboard doors w/scroll-carved corners above a pair of round-fronted bottom drawers w/bail pulls, on ogee bracket feet, original hardware, refinished, ca. 1900, 18 x 30", 5' h. (ILLUS.)...................... **2,000**

Nicely Carved Oak Slant-front Desk

Victorian Golden Oak slant-front desk, quarter-sawn oak, the superstructure w/a low scroll-carved crestrail over a narrow shelf & incurved side brackets backed by wainscoted boards over the narrow rectangular top above the hinged slant front ornately carved w/a central diamond framed by leafy scrolls over a single long leaf-carved drawers flanked by pullout supports above incurved sides backed by wainscoted boards & flanking two narrow open shelves, arched boot jack ends, refinished, ca. 1900, 16 x 30", 4' 2" h. (ILLUS.) **600**

Unusual Renaissance Fall-front Desk

Victorian Renaissance Revival country-style fall-front desk, walnut & bird's-eye maple, the superstructure composed of a narrow top shelf w/an ornately pierce-carved back rail & scroll-cut end brackets supported on slender turned spindles & back brackets flanking another pierced rail on the rectangular top over the flat fall front w/four recessed bird's-eye maple panels flanked by scroll-cut brackets, the stepped-out base w/a long drawer w/two recessed maple panels & small ring pulls above an arched & serpentine apron w/two trefoil cutouts, on ring-turned tapering legs, paneled sides, original hardware, refinished, ca. 1870s, 20 x 32", 5' 8" h. (ILLUS.) **850**

Nice Renaissance Davenport Desk

Victorian Renaissance Revival Davenport desk, walnut & burl walnut, a low pierced scroll-carved gallery above the gently slanted writing surface w/leather inset opening to a well, a tiny drawer at the side of the case, the stepped-back lower case w/two raised burl panels flanked by pierced scroll-cut & leaf-carved brackets, the side fitted w/a stack of four paneled drawers w/leaf-carved pulls, molded bas w/projecting feet, refinished, ca. 1870s, 22 x 28", 40" h. (ILLUS.) **1,600**

Quality Renaissance Fall-front Desk

Victorian Renaissance Revival fall-front desk, walnut & ebonized wood, a high arched & scroll-carved crestrail flanked by scroll-ends & centering a pointed oblong carved cartouche above the narrow rectangular top over the hinged flat fall front w/a rectangular center panel w/another carved cartouche, opening to a fitted interior of bird's-eye maple, the stepped-out lower case w/a pair of drawers w/line-incised decorated & brass ring pulls above a molding projecting above a pair of paneled cupboard doors each centered by a large carved shield-style cartouche flanked by block- and scroll-carved side brackets on the flat molded base, overall ebonized trim molding, paneled sides, original finish, ca. 1875, 20 x 32", 4' 8" h. (ILLUS.) **2,000**

William & Mary Revival Partner's Desk

High-quality Wooton Desk

Victorian Rococo Fall-front Desk

Victorian Renaissance Revival 'patent' desk, walnut & burl walnut, the ornate carved crest w/applied designs & bulbous urn finials above a similar gallery over an outset rectangular case w/projecting quarter-round upper section fitted w/two conforming & paneled doors w/applied ornament, each door w/a letter slot, one marked "Letters," the other "Manufactured by the Wooton Desk Co., Indianapolis, Inc. Pat. Oct. 6, 1874," the doors opening to reveal a compartmented interior w/hinged writing surface opening to reveal a further compartmented interior, all over a shaped skirt, on paired downscrolling legs on casters, ca. 1874, 32 x 45 1/4", 6' 6 1/2" h. (ILLUS.) **12,925**

Victorian Rococo fall-front desk, walnut & bird's-eye maple, the high superstructure w/a central arched crest over an oval mirror flanked by ornate pierced scroll-carved rails & side brackets flanking quarter-round corner shelves over two recessed oval panels above the rectangular top w/molded edges & rounded front corners, the flat fall front opening to a bird's-eye- maple interior fitted w/small drawers, letter slots & a central compartment al flanked by turned half-round side drops & carved brackets, raised on heavy molded cabriole legs joined by a serpentine medial shelf w/a low scroll-pierced crest above a conforming line-incised drawer, refinished, ca. 1860, closed 22 x 40", 6' h. (ILLUS. open) **400**

Exceptional Colonial Revival Dining Room Suite

William & Mary Revival partner's desk, walnut, the wide rectangular top inset w/leather w/embossed edging, each side fitted w/a long center drawer w/a roundel above the kneehole opening flanked by deeper drawer w/scalloped & scroll-carved bases, raised on eight trumpet-and-ring-turned legs joined by H-stretchers, bun feet, old refinish, early 20th c., 32 x 54", 30" h. (ILLUS., top of previous page) **1,200**

Dining Room Suites

Colonial Revival: dining table, sideboard, server, china cabinet & five side chairs & one armchair; inlaid mahogany & mahogany veneer, the Chippendale-style chairs w/an arched shell-carved crestrail over pierced carved vasiform back splat, over-upholstered seat on cabriole legs; the oval extension dining table raised on heavy C-scroll legs ending in bun feet, the two-part D-form china cabinet w/the upper section centered by a large curved door w/a large oval reserve w/inlaid floral decoration, matching details on the long sideboard & small server, Rockford Republic Furniture Co., ca. 1920s, the suite (ILLUS., top of page) **10,450**

Modern Style Iron Dining Suite

English Cast-Iron Garden Chairs

Modern style: dining table & four side chairs; cast iron & glass, the table w/a rectangular glass top set in a green-painted iron frame of scrolling vines w/rosettes raised on a double pedestal base w/a stretcher & arched legs, the chairs w/upright rectangular backs w/pierced floral splats, rectangular seats w/cushions & raised on slender iron bar legs, mid-20th c., table 30 x 48", 29 1/2" h., the suite (ILLUS., bottom previous page) **414**

Modern style: table & eight chairs; walnut, the circular table w/natural burl on a cross-stretcher base w/rectangular uprights joined by cross tie, the 'Conoid' chairs w/tall spindled backs topped by a narrow curved overhanging crestrail above cantilevered seats, each marked w/the client's name under the base, by George Nakashima, ca. 1969, table 66" d., 28" h., the suite **42,300**

Garden & Lawn

Cast iron unless otherwise noted.

Armchairs, a rounded molded & floral-designed back depicting the seasons, flanked by pierced scrolling arms over a pierced seat w/serpentine front w/a pierced leaf design apron, raised on scroll-trimmed cabriole legs joined by leafy vine stretchers, black paint, England, early 20th c., some rust & paint loss, 37" h., set of 4 (ILLUS. of part, top of page).. **2,415**

Bench, twig & leaf open design, signed "Mfg. By The Kramer Bros. Fdry. Dayton, O," late green paint, early Ohio, 22 x 37 1/2", 31" h. (some old welded restoration).. **715**

Garden Settee with C-scroll Back

One of Two Iron Garden Settees

Settee, a serpentine scroll-cast crestrail over a pierced back composed of small C-scrolls, the stepped arms w/tall looped scrolls flanking the seat w/a new pad, raised on scrolling cabriole legs w/scrolling leaf returns, painted green, American, 19th c., 35" l., 41" h. (ILLUS., bottom previous page) **1,380**

Settee, wire camelback settee w/"X" stretchers & sunray & S-scroll frets at front legs, "OHIO" spelled out on seat back, manufacturer tag reads "The Bromwell Co - Cincinnati, O," old white paint, 36 1/4" h. (some wear to paint) **1,045**

Settees, Rococo-style, the arched curved back continuing to form the arms cast overall in a pierced grapevine design, oblong pierced lattice seat w/a grapevine apron & raised on outswept grapevine legs joined by a cross-stretcher, dark green paint, early 20th c., 23 x 34", 31" h., pr. (ILLUS., bottom of page) **1,495**

Settees, the back composed of three stepped rectangular sections, the taller center section w/a sunburst & florette crest over a narrow lattice back above the ornate pierced scroll back, the lower side sections w/similar decor, simple scrolled bar arms over the pierced seat w/a flat pierced apron, on simple iron bar legs, worn old paint, American, 19th c., 45" l., pr. (ILLUS. of one, top of page) **978**

Two Grapevine Garden Settees

Hall Racks & Trees

Wrought-iron & Tile Hall Rack

Hall rack, wrought-iron & tile, a long narrow rectangular form w/iron bars above & below seven coat hooks separating a row of six colorful French faience tiles decorated w/figurines, an ornate scrolling wrought-iron crest across the top, probably France, 19th c., 5 3/4 x 39 1/2", 13" h. (ILLUS.)... **1,725**

Hall tree, Federal style, cherry & birch, turned central column w/spiral & ring detail topped w/a small urn finial, fourteen hooks w/ball finials w/old gold paint, high tripod spider base, 77 1/2" h. (one hook broken, base restored) **2,310**

Late Victorian Cherry Hall Tree

Hall tree, late Victorian style, cherry, a high serpentine crestrail w/a large fan-carved crest & fan-carved ears above a tall rectangular beveled mirror flanked by wide serpentine sides mounted w/four double pierced iron scrolling hooks above a lower back panel w/a leaf-carved band flanked by arms composed of spindled bands joined to flat S-scroll arm supports continuing down to form the front legs, rectangular lift seat above a well, delicate beaded & scrolled apron band, old refinish, ca. 1895, 18 x 36", 7' 4" h. (ILLUS.) **1,800**

Cherry & Leather Ornate Hall Tree

Hall tree, Victorian Aesthetic Movement style, cherry, a high oval crestrail centered by scroll carving & enclosing small spindles above a flat molded crestrail over a circle-incised frieze band above a large rectangular beveled mirror flanked by shaped sides w/tall slender outside columns, a large scroll-embossed leather panel below the mirror & above a pierced scroll lower rail, mounted w/six brass hooks, low shaped arms flank the rectangular seat over an arched spindled apron, a bottom open shelf w/one end projecting out to support a metal drip pan below a rectangular metal bracket, original finish, ca. 1890s, 17 x 36", 7' 4" h. (ILLUS.) **1,500**

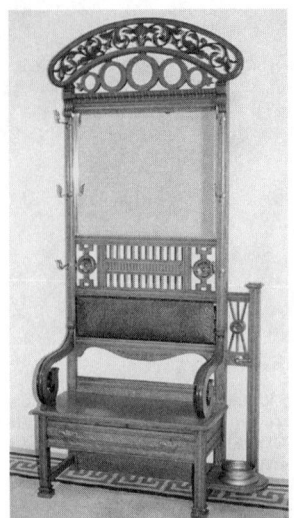

Ornately Pierced Aesthetic Hall Tree

Hall tree, Victorian Aesthetic Movement style, oak, a long arched oval crestrail enclosing ornate pierced leafy scrolls above an arched panel w/graduated rings above the flat molded rail & sides enclosing a large rectangular beveled mirror, each side mounted w/three cast-brass hooks, a pierced lattice panel below the mirror & above a narrow rectangular padded back panel, heavy C-scroll arms on the narrow rectangular seat over a long line-incised drawer w/stamped brass pulls, a projecting post & lattice panel at one side supporting a projecting rounded shelf w/a brass drip pan, square stile legs, original finish, ca. 1895, 20 x 42", 7' 6" h. (ILLUS.) **2,000**

Oak Aesthetic Movement Hall Tree

Hall tree, Victorian Aesthetic Movement style, oak, a wide flaring stepped cornice above a framework of slender square stiles & rails, a top panel w/a narrow almond-shaped panel carved w/scrolls flanking a central lion mask, a large rectangular beveled mirror over a narrow carved & pierced band above the large rectangular back panel carved w/ornate scrolls, the sides mounted w/six double scrolling iron hooks, simple shaped arms over the rectangular seat above a long narrow drawer w/stamped brass pulls, square slightly curved front legs, a pierced half-round side shelf at each side of the base for holding missing drip pans, original finish, ca. 1890s, 18 x 44", 7' 4" h., as is (ILLUS.) **2,400**

Fancy Large Baroque Style Hall Tree

Hall tree, Victorian Baroque Revival style, quarter-sawn oak, a high arched & pierce-carved crest on the overhanging crestrail supported by ornate heavy carved S-scroll dragon-form brackets above the very large rectangular beveled mirror over a lower scroll-carved back panel, solid rounded arms flank the rectangular lift-seat over a deep well, mounted w/four double cast-metal hooks, flat incised apron flanked by paw feet, refinished, ca. 1900, 22 x 50", 7' 8" h. (ILLUS.) **3,500**

Hall tree, Victorian Eastlake style, oak, the pierced & upswept crest on a narrow flaring crestrail over a delicately-pierced narrow almond-shaped panel above a small vertical rectangular mirror beside a narrow vertical pierced panel w/flat short rails flanked a figural carved crescent moon face, a large lower splat w/incurved sides & pierced narrow splat sections flanking a leaf-incised panel above a solid lower back panel flanked by narrow flat open arms on shaped supports over the rectangular seat, tapering turned front legs & a projecting rounded shelf w/metal drip pan at one side, the top mounted w/six brass hooks, refinished, ca. 1890s, 18 x 26", 7' h. (ILLUS., below) **1,200**

Tall Narrow Eastlake Hall Tree

Hall tree, Victorian Eastlake style, walnut & burl walnut, the high rectangular slightly projecting crest w/a flat key-pierced rail divided by four molded blocks ending in short turned bulbous spindles & two topped by angular leaf finials, two narrow burled frieze bands above the tall rectangular beveled mirror flanked by wide sides w/narrow burl panels incised w/stylized angular urn designs, the lower section w/a rectangular white marble center section over a single drawer & flanked by square frameworks for canes & umbrellas all supported on square reeded legs w/small corner ball finials, a lower paneled back above a bottom shelf joined by a flat molded base on thick wedge feet, fitted w/four projecting peg hooks on each side, refinished, ca. 1880, 14 x 48", 8' h. **3,500**

Hall tree, Victorian Golden Oak style, a wide serpentine crestrail w/carved center arch over a rosette & rounded scroll-carved ears above a framework w/pierced scroll-carved brackets forming a circle centered by a diamond-shaped beveled mirror above another lower rectangular panel w/two large pierced scroll-carved corner brackets & a spindled angled center rail, simple open arms flanked by lift-seat, square stile legs w/knob feet, six cast-iron hooks,

refinished, ca. 1890s, 18 x 30", 7' 4" h. (ILLUS., below).. **1,500**

Oak Hall Tree with Pierced Panels

Ornately Spindled Oak Hall Tree

Hall tree, Victorian Golden Oak style, oak, a large serpentine scroll-carved crestrail on the flaring cornice above a dentil-carved band & a turned spindle rail above a large square beveled mirror flanked by side panels w/a shell carving over three tall slender spindles above another turned spindle rail over a row of five vasiform scroll-carved splats, mounted w/six cast-brass hooks, open shaped arms flanking the rectangular seat over a single long drawer w/stamped brass pulls, turned tapering front legs w/knob feet joined to square back legs w/square stretchers, a side base half-round rail for the wooden drip pan, upper support arm missing, refinished, ca. 1890s, 16 x 44", 7' 10" h. (ILLUS.) **2,400**

Scrolling Pierced Oak Hall Tree

Hall tree, Victorian Golden Oak style, oak, the ornate upper section w/a high peaked & scroll-carved center crest & outscrolled scroll-carved ears above serpentine pierced sides enclosing a round beveled mirror & above a pierced & scroll-carved splat above a row of slender turned spindles, flat side stiles, mounted w/four ornate cast-brass double coat hooks, shaped open arms on flat S-scroll arms supports above the lift-seat over a deep wells, flat serpentine front legs & serpentine apron, refinished, ca. 1900, 20 x 30", 7' h. (ILLUS.) **1,500**

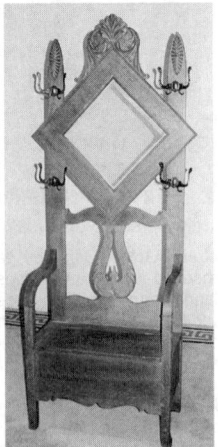

Oak Hall Tree with Diamond Mirror

Hall tree, Victorian Golden Oak style, quarter-sawn oak, a large flat diamond-shaped frame enclosing a beveled mirror below a high arched scroll-carved crest, supported on flat pointed stiles w/carved ovals at the peaks, a serpentine mid-rail above a pierced & scroll-trimmed lower splat, rounded open arms above the lift-seat above a scalloped apron, refinished, ca. 1890s, 18 x 24", 6' 10" h. (ILLUS.) **1,250**

Very Fine Eastlake Hall Tree

Hall tree, Victorian Golden Oak style, quarter-sawn oak, a large wide top w/an arched molded crestrail centered by scroll-carved crest flanked by scroll-carved corner finials above rounded side columns flanked the wide flat panels enclosing the arched & shaped rectangular beveled mirror w/a bottom section of arched carved scrolls, mounted w/four ornate cast-metal double coat hooks, a rectangular top above a deep long drawer w/stamped-brass pulls raised on spiral-turned spindles above a rectangular pullout bench on flat arched front legs w/scroll-carved trim & supported on square tapering frame legs, the back of the framework w/flattened scroll-carved legs w/paw feet, refinished, ca. 1890s, 30 x 34", 7' h. (ILLUS.) **1,600**

Very Large Ornate Oak Hall Tree

Hall tree, Victorian Golden Oak style, quarter-sawn oak, a wide arched crestrail w/ornate leafy scroll carving centered by an oval medallion & flanked by wide sides w/rounded scroll-carved tops all enclosing a large rectangular beveled mirror w/a gently arched top & flanked by four cast-brass double hooks, a wide lower back panels w/applied scroll carving & a serpentine bottom edge flanked by heavy serpentine arms w/scroll hand grips & leaf-carved incurved arm supports flanking the wide rectangular seat over a grouping of four scroll-carved drawers, scroll-carved front feet, original finish, ca. 1890s, 22 x 46", 7' 6" h. (ILLUS.)................. **4,000**

Fancy Gothic Revival Hall Tree

Hall tree, Victorian Gothic Revival style, chestnut, a high arched, scroll-carved & pierced crestrail on a molded arched rail over two arched oblong cutout flanked by corner drops & mounted w/iron hooks above an arched center mirror flanked by ornate scroll-carved & C-form cutout sides mounted w/further hooks over an ornately cutout panel above a center small white marble shelf w/curved front above a conforming small drawer flanked by round wood rings above long slender serpentine support brackets on the tall base section w/scroll-cut sides & fancy shaped cutouts over a molded base w/two round side rings enclosing cast-iron drip pans, refinished, ca. 1860, 16 x 44", 7' h. (ILLUS.)................................. **1,600**

Slender Pierce-carved Hall Tree

Hall tree, Victorian Renaissance Revival style, walnut, a small arched top cornice w/a fleur-de-lis-carved center crest over a pierce carved arched panel above the scroll-cut wide oval framework w/narrow pierced leafy scroll-carved curved panels framing an oval mirror within a raised molded frame, mounted w/seven coat pegs, raised above a small white marble rectangular shelf over a small drawer w/leaf-carved pulls flanked by open side rings & raised on slender ring-turned columns, the oblong base platform fitted at the sides w/round cast-iron drip pans, ca. 1870, 16 x 36", 7' h. (ILLUS.)...................... **1,400**

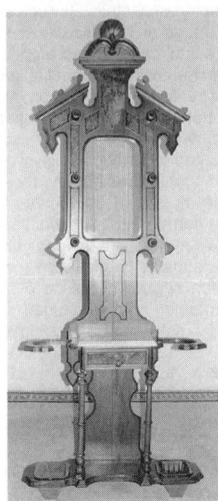

Slender Renaissance Hall Tree

Hall tree, Victorian Renaissance Revival style, walnut & burl walnut, a tall central crest w/a carved shell atop an arched molding & cornice raised above canted side cornices w/scallop-cut crests over raised burl panels across the top & down the sides of the framework mounted w/six coat pegs & centering a rounded rectangular mirror, a waisted lower section w/a raised burl panel above a rectangular white marble shelf over a small burl-paneled drawer flanked by C-form supports at the sides & raised on slender ring-turned supports above the oblong platform base w/rectangular cast-iron drip pans, refinished, ca. 1875, 15 x 30", 7' 4" h. (ILLUS.) **1,200**

Renaissance Hall Tree with Lady

Hall tree, Victorian Renaissance Revival style, walnut & burl walnut, the high top w/a molded, arched crestrail over a flaring molded cornice over angled side panels & blocks centered by an oval medallion carved in relief w/a classical lady's head, flaring side cornices above wide shaped sides w/narrow burl panels & mounted w/six brass hooks above a rectangular red marble top over a long narrow burl-paneled drawer above an arched & burl-paneled support, curled flat side supports & a shaped thick base platform fitted at the sides w/cast-iron drip pans, ca. 1870s, 17 x 48", 8' h. (ILLUS.) **3,500**

Victorian Rococo Walnut Hall Tree

Hall tree, Victorian Rococo style, walnut, a wide rounded molded frame w/grape-carved crest w/finial & eight wooden pegs encloses large round mirror above flat side stiles & a scroll-carved center splat above the white marble serpentine shelf above a carved serpentine apron supported on cabriole front legs & the flat back stiles, serpentine base platform w/round drip pans at each end, second half 19th c., 16 x 42", 7' h. (ILLUS.) **1,800**

Hall tree, Victorian Rococo style, walnut, the wide shield-form top frame composed of flat C- and S-scrolls mounted w/coat pegs above a small oval mirror raised on a center splat w/a cutout heart-shaped top curving down top figural swan's neck-carved side rails w/pegs & continuing down to a wide flat vasiform back behind a tall rectangular open framework composed of slender bobbin-turned rails above the rectangular base fitted w/a rectangular metal drip pan, original dark finish, ca. 1860, 12 x 28", 6' 6" h. (ILLUS., top of next page).. **650**

Swan head-carved Rococo Hall Tree

Simple Early Oak Ice Box

Ice Boxes

Early 20th century, oak, the upright case w/a rectangular top over two long rectangular three-panel doors w/original nickel-plate hardware, flat molded base, paneled sides, refinished, ca. 1910, 20 x 24", 40" h. (ILLUS., top next column).................... **400**

Victorian Golden Oak style, rectangular top w/a deep flaring cornice above a long rectangular scroll-carved panel over a pair of paneled scroll-carved doors over the scalloped apron & block feet, paneled sides, original heavy brass hardware, zinc-lined w/wire shelves, old worn fish, ca. 1890s, 20 x 28", 40" h., as is (ILLUS., to the right) **450**

Fancy Oak Ice Box with Worn Finish

Love Seats, Sofas & Settees

"Chesterfield" Style Chaise Lounge

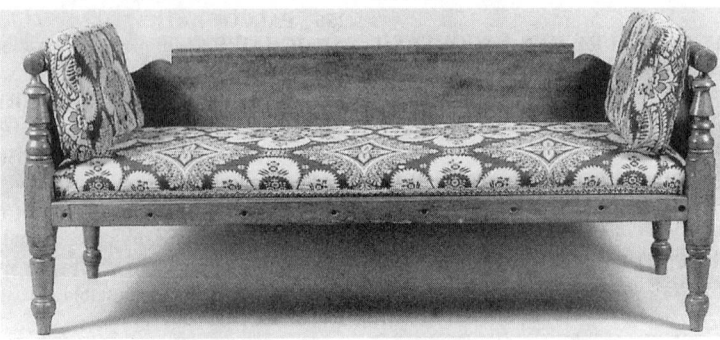

Early Country-style Daybed

Chaise lounge, Victorian-style "Chester-field" design, an high angled adjustable back rest at one end above the long rectangular seat w/a deep flat apron, overall tufted brown leather upholstery w/tack trim, on casters, early 20th c., 62" l. (ILLUS., bottom previous page) **2,990**

Daybed, Early American country-style, tiger stripe & bird's-eye maple, a low backboard w/a flat top & serpentine ends flanked by turned rod end arms raised on ring-and-baluster-turned arm supports above the seat w/an added slip seat, raised on turned & tapering legs w/tapering ovoid feet, early 19th c., 71" l. (ILLUS., top of page) **863**

Daybed, Louis Philippe style, mahogany, a sleigh-bed form w/solid outscrolled head- and foot boards joined by deep rails & flat legs w/ormolu mounts, France, second quarter 19th c., 44 1/2 x 77", 40" h. (ILLUS.) **920**

Early French Duchesse Brisee

Duchesse brisee, Louis XVI style, beech-wood, two-part construction, one section w/a high barrel-form upholstered back over a long cushion seat raised on a conforming frame w/simple turned tapering fluted legs, the second section formed as a similar low-backed chair curved at the foot to align w/the first section, France, late 18th c. (ILLUS.) **3,738**

Louis Philippe "Sleigh-form" Daybed

Delicate Decorated Federal Recamier

Rare Aesthetic Movement Recamier

Recamier, Federal style, painted & decorated wood, the delicate frame w/a high backswept scrolling end w/a pierced panel set w/three gilt knobs over a curved gilt-stenciled panel & backed by a long slender scroll-ended arm above the long seat composed of three caned panels, the foot w/a low inward curved solid C-scroll footboard, raised on four flat outswept scrolled legs on knob feet, decorated overall w/dark grain painted background highlighted w/gilt banding & gilt-stenciled classical details, possibly the Finley Shop, Baltimore, Maryland, ca. 1815, 80" l. (ILLUS., bottom previous page) **3,600**

Fine Neoclassical Recamier

Recamier, Neoclassical style, mahogany, one end w/a high out-scrolled upholstered arm supported by a scroll-and-fan-carved front rail, a matching lower arm at the opposite end, joined by a tapering serpentine crestrail on the upholstered back, upholstered seat on the reeded seatrail, raised on outswept cornucopia-carved legs w/paw feet on casters, Europe, second quarter 19th c., 25 x 69", 38" h. (ILLUS.) **1,955**

Recamier, Victorian Aesthetic Movement style, inlaid mahogany, a two-panel rectangular back behind a wide rolled upholstered end arm w/a fan-carved arm support, the long upholstered seat on a flat seatrail delicately inlaid w/tiny sunflower blossoms, on heavy tapering block feet, attributed to Herter Brothers, New York,

New York, ca. 1870-90, 76" l. (ILLUS., top of page) **10,575**

Fine Chippendale-Style Settee

Settee, Chippendale-Style, mahogany, a double-chairback style w/two serpentine crestrail above scrolling foliate-pierced & carved splats, shaped open arms w/scrolled hand grips on incurved arm supports above the long upholstered seat, three front cabriole legs w/leaf-carved knees & ending in claw-and-ball feet, late 19th c., 20 x 45", 40 1/2" h. (ILLUS.) **748**

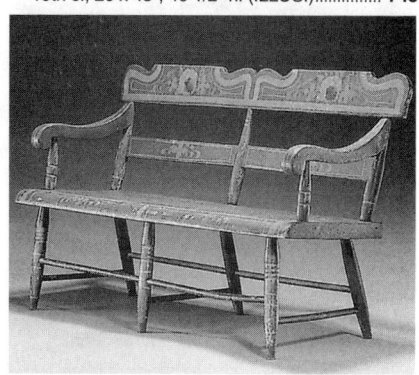

Rare Decorated Miniature Settee

Settee, Early American country-style, miniature, painted & decorated, the double arched crestrail above three turned stiles & double rails flanked by downswept arms on turned supports over the long plank seat, on six ring-turned cylindrical legs joined by round stretchers, original green-painted surface w/yellow & red painted florals & banding on the crests, rails & seat, possibly Pennsylvania, mid-19th c., 9 1/4 x 26", 16 1/2" h. (ILLUS.).. **5,288**

Rare Windsor Child's Settee

Settee, Windsor child's size, a flat crestrail & flat even arms over 21 canted swelling cylindrical spindles over a rectangular plank seat w/molded edges, on four splayed ring-incised & baluster-turned legs, old natural finish, New England, 19th c., 13 1/2 x 27", 18 1/2" h. (ILLUS.)... **3,760**

One of Two Classical Settees

Settees, Classical style, mahogany, the serpentine back w/a leaf-carved center crest flanked by long scrolled serpentine rails arched down to frame to long tufted upholstered back, the long serpentine upholstered seat w/a deep conforming apron w/scroll-carved corner returns, on casters, American, second quarter 19th c., 27 x 61", 38" h., pr. (ILLUS. of one) **2,300**

Rare Early Painted Child's Settle

Settle, Early American child's country-style, painted & decorated pine, the high rectangular flat back flanked w/downswept end arms flanking the long lift-top seat over a deep box base, overall painted red ground decorated w/bold black arches, scrolls & dashes, New England, early 19th c., 14 1/2 x 40", 29 3/4" h. (ILLUS.).... **9,600**

Early Biedermeier Walnut Sofa

Sofa, Biedermeier style, walnut, a narrow flat ormolu-mounted crestrail above the upholstered back flanked by outswept scroll arms within a conforming frame above the long upholstered seat on a ormolu-mounted flat seatrail, outswept flattened scroll legs, Europe, first half 19th c., 26 x 80 1/2", 35 1/2" h. (ILLUS.) **1,725**

Fancy Chippendale Revival Sofa

Sofa, Chippendale Revival style, walnut, the high upholstered back w/an arched & scalloped crestrail flanked by low outscrolled upholstered arms flanking the long upholstered seat w/a flat seatrail raised on three cabriole front legs w/shell-carved knees & drake feet, early 20th c., 81" l., 49" h. (ILLUS.) **2,475**

Unmarked Mission-Style Sofa

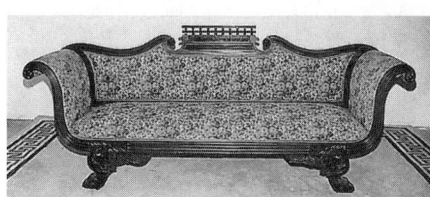

Classical Sofa with Unusual Crest

Sofa, Classical style, mahogany, the broken-scroll serpentine crestrail centered by a raised spindled crest over narrow bands above the upholstered back, the outscrolled deep arms w/reeded rosette-tipped supports continuing down to the seatrail w/leaf-carved blocks above the carved paw feet w/wing-carved returns, refinished, ca. 1840s, later upholstery, 29 x 80", 36" h. (ILLUS.) **1,200**

Sofa, Classical style, mahogany, the flat bar-topped crestrail w/leaf-carved scroll ends raised above serpentine rails above the long upholstered back flanked by high incurved padded arms w/bolsters & cornucopia-carved arm supports, the flat seatrail centered by a rectangular stenciled panel, raised on heavy paw front legs w/long fruit-carved returns, on casters, original polished finish, ca. 1830s, 30 x 76", 34" h. **3,600**

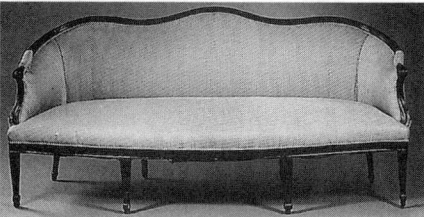

Fine George III-Style Sofa

Sofa, George III-Style, ebonized wood, the long narrow serpentine crestrail above the upholstered back curves down to from the padded & upholstered arms, the long upholstered seat raised on four square tapering front legs w/spade feet, England, ca. 1900, 29 x 87", 39 1/2" h. (ILLUS.) **2,300**

Fine Louis-XVI-Style Sofa

Sofa, Louis XVI-Style, giltwood, a narrow beaded & rope-carved oval frame encloses the upholstered back flanked by open padded arms on rope-carved incurved supports above the upholstered seat, a guilloche-carved seatrail raised on four stop-fluted tapering front legs on peg feet, France, ca. 1900, 26 1/2 x 68", 39 1/2" h. (ILLUS.) **2,530**

Sofa, Mission-style (Arts & Crafts movement), oak, the long gently arched crestrail over a back w/multiple slats between square stiles & flat drop arms over five slats, the replaced cushion seat w/a wide seat rail., square stile front legs, medium brown finish, water damage to rear legs, early 20th c., 26 1/2 x 69", 37 1/2" h. (ILLUS., top of page) **1,150**

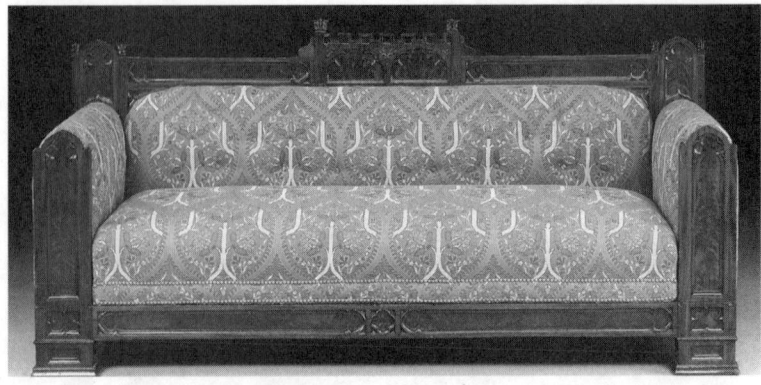

Unusual Gothic Revival Sofa

Carved Victorian Eastlake Sofa

Sofa, Victorian Eastlake style, ebonized wood, an arched crestrail over a leafy vine-carved panel above a leafy scroll-carved central back splat separating two square upholstered back panels, low outscrolled arms w/carved supports flank the wide upholstered seat on simple seat rail & blocked & turned tapering front legs, ca. 1880s, 68" l. (ILLUS.) **200-300**

Sofa, Victorian Gothic Revival style, mahogany, the molded & carved crestrail centered by a raised panel w/Gothic style carved designs flanked by rounded stiles carved w/Gothic arches, the low upholstered back flanked by rounded upholstered arms w/wide paneled & Gothic arch-carved front supports continuing down to from the paneled block feet, the flat paneled seatrail w/carved Gothic details, New York City, ca. 1840-60, 28 x 84", 40 1/2" h. (ILLUS., top of page) **4,780**

Inlaid Rosewood Renaissance Sofa

Sofa, Victorian Renaissance Revival, inlaid rosewood, the upholstered arched & stepped crestrail above the upholstered back flanked by closed upholstered arms w/incurved arm supports, the narrow bowed seatrail inlaid w/a band of anthemion, on gilt-trimmed fluted turned tapering legs on casters, ca. 1870, 72" l. (ILLUS.)..... **1,265**

Fine Renaissance Revival Rosewood Sofa

Triple-back Belter-style Sofa

Sofa, Victorian Renaissance Revival style, carved rosewood, a triple-panel back, the high upholstered central panel w/pierced scroll-carved crestrail flanked by slender colonettes w/turned finials flanked by the lower upholstered side panels each w/side stiles topped by gilt-bronze inset disks w/Classical heads & trimmed w/leaf carving, the padded open arms w/arm supports carved w/figural maiden heads, long oval upholstered seat w/a conforming seatrail w/fan-carved trim & a scroll-carved center drop, on four turned & tapering front trumpet legs on casters, ca. 1870s, New York City, 31 x 82", 43" h. (ILLUS., bottom previous page)................. **1,150**

Sofa, Victorian Rococo style, carved & laminated rosewood, a long triple-back style w/high chair back corseted sections at each end enclosed by wide ornate pierced scroll-carved arching rails, rails continue down & up around the lower arched central section w/a similarly carved crestrail, the side rails continue down over the half-length closed upholstered arms w/incurved arm supports, the long serpentine-fronted seat w/a conforming seatrail carved w/scrolls & a central floral reserve, on demi-cabriole front legs on casters, attributed to John Henry Belter, New York City, ca. 1855, 31 x 88", 41" h. (ILLUS., top of page)...... **16,675**

Fine "Stanton Hall" Rococo Sofa

Sofa Attributed to Alexander Roux

Sofa, Victorian Rococo style, carved & laminated rosewood, the ornate pierce-carved crestrail centered by a higher peaked section w/a flower cluster flanked by beaded bands, the lower curved side rails curve down around to the closed upholstered arms w/incurved arm supports, long serpentine-front seat w/a conforming seatrail carved w/a center blossom, demi-cabriole front legs on casters, "Stanton Hall" patt. by Meeks of New York City, ca. 1855, original finish, 36 x 66", 4' h. (ILLUS., bottom of previous page)... **5,500**

Sofa, Victorian Rococo style, carved & laminated rosewood, the wide serpentine crestrail centered by a high arched & pierced crest w/asymmetrical scrolls & continuing to rounded corner crests w/matching carving, closed upholstered arms w/incurved arm supports, serpentine-fronted seat w/a conforming seatrail carved w/ornate scrolls, demi-cabriole front legs on casters, attributed to Alexander Roux, New York City, ca. 1850s, original finish, later upholstery, 32 x 72", 44" h. (ILLUS., top of page)........................ **5,000**

Rococo 'Inverted Heart' Back Sofa

Sofa, Victorian Rococo style, walnut, a central 'inverted heart' tufted upholstered back panel w/a grape-carved crest flanked by high rounded side rails w/further grape carving, rolled upholstered closed arms w/S-scroll carved arm supports, long seat w/serpentine front above a conforming seatrail centered by a carved grape cluster, on demi-cabriole front legs, original finish, ca. 1865, 28 x 72", 40" h. (ILLUS.).............................. **1,800**

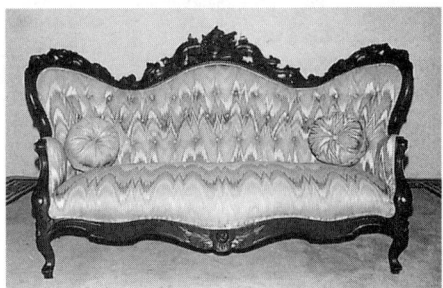

Nicely Carved Walnut Rococo Sofa

Sofa, Victorian Rococo style, walnut, the double serpentine crestrail centered by a pierced scrolled leaf & fruit-carved crest w/similar carving on the rounded rail corners continuing down to the closed upholstered arms w/incurved arm supports, a tufted upholstered back & long serpentine seat w/a conforming seatrail carved in the center w/a blossom & leaves, on demi-cabriole front legs w/peg feet, refinished, new upholstery, ca. 1860, 28 x 70", 38" h. (ILLUS.).............................. **2,500**

Fine William IV M ahogany Sofa

Sofa, William IV style, mahogany, a thin flat crestrail w/rounded corners above the long upholstered back, wide upholstered arms w/wide lotus-carved front supports, a long cushion seat above an ogee apron, heavy tapering knob-and-ring-turned legs w/peg feet on casters, England, second quarter 19th c., 25 1/2 x 79", 34 1/2" h. (ILLUS.) **978**

Mirrors

Lovely Adams-Style Gesso Mirror

Adams-Style wall mirror, gilt gesso & paint, a large narrow oval frame topped by a high arched pierced crest composed of ornate leafy scrolls, draperies & side floral swags centered at the peak by a small oval h.p. medallion of a woman in classical dress, original finish, minor damage, late 19th - early 20th c., 30" w., 4' 10" h. (ILLUS.) **650**

Classical Child's Cheval Mirror

Classical cheval mirror, child's size, mahogany, a tall rectangular mahogany frame w/brass button corner mounts swiveling between tapering columnar uprights w/flame finials raised on a trestle-form base w/outswept legs w/knob finials above knob feet, early 19th c., 15 x 18", 38" h. (ILLUS.) **1,035**

Classical Giltwood Overmantel Mirror

Classical overmantel mirror, carved giltwood, a long rectangular frame composed of half-round columns w/ring-turned segments alternating w/sections of delicate scrolls, corner blocks w/molded rosettes, American, second quarter 19th c., scattered minor gilt loss, 38 1/4 x 58" (ILLUS.) **1,840**

Small Classical Giltwood Mirror

Classical wall mirror, carved giltwood, a rectangular frame w/the outer band joining large ornate scroll-carved corners enclosing an inner frame composed of half-round ring-and-baluster-turned columns & corner blocks w/rosettes, American, second quarter 19th c., 19 x 32" (ILLUS.) **748**

Classical Giltwood Pier Mirror

Classical pier mirror, giltwood, rectangular frame w/half-round ring-and-baluster-turned columns joined by rosette-carved corner blocks, America, 1820-40, 20 1/2 x 31 1/4" (ILLUS.) **940**

Giltwood and Mahogany Federal Mirrors

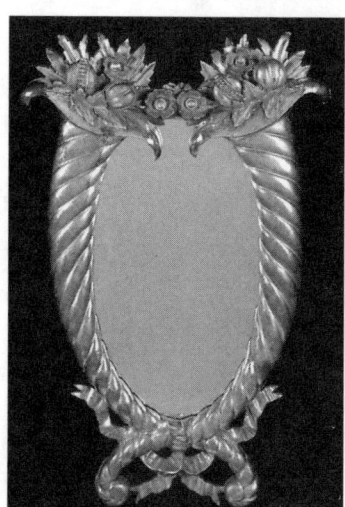

Rare Classical Cornucopia Mirror

rosettes joined by a ring-and-knob-turned half-column, the upper mirror probably replacing original reverse-painted pane, ca. 1830s, 20 x 40" (ILLUS. right with small giltwood mirror) **450**

Federal wall mirror, giltwood, the flat flaring pediment w/blocked ends above a band of small suspended spheres above the narrow reeded frame enclosing an upper rectangular reverse-painted glass panel w/a scene of a fisherman above the rectangular mirror, small corner blocks at the bottom, ca. 1830, 18 x 32" (ILLUS. left, top of page) **350**

Classical wall mirror, giltwood, a large oval mirror enclosed by two long entwined rope-twisted cornucopias issuing fruit & foliate at the top & w/a ribbon-tied base, New York City, 1820-30, 24 x 35 1/2" (ILLUS.) **8,225**

Federal wall mirror, carved mahogany, the flat pediment w/rounded corners & a bowed center above a band of small spheres over a scroll-inlaid frieze band flanked by corner blocks w/metal rosettes, bold ring-and-baluster-turned & leaf-carved side columns flanking a small rectangular mirror above a tall rectangular mirror, bottom corner blocks w/metal

Fancy Louis XVI-Style Pier Mirror

Louis XVI-Style pier mirror, giltwood, the gently arched crest ornately molded w/delicate flowers & ribbons above suspended floral swags across the top of the mirror, narrow scroll-molded frame w/rounded corners, France, late 19th - early 20th c., 34 x 6' 6" h. (ILLUS.)............ **1,495**

Ornate Louis XVI-Style Mirror

Louis XVI-Style wall mirror, giltwood, the arched crest centered by a shell-and-acanthus cast openwork crest flanked by corner scrolls w/bird finials, the arched mirror surrounded by an annulated slip, mirrored panels & an egg-and-dart-molded frame, France, late 19th c., 60 1/2 x 94" (ILLUS.) **3,450**

Napoleon III Mirror with Urn Finial

Napoleon III overmantel mirror, giltwood, the tall narrow rectangular molded frame

topped by an urn finial flanked by laurel leaf garlands & oak leaf sprays, France, third quarter 19th c., 46 x 78 3/4" (ILLUS.) **920**

Italian Neoclassical Cheval Mirror

Neoclassical cheval mirror, walnut, surmounted by a gilded and pierced palmetto crest flanked by gilt urn-form finials, the large rectangular mirror enclosed by a floral-, urn- and griffin-inlaid frame & supported on each side by two columns also inlaid, raised on arched inlaid base supports, Italy, late 18th c., 45" w., 7' 1" h. (ILLUS.) **6,900**

Fancy Neoclassical-Style Pier Mirror

Neoclassical-Style pier mirror, gilt gesso, the tall rectangular frame topped by an ornate pierced crest centered by a pineapple & leaf finial over a large oval plaque embossed w/the figure of a classical woman, flanked by standing winged griffins, the molded crestrail w/a leaf band, openwork leafy swags across the top of the tall rectangular mirror flanked by side rails w/tall urns above caryatids & squared pilasters down the sides, deep molded base rail w/ornate scrolls, original finish, late 19th c., 30 x 66" (ILLUS.) ... **2,500**

Early Queen Anne Wall Mirror

Queen Anne wall mirror, walnut, the scrolling cutout crest above the arched mirror incised at the top w/a star, a narrow molded frame w/a wide serpentine base drop, early 18th c., 16 3/4" w., 39" h. (ILLUS.) **2,070**

Regency Classical Wall Mirror

Regency wall mirror, giltwood, the flat narrow overhanging crest w/blocked corners above a row of small spheres above a wide frieze panel molded w/a mythological harvest scene flanked by leaf-embossed side panels, narrow half-round side cluster columns flank the tall rectangular mirror, a narrow molded base band w/small corner blocks w/rosettes, England, first quarter 19th c., 26 x 38 1/2" (ILLUS.) **1,035**

Venetian Rococo Wall Mirror

Rococo-style wall mirror, giltwood & paint, wide rectangular frame molded w/large openwork scrolling acanthus leaves against a red-painted ground, Italy, early 20th c., 26 1/2 x 30 1/4" (ILLUS.) **1,035**

Finely Engraved Venetian Mirror

Venetian wall mirror, giltwood, the wide cartouche-shaped frame set w/curved engraved mirror panels enclosing the shaped mirror finely engraved w/a large classical maiden, Italy, mid-18th c., 23 1/4 x 31 1/2" (ILLUS.) **3,910**

Ornate Baroque Revival Mirror

Victorian Baroque Revival wall mirror, gilt gesso, a wide flaring flat pediment centered by an scalloped & arched crest decorated w/ornate scrolls & flanked by pointed shell-molded corner ears, the cornice, wide sides & blocked base band molded overall w/ornate scrolling baroque designs, original surface, late 19th - early 20th c., 20" w., 36" h. (ILLUS.)............ **400**

Late Victorian Cheval Mirror

Victorian country-style cheval mirror, walnut, a tall narrow rectangular mirror frame topped w/corner brackets composed of carved pyramidal blocks centering carved fruit & leaves, enclosing a beveled mirror swiveling between tall

rope-twist-turned side supports raised on arched & outswept legs w/brass claw & glass ball mounts, joined w/by ropetwist stretcher & brackets, late 19th c., refinished, 14 x 26", 6' h. (ILLUS.) **750**

Rare Country Victorian Mirror

Victorian country-style wall mirror, tiger stripe maple, rectangular wide sides of figured maple within a narrow black molding, each side panel centered by a small ivory or bone disk w/inlaid corner blocks each w/another disk, American, 19th c., 18 1/2 x 22 1/2" (ILLUS.) **5,640**

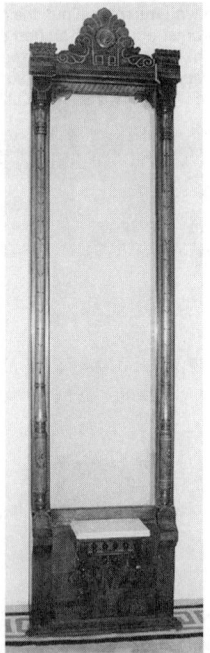

Tall Victorian Eastlake Pier Mirror

Golden Oak Mirror with Fancy Crest

Victorian Eastlake style pier mirror, walnut, a high arched fan-carved crest centered by a roundel & flanked by notched corner blocks above slender half-round turned columns flanking the tall rectangular mirror above a small white marble shelf supported on a spindled apron & brackets above a large line-incised base panel, refinished, ca. 1885, 12 x 28", 9' 8" h. (ILLUS., bottom previous page) **1,600**

Victorian Golden Oak style hall mirror, quarter-sawn oak, the wide rectangular frame w/an ornate pierce-carved crest w/facing griffins flanking an oval cartouche, the sides mounted w/four metal coat hooks, enclosing a beveled mirror, refinished, ca. 1900k 30 x 48" (ILLUS., top of page).. **900**

Victorian Rococo style overmantel mirror, giltwood, a long molded oval frame w/a pierce-carved crest of leafy scrolls centering a cartouche finial, large pierced & scroll-carved base brackets, burnished highlights, American, mid-19th c., 56 x 65" (ILLUS., below)............................. **2,760**

Fancy Victorian Overmantel Mirror

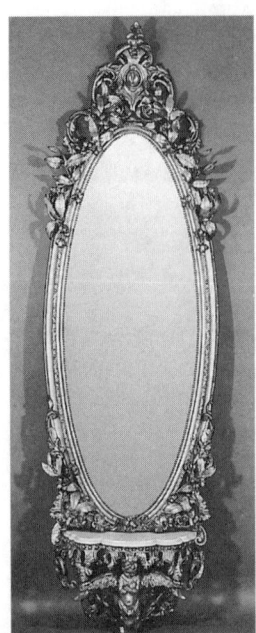

Rare Victorian Rococo Pier Mirror

Victorian Rococo style pier mirror, gilt-wood, a tall narrow molded oval frame topped by a very high openwork leafy scroll crest centering a large cartouche, ornate leafy scroll base brackets above the half-round scalloped white marble shelf raised on an ornate scroll-carved bracket centered by a full-figure cherub, mid-19th c., 15 x 34", 9' h. (ILLUS.) **11,213**

Victorian Rococo Shaving Mirror

Victorian Rococo style shaving mirror, walnut & burl walnut, table model, a wide rectangular flat frame w/incised leaf bands mounted w/an ornate pierced scroll-carved crest centering a flower basket all enclosing a mirror swiveling between scroll-carved uprights w/scroll brackets above the serpentine platform w/projecting corners & burl veneer above a pair of narrow serpentine burl veneer drawers w/original brass knobs, original finish, mid-19th c., 12 x 20", 28" h. (ILLUS.) **1,200**

Victorian Rococo Wall Mirror

Victorian Rococo style wall mirror, gilt gesso, the wide cove-molded rectangular frame decorated at each corner w/ornate leafy-scroll brackets & swags, thin inner beaded band around the two-part mirror, original finish, mid-19th c., 20 x 48" (ILLUS.) **950**

Parlor Suites

Bentwood: settee & two armchairs; settee w/serpentine crestrail over three loop-framed caned panels over corner scrolls, scrolled open arms on the long oval seat raised on four simple turned & slightly curved legs joined by an oval bentwood stretcher, signed "Kohn," Austria, late 19th c., settee 58" l., the set (ILLUS. of settee, top of next page) **978**

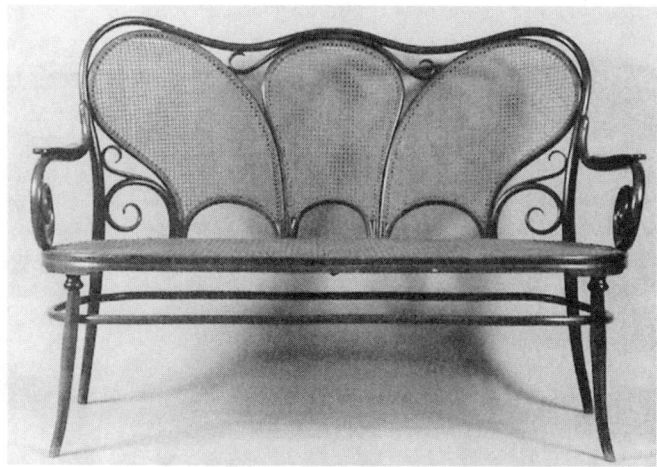

Early Bentwood Settee from a Suite

Part of Louis XV-Style Parlor Suite

Louis XV-Style: settee & four armchairs; painted wood, the settee w/a long oval upholstered back
within a narrow molded & floral-trimmed rail raised above the long overupholstered seat flanked by
padded open arms, serpentine seatrail w/delicate scrolls, raised on cabriole legs, matching armchairs w/squared balloon backs, painted beige, France, late 19th - early 20th c., the set (ILLUS. of
part) **2,185**

Part of Louis XVI-Style Giltwood Suite

A Portion of an Eastlake Parlor Suite

Louis XVI-Style: settee & four armchairs; giltwood, the settee w/a gently arched incurving delicately carved crestrail continuing to form the tops of the arms supported on incurved arm supports above the long upholstered seat on a dentil-carved seat rail on round tapering stop-fluted legs, each chair w/an oval upholstered back, France, late 19th c., settee 53" l., the set (ILLUS. of part, bottom, previous page) **2,530**

Mission-style (Arts & Crafts movement): armchair, settle & rocking chair w/arms; oak, the settle w/arched crestrail over ten vertical back slats centered w/a wide back slat, shaped arms over one wide & two narrow slats, curved seatrails, brown leather spring cushion seat, armchair & rocker w/a curved crestrail over two further rails above & below five vertical back slats, shaped arms, brown leather spring cushion seats, medium brown finish, rocker & settle w/original brass Stickley Brothers Quaint Furniture tags, early 20th c., settle 54 1/4" w., the set (minor wear) **1,495**

Victorian Eastlake style: settee, armchair, platform rocker & four side chairs; walnut, each piece w/an arched crestrail carved w/scrolls & a narrow fan-carved reserve atop the line-incised back frame w/top corner brackets, padded upholstered open arms, squared upholstered seats, ring-and-baluster-turned front legs on casters, settee 52" l., ca. 1880, the set (ILLUS. of part, top of page) **805**

Fine Renaissance Sofa from a Set

Victorian Renaissance Revival style: sofa, two armchairs & one side chair; walnut & burl walnut, the sofa w/a triple-panel back, the vertical oval center upholstered panel within a block-carved frame topped by a high crown-form crest centered by a medallion carved w/a woman's head, the horizontal oval side panels in simple oval frames w/peaked scroll-carved crests, curved padded open arms w/the supports carved w/ladies' heads, long seat w/a short carved drops, raised on tapering trumpet legs on casters, the chairs w/matching backs, attributed to John Jelliff, Newark, New Jersey, ca. 1870, original finish, later upholstery, sofa 72" l., the set (ILLUS. of sofa) **7,500**

Chairs in the Rare "Bird" Pattern

Victorian Rococo style: armchair & two side chairs; carved & laminated rosewood, each back w/a central upholstered figure-8 panel enclosed w/a wide framed ornately pierced & carved w/leafy scrolls, the arched top of the sofa w/a scroll-and-floral-carved crest w/a bird, armchair w/padded open arms, wide rounded seats w/serpentine seatrails w/ornate carved scrolls, demi-cabriole front legs on casters, "Bird" patt. but bird only found on armchair crest, unknown maker, ca. 1855, refinished, armchair 46" h., the set (ILLUS.) **18,000**

Belter "Fountain Elms" Chairs

Victorian Rococo style: armchair & two side chairs; carved & laminated rosewood, the armchair w/a high arched back w/an oval tufted upholstery panel enclosed by a wide pierced scroll-carved framed w/an arched floral-carved crestrail, serpentine wood open arms on incurved arm supports above the wide upholstered seat, serpentine seatrail w/ornate scroll carving, demi-cabriole front legs on casters, matching side chairs, "Fountain Elms" patt. by John H. Belter, New York City, ca. 1855, refinished, new upholstery, armchair 46" h., the set (ILLUS.) **28,000**

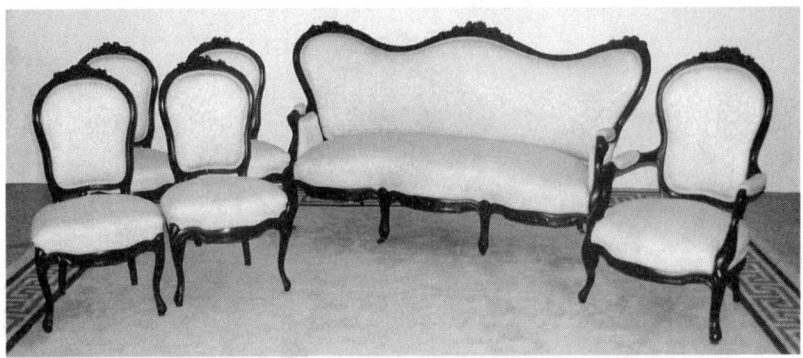

Restrained Rococo Rosewood Parlor Suite

Victorian Rococo style: sofa, armchair & four side chairs; carved rosewood, the sofa w/a long upholstered serpentine back w/a narrow conforming crestrail w/low carved crests, padded & closed upholstered arms w/incurved arm supports, long serpentine seatrail w/a carved trim above four demi-
carbriole front legs, matching chairs w/shaped balloon backs, original finish, ca. 1860, sofa 66" l.,
the set (ILLUS.) **2,300**

Rococo Sofa from Rare Baudouine Set

Victorian Rococo style: sofa, armchair & two side chairs; pierce-carved rosewood, the triple-back
sofa w/tall upholstered balloon-shaped end backs enclosed by wide very ornate serpentine arched
frames w/pierce-carved scrolls & a top crest carved w/a female face, the lower arched upholstered
center back section w/a similar carved crestrail & arched crest, padded open arms w/incurved arm
supports, the long upholstered seat w/a serpentine scroll-carved seatrail on demi-cabriole legs, the
chairs w/balloon backs w/frames matching the end sections of the sofa, Charles Baudouine, New
York City, ca. 1855, sofa 80" l., the set (ILLUS. of sofa) **30,000**

Fine Rococo Set Attributed to Meeks

Victorian Rococo style: sofa & two side chairs; carved & laminated rosewood, sofa w/a serpentine crestrail w/pierced carving consisting of scrollwork, leaves & grape clusters, the center section surmounted by a gadrooned molding centering a floral-carved cartouche, all above the upholstered back flanked by closed molded & outward scrolling arms w/incurved arm supports, serpentine seatrail carved w/scrolled cartouches, demi-cabriole front legs on casters, matching armchairs, attributed to J. & J. W. Meeks, New York City, ca. 1859, sofa 74" l., the set (ILLUS., bottom previous page) **7,638**

Screens

Painted Louis XVI-Style Firescreen

Firescreen, Louis XVI-Style, painted wood & gesso, the narrow upright rectangular frame w/an arched & scroll-carved crestrail centered by a cartouche above a solid panel h.p. w/large colorful flowers in pink & white against a blue ground, on arched trestle legs, ca. 1920s, 20" w., 28" h. (ILLUS.) **250**

Renaissance Revival Firescreen

Firescreen, Victorian Renaissance Revival style, walnut, the slender bobbin-and-rod-turned top rail surmounted by a large arched scroll-carved crest centered by a carved lion mask, the rail raised atop slender ring-turned columnar supports w/urn finials enclosing a square frame w/line-incised decoration & blocked corners around the machine-made tapestry panel, a lower ring-and-rod-turned stretcher joins the high arched flattened outswept legs, refinished, ca. 1875, 30" w., overall 46" h. (ILLUS.) **950**

Fine Victorian Rococo Firescreen

Firescreen, Victorian Rococo style, carved rosewood, a large serpentine-sided frame carved w/a shell at the center top & bottom encloses the original figural needlepoint panel, raised on scroll-carved supports joined by a scroll-carved stretcher & raised on four cabriole legs, original finish, mid-19th c., 12 x 24", 46" h. (ILLUS.) **750**

Fine Carved Japanese Screen

Folding screen, two-fold, carved hardwood, lacquer, ivory & mother-of-pearl, the central rectangular panels w/floral-painted red lacquer border bands around black panels decorated in high-relief w/ivory & mother-of-pearl birds among flowering branches, the dark outer frame ornately carved w/Oriental motifs include birds & leaves in the crests & further designs in the rectangular bottom panels, Japan, Meiji Period, late 19th c., overall 68" w., 6' 4" h. (ILLUS.) **4,830**

Ornate Scenic Indian Folding Screen

Folding screen, three-fold, inlaid carved hardwood, a wide central panel flanked by narrower side panels, each w/a large central panel, the center panel depicting a scene of the Taj Mahal done in mother-of-pearl, abalone, lacquer & paint, the side panels continue this scene, the frame of each panel w/an pierced, arched & ornately carved crest rail w/an exotic flying bird among flowering vines, the solid bottom panels w/similar carving, India, late 19th c., overall 73" w., 6' 1 1/2" h. (ILLUS.) **748**

Ornate Chinese Lacquer Screen

Folding screen, four-fold, decorated red lacquer, the panels decorated w/a contin-

uous landscape scene w/Chinese figures in gardens w/houses & temples in the foreground & upper background, done in gilt & polychrome paints, the reverse decorated w/colorful Oriental plants & animals, China, ca. 1900, overall 64" w., 5' 11 1/4" h. (ILLUS.) **1,150**

Unique Fornasetti Folding Screen

Folding screen, four-fold, hand-painted & lithographically-printed wood, the front in the "Uccelli" patt. depicting a continuous scene of multi-paned windows looking out to slender trees filled w/colorful birds, faux panels at the bottom, all on a creamy white ground, the reverse painted in a monochromatic "Libreria" patt. depicting library shelves filled w/leather-bound books, trophies & knickknacks, raised on casters, designed by Piero Fornasetti, Italy, ca. 1950s, each panel 19 5/8" w., overall 6' 4 1/2" h. (ILLUS.) **6,463**

Fine English Victorian Screen

Folding screen, four-fold, mahogany & fabric, the simple mahogany framework enclosing two yellow damask panels in each section, the reverse w/claret damask panels, England, third quarter 19th., overall 100" w., 6' h. (ILLUS.) **1,380**

Lacquer Screen with Figural Panels

Folding screen, four-fold, painted lacquer, each panel on the front w/a black lacquer ground, a tall upper panel in each panel painted w/a standing figure of a Japanese man or woman, a small square bottom panel decorated w/a bird perched among pine boughs, the whole framework painted in gold w/a chain-like design, the reverse in red lacquer decorated w/Oriental foliage, Japan, ca. 1900, overall 72" w., 5' 3" h. (ILLUS.) **978**

Six-fold Chinese Lacquer Screen

Folding screen, six-fold, decorated black lacquer, the front w/narrow black lacquer panels decorated w/a continuous scene of small applied mother-of-pearl Chinese figures w/a temple & trees, enclosed in narrow gilt banding, the reverse w/overall gilt foliate decoration, China, ca. 1900, overall 108" w., 8' h. (ILLUS.) **1,495**

Folding screen, six-fold, tooled leather, each panel decorated w/richly tooled floral leather on one side & birds among flowering branches on the other, Spain, second quarter 19th c., overall 126" w., 6' 6" h. (ILLUS., top of next column) **1,150**

Fine Tooled Leather Spanish Screen

Ornate Chinese Coromandel Screen

Folding screen, eight-fold, Coromandel-type, in the Ch'ien Lung taste, the primary facade decorated w/"Precious Objects" borders & "Boys at Play on a Mountain Lake" central scene, the reverse w/"Bamboo-and-Rocks" design, signed on the reverse right in vermilion calligraphy, scattered minor losses in the lacquer, China, overall 144" w., 8' h. (ILLUS.) **2,070**

English Mahogany Pole Screen

Pole screen, mahogany, the shield-shaped screen decorated w/floral découpage on a red ground, raised on a turned & foliate-carved standard above a tripod base w/cabriole legs ending in acanthus-carved feet, George III period, England, last quarter 18th c., 44" h. (ILLUS.)............... **518**

Secretaries

Early Biedermeier Secretary

Biedermeier secrétaire à abattant, mahogany & mahogany veneer, the rectangular grey marble top w/rounded front corners on a deep ogee cornice above the wide rectangular fold-down writing surface opening to an interior fitted w/an arrangement of small drawers over a long narrow drawer, the lower case w/three long drawers w/bold crotch-grained veneer, original finish, Europe, ca. 1830s, 18 x 38", 5' 4" h. (ILLUS.)... **1,800**

Chippendale Mahogany Secretary

Chippendale secretary, mahogany, two-part construction: the upper section w/a broken-scroll pediment centered by a ball finial above a pair of arched mirrored doors w/ornate engraving opening to a large interior fitted w/numerous pigeon-holes & small drawers; the lower section w/fold-down slant-top opening to an interior centered by a small square mirrored door flanked by small pigeonholes & drawers, the lower case w/a pair of drawers over two long drawers, molded back on bracket feet, old refinish, original oval brass pulls, late 18th c., Europe, possibly England, 26 x 46", 8' h. (ILLUS.) **7,500**

Fine Chippendale Revival Secretary

Chippendale Revival secretary-bookcase, mahogany & mahogany veneer, two-part breakfront-style: the upper section w/a tall stepped-out central section w/a pierced & scroll-carved broken-scroll pediment centered by a raised block on the flaring coved cornice above a single large glazed door w/ornate applied scrolling grillwork & opening to shelves above a narrow rectangular molded panel folding-down to form the writing surface & expose the fitted interior, the lower sections each w/a scroll-pierced gallery on the coved cornice above a tall narrow glazed door w/applied scrolling grillwork & opening to shelves; the matching lower section w/a mid-molding above a pair of central doors w/serpentine scroll banding flanked by matching narrow side doors, deep molded flat base, original finish, ca. 1920s, 24 x 60", 7' 8" h. (ILLUS.) **3,000**

Classical Secretary with Scroll Feet

Classical secretary-bookcase, mahogany & mahogany veneer, two-part construction: the upper section w/a rectangular top w/a wide flat flaring cornice above a pair of tall 6-pane glazed doors opening to shelves above two narrow drawers w/wooden knobs; the stepped-out lower section w/a fold-out writing surface above a plain long & slightly overhanging drawer above two long lower drawers w/wooden knobs flanked by long serpentine brackets w/heavy C-scroll front feet, short turned rear legs w/knob feet, refinished, ca. 1840, 21 x 40", 7' h. (ILLUS.) **1,200**

Simple Classical Secretary-Bookcase

Classical secretary-bookcase, mahogany & mahogany veneer, two-part construction: the upper section w/a rectangular top w/a deep flaring ogee cornice w/rounded corners above a pair of two-pane glazed doors opening to shelves above a wide rectangular fold-down writing surface opening to an interior fitted w/numerous pigeonholes & small drawers; the stepped-out lower case w/three long graduated drawers w/original glass pulls, serpentine apron & bracket feet, original finish, ca. 1850, 20 x 42", 7' h. (ILLUS.) **2,000**

Fancy Classical Secretary-Bookcase

Classical secretary-bookcase, mahogany & mahogany veneer, two-part construction: the upper section w/a rectangular top w/a long serpentine & scroll-cut crestrail above the deep coved cornice over a pair of tall glazed doors w/scalloped arch tops opening to shelves; the lower section w/a thick fold-out writing surface opening to a row of small narrow drawers above a pair of paneled cupboard doors w/scalloped arch tops, scroll-cut bracket feet, original finish, ca. 1840, 22 x 44", 8' 2" h. (ILLUS.) **2,500**

Colonial Revival secretary, mahogany & mahogany veneer, two-part construction: the low top section w/a rectangular top above a pair of short rectangular glazed doors w/ornate applied scrolling grillwork & divided by a scroll-carved panel, a pair of small columns at each outside corner; the lower section w/a wide hinged slant-top w/an inlaid design of a floral wreath w/plume suspended on a bow & opening to a fitted interior above a case w/three long serpentine drawers surrounded by bands of carved scrolls flanked by free-standing corner columns w/bronze capitals & bases, molded serpentine base on tall ogee feet, refinished, ca. 1900, 20 x 34", 5' 6" h. (ILLUS., below) **1,800**

Ornate Colonial Revival Secretary

Rare Southern Federal Secretary

Federal secretary-bookcase, cherry, curly maple & mahogany flame veneer, two-part construction: the upper section w/a

broken-arch pediment w/star inlay medallions at the ends of the scrolls & a central urn-form finial & matching corner finials above the flaring coved corner over two tall doors w/Gothic panels, three adjustable interior shelves; the stepped-out lower section w/a reeded edge above a flat fold-down writing surface opening to an interior fitted w/a central square door w/variegated star inlay flanked on each side w/a hidden compartment faced to resemble a book binding, a row of small pigeonholes & four small drawers on each side, the lower case w/a pair of doors w/matching recesses forming a single large Gothic arch, tall narrow front panels each w/a narrow Gothic arch above a quatrefoil, short ring-and-knob-turned legs, possibly Southern (Kentucky), expertly restored, replacements include backboard & finials, pieced repairs along hinge rail & to veneer (ILLUS.) **8,800**

Inlaid Mahogany Federal Secretary

Federal secretary-bookcase, inlaid mahogany, two-part construction: the upper section w/a rectangular top w/a pierced broken swan's-neck pediment centered by a carved urn finish above a Greek key-carved cornice & narrow frieze band inlaid a central fan flanked by narrow banded veneer panels over a pair of tall geometrically-glazed doors opening to shelves; the lower section w/a hinged slant-front centered by an inlaid fan & opening to a fitted interior above a pair of narrow pullout supports flanked a narrow top drawer over three long graduated drawers all w/simple bail pulls, molded base w/scroll-cut ogee bracket feet, American, late 18th - early 19th c., 22 1/2 x 47 1/2", 7' 7" h. (ILLUS.) **9,400**

Top Quality Federal Secretary

Federal secretary-bookcase, mahogany & mahogany veneer, two-part construction: the upper section w/a rectangular top w/a broken-scroll pediment centered by a fluted panel & flanked by small fluted corner blocks above a frieze molding over a pair of triple-arched glazed doors opening to shelves; the stepped-out lower section w/a fold-out writing flap above narrow pullout supports flanking a long drawer above two long drawers all w/original round brass pulls, ring-turned & fluted leaf-carved tapering legs w/knob feet, possibly by Joseph Short, Newburyport, Massachusetts, 1810-20, 19 x 38", 6' 1" h. (ILLUS.) **7,638**

Fine Georgian Revival Secretary

Georgian Revival secretary-bookcase, walnut, oyster-grain walnut veneer & mahogany, one-piece construction, the rectangular top w/a high arched central coved cornice flanked by flat side cornices, above a case w/a central high arched bi-fold door w/fine veneer opening to shelves & flanked by tall narrow matching doors opening to shelves, the stepped-out lower case w/a hinged fold-out writing surface above a case w/an arrangement of eight horizontal & vertical banded veneered drawers w/brass teardrop pulls, on simple cabriole legs w/pad feet, original finish, Europe, early 20th c., 16 x 28", 5' h. (ILLUS.) **850**

Very Fine Aesthetic Inlaid Secretary

Victorian Aesthetic Movement secretary-bookcase, walnut & inlaid burl walnut, two-part construction: the upper section w/a rectangular top fitted w/a tall ornate front crestrail centered by a pointed leaf-carved crest over a burl panel inlaid w/an urn flanked by narrow vertical blocks flanked by pierced side panels carved w/stylized sunflowers below a dentil-carved band, resting on the flaring cornice above a pair of tall glazed doors opening to shelves & decorated w/carved & incised sunflowers at the top corners & flanked by blocked & line-incised side moldings; the slightly stepped-out lower section w/a hinged slant-front door w/two recessed burl panels each finely inlaid w/stylized sunflowers & leaves & flanked by carved side moldings, opening to a fitted interior above a mid-molding over three long graduated drawers w/line-incised banding &

centered by a narrow burl panel inlaid w/pairs of stylized sunflowers & leaves, original hinged brass pulls & keyhole escutcheons, blocked & carved side moldings, flat molded base, refinished, ca. 1885, 22 x 42", 8' h. (ILLUS.) **3,400**

Country Gothic Secretary-Bookcase

Victorian country-style secretary-bookcase, butternut, two-part construction: the upper section w/Gothic Revival influences including a narrow Gothic arch scalloped drop cornice above a pair of tall two-pane doors w/a Gothic arch grill in the top pane, flanked by applied serpentine bands down the outside edges; the lower section w/a hinged slant-front w/two recessed panels each centered by carved leaves & grape clusters, opening to a fitted interior above three long graduated drawers w/carved fruit & leaf pulls, short scalloped apron & block feet, Norwegian-American workmanship, Midwest, ca. 1870, 26 x 42", 7' h. (ILLUS.) **3,000**

Ornate Baroque Revival Secretary

Victorian Baroque Revival secretary-bookcase, carved walnut, two-part construction: the tall upper section w/a very high arched & deeply molded cornice topped by a large crest composed of carved full-figure seated cherubs flanking a large shield, above a wide arched band at the front ornately carved w/cherubs climbing grapevines & centered at the top w/a carved lion mask all enclosing the pair of tall arched glazed doors opening to shelves; the lower section w/a raised rectangular central section w/a long rectangular fold-down writing surface carved on the front w/a panel of frolicking cherubs flanked at each corner by carved full-figure seated cherubs atop the stepped-out bottom section which features a central stack of three small drawers flanked by cupboard doors w/a round raised center molding enclosing carved cherub scenes, ornately carved end panels, all on a molded base w/large bracket feet, Europe, late 19th c., original dark finish, 22 x 50", 9' 9" h. (ILLUS.) **35,000**

Outstanding Country Secretary

Victorian country-style secretary-book-case, cherry & mixed woods, two-part construction: the upper section w/an arched, pierced & scroll-cut crestrail centered by a inlaid starburst & flanked by trefoil corner finials over the deep stepped & flaring cornice w/angled corner blocks above a pair of cupboard doors each w/a recessed oblong panels w/molded edges centered by an inlaid starburst & flanked by chamfered front corners w/carved drops & a raised narrow diamond all above a wide hinged slant-front w/a large oblong recessed panel centered by another large inlaid starburst & opening to an interior w/numerous small inlaid drawers & pigeon-holes; the slightly stepped-out lower section w/a rectangular top w/a flaring stepped cornice w/corner blocks flanking a narrow ogee-fronted drawer above another pair of doors w/octagonal recessed panels centered by inlaid starbursts, recessed panels at the sides, on a flat molded base w/a raised carved diamond at the front center & projecting block corners carved w/pyramidal blocks, original finish, Norwegian-American workmanship, Midwest, ca. 1870s, 22 x 40", 7' 6" h. (ILLUS.) **5,000**

Fine Victorian Eastlake Secretary

Victorian Eastlake 'cylinder-front' secretary-bookcase, walnut, the tall upper section w/a high arched crest over a leaf-carved panel flanked by block-carved panels over the coved cornice above a

pair of tall glazed cupboard doors w/rounded corners flanked by quarter-round corner columns above the large cylinder front w/two recessed burled panels opening to a fitted interior, bird's-eye maple interior, a projecting mid-molding above the lower case w/a long narrow drawer slightly projecting over two long drawers flanked by small round columns, flat molded base, paneled sides, original hardware & finish, ca. 1880, 22 x 40", overall 8' 2" h. (ILLUS.) **4,500**

Fancy "Cylinder-front" Secretary

Victorian Golden Oak style "cylinder-front" secretary-bookcase, quarter-sawn oak, two-part construction: the upper section w/a high crestrail w/a band of three pierced round holes centered by an arched & pierced crest carved w/leafy scrolls & daisy-like blossoms above the narrow curved cornice w/incised lines centered by a small rectangular leaf-carved panel over a frieze band w/two applied bands of leafy scrolls, the case w/a pair of tall glazed doors opening to adjustable shelves; the lower section w/a two-panel cylinder front w/each panel boldly carved w/leafy scrolls, opening to a pullout writing surface & fitted w/a desk interior above a long drawers slightly projecting over two shorter drawers beside a small paneled cupboard door carved w/a rayed design, flat molded base, original stamped brass hardware, original dark finish, ca. 1890, 22 x 40", 7' 10" h. (ILLUS.).............. **4,000**

Rare Double Side-by-Side Secretary

Oak Secretary with Leaded Doors

Victorian Golden Oak style secretary-bookcase, oak, side-by-side-style, the superstructure w/an arched crest centered by pierced scrolls above a narrow shelf raised on winged scroll supports also supporting small side shelves all backed by a long narrow beveled mirror, the case w/a tall bow-fronted glass door opening to shelves beside a pair of short doors w/leaded & stained flora-form glass panes above a flat hinged fall-front decorated w/an applied oval band of molding w/a grotesque face opening to a fitted interior, a stack of three bow-fronted drawers below w/simple bail pulls, molded base on tall bracket feet, original dark finish, ca. 1895, 18 x 44", 6' 6" h. (ILLUS., at left).. **2,800**

Victorian Golden Oak style secretary-bookcase, quarter-sawn oak, rare double side-by-side-style, a pair of tall serpentine curved glass doors at each side of a wide central section, the center w/an arched & scroll-carved crestrail above a large arched rectangular beveled glass mirror above two small projecting open shelves raised above a narrow shelf on the long rectangular hinged fall-front above a pair of deep serpentine-fronted drawers w/pierced brass pulls above a long deep bottom drawer w/top rounded brackets below each of the upper drawers, narrow serpentine apron w/scroll-carved trim, raised on tall simple cabriole legs, original hardware, refinished, ca. 1900, 20 x 68", 6' h. (ILLUS., top of page) **3,500**

Renaissance "Breakfront" Secretary

Oak Secretary with Stepped Cornice

Victorian Golden Oak style secretary-bookcase, quarter-sawn oak, side-by-side-style, a two-part stepped cornice above the two-part cabinet, the left side w/a flat rolled crestrail above a narrow rectangular leafy scroll-carved panel flanked by shaped brackets on the bow-front top & tall bowed glass door opening to wooden shelves, the right side w/a stepped scroll-carved crestrail above a narrow top shelf w/scroll-cut front brackets over a tall open compartment backed by a large rectangular arch-topped bev-eled mirror & a small side shelf all above the wide flat fall-front decorated w/a scroll-carved heart-shaped panel above a long ogee-front drawer & two long flat drawers all w/highly figured oak & pierced brass pulls, raised on ogee bracket feet on casters, refinished, ca. 1890s, 16 x 40", 6' h. (ILLUS.) **2,000**

Victorian Renaissance Revival style secretary-bookcase, walnut & burl walnut, breakfront-style, the wide stepped-out center cabinet w/a high peaked broken-scroll pediment centered by a square burl panel w/rosette below a fan-carved crest, the sides of the pediment w/curved molding over small triangular burl panels flanked by flat arched corner ears above a flaring stepped flat cornice above a pair of tall glazed doors opening to shelves & flanked by narrow blocks & burl panels down the sides all atop a long two-panel false drawer decorated w/raised pull panels & leaf-carved pulls opening to reveal a pullout writing surface & storage slots, a pair of large square paneled doors at the base centered by raised round medallions enclosing facing profile portraits of classical woman, a flat molded base; the narrow stepped-back side cabinets each w/a half-round curved crest w/burl panel above a flaring stepped cornice over a tall narrow glazed door opening to shelves & w/narrow blocks & burl panels down the outer edge, a small raised burl panel door at the bottom of each side above the molded flat base, old refinished, ca. 1870s, 24 x 90", 9' 3" h. (ILLUS., top of page) **9,500**

Simple Renaissance Walnut Secretary

Victorian Renaissance Revival style secretary-bookcase, walnut, two-part construction: the upper section w/a high arched serpentine crestrail centered by a cluster of carved fruit above a deep coved cornice w/rounded corners above a pair of tall glazed doors w/a small block carving at the top center & opening to adjustable shelves above a pair of long narrow drawers w/fruit-and-leaf-carved pulls; the stepped-out lower section w/a fold-out writing surface above a long drawer w/carved fruit-and-leaf-carved pulls over a pair of paneled cupboard doors, deep flat molded base, ca. 1865, refinished, 18 x 42", 8' h. (ILLUS.) **2,300**

Victorian Rococo style "butler's" secretary-bookcase, carved mahogany, two-part construction: the upper section w/a high boldly arched & scroll-carved crestrail topped by a full-figure head of Shakespeare above the deep flaring & stepped cornice over a scroll-carved frieze band w/carved fruit at the corners above a pair of tall cupboard doors centered by tall oval mirrors framed w/scroll-carved corners all above a pair of long narrow drawers w/scroll-carved pulls; the stepped-out lower section w/a narrow rectangular white marble top w/a serpentine front above a conforming scroll-carved long drawer pulling out to reveal a writing surface & storage all above a pair of large square cupboard doors centered by large round moldings enclosing rounded carved cartouches, scroll-carved bands at the sides, on a molded base w/flat block feet, original dark finish, ca. 1855, 24 x 55", 8' 9" h. (ILLUS., below) **8,000**

Fine Rococo "Butler's" Secretary

Rosewood Rococo Secretary-Bookcase

Victorian Rococo style secretary-book-case, carved rosewood, two-part construction: the upper section w/a long peaked crest rail w/carved scroll edging & a carved shell finial, the long canted corners above a conforming coved cornice above scroll-carved chamfered sides flanking a pair of tall glazed cupboard doors w/scroll-carved corners above a flat fall-front opening to a series of pigeonholes & small drawers w/bird's-eye maple veneer; the lower stepped-out case w/a pair of long drawers w/raised oval molding above a row of three cupboard doors each w/rectangular panels formed by raised scroll molding & flanked by chamfered sides, flat molded base on short block feet, original dark finish, ca. 1855, 24 x 48", 9' 2" h. (ILLUS.) **8,000**

Rococo Slant-front Secretary

Victorian Rococo style secretary-book-case, mahogany & mahogany veneer, two-part construction: the upper section w/a broken-scroll pediment centered by a carved fleur-de-lis & grape-carved finial & w/turned urn corner finials above a pair of tall arched glazed doors opening to shelves; the lower section w/a hinged slant-front ornately carved w/scrolls & opening to a fitted interior above a case w/three long graduated drawers each decorated w/scroll-carved pulls & bands, molded base, original dark finish w/some veneer damage on base, ca. 1860, 22 x 40", 8' 4" h. (ILLUS.)............................. **3,000**

Sideboards

Attractive Arts & Crafts Sideboard

Arts & Crafts sideboard, quarter-sawn oak, the superstructure w/an arched center crest above a large beveled mirror flanked by small cupboards w/clear & blue leaded glass doors raised on sides w/heart cutouts above the long rectangular top overhanging corner corbels on the case, two long narrow drawers above a long drawer above a pair of short leaded glass doors flanked by tall narrow cupboard doors w/incised bands, a long drawer across the bottom, raised on squared tapering legs on casters, original wooden pulls, old refinish, ca. 1910, 20 x 54", 6' h. (ILLUS.)................................ **1,500**

Nice Mahogany Classical Server

Classical server, mahogany & mahogany veneer, a high flat-topped backsplash surface-carved w/a large basket flanked by carved fans between flat corner blocks, the rectangular top above a case w/a pair of drawers w/oval brasses flanked by side panels & projecting above a pair of cupboard doors w/panels combining to form a large Gothic arch, a tapering freestanding column w/scroll-carved capital at each side, flat apron on scroll-carved heavy paw front legs, refinished, ca. 1830s, 24 x 48", 4' 4" h. (ILLUS.).. **1,200**

Large Carved Classical Sideboard

Classical sideboard, mahogany & mahogany veneer, a high back rail centered by a tall plain rolled panel flanked by serpentine panels carved w/cornucopias, the drop-well top w/blocked front corners, the tall side sections w/a round-fronted drawer over a tall raised panel cupboard door, the dropped center section w/a long round-fronted drawer above a pair of shorter raised panel drawers, the facade divided by four tall turned & tapering freestanding columns above bulbous leaf-carved & ring-turned legs w/knob feet, original finish, ca. 1830s, 24 x 72", 5' h. (ILLUS.).. **2,500**

Classical Sideboard with Gallery Top

Classical sideboard, mahogany & mahogany veneer, a three-quarters low gallery w/shaped sides on the rectangular top w/blocked corners & gadroon-carved edges above the case w/a pair of drawers w/original ornate pierced brass butterfly pulls above a pair of large paneled cupboard doors all flanked by large spiral-turned side columns w/carved capitals & resting on shell-carved blocks above the heavy paw feet, original dark finish, ca. 1840s, 22 x 52", 4' h. (ILLUS.) **1,600**

Federal country-style corner sideboard, cherry, two-board top w/scalloped gallery dovetailed at corners, above two dovetailed drawers flanked by angled false drawer fronts above two tall paneled doors w/turned wooden pulls & locks opening to a shaped interior shelf & flanked by semi-curved side panels, all doors & drawers w/incised beading, three turned & tapering front legs & two tapered rear legs, chalk initial on base "N.E.," original reddish brown finish, Ohio or Kentucky, early 19th c., 25 x 56", 4' 2" h. **6,600**

Baltimore Federal Sideboard

Federal sideboard, mahogany & mahogany veneer, rectangular top on a case w/a pair of long drawers w/oval brass pulls projecting slightly over a pair of two-panel cupboard doors centered by a stack of two narrow bottle drawers, ring-turned freestanding columns at outside corners above beehive-turned front legs on tiny paw feet, Baltimore, ca. 1820-30, 25 x 61", 45 3/4" h. (ILLUS.) **2,352**

Serpentine-fronted Federal Sideboard

Nice Federal-Style Service

Federal sideboard, mahogany & mahogany veneer, the rectangular top w/convex ends & a concave center above a case w/bow-fronted end cupboard doors flanking a concave-fronted long drawer over a pair of concave cupboard doors, front divided by four leaf-carved & reeded columns continuing down to form the reeded legs on peg feet, refinished, ca. 1820, 22 x 60", 36" h. (ILLUS., bottom, previous page).. **1,400**

Federal-Style server, mahogany & mahogany veneer, a high gallery composed of brass rods & urn finials above the long rectangular top above a row of three drawers w/simple brass bail pulls raised on ebonized columns over a full lower shelf over a pair of drawers flanking a pair of long & low reeded cupboard doors, on tapering turned feet w/brass caps, original hardware, ca. 1920s, refinished, 20 x 64", 4' 10" h. (ILLUS., top of page) **1,000**

Victorian Baroque Revival sideboard, ebonized oak, two-part construction: the upper tall section w/a serpentine scroll-carved crestrail centered by an oval medallion above the egg-and-dart-carved cornice over an upper three-section frieze band carved w/acanthus leaves over lower three-section arched frieze band carved w/scrolls, each section separated by a carved lion masks, the top projecting over the tall back & supported by tall block-reeded baluster-and-reeded knob-turned columns, the tall back divided into two horizontal sections, the upper section divided into three rectangular panels each carved w/scrolls surrounded a ring & diamond motif, the long lower panel carved overall w/leafy scrolls; the lower section w/a rectangular top w/molded edges over a case w/a row of three plain drawers each separated by a carved lion mask above a beaded band & three paneled lower doors carved w/scrolls & the ring & diamond motif, each door separated by a large carved caryatid, a long narrow drawer across the bottom, narrow flat reeded apron w/blocked end feet, original finish, Europe, ca. 1880s, 22 x 60", 8' h. (ILLUS., below)... **3,200**

Ebonized Oak Baroque Sideboard

Huge Ornate Baroque Sideboard

Victorian Baroque Revival sideboard, oak, the large superstructure w/a high broken-scroll pediment w/the peaked center section carved in bold relief w/a satyr face above grapevine swags continuing to the high flanking scrolls all above a long narrow rectangular shelf raised on seated griffin supports flanking a large rectangular back panel boldly carved w/grapevines centered by another large satyr mask, the rectangular top over a row of three scroll-carved drawers separated by carved satyr mask-carved blocks & projecting slightly over a three large paneled doors, the central door carved in full-relief w/dead game & the matching side doors carved in full-relief w/fruit clusters, the doors separated by columns carved in full-relief w/bands of fruit, the blocked & flaring base band w/leaf & dart carving, raised on four flattened bun feet, refinished, Europe, ca. 1880, 24 x 76", 6' 8" h. (ILLUS.) **9,500**

Unusual Eastlake Cherry Sideboard

Victorian Eastlake style sideboard, cherry, the tall superstructure w/a long narrow rectangular shelf w/spindled gallery at the ends & front topped by turned finials raised on arched front & side brackets above two slender ring-, rod- and baluster-turned spindles resting on low spindled galleries enclosing another long shelf backed by a very large rectangular beveled mirror, a narrow paneled lower back section above the wide projecting top on the case, the case fitted w/a long narrow drawer beside a shorter narrow drawer above an asymmetrical arrangement of four drawers & two paneled scroll-carved doors, on short ring-turned front legs, original finish, ca. 1890, 20 x 52", 6' 6" h. (ILLUS.) **1,500**

Tall Carved Eastlake Sideboard

Victorian Eastlake style sideboard, walnut & burl walnut, the very tall superstructure w/a high notched and panel-cut crestrail flanked by roundels above a molded corner of shaped blocks above a large long rectangular panel boldly carved w/sprays of fruit & leaves centered by an urn, flanked by incurved side brackets on a long narrow open shelf supported by curved brackets & baluster- and ring-turned columns, a large rectangular beveled mirror at the back above rectangular pink marble top above the case w/a pair of burl veneer drawers w/angular brass pulls over a pair of cupboard doors w/raised burl panels, reeded pilasters down the sides, flat base w/blocked feet, original finish & hardware, ca. 1885, 22 x 48", 7' 6" h. (ILLUS.) **2,800**

Fine Oak Server with Leaded Glass

Victorian Golden Oak style server, quarter-sawn oak, a flat crest rod above a long narrow oval beveled mirror flanked by curved scrolls above the long rectangular top w/rounded corners over a rounded frieze w/two long drawers above a pair of large cupboard doors w/fan-shaped leaded glass panels flanking an ornate scroll-carved center door, long round-fronted drawer across the bottom, the canted front corner headed by carved lion masks above scroll-carved tapering columns continuing to form the front legs ending in paw feet, original hardware, refinished, ca. 1895, 22 x 50", 4' 6" h. (ILLUS.) **2,400**

Unique Oak Sideboard-Curio Cabinet

Victorian Golden Oak style sideboard, quarter-sawn oak, the superstructure w/an oblong top w/rounded ends & a bowed center section w/an arched & scroll-carved crest, the top above rounded glass display sections at each end centered by a long bow-front glass door opening to the long mirrored interior, all raised on cabriole legs w/paw feet & overhanging a long narrow rectangular beveled mirror, the top of the base w/rounded front corners above quarter-round glass doors opening to shelves & flanking the long flat central section w/a long concave-fronted drawer over a long rounded-front drawer over long deep bottom drawer w/carved scroll trim, carved cabriole front legs ending in paw feet on casters, original hardware, refinished, ca. 1890s, 24 x 56", 6' 6" h. (ILLUS.) **2,600**

Oak Sideboard with High Back

Victorian Golden Oak style sideboard, quarter-sawn oak, the tall superstructure w/a high arched & ornately scroll-carved crestrail over a long narrow shelf w/a narrow serpentine scroll-carved apron raised on tall simple columns flanking a large oblong beveled mirror w/a small shelf at each side, the rectangular top w/a double-serpentine front over a conforming case w/a pair of drawers over a single long drawer above a pair of long rectangular cupboard doors w/applied scrolls, bottom corner scrolls above the large paw feet on casters, original brass hardware, refinished, ca. 1895, 22 x 44", 6' 8" h. (ILLUS.) **1,800**

Handsome Renaissance Server

Victorian Renaissance Revival server, walnut & burl walnut, the superstructure w/a peaked pediment centered by a large fleur-de-lis finial & small raised burl panels above a flaring molding above a wide panel w/incurved sides centered by a large round raised burl panel w/a carved sunburst & shaped raised burl panels over a long narrow rectangular shelf w/rounded corners & flanked by small turned finials, the shelf supported on high pierced & scroll-cut brackets flanking a wide panel centered by a raised oval banding enclosing burl veneer, all atop the rectangular white marble top w/rounded front corners over a conforming case, the case w/a pair of drawers w/oval burl panels above a pair of cupboard doors w/large oval sunken panels w/burl veneer, deep molded flat base on casters, original finish, ca. 1875, 20 x 42", 7' 4" h. (ILLUS.) **2,600**

Victorian Renaissance Revival sideboard, chestnut, walnut & walnut veneer, the tall superstructure topped by a wide peaked scroll-carved crest w/a fan-carved finial above an arched molding above a long arched burl panel flanked by side scrolls & narrow burl panels over a long rectangular shelf w/rounded corners supported on tall blocked brackets w/turned drop finials above a long narrow rectangular mirror & scrolled side brackets, the long rectangular white marble top w/rounded front corners above a conforming case, the case w/a central stack of five small molded drawers flanked at each side w/a burled drawer w/brass ring pulls over large cupboard doors w/a rectangular raised burl panel & notch-carved dark border molding, flat molded base, original finish, 1870s, 22 x 52", 8' h. (ILLUS., top of column) **2,400**

Chestnut & Walnut Tall Sideboard

Extra Wide Renaissance Sideboard

Victorian Renaissance Revival sideboard, walnut & burl walnut, massive size, the tall & wide superstructure w/a high arched central section w/a long pierced crest centered by a carved palmette & scrolls above further carved scrolls & an arched molding, the matching broken-scroll side crest above tall & wide carved & burl-veneered side panels w/large half-round candleshelves flanking the large arched mirror which rests above narrow burl-paneled drawers on the long rectangular white marble top w/blocked corners & projecting center section, a conforming case w/a large stepped-out center paneled door w/burl veneer & a carved oblong medallion flanked by blocked side pilasters, each side section w/a paneled drawer over a smaller cupboard door w/burl veneer & a large raised diamond-shaped panel, blocked pilasters at the outside corners, wide blocked flat base band, original dark finish, ca. 1875, 24 x 68", 8' 6" h. (ILLUS.) **6,500**

Walnut Sideboard with High Crest

Victorian Renaissance Revival sideboard, walnut & burl walnut, the superstructure w/a very high arched broken-scroll pediment centered by a large pointed & carved finials above the wide smooth panel centered w/a carved cluster of fruit & two triangular raised panels, all above a long narrow shelf supported on ornate S-scroll brackets above a long narrow oval mirror over the half-round white marble top w/wide rounded corners & flat center section, on a conforming case w/a long burled drawer w/black pear-shaped drops flanked by curved side panels above a pair of flat paneled cupboard doors centered by carved fruit clusters & flanked by curved side panels w/matching carved fruit, deep molded flat base on wafer feet, refinished, ca. 1875, 20 x 48", 7' h. (ILLUS.) **2,400**

Victorian Renaissance Revival sideboard, walnut & burl walnut, the tall superstructure w/an arched crestrail centered by a curved fanned crest & blossom-carved bands on a scroll-carved crest above narrow raised burl panels & rounded corners above brackets & tall reeded columns flanking a tall rectangular mirror w/rounded top corners, a large half-round candle shelf at each side

backed by a quarter-round panel & disk-turned finials, each shelf on a large pierced C-scroll bracket ending in a vertical raised burl panel flanked by narrow burl panels all above the half-round grey marble top w/a flat central section, the conforming case w/a long narrow center drawer w/raised burl panel & two black pear-shaped drop pulls flanked by rounded matching swing-out side trays w/pulls, the lower case w/three large cupboard doors each w/a large fine feather-grained panel, the center door carved in relief w/a group of dead game, the doors separated by large ring-turned spool over a narrow burl panel, conforming molded base, ca. 1875, 22 x 60", 8' 5" h. (ILLUS., below) **8,000**

Renaissance Sideboard with Mirror

Victorian Rococo style server, walnut & burl walnut, the tall superstructure w/an arched crestrail decorated w/an ornate pierced & scroll-carved crest centered by a carved fruit clusters above an arched panel centered by another carved fruit cluster & flanked by turned finials above a narrow serpentine shelf supported small shaped brackets above a longer serpentine shelf supported on a large scroll-carved center bracket flanked by a pair of oblong mirrors, deeply cut scallops down the outer sides, the rectangular white marble top w/rounded corners above a conforming case w/a pair of drawers w/recessed burl oval panels centered by a scroll-carved pull flanked by black teardrop pulls, tow large cupboard doors below each w/a large recessed serpentine-sided burl panel centered by a large carved fruit clusters & w/carved leaf sprigs at each corner, rounded front corners & a shallow serpentine apron, refinished, ca. 1860, 20 x 44", 7' 6" h. (ILLUS., top next page)... **2,400**

Fine Rococo Walnut Server

Fine Rococo Mahogany Sideboard

Victorian Rococo style sideboard, carved mahogany, the high superstructure w/an arched crestrail carved w/bands of fruit centering a large scroll cartouche & flanked by turned urn corner finials above an arched panel carved w/a large cluster of fruit & scrolls flanked by triangular raised panels above a long narrow shelf w/rounded corners supported by ring-and-rod-turned spindles above a long narrow rectangular back panel & another slightly longer shelf supported on bold scroll-cut brackets, pierced scroll brackets at the sides above the long rectangular white marble top w/rounded corners above a conforming case, the case w/a pair of drawers w/raised oval molding & turned wood knobs flanked by rounded corner panels above the pair of large cupboard doors w/rectangular arch-topped molding centering a boldly carved cartouche, plain curved side panels, molded flat base on casters, refinished, ca. 1855, 23 x 56", 8' h. (ILLUS.) **8,500**

Stands

Early Chippendale Candlestand

Candlestand, Chippendale, walnut, the large round dished top tilting above a ring-and-urn-turned pedestal on a tripod base w/three cabriole legs ending in raised snake feet, Pennsylvania, ca. 1790, old refinish, 16" d., 30" h. (ILLUS.)........................ **800**

Simple Federal Cherry Candlestand

Candlestand, Federal country-style, cherry, round top on a heavy baluster-turned pedestal on a tripod base w/simple flattened cabriole legs on button feet, original finish, early 19th c., 18" d., 28" h. (ILLUS.) **300**

Rare Federal Painted Candlestand

Candlestand, Federal country-style, painted maple, a nearly square top raised on a ring-and-baluster-turned pedestal on a tripod base w/flattened cabriole legs w/snake feet, old green paint, coastal Long Island Sound, New York, early 19th c., 17 1/2 x 18", 25 3/4" h. (ILLUS.) **14,100**

Simple Federal Candlestand

Candlestand, Federal, mahogany, the rectangular top w/rounded corners tilting above a bold ring-and-baluster-turned pedestal on a tripod base w/outswept legs ending in knob feet, original dark finish, first quarter 19th c., 18 x 24", 28" h. (ILLUS.) **350**

Ornate Rococo Cane Stand

Cane stand, Victorian Rococo style, mahogany, the arched scroll-carved crest w/pierced scroll panels above a serpentine rail raised on ring-and-rod-turned columns over the tall waisted lower back trimmed w/ornate scrolls & centered by a large heart-shaped scroll-pierced panel above the serpentine-sided platform base centering a cast-iron shell-shaped drip pan, mid-19th c. (ILLUS.)............................. **1,320**

Baroque Display Stand with Busts

Display stand, Victorian Baroque Revival style, walnut & composite material, a square top w/a flaring edge over an apron w/each side decorated w/two small panels enclosing a rosette & flanking a round wreath enclosing a profile bust made from a molded composite material, the tapering rectangular sides w/molded leaf bands down each corner & two sides molded w/large busts & two sides w/floral wreaths, a lower rail over a molded base band above a molded apron & simple bracket feet, original dark finish, ca. 170s, 16" w., 36" h. (ILLUS.).. **750**

Unusual Odd Fellows Display Stand

Display stand, Victorian Renaissance Revival style, walnut, made for an Odd Fellows lodge, the rectangular upholstered top w/a flaring cornice above a dentil-carved band over a narrow frieze band carved in-relief w/the Odd Fellows symbol above a mid-molding over sides centered by rectangular molding-trimmed panels w/grain painting, widely flaring block-incised apron on a flat platform base on later casters, original finish, ca. 1880, 18 x 26", 34" h. (ILLUS., w/separate statue)................... **500**

Federal country one-drawer stand, cherry, two-board top over a dovetailed drawer fitted w/original wooden pull, turned legs, 18 1/2 x 18 3/4", 27" h. (slight warp in top, newer screws beneath, small corner repair)... **935**

Unique Ornate Inlaid Music Stand

Music stand, Victorian Aesthetic Movement style, walnut & maple, the rectangular top w/lightly scalloped edges above a cabinet w/two paneled doors inlaid w/a stylized lyre & cross horns, paneled sides, on a lightly scalloped band above a row of four ornately pierced & carved lyres forming four tall slots above a rectangular base w/overall lattice carving, a drawer w/small ring pulls at one side, tall tapering bracket feet on casters, original finish, last quarter 19th c., 14 x 22", 40" h. (ILLUS.) **750**

Ornately Pierce-carved Music Stand

Music stand, Victorian Baroque Revival style, mahogany, high rectangular slightly flaring side panels ornately pierce-carved w/phoenixes & leafy scrolls centered by a grotesque mask, rotating above a tripod-base w/cabriole legs carved at the knees w/a lion mask & ending in paw feet, the legs joined by a small triangular stretcher, original finish, late 19th c., 10 x 18", 25" h. (ILLUS.).. **1,250**

Victorian Eastlake Music Stand

Music stand, Victorian Eastlake style, oak, the flaring rectangular sides decorated w/a border band of incised leaf bands & a roundel enclosing a central rectangular panel inlaid w/musical instruments, each side attached by slender chains to a center panel topped by an open angular handle, raised on a trestle-type base w/a narrow leafy-vine-incised apron & flat flared end legs w/incised stylized flowers & leaves joined by a medial shelf, refinished, ca. 1890, 16 x 20", 30" h. (ILLUS.).. **400**

Music stand, Victorian Renaissance Revival style, inlaid ebonized wood, the rectangular top w/a low spindled gallery centered by a small arched crest, a top drawer inlaid w/a light band of stylized flower heads above inlaid side rails flanking a cabinet door ornately inlaid w/a rectangular panel w/pointed corners enclosing an ornate musical instrument trophy cluster, flat molded base, original finish, ca. 1875, 14 x 22", 44" h. (ILLUS., top of column)...... **1,000**

Finely Inlaid Ebonized Music Stand

Rare Aesthetic Movement Stand

Night stand, Victorian Aesthetic Movement style, inlaid mahogany, the square top w/reeded edges above an apron w/reeded moldings raised on ring-and-rod-turned supports on a matching rectangular shelf above the long rectangular paneled door decorated w/line-incised bands centering a wide band inlaid w/light stylized blossoms, reeded stiles at the sides & a reeded base rail, raised on short turned legs on brass casters, attributed to Herter Brothers, New York City, ca. 1870-80, 18" sq., 28 1/2" h. (ILLUS.) **10,575**

Fancy Louis XV Revival Night Stands

Night stands, Louis XV Revival, walnut, demi-lune form, the half-round white marble top on a deep rounded case w/a stack of three drawers, the top drawer w/an ornate scroll-carved panel, the bottom two drawers carved w/a continuous design of a large shell, scroll-carved serpentine apron, raised on scroll-carved cabriole legs w/scroll feet, refinished, ca. 1920s, 14 x 26", 30" h., pr. (ILLUS., bottom of previous page)... **1,600**

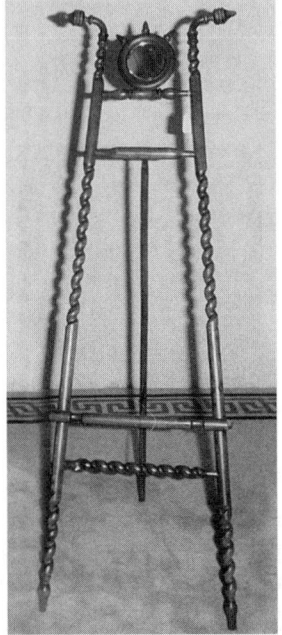

Turned Golden Oak Picture Stand

Picture stand, easel-type, Victorian Golden Oak style, oak, the tall slender inwardly canted front legs w/decorative spiral-twist carving & ending in angled pointed knob finials flanking a small round beveled mirror, a plain support rail lower on the front legs above a spiral-twist stretcher, a short plain upper rail attached to the plain adjustable rear leg, original brass chain, refinished, ca. 1900, 20" w., 4' 4" h. (ILLUS.)...................... **300**

Picture stand, easel-type, Victorian Renaissance Revival style, walnut & ebonized mixed woods, the two long inwardly slanting front legs joined at the top at a high pierced scroll-carved finial centered by a small ebonized roundel inlaid w/musical instruments, a slender notch-cut support rail below & a large rectangular folio compartment w/the fold-out front in ebonized wood decorated w/inlaid musical instruments & gilt trim, canted scroll-carved front feet, a medial rail at the front & a plain adjustable rear leg, original decoration, ca. 1875, 24" w., 6' 4" h. (ILLUS., top of column) **4,700**

Ornate Renaissance Picture Stand

Very Ornate Rococo Picture Stand

Picture stand, easel-type, Victorian Rococo style, carved walnut, the simple inwardly slanted front legs joined by an ornate scroll-carved lower stretcher & a plain upper stretcher w/a wide support rail w/delicate scroll carving, the large top crest rounded & ornately pierce-carved overall w/leafy scrolls, the front legs ending in incurved C-scroll carved feet, a plain adjustable back leg, ca. 1860, original finish, 26" w., 5' 10" h. (ILLUS.)................................ **1,800**

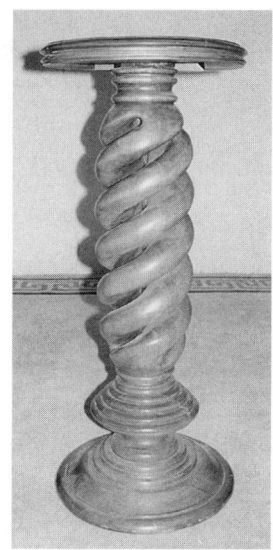

Ornately Turned Plant Stand

Classical Country Plant Stand

Plant stand, Classical country-style, painted pine, the octagonal top w/a stepped molding raised on an octagonal column w/a flaring base resting on a square platform, original overall grain-painting, ca. 1850, 10" w., 32" h. (ILLUS.)....................................... **300**

Plant stand, late Victorian style, walnut-stained maple, a wide round top above a pierced & spiral-turned heavy pedestal w/a stepped flaring ring above the wide disk foot, original finish, ca. 1900, 15" d., 36" h. (ILLUS.) **650**

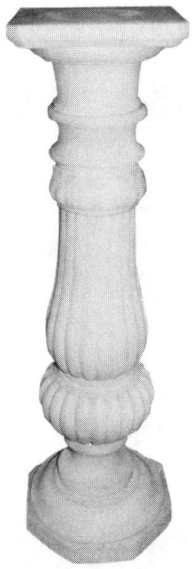

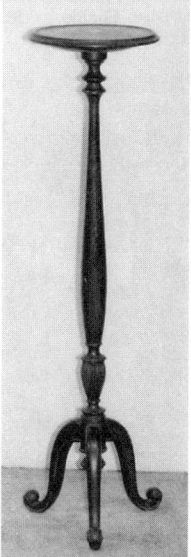

Delicate Queen Anne Revival Stand

Fine Classical Alabaster Stand

Plant stand, Classical Revival style, carved alabaster, columnar-form w/a square top above a ringed & reeded baluster-form pedestal on an octagonal foot, ca. 1890, 12" w., 34" h. (ILLUS.)...................................... **500**

Plant stand, Queen Anne Revival, mahogany & mahogany veneer, a small round top w/molded edge raised on a slender baluster-turned pedestal above a tripod base w/cabriole legs ending in scroll feet, original finish, ca. 1920s, 12" d., 36" h. (ILLUS.) **300**

Figural Baroque Revival Plant Stand

Plant stand, Victorian Baroque Revival style, mahogany, the large round top w/incised apron raised on a finely carved full-figural standing putti swagged in a drapery, on a lappet-and-scroll-carved X-form base, original finish, Europe, ca. 1890, 15" d, 32" h. (ILLUS.) **2,600**

Oak Eastlake Plant Stand

Plant stand, Victorian Eastlake style, oak, a square top w/molded edges above a deep line-incised apron w/curved & reeded corner brackets raised on ring-

and-rod-turned legs joined by two small square shelves, square outswept lower legs, refinished, ca. 1880s, 12" w., 36" h. (ILLUS.) **450**

Decorated Golden Oak Plant Stand

Plant stand, Victorian Golden Oak style, oak, a thick round top raised on a round pedestal w/four vertical panels of pressed leafy scrolls & beading, stepped round base on small arched feet, refinished, ca. 1900, 14" d., 34" h. (ILLUS.) **400**

Unusual Molded Renaissance Stand

Plant stand, Victorian Renaissance Revival style, mahogany & molded plaster, the square top w/molded edges above a shallow scalloped apron pierced w/small opening holding small balls, raised on a square waisted top pedestal section resting on a molded plaster band w/two leaves on each side above a tall square tapering pedestal w/each side decorated w/a large molded plaster grotesque face, the flaring pedestal base on a shell-molded band raised on a square platform w/cut-corners over flared block feet, original finish, ca. 1880, 14" w., 36" h. (ILLUS.) **500**

Simple Renaissance Plant Stand

Plant stand, Victorian Renaissance Revival style, walnut, a round white marble top above a coved apron w/two low arched & scalloped drops, raised on a baluster- and ring-turned pedestal flanked by three scalloped S-scroll legs w/outswept scroll feet, original finish, ca. 1870s, 16" d., 34" h. (ILLUS.) **350**

Plant Stand with Carved Putti

Plant stand, Victorian Rococo style, carved oak, a wide thin round dished top raised on a slender round pedestal carved in full-relief w/twining grapevine & two full-figure putti above a round platform issuing four outswept long scroll-carved legs each topped by a carved boar head, Europe, ca. 1870, original finish, 16" d., 26" h. (ILLUS.) **2,000**

Fine Classical Revival Plant Stands

Plant stands, Classical Revival style, mahogany, a square top w/a tapering pointed drop finial at each corner, raised on a heavy tapering columnar pedestal w/a ring of beads above a heavy baluster-turned base section resting on a square platform w/tiny ball feet, original dark finish, late 19th c., 14" w., 40" h., pr. (ILLUS.) **2,800**

Plant Stand with Carved Dolphins

Plant stands, Victorian Baroque style, carved mahogany, square small top w/gadrooned edges above a deep apron carved w/a band of stylized blossoms & an animal head at each corner, raised on a pedestal w/a divided ovoid reeded post atop a lower pedestal flanked by four figural dolphins resting on a cross-form base w/carved paw feet, original dark finish, probably Europe, late 19th c., 14" w., 38" h., pr. (ILLUS. of one) **1,800**

Plant Stands with Figural Mermaids

Plant stands, Victorian Baroque style, ebonized fruit wood, a small octagonal top w/a shallow scalloped & carved apron raised on a slender pedestal mounted w/a full-figure mermaid w/arms outstretched, the forked tail wrapping around the lower pedestal above leafy vines & a tripod base w/outswept scroll-carved legs, Europe, late 19th c., original finish, 15" w., 36" h., pr. (ILLUS.) **3,000**

One Ornate Renaissance Stand

Plant stands, Victorian Renaissance Revival style, ebonized & inlaid walnut, a round top raised on a large bulbous ebonized urn w/large gilt-incised shells resting on a

square platform w/notched corner brackets above a heavy square tapering pedestal, each side centered by a tall tapering arch-topped ebonized panel ornately inlaid a basket, bird, bow & flowering vines, on a ringed band on the square platform base w/short bracket feet, original finish, ca. 1875, one w/a round white marble top, 14" d., 36" h., pr. (ILLUS. of one without marble top) **2,000**

Finely Veneered Classical Stand

Sewing stand, Classical style, mahogany & mahogany veneer, the rectangular top w/rounded corners lifting above an interior fitted w/an outside band of small compartments centered by a lidded center well, the sides of the well form the square tapering base of the case resting on a notch-carved band above a square short pedestal w/another carved band raised on a square panel & cross-form platform w/incurved C-scroll feet, fine figured veneering, original finish, ca. 1830s, 18 x 20", 30" h. (ILLUS. open).. **750**

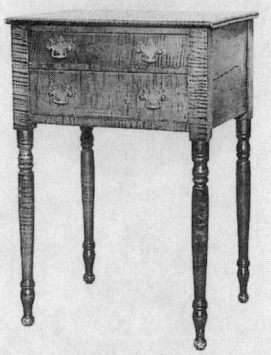

Rare Country Federal Sewing Stand

Sewing stand, Federal country-style, curly maple & curly maple veneer, a rectangular top above a case w/two drawers w/replaced batwing brasses, the top drawer fitted w/11 compartments, raised on ring, rod- and knob-turned tapering legs w/knob feet, early 19th c., 15 1/2 x 20", 28 1/2" h. (ILLUS.) **2,530**

Sewing stand, Federal, mahogany, rectangular top & flanking drop leaves w/molded edges, thin applied molding around lower apron, two dovetailed drawers w/old Rockingham glazed pottery pulls, top drawer w/divider along one side w/hollowed-out insert, ropetwist legs w/ring turnings end in brass caps w/casters, 17" sq. (plus 8" leaves), 29" h. (two loose pulls, minor chip, small pieced repair) **1,760**

Aesthetic Movement Shaving Stand

Fancy Labeled Rococo Sewing Stand

Sewing stand, Victorian Rococo style, carved walnut, the rectangular top flanked by rounded end drop leaves above a case w/two narrow drawers w/scroll-carved pulls over a thin pullout slide w/carved pulls supporting the deep cloth bag below, trestle-style supports w/forked heavy scroll-carved uprights raised on blocked shoe feet joined by a flat scroll-carved stretcher w/a central medallion, retailer's label for George Crome Furniture Co. of Boston but produced by Mitchell & Rammelsberg, Cincinnati, Ohio, ca. 1850s, refinished, 16 x 20", 30" h. (ILLUS.)................. **1,400**

Shaving stand, Victorian Aesthetic Movement style, walnut, the superstructure w/a flat cornice over a pierced narrow band of knobs & dentil carving between the side rails flanking the square swiveling mirror above the rectangular white marble top on a case w/two narrow drawers over a narrow shaped apron & corner drops, raised on four slender square supports, the front two joined by a slender turned towel bar above a lower rectangular shelf w/a low geometrically-pierced gallery, outswept front lower legs, refinished, ca. 1880s, 16 x 20", 5' 4" h. (ILLUS., top of column).... **1,500**

Fancy Eastlake Shaving Stand

Shaving stand, Victorian Eastlake style, walnut & burl walnut, the tall superstructure w/an arched & bobbin-pierced crestrail flanked by corner blocks w/pointed finials above bamboo-turned uprights flanking the tall swiveling rectangular mirror above another bobbin-pierced rail, the rectangular pink marble top above a single narrow burl-veneered drawer w/a rectangular brass pull flanked by corner blocks over drop finials flanking a scalloped narrow apron, the side of the case fitted w/a small drawer, raised on turned front spindles & flat back stiles above a lower shelf w/a bobbin-turned gallery over a small rectangular door w/a recessed burl panel, arched front legs, original finish, ca. 1880s, 16 x 18", 6' h. (ILLUS.).... **3,200**

Fine Renaissance Shaving Stand

Shaving stand, Victorian Renaissance Revival style, walnut & burl walnut, a rectangular mirror in a molded frame w/corner blocks & a scroll-and-shell-carved crest swiveling between scroll-tipped uprights & a pierced tapering panel over a small half-round shelf, the rectangular white marble top w/molded edges above a narrow burl veneered drawer, raised on a slender rod-and urn-turned pedestal on center post supported by four arched & scroll-trimmed legs, refinished, ca. 1870s, 14 x 16", 5' 10" h. (ILLUS.) **2,800**

Simple Golden Oak Shaving Stand

Shaving stand, Victorian Golden Oak style, quarter-sawn oak, a rectangular beveled mirror in a narrow frame w/a scroll-carved crest swiveling between slender scrolled uprights over the rectangular top over two plain doors, raised on four slender square tapering legs joined by a lower shelf, original finish, ca. 1900, 14 x 16", 5' 6" h. (ILLUS.) **750**

Rare Baudouine Shaving Stand

Wide Federal Mahogany Washstand

Shaving stand, Victorian Rococo style, figured maple, a small oval mirror swiveling above a U-form bracket supported w/a slender turned column flanked by ornate pierced carved scrolls, the rectangular tan marble top w/rounded front corners & bowed front above a serpentine drawer w/scroll-carved trim & turned corner drop pendants, raised on a columnar pedestal w/gadrooned base above a round post enclosed w/four scroll-carved arching legs, original finish, Charles Baudouine, New York City, ca. 1850s, 16 x 18', 5' 4" h. (ILLUS., previous page) **10,000**

crest over the long rectangular white marble top above a long ogee-fronted drawer, raised on heavy S-scroll front supports & flat back supports over a rectangular shelf, C-scroll front legs on casters, ca. 1840, refinished, 18 x 30", 38" h. (ILLUS.) **850**

Washstand, Federal style, mahogany & mahogany veneer, a galleried top w/an arched crestrail & flaring stepped side rails flanking the rectangular top w/two large round cutout & a bowed front, solid sides w/concave-cut fronts flank a lower shelf over a pair of narrow drawers w/butterfly brasses, on short knob-and-ring-turned feet, original finish, ca. 1820s, 20 x 48", 38" h. (ILLUS., top of page) **1,400**

Veneered Classical Washstand

Washstand, Classical style, mahogany & mahogany veneer, a high rectangular splashback w/an arched & scroll-carved

Louis XVI Revival Fancy Washstand

Washstand, Louis XVI Revival style, figured rosewood veneer, the square top inset w/white marble above the apron w/projecting round corners & a narrow paneled drawer w/wooden knob raised on four ring-turned & reeded columns above a panel-veneered shelf over a small rectangular panel-veneered door & matching sides, serpentine apron raised on short scroll-carved legs on metal casters, original finish, early 20th c., 16" sq., 30" h. (ILLUS., previous page)...................... **650**

Fancy Golden Oak Washstand

Grain-painted Country Washstand

Washstand, Victorian country-style, painted & decorated pine, an ornate galleried splashback, the high serpentine back centered by a tall scroll-cut finial & flanked by stepped low sides over the rectangular top above the apron w/a small oval-fronted drawer w/porcelain knob, raised on flat serpentine front supports & turned tapering rear legs joined by a lower shelf w/a serpentine front, simple flat front feet, original mahogany-grained decorating w/yellow trim, mid-19th c., 18 x 25", 42" h. (ILLUS.)................... **400**

Washstand, Victorian Golden Oak style, oak, a large oval beveled mirror swiveling between slender S-scroll uprights w/a small towel bar to one side supported on a shorter S-scroll upright all on a serpentine backsplash over the rectangular top w/serpentine sides, the case w/a long serpentine drawer over a stack of two flat drawers beside a paneled cupboard door, serpentine apron between short shaped front feet on casters, original hardware, refinished, ca. 1900, 18 x 32", 5' h. (ILLUS., top next column) **650**

Simple Golden Oak Washstand

Washstand, Victorian Golden Oak style, quarter-sawn oak, a slender towel bar raised between tall S-scroll supports above the rectangular top w/rounded corners & a bowed front, the conforming case w/two long bowed drawers w/brass pulls above a pair of flat cupboard doors, simple cabriole front legs, refinished, ca. 1890s, 19 x 32", 4' 4" h. (ILLUS.).................... **500**

Washstand with Marble Splashback

Washstand, Victorian Renaissance Revival style, walnut & burl walnut, a tall arched white marble splashback fitted w/two small shelves above the rectangular white marble top w/notched front corners, the case w/a long narrow drawer w/a raised burl oblong panel & black teardrop pulls flanked by blocks at the angled corners above a pair of paneled cupboard doors each centered by a square raised burl panel & flanked by blocked angled front corners, flat molded base w/wafer feet, original finish, ca. 1870s, 17 x 30", 38" h. (ILLUS.)... **1,350**

Marble-topped Walnut Washstand

Washstand, Victorian Renaissance Revival style, walnut & burl walnut, the high peaked white marble splashback mounted w/two small shelves above the rectangular white marble top w/angled front corners over a conforming case, a long top drawer centered by a burl roundel flanked by shaped rectangular raised burl panels w/cartouche-carved pulls, two paneled cupboard doors w/arched raised burl panels above the flat molded base w/wafer feet on casters, refinished, ca. 1870s, 18 x 28", 38" h. (ILLUS.) **1,200**

Fancy Victorian Rococo Washstand

Washstand, Victorian Rococo style, figured walnut, the high arched splashback w/a fancy fruit- and scrolling leaf-carved crest & flanked by scroll-cut sides on the rectangular white marble top w/projecting corners over scroll-carved blocks flanking a long figured walnut drawer w/a raised oval band & fruit- and leaf-carved pulls over a pair of cupboard doors w/large figured walnut oval panels surrounded by carved scrolls, angled front corners w/scroll-carved base blocks over the molded base w/rounded corners & a low scroll-carved apron, refinished, ca. 1860, 18 x 30", 42" h. (ILLUS.) **1,800**

Stools

Classical Curule-form Stool

Classical stool, mahogany, curule-style, rectangular upholstered slip seat on a frame raised on X-form scrolled legs joined by a turned stretcher, ca. 1830, 19" h. (ILLUS.) **633**

English George III Upholstered Stool

George III stool, mahogany, the rectangular over-upholstered needlepoint top raised on cabriole legs w/scroll feet, England, first quarter 19th c., 18 x 22", 19" h. (ILLUS.) **748**

Jacobean-Style Oak Joint Stool

Jacobean-Style joint stool, oak, rectangular top centered by a small heart-shaped cutout above a narrow frame raised on knob-, ring- and rod-turned tapering legs ending in blocks on knob feet & joined by a turned H-stretcher, 19th c., 23" h. (ILLUS.) **546**

Louis XV-Style Upholstered Stool

Louis XV-Style stool, carved fruitwood, the rectangular needlepoint top w/serpentine sides on a conforming apron w/a carved shell at each side, raised on cabriole legs w/shell-carved knees & ending in scroll-and-peg feet, France, third quarter 19th c., 16 x 17 1/2", 16 1/4" h. (ILLUS.) **920**

Napoleon III Giltwood Stool

Napoleon III stool, giltwood, square padded top raised on giltwood faux bamboo tapering & slightly outswept legs w/lattice brackets at the top corners & joined by a cross-stretcher centered by a square, France, third quarter 19th c., 12" w., 16" h. (ILLUS.) **575**

Victorian Chippendale Piano Stool

Victorian Chippendale Revival piano stool, mahogany, the rectangular needlepoint top opening to a storage space, the deep apron frame & square legs carved in the Chinese Chippendale taste w/lattice-work along the apron & down each leg, on block feet, legs joined by a pierced H-stretcher, probably England, late 19th c., 14 x 19 1/2", 20" h. (ILLUS.) **690**

William & Mary-Style Footstool

William & Mary-Style footstool, walnut, rectangular over-upholstered gros point top above ring-, knob- and rod-turned legs on blocks joined by a baluster-turned H-stretcher, flattened knob feet, 19th c., 17" h. (ILLUS.).. **805**

Windsor stool, circular seat on four canted legs w/four stretchers, old red graining over a brownish red base coat, yellow detail in incised turnings, attributed to the state of Maine, 16 1/2" h. (wear) **825**

Tables

Arts & Crafts library table, oak, rectangular top above an apron w/a long center drawer w/square wood pulls above the arched kneehole opening flanked by front & back panels w/cutout pairs of ovals over a circle, front & back panels joined by a shelf & side rail, square legs, dark brown finish, early 20th c., 26 x 40", 30 1/8" h. (imperfections)... **345**

Baroque Bird-carved Coffee Table

Baroque Revival coffee table, carved walnut, the rectangular top w/inset marble raised on large end supports carved in bold relief as spread-winged phoenixes above serpentine shoe feet, original

finish, ca. 1920s, 16 x 26", 21" h. (ILLUS.)... **950**

Baroque Revival Side Table

Baroque Revival side table, walnut, a rectangular top w/rounded ends w/wide scroll-carved bands & flanked by oblong drop leaf carved to continue the scroll band & forming an oblong top when raised, on slender ring- and-rod-turned legs joined by bobbin-turned stretchers, two matching swing-out support legs, original dark finish, ca. 1920s, 20 x 30" open, 26" h. (ILLUS. open)... **650**

Fine Chippendale Revival Side Table

Chippendale Revival side table, mahogany, a rectangular top w/gadrooned ends flanked by half-round drop leaves above a deep apron w/a stack of two cock-beaded end drawers w/round brass pulls, cabriole legs w/scroll-carved knees & ending in claw-and-ball feet, original finish, 19th c., 16 x 20" closed, 30" h. (ILLUS.).................... **1,400**

Chippendale Revival Tea Table

Chippendale Revival tea table, mahogany, large round top w/piecrust edge tilting above a turned pedestal on a tripod base w/three outstretched cabriole legs ending in claw-and-ball feet, original dark finish, late 19th c., 24" d., 30" h. (ILLUS.) **500**

Fine Classical Breakfast Table

Classical breakfast table, mahogany & mahogany veneer, the wide rectangular top flanked by deep half-round drop leaves above a veneer-banded apron w/corner drops, raised on a heavy bulbous acanthus leaf-carved pedestal on a block platform over four outstretched leaf-carved legs w/paw feet, old refinish, ca. 1840, 24 x 48" closed, 30" h. (ILLUS.) **1,400**

Fine Round Classical Dining Table

Classical dining table, mahogany & mahogany veneer, extension-type, round top w/a deep crotch-veneered apron, raised on a cluster of four columns over a cross-form base w/arch-topped flattened legs on disk feet on casters, old refinish, w/six leaves, ca. 1840, 60" d., 30" h. (ILLUS.)...... **4,000**

Quality Classical Dressing Table

Classical dressing table, mahogany & mahogany veneer, the superstructure w/a large vertical rectangular mirror mounted in a wide frame w/half-round column sides joined by corner blocks w/brass rosettes, swiveling between ornate turned & acanthus leaf-carved uprights joined at the top w/a plain pointed crestrail, the columns resting on a pair of long shallow handkerchief drawers set back on the rectangular white marble top, the case w/a long round-fronted veneered drawer over two shorter round-fronted drawers flanking an arched central panel, raised on four spiral-turned acanthus leaf-carved legs joined by a wide medial shelf w/a serpentine front, on small double-knob feet on brass casters, original hardware, refinished, ca. 1830s, 19 x 36", 6' 2" h. (ILLUS.)............................ **2,000**

Classical Inlaid Game Table

Classical game table, inlaid mahogany, the rectangular fold-over top w/rounded corners above a conforming apron centered by an inlaid feathered maple rectangular panel, raised on a heavy pedestal boldly carved w/acanthus leaves above a round platform w/a carved border raised on four outswept legs w/leaf-carved knees & large paw feet, original finish, ca. 1830, 18 x 36" closed, 30" h. (ILLUS.) **1,200**

Philadelphia Classical Game Table

Classical game table, mahogany & mahogany veneer, the rectangular fold-over top w/a gadrooned edge & rounded corners opening to a plain top w/a narrow half-round apron w/florette-carved front corners, raised on a pedestal composed of a cluster of columns resting on a long quadripartite platform base raised on carved paw feet, Philadelphia, ca. 1830s, original finish, 18 x 36", 30" h. (ILLUS.) **3,000**

Game Table on Ornate Carved Base

Classical game table, mahogany & mahogany veneer, the rectangular fold-over top w/rounded corners & a flat projecting front section opening over a conforming veneered apron, raised on a heavy cylindrical column boldly carved w/rings of acanthus leaves atop w/sawtooth-carved disk supported by outswept animal legs w/leaf-carved knees & large paw feet, original finish, ca. 1830s, 20 x 40", 30" h. (ILLUS.)... **2,000**

Late Classical Parlor Table

Classical parlor center table, mahogany & mahogany veneer, the rectangular top w/serpentine edges above a conforming deep scalloped apron, raised on a bulbous baluster-form octagonal pedestal resting on a domed, stepped paneled base w/notch-carved bands, raised on four flaring ogee bracket feet, refinished, ca. 1840s, 20 x 32", 30" h. (ILLUS.) **500**

Unusual Classical Pier Table

Classical pier table, mahogany & mahogany veneer, the rectangular white marble top above a coved apron, supported at the front by large square tapering columns w/carved acanthus leaves & gadrooning & resting on turned disk feet supported by projecting side platforms backed by matching half-columns centering a large arched mirror above a half-round acanthus leaf-carved disk which appears round in the mirror reflection, compressed carved round feet, probably Baltimore, original finish, ca. 1830s, 18 x 42", 34" h. (ILLUS.) **3,500**

Labeled Classical Pier Table

Classical pier table, mahogany & mahogany veneer, the rectangular white marble top over a concave frieze band decorated w/stylized acanthus leaves & other foliage, supported on a pair of veneered columns w/gilt-brass capitals & bases, the edge of the lower shelf stenciled w/a classical design, a rectangular mirror in the back panel, on ebonized carved front paw feet crowned w/gilded vertical gadrooning, simple turned rear legs, on casters, original finished except lower shelf, stenciled label of Cook & Parkin, Philadelphia, first quarter 19th c., 20 x 47 3/4", 40 3/4" h. (ILLUS.) **6,900**

Mahogany Classical Sewing Table

Classical sewing table, mahogany & mahogany veneer, the rectangular top w/chamfered edges lifting over a shallow fitted interior above a deep ogee-fronted drawer, raised on a tall waisted octagonal pedestal resting on an octagonal platform w/four projecting blocked & paneled feet w/disk finials, original finish, ca. 1830, 18 x 20", 30" h. (ILLUS.) **1,400**

Classical Maple-inlaid Work Table

Classical work table, mahogany & figured maple, the rectangular top w/rounded corners above a conforming deep case w/a very narrow top drawer w/a figured walnut veneer panel, brass knob pulls & a brass keyhole escutcheon above two graduated matching drawers, raised on a heavy baluster-turned & acanthus leaf-carved pedestal on outswept leaf-carved legs ending in hairy paw feet on casters, polished original finish, ca. 1830s, 16 x 22", 30" h. (ILLUS.) **1,600**

Large Classical Revival Round Dining Table

Basket-based Classical Work Table

Classical work table, mahogany & mahogany veneer, rectangular top over a deep case w/a concave-fronted plain drawer above a flat drawer w/large rosette & ring pulls flanked by half-round ring-turned drops, raised on a bulbous pedestal carved in the form of a fruit-filled basket resting on a quadripartite platform raised on outswept fluted scroll feet on casters, refinished, ca. 1835, 16 x 20", 28" h. (ILLUS.)... **850**

Classical Revival dining table, mahogany & mahogany veneer, expandable, the large round top opening in the center above a large round column flanked by heavy curved leaf-carved brackets & carved dolphin heads on the cross-form

base w/heavy paw feet, refinished, w/10 leaves, late 19th c., closed 60" d., 30" h. (ILLUS., top of page)..................................... **6,500**

Classical Revival Work Table

Classical Revival work table, mahogany & mahogany veneer, rectangular top w/gadrooned edges flanked by half-round drop leaves over a case w/two round-fronted drawers w/original brass knobs flanked by leaf-carved side panels, raised on a baluster-turned leaf-carved pedestal on four outswept leaf-carved legs ending in paws on casters, refinished, late 19th c., 16 x 18", 30" h. (ILLUS.) **750**

Fine Classical Revival Mahogany Dining Table

Colonial Revival dining table, mahogany & mahogany veneer, expandable, the long rectangular top w/rounded corners above deep apron w/a thin gadroon-carved edge band, raised on six cabriole legs w/leaf-carved knees & ending in scroll feet on pads, original finish, late 19th c., w/six leaves opens to 16', closed 50" l., 30" h. (ILLUS., above)................................... **6,500**

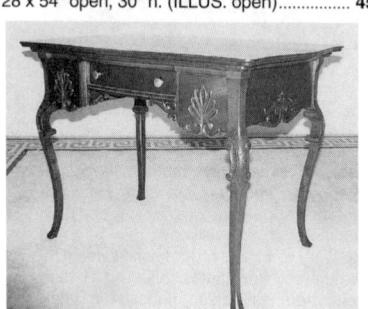

Oak Colonial Revival Dining Table

Colonial Revival dining table, quarter-sawn oak, the rectangular top flanked by wide D-form drop leaves raised on simple trumpet-turned legs joined by box stretchers, on ball feet on casters, two swing-out support legs, refinished, early 20th c., 28 x 54" open, 30" h. (ILLUS. open)................ **450**

Colonial Revival Library Table

Colonial Revival library table, cherry, the rectangular top w/serpentine edges over-hanging a case w/a center drawer above an arched opening flanked by panels carved w/large palmette leaves, scroll-carved side aprons, on simple cabriole legs w/scroll-carved knees, refinished, late 19th c., 28 x 48", 30" h. (ILLUS.).............. **600**

Colonial Revival Sewing Table

Colonial Revival sewing table, heavily fig-ured cherry, the rectangular top opening to a deep divided well, the serpentine apron w/a small carved shell on each side, raised on slender cabriole legs w/leaf-carved knees & paw feet, refinished, ca. 1900, 16 x 18", 30" h. (ILLUS. open).. **450**

Federal Table with Unusual Top

Federal card table, cherry & mahogany veneer, the hinged half-round top w/projecting scroll-carved front corners above a matching a conforming apron w/mahogany veneer, raised on ring- and knob-turned legs w/a long spiral-turned section above the ring- and baluster-turned feet, old refinish, ca. 1820, 18 x 40", 30" h. (ILLUS.) **1,800**

Fine Federal Inlaid Game Table

Federal card table, inlaid mahogany, the half-round hinged top above a conforming apron inlaid w/a leaf & line design, on square tapering legs w/similar line inlay, Rhode Island, 1790-1810, swing-out leg pieced, 17 3/4 x 36", 29 1/4" h. (ILLUS.)..... **3,055**

Federal card table, refinished mahogany & figured veneer, double inlay on edges of fold-over top w/serpentine sides & slightly bowed front w/bird's-eye rectangular panels & oval at center, turned & reeded legs w/line border inlay around bottom of aprons, attributed to Salem, Massachu-

setts, early 19th c., 18 x 37", 30 1/2" h. (old break at dovetail on back right corner).. **4,400**

Federal Country Dressing Table

Federal country-style dressing table, painted mahogany, a scroll-cut crestrail above a narrow rectangular shelf over a pair of handkerchief drawers on the rectangular top over a single long drawer, ring-and-spiral-twist-turned legs on knob feet, old green repaint, replaced wood pulls, ca. 1830, sold refinished, 18 x 34", 40" h. (ILLUS.) **800**

Fine Federal Pembroke Table

Federal Pembroke table, mahogany, the wide rectangular top flanked by half-round shaped drop leaves over the wide apron w/a working drawer w/brass knob at one end & a sham drawer at the other end, on ring-turned reeded legs on double-knob feet on casters, New York City, 1815-25, 36 x 47" open, 28 1/2" h. (ILLUS.)............... **5,288**

French Provincial Long Work Table

Federal Two-Drawer Work Table

ets flanked by fluted sides, raised on turned tapering reeded supports joined by a scroll-carved cross-stretcher mounted w/a square central shelf carved w/a large rosette, on ring-turned tapering legs w/outswept brass caps, original finish, late 19th c., 18 x 20", 30" h. (ILLUS., below).. **800**

Federal Revival Side Table

Federal work table, mahogany, the square top w/ovolo corners above leaf-carved projecting corners flanking a pair of cockbeaded drawers w/original round brass pulls, raised on ring- and spiral-twist-turned legs w/a leaf-carved knob resting on peg feet w/disk angles, original brass casters, original finish, top repairs, attributed to the school of Samuel McIntyre, Salem, Massachusetts, early 19th c., 18" w., 30" h. (ILLUS.).................................. **2,000**

Federal Revival side table, mahogany, the rectangular top flanked by half-round drop leaves w/leaf-carved corners above an apron w/a single paneled end drawer w/butterfly brass over line-incised brack-

French Provincial work table, apple wood, pegged construction, rectangular top w/rounded corners over a dovetailed apron w/two drawers along one side, on simple cabriole legs, old refinish, France, mid-19th c., 34 x 72", 29" h. (ILLUS., top of page).. **750**

Rare Gothic Revival Library Table

Gothic Revival library table, carved rosewood, the rectangular top inset w/variegated white marble over a wide apron w/a band of quatrefoil cutouts, raised on angled naturalistic animal legs w/scrolled hair at the top & ending in cloven hoof feet, mid-19th c., 25 1/4 x 43 1/2", 28" h. (ILLUS.).. **16,675**

Harvest table, birch & pine, rectangular one-board top flanked by narrow drop leaves, on turned legs w/applied pads, old alliga-tored light brown surface, 19th c., 20 1/4 x 66" (w/10" leaves), 27" h. (postage stamp-size repair on one leaf & larger one on top, probably done by original craftsman, leaves refinished) **825**

Harvest table, pine, a very long rectangular two-board to raised on flattened X-form end supports joined by a flat through-tenoned stretcher, first half 19th c., 29 1/4 x 108", 27 1/4" h. (ILLUS., below).. **12,925**

Very Rare Pine Harvest Table

Scarce Early Painted Hutch Table

Hutch (or chair) table, painted pine, the large round top titled above a box seat base on trestle feet, old red paint, New England, 18th c., 47 1/2" d., 29" h. (ILLUS.).. **8,225**

Fancy Late Victorian Side Table

Late Victorian side table, oak, a square top w/molded edges raised on canted legs w/ornate pierce-carved C-scrolls enclosing a slender rod all joined by a square medial shelf & ending in a brass eagle claw w/glass ball foot, original finish, ca. 1900, 20" sq., 30" h. (ILLUS.)........................... **400**

Finely Carved Chinese Side Table

Oriental side table, carved hardwood, the round top inset w/a Rose Medallion patt. porcelain plaque surrounded by a carved lappet band above a gadrooned band over the curved apron ornately pierce-carved w/branches of leaves & berries, raised on cylindrical legs carved w/flower swags at the top & ending in leafy scroll feet, joined by a lower round carved stretcher centered by a carved openwork diamond, China, late 19th c., 24" d., 30 1/2" h. (ILLUS.).. **2,185**

Queen Anne country-style tavern table, maple & pine, rectangular one-board top w/breadboard ends, molded stretcher base & pegged construction, well-turned legs & molded edge around bottom of apron, turned feet, w/thin old salmon paint on base, scrubbed top, New England, 28 x 46 3/4", 27 1/2" h. (old splits, wear)..... **4,125**

Rare Queen Anne Dining Table

Queen Anne dining table, mahogany, the rectangular top w/rounded ends flanked by wide half-round drop leaves, the apron raised on simple cabriole legs ending in padded disc feet, Massachusetts, 1740-60, 43" d. open, 28" h. (ILLUS. closed)..... **14,100**

Rare Queen Anne Tavern Table

Queen Anne tavern table, painted maple, the oval top overhanging a rectangular

apron, raised on round tapering legs ending in pad feet, old red paint, New England, 1740-60, 25 1/2 x 33 1/2", 27" h.
(ILLUS., previous page) **16,450**

Queen Anne Tea Table & Queen Anne
Revival Dressing Table

Queen Anne tea table, mahogany, a large
single-board octagonal top tilting above a
turned pedestal on a tripod base w/three
outswept cabriole legs ending in pad feet,
possibly original finish, 32" w., 30" h.
(ILLUS. right with Queen Anne Revival ta-
ble) **1,800**
Queen Anne Revival dressing table, ma-
hogany & mahogany veneer, a rectangular top above a case w/a row of three small
drawers over two deeper drawers flanking
an arched apron, on cabriole legs w/shell-
carved knees & pad feet, original teardrop
brasses, original finish, ca. 1920s,
16 x 26", 30" h. (ILLUS. left with tea
table) **400**

Very Ornate Rococo Coffee Table

Rococo Revival coffee table, carved walnut, the oblong tray top ornately carved
w/a wide serpentine border of leafy scrolls
w/loop end handles & an oval glass center
inset, raised on a serpentine pierce-
carved apron w/scrolls centering a large
shell, leaf-carved S-scroll legs w/scroll
feet joined by a scroll-carved cross
stretcher centered by a scroll-carved disk,
original finish, ca. 1920s, 24 x 32", 20" h.
(ILLUS.) **750**

Angel-carved Rococo Side Table

Rococo Revival side table, carved mahogany, a black marble 'turtle-top' inset into a
widely flaring conforming apron carved
w/leaves, raised on cabriole legs, each
topped by a large carved angel head
w/wings & tapering down to a scroll foot,
joined by a baluster-turned cross stretcher
centered by a turned finial, original
finish, ca. 1920s, 20" w., 20" h.
(ILLUS.) **600**

Very Fine Rococo Revival Side Table

Rococo Revival side table, carved mahogany, a rectangular black marble top set
into a molded frame w/ovolo corners
above a deep serpentine ornately pierce-
carved apron w/leafy scrolls & florettes
centering an large oblong lattice-inlaid
panel, raised on cabriole legs, each
topped by a carved full-figure putto & ending in a scroll foot, joined by an arched
cross-stretcher centered by a carved flower basket finial, original finish, by Flint &
Horner, New York City, ca. 1920s,
18 x 24", 30" h. (ILLUS.) **1,800**

Victorian Aesthetic Dining Table

Victorian Aesthetic Movement dining table, mahogany, expandable, the wide round top over a deep apron carved w/a lappet band, raised on four heavy square stop-fluted & tapering legs on casters, joined by a heavy cross-stretcher centered by four heavy solid scroll-shaped brackets w/oval carved rosettes, refinished, ca. 1890, w/six leaves, 60" d. closed, 30" h. (ILLUS.) **2,000**

Rare Horner Baroque Dining Table

Victorian Baroque Revival dining table, carved mahogany, expandable, the round top w/a deep scroll-carved apron, raised on a large center post flanked by four supports carved as large seated winged griffins on the cross-form base, by Horner Furniture Co., New York City, late 19th c., refinished, w/eight leaves, 60" d., 30" h. (ILLUS.) **10,000**

Baroque Table with Large Pedestal

Victorian Baroque Revival dining table, oak, expandable, the round top above a plain apron, raised on a large round reeded squatty disk above a large cylindrical base issuing four large animal legs w/paw feet on casters, original finish, w/six leaves, ca. 1895 54" d., 30" h. (ILLUS., at left with leaves on the top) **3,000**

Fine Horner Library Desk with Carved Griffin Legs

Victorian Baroque Revival library table, carved mahogany, partner's-type, the rectangular top w/a wide scroll-carved border band above the deep rounded apron carved overall w/leafy scrolls & centered on each side by a long drawer, raised at each corner by a large full-figure carved seated griffin on a narrow platform connecting to a raised rectangular center shelf w/incurved beaded edges, Horner Furniture Co., New York City, ca. 1880s, 28 x 52", 30" h. (ILLUS., above) **5,500**

of carved blocks over a bulbous turned knob over a smaller block over slender turned legs w/paw feet, the legs joined across the ends by a lattice-bar design centered by a pierced scroll-carved panels, a shaped flat stretcher shelf from end to end, sold refinished, ca. 1890, 24 x 40", 30" h. (ILLUS.) **2,000**

Library Table with Paneled Ends

Victorian Baroque Revival library table, carved oak, rectangular top w/a wide border band carved w/leafy vines w/pineapple-like fruits, the edge carved w/a raised dash design, scroll-carved corner brackets, the ends supported w/legs composed

Unique Folk-carved Parlor Table

Victorian Baroque Revival parlor table, carved walnut, the rectangular top fitted w/two fold-out leaves carved w/pairs of scroll-carved bands on the top side, the deep rectangular case below carved on three sides w/primitive geometric designs, one long side fitted w/a paneled door centered by a panel carved w/a round medallion carved w/a primitive bust profile of a woman flanked leaf-carved columns, a projecting medial band raised on four heavy square legs carved w/geometric designs & resting on a lower shelf above simple carved paw feet, original finish, ca. 1890-1900, 15 x 20" closed, 31" h. (ILLUS.)..................... **650**

Ornately Carved Parlor Table

Victorian Baroque Revival parlor table, carved walnut, the rectangular top w/a wide ornate scroll-carved border band & carved beveled edge overhanging a deep scroll-carved apron w/sunburst-carved corner blocks all overhanging a case w/a group of four paneled & scroll-carved drawers on each side & matching carved end panels, the projecting corners w/bold leaf-carved & ring-turned freestanding columns above blocks on bun feet, probably an exhibition piece, original finish, ca. 1870s, 22 x 40", 30" h. (ILLUS.)................... **4,500**

Octagonal Baroque Parlor Table

Victorian Baroque Revival parlor table, oak, the octagonal top above a deep line-incised octagonal apron supports four slender legs w/a bulbous scroll-carved top

over a fluted section resting on a block above a short ring-carved legs on a claw-and-ball foot, the legs joined by a squared pierce-carved medial shelf, original finish, ca. 1890s, 22" w., 30" h. (ILLUS.)........ **650**

Unusual Country-style Game Table

Victorian country-style game table, oak w/maple top, the square top w/a window in the center allowing a view of a numbered scorekeeping devices, the apron w/knobs on each side used to change the score, a small square drawer in one corner of the apron, top also w/a flush-mounted button which rings a bell when pressed, heavy ring-, rod- and baluster-turned legs, original finish, ca. 1900, 34" w., 30" h. (ILLUS.)... **600**

Victorian Painted Country Table

Victorian country-style work table, painted pine, the oval top widely overhanging one end, the apron centered by a small drawer w/wooden pull, on square tapering legs, original crackled light blue paint w/white on legs, ca. 1900, 18 x 28", 30" h. (ILLUS.)... **175**

Fine Eastlake Oak Library Table

Six-legged Eastlake Dining Table

Victorian Eastlake style dining table, walnut, extension-type, square top w/rounded corners above a conforming block-incised apron, raised on six heavy legs w/large gadrooned & fluted bulbous knobs or ring-turned & fluted knobs over long incurved block-incised side stretchers flanking a shorter center stretchers, on bun feet on casters, original finish, ca. 1890, w/four leaves, 52" w., 30" h. (ILLUS.) **1,800**

Eastlake Dining Table with Bobbins

Victorian Eastlake style dining table, walnut, extension-type, square top w/rounded corners over a simple apron raised on six ring- and knob-turned legs, the outer pairs of legs joined by concave stretchers mounted w/high bobbin-turned bands between blocks, the flat center stretchers joining the center two legs, original porcelain casters, original finish, w/six leaves, ca. 1890, 48" w., 30" h. (ILLUS.)... **1,500**

Victorian Eastlake style library table, oak, partner's-type, the rectangular top w/molded edge over an apron w/a working drawer next to a false drawer on each side, each section w/a lightly carved center panel w/brass keyhole escutcheon flanked by diamond point-carved narrow panels, raised on four reeded block corner legs w/turned rings at the top & base, resting on blocked outswept legs, joined by a cross: stretcher fitted w/a rectangular shelf w/a long gallery & turned corner finials, on casters, refinished, ca. 1890, 24 x 48", 30" h. (ILLUS., top of page) **650**

Eastlake Mahogany Parlor Table

Fine Golden Oak Dining Table with Square Pedestal

Victorian Eastlake style parlor table, mahogany, the rectangular top w/a narrow shell-carved band at the molded edge above the line-incised apron w/a gently arched apron, raised on knob-, ring- and rod-turned legs curving out at the base, scroll-carved end stretchers joined by flat cross-stretchers centered by a small disk finial, original finish, ca. 1885, 18 x 30", 30" h. (ILLUS., bottom previous page)........... **450**

Square Golden Oak Dining Table

Victorian Golden Oak style dining table, oak, expandable, the square top w/small rounded corners above an apron w/a notch-carved border, raised on five heavy columnar legs w/bulbous reeded central knobs above large bun feet on casters, the corner legs joined by a high concave panel stamped w/pairs of scrolls, a central support leg, w/four leaves, refinished, ca. 1900, 52" w., 30" h. (ILLUS. open) **2,800**

Claw-footed Oak Dining Table

Victorian Golden Oak style dining table, oak, extension-type, round top w/simple apron raised on a heavy split post pedestal w/three incised rings flanked by four outstretched shaped legs ending in large paw feet on casters, refinished, w/four leaves, ca. 1900, 48" d., 30" h. (ILLUS.)...... **1,250**

Victorian Golden Oak style dining table, quarter-sawn oak, extension-type, the round top w/scallop-carved edge over a plain apron & a large square split pedestal w/a fruit-carved panel on each side & spiral-carved columns at each corner, supported on a cross-form platform on tapering knob feet, w/three leaves, original finish, ca. 1890s, 60" d., 30" h. (ILLUS. with leaves on the top, top of page) **3,500**

Golden Oak Library Table with Long Drawer

Victorian Golden Oak style library table, quarter-sawn oak, rectangular top w/molded edge above an apron w/a single very long drawer w/small brass pulls & a carved scroll at the center, each end w/a raised scroll-carved block, a narrow gadrooned edge band above the boldly ring-turned & reeded columnar supports joined by a wide flat barbell-shaped shelf-stretcher, on ring-turned short legs on lobed paw feet, refinished, ca. 1900, 26 x 42", 30" h. (ILLUS.) **650**

flat stretcher, ca. 1900, refinished, 22 x 42", 30" h. (ILLUS.) **950**

Fancy Golden Oak Side Table

Shell-carved Oak Library Table

Victorian Golden Oak style library table, quarter-sawn oak, rectangular top w/wide round corners overhanging an apron w/a long drawer w/stamped brass pulls on one side, curved & shaped scroll-carved corner blocks, solid end panels carved w/a large shell within an arched band, flat slightly slanted legs ending in carved paw feet on casters, a barbell-shaped lower

Victorian Golden Oak style side table, oak, square top w/serpentine edges above a serpentine scroll-carved apron w/a center fleur-de-lis on each side, raised on slender serpentine scroll- and bead-carved legs joined by arched scroll-carved cross stretchers supporting a small four-lobed shelf, original finish, ca. 1900, 16" w., 30" h. (ILLUS.) **350**

Renaissance Revival Square Oak Dining Table

French Gothic Revival Game Table

New York City, 1875-90, 22 3/4 x 31", 4'
7" h. (ILLUS., below) **5,640**

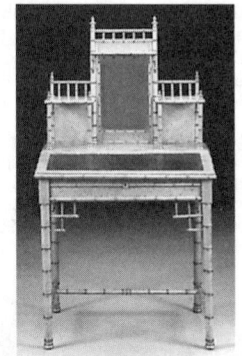

Rare Faux Bamboo Dressing Table

Victorian Gothic Revival game table,
carved & inlaid fruitwood, the square top
w/beveled corners over a deep apron
w/swing-out arms containing the wells for
the gaming pieces, a large arched &
pierced bracket at each corner, raised on
flattened slightly tapering canted legs
w/panels carved w/Gothic arches above a
trefoil-cut foot, lift-off top, France, ca.
1900, 29 1/2" w., 28 1/2" h. (ILLUS.).......... **1,150**

Victorian novelty dressing table, maple
faux-bamboo-style, the superstructure
w/a tall framework of faux bamboo w/a low
bobbin-turned rail above a rectangular
mirror flanked by lower side panels
w/matching rails over narrow shelves, the
slightly slanted hinged top w/inset panel
opening to a fitted interior, on four bamboo-turned legs joined by an H-stretcher,
bamboo-form lattice brackets under front
corners, possibly by R. J. Horner & Co.,

Unusual Pyrographic Side Table

Exceptional Herter Bros. Renaissance Revival Library Table

Victorian novelty side table, folding-type, pyrographic decoration, the round top hinged at the center over intersecting flattened & shaped legs w/Moorish-style cutouts & floral & leaf pyrographic decoration outlined in red, black & gold stain, early 20th c., wear, scratches, 24 1/4" d., 25 1/4" h. (ILLUS., bottom of previous page)... **518**

Victorian Renaissance Revival style dining table, oak, extension-type, square top w/rounded corners above a line-incised apron raised on a heavy paneled central column fitted w/four half-round fluted columns issuing angled heavy fluted legs w/carved roundels & supporting full-round & fluted column supports, on casters, old refinish, w/five leaves, ca. 1880, 52" w., 30" h. (ILLUS., top of previous page) **2,000**

Renaissance Walnut Dining Table

Victorian Renaissance Revival style dining table, walnut & burl walnut, a square

top w/wide rounded corners over a burl-banded apron, raised on a large square center posted issuing four downswept carved legs ending in octagonal ends carved w/rosettes & raised on rectangular platform feet, w/four leaves, ca. 1875, 53 1/2" w., 30 1/2" h. (ILLUS.)...................... **3,300**

Victorian Renaissance Revival style library table, marquetry-inlaid rosewood, the rectangular top w/rounded ends centered by a marquetry panel using various inlaid woods, ivory & brass & depicting a central Grecian urn draped w/ribboned garlands raised on poles grasped by wing griffins, against an ebonized ground encircled by line stringing, foliate & repeating banded marquetry around the border, the apron centered on the long sides by a turret w/gilt-incised carving flanked by a repeating marquetry band, each rounded end fitted w/a full-width drawer, the concealed interior beneath one end drawer bears the name "Schulte" or "Schatte" in pencil, raised on trumpet-turned legs w/incised carving & marquetry banding of hexagonal panels decorated w/alternating light & dark wood triangles, the base knobs above bun feet on casters, the legs joined by flattened U-shaped stretchers connected by a flattened roundel-centered stretcher w/a turned finial, stamped mark of Herter Bros., New York City, third quarter 19th c., 33 1/4 x 52", 30" h. (ILLUS., top of page) **41,400**

Fine Renaissance Revival Burl Walnut Library Table

Victorian Renaissance Revival style library table, walnut & burl walnut, the rectangular top w/wide rounded ends & inset center panel above a deep conforming apron w/large corner blocks w/turned drops, a long drawer centered by a bold oblong scroll-carved burl & roundel keyhole escutcheon, raised on a trestle-style base, w/pairs of square burl posts flanking large urn-turned supports raised on angled squared legs w/scroll feet on casters, a scroll-ended slender stretcher centered by a squatty bulbous turned finial, ca. 1875, 31 x 55", 30" h. (ILLUS.).. **1,610**

Walnut Renaissance Parlor Table

Victorian Renaissance Revival style parlor table, walnut, the oblong white marble top w/notched corners above a molded apron w/spearpoint-carved drops raised on four S-scroll incurved supports ending in turned finials & joined to a center post w/a slender ring-turned pedestal, all raised on four outswept shaped & molded legs on casters, refinished, ca. 1875, 20 x 32", 30" h. (ILLUS.) **750**

Carved Rosewood Rococo "Turtle-top" Parlor Table

Victorian Rococo parlor table, carved rosewood, a white marble "turtle-top" above a conforming apron carved in the center of each side w/a large scroll cluster, the blocked corners above heavy S-scroll legs w/leaf-carved knees & raised on casters, C-scroll-carved cross stretcher centered by a squatty ribbed urn finial, original finish, ca. 1860, 26 x 48", 30" h. (ILLUS.).. **2,500**

Fine Floral- and Disk-carved Meeks Rococo Parlor Table

Victorian Rococo parlor table, carved rosewood, a white marble "turtle-top" above a conforming apron ornately pierce-carved w/scrolls centered a floral cluster, raised on S-scroll legs w/the knees carved w/large floral clusters, scroll feet on casters, joined by a scroll-carved serpentine cross stretcher centered by a reeded carved disk finial & smaller disk drop finial, by J. & J. Meeks of New York City, original finish, ca. 1855, 25 x 48", 30" h. (ILLUS.).. **15,000**

Simple Rococo Walnut Parlor Table

Victorian Rococo parlor table, walnut, a wood "turtle-top" above a conforming narrow molded apron w/large leaf-and-grape cluster drops at each side, raised on simple heavy cabriole legs w/grape-carved knees & joined by a simple arched cross stretcher centered by a small urn-turned finial, on original brass casters, ca. 1865, original finish, 20 x 34", 30" h. (ILLUS.)........... **500**

Ornate Rococo Console Table

Victorian Rococo style console table, mahogany, the half-round top w/serpentine sides & a low arched & scroll-pierced crestrail above a conforming apron w/a long drawer at the front decorated w/a scroll-carved cartouche, ornate double-scroll front legs carved w/rose clusters, flat serpentine rear legs, joined by a half-round medial shelf & a rectangular base platform w/incurved front & sides on thin bun feet, original finish, ca. 1860, 14 x 28", 34" h. (ILLUS.) **1,800**

Large Walnut Rococo Game Table

Victorian Rococo game table, walnut, the octagonal top inset w/replaced green felt, the deep apron fitted w/four drawers alternating w/round panels, all centered by a carved cartouche & scrolls, raised on four heavy scroll-carved supports centered by a squatty bulbous finial all resting on a platform issuing four thick outstretched scroll-carved legs, old refinish, ca. 1865, 34" w., 30" h. (ILLUS.) **1,500**

Fine "Turtle-top" Rosewood Table

Victorian Rococo parlor table, carved rosewood, a white marble "turtle-top" above a conforming apron carved w/large floral & scroll clusters & a border of heavy scrolls, raised on heavy cabriole legs w/fruit- and scroll-carved knees & ending in scrolled leaf feet on casters, joined by a serpentine cross stretcher centered by a gadrooned urn finial, original finish, ca. 1850s, 24 x 44", 30" h. (ILLUS.) **3,600**

Rococo Table Attributed to Mallard

Victorian Rococo parlor table, carved rosewood, a white marble "turtle-top" above a conforming apron ornately carved w/scrolls, beaded panels & large fruit-carved reserves, raised on bold S-scroll legs on casters joined by a delicate S-scroll cross stretcher centered by a large bulbous spiral-turned urn finial, attributed to Prudent Mallard, New Orleans, Louisiana, 1850s, original finish, 28 x 50", 30" h. (ILLUS.) **6,500**

Fine Pierce-carved Parlor Table

Victorian Rococo parlor table, rosewood, the oblong white marble top w/notched corners above a conforming deep apron pierce-carved w/long narrow bands of scrolls over scroll-carved drops, raised on forked scroll supports joining tall C-scroll supports above a serpentine cross stretcher centered by a low carved reeded dome, on squatty disk feet, refinished, ca. 1850, 24 x 44", 30" h. (ILLUS.) **3,600**

Wardrobes & Armoires

European Walnut Armoire

Armoire, Baroque Revival, carved walnut, the rectangular top w/a low spindled gallery above the deep flaring cornice w/a scroll- and rosette-carved frieze band above a pair of tall doors, each door w/a long panel carved w/leafy scrolls & a round central medallion above a small rectangular panel over a square scroll-carved bottom panel centered by a large roundel, three slender columns across the front, each turned & fluted w/a scroll-carved capital & urn-turned base on a block, two carved drawers at the bottom w/brass pulls, flat molded base, plain matching panels down the sides, bun feet, opens to a shelved interior, Europe, original finish, late 19th c., 22 x 48", 7' 8" h. (ILLUS.) **2,400**

Fine Mahogany Veneer Armoire

Armoire, Classical, mahogany & mahogany veneer, demountable, rectangular top w/a widely flaring stepped cornice above a pair of tall paneled doors w/fine crotch-grain veneering & brass keyhole escutcheons opening to an interior w/shelves & hangers, flat base on bulbous tapering legs on brass caps, refinished, considerable restoration, ca. 1830, 24 x 64", 8' 4" h. (ILLUS.) **3,500**

Classical Armoire with Wreaths

Armoire, Classical, mahogany & mahogany veneer, rectangular top above a deep cornice w/a half-round band above a pair of tall paneled doors each centered by carved oval floral wreath, flat base on scroll-carved bracket feet on casters, the back w/an old label from an antique dealer in Virginia, ca. 1840, 21 x 57", 7' 5" h. (ILLUS.) **1,725**

Mallard-style Classical Armoire

Armoire, Classical, mahogany & mahogany veneer, the rectangular top w/a deep flaring beaded & molded cornice over a tall cyma-molded mirrored door framed by a similar molded frame, the interior w/original central drawer, the front corners w/spiral-turned edging, a long drawer at the bottom above the deep molded flat base, attributed to Prudent Mallard, New Orleans, mid-19th c., 25 x 53", 8' 4" h. (ILLUS.).. **6,613**

Empire Revival Ebonized Armoire

Armoire, Empire Revival, ormolu-mounted ebonized wood, the rectangular top w/an arched crest centered by an ormolu wreath above a wide frieze band centered by a band of ormolu & small ribbon & wreath ormolu mounts at each corner, above a large beveled glass mirrored door flanked by slender fluted columns w/gilt trim, a long molded drawer at the bottom w/an ormolu keyhole escutcheon, the flat base band w/two ormolu swag mounts, gilt-incised bun feet, Europe, ca. 1900, 22 1/2 x 48", 7' 10" h. (ILLUS.)........ **2,300**

Armoire, French Provincial, mahogany demountable, the rectangular top w/a high arched crestrail centered by a pierced scroll-carved crest over molded scrolls & a frieze band w/lattice-incised triangular panels above the pair of tall arched doors, each door w/a tall shaped raised panel topped by a scroll-carved drop over a short lower panel w/similar scroll-carved trim, front corners w/quarter-round colonettes, a long oval-paneled base drawer above the flat base on short

scroll-carved bracket feet, interior shelves, original hardware, refinished, France, third quarter 19th c., 24 x 48", 7' 6" h. (ILLUS., below) **6,000**

Fine French Provincial Armoire

Flat-topped Golden Oak Armoire

Armoire, Victorian Golden Oak style, quarter-sawn oak, demountable, rectangular top w/a flat narrow flaring cornice above a scroll-carved frieze band above a pair of tall beveled glass mirrored doors w/shaped tops trimmed w/carved scrolls, half-round columns down the center & at each side, the stepped out base w/a pair of bow-fronted drawers over a long bow-fronted drawer, flat shaped sides w/block feet, open interior, mix or old & new hardware, ca. 1900, refinished, 24 x 56", 7' 8" h. (ILLUS.) **3,500**

Scroll-carved Golden Oak Armoire

Armoire, Victorian Golden Oak style, quarter-sawn oak, demountable, rectangular top w/low arched crestrail carved w/scrolls centering a wide smooth, curved panels flanked by further scroll carving & an arched molding, above a pair of tall beveled glass mirrored doors w/arched scrolls above the rounded top, a half-round smooth column down the center & half-round columns w/reeded capitals at the sides, a mid-molding over a pair of flat-front drawers over a single long double-serpentine bottom drawer, molded flat base on ogee bracket front feet, refinished, ca. 1895, 22 x 54", 8' h. (ILLUS.)... **4,000**

Armoire, Victorian Golden Oak style, quarter-sawn oak, demountable, the rectangular top w/a high arched crest board w/heavy molding & centered by a large shell-carved crest, scroll-carved rounded ears, a scroll-carved frieze band above a pair of tall beveled glass mirrored doors w/carved scrolls across the top, centered by a half-round colonette w/quarter-round colonettes down each front corner, stepped-out lower section w/a pair of bow-fronted shallow drawers over a very long bow-fronted drawer all w/brass

pulls, scroll-carved front corners continuing to form short flared block feet on casters, shelved interior, original hardware, refinished, ca. 1890s, 24 x 60", 8' 4" h. (ILLUS., below)... **3,800**

Shell-crested Golden Oak Armoire

Renaissance Revival Armoire

Armoire, Victorian Renaissance Revival style, walnut & burl walnut, demountable, a high long arched crestrail centered by a large carved shell flanked by gadrooned moldings over carved serpentine leafy vines, all on a flaring stepped cornice above a serpentine scroll-carved burl band flanked by blocked corners over a pair of tall beveled glass mirrored doors each w/a shaped burl panel at the top & flanked by reeded pilasters, the slightly stepped-out lower case w/a pair of burl veneered drawers w/pierced brass pulls, molded base w/low serpentine apron & block feet, refinished, ca. 1875, 23 x 58", 8' 6" h. (ILLUS.) **3,500**

Ornately Carved Rococo Armoire

Armoire, Victorian Rococo style, mahogany & mahogany veneer, the rectangular top w/a deep flaring cyma- and cove-molded cornice w/angled corners above a conforming case w/a pair of narrow raised molding panels in the frieze band above a pair of tall doors, w/rectangular mirrors framed w/floral & scroll carving above a raised rectangular band of carved florals & scrolls, the beveled front sides w/a floral-carved bracket at the top & a scroll-carved bracket at the bottom, a pair of bottom drawers w/raised oblong molding enclosing leaf-carved pulls, molded base w/serpentine scroll-carved apron & angled block feet, mid-19th c., 29 x 74", 8' 4" h. (ILLUS.) **6,613**

Armoire, Victorian Rococo style, mahogany, wooden peg construction, the rectangular top w/an arched scroll-carved crest centered by a rounded fleur-de-lis & shell crest above a narrow scroll-carved frieze band continuing around the sides, a single tall door w/a beveled glass mirror w/a serpentine top above a narrow scroll-carved panel, a mid-molding over a long

base drawer w/brass hardware, curved serpentine apron on cabriole front legs w/paw feet, drawers & shelves inside, original finish, probably Europe, ca. 1860, 17 x 30", 7' 8" h. **2,200**

Massive Walnut Rococo Armoire

Armoire, Victorian Rococo style, walnut, demountable, rectangular top w/an arched cove-molded cornice w/rounded corners above a conforming frieze band centered w/carved oval panel flanked by narrow triangular scroll-carved panels above a pair of wide arched doors w/leaf-carved sprigs above a large arched scroll-topped door flanking a narrow fruit- and block-carved middle column & flanked by matching angled corner columns, scroll-carved serpentine apron & feet, possibly Philadelphia, ca. 1860, refinished, 22 x 62", 8' h. (ILLUS.) **4,500**

Fancy Painted European Wardrobe

Wardrobe, country-style, painted & decorated pine, rectangular top w/a narrow flaring cornice above a pair of wide flat doors decorated w/a large white-painted oval reserve enclosed by a green ground decorated w/dark green, yellow & blue scrolls, tall narrow recessed panels down the sides, the green ground painted w/small yellow ovals & dark green scrolls, a long green paneled drawer across the bottom painted w/small yellow ovals & dark green scrolls, flat molded base, open interior, Europe, ca. 1840, 20 x 62", 7' h. (ILLUS.) **4,500**

Wardrobe, country-style, pine & poplar, cove molded cornice over a pair of two panel doors flanked by chamfered corners, over two deep dovetailed drawers w/turned wooden pulls, interior shelf & pegs, tapered round feet w/molded base, original red paint, Ohio, 19th c., 21 x 60", 6' 7 1/2" h. **2,640**

Country Gothic Walnut Wardrobe

Wardrobe, Gothic Revival country-style, walnut, the rectangular top w/a high serpentine crestrail w/slender projecting small scrolls above the coved cornice over a pair of tall Gothic arched feather-grained doors over a pair of deep drawers w/wooden knobs, flat apron on scroll-cut bracket feet, refinished, found in Missouri, ca. 1850, 20 x 52", 7' 2" h. (ILLUS.) **1,800**

Wardrobe, Late Victorian, walnut, demountable, the high serpentine crestrail carved w/scrolls & centered by a large carved florette above a narrow coved cornice over a scroll-trimmed frieze band above a pair of tall beveled glass mirrored doors w/curved top edge trimmed w/carved scrolls, a mid-molding over a pair of line-incised bottom drawer w/brass pulls, flat molded base, open in-

terior, original finish, ca. 1890, 20 x 54", 8' h. (ILLUS., below) **2,400**

Late Victorian Walnut Wardrobe

High-crested Victorian Wardrobe

Wardrobe, Victorian country-style, walnut, rectangular top w/wide arched crestrail centered by a pierced fan-carved crest over scrolls & w/pointed corner ears w/pierced scrolls, a pair of wide Gothic arch paneled doors opening to a shelved interior, flat base on ring-turned feet, original finish, ca. 1850s, 18 x 52", 7' 8" h. (ILLUS.) **2,000**

Country Eastlake Walnut Wardrobe

Wardrobe, Victorian Eastlake country-style, walnut, the rectangular top w/a flaring stepped cornice above frieze band carved w/roundels & incised leafy bands above a pair of tall paneled doors centered by a large rosette & incised leafy scrolls & blossoms, a pair of paneled drawers w/brass pulls at the bottom, flat molded base w/cutout apron & bracket feet, refinished, ca. 1885, 18 x 48", 7' 2" h. (ILLUS.) **2,400**

Victorian Eastlake Wardrobe

Wardrobe, Victorian Eastlake style, walnut & burl walnut, demountable, the rectangular top w/a wide flaring cornice above a narrow burl frieze band over a pair of tall beveled glass mirrored doors topped by narrow raised burl panels, a slender half-round colonette down the center & flanking the doors, a pair of burl veneered drawers w/stamped brass pulls at the bottom, flat molded base w/wafer feet, original hardware, refinished, ca. 1875, 20 x 52", 7' 4" h. (ILLUS.) **2,400**

Crested Golden Oak Wardrobe

Wardrobe, Victorian Golden Oak style, oak, demountable, a high scroll-cut & scroll-carved crestrail above the flaring cornice above a pair of tall doors w/recessed panels w/rounded corners, a mid-molding over the long line-incised bottom drawer, paneled sides, original brasses, original finish, ca. 1900, 20 x 48", 7' 10" h. (ILLUS.) **2,000**

Country Renaissance Wardrobe

Wardrobe, Victorian Renaissance Revival country-style, butternut, one-piece construction, the rectangular top w/an arched & notch-cut crestrail centered by a walnut fruit cluster above the flaring cornice over a pair of tall doors w/arched molded panels, a pair of drawers w/small wood knobs at the bottom above the notch-cut apron w/bracket feet, possibly Norwegian-American influence, Midwest, ca. 1870s, refinished, 20 x 50", 7' 4" h. (ILLUS.) **1,500**

Massive Renaissance Wardrobe

High-crested Walnut Wardrobe

Wardrobe, Victorian Renaissance Revival style, walnut, demountable, the rectangular top w/a high arched crestrail w/molding flanking a large scroll- and leaf-carved center crest, rounded stepped ears at the rounded top corners above a pair of wide paneled doors w/carved scrolls across the top, open interior, flat base w/cut-down bracket feet, original finish, ca. 1875, 21 x 56", 8' h. (ILLUS.)... **1,500**

Wardrobe, Victorian Renaissance Revival style, walnut, demountable, the rectangular top w/a high arched & deeply molded crestrail above an arched panel centered by a carved ring over a pair of tall arch-paneled doors centered by a narrow tall oval panel, flat molded & flaring base, open interior, refinished, ca. 1875, 22 x 60", 7' 10" h. (ILLUS., top next column) **2,400**

Scroll-carved Rococo Wardrobe

Wardrobe, Victorian Rococo style, walnut & burl walnut, demountable, rectangular top w/an arched molded cornice fitted w/a high arched & pierced scroll-carved crestrail above a scroll-carved frieze band above a molding over a pair of tall arched doors w/burl panels above a molding over a pair of drawers w/a raised oval banding enclosing fan-carved pulls & a carved keyhole escutcheon, deep molded base, refinished, ca. 1860, 20 x 60", 7' 6" h. (ILLUS.)............................ **3,200**

Rococo Paneled-door Wardrobe

Wardrobe, Victorian Rococo style, walnut, demountable, the rectangular top w/an arched scroll-cut & scroll-trimmed crestrail above the flaring ogee cornice above a pair of tall doors, each w/a pair of tall narrow rectangular panels w/carved scrolls at the top of each panel, a pair of drawers w/simple wood knobs below, open interior, scalloped narrow apron w/bracket feet, refinished, ca. 1860, 20 x 54", 7' 10" h. (ILLUS.) **2,500**

Whatnots & Etageres

Late Victorian Etagere-Curio

Etagere, late Victorian style, mahogany, the superstructure w/a large arched & beveled mirror flanked by slender tapering spiral-turned spindles above the half-round case over a pair of large curved glass doors centered by a narrow arched coved panel & opening to a mirrored interior, supported on flat corner supports & a single slender tapering spiral-turned center spindle on the half-round lower shelf, squared slightly curved front legs, original dark finish, ca. 1890s, 18 x 28", 6' h. (ILLUS.)... **1,200**

Fancy Open-based Rococo Etagere

Etagere, Victorian Rococo style, carved & laminated rosewood, the superstructure w/a high arched & ornately scroll-carved stepped crestrail centered by a rose-carved medallion crest, a large arched center mirror flanked by smaller arched mirrors each fronted by three small half-round open shelves w/pierced scroll-carved aprons, resting on the half-round serpentine-sided base w/a wide flat central section above a conforming apron centered by a long paneled scroll-carved drawer flanked by raised side panels, raised on four S-scroll legs w/fruit-carved knees, joined by a delicate scroll-carved H-stretcher, attributed to John H. Belter, New York City, ca. 1855, original finish, 20 x 50", 8' h. (ILLUS.).............................. **16,000**

Extraordinary Carved Rosewood Signed Rococo Etagere

Fine Meeks Rosewood Etagere

Etagere, Victorian Rococo style, carved rosewood, the tall superstructure w/a high arched pierced & scroll-carved crest flanked by tall baluster- and ring-turned finials & scroll-carved corners, a tall arched central mirror flanked by narrow arched mirrors fronted by small half-round open shelves supported by slen- der ring- and rod-turned spindles & flanked by graduated scroll-carved bor- der brackets, the half-round white marble base w/serpentine edges above a con- forming pierced & scroll-carved apron supported on a pair of large ornately turned columns above the conforming serpentine platform base w/a scroll- carved apron & centered by a rectangular mirror flanked by wide serpentine scroll- carved sides, on small knob feet, by J. & J. Meeks, New York City, ca. 1855, refin- ished, 22 x 48", 8' h. (ILLUS.) **20,000**

Etagere, Victorian Rococo style, carved rosewood, the upper section w/a faceted, domed cornice surmounted by a pierced scrolling foliate-carved crest w/a center finial flanked by carved recumbent putti, projecting over a large mirror flanked by narrower mirrors fronted by four half- round open shelves supported on slen- der ring- and baluster-turned spindles, the half-round serpentine-fronted base w/a molded edge over a conforming deep apron elaborately pierce-carved w/leafy carved vines w/grape clusters & a bird, supported on four bold C-form fruit- and leaf-carved brackets joined to tapering turned spindles w/finials above the half- round serpentine lower platform backed by a mirror, a serpentine scroll-carved apron on disk feet, signed & dated by Th- omas Brooks, Brooklyn, New York, 1860, 22 1/2 x 71", 9' 3" h. (ILLUS., top of page) **105,900**

Elaborate Rosewood Etagere Base

Etagere base, Victorian Rococo style, carved & laminated rosewood, the half-round white marble top w/serpentine edges above a deep conforming case w/a pair of bowed doors ornately pierce-carved w/delicate scrolls in a rectangular scroll-bordered panel, matching pierced side panels above the pierced floral garland-carved swags across the apron, raised on S-scroll legs w/leaf-carved knees, attributed to Meeks of New York City, ca. 1855, base only, 20 x 46", 36" h. (ILLUS.).. **4,000**

GAMES & GAME BOARDS

Checkerboard, painted, double-sided, constructed of two boards mortise & tenoned together, obverse & reverse w/81 & 144 squares outlined in black, late 19th c., 16 x 18".. **1,035**

Checkerboard, painted wood, red & black game area framed by a white rectangular ground w/applied frame edge, first half 20th c., 19 x 24 1/2" (ILLUS. bottom left w/other game boards, bottom of page) **1,265**

Checkerboard with Original Paint

Checkerboard, pine, black & cream checkerboard w/putty band & butternut scallops, green line accents, all on black ground, original paint, some wear, 17 1/4 x 17 3/8" (ILLUS.) **1,210**

Checkerboard, single wide board w/applied moldings on one side & a narrow strip on the top & bottom of the back, old painted red & black blocks divided by yellow lines, additional yellow decoration on either end painted in thin lines & arcs, 18 1/2 x 24 1/2" (edge wear & a scrape)....... **880**

Five Early Painted Game Boards

Painted Slate Checkerboard

Checkerboard, slate, incised geometric design h.p. to resemble hardstone in shades of marbleized green & red w/solid dark red checks on a shaded yellow ground, mottled black border, New England, late 19th c., 19 1/2" sq. (ILLUS.)..... **1,645**

Dart board, painted canvas & wood, red, white & blue painted canvas over a square pine board, Midwest, ca. 1930, 18 1/4 x 19 1/4".. **1,840**

Double-sided, checkerboard on one side w/black squares & white & black scrolled border, backgammon on the other side w/black & mustard points, original medium blue ground, applied edge molding w/assorted old nails, 17" sq. (minor wear, old varnish has yellowed)............................ **5,060**

Double-sided, checkers on one side & Parcheesi on the other, original paint on old board w/gallery rim, black borders w/gold striping, green corner fans, multiple shades of gold for playing fields, 22 1/2" sq. (wear, faint numbers have been scratched into the checkerboard)........ **495**

Double-sided Game Board

Double-sided, checkers on one side & Parcheesi on the other, single wide board w/applied molding around edge, original tomato red, gold, green & pink paint on dark red ground, old protective coat of overvarnish crackled, small areas of wear, chips to moldings, 21 1/2 x 35" (ILLUS.)................... **3,850**

Double-sided, incised checkerboard in colors of red, lime green, yellow & black under glass, the reverse painted in red, white & blue, framed, America, 20th c., 17 1/2 x 21 1/2" (paint wear)...................... **646**

Double-sided, incised & polychrome-painted, the obverse w/a Parcheesi board flanked by two tin-lined compartments w/sliding lids, carved w/clover & quatrefoil designs, wells w/incised initials "A" & "F," reverse w/orange & black checkerboard, possibly Canada, early 20th c., 19 x 31".. **5,750**

Double-sided, painted wood, folding-type, the obverse w/a checkerboard, the interior w/a Parcheesi board in green, red & yellow, breadboard ends, late 19th c., open 21" sq. (ILLUS. previous page bottom right with other game boards)............. **1,840**

Parcheesi Board/Checkerboard

Double-sided, rectangular w/polychrome Parcheesi game on one side, red & black checkerboard on reverse, late 19th - early 20th c., 22 x 28 3/4" (ILLUS.).................. **1,880**

Double-sided, round painted wood, the obverse stenciled "Railroad Game or Trip Around the World," the reverse w/red & white checkerboard on orange ground, applied metal frame, ca. 1900, 22" d. (ILLUS. previous page, center with other game boards)............................ **2,530**

Parcheesi, painted paper on wood, the playing surface in dark blue, red, black & yellow on a white ground, applied frame edge, overall wear, late 19th c., 18" sq. (ILLUS. previous page, top left with other game boards)... **1,265**

Parcheesi, painted wood, double-sided, Parcheesi side in red, white & black, the reverse w/an incised fox & geese game, breadboard ends, late 19th c., 18" sq. (ILLUS. previous page, top right with other game boards)...................................... **2,300**

Pine Parcheesi Board

Parcheesi, pine, decorated in original red, green, yellow & black, "HOME" stenciled in center, minor paint alligatoring & wear, 19 x 19 3/8" (ILLUS.) **3,575**

Parcheesi, pine, three-panel board w/old painted surface in red, green & yellow playing field on light blue ground, America, 19th c., 33 x 36" **823**

GLASS

Also see: Antique Trader Books American Pressed Glass & Bottles Price Guide and Antique Trader Books American & European Decorative Art Glass Price Guide.

Amberina

Amberina was developed in the late 1880s by the New England Glass Company and a pressed version was made by Hobbs, Brockunier & Company (under license from the former). A similar ware, called Rose Amber, was made by the Mt. Washington Glass Works. Amberina-Rose Amber shades from amber to deep red or fuchsia and cut and plated (lined with creamy white) examples were also made. The Libbey Glass Company briefly revived blown Amberina, using modern shapes, in 1917.

Amberina Label

Bowl, 4 1/2" d., 1 3/8" h., plain rim, polished pontil, light Inverted Thumbprint patt............. **$60**

Bowl, 5 1/2" d., 2 3/4" h., squat body w/widely flared ruffled rim, polished pontil...... **100**

Celery vase, slightly waisted form w/pinched rim, polished pontil, Inverted Thumbprint patt., 6 1/2" h. **300**

Creamer, ovoid body, square top, applied amber reeded handle, polished pontil, Inverted Thumbprint patt., 4 1/2" h. **110**

Goblet, Inverted Thumbprint patt., 6 1/4" h......... **80**

Ice cream dish, square, quatrefoil shape, pressed, Daisy and Button (Hobbs No. 101 patt.,), Hobbs, Brockunier & Co., 5 3/4" sq., 1 1/4" h. **70**

Novelty dish, canoe-shaped, pressed, Daisy and Button (Hobbs No. 101) patt., Hobbs, Brockunier & Co., 3 x 8 1/4", 3 1/2" h. **100-300**

Pitcher, 6 1/2" h., ovoid body, square top, amber applied reeded handle, Inverted Thumbprint patt. **190**

Pitcher, water, 7 1/4" h., ruffled turned-down rim, bulbous ovoid body w/molded alternating vertical rows of flowers & leaves, applied amber reeded handle, polished pontil... **150**

Pitcher, water, 7 1/2" h., bulbous, applied amber handle, polished pontil, Hobnail patt. **375**

Pitcher, water, 7 3/4" h., bulbous body w/pinched sides, applied amber square handle & polished pontil, Inverted Thumbprint patt. **210**

Inverted Thumbprint Amberina Pitcher

Pitcher, 8 1/2" h., 6 1/2" d., Inverted Thumbprint patt., nearly spherical body w/a tall tri-lobed neck, applied amber handle (ILLUS.) **230**

Toothpick holder, cylindrical w/rounded bottom raised on a short pedestal foot, Inverted Thumbprint patt........................ **150-190**

Vase, 2 1/4" h., 4" d., mushroom form w/widely flaring flattened rim, polished pontil.. **650**

Vase, 6 1/2" h., spherical w/pinched sides tapering to flaring neck w/polished rim, Inverted Thumbprint patt............................ **150**

Animals

Americans evidently like to collect glass animals. For the past sixty years, American glass manufacturers have turned out a wide variety of animals to please the buying public. Some were produced for long periods and some were later reproduced by other companies, while others were made for only a short period of time and are rare. We have not included late productions in our listings and have attempted to date the productions where possible. Evelyn Zemel's book, American Glass Animals A to

Z, will be helpful to the novice collector. Another helpful book is Glass Animals of the Depression Era *by Lee Garmon and Dick Spencer Collector Books, 1993.*

Airedale Dog, clear frosted, unmarked,
6 1/2" l., 5 3/4" h **$600**
Angelfish, book end, clear, A.H. Heisey &
Co., 2 1/4 x 3 1/2" wave base, 7" h............. **185**
Chinese Pheasant, blue, Paden City Glass
Mfg. Co., ca. 1940, 13 3/4" l., 5 3/4"h. **175**
Elephant, book end, clear, New Martinsville
Mfg. Co., 3 1/4 x 5 1/4" base, 6 1/4" l.,
5 1/4" h... **95**
Elephant, figure w/trunk up, clear, A.H.
Heisey & Co., 1944-53, large, 6 1/2" l.,
4 1/4" h... **500**
Elephant, book end, clear, No. 237, New
Martinsville Glass Co., 5 1/2" h........................ **95**

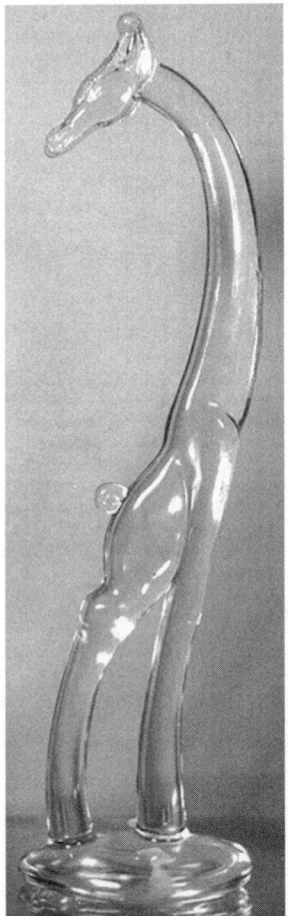

Heisey Giraffe

Giraffe, clear, A.H. Heisey & Co., 1942-52,
3" l., 10 3/4" h. (ILLUS.)................................. **300**
Goose, figure, wings up, clear, A.H. Heisey
& Co., 1947-53, 7" h **125**
Goose, wings up, clear, A.H. Heisey & Co.,
1942-53, 7 1/2" l., 6 1/2" h. **125**

Horse, Pony, standing, clear, A.H. Heisey &
Co., 1940-52, 1 1/2 x 2 1/4" base, 3" l.,
5" h. **110**
Horse, Plug (Oscar), clear, A.H. Heisey &
Co., 1941-46, 3 1/2" l., 4 1/4" h. **150**
Horses, Clydesdale, clear, A.H. Heisey &
Co., 1942-48, 8" l., 8" h., pr........................... **500**
Pelican, clear, No. 761, New Martinsville
Glass Co., 8" h. **100**
Pouter Pigeon, book ends, clear, Paden
City Glass Mfg. Co., 3 x 3 3/4" base,
6 1/2" h., pr.. **150**
Seal, w/ball candleholders, clear, New Martinsville Glass Mfg. Co., 7 1/4" h., pr............ **100**
Starfish, book end, clear, Paden City Glass
Mfg. Co., 2 3/4 x 6 1/4" base, 7 3/4" h......... **200**
Tiger, Head Up, clear, New Martinsville
Glass Co., 6 1/2" h... **180**

Cambridge

The Cambridge Glass Company was founded in Ohio in 1901. Numerous pieces are now sought, especially those designed by Arthur J. Bennett, including Crown Tuscan. Other productions included crystal animals, "Black Amethyst," "blanc opaque," and other types of colored glass. The firm was finally closed in 1954. It should not be confused with the New England Glass Co., Cambridge, Massachusetts.

Cambridge Marks

Ashtray, Statuesque line, Royal Blue (dark
blue) bowl, clear Nude Lady stem............... **$145**
Banana bowl, pressed Caprice patt., Crystal.. **60**
Bonbon, handled, Inverted Strawberry
patt., clear, 5 1/2" **25**
Bonbon, upright handles, pressed Caprice
patt., Crystal, 5" sq. **22**
Bowl, 11", etched Chantilly patt., No. 400,
Crystal... **110**
Bowl, 12 1/2" d., bellshaped, four-footed,
pressed Caprice patt., Moonlight........ **95**
Bowl, 12" d., crimped rim, footed, Caprice
patt., Moonlight (pale blue)............................ **120**
Bowl, 12" d., etched Rose Point patt., Crystal.. **110**
Bowl, 5 3/4" d., Strawberry (No. 2780) line,
clear.. **35**
Bowl, 6" d., Inverted Strawberry patt., clear........ **35**
Bowl, & underplate, 9 1/2" d. bowl w/ruffled
rim, 10 1/2" d. underplate; Strawberry
(No. 2780) line, clear, 2 pcs. **95**
Brandy, Tally-Ho line, Carmen (ruby red)
bowl, clear stem **42**

Butter dish, cov., pressed Caprice patt.,
Crystal 325

Candlesticks, w/ramsheads', etched Rose
Point patt., No. 3500/74, Crystal, 4" h.,
pr. 200

Candy box, cover w/sterling silver finial,
three-part, etched Chantilly patt., Crystal,
7" l. 120

Champagne, etched Rose Point patt., Crys-
tal 35

Champagne, Statuesque line, Carmen
bowl, clear Nude lady stem 135

Cocktail, etched Chantilly patt., Crystal 30

Cocktail, etched Wildflower patt., Crystal 45

Cocktail, Statuesque line, Carmen bowl,
clear Nude Lady stem 130

Cocktail, Statuesque line, Royal Blue bowl,
clear Nude Lady stem 125

Compote, open, 7" d., 9 1/2" h., Statuesque
line, Carmen bowl, clear Nude Lady stem 170

Cordial, etched Apple Blossom patt., Topaz
(vaseline) bowl w/Amber stem 95

Cordial, etched Rose Point patt., Carmen
bowl w/clear embossed base 170

Cordial, etched Rose Point patt., No. 3500,
Crystal, 1 oz. 120

Cordial, etched Wildflower patt., No. 3121,
Crystal, 1 oz., set of 6 420

Cordial, pressed Caprice patt., Moonlight,
1 oz., set of 12 240

Cordial, Statuesque line, Topaz bowl, clear
Nude Lady stem 225

Creamer, individual size, etched Chantilly
patt., Crystal 15

Creamer, & open sugar bowl, Decagon line,
Crystal, 2 pcs. 20

Creamer, & open sugar bowl, etched Wildflower patt., No. 3900/41, Crystal, pr. 90

Creamer, & open sugar bowl, individual
size, Gadroon (No. 3500) line, Crystal,
2 pcs. 24

Creamer, & open sugar bowl, individual
size, pressed Caprice patt., Moonlight,
pr. 60

Creamer, & open sugar bowl, individual
size, pressed Caprice patt., No. 40, Crys-
tal, pr. 30

Creamer, sugar bowl & underplate, Decagon line, Ebony, (black), 3 pcs. 70

Crown Tuscan, cake plate w/open handles,
Gadroon (No. 3500) line, 13" d. 100

Crown Tuscan, candy dish, cov., three-
part, Gadroon (No. 3500/57) line 65

Crown Tuscan bowl, flower or fruit,
10 1/2" l., footed, Statuesque line, Flying
Lady patt., seashell bowl w/nude lady at
one end, h.p. roses & floral bands, No.
30011/40 325

Crown Tuscan cocktail, Statuesque line,
Nude Lady stem 135

Crown Tuscan compote, open 7" w., Sea
Shell line 90

Crown Tuscan vase, 7" h., Sea Shell line 125

Cruet, w/original stopper, Strawberry (No.
2780) line, Crystal 45

Cruet, w/original stopper & undertray,
pressed Caprice patt., Moonlight, 2 pcs. 110

Cruet set, two cruets w/original stoppers &
underplate; pressed Caprice patt., Crys-
tal, 3 pcs. 75

Cup & saucer, etched Cleo patt., Emerald
(light green) 27

Cup & saucer, Mt. Vernon line, Crystal 12

Decanter, w/original stopper, etched Rose
Point patt., No. 1321, Crystal 380

Decanter, w/original stopper, footed, No.
1321, Crystal, 28 oz. 45

Decanter, w/original stopper, Mt. Vernon
line, Crystal, 40 oz. 45

Decanter, w/original stopper, Nautilus line,
Crystal, Cobalt Blue, 80 oz. 150

Figure flower holder, "Draped Lady," yel-
low, 8 1/2" h. 275

Goblet, Martha Washington line, Crystal 10

Goblet, pressed Caprice patt., Crystal,
7 1/2" h. 17

Goblet, pressed Caprice patt., No. 300,
Moonlight, 9 oz. 45

Goblet, water, etched Wildflower patt.,
Crystal w/gold trim 50

Ice bucket, etched Cleo patt., pink 110

Ice bucket, w/chrome handle & tongs,
etched Rose Point patt., Crystal, 2 pcs. 270

Ivy ball w/keyhole stem, Carmen 70

Lemon plate, handled, pressed Caprice
patt., Crystal 6 1/2" d. 15

Mayonnaise dish & ladle, etched Rose
Point patt., Crystal, 2 pcs. 75

Model of a swan, Dianthus, (light pink)
6 1/2" l. 95

Model of a swan, Ebony, 6 1/2" l. 85

Mustard jar, cov., etched Rosepoint patt.,
Crystal 150

Oyster cocktail, etched Rose Point patt.,
Crystal 25

Plate, 14" d., Mt. Vernon line, Crystal 22

Plate, 7 1/2" d., etched Wildflower patt.,
Crystal 24

Plate, 7 3/4" d., etched Cleo patt., Crystal 10

Plate, 7 3/4" w., Decagon line, Moonlight 8

Plate, 8 1/2" d., etched Apple Blossom
patt., Mandarin Gold (light yellow) 24

Plate, 8 1/2" d., etched Rose Point patt.,
Crystal 25

Plate, 8" d., etched Elaine patt., Crystal 14

Plate, bread & butter, 6 1/2" d., etched
Rose Point patt., Crystal 18

Plate, torte, 13" d., three-footed, etched
Chantilly patt., Crystal 200

Plates, salad, 7 1/2" d., Caprice patt., Crys-
tal, set of 7 95

Relish, pressed Caprice patt., Crystal, 12" l. 60

Relish, two-part, etched Elaine patt., Crys-
tal, 9" l. 40

Relish dish, etched Apple Blossom patt.,
Crystal, 9" l. 30

Relish dish, five-part, etched Chantilly
patt., Crystal 80

Relish dish, five-part, etched Portia patt.,
Crystal, 12" 90

Salt & Pepper shakers w/original tops,
etched Chantilly patt., Crystal, pr. 60

Sherbet, low, etched Rose Point patt., Crys-
tal 28

Sherbet, pressed Caprice patt., Moonlight,
5 3/4" h. #200 40

Sherbet, tall, etched Cleo patt., Crystal **18**
Tumbler, footed, etched Cleo patt., Crystal, 5 1/2" h., 12 oz................. **35**
Tumbler, footed, pressed Caprice patt., Moonlight, 12 oz................. **50**
Tumbler, iced tea, etched Rose Point patt., Crystal................. **45**
Tumbler, whiskey, pressed Caprice patt., Crystal................. **25**
Vase, 10 1/2" h., pressed Block Optic patt., Rubina (ruby blending to blue then green)................. **170**
Vase, 12" h., etched Wildflower patt., Crystal................. **125**
Vase, 3 1/2" h., pressed Caprice patt., Amber.................
Water set: 32 oz. pitcher & six 5 oz. tumblers; pressed Caprice patt., Moonlight, 7 pcs................. **650**
Wine, etched Rose Point patt., Crystal............... **50**
Wine, Statuesque line, Carmen bowl, clear Nude Lady stem, 7 3/4" h. **145**

Chocolate

This glass is often called Caramel Slag. It was made by the Indiana Tumbler and Goblet Company of Greentown, Indiana, and other glasshouses, beginning at the turn of the 20th century. Various patterns were produced, highly popular among them being Cactus and Leaf Bracket.

Animal covered dish, Cat on Hamper, Indiana Tumbler & Goblet Co., 5" h., 3 1/4" sq. **$550**
Animal covered dish, Dolphin, w/sawtooth rim, Indiana Tumbler & Goblet Co................... **80**
Berry set: 8" d. footed master bowl w/six 4 1/2" d. footed berry bowls; scalloped rims, Leaf Bracket patt., 7 pcs. (master bowl w/rim chips, flakes to berry bowls) **130**
Compote, open, jelly, 4 1/2" d., 3 1/2" h., scalloped rim, Geneva patt., McKee & Bros. **110**
Compote, open, 4 1/2" d., 4 3/4" h., Chrysanthemum Leaf patt............................. **230-300**
Compote, open, 9 1/4" d., 8 1/2" h., high standard, scalloped rim, Cactus patt., Indiana Tumbler & Goblet Co. (two chips) **150**
Creamer, child's, stippled background, Wild Rose with Scrolling patt. (flake on rim point) **150**
Creamer, Shuttle patt., tall cylindrical form w/raised spout & slightly scalloped rim, applied handle, Indiana Tumbler & Goblet Co., 6" h.................. **170**
Dresser tray, Venetian patt., rectangular w/rounded corners, McKee & Bros., 8 x 10"................. **425**
Pitcher, tankard-type, 4 1/4" d., 8 1/4" h., Indoor Drinking Scene patt., Indiana Tumbler & Goblet Co..................... **425**
Pitcher, water, 8 3/4" h., slightly tapered cylindrical form w/high arched spout, disc foot, applied handle, Squirrel patt., Indiana Tumbler & Goblet Co. (ILLUS., top next column)... **700**
Tumbler, Cactus patt., Indiana Tumbler & Goblet Co. (pattern flake)................... **35**

Squirrel Water Pitcher

Tumbler, Fleur-de-lis patt., Indiana Tumbler & Goblet Co. (semicircular annealing separation under base)...................... **60**
Tumbler, Geneva patt., McKee & Bros., 3 7/8" h. **110**
Tumbler, Leaf Bracket patt., Indiana Tumbler & Goblet Co. (circular annealing separation under base).......................... **25**
Tumbler, Sawtooth patt., Indiana Tumbler & Goblet Co., 3 3/4" h. **60**
Tumbler, Scalloped Flange patt., Indiana Tumbler & Goblet Co., 3 7/8" h..................... **100**
Tumbler, Shuttle patt., Indiana Tumbler & Goblet Co., 3 7/8" h. **50**

Chocolate Uneeda Biscuit Tumbler

Tumbler, Uneeda Biscuit advertising, tall (ILLUS.) **120-125**
Tumbler, Water Lily & Cattails patt., Fenton Art Glass Co., 4" h. **250**
Tumbler, Wild Rose with Bowknot patt., McKee & Bros... **100**
Vase, 6" h., slightly ovoid body w/scalloped rim & flared scalloped base, Cactus patt., Indiana Tumbler & Goblet Co. **475**

Consolidated

The Consolidated Lamp and Glass Company of Coraopolis, Pennsylvania, was founded in 1894. For a number of years it was noted for its lighting wares but also produced popular lines of pressed and blown tablewares. Highly collectible glass patterns of this early era include the Cone, Cosmos, Florette and Guttate lines.

Lamps and shades continued to be good sellers, but in 1926 a new "art" line of molded decorative wares was introduced. This "Martelé" line was developed as a direct imitation of the fine glasswares being produced by René Lalique of France, and many Consolidated patterns resembled their French counterparts. Other popular lines produced during the 1920s and 1930s were "Dancing Nymph," the delightfully Art Deco "Ruba Rombic," introduced in 1928, and the "Catalonian" line, which debuted in 1927 and imitated 17th-century Spanish glass.

Although the factory closed in 1933, it was reopened under new management in 1936 and prospered through the 1940s. It finally closed in 1967. Collectors should note that many later Consolidated patterns closely resemble wares of other competing firms, especially the Phoenix Glass Company. Careful study is needed to determine the maker of pieces from the 1920-40 era.

A book that will be of help to collectors is Phoenix & Consolidated Art Glass, 1926-1980, *by Jack D. Wilson (Antique Publications, 1989).*

Consolidated Martelé Label

Bulging Loop

Salt & pepper shakers, w/period tops, pigeon blood, pr. (wear to ribs of one) $80
Tumbler, yellow cased (two exterior rim flakes) 120
Water set: 9" h. pitcher & six tumblers; pigeon blood, the pitcher w/clear applied handle, 7 pcs. 550
Pitcher, water, cased pink 500
Tumbler, cased yellow 120

Cone

Pickle castor, cased pink, ornate silver plate frame, elaborate side & top trim, w/tongs 600
Pickle castor, cased yellow, silver plate frame 650
Sugar shaker, w/original top, cased blue satin 275
Sugar shaker, w/original top, cased pink, glossy finish 275
Sugar shaker, w/original top, green opaque 285
Sugar shaker, w/original top, squatty form, opaque blue 130

Sugar shaker, w/original top, squatty form, pink cased 170
Syrup pitcher, w/lid, cased pink (crack at top of handle) 140
Syrup pitcher, w/lid, opaque blue 220
Syrup pitcher, w/original lid w/detached hinge, cased blue (tiny crack in body at upper handle) 90
Syrup pitcher, w/original top, squatty, cased blue 240
Syrup pitcher, w/original top, squatty, cased pink 275
Syrup pitcher, w/original top, tall, blue opaque 315
Toothpick holder, cased pink 85
Tumbler, butterscotch cased 80
Tumbler, butterscotch cased satin 50
Tumbler, light blue cased 50
Water set: pitcher & four tumblers; blue opaque, 5 pcs. 550

Cosmos

Salt & pepper shakers w/period tops, pink cased, pr. (minor top dents) 120

Florette

Butter dish, cov., cased pink satin 250
Cracker jar, w/original silver plate rim, lid & bail handle, cased pink 350
Creamer, cased pink satin, 2 3/4" h. 60
Cruet, w/original frosted stopper, frosted handle, cased pink satin 210
Cruet, w/original stopper, pink 210
Mustard pot, w/hinged metal lid, cased yellow satin 150
Pitcher, water, pink satin 400
Salt shaker, w/original top, cased pink 100
Spooner, cased pink, metal rim & handles 95
Sugar bowl, cov., cased pink 150
Sugar bowl, cov., cased pink satin 150
Syrup pitcher, w/original ornate silver plate hinged lid & handle, cased pink satin 310
Toothpick holder, cased blue 135
Toothpick holder, cased green 140
Toothpick holder, cased pink 140

Guttate

Celery vase, cased pink 175
Pitcher, water, 9 1/2" h., applied clear handle, cased pink satin 425
Pitcher, water, 9 1/4" h., pink cased w/clear applied handle 700
Salt & pepper shakers, cased pink, pr. 185
Salt shaker, w/brass top, cased blue 95
Spooner, cased pink 120
Sugar shaker, w/original top, cased pink satin 250
Sugar shaker, w/top, cranberry 500
Syrup pitcher, w/lid, pink cased 325
Syrup pitcher, w/original top, cased pink 400
Table set, cov. butter dish, sugar bowl, creamer & spooner; white w/gold trim, 4 pcs. 650

Later Lines

Banana boat, oblong, Love Birds patt., Martelé line, three-color decoration on custard ground 600
Bowl, 13" d., Cockatoo patt., Martelé line, gold wash 185

Bowl, 13" d., Cockatoo patt., Martelé line, green wash 210

Bowl, 15" d., Fish patt., Martelé line, green wash 400

Bowl, 9" d., 4" h., Catalonian line, yellow 95

Candlesticks, Catalonian line, emerald green, pr. 60

Cookie jar, cov., Con-Cora line, roses decoration on a milk white ground, 6 1/2" h. 90

Cookie jar, cov., Con-Cora line, violets decoration on a milk white ground, 9" h. 120

Creamer & open sugar bowl, Catalonian line, pink, pr. 60

Ruba Rombic Dresser Jar

Dresser jar, cov., oblong, Ruba Rombic line, frosted amber, some staining, 5 1/2" w., 4" h. (ILLUS.) 550

Plate, 10" d., Dancing Nymph line, green frosted 200

Plate, 8 1/2" d., Dancing Nymph line, clear frosted 80

Plate, snack-type, pear-shaped, Five Fruits patt., Martelé line, jade green wash, 9 1/4" d. 40

Ruba Rombic Tumbler

Tumbler, conical, Ruba Rombic line, opal green, 7 1/4" h., (ILLUS.) 425

Vase, 10 1/2" h., Dogwood patt., Martelé line, tan decoration on a custard ground 220

Vase, 10 1/2" h., Dogwood patt., Martelé line, three-color decoration on a white ground 170

Vase, 10" h., triangular, Catalonian line, red wash 120

Vase, 11 1/2" h., Dancing Girls patt., Martelé line, blue figures on a custard ground 525

Vase, 11 1/2" h., Dancing Girls patt., Martelé line, clear figures on a frosted background 400

Vase, 6 1/2" h., Chickadee patt., Martelé line, satin milk white 110

Vase, 6" h., ovoid, Dragonfly & Cattails patt., Martelé line, brown & coral decoration on a milk white ground 110

Vase, 6" h., ovoid, Dragonfly & Cattails patt., Martelé line, milk white w/gold trim 85

Vase, 8 1/2" h., 9" d., Cockatoo patt., Martelé line, three-color decoration on a white ground 250

Vase, 8" h., 9" d., Catalonian line, amethyst wash 125

Vase, 9 1/2" h., baluster-form, Bittersweet patt., Martelé line, two-color decoration on white ground 135

Vase, 9 1/2" h., Bittersweet patt., Martelé line, purple berries & brown leaves on a creamy white ground 135

Vase, 9 1/2" h., Bittersweet patt., Martelé line, three-color decoration on custard ground 150

Vases, 6 3/4" h., Ruba Rombic line, tall conical body on a flaring foot, green, pr. 850

Water set: pitcher & six tumblers; Five Fruits patt., Martelé line, yellow wash, 7 pcs. 485

Cruets

Apple green, ovoid base tapering to waisted neck, arched spout, clear disc stopper, Jeweled Heart patt., 6" h. (wear to pattern, stopper not original) 40

Apple green, ovoid body, tapering shoulder, ringed neck, arched spout, clear stopper, Double Circle (Jefferson No. 231) patt., 7" h. (some interior residue, stopper not original) 110

Blue, tapering cylindrical base, ringed neck, applied scroll handle, pointed paneled stopper, Reflecting Fans patt., 6 1/4" h. 180

Cranberry, clear reeded handle, clear cut faceted stopper, Inverted Thumbprint patt., 7 1/4" h. 50

Cranberry, ovoid base w/polychrome & gilt floral decoration, waisted neck, arched spout, clear applied reeded handle, clear cut faceted flame-shaped stopper, Inverted Thumbprint patt., 7" h. (chip on bottom of stopper) 180

Green, tapering ovoid base, waisted neck, arched spout, flame stopper, applied handle, Beaded Grape (California) patt., 6 3/4" h. (roughness on point of stopper) 40

Opalescent mold-blown, blue opalescent ovoid body, cylindrical neck, tricorner rim, applied transparent blue handle, clear unpatterned bulbous stopper, Reverse Swirl patt., 6" h. (crack at top of handle where it attaches to cruet) 180

Opalescent mold-blown, blue opalescent tapering cylindrical body, short neck w/tricorner rim, applied transparent blue handle, clear cut faceted stopper, Ribbed Opal Lattice patt., 6 3/4" h. (crack in handle at upper end, stopper slightly ill-fitting) 130

Opalescent mold-blown, blue satin finish, stepped ovoid base, cylindrical neck, ruffled rim, applied handle, clear faceted stopper, Chrysanthemum Base Swirl patt., 6 1/2" h. 180

Opalescent mold-blown, bulbous body, cylindrical neck, arched spout, clear applied handle, clear faceted stopper, Daisy & Fern patt., 6 1/4" h. 110

Opalescent mold-blown, ruby opalescent ovoid base, double-ring cylindrical neck, ruffled rim, applied clear handle, clear faceted stopper, polished pontil, Hobbs Hobnail (No. 323 Dew Drop) patt., 7 3/4" h. (one hob w/chip, stopper not original) 130

Opalescent mold-blown, white opalescent, clear handle & cut faceted stopper, polished pontil, Hobbs Hobnail (No. 323 Dew Drop) patt., 7 3/4" h. (stopper not original) 70

Opaque white w/purple, cylindrical base tapering to waisted neck, arched spout, w/gilt beaded swag decoration, clear faceted stopper, 6 1/4" h. (some wear to decoration) 100

Rubina, squatty ovoid base, arched spout, clear applied handle, clear cut faceted stopper, Inverted Thumbprint with Swirl patt., 5 1/4" h. (missing handle curl, probably removed at factory) 100

Vaseline, ovoid base, waisted neck, pinched spout, applied handle, original faceted stopper, Daisy & Button patt., 7 1/4" h. 130

Vaseline, tapering cylindrical base, long waisted neck, applied handle, patterned cube stopper, Bagware (No. 800) patt., 6 1/4" h. (stopper not original) 100

Custard

This ware takes its name from its color and is a variant of milk white glass. It was produced largely between 1890 and 1915 by the Northwood Glass Co., Heisey Glass Company, Fenton Art Glass Co., Jefferson Glass Co., and a few others. There are 21 major patterns and a number of minor ones. The prime patterns are considered Argonaut Shell, Chrysanthemum Sprig, Inverted Fan and Feather, Louis XV and Winged Scroll. Most custard glass patterns are enhanced with gold and some have additional enameled decoration or stained highlights. Unless otherwise noted, items in this listing are fully decorated.

Argonaut Shell (Northwood)
Tumbler w/gilt decoration $60

Beaded Circle (Northwood)
Tumbler polychrome & gilt decoration 130

Cherry & Scale or Fentonia (Fenton)
Tumbler w/nutmeg stain 35

Chrysanthemum Sprig (Northwood's Pagoda)
Tumbler w/green, pink & gilt decoration 40

Everglades or Carnelian (Northwood)
Tumbler w/green & gilt decoration 120

Fan (Dugan)
Tumbler w/gilt decoration 60

Geneva
Tumbler, w/green & gilt decoration 80
Tumbler, w/polychrome decoration 35

Grape & Gothic Arches (Northwood)
Tumbler, iridized w/gilt decoration 20
Tumbler, w/blue stain 140

Intaglio (Northwood)
Tumbler, w/blue & gilt decoration 80

Inverted Fan & Feather (Northwood)
Tumbler, w/pink & gilt decoration 40

Maple Leaf (Northwood)
Tumbler, w/green & gilt decoration 150

Northwood Grape, Grape & Cable or Grape & Thumbprint
Tumbler, w/nutmeg stain 15

Ribbed Drape (Jefferson)
Tumbler, w/multicolor decoration 35

Ring Band (Heisey)
Toothpick holder, w/floral decoration (some wear to decoration)................................. 45

Victoria (Tarentum)
Tumbler, w/gilt decoration 35

Winged Scroll (Heisey)
Toothpick holder, ovoid body tapering to scrolled rim & ring base, w/gilt decoration on scallops & sides of body........................... 120
Tumbler, w/gilt decoration (wear to gilt) 35

Miscellaneous Patterns

Dart Bar Variant
Tumbler 50

Delaware
Tumbler, w/blue stain 70
Tumbler, w/green decoration 54-60
Tumbler, w/red stain 60

Grape Arbor (Northwood)
Tumbler, w/blue stain, satin finish 90
Tumbler, w/nutmeg stain 90
Tumbler, w/pink stain, satin finish 120

Ribbed Thumbprint (Jefferson)
Tumbler, w/polychrome & gilt decoration 15

Vermont
Tumbler, w/polychrome decoration & green stain... 50

Wild Bouquet
Tumbler, w/polychrome & gilt decoration 90

Depression

The phrase "Depression Glass" is used by collectors to denote a specific kind of transparent glass produced primarily as tablewares, in crystal, amber, blue, green, pink, milky-white, etc., during the late 1920s and 1930s when this country was in the midst of a financial depression. Made to sell inexpensively, it was turned out by such producers as Jeannette, Hocking, Westmoreland, Indiana and other glass companies. We compile prices on all the major Depression Glass patterns. Collectors should consult Depression Glass references for information on those patterns and pieces which have been reproduced.

Floral or Poinsettia, Jeannette Glass Co., 1931-35 (Process-etched)

Bowl, berry, 4" d., Delphite	$60
Bowl, berry, 4" d., green	24
Bowl, berry, 4" d., pink	20
Bowl, cream soup, 5 1/2" d., green	800
Bowl, cream soup, 5 1/2" d., pink	750
Bowl, salad, 7 1/2" d., Cremax	85
Bowl, salad, 7 1/2" d., Delphite	65
Bowl, salad, 7 1/2" d., green	35
Bowl, salad, 7 1/2" d., pink	30
Bowl, cov. vegetable, 8" d., Delphite	75
Bowl, cov. vegetable, 8" d., green	65
Bowl, cov. vegetable, 8" d., pink	55
Bowl, 9" oval vegetable, green	28
Bowl, 9" oval vegetable, pink	24
Butter dish, cov., green	100
Butter dish, cov., pink	95
Candlesticks, green, 4" h., pr.	95
Candlesticks, pink, 4" h., pr.	85
Candy jar, cov., green	85
Candy jar, cov., pink	75
Coaster, green, 3 1/4" d.	18
Coaster, pink, 3 1/4" d.	16
Compote, 9" d., green	1,100
Compote, 9" d., pink	950
Creamer, Cremax	65
Creamer, Delphite	85
Creamer, green	18
Creamer, pink	16
Cup & saucer, green	24
Cup & saucer, pink	22
Flower frog for vase, green	750
Ice tub, oval, green, 3 1/2" h.	850
Ice tub, oval, pink, 3 1/2" h.	800
Lamp, green	300
Lamp, pink	275
Pitcher, 5 1/2" h., 24 oz., green	575
Pitcher, 8" h., 32 oz., cone-shaped, green	42
Pitcher, 8" h., 32 oz., cone-shaped, pink	38
Pitcher, lemonade, 10 1/4" h., 48 oz., green	275
Pitcher, lemonade, 10 1/4" h., 48 oz., pink	245
Plate, sherbet, 6" d., green	8
Plate, sherbet, 6" d., pink	6
Plate, salad, 8" d., green	15
Plate, salad, 8" d., pink	14
Plate, dinner, 9" d., Delphite	175
Plate, dinner, 9" d., green	24
Plate, dinner, 9" d., pink	20
Plate, grill, 9" d., green	275
Platter, 10 3/4" oval, Delphite	175
Platter, 10 3/4" oval, green	24
Platter, 10 3/4" oval, pink	22
Platter, 11" oval, scalloped edge, pink	125
Powder jar, cov., green	250
Refrigerator dish, cov., green, 5" sq.	75
Refrigerator dish, cov., Jadite, 5" sq.	55
Relish, two-part, oval, green	24
Relish, two-part, oval, pink	22
Rose bowl, three-footed, green	575
Salt & pepper shakers, footed, green, 4" h., pr.	60
Salt & pepper shakers, footed, pink, 4" h., pr.	50

Salt & pepper shakers, flat, pink, 6" h., pr.	60
Sherbet, Delphite	75
Sherbet, green	20
Sherbet, pink	18
Sugar bowl, cov., green	38
Sugar bowl, cov., pink	35
Sugar bowl, open, Cremax	65
Sugar bowl, open, Delphite	85
Sugar bowl, open, green	18
Sugar bowl, open, pink	16
Tray, closed handles, green, 6" sq.	24
Tray, closed handles, pink, 6" sq.	20
Tray, dresser, green, 9 1/4" oval	225
Tumbler, footed, green, 3 1/2" h., 3 oz.	175
Tumbler, juice, footed, green, 4" h., 5 oz.	24
Tumbler, juice, footed, pink, 4" h., 5 oz.	20
Tumbler, water, footed, green, 4 3/4" h., 7 oz.	24
Tumbler, water, footed, pink, 4 3/4" h., 7 oz.	22
Tumbler, green, 4 1/2" h., 9 oz.	195
Tumbler, lemonade, footed, green, 5 1/4" h., 9 oz.	60
Tumbler, lemonade, footed, pink, 5 1/4" h., 9 oz.	50
Vase, 6 7/8" h., octagonal, clear	350
Vase, 6 7/8" h., octagonal, green	550

Lorain or Basket or Number 615, Indiana Glass Co., 1929-32 (Process-etched)

Bowl, cereal, 6", clear	20
Bowl, cereal, 6", green	45
Bowl, cereal, 6", yellow	65
Bowl, salad, 7 1/4", clear	22
Bowl, salad, 7 1/4", green	48
Bowl, salad, 7 1/4", yellow	70
Bowl, berry, 8", clear	50
Bowl, berry, 8", green	120
Bowl, berry, 8", yellow	175
Bowl, 9 3/4" oval vegetable, green	60
Bowl, 9 3/4" oval vegetable, yellow	65
Creamer, footed, clear	10
Creamer, footed, green	20
Creamer, footed, yellow	30
Cup & saucer, clear	9
Cup & saucer, green	18

Lorain Cup & Saucer

Cup & saucer, yellow (ILLUS.)	23
Plate, sherbet, 5 1/2", clear	4
Plate, sherbet, 5 1/2", green	10
Plate, sherbet, 5 1/2", yellow	12
Plate, salad, 7 3/4", clear	5
Plate, salad, 7 3/4", green	12
Plate, salad, 7 3/4", yellow	16
Plate, luncheon, 8 3/8", clear	8

Plate, luncheon, 8 3/8", green.............................. 18
Plate, luncheon, 8 3/8", yellow......................... 30
Plate, dinner, 10 1/4", clear................................ 35
Plate, dinner, 10 1/4", green.............................. 75
Plate, dinner, 10 1/4", yellow............................ 85
Platter, 11 1/2", clear.. 15
Platter, 11 1/2", green... 35
Platter, 11 1/2", yellow.. 48
Relish, four-part, clear, 8"................................... 12
Relish, four-part, green, 8".................................. 26
Relish, four-part, yellow, 8"................................. 38
Sherbet, footed, clear... 10
Sherbet, footed, green.. 24
Sherbet, footed, yellow....................................... 32
Sugar bowl, open, footed, clear........................ 10
Sugar bowl, open, footed, green...................... 20
Sugar bowl, open, footed, yellow..................... 30
Tumbler, footed, clear, 4 3/4" h., 9 oz.............. 10
Tumbler, footed, green, 4 3/4" h., 9 oz. 24
Tumbler, footed, yellow, 4 3/4" h., 9 oz. 32

Moderntone, Hazel Atlas Glass Co., 1934-42, late 1940s & early 1950s (Press-mold)

Ashtray w/match holder, cobalt blue,
    7 3/4" d.. 175
Ashtray w/match holder, pink, 7 3/4" d............. 85
Bowl, cream soup, 4 3/4" d., amethyst 25
Bowl, cream soup, 4 3/4" d., cobalt blue 26
Bowl, cream soup, 4 3/4" d., platonite............... 8
Bowl, berry, 5" d., amethyst.................................. 28
Bowl, berry, 5" d., cobalt blue.............................. 30
Bowl, berry, 5" d., platonite................................... 6
Bowl, cream soup w/ruffled rim, 5" d., ame-
    thyst.. 50
Bowl, cream soup w/ruffled rim, 5" d., cobalt
    blue.. 65
Bowl, cream soup w/ruffled rim, 5" d., plato-
    nite.. 12
Bowl, cereal, 6 1/2" d., amethyst...................... 85
Bowl, cereal, 6 1/2" d., cobalt blue 95
Bowl, cereal, 6 1/2" d., platonite........................ 8
Bowl, soup, 7 1/2" d., amethyst......................... 120
Bowl, soup, 7 1/2" d., cobalt blue...................... 185
Bowl, soup, 7 1/2" d., platonite.......................... 18
Bowl, large berry, 8 3/4" d., amethyst 48
Bowl, large berry, 8 3/4" d., cobalt blue 60
Bowl, large berry, 8 3/4" d., platonite 12
Butter dish w/metal lid, cobalt blue 120
Cheese dish w/metal lid, cobalt blue, 7" d....... 475
Creamer, amethyst... 14

Moderntone Pieces

Creamer, cobalt blue (ILLUS.)............................. 16
Creamer, platonite... 6
Cup & saucer, amethyst 18
Cup & saucer, cobalt blue 20
Cup & saucer, platonite... 7
Custard cup, amethyst... 24
Custard cup, cobalt blue...................................... 28
Plate, sherbet, 5 7/8" d., amethyst 6
Plate, sherbet, 5 7/8" d., cobalt blue 8
Plate, salad, 6 3/4" d., amethyst......................... 12
Plate, salad, 6 3/4" d., cobalt blue....................... 15
Plate, salad, 6 3/4" d., platonite........................... 5

Plate, luncheon, 7 3/4" d., amethyst................... 10
Plate, luncheon, 7 3/4" d., cobalt blue............... 12
Plate, luncheon, 7 3/4" d., platonite..................... 6
Plate, dinner, 8 7/8" d., amethyst........................ 16
Plate, dinner, 8 7/8" d., cobalt blue..................... 20
Plate, dinner, 8 7/8" d., platonite 8
Plate, sandwich, 10 1/2" d., amethyst................ 50
Plate, sandwich, 10 1/2" d., cobalt blue 85
Plate, sandwich, 10 1/2" d., platonite 24
Platter, 11" oval, amethyst................................... 45
Platter, 11" oval, cobalt blue............................... 50
Platter, 11" oval, platonite.................................... 20
Platter, 12" oval, amethyst................................... 60
Platter, 12" oval, cobalt blue............................... 85
Platter, 12" oval, platonite................................... 24
Salt & pepper shakers, amethyst, pr................. 45
Salt & pepper shakers, cobalt blue, pr.
    (ILLUS. w/creamer)... 48
Salt & pepper shakers, platonite, pr. 15
Sherbet, amethyst.. 12
Sherbet, cobalt blue.. 12
Sherbet, platonite.. 5
Sugar bowl, open, amethyst 14
Sugar bowl, open, cobalt blue (ILLUS.
    w/creamer).. 16
Sugar bowl, open, platonite 6
Sugar bowl w/metal lid, cobalt blue................... 42
Tumbler, whiskey, clear, 1 1/2 oz....................... 10
Tumbler, whiskey, cobalt blue, 1 1/2 oz............. 45
Tumbler, whiskey, platonite, 1 1/2 oz................. 12
Tumbler, juice, amethyst, 5 oz............................ 45
Tumbler, juice, cobalt blue, 5 oz......................... 60
Tumbler, juice, platonite, 5 oz............................. 15
Tumbler, water, amethyst, 4" h., 9 oz................. 40
Tumbler, water, cobalt blue, 4" h., 9 oz.............. 45
Tumbler, water, platonite, 4" h., 9 oz.................. 15
Tumbler, iced tea, amethyst, 12 oz..................... 95
Tumbler, iced tea, cobalt blue, 12 oz................. 145
Little Hostess Party Set, cup & saucer,
    dark... 22
Little Hostess Party Set, cup & saucer,
    pastel... 15
Little Hostess Party Set, creamer,
    1 3/4" h., dark 15
Little Hostess Party Set, creamer,
    1 3/4" h., pastel.. 14
Little Hostess Party Set, sugar bowl,
    1 3/4" h., dark 15
Little Hostess Party Set, sugar bowl,
    1 3/4" h., pastel.. 14
Little Hostess Party Set, teapot, cov.,
    3 1/2" h., dark 195
Little Hostess Party Set, teapot, cov.,
    3 1/2" h., pastel.. 145
Little Hostess Party Set, plate, 5 1/4" d.,
    dark... 12
Little Hostess Party Set, plate, 5 1/4" d.,
    pastel... 10

Parrot or Sylvan, Federal Glass Co., 1931-32 (Process-etched)

Bowl, berry, 5" sq., amber................................... 22
Bowl, berry, 5" sq., green.................................... 28
Bowl, soup, 7" sq., amber.................................... 38
Bowl, soup, 7" sq., green..................................... 50
Bowl, large berry, 8" sq., amber......................... 80
Bowl, large berry, 8" sq., green........................... 98
Bowl, 10" oval vegetable, amber 72
Bowl, 10" oval vegetable, green 68
Butter dish, cov., amber................................... 1,350

Parrot Butter Dish

Butter dish, cov., green (ILLUS.)	425
Creamer, footed, amber	60
Creamer, footed, green	55
Cup & saucer, amber	63
Cup & saucer, green	60
Hot plate, green, scalloped edge	950
Hot plate, green, 5" d.	850
Jam dish, amber, 7" sq.	40
Pitcher, 8 1/2" h., 80 oz., green	2,950
Plate, sherbet, 5 3/4" sq., amber	28
Plate, sherbet, 5 3/4" sq., green	38
Plate, salad, 7 1/2" sq., green	40
Plate, dinner, 9" sq., amber	48
Plate, dinner, 9" sq., green	58
Plate, grill, 10 1/2" sq., amber	45
Platter, 11 1/4" oblong, amber	75
Platter, 11 1/4" oblong, green	62
Salt & pepper shakers, green, pr.	295
Sherbet, footed, cone-shaped, amber	24
Sherbet, footed, cone-shaped, blue	245
Sherbet, footed, cone-shaped, green	30
Sherbet, green, 4 1/4" h.	1,300
Sugar bowl, cov., amber	550
Sugar bowl, cov., green	275
Sugar bowl, open, amber	60
Sugar bowl, open, green	50
Tumbler, amber, 4 1/4" h., 10 oz.	125
Tumbler, green, 4 1/4" h., 10 oz.	165
Tumbler, footed, amber, 5 1/2" h., 10 oz.	150
Tumbler, footed, cone-shaped, amber, 5 3/4" h.	120
Tumbler, footed, cone-shaped, green, 5 3/4" h.	145

Duncan & Miller

Duncan & Miller Glass Company, a successor firm to George A. Duncan & Sons Company, produced a wide range of pressed wares and novelty pieces during the late 19th century and into the early 20th century. During the Depression era and after, they continued making a wide variety of more modern patterns, including mold-blown types, and also introduced a number of etched and engraved patterns. Many colors, including opalescent hues, were produced during this era, and especially popular today are the graceful swan dishes they produced in the Pall Mall and Sylvan patterns.

The numbers after the pattern name indicate the original factory pattern number. The Duncan factory was closed in 1955. Also see ANIMALS.

Ashtray, Caribbean patt. (No. 112), ruby	$40
Ashtray, model of a duck, ruby	140
Bowl, 10" d., Murano patt., milk white	180

Bowl, 4 3/4" d., Puritan patt., pink	12
Bowl, 6 1/2 x 11 1/2", model of a Viking boat, clear	240
Bowl, 6" d., handled, Teardrop patt. (No. 301), clear	15
Bowl, 7" d., Murano patt. (No. 127), pink opalescent	65
Bowl, 9" oval., Canterbury patt. (No. 115), clear	30
Candelabrum, three-light, No. 14, w/prisms, clear, 10" h., 8" w.	65
Candlesticks, Terrace patt. (No. 111), amber, pr.	120
Candlesticks, two-light, etched First Love patt., clear, 6" h, pr.	125

Teardrop Champagne

Champagne, Teardrop patt. (No. 301), clear, 5" h., 5 oz. (ILLUS.)	10
Cheese stand, Caribbean patt., blue, 3 1/2" h.	95
Cigarette box, cov., Caribbean patt., blue	95
Cocktail, Caribbean patt., blue, 4 3/4" h., 3 oz.	225
Cologne bottle w/original stopper, Hobnail patt. (No. 118), blue	65
Compote, Canterbury patt., ruby w/clear base, 5 1/2" h.	95
Compote, Teardrop patt., clear 5" d., 3" h.	20
Console set: bowl & candlesticks; American Way patt. (No. 71), ruby red, 3 pcs.	170
Cordial, Mardi Gras patt. (No. 42), clear	50
Cornucopia-vase, etched First Love patt., clear, 8" h.	75
Creamer & open sugar bowl, Georgian patt. (No. 103), pink, pr.	40
Creamer & open sugar bowl, individual, etched Language of Flowers patt., clear, pr.	80
Creamer & sugar bowl, large, etched Language of Flowers patt., clear, pr.	90
Cruet, w/original stopper, Bag Ware (No. 800), vaseline, large, ca. 1880s	145
Cup & saucer, Teardrop patt., clear	35
Deviled egg plate, Early American Sandwich patt., green, 12" d.	90
Goblet, Canterbury patt., clear	10
Goblet, Early American Sandwich patt., blue	30
Goblet, Early American Sandwich patt., clear, 9 oz., 6" h.	18
Goblet, water, Hobnail patt., clear	8

Goblet, etched First Love patt., clear,
6 3/4" h... 50
Ivy bowl, footed, Hobnail patt., blue opalescent, 6 1/2" d...................................... 52
Model of a goose, door stop-type, clear, 4
lb.. 425
Model of a swan, Pall Mall patt. (No. 30),
ruby, 7" l... 85
Model of a swan, spread wing-type, green,
12" w., 11" h... 120
Model of a swan, Sylvan patt., blue opalescent, 12" l... 295
Model of a swan, Sylvan patt. (No. 122),
blue opalescent, 7" l.................................. 90
Model of a swan, Sylvan patt. (No. 122),
milk white w/ruby neck & head, 7" l.......... 385
Model of a swan, Sylvan patt., pink opalescent, 12" l... 295
Mustard jar, cov., Caribbean patt., clear.......... 25
Olive dish, Teardrop patt., clear, 7" l................. 10
Pitcher, w/applied amber handle, Teardrop
patt., clear.. 100
Plate, 8 1/2" d., Spiral Flutes patt., green.......... 12
Plate, 8 1/2" d., Spiral Flutes patt., (No. 40),
clear... 6
Plate, salad, 8" d., Early American Sandwich patt., clear................................... 12
Punch set: punch bowl, 18" d., underplate
& twelve cups; Caribbean patt., clear,
cups clear w/applied ruby red handles,
14 pcs.. 265
Relish dish, five-part, Teardrop patt., clear,
12" d... 45
Relish dish, Sylvan patt., milk white w/ruby
handles, 10" l.. 180
Relish dish, three-part, Sylvan patt., yellow
opalescent, 10 x 13"..................................... 90
Relish dish, two-part, Caribbean patt., blue,
6" d... 75
Salt & pepper shakers w/original tops,
Mardi Gras patt., clear, pr.............................. 60
Salt & pepper shakers w/original tops,
Teardrop patt., clear, pr................................. 30
Sherbet, crimped rim, Canterbury patt.,
clear, 5 1/2" h.. 12
Sherbet, Teardrop patt., clear, 3 1/2" h................. 8
Sugar bowl, cov., Bag Ware (No. 800),
vaseline, ca. 1880s...................................... 110
Tumbler, Canterbury patt., clear, 5 1/4" h........... 10
Tumbler, Canterbury patt., yellow opalescent, 5 1/2" h... 60
Tumbler, footed, Caribbean patt., blue,
5 1/2" h.. 50
Tumbler, hi-ball, flat, Teardrop patt., clear,
4 3/4" h.. 10
Tumbler, iced tea, Early American Sandwich patt., clear, 5 1/4" h......................... 18
Tumbler, old fashioned, Canterbury patt.,
clear, 8 oz.. 10
Tumbler, whiskey, footed, Teardrop patt.,
clear, 3" h.. 17
Vase, 10 1/2" h., Teardrop patt., clear............... 35
Vase, 10 1/2" h., Venetian patt., (No. 126),
ruby red... 170
Vase, 2 1/2" h., Chanticleer patt., green
opalescent... 110
Vase, 5" h., Canterbury patt., clear..................... 10
Vase, 8" h., ruffled rim, Hobnail patt., blue
opalescent... 65
Vase, (cigarette holder), 3 1/2" h., Grecian
Urn line (No. 538), clear................................ 15

Violet bowl, Canterbury patt., clear,
4 1/2" d... 20
Wine, Mardi Gras patt....................................... 30
Wine, Teardrop patt., clear, 4 3/4" h., 3 oz. 15

Fostoria

Fostoria Glass company, founded in 1887, produced numerous types of fine glassware over the years. Its factory in Moundsville, West Virginia, closed in 1986.

Fostoria Label

Ashtray, American patt., clear, 2 7/8" d............ $10
Ashtray, Coin patt., olive green, 5"...................... 15
Bonbon, three-toed, American patt., clear......... 15
Bouillon cup, Fairfax patt., pink......................... 15
Bouillon cup, footed, Versailles etching,
blue.. 42
Bowl, 10 1/2" d., three-footed, American
patt., clear... 45
Bowl, 10" d., Romance etching, clear................. 80
Bowl, 11 1/2" d., flared rim, Chintz etching,
clear... 130
Bowl, 11 1/2" oval, American patt., clear............ 48
Bowl, 11" d., flared rim, Navarre etching,
clear... 65
Bowl, 12 1/2" oval, 2 7/8" h., Flame patt.,
Navarre etching, clear.................................... 65
Bowl, 12" d., flared rim, Shirley etching,
clear... 65
Bowl, 12" d., three-footed, Oak Leaf etching, pink.. 110
Bowl, 13" l., oblong, Heirloom cutting, blue....... 55
Bowl, 6 1/4" d., handled, Raleigh patt., Laurel cutting, clear.. 15
Bowl, 9 1/4" oval, Pioneer patt., green............... 25
Bowl, cov., fruit, footed, Coin patt., blue............ 95
Bowl, cream soup, w/underplate, Fairfax
patt., blue.. 35
Bowl, cream soup, w/underplate, June
etching, blue.. 70
Bowl, fruit, 12" d., footed, American patt.,
clear... 200
Cake plate, two-handled, Baroque patt.,
Meadow Rose etching, clear, 10" d............... 70
Cake plate, two-handled, Chintz etching,
clear, 10" d.. 85
Cake stand (or salver), American patt.,
clear, 10" sq., 7 1/4" h.................................... 95
Candelabra, w/bobeches & prisms, twolight, Baroque patt., clear, pr...................... 110
Candlesticks, one-light, Romance etching,
clear, 5", pr... 90
Candlesticks, two-light, Meadow Rose
etching, clear, pr... 75
Candy dish, cov., Coin patt., clear...................... 45
Candy dish, cov., three-part, Chintz etching, clear... 165
Candy dish, cov., three-part, Shirley etching, clear.. 95

Candy jar, cov., urn-shaped, Coin patt., emerald green, 12 1/2" h. 250
Celery dish, Baroque patt., yellow, 11 1/4" l. 35
Celery dish, handled, Sunray patt., clear, 10" l. 15
Celery dish, Trojan etching, yellow, 11 1/2" l. 45
Champagne, Chintz etching, clear 35
Champagne, Holly cutting, clear 35
Champagne, Navarre etching, blue 50
Cheese & cracker set, Navarre etching, clear, 2 pcs. 75
Cocktail, Colony patt., clear, 3 1/2" oz. 18
Cocktail, Holly cutting, clear, 5 1/4" h. 25
Compote, 8 1/2" h., Coin patt., frosted ruby 110
Compote, cov., 6 1/2 h", Colony patt., clear 40
Console bowl, footed, Versailles etching, blue 85
Console set: bowl & pr of 3 1/2" h. candlesticks; June etching, blue, 3 pcs., the set 250
Cordial, Chintz etching, clear, 1 oz. 70
Cordial, Christiana cutting, clear 50
Cordial, Trojan patt., yellow 95
Cordial, Wheat cutting, clear 40
Creamer, footed, Fairfax patt., pink 15
Creamer, individual size, Baroque patt., blue 35
Creamer & open sugar bowl, flared rim, footed, American patt., clear, pr. 40
Creamer & open sugar bowl, individual size, Baroque patt., blue, pr. 70
Creamer & open sugar bowl, Queen Anne etching, clear, pr. 30
Creamer, open sugar bowl & undertray, Navarre etching, clear, 3 pcs. 65
Cruet w/original stopper, Fairfax patt., pink 120
Cup & saucer, Baroque patt., clear 15
Cup & saucer, demitasse, Vernon etching, green 40
Cup & saucer, Fairfax patt., pink 15
Goblet, Arcady etching, clear, 9 oz. 30
Goblet, Buttercup etching, clear, 10 oz. 25
Goblet, Colony patt., clear, 5 1/4" h., 9 oz. 20
Goblet, Corsage etching, clear, 7 3/8" h. 32
Goblet, Florentine etching, clear bowl w/yellow stem. 35
Goblet, June etching, topaz 38
Goblet, Lido etching, clear, 12" h., 12 oz. 28
Goblet, Navarre etching, clear 60
Ice bucket, Baroque patt., topaz 120
Ice bucket, Versailles etching, blue 120
Ketchup (condiment) bottle w/stopper, American patt., clear 135
Marmalade jar, cov., handled, American patt., clear, 5 1/2" 95
Oyster cocktail, Beverly etching, amber 8
Parfait, Fairfax patt., topaz, 7 oz. 12
Pitcher, 5" h., American patt., clear 30
Pitcher w/ice lip, 6 1/2" h., footed, American patt., clear, 3 pt. 85
Pitcher w/ice lip, Colony patt., clear, 2 qt. 135
Plate, 9 1/2" d., Baroque patt., clear 30
Plate, bread & butter, 6" d., Lido etching, clear 15
Plate, bread & butter, 6" d., Trojan etching, pink 10
Plate, dinner, 10 1/4" d., Fairfax patt., blue 50
Plate, dinner, 10" d., Seville patt., amber 35
Plate, dinner, 9 1/2" d., Chintz etching, clear 65

Plate, dinner, 9 1/2" d., Navarre etching, clear 55
Plate, dinner, 9" d., Colony patt., clear 25
Plate, luncheon, 8 1/2" d., Holly cutting, clear 35
Plate, luncheon, 8 1/2" d., Meadow Rose etching, clear 25
Plate, luncheon, 8" d., Fairfax patt., topaz 12
Plate, salad, 7 1/2" d., Chintz etching, clear 20
Plate, salad, 7 1/2" d., June etching, topaz 12
Plate, salad, 7 1/2" d., Navarre etching, clear 18
Plate, salad, 7 1/2" d., Versailles etching, blue 15
Plate, salad, 7" d., American patt., clear 12
Plate, torte, 14" d., American patt., clear 45
Plate, torte, 20" d., American patt., clear 175
Punch bowl & base, American patt., clear, 14" d. bowl, 2 pcs. 275
Punch set: punch bowl, base & ten cups; Coin patt., clear, 12 pcs. 750
Relish, three-part, Romance etching, clear, 10" l. 45
Relish dish, boat-shaped, American patt., clear, 8 1/2" l. 22
Relish dish, divided, oval, Versailles etching, green, 8 1/2" l. 30
Relish dish, five-part, Navarre etching, clear, 13 1/4" l. 100
Relish dish, three-part, American patt., clear, 6 x 9 1/2". 40
Relish dish, three-part, Fairfax patt., amber, 11 1/2" l. 18
Relish dish, two part, Baroque patt., blue, 6 1/2" l. 32
Relish dish, two-part, Holly cutting, clear, 6 1/2" 40
Salt & pepper shakers w/original tops, Baroque patt., topaz, pr. 120
Salt & pepper shakers w/original tops, Fairfax patt., pink, pr. 60
Salt & pepper shakers w/original tops, footed, Navarre etching, clear, pr. 150
Sandwich server w/center handle, Chintz etching, clear, 12" d. 65
Sandwich server w/center handle, Colony patt., clear. 32
Sauceboat & underplate, American patt., clear, 2 pcs. 85
Sauceboat & underplate, Fairfax patt., topaz, 2 pcs. 52
Sauceboat w/attached underplate, Pioneer patt., green 45
Sherbet, Coin patt., ruby 55
Sherbet, Colony patt., clear, 5 oz. 10
Sherbet, Jamestown patt., green, 7 oz. 15
Sherbet, Lido etching, clear, 6 oz. 15
Sherbet, low, Cynthia cutting, clear 18
Sherbet, low, Florentine etching, clear, 7 oz. 12
Shrimp bowl, American patt., clear, 12 1/4" d. 375
Syrup pitcher w/original glass top & underplate, American patt., clear, 10 oz., 3 pcs. 150
Tumbler, Cameo patt., opaque white w/multicolor decoration 45
Tumbler, footed, Colony patt., clear, 5 3/4" h., 12 oz. 22
Tumbler, footed, Fairfax patt., blue, 6" h., 12 oz. 25

Tumbler, footed, June etching, clear, 6" h., 12 oz.. 35

Tumbler, footed, Lido etching, clear, 9 oz........... 20

Tumbler, ice tea, footed, American patt., clear, 5 1/2" h., 12 oz. (ILLUS.)....................... 18

Tumbler, iced tea, footed, Chintz etching, clear, 12 oz... 40

Tumbler, iced tea, Holly cutting, clear, 12 oz... 32

Tumbler, juice, Colony patt., clear, 3 5/8" h., 5 oz.. 18

Tumbler, juice, Jamestown patt., green.............. 18

Tumbler, Versailles etching, green, 5 1/4" h., 9 oz.. 28

Tumbler, water, Cynthia cutting, clear 18

Vase, 10" h., flared rim, American patt., clear.. 75

Vase, bud, 8" h., Coin patt., frosted blue............. 45

Water set: pitcher & six tumblers; Rosby patt., clear, 7 pcs................................ 220

Wine, Coin patt. clear.................................. 35

Wine, Corsage etching, clear, 5 1/2" h................ 35

Wine, footed, American patt., clear, 4 3/8" h., 2 1/2 oz........................... 15

Wine, Lido etching, clear, 3 oz...................... 32

Wine, Navarre etching, clear.......................... 60

Heisey

Numerous types of fine glass were made by A.H. Heisey & Co., Newark, Ohio, from 1895. The company's trademark, an H enclosed within a diamond, has become known to most glass collectors. The company's name and molds were acquired by Imperial Glass Co., Bellaire, Ohio, in 1958, and some pieces have been reissued. The glass listed below consists of miscellaneous pieces and types. Also see ANIMALS and CUSTARD GLASS.

Banana split dish, footed, Greek Key patt., clear.. $35

Basket, Lariat patt., clear 8 1/2" h...................... 230

Bowl, cov., 5 1/2" d., Ridgeleigh patt., clear........ 50

Cake salver, Plantation patt., clear, 13" d......... 245

Cake stand, Waverly patt., Orchid etching, clear, 12" d.. 275

Candlesticks, two-light, No. 134 Orchid etching, clear, pr............................... 130

Candy dish, cov., w/sea horse handles, Waverly patt., Rose etching, clear............... 210

Celery tray, oval, Coarse Rib patt., clear, 9" l....................................... 18

Champagne, Kohinoor patt., clear, 3 oz. 35

Champagne, Rose etching, clear 55

Champagne, saucer-type, Spanish patt., Killarney cutting, clear 42

Champagne, saucer-type, Victorian patt., clear... 20

Champagne, Spanish patt., cobalt blue bowl w/clear stem, 5 1/2" oz.................... 115

Cigarette box, cov., w/small horsehead finial, Puritan patt., No. 1489, clear 125

Cocktail, Gascony patt., Tangerine (orange) 110

Cocktail, Orchid etching, clear, 5 5/8" h., 4 oz.. 55

Cocktail shaker, cov., Orchid etching, clear, sterling silver top & base.................... 295

Cocktail shaker, w/original stopper, Coronation patt., clear.............................. 75

Compote, jelly, 6 3/4" h., Rose etching, clear.. 70

Console set: bowl & pair of candle vases w/prisms & inserts; Ipswich patt., clear, bowl 11 1/2" d., 5" h., 3 pcs...................... 600

Cordial, Lariat patt., w/Moonglo cutting, clear.. 150

Creamer & sugar bowl, Crystolite patt., clear, pr.. 50

Creamer & sugar bowl, Petal patt., Moongleam (light green), pr..................... 110

Creamer & sugar bowl, Queen Ann patt., Danish Princess etching, clear, pr............ 120

Cruet w/original stopper, Empress patt., Sahara (yellow) 160

Cruet w/original stopper, Pleat & Panel patt., Flamingo (pink)............................... 90

Crushed fruit jar, cov., Greek Key patt., clear.. 500

Cup & saucer, Orchid etching, clear.................. 60

Domino sugar tray, Narrow Flute patt., Moongleam.. 160

Goblet, Carcassonne patt., Sahara, 9 oz. 50

Goblet, Impromptu patt., clear........................... 45

Goblet, Ipswich patt., clear, 8 oz. 25

Goblet, Old Dominion patt., Alexandrite (lavender)... 300

Ice bucket, cov. w/tongs, Empress patt., Alexandrite.................................... 325

Ice bucket, Queen Ann patt., Orchid etching, clear... 250

Ice bucket, Waverly Orchid etching (No. 1519), clear... 280

Ice tub, Puritan patt. (No. 341), clear, 6" d........ 120

Lamps, hurricane-type, Plantation patt., clear, 15" h., pr................................... 1,200

Lemon dish, cov., Tudor patt., clear w/cutting.. 35

Luncheon set: four cups & plates & dolphin-footed creamer & sugar bowl; Empress patt., Sahara, 10 pcs. 325

Marmalade jar, cov., Crystolite patt., clear, 6" h.. 50

Marmalade jar, cov., Minuet etching, clear....... 170

Matchbox, cov., Banded Flute patt., clear 250

Mayonnaise bowl & spoon, Minuet etching, No. 1509, clear...................................... 100

Mug, eight-sided w/elephant head & trunk forming handle, amber...................... 925

Mugs, Pineapple & Fan patt., emerald green.. 90

Mustard jar, cov., Crystolite patt., clear............. 35

Mustard jar, cov., Narrow Flute patt., clear 50

Nappy, Whirlpool (Provincial) patt., clear, 5 1/2"... 15

Nut cup, Empress patt., Flamingo...................... 35

Nut dishes, Octagon patt., Moongleam, set of 7.. 120

Oyster cocktail, Victorian patt. (No. 1425) clear, 5 oz.. 16

Parfait, Old Glory patt., clear............................. 30

Perfume bottle w/stopper, Ridgeleigh patt., clear.. 200

Pitcher, Minuet etching, No. 4164, 1/2 gal., clear.. 350

Pitcher, tankard, Bead Swag patt., ruby-stained, late 1890s.................................. 150

Pitcher, water, Puritan patt., clear, 3 qt.
(ILLUS.).. 250
Plate, 13" d., Ridgeleigh patt., clear..................... 50
Plate, 6" d., Tudor patt., clear 10
Plate, 7 1/2" d., Empress patt., Sahara............... 25
Plate, 7" d., Empress patt., clear 12
Plate, 7" d., Minuet etching, clear......................... 22
Plate, 8 1/2" d., Empress patt., Tangerine......... 150
Plate, 8 1/4" d., Rose etching, clear..................... 28
Plate, 8" d., Ipswich patt., Sahara 35
Plate, 8" d., Orchid etching, clear......................... 28
Plate, dinner, square, Old Colony etching,
Empress patt., clear...................................... 140
Plate, torte, 13" d., rolled rim, Lariat patt.,
clear.. 40
Plate, torte, 14" d., Orchid etching, clear 100
Plate, torte, 14" d., Rose patt., clear 100
Plate, torte, 14" d., Waverly patt., w/Orchid
etching, clear.. 43
Plates, 8" d., Crystolite patt., clear, set of 8....... 110
Puff box, cov., Winged Scroll patt., emer-
ald, green,late 19th c. 185
Punch bowl & base, Banded Flute patt.,
clear, 2 pcs. 395
Punch bowl & base, Greek Key patt., clear,
2 pcs.. 600
Punch cup, Pillows patt., clear, ca. 1900 35
Punch cup, Pinwheel & Fan patt., clear 25
Punch cup, Prince of Wales patt., clear,
early 1900s... 20
Punch cup, Prison Stripe patt., No. 357,
clear.. 35
Punch cup, Victorian patt., clear........................... 15
Punch set: bowl, base & eleven cups;
Greek Key patt., clear, 13 pcs...................... 900
Punch set: bowl, base & ten cups; Beaded
Panel & Sunburst patt., No. 1235, clear,
12 pcs.. 425
Punch set: bowl, ten cups & ladle;
Ridgeleigh patt., clear, 12 pcs...................... 400
Punch set: bowl, twelve cups; Puritan patt.,
clear, 13 pcs. 320
Relish dish, Crystolite patt., clear, 6" oval 25
Relish dish, five-part, Colonial patt., clear 95
Relish dish, five-part, Old Williamsburg
patt., clear 43
Relish dish, three-part Fern patt., Zircon
(blue green)... 275
Relish dish, three-part, Lariat patt., clear,
10" l... 45
Relish dish, three-part, Orchid etching,
clear, 11 1/4" l.. 80
Relish tray, five-part, Crystolite patt., clear.......... 45
Rose bowl, Fancy Loop patt., clear, late
1890s, 4" h. 65

Heisey Pillows Rose Bowl

Rose bowl, footed, Pillows patt. (No. 325),
clear (ILLUS.)... 275
Salt dip, individual size, Ridgeleigh patt.,
clear.. 15
Salt & pepper shakers w/original metal
tops, Pineapple & Fan patt., clear, late
1890s, pr. 100
Salt & pepper shakers w/original metal
tops, Pineapple & Fan patt., emerald
green w/gold, late 1890s, pr........................... 300
Salt & pepper shakers w/original tops,
Bead Swag patt., clear, late 1890s, pr. 50
Salt & pepper shakers w/original tops,
Empress patt., Sahara, pr.............................. 150
Salt & pepper shakers w/original tops,
Rose etching clear, pr. 95
Salt shaker w/original top, Bead Swag
patt., souvenir, milk white, late 1890s............. 55
Salt shaker w/original top, Winged Scroll
patt., green w/gold trim, late 1890s.............. 110
Sherbet, low, Rose etching, clear......................... 50
Spooner, Pineapple & Fan patt., emerald
green w/gold trim, late 1890s........................ 120
Spooner, Queen Anne patt. (No. 365), clear....... 95
Sugar bowl, open, individual, Twist patt.,
Moongleam 90
Sugar bowl, open, Minuet etching, clear............... 60
Syrup pitcher w/original top, Bead Swag
patt., milk white, late 1890s........................... 160
Table set: creamer, cov. sugar bowl, cov.
butter dish & spooner; Pineapple & Fan
patt., emerald green w/gold trim, 4 pcs. 550
Toothpick holder, Bead Swag patt., milk
white w/floral decoration, late 1890s.............. 150
Toothpick holder, Bead Swag patt., ruby-
stained, late 1890s... 60
Toothpick holder, Fancy Loop patt., clear,
late 1890s.. 85
Toothpick holder, Fancy Loop patt., emer-
ald green w/gold trim, late 1890s 285
Toothpick holder, Pineapple & Fan patt.,
emerald green, late 1890s............................. 295
Tray, Empress patt., Sahara, 13" d. 60
Tumbler, iced tea, footed, Rose etching,
clear, 12 oz. 60
Tumbler, iced tea, footed, Twist patt., (No.
1252), Marigold, 8 oz..................................... 75
Tumbler, iced tea, Plantation patt., clear, 12
oz.. 50

Tumbler, juice, footed, Rose etching clear,
5 oz.. 45
Tumbler, Minuet etching, clear, 12 oz................ 55
Tumbler, Pineapple & Fan patt., clear
w/gold trim, late 1890s 35
Tumbler, whiskey, Victorian patt., clear.............. 35
Vase, 8" h., dolphin-footed, Empress patt.,
Alexandrite 600
Vase, 8" h., Empress patt., Sahara................... 155
Vase, 8" h., Fancy Loop patt., clear late
1890s.. 95
Vase, 8" h., Pineapple & Fan patt., emerald
green w/gold trim, late 1890s 50
Vases, 7 1/2" h., Ipswich patt., No. 1405,
w/12 prisms each, clear, & inserts, pr............ 550
Water set: pitcher & four tumblers; Narrow
Flute patt., clear, early 20th c., 5 pcs............ 200
Wine, Minuet etching, clear, 2 1/2 oz. 80
Wine, New Era patt., clear................................. 40
Wine, Orchid etching, clear, 3 oz. 95
Wine, Spanish patt., cobalt blue 225

Hobbs, Brockunier & Co.

The Hobbs Company originated about 1845 in Wheeling, West Virginia with the founding of Hobbs, Barnes & Co. by John L. Hobbs and James B. Barnes, both former employees of the New England Glass Company. Their sons eventually joined the firm and in 1863 the company became Hobbs, Brockunier & Co. when John L. and John H. Hobbs and Charles Brockunier took over. That year they hired William Leighton Sr., former superintendent of the New England Glass Company. Leighton took charge of production and in 1864 he revolutionized the American glass industry by devising a formula for soda lime glass, a cheaper method of producing clear glass which didn't require lead oxide. By the 1880s Hobbs was producing a number of decorative glassware lines including Peach Blow, Spangled, pressed Amberina and various opalescent patterns. The plant closed in the 1890s. Also see CRUETS and OPALESCENT GLASS.

Butter dish, cov., sapphire blue, Hobnail
(323 Dew Drop) patt., polished pontil,
5" d. (several flakes under lid)....................... $35
Celery vase, canary opalescent, Hobnail
(323 Dew Drop) patt., applied hobnail
prunt under base, 6 1/2" h. 210
Celery vase, cranberry opalescent, Hobnail
(323 Dew Drop) patt., polished pontil,
6 1/2" h... 230
Child's water set: No. 0 jug-type 4" h.
pitcher, four 2 1/2" h. tumblers, round
tray; amber, Hobnail (323 Dew Drop)
patt., 6 pcs. (several minor hob flakes).......... 400
Child's water set: No. 0 jug-type 4" h.
pitcher, four 2 1/2" h. tumblers, round
tray; clear w/Frances decoration, Hobnail
(323 Dew Drop) patt., 6 pcs. (one tumbler
w/amethyst tint) 475
Child's water set: No. 1 jug-type 4 1/4" h.
pitcher, four 2 1/2" h. tumblers, round
tray; blue, Hobnail (323 Dew Drop) patt.,
6 pcs. (several minor hob flakes)................... 325
Lamp, tapering cylindrical hobnail shade in
Hobbs Hobnail (No. 323 Dew Drop) patt.
w/Frances decoration, w/ovoid brass font
marked "The Rochester," & "Columbia"
central draft burner, 4" fitter 275

Pitcher, No. 0 jug type, 3 7/8" h., cranberry
opalescent, Hobnail (323 Dew Drop)
patt., applied clear handle, polished pon-
til (chipping to several base hobs)................. 160
Pitcher, No. 0 jug type, 4" h., blue plated,
Hobnail (323 Dew Drop) patt., blue ap-
plied handle, polished pontil 110
Pitcher, No. 0 jug type, 4" h., carnary light
opalescent, Hobnail (323 Dew Drop)
patt., applied vaseline handle, polished
pontil (one hob chipped) 180
Pitcher, No. 0 jug type, 4" h., rubina verde
light opalescent, Hobnail (323 Dew Drop)
patt., applied vaseline handle, polished
pontil.. 500
Pitcher, No. 1 jug type, 4 1/2" h., blue, Hob-
nail (323 Dew Drop) patt., blue applied
handle, polished pontil (chipping to sev-
eral base hobs)... 200
Pitcher, No. 1 jug type, 4 1/2" h., Hobnail
(323 Dew Drop) patt., canary satin, ap-
plied canary handle, polished pontil.............. 220
Pitcher, No. 1 jug type, 4 1/2" h., Hob-
nail/323 Dew Drop patt., vaseline plated,
applied vaseline handle, polished pontil....... 220
Pitcher, No. 2 or 3 jug type, 5 1/2" h., vaseline plated, Hobnail (323 Dew Drop) patt.,
applied carnary handle, polished pontil 170
Pitcher, No. 3 jug type, 5 3/4" h., Hobnail
(323 Dew Drop) patt., Frances decoration, applied handle, polished pontil
(flake & bruise to several base hobs) 200
Pitcher, No. 4 jug type, 6 3/4" h., Hobnail
(323 Dew Drop) patt., crystal opalescent,
applied clear handle, polished pontil.............. 90
Pitcher, No. 4 jug type, 7" h., Hobnail (323
Dew Drop) patt., frosted, polished pontil
(several hobs chipped).................................... 50
Pitcher, water, 7 1/2" h., Polka Dot patt., rubina verde, applied vaseline handle, pol-
ished pontil.. 475
Pitcher, No. 5 jug type, 7 3/4" h., cranberry
opalescent, Hobnail (323 Dew Drop)
patt., clear applied handle, polished pon-
til 600
Pitcher, No. 5 jug type, 7 3/4" h., rubina ver-
de opalescent, Hobnail (323 Dew Drop)
patt., applied vaseline handle, polished
pontil (chip on one hob) 700
Pitcher, No. 5 jug type, 8" h., Hobnail (323
Dew Drop) patt., Frances decoration, applied handle, polished pontil (one hob off
& frosted over, several hob flakes)................ 170
Tumbler, cranberry opalescent, Hobnail
(323 Dew Drop) patt., polished pontil 70
Tumbler, Hobnail (323 Dew Drop) patt.,
sapphire blue opalescent, polished pontil 70

Imperial

Imperial Glass Company, Bellaire, Ohio was organized in 1901 and was in continuous production, except for very brief periods, until its closing in June 1984. It had been a major producer of Carnival Glass early in the 20th century and also produced other types of glass, including an art glass line called "Free Hand Ware" during the 1920s and its "Jewels" about 1916. The company acquired a number of molds of other earlier factories, including the Cambridge and A.H. Heisey Companies, and reissued numerous items through the years.

Candlewick

Ashtray, heart-shaped, No. 400/172, clear, 4 1/2".. $12
Bonbon dish, heart-shaped, No. 51H, clear w/gold trim, 6" w. 25
Bowl, 7" d., No. 400/5F, blue 65
Bowl, 7" d., two-handled, No. 400/62B, red 165
Bowl, 9" d., four-toed, square crimped, No. 400/74SC, black amethyst............................ 220
Bowl, fruit, 5" d., 400/1F, clear 10
Candleholders, footed urn shape, No. 400/129R, clear, 6" h., pr. 200
Candleholders, mushroom, No. 400/86, clear w/gold beading, pr. 70
Candleholders, three-light, No. 400/115, clear, pr. 250
Candleholders w/applied handle, No. 400/90, clear, 5" pr. 100
Candy box, cov., No. 400/259, clear, 7" d. 130
Champagne, saucer-type, No. 3400, clear, 6 oz. 16
Cheese & cracker server, No. 400/88, clear... 45
Compote, 4 1/2" d., No. 400/63B, clear.............. 18
Compote, 8", No. 400/48F, clear 85
Cordial, No. 3400, clear.. 45
Cream soup bowl w/underplate, two-handled, No. 400/50, clear, 5" d. bowl & 6 3/4" d. underplate, 2 pcs. 58
Creamer & open sugar bowl, No. 400/18, clear, pr. 120
Creamer & open sugar bowl, pedestal base, No. 400/31, clear, pr. 40
Cruet w/original stopper, applied handle, No. 400/279, clear, 6 oz. 65
Cup & saucer, clear 15
Goblet, water, No. 3400, clear, 9 oz. 25
Mayonnaise bowl & underplate, No. 40, blue, 2 pcs. 65
Mustard jar, spoon & underplate, No. 400/156, clear, 3 pcs. 50
Pitcher, water, 80 oz., No. 400/24, clear 125
Plate, 10" d., two-handled, No. 400/72D, clear.. 35
Plate, 10" d., two-handled, No. 400/72D, ruby.. 90
Plate, 14" d., two-handled, No. 400/113D, clear.. 50
Plate, 8 1/2" d., handled, crimped rim, No. 400/62C, clear 22
Plate, bread & butter, 6" d., No. 400/1D, clear 8
Plate, luncheon, 8" d., No. 400/5D, clear............ 12
Plate, salad, 7" d., No. 400/3D, clear.................. 10
Platter, 16" oval, No. 400/131D, clear................ 190
Punch bowl & underplate, 13" d. bowl No. 400/20B & 17" d. underplate No. 400/20V, clear, 2 pcs. 175
Relish dish, five-part, No. 400/209, clear, 13 1/2" d. 70
Relish dish, three-part, No. 400/208, clear, 10" l. 95
Relish tray, four-part, No. 400/55, clear, 8 1/2" d. 20
Relish tray, three-part, No. 400/56, clear, 10 1/2" d. 65
Salt & pepper shakers, No. 400/96, clear, pr. 15
Sandwich server, center handle, No. 68D, clear, 11 1/2" d. 42
Seafood cocktail, footed, 400/190, clear........... 35
Sugar bowl, open, No. 400/122, clear 10

Teacup & saucer, mallard cutting, No. 400/35, clear 20
Tray, heart-shaped center handle, No. 400/149D, clear, 9" d.. 45
Tray, pastry, heart-shaped center handle, No. 400/68D, clear, 11 1/2" d. 38
Tumbler, juice, No. 400/19, clear, 5 oz............... 15
Vase, 8" h., fan-shaped, etched stars design, No. 400/87F, clear................................. 45
Vase, 8" h., flip-type, ruffled rim, No. 400/143C, clear....................................... 75
Vase, bud, 5 3/4" h., No. 400/107, clear 65
Water set: 80 oz. pitcher No. 400/24 & six 12 oz. tumblers No. 400/19; clear, 7 pcs. 300

Cape Cod

Ashtray, No. 160/134/1, clear, 4" d. 12
Bowl, 10" d., footed, No. 160/137B, clear 70
Bowl, cream soup, 5 1/2" tab-handled, No. 160/198, clear 40
Bowl, fruit, 9" d., footed, No. 160/67F, clear 65
Box, cov., handled, clear.................................... 35
Cake stand, round, footed, No. 160/67D, clear 10 1/2" d. 55
Comport, clear, 4 1/2" d. 22
Compote, 6", cov., footed No. 160/140, clear... 65
Cruet w/original stopper, No. 160/119, amber, 4 oz. 35
Egg cup, No. 160/225, clear................................ 22
Epergne, plain center, No. 160/196, clear, 2 pcs. 190
Goblet, water, stemmed, No. 1600, clear, 10 oz. 20
Pitcher w/ice lip, No. 160/239, clear, 60 oz. 80
Plate, 16" d., cupped, No. 160/20V, clear........... 50

Cape Cod Dinner Plate

Plate, dinner, 10" d., No. 160/10D, clear (ILLUS.) 35
Punch cup, clear.. 8
Punch set: punch bowl, underplate & twelve cups; clear, 14 pcs. 175
Salt & pepper shakers w/original tops, cobalt blue, pr. 100
Sherbet, No. 1600, clear, 6 oz. 15
Tom & Jerry punch bowl, footed, No. 160/200, clear.. 290
Tumbler, flat, No. 160, clear, 10 oz. 10
Wine, No. 160/27, clear, 4 1/2" h. 10

Miscellaneous Patterns & Lines

Animal covered dish, lion on lacy base, caramel slag.. 150
Animal covered dish, rooster on lacy base, jade green 140
Animal covered dish, rooster on lacy base, purple slag.. 200

Bowl, Cathay line, Phoenix patt., blue satin 110
Pitcher, Mt. Vernon patt. 25
Urn, Snake Dance patt., pink, 8 1/2" h. 95
Vase, 8 1/2" h., model of a dancing lady, red
slag 120

Free-Hand Ware
Decanter w/original stopper, ship decoration, peach blow, w/original label 180
Vase, 10" h., baluster-form w/flaring foot &
rim, opaque white heart & vine decoration on a translucent cobalt blue ground 525
Vase, 10" h., iridescent yellow orange exte-
rior, blue interior... 150
Vase, 7 3/8" h., 3 1/2" d., cushion footed
baluster-form w/flared rim, overall white
decoration on butterfly blue iridescent
ground, ca. 1924 400
Vase, 7" h., iridescent orange w/dark
threading.. 195
Vase, 8 1/2" h., blue iridescent ground, gold
iridescent interior.. 140
Vase, 8 1/2" h., cylindrical shape, white
drape design over mustard ground, or-
ange iridescent interior................................... 165
Vase, 9 3/4" h., iridescent orange over
opaque white.. 65

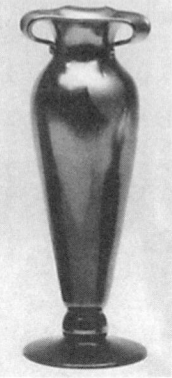

Graceful Free-Hand Vase

Vase, 9 3/4 h., iridescent orange over
tooled trefoil rim, dark iridescent body
decorated w/orange hearts & vines
(ILLUS.) 690

Le Verre Francais
Cameo vase, 17 3/4" h., round cushion foot
supporting a tall trumpet-form body
swelled at the top & w/a closed rim, shaded orange overlaid in mottled brown &
etched & cut w/cascading stylized fruit &
leaves, inscribed mark on the foot, ca.
1920s 1,265

Libbey
Tumbler, w/blue & gilt leaves 140

Maize (Libbey)
Celery vase, off white w/green leaves,
6 1/2" h. 90

Milk Glass
Opaque white glass, or "opal," has been called
"milk-white glass" perhaps to distinguish it from trans-
parent or "clear-white glass." Resembling fine white
porcelain, it was viewed as an inexpensive substitute.
Opacity is obtained by adding bone ash or oxide of tin to
clear molten glass. By the addition of various coloring
agents, the opaque mixture can be turned into blue milk
glass, or pink, yellow, green, caramel, even black milk
glass. Collectors of milk glass now accept not only the
white variety but virtually any opaque color and color
mixtures, including slag or marbled glass. It has been
made in numerous forms and shapes in this country and
abroad from about the first quarter of the 19th century.
Many of the items listed here were also made in colored
opaque glass, which collectors call blue or green or
black "milk glass." It is still being produced, and there
are many reproductions of earlier pieces. Pieces are all-
white unless otherwise noted.

Animal covered dish, "American Hen," eagle w/eggs inscribed "Porto Rico," "Cu-
ba," & "Philippines," 6" l., 4" h. **$55**
Animal covered dish, Bull's Head mustard
jar, w/separate tongue spoon, original
paint, Atterbury 250

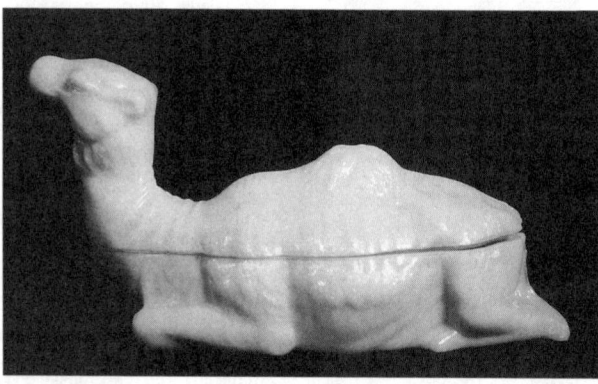

Camel Covered Dish

Animal covered dish, Camel/Dromedary,
light caramel, Vallerysthal, 7" l. (ILLUS.)... **1,800**
Animal covered dish, Cat on Drum,
Portieux, France, 4 5/8" d. **110**
Animal covered dish, Cat on lattice base,
blue glass eyes, Westmoreland Specialty
Company, early 20th c. **110**

Cat on Split-Ribbed Base Dish

Animal covered dish, Cat on split-ribbed
base, signed "McKee," 5 1/2" l. (ILLUS.) **375**
Animal covered dish, Cow on oval paneled
base, maker unknown, 6 1/4" l. **350-400**
Animal covered dish, Crawfish on two-
handled oblong base, overall 7 1/2" l. **160**
Animal covered dish, Deer on fallen tree
base, Flaccus, 6 3/4" l. **250-275**
Animal covered dish, Dog on oval wide rib
base, blue head, Westmoreland Special-
ty Company, early 20th c., 5 1/2" l. **55-60**

Pekinese Covered Dish

Animal covered dish, Dog, Pekinese (also
known as Spaniel or Pomeranian), attributed to Boston & Sandwich Glass Co.,
4 3/4" l. (ILLUS.) **600-700**

Setter Dog on Square Base Dish

Animal covered dish, Dog, Setter on
square base, Vallerysthal (ILLUS.) **200-250**
Animal covered dish, Dove on split-ribbed
base, signed "McKee" **275**

Duck on Flange Base Covered Dish

Animal covered dish, Duck on flange
base, blue w/white head, L.G. Wright,
6 1/2" l. (ILLUS.) **75-90**

Cold-painted Duck Covered Dish

Animal covered dish, Duck on ovoid basketweave base, cold painted, marked
"SV" inside cover, 5" l. (ILLUS.) **185**
Animal covered dish, Duck w/amethyst
head, Atterbury, 11" l., 5" h. **350-400**
Animal covered dish, Duck w/wavy base,
glass eyes, Challinor, Taylor & Co.,
5 1/4" h. **95-125**

Elephant on Split Ribbed Base Dish

Animal covered dish, Elephant on split-
ribbed base, signed "McKee" inside cov-
er & base (ILLUS.) **2,800**

Elephant with Rider Dish

Animal covered dish, Elephant w/rider, signed "Vallerysthal," France (ILLUS.) . **450-550**

Entwined Fish Covered Dish

Animal covered dish, Fish, Entwined Fish on lacy-edge base, shell finial, Atterbury, 7 1/2" d. (ILLUS.).. **200-225**

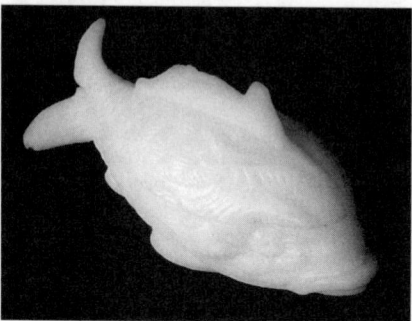

Vallerysthal Fish Covered Dish

Animal covered dish, Fish, Vallerysthal, 7" l. (ILLUS.)... **225**

"Walking Fish" Covered Dish

Animal covered dish, Fish, "Walking Fish," w/attached red glass eyes, attributed to Challinor, Taylor (ILLUS.).............................. **290**

Fox on Ribbed Base Covered Dish

Animal covered dish, Fox on ribbed base, red glass eyes attached, Atterbury patent dated Aug. 6, 1889 inside cover, 6 3/8" l. (ILLUS.) **175-200**

Animal covered dish, Fox on ribbed top & lacy-edge base, Atterbury, 7 3/4" l. **200**

Animal covered dish, Frog sitting, mouth slightly open, signed "Vallerysthal"........ **225-250**

Animal covered dish, Hen on basketweave base, Challinor, Taylor & Co., 7" l. **70**

Challinor, Taylor Hen & Rooster Dishes

Animal covered dish, Hen on basketweave base, fired-on colors, Challinor, Taylor, 7 1/8" l. (ILLUS. right w/Rooster) **225-250**

Animal covered dish, Lion on scroll base, 5 3/4" l. (ILLUS.).. **75**

Rare Monkey On Grass Mound Dish

Animal covered dish, Monkey on Grass Mound w/leaf & scroll patt. base, 6 1/4" l. (ILLUS.) **1,800-2,000**
Animal covered dish, Owl Head on split-ribbed base, McKee.............................. **800-1,000**

Hen on Basketweave Base Dish

Animal covered dish, Hen on basketweave base, red painted comb & eyes, Fostoria (also comes in pink & aqua), 7 1/8" (ILLUS.)... **120**
Animal covered dish, Hen w/amethyst head, lacy base, Atterbury...................... **200-225**
Animal covered dish, Horse on split-ribbed base, McKee **275-300**

Pintail Duck Covered Dish

Animal covered dish, Pintail Duck on basketweave base, Westmoreland Specialty Co., 5 1/4" l. (ILLUS.) **90**
Animal covered dish, Rabbit, Flat-Eared Rabbit on split-ribbed base, McKee, 5 1/2" l. **300**

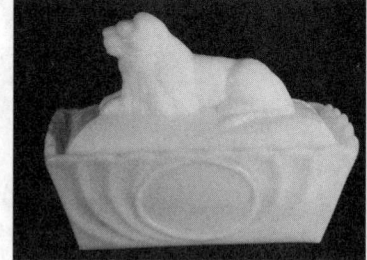

Blue & White Lamb Covered Dish

Animal covered dish, Lamb on picket base, blue body & white head, Westmoreland Specialty Co., 5 1/2" l. (ILLUS.).......... **120**
Animal covered dish, Lion, Majestic Lion, molded bird & foliage base, 6 3/4" h. **2,600**

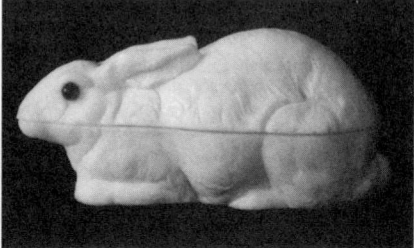

Atterbury Rabbit Dish

Animal covered dish, Rabbit, original red glass eyes, patent date stamped on bottom, Atterbury, 9" l. (ILLUS.) **250-275**
Animal covered dish, Robin on pedestal nest, signed "Vallerysthal" **200-225**
Animal covered dish, Rooster on basketweave base, fired-on colors, Challinor, Taylor, 7 1/8" l. (ILLUS. left w/Hen)... **450-475**
Animal covered dish, Rooster on wide rib base, Westmoreland Specialty Company, 5 1/2" l. **45**

Lion on Scroll Base Dish

Standing Rooster Covered Dish

Animal covered dish, Rooster, standing, blue, signed "Portieux" (ILLUS.) **110**

Snail on Strawberry Covered Dish

Animal covered dish, Snail on Strawberry, traces of paint, Vallerysthal, France, 5 1/8" (ILLUS.) **125**

Covered Dish with Squirrel Finial

Animal covered dish, Squirrel as finial on baroque-style lid & base, Portieux, France, 5" l. (ILLUS.)................................ **95-100**

Squirrel on Acorn Covered Dish

Animal covered dish, Squirrel as handle on acorn-form dish w/oak leaf base, L.G. Wright, 7 1/4" l. (ILLUS.) **75**

Animal covered dish, Squirrel on acorn-shaped base, signed "Vallerysthal," 7 1/4" l. **255**

Portieux Swan Covered Dish

Animal covered dish, Swan, "Cere," un-marked, Portieux, France, 5 1/4" l. (ILLUS.) **300-325**

"Square Block Swan" Covered Dish

Animal covered dish, Swan, "Square Block Swan," w/original blue eyes w/black pupils, Challinor, Taylor, 7" l. (ILLUS.)................ **350**

Animal covered dish, Swan w/raised wings & glass eyes on lacy-edged base, Atterbury, 9 1/2" l.................................... **150-175**

Animal covered dish, Turkey on ribbed base, McKee, 5 1/2" l. **85**

Animal covered dish, Turkey on split-ribbed base, McKee............................... **250-275**

Animal covered dish, Turtle on two-handled oblong base, Westmoreland Specialty Co., overall 7 1/2" l. **225-250**

Basket, chick emerging from egg on cover, two-handled.. **75**

Bowl, 7" d., 5" h., Chain & Petal Edge patt. **35**

Bowl, 8" d., footed Wide Weave Basket design, Atterbury, open.......................... **60**

Bowl, 8 3/4" d., 3 1/2" h., Crinkled Lacy Edge patt. **38**

Rectangular Open Edge Bowl

Bowl, 8 3/4 x 9 1/4", rectangular w/open edge loop border (ILLUS.) **55-60**

Bowl, 10" d., 4 1/2" h., Acanthus Leaf patt., all-white.. **75**

Bowl, 10" l., 5 3/4" h., oblong, Shell patt., two ribbed & two petal feet **55**

Box, cov., heart-shaped, embossed floral design highlighted w/touches of blue & gold, McKee **35**

Rabbit in Egg Covered Box

Box, cov., in the form of an egg, w/the head of a brown painted rabbit breaking out of the shell forming the handle of the lid, some floral & clover decoration also on lid, Gillinder, 3 3/4" h. (ILLUS.)...................... **135**

"Three Kittens" Covered Box

Box, cov., rectangular, w/scroll & bead decoration around rim, raised oval in center of lid featuring embossed "Three Kittens" design, traces of paint, hairline crack in lid, 5 1/2" (ILLUS.) **55**

Bread tray, Basketweave patt., Atterbury, patent-dated 1874, 9 3/4 x 12"........................ **65**

Bust of Admiral Dewey

Bust, Admiral Dewey, satin finish, 5 1/2" h. (ILLUS.) **175**

Butter dish, cov., Blackberry patt........................ **75**

Butter dish, cov., Daisy & Tree of Life patt. **175**

Cake stand, Lacy Edge patt., Atterbury, 12" d., 2 3/4" h.. **55**

Challinor, Taylor "Scroll" Compote

Compote, 8" h., round, "Scroll," on stepped base, Challinor, Taylor (ILLUS.) **210**

Compote, cov., Melon with Leaf & Net patt., small size **75-90**

Compote, open, 7 1/2" h., Jenny Lind figural bust pedestal, ribbed bowl **85**

Goddess of Liberty Compote

Compote, open, 7 5/8" h., Goddess of Liberty patt., figural stem (ILLUS.) **125-150**

Covered dish, Admiral Dewey on round basket base, "Dewey" on cover, 5 1/2" h. **300-350**

Covered dish, Automobile, signed "Portieux," France **175**

Covered dish, Battleship "Maine," 7 1/2" l., 3 1/2" h. **53**

Admiral Dewey Covered Dish

Covered dish, bust of Admiral Dewey on scroll base, possibly Flaccus, 5 1/2" l. (ILLUS.) **175**

Covered dish, Hand & Dove on lacy-edged base, Atterbury, 8 3/4" l., 4 3/4" h. **125-150**

Pear Covered Dish

Covered dish, Pear, lid in the form of the stem end of a pear set into a leaf-form dish (also found as apple, usually w/traces of paint), Westmoreland Specialty Co. (ILLUS.) **75**

Covered dish, Santa Claus, Santa on Sleigh base, large head, Westmoreland Specialty Company, early 20th c., 5 1/2" l. **90-125**

Covered dish, Snare Drum w/Cannon finial, 4 1/2" d., 4" h. **70-90**

Creamer, Apple Blossom patt., decorated & w/yellow band **25**

Creamer, "Oval Panel," Challinor, Taylor (ILLUS. on page 744left w/Sugar & Spooner) **70**

Creamer, Paneled Flower patt. **85**

Creamer, Swan patt., 5" h. **50-60**

Creamer, miniature, Owl w/glass eyes, 3 1/2" h. **40**

"Diapered Flower" Creamer & Sugar

"Paneled Forget-Me-Not" Creamer & Sugar

Creamer & sugar, cov., "Diapered Flower" patt., grey-blue w/gold accents, the set (ILLUS., bottom previous page) **90**

Creamer & sugar, cov., "Paneled Forget-Me-Not" patt., Westmoreland Specialty Co., the set (ILLUS., top of page) **90**

Creamer & sugar, cov., "Primrose" ("Primula") patt., w/traces of gold paint, Westmoreland Specialty Co., the set (ILLUS., bottom of page) **45-55**

Dresser bottles w/stoppers, Leaf patt., green & gold decoration, 10" h., pr. **50**

Dresser jar, cov., Versailles patt., 3 x 3 1/2" **65**

Dresser tray, Actress patt., Fostoria Glass Co. **55-65**

Egg, blown, w/multicolored floral decoration & legend "An Easter Anthem," 7 3/4" l. (ILLUS., to the right) **85**

Inkwell, model of a Minstrel boy **125-135**

Jar, cov., embossed British royal arms on sides, figural bust portrait of Queen Victoria on cover. **125**

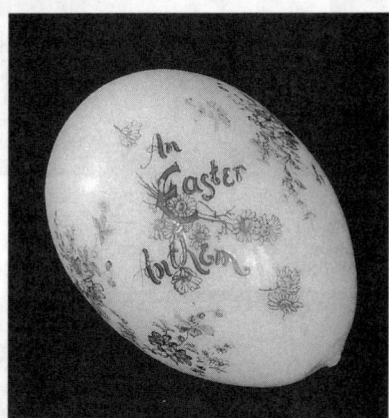

"An Easter Anthem" Decorative Egg

"Primrose" Creamer & Sugar

Miniature Oil Lamp

Lamp, figural miniature, oil-type, "Reclining Elephant" base, original shade, some paint, 7 3/4" h. (ILLUS.).......................... **750-800**

Indian Head Match Holder

Match holder, Indian Head, in feathered headdress, satin finish, Challinor, Taylor, 4 3/4" h. (ILLUS.).. **95**

Match holder, model of bulldog head w/striker on back of head, possibly McKee, 2 1/4" h. **125-150**

Match holder, pierced for hanging, basket-shaped w/scrolls & relief-molded painted rabbit & chick, attributed to Eagle Glass Co. **125**

Mug, Swan & Cattails patt. **45**

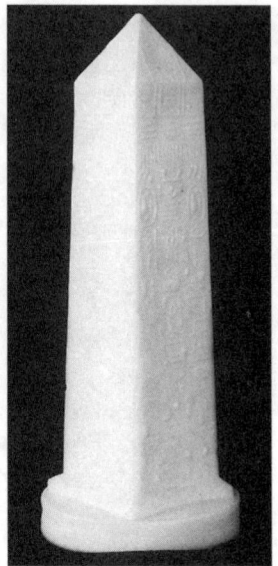

Cleopatra's Needle Obelisk

Obelisk, in the form of Cleopatra's Needle, unknown maker, possibly English, 8 1/2" h. (ILLUS.) **120**

Pickle dish, model of a fish, Atterbury, 5 1/4 x 8" **32**

Challinor, Taylor Fish Pickle Dish

Pickle dish, model of a fish on base, waffle pattern on sides, glass or molded eyes, Challinor, Taylor & Company, 9" l., 3" h. (ILLUS.) **125**

"Birds on Branch" Pitcher

Pitcher, 5 3/4" h., "Birds on Branch," paint on embossed elements, maker unknown (ILLUS.) 145
Pitcher, milk, 7" h., Block Daisy patt. 70
Pitcher, water, Wild Iris patt. 75
Pitcher, tankard-type, Opaque Scroll patt. 125
Plate, 4 3/8" d., Rising Sun patt. 50
Plate, 6" d., Three Puppies patt., open leaf border, Westmoreland Specialty Company, early 20th c. 125
Plate, 6 3/4" d., Easter Rabbits, in cabbage patch, old paint 45
Plate, 7" d., Challinor's Forget-Me-Not patt. 40
Plate, 7" d., Roger Williams Memorial, flag, fleur-de-lis & eagles border 150-160

Three Bears Plate

Plate, 7" d., Three Bears patt., traces of original brown, green & gilt paint (ILLUS.) 65
Plate, 7 1/4" d., "Easter," rabbits & eggs, scroll border 38
Plate, 7 1/4" d., Lacy-Edge Indian patt., good paint 50-75
Plate, 7 1/4" d., Pansy patt., molded openwork border 50-75
Plate, 7 1/2" d., Crown Border patt. 30
Plate, 7 1/2" d., Hare & Cloverleaf patt., scalloped & beaded border 70-90
Plate, 7 1/2" d., Yoked Slatted Border patt. 30-40
Plate, 6 1/2 x 7 3/4", Horseshoe & Anchor patt., patent-dated on back "December 10, 1901" 55
Plate, 8" d., Fan & Circle Border patt., Atterbury 30
Plate, 8" d., Single Forget-Me-Not patt., openwork border 20
Plate, 8" sq., Backward-C Border patt. 45

Lattice Edge Plate with Decoration

Plate, 9" d., Lattice Edge Border patt., painted trumpet vine center decoration (ILLUS.) 45-65

Lincoln on Backward C Border Plate

Plate, 9 1/4" d., Lincoln on Backward C Border, embossed "Lincoln" under profile, L.E. Smith (ILLUS.) 65
Plate, 11" d., Pinwheel Border patt., shallow pedestal, h.p. center 50
Platter, 10 1/2 x 13 3/4", model of a fish, flattened form w/scale details, Atterbury, patent-dated "June 4, 1872" 125-150
Relish dish, model of a bird, flattened form w/oval dished center, attributed to Hemingray Glass Company, ca. 1876, 5 x 10 3/4", 2" h. 95
Salt dip, footed, Strawberry patt. 40
Salt dip, model of a basket w/handle, Atterbury, patent-dated, excellent, 3 3/4" l. 45-50

Swan Salt Dip

Salt dip, model of a swan, signed "Meisenthal" inside, 4" l. (ILLUS.) 75
Salt & pepper shakers w/original tops, Heron & Lighthouse patt., each 75
Salt & pepper shakers w/original tops, Scroll patt., pr. 50
Salt shaker w/original top, Twisted Scroll patt. 20
Smoke bell, cranberry trim on fluted rim, w/original brass chain, 7" h. 120
Spooner, Acanthus Leaf patt., base marked "Pat'd Apr. 23, '78," 4 5/8" h. 55
Spooner, Blackberry patt. 50
Spooner, Flower & Panel patt. 40
Spooner, "Oval Panel," Challinor, Taylor (ILLUS. right w/Creamer & Sugar, top next page) 60

"Oval Panel" Creamer, Covered Sugar & Spooner

Sugar bowl, cov., Melon with Leaf patt., patent-dated 1878...................................... **90-110**

Sugar bowl, cov., model of a beehive, Vallerysthal.. **85**

Sugar bowl, cov., "Oval Panel," Challinor, Taylor (ILLUS. center w/Creamer & Spooner, top of page).. **95**

"Ovale Sucrier" Sugar Bowl

Sugar bowl, cov., "Ovale Sucrier," Portieux, France, 6 3/4" h. (ILLUS.)............................... **80**

Roman Cross Sugar Bowl

Sugar bowl, cov., Roman Cross patt. (ILLUS.)... **65**

Sugar bowl, cov., Versailles patt., pink decoration, 6" h.. **45**

Sugar shaker w/original top, Challinor's Forget-Me-Not patt. **110**

Sugar shaker w/original top, Little Shrimp patt. **75**

Atterbury Syrup Pitcher

Syrup pitcher, w/clip-on metal lid, Atterbury, 5 1/2" h. (ILLUS.) **145**

Syrup pitcher w/original top, Challinor's Banded Shells patt., h.p. apple blossoms & green shells.. **95**

Syrup pitcher w/original top, Heavy Scroll patt. **75**

Syrup pitcher w/original top, Torquay patt., h.p. yellow stripes **150**

Toothpick holder, Horseshoe & Clover patt. **40-50**

Hand Holding Fan Tray

Tray, Hand Holding Fan, attached red stone in ring on finger, Atterbury, 9 1/2" l. (ILLUS.).. **125**
Tray, Dahlia (in corners) patt., 8 x 10 1/4" **50**
Tray, Diamond Grill patt. center, "Give Us This Day" border, 10 x 12"................................ **25**

Miniature Covered Tureen

Tureen, cov., miniature, notched, Gillinder, 4" l. (ILLUS.)... **38**

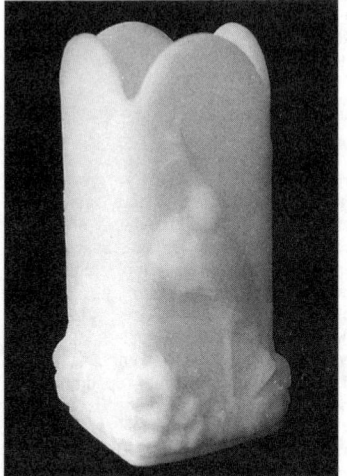

Stork Vase

Vase, 4 1/4" h., Stork, designed by Joseph Locke, New England Glass Co., ca. 1884, also found in art glass Amberina (ILLUS.) **275-300**

Scroll Pattern Water Set

Water set: tankard-type pitcher & four tumblers; Scroll patt., Challinor, Taylor & Company, 1880s, 5 pcs. (ILLUS.)................. **245**
Whimsey, model of a canoe, enameled flowers & gold trim, 6" l. **15**
Whimsey, model of a Straw Hat (College Hat), w/old paint, McKee, 4" d. **55**
Whimsey, model of Uncle Sam's Hat, color decoration, w/coin bank closure inside brim **90**
Whimsey vase, model of a hand holding a cornucopia, ruffled rim, 8 1/2" h....................... **90**

Opalescent

Presently, this is one of the most popular areas of glass collecting. The opalescent effect was attained by adding bone ash chemicals to areas of an item while still hot and refiring the object at tremendous heat. Both pressed and mold-blown patterns are available to collectors and we distinguish the types in our listing below. Opalescent Glass from A to Z by the late William Heacock is the definitive reference book for collectors.

Mold-blown Opalescent Patterns

Arabian Nights
Pitcher, 9" h., bulbous ovoid body, short cylindrical ringed neck w/ruffled rim, applied handle, clear... **$650**
Pitcher, 9" h., bulbous ovoid body, short cylindrical ringed neck w/ruffled rim & arched spout, applied handle, cranberry w/clear applied handle **3,000**
Tumbler, blue.. **140**
Tumbler, cranberry **350**
Tumbler, satin finish, blue.................................. **160**

Big Windows
Pitcher, 9" h., spherical body w/slightly tapering cylindrical neck, flat rim w/pinched spout, blue w/translucent blue applied handle (interior residue).................................. **475**

Big Windows Swirl
Celery, ovoid body w/short, slightly tapered neck, blue (bruises & flaking to rim).............. **140**

Water bottle, spherical body w/cylindrical neck flaring out at rim, blue (flat chip on outside rim) 130

Blown Drapes
Pitcher, 9 3/8" h., bulbous ovoid body, short cylindrical neck, flaring ruffled rim, blue w/translucent blue applied handle 425
Tumbler, clear 80
Tumbler, cranberry 200
Tumbler, cranberry, vertical stripes connect drapery 170

Buttons & Braids
Tumbler, blue 90
Tumbler, cranberry 200
Tumbler, green 60
Water set: 9 3/4" h. pitcher & four tumblers; pitcher w/bulbous ovoid body, short cylindrical neck & flaring ruffled rim, tumblers w/cylindrical shape tapering out slightly at rim, blue, 5 pcs. (rim chip to one tumbler) 550

Christmas Snowflake
Tumbler, cranberry 200

Christmas Snowflake (L.G. Wright)
Sugar shaker w/original top, cobalt, 4 3/4" h. 120

Christmas Snowflake, Ribbed
Pitcher, 9" h., slightly ovoid body w/tapering shoulder, cylindrical neck & ruffled rim, cranberry w/clear applied handle **2,400**
Tumbler, blue 160
Tumbler, cranberry (open bubble on rim) 170

Chrysanthemum Swirl
Butter, cov., short, slightly tapering cylindrical base w/domed lid tapering to clear knob finial, cranberry (small open bubble on base interior) 400
Pitcher, 8 7/8" h., tapering cylindrical body on squatty ovoid base, short neck, flat rim w/pinched spout, applied handle, blue **1,000**
Spooner, cranberry, slightly tapering body on squatty lobed base, light opalescence 300
Tumbler, blue 100
Tumbler, cranberry 170

Chrysanthemum Swirl Variant
Pitcher, water, 10 3/4" h., tankard type, flat rim w/pinched spout, cranberry w/clear applied handle **2,800**

Coin Spot
Pitcher, water, 8" h., bulbous body, no neck, hexagonal ruffled rim, clear w/light tint 90
Pitcher, water, 9 1/2" h., bulbous ovoid body w/cylindrical neck, flaring crimped rim, applied handle, green 240

Coin Spot Nine-Panel
Sugar shaker w/period lid, blue, 4 3/4" h. 210

Coin Spot & Swirl
Syrup w/period lid, blue, 6" h. 140
Tumbler, butterscotch amber shading to clear 80

Criss Cross
Tumbler, light cranberry ....
Tumbler, rubina 210
Tumbler, satin finish, cranberry 200

Daffodils
Tumbler, blue 200
Tumbler, clear (rim chip) 140
Tumbler, green 190

Daisy & Fern
Pitcher, 8 5/8" h., spherical body, short cylindrical neck, flaring crimped rim, light blue w/translucent blue applied handle 230
Rose bowl, bulbous ovoid body on short disc foot, ruffled, incurved rim, cranberry, 3 3/4" h. 200
Syrup w/period lid, blue, WVA Optic mold, w/patent date, 6 1/2" h. (small split in lid) 275
Tumbler, Swirl mold, blue, 3 3/4" h. 110
Water set: 8 1/2" h. pitcher & five tumblers; the pitcher w/spherical bulbous body, short cylindrical neck, flared ruffled rim, applied clear handle, the tumblers cylinder-shaped tapering very slightly at rim, cranberry, strong opalescence, 6 pcs. (one tumbler w/rim crack, one w/exterior rim chip) 900

Daisy in Criss-Cross
Pitcher, 9" h., bulbous ovoid body, short cylindrical ringed neck, widely flaring ruffled rim, green light opalescence w/translucent green applied handle 550
Pitcher, 9" h., bulbous ovoid body, short cylindrical ringed neck, widely flaring ruffled rim, green milky swirled opalescence w/translucent green applied handle 900
Tumbler, blue 100
Tumbler, clear 80
Tumbler, cranberry 250
Tumbler, green, light opalescence 170

Diamonds
Punch cup, blue, crackled finish, translucent blue applied handle 25
Tumbler, blue, crackle finish 80
Tumbler, reverse rubina (flake & tiny bruise on rim) 90

Fern
Creamer, squatty bulbous body w/slightly arched spout, applied handle, clear 150
Pitcher, 8 1/2" h., bulbous ovoid body w/cylindrical neck & square top, cranberry, clear applied handle **2,100**
Pitcher, 8 3/4" h., ovoid body, cylindrical neck tapering to slightly ruffled rim, blue w/translucent blue applied handle 650
Salt shaker w/inappropriate top, cranberry 180
Salt shaker w/period top, blue 130
Tumbler, blue 140
Tumbler, cranberry 210

Herringbone
Pitcher, 8 3/4" h., ovoid body, cylindrical neck, flared spout, blue w/translucent blue applied handle **1,150**

Herringbone Mold-blown Pitcher

Pitcher, 9" h., ovoid body, cylindrical neck, flared spout, cranberry w/clear applied handle (ILLUS.) **5,000**
Tumbler, blue 70
Tumbler, cranberry... 210

Herringbone Plain
Tumbler, Canary, without ribs 230

Honeycomb
Pitcher, 7 1/2" h., spherical bulbous body, cylindrical neck, flaring crimped rim, blue, clear reeded applied handle, light opalescence (tiny flake to body)................................ 160
Tumbler, canary w/enamel floral decoration, polished base... 140

Mold-blown Opalescent patterns

Opaline Brocade, Spanish Lace
Barber bottle, waisted body w/long, slender cylindrical neck flaring at lip, cranberry, 7 1/2" h... **1,900**
Butter dish, cov., clear & opalescent round scalloped base, cranberry dome lid w/closed bubble, 5 1/2" h. (flakes to rim of cover)... **1,000**
Celery vase, cylindrical form on bulbous squatty base, wide, deeply ruffled rim, canary, 6" h.. 180
Celery vase, cylindrical form on bulbous squatty base, wide, deeply ruffled rim, cranberry, 6" h... 425
Finger bowl, deep rounded body, flat rim, blue, 2 3/4" h... 90
Pitcher, 8 1/2" h., squat mold, wide cylindrical body tapering to cylindrical neck w/ruffled rim, applied handle, blue................. 600
Rose bowl, bulbous ovoid body on disc foot, incurved ruffled rim, canary, 3 3/4" h.. 70
Salt & pepper shakers w/period tops, ribbon tie mold, clear, 3" h., pr........................... 100
Tumbler, blue.. 60
Tumbler, canary... 120
Tumbler, cranberry.. 160
Tumbler, cranberry, unusual ridge on interior.. 90
Tumbler, green 60-65

Water bottle, bulbous ovoid body, waisted neck ringed at shoulder & flaring at rim, quadruple plated mount, cranberry, 8" h....... **500**
Water set: 9 1/2" h. pitcher & five tumblers; the pitcher w/bulbous body tapering at base & neck, deeply ruffled rim, clear reeded applied handle on pitcher, the tumblers slightly tapering cylinder shape, cranberry, 6 pcs. (two tumblers w/exterior rim flakes) **950**

Poinsettia
Tumbler, blue.. 200
Tumbler, clear.. 140
Tumbler, cranberry 240
Tumbler, green 130-160
Tumbler, satin finish, blue................................... 110

Polka Dot
Tumbler, blue.. 140

Reverse Swirl
Celery, slightly ovoid form w/short cylindrical neck, blue, 4 1/2" d., 6" h. (small bruise)... 110
Covered butter, short, squatty base & lid, transparent knob finial, blue, 5 3/4" d., 4 1/2" h. (lid slightly darker shade than base) 210
Covered sugar, slightly ovoid body, short squatty lid w/transparent finial, blue, 6" d., 6 1/4" h... 300
Creamer, slightly ovoid body, short cylindrical neck, flat rim w/pinched spout, blue w/transparent blue applied handle, 5 1/2" h.. 100
Finger bowl, squatty bulbous body, short cylindrical neck, blue, 4 1/2" d., 2 1/4" h. (small inner rim chip) 90
Pitcher, water, 9" h., blue, w/translucent blue applied handle (horizontal base crack)... 60
Punch cup, blue, transparent blue applied handle, 2 1/2" d., 2" h. 30
Salt & pepper shakers w/period lids, blue, 2" d., 2 1/4" h., pr. 130
Spooner, slightly ovoid body, short slightly tapering neck, blue, 3 1/4" d., 4" h. 80
Sugar shaker w/period top, blue, 4 3/4"h. 230
Sugar shaker w/period top, pale canary opalescent, 4 1/2" h.................................. 220
Syrup w/period lid, blue w/transparent blue applied handle, silver-plate lid w/patent date, 7" h.. 350
Syrup w/period lid, pale canary opalescent, 6 1/2" h.................................. 350
Toothpick holder, blue, ovoid shape 60
Tumbler, blue (rim flake).. 50
Tumbler, canary 100
Tumbler, cranberry 150
Tumbler, satin finish, blue w/white speckles 80
Water bottle, spherical body w/cylindrical neck tapering at ringed shoulder & slightly flaring rim, blue, 4 1/4" d., 7" h................ 50
Water bottle, spherical body w/cylindrical neck tapering at ringed shoulder & slightly flaring rim, cranberry, 5 1/4" d., 8 1/4" h. 425

Ribbed Opal Lattice

Pitcher, water, 10" h., tankard-type, blue w/translucent blue applied handle 550
Pitcher, water, 10 1/8" h., tankard-type, cranberry w/clear applied handle **1,700**
Salt & pepper shakers w/period lids, cranberry, 3 1/8" h., pr. (tops w/minor damage) 180
Sugar shaker w/period lid, blue, 4 1/2" h. 190
Sugar shaker w/period lid, cranberry, 4 1/2" h. 400
Syrup w/period lid, blue, 6 3/4" h. 375
Tumbler, blue 70
Tumbler, cranberry 100-135

Scottish Moor

Scottish Moor Water Pitcher

Pitcher, water, 8 1/4" h., cranberry, waisted form w/arched spout, applied reeded handle, polished pontil (ILLUS.) **5,300**
Tumbler, cranberry (rim flakes) 220

Seaweed

Pitcher, 9" h., bulbous body w/triangular crimped rim, cranberry w/clear applied handle (some exterior scratches & surface flake left of the lower handle attachment) 850
Pitcher, 9" h., bulbous ovoid body w/triangular crimped rim, arched spout, blue w/translucent blue applied handle 500
Sugar shaker w/period lid, cranberry, satin finish, 5" h. (tiny surface flake to body) **1,000**
Tumbler, cranberry 120-150
Tumbler, satin finish, blue 90
Tumbler, satin finish, cranberry 140

Stars & Stripes

Barber bottle, bulbous body tapering to tall cylindrical neck, flaring at lip, blue, polished pontil, 7" h. 275
Barber bottle, bulbous body tapering to tall cylindrical neck, flaring at lip, period spout, cranberry, polished pontil, 7" h. 425

Stars and Stripes Tankard

Pitcher, tankard-type, cranberry w/clear applied handle, 8 1/4" h. (ILLUS.) **4,700**
Tumbler, clear 300

Stars & Stripes Tumbler

Tumbler, cranberry (ILLUS.) 300

Stripe

Pitcher, 9 1/2" h., spherical body, short cylindrical neck w/tricorner rim, canary w/translucent canary applied ribbed handle w/unique faint opalescent striping within 800
Pitcher, 9 1/4" h., tapering ovoid body, ring neck, ruffled rim, cranberry w/clear applied handle **1,600**
Pitcher, 9 1/2" h., bulbous ovoid body tapering to neck, flared crimped rim, light blue w/translucent blue applied handle 600
Tumbler, blue, wide area between stripes 60
Tumbler, cranberry 90

Swastika

Tumbler, clear 325
Tumbler, green (polished rim w/interior flake) 350

Swirl

Barber bottle, blue, polished pontil, 7 1/4" h. 180
Pitcher, water, 8 1/4" h., blue ball form w/short neck, square top w/three crimps on each side 275
Pitcher, 8 1/2" h., ovoid body tapering to square top, cranberry w/clear applied handle 600

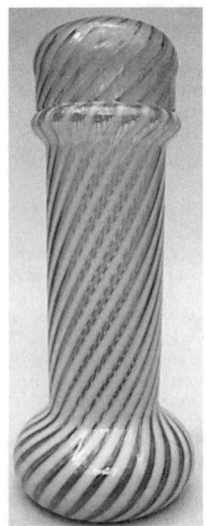

Swirl Covered Straw Jar

Straw jar, cov., cylinder shape on squat bulbous base, short tapered rim, dome lid, blue, small flakes on interior rim of cover, 11 1/4" h. (ILLUS.) **4,100**

Tankard, flat rim w/pinched spout, cranberry w/clear ribbed applied handle, 9" h........ **2,800**

Tumbler, blue **80**

Tumbler, cranberry (polished rim) **110**

Tumbler, green (polished rim).............................. **40**

Tumbler, rubina.. **90**

Tumbler, satin finish, blue (flake on rim interior) **40**

Vase, 7 3/4" h., bulbous shape, short cylindrical neck w/rolled-over rim, small rough pontil, clear w/light tint **130**

Water set: 8 1/2" h. pitcher & five tumblers; the pitcher w/bulbous ovoid body tapering to flared square top, the tumblers slightly tapering cylinder shape, blue, 6 pcs. (one tumbler damaged) **400**

Swirling Maze

Bowl, 3 3/4" h., w/ruffled, crimped edge, cranberry.. **150**

Tumbler, blue **80**

Tumbler, clear **160**

Tumbler, cranberry.. **130-160**

Twist, Blown

Sugar shaker w/period lid, blue, 4 3/4" h....... **250**

Tumbler, blue **110**

Tumbler, cranberry.. **275**

Tumbler, green (underfill w/undissolved metal on interior) **210**

Wide Stripe

Tumbler, cranberry.. **110**

Windows (Hobbs No. 333)

Condiment set: two shakers w/two-part tops, mustard pot w/two-part hinged lid, one bottle w/clear blown hollow stopper, all fitted into unmarked quadruple plate 9 1/4" h. Victorian frame; blue, the set **1,500**

Pitcher, 8 5/8" h., tapering ovoid body, flaring tricorner rim, blue w/deep translucent blue applied handle.. **350**

Pitcher, water, 8 5/8" h., bulbous ovoid body w/flaring square top, blue w/deep translucent blue applied handle.................... **425**

Pitcher, water, 9" h., slightly ovoid body w/tapered shoulder, cylindrical neck flaring to tricorner crimped rim, cranberry, heavy opalescence.................................... **850**

Tumbler, blue **70**

Tumbler, clear **100**

Tumbler, cranberry.. **100**

Windows Swirl

Celery, gently ovoid form w/short tapered neck w/crimped rim, blue, 3 1/2 x 4", 6" h. **100**

Covered sugar, squatty bulbous base, cylindrical lid tapering to faceted finial, cranberry, 5 1/2" h. (short crack in lid) **60**

Sugar shaker w/period lid, clear opalescent, 5" h. (dents to top)................................. **180**

Tumbler, blue **110**

Tumbler, cranberry.. **120**

Pressed Opalescent Patterns

Argonaut Shell

Tumbler, blue.. **60**

Beatty Honeycomb

Celery vase, cylindrical form, flat rim, blue, 6 1/4" h.. **60**

Sugar shaker w/period lid, clear opalescent, 4" h. **160**

Tumbler, blue.. **70**

Beatty Rib

Tumbler, blue (tiny bubble on two ribs) **40**

Beatty Swirl

Celery, cylindrical form, scalloped rim, blue (small flake, interior sickness).................... **90**

Pitcher, water, 7 3/4" h., cylindrical form w/scalloped rim & raised spout, angled applied handle, pale canary **240**

Circled Scroll

Compote, jelly, 4 3/4" d., 4 1/2" h., blue **90**

Tumbler, clear.. **35**

Tumbler, green (three pattern flakes) **40**

Diamond Spearhead

Syrup pitcher w/period top, green opalescent, 5 1/2" h. (lid w/worn surface)................ **900**

Tumbler, canary **90**

Tumbler, cobalt blue.. **160**

Tumbler, green **50**

Dolly Madison

Tumbler, green (tiny flake on one rib)................. **45**

Double Greek Key

Tumbler, clear.. **80**

Duchess

Tumbler, clear.. **30**

Flora

Tumbler, canary (flaking, roughness on edge of base).. **80**

Intaglio
Tumbler, blue w/traces of gilt decoration............. 50

Inverted Fan & Feather
Tumbler, blue w/gilt decoration 60
Tumbler, clear w/gilt decoration (rough-
ness, flakes on base).. 25

Iris With Meander
Tumbler, canary.. 60

Jewel & Flower
Tumbler, blue w/gilt decoration 80
Tumbler, canary w/gilt decoration...................... 100

Jeweled Heart
Tumbler, apple green... 40

Lustre Flute
Tumbler, clear... 45

Over-All Hob
Bone dish, scalloped rim, clear,
3 1/4 x 6 1/2", 1 3/8" h. 20
Tumbler, amethyst (chips under base) 100

Palm Beach/#15119
Tumbler, blue 40
Tumbler, canary.. 160

Panelled Holly
Tumbler, blue w/gilt decoration 60

Regal (Northwood)
Tumbler, green (several flakes under base)........ 40

Ribbed Opal Rings
Tumbler, blue 130
Tumbler, cranberry... 200

Ribbed Spiral
Tumbler, blue (flake on edge of base) 70
Tumbler, canary (chip & flake on edge of
base) 70

S-Repeat
Tumbler, blue.. 45-55

Shell (New York)
Tumbler, blue... 45

Sunburst-on-Shield
Tumbler, blue... 100

Swag With Brackets
Tumbler, blue... 40

Swag with Brackets
Tumbler, green (flakes under two feet).............. 90

Water Lily & Cattails
Tumbler, amethyst (pattern flake)........................ 60
Tumbler, blue 40
Tumbler, green (chip on fin above pattern)........ 30
Tumbler, light cobalt blue.................................... 40

Wild Bouquet
Tumbler, blue 60
Tumbler, clear 50
Tumbler, green 70

Wreath & Shell
Tumbler, collared, canary 50
Tumbler, footed, canary 150

Tumbler, footed, clear (pattern flakes & mi-
nor roughness) 30

Miscellaneous Pressed Novelties
Diamond Point vase, 13 1/2" h., tall waisted cylindrical form on disc base, ruffled
rim, clear, swung... 60

Overshot

*Popular since the mid-19th century, Overshot glass
was produced by having a gather of molten glass rolled
in finely crushed glass to produce a rough exterior finish. The piece was then blown to the desired size and
shape. The finished piece has a frosted or iced finish and
is sometimes referred to as "ice glass." Early producers
referred to this glass as "Craquelle" and, although
Overshot is sometimes lumped together with the glass
collectors now call "crackle," that type was produced
using a totally different technique.*

Cologne bottle, clear body & stopper
w/three blue applied reeded feet,
8 3/4" h. $190
Goblet, blown, clear w/gilded rim, 6" h. 20
Pitcher, water, 8" h., bulbous ovoid body
w/cylindrical neck, flat rim, applied reeded handle, polished pontil, cranberry.............. 90
Pitcher, water, tankard-type, 10" h., blue
waisted body w/applied amber rigaree
rim & reeded handle, polished pontil 230
Pitcher, champagne, 12" h., ewer shape
w/ice bladder opening at the back, cranberry w/clear applied handle & rigaree,
polished pontil.. 500
Plates, 8 3/4" d., cranberry w/gilt scalloped
rims, set of 6 (small rim chips) 100

Pattern

*Though it has never been ascertained whether glass
was first pressed in the United States or abroad, the
development of the glass pressing machine revolutionized the glass industry in the United States, and this
country receives the credit for improving the method to
make this process feasible. The first wares pressed were
probably small flat plates of the type now referred to as
"lacy," the intricacy of the design concealing flaws.*

*In 1827, both the New England Glass Co., Cam-
bridge, Mass., and Bakewell & Co., Pittsburgh, took out
patents for pressing glass furniture knobs; soon other
pieces followed. This early pressed glass contained red
lead, which made it clear and resonant when tapped
(flint.) Made primarily in clear, it is rarer in blue, amethyst, olive green and yellow.*

*By the 1840s, early simple patterns such as Ashbur-
ton, Argus and Excelsior appeared. Ribbed Bellflower
seems to have been one of the earliest patterns to have
had complete sets. By the 1860s, a wide range of patterns was available.*

*In 1864, William Leighton of Hobbs, Brockunier &
Co., Wheeling, West Virginia, developed a formula for
"soda lime" glass that did not require the expensive red
lead for clarity. Although "soda lime" glass did not have
the brilliance of the earlier flint glass, the formula came
into widespread use because glass could be produced
cheaply.*

An asterisk (*) indicates a piece which has been reproduced.

Ashman
Cake stand, round plate on stepped square base, apple green, 9" d., 6 1/4" h. (two small flakes under rim) **$230**

Atlanta (Lion or Square Lion's Head)
Tumbler, clear **50**

Bellflower
Tumbler, fine rib, single vine, flint, vines flow to right, ribbed to rim, 3 1/2" h. **70**

Cord Drapery
Compote, open, jelly, deep round bowl w/small flared rim, disc base, 4 1/2" d., 4 1/4" h., blue (two rim chips) **130**
Tumbler, blue **125-170**

Croesus
*Tumbler, green w/gilt decoration **35-75**
*Tumbler, purple w/gilt decoration **50-75**

Cupid & Venus (Guardian Angel)
Bread plate, amber, round w/tab handles, 10 1/2" d. (small rim chip, minor wear) **35**

Currier & Ives
Tumbler, footed, amber **30**

Daisy & Button
Compote, open, jelly, 6" d., 5" h., high standard, canary (minor flakes) **140**
Lamp shade, amber, round, flaring out to scalloped rim, 5" d. fitter, 9 1/2" d., 4" h. (minor flakes, mold roughness to fitter) **40**
Pitcher, milk, 8" h., tankard-type, flat rim, applied reeded handle, canary **170**

Daisy & Button (Hobbs No. 101)
Ice cream set: oblong master tray & six square saucers; canary, tray 9 x 14", saucers 5 3/4" sq., the set **350**
Tray, clover-shaped, canary, 12 3/4 x 12 3/4" **110**

Daisy & Button with Thumbprint Panels
Cake stand, round plate, tapering quatrefoil base, canary, 10 1/2" d., 7 1/2" h. (chips & flakes) **220**
Creamer & cov. sugar bowl, canary, 7 3/4 & 5 1/2" h., pr. (some chips & flakes) **190**
Water set: 9" h. pitcher & 6 tumblers; canary, 7 pcs. (pitcher w/spout & foot flakes, one tumbler cracked) **350**

Dewey
Mug, Nile green (flake on rim, chip on foot) **190**
Tumbler, amber **25**
Tumbler, emerald green **35**

Gonterman
Tumbler, blue top, frosted base **120**

Hobnail
Toothpick holder, apple green, cylindrical, Hobbs, Brockunier & Co. **40**
Toothpick holder, canary, cylindrical, Hobbs, Brockunier & Co. (one hob w/flake) **50**

Toothpick holder, clear w/ruby-plated interior, cylindrical, Hobbs, Brockunier & Co. **90**

King's 500
Bowl, 8" d., blue **50**

Log Cabin

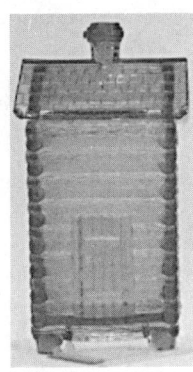

Log Cabin Covered Pickle/Jam Jar

Pickle/jam jar, cov., blue, minor flake & mold roughness on base rim, crack & corner chips on cover, base 2 5/8 x 3 1/8", 6 3/4" h. overall (ILLUS.) **1,050**

Medallion Sprig
Butter dish, cov., clear to cranberry, satin finish, knob lid handle, 7 1/8" d., 6 1/4" h. (some flakes) **80**
Tumblers, amethyst to clear, 3 3/4" h., set of 4 .... **120**

Pineapple & Fan
Tumbler, green **70**

Pleat & Panel
Bread tray, octagonal, closed angled handles, blue, 8 1/2 x 13" **150**

Priscilla
Tumbler, green w/gilt decoration **40**

Royal Ivy (Northwood)
Sugar shaker w/period top, frosted w/amber (dent to top) **750**
Sugar shaker w/period top, frosted rainbow craquelle, 4 1/8" h. **375**
Syrup pitcher w/period top, rubina, 6 1/4" h. (crack in upper handle) **150**
Toothpick holder, rubina crystal **60-85**
Tumbler, rubina (inner rim bruise) **25**
Tumbler, satin rubina **45-90**

Royal Oak (Northwood)
Pitcher, water, 8" h., satin rubina (small crack at base of handle) **180**

S-Repeat
Set: 7 1/2" h. cruet w/original stopper, salt & pepper shakers w/metal lids, toothpick holder, 6 3/4" d. round footed tray w/scalloped rim & skirt; blue, S-Repeat patt., 5 pcs. (one shaker w/interior residue, tray w/chip causing loss of one scallop on skirt) **350**

Teardrop & Tassel
Tumbler, Type 1, cobalt blue 50
Tumbler, Type 1, Nile green 375

Three Face

Three Face & Shell & Tassel Compote

Compote, open, 7 1/2" sq., 8 1/2" h.,
square Shell & Tassel bowl & Three Face
high standard molded in one piece, extremely rare, tiny flake on two foot points
(ILLUS.)...................................... **5,200**

Tree of Life - Portland
Waste bowls, cranberry lead glass, polished bases, 4 3/4" d., 2 3/4" h., pr. 70

Two Panel (Daisy in Panel)
Compote, cov., high standard, canary,
7 1/2 x 9 1/8", 12 3/4" h. (chip on interior
of lid flange)...................................... 170

Valencia Waffle (Block & Star)
Syrup w/period top, blue, 8" h. (light interi-
or residue, lid missing tab).............................. 100

Water Lily & Cattails
Tumbler, blue 35

Willow Oak
Cake stand, amber, 11" d., 5 1/4" h. 40

Ruby- & Amber-Stained

*This name "ruby-stained" derives from the color of
the glass, a deep red. The red staining was thinly painted
on clear pressed glass patterns and refired at a low temperature. Many pieces were further engraved as souvenir items and were very popular from the 1890s into the
1920s. This technique should not be confused with
"flashed" glass where a clear glass piece is actually
dipped in molten glass of a contrasting color. See PAT-
TERN GLASS.*

Amber
Bowl, cov., 8 1/2" d., 8" h. overall, Amber-
ette patt., George Duncan & Sons. (chip
& flakes)...................................... $130
Celery, Fine Cut & Block patt., turned-up
sides, 4 3/4 x 11 1/4", 3" h.............................. 50
Salt & pepper shakers w/period tops,
squat form, frosted w/amber, Klond-

ike/Amberette patt., pr. (one w/minor cor-
ner wear) 170
Tumbler, clear w/amber, Swirl patt.
Francesware...................................... 30
Tumbler, frosted w/amber stain, satin finish,
Klondike patt., Dalzell, Gilmore & Leight-
on...................................... 110
Tumbler, Superior patt., etched floral deco-
ration, 3 7/8" h. 150

Ruby
Pitcher, water, 11 3/4" h., tankard-type,
Pavonia patt., engraved foliate decora-
tion...................................... 300
Pitcher, water, 8 3/4" h., Broken Column
patt. 600
Pitcher, water, 12 1/4" h., tankard type,
Box-in-Box (Riverside No. 420) patt., Riv-
erside Glass Works (tiny pattern nicks)........ 350

Ruby-Stained Sugar Shaker

Sugar shaker, cov., Chandelier patt., w/pe-
riod brass lid, two short annealing lines
concealed by top, very minor wear to
prisms, 4 3/4" h. (ILLUS.) **2,500**
Tumbler, Art Navo patt., w/gilt decoration,
4" h. 45
Tumbler, Box-in-Box (Riverside No. 420)
patt., Riverside Glass Works (tiny pattern
nicks)...................................... 25
Tumbler, Cathedral patt., Bryce Bros. 50
Tumbler, Dakota patt., 3 5/8" h. 45
Tumbler, Eureka patt., National Glass Co. 180
Tumbler, Fleur-De-Lis patt., w/gilt decora-
tion, Bryce, Higbee & Co. (flake, some
wear to gilding) 60
Tumbler, Lorraine patt., New Martinsville
Glass Mfg. Co....................................... 45
Tumbler, Millard patt., engraved decora-
tion, 3 3/4" h. 50
Tumbler, Nail patt., 3 5/8" h....................... 50
Tumbler, Nearcut Daisy patt., w/gilt decora-
tion, Cambridge Glass Co. (nick under
one foot) 60
Tumbler, Nearcut Star patt., traces of gilt
decoration, 4" h. 50
Tumbler, New Jersey patt., 4" h. 300
Tumbler, Pleating patt., 3 1/2" h. 50
Tumbler, Shoshone patt., United States
Glass Co....................................... 35
Tumbler, Snail patt., 3 1/2" h.............................. 350

Tumbler, Torpedo patt., Thompson Glass Co. (bruises on line above pattern) **70**
Tumbler, Victoria patt., 3 1/2" h. **140**
Water set: 8 5/8" h. pitcher & six tumblers; Lorraine patt., the pitcher w/clear molded handle, New Martinsville Glass Mfg. Co., 7 pcs. **300**

Spatter

This variegated-color ware is similar to Spangled glass but does not contain metallic flakes. The various colors are applied on a clear, opaque white or colored body. Much of it was made in Europe and England. It is sometimes called "End Of Day."

Pitcher, water, 7 1/2" h., bulbous body w/short cylindrical neck, Ribbed Swirl patt., cased multicolor w/clear applied reeded handle, polished pontil **$150**
Pitcher, water, 7 3/4" h., bulbous ovoid base, flaring rim, blue & white w/applied clear reeded handle, polished pontil **160**
Pitcher, water, 7 3/4" h., spherical base w/cylindrical neck tapering out to tricorner rim, blood red & opal w/applied clear reeded handle, polished pontil **130**
Syrup pitcher w/reproduction lid, Royal Ivy patt. in pink & white, clear applied handle, 6 1/4" h. (crack in upper handle) **325**
Toothpick holder, Ribbed Pillar patt.,cranberry & opal spatter, satin finish (bruise on exterior of rim) **50**
Tumbler, overshot ruby & opal, Hobbs, Brockunier & Co. **100**
Water set: 8 1/2" h. pitcher & six tumblers; cranberry & opal, the pitcher w/bulbous base, ruffled rim & applied clear handle, 7 pcs. **350**

Tiffin

A wide variety of fine glasswares were produced by the Tiffin Glass Company of Tiffin, Ohio. Beginning as a part of the large U.S. Glass Company early in the 20th century, the Tiffin factory continued making a wide range of wares until its final closing in 1984. One popular line is now called "Black Satin" and included various vases with raised floral designs. Many other acid-etched and hand-cut patterns were also produced over the years and are very collectible today. The three "Tiffin Glassmasters" books by Fred Bickenheuser, are the standard references for Tiffin collectors.

Carafe, etched Roses patt., clear........................ **$80**
Champagne, etched Flanders patt., pink **42**
Champagne, etched June Night patt., clear, 6 oz. **40**
Cocktail, etched Cordelia patt. **20**
Compote, 7 1/2" twist stem, No. 315, vaseline satin.. **20**
Console set: 13" d. bowl w/deep everted rim & pair of candleholders; Fontaine etching, bowl No. 8153, candleholders No. 9758, twilite, 3 pcs. **400**
Creamer & sugar bowl, etched Fuchsia patt., clear, pr. **70**

Creamer & sugar bowl, etched June Night patt., clear, pr.. **80**
Flower bowl, cut Twilight patt., No. 9153-108, clear, 10" d. **180**
Goblet, Diamond Optic patt., All Rose-Pink, 10 oz. **25**
Goblet, etched Classic patt., clear...................... **35**
Goblet, etched Flanders patt., pink **60**
Goblet, etched Persian Pheasant patt., clear.. **38**
Goblet, water, etched Fuchsia patt., clear 7 5/8" h. **45**
Plate, 8 1/8" d., etched Fuchsia patt., clear........ **20**
Plate, 8" d., etched Flanders patt., yellow **17**
Rose bowl w/three ball feet, Copen blue, medium **70**
Sherbet, etched Fuchsia patt., clear **20**
Tumbler, footed, etched June Night patt., clear, 10 1/2 oz. **38**
Tumbler, iced tea, footed, Fuchsia patt., clear.. **35**
Tumbler, juice, footed, etched Persian Pheasant patt., clear, 5 oz. **25**
Vase, 5" h., etched Poppy patt., black amethyst **75**
Vase, 6 1/2" h., Black Satin ground w/alternating glossy stripes **65**
Vase, 6" h., four-footed, cut Twilight patt., clear... **185**
Vase, bud, 10" h., etched Cherokee Rose patt., clear.. **70**
Wine, etched June Night patt., clear................... **50**

Wall Pocket Vases

Amber, satin finish, style No. 16258 by Tiffin Glass Co., 3 7/8 x 9 1/4" **95-125**

Amethyst, morning glory shape, 7 3/4" l. **50-75**
Black, satin finish, Kimberley decoration, No. 320, Tiffin Glass Company, 3 3/8" w., 9 1/8" l. **75-95**
Black, satin finish, No. 320, Tiffin Glass Company, 3 3/8" w., 9 1/8" l. **75-95**
Black, satin finish, No. 320, Tiffin Glass Company, Echec's decoration w/gold trim, 3 3/8" w., 9 1/8" l. **75-95**
Green, paneled conical form w/ribbed top, flat base w/scalloped design, Czechoslovakia, 5 1/4 x 6 1/2" **100-125**
Marigold carnival, conical form, raised leaf & grape pattern & bird, 7 x 7 3/4" **65-85**
Peacock blue, conical form w/applied gold trim, 4 x 6 1/2" **135-175**
Peacock blue, morning glory shape, 7 3/4" l. **50-75**
Red, brilliant finish, slender conical form w/pointed end finial, Style No. 320 by Tiffin Glass Co., 3 3/8 x 9 1/8" **150-185**
Vaseline, conical form w/molded scroll design, pointed end finial, U.S. Glass Co., 5 x 6" **65-85**
White milk glass, wide conical shape w/pointed end finial & scalloped rim, Panelled Grape patt., Westmoreland Glass Co., 5 x 8" **150-200**

HALLOWEEN COLLECTIBLES

Dennison Book on Crepe Paper Costumes

Book, "Easy-to-Make Colorful Costumes of Dennison Crepe Paper," Dennison, ca. 1950s (ILLUS.)... **$25-45**

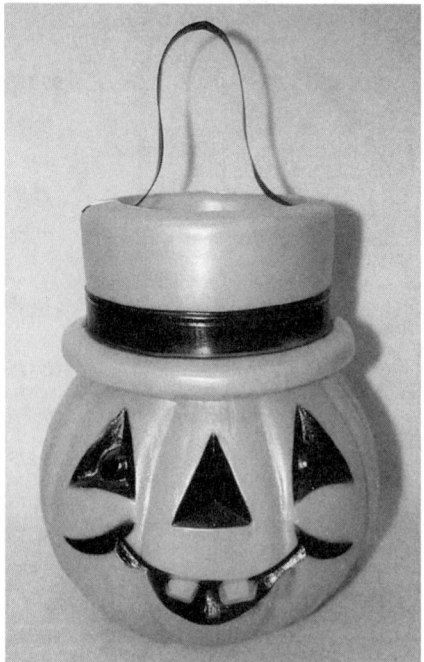

Jack-O'-Lantern with Hat Bucket

Bucket, plastic, jack-o'-lantern w/hat, ca. 1950s-60s, 9" l. (ILLUS.)............................... **10-15**

Figural Cat Cake Topper

Cake topper, plastic, cat on round base, painted orange, 2" h. (ILLUS.)...................... **8-12**

Cat Face and Paws Shaped Cake Topper

Cake topper, plastic, light vacu-formed cat face & paws, ca. 1960s 4 1/4" l. (ILLUS.) **5-10**

Figural Scarecrow Cake Topper

Cake topper, plastic, scarecrow on round base, painted orange, Hong Kong, 1 1/2" l. (ILLUS.)... **10-15**

Variety of Halloween Cake Toppers

Cake toppers, plastic, spiked,bat, skull, crossbones, & other shapes, ca. 1960s-70s, 2 1/2" h., each (ILLUS., top of page)....... **2-5**

Halloween Theme Cake Toppers

Cake toppers, plastic, spiked, cat, witch, or jack-o'-lantern painted orange, ca. 1950s-60s, each (ILLUS.)................................ **4-8**

Cat on Fence Candle

Candle, cat on fence w/moon behind, Gurley, ca. 1950s, 3 1/2" h. (ILLUS.)............. **5-8**

Cat in Mouth of Jack-O'-Lantern Candle

Candle, cat in jack-o '-lantern mouth, Gurley, ca. 1950s, 2" h. (ILLUS.).................... **5-8**

Figural Witch with Cat Candle

Candle, figural witch w/cat, Gurley, ca. 1950s-60s, 3 1/2" h. (ILLUS.) **5-8**

Ghost with Jack-O'-Lantern Candle

Candle, ghost w/jack-o'-lantern, Gurley, ca. 1950s, 3 1/4" h. (ILLUS.) **5-8**

Jack-O'-Lantern Wizard Candle

Candle, jack-o'-lantern wizard, Gurley, ca. 1960s, 4" h. (ILLUS.) **5-8**

Figural Owl Candle

Candle, owl, ca. 1960s, 3 1/4" h. (ILLUS.) **5-8**

Pumpkin Man Candle

Candle, pumpkin man, red & orange, Gurley, ca. 1950s, 5" h. (ILLUS.) **6-10**

Pumpkin Man with Hat Candle

Candle, pumpkin man w/green hat, Gurley, ca. 1950s, 3" h. (ILLUS.) **5-8**

Wax Black Cat Candleholder

Candleholder, wax, black cat, Gurley, ca. 1950s, 2 1/2" h. (ILLUS.) **7-12**

Wax Jack-O'-Lantern Candleholder

Candleholder, wax jack-o'-lantern, Gurley, ca. 1950s, 1 1/2" h. (ILLUS.) **6-9**

"Trick or Treat" Candy Bucket

Candy bucket, paper, w/plastic handle, "Trick or Treat," Lily Nestrite, 1960s, 6" h. (ILLUS.) **8-12**

Plastic Basket with Witch Handle

Candy holder, plastic, basket w/witch handle, Best, ca. 1950s, 3" h. (ILLUS.) **12-20**

Jack-O'-Lantern on Cat Candy Holder

Candy holder, plastic, jack-o'-lantern on cat, painted black, Rosbro Plastics, ca. 1950s-60s, 2 1/2" h. (ILLUS.) **20-30**

Plastic Jack-O'-Lantern Candy Holder

Candy holder, plastic, jack-o'-lantern w/handle, 1940s, 3 1/2" h. (ILLUS.) **50-55**

Scarecrow Candy Holder

Candy holder, plastic, scarecrow, Rosbro Plastics, ca. 1950s, 4 3/4" h., (ILLUS.) **50-70**

Candy holder, plastic, witch on motorcycle, wheels turn, Rosbro, ca. 1950s, 5 x 7" h. **200-350**

Blue and Red Owl Clicker

Clicker, owl, blue & red, Japan, ca. 1960s, 2 1/4" h. (ILLUS.) **15-20**

"Life of the Party" Owl Clicker

Clicker, owl, "Life of the Party Products," Kirchof, ca. 1940s, 3" h. (ILLUS.) **20-30**

Die-cut Bat with Jack-O'-Lantern

Decoration, die-cut cardboard, bat w/jack-o'-lantern, ca. 1950s-60s (ILLUS.) **5-10**

Cat Howling at Jack-O'-Lantern

Decoration, die-cut cardboard, cat howling at jack-o'-lantern, H.E. Luhrs, ca. 1950s (ILLUS.) **8-12**

Cat Inside Pumpkin Decoration

Decoration, die-cut cardboard, cat inside pumpkin, ca. 1960s, 11" h. (ILLUS.) **4-6**

Glow-in-the Dark Three-piece Set

Decoration, die-cut cardboard, glow-in-the dark three-piece set, owl, skeleton & cat, ca. 1950s, 5 1/2" h., the set (ILLUS.).. **15-25**

Die-cut Gypsy Witch

Decoration, die-cut cardboard, gypsy witch, USA, ca. 1930s, 10" h. (ILLUS.)...... **30-45**

Happy Cat with Jack-O'-Lantern Die-cut

Decoration, die-cut cardboard, happy cat w/jack-o'-lantern, two-color, ca. 1970s, 16" h. (ILLUS.) **5-10**

Die-cut Cardboard Haunted House

Decoration, die-cut cardboard, haunted house, H.E. Luhrs, 1950s (ILLUS.) **8-12**

Jack-O'-Lantern Die-cut Decoration

Decoration, die-cut cardboard, jack-o'-lantern, ca. 1950s, 5 1/4" h. (ILLUS.) **3-6**

Die-cut Jack-O'-Lantern with Pipe

Decoration, die-cut cardboard, jack-o'-lantern w/pipe, H.E. Luhrs, ca. 1950s (ILLUS.) **8-12**

Scarecrow Head Jack-O'-Lantern

Decoration, die-cut cardboard, jack-o'-lantern w/scarecrow head, H.E. Luhrs, ca. 1950s (ILLUS.).. **8-12**

Die-cut Jack-O'-Lantern with Scarf

Decoration, die-cut cardboard, jack-o'-lantern w/scarf, USA, ca. 1930s, 10" h. (ILLUS.)... **20-30**

Die-cut Large Embossed Pumpkin

Decoration, die-cut cardboard, large embossed pumpkin, Luhrs, early 1940s, 9 1/2" h. (ILLUS.).. **25-45**

Die-cut Cat with Checkered Pants

Decoration, die-cut cardboard, large jointed cat w/checkered pants, Japan, ca. 1940s (ILLUS.) **44-65**

Mad Cat with Jack-O'-Lantern Die-cut

Decoration, die-cut cardboard, mad cat w/jack-o'-lantern, ca. 1950s, 5" h. (ILLUS.) **5-10**

Mean Flying Witch Die-cut Decoration

Decoration, die-cut cardboard, mean flying witch, America, ca. 1940s, 14 1/2" h. (ILLUS.) **10-20**

Owl on Branch Die-cut

Decoration, die-cut cardboard, owl on branch, H.E. Luhrs, ca. 1950s (ILLUS.)....... **8-12**

Dennison Die-Cut Owl

Decoration, die-cut cardboard, owl, orange & black, Dennison, ca. 1940s, 9" h. (ILLUS.).. **15-25**

Die-cut Cardboard Owl with Moon

Decoration, die-cut cardboard, owl w/moon, ca. 1960s, 16" h. (ILLUS.) **5-10**

Die-cut Cardboard Scarecrow

Decoration, die-cut cardboard, scarecrow, USA, ca. 1930s, 10" h. (ILLUS.)................ **20-30**

Screaming Cat Die-cut Decoration

Decoration, die-cut cardboard, screaming cat w/big orange eyes, USA, ca. 1940s, 21" h. (ILLUS.)... **12-20**

Owl and Scarecrow Die-cut Set

Decoration, die-cut cardboard, silver metallic owl & scarecrow two-piece set, early 1940s, the set (ILLUS.) **12-20**

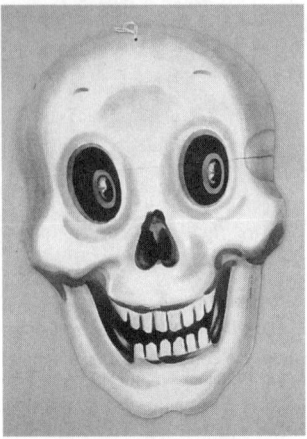

Skull with Blue Eyes Decoration

Decoration, die-cut cardboard, skull w/blue eyes, ca. 1960s, 14 1/2" h. (ILLUS.) **10-20**

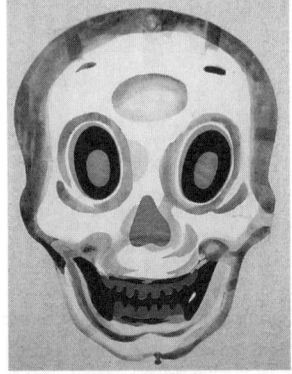

Diecut Skull with Crepe Paper Inserts

Decoration, die-cut cardboard, skull w/crepe paper inserts, Japan, ca. 1950s, 14 1/2" h. (ILLUS.) **15-25**

Die-cut Skunks with Pumpkin

Decoration, die-cut cardboard, skunks w/pumpkin, ca. 1940s, 8" h. (ILLUS.) **15-25**

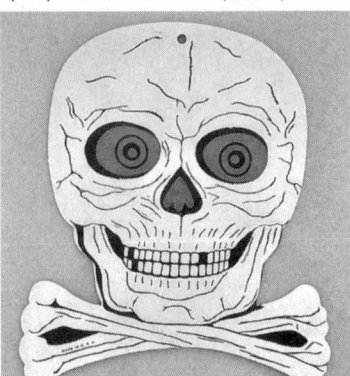

Die-cut White Skull and Crossbones

Decoration, die-cut cardboard, white skull & crossbones, USA, ca. 1940s, 8 1/2" h. (ILLUS.) **10-20**

Witch with Bulging Eyes Die-cut

Decoration, die-cut cardboard, witch w/bulging eyes, ca. 1950s, 5 1/2" h. (ILLUS.) **5-10**

Witch with Moon & Jack-O'-Lantern

Decoration, die-cut cardboard, witch w/moon & jack-o'-lantern, ca. 1950s, 5 1/4" h. (ILLUS.)... **5-10**

Elvira Electric Halloween Lights

Decoration, electric lights, Elvira Halloween lights, boxed set of 50, limited production, mid-1990s (ILLUS.)........................ **35-55**

Skeleton, Witch and Zombie Plastic Figures

Figures, plastic PVC, skeleton, witch & zombie, Palmer Plastics, ca. 1960, 2 1/2" h., each (ILLUS.)................................ **10-15**

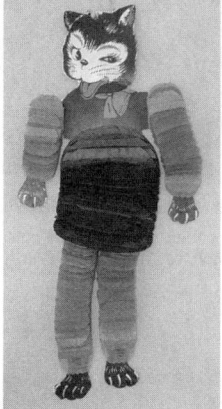

Honeycomb Paper Cat

Decoration, honeycomb paper, winking cat w/accordion-style legs, USA, ca. 1940s, 25" h. (ILLUS.) **25-40**

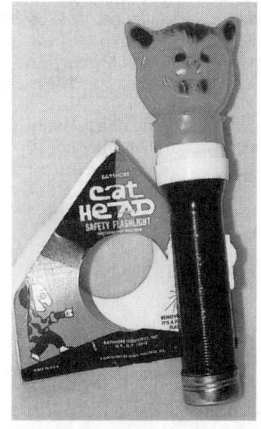

Cat Head Top Safety Lantern Flashlight

Flashlight, plastic, safety lantern with plastic cat head top, Bayshore Industries, ca. 1960s, 10" h. (ILLUS.).................................. **30-45**

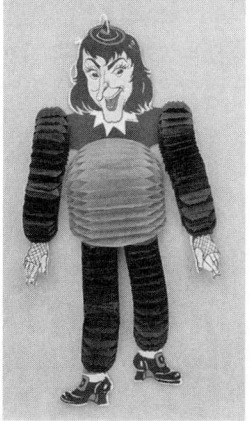

Honeycomb Paper Witch

Decoration, honeycomb paper, witch w/fishnet gloves & accordion-style legs, USA, ca. 1940s, 20" h. (ILLUS.) **20-40**

"Ring-A-Tail Game"

Game, cardboard, glass & metal, Ring-A-Tail Game, w/black cat, A.C. Gilbert Co., ca. 1940s, 4 1/4" h. (ILLUS.) **25-40**

"I'm a Dumb Skull Stunt" Game

Game, cardboard, "I'm A Dumb Skull Stunt", in envelope, Beistle, ca. 1920s-30s, 13" h. (ILLUS.) **30-60**

Game, cardboard, "Witch's Mystery Answer Game," Beistle, ca. 1920s-30s, 12 1/4" h. **50-75**

Garland, cardboard, hinged segments, bat, ghost, moon decorations, Japan, 1940s **75-125**

Cardboard & Crepe Paper Cone-Shaped Hat

Hat, cardboard & crepe paper, cone-shaped, orange and black hat, ca. 1920s, 15" h. (ILLUS.) **20-30**

Crepe Paper and Die-cut Hat

Hat, crepe paper & die-cut cardboard, devil, ca. 1940s (ILLUS.) **15-25**

Crepe Paper Die-Cut Hat with Owl

Hat, crepe paper & die-cut cardboard, owl, ca. 1940s (ILLUS.)............................... **10-20**

Crepe Paper and Metallic Witch Hat

Hat, crepe paper & metallic die-cut cardboard, witch, ca. 1940s (ILLUS.) **10-20**

Crepe Paper and Die-Cut Cat Hat

Hat, die-cut cardboard & crepe paper, black cat, ca. 1940s (ILLUS.) **15-25**

Scared Jack-O'-Lantern

Lantern, cardboard, scared jack-o'-lantern w/paper inserts, late 1950s, 6 1/2" h. (ILLUS.).. **50-75**

Papier-Maché Lantern

Lantern, papier-mâché, jack-o'-lantern shaped w/paper insert, ca. 1940s, 5" h. (ILLUS.).. **95-125**

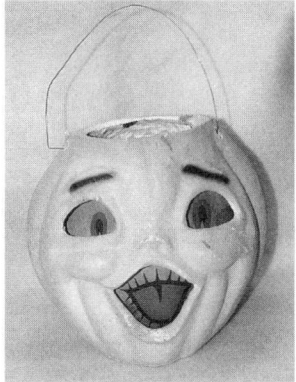

Papier-Maché Jack-O'-Lantern

Lantern, papier-mâché, jack-o'-lantern w/paper inserts, wire handle, ca. 1940s, 7 1/2" h. (ILLUS.).. **75-125**

Plastic Blinking Jack-O'-Lantern

Lantern, plastic, blinking jack-o'-lantern, Bayshore Industries, ca. 1960s, 7" h. (ILLUS.) **10-20**

"Elvira Look-A-Like Make-Up-Kit"

Make-up kit, "Elvira Look-a-Like Make-up Kit," Imagineering, 1990s (ILLUS.)............. **15-20**

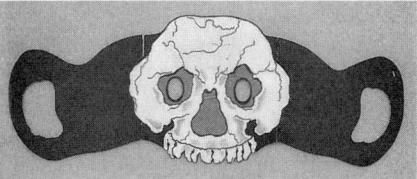

Paper Skull Mask

Mask, paper, skull, from cereal box, ca. 1960s, 5" h. (ILLUS.).................................. **20-30**

Witch and Cat Design Paper Napkin

Napkin, paper, cat over pumpkin patch, witch over moon, small size, 1950s-60s (ILLUS.) **5-10**

Halloween Paper Napkin

Napkin, paper, cat, witches, jack-o'-lanterns, 1950s-60s, 7" h. (ILLUS.) **5-10**

Noisemaker by NuWay Spinning Co.

Noisemaker, cardboard horn, orange & black, NuWay Spinning Co., ca. 1930s, 6 1/2" h. (ILLUS.) **15-25**

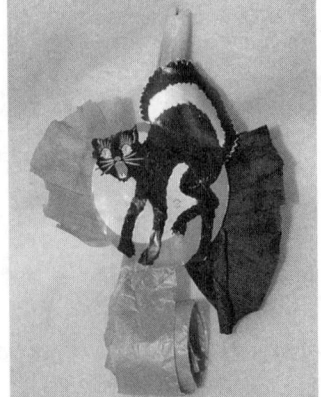

Paper Blower Noisemaker with Screaming Cat

Noisemaker, paper blower w/screaming cat, USA, ca. 1930s (ILLUS.) **20-25**

Bell-shaped Noisemaker

Noisemaker, plastic & metal, bell-shaped w/plastic handle, US Metal Toy, ca. 1950s-60s, 3 1/2" h. (ILLUS.) **10-20**

Tin Noisemaker with Plastic Mouthpiece

Noisemaker, tin horn lithographed w/plastic mouthpiece, US Metal Toy, ca. 1950s-60s, 9" l. (ILLUS.) **15-25**

Tin Lithographed Horn Noisemaker

Noisemaker, tin horn, lithographed, white base, US Metal Toy, ca. 1950s-60s, 6" l. (ILLUS.).. **10-20**

Winking Owl Tin Noisemaker

Noisemaker, tin lithographed winking owl w/plastic handle, US Metal Toy, ca. 1950s, 4 3/4" h. (ILLUS.)............................. **20-40**

Witch with Fangs Tin Noisemaker

Noisemaker, tin round, lithographed witch w/fangs, w/wooden handle, 4" l. (ILLUS.).. **20-30**

Round Tin Litho Noisemaker

Noisemaker, tin, round, w/green plastic handle, cat in center, US Metal Toy, 3 1/2" h. (ILLUS.).. **15-25**

Paper Plate with Bobbing for Apples Design

Paper plate, cat bobbing for apples w/pumpkin people, ca. 1950s, 9" l. (ILLUS.)............ **12-20**

Paper Plate with Trick-Or-Treating Children

Paper plate, children trick-or-treating, ca. 1950s, 9" l. (ILLUS.) **12-20**

Halloween Scene on Paper Plate

Paper plate, design of cats, jack-o'-lantern & haunted house, ca. 1950s, 9" l. (ILLUS.).... **10-20**

Howling Cat with Bats on Paper Plate

Paper plate, howling cat w/bats & jack-o' - lanterns, ca. 1950s, 9" l. (ILLUS.)............... **12-20**

Paper Plate with Scarecrow & Screaming Cat

Paper plate, scarecrow, screaming cat & jack-o'-lantern, ca. 1960s, 6 1/2" l. (ILLUS.).. **7-12**

Jack-O'-Lantern Design Paper Plate

Paper plate, small jack-o'-lantern w/donuts & cider, 1950s (ILLUS.).............................. **10-20**

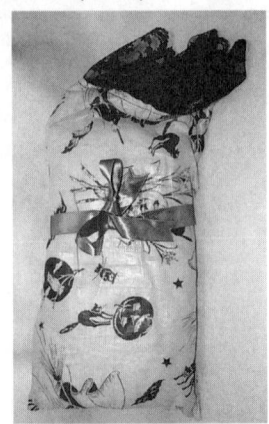

Vintage Halloween Fabric Pillow

Pillow, vintage Halloween fabric w/black lace, ca. late 1940s - early 1950s, 20" l. (ILLUS.) **25-35**

Colorful Cylindrical Rattle

Rattle, tin lithographed cylinder w/green plastic handle, US Metal Toy Co., 1950s-60s, 3 1/4" h. (ILLUS.)................................. **20-30**

Round-topped Rattle

Rattle, tin & plastic, lithographed w/black cats on round top w/plastic handle, US Metal Toy, ca. 1950s-60s, 4" l. (ILLUS.).... **10-15**

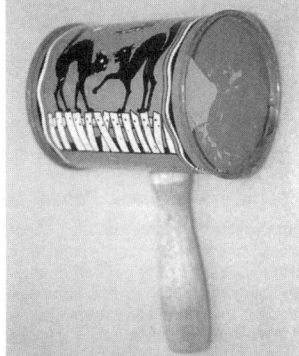

Rattle with Black Cats

Rattle, tin & wood lithographed cylinder w/black cats, on wooden handle, USA, ca. 1930s-40s (ILLUS.)...................... **25-45**

Ghost and Cats on Round Rattle

Rattle, tin & wood lithographed w/ghost and cats, round top on wooden handle, USA, 4 1/4" l. (ILLUS.).. **12-20**

Fat Albert Halloween Record

Record, vinyl, LP Halloween record starring Fat Albert, Kid Stuff, ca. 1960s (ILLUS.)... **20-30**

Dennison Crepe Paper Table Cloth

Table cloth, crepe paper, large folding cloth, orange w/black border design, Dennison, ca. 1950s (ILLUS.)................... **30-40**

Tambourine, tin litho decorated w/images of gypsies, US Metal Toy Co., ca. 1950s, 6 1/4" h. **10-20**

Tambourine, tin, orange & black Halloween party decoration, J. Chein Co., early 1900s, 7" h. **150-200**

INDIAN ARTIFACTS & JEWELRY

Bag, Great Lakes Chippewa/Ojibwa, yarn twined bag w/colorful horizontal bands & central geometric design in red, black & gold, cloth band rim w/long tie, bottom has beaded drops w/colorfully dyed horsehair tassels, early 20th c., 5 1/2" w., 6" h. (wear).. **$303**

Belt, Navajo, sterling silver concho belt, stamped & formed w/fifteen 2" l. bow & 8 1/8" l. oval conchos, intricate buckle, mounted on leather belt w/copper hanks...... **468**

Blanket strip, Northern Plains, white bead ground w/interspersed blocks & double diamond designs in translucent dark blue & rose beads w/yellow, spot stitched, yellow ochre stained twisted rawhide tassels hang from center of each set of joined double diamonds, rawhide backing, 2 3/8" w., 53 1/2" l. **880**

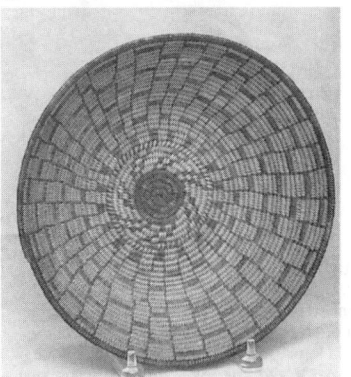

Apache Basketry Bowl

Bowl, Apache, basketry, willow w/radiating interlocked design in dark martynia, three or four rim stitches missing, 11 1/4" d., 3 1/4" h. (ILLUS.).. **935**

Miwok Basketry Bowl

Bowl, California Miwok, basketry, flaring straight sided bowl w/typical rectangular design in dark dyed fiber w/reddish areas, one rod coil, several small fiber breaks in body, 13 3/4" d., 6 3/4" h. (ILLUS.).. **715**

Maidu Basketry Bowl

Bowl, Maidu, basketry, finely woven on three-rod coil w/stepped dark rectangular design elements surmounted w/a cross on the outer side, California, 10" d., 5" h. (ILLUS.).. **990**

Doll, Plains, leather & beaded figure of brave, w/intricately beaded clothing, moccasins, knife sheath, quiver, etc., braided hair w/quilled ornament, metal & horsehair tassels, trade cloth breech, 16" h. (older reproduction, minor damage & stains)... **1,430**

Southwestern Pueblo Dough Bowl

Dough bowl, Southwestern Pueblo, probably San Ildefonso, pottery, round, polished creamy slip w/brick-orange & black decoration, attributed to a member of the Da family, early 20th c., minor paint wear, small glaze chip on interior, hairline on base does not go through, 13" d., 5 1/4" h. (ILLUS.) **1,980**

Southwestern Pueblo Pottery Jar

Jar, Southwestern Pueblo, probably Acoma, possibly Laguna, pottery, ovoid form decorated w/bold umber painted double-headed birds w/smaller birds & floral elements on a thin white slip ground, some wear, 7" d., 7" h. (ILLUS.).............................. **935**

Hopi Cow Kachina

Kachina, Hopi, Wakas or Cow, case mask in faded turquoise, red & black, cow horns on top, cow ears sticking straight out to sides, arms integral w/body, muted color, holes for string hanger, minor wear, age crack on back, 12 1/4" h. (ILLUS.)............... **3,630**

Sioux Beaded Moccasins

Moccasins, Sioux, beaded leather, classic design in dark green & white w/red, blues & yellow, cuff seam loose, 10 5/8" l. (ILLUS.) **325**

Pima Basketry Olla

Olla, Pima, basketry, willow body w/overall bands of triangles in dark martynia, minor breaks in stitching, 7" d., 6" h. (ILLUS.)......... **715**

Pima Basketry Olla

Olla, Pima, basketry, willow & martynia w/overall stepped geometric design, 8" d., 9 7/8" h. (ILLUS.) **1,650**

Northwest Coast Totem Pole

Totem pole, wood, Northwest Coast, possibly Kwakiutl, graphically carved & polychrome painted figures of beaver, frog, raven & clan crest figure, late 19th - early 20th c., 32" h. (ILLUS.)................................. **2,860**

Zuni Figural Pottery Vessel

Vessel, Zuni, pottery, polychrome male figure wearing painted cross necklace, typical male wrap hairstyle, ceremonial face markings, turquoise earrings attached through holes in ears, whimsical expression w/open mouth, polished white slip body w/ochre & umber decoration, small opening at top of head, minor pitting & glaze flecks, one earring missing, 10 1/8" h. (ILLUS.) **4,510**

IVORY

Carved Ivory Figural Group

Figural group, carved female forms under tree posing w/objects, on oval base, Chinese, ca. 1900, 6 1/2" h. (ILLUS.)......... **$336**

Figure of a Japanese Man

Figure of man, dressed in kimono & hat, w/long beard, kneeling & resting head on drum-like object w/carving resembling basketweave, Japanese, ca. 1900, 3" h. (ILLUS.) **900**

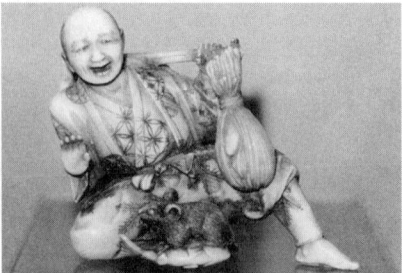

Carved Ivory Figure of Sitting Man

Figure of man, w/open mouth, dressed in kimono, sitting w/one leg tucked under him & the other extended, holding sack & gesturing at figure of rat-like animal clutching fish, Japanese, early 20th c., 2 1/2" h. (ILLUS.) **650**

Carved Ivory Mandolin Players

Figures of mandolin players, carved ivory figures in 18th c. dress, man holding mandolin at side, woman playing mandolin, each on turned wood base, late 19th c., 7" h., pr. (ILLUS.) **3,738**

Carved Ivory Two-case Inro

Inro, cov., rectangular, two-case example carved w/stylized figures of two men, w/black cord w/bead & ending in carved ivory figure of man, Japanese, ca. 1900, 3 3/4" l. (ILLUS.).. **400**

Model of tortoise, back fitted w/a monkey, baby tortoises & rodents, ca. 1900, 2 1/4 x 3 1/2" **616**

One of a Pair of Carved Ivory Plaques

Plaques, rectangular, carved & inlaid high-relief scenes of Chinese interiors w/three female figures, Chinese, late Ch'ing dynasty, 4 1/4 x 7 1/2", pr. (ILLUS. of one) **1,568**

Seal set, in the form of a figure seated over a basket w/toad, fitted w/two seals, Oriental, early 19th c., 1 1/2" sq., 3" h. **146**

Wonder ball, intricately carved ball w/ten spheres, one inside the other, interior ones carved in pierced patterns, the outer carved w/dragon & flowers, ca. 1890, 2" d. **504**

JEWELRY

American Painted Porcelain

American painted porcelain jewelry comprises a unique category. While the metallic settings and porcelain medallions were inexpensive, the painted decoration was a work of fine art. The finished piece possessed a greater intrinsic value than costume jewelry of the same period because it was a one-of-a-kind creation, but one that was not as expensive as real gold and sterling silver settings and precious and semiprecious jewels. Note that signatures are rare, backstamps lacking. To learn more about identification, evaluation, history, and appraisal, the following book is recommended: Painted Porcelain Jewelry and Buttons: Identification & Value Guide *by Dorothy Kamm.*

Bar pin, gold-plated bezel, geometric design in blues on a burnished gold ground, ca. 1900-1915, 3" w. **$50**

Belt buckle brooch, oval, w/a stylized tiger lily, buds & greenery outlined in gold, burnished gold border, gold-plated bezel, ca. 1900-1917, 1 5/8 x 2 1/8" w. **200**

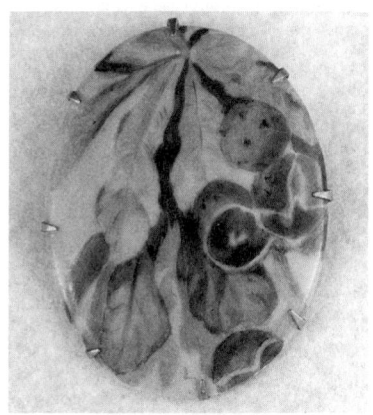

Oval-shaped Belt Buckle Brooch

Belt buckle brooch, oval, w/horse chestnut branch on baby blue ground, gold-plated bezel, ca. 1900-1917, 2" x 2 1/2" (ILLUS.)... **150**

Belt buckle brooch, oval, w/water lilies & cattails in a waterscape, w/dark blue green border, white enamel highlights, burnished gold rim, ca. 1900-1917, 1 5/8 x 2 1/8" w... **175**

Brooch, heart-shaped, w/violets & leaves on a pastel polychrome ground, white enamel highlights, burnished gold rim, major gold wear, gold-plated bezel, ca. 1890 - 1910, 7/8" x 1" **45**

Brooch, lozenge-shaped, w/forget-me-nots on a polychrome ground, white enamel highlights, burnished gold border, gold-plated bezel, ca. 1890-1920, 15/16" x 15/16" **30**

Brooch, oval, decorated w/a water lily and waterscape, white enamel highlights, burnished gold border, gold-plated bezel, ca. 1925-1945, 1 3/16" x 15/16"............ **55**

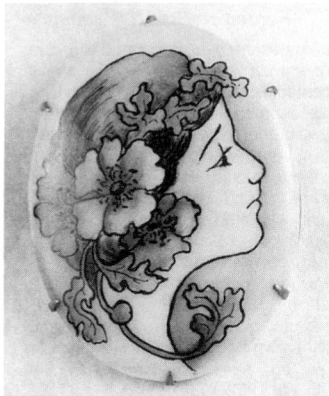

Art Nouveau-style Brooch

Brooch, oval, decorated w/an Art Nouveau-style woman's bust, w/poppies in her hair, gold-plated bezel, 1900-1915, 1 1/2" w x 2" (ILLUS.) **90**

Oval Brooch with Columbine

Brooch, oval, decorated w/columbine & greenery on a polychrome ground, burnished gold rim, gold-plated bezel, ca. 1900-1920, 1 13/16" x 2 3/16", (ILLUS.)......... **75**

Pink Roses on Oval Brooch

Brooch, oval, decorated w/pink roses & greenery on a pastel polychrome ground, accented w/white enamel, edged w/burnished gold on one side, gold-plated bezel, ca. 1890-1920, 1 1/16" x 1/3/8" (ILLUS.) **45**

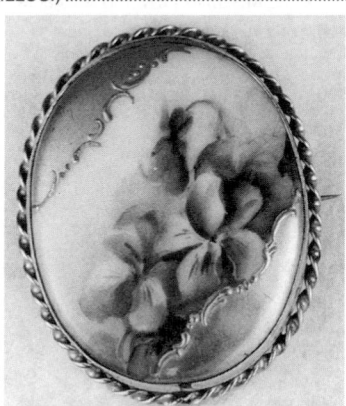

Brooch with Violets and Leaves

Brooch, oval, decorated w/violets & leaves on a polychrome ground, framed by diagonals of burnished gold bordered w/raised paste scrolls & dots, gold-plated box setting w/twisted rope border, ca. 1880-1920, 1 3/4" x 2 1/8", (ILLUS.) **100**

Oval Brooch with Violets

Brooch, oval, decorated w/violets on an ivory ground, burnished gold border superimposed w/a black line border design of violets & vines, ca. 1900-1915, 1 1/2" x 2" (ILLUS.) **75**

Porcelain Medallion Brooch with Roses

Brooch, porcelain medallion, oval, inset in black plastic, decorated w/ruby roses & greenery on an ivory ground, ca. 1910-1930, 1 3/8" x 1 3/4", (ILLUS.) **50**

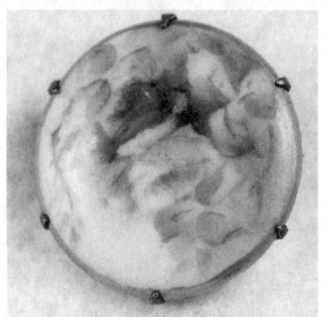

Brooch with Pink & Ruby Roses

Brooch, round, decorated w/a pink & a ruby rose & greenery on a pastel polychrome ground, burnished gold rim, gold-plated bezel, ca. 1890-1910, 1 3/16" d. (ILLUS.) **40**

Brooch with Forget-me-nots

Brooch, round, w/forget-me-nots & leaves, border of raised paste dots covered w/burnished gold, gold-plated bezel, ca. 1890-1910, 1 1/8" d. (ILLUS.) **35**

Portrait on Brooch/Pendant

Brooch/pendant, oval, decorated w/an elegant woman wearing a pale blue shawl, accented w/turquoise jeweled necklace, white enamel pearls in headband & on shawl, bordered by raised paste scrolls & dots covered w/burnished gold & accented by turquoise enamel jewels, polychrome ground, set in gold-plated box setting w/twisted rope border, ca. 1880-1920, 2 1/16" x 2 1/2" (ILLUS.) **200**

Cuff pin, decorated w/a forget-me-not on burnished gold ground, gold-plated bezel, ca. 1880-1920, 1" x 1/4" **15**

Flapper pin, oval, decorated w/a stylized, wavy brown-haired flapper w/a blue corsage on her shoulder, gold-plated bezel, ca. 1922-1930 .... **65**

Handy pin, crescent shape, asymmetrically decorated w/a purple pansy on an ivory ground, burnished gold tip, gold-plated bezel, ca. 1880-1915 .... **35**

Handy pin, crescent-shaped, decorated w/forget-me-nots & leaves on a burnished gold ground, gold-plated bezel, ca. 1890-1915, gold wear, 1 13/16" w. **30**

Handy pin, crescent-shaped, decorated w/forget-me-nots & leaves on a burnished gold ground, bold-plated bezel, ca. 1880-1915, 1 13/16" w. **50**

Handy pin, crescent-shaped, decorated w/pink & ruby roses & green leaves on an ivory ground, w/white enamel highlights & one burnished gold tip, gold-plated bezel, ca. 1890-1915, 2 3/16" w. **45**

Handy pin, crescent-shaped, decorated w/pink & ruby roses & leaves on an ivory ground, white enamel highlights, burnished gold tip, gold-plated bezel, ca. 1880-1915, 1 3/16" w. **40**

Hatpin, circular head, decorated w/a conventional geometric design in raised paste dots & scrolls, covered w/burnished gold, turquoise enamel jewels, cobalt blue flat enamel, gold-plated bezel, ca. 1905-20, 1" d., 6 3/8" shaft **110**

Hatpin, circular head, decorated w/pink roses & greenery on a pale blue & yellow ground, burnished gold border, gold-plated bezel, ca. 1890-1920, some gold wear, 1" d., 7 3/4" shaft **115**

Hatpin Head with Wild Roses

Hatpin, circular head, decorated w/pink wild roses & greenery on a yellow ground, burnished gold rim, gold-plated filigree setting, head 1 1/16" d., shaft 9" l. (ILLUS. of head) **135**

Hatpin Head with Ruby Roses

Hatpin, circular head, decorated w/ruby roses & green leaves, embellished w/burnished gold scrolls, gold-plated bezel, head 1 3/8" d., shaft 7 3/4" l. (ILLUS. of head) **125**

Hatpin with Roses

Hatpin, decorated w/yellow roses & leaves on a yellow, yellow brown, & brown background, gold-plated bezel, ca. 1890-1920, 1 1/4" d., 7 3/4" shaft (ILLUS.) **115**

Pendant, heart-shaped, decorated w/pink roses & greenery on a polychrome ground, gold-plated bezel, ca. 1900-1930, 1 13/16" x 2" **80**

Scarf pin, medallion, decorated w/violets, gold-plated bezel & shank, ca. 1880-1920, 1 1/4" d., 3" shank.............................. **50**

Shirtwaist button, decorated w/a conventional design in raised paste & pastel-colored enamel on a cobalt ground, burnished gold rim, 1" d.. **14**

Shirtwaist button, decorated w/forget-me-nots & greenery on a polychrome ground, white enamel highlights, burnished gold rim & asymmetrical ground outlined w/black scrolling, signed "McCullam, '05," 1 5/16" d. **40**

Shirtwaist buttons, three, decorated w/purple flowers & greenery on a lavender ground, w/black borders & rims, white enamel highlights, 1 1/16" d. w/shank, the set **60**

Shirtwaist set, decorated w/ruby roses & greenery on a light yellow ground, burnished gold rims, one 1 3/8" d., three 1" d. w/shanks, the set **100**

Antique (1800-1920)

Bar pin, gold (14k) & carnelian, centered by a carnelian intaglio of three cherubs within a wirework frame, applied floral, bead, & ropetwist design, Victorian.......................... **411**

Bar pin, moonstone & diamond, round moonstone carved w/head of a classical warrior, further set w/eighteen old mine-cut diamonds, 18kt gold mount, signed "C. & C.," no. 7653, Edwardian.................... **2,070**

Bar pin, pearl & diamond, centered pearl framed w/twelve old mine-cut diamonds, bezel-set old mine-cut diamond terminals, silver-topped mount.............................. **264**

Bar pin, pearl & diamond, set w/twelve rose-cut diamonds, surmounted by three pearls of purple & ivory hue, silver & gold mount, French hallmarks, Edwardian, England.. **88**

Bar pin, pearl & gold (14k), designed as five 14k gold interlocking links each centering a pearl, 10k gold pin stem & safety chain, Edwardian, England **144**

Gold Charm Bracele

Bar pin, sapphire, diamond & gold (14k), set w/nine circular-cut sapphires interspersed w/diamonds, platinum-topped 14k gold mount, Austrian hallmarks **432**

Barrette, gold (18k), ribbed, shaped barrette surmounted by ribbon design in green gold, French hallmarks, Edwardian (losses to gold) **202**

Bracelet, charm, gold, pearl, enamel, platinum, onyx & diamond, fifteen charms including an Edwardian pavé pearl heart locket, enameled elephant, Buddha, thermometer, schnauzer, platinum, onyx, & diamond pig, gold stirrups, etc. suspended by a 14k gold, green & white enamel baton link bracelet, Edwardian, England, 7" l., heart locket missing one pearl (ILLUS., top of page) **1,410**

Bracelet, gold (14k), bangle-type, hinged, Art Nouveau style, bangle centering a lion's head w/red stone eyes clutching an old mine-cut diamond in its jaws, flanked by scroll design **867**

Bracelet, gold (14k), enamel & diamond, embossed crescent-form links completed by a box clasp surmounted by a knot decorated w/blue & green enamel flowers & centered by an old mine-cut diamond, 6" l. **499**

Bracelet, gold (14k), enamel & pearl, shield-shaped slide decorated w/black tracery enamel & seed pearls, supported by a brickwork band w/fox tail fringe terminal, Victorian **345**

Bracelet, gold (14k), Retro style, yellow gold oval links connected by domed half links alternating w/gadrooned pink gold links, European hallmark, 8 1/4" l. **489**

Bracelet, gold (14k) & sapphire, openwork bangle-type set w/three square-cut sapphires within a delicate wiretwist mount, Edwardian **374**

Bracelet, gold (14k), woven wire braided style, ending w/an oval box clasp surmounted by an oval plaque decorated w/a green, yellow & rose gold applied bird, clasp flanked by crescents of bead & wiretwist, Victorian, 7 1/4" l. **748**

Art Nouveau Style Bracelet

Bracelet, gold (18k), diamond & ruby, Art Nouveau style, pierced floral oval links highlighted by old European-cut diamonds & rubies alternating w/shaped floral links, European assay marks, 8 3/4" l. (ILLUS.) **1,610**

Bracelet, gold (18k) & pearl, Art Nouveau design w/floral & elliptical links highlighted by five button pearls, French assay marks, 7 1/2" l. **690**

Gold Hinged Bangle Bracelet

Bracelet, gold (18k) & pearl, bangle-type, hinged, spiral design, surrounded by a diagonal row of freshwater pearls, French hallmarks, Victorian (ILLUS.) **646**

Bracelet, white gold (14k) & diamond, openwork filigree links surmounted by seventeen box-set w/old min- & European-cut diamonds & single-cut diamonds, 6" l. **705**

Bracelet w/locket, gold (15k) & enamel, tapering, interlocking infinity links centering a round, engraved blue enamel locket set w/a circular-cut diamond, English registry mark, Victorian, 7 1/2" l. (ILLUS., below) **920**

Gold, Enamel Bracelet with Locket

Bracelets, gold (14k) & enamel, bangle bracelets decorated w/black tracery enamel in a bold scalloped design, ca. 1865, pr....... **1,093**

Brooch, amethyst & diamond, faceted oval amethyst centered by a bead-set cushion-shape rose-cut diamond, 14k gold mount w/rose-cut diamond accents **382**

Brooch, amethyst, turquoise, & pearl, the shell design mount centered by a mixed-cut amethyst & decorated w/four pearls & four turquoise beads, Georgian, England...... **288**

Brooch, coral & rose-cut diamond, oval coral framed by rose-cut diamonds, pierced gallery, gold mount.. **345**

Brooch, diamond & pearl, starburst design set w/eight old mine-cut diamonds & nine cultured pearls, 18k gold mount, Edwardian **1,265**

Brooch, diamond & pearl, yellow, champagne, brown & colorless old European-cut diamonds set in 18k yellow gold & silver scrolls, suspending an ovoid yellow cultured pearl of later origin **3,819**

Brooch, diamond, platinum & gold (14k), circular design, crescent & star set w/twenty old European & transitional-cut diamonds, approx. total wt. 1.32 cts., platinum & 14k gold mount, Edwardian, England............................... **881**

Brooch, diamond, ruby & emerald figural bee, body & wings set w/old mine- & European-cut diamonds, further set w/bands of cabochon rubies, cabochon emerald eyes, silver & 18k yellow gold mount **4,025**

Brooch, diamond & ruby, ribbon design suspending three pendant florets, set throughout w/rose-cut diamonds, ruby & millegrain accents, gold mount, Victorian (missing two rubies, one diamond & pin stem) **345**

Brooch, diamond, ruby, seed pearls & 14k yellow gold, floral form centered by prong-set diamond surrounded by five cultured pearls & small prong-set diamonds w/gold petals on gold stem w/two clusters of eight rubies each & two gold leaves, first half 20th c., 1 3/4 x 2 1/4"....... **1,456**

Emerald, Gold and Diamond Brooch

Brooch, emerald, gold & diamond, concentric design of square- & emerald-cut emeralds set in crimped 18k gold bezels, further highlighted by rose-cut diamonds mounted in silver bezels (ILLUS.) **2,820**

Art Nouveau Flower Brooch

Brooch, enamel, Art Nouveau style, designed as an orchid & decorated w/pale pink & yellow iridescent enamel, the stamen set w/two old European-cut diamonds & pearls, 14k gold mount, hallmark for Whiteside and Blank (ILLUS.)...... **2,350**

Brooch, enamel, diamond, pearl & gold, figural swallow, body decorated w/cobalt blue enamel, wings edged w/rose-cut diamonds, baroque pearl body, red enamel eyes, 18k yellow gold & silver mounting (chip to enamel).. **288**

Enamel and Diamond Brooch

Brooch, enamel & diamond, young fair-haired woman depicted in three-quarter profile wearing a diadem w/star-set old mine-cut diamond against shades of lavender & blue, framed by twenty-eight old mine-cut diamonds, 18k gold mount, French guarantee stamp (ILLUS.)............... **1,840**

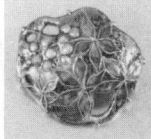

Arts & Crafts Tiffany Enamel Brooch

Brooch, enamel & gold, Arts & Crafts style, the freeform mount decorated w/polychrome enamel in green, lavender & gold in a flower & berry design, the reverse engraved "B.M.W.," designed by Louis Comfort Tiffany & signed by Tiffany & Co. (ILLUS.) **36,425**

Brooch, enamel, polychrome & gold (18k), set w/an octagonal polychrome plaque depicting a girl & her lap dog in garden w/baroque fountain, framed by floral & swag design, later 18k gold mount............. **1,265**

Brooch, enamel & rose-cut diamond, polychrome enamel portrait of a woman framed by rose-cut diamonds, silver-topped 14k gold mount................................ **1,093**

Brooch, garnet, shell, mine-cut diamond & gold (14k), Art Nouveau style, gem-set brooch depicting a woman w/flowing hair & a dolphin w/a demantoid garnet eye amid waves within a chased & engraved scallop shell, old mine-cut diamond moon, 14k gold mount...................................... **382**

Victorian Garnet Brooch

Brooch, garnet & silver, silver circular-shape set w/nine garnets between enam-eled figures, ca. 1900 (ILLUS.) **168**

Arts & Crafts Gold Brooch

Brooch, gold (14k), Arts & Crafts style, oval openwork form depicting a chased & en-graved maple leaf & seeds within a twig design frame, stamped by Potter Studio (ILLUS.).. **1,293**

Gold and Enamel Brooch

Brooch, gold (14k) & enamel, portrait style, depicting enameled portrait of a gentle-man in Renaissance dress w/a rose-cut diamond highlight, framed by seed pearls (ILLUS.)... **588**

Brooch, gold (14k), ruby & diamond, the scrolled gold mount w/millegrain accents centered by a ruby & rose-cut diamond flowerhead.. **823**

Brooch, gold (14k), turquoise & diamond, oval cabochon turquoise surrounded by gold filigree frame inset w/four diamonds, ca. 1900, approx. 3/4 x 1 1/8"...... **336**

Brooch, gold (18k) & micromosaic, the cen-ter oval plaque depicting the Greek let-ters alpha & omega & the symbol for Pax Christi on a brick red ground, framed by tessarae in a white, red & black geomet-ric design, gold mount w/wiretwist deco-ration **345**

Brooch, gold (18k) & opal, oval opal cen-tered in a platinum bezel flexibly set with-in a floral wreath flanked by griffins hold-ing swags & seated on cornucopia-form pedestals joined by a bow, hallmark for Gaston Lafette, No. 3058............................ **1,998**

Brooch, hardstone & gold (14k), pietra dura brooch w/pink, white & green stone rose on black hardstone ground, applied wire-work, 14k gold mount **264**

Brooch, micromosaic, gold & onyx, multi-colored tesserae depicting a spaniel seated in a classical landscape within an onyx ground, frame w/applied wiretwist decoration, 18k gold mount (later clasp).... **4,818**

Gold and Enamel Mourning-type Brooch

Brooch, mourning-type, gold & enamel, rib-bon & buckle design, ribbon decorated w/light blue & black enamel, centering a glass locket compartment within a gar-net-set buckle, Victorian (ILLUS.).................. **259**

Brooch, sapphire, diamond & gold, horse-shoe shaped bezel set w/seven round faceted sapphires, spaced by six old mine-cut diamonds in a crossover de-sign, platinum & 14k yellow gold mount, ca. 1915.. **529**

Sapphire and Pearl Brooch

Brooch, sapphire & pearl, centered by an oval mixed-cut sapphire measuring ap-prox. 14.20 x 12.20 mm, framed by two rows of split pearls, 14k gold, closed back mounting, Edwardian, England, missing one pearl (ILLUS.).. **1,410**

Brooch, sapphire & pearl, crescent-shaped brooch set w/ten graduated faceted sap-phires alternating w/eleven pearls, 14k gold mount, Edwardian, England **588**

Brooch, sterling silver, shaped pendant set w/two oval green agates, Jugendstil de-sign, stamped on the reverse "MiG, TF,

900, depose for Max Joseph Gradl, Theodor Fahrner" **881**

Brooch, turquoise & gold (18k), Art Nouveau style, rectangular turquoise w/rounded edges enclosed in an 18k gold mount designed as two sinuous vines **317**

Brooch, white gold (14k) & diamond, openwork shield-form designed w/a bow flanked by flowers centering a flexibly-set old European-cut diamond, set throughout w/single-cut diamonds **863**

Brooches, amethyst, both set w/oval faceted amethyst, the first framed by seed pearls, Birmingham hallmark, the second in a chased & engraved floral & foliate frame, 14k gold mounts, Victorian, pr. **411**

Buckle brooch, diamond & pearl, gem-set buckle brooch, perimeter set w/rose & old mine-cut diamonds, four pearl accents, 18k gold mounting (lead solder on reverse) **575**

Cameo brooch, coral cameo & gold (15k), shield-shaped brooch surmounted by a coral cameo carved w/image of a classical woman w/grape leaf design, 15 k gold mount, Victorian.. **382**

Cameo brooch, onyx, gold (18k) & pearls, depicting profile of a woman wearing a flower in her hair, 18k gold ropetwist frame set w/split pearls............................... **1,035**

Shell Cameo Brooch

Cameo brooch, shell & gold, carved shell depicting an allegorical scene, 10k gold wiretwist mount (ILLUS.)................................. **499**

Cameo brooch/pendant, hardstone, gold & pearl, depicting a woman's profile within a 14k gold scrolled mount highlighted w/pearls, reverse glass locket compartment, Victorian.. **863**

Cameo brooch/pendant, shell & gold, large circular-form depicting four female classical bathers, polished gold frame accented by wiretwist, retractable bail, the reverse possibly signed Lev, Victorian... **863**

Cameo earrings, gold (18k) & shell, cameo tops suspending oval drops depicting profile of a classical woman in an independent frame, flanked by brushed gold leaves, Victorian (later findings), pr.............. **575**

Chain, gold (14k), composed of textured & polished fancy links completed by a barrel clasp surmounted by flowerhead decoration, w/original fitted box, 46 1/2" l,....... **7,590**

Chain, gold (14k) & enamel, Art Nouveau style, alternating baton, trace & guilloché blue enamel navette-shaped links suspending a pliquè-a-jour enamel decoration, 22" l.. **575**

Chain, gold (18k), chain consisting of navette-shaped links pierced in a floral design & joined by curb links, French hallmarks & guarantee stamp, 61" l. **1,380**

Chain, gold (18k) & enamel, Art Nouveau style, navette-shaped white enamel links engraved w/a flowerhead design alternating w/baton links & seed pearls, European hallmarks, 21" l. **632**

Chain, gold (18k), link-style, Art Nouveau design w/fancy intertwined oval & navette-shaped links centering a wiretwist scroll decoration, French hallmarks, 59" l. **1,840**

Chain, platinum, sapphire & pearl, bead chain designed w/ten sapphire beads flanked by freshwater pearls, joined by pierced navette-shaped links, Edwardian, England, 44" l. (ILLUS., bottom of page)... **3,525**

Chain & slide, gold (14k), enamel & hardstone, double fancy trace link chain supporting a shield-shaped slide decorated w/black tracery enamel, surmounted by a bezel-set hardstone cameo, Victorian **823**

Clasp, gold (14k) & pearl, depicting miniature of a young woman w/garland of roses, frame decorated w/gold beads, clasp designed to hold up to eight strands of pearls, back w/added pin stem.. **529**

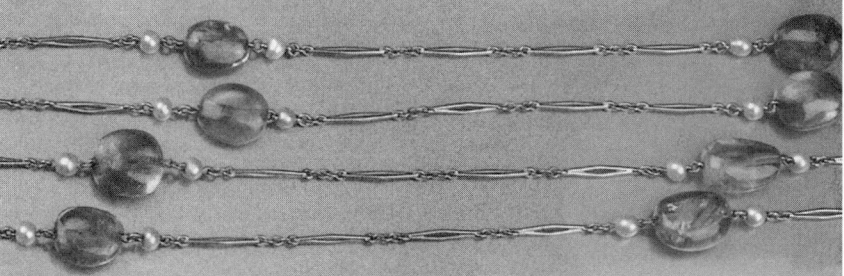

Platinum, Pearl and Sapphire Bead Chain

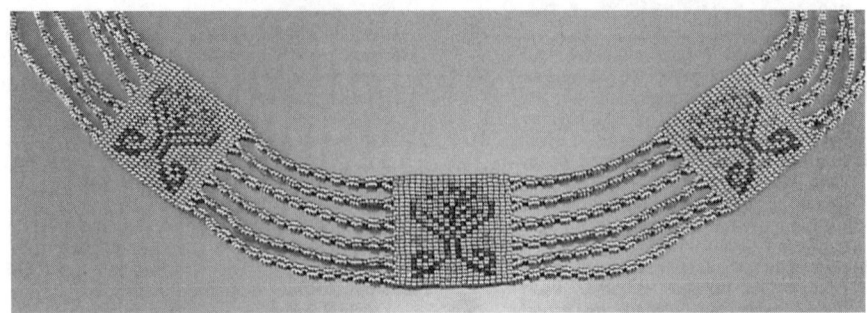

Beadwork and Silver Collar

Clasp, gold tricolor (14k), Art Nouveau, the shaped plaque surmounted by a bird & foliate design in green, yellow & rose gold, plunger clasp & jump ring finders, ca. 1900 .... **431**

Collar, beadwork & silver, Arts & Crafts style, composed of silver, gold, green & yellow beads designed as five square woven plaques w/floral design, each joined by six strands of beads, completed by a silver metal slide clasp, possibly Wiener Werkstatte, ca. 1908, 13" l., (ILLUS., top of page) **3,565**

Cuff links, gold (14k) & diamond, designed w/oval & elliptical chased edge links, the oval link set w/an old mine-cut diamond, 14k & 18k gold, Victorian, pr. **87**

Cuff links, gold (14k) & diamond, oval links w/chased edges, one link of the pair set w/an old European-cut diamond, Victorian, pr. **173**

Cuff links, gold (18k), Art Nouveau style, elliptical form links decorated w/a laurel & ribbon design in repoussé, French hallmarks, pr. **288**

Earrings, diamond & enamel, bow-form tops suspending oval enamel pendants depicting a fashionable woman, set throughout w/rose-cut diamonds, silver-topped 18k gold mount, pr. **1,094**

Earrings, enamel & diamond, pendant-type, sky blue enamel bosses centering a star-set rose-cut diamond, 14k gold mounts, w/early box, pr. **374**

Earrings, gold (14k) & diamond, drop-style w/old European-cut diamonds, pr. **7,188**

Earrings, gold (14k), openwork oval tops w/wiretwist decoration suspending an oval medallion surmounted by the profile of a classical male within similarly decorated wiretwist frames, fringe terminals, ca. 1810, pr. (ILLUS. of one, top of next column) **690**

Earrings, gold (18k), hoop-style earrings w/tapering ends, pr. **201**

Earrings, gold (18k), poissarde earrings designed as sunbursts flanked by trefoil design, French hallmarks, ca. 1800, pr. (evidence of solder) **317**

Earrings, paste & gold (18k), poissarde earrings set w/rectangular cushion-shaped pastes resembling topaz, ropetwist & star accents, pr. **345**

Gold Earring with Profile

Earrings, pearl & diamond, shield-form tops w/three strands of pearls (probably natural) suspended, w/bow design terminal, further suspending three baroque pearls, set throughout w/rose-cut diamonds, 18k gold & silver mount, French import marks, pr. **1,495**

Earrings, turquoise & gold, round pendant surmounted by turquoise boss centering a star & rose-cut diamond, framed by a spiral wiretwist, Victorian, pr............................ **316**

Lavaliere, pearl & diamond, openwork shield-shaped form set throughout w/old European & single-cut diamonds w/six small pearl accents, semi-baroque pearl terminal, suspended from a platinum & pearl trace link chain, Edwardian, England, 17 1/2" l.. **1,528**

Lavaliere, platinum, aquamarine & pearl, heart-shaped aquamarine suspended by two collet-set old European-cut diamonds w/pear-shaped aquamarine terminal, three pearl accents, completed by a fine 14k white gold ropetwist chain, Edwardian, England **1,410**

Platinum and Pearl Chain Lavaliere

Lavaliere, platinum, synthetic ruby & diamond, delicate platinum & pearl chain centering an openwork plaque set w/old European & transitional-cut diamonds, suspending a collet-set ruby simulant framed by a single-cut diamond foliate wreath above a briolette red stone drop w/diamond, Edwardian, approx. 20 1/2" l. (ILLUS.)... **1,955**

Locket, enamel & gold (14k) chased & engraved oval case decorated w/champlevé enamel sprays of pansies & bachelor's buttons, opens front & back **863**

Gold Gem-set Locket

Locket, gold (18k), pearl, turquoise & diamond, ovoid form surmounted by seed pearls, calibré-cut turquoise & rose-cut diamonds in fleur-de-lis & circle design, opens to reveal a glass compartment, Victorian (ILLUS.).. **1,058**

Locket, sterling silver, round w/Art Nouveau leaves on upper half, Victorian, on 18" chain, 1" d. **80-115**

Gold and Pearl Locket and Chain

Locket & chain, gold (18k) & pearl, oval reeded, trace link chain suspending a locket surmounted by a pearl, opens to reveal a compartment containing a lock of hair, w/bill of sale dated May 20, 1878, Tiffany & Co., 20" l. (ILLUS.)........................ **1,763**

Locket/pendant, gold & enamel, high carat hexagonal-form w/hinged top depicting an enameled design of a knight trampling a vanquished knight within a pierced polychrome floral & vine case, reverse of similar design, European hallmarks, possibly 17th c. **3,450**

Necklace, Berlin ironwork & polished steel, festoon-style necklace, delicate spirals of wirework links suspend an oval polished steel plaque surmounted by a low-relief classical standing figure, possibly Athena, 15 " l. (ILLUS, bottom of page.)............. **1,265**

Necklace, coral, composed of a triple strand of coral beads, 14 1/2" l. **176**

Berlin Ironwork Festoon-style Necklace

Pearl and Diamond Necklace

Necklace, diamond, set w/sixty-four graduated old mine-cut diamonds ranging in
size from approx. 0.07 to 2.25 cts., approx. total weight 15.00 cts., silver-
topped gold mounting, 14" l....................... **17,250**

Necklace, gold (14k) & faceted beads, composed of forty-two faceted beads completed by a round chased & engraved floral box clasp, inscribed "1889" (some
beads w/dents) **345**

Necklace, gold (14k), necklace composed
of 14k gold beads, 6.70 mm, 14 1/2" l. **176**

Necklace, gold (14k), turquoise & pearl, festoon-style, delicate trace link chain suspended by festoons decorated w/eight
prong-set square turquoise, each framed
w/freshwater pearls, the center suspended by three bezel-set teardrop-shape turquoise, the back etched w/hieroglyphic
design, Edwardian, England, 17" l. (re-
placed clasp) **1,880**

Necklace, gold (18k), designed as a spiraling mesh link flexible rope in tubular form,
10.7 dwt., ca. 1870, 17 1/2" l. **460**

Necklace, gold & pearl, Art Nouveau style,
composed of delicate pierced swag-form
links spaced by four pearls, 17" l. **230**

Necklace, pearl & diamond, alternating
round & floret links centered by nineteen
pearls (probably natural) & set throughout w/rose- & old mine-cut diamonds, silver-topped 14k gold, converts into one
7" l. bracelet by detaching two elements,
necklace 14 1/4" l. (ILLUS. top of page.)... **9,775**

Pendant, amethyst & diamond, floral &
scroll design centered by an oval amethyst & set throughout w/old mine- &
rose-cut diamonds, the bottom section
flexibly set w/pear-shaped amethyst terminal, silver-topped gold mount
(ILLUS., top next column) **1,175**

Pendant, amethyst, diamond & platinum,
faceted oval bezel-set amethyst framed
by a rose-cut diamond bow & flowering
vines, platinum-topped 18k gold mount,

suspended from platinum trace link
chain, Edwardian, England, 23" l. **2,115**

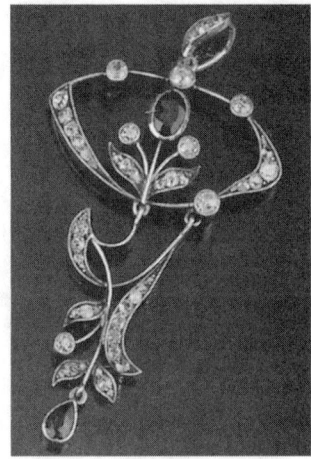

Amethyst and Diamond Pendant

Pendant, amethyst & gold (14k), faceted,
teardrop-shaped pendant carved in the
form of a sphinx's head, 14k gold cap &
bail, Egyptian Revival..................................... **690**

Enamel and Pearl Pendant

Pendant, enamel & pearl, depicting a seated woman in a landscape holding a rose, within an oval frame suspended from bail & swags all set w/seed pearls, the reverse w/glass locket compartment, 10k gold mount (ILLUS.) **173**

Pendant, gold (14k), opal & enamel, Art Nouveau style, oval opal framed by a pink guilloché enamel lotus design, two diamond accents, suspended by a 14k gold trace link chain, hallmark for Krementz & Co. (crack to opal) **705**

Pendant, mourning-type, black onyx & rose gold pendant inscribed, "Charles Lord Southampton, obt 22 March 1797" & "George Lord Southampton, obt 24 June 1810," centering a glass compartment containing locks of hair, enameled crown design bail, early 19th c. **259**

Pendant, silver, ivory & coral, designed as cluster of silver leaves & scrolling tendrils w/two fluted ivory bellflowers suspended, accented by three coral beads (probably designed by Dagobert Peche), Wiener Werkstatte, Austria, early 20th c. **3,525**

Pendant necklace, sterling silver, Art Nouveau style, tripartite abstract form pendant decorated en plein w/blue & green enamel, suspended from a baton-link chain, hallmarks for Chester, letter date for 1911, maker "C.H.," England **323**

Pendant necklace, sterling silver & green agate, shaped pendant centered by an oval green agate, suspended from a silver paper clip chain, pendant stamped on reverse "TF for Theodor Fahrner, 935, Depose," 21" l. **1,528**

Gem-set Bloodstone Pendant Brooch

Pendant/brooch, bloodstone, rose-cut diamond, ruby & gold (18k), the oval bloodstone surmounted by a rose-cut diamond & cabochon ruby floral design, within an 18k gold pierced, chased & engraved floral & foliate frame set w/rose-cut diamonds & rubies, French import stamp, Victorian (ILLUS.) **489**

Pendant/brooch, chalcedony, ruby & enamel, oval chalcedony carved w/four intaglio classical figures within a Holbeinesque polychrome floral enamel frame set w/three circular cut rubies, 18k gold mount **1,840**

Pendant/brooch, diamond, bow design w/five loops each set w/nine old mine-cut diamonds & centered by an old European-cut diamond, 18k gold mount, ca. 1895 .... **1,955**

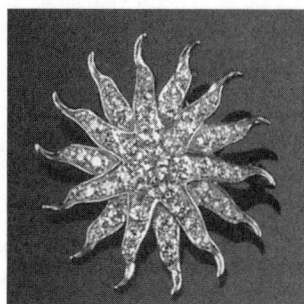

Starburst Pendant/Brooch

Pendant/brooch, diamond & gold (14k), starburst shaped pendant/brooch set w/fifty old mine-cut diamonds, 14k gold mount, hallmark for Krementz & Co., ca. 1900 (ILLUS.) **2,990**

Tiffany Starburst Pendant/Brooch

Pendant/brooch, diamond & gold (18k), starburst design, set w/fifty-five old European-cut diamonds, 18k gold mount, signed "Tiffany & Co." (ILLUS.) **7,168**

Diamond and Gold Pendant/Brooch

Pendant/brooch, diamond & gold, oval frame containing portraits of young girls painted front & back, silver-topped 18k gold mount designed as a bow set w/old mine-cut diamonds, Edwardian, England (ILLUS.).. **1,410**

Pendant/brooch, diamond, ruby & gold, the pinwheel design centered by an old European-cut diamond weighing approx. .35 cts., set throughout w/36 old European-cut diamonds & six rubies, 14k white gold mount, partially obliterated European hallmarks **1,116**

Pendant/brooch, enamel, Art Nouveau style, a large six-petal pale orange blossom encircled by a sinuous green vine & centering an old mine-cut diamond, pearl accent, 14k gold mount, hallmark for Carter, Howe & Gough.................................... **999**

Pendant/brooch, enamel & gold, Art Nouveau style, a pansy decorated w/cobalt blue, light blue, white, yellow & brown enamel, centering a pearl, partially obliterated hallmark, possibly by Larter & Sons **441**

Pendant/brooch, gold (14k), coral & pearl, centered by angelskin coral bead, framed by ribbon & crown design mounted w/seed pearls, together w/bracelet of chased & engraved shaped gold plaques interspersed w/gold beads, mounted w/profile cameos, 14k gold mount, Edwardian, England... **764**

Early Gold & Quartz Pendant/Brooch

Pendant/brooch, gold & gold quartz, the circular form decorated w/black & white tracery enamel intersected by a rectangular gold quartz plaque trimmed w/seed pearls, Victorian (ILLUS.)................................ **881**

Pendant/brooch, pearl, sapphire, diamond & gold (18k), a center design of nine old European-cut diamonds & eight sapphires set within an 18k gold, white enamel & pearl spiral mounting, Edwardian, England **1,058**

Heart-shaped Pendant/Brooch

Pendant/brooch, portrait-type, heart-shaped mount enclosing a painted image of three cherubs, frame set w/rose-cut diamonds & surmounted by butterflies, backed w/mother-of-pearl & engraved initials, silver-topped gold mount, missing two stones (ILLUS.) **1,645**

Pendant/brooch, seed pearl & diamond, designed as an openwork flower w/six seed pearl petals centering an old European-cut diamond, 14k gold mount, Edwardian **558**

Pendant/brooch, silver-gilt & stone, silver-gilt mount of scrolling vines set w/oval & pear-shaped closed-back red stones............ **323**

Pendant/necklace, gold, Cannetille pendant necklace, the central pendant comprised of floret & scroll design, highlighted by diminutive gold spherules suspending three similar drops completed by a spiraling double ropetwist chain supporting two slides, French gold guarantee stamp, 19" l. **2,185**

Pin, emerald & rose-cut diamond, railroad spike- shaped pin, centering a prong-set square-cut emerald, further set w/rose-cut diamonds, silver-topped gold mount, Victorian.. **633**

Pin, enamel, diamond & gold (18k), centered by an old mine-cut diamond within a gold foliate surmount framed by white & blue guilloché enamel, gold foliate accents, 18k gold mount, Edwardian, England **575**

Gold and Pearl Pin

Pin, gold (18k) & pearl, designed as a chased & engraved open pod w/five pearl peas inside, French guarantee stamp, fitted box (ILLUS.) **353**

Pin, sterling silver, octagonal w/applied bird w/long tail on etched background, ca. 1910, 1 1/2 x 1 3/4"................................. **125-150**

Ring, diamond, old mine-cut diamond flanked by fourteen old mine-cut diamonds, pierced floral gallery & shoulders, platinum mount, Edwardian, England, size 6 1/2 .... **17,250**

Ring, diamond, set w/a double row of eighteen old mine-cut diamonds, silver-topped gold mount, size 7 .... **940**

Ring, emerald & gold (14k), centering a bezel-set rectangular step-cut emerald, within a floral chased & engraved 14k gold mount, size 5 1/2 .... **489**

Ring, gold (18k), goldstone, white jasper, carnelian, lapis, malachite & turquoise, five rectangular hardstone plaques interspersed w/green & blue turquoise beads, chased & engraved 18k gold mount, size 6 1/2.. **633**

Ring, gold (18k), ruby & diamond, set w/a faceted round ruby weighing approx. 0.75 cts., flanked by old mine-cut diamonds, approx. total wt. 0.60 cts., within a handmade scroll design, size 6 .... **940**

Ring, mourning-type, gold (18k) & enamel, centering a white enamel plaque picturing a neoclassical urn en grisaille, the black enamel shank reading "Jane Pritchard OB: 17th Dec: 1780 AE: 35," probably English, ca. 1780, size 6 1/4, (slight wear to shank) **345**

Ring, pearl, diamond & platinum, set w/a cream-colored & a grey pearl, the shank set w/old mine- & single-cut diamonds, platinum & 18k gold mount, Edwardian, England, size 7 .... **1,610**

Ring, platinum & diamond, set w/one old mine- & three European-cut diamonds within a shaped & scrolled navette-shaped millegrain mount, approx. total wt. 3.32 cts., Edwardian, England, size 4 3/4.. **4,583**

Ring, ruby & gold (14k), set w/five graduating cushion-cut rubies, 14k gold mount, w/box, size 4 .... **264**

Ring, sapphire, diamond & gold, set w/a cabochon sapphire weighing approx. 11.00 cts., within a scrolled platinum basket mount, single-cut diamond shoulders, 18k gold shank, Edwardian, England, size 6 1/2 .... **3,055**

Ring, wood & crystal, centered by the enamel image of a wild mushroom under a circular crystal in a silver collet, ebonized wood shank, size 6 3/4 .... **316**

Sash pin, gold plate & stone on copper, early angular design, center green cabochon stone, embossed flowers & squares, ca. 1910, 2 x 2 1/2"..................... **75-100**

Stickpin, diamond & banded agate, carved as a naturalistic human eye centering a bezel-set old mine-cut diamond, 14k gold mount **2,415**

Stickpin, gold (14k) & diamond, 14k gold figural bulldog set w/old European-cut diamond in mouth & cabochon ruby eyes **323**

Stickpin, gold (14k) & peridot, briolette-cut peridot within a vine & scroll design, mount supported by a seed pearl, signed "Kuhn," Edwardian, England **144**

Stickpin, gold (18k) & agate, surmounted by the carved head of a saint wearing a bead-set rose-cut diamond crown, French hallmarks, signed "LS" & "L Roussel," w/original box **230**

Stickpin, gold (18k), diamond & enamel, designed as a figural coiled serpent w/green enamel wings, head & flexible tongue set w/five rose-cut diamonds, French hallmarks **173**

Stickpin, jasper & gold (18k), carved bust of a pharaoh, 18k gold mount, French guarantee stamp, Egyptian Revival **690**

Stickpin, pearl & diamond, old mine-cut diamond petals set around a small pearl, platinum-topped 14k gold mount, Edwardian, England... **144**

Stickpin, sapphire, enamel & gold, Art Nouveau style, designed as a flower set w/a cabochon sapphire measuring approx. 3.1 x 3.8 x 6.0 mm, blue enamel accents, 14k gold mount.. **230**

Stickpin Brooch

Stickpin-brooch, diamond & gold, composed of nine stickpins, including two bulldogs, two diamond knots, a shield dated 1905 (ILLUS.) **411**

Sets

Bracelet & brooch, gold (10k) & paste, bracelet centered by three faceted orange-pink pastes within collet mounts edged by floral vines & joined by a lattice-style strap, clasp engraved "MA Doll," 6 1/2" l., together w/a similarly set oval brooch, the set... **176**

Brooch & earrings, gold (14k) demi-parure, the brooch w/an engraved scroll design suspended loop set w/seed pearls suspended within a trapezoid, earrings ensuite, Victorian, the set..................... **335**

Brooch, lapel pin & bracelet pendant, gold (14k) ribbed circle brooch draped w/a pierced ribbon; bracelet articulated 14k gold w/rectangular plaques formed of elongated links, 6 1/2" l.; lapel pin 10k gold openwork designed as a profile of woman encircled by leaves & flowers w/circular pendant suspended, each set w/an old mine-cut diamond, the set **382**

Pendant/brooch & lapel pins, onyx & diamond, oblong onyx pendant/brooch set w/thirty-five old mine-cut diamonds in a knot design, two lapel pins ensuite, 14k gold mounts, signed "Tiffany & Co.," fitted box, the set... **4,230**

Art Deco Rhinestone Bracelet

Costume

Costume jewelry, unlike precious jewelry, is made of inexpensive materials. It is valued for its art, design and craftsmanship, and as part of the history of another era. It was originally made to accessorize designers' clothing collections, and even though it was meant to be discarded when that clothing went out of style, women saved it, and a large selection is available for today's collectors. It is as affordable today as it was in its time, but even so, some costume jewelry has become so collectible and so in demand that it even surpasses precious jewelry in cost.

Bar pin, rhinestones set in white metal, Art Deco openwork design, 2 1/2" w., 1/2" l.. **$45-65**

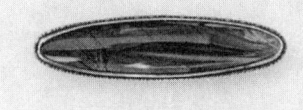

Iridescent Blue Butterfly Bar Pin

Bar pin, sterling silver, iridescent blue butterfly wing under glass, oval shape, 2" w., 1/2" h. (ILLUS.) **65-90**

Bar Pin with Openwork Leaves

Bar pin, sterling silver, openwork leaves design w/center rhinestone on each leaf, 2 3/4" w., 3/8" l. (ILLUS.)............................. **60-85**

Bar pin, sterling silver, V-shaped design w/three hanging stirrups on chains, 2" l..... **65-85**

Bracelet, Bakelite, bangle-type, cranberry red, raised carved scallops all around the edges, 3/8" thick, 1/2" w.............................. **75-90**

Bracelet, Bakelite, bangle-type, moss green, carved stars design, 1/4" thick, 7/8" w. **100-125**

Bracelet, black enamel on gold plate, bangle-type, hinged, in the form of a belt w/a buckle, 3/8" w... **45-65**

Bracelet, brass, bangle-type, hinged, thick black Bakelite circles in front w/densely carved leaves on the sides, 1 1/8" w. in front **135-155**

Bracelet, charm-type, gold plate & enamel, nine Christmas design charms in enamel, rhinestones accents................................ **40-55**

Bracelet, gold plated, six flattened snake chains w/gold drops at end, pulled through an oval gold slide, lengthened or shortened by pulling each chain through the center slide, signed "Monet" on clasp & attached tiny tag, 1 1/4" w. **100-125**

Bracelet, gold-filled, Retro-style, circles alternating w/cabochon set large rectangular royal blue stones, ca. 1950................. **95-120**

Bracelet, gold-filled, Retro-style, triple bar design links alternating w/three cabochon set topaz stones, 3/8" w............... **135-160**

Bracelet, Lucite, hinged bangle, overlapping tapered front, blue glitter & gold threads inside, front 2 1/4" w...................... **75-90**

Bracelet, pink gold on sterling silver, Retro-style, large wide links w/a slanted coiled design atop each link, signed "Napier," 1 1/8" w.. **150-175**

Bracelet, rhinestone, Art Deco style, triple row open back set w/individual blue oval crystal stones, clear round, baguette rhinestone clasp, signed "Czechoslovakia," 5/8" w. (ILLUS., top of page).. **175-2000**

Bracelet, rhinestone, expansion-type, covered w/large emerald-cut clear rhinestones, ca. 1950s, 1/2" w................. **85-115**

Bracelet, rhinestone & gold plate, Retro style, curved center design w/two rows of curved baguette rhinestones, sides composed of small flexible hinged links resembling basketweave, signed "Trifari," 1" w. **150-175**

Bracelet, rhinestone, lavender stones individually set in square white metal setting, 1/4" w.. **40-65**

Bracelet, turquoise enamel, hinged bangle, w/gold ribbon-style X designs going all around, signed "Pauline Rader," 1/2" w. **75-95**

Bracelet/watch, enameled hinged bangle, individual blossoms in red, white & blue enamel w/pearl centers, center blossom opens to a 17-jewel Swiss watch, 7/8" w. **125-150**

Clip, dress-type, Bakelite, Art Deco design in moss green, circle shape w/center white metal multiple-circle design, 1 1/4" d. **50-70**

Clip, dress-type, Bakelite & rhinestone, Art Deco design of green Bakelite canoe-shaped base w/white metal triangular design above pavé set rhinestones, 1 3/8" h. **35-55**

Clip, dress-type, rhinestone, red, blue, green & yellow rhinestones set into Art Deco white metal design, 1 3/4" h............. **50-75**

Clip, fur-type, enamel, bouquet of red & blue enamel flowers w/clear rhinestone centers, flanked by white enamel lace & green leaves, signed "Trifari," 2 1/4" l. **65-90**

Clip, fur-type, enamel on gold plated sterling, exotic bird on branch in detailed workmanship w/pavé rhinestone trim, enamel in yellow, red & green, signed "Coro Craft," 2 1/4 x 2 1/2" **195-225**

Clip/pendant, gold plated, Retro design, swirled ribbons w/rhinestone bands, clip converts to pendant, 1 1/2" x 2 3/4 .... **85-120**

Clips, black glass, carved rectangular Art Deco designs, 1" h., pr. **65-85**

Clips, chatelaine-type, turquoise inlaid in white metal shield-shaped forms connected w/a 4" double chain, clips marked "Made in India" **65-95**

Clips, duette-type, rhinestone, Art Deco sunburst style w/baguettes, clips convert to dress clips, marked "Clipmates" (Trifari trademark), 1 1/2 x 2 1/2" **165-195**

Clips, duette-type, rhinestone, Art Deco trapezoidal-shaped design w/baguettes, emerald green baguette accents, 1 x 2 1/4"... **120-140**

Gold Plate & Glass Art Deco Clips

Clips, gold plate & art glass, Art Deco arrangement w/four leaves in sunburst design, large 1 1/4" green oval glass cabochon at the side, 2" w., 3" h., pr. (ILLUS.)... **135-160**

Earrings, amber & sterling silver, teardrop-shaped brownish-orange amber on sterling silver screw backs, original tag w/"natural Danish amber," w/original box, 5/8", pr. **55-75**

Tiffany-style Glass Earrings

Earrings, art glass, red Tiffany-style iridescent large bead centers surrounded by red beads & tiny yellow bead accents, West Germany, 1 1/4"d., pr. (ILLUS). **35-55**

Earrings, enamel, hanging hoops in bright turquoise enamel, clip-on-type, 2", pr. **40-65**

Earrings, enamel, pearl & rhinestone, fish-shaped in turquoise enamel accented w/royal blue enamel, gold, rhinestones & hanging pearls, turquoise beads on bottom, post, 2", pr..................................... **45-65**

Earrings, enamel & rhinestone, inverted curved triangular Art Deco revival design, black enamel center, clear rhinestone border w/clear square rhinestone on top, clip-on-type, 7/8", pr. **45-65**

Earrings, gold plate, enamel & rhinestone, curved button style in openwork basketweave design, alternating black enamel strips w/rhinestone-set strips in gold borders, clip-on-type, 1" d., pr........... **35-55**

Earrings, gold plate & rhinestone, cluster of flowers w/red & clear rhinestone-set centers, baroque pearl accent, signed "Miriam Haskell," clip-on-type, 1 1/8" d., pr. **50-75**

Earrings, gold plate, scallop shell design, signed "Napier," clip/screw-on-type, 7/8", pr.. **40-65**

Earrings, marcasites set in sterling silver, heart-shaped drops completely pavé set w/marcasites, signed "KD," screw-back-type, 1 1/4" l., pr..................................... **75-100**

Earrings, rhinestone, Art Deco design of clear rhinestones set in white metal drop, hanging from single rhinestone screw-back type, 1 1/4" l., pr.................................. **40-55**

Earrings, rhinestone, black w/Aurora Borealis finish, set in leaves w/large black center stone, signed "Miriam Haskell" on horseshoe-shaped plate, 1 1/4" l., pr........ **65-90**

Earrings, rhinestone, fleur-de-lis shape handset w/round, marquise green stones w/clear rhinestone trim, signed "Eisenberg," clip-on-type, 1" l., pr. **85-120**

Earrings, turquoise inlaid in 800 silver, star-shaped, clip-on-type, 7/8", pr. **65-90**

Earrings, white metal & glass, drop-shaped w/four rows of raised dots, center teardrop of white opaline glass, clip-on-type, 1 1/4", pr... **25-40**

Bead and Rhinestone Earrings

Earrings, wood & plastic beads w/rhinestones, plastic coral & turquoise beads w/center orange plastic scallop shells flanking a large yellow bead, a ring of rhinestones flank shells, signed "Haskell," drop-style w/clip/screw-on mounts, 3 3/4" l., pr. (ILLUS.)................. **150-175**

Necklace, bead, African-style, triple strand of plastic beads in orange, medium coral-red, tan & black flat beads, 16" l. **30-45**

Necklace, bead, graduated coral & red beads strung on sterling silver chain, 16" l. **150-175**

Necklace, bead, graduated faceted garnet beads, garnet bead clasp, 16" l. **175-200**

Necklace, bone beads, graduated rose-carved beads, natural color, 20" l. **35-55**

Art Glass Four Strand Necklace

Necklace, faceted glass beads, four graduated strands of shaded red beads w/black spacers, ornate clasp w/red & yellow beads on gold filigree, 15-18" l. (ILLUS.) **160-185**

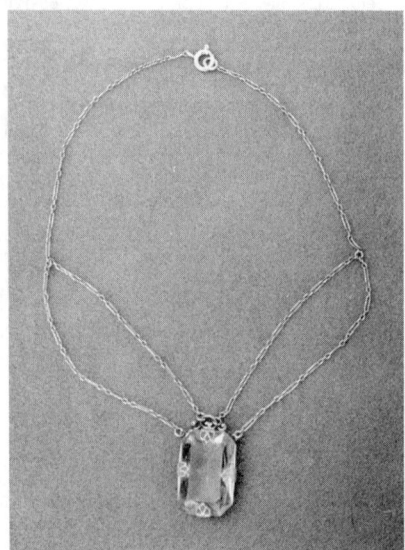

Art Deco Faux Citrine Necklace

Necklace, faux citrine & sterling silver, Art Deco style, large emerald-cut faux citrine stone suspended on swag-style sterling silver chain, 15" l., stone 1 1/4" (ILLUS.) **65-85**

Necklace, glass bead, Art Deco style w/small multistrands of small coral beads alternating w/large black cylindrical beads w/greyish-blue African-style designs, ca. 1935, 24" l........................... **165-185**

Necklace, glass beads & gold metal, collar-style, individual black glass beads, gold collar w/attached moving individual glass beads, signed "Trifari," adjustable 14-16" l. **295-325**

Necklace, glass beads, large green beads marbleized w/red & black veining, alternating w/gold metal beads & gold metal filigree designs, signed "Miriam Haskell," 30" l. **275-300**

Necklace, gold plate, gold pierced work w/six rows of inverted crescent moon design in graduated bib-style, paper tag w/"Matisse," adjustable clasp, 24" l........... **50-65**

Necklace, pearl & rhinestone, double strand of small & medium size baroque pearls, ornate center, gold plate filigree-style design w/seed pearl flowers, baguette & marquise rhinestones, blue, clear & garnet rhinestone trim, signed "Denbe," adjustable 12-15" l... **75-100**

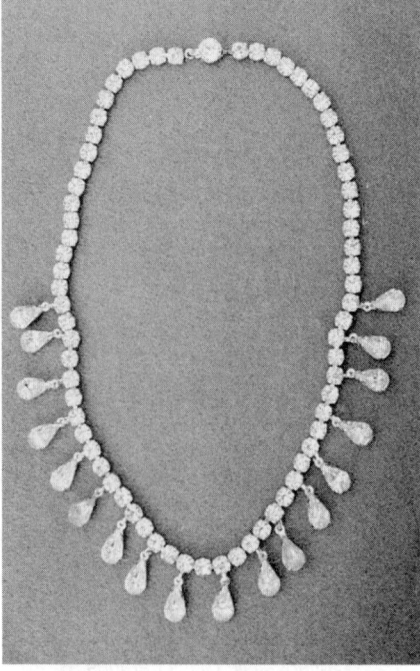

Coro Rhinestone Silver Necklace

Necklace, rhinestone, sterling chain set w/medium sized clear rhinestones, suspending 18 handset teardrops, signed "Coro Sterling" 14" l. (ILLUS.) **125-150**

Enameled Cherry Pendant on Chain

Pendant, enamel & white metal, cluster of red enamel cherries below antiqued white metal leaves on white metal chain w/scattered matching red glass beads, ca. 1935, 24" l. (ILLUS.)............. **75-1,000**

Pendant, gold-filled metal, amethyst & cultured pearls, oval openwork pendant w/flowers, leaves & amethyst bud, three hanging gold-filled drops w/cultured pearls, two 8" chains, 2" drop.................. **150-175**

Pendant, sterling silver & marcasite, Art Deco style, marcasites in openwork design w/large hematite stone, no chain, 1 3/4" l. **95-120**

Pendant, white metal, filigree cylindrical shape, one end opens for placement of money or perfumed cotton, no chain, 2 1/8" w. **40-65**

Pin, bead & gold plate, pair of flowers w/coral bead centers & clear rhinestone tops, signed "HAR," 2" h. **55-70**

Pin, colored stones & gold plate, antique ornate three-dimensional design of flowers w/tiny purple stone-set centers & leaves surrounding a very large center oval cabochon purple stone, ca. 1910, 1 1/2" x 2".. **70-95**

Pin, enamel on gold plate, figural clown playing flute, white squares on navy blue enamel, legs swing side to side, w/original blue grosgrain case, 1 3/4" h. **30-50**

Pin, garnet, crystal & sterling silver, Retro style bow design, fan shape over a flower set w/garnets above sterling silver bow set w/crystals, 2 7/8" w............................ **350-375**

Pin, glass stone & gold plate, stylized crescent shape w/black three-dimensional marquise-cut glass stone, signed "Sarah Coventry," 1 1/2"... **35-50**

Rhinestone, Pearl and Art Glass Pin

Pin, gold plate, rhinestone & pearl, antiqued finish, very ornate design set w/large & small red & green rhinestones, pearls & green art glass, ornate bar w/seven chain drop in diamond-shape, unsigned Czechoslovakian, 4 1/8" h. (ILLUS)....... **150-175**

Pin, micromosaic, center white & blue flowers, outside border w/white, green, red & black designs, Victorian, 1 1/4" d. **145-165**

Pin, rhinestone, Art Deco design, white metal, winged design set w/two large royal blue square stones in center, center row of blue baguettes, remainder of pin set w/blue round stones, 2 1/4" w.................... **65-85**

Pin, rhinestone & gold plate, figural bird w/pavé-set rhinestone body, neck & crest w/large green cabochon stone eye, body rotates to flat coral stones set in textured gold, signed "K.J.L." 2 1/2" h.................. **245-285**

Pin, rhinestone & gold plate, figural lion running w/amber rhinestone-set mane & tail, clear rhinestones on silver colored body, green rhinestone eyes, can stand as figurine, 1 3/4" x 4 1/4".............................. **125-150**

Pin, rhinestone & gold plate, figural spread-winged eagle, pavé-set w/clear rhinestones, signed "Kramer," 3 1/2" w......... **125-150**

Freeform Gold Plated & Bead Pin

Pin, rhinestone, gold plate & pearl, freeform granular textured design set w/turquoise stones & pearls, overlapping two large white glass teardrops, signed "Mimi di N." 2" l. (ILLUS.)... **70-95**

Pin, rhinestone & gold plate, Retro style, marquise & baguette rhinestones in swirled three-dimensional design, signed "Trifari," 2" h. **75-95**

Pin, rhinestone & sterling silver, openwork bow design, sterling silver bow set w/marquise-cut & round stones, center row of baguettes, signed "Coro Craft," 2 1/8" w... **75-95**

Pin, rhinestone & white metal, long narrow sword design set w/rhinestones, ca. 1940, 4 1/2"...................................... **45-60**

Pin, sterling silver & enamel, etched Siamese dancer on black enamel background, signed "Siam Sterling," 1 3/4" sq... **65-90**

Pin, sterling silver, figural bird w/open wings eating a berry, signed "Black, Starr & Gorham," also designer-signed "C. Ruopoli," 2 1/4 x 2 3/8".......................... **165-185**

Pin, sterling silver, Retro style, abstract form, w/pleated fabric design, signed "Christian Dior," Germany, 2 1/2" **145-165**

Pin, white metal, figural dinosaur, 2 1/2" h. x 3 3/4" w. **75-100**

Pin/pendant, cut glass & gold plate, seven intaglio-cut topaz-colored glass circles w/profiles of women set in gold plate frames, set in a circle w/flower-like center, unsigned **75-1000**

Pin/pendant, sapphire, emerald, ruby & sterling silver, flower basket form set w/sapphire, emerald & ruby flowers, entire basket & leaves set w/marcasites, 1 1/2".. **325-350**

Pin/pendant, white metal, scene of Egyptian charioteer w/bow & arrow set in openwork ornate frame, 1 3/4" d. **45-70**

Figural Ship's Wheel Lapel Watch

Watch, lapel-style, gold plate & rhinestone, figural ship's wheel set w/baguettes on the spokes, suspended on a chain from a rhinestone-set bow design, sweep seconds hand, signed "Pierce," 2" l. (ILLUS.)... **145-170**

Watch, lapel-style, gold plated case w/three-dimensional flower w/center

pearl, iridescent dial face, signed "Bercona," 2 1/2" d. **150-175**

Watch, lapel-style, sterling silver set w/marcasites, suspended from a Retro- style swirl design bar pin, marcasite-set leaves framing watch, signed "Croton," 2 1/2" l. **230-255**

Sets

Necklace, bracelet, & earrings, enameled metal, red w/gold cross design, matching bangle bracelet, solid metal collar-style necklace, clip-on earrings, signed "YSL" (Yves St. Laurent), the set........................ **95-125**

Seashell Design Necklace & Earrings

Necklace & earrings, gold plate & pearl, gold plate seashell design w/pearl accents in center, necklace w/14" pearl adjustable chain, screw back-type earrings, 1 1/2" l. earrings, the set (ILLUS.).............. **50-75**

Necklace & earrings, rhinestone, center composed of large multicolored stones, large earrings w/matching design, the set.. **80-115**

Pin & earrings, rhinestone, figural butterfly pin, marquise-cut & art glass stones set in four trembling wings mounted on springs, round & square citrine-colored stones & gold-flecked art glass beads, topaz, 1 1/2" l. earrings do not repeat butterfly design, signed "Schreiner," pin 2" h., the set.. **225-250**

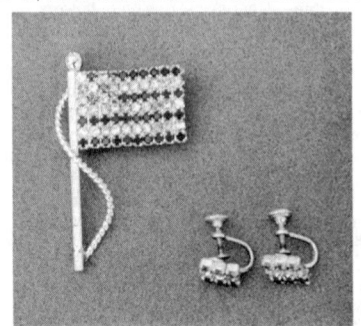

Rhinestone American Flag Set

Art Deco Style Bar Pin

Art Deco Style Bracelet

Pin & earrings, rhinestone & gold plate, model of American flag set w/red, clear & blue rhinestones, matching 2" h. square screw back earrings, ca. 1955, 3/8" l. pin, the set (ILLUS.) **40-65**

Pin & earrings, rhinestone & sterling silver, cluster of leaves set w/clear rhinestones, 1 3/4" d. earrings, signed "Carl-Art," w/original box, 1 1/8" l. pin, the set........ **100-125**

Pins, gold plated 800 silver, figural filigree butterflies, 1 1/4 x 2", the set.................... **95-125**

Modern (1920-1960s)

Bar pin, platinum & diamond, Art Deco style, set throughout w/thirty-nine old European-cut diamonds, approx. total wt. 1.75 cts., millegrain accents **1,880**

Bar pin, platinum & diamond, Art Deco style set w/seven collet-set old European-cut diamonds, within a lattice design mount (ILLUS., top of page) **1,380**

Bar pin, sapphire, diamond & gold (14k), Art Deco style, set w/sixteen bead-set old European-cut diamonds & eight calibré-cut sapphires within a filigree platinum mount, pierced gallery, 14k yellow gold pin stem **646**

Bracelet, diamond & sapphire, Art Deco style, centered by an old European-cut diamond, set throughout w/seventy-four bead-set old European-, old mine- & single-cut diamonds, calibré French-cut sapphire highlights, millegrain accents, platinum mount, 7" l. **3,795**

Bracelet, gold (14k), Art Moderne style, bi-color 14k gold, large square openwork yellow gold links joined by domed rose gold links... **1,880**

Bracelet, gold (14k), bicolor gold, flexible tubular links of yellow & rose gold edged w/brickwork links, signed "Tiffany & Co.," ca. 1940, 7 1/2" l. **1,763**

Bracelet, gold (14k) & diamond, double "tubogas" style surrounded by bezel & bead-set old European-cut diamonds, set in silver flowerheads, stems incorporating initials "H & L," French hallmarks, ca. 1940... **411**

Bracelet, gold (14k), flexible tubular links of yellow & rose gold edged w/brickwork links, ca. 1940, 7 1/2" l. **823**

Bracelet, gold (14k) & green stone, openwork gold double fan design links spaced by rectangular floral-carved green stone links, possibly dyed green onyx, Czechoslovakian import mark, ca. 1940, 7 3/4" l. **235**

Bracelet, gold, ruby & diamond, hexagonal links, Retro style, each decorated w/a star-set ruby, centered by an abstract ribbon design of rubies & diamonds, 6 3/4" l... **2,938**

Bracelet, paste, hardstone & sterling silver, Art Deco style, floral design w/multiple hinged plaques set w/colorless pastes highlighted by a geometric design of green & black stones, silver mount, French hallmarks, 7" l................................. **1,175**

Bracelet, platinum & diamond, Art Deco style, designed w/interlocking circles spaced by lozenge-form links, set throughout w/approx. 324 old European, transitional & single-cut diamonds, approx. total wt. 8.00 cts., original fitted box, 7 5/8" l.. **12,925**

Bracelet, platinum, diamond & pearl, Art Deco style, composed of three rows of 3.90 mm pearls completed by a platinum & diamond clasp, signed "Cartier," 8" l....... **2,115**

Bracelet, platinum, diamond & sapphire, Art Deco style, link bracelet w/thirty-five flexible openwork links, each centered w/a box set of old European-cut diamond calibre-cut sapphire accents, engraved gallery, 7 1/4" l. **1,880**

Bracelet, platinum, diamond & sapphires, Art Deco style, designed w/a double row of flexible pierced filigree plaques alternating w/links set w/single-cut diamonds & triangle-cut sapphires, gallery pierced in a heart design, millegrain accents, 6 1/2" l.. **1,763**

Bracelet, platinum & sapphire, Art Deco style link, composed of forty French-cut sapphires, engraved gallery, millegrain accents, 6 3/4" l.. **3,643**

Bracelet, sapphire & diamond, Art Deco style, set w/119 circular-cut diamonds, highlighted by forty-two calibré-cut sapphires, platinum mount, 7" l. (ILLUS., second from top of previous page)............ **5,865**

Bracelet, sterling silver & coral, six circular links decorated w/abstract design, each link bezel-set w/a coral highlight, signed "Georg Jensen, No. 19," 7" l........................ **1,645**

Brooch, gold (14k), ruby & diamond, Retro style, abstract ribbon design set w/eight oval cabochon rubies & nineteen single-cut diamond accents, signed "Reflections by Mauboussin"..................................... **1,410**

Brooch, gold (18k), ruby & diamond, Retro style, designed as floral spray set w/eleven oval & two circular-cut rubies, further set w/eighteen single & six full-cut diamonds, marker's mark "TW"........................... **588**

Brooch, gold, ruby & diamond, Retro style, green & pink gold bow centered by a line of channel-set square-cut rubies flanked by four single-cut diamonds, hallmark **940**

Brooch, jadeite jade & diamond, Art Deco style, the floral-carved & pierced jade oval plaque centering a bezel-set marquise-cut yellow diamond within a scalloped black enamel frame set w/four baguettes, millegrain accents, 18k white gold mount....................... **1,293**

Brooch, platinum & diamond, Art Deco style, openwork form bead-set w/ninety old mine-, full- & single-cut diamonds, millegrain accents, approx. total wt. 5.26 cts. **3,290**

Brooch, platinum & diamond, Art Deco style, openwork mount w/millegrain accents set throughout w/approx. 103 old European-, transitional- & single-cut diamonds, approx. total wt. 3.05 cts............... **1,998**

Brooch, platinum, diamond & sapphire, Art Deco style, openwork brooch set throughout w/thirty-four old European-, transitional- & single-cut diamonds, w/line of centered square-cut sapphires, millegrain accent (missing one sapphire).. **1,763**

Brooch, platinum, diamond & tourmaline, designed w/two flowers each set w/an old European-cut diamond total wt. approx. 6.00 cts., flanked by carved pink tourmaline petals set entremblant, highlighted throughout w/twelve prong-set diamonds on a flexible spray branch set w/110 single & brilliant-cut diamond petals, approx. total wt. 5.40 cts., platinum & 18k white gold mount, French assay marks & obliterated marker's mark (one diamond melée missing)... **21,150**

Art Deco Brooch

Brooch, platinum, sapphire & diamond, Art Deco style, decorated w/a sapphire set within a bow design on a rectangular openwork frame set w/thirty-six old mine- & old European-cut diamonds, millegrain accents (ILLUS.)........................... **1,763**

Brooch, ruby, diamond & gold (14k), Retro style, pink & yellow 14k gold bowknot centered by a cluster of bead-set rubies, twelve diamond accents............................... **1,410**

Brooch, ruby, garnet & diamond, Retro style floral spray brooch, flowerheads set w/rubies & framed w/demantoid garnets, three old European-cut diamond accents, joined by a rose gold ribbon **920**

Brooch, sterling silver, long undulating abstract form surmounted by a raised circular line design & set w/green & pink stones, partially oxidized finish, hallmark of Sam Kramer, ca. 1950s........................... **1,116**

Gold & Turquoise Insect Brooch

Brooch, turquoise, pearl & gold, insect form, w/14k yellow gold legs & wings, turquoise body, pearl head & garnet eyes, ca. 1930 (ILLUS.) **280**

Chain, platinum & diamond, the cross set w/four kite-cut, twenty baguette & twenty-eight single-cut diamonds, suspended from an Art Deco trace link chain interspersed w/twenty-four old European-cut diamonds, approx. total wt. 2.50 cts., 16 1/2" l.. **5,875**

Clip, gold (18k), enamel & crystal, Art Deco style, scallop design decorated w/cobalt blue enamel highlighted by a circular-cut diamond, signed "Cartier," no. 3016076..... **2,350**

Clips, dress-type, diamond & platinum, Art Deco style, two detachable triangular clips set throughout w/35 baguettes, two kite-shape & 174 single- & full-cut diamonds, w/convertible white metal frame attachment, pr. **3,408**

Clips, dress-type, gold (14k), Retro style, bicolor 14k gold, triangular shaped forms consisting of domed links, signed "WAB" for Wordley, Allsopp & Bliss............................ **705**

Platinum and Diamond Dress Clips

Clips, dress-type, platinum & diamond, designed as scrolling bouquet, each set w/fifty-six old European-, circular-, square- & baguette-cut diamonds, plati-

num mount, ca. 1950, missing one small
diamond, pr. (ILLUS.) **2,526**
Earrings, platinum & diamond, Art Deco
style, drop-style, set w/line of twenty-four
transitional & single-cut diamonds, approx. total wt. 0.68 cts., millegrain, posts,
pr. **1,116**

Art Deco Style Lavaliere

Lavaliere, platinum, diamond & sapphire,
Art Deco style w/a cushion-cut sapphire
within an openwork, geometric mount set
throughout w/old European-cut diamonds, millegrain accents, suspended
by a delicate trace-link chain, signed "Tif-
fany & Co.," 16 1/4" l. (ILLUS.) **4,370**

Agate and Diamond Lorgnette

Lorgnette, agate & diamond, Art Deco
style, designed w/a hexagonal agate
plaque both framed & surmounted by single-cut diamonds, millegrain accents,
suspended by a silver chain (ILLUS.) **2,350**
Necklace, moonstone, sapphire, & emerald, composed of round pierced foliate
design set w/sixteen cushion & circular-
cut sapphires, twenty-five moonstones, &
twenty-two circular-cut emeralds completed by an adjustable curb-link chain,
14k gold mount, signed "F.W.L. Inc.," ca.
1940, adjustable 15-17" **2,645**

Necklace, pearl & gold (18k), composed of
nineteen pearls measuring approx. 4.2
mm spaced by gold curb & fancy
links, ca. 1925, 22" l. **230**
Pendant, coin (14k) & diamond, set w/a
twenty dollar standing liberty coin, the reverse w/double eagle, within a basketweave mount set w/six diamond
melée, America, ca. 1927 .... **403**
Pendant, coral & gold (14k), Art Deco style,
swelled rectangular shape, the upper half
carved in a flowerhead design, 14k gold
mount, European hallmarks **374**

Egyptian Revival Beetle Pendant

Pendant, gold, enamel & Favrile glass,
Egyptian Revival beetle pendant, centered by a blue favrile glass beetle set
within a rectangular plaque decorated
w/dark blue-green enamel corners,
signed "Tiffany & Co., no. 379," also
stamped "Gold & Other Metals," ca.
1920, minor chips to enamel (ILLUS.) **18,800**
Pendant, onyx & diamond, tassel pendant,
Art Deco style, bombé-form onyx pendant
set w/rose-cut diamond & triangular-cut
onyx accents suspending a seed pearl
fringe, millegrain accents, Continental hallmarks, silver & 14k gold mount **1,175**

Art Deco Platinum and Diamond Pendant

Pendant, platinum, diamond & crystal, Art
Deco style, rectangular crystal plaque
carved w/an intaglio image of a classical
woman playing a flute, platinum mount
set w/single-cut diamonds, engraved gallery, back mirrored, suspended by plati-
num chain (ILLUS.) **1,880**

Silver and Enamel Art Deco Pendant

Pendant, silver & enamel, Art Deco style, square plaque w/clipped corners surmounted by an urn & flower design on a green & black enamel ground, hallmark for David (ILLUS.) **1,725**

Pendant/brooch, platinum, diamond & emerald, Art Deco style, openwork plaque set w/twenty-three old European- & single-cut diamonds & eighteen emerald & green stone accents, deployant bail, millegrain accents.. **2,938**

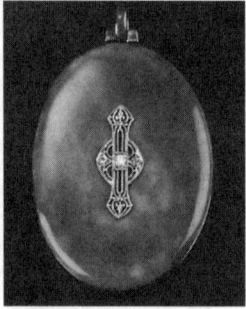

Art Deco Enamel Pendant/Locket

Pendant/locket, platinum, diamond & faux green jade enamel, Art Deco style oval locket w/millegrain platinum mount set w/three circular-cut diamonds, faux green jade "en plein" enamel surface (ILLUS.).. **920**

Silver and Marcasite Pendant

Pendant/necklace, sterling silver, marcasite & glass baguettes, Art Deco style, pierced rectangular pendant set w/carved blue & pink flowerheads over a row of clear glass baguettes, set throughout w/marcasites, completed by a baton-link chain, one marcasite missing, chain not silver, 32" l. (ILLUS.)................................ **489**

Art Deco Diamond Solitaire Ring

Ring, diamond, Art Deco style diamond solitaire, set w/a pear-shaped diamond weighing approx. 2.35 carats further set w/six straight baguettes, nine single- & six transitional-cut diamonds, platinum mount signed "Shreve & Co., no. B9550," size 8 (ILLUS.)... **17,625**

Ring, diamond, Art Deco style, set w/three old European-cut diamonds, approx. total weight .60 cts., within a pierced & engraved platinum mount set w/four single-cut diamonds, millegrain accents, size 6 3/4 .... **881**

Ring, diamond, Art Deco style, three-stone diamond ring box-set w/three old European-cut diamonds, gallery & shoulders pierced in a scroll design, platinum mount, size 6 .... **8,338**

Ring, diamond & gold, Art Deco style,14k white gold filigree mounting w/one marquise diamond, ca. 1920........................... **11,200**

Ring, diamond & platinum, Art Deco style, centered by a bezel-set cushion-shape old mine-cut diamond weighing approx. .81 cts., framed by 18 old mine-cut diamonds, platinum openwork mount w/millegrain accents, size 5 3/4 .... **1,528**

Ring, diamond & sapphire, Art Deco style, openwork pierced platinum mount w/millegrain accents centered by a collet-set circular-cut sapphire, framed by eight old mine-cut diamonds, size 6 1/2 .... **863**

Ring, diamond solitaire, Art Deco style, centering a transitional-cut diamond weighing approx. .94 cts., framed by 12 circular-cut diamonds, shoulders set w/six circular-cut diamonds, millegrain accents, incised shank, size 5 1/4 .... **2,350**

Ring, emerald & diamond, Art Deco style, 18k yellow gold, silver wash, emerald & diamond, silver washed crown holds a center oval cabochon emerald surrounded by two rows of round diamonds flanked on each side by round diamonds, ca. 1930 .... **896**

Ring, gold (18k), diamond & platinum, Retro style, two old European-cut & six single-cut diamonds, vertically set in platinum, tiered shoulders, size 6 .... **294**

Ring, opal, Art Deco style, black oval opal centered within a hand-engraved, pierced platinum mount, signed "Marcus & Co.," size 4 (shank out of round) **4,715**

Ring, platinum & diamond, Art Deco style, centered by a bezel-set old European-cut diamond weighing approx. 1.00 cts., further set w/thirty-two full-cut & twelve calibré-cut sapphires in an openwork scroll design, size 7 1/2 .... **2,468**

Ring, platinum & diamond, Art Deco style, geometric mount set w/twenty-one European-, transitional- & single-cut diamonds, center three stones set in a navette shape framed by calibré-cut emeralds, millegrain accents, size 3 3/4 .... **529**

Ring, platinum & diamond, Art Deco style, set w/five old European-cut diamonds, approx. total wt. 1.15 cts., within an openwork filigree mount, size 10 1/2 .... **999**

Art Deco Diamond Ring

Ring, platinum & diamond, Art Deco style, three collet-set old European-cut diamonds set within a filigree & old European-cut diamond mount, size 6 (ILLUS.) **1,265**

Ring, platinum, ruby & diamond, Art Deco style, centered by a round, faceted ruby, flanked by two old European-cut diamonds, in a pierced platinum mount w/six marquise- and six single-cut diamond accents, size 2 1/4 .... **2,990**

Ring, platinum, sapphire & diamond, Art Deco style, vertically set w/cushion-cut sapphire measuring 7.60 x 7.42 x 5.46 mm & weighing 2.39 cts., flanked by old European-cut diamonds, approx. total wt. 2.26 cts., pierced & scrolled shoulders set w/twenty-six old mine-& old European-cut diamonds, millegrain accents, size 3 1/4 .... **18,800**

Ring, ruby & citrine, Retro style, set w/large emerald-cut citrine, shoulders designed as an openwork loop set w/a curved row of channel-set rubies, 14k gold mount, size 5 1/2 .... **646**

Ring, ruby, diamond & gold, Art Deco style, centered by octagonal step-cut ruby measuring approx. 7.39 x 7.08 x 4.60 mm, flanked by pentagonal-cut diamonds, approx. total wt. 1.50 cts., all collet-set in an 18k yellow gold mount, together w/original platinum mounting signed "Yard," size 7 1/2 .... **34,075**

Ring, ruby & diamond, Retro style, bow-form channel-set w/nineteen calibré-cut rubies & sixteen bead-set circular diamonds, 14k gold mount, stamped "H" for J. & L. Hartzberg, size 5 .... **1,410**

Ring, sapphire & diamond, Art Deco style, bezel-set w/a rectangular-cut synthetic sapphire flanked by openwork shoulders enhanced w/baguette & circular-cut diamonds, millegrain accents, platinum mount, stamped "M.S. Bowman," size 4 1/2 .... **441**

Ring, sapphire & diamond, Art Deco style, centered by a faceted round sapphire measuring approx. 8.29 x 5.59 mm in a

vertical chased & engraved platinum mounting set w/two old European-cut diamonds each weighing approx. 0.75 ct., openwork shoulders & gallery further enhanced w/twenty-two old European- & full-cut diamonds, millegrain accents, signed "Tiffany & Co.," boxed, size 6......... **8,225**

Ring, sapphire & diamond, Art Deco style, three-stone ring centered by a cushion-cut sapphire measuring approx. 7.20 x 6.00 x 3.95 mm, flanked by old European-cut diamonds, approx. total wt. 1.15 cts., platinum mount set w/straight baguettes, engraved gallery, boxed, size 6 (chip to girdle of one diamond) **2,585**

Ring, sapphire, ruby & diamond, Retro style, set w/a square yellow sapphire w/clipped corners, flanked by a row of channel-set square-cut rubies, further set w/three full-cut diamonds set in a white gold raised triangle design, 18k yellow gold mount, size 6 3/4 .... **999**

Ring, turquoise, diamond & enamel, Art Deco style, centered by a round turquoise flanked by rose-cut diamonds set in platinum, millegrain & black enamel accents, 18k gold gallery & shank, French import stamps, size 4 1/4 .... **920**

Sets

Retro-style Brooch

Brooch & earrings, bicolor gold (14k), Retro style, brooch designed as a stylized pink & yellow gold flower bouquet w/full-cut diamond highlights, earrings set w/cluster of six aquamarines, American hallmark, the set (ILLUS. of brooch only)...... **588**

Necklace & earrings, gold (14k), Retro style, necklace w/five abstract geometric form pendants interspersed w/gold beads suspended from snake link chain, earrings ensuite, ca. 1940, 14 3/4" l., the set.. **441**

Pendant/brooch & earrings, tourmaline & gold (14k), Retro style, circular polished gold, surmounted by a fan-shaped ornament set w/an octagonal green tourmaline, together w/flowerhead earrings, centered by circular-cut green tourmalines, hallmark for F. & F. Felger, Inc., the set.. **588**

KEWPIE COLLECTIBLES

Rose O'Neill's Kewpies were so popular in their hey-day that numerous objects depicting them were produced and are now collectible. Bisque figures made in Germany were widely made in various poses. Following is a sampling of vintage Kewpie items.

Chamber set: pitcher & bowl, cov. tooth-brush dish, chamber pot, cov. soap dish; porcelain, each w/color transfers of various action Kewpies, marked "Rose O'Neill - Kewpie - Germany," early 20th c., the set **$1,600**

Doll, all-bisque, stiff neck, painted black eyes to left, dash brows, closed smiling mouth, molded & painted tufts of hair, body jointed at shoulders only, molded blue wings at shoulders, "O'Neill" incised on bottom of feet, marked "Kewpie - Germany" on paper heart label on chest & "Design - Patented" on partial round label on back, 8" **235**

Doll, bisque head w/stiff neck, large side-glancing eyes, dash brows, closed smiling mouth, molded & painted tufts of hair, bisque body jointed at shoulders only, molded & painted blue wings, wearing antique knit red & white dress, marked "O'Neill" on bottom of feet, partial Kewpie heart label on chest, partial round Kewpie label on back, 10" **400**

Cloth Kewpie Doll

Doll, cloth, mask face w/eyes painted to side, dash brows, painted button nose, closed smiling mouth, red nylon body w/shaped wings, "'Kewpie' - Reg. U.S. Pat. Off. - Rose O'Neill - © - Krueger N.Y. - Reg. U.S. Pat. Off. - Made in U.S.A." on tag on right side seam, 10" (ILLUS.).............. **135**

Figurine, all-bisque, w/painted side-glancing eyes, dash brows, closed smiling mouth, molded & painted tufts of hair, molded blue wings at shoulders, unjointed body in sitting position, w/black flocked cat on Kewpie's lap, "©" on bottom, 3 1/4" (ILLUS., top next column)............ **375**

Kewpie Figure with Cat

Kewpie Farmer Figure

Figurine, all-bisque unjointed farmer doll, eyes painted to side, dash brows, closed smiling mouth, molded bisque farmer's straw hat, molded blue wings, right hand molded to hold rake, left arm molded behind back, "O'Neill" incised on bottom of feet, "Copyright - Rose O'Neill" on round label on back, rake missing, 4" (ILLUS.) **405**

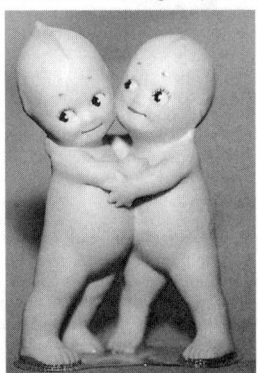

Kewpie Huggers Figure Group

Figure group, Kewpie Huggers, on a base, Germany, 1913, 3 1/2" h. (ILLUS.) **200-225**

Pincushion, a bisque Kewpie w/jointed arms wearing peach silk jacket & hat & attached to a thick round peach silk-covered pincushion, paper label on chest, early 20th c., figure 5 1/4" h. (clothing fragile) **288**

Salt & pepper shakers, figural, china, Rose O'Neill label, 2 1/4" h., pr. **550**

KITCHENWARES

Coffee Mills

Coffee mills, commonly called grinders, are perfectly collectible for many people. They are appealing to the eye and are frequently coveted by interior decorators and today's coffee-consuming homeowners. Compact, intricate, unique, ornate, and rooted in early Americana, coffee mills are intriguing to everyone and are rich and colorful.

Coffee milling devices have been available for hundreds of years. The Greeks and Romans used rotating millstones for grinding coffee and grain. Turkish coffee mills with their familiar cylindrical brass shells appeared in the 15th century, and perhaps a century or two later came the earliest spice and coffee mills in Europe. Primitive mills were handmade in this country by blacksmiths and carpenters in the late 1700s and the first half of the 19th century. These were followed by a host of commercially produced mills, which included wood-backed side mills and numerous kinds of box mills, many with machined dovetails or finger joints. Characterized by the birth of upright cast-iron coffee mills, so beautiful with their magnificent colors and fly wheels, the period of coffee mill proliferation began around 1870. The next 50 years saw a staggering number of large and small manufacturers struggling to corner the popular home market for box and canister-type coffee mills. After that, the advent of electricity and other major advances in coffee grinding and packaging technology hastened the decline in popularity of small coffee mills.

Value-added features to look for when purchasing old coffee grinders include:

• good working order and no missing, broken, or obviously replaced parts

• original paint

• attractive identifying markings, label or brass emblem

• uncommon mill, rarely seen, or appealing unique characteristics

• high quality restoration, if not original.

—Mike White

Box Mills

Advertising Coffee Mill

Box mill, advertising mill w/colorful litho printing made for Hoffmann's Old Time Coffee, based on Arcade's Telephone Mill (ILLUS.) **$1,350**

Rare Metal Mill with Sliding Door

Box mill, rare metal model w/sliding door on front by Parker, Brown's 1860 patent (ILLUS.) **1,100**

Peck, Stow & Wilcox Box Mill

Box mill, w/decorative iron top & open hopper, Peck, Stow & Wilcox (ILLUS.)............ **280**

No. 1100 Quick Grinder

Box mill, w/iron top & cover, No. 1100 Quick Grinder by Landers, Frary & Clark (ILLUS.).. **150**

Arcade Box Mill with Raised Hopper

Box mill, w/raised hopper, patented partial cover design, Arcade (ILLUS.)....................... **130**

Parker Eagle No. 314 Coffee Mill

Box mill, w/raised tin hopper, Parker Eagle No. 314 (ILLUS.).. **110**

Arcade No. 777 Box-style Coffee Mill

Box mill, wooden, w/decorative iron top & pivoting lid embossed "IXL, Arcade Mfg. Co.," side crank, Home Coffee Mill No. 777, 11" h. (ILLUS.)... **500**

Primitive Coffee Mills

Early Blacksmith's Mill

Blacksmith's mill, iron & steel, 9" hopper, mounted on post, ca. 1790 (ILLUS.) **800**

Primitive Belgian Box Mill

Box mill, w/brass hopper & Moravian base, crank on back, Belgium (ILLUS.) **320**

Wooden French Wall Canister Mill

Wall canister mill, wooden, 5 x 10" rectangular hopper, metal inserts used as grinding blades, ca. early 1800s, France (ILLUS.) **900**

Side Mills

Sunflower Design Coffee Mill

Side mill, bronzed cast iron, hanging model, sunflower design, No. A-17, 7" h. (ILLUS.) **250**

Parker No. 370 Coffee Mill

Side mill, cast iron w/wood backing board, decorative, Parker No. 370; smaller sizes No. 350 & 360 were also made (ILLUS.) **250**

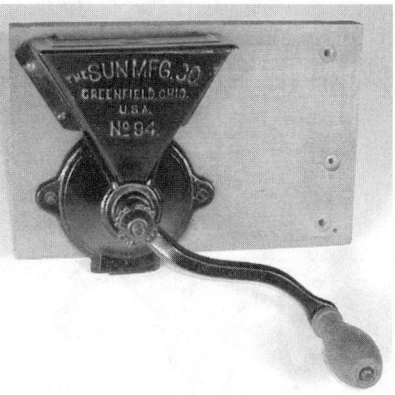

Sun Mfg. Co. No. 94 Side Mill

Side mill, w/tin hopper & lid, Sun Mfg. Co. No. 94, ca. early 1900s (ILLUS.) **150**

Peck, Stow & Wilcox Coffee Mill

Side mill, w/wood backing, brass emblem embossed w/the script logo "PS&W" for Peck, Stow & Wilcox, American (ILLUS.)...... **150**

Upright mills

Enterprise No. 3 Upright Mill

Upright mill, cast iron, w/11" wheels, pivoting cover on hopper, all original, Enterprise No. 3 (ILLUS.) **1,050**

Star No. 7 by Troemner

Upright mill, cast iron, w/15" wheels, all original, Star No. 7 by Troemner (ILLUS.).. **1,250**

Upright mill, cast iron, w/17" wheels, pivoting cover on hopper, original red paint, decals & pin striping, 1898 patent date marked on grinding burrs, Enterprise #7 .... **1,400**

Upright mill, cast iron, w/nickel-plated brass hopper, 10 3/4" wheels, Enterprise No. 4 (ILLUS.).. **1,500**

Charles Parker No. 3000 Coffee Mill

Upright mill, cast iron, w/sliding hopper cover & flower decals, 10 3/4" wheels, Charles Parker No. 3000 (ILLUS.) **1,600**

Wall Canister Mills

Arcade's Crystal No. 3 Coffee Mill

Wall canister mill, Arcade's Crystal No. 3, the most popular coffee mill ever produced, the glass to catch the ground coffee is marked "Arcade Mfg. Co., 3" (ILLUS.) **325**

Brighton Queen No. 150

Wall canister mill, decorative, w/embossing on glass canister, Brighton Queen No. 150 by Logan & Strobridge, 16" h. (ILLUS.).. **750**

Steel Wall Canister Coffee Mill

Wall canister mill, steel, w/oval window & tin cup, Bronson-Walton Oplex No. 10 (ILLUS.) **325**

Peugeot Freres Porcelain Coffee Mill

Wall canister mill, porcelain, colorful graphics, made by Peugeot Freres, France, ca. 1936, one in a set of ten (ILLUS.).. **375**

"X-Ray Coffee Mill No. 1"

Wall canister mill, wood, glass & metal, w/blue paper label that reads "X-Ray Coffee Mill No. 1, Manufactured by Arcade Mfg. Co.," detachable cast-iron catch cup (ILLUS.).. **250**

Miscellaneous

Child's Box-type Coffee Mill

Child's box mill, A.C. Williams Daisy No. 867, 2 1/2 x 2 1/2" base, same size as Arcade's Little Tot, but metal castings are different (ILLUS.)... **150**

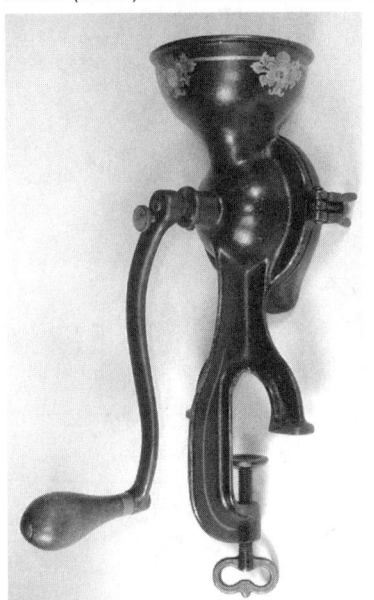

Clamp-on Enterprise No. 0

Shelf clamp-on, cast iron, Enterprise No. 0, 12" h. (ILLUS.).. **150**

Parker No. 3 Planters' Mill

Wall-mounted corn & coffee grinder, cast iron, 17" wheel, Parker No. 3 Planters' Mill (ILLUS.)... **500**

Egg Cups

Ceramic egg cups were a common breakfast table accessory beginning about the mid-19th century and were used for serving soft-boiled eggs. Ceramics egg "hoops" or "rings" were used for many years before the cup-form became common. Egg cups continue to be produced today, and modern novelty and souvenir types are especially collectible.

The descriptions and values listed here were provided by collector Dr. Joan M. George, who notes that values for older egg cups are based on their marks, rarity and recent sales results.

Bucket-style, blue monogram "EIIR," for Queen Elizabeth II, England, 1950s **22**
Bucket-style, commemorates death of Princess Diana, England, 1997 .... **35**
Bucket-style, souvenir of Portsmouth, England w/picture of the HMS Victory, England, 1996 .... **8**

English Gollywog Egg Cup

Bucket-type, colored design of a Gollywog pointing to a stove, Robertsons & Sons, England, ca. 1960s (ILLUS.)............................ **50**

Bjorn Wiinblad Designed Egg Cup

Bucket-type, colorful stylized modernistic design, Bjorn Wiinblad, Rosenthal, Germany, 1985 (ILLUS.)... 45
Double, decorated w/a chick & a green stripe, Roseville Pottery, ca. 1919.................. 250
Double, Garland patt., dark red flower on a grey ground, Stangl Pottery, ca. 1960s........... 20
Double, Luckenbach Line, pennant w/logo, unmarked, American-made............................. 50
Double, Mexicana patt. by Homer Laughlin, ca. 1930s... 30

Singapore Bird Pattern Egg Cup

Double, Singapore Bird patt., Oriental-style design of birds & flowering branches on a celadon green ground, Adams, England, ca. 1950s (ILLUS.)............................ 20
Double, souvenir of Caesar's Palace, Las Vegas, Nevada, brown design, 1993.............. 18

French Child's Egg Hoop

Hoop-style, child's, pink band & red stripes around upper half, stylized animals around the lower half, France, 1930s (ILLUS.) 35

Early Staffordshire Egg Hoop

Hoop-style, green transfer-printed design of people & houses, Staffordshire, England, 19th c. (ILLUS.) 65

Haviland Porcelain Egg Hoop

Hoop-style, white decorated w/green garland band & gilt scrolls, Haviland, Limoges, France, 1990s (ILLUS.) 85

W.H. Goss Crest Egg Cup

Single, banner w/crest marked "Ye Ancient Port of Seaford," W.H. Goss, England, 1930s (ILLUS.) 45

French Bart Simpson Egg Cup

Single, Bart Simpson bust, yellow w/blue base, France, 1997, large (ILLUS.).................. **35**
Single, Bayeux Tapestry, white ground w/a picture showing a portion of the tapestry, Limoges, France, 1998..................................... **15**

French Bellhop Egg Cup

Single, bellhop wearing blue hat & coat, cigarette in his mouth, France, ca. 1920 (ILLUS.)... **70**

Rare Betty Boop Egg Cup

Single, Betty Boop head, red dress, grey lustre hair, Germany, ca. 1930s (ILLUS.)...... **200**

Minton Blue Delft Pattern Egg Cup

Single, blue floral Delft patt., gold band trim, Minton, England, 1990s (ILLUS.) **85**
Single, Booth's "Pompadour" patt., multicolored flowers, Silicon China, England, ca. 1920s **30**

Figural Bugs Bunny Egg Cup

Single, Bugs Bunny head, grey & white, part of a set including Tweety Bird, Tasmanian Devil & Sylvester the Cat, unmarked, large size, 1980s, each (ILLUS.) **35**

Handled Quaker Oats Man Egg Cup

Single, bust of the Quaker Oats Man, handled, tall, England, 1920s (ILLUS.) **65**

Single, CAAC insignia of star & wings, small, current, China.. **12**

Mona Lisa Egg Cup

Single, color copy of the Mona Lisa on a white cup, unmarked, France, 1998 (ILLUS.).. **10**

New York-Brooklyn Bridge Egg Cup

Single, color scene of bridge w/"New York & Brooklyn Bridge," Germany, early 20th c. (ILLUS.).. **40**

Souvenir Cup with Dutch Children

Single, color scene of Dutch children around the sides, printed in gold at the top "Souvenir Holland," unmarked, 1930s (ILLUS.).. **32**

Early Goebel Boy's Head Egg Cup

Single, comical boy's head, painted features, high collar below chin, Goebel, Germany, ca. 1930s (ILLUS.) **100**

Goebel Girl's Head Egg Cup

Single, comical girl's head, painted features, ruffled collar & pink hair band, Goebel, Germany, ca. 1930s (ILLUS.) **100**
Single, commemorates the wedding of Princess Grace & Prince Rainier of Monaco, France, 1956... **95**

Charles & Diana Divorce Egg Cup

Single, commemorating the divorce of Prince Charles & Princess Diana, Coronet Pottery, England, 1996 (ILLUS.)............... **30**

Rare Baby Doll Figural Egg Cup

Single, cov., baby doll head & shoulders painted in natural colors form the top, the footed base shows the hands & feet, unmarked, probably American-made, ca. 1930s, rare (ILLUS., of base)............................ **150**

Single, cov., full-figure English Beefeater guard, England, 1999 .... **15**

English Davenport Egg Cup

Single, decorated by hand w/blue scroll arches trimmed w/gold, Davenport, England, 1887 (ILLUS.) **85**

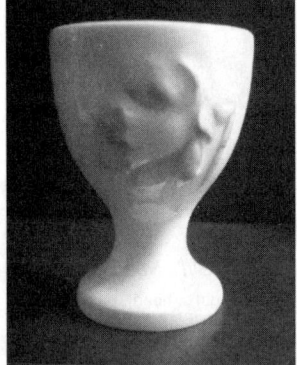

Goebel Daffodil Egg Cup from Series

Single, daffodil blossom, one of an annual series of flowers, birds & animals by Goebel of Germany, 1982 (ILLUS.) **20**

Meissen Blue Orchid Egg Cup

Single, deeply scalloped rim, Blue Orchid patt., Meissen, Germany, 1988 (ILLUS.)......... **95**

Jasper Ware Egg Cup Souvenir

Single, dark blue jasper ware w/white coat-of-arms of the Dominion of Canada, England, ca. 1950 (ILLUS.) **35**

French Faience Egg Cup

Single, faience, h.p. w/colorful blue & yellow florals & scrolls, France, ca. 1920s (ILLUS.) **45**

Swee'pea Figural Egg Cup

Single, figural Swee'pea, from Popeye cartoons, KFS Vandor Imports, Japan, 1980, large size (ILLUS.) **55**

English Ugly Face Egg Cup

Single, figural ugly man's face in grey clay, large nose & blue & white eyes, England, 1999 (ILLUS.) **15**

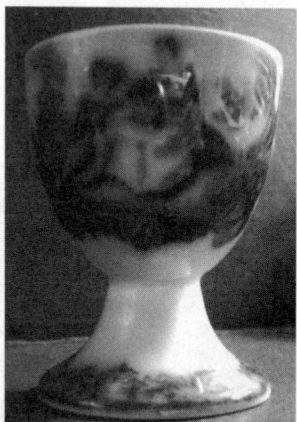

Doulton Watteau Pattern Egg Cup

Single, flow blue Watteau patt., two figures in landscape having a picnic, Doulton, Ltd., England, ca. 1900 (ILLUS.) **85**

Figural Staffordshire Egg Cup

Single, "Ham and Eggs," model of a pig seated at a table that forms the egg cup, Staffordshire bone china, England, ca. 1980s (ILLUS.) **35**

Early Mintons Floral Egg Cup

Single, hand-decorated w/a colorful floral & geometric border band above floral garlands, Mintons, England, ca. 1890s (ILLUS.) **50**
Single, hand-decorated w/a face, Desimone, Italy, ca. 1980s.. **40**

Harrod's Bear Egg Cup

Single, Harrod's bear mascot, standing wearing trademark green Harrod's sweater, tall, England, 1999 (ILLUS.) **35**

Unusual Humpty Dumpty Egg Cup

Single, Humpty Dumpty body in blue, sitting on a wall titled "Humpty Dumpty Egg Cup," egg would form the head, unmarked, ca. 1920s (ILLUS.) **60**

Jemima Puddleduck Egg Cup

Single, Jemima Puddleduck standing beside a bush-form cup, one from a set of Beatrix Potter characters, Enesco, 1999, each (ILLUS.) **35**

Single, King Edward VII coronation commemorative, portrait wearing crown, England, 1901 .... **85**

Single, King George V of England coronation commemorative, England, 1911 .... **65**

Royal Albert, England Egg Cup

Single, Lady Carlyle patt., decorated w/large clusters of flowers below a scal-

loped pink rim band, Royal Albert, England, ca. 1950s (ILLUS.) **35**

Longwy Pottery Egg Cup

Single, large bright pink blossoms & branches on a light blue ground w/dark blue foot & rim, Longwy, France, ca. 1920s (ILLUS.) **65**

Hutschenreuther "March" Egg Cup

Single, lightly scalloped rim, colorful design of exotic bird & flowering branches, one of a series representing the months, marked "MARZ - Hutschenreuther," Germany, 1980s (ILLUS.) **45**

Single, Marilyn Monroe picture transfer-printed on hollow cup, England, 2002 .... **10**

Rare Early Minnie Mouse Egg Cup

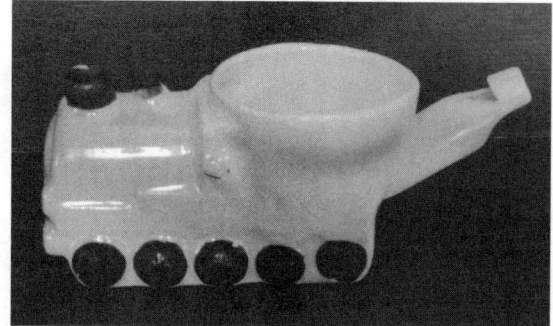

Unusual Train Egg Cup - Whistle

Single, Minnie Mouse, pointed nose & large ears, wearing orange skirt & blue blouse on a green base, Japan, ca. 1930s (ILLUS.).. **90**

Modern Cow-form Egg Cup

Single, model of a cow, round, painted black & white over green grass, Knobler, U.S., 1987 (ILLUS.).. **15**

English Lion-form Egg Cup

Single, model of a lion supporting the cup on its back, tan lustre glaze, Royal Fenton, Staffordshire, England, ca. 1930s (ILLUS.).. **25**

Single, model of a peacock, colorful bird supporting the cup on its back, Sarreguemines, France, ca. 1930s **50**

Franklin Mint Raccoon Egg Cup

Single, model of a raccoon beside a picnic basket, natural colors, part of the "Forest Friends" set, Franklin Mint, 1986, each one in set (ILLUS.).. **45**

Single, model of a train engine w/whistle at end, marked "Foreign" in a circle on the base, Germany, ca. 1920s (ILLUS., top of page).. **175**

Figural Noah's Ark Egg Cup

Single, model of Noah's Ark w/cup on the roof, England, ca. 1920s (ILLUS.)................... **75**

Single, Muppets, either Statler, Waldorf, Sam or Zoot, American-made, 1981, each... **50**

Royal Doulton Nanking Egg Cup

Single, Nanking patt., band of stylized colorful flowers & blue ribbons, Royal Doulton, England, ca. 1930s (ILLUS.) **28**

Single, Niagara Falls picture titled "Niagara Falls Prospect Point Canada," Japan, 1930s.. **28**

Royal Doulton Egg Cup in Orange

Single, orange rim band of stylized floral panels above floral sprigs, gold rim band, Royal Doulton, England, ca. 1930s (ILLUS.)... **35**

Mintons Egg Cup

Single, overall dark blue branching design on exterior & interior, gold rim stripes, Mintons, England, ca. 1910 (ILLUS.).............. **50**

Single, painted sea gull & "Torquay" on a dark blue ground, Torquay, England, 1985 .... **45**

Royal Delft Floral-Painted Egg Cup

Single, painted w/small stylized blue flower sprigs, Royal Delft, Germany, 1967 (ILLUS.) **55**

Single, picture of Queen Elizabeth of England as a child, England, 1937 .... **90**

Early Tower of London Egg Cup

Single, pink lustre ground around a white reserve w/a black transfer-printed scene of the Tower of London, Germany, early 20th c. (ILLUS.) **35**

Single, pirate wearing tricorner hat & eye patch, unmarked, American-made, modern **12**

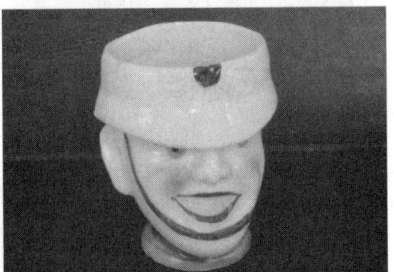

Smiling Policeman Egg Cup

Single, policeman, smiling & wearing a helmet w/a chin strap, unmarked, ca. 1930 (ILLUS.) **40**

Early Figural Popeye Egg Cup

Single, Popeye full-figure, standing wearing
a white suit w/blue trim & anchors, Japan,
1930s (ILLUS.).. **125**

Blessed Mother Shrine Souvenir

Single, portrait of the Virgin Mary, Blessed
Mother Shrine, marked "Present from
Carfin" (Scotland), made in Czechoslo-
vakia, 1930s (ILLUS.) **35**
Single, Prince Charles, "Spitting Image,"
Luck & Flaw, England, 1980s............................ **65**
Single, Prince William birth commemora-
tive, family portrait, Coronet, England,
1982... **30**
Single, Queen Elizabeth II 70th birthday
commemorative, England, 1996 .... **25**
Single, Queen Elizabeth II Golden Jubilee
commemorative w/portrait & royal crest,
England, 2002.. **25**
Single, Queen Mary of England coronation
commemorative, mate to George V cup,
England, 1911.. **65**
Single, Rhodes, Greece, white w/picture,
2000.. **6**

Modern Wedgwood Egg Cup

Single, rim band in blue & gold w/tiny red
blossoms, Wedgwood, England, 1990s
(ILLUS.) **25**
Single, Royal Copenhagen "Flora Danica"
patt., hand-painted, Denmark, current.......... **475**
Single, Royal Doulton example decorated
w/roses & gold garlands, England, 1927........ **50**

Chintz "Welbech" Pattern Egg Cup

Single, Royal Winton Chintz "Welbech"
patt., England, 1999 (ILLUS.) **35**
Single, "Running Legs," white cup attached
to legs w/yellow shoes, Carlton Ware,
England, 1970s **40**
Single, scalloped bottom, black transfer-
printed scene of "Porta Nigra, Tier," old-
est city in Germany, Germany, 1998 .... **15**

Rare Disney Snow White Egg Cup

Single, Snow White, standing beside cup marked w/her name, Walt Disney Enterprises, part of a set, Japan, 1937 (ILLUS.).. **250**

The Drunk Figural Egg Cup

Single, The Drunk, silly face of a man w/half-closed eyes & tongue hanging out, unmarked, ca. 1930s (ILLUS.) **75**
Single, Union Pacific Railroad "Winged Streamline" design, Scammell China, 1930s... **65**

Egg Cup Decorated with Chickens

Single, upper section decorated in color w/scenes of chickens, yellow foot, gold rim bands, unmarked, 1930s (ILLUS.)............. **35**
Single, white ground w/a flag in an oval, titled "Nova Scotia," Canada, 2001 .... **7**

Winston Churchill-VE Day Egg Cup

Single, Winston Churchill portrait against the Union Jack, commemorates 50th Anniversary of VE Day, Norwich Bone China, England, 1995 (ILLUS.).............................. **55**

Shy Lady Egg Cup by Goebel

Single, woman w/center-parted brown hair pulled into a bun, shy smile & side-glancing eyes, yellow bow at neck, Goebel, Germany, ca. 1930s (ILLUS.) **100**

Egg Timers

A little glass tube filled with sand and attached to a figural base measuring between 3" and 5" in height was once a commonplace kitchen item. Although egg timers were originally used to time a 3-minute egg, some were used to limit the length of a telephone call as a cost saving measure.

Many beautiful timers were produced in Germany in the 1920s and later in Japan, reaching their heyday in the 1940s. These small egg timers were commonly made in a variety of shapes in bisque, china, chalkware, cast iron, tin, brass, wood or plastic.

Egg timers had long been considered an essential kitchen tool until, in the 1920s and 1930s, a German pottery company, W. Goebel, introduced figural egg timers. Goebel crafted miniature china figurines with attached glass vials. After the Great Depression, Japanese companies introduced less detailed timers. The Goebel figural egg timers are set apart by their trademark, delicate painting and distinctive clothes. It is best to purchase egg timers with their original tube, but the condition of the figure is most important in setting prices.

Goebel Baker Egg Timer

Baker, ceramic, Goebel (ILLUS.) **65**

Bellhop, ceramic, Oriental, wearing red outfit, marked "Germany" **50**

Bellhop, ceramic, talking on telephone, marked "Japan," 3" h. **45**

Bellhop, ceramic, wearing green uniform, marked "Japan," 4 1/2" h. **70**

Bird, ceramic, sitting on nest, wearing white bonnet w/green ribbon, Josef Originals sticker **55**

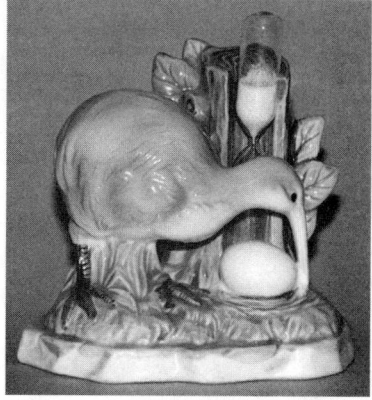

Bird & Egg Near Stump Egg Timer

Bird, ceramic, standing next to stump w/egg at base, shades of brown w/green grassy base & leaves on stump, Japan (ILLUS.) **65**

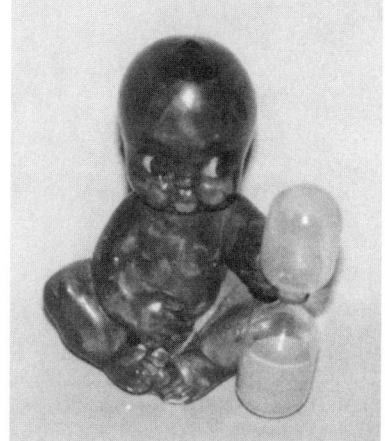

Black Baby Egg Timer

Black baby, ceramic, sitting w/left arm holding timer (ILLUS.) **95**

Black boy, holding timer in right hand & sitting on chamber pot, marked "Foreign" **85-110**

Black chef, ceramic, sitting w/arm up holding timer, variety of sizes, Germany **85-100**

Black chef, ceramic, standing w/large fish, timer in fish's mouth, Germany, 4 3/4" h. **100**

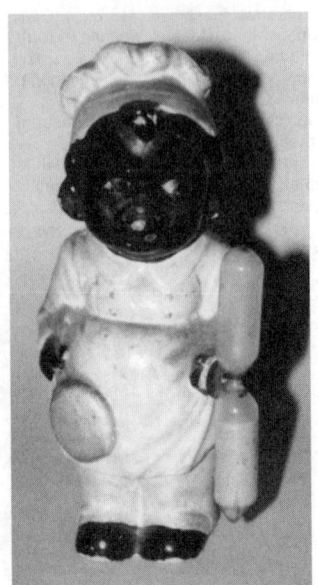

Black Chef w/Frying Pan Egg Timer

Black chef with frying pan, composition,
Japan (ILLUS.).. **100**
Black lady chef, ceramic, sitting,
Germany **95-125**

Bo-Peep Egg Timer

Bo-Peep, ceramic, "Bo-Peep" on base, Ja-
pan (ILLUS.)... **100**
Boy, ceramic, holding rifle, marked "Germa-
ny".. **50**
Boy, ceramic, skiing pose, marked "Germa-
ny," 3" h... **50**

Swiss Boy Egg Timer

Boy, composition, wearing Swiss outfit,
marked "Germany" (ILLUS.)...................... **65-75**
Boy, wood, w/red cap, standing & holding a
glass tube in each hand, unmarked,
4 1/2" h. **25-45**
Boy, Mexican, playing guitar, ceramic, Ger-
many, 3 1/2" h. **55**

Boy Chef Egg Timer

Boy chef, ceramic, sitting w/raised arm,
Germany (ILLUS.)... **95**
Boy & girl, ceramic, flanking timer on ob-
long base, boy w/white pants, dark blue
coat & yellow cap, girl in red dress
w/white apron & large dark blue hat,
Goebel, Germany **125**

Buccaneer Egg Timer

Buccaneer, ceramic, hanging-type, w/white polka-dotted red scarf, Germany (ILLUS.).. **100-150**

Wooden Cat Egg Timer

Cat, wooden, black cat w/yellow eyes & red collar on domed yellow base, timer lifts out of back (ILLUS.)... 35
Cat, ceramic, standing by base of grandfather clock, Germany, 4 1/2" h.......................... 50
Chef, ceramic, holding blue spoon, marked "Germany" 65
Chef, ceramic plate w/hole to hold timer, which removes to change, Japan..................... 50
Chef, ceramic, winking, white w/black shoes & trim, turn onto head to activate sand, 4" h. 50
Chef, composition board, black chef holding platter of chicken, w/pot holder hooks 50

Chef, composition, w/cake, Germany 75

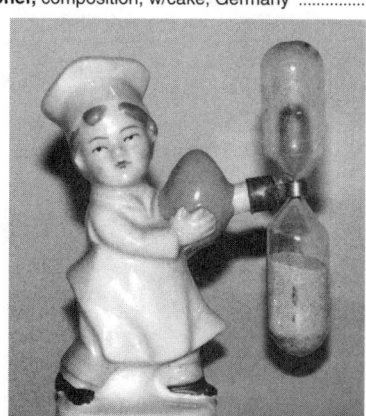

Egg Timer with Chef Holding Egg

Chef, porcelain, white & blue, holding reddish orange egg, supporting timer, Germany (ILLUS.) 65
Chef, wood, "Time Your Egg" 25
Chef, standing in blue w/white apron, towel over right arm, timer in jug under left arm, Japan, 4 1/2" h. 50
Chefs, ceramic, man & woman, Goebel, Germany, 4" h. 100
Chick, ceramic, white, yellow & purple chick, marked "Japan"...................................... 50
Chick with cap, ceramic, Josef Originals 55
Chicken, ceramic, white w/black wings & tail feathers, marked "Germany"...................... 65
Chicken, on nest, green plastic, England, 2 1/2" h. 25
Chicken, wings hold tube, ceramic, Germany, 2 3/4" h. 65

Chimney Sweep Egg Timer

Chimney sweep, ceramic, Goebel, Germany (ILLUS.) 75

Chimney sweep, ceramic, wearing black outfit w/top hat, carrying ladder, Germany 65

Chimney sweep, ceramic, carrying ladder, Germany, 3 1/4" h. 65

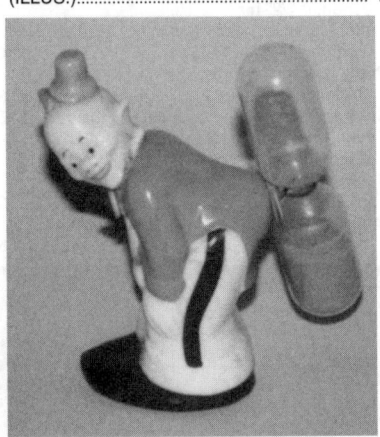

Clockman Planter

Clock, ceramic, clock face, w/man's plaid suit & tie below, w/planter in back, Japan (ILLUS.) 40

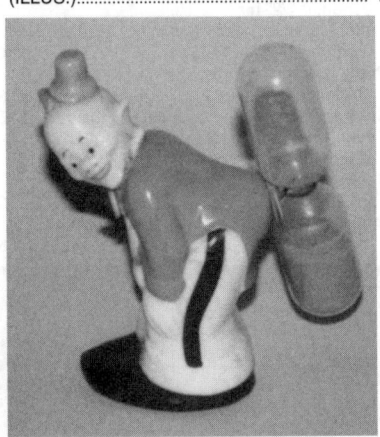

Clown Egg Timer

Clown, ceramic, Germany (ILLUS.) 85

Clown on phone, ceramic, standing, full-figured, Japan 60

Clown on phone, ceramic, standing, yellow suit, Japan, 3 3/4" h. 60

Colonial man, ceramic, yellow & white, Japan 55

Colonial man in knickers, ruffled shirt, ceramic, Japan, 4 3/4" h. 75

Colonial woman with bonnet, ceramic, variety of dresses & colors, Germany, 3 3/4" h., each 60

Dog, ceramic, black Poodle, sitting, Germany 65

Dog, ceramic, Dachshund, red w/hole in back for timer, label on back reads "Shorty Timer" 40

Green Dog Egg Timer

Dog, ceramic, green, looking at his tail (ILLUS.) 55-85

Dog, ceramic, Pekingese, standing brown & white dog, marked "Germany" 55

Dog Egg Timer

Dog, ceramic, sitting, white w/brown tail & ears, timer in head, Germany (ILLUS.) 55

Dog, chalkware, white Scottie 45-65

Lustreware Dog

Dog, white w/brown ears & tail, lustre ware,
Japan (ILLUS.)... 65
Dogs, ceramic, Scotties, brown, standing
facing each other holding timer in paws,
marked "Germany".. 65
Duck, wood, hanging-type, duck sitting on
green egg, marked "Germany".......................... 35
Dutch boy, ceramic, wearing blue & white
sailor outfit, Germany, small............................. 50
Dutch boy, ceramic, yellow pants, brown
shoes, hat, scarf, Japan.................................... 45

Dutch Boy Egg Timer

Dutch boy, composition, blue pants & hat,
red shirt, white tie w/blue polka dots, Ger-
many (ILLUS.).. 45
Dutch boy & girl, ceramic, double-type, un-
known modeler, timer marked w/3-, 4- &
5-minute intervals, Goebel, Germany,
1953.. 95
Dutch boy kneeling, ceramic, Japan,
2 1/2"... 50
Dutch girl, ceramic, talking on telephone,
Japan.. 45
Dutch girl, ceramic, w/red heart on apron,
Germany... 45
Dutch girl, ceramic, white w/blue apron &
trim, Germany 65-85
Dutch girl, ceramic, yellow 45-65
Dutch girl w/flowers, chalkware, walking,
unmarked, 4 1/2" h.. 65
Elephant, ceramic, white, sitting w/timer in
upraised trunk, marked "Germany"................. 65
Elf by well, ceramic, Manorware, England.......... 35

English Bobby Egg Timer

English Bobby, ceramic, Germany
(ILLUS.) 95

Lustreware Fish Egg Timer

Fish, ceramic, lustre ware, burgundy, yellow
& green, Germany (ILLUS.)............................... 85

Fisherman Egg Timer

Fisherman, ceramic, standing, wearing
brown jacket & hat, tall black boots, carrying a large white fish on his shoulders,
timer attached to mouth of fish, Germany
(ILLUS.) 95
Friar Tuck, ceramic, single, Goebel, Ger-
many, 4" h. 65
Frog, ceramic, multicolored frog sitting on
egg, marked "Japan".. 65

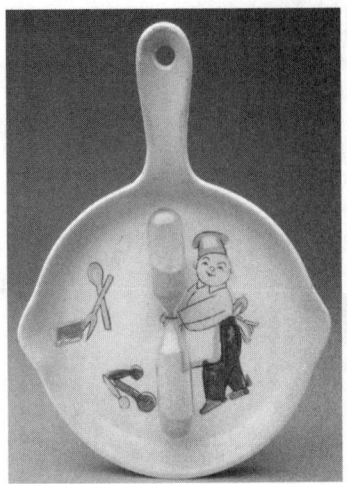

Frying Pan Egg Timer

Frying pan, ceramic, hanging-type, w/picture of chef & cooking utensils, Japan (ILLUS.).. **25-45**

Genie, w/recipe holder in back **75-95**

Gollywog, bisque, England, 4 1/2" h., minimum value.. 150

Gollywog, ceramic, character-type, marked "FOREIGN"... 125-150

Grandfather clock, composition, Manorware, England 45-55

Happy the Dwarf, ceramic, from "Snow White & the Seven Dwarfs," Maw Co., England.. 100

Honey bear, ceramic, brown & white, w/timer in mouth made to resemble milk bottle, Cardinal China Co., No. 1152 65

House with clock face, ceramic, yellow & gold, Japan.. 35

Huckleberry Finn, ceramic, sitting in front of post, Japan 95

Humpty Dumpty, ceramic, wearing hat & bow tie, turn onto head to activate sand, marked "California Cleminsons" 40

Indian Egg Timer

Indian, ceramic, kneeling, white, wearing headdress w/red, blue & green feathers, holding timer in one hand, marked "Germany," rare (ILLUS.).. **125**

Leprechaun, glazed chalkware, sitting on wishing well, "Porkush" on front base, marked "Manorware," England 35

Leprechaun, shamrock on base, brass, Ireland, 3 1/4" h.. 35

Lighthouse, ceramic, blue, cream & orange lustre ware, Germany, 4 1/2" h. 75

Little Boy Egg Timer

Little boy, ceramic, standing wearing black shorts & shoes & large red bow tie, Germany (ILLUS.) 75

Little girl on phone, ceramic, sitting w/legs outstretched, pink dress, Germany 65

Little girl with chick on her toes, ceramic, Goebel, Germany 100

Mammy, tin lithographed, mammy cooking on gas stove, w/pot holder hooks, unmarked, 7 3/4" h... 145

Minuteman, ceramic, holding rifle & leaning against stone wall, "Kitchen Independence" on front base, marked "Enesco" & "Japan"... **25-35**

Mother Rabbit Egg Timer

Mother rabbit, ceramic, holding carrot w/basket, Japan (ILLUS.)................................ **60**

Mouse Chef Egg Timer

Mouse, ceramic, sitting & holding timer, brown w/white apron marked "Chef" in red letters, Josef Originals (ILLUS.)........... **35-45**
Mouse, chalkware, yellow & green, Josef Originals, Japan, 1970s, 3 1/4" h. **35**
Mr. Pickwick, ceramic, double-type, green, Germany, 4" h.. **165**

Mrs. Claus Egg Timer

Mrs. Claus, ceramic, in yellow dress w/green collar, cuffs & hem, w/red bag full of gifts & black bag w/timer (ILLUS.) **65**
Newspaper boy, ceramic, Japan, 3 1/4" h.......... **55**
Oliver Twist, ceramic, wearing red pants & vest, brown jacket, black hat, marked "Germany" **95**

Goebel Owl Egg Timer

Owl, ceramic, Goebel, Germany (ILLUS.).......... **75**
Parlor maid with cat, ceramic, Japan................ **65**
Penguin, glazed chalkware, standing on green & white base w/"Bagnor Regis" painted on front, marked "Manorware, England".. **50**
Penguin, chalkware, England, 3 3/4" h. **50**
Pixie, ceramic, Enesco, Japan, 5 1/2" h............. **40**
Prayer lady, ceramic, pink & white, Enesco **95**

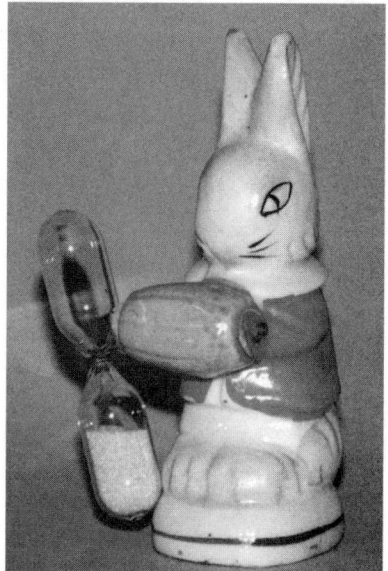

Rabbit with Carrot Egg Timer

Rabbit, ceramic, sitting, white w/red jacket, holding carrot that supports the timer, Germany (ILLUS.).. **65**
Rabbit with floppy ears, ceramic, standing, tan, Germany **75**
Rabbits, ceramic, double-type, various color combinations, Goebel, Germany, 4" **75**
Rooster, wood, multicolored, standing on thick base **25**
Rooster, wood, red wattle & comb, blue on tail, upturned head, Germany **35-45**

Roosters Egg Timer

Roosters, ceramic, double-type, modeled by Horst Ashermann, timer marked w/3-, 4- & 5-minute intervals, Goebel, Germany, 1953 (ILLUS.) **85-100**

Sailboat Egg Timer

Sailboat, ceramic, lustre ware, tan boat w/white sails, Germany (ILLUS.) **75**
Sailboat with sailor, ceramic, lustre ware, Germany... **75**
Sailor, ceramic, blue, Germany............................ **85**
Santa Claus, ceramic, sitting, unmarked....... **50-75**
Santa Claus w/present, ceramic, Sonsco, Japan, 5 1/2" h.................................... **85**
Scotsman with bagpipes, plastic, England, 4 1/2" h.................................... **50**

Sea gull, iron, white & tan bird w/red beak & legs, on black & white branch that is also

Sea Gull Egg Timer

Sea gull, ceramic, timer in beak, Germany (ILLUS.) **75**

Sea Gull Egg Timer with Bottle Opener

a bottle opener (ILLUS.)...................................... **25**

Swiss woman, ceramic, w/multicolored striped apron, marked "Germany" 65
Telephone, candlestick tube on base w/cup for timer, wooden, Cornwall Wood Products, South Paris, Maine 25
Telephone, ceramic, black, Japan...................... 35
Telephone, black glaze on clay, Japan, 2" h. 25

"Timothy Timer" Egg Timer

"Timothy Timer," ceramic, w/upraised arms, label reads "Conley Lilley, Cape May, N.J., Chester, Pa.," turn onto head to activate sand (ILLUS.) **45-65**
Vegetable person, ceramic, Japan..................... 95
Veggie man or woman, bisque, Japan, 4 1/2" h., each.. 75

Waiter Egg Timer

Waiter, ceramic, standing next to ovoid holder for timer, black & white, Germany (ILLUS.)... 65
Welsh woman, ceramic, Germany, 4 1/2" h.. 65

Windmill with Pigs Egg Timer

Windmill, ceramic, w/pigs on base, Japan, 3 3/4" h. (ILLUS.) 85
Windmill, yellow w/bird on top, ceramic, unmarked, 4" h.. 75
Windmill, ceramic, w/dog on base, Japan, 3 3/4" h. 85
Woman in cap, composition, Josef Originals **25-45**

Kitchen Utensils

Apple peeler, cast iron, Keen Kutter, "Pat. May 24, 1898, E.C. Simmons Keen Kutter".. 100
Apple peeler, cast iron, "Pat June 9, 1872 Mfd by G. Bergner Washington, MO," no segmenter 1,500
Apple peeler, cast iron, "The Favorite L.A. Sayre Newark, N.J." 250
Apple peeler, cast iron, "The Jersey Pat. Pending".. 650
Apple peeler, cast iron, "White Mountain Apple Made by Goodell Co. Antrim, N.H. USA".. 35
Apple slicer, cast iron w/brass blades, "Sun Pat. June 10, 1890 C.M. Heffron Rochester".. 750
Butter churn, cast-iron gear on tin top w/fruit jar base, "Schmidt Bros. Lancaster, PA".. 400
Butter churn, Dazey Churn No. 80, "Patented Feb. 14, 11 / Dazey Churn & Mfg. Co. St. Louis, MO. Made in USA".................. 200
Butter churn, tin & cast-iron top w/unmarked glass jar, "The Home Butter Maker, Kohler Die & Specialty Co. Dekalb, Ill USA" (ILLUS., top next page) 125
Can opener, cast iron, swings open, "Universal Dazey Americana New Britain, Conn. USA Patent Applied For"..................... 100
Cherry pitter, cast iron, plunger style, "Goodell Co Antrim NH" 30
Cherry pitter, cast iron, "The Rapid Mfd By Ed Parker Co Springfield Ohio Pat Pend" .. 1,000
Cherry pitter, cast iron w/nickel plate, "Rollman Mfg. Co. Mount Joy PA. USA" 45

"The Home Butter Maker" Churn

Cookie cutter, tin, early handmade design in form of dove, spot soldered, 4 1/4 x 4 3/4" **65**

Cookie cutter, tin, early handmade design in form of hand, strap handle, 3 1/4 x 4 1/2" **145**

Egg beater, cast iron, "Dover Egg Beater Pat May 6th Apr 3d 1888 Nov 24th 1891," small tubular dashers, 10" **80**

Egg beater, cast iron, "Dover Pat. July 14 '85. U.S.A.," 10 1/2" **45**

Egg beater, cast iron, "Family. Egg. Beater. Pat Sep 26, 1876," 10" **800**

Egg beater, cast iron w/nickel plate, "Genuine Dover - Dover Stamping Co." on D-form handle, 12" **55**

Master Egg Beater

Egg beater, cast iron w/nickel plate, "Master Pat. Aug. 24-09," 10 3/4" (ILLUS.)........ **1,500**

Egg beater, steel, "Minute Maid Henderson Corp. Pat Pend Seattle U.S.A.," 11 1/2"........ **250**

Egg beater, tin w/wood handle, "Super Speed A&J Spinnit Cream and Egg Whip," 11 1/2" **35**

Egg beater, wire, Archimedes type, "20th Century Egg & Cream Whip"........................... **275**

Egg poacher, "Perfect Egg Poacher - pat 1921, Chicago".. **200**

Egg scale, "Jiffy Way - Mfg. by Kuhl Corporation Flemington, New Jersey," red or green **35**

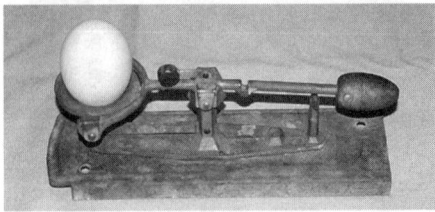

Egg Scale

Egg scale, "Reliable Mfg Co./Los Angeles Calif," 8 3/4" (ILLUS.) **60**

Egg separator, tin, advertising "Corby's Mothers Bread Hot 3 Times A Day At Your Grocers / 100% Pure"............................... **45**

Egg separator, tin, advertising "Roberts Perfect Egg Separator" **25**

Egg separator, tin, advertising "Use Putnam Fadeless Dyes / None Better"................. **35**

Jar lid reformer, cast iron, "Home Supply Mfg. Co Rockford, IL," 6 1/4"............................. **50**

Jar lid reformer, cast iron, "Warren Novelty Co, Warren O," 7" **35**

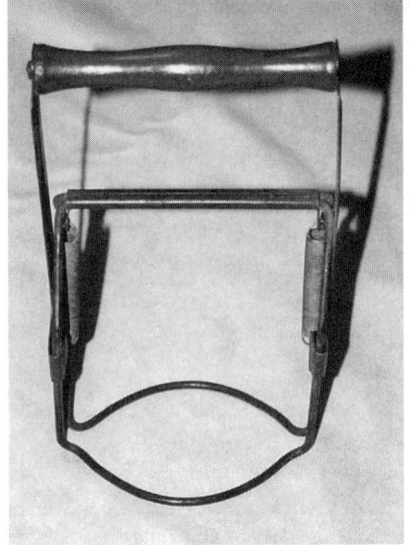

Jar Lifter with Wooden Handle

Jar lifter, steel w/wood handle, "Pat Pend," 8 1/2" (ILLUS.)... **30**

Jar lifter, wire, scissors type, no markings, 12" **15**

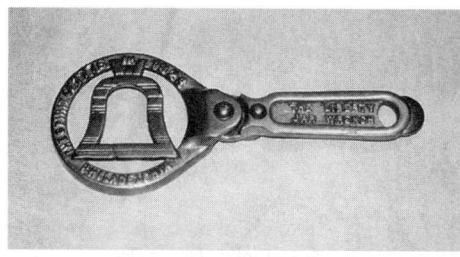

Liberty Jar Opener

Jar opener, cast iron w/nickel plate, opener w/outline of bell in center & "The Spirit of 1776 in 1926 Philadelphia" around rim, handle marked "The Liberty Jar Wrench," 7" (ILLUS.).. 75
Jar opener, steel, "Gilhoolie - Pat. No. 2669142 Others Pend. Riswell, Inc Greenwich, Ct.," 9".. 15
Jar opener, steel w/wood handle, "Grip-All Screw Cap Opener Pat Appl'd," 8".................. 15

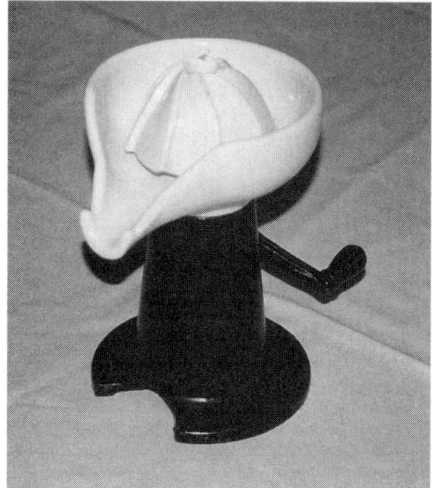

Lemon Juicer/Reamer

Lemon juicer/reamer, cast iron & porcelain, "Handy Equipment Corp. Bridgeport Conn," 7 3/4" h. (ILLUS.)................................ 300
Mayonnaise mixer, cast iron & glass, "Universal Mayonnaise Mixer and Cream Whipper Made by Landers, Frary & Clark, New Britain, Conn. USA"..................... 450
Mayonnaise mixer, tin & glass, "Wesson Oil Mayonnaise Maker," 8 1/2".......................... 35
Nut chopper, tin top w/glass jar, "Pat. No. 2,901,073," 6 1/2" h. 15
Nutmeg grater, cast iron, bellows-shaped, hinged w/pin, marked "Patented June 7, 1870".. 350
Nutmeg grater, tin w/wood slide & end, 2 1/2 x 4".. 135
Pie crimper, brass, crimping wheel on both ends, 5 1/2" 35
Pot scraper, graniteware, "Sharples Cream Separator".. 250

Raisin seeder, cast iron, "PAT US Mar 26, CT. BN. Mar. 12, CA May 10, 1895 Lightning Raisin Seeder," 8" 50
Rolling pin, bird's-eye maple w/nice patina, one piece, 16 1/2"... 50
Rolling pin, ceramic, Harker, advertising "The Kelvinator," 15"... 100
Tea strainer, tin, marked "All Allen's Teas & Coffees Strictly Guaranteed".......................... 25
Tea strainer, tin, marked "Use Big Jo Flour - The Best In The World" 30

Napkin Dolls

Ceramic, figure of angel, blonde, wearing blue & white dress w/gold trim, holding maroon flowers w/green leaves, gold halo on head, two slits in shoulders for napkins to form "wings," 5 3/8" h. **100-115**
Ceramic, figure of bartender/waiter, w/black mustache, red & white checked apron, black bow tie & shoes, holds a tray that serves as candleholder, foil sticker w/"Viking Handmade, Made in Japan," 8 3/4" h. **85-100**
Ceramic, figure of genie, dressed in white robes trimmed in gold, jewel-decorated turban, holds a gold lantern, label reads "Genie at Your Service," Enesco, 8" h. **100-135**

Byron Molds Napkin Doll

Ceramic, figure of girl holding flowers, red hair, yellow dress w/matching hair bow, arms clutch flowers to chest, marked "copyright Byron Molds," 8 1/2" h. (ILLUS.) **65-85**

Atlantic Mold Napkin Doll

Ceramic, figure of girl holding lily, mouth open as if singing, brown bobbed hair w/yellow headband, bright yellow dress w/green leaf design, holds a blue lily in arms, Atlantic Mold, 11" h. (ILLUS.).......... **65-75**

Ceramic, figure of "Miss Versatility," woman in red & white dress w/red scallop trim & matching red picture hat that serves as candleholder, one hand held behind back, California Originals, 13" h. **75-95**

Ceramic, figure of Santa Claus, in red suit w/black belt & shoes, toothpick holes in hat, marked "Japan," w/a "Sage Store" label, 6 3/4" h. **95-150**

Ceramic, figure of Spanish dancer w/black hair, handmade pink dress w/flowers on skirt, holding tambourine overhead, 17" h. **130-150**

Holt Howard Napkin Doll

Ceramic, figure of "Sunbonnet Miss," red-haired little girl in yellow dress w/white shoulder ruffle, matching yellow picture hat w/pink rose serves as candleholder, one hand pats hair, other arm is extended, marked "© Holt Howard 1958" (ILLUS.) **125-150**

Napkin Holder/Toothpick Holder

Ceramic, figure of woman holding tray, blonde, wearing black off-the-shoulder dress, one hand on hip, other holding pink covered tray, the lid w/holes to hold toothpicks, 8 1/2" h. (ILLUS.) **95-110**

White Ceramic Napkin Doll

Ceramic, figure of woman in a white dress w/yellow trim, holding a toothpick basket over her head, foil label "California Originals USA," 13 3/4" h. (ILLUS.) **65-85**

Woman in Hat Napkin Holder

Ceramic, figure of woman in hat, in dress w/yellow drop waist & purple skirt, yellow & purple hat w/upturned brim, marked "Cal. Cer. Mold," 12 1/2" h. (ILLUS.).......... **65-85**

Ceramic, figure of woman in pink, flowers on bodice, hat brim masks candleholder in head, 9" h. **60-75**

Holland Mold Napkin Holder

Ceramic, figure of woman w/daisy, black hair w/bangs, dressed in blue & white dress & long white gloves, one hand fixes daisy behind ear, ca. 1958, marked "Holland Mold," 7 1/4" h. **75-95**

Napkin Doll Holding Fan

Ceramic, figure of woman w/fan, in 18th-c. white dress w/blue trim on bodice & sleeves & blue bows on front of dress & in her dark hair, one hand holds up white fan w/blue trim, marked "Jam. Calif. ©" (ILLUS.).. **55-65**

Ceramic, figure of woman w/hands clasped in front, black hair in bun, pink dress, ca. 1998, incised "Made Exclusively for Lillian Vernon," 9" h. **10**

Ceramic, figure of woman w/poodle,blonde, dressed in pink dress trimmed in black, matching hat serves as candleholder, blue jeweled eyes, crystal jeweled necklace & red jewel on finger, holds a white poodle, marked "Kreiss & Co.," 10 3/4" h. **100-125**

Ceramic, figure of woman w/toothpick tray, bobbed hair, white dress w/yellow scalloped trim, holds oblong toothpick tray attached at waist, 10 3/4" h. **75-85**

Woman with Bird Napkin Doll

Ceramic, figure of woman w/toothpick tray, brown hair, green lustre dress decorated w/pink roses, one arm holds a toothpick tray w/similar decoration on her head, pink bird perches on other arm, 10 1/2" h. (ILLUS.).. **75-95**

Ceramic, figure of woman wearing off-the-shoulder dress w/flowers on front, floppy-brimmed hat w/candleholder, green, stamped "Kreiss and Company," 10" h. ... **65-85**

Ceramic, figure of woman wearing off-the-shoulder dress w/flowers on front, floppy-brimmed hat w/candleholder, pink, stamped "Kreiss and Company," 10" h. ... **65-85**

Ceramic, figure of young girl peeking over her shoulder, in pink & white dress w/gold trim, w/daisy over her ear & holding a hat in one hand, Holland Mold "Daisy," No. 514, ca. 1958, 7 1/4" h. **75-95**

Ceramic, figure of young girl w/surprised expression, yellow ruffled dress, large-brimmed black hat, carrying basket of flowers over one arm, 6 1/2" h. **90-110**

Ceramic, model of rooster, black w/yellow & white trim, red comb & wattle, yellow beak & feet, paper label w/"Made in Japan," 10 1/4" h. **35-45**

Wood, figure of woman in black dress w/multicolored striped apron, wearing pointed hat, 12 1/4" h. **40-50**

Wood, figure of woman w/moveable arms, pink, blue & white, strawberry w/toothpick holes on top of head, 8" h. **60-75**

Napkin Doll with Striped Dress

Wood, figure of woman, yellow, ca. 1949, Finland, 10 1/2" h. **40-50**

Wood, half-figure of woman, white blouse & red jacket, small red & white hat, 11 1/4" h. **35-45**

Pie Birds

Wide Mouth English Pie Bird

Bird, ceramic, black w/wide mouth, wide shape, England (ILLUS.)......................... **175-225**

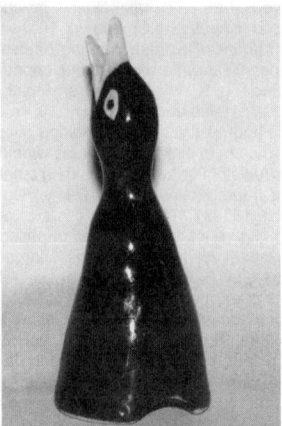

English Pie Bird

Bird, ceramic, black w/yellow beak & eyes, narrow, England (ILLUS.) **150**
Bird, ceramic, grey, England................................. **95**

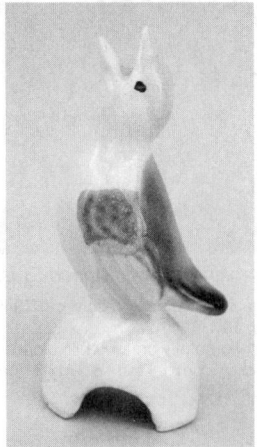

"Patch" Pie Bird

Bird, ceramic, "Patch," white, yellow, green & pink, Morton Pottery (ILLUS.).................. **35-50**
Bird, ceramic, two-piece, blue & white on white funnel, Royal Worcester, England **85**

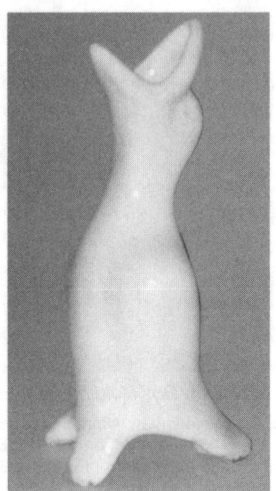

English White Pie Bird

Bird, ceramic, white w/wide mouth, England (ILLUS.) **50-60**

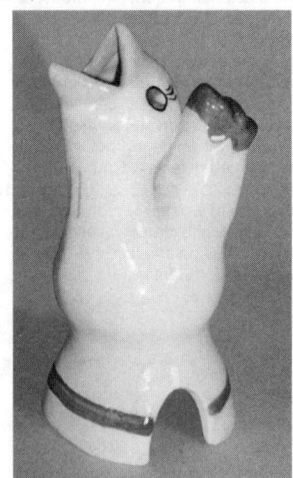

White & Blue Pie Bird

Bird, ceramic, white w/yellow beak, blue trim on tail & base, made in California, 1950s (ILLUS.) **300-500**

"Yankee Pie Bird"

Bird, ceramic, "Yankee Pie Bird," black & brown, made in New England, 1960s (ILLUS.) **40-50**

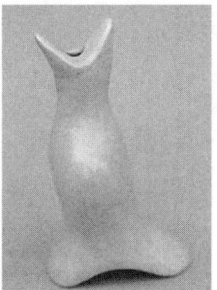

Yellow Pie Bird

Bird, ceramic, yellow w/wide mouth, England (ILLUS.)... **50-75**
Black chef, ceramic, full-figure, yellow smock w/white hat, USA **95**
Brown chef, ceramic, half-figure, England........ **115**

Taunton Chefs Pie Birds

Chefs, ceramic, all-white, man & woman, Taunton, England, each (ILLUS.)........... **125-150**

Australian Pie Bird

Clown/Dopey, ceramic, white bust, Australian (ILLUS.) .... **300+**

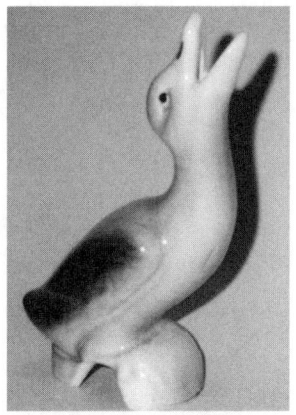

Blue Duck Pie Bird

Duck, ceramic, long neck, blue, USA (ILLUS.) **65-95**

Solid-colored Duck Pie Bird

Duck, ceramic, solid-colored, USA, each (ILLUS.) **150-200**
Duck, ceramic, yellow beak, white w/black detail, England... **100**

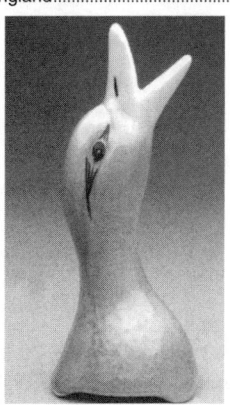

Duck Head Pie Bird

Duck head, ceramic, beige w/black detail, England (ILLUS.)... **125**

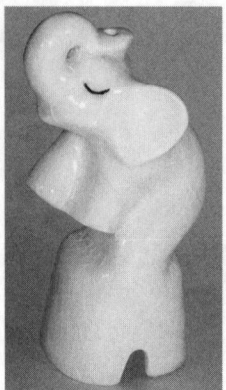

Standing Elephant Pie Bird

Elephant, ceramic, all-white, standing on back legs, trunk over head, England (ILLUS.)... **100**
Elephant, ceramic, dark grey w/yellow glaze inside, England **100**
Elephant, ceramic, grey, Nutbrown, England.. **200+**
Elephant, ceramic, incised "CCC" on back, USA .... **200+**

Elephant Pie Bird

Elephant, ceramic, white, Nutbrown, England (ILLUS.)... **55**

Aluminum Funnel Pie Bird

Funnel, aluminum, marked "Swan Brand," England (ILLUS.) **50-75**

Wheat Stalk Funnel Pie Bird

Funnel, ceramic, model of wheat stalk, cream & white, England, ea. (ILLUS.) **75-100**

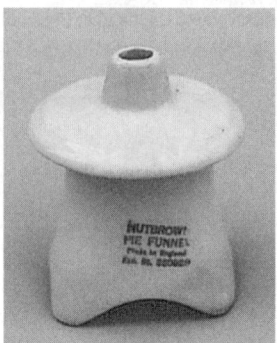

Nutbrown Funnel Pie Bird

Funnel, ceramic, Nutbrown, England (ILLUS.) **75-95**
Funnel, ceramic, plain white, England................ **22**

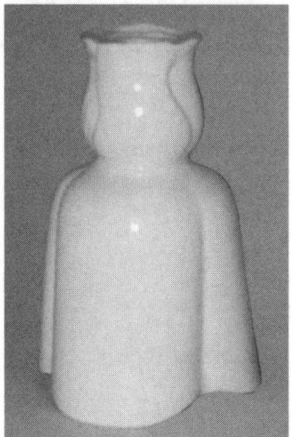

Rosebud Funnel Pie Bird

Funnel, ceramic, rosebud, white, England (ILLUS.) **150-175**

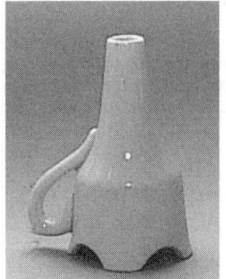

Funnel Pie Bird with Handle

Funnel w/handle, ceramic, England
(ILLUS.).. **125-150**

Gourmet Pie Cup

Gourmet pie cup, ceramic, England
(ILLUS.).. **75-95**
Rooster, ceramic, multicolored, Cleminson,
USA **50**
Rooster, ceramic, Pearl China, USA............ **95-200**

Rooster Pie Bird

Rooster, ceramic, white, brown, yellow &
green, Provincial Pottery (ILLUS.).......... **350-450**

Songbird, ceramic, blue & yellow, American Pottery Company, 1940-50 .... **40-50**

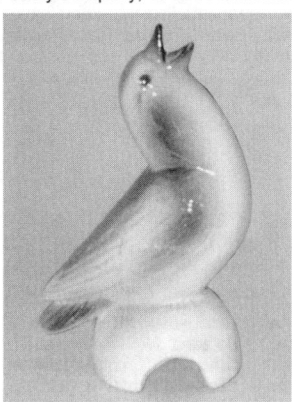

Sweet Songbird Pie Bird

Songbird, ceramic, Sweet Songbird, Amer-
ican, white, yellow, grey & green (ILLUS.) ... **400+**
Songbirds, ceramic, beige, blue, and pink,
USA, each **35-50**
Songbirds, ceramic, gold beaks and feet,
Lapiere (Ohio), USA **100-150**

Welsh Woman Pie Bird

Welsh woman, ceramic, brown w/large
black hat, 1969, commemorating investi-
ture of Prince Charles (ILLUS.).................... **200+**

Reamers

Floral Ceramic Reamer

One-piece, saucer shape w/lipped spout and shell-form handle, white ground w/pink & magenta flowers, green leaves & gold bead trim, marked "Hand Painted Japan" (ILLUS.) **150-175**

Reamer with Lattice Strainer

One-piece, saucer shape w/spout & side handle, round seed dam w/lattice strainer, white ground w/design of red cherries & green leaves, gold trim, 3" h. (ILLUS.). **85-115**

Gold-trimmed Reamer

One-piece, saucer shape, white w/gold trim, w/figures of tree, swan, butterfly & flowerpot, marked "Made In France - Limoges France," 3 1/2" d. (ILLUS.)............ **95-125**

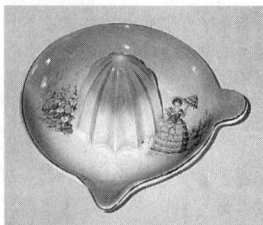

Hall Ceramic Reamer

One-piece, simple round shape w/lip & side tab handle, green outside, white inside, marked "Hall," 6" h. (ILLUS.) **550-600**

Souvenir Ceramic Reamer

One-piece, souvenir, saucer shape w/spout & side handle, blue, rust & cream, w/painted image of Victorian woman w/parasol on one side of bowl & mass of flowers on the other, marked "Made in England, A Present From Dobercourt," 3 1/4" d. (ILLUS.).. **85-125**

Three-piece, teapot shape, orange & white w/gold trim, cone sits under gold-handled lid, 3 1/2" h. **75-85**

Three-piece w/tray, ceramic w/sterling silver trim, white ground w/orange flowers, green leaves, rust trim, marked "France," 5" h. **225-250**

Two-piece, figure of duck w/white lustre body, blue head, orange beak, yellow top knot, marked "Made In Japan," 2 3/4" h.... **35-50**

Oriental Man's Head Reamer

Two-piece, in the shape of an Oriental man's head, w/collar as base, hat as lid/reamer, light blue w/dark grey highlights, incised "9496," 5 3/4" h. (ILLUS.) **95-125**

Two-piece, model of lemon slice, yellow w/green handle, marked "Japan," 6 3/4" h. **40-50**

Reamer with Basketweave Design

Two-piece, pitcher shape w/C-form handle, basketweave design in dark green w/orange & maroon flowers & light green leaves, yellow top & cone, black trim, marked "Maramotoware Hand Painted Japan," 4" h. (ILLUS.).................................. **40-50**

Squat Pitcher-form Reamer

Two-piece, squat pitcher form w/lip & circular handle, white ground w/maroon & yellow flower design, gold trim, marked "Hand Painted Japan," 3 3/4" h. (ILLUS.) **125-150**

Tall Pitcher-form Reamer

Two-piece, tall pitcher form w/lip, C-form handle & short outcurved base, pale pink ground w/painted floral decoration in pinks, blues, yellows & greens, thin green rim decoration, marked "Pantry Bak-In Ware by Crooksville," 8 1/4" h. (ILLUS.).. **125-175**

Two-piece, teapot shape on three legs, white ground w/color photograph of Westminster Abbey, marked "Foreign," 3 1/2" h.. **100-125**

Figural Painted Ceramic Reamer

Two-piece, teapot shape, with earthtone & purple pansy-type flowers on white ground, green lustre trim on handle & rim of body, lid & spout, ribbed lid w/holes for liquid to pass through, reamer in the form of a head with yellow ribbed cone hat, marked "Made in Japan," 6" h. (ILLUS.).. **75-125**

Salt & Pepper Shakers

Range Shaker Sets
Herb shakers, white milk glass w/red metal caps, blue figures of Dutch people in various scenes on front, paper labels on reverse, 3 1/4" h., each..................................... **8-10**

Variety of Pepper Shakers

Pepper shaker, fired-on green, metal cap, Hocking Glass Company, 4 7/8" h. (ILLUS. center) **18-25**

Pepper shaker, white milk glass, black Dutch girl & windmill design, aluminum cap (ILLUS. right, w/other milk glass shakers).. **18-22**

Milk Glass Pepper Shakers

Pepper shaker, white milk glass, black scroll design & "White Pepper" on front, 3 1/4" h. (ILLUS. center) **12-15**

Pepper shaker, white milk glass w/aluminum cap, blue Dutch girl & windmill design, 3 1/8" h. (ILLUS. left, w/other milk glass shakers) **18-22**

Pepper shaker, white milk glass w/yellow metal cap, black basket w/red flower design, 4" h. (ILLUS. left, w/other pepper shakers).. **15-20**

Pepper shaker, white milk glass w/yellow metal cap, black & red Scottie dog design, 3 1/4" h. (ILLUS. right, w/other pepper shakers)... **18-22**

Salt, pepper, flour & sugar shakers, white milk glass w/red metal caps, in black metal holder, red cherry design, marked "Tipp USA," 2 3/4" h., the set.................... **30-40**

Orange Hocking Shakers

Salt & pepper shakers, fired-on orange w/metal caps, round w/ribbed design, black lettering, Hocking Glass Company, 4 3/4" h., each (ILLUS.)............................... **15-20**

Green Salt & Pepper Shakers

Salt & pepper shakers, green transparent glass w/metal caps, embossed "Salt" & "Pepper," each (ILLUS.) **45-55**

Salt & pepper shakers, green transparent w/aluminum dome caps, "Salt" & "Pepper" embossed on front, 4 3/8" h., each (Beware: these have been reproduced in green, pink & cobalt blue) **50-55**

Shakers with Hat Decoration

Salt & pepper shakers, white milk glass, red & blue design of "Uncle Sam" hats, 3 1/8" h., pr. (ILLUS.) **25-30**

Shakers with Gate & Tree Design

Salt & pepper shakers, white milk glass w/aluminum caps, black gate w/red & black tree & flower design, 3 1/8" h., each (ILLUS.) **18-25**

Shakers with Dutch Scenes

Salt & pepper shakers, white milk glass w/aluminum caps, in aluminum holder, salt w/blue design of Dutch girl & wind-

mill, pepper w/red design of Dutch boy & windmill, 3 3/8" h., pr. (ILLUS.) **25-30**

Shakers with Apple

Salt & pepper shakers, white milk glass w/black caps, decorated w/red apple & green leaves, 3 1/4" h., each (ILLUS.) **15-20**

Advertising Shakers

Salt & pepper shakers, white milk glass w/black caps, red Dutch boy & windmill design on front, back marked "Good [logo] Year - Bob Black Stores Inc. - 6220 Broadway," 3 3/8" h., each (ILLUS.) **18-25**

Salt & pepper shakers, white milk glass w/black plastic caps, fired-on blue & yellow image of Tappan chef on front, 3 3/4" h., each **10-12**

Shakers with Blue Circle Design

Salt & pepper shakers, white milk glass w/metal caps, decorated w/blue circles, 3 5/8" h., pr. (ILLUS.) **20-25**

Shakers with Flower Design

Salt & pepper shakers, white milk glass w/metal caps, red, black & yellow flower design, 2 5/8" h., each (ILLUS.).................. **15-20**

Shakers with Black Flower Design

Salt & pepper shakers, white milk glass w/red metal caps, black flowers on stem design, 4 3/4" h., each (ILLUS.).................. **18-25**

Shakers with Sailboats

Salt & pepper shakers, white milk glass w/red metal caps, blue sailboats w/red "Salt" & red sailboats w/blue "Pepper," 3 1/8" h., each (ILLUS.).............................. **20-25**

Shakers with Windmill Design

Salt & pepper shakers, white milk glass w/red metal caps, blue windmill design on front, "Salt" & "Pepper" written in red below, marked "Tipp USA," 3 1/8" h., pr. (ILLUS.) **10-12**

Shakers with Roosters

Salt & pepper shakers, white milk glass w/red metal caps, red, black & green rooster design, 2 3/4 to 4 1/2" h., each (ILLUS.) **12-15**

Salt shaker, white milk glass w/aluminum cap, black bird on green-leafed branch on front, 5" h. **10-15**

Salt shaker, white milk glass w/aluminum cap, "Salt" in green on front, Hocking Glass Co., 4 1/2" h. **10-12**

Salt Shaker with Ship Design

Salt shaker, white milk glass w/red cap, red ship design, 3" h. (ILLUS.)........................... **15-20**

Salt shaker, white milk glass w/red metal cap, Roman Arch style w/red sailboat & anchor design, McKee Glass Co., 3 1/8" h. **20-25**

Spice shakers, "The Herb Chest," white milk glass w/blue designs on front, red metal caps, 3 3/16" h., each **8-10**

A Variety of Sugar Shakers

Sugar shaker, forest green transparent glass w/domed metal cap, Owens, Illinois, square shape, 4" h. (ILLUS. left) **12-15**

Sugar shaker, white milk glass w/red metal cap, image of black Scottie dog w/red bow sitting on red blanket, 3 1/4" h. (ILLUS. center, w/other sugar shakers) **15-20**

Sugar shaker, white milk glass w/red metal cap, multicolored horn of plenty decal, 4 3/8" h. (ILLUS. right, w/other sugar shakers) **18-22**

String Holders

String holders were standard equipment for general stores, bakeries and homes before the use of paper bags, tape and staples became prevalent. Decorative string holders, mostly chalkware, first became popular during the late 1930s and 1940s. They were mass-produced and sold in five-and-dime stores like Woolworth's and Kresge's. Ceramic string holders became available in the late 1940s through the 1950s. It is much more difficult to find a chalkware string holder in excellent condition, while the sturdier ceramics maintain a higher quality over time.

Apple, ceramic, handmade, 1947 .... **35-55**
Apple w/face, ceramic, "PY" **135**
Apple with berries, chalkware, common **15-35**

Apple with Worm String Holder

Apple with worm, chalkware, "Willie the Worm," ca. 1948, Miller Studio (ILLUS.) **65**

Art Deco Woman String Holder

Art Deco woman, chalkware, green beret & scarf (ILLUS.) **150**

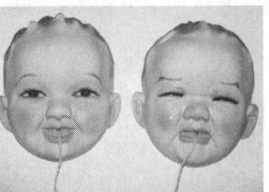

Baby Face String Holders

Babies, ceramic, heads only, one crying, one happy, Lefton, pr. (ILLUS.) **250**

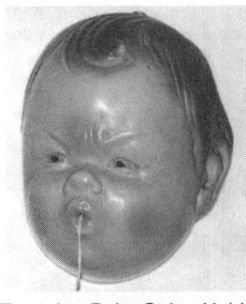

Frowning Baby String Holder

Baby, chalkware, frowning (ILLUS.) **225-275**
Balloon, ceramic, variety of colors, each **45**

Bananas String Holder

Bananas, chalkware, ca. 1980s-present (ILLUS.) **25-50**

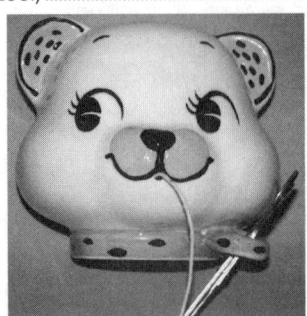

Bear with Scissors In Collar

Bear, w/scissors in collar, ceramic, Japan (ILLUS.).. **50**

Betty Boop String Holder

Betty Boop, chalkware, original (ILLUS.).......... **500**
Bird, ceramic, green, "Arthur Wood, England," also found in blue & brown.................. **25**

"String Swallow" Bird String Holder

Bird, ceramic, in birdhouse, "String Swallow" (ILLUS.)... **45**
Bird, ceramic, yellow bird on green nest, embossed "String Nest Pull," Cardinal China, U.S.A. **50**
Bird, chalkware, in birdcage.............................. **100**
Bird, chalkware, peeking out of birdhouse **175**
Bird & birdhouse, wood & metal......................... **35**
Bird on birdhouse, chalkware, cardboard, "Early Bird," bobs up & down when string is pulled, handmade.................................... **45-55**
Bird on branch, ceramic, Royal Copley.............. **60**
Bird on branch, ceramic, scissors in head........ **85**
Bird on nest, ceramic, countertop-type, Josef Originals **75-95**
Bonzo, ceramic, comic character dog w/bee on chest **135**

Bonzo Face String Holder

Bonzo face, ceramic, comic character dog, marked "Japan," rare (ILLUS.)....................... **350**

Boy with Tilted Cap

Boy, w/tilted cap, chalkware (ILLUS.) **100**
Boy, w/top hat and pipe, eyes to side, chalkware... **50**

Man & Woman String Holder

Brother Jacob and Sister Isabel, chalkware, newer vintage, each (ILLUS.).......... **55-60**
Bunch of balloons, ceramic, green, pink & blue, ca. 1983, Fitz & Floyd............................. **50**
Bunch of fruit, chalkware **195**
Butler, ceramic, black man w/white lips & eyebrows, Japan, hard to find...................... **350+**

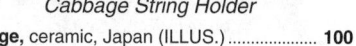

Cabbage String Holder

Cabbage, ceramic, Japan (ILLUS.)................... **100**

Campbell Soup boy, chalkware, face only.... **500+**

Black Cat with Gold Bow

Cat, ceramic, black w/gold bow, handmade
(ILLUS.)... **50**
Cat, ceramic, climbing a ball of string.................. **65**
Cat, ceramic, full-figured w/flowers & scis-
sors **25-45**

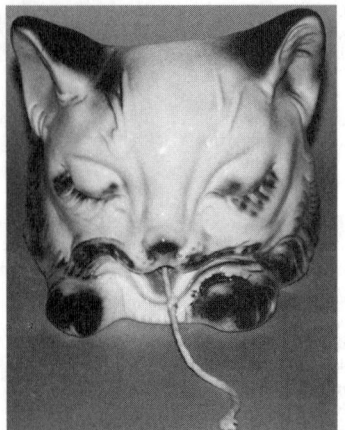

"Knitter's Pal" String Holder

Cat, ceramic, "Knitter's Pal" (ILLUS.) **45**
Cat, ceramic, w/matching wall pocket.................. **95**

Cat with Plaid Collar

Cat, ceramic, w/plaid collar, space for scis-
sors, Japan (ILLUS.).. **50**
Cat, ceramic, w/scissors in collar, "Babba-
combe Pottery, England" **25**
Cat, ceramic, white face w/pink & black pol-
ka dot collar.. **50**
Cat, ceramic, white, full-figured on top of
ball of string... **55-85**

Cat Face String Holder

Cat, ceramic, white, w/large green eyes,
scissors hang on bow (ILLUS.)........................ **35**

Cat on Ball of String String Holder

Cat, chalkware, grinning, on a ball of string,
Miller Studio, 1952 (ILLUS.) **50**
Cat, chalkware, w/bow, holding ball of string **40**
Cat, composition, sitting yellow cat w/red
ball of string, marked "Lorrie Design, Ja-
pan" **35**
Chef, ceramic, "Gift Ideas Creation, Phila.,
Pa.," w/scissors in head.................................... **35**

Chef with Rosy Cheeks

Chef, ceramic, w/rosy cheeks, marked "Japan" (ILLUS.) **50**
Chef, chalkware... **65**
Chef, chalkware, baby face w/chef's hat............ **200**

Chef with Spoon & Box String Holder

Chef, chalkware, full-figured black chef w/spoon & blue box (ILLUS.)............................ **275**
Chef, chalkware, Rice Crispy............................... **145**

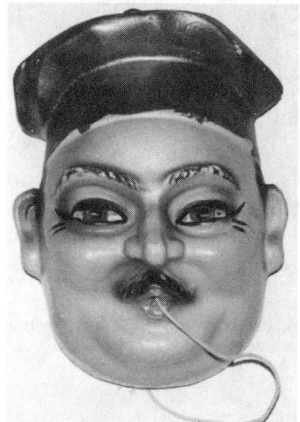

Chef with Bushy Eyebrows

Chef, chalkware, unusual version of chef w/bushy eyebrows (ILLUS.) **150**

Chef with Large Hat

Chef, chalkware, w/large hat facing left (ILLUS.) **150**

Chef with Bottle, Glass String Holder

Chef w/bottle & glass, ceramic, full-figured, Japan (ILLUS.) **175**
Chef's head, ceramic, light-skinned, hard to find **295**

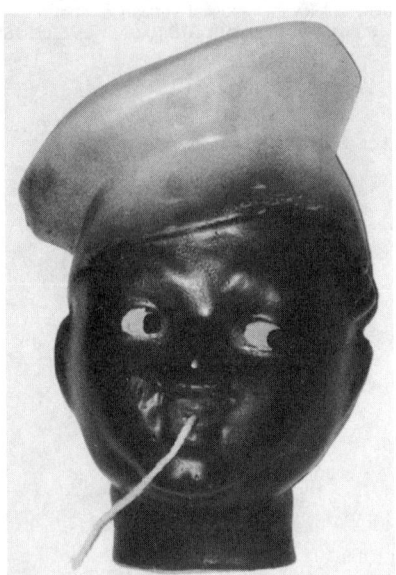

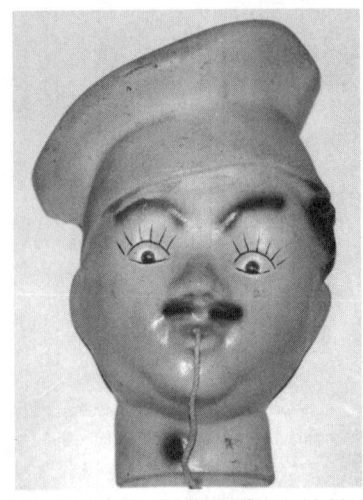

Chalkware Chef's Head String Holder

Chef's head, chalkware, common (ILLUS.) **60**
Chef's head, chalkware, "Little Chef," Miller
   Studio **150**
Cherries, chalkware **175**
Chicken, ceramic, "Quimper of France,"
   found in several patterns, still in produc-
   tion **65-85**
Chicken, ceramic, unmarked **40-50**

Black Chef's Face String Holder

Chef's head, chalkware, black face, white
   hat (ILLUS.) **200**

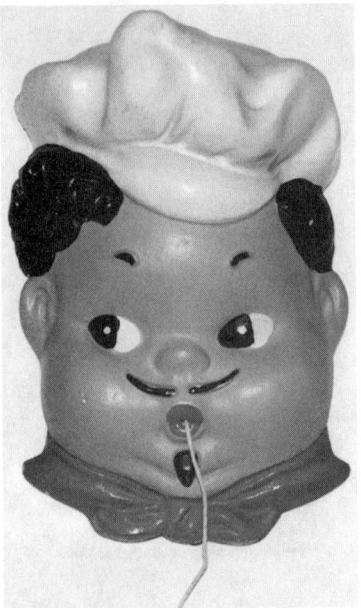

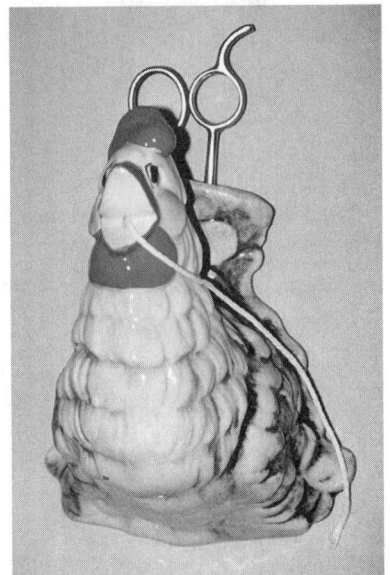

Rare Chef String Holder

Chef's head, chalkware, "By Bello, 1949,"
   chubby-faced, rare (ILLUS.) **450**

French String Holder

Chicken, ceramic, yellow & green w/red
   trim, scissors in tail, France (ILLUS.) **95-125**

Chipmunk String Holder

Chipmunk's head, ceramic, white & brown, red & white striped hat & bow, bow holds scissors, Japan (ILLUS.) 55
Clown, ceramic, full-figured, "Pierrot," hand holds scissors 85

Jo-Jo the Clown String Holder

Clown, chalkware, "Jo-Jo," ca. 1948, Miller Studio (ILLUS.) 200
Clown, chalkware, w/string around tooth........... 125

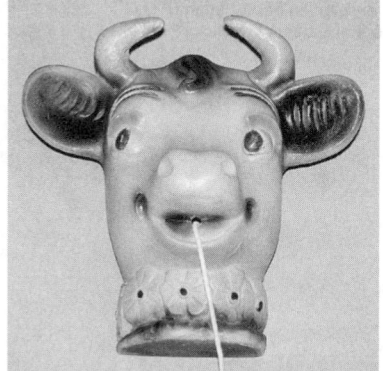

Elsie the Cow String Holder

Cow head, chalkware, Elsie the Cow (ILLUS.) 450

Crock, ceramic, "Kitchen String," by Burleigh Ironstone, Staffordshire, England, w/scissors in top 50

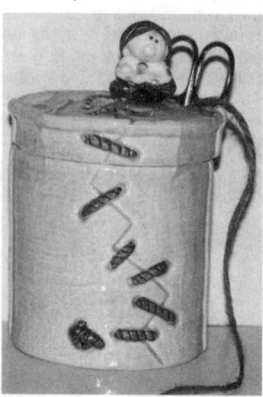

"The Darned String Caddy"

"Darned String Caddy (The)," ceramic, marked "Fitz & Floyd, MCMLXXVI" (ILLUS.) 35
Delicious apple, chalkware, w/stem & leaves.. 25-50
Dog, ceramic, Boxer.. 95
Dog, ceramic, Collie, "Royal Trico," Japan........ 135
Dog, ceramic, German Shepherd, "Royal Trico, Japan"... 135

Dog String Holder

Dog, ceramic (ILLUS.) 100
Dog, ceramic, Schnauzer 135

Scottie String Holder

Dog, ceramic, Scottie, marked "Royal Trico, Japan" (ILLUS.) 135
Dog, ceramic, w/diamond-shaped eyes **85-100**
Dog, ceramic, w/puffed cheeks **35-55**
Dog, ceramic, w/scissors as glasses, marked "Babbacombe Pottery, England" 25
Dog, chalkware, Bulldog w/studded collar, ca. 1933 100
Dog, chalkware, w/chef's hat, "Conovers Original" 275

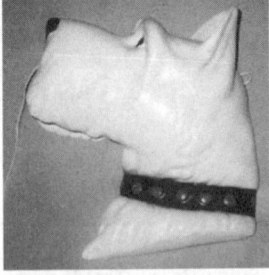

Westie with Studded Collar

Dog, chalkware, Westie, white w/studded color (ILLUS.) 125
Dog, wood, "Sandy Twine Holder," body is ball of string 35

Dog with Black Eye

Dog w/black eye, ceramic, w/scissors holder in collar, right eye only circled in black, England (ILLUS.) 45
Dove, ceramic, Japan 45
Dutch Boy, chalkware, w/cap 125

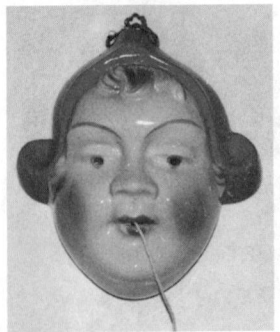

Ceramic Dutch Girl String Holder

Dutch Girl, ceramic, head only, Japan (ILLUS.) 50
Dutch girl, chalkware, head only, w/hat 65
Elephant, ceramic, "Hoffritz, England" 40

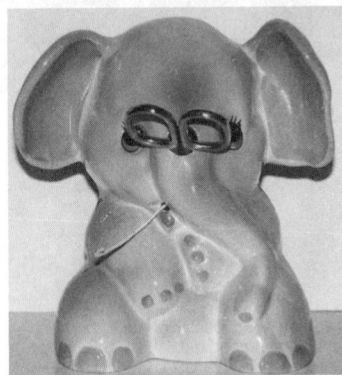

English Elephant String Holder

Elephant, ceramic, marked "Babbacombe Pottery, England," scissors as glasses (ILLUS.) 25
Elephant, ceramic, white 30-40

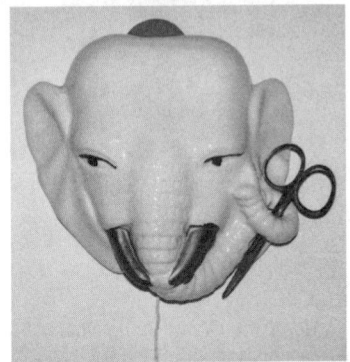

Elephant Pincushion-String Holder

Elephant, ceramic, white w/gold tusks, pincushion on head, Japan (ILLUS.) 50
Elephant, ceramic, yellow, England 75

Father Christmas String Holder

Father Christmas, ceramic, Japan
(ILLUS.).. **175**

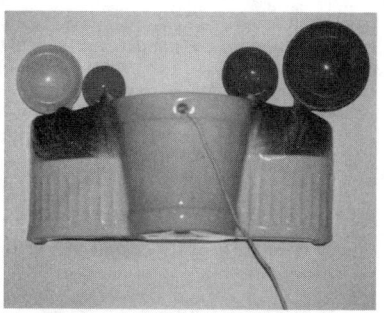

Flowerpot Spoon & String Holder

Flowerpot, ceramic, yellow, w/measuring
spoon holder (ILLUS.) **75**

French Chef String Holder

French chef, ceramic, newer vintage
(ILLUS.).. **35-40**

Chalkware Chef String Holder

French chef, chalkware, w/scarf around
neck (ILLUS.).. **185**

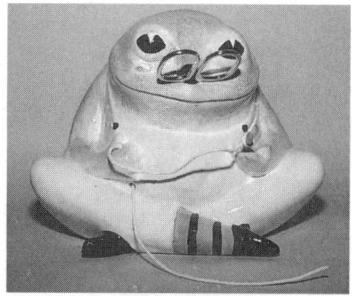

Frog String Holder

Frog, ceramic, countertop-type, Babba-
combe Pottery, England (ILLUS.).............. **45-65**
Funnel-shaped, w/thistle or cat & ball, ce-
ramic **75**
Girl in bonnet, chalkware, eyes to side.............. **65**
Gourd, chalkware **150**

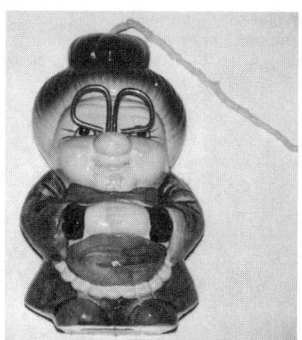

Granny String Holder

Granny, ceramic, full-figured, top of nose
holds scissors that look like glasses
(ILLUS.) **50**

Granny in Rocking Chair String Holder

Granny in rocking chair, ceramic, marked
"PY," Japan (ILLUS.)....................................... **125**

Grapes String Holder

Grapes, chalkware, bunch (ILLUS.)................... **150**
Green pepper, ceramic, Lego sticker.................. **65**

Puffed Heart String Holder

Heart, ceramic, puffed, heart reads "You'll always have a 'pull' with me!" California Cleminsons (ILLUS.)... **50**
House, ceramic, California Cleminsons............. **125**

Humpty Dumpty String Holder

Humpty Dumpty, ceramic, sitting on wall, white & yellow (ILLUS.)...................................... **65**

Indian w/headdress, chalkware........................ **300**
Iron w/flowers, ceramic **75**
Jester, chalkware **95**
Kitten w/ball of yarn, ceramic, handmade........ **40**
Kitten w/ball of yarn, chalkware **65**
Ladybug, chalkware **225-275**

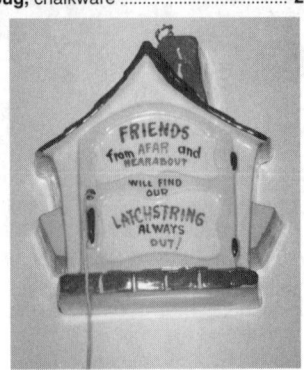

Cleminsons House String Holder

Latchstring house, ceramic, California Cleminsons (ILLUS.) **100**

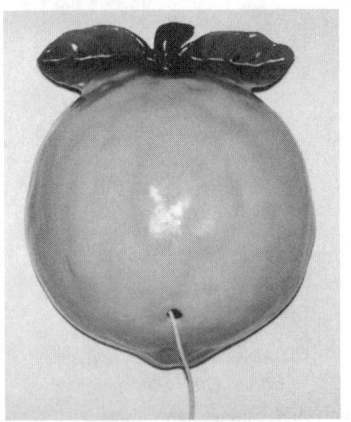

Lemon String Holder

Lemon, ceramic, Japan (ILLUS.)......................... **95**

Little Bo Peep String Holder

Little Bo Peep, ceramic, white w/red & blue trim, marked "Japan" (ILLUS.) **175**
Little Red Riding Hood, chalkware, head wearing hood **250**

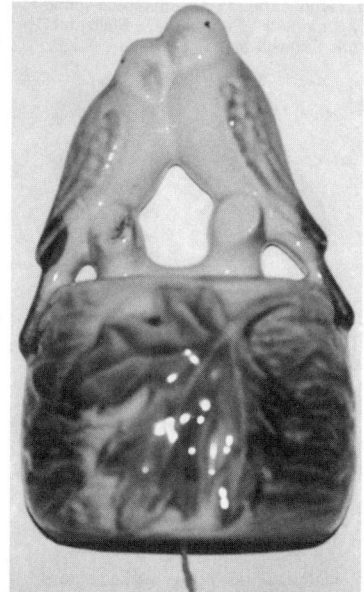

Lovebirds String Holder

Lovebirds, ceramic, Morton Pottery (ILLUS.) **50**
Maid, ceramic, Sarsaparilla, 1984 .... **65**
Mammy, ceramic, full-figured, plaid & polka dot dress, Japan **100**

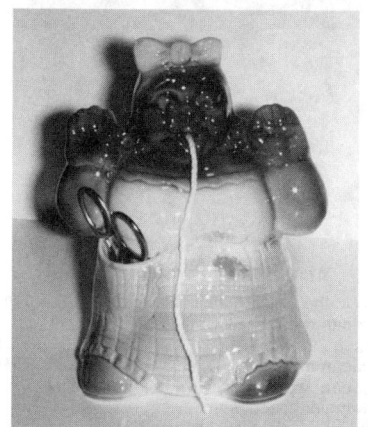

Mammy String Holder

Mammy, ceramic, full-figured, w/arms up & scissors in pocket (ILLUS.) **225**

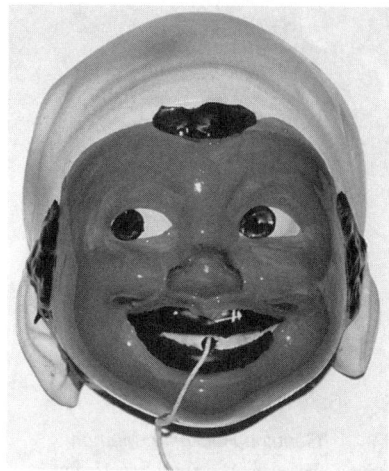

Mammy Face String Holder

Mammy, ceramic, head only, Japan (ILLUS.) **250**

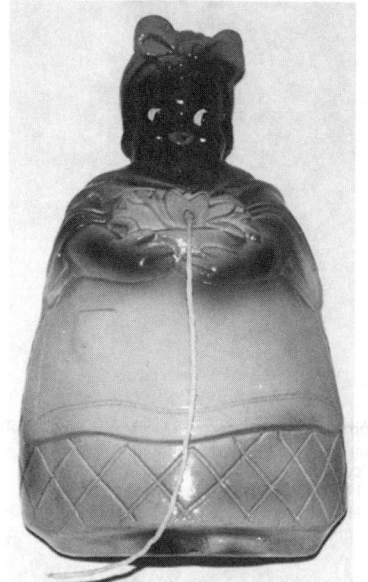

Mammy Holding Flowers

Mammy, chalkware, full-figured, holding flowers, marked "MAPCO" (ILLUS.) **175**
Mammy, chalkware, head only, many variations .... **200+**
Mammy, chalkware, head only, marked "Ty-Me" on neck **250**

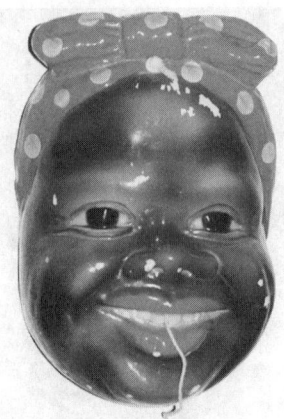

"Genuine Rockalite" Mammy

Mammy, chalkware, head only, w/polka-dot bandana, marked "Genuine Rockalite," made in Canada (ILLUS.) **200**

Mammy String Holder

Mammy, cloth & wood (ILLUS.) **50-75**
Mammy, cloth-faced, "Simone," includes card that reads "I'm smiling Jane, so glad I came to tie your things, with nice white strings," rare **150-195**

Coconut Mammy

Mammy, coconut, w/red and blue floral scarf (ILLUS.) **35**
Mammy, felt, head only, w/plastic rolling eyes **50-75**
Man, ceramic, head only, drunk, designed by & marked "Elsa" on back, Pfaltzgraff, York, Pennsylvania **95**

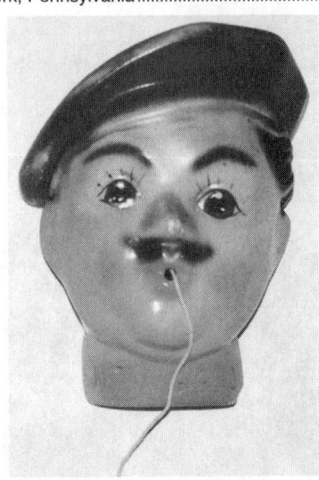

Gigolo Man String Holder

Man, chalkware, head only, marked across collar, "Just a Gigolo" (ILLUS.) **100**

Man in the Moon String Holder

Man in the Moon face, chalkware (ILLUS.) **150**
Mexican man, chalkware, head only, common **50**
Mexican man, chalkware, w/ornate hat **85-100**
Mexican woman, chalkware, head only, w/braids & sombrero **150**
Monkey, chalkware, sitting on ball of string, found in various colors **225-275**
Mouse, ceramic, countertop-type, Josef Originals sticker **50**
Mouse, ceramic, England **75**
Mouse, ceramic, sitting, Josef Original **85**
Oriental man, ceramic, w/coolie hat, Abingdon **400**
Owl, Babbacombe Pottery, England **25**
Owl, ceramic, full-figured, Josef Originals **35**

Pancho Villa String Holder

Pancho Villa, chalkware (ILLUS.)...................... **275**
Parlor maid, ceramic, marked "Sarsasparil-
la," early 1980s **65**
Parrot, chalkware, brightly colored **125-175**
Peach, ceramic.. **60**
Pear, chalkware.. **45**

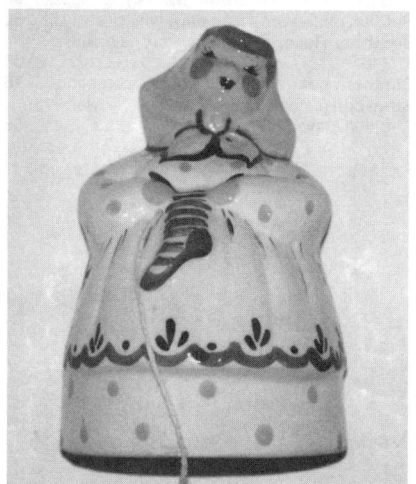

Peasant Woman Knitting String Holder

Peasant woman, ceramic, full-figured, knitting sock, sticker reads "Wayne of Holly-
wood" (ILLUS.)... **175**
Penguin, ceramic, full-figured w/scissors
holder in beak, marked "Arthur Wood,
England" **85**

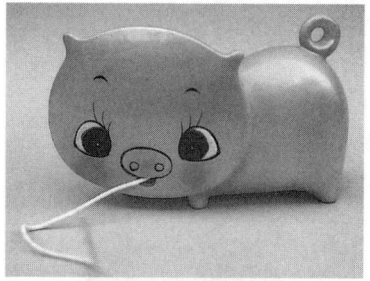

Pink Pig String Holder

Pig, ceramic, hanging or countertop-type,
pink (ILLUS.)... **50**

Pig String Holder

Pig, ceramic, Holt Howard (ILLUS.)..................... **75**

Floral Decorated Pig String Holder

Pig, ceramic, white w/red & yellow flowers &
green leaves decoration, scissors holder
on back near tail, Arthur Wood, England
(ILLUS.) **50**
Pig w/flowers, ceramic.. **145**
Pineapple, chalkware, "Prince Pineapple,"
by Miller Studio... **250**
Pirate & gypsy, wood fiber, pr. **150**

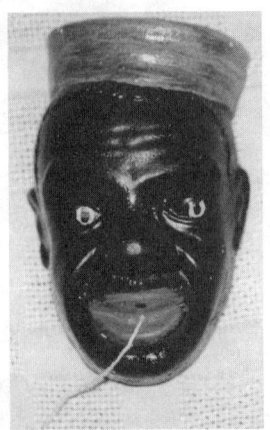

Porter String Holder

Porter, clay, without teeth, marked "Fredericksburg Art Pottery, U.S.A." (ILLUS.) **145**
Prayer lady, ceramic, by Enesco **175**

R2D2 String Holder

Robot R2D2, ceramic, countertop, newer vintage, marked "Sigma" (ILLUS.) **95-135**
Rooster, porcelain, head only, Royal Bayreuth .... **350+**

Chalkware Rose String Holder

Rose, chalkware (ILLUS.) **135**
Sailor Boy, chalkware **150**
Sailor Girl (Rosie the Riveter), chalkware....... **225**
Senor, chalkware.. **65**
Senora, chalkware.. **75**
Shaggy dog, ceramic, full-figured, w/scissors as glasses, marked "Babbacombe Pottery, England" **25**

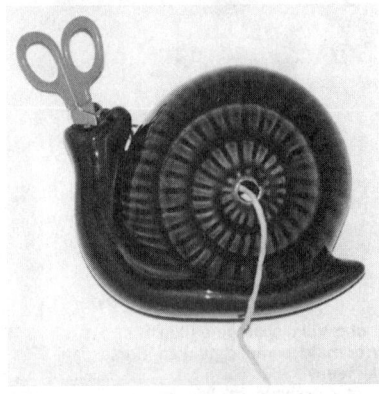

Snail String Holder

Snail, ceramic, dark brown (ILLUS.).................... **35**
Soldier, chalkware, head only, w/hat **50**
Southern Belle, ceramic, w/very full skirt, Japan **65**
Southern gentleman with ladies, ceramic........ **75**
Strawberry, chalkware, w/white flower, green leaves & no stem **55**

Sunfish String Holder

Susie Sunfish, chalkware, Miller Studio, 1948 (ILLUS.) **225-275**
Teapot, ceramic, Japan, w/parakeet.................... **65**
Teddy bear, ceramic, brown, marked "Babbacombe Pottery, England," hole for scissors in bow at neck **25**
Thatched-roof cottage, ceramic **35**
Tom cat, ceramic, "Takahashi, San Francisco," Japan.. **35**

Tomato String Holder

Tomato, ceramic (ILLUS.).................................... 55
Tomato, chalkware.. 50

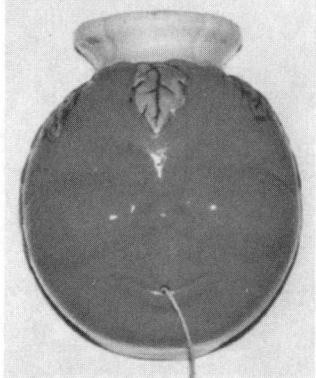

Tomato Chef String Holder

Tomato chef, ceramic, "Japan," eyes
 closed (ILLUS.)... 100

Westie String Holder

Westie, chalkware (ILLUS.)................................ 200
Witch in pumpkin, ceramic, winking................. 100

Woman in Flowered Dress String Holder

Woman, ceramic, full-figured, blue dress
 w/white & red flowers, Japan (ILLUS.) 85
Woman, ceramic, head only, arched eye-
 brows.. 125

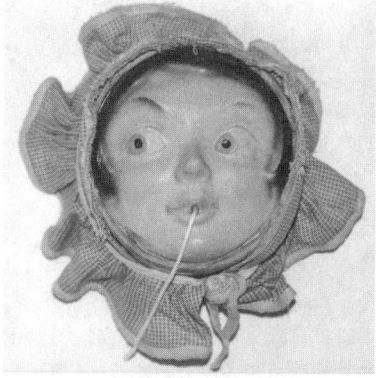

Chalkware, Cardboard & Cloth String Holder

Woman's face, chalkware on cardboard
 box w/cloth bonnet (ILLUS.).......................... 100

Young Girl String Holder

Young black girl, ceramic, w/surprised
 look, Japan (ILLUS.)................................ 250-295

LAUNDRY ROOM ITEMS

Clothes Sprinkler Bottles

To remove wrinkles from clothes, water was distributed through the fabric and rolled-up clothes were then ready to be ironed.

Although many people used a soda bottle with an attached sprinkler head, many whimsical bottles produced for this purpose were either purchased or created in ceramic class.

The variety of subjects depicted by figural sprinkler bottles run from objects related to ironing to the people who did the ironing.

Cat, ceramic, homemade, variety of colors & designs.. **$75-250**
Cat, ceramic, Siamese, tan **125**
Cat, ceramic, w/marble eyes, American Bisque **250**

Mr. & Mrs. Cat Sprinkler Bottles

Cats, ceramic, handmade, Mr. & Mrs. Cat, the set (ILLUS.) **500**

Variety of Chinese Man Sprinkler Bottles

Chinese man, ceramic, homemade, variety of designs & colors, each (ILLUS. of three) **75-125**
Chinese man, ceramic, Sprinkle Plenty, white, green & brown, holding iron **150-200**

Chinese man, ceramic, Sprinkle Plenty, yellow & green, Cardinal China Company **40**
Chinese man, ceramic, white w/aqua & black trim, California Cleminsons.................... **40**
Chinese man, ceramic, white w/aqua & black trim, w/original shirt tag hanging around neck, California Cleminsons................ **85**
Clothespin, ceramic, aqua, yellow & pink, with smiling face... **225**
Clothespin, plastic, red, yellow or green............. **40**
Dutch Boy, ceramic, green & white **200**
Dutch Girl, ceramic, mate to Dutch boy **200**
Elephant, ceramic, pink & grey **65**
Elephant, ceramic, trunk used for handle, American Bisque **600**

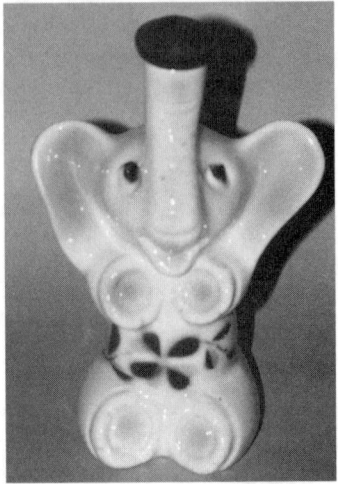

Elephant with Clover

Elephant, ceramic, white w/pink w/clover on tummy (ILLUS.) **100**

Variety of Emperor Sprinkler Bottles

Emperor, ceramic, variety of colors & designs, homemade, each (ILLUS. of three).. **100-200**
Fireman, ceramic, California Cleminsons, rare .... **1,500+**
Iron, ceramic, blue flowers **125**
Iron, ceramic, farm couple **250**

Iron-Shaped Aquarena Springs Bottle

Iron, ceramic, souvenir of Aquarena Springs, San Marcos, Texas (ILLUS.)... **250**

Iron, ceramic, souvenir of Florida, w/pink flamingo, marked "A touch of sun, a drop of rain, helps your clothes feel fresh again" **300**

Iron, ceramic, souvenir of Wonder Cave............ **300**

Iron, ceramic, w/ironing housewife dressed in red skirt & green blouse................................. **65**

Iron, ceramic, white w/green ivy decorations, black cap.. **75**

Iron, plastic, green.. **40**

Mammy, ceramic, unmarked................................ **325**

Mary Poppins, ceramic, California Cleminsons.. **350**

Merry maid, plastic, all colors, Reliance........ **25-40**

Myrtle, ceramic, Pfaltzgraff.................................... **250**

Myrtle Sprinkler Bottles

Myrtle, homemade, each (ILLUS. of two).......... **150**

Poodle, ceramic, grey, pink or white, each....... **225**

Rooster, ceramic, red, white & green................. **125**

Irons

What is the spark that inspires an interest in accumulating antique pressing irons? Once the mysterious process is in action, you are changed to the dedicated and possessed individual known as a collector.

One iron is not a collection. It seems lonely by itself. Perhaps it would be happier if others joined it. A collection begins to coalesce.

Most beginners start with common irons. Some remain at the entry level without moving to explore the higher delights of collecting. There is a tendency to acquire only one iron of a type and this is a common mistake. A representative collection should include a range of irons. Look for scarcity, attractiveness, interest and condition; emphasize quality. If you have pride in your collection, insist on the best and don't buy anything broken.

A quest for irons will lead to antiques shows, auctions and flea markets. These are chances to be exposed to various kinds of irons, possibly seeing one that will lead in an entirely new direction. Do not overlook any opportunity to get acquainted with the market. The real education begins by talking to other collectors, reading books and periodicals.

Traditionally, irons are used as book ends and doorstops and they look especially at home on the hearth or mantel. The more decorative pieces are proudly displayed where they can be seen in the entryway, living and dining rooms. Some of the finer irons were originally designed to be shown and admired. Today they still fulfill that purpose as well as they did when originally made a century or two ago.

By collecting irons, you are not only engaging in an absorbing hobby, but you are preserving the cultural and historical interest of antique pressing irons.

-Jimmy Walker

Bless & Drake "Salamander" Box Iron

Box iron, Bless & Drake "Salamander," w/slug (ILLUS.)... **450**

Box iron, brass sole, lift gate, single post, w/slug, Germany **300**

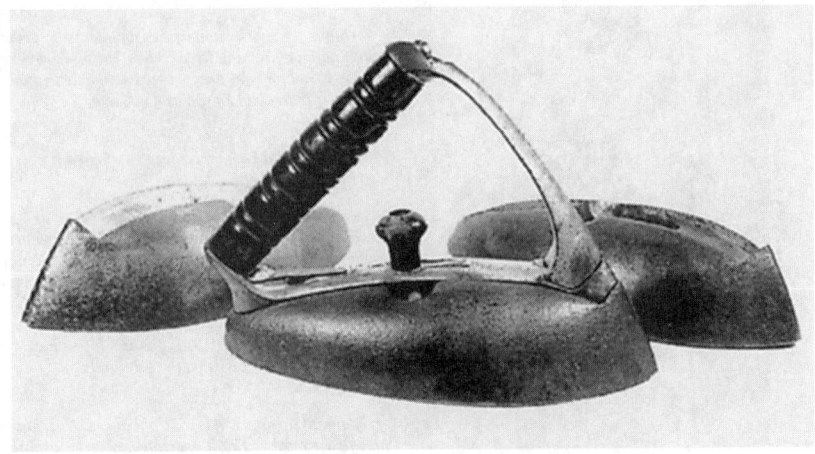

Three-base Slant-handle Iron

Box iron, brass sole, lift gate, w/slug, England.. **225**

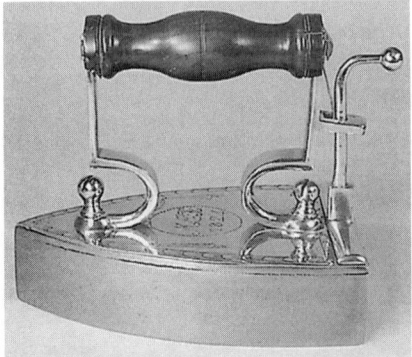

Engraved Box Iron

Box iron, lift gate, steel base, brass uprights & top w/engraved decoration & "1824," wooden handle, w/slug (ILLUS.)....... **700**

"Only One" Charcoal Iron

Charcoal iron, "Only One," patents 1914 & 1916 (ILLUS.) **150**

Charcoal iron, w/thermometer mounted on top, pat. July 9, 1889 .... **2,000**

Charcoal iron, box, side dampers & liftoff top, marked "The Marvel, Patented Dec 30, 1924," 6 5/8" l.. **125**

Combination iron, box w/slug, "Magic No. 1," w/fluter bed & roller **900**

"Ladies Friend" Combination Iron

Combination iron, "Ladies Friend," box w/slug (ILLUS.).. **1,300**

Combination iron, "Patent Home Iron," separate fluter bed attached to iron w/wire bail & screw **800**

Detachable handle iron, "Sensible No. 4," N.R.S. & Co. **40**

Detachable handle iron set, three bases, slant handle, the set (ILLUS., top of page).. **200**

Detachable handle iron set, w/three bases & trivet, "Wapak," the set **125**

Egg iron, electric, "Tommy Iron," patent 6-6-22, w/flat iron attachment............................ **275**

Egg iron, on tripod stand **250**

Shepard Hand Fluter Model No. 85

"Paris" Egg Set

Egg set, six assorted sizes w/stand, "Paris,"
   the set (ILLUS.) **1,000**
Electric iron, A.C. Williams, double-point
   side connection.. **100**

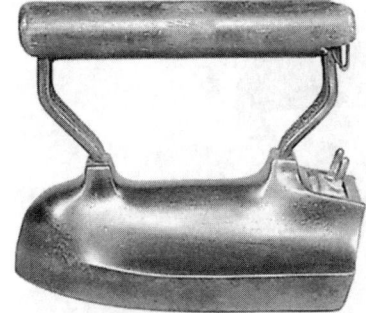

Early GE F10 Iron

Electric iron, early, GE F10 model, patent
Nov. 7, 1905 (ILLUS.)... **50**

Electric iron, "Proctor Snap Stand Speed
   Iron," chrome w/cork grip, early **200**
Fluter, hand, "Elgin," rocking type...................... **300**
Fluter, hand, Shepard "Model No. 85"
   (ILLUS., top of page) **175**
Fluter, hand, Street's transverse rolling type **400**
Fluter, machine, "Crown," patent Nov. 2,
   1875, reissued March 23, 1880 .... **150**

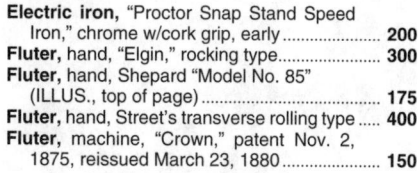

Dudley Machine Fluter

Fluter, machine, "Dudley," patent Nov. 14,
   1876 (ILLUS.) **950**
Fluter, machine, "Eagle," 5" rollers, patent
   Nov. 2, 1875.. **150**

Coleman "Model No. 5" Fuel Iron

Fuel iron, porcelain, Coleman "Model No. 5," green (ILLUS.) **200**

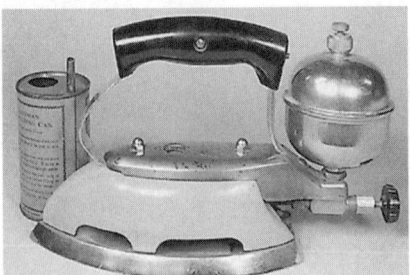

Coleman Model No. 611 Fuel Iron

Fuel iron, porcelain, Coleman Model No. 611, turquoise, Canada (ILLUS.) **175**

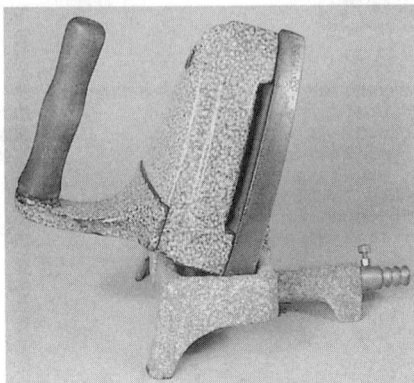

Wrights Eureka Granite Gas Iron

Gas iron, graniteware, "Wrights Eureka No. 350," on special stove, wooden handle, grey, England (ILLUS.) **300**

Gasoline iron, "Diamond," Akron Lamp Co........ **60**

Gasoline iron, "Monitor," patented in 1903........ **90**

Goffering iron, cast iron, paw feet, w/heater, 1840 .... **500**

Goffering iron, cast iron, "S" standard w/heater **500**

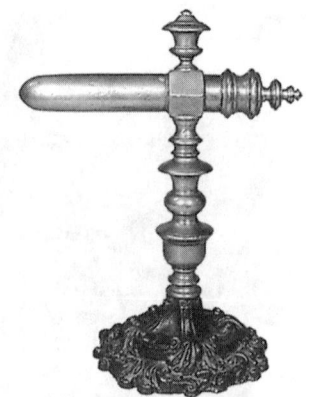

Victorian Goffering Iron

Goffering iron, single barrel w/plug, brass, Victorian (ILLUS.) **600**

Hat iron, brass, foot tolliker (so called because it resembles a foot) **225**

Hinged-shackle Hat Iron

Hat iron, hinged shackle (ILLUS.) **250**

Hat iron, tolliker, two grooves on base **125**

Dover "A-BEST-O No. 602" Iron

Metal Ivory Pan Iron

Little iron, Dover flat latch, "A-BEST-O No. 602," 3 3/8" l. (ILLUS., bottom previous page) 60
Little iron, Potts type, detachable handle, 3 3/4" 80
Little iron, "Sensible No. 6," N.R.S. & Co., 3 3/4" 150

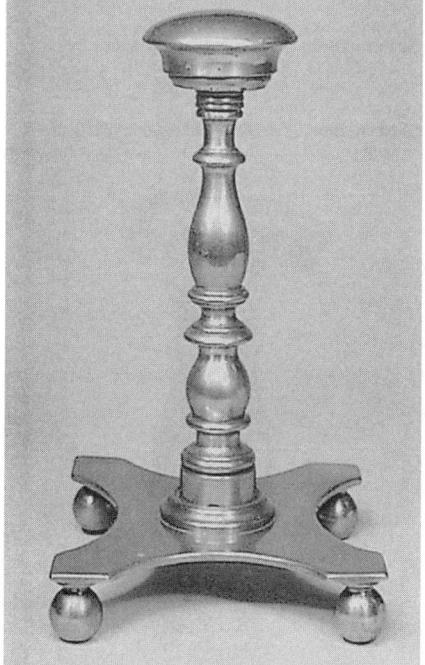

Brass Mushroom Iron

Mushroom iron, brass, heated w/slug, England (ILLUS.) 1,700
Natural gas iron, "Central Mfg. Co.," chimney w/openings on each side, closed on front 700

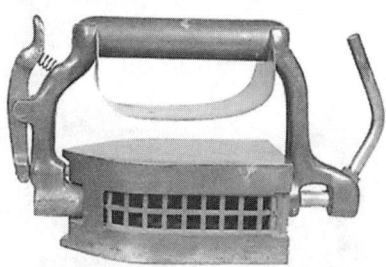

Comfort Reversible Gas Iron

Natural gas iron, "Comfort," reversible (ILLUS.) 900
Natural gas iron, "Nu-Style La Rue Gas Iron," 8-lb. iron w/2-lb. slide-out top 700
Pan iron, brass, inside liner, Japan 250
Pan iron, metal, ivory handle in the shape of a dragon head, Chinese (ILLUS., top of page) 1,200
Pan iron, vent opening in front, Philippines 160
Polisher, "Bubble" sole, France 300
Polisher, "Geneva," Howell Co., Geneva, Illinois 35

M.A.B. Cook Polisher

Polisher, "M.A.B. Cook," pantented in 1848 (ILLUS.) 250

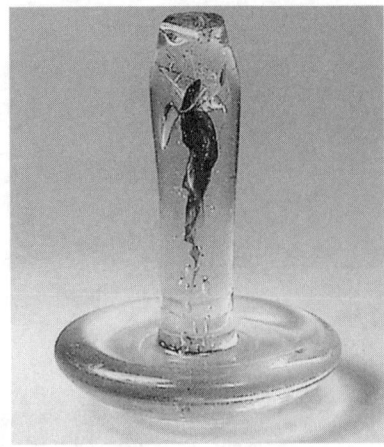

Glass Slickenstone

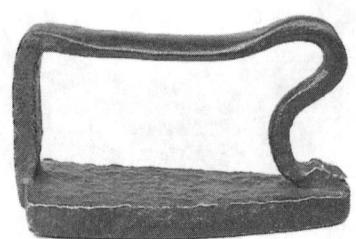

Primitive Iron with Serpent Grip

Sleeve iron, "Geneva," thick toe holds heat, Howell Co., Geneva, Illinois (ILLUS.) **200**
Sleeve iron, "Ober No. 2" **200**
Sleeve iron, "Sensible No. 1," w/detachable handle **85**
Slickenstone, clear glass w/red spiral in grip (ILLUS., top of page) **800**
Slickenstone, hand-blown amber glass, made without grip **300**
Slickenstone, hand-blown green glass, w/grip **400**

Primitive, serpent grip (ILLUS.) **175**
Primitive, "Slave" iron, pebble in handle makes ringing sound **200**

Primitive Iron with Twist Handle

Primitive, twist handle (ILLUS.) **200**

"Geneva" Sleeve Iron

Lignum Vitae Slickenstone

Slickenstone, lignum vitae (ILLUS.) **400**
Tailor iron, 20 lbs., unmarked **40**
Tailor iron, box, "New England Butt." **350**

Travel Iron in Case

Ober 20-pound Tailor Iron

Tailor iron, Ober, 20-pound (ILLUS.) **175**

Travel iron, "Meta Fuel," England **75**

Travel iron in case, "Betsy Ross EZ Way," w/padded case, Central Flatiron Co., U.S.A. (ILLUS., top of page) **190**

Travel iron in case, "Sunbeam No. 52," metal carrying case... **75**

Travel iron set, "Hot Point Utility," w/trivet, curling iron, pan & lid (ILLUS., bottom of page) **400**

Miscellaneous

Washboard, "Pearl," w/glass scrubbing surface, 1900, 8 1/2 x 16" **40**

Travel Iron Set

LEHN WARE

Wooden items made and decorated by Joseph Lehn, Lancaster County, Pennsylvania, command high prices today. To supplement his income from farming, Lehn began making barrels for local gristmills in the mid-1850s and, a few years later, began to turn small wooden items as gifts for family and friends. The popularity of the small wooden items led him to begin to decorate these items for local stores in Lititz and New Euphrata, Pennsylvania. Today these turned wooden bowls, buckets, boxes and covered footed bowls - enhanced with hand-painted colorful stripes, stylized borders, floral or fruit designs, almost always on a salmon or dusty pink ground - do not often come on the market, especially in top condition with no wear or damage.

Jar, cov., wooden, straight sides, salmon ground w/red, white & green flowers, red & green stripes & worn black paint on finial, lid has strawberries, inside is marked "M.M. Grubaker Lititz, PA 1865," heavy varnish, 4 5/8" h.. **$220**

Saffron jar, cov., wooden, w/pedestal base, decorated w/delicate red & green flowers on light peach ground, lid w/strawberries, red & green stripes & black finial, 4 3/4" h. (some wear & light alligatoring)....... **660**

Saffron jar, cov., wooden w/pedestal base, decorated w/red & green flowers on peach ground, lid w/strawberries, red & green stripes w/black finial, bright colors, 4 5/8" h.. **220**

Saffron jar, cov., wooden, w/pedestal base, painted in dark pink w/red three-petal flowers & green leaves, lid w/strawberries, red & green stripes, black finial, 5 3/8" h. (small putty-filled chips, minor paint flakes, possible repaint to finial)............ **550**

LIGHTING DEVICES
Also see Antique Trader Lamps & Lighting Price Guide.

Early Non-Electric Lamps & Lighting

Fairy Lamps
These are candle burning night lights of the Victorian era. Best known are the Clarke Fairy Lamps made in England, but they were also made by other firms. They were produced in two sizes, each with a base and a shade. Fairy Pyramid lamps usually have a clear glass base and are approximately 2 7/8" d. and 3 1/4" h. The Fairy Lamps are usually at least 4" d. and 5" h. when assembled. These may or may not have an additional saucer or bottom holder to match the shade in addition to the clear base.

Blue Hobnail Fairy Lamp

Blue Hobnail patt. shade, pyramid-size, in a clear Clarke lamp cup, 3" d., 4" h. (ILLUS.) **$150**

Blue Mother-of-Pearl & Swirl Lamp

Blue mother-of-pearl satin shade, fairy-size, Diamond Quilted patt. cased in white & w/an overall embossed reverse swirl mold design, matching smooth-shouldered lamp cup, 3 3/4" d., 5" h. (ILLUS.) **250**

Mother-of-Pearl Shade on Plateau

Blue mother-of-pearl satin shade, pyramid-size, Diamond Quilted patt., cased in white, in a Clarke glazed creamware lamp cup w/gold trim marked by Taylor, Tunnicliffe & Co. on the bottom, cup fits in the ring of an ormolu stand attached to a beveled mirror plateau, 4 1/2" d., 5 1/2" h. (ILLUS.) **450**

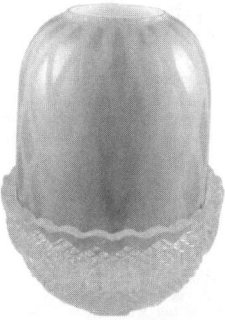

Blue Diamond Quilted Satin Lamp

Blue mother-of-pearl satin shade, pyramid-size, Diamond Quilted patt. cased in white, in a clear Clarke Fairy Pyramid lamp cup (ILLUS.) **200**

Blue Opaque Building Fairy Lamp

Blue opaque figural shade, modeled as a tall six-sided building w/embossed windows, doors & shingle roof, on a conforming base w/stone block design & containing an integral candle cup, 4" w., 6" h. (ILLUS.) **150**

Decorated Blue Satin Shade & Stand

Blue satin decorated shade, pyramid-size, the blue ground enameled w/white flowers, leaves & a decorative ring around the top opening, on a clear Clarke lamp cup, cup fits into an ormolu stand w/openwork trim attached to a blue plush mirror plateau base, 4 7/8" d., 8 7/8" h. (ILLUS.).. **600**

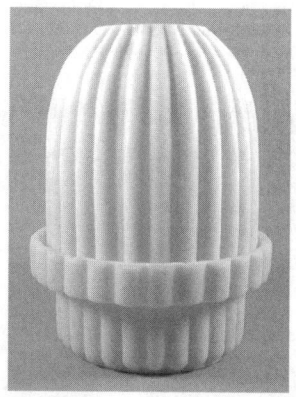

Blue Satin Ribbed Fairy Lamp

Blue satin ribbed shade, fairy-size, narrow vertical ribbing, in a smooth-shouldered matching lamp cup, 3 5/8" d., 4 5/8" h. (ILLUS.) **250**

Satin Glass Fairy Lamp-Vase Epergne

Blue shaded satin shade, epergne-style, blue shaded to white, a fairy-size central shade cased in creamy white in a clear Clarke lamp cup, the cup resting on the inward-turned crimped rim of the matching bowl, bowl rests in an ormolu frame attached to a round mirror plateau w/beveled & notched edge, each frame arm supporting a matching bulbous satin glass bud vase w/flared & scalloped rim & applied opaque berry prunt, 10 1/4" d., 6 1/2" h. (ILLUS.) **2,000**

Blue & White Candy Stripe Fairy Lamp

Blue & white candy stripe shade, fairy-size, shade embossed w/reverse swirl design, in a clear Clarke lamp cup, 4" d., 4 1/2" h. (ILLUS.)... **300**

Frosted Blue & White Swirl Lamp

Blue, white & clear frosted Cleveland Swirl patt. shade, fairy-size, in a matching lamp cup w/crimped rim & raised on a matching base w/upturned fluted rim, 6 1/2" d., 6 1/4" h. (ILLUS.)............................. **750**

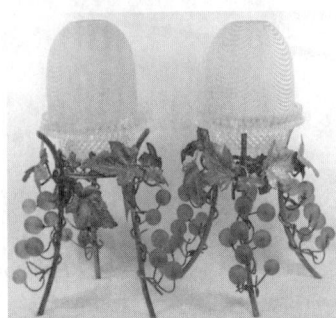

Lamps in Stands with Nailsea Shades

Blue & white Nailsea-style shade, fairy-size, blue w/white loopings, on a clear Clarke lamp cup resting in a three-legged brass stand decorated w/glass green grape leaves & frosted green grapes, 10" h., pr. (ILLUS.) **1,500**

Blue Nailsea & Creamware Lamp

Blue & white Nailsea-type shade, fairy-size, blue ground w/delicate overall blue loopings, resting on the ribbed shoulder of a creamware lamp cup trimmed in blue & gold & marked "S. Clarke's Patent Trade Mark Fairy" raised on the integral post of a Tapestry Ware flower bowl base w/incurved ruffled rim marked "Taylor, Tunnicliffe & Co.," 8 1/8" d., 7 1/2" h. (ILLUS.) **750**

Tall Marked Burmese Epergne-Lamp

Burmese decorated shades, epergne-style, pyramid-size, satin finish, four shades decorated in the woodbine design in clear Clarke lamp cups, the center lamp elevated, alternating w/three undecorated satin finish Burmese bud vases w/fluted, flared rims w/rings & berry prunts fitted into the metal rings of a seven-armed ormolu frame rising above a miniature Burmese rose bowl, all supported by an ormolu fitting on a tubular trumpet-form center pedestal of unrefired Burmese, the frame marked "Clarke's Trade Mark Cricklite," 8 1/2" d., 12" h. (ILLUS.) **3,000**

Marked Webb Burmese Fairy Lamp

Burmese shade, fairy-size, satin finish, in a clear ribbed Clarke lamp cup marked "Fairy Lamp Patent Nov 9, 1886 - 352296 American Patent," resting on a Webb Burmese reversible base w/upturned ruffled rim marked "Thomas Webb & Sons -

Queen's Burmese Ware Patented" & "S. Clarke's Patent Trade Mark Fairy," 7 1/4" d., 5 1/2" h. (ILLUS.)............................. **500**

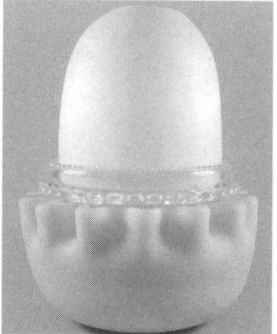

Webb Burmese Shade & Base

Burmese shade, fairy-size, satin finish, in a clear ribbed lamp cup resting on a matching satin-finish Burmese base w/a deep rounded bottom & upright fluted rim, base acid-stamped "Thomas Webb & Sons," 5" d., 6" h. (ILLUS.) **750**

Webb Burmese Marked Fairy Lamp

Burmese shade, fairy-size, undecorated satin finish shade resting in a Clarke pressed glass lamp cup, fitted in a reversible matching Burmese base w/fluted downturned rim marked "Thomas Webb & Sons - Queen's Burmese Ware - Patented" & "S. Clarke's Patent Trade Mark Fairy," 7 1/4" d., 6" h. (ILLUS.) **500**

Clear Ribbed Glass & Brass Lamps

Clear ribbed shade, fairy-size, in a Clarke spun brass handled lamp cup w/porcelain candle cup, holder & candle cup printed & embossed w/Clarke advertising, 4" d., 3 1/2" h., each (ILLUS. of two) **200**

Cranberry & Clear Wee Fairy Lamp

Cranberry & clear shade, a wee-size shade w/three rows of applied clear tooled petals, in a Clarke clear swirl design lamp cup embossed "Clarke's Patent Wee Fairy," 2 1/2" d., 3" h. (ILLUS.) **600**

Two Embossed Shades on Bases

Cranberry or green waffle-embossed shade, pyramid-size, each w/an applied brass ring around the top opening, each fitted into a brass lamp cup w/slotted openwork design & depression for candle, 4 3/4" d., 3 3/4" h., each (ILLUS. of two)... **200**

Bisque Monkey Figural Fairy Lamp

Figural bisque shade, pyramid-size, molded & hand-colored full-relief figure of a monkey in clothing playing a mandolin while seated on a crescent Man-in-the-Moon w/pierced star openings, impressed fleur-de-lis design on the unpainted back, 3 1/2" w., 3 1/2" h. (ILLUS.)............................. **350**

Figural Green Owl Head Fairy Lamp

Figural frosted green glass shade, modeled as a two-faced owl head w/red-painted eyes, in a clear Clarke pyramid lamp cup, 4" d., 4 1/2" h. (ILLUS.) **200**

Royal Worcester Figural Fairy Lamp

Figural porcelain fairy lamp, a Royal Worcester porcelain figural Water Carrier, Model No. 125, trimmed in orange & gold & date coded for 1903, supporting a single pegged clear Clarke lamp cup & stamped "Trade Mark Cricklite," the clear Clarke shade w/a replacement beaded shade, figure 10 1/2" h., overall 19" h. (ILLUS.) **3,500**

Porcelain Lion Head Fairy Lamp

Figural porcelain shade, model of a lion head, translucent & painted in shades of brown & tan, number "4" incised in base, 4 5/8" w., 3 1/2" h. (ILLUS.) **250**

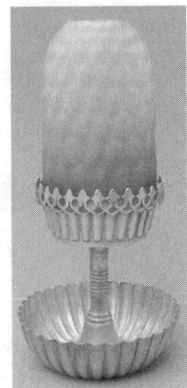

Clear to Cranberry Shade on a Base

Frosted clear shading to cranberry shade, fairy-size, embossed w/a honeycomb design, resting in a punched brass cup atop a center column of pressed brass attached to an upturned fluted base, base marked "Samuel Clarke Trade Mark Fairy - US Pat. Appl'd For," 4 1/4" d., 8 1/2" h. (ILLUS.) **600**

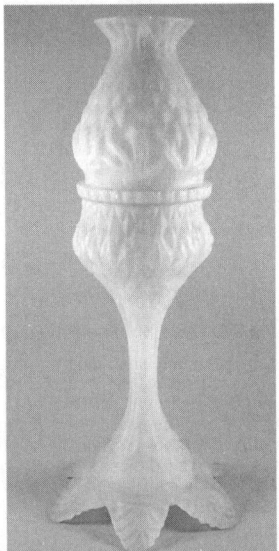

Frosted Lime Green Fairy Lamp

Lime green frosted shade, pyramid-size, an embossed leaf & diamond design, on a matching ribbed lamp cup sitting atop a frosted green shading to clear slender pedestal w/six applied leaves forming the feet, 2 3/4" d., 9 5/8" h. (ILLUS.) **350**

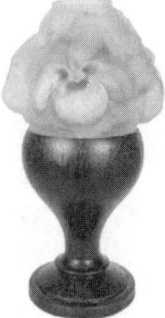

Pairpoint Puffy Pansy Fairy Lamp

Pairpoint "Puffy" Pansy shade, tapering form molded w/blossoms & reverse-painted w/naturalistic colors, raised on a turned walnut standard, 4 1/4" d., 7 5/8" h. (ILLUS.)... **1,500**

Pink Cased & Ribbed Fairy Lamp

Pink cased & ribbed shade, fairy-size, cased in white, in a clear Clarke lamp cup resting on the center post of a matching pink cased base w/a fluted rim, shade acid-marked "Rd 50725" & "Trade Mark Fairy," 6 2/3" d., 4 3/4" h. (ILLUS.) **500**

Pink Satin & Flower Bowl Fairy Lamp

Pink mother-of-pearl satin shade, pyramid-size, Diamond Quilted patt., in a clear Clarke Patent Trade Mark flower

bowl base w/integral two-shoulder lamp cup, 6" d., 3 5/8" h. (ILLUS.) **250**

Pink Opalescent Fairy Lamp

Pink opalescent shade, pyramid-size, a tapering light pink blossom form w/opalescent upper half, w/six upturned applied petals, on a matching base w/six downturned applied petals & an integral candle cup, 3 1/2" d., 3 3/4" h. (ILLUS.).................... **350**

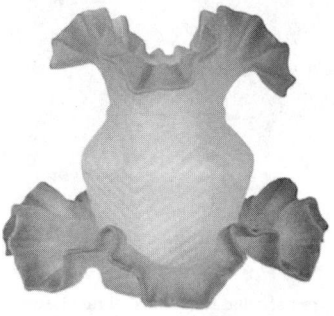

Pink Shaded Chimney-style Lamp

Pink shading to white frosted shade, chimney-style, ovoid form w/widely rolled & ruffled top opening & embossed w/opposing diagonal ribs, rests on a matching deeply fluted & ruffled low base, 7 1/2" d., 5 3/4" h. (ILLUS.) **500**

Flower-decorated Rose Fairy Lamp

Rose amethyst decorated shade, pyramid-size, h.p. w/large white & blue blossoms w/yellow centers & shaded green leaves, in a clear Clarke Fairy Pyramid lamp cup, 2 3/4" d., 3 1/4" h. (ILLUS.) **150**

Rose Red Berry-form Fairy Lamp

Rose red berry-form shade, pyramid-size, bumpy surface overshot in clear, in clear Clarke Fairy Pyramid lamp cup, 2 3/4" d., 3 3/4" h. (ILLUS.)... **150**

Three Rose Red Shaded Fairy Lamps

Rose red shaded to creamy white shade, fairy-size, enamel-decorated in green in the Wild Rose patt., on a clear Clarke lamp cup, 4" d., 5" h., each (ILLUS. back left & right) **250-300**

Rose red shaded to creamy white shade, pyramid-size, enamel-decorated in green in the Wild Rose patt., on a clear Clarke lamp cup, 3" d., 3 1/2" h. (ILLUS. front with two matching fairy-size lamps) **200-300**

Ruby Red Swirl Fairy Lamp

Ruby red embossed Swirl shade, pyramid-size, in a clear Clarke Fairy lamp cup, 3" d., 3 5/8" h. (ILLUS.) **150**

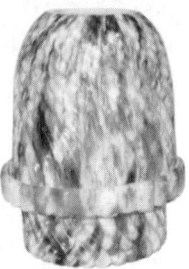

Spatter Reverse Swirl Fairy Lamp

Spatter glass shade, fairy-size, mottled brown, yellow & pink w/embossed reverse swirl design cased in white, resting in a matching lamp cup, 3 3/4" d., 4 1/2" h. (ILLUS.) **300**

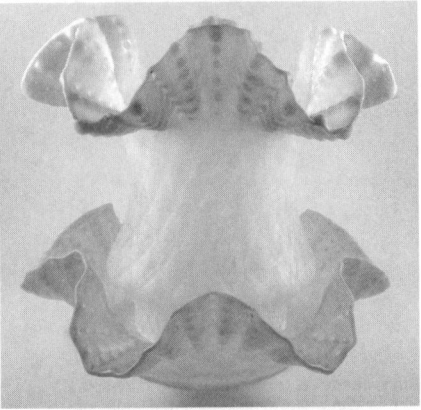

Shaded Turquoise Blue Fairy Lamp

Turquoise blue shading to frosted clear shade, chimney-style, the shade w/an embossed diamond quilted design shading from a deeply ruffled & crimped rim to frosted sides, in a matching saucer base w/matching fluted rim, 6 1/2" d., 5 1/2" h. (ILLUS.) **350**

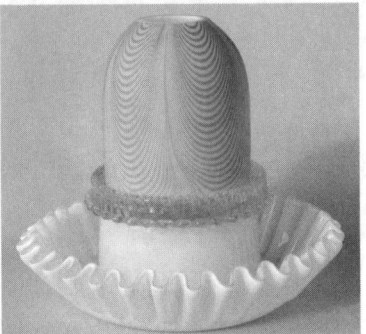

Blue & White Nailsea-style Lamp

White & blue Nailsea-style shade, fairy-size, white ground w/delicate overall royal blue loopings, on a clear Clarke lamp cup marked "U.S. Patent Nov 9, 1886 - #352296 - S. Clarke Patent Trade Mark Fairy," cup resting on the raised column of a reversible glossy white base w/upright petticoat rim, 7" d., 5 1/2" h. (ILLUS.) 750

Miniature Lamps

Our listings are generally arranged numerically according to the numbers assigned to the various miniature lamps pictured in Frank R. & Ruth E. Smith's book Miniature Lamps, *now referred to as Smith's Book I, and Ruth Smith's sequel,* Miniature Lamps II. *All references are to Smith's Book I unless otherwise noted. Lamps are glass unless otherwise noted.*

Amberina glass, ribbed optic, cylindrical waisted base w/matching chimney tapering to rim, brass #1 collar, Hornet burner, 8" h., No. 439 .... $600

Blue transparent glass, cylindrical base ringed at top & bottom, ball shade, contemporary #1 collar, Pet Ratchet burner w/cap & chain, 8" h. 250

Clear glass, spherical base w/vertical opalescent stripes, slender cylindrical chimney tapering out slightly at base, patent dated Nutmeg burner "FEB. Y 27. 1877," 7 1/2" h. (no shade) 70

Custard glass, "Leon's Rib" or "Quarter Dollar Leader Lamp," bulbous paneled base, bell-form shade/chimney w/ribbed top, Acorn burner, 5 3/4" h., No. 177 425

Opaque white glass, bulbous base tapering in to blue crimped rim, squatty bulbous shade w/decorative blue crimped rings at top & bottom, painted reddish-pink & green floral decoration over all, clear chimney, Nutmeg burner, "Little Jewel" embossed on underside of base, 7" h., No. 196 300

Opaque white glass, bulbous base & shade, both w/multicolored embossed floral & leaf decoration over a swirled net field, clear chimney, Nutmeg burner, 7 1/8" h., No. 195 (flake to top of chimney) 400

Opaque white glass, cylindrical base, chimney/shade w/bulbous base & cylindrical neck, both decorated w/light brown staining, embossed swag & bead pattern & painted flowers, brass #1 collar, Hornet burner, 8" h., No. 183 (some paint loss) 180

Opaque white glass, bulbous base & shade, both w/embossed multicolored flower & leaf decoration over a lattice field, clear chimney, Nutmeg burner, 8 1/8" h., No. 229 (some paint loss) 250

Opaque white glass, bulbous base tapering in to slightly flaring top, ball shade, both w/blue painted vertical ribbing & panels of embossed multicolored floral & leaf decoration over a lattice field, clear

chimney, Nutmeg burner, 8 1/2" h., No. 232 210

Opaque white glass, opaque white bulbous pedestal base & ovoid shade, both decorated w/purple stain & painted flowers, clear chimney, brass #1 collar, Hornet burner, 9" h., No. 219 150

Opaque white glass, opaque white bulbous pedestal base & ovoid shade, both decorated w/blue stain & painted flowers, clear chimney, brass #1 collar, Hornet burner, 9" h., No. 219 180

Opaque white glass, bulbous font on tapering cylindrical base, ball shade, all w/embossed multicolored flower & shell decoration, clear chimney, Nutmeg burner, 9 1/4" h., Book II, pg. 12 (shade ring is contemporary replacement, some paint loss) 120

Opaque white glass, cylindrical base tapering out at bottom, ball shade, both w/embossed multicolored floral & leaf decoration, clear chimney, Nutmeg burner, 9 1/2" h., No. 241 (some paint loss) 220

Opaque white glass, melon-shaped base & shade in "Pink Toy Rose" patt., w/vertical panels decorated w/pink flowers & green leaves, Nutmeg burner, L.G. Wright & Co., 9 1/2" h., No. 241 (some paint loss) 50

Opaque white glass, ball base & shade w/embossed swirl pattern & decoration, lime green trim & chimney, decorated w/red roses & green leaves, brass #1 collar, contemporary burner, 10 1/4" h., No. 177 275

Red satin glass, bulbous base tapering at bottom & petal-form shade, both w/embossed decoration, clear chimney, Nutmeg burner, 10 1/4" h., No. 284 (some scratching to finish, flakes to top of shade) 70

Vaseline glass, squatty font on pedestal base, clear chimney, period burner, 3 1/4" h. to top of collar, Book II, No. 88 80

Kerosene Lamps & Related Lighting

Kerosene Lamps

Banquet lamp, bulbous cranberry glass shade w/ground finished base, tapering to flaring ruffled rim, brass font w/5" shade ring, filler cap & "Chautauqua" burner, clear chimney, patent dated cast-spelter font holder w/"PAT.D Mar 19, 1895," over oval marble insert, patternless brass stem & nickel-plated cast-brass base, Bradley & Hubbard, 19 1/2" h. (shade ring repaired, two set screws replaced) 250

Banquet lamp, glass ball shade in deep red decorated w/gilt & enameled florals, above a rounded brass font raised on a serpentine scroll-trimmed iron base w/claw-form feet, Reform-Kosmos-Brenner Patent burner, late 19th c., overall 17" h. 275

Consolidated Monarch Banquet Lamp

Banquet lamp, Monarch model, a cased yellow glass ball shade on a tall burner & brass shoulder over a bulbous matching glass font on a pierced metal cupped connector on the tall baluster-form matching glass pedestal base raised on a pierced cast metal domed foot, Consolidated Lamp & Glass Co., ca. 1890, overall 37 1/2" h. (ILLUS.) **770**

Banquet lamp, squatty cased pink glass font w/embossed floral decoration, enameled & gilded stem on round black fired earthenware base, deep cranberry quilted pattern shade w/ruffled rim, contemporary cranberry stained chimney, British double-wick burner, brass collar, connector & base cap, Europe, 18 3/4" h. (losses to burner & stem gilding) **350**

Banquet lamp, tapering cylindrical cased pink glass font w/embossed floral decoration & ribbing, reeded brass stem on round black fired earthenware base, deep cranberry shade w/ruffled rim, "British Made Duplex" double-wick burner, brass collar & connector, Europe, 18" h. (chips to upper portions of base) **400**

Chandelier, cast-iron four-arm frame w/ornate scroll detail & central shaft, four clear glass fonts in cups, electrified, ca. 1880, 21" w., 35" h. **385**

Cut-overlay Lamp on Ornate Base

Cut-overlay table lamp, amethyst cut to clear cylindrical font tapering slightly to the collar, on an applied glass collar above an elaborate cast-brass base w/curled leaves above a ribbed urn standard & foot on a stepped black marble base w/brass trim, New England, ca. 1850-60, 13 3/4" h. (ILLUS.) **2,475**

Blue Hobnail Hall Hanging Lamp

Hall hanging lamp, a bulbous blown glass blue Hobnail patt. shade, fitted in a brass frame w/base & crown & four long chains to the ceiling plate, ca. 1890, shade 7" h. (ILLUS.) **264**

Hall hanging lamp, a bulbous tapering molded blown pink opalescent shade in the Lattice patt., in a brass frame w/chains & ceiling plate, original font, ca.

1890, shade 7" h. (ILLUS. right with ruby hall lamp) **242**

Two Victorian Hanging Hall Lamps

Hall hanging lamp, an ovoid egg-shaped deep ruby glass optic ribbed shade fitted in a brass frame w/bottom pull ring, flared crown & four hanging chains to ceiling plate, chip on base of shade hidden by frame, ca. 1890, shade 8 3/4" h. (ILLUS. left) **209**

Satin Peg Lamp on Figural Base

Peg lamp, a squatty bulbous cased pink satin glass font in the Prism & Diamond patt., attached to a socket held aloft by a white metal figure of a young man in Napoleonic dress standing on a high, round socle base, base w/a plaque reading "Depart Pour La Promenade - Par Rancoulet," w/a pink shading to clear shade reverse acid-etched w/lilies, base w/old, dull brass colored repaint, overall 20" h. (ILLUS. without shade) **385**

Peg lamp, a squatty bulbous optic-ribbed shaded dark to light cranberry font decorated w/colorful enameled blossoms, fitted in a period brass beehive design candlestick, the burner fitted w/a tulip-form cranberry shade w/a deeply crimped & ruffled rim w/tiny enameled floral beading around the top, late 19th c., overall 16 3/4" h. **413**

Peg lamp, squatty bulbous cranberry cut to clear glass font w/two rows of thumbprints, attached to a period brass beehive-design candlestick, w/a tulip-form cranberry glass shade w/applied white threading around the flaring ruffled rim, overall 16 1/2" h. **198**

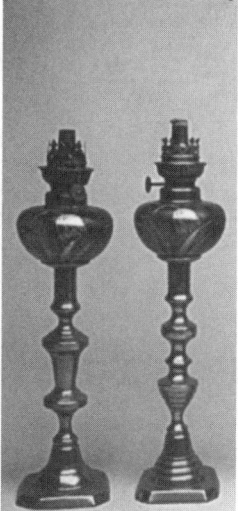

Decorated Cranberry Peg Lamps

Peg lamps, a bulbous squatty cranberry glass font w/a satin finish, decorated w/bright gilt tulip-like flowers & leaves, fitted on slightly differing period brass candlesticks, w/matching burners, late 19th c., overall 14 1/2" & 15" h., pr. (ILLUS.) **358**

Peg lamps, a squatty bulbous amber iridescent Loetz-type font w/applied random threading, fitted on a period brass ring-turned candlestick, fitted w/a creamy iridescent tulip-form shade w/a random crackled finish & a flat, flaring rim, late 19th c., overall 15" h., pr. **275**

Table lamp, Amberina shade w/ruffled & crimped rim, brass base in honeycomb pattern w/spelter center bead band & paw feet, brass font stamped "Bradley &

Hubbard Mfg. Co.," E.M. Miller solar burner, 4" shade ring & chimney, 9" h. 350

Table lamp, blown glass Hobb's Snowflake patt., the squatty squared blue opalescent font raised on a clear stem w/round scalloped foot, Hobbs, Brockunier & Co., ca. 1890, two holes in metal connector, w/burner, 9 1/2" h. 440

Table lamp, blue glass font, cast-iron base w/copper colored highlights, brass collar & connector & burner, chimney, Europe, 8 5/8" h. 220

Table lamp, cranberry glass, squatty font on cast-iron brass-plated base, shade w/gauffered rim that fades to graduating shades of pink & floral acid etching, brass collar & connector, brass double-wick burner w/snuffers & 4" shade ring, Europe, 11 3/4" h. (font crack radiating from collar & extending across shoulder, burner shows damage to center divider of deflector) 100

Table lamp, ovoid cranberry Hobnail shade w/widely ruffled rim, two-tone brass & plated cast-iron base, brass squatty urn-style footed vase w/brass font, plated & applied twisted iron handles, 5" shade ring & brass "Success" burner, 16 1/4" h. (font & burner electrified) 375

Fine Cut Velvet Kerosene Table Lamp

Table lamp, spherical opalescent glass ball shade on a burner & wide brass collar fitted on a large ovoid melon lobed Cut Velvet Diamond Quilted patt. base in deep pink shaded to white, on a high brass foot cast w/an acanthus leaf band & blocked feet w/classical details, w/chimney, late 19th c., 17" h. (ILLUS.) 495

Table lamp, squatty blue glass font, amber glass waisted base on quatrefoil foot, Moon & Star patt., brass #2 collar, contemporary burner & chimney, 11 7/8" h. (collar dents & foot flakes) 120

Tall Green Glass Kerosene Lamp

Table lamp, wide squatty mushroom-shaped shade tapering to a flared cylindrical top opening, in deep green glass w/a frosted interior & decorated w/dainty enameled flowers & gilt trim, raised on a shade ring above a burner & brass shoulder w/a drop-in font, a tall baluster-form matching base resting on a round brass foot, w/a Success burner, ca. 1890, shade 10" d., overall 22" h. (ILLUS.) 303

Lamps, Miscellaneous

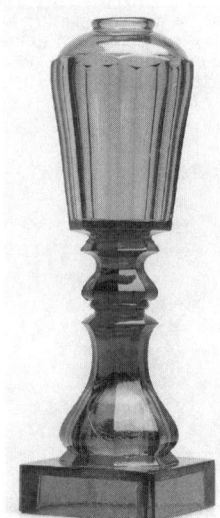

Rare Paneled Pressed Glass Lamp

Fluid burning lamp, pressed flint glass, a slightly tapering octagonal font on a baluster- and knob-form paneled standard & square base, bright teal bluish green, attributed to Boston & Sandwich Glass Co., ca. 1840-60, 10 1/2" h. (ILLUS.)......... **6,600**

Powder Blue "Onion" Table Lamp

Fluid burning lamp, pressed flint glass, "Onion" lamp, a squatty bulbous finely ribbed font w/collar raised on a ringed metal connector to the tall slender ribbed standard & widely flaring ribbed foot, powder blue, complete w/12" d. frosted clear floral-engraved shade, original double brass burner, mid-19th c., overall 21 1/2" h. (ILLUS. of base) **2,090**

Fluid burning lamp, pressed flint glass, Three-Printie Block patt., waisted paneled standard & square foot, original pewter whale oil burner, sapphire blue, Boston & Sandwich Glass Co., 9 3/4" h. **3,300**

Fluid burning lamp, pressed flint glass, Waisted Loop patt. font, on a pressed octagonal base, canary yellow, possibly Boston & Sandwich Glass Co., ca. 1840-60, 10 1/2" h. **1,980**

French Brass Lantern Night Light

Night light, brass, glass & cast white metal, a tall twisted brass upright w/arched top suspending on chains a squared brass filigree lantern w/a ruby jewel set in the front & holding a ruby glass candle cup, the ornate scroll-cast footed base in white metal, France, late 19th c., overall 12 1/4" h. (ILLUS.) **275**

Parlor vase lamp, spatter glass in cranberry & opaque white, pedestal vase w/clear applied glass petals at shoulder, floral & foliate enamel decoration to vase & removable glass oil font, American brass #2 collar plastered over a second larger collar, 14 1/4" h. (lacking burner & shade) **275**

Rush lamp, wrought iron & wood, a wrought-iron upright w/rush holder top, a short side upturned arm w/candle socket, inserted in a rounded wooden block base, early, 11" h. **385**

Electric Lamps & Lighting

Handel Lamps

The Handel Company of Meriden, Connecticut (1885-1936), began as a glass and lamp shade decorating company. Following World War I it became a major producer of decorative lamps that have become very collectible today.

Boudoir lamp, 8" d. domed reverse-painted shade w/a scalloped edge, painted w/a small basket of colorful flowers against a pale yellow ground w/a scalloped orange border band painted to resemble basketweave, raised on a slender painted metal base also resembling a wide basketweave design, shade signed "Handel 7969," base w/felt tag **1,792**

Handel Desk Lamp & Leaded Shade

Desk lamp, 5" d. six-sided leaded shade w/green floral design on a cream background, on an adjustable bronzed metal base, base signed w/felt tag, shade unsigned, original patina, 18" h. (ILLUS.)......... **748**

Table lamp, 14" d. domical reverse-painted shade, decorated w/a border band of pink & rose-colored dogwood blossoms & green leaves against a solid light peach background, shade signed "Handel 6980," on a slender bronzed metal standard on a round flattened foot w/lappet rim band, base signed w/felt tab **3,080**

Table lamp, 14" d. mushroom-shaped open-topped bent-panel slag glass shade, the wide rolled sides tapering to a flared & serrated top opening, composed of large & small panels of streaked deep maroon, green & white slag glass w/a band of red diamond-shaped inserts around the lower border, on a slender gilt bronzed metal lappet-embossed Handel shade **2,184**

Scarce Handel Wisteria Table Lamp

Table lamp, 15" d. domical reverse- and obverse-painted shade, decorated on the exterior w/dark & light green leaves suspended from the upper rim, the interior painted w/large clusters of deep purple & deep red wisteria blooms, all above a mottled frosted white & pale yellow ground, on a slender Handel bronzed metal paneled standard w/a wide round paneled foot, signed on shade ring (ILLUS.) **6,720**

Table lamp, 16" d. domical reverse-painted shade decorated w/a small flock of dark blue swallow-like birds flying above tall green grasses w/a dark tan to pale yellow mottled sky in the background, shade signed "Handel 6425 F.C.," on a slender bronzed metal base w/a round foot **5,320**

Aquarium Pattern Handel Lamp

Table lamp, 16" l. rectangular reverse-painted shade w/cut-corners, decorated w/a unique Aquarium patt., the long flat sides & end panels painted in autumn colors w/tropical fish swimming among sea grasses & seaweed, in shades of yellow, tan, orange, brown, purple & red, raised on a slender central shaft flanked by a pair of upturned candle socket-style sockets above a domed leaf-cast foot, two panels w/stress cracks (ILLUS.) **36,400**

Table lamp, 18" d. conical reverse-painted shade decorated w/a mound of trees surrounded by choppy water forming waves in the background, shades of green, brown, cream & black, on felt tab-signed Handel urn-form base **6,440**

Arts & Crafts Style Handel Lamp

Table lamp, 18" d. conical reverse-painted shade decorated w/an Arts & Crafts style design of long slender blades of grass in shades of green & blackish green against a yellow ground, raised on a slender signed bronzed metal base, shade signed "#5357" (ILLUS.)............................ **12,320**

Table lamp, 18" d. conical reverse-painted shade, decorated w/large leafy trees in the foreground w/dark green foliage & brown trunks, green shrubbery & small trees under the large trees w/a yellow, orange & red sunset sky in the background, shade signed "Handel 6434," large bronzed metal baluster-form ribbed base w/a round scalloped foot also marked..... **14,000**

Handel Lamp with Countryside Scene

Table lamp, 18" d. domical reverse-painted shade decorated w/a continuous countryside landscape of grassy fields & a stream w/large trees & rail fences in the center ground & woodlands in the background, shade signed "Handel 6754 R," on a slender signed bronzed metal tree trunk base (ILLUS.)...................................... **7,840**

Table lamp, 18" d. domical reverse-painted shade decorated w/a continuous very detailed landscape scene, pairs of tall realistic leafy trees in the foreground on a grassy hilltop w/clusters of lower trees beyond & water & mountains in the distance, a yellow & brown cloud-streaked sky w/the mountains & water in purple & dark blue & the trees in shades of green, dark & light brown, black & umber, a pathway through the foreground w/small painted figures, raised on a heavy bronze metal ovoid base cast w/a wide raised band & tapering to a ringed & domed round foot, shade signed "Handel 6823".. **14,000**

Table lamp, 18" d. domical reverse-painted shade, painted on the interior w/a continuous landscape of groups of tall fir trees in a rocky landscape w/other trees in the distance, in shades of dark green, tan, brown & cream, shade signed "Handel

6323," on a signed base w/three slender scrolled legs resting on a stepped round foot... **7,280**

Interior- & Exterior-painted Handel

Table lamp, 18" d. domical reverse-painted shade, painted on the interior w/a continuous landscape w/clusters of delicate trees & shrubbery in greens w/distant trees & shrubs in lavender & pinks against a creamy yellow ground, the trees also painted green on the exterior, shade signed "7117 Handel" & artist-signed, on a signed base w/three slender scrolled legs on a stepped round foot (ILLUS.) **8,400**

Handel Two-arm Table Lamp

Table lamp, double arms supporting hanging lanterns w/metal overlay at border in dark green over caramel slag panels, original patina, base & shade signed, 21" w., 21" h. (ILLUS.).................................... **3,335**

Motion Lamps

There were three major manufacturers of motion lamps in the period of the 1920s to the early 1970s. Two

of the companies were located in Chicago, and the third was in Los Angeles.

The Scene in Action of Chicago operated from 1927 to 1936. Its motion lamps featured fancy metal framework bases and beautiful, brightly colored glass or lithograph panels.

The L.S. Goodman Company operated in Chicago from 1955 to 1972. In that time the company manufactured 50 different models of 8"-high lamps.

The Econolite Company operated out of Los Angeles from 1946 to 1963. Many of the company's products bear the name wLamps, Miscellaneous wLamps, Miscellaneous "Aubrey B. Leach," who was the graphic artist and designer of the majority of its lamps. Econolite lamps usually stand 11" tall. The company made many unique promotional and advertising lamps for other companies (including those that sold liquor, beer or auto parts).

Two types of lamps were made: oval and round, with oval being the more panoramic.

Bases on motion lamps changed over the years. Scene in Action lamps had very heavy, ornate brass bases and tops. Later, Econolite and L.A. Goodman bases became very plain and often stood on three ball feet. Materials changed from metal or Bakelite to plastic or, in some instances, paper inserts.

In the 1920s and '30s chalk material was employed for making figures of famous comic strip characters such as Superman, the Lone Ranger and others. They were commonly given away at carnivals as prizes for winning at games of chance. Some of the chalk lamps listed here may have been sold through carnival outlets or been used as special giveaways.

In recent years, new motion lamps have appeared on the market, selling in the area of $45. Some of the scenes, such as racing trains or Niagara Falls, mirror those of the old lamps, but the new ones do not have the same bright colors or detail of the older ones.

It is possible to order replacement parts for lamps today. The main piece that usually breaks is the spinner inside that causes the motion. These spinners usually sell for $45-65. There are a few replacements manufactured of the inside plastic core (which had the holes to match the pattern of the outside painted lamp & which revolved, making the outside design appear to move). Replacements of the outside sell for $90-100.

Antique Road Race, 1914 Stutz Bearcat & 1912 Motel T Ford appear to race (wheels turn, scenery whizzes by), Econolite, 1957 .... **250**

Bathing Beauties, white Bakelite shade embossed w/four bathing beauties, one on each of four panels, L.A. Goodman, 1950s **275**

Beacon Light, wooden frame, scene of trees, water, white clouds, National, 1930s **400**

Boy at Pond, image of boy w/straw hat & fishing pole standing at edge of pond & relieving himself (a separate "preacher shade" was sold to insert into the lamp when guests who might be offended by the scene were expected), plastic base, Econolite, 1954 (ILLUS., next column) **275**

Boy Scout, chalkware figure of Boy Scout sitting by campfire that appears to flicker, Gritt Manufacturing, rare, 1920s **700**

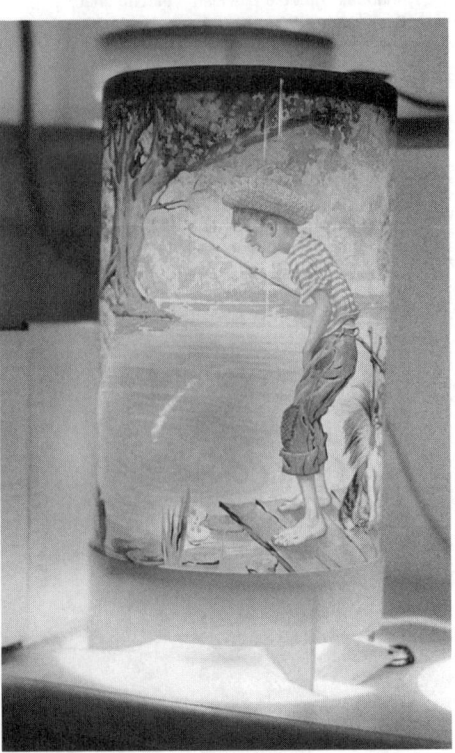

Boy at Pond Lamp

Butterflies with Flowers, butterflies appear to be flying & landing on flowers (also comes w/tripod base), L.A. Goodman, 1956 .... **250**

Chicago Century of Progress, scene of fireworks erupting over World's Fair in Chicago, Scene in Action, rare, 1933 .... **800**

Christmas Tree, blue, Christmas tree-shaped lamp sits on white base, light from blue-green bulb inside shows through holes in tree, appearing as Christmas tree lights, as lamp revolves, Econolite, 1950s, 15" h. **110**

Christmas Tree, red, Christmas tree-shaped lamp sits on white base, light from red bulb inside shows through holes in tree, appearing as Christmas tree lights, as lamp revolves, Econolite outlet in Canada, 1950s, rare, 15" h. **225**

Christmas Tree, white, Christmas tree-shaped lamp sits on white base, as lamp revolves light from red bulb inside shows through holes in tree on snow flakes, deer, Santa Claus, elves & a star at top, Econolite, 1950s, 15" h. **195**

Circus, cylinder features scene of Big Top w/elephant & ringmaster, top lifts off compartment for heating peanuts, L.A. Goodman, 1950s **575**

Colonial Fountain, cast iron & glass, water cascades & ripples in fountain, meant to be placed on radio for visual interest, Scene in Action, 1931, 9 1/2" h. **260**

Cover Girl, featured artwork of pinup artist Gil Elvgen, Econolite, rare, 1955 .... **750**

Davy Crockett, outer shell w/black & brown trees, second spinner features Davy, Indian & bear, all appearing to run through trees when lamp heats up, L.A. Goodman, rare, 1955 .... **425**

Disneyland, tin lithograph base decorated w/Disney characters, yellow or red plastic top, when lamp is lit Disney characters appear to ride carousel horses, tie-in w/grand opening of Disneyland, Econolite, 1955 .... **225**

Ducks in Flight, ducks & Canada geese flying, only appear when lamp is lit, on metal base w/ball feet, Econolite, 1955 .... **375**

Fish in the Window, cylindrical shape on base, fish appear to swim by small oval window, Lacolite, 1957 .... **150**

Fish in Water, on candy dish base, fish appear to swim & water to flow, rare, Econolite, 1954 .... **225**

Fish lamp shade, original green glass shade for fish lamp by Scene in Action, 1930s, shade only **95**

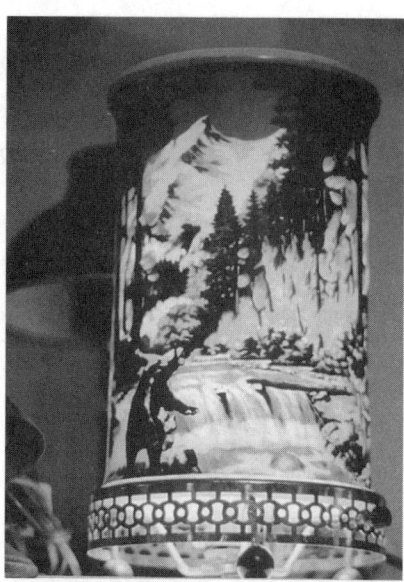

Forest Fire Lamp, 1955

Forest Fire, Econolite, 1955 (ILLUS.) **295**

Forest Fire Lamp, 1931

Forest Fire, cast-iron base & top, glass w/paper shade, Scene in Action, 1931, 10" h. (ILLUS.) **250**

Forest Fire Lamp, 1950

Forest Fire, Econolite Roto Vue Jr., 1950 (ILLUS.) **135**

Forest Fire, round shape, fire appears to rage through forest w/bear, deer, fox & flowing stream, Econolite, 1955 .... **210**

Forest Fire, scene of deer standing in stream as a fire appears to rare in the distance, consuming a cabin, L.A. Goodman, 1956 .... **190**

Fortune Teller, h.p. figure w/three red jewels around neck, flanked by elephant heads w/purple teardrop prisms, small cup in front of figure for incense, face is illuminated when lamp is on, smoke from incense adds air of mystery, S&S Manufacturing Company, Milwaukee, Wisconsin, 1926, 16" h. **500**

Fountain of Youth Motion Lamp

Fountain of Youth, image of boy w/straw hat & fishing pole standing at edge of pond & relieving himself (a separate "preacher shade" was sold to insert into the lamp when guests who might be offended by the scene were expected), metal filigree base on three ball feet, Econolite Roto-Vue Lamp, 1950s (ILLUS.) **225**

Fountains of Rome, scene of St. Peter's Square & Fountain, fountain appears to shoot water into air, Econolite, 1950s **625**

Hawaii, tropical scene of trees, sandy beach, ocean & water falls, Econolite, 1959 .... **600**

Hearth Motion Lamp

Hearth, half of cylinder features woman at a spinning wheel, the other half a man smoking a pipe before the fire, fire flickers, steam rises from kettle hanging over fire, spinning wheel spins, metal filigree base on three ball feet, Econolite, 1958 (ILLUS.) **260**

Hopalong Cassidy, scene of Hopalong Cassidy on Topper & other cowboys chasing stagecoach, clear plastic outer shell decorated w/Bar-20 Ranch symbols, base & top are red, w/air vents in top, Econolite, 1950, 6" d., 9" h., rare yellow & blue version $700, this version **600**

Indian Chief, chalkware, h.p. flames appear to flicker in campfire at which tall figure of chief stands, Gritt Manufacturing, 1920s, 12" h. (difficult to find in mint condition due to wear to chalkware) **300**

Japanese Twilight, scene of Mt. Fuji w/lake water gently lapping at the shores of a lake in the foreground base, Scene in Action, 1931 .... **250**

Jets, scene of early jet passenger aircraft w/orange exhaust that appears to flame & leave vapor trails, Econolite, 1958 .... **775**

Ku Klux Klan, wood, metal & glass, features blazing cross, probably special order, Scene in Action, rare, 1920s, 17 x 28" **2,000**

Marine Scene, lighthouse beacon searches waters around rocky island & waves

move against tall sailing ship out at sea,
Scene in Action, 1931....................................... **350**

Miller High Life Motion Sign

Miller High Life advertising, rectangular,
beer appears to flow from bottle of Miller
High Life beer to glass, "Miller High Life -
The Champagne of Bottled Beer" on
front, maker unknown, 1950s, 13 x 16"
(ILLUS.)... **100**

Moonlight, scene of moon shining on lake,
Scene in Action, very rare, 1931.................... **275**

Niagara Falls Motion Lamp, 1931

Niagara Falls, cast-iron base & top, paper
scene is attached to glass cylinder,
Scene in Action, 1931, 10" h. (ILLUS.).......... **250**

Niagara Falls Lamp, 1957

Niagara Falls, L.A. Goodman, 1957
(ILLUS.) **155**

Niagara Falls Motion Lamp, 1970s

Niagara Falls, Lacolite Lamp, 1970s, hard to find (ILLUS.).. **80**

Niagara Falls, wooden frame covered w/gold plaster, National of Canada **275**

Nursery Rhymes, brass frame, scene of Jack & Jill falling down the hill, the well in the background, Little Bo Peep & her sheep, & a child reading a book of nursery rhymes, L.A. Goodman, 1957.................. **600**

Old Ironsides, famous ship appears to move through water, Econolite, 1958 .... **475**

Old Mill, plastic figural base, water appears to run over water wheels into small waterfall, Econolite, 1961.. **550**

Pabst Blue Ribbon Beer, wall-hanging type w/antique-style shade, beer bubbles rise as lamp heats up, Embossograph Display Manufacturing Company, 1960........ **125**

Peanut Lamp, cov., pewter metal finish, six-sided, features compartment to heat peanuts as lamp heats up, flames painted on panels to indicate function, lid w/molded peanut handle, Scene in Action, 1920s **725**

Pot Belly Stove Motion Lamp/Clock

Pot Belly Stove lamp/clock, metal, black pot belly stove attached to square shelf clock, fire appears to flicker through door of stove, United Manufacturing Company, 1962 (ILLUS.) **200**

Psychedelic lamp, abstract designs ripple & appear to move in all directions, one of many different models made, L.A. Goodman, 1969-70... **150**

Psychedelic lamp, multicolored abstract designs swirl when lamp heats up, Visual Effects Company, 1970s................................. **85**

Racing Trains, Civil War era trains the General & the John Bull appear to race each other down the track, smoke billows, headlamp on front of smokestack flickers, & wheels turn, scenery flies by, Econolite, 1956............................... **275**

Racing Trains Motion Lamp

Racing Trains, L.A. Goodman (ILLUS.)............ **195**

Racing Trains, three Civil War era trains appear to race neck & neck down the track, smoke billows, headlamp on front of smokestack flickers, & wheels turn, Econolite, 1957.. **275**

Raytheon TV Tubes & Services, advertising lamp, graphics of TV tube, tube box & picture tube glimmer when lamp is on, maker unknown, rare, 1950s.......................... **500**

Roy Rogers, scene of Roy Rogers standing at gate to Double R Bar ranch, bucking broncos in the background, tall base, Pearson & Company, rare, 1950s................ **900**

Seattle World's Fair, scene of 1962 Fair w/Space Needle in motion when lamps is lit, Econolite, 1962... **550**

Statue of Liberty, shows upper part of statue w/New York skyline & harbor in background, light appears to radiate from torch, Econolite, 1940 .... **250**

Village Blacksmith, metal case w/glass panel showing tall figure of blacksmith, Gritt Manufacturing, 1920s, 12" h.................. **300**

Winter Scene, snow appears to fall on a country church, Econolite, 1950s................. **200**

Pairpoint Lamps

Well known as a producer of fine Victorian art glass and silver plate wares between 1907 and 1929, the Pairpoint Corporation of New Bedford, Massachusetts, also produced a wide range of decorative lamps.

"Puffy" with Portsmouth Shade

Boudoir lamp, 8" d. "Puffy" pyramidal re-verse-painted closed-top 'Portsmouth' shade, each wide tapering panel re-verse-painted w/large blossoms, includ-ing pansies, in shades of red, yellow, blue, orange & green on a pale mottled green ground, narrow pale orange border bands between the panels & on the top, raised on a slender flaring gilt-metal stan-dard on an oval dished foot, base signed (ILLUS.) **4,200**

Boudoir lamp, 8" d. "Puffy" reverse-painted flat-topped domical 'Floral' patt. shade, decorated around the lower border w/pairs of large rose blossoms alternat-ing w/five-petal blossoms & leaves, in shades of orangish red, purple & yellow against a frosted white & yellow lattice background, on a slender gilt-metal base w/round, lobed foot **6,720**

Boudoir lamp, 8" d. "Puffy" reverse-painted 'Papillon' shade w/groups of large red, yellow & purple blossoms w/green leaves around the scalloped lower body w/a large colorful butterfly above each group of flowers, raised on a gilt-metal tree trunk base, base signed **3,360**

Boudoir lamp, 9" d. "Puffy" tapering cylin-drical flat-topped reverse-painted 'Strat-ford' shade, decorated w/the "Floral" de-sign, the sides w/pairs of large roses, daisies & other blossoms in deep rose, yellow & blue w/green leaves against a black ground, the flat top in yellow, raised on a slender gilt-metal baluster-form standard on a disk base w/small scroll feet **3,920**

Boudoir lamp, 10" d. "Puffy" domical shade molded w/large clusters of rose blos-soms reverse-painted in red & yellow w/green & blue leaves against a frosted background, on a slender bronze metal shaft on a squared flattened base, shade signed **3,360**

Pairpoint Lamp with Papillon Shade

"Puffy" Stratford Shade & Lamp

Table lamp, 14" d. "Puffy" reverse-painted 'Papillon' shade in the Butterfly & Roses patt., large clusters of red & pink roses around the border w/green leaves & large colorful butterflies against a white & green-streaked background, on a signed Pairpoint base w/a slender square shaft & rectangular dished foot (ILLUS., bottom previous page) **13,440**

Table lamp, 14" d. "Puffy" reverse-painted 'Stratford' shade, a wide border of large colorful roses & flying hummingbirds against a mottled mauve & black background, on a signed Pairpoint base w/a slender swelled standard on a round multi-lobed foot (ILLUS., top of page)...... **7,280**

Table lamp, 14" d. reverse-painted 'Palermo' shade, decorated w/wide stripes of leafy scrolls against a finely striped reddish brown ground alternating w/wide white stripes decorated w/delicate colorful floral stripes, on a signed worn silver plated Pairpoint base w/a slender squared shaft w/a bulbed bottom over the flaring hexagonal foot (ILLUS., to right) **4,200**

Pairpoint Lamp with Palermo Shade

Table lamp, 16" w. six-sided tapering reverse-painted shade, the flat panels decorated alternately w/an overall rose design in orange & dark brown on a tan ground or a single small rose blossom & leaf design on a tan ground, narrow yellow border bands, raised on a gilt-metal base w/a slender central handle shaft surrounded by three electric candle sockets all on a triangular onyx plinth set in a conforming metal frame w/small inscrolled feet, base signed **2,240**

Tiffany Lamps

Tiffany Dogwood Shade & Lamp Base

Table lamp, "Dogwood," 18" d. domical leaded glass shade, decorated w/a wide band of pink, white, yellow & crimson mottled blossoms w/green striated & mottled leaves against an opalescent & mottled white block background, on a rare gilt-bronze cylindrical base cast w/flowering branches above a ringed & domed matching foot, shade signed, base signed "Tiffany Studios 629" (ILLUS.) **44,800**

Tiffany Greek Key Table Lamp

Table lamp, "Greek Key," 16" d. leaded glass shade composed of graduated tiles of mottled yellowish green above a wide border band of Greek Key in mottled yellowish green, the bronze base w/slender scroll-trimmed standard above a knobby cushion base w/curled feet, base stamped w/Tiffany Glass & Decorating Co. monogram & "TIFFANY - STUDIOS - NEW YORK - 28617," ca. 1910, 22 7/8" h. (ILLUS.) **18,880**

Unique Tiffany Glass & Bronze Lamp

Tiffany Turtleback Tile Border Lamp

Table lamp, "Leaf & Berry," a unique pyramidal leaded glass & bronze filigree shade decorated w/a wide border band leaded w/emerald green leaves & yellow & red berries meandering on a deep cobalt blue & purple striated & rippled glass ground, the upper shade w/a swelled pierced filigree band of stylized Queen Anne's Lace blossoms below an upper band of entwined pierced lattice, raised on four arm supports above the large matching urn-form base w/matching bands of floral decoration, shade signed "Tiffany Studios - New York - 783 SX," base signed "27476 - Tiffany Studios - New York" (ILLUS., bottom previous page) **235,200**

Table lamp, "Lily," eighteen-light, a rounded full-relief lily pad bronze base centered in a cluster of tall slender stems w/arched tops ending in petal-form sockets each fitted w/a long lightly ribbed golden iridescent lily-form shade, all shades & base signed **56,000**

Table lamp, "Pulled Feather," a 14" d. blown bell-shaped shade of gold iridescence w/a gold & white pulled feather design, on Tiffany gold doré slender standard & round dished & footed base (ILLUS., to the right) **3,920**

Table lamp, "Tulip," 14" d. domical leaded glass shade, composed of an overall design of dark mottled red & violet tulip blossoms on mottled light green & amber stems w/leaves against a mottled dark green & brownish green ground, on a signed Tiffany tree trunk base w/original green patina **78,400**

Table lamp, "Turtleback Tile Border," 20 1/8" d. leaded glass shade composed of an overall design of graduated mottled yellowish green tiles w/a border band of iridescent green turtleback tiles, shade tag stamped "TIFFANY STUDIOS - NEW

YORK," base stamped "TIFFANY STUDIOS - NEW YORK - D806" w/Tiffany Glass & Decorating monogram, ca. 1910, 25" h. (ILLUS., top of page)............ **35,250**

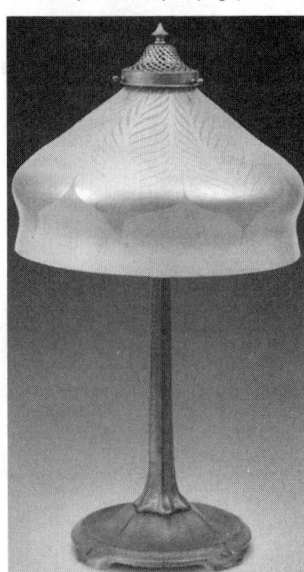

Tiffany Pulled Feather Shade & Lamp

Lamps, Miscellaneous

Duffner & Kimberly table lamp, 16" d. domical leaded glass shade, the center top w/radiating panels of green slag glass above a wide border band of entwined green & white slag leaves against a mottled dark brown ground, on a bronzed metal slender ovoid standard raised on a tripod base over a round platform foot........ **5,600**

Duffner & Kimberly Leaf Cluster Lamp

Duffner & Kimberly table lamp, 16" d. domical leaded glass shade w/a scrolled border composed of dark & light green & white slag scrolls w/dark amber fanned shells, the upper body composed of graduated blocks of mottled white & green & white slag glass, raised on a slender bulbed ribbed signed base w/a four-lobed flattened foot **5,600**

Duffner & Kimberly table lamp, 20" d. mushroom-shaped leaded glass shade, decorated w/large tall leafy clusters in mottled shades of light & dark green alternating w/large spear point leaf motifs in similar colors all on a striated light blue to deep purple ground, raised on a Duffner & Kimberly slender reeded shaft w/bottom bulb above a flaring paneled & scalloped foot (ILLUS., top of page).......... **8,960**

Floor lamp, enameled aluminum, a weighted round disk black base centered by a slender cylindrical shaft topped by three adjustable metal arms each fitted w/a long conical aluminum shade each in a different color, yellow, green or orange, ca. 1955, wear, corrosion, 5' 11 1/2" h. **184**

Floor lamp, wood covered w/gesso & gilding, colorful polychrome fruit at base, relief scrolled feet & openwork base w/acanthus leaves, crossed arrows & relief floral work near top of column, four branches at top w/center finial, all w/simulated candles & internal electric sockets, 76" h. (one socket chipped) **1,650**

Pittsburgh Lamp and Seascape Shade

Pittsburgh table lamp, 16" d. domical reverse-painted shade decorated w/a wide seascape w/a cloudy moonlit sky flanked on each side by a shoreline w/tall leafy trees, in dark shades of blue, white, black, brown, maroon & yellow, on a tall slender bronzed metal standard w/a round paneled foot & a pair of small loop handles at the top (ILLUS.) **3,416**

Rookwood Table Lamp

Rateau Table Lamp

Rateau table lamp, patinated bronze w/shade, reeded baluster base stamped

"A.A. RATEAU 1392," France, ca. 1921, 23" h. with shade (ILLUS.)......................... **49,350**

Riviere table lamp, 21" d. domical leaded glass shade composed of segments forming an overall design of leafy morning glory vines w/blossoms in shades of red, pink & blue w/textured green glass leaves all against a pale caramel slag ground, raised on a slender square bronze standard w/four leaves spaced around the round foot, early 20th c. **7,840**

Rookwood pottery table lamp, Iris glaze w/painted & carved decoration of pink flowers & green leaves against a grey background, base executed by John Wargham in 1905, impressed mark #S1738, shade is period multicolored leaded & stained glass w/same decoration of flowers & leaves as base, shade 15 1/2" d., overall height 25", mint (ILLUS., top of page) **5,750**

Slag glass table lamp, a high domical shade composed of six bent-glass caramel slag panels divided by metal bands and decorated around the lower border w/florette metal filigree, raised on a bronzed metal waisted & paneled base, early 20th c. **840**

Other Lighting Devices

Chandeliers

Arts & Crafts Five-light Chandelier

Arts & Crafts, five lanterns w/a pyramidal top & geometric designs over caramel slag glass, suspended by original chain in brass, original ceiling cap & chains, overall, worn original patina, some roughness, 14" w., 52" h. (ILLUS.)............... **575**

Czechoslovakian Glass Chandelier

Czechoslovakian glass, twelve-light, a painted metal ceiling mount suspending a baluster- and ring-form long yellowish green glass standard supporting twelve yellowish green glass arms each fitted w/a shallow cupped bobêche & candle-form socket, ca. 1930, 28 1/2" d., 23" h. (ILLUS.)... **748**

Stylized Flowers on D&K Chandelier

Duffner & Kimberly-signed, 25" d. domical leaded glass shade, composed of pairs of large stylized striated white, pink & tan blossoms around the scalloped lower border against a dark brown & tan slag ground w/delicate undulating stems in pale yellow (ILLUS.) **14,000**

Handel Bent Glass Slag Chandelier

Handel-signed, 24" d. domical bent-panel shade w/a flaring open crown top w/green slag pointed segments above the long pointed leaf-form green slag panels w/pointed tips, the leaf tips alternating w/white slag diamonds (ILLUS.)...... **2,632**

Jasper Ware Three-Light Chandelier

Jasper ware & brass, three-light, a brass tall pointed leaf-cast crown & connector above an ovoid blue jasper ware bulb w/applied white relief classical figures &

leaf & scroll devices above a long ring-turned brass connector issuing three long S-scroll leaf-cast arms each ending in a socket above the dished matching jasper ware lower bowl w/a wide rolled rim & a brass knob drop, unmarked Wedgwood, England, late 19th c., overall 19 1/4" h. (ILLUS.) **1,093**

Lalique Champs Elysées Chandelier

Lalique, "Champs Elysées" patt., a large ball-shaped shade in frosted clear glass molded in high relief w/overall acanthus-style leaves, suspended in a brass mount w/arched & pierced fruit-design crest suspended from three chains, model introduced in 1926, unsigned, 16" d. (ILLUS.)... **5,175**

Unsigned Leaded Glass Chandelier

Leaded glass, 22 1/2" d. conical leaded glass shade w/a wide flat drop apron, the top section w/hexagonal segments in striated green & caramel slag, the deep apron w/an irregular border decorated w/eight large red & orange striated glass stylized flowers on a curvilinear green & caramel slag ground, three-light fixture, unsigned, a few cracked segments, early 20th c., 11" h. (ILLUS.)................................... **460**

Louis XV-Style Chandelier with Prisms

Louis XV-Style, six-light, gilt-metal & cut glass, the pierced baluster-form central standard issuing a corona & six scrolling arms w/candle sockets & bobêches, densely hung w/shaped cut prisms & a pendant glass drop, drilled for electricity but unwired, late 19th c., Europe, 38" h. (ILLUS.).. **2,520**

Louis XVI-Style, six-light, ormolu & blued steel, the ribbon-tied corona supporting a central stem & quiver of arrows mounted w/Bacchic masks, supporting acanthus-sheathed reeded branches, each mounted w/a bird & terminating in a ram's mask, in the manner of Pierre Gouthière, France, 20th c., 33 1/2" h. **6,463**

Neoclassical-style, eighteen-light, ormolu & cut glass, w/a domed acanthus-case corona, above a band set w/square lozenges & hung w/drop festoons, above spreading drop chains supporting a similar central band surmounted by anthemion-crested drop-set laurel wreaths, above ten graduated tiers of drops, w/faceted ball terminal, Europe, ca. 1900, 70" h... **8,813**

Neoclassical-style, fifteen-light, ormolu & cut glass, the scrolled acanthus-cast corona above a band alternately cast w/acanthus-flanked baskets of flowers & flambeaux flanked by adorsed dolphins, above tapering husk-cast straps & further glass drop chains, w/fruit terminal, electrified, Europe, ca. 1900, 51 1/2" h.............. **6,463**

Five-arm Neoclassical Chandelier

Neoclassical-style, five-light, gilt-bronze, a tall trumpet-form central standard w/cast leaf detail above a broad disk issuing five wide upswept & tapering arms ending in leaf-trimmed sockets & w/a cast tassel, the panel-cast lower surface w/a central floral drop, possibly by E. F. Caldwell & Co., New York, New York, early 20th c., 23" h. (ILLUS.) **2,400**

Quezal Bowl-form Chandelier

Quezal-signed, a large 13 3/4" d. bowl-form glass shade in iridescent ivory dec-

orated w/radiating iridescent gold & green leaf decorations, supported on a brass ring suspended from three ball chains & a two-socket fixture, shade signed, overall 21 1/2" h. (ILLUS.) **6,325**

Quezal-signed, five-light, bronze & glass, a heavy metal baluster-turned drop shaft supporting a large inverted-dome disk suspending five long conical sockets each fitted w/a signed trumpet-form Quezal shade w/a ruffled rim, each exterior in iridized white w/a gold band, each shade 5" d. **2,240**

Paneled Slag Glass Chandelier

Slag glass, domical form w/ten curved caramel slag panels set in a frame above a wide blue slag flat apron band overlaid w/an embossed metal filigree design of windmills alternating w/clumps of trees & cottages, ca. 1920, one panel w/hairline, hanging cap & chain, 24" d. (ILLUS.) **575**

Steuben-signed, six-light, designed by Oscar Bach, a gilt-bronze framework w/a domed ceiling cap suspending five chains composed of metal rings alternating w/long gold iridescent glass waisted tubes, four outer chains suspending a wide pierced metal ring cast w/round scrolls enclosing different designs including birds, squirrels & flowers, the ring mounted w/five downcurved short arms each suspending a bell-shaped ribbed iridescent gold Steuben shade, a central chain suspending a sixth matching shade, each shade 6 x 6" (ILLUS., below) **12,800**

Unique Steuben Glass Chandelier

Tiffany Daffodil Chandelier

Tiffany-signed, "Daffodil," a wide leaded glass inverted dome shape, composed of two amber-brown border bands, clusters of mottled yellow daffodils & bluish green spiked leaves on an amber fractured glass ground, closed center w/leaded symmetrical circle, the interior fitted w/four hooks, circlet & hooks later added by Tiffany Studios, metal rim tags impressed "Tiffany Studios - New York - 144...," all suspended from a patinated metal ceiling mount w/four chains, shade 16" d., drop 21" (ILLUS.)............................ **32,200**

Tiffany Five-light Chandelier

Tiffany-signed, five-light, a bronze domed ceiling plate suspending a long slender reeded shaft to a large ball issuing five downturned arms each ending in a socket w/a ribbed tulip-shaped gold iridescent signed shade, 16" w., 34" h. (ILLUS.)........ **9,775**

Unique Venetian Glass Chandelier

Venetian glass, eight-light, in green & white glass w/gold inclusions, the knopped central standard surrounded by delicate leaves & scrolls set w/applied swans, the long down-turned lily-form socket arms w/applied clear sawtooth edging, early 20th c., 48" d., 42" h. (ILLUS.)..................... **3,163**

Shades

Lime Green Optic Ribbed Shade

Art glass, flora-form, lime green optic ribbed form w/widely flaring ruffled rim, enameled w/large pink & white stylized blossoms & aqua & white leaves on thin white branches, 6 1/4" d., 5 1/2" h. (ILLUS.) **145**

Acid-etched & Enameled Shade

Art glass, tulip-shaped w/flaring ruffled rim, a frosted acid cut-back overall design w/the smooth areas painted as deep maroon & yellow blossoms on gold-trimmed leaves & stems, dark green border band, 7" d., 5 1/2" h. (ILLUS.) **225**

High-quality Large Leaded Shade

Ball shade, spherical pink cased glass, decorated w/a large gilt rampant lion & fleur-de-lis designs, possibly Consolidated Lamp & Glass Company, ca. 1900, 8" h. **440**

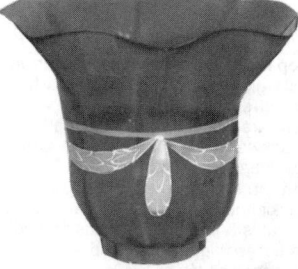

Decorated Cranberry Glass Shade

Cranberry glass, flora-form, optic-ribbed w/a widely flaring ruffled rim, decorated around the middle w/a gold & white painted swag & tassel band, 7" d., 5 1/2" h. (ILLUS.)... **195**

Ornate Pink Cased Hall Lamp Shade

Hall lamp shade, large ovoid form w/a wide flared top rim, cased glass in light pink shading down to dark pink, a molded blown design of overall scales w/a band of acanthus leaves around the top & scrolls & medallions around the bottom, 4 1/4 x 6", 11" h. (ILLUS.) **165**

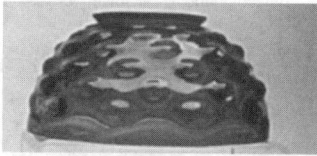

Cranberry Hobnail Hanging Shade

Hanging parlor lamp shade, high domed form w/an open top, mold-blown cranberry Hobnail patt.,10" d. base, 4 1/2" h. (ILLUS.) **440**

Lamp shades, tapering hexagonal shape w/painted brown & peach gothic-style decoration, 6" fitter bases, 16 1/4" h., pr. (one w/fitter chip, both w/minor paint loss)... **90**

Leaded glass, 24" d. wide domical open-topped shade composed of oblong panels of graduated creamy yellow glass segments between scrolls in mottled shades of blues, greens & browns w/large green & yellow shell designs around the scalloped lower border, possibly by Duffner & Kimberly (ILLUS., top of page)................................... **6,720**

Puffy Pairpoint Pisa Shade

Pairpoint-signed, 16" w. "Puffy" paneled "Pisa" shade, reverse-painted in the panels w/an overall design of deep red & pink rose blossoms & green leaves trimmed w/a gold scrolling border, the low domed closed top w/a rayed band design, black

border bands, minor chips, signed
(ILLUS.).. **5,175**
Quezal-signed, bulbous ovoid dome w/tiny
pointed tip, overall gold iridescent King
Tut patt. on cream ground, 5 3/8" h. (mi-
nor scratches) **690**

Tiffany Fleur-de-Lys Pattern Shade

Tiffany-signed, "Fleur-de-Lys," 16" d. domical leaded glass shade composed of
graduated blocks of caramel slag glass
above a wide band of dark green fleur-
de-lis devices above a lower border
w/bands of caramel slag (ILLUS.) **10,080**

Williamson Leaded Glass Chandelier

Williamson-signed, 24" d. wide bell-
shaped leaded glass shade, the open
center top w/a band of oval caramel slag
segments over a metal ring, the top of

the shade in caramel slag segments arranged in a honeycomb design above
the wide curved apron decorated
w/large rose blossoms in deep purple &
deep rose w/alternating matching bud
clusters & smaller scattered blossoms
all on a background of green slag leaves
(ILLUS.).. **3,920**

MAGIC COLLECTIBLES

Animation cel, from Disney movie "Fantasia," Scene 9, Sorcerer's Apprentice,
1940s **$18,000**

Magician's Black Hat with Rabbit

Black top hat toy, plastic, sits upside down
w/white gloves covering opening, white
rabbit on spring pops out of hat when
gloves are moved, manufactured by
Commonwealth Plastics Corp. USA,
1960s, 3 3/4 x 1 1/2" h. (ILLUS.) **5**
Blackout kit, Kix cereal Lone Ranger pre-
mium, kit endowed "Lone Ranger Volunteer" status & included luminous "magic"
items accessible only to those w/the se-
cret for opening them, 1940s **300**

"Kreskin's ESP" Game

Board game, "Kreskin's ESP," box lid shows image of spectacled figure swinging pendulum w/text
"Will the MYSTERY PENDULUM answer your questions about LOVE? CAREER? FINANCE?
TRAVEL?", Milton Bradley, 1966 (ILLUS.) **40**

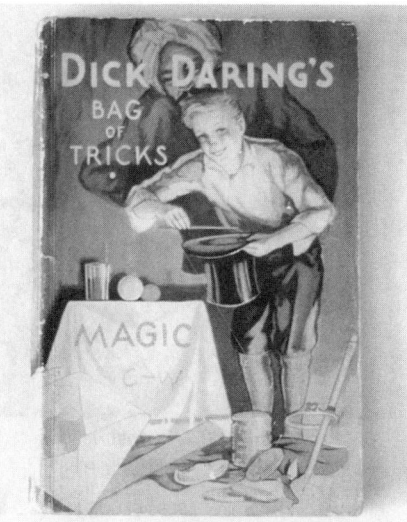

"Dick Daring's Bag of Tricks" Book

Book, "Dick Daring's Bag of Tricks," Quaker Oats (sponsor of Dick Daring radio show) premium, 64 pages of simple magic tricks (how to make an ace disappear in a deck of cards), cover w/color image of boy waving wand over top hat amid magic paraphernalia while turbaned figure looks over his shoulder, 1933, 5 x 7 1/2" (ILLUS.) 50

Book, "Dick Daring's New Bag of Tricks," Quaker Oats premium, follow-up to original book, 1934 35

Houdini Book

Book, "Houdini His Legend and His Magic," by Doug Henning with Charles Reynolds, hard bound, 1977, New York Times Book Company, 8 3/4 x 11" (ILLUS.) 45

Book, "Houdini's Big Little Book of Magic," by Harry Houdini, Whitman, American Oil Company premium, 192 pages, 1927.............. 40

Book on Houdini

Book, "Presenting Houdini His Life and Art" by The Amazing Randi and Bert Randolph Sugar, paperback, Grosset and Dunlap, New York City, 1976, 8 x 10 1/2" (ILLUS.) 40

Blackstone Book

Book, "The Blackstone Book of Magic & Illusion," by Harry Blackstone, Jr., son of famous magician, filled w/pictures of family & tours from 1920s, blurb on cover states "For the first time, America's premier prestidigitator tells the Blackstone story and examines the history, science, and art of illusion," foreword by Ray Bradbury, hard bound, Newmarket Press, New York (ILLUS.)... 35

Book, "The Life of Robert Houdini - King of the Conjurers," Rochester Publications, 1859 65

Booklet, "Easy Magic for Everyone," published by Arthur Felsman of Chicago, 16 pages, w/drawings showing how to do magic tricks, 1920 20

Card set, Harry Blackstone Magic Tricks, Philadelphia Chewing Gum Company, each card w/explanation of magic trick, 1953, 2 x 3 1/2", set of 24 95

Card set, Magic Picture series, a "magic screen" placed over the pictures revealed the image on the card, 40 cards in series, 1950s, 2 1/2 x 3 3/4", wrapper $10, each card 1

Comic book, "Mandrake the Magician," 1938.. 120

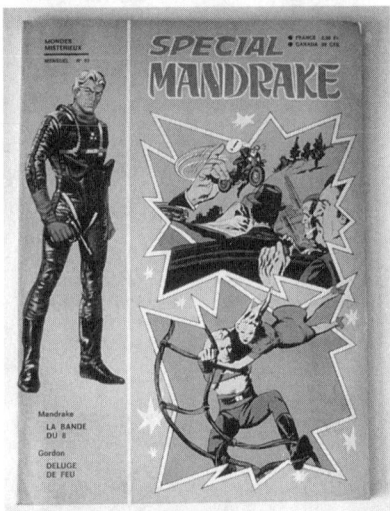

"Mandrake the Magician" Comic Book

Comic book, "Mandrake the Magician," 1968, 7 1/2 x 10 1/4" (ILLUS.)........................... 15

Sorcerer's Apprentice Mickey Mouse

Figure of Mickey Mouse as Sorcerer's Apprentice from "Fantasia," fast food giveaway, 1990s, 2" h. (ILLUS.) 2

Fortunetelling cards, Dietz's Magic Fortune Cards, cards had to be moistened to reveal fortune, believed to be 80 in set, 1930s, about 1/2 x 2 1/2", rare, each................ 5

Gumball charm, Mandrake the Magician, small flicker charm of Mandrake in black top hat, 1950s.. 25

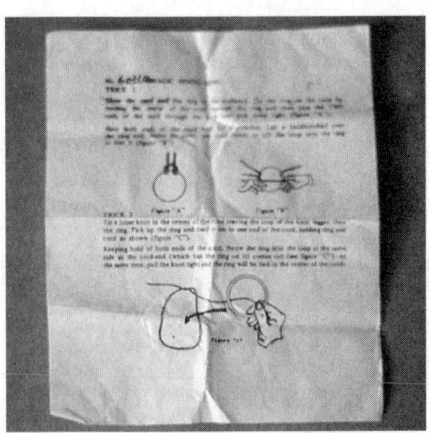

Magic Hindu Ring Trick Instructions

Instruction sheet, for Magic Hindu Ring trick, text & line drawings, probably from gum vending machine, 1960s (ILLUS.)............. 3

Leaflet, for Mandrake the Magician Magic Kit, distributed by Suchard Chocolate Bars, offered magic trick premiums for candy bar wrappers, 1948................................ 30

Magic kit, in box, 25 simple tricks w/instructions, 1963, 11 x 15"...................................... 40

Magic kit, "The Young Magician's Easy Conjuring Tricks Kit" in colorful box, open box reveals compartments filled w/tricks & equipment, 1910, 13 x 17"............................ 85

Movie poster, "Chandu the Magician," based on the radio show character, w/stars Bela Lugosi & Edmund Lowe, Fox, one-sheet, features image of Lugosi as Chandu in turban & robes, printed by Graven Images, 1932, 27 x 41"................. 3,000

Movie poster, "Houdini," w/stars Tony Curtis & Janet Leigh, Paramount Pictures, one-sheet, 1953, 27 x 41"............................... 50

Movie poster, "The Mad Magician," w/stars Vincent Price, Eva Gabor & Mary Murphy, Columbia, one-sheet, 1954, 27 x 41"... 200

Movie poster, "The Magician," w/stars Alice Terry & Paul Wegener, M-G-M, one-sheet, 1928, 27 x 41".................................. 1,200

Movie poster, "The Magician," w/stars Max von Sydow & Ingrid Thulin, one-sheet, 1958, 27 x 41"... 200

Poster, "Alexander - The Man Who Knows," three-sheet, image of Alexander in striped outfit w/feathered turban, holding crystal ball, 1920s, 41 x 81" 2,000

Poster, "Carter the Great," one-sheet, image of Carter riding camel w/Sphinx in the background, "Carter the Great - Sweeps the Secrets of the Sphinx and Marvels of the Tomb of Old King Tut to the Modern World," Otis Lithograph Company, 1920s, 27 x 41" 900

Poster, "Chung Ling Soo - A Gift From the Gods to Mortals on Earth to Amuse and Mystify," half-sheet, image of Chung Ling Soo framed in sunlight appearing through a break in the clouds, James Lipton Company, Birmingham, England, 1905-1920, 22 x 28"..................................... 8,000

Poster, "Chung Ling Soo - Marvelous Chinese Conjurer," three-sheet, image of Chung Ling Soo in center, with other images in corners, James Lipton Company, Birmingham, England, 1905-1920 .... **6,000**

Poster, "Chung Ling Soo," three-sheet, sepia image of Chung Ling Soo w/his name spelled out in dragons, James Lipton Company, Birmingham, England, 1905-1920, 41 x 81" **2,800**

Poster, for the 12-chapter serial "Mandrake the Magician, Solver of Crimes," w/stars Warren Hull & Doris Weston, Colombia Pictures, one-sheet, based on King Feature Syndicate newspaper comics character, 1939, 27 x 41" **125**

Poster, "Germain the Wizard in the Witch's Cauldron," three-sheet, image of Germain in center, w/a witch & broom & a black cat in corners, by Schmidt Horning Litho Company, 1913-1919, 41 x 81" **3,000**

Poster, "Harry Houdini," three-sheet, sepia image of Houdini, printed by Strobridge Lithography Co., 1900, 41 x 81" **20,000**

Poster, "Kellar," half-sheet, image of Kellar levitating woman, w/Egyptological objects in background, Strobridge Lithography Company, 1898, 22 x 28" **6,000**

Poster, "Kellar & Thurston," half-sheet, image of Thurston in turban & cape, Strobridge Lithography Company, 1906, 22 x 28" **4,000**

Poster, "The Great Brindamour Magician," one-sheet, picture of woman being levitated as what appear to be electrical impulses spring from magician's fingers, amid images of hatted imps, 1913, 27 x 41" **1,800**

Poster, "The Great Levante, The Famous Australian Illusionist," one-sheet, picture of illusionist, other cast members, & images of clocks, skeletons, other occult objects, Central Printing Company, United Kingdom, 1920s, 27 x 41" **800**

Poster, "Thurston Famous Magician - East-Indian Mysteries - the Wonder Show of the Universe," 20-sheet, image of Thurston in black suit w/elephants, fire eaters, a woman, and native assistants, Otis Lithograph Company, 1920s, 11 x 20" **5,000**

Poster, "Thurston the Great Magician," one-sheet, image of Thurston w/imp whispering in ear & another looking over his shoulder, Otis Lithograph Company, 1920s, 27 x 41" **1,200**

Premium, Popsicle Pete's Mystery Box with Mystery Prize, Popsicle Pete appears on packaging wearing a Halloween mask, contained prize & popsicle stick good for other giveaways, 1940s **55**

Radio premium, celluloid club member button, from radio show featuring Chandu the Magician, w/image of Chandu in turban & robes, 1930s, rare **275**

Radio premium, "Chandu - Svengali Mind Reading Trick" in box, from radio show featuring Chandu the Magician, Beech-Nut Gum premium, 1930s............................. **100**

Radio premium, "Chandu White King of Magic" complete trick boxed set, from radio show featuring Chandu the Magician, box features image of Chandu holding hands over a crystal ball, w/girl & dog looking on, "Simple Enough for a Child to Master - Perplexing Enough to Interest the Grownups - Instructive, Entertaining, Interesting," White King Soap premium, 1930s **300**

Radio premium, "Chandu's Ball and Base Magic Trick" w/instructions, from radio show featuring Chandu the Magician, Beech-Nut Gum premium, 1930s.................... **75**

Ring, Magic Pup, Ralston Wheat Chex premium, magnet moves head of Magic Pup, 1951 .... **130**

Souvenir pamphlet, 1876 U.S. Centennial, "Parlour Magic Without Apparatus," two-sided, published by Robert Nickle, 1876........ **40**

Mickey Mouse Pop Pal

Toy, Mickey Mouse Pop Pal, plastic, black top hat, top of hat opens at the push of a button & bust of Mickey Mouse rises from inside, 1960s, 2 1/2 x 4" (ILLUS.).................... **20**

Mysterious Panel Board Trick

Toy, Mysterious Panel Board Trick, wooden board divided into 36 squares, "Coins placed on this board and covered with a box, sheet of paper, or handkerchief will pass through the board or will entirely disappear. A dandy pocket trick that is easy to do. Full instruction are included," w/instructions in text & graphics, 1940s, 3 3/4 x 3 3/4" (ILLUS.) **15**

METALS

Also see: Antique Trader Metalwares Price Guide, 2nd Edition.

Aluminum

Cast Aluminum Art Deco Ashtray

Ashtray, cast, figural, an Art Deco design w/an angular terrier seated at the edge of a fanned angular tray, 3 1/4 x 5 1/8", 4 3/8" h. (ILLUS.) **$65**

Ashtray, hammered, large center flower, wrap-around platform base forms cigarette rests, Buenilum, 4 1/2" d. 25

Ashtray, hammered, bittersweet decoration, Wendell August #60, 5 1/2" d. 15

Ashtray, cast, horsehead decoration, Bruce Fox, 5 1/2 x 5 1/2" 25

Basket, bread, hammered, oval w/twisted handle, duck on pond decoration, Cromwell 12

Basket, hammered aluminum frame w/flower clusters, Paden City glass insert, looped handle, fluted edge, Cromwell, 14" d. 35

Basket, hammered, china plate insert, morning glories on frame, square w/rolled sides, looped diagonally-placed handle, Wrought Farberware, 12" w. 38

Basket, hammered, double-style, handle w/square knot, fern & flowers decoration, Canterbury Arts, 9" w. 12

Basket, hammered, twisted handle, sailing ship decoration, Hand Forged #29, 10" d. 8

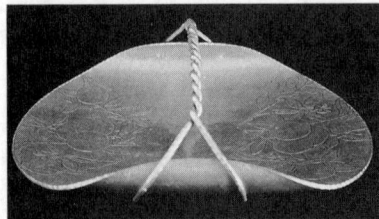

Rare Orange Pattern Basket

Basket, oval w/turn-in sides joined by a double twist handle, orange design, Arthur Armour, rare, 14 x 18" (ILLUS.) .. **295-350**

Basket, polished aluminum frame w/stamped rose design, fluted, etched glass insert, double aluminum strand handle, twisted in center, Farber & Shlevin, 9 1/2" d. 20

Basket, polished aluminum, frame w/stamped rose pattern, twisted handle, pottery insert, Farber & Shlevin, 7" d. 18

Basket, polished w/stamped flowers, unmarked, 7" d. 5

Book ends, hammered, applied horseshoe, Everlast, pr. 95

Book ends, hammered, chopped corners, daisy decoration, Wendell August, pr. 150

Bowl, cov., hammered, cast aluminum "baker man" on cover, Cellini Craft 85

Bowl, hammered, petal design w/grape cluster in center, Wendell August #807 85

Bowl, polished, repoussé flower design in center, butterfly handles, Hand Forged 12

Bowl, hammered, blackbird & fledglings decoration, De Ponceau, 5 3/4" d. 30

Bowl, machine-embossed pattern, Wrought Aluminum, 7" d. 5

Bowl, hammered, Big Horn sheep decoration, Hand Forged #2, 8 3/4" d. 5

Bowl, hammered, intaglio band of stylized daisy, Everlast, 9" d. 5

Bowl, hammered, Bromeliad-like flowers, Buenilum, 9 1/4" d. 15

Bowl, hammered, footed, flat, scalloped edge w/tiny berries between scallops, Cellini Craft, 11 1/2" d. 33

Bowl, hammered, fruits decoration, Everlast, 12 1/2" d. 12

Bowl, hammered, scalloped edge, oak leaves & acorns decoration, Everlast, 13" d. 12

Bowl, hammered, hunter scene, LA Handwrought (bell symbol), 15" d. 95

Box, cov., cigarette, hammered, applied leaves & rosette on cover, World 40

Box, cov., cigarette, hammered, pine decoration, Wendell August 95

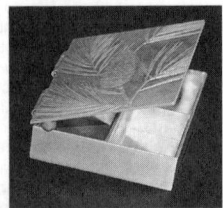

Wendell August Pine Motif Box

Box, cov., flattened square form, pine bough design on the cover, opens to three compartments, Wendell August (ILLUS.) 125

Box, cov., hammered square w/sturdy hinged cover, schooner decoration, Arthur Armour 125

Bread tray, hammered, anchor decoration, Everlast 12

Bread tray, hammered, chrysanthemum decoration, applied leaves, Continental 14

Bread tray, hammered, grape clusters, handles w/leaves, World 10

Bread tray, hammered, scalloped edges, tulip decoration, Rodney Kent 15

Bread tray, hammered, wild rose decoration, Continental 9

Bread tray, machine-embossed, pansy decoration, National Silver Co. 5

Bread tray, polished, stamped wild rose decoration, unmarked 5

Butter dish, cov., deep glass dish in crisscross design, aluminum undertray & cover w/tulip finial, Rodney Kent 20

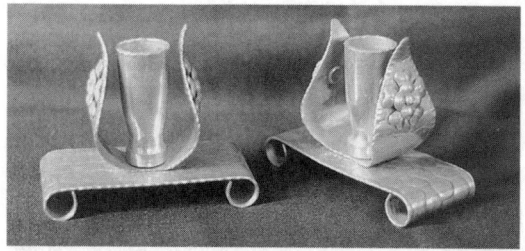

World Handforged Candleholders

Butter dish, cov., machine-embossed chrysanthemum on aluminum cover, floret finial, pressed glass base, Forman Family **18**

Butter dish, cov., polished, glass insert for 1/4 lb., looped finial, Buenilum **18-20**

Butter dish, cov., polished, round w/glass insert, looped finial on domed cover, undertray w/beaded edge, Buenilum, 6 1/2" d. **18-20**

Butter dish, cov., polished, stamped Bali Bamboo patt., crisscross patterned glass insert for 1/4 lb., Everlast #B55 .... **25**

Candelabra, hammered, holds three candles on a thick bar w/large center loop, Buenilum, 14" w., 6" h., pr. **125**

Candelabra, hammered, two-light, rectangular base w/scrolled band, Wendell August #840, pr. **150**

![Buenilum Three-light Candelabrum]

Buenilum Three-light Candelabrum

Candelabrum, three-light, each cylindrical socket w/a flat round drip tray, on two looped arms & a tall twisted strand stem on a slightly domed round foot, Buenilum, 13 1/2" h. (ILLUS.) **85-125**

Candleholder, applied leaves on stem, Continental, 4 1/2" h. **30**

Candleholder, hammered, scalloped base, Everlast, 4" w., 3 1/2" h. **20**

Candleholders, anodized (polished), crystal ball, Kensington, pr. **35**

Candleholders, hammered, deep saucer base, twisted stem, Wendell August, 6" w., 8" h., pr. **125**

Candleholders, hammered, double platform base, three cupped lotus leaves, holds one candle, Wendell August, pr. **225**

Candleholders, hammered, flower sprigs, Findley, 5" w., 3 1/2" h., pr. **35-40**

Candleholders, simulated hammer marks, the tall socket flanked by pairs of upright leaves w/an applied floret on each, on a wide flat base w/inwardly scrolled feet, World Handforged, pr. (ILLUS., top of page) **25**

Candy dish, cov., hammered aluminum cover, fruits decoration, pear finial, thick glass base dish, unmarked Everlast **35-45**

Candy dish, cov., hammered, aluminum cover w/chrysanthemum & floret, footed pressed glass base dish, Continental, 6" d. **35**

Candy dish, cov., hammered aluminum cover w/flower sprigs & "spoon handle" curl, footed etched glass base dish, Buenilum, 6" d. **35-45**

Candy dish, cov., hammered aluminum holder & cover w/applied ribbon decoration, tulip finial, ribbon & flower decorative handles extending into feet, divided glass insert dish, Rodney Kent, 6" d. **35**

Casserole, cov., hammered, Bali Bamboo patt., baking dish insert, stylized bamboo cover finial, Everlast, 7" d. **15**

Casserole, cov., hammered, butterfly & dogwood decoration & ring handle on cover, baking dish insert, grooved handles, Arthur Armour, 9" d. **95-125**

Casserole, cov., hammered, intaglio design of stylized leaves & flowers, flattened cover knob, side handles, baking dish insert, Everlast, 9 1/4" d. **10**

Casserole, cov., hammered, leafy vine & open pea pod cover finial, baking dish insert, Everlast #1038, 7"d. **12**

Casserole, cover & undertray, hammered, Bittersweet patt., twisted bar handle on cover, baking dish insert, Wendell August #735, 9 x 13 1/2" undertray, 3 pcs..... **125**

Chafing dish, cov., hammered, black handle & knob finial on cover, Spain **12**

Chafing dish, cov., hammered, grape cluster design around cover w/beaded knob surrounded w/leaves, baking dish insert, Everlast, 10" d. **25**

Chafing dish, cov., hammered, tulip decoration, decorative ribbon & flower handles & legs, baking dish insert, Rodney Kent **30**

Coaster, hammered, tropical fish decoration, Wendell August w/old mark **15**

Coasters, embossed, chrysanthemum pattern, in caddy w/decorative leaves, Continental, set of 8 .... **25**

Rodney Kent Condiment Server

Coasters, embossed tulip motif, in caddy w/decorative ribbon & flower design handle, Rodney Kent, the set................................... 30

Coasters, hammered, rose decoration, in caddy w/curled handle, Everlast, set of 6.. **16-20**

Coasters, hammered, spiral design, Everlast, set of 6... 16

Coasters, polished, beaded edge, in caddy w/double looped handle, Buenilum, set of 8 25

Cocktail shaker, cov., double looped finial on cover, Buenilum, 9 1/2" h. **85-95**

Condiment server, hammered, apple blossom design on undertray & slotted cover on glass jar, Wendell August #592, the set **35-50**

Condiment server, hammered, Ferris-wheel style, three "baskets" holding dishes, Continental.. 55

Condiment server, hammered, revolving-type, cruets & covered jars in apple design, twisted center handle, Continental......... 45

Condiment server: oval handled tray & two cov. glass containers; the hammered tray w/an arched & pierced central handle w/a ribbon & flower design, lids on containers w/spoon slots & bud finials, Rodney Kent, the set (ILLUS., top of page) 50

Cast Aluminum Turtle Corkscrew

Corkscrew, cast, model of a turtle w/a cork screw tail, original worn paint, 2 1/4 x 4 1/4" (ILLUS.)....................................... 95

Crumber set: brush & rectangular tray; the tray w/a rolled handle w/applied blossoms & leaf spring & an engraved tulip cluster in tray, the brush w/a wooden handle applied w/a blossom & leaf sprig, Rodney Kent 3444, tray 3 1/4 x 8 1/2", 2 pcs. **25-35**

Crumber set: scraper & tray; hammered, scalloped edges, grape decoration on each piece, Everlast, the set 35

Crumber set: tray & brush; hammered, looped handles, Buenilum, the set **35-40**

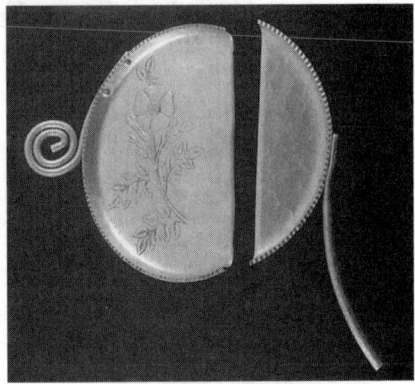

Crumber Set with Wild Rose Design

Crumber set: tray & scoop; the two pieces forming a disc, the larger tray section w/a tight curl handle, stamped wild rose sprig decoration, the scoop w/a long curved bar handle, Continental #725, 2 pcs. (ILLUS.) **18-25**

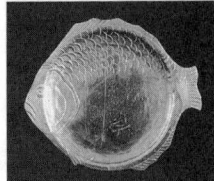

Small Fish-shaped Dish

Dish, rounded flattened model of a fish, old circular Everlast mark, small (ILLUS.)....... **25-40**

Dresser set: two covered glass dishes on a tray; hammered, covers w/tulip finials, ribbon & flower design caddy handles extend to form feet, Rodney Kent #403, tray 6 x 12", the set... 45

Drink mixer, hammered, one-piece construction, large hole for long-handled stirring spoon, Everlast, 7" h............................ **50-60**

Gravy boat on attached undertray, hammered, w/ladle, looped handles, Buenilum.. 35

Gravy boat on attached undertray, hammered, wrapped handle w/decorative

leaf, w/aluminum ladle, chrysanthemum decoration, Continental #610 .... **35-45**
Ice bucket, cov., hammered, handled, cover w/applied leaves under knob, Everlast Ice Cooler (with polar bear) #5008 .... **20**
Ice bucket, cov., hammered, side handles, roses decoration, hammered ball cover knob, Everlast, 9 1/2" h. **25-35**
Ice bucket, cov., hammered, thin aluminum, handled, Nassco **6**
Ice bucket, cov., hammered, tulip cover finial, ribbon & flower handles, Rodney Kent **35**
Ice bucket, cov., polished, footed, large looped cover finial, Knight Kraft **18**

Two Everlast Pendants

Jewelry, pendant, domed round form w/flat fluted rim enclosing center w/raised embossed floral design, w/chain, unmarked Everlast (ILLUS. left) **45**
Jewelry, pendant, flattened oval shape w/embossed leafy design, w/chain, unmarked Everlast (ILLUS. right) **45**
Lamp, table, hammered, walnut decoration, aluminum shade, Wendell August ... **1,700-1,900**
Lamp, table, hammered, zinnia design, silk shade, Wendell August **1,000-1,200**
Magazine rack, hammered, thick aluminum, world map decoration, Arthur Armour **350**
Match box cover, hammered, "penny box" size, Wendell August **35**
Match box cover, polished, kitchen-size, stylized fish & water design, Palmer-Smith **55**
Match folder cover, polished, ducks decoration, unmarked **5**
Meat server, hammered, well & tree-type, curved band supports each end, floret & leaves decoration, Continental #544, 11 x 15 1/2" **35-50**
Napkin holder, hammered, decorative ribbon & flower band forms feet, Rodney Kent **27**
Napkin holder, hammered, trefoil shape, roses decoration, Everlast **25**
Napkin holder, polished, cactus decoration, Farber & Shlevin **12**
Napkin holder, polished, machine-embossed roses, World **15**
Nut bowl & picks, hammered, fruits & flowers decoration, looped handles, pedestal base, Cromwell, 10" d., the set **15-20**

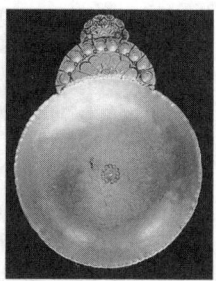

Unique Round Nut Dish

Nut dish, shallow round bowl w/a tiny floret in the center & a unique stamped tab side handle, Florence Kimbell (ILLUS.) **30-40**

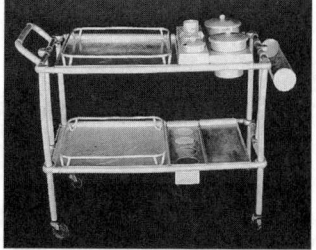

Everlast Patio Cart

Patio cart, hammered, intaglio leaves decoration, complete w/serving pieces, wheels & push handle, Everlast (ILLUS.) **650**

Cast Aluminum Pencil Sharpener

Pencil sharpener, cast, figure of colonial woman holding tray, marked on reverse "Baker Chocolate Girl - reg. U.S. patent office," w/original red, white & blue paint, 1/2 x 1", 1 7/8" h. (ILLUS.) **135**
Pitcher, hammered, applied floret & leaves on body, World **25-30**
Pitcher, hammered, flared at top, Everlast **15**
Pitcher, hammered, grooved bulbous form, berry & leaf decoration on handle, Cellini Craft **75**
Pitcher, hammered, looped & twisted handle, Buenilum **25**
Pitcher, hammered, mums decoration, handle w/leaf decoration, Continental **35**
Pitcher, hammered, thin aluminum, grooved band around center, Italy **10**

Art Deco Aluminum Punch Bowl

Pitcher with Signed Floral Decor

Pitcher, oval cylindrical body w/embossed flower & leaf design up the sides, angled handle, artist-signed within decoration, Canterbury Arts (ILLUS.) **75**

Pitcher, polished, straight sides, twisted handle, Buenilum.. **15**

Pitcher, w/ice guard spout, hammered, Bali Bamboo patt., Everlast...................................... **65**

Pitcher, w/ice guard spout, hammered, pine decoration, Wendell August #760.................... **85**

Pitcher, w/ice guard spout, hammered, tulip decoration, tiny tulips on ice guard, ribbon-styled handle, Rodney Kent................ **35-45**

Pitcher, hammered, intaglio band of stylized daisies, double twisted handle of large rods, Everlast, 6" h............................ **35-45**

Punch bowl & ladle, hammered, grapes decoration, Wendell August, 2 pcs................ **350**

Punch bowl, tray & ladle, hammered w/blue crock liner, ring handles, Keystone, the set **125**

Punch bowl, undertray & ladle, a deep flaring bowl w/geometric Art Deco designs on a wide round matching undertray, Laird, underplate 20" d., bowl 14" d., the set (ILLUS., top of page) **450-475**

Serving utensil, punch ladle, polished, twisted double looped handle, unmarked Buenilum.. **35-45**

Serving utensils, salad fork & spoon, hammered, twisted handles, unmarked Wendell August, pr.. **65**

Serving utensils, salad fork & spoon, wooden w/bamboo design section at each end, unmarked, pr. **25**

Serving utensils, salad fork & spoon, wooden w/decorative aluminum inset on handle in an Everlast pattern, unmarked, pr.. **15**

Silent butler, hammered, cattails decoration, unmarked, 5 x 6"... **15**

Everlast Silent Butler with Flowers

Silent butler, oblong dish w/scalloped edge & slightly domed hinged cover embossed w/stylized lilies & leaves, flat hammered handle, Everlast (ILLUS.)................................. **25**

Silent butler, oval, hammered, flower cluster decoration, Henry & Miller, 4 1/2 x 6" **15**

Silent butler, oval, hammered, fruits decoration, Everlast, 7 x 9" **20**

Fern & Berry Decor on Silent Butler

Silent butler, round dish w/embossed Fern & Berry pattern on the hinged lid, flat hammered handle, Canterbury Arts (ILLUS.) **27-35**

Sugar, creamer & tray, hammered, chrysanthemum decoration on sugar & creamer, plain tray w/scalloped edges, Continental #515, 3 pcs. **25-35**

Sugar, creamer & tray, plain sugar & creamer, grape decoration on tray, Everlast, 3 pcs..................................... **20-25**

Sugar, creamer & tray, plain, World, 3 pcs. **20**

Tidbit tray, hammered, tiered w/three trays, grape decoration, center standing w/ring handle, Everlast, 14" h. **22**

Tidbit tray, machine-embossed, tiered, unmarked 10

Tidbit tray, polished, floral decoration, side handle, Hammercraft 7

Toast rack, hammered, wheat decoration, Wendell August #709 65

Toast rack, w/two each covered butter & jam jars, hammered, center toast rack, Rodney Kent 55

Tray, hammered, rope pattern, ring handles w/small balls, Palmer-Smith #18, 10" d. 95

Tray, hammered, intaglio design of stylized daisies, ribbed tab handles, Everlast, 9 x 11" 12

Tray, hammered, square, rose bouquet decoration, Everlast, 12" w. 15

Tray, machine-embossed flowers, Wright Aluminum, 12" d. 10

Tray, oval, smooth, stamped wild roses decoration, fluted, unmarked, 12 1/4" l. 8

Tray, hammered, grooved bar handles, scenic design of horseback riders & lake, Arthur Armour, 9 x 13" 125

Tray, hammered, twisted handles, Wild Rose patt., fluted edge, Continental #703, 13 1/2" d. 15

Tray, hammered, tab handles, heron & marsh scene, Leroy DeLoss, 8 x 13 1/2" 100-150

Tray with Celtic Knot Design

Tray, rectangular w/tab end handles, intaglio curvilinear or Celtic Knot design, Canterbury Arts, 9 1/2 x 13 1/2" (ILLUS.) 14-16

Tray, hammered, tab handles, oak leaves decoration, Wrought Farberware, 10 1/2 x 13 1/2" 10

Tray, hammered, daisies or sunflowers decoration, DePonceau, 14" d. 35-45

Tray, hammered, handled, tulip decoration, Rodney Kent, 14" d. 25

Tray, hammered, handled, nautical motif, Lehman, 9 x 14" 35

Tray, hammered, tab handles, tropical fish decoration, Everlast, 9 x 14" 45

Tray, machine-embossed, handles, hunt scene, crimped edges, Beautyline Designed Aluminum, 11 1/2 x 16 1/2" 10

Tray, hammered, bar handles, hunt scene, Keystone, 13 x 17" 35-45

Tray, hammered, handled, oak leaf & acorn decoration, Continental #520, 17 1/2" l. 30

Tray, hammered, coach & four decoration, Clayton Sheasley, 7 1/2 x 17 1/2" 65-75

Tray, hammered, floral decoration, Clayton Sheasley, 7 1/2 x 17 1/2" 40-60

Tray, hammered, small hand-stamped flowers, Palmer-Smith #33, 9 1/2 x 20" 125

Tray, hammered, polo players decoration w/trophy inscribed with winners' names, dated "4-23-39," Wendell August, 8 x 23" 95

Trivet, hammered, oval, cork pads, leaves decoration, Everlast, 5 1/2 x 7" 10

Trivet, hammered, cork pads, wildflowers decoration, Everlast, 10" d. 12

Trivet, hammered, cork pads, ivy decoration, Everlast, 8 x 11" 12

Trivet, hammered, cork pads, Tapestry patt., Arthur Armour, 8 1/2 x 11" 20-30

Tumbler, hammered, applied floret & leaves, World, 20 oz. 10

Tumbler, hammered, bamboo joint design, Everlast 10

Tumbler, hammered, beaded base, Buenilum 6

Tumbler, hammered, footed, chrysanthemum decoration, Continental 18-25

Tumbler, hammered, plain, Buenilum 5

Tumbler, hammered, plain, Everlast 5

Tumbler, hammered, plain, Leumas 4

Tumbler, hammered, stemmed base, lightweight, unmarked 6

Tumbler, spun, wheat decoration, West Bend 4

Vase, hammered, fluted top, World, 8" h. 45

Continental #630 Vase

Vase, hammered, flared foot & slightly flaring cylindrical body w/incurved rim, chrysanthemum decoration, Continental #30, 10" h. (ILLUS.) 55

Vase, hammered, hollyhock decoration, Wendell August #858, 12" h. 300

Vase, hammered, urn-shaped w/handles, World #207, 12" h. 125

Large Wendell August Vase

Vase, wide slightly flaring cylindrical form w/rolled rim, zinnia decoration, Wendell August, 12" h. (ILLUS.) 275-300

Wastebasket, hammered, fluted top, apple blossoms decoration, Wendell August #900 95

Wastebasket, hammered, lightweight, water lilies stamped design, West Bend 10

Wastebasket Signed in the Design

Wastebasket, hammered, oval cylindrical form, embossed detailed floral bouquet design, signed in the pattern "CC Pflanz," Canterbury Arts (ILLUS.) **195**

Brass

Andirons, Federal style, a knop finial above a small flaring urn over a spherical & ring-turned shaft above a ring-and-column-turned shaft, on spurred cabriole front legs w/ball feet, together w/two shovels, a pair of tongs & a brass & wire fire-screen, New York, New York, ca. 1800-1820, andirons 22 1/2" h., the set **3,525**

Trench Art Ashtray

Ashtray, Trench art-type, round base of a 105 mm shell casing w/the central pierced stem, World War I era, 4" d. (ILLUS.) **15**

Early Engraved Book-shaped Box

Box, hand-forged, book-shaped, the covers engraved overall w/biblical scenes, Europe, ca. 1750, 2 1/2 x 4 3/4", 1" h. (ILLUS.) **1,500**

Brass Gorham Candleholders

Candleholders, round wide foot w/ga-drooned band tapering to a tulip-form

socket w/a gadrooned band, marked "Gorham Giftware L17," 3 3/4" h., pr. (ILLUS.) **40**

Drink Heating Set

Drink heating set, Arts & Crafts style, a Colonial Revival design w/a tall square brass lidded tankard w/strap handle & a long-handled heating rod w/egg-shaped tip, on a square iron base marked "Cape Cod Trademark" & w/an embossed image of a fish, probably for mulling wine, early 20th c., 12" h., the set (ILLUS.)............. **295**

Fireplace fender, brass & wire, long slender upper & lower brass rails curving at the ends to form fender & enclosing a decorative latticework wire band above a fine wire lower vertical band interwoven w/wire scrolls, America or England, late 18th - early 19th c., 15 x 49 1/2", 10" h. **2,875**

Fireplace set: andirons & tools; each andiron modeled as a half-round lighthouse on an articulated base w/lighthouse form log stop, billet bars marked "Rostand N.," together w/a matching tool set including a poker, shovel & tongs each w/a lighthouse-form handle, on a matching stand w/lighthouse & rock-form base, stamped on the bottom w/the Rostand trademark, Rostand Mfg. Co., Milford, Connecticut, early 20th c., andirons, 29 3/4" h., the set **7,050**

Masonic Emblem Picture Frame

Frame, cast, table model, in the form of the Masonic emblem w/a picture opening in the center, swing-out wire back support, gilt finish, patent-dated in October 1899, 7" w., 9 5/8" h. (ILLUS.) **145**

Frame, stamped, table model, delicate pierced designs of flowers, leaves & branches across the top & base, late 19th c., 5 x 8 1/4" **58**

Oval Victorian Frame with Scrolls

Frame, stamped, table model, horizontal oval form supported by ornate pierced scrolls at the sides, late 19th c., 6 1/4 x 10 1/4" (ILLUS.) **65**

Cast Brass Incense Burner

Incense burner, cast, classical urn shape w/pagoda form lid, raised on three slender legs joined by stretchers, early 20th c., 2 1/4" d., 4 3/4" h. (ILLUS.) **40**

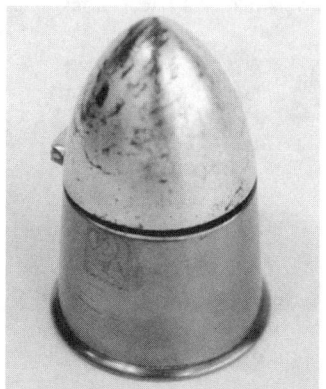

Brass Bullet-shaped Inkwell

Inkwell, bullet-shaped w/ring foot, hinged plated top, English, 2 1/4" d., 3 1/4" h. (ILLUS.) **175**

Roycroft Hammered Brass Inkwell

Inkwell, cov., hammered, round on spreading foot, w/glass insert, cover w/rounded finial, maker's mark on bottom, Roycroft, 3 1/4" d., 3 1/4" h. (ILLUS.) **950**

Jamb hooks, two-part construction, the hooks w/belted urn finials, the back plates of a conforming shape, America or England, late 18th c., 4 x 4 1/2", pr. (one back plate w/mold imperfections) **460**

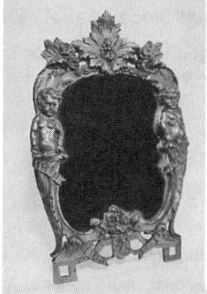

Mirror in Fancy Cast Frame

Mirror, cast, table model, the upright oblong frame cast at each side w/a putto, leaves, grape cluster & roses across the top & scrolls & a basket of flowers across the bottom, goldtone finish, late 19th - early 20th c., 8 x 12 1/4" (ILLUS.) **165**

Brass Rococo Design Mirror Frame

Mirror frame, hanging-type, an ornate rectangular rococo design composed of pierced scrolls & a tall scroll finial, early 20th c., 11 1/2 x 16 1/2" (ILLUS.) **145**

Brass Spring-loaded Scale

Small Model of an Airedale

Model of a dog, stylized Art Deco seated Airedale on oval base, 2" h. (ILLUS.).............. **50**

Unusual Duck Head Paper Clamp

Paper clamp, cast, hanging-type, figural, model of a mallard duck head, painted w/red glass eyes, spring-loaded, late 19th - early 20th c., 5" l. (ILLUS.) **125**

Figural Fox Paperweight

Paperweight, cast, figural, a walking fox atop a thin rectangular plaque raised on scrolls over a round base, 2 1/4 x 5 3/4", 4 3/4" h. (ILLUS.)................................ **45**

Planter, table top type, oval w/deep upright sides raised on four short scroll-cast feet, molded top & bottom edges & decorated around the sides w/continuous wide band of classical urns & leaf clusters, France, ca. 1865, 7 x 9 1/2", 6 1/4" h. **380**

Scale, spring-loaded, w/ring handle and stamped w/company name and weight measures, Frary, 1 x 1 3/4", 10" h. (ILLUS., top of page) **15**

School bell, handheld type, simple turned-wood handle, 8" h. **69**

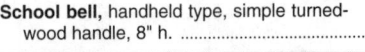
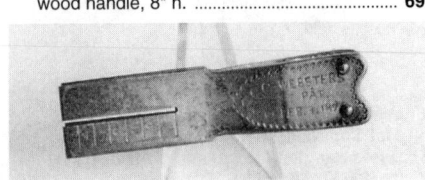

Brass Sewing Clip

Sewing clip, marked "Webster's patented Feb. 3, 1874," 5/8 x 2 1/2" (ILLUS.)................. **75**

Bronze

Bronze Racehorse Book Ends

Book ends, gold finish, marbled onyx bases hold models of racehorses, 3 x 9 1/4", 8" h., the pr. (ILLUS.)...................................... **475**

Book ends, Zodiac patt., dark brown & green patina, marked "Tiffany Studios New York 1091," 4 3/4" w., 6" h., pr.............. **489**

Egyptian Revival Candleholder

Candleholder, Egyptian Revival style, trapezoidal footed base w/two rectangular inserts of turquoise or enamel chips, angled shaft supports candle socket w/bobêche, all decorated w/Egyptian symbols & designs, 4 1/2" h. (ILLUS.) **250**

Art Deco Glass & Bronze Chandelier

Chandelier, Art Deco style, a cast-bronze paneled ceiling mount & lower shade mount cast w/a border of angular designs, the center w/a frosted glass bowl-form shade w/molded stylized flowers & geometric designs, four angled & pointed arms each suspending a conical frosted glass shade w/a molded geometric floral design, ca. 1930, 30" d., overall 26 1/2" h. (ILLUS.) **2,300**

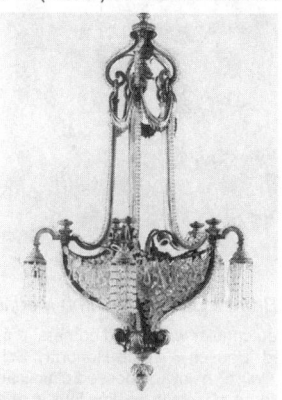

Louis XVI-Style 15-light Chandelier

Chandelier, Louis XVI-Style, fifteen-light, gilt-bronze & glass, the top section w/five C-scrolled glass-trimmed arms supporting five long glass-trimmed arms, each arm ending w/one upturned socket & one exterior downturned socket w/beaded trim, a lower metal basket-form framework densely trimmed w/prisms & enclosing five additional sockets, a scroll-decorated base w/a pineapple drop, Europe, early 20th c., 54" h. (ILLUS.) **5,100**

Neoclassical-style Chandelier

Chandelier, Neoclassical-style, eight-light, the trumpet-form fluted central standard topped by flat leaves, flaring outward to the eight fluted cornucopia-shaped candlearms w/squat ovoid fluted nozzles, the standard ending in a similar ovoid form, finishing in an inverted pineapple finial, electrified, late 19th c., 28" w., 28" h. (ILLUS.) **3,450**

Bronze Incense Burner on Base

Incense burner on base, cov., Oriental style w/finely detailed casting, stump base w/character signature (foundry mark?), old painted signature inside domed lid reads "Gruschwitz," footed pot w/relief turtle & dragon medallions, patina, 14 1/2" h. (ILLUS.) **495**

Bronze & Wood Pheasant Ink Blotter

Ink blotter, curved wooden base topped w/polychrome image of a pheasant on irregular surface, 3 x 5, 4" h. (ILLUS.) **695**

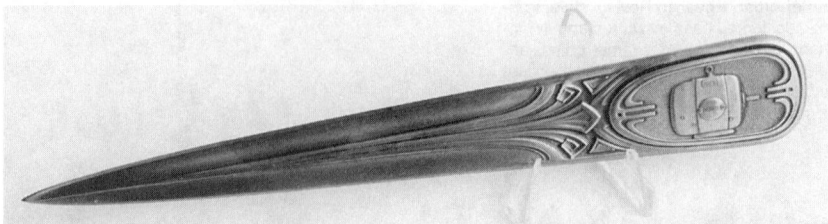

Art Deco Advertising Letter Opener

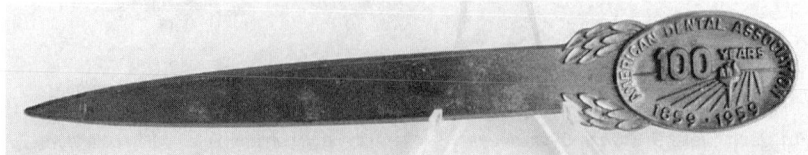

Bronze Commemorative Letter Opener

Elaborate Bronze Lamp

Lamp, electric, cold-painted, base a thin sheet representing a carpet, holds figure of Arab holding writing tablet & sitting next to small round table w/Arabic-style coffee urn, background of bamboo branches, decorated w/round shield & crossed sword & rifle, holds rectangular Moorish-style lighting unit w/domed roof, notched upper & lower rims and crescent moons dangling from corners and sitting atop dome, red & green glass inserts, bottom marked w/"B" in a vase and "Namgreb," made in Austria, 19 x 19 1/2" (ILLUS.).. **2,950**

Letter opener, gold finish, overall Art Deco design, advertising Howell projectors, indistinct mark on reverse, 9 1/4" l. (ILLUS., top of page) **55**

Letter opener, oval head embossed "100 Years - American Dental Association - 1859-1959," reverse marked "With compliments of Ritter & Co., Rochester NY," feathered wings "grip" envelope slicer,

6 5/8" l. (ILLUS., top second from of page).. **18**

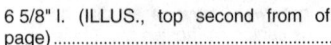

Bronze Bausch & Lomb Medal

Medal, rectangular w/rounded corners, embossed "Bausch & Lomb Honorary Science Award" below embossed classical-style figure of woman holding lens in one hand & garland in other, 1 3/4 x 2 1/4" (ILLUS.) **35**

Cast Bronze Commemorative Medallion

Medallion, cast, commemorative, bordered rectangle w/"Massachusetts Bay Tercentenary in New England - 1630-1930" on one side and detailed scenes depicting Native Americans, Pilgrims, a flying witch, a plane, Priscilla & John Alden, etc., on reverse, all in relief, 2 5/8 x 3 1/2" (ILLUS.)... **145**

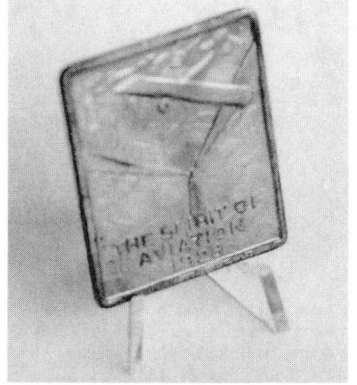

Bronze Aviation Medallion

Medallion, commemorative, bordered rectangle w/embossed decoration of plane flying over beacon and "The Spirit of Aviation - 1928" on front, marked on reverse "Chicago Central Aerial Beacon, Roanoke Tower, LaSalle and Madison Streets, erected and maintained by Greenebaum & Sons Investment Co., founded 1855," 1 1/4 x 1 3/4" (ILLUS.)............ **45**

Bronze Commemorative Medallion

Medallion, commemorative, round, heavily embossed stylized Eastern cross on right, writing at left, to honor the 1985 national gathering in Washington, D.C. of the survivors of the Armenian genocide by the Ottoman Empire in 1915, 2 3/8" w. (ILLUS.)... **65**

Dental Congress Medallion

Medallion, commemorative, round, in honor of 4th International Dental Congress held in St. Louis in 1904, front features eagle perched on scroll holding olive branch, reverse shows figure of woman holding olive branch, 2 1/4" d. (ILLUS.)......... **125**

Pittsburgh Bicentennial Medallion

Medallion, commemorative, round, in honor of bicentennial of Pittsburgh, front embossed w/image of city spread out under the words "Pittsburgh Bicentennial - 1758-1958," reverse features image of Fort Pitt, 3" d. (ILLUS.)..................................... **75**

Benjamin Franklin Medallion

Medallion, commemorative, round, w/embossed bust of Benjamin Franklin in profile encircled by his name and birth date, 1 7/8" d. (ILLUS.) **55**

Union Medallion

Medallion, commemorative, round, w/embossed likenesses of George Meany & William Schnitzler above "George Meany - President," "Wm. Schnitzler, Secretary & Treas." and "Amalgamated Meat Cutters & Butcher Workmen of North America, A. F. of L.," 3" d. (ILLUS.) **55**

Columbian Exposition Medallion

Medallion, commemorative, round w/raised rim, "World's Columbian Exposition - 1892-93" in banner across front & decorated w/embossed images of a spread-winged eagle, Christopher Columbus, George Washington & the signing of the Declaration of Independence, 2 1/4" d. (ILLUS.) **125**

U.S.S. Enterprise Medallion

Medallion, commemorative, silver finish, embossed w/image of U.S.S. Enterprise aircraft carrier surrounded by "U.S.S. Enterprise - World's Largest Ship - First Nuclear Powered Aircraft Carrier," commemorates its launching on Sept. 14, 1960 at Newport News, Va., 2 1/2" d. (ILLUS.) **45**

Chester A. Arthur Medallion

Medallion, commemorative, w/embossed profile of 21st president of United States in center surrounded by "Chester A. Arthur," dated Sept. 20, 1881, 3" d. (ILLUS.) **135**

Graf Ferdinand Zeppelin Medallion

Medallion, memorial for Graf Ferdinand Zeppelin, w/embossed profile of him on front surrounded by "Graf Ferdinand V. Zeppelin [star] 8 Juli 1838 - 8 Marz 1917" around rim, reverse shows figure of Mercury holding zeppelin, 2 5/8" d. (ILLUS.) **35**

Bronze Medallion with Bust

Medallion, round w/relief-cast bust of a Classical goddess, 5 3/4" d. (ILLUS.) **350**

Small Bronze Airedale Model

Model of a dog, stylized walking Airedale on a thick rectangular base, 1 1/2 x 4", 2 7/8" h. (ILLUS.).. **90**

Bronze Fairy Paperweight

Paperweight, circular base printed w/"The Good Fairy," holds figure of girl w/long hair & outstretched arms dressed in short dress that appears to be blowing in the wind, 2 x 3", 6" h. (ILLUS.) **145**

Milk Bone Elephant Paperweight

Paperweight, model of an elephant w/a large Milk Bone Dog Biscuit in its trunk, used as an advertising premium, 20th c., 4 1/4 x 5" (ILLUS.).. **250**

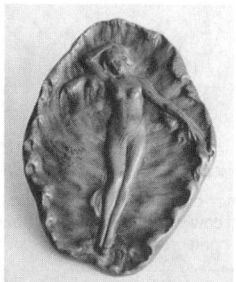

Art Nouveau Bronze Plaque

Plaque, Art Nouveau design, shallow oblong form cast w/a relief figure of a female nude standing in billowing surf, back marked "Extra" w/indistinct mark, 5 x 7" (ILLUS.) **300**

Chrome

Art Deco Chrome Ashtray Set

Ashtray set, a flat square chrome base w/rolled-under edges & an upright center handle holds a stack of three clear glass rectangular ashtrays, a cast-metal bronzed figure of an Art Deco nude at the back, 5" sq., 6 3/4" h., the set (ILLUS.).......... **85**

Glass & Chrome Basket

Basket, shallow round purple glass bowl fitted in a pierced & arched chrome frame w/a rounded foot ring, arched & pointed chrome swing bail handle, Farber Bros. mark on base, 5 3/8 " d., 2" h. plus handle (ILLUS.)... **30-40**

Cow Bottle Opener/Corkscrew

Bottle opener-corkscrew, figural, model of a stylized cow w/bottle opener on head & the tail a corkscrew, overall 5 1/4" l. (ILLUS.).. **75**

Glass & Chrome Candlesticks

Candlesticks, thick clear glass candle socket w/flattened, flaring rim fitted in a pierced lacy chrome stem w/flaring ringed foot, "Krome Kraft - Farber Bros." mark on base, 4 3/4" h., pr. (ILLUS.) **80-90**

Glass & Chrome Cocktail Glass

Cocktail, rounded purple insert in pierced chrome stem by Farber Brothers, 5 3/8" h. (ILLUS.)... **30**

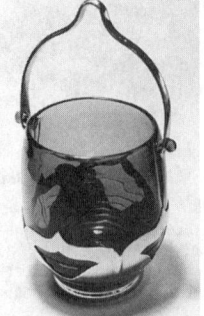

Glass & Chrome Ice Bucket

Ice bucket, high swing bail handle, deep round cylindrical emerald green glass bowl set in a pierced & arched chrome base, Farber Bros. mark on base, 4 1/2" d., 6" h. plus handle (ILLUS.)........ **75-100**

Letter rack, chromed bronze, Art Deco style, four tiers of rectangular upright frames fitted w/curved sheet dividers, attributed to Jacques-Emile Ruhlmann, France, ca. 1925, 19 5/8" l., 8 1/4" h. **11,750**

Glass & Chrome Salt & Peppers

Salt & pepper shakers, bulbous green glass body tapering to a short neck w/applied green shoulder handle, chrome cap & pierced & arched chrome frame, Farber Bros. mark, 3 1/2" h., pr. (ILLUS.)....... **20-25**

Green Glass & Chrome Server

Server, cov., ovoid green glass body w/paneled sides & applied green glass handle, chrome collar w/spout & hinged cover w/pointed finial, 5" d., 10" h. (ILLUS.) **125-150**

Chrome & Glass Silent Butler

Silent butler, shallow round purple glass bowl fitted in a pierced & arched chrome frame w/thick round foot, hinged low domed chrome cover w/engraved sunburst & thumb rest, turned wood handle, Farber Bros. mark, 5 1/4" d. w/4 3/4" l. handle, 2 3/4" h. (ILLUS.) **85-95**

Copper

Copper & White Metal Coffeepot

Coffeepot, cov., footed cylindrical body w/a wide shoulder to the short neck & hinged domed cover w/urn finial, cast white metal scroll handle, spout & shoulder band, late 19th - early 20th c., 10" h. (ILLUS.) **45**

Dish, ten-sided tray-form "Dinanderie," dish, Art Deco style, patinated copper w/inlaid silver geometric designs, stamped "3960 - Jean Dunand," France, ca. 1925, 14 1/4" w. **8,813**

Unusual Copper Funnel

Funnel, deep rounded, ringed bowl w/slender tapering spout, riveted strap side handle w/spring-loaded thumb control, marked on handle "Patent Allowed," overall 8" w., 7 3/4" l. (ILLUS.) **85**

Teakettle, cov., dovetailed construction, domed cover w/brass finial, gooseneck spout, concave strap handle stamped "Hunneman Boston," ca. 1825, base 6 1/2" d., 10" h. (imperfections)...................... **460**

Weathervane, copper & iron, molded copper figure of the Statue of Liberty wearing a radiating crown & holding a torch in an extended hand, on a rectangular platform, the arrow below w/a corrugated copper tail, mounted on iron directionals & two copper spheres, no stand, several dents, minor loss on tail, American, ca. 1886, 56 1/2" h. **23,500**

Weathervane, molded copper model of a steam-driven locomotive & tender car, overall verdigris patina, mounted on a hollow copper rod, no stand, American,

late 19th c., minor dents, 75" l., 29 1/2" h. **237,000**

Weathervane, molded & gilded model of a steeplechase horse, molded in two parts, the horse w/hole-eyes, notched mouth, windswept, stamped & serrated mane & tail, leaping w/forelegs tucked under & rear legs extended over a stamped sheet metal fence on a vertical rod support, A.L. Jewell, Waltham, Massachusetts, mid-19th c., on modern base, 37" l., 34" h. **94,600**

Weathervane, sheet copper & zinc, silhouetted figure of a Native American w/a zinc left arm drawing a bow w/arrow, traces of yellow paint, attributed to A.L. Jewell, Waltham, Massachusetts, mid-19th c., 16 1/2" w., 26" h. **11,750**

Gold

Gold Pin

Pin, commemorative, ornate 14k decoration surrounds words "Waukesha Fire Department" in circle around "Asst Chief" in middle, in honor of Charles H.R. Kranich, appointed assistant fire chief of Waukesha, Wisconsin Fire Department in 1916, retired 1942, w/leather case, 3/8 x 1 1/8" (ILLUS.) **150**

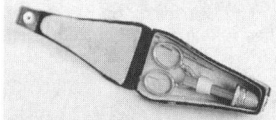

Gold-plated Sewing Kit

Sewing kit, plated, set includes scissors, thimble & tubular needle case in leatherette snap-closure case, closed size 1 x 2", 4 1/4" l. (ILLUS.) **135**

Iron

Andirons, cast, figure of an African-American man standing w/hands on bent knees, early paint w/white shirt, red paints, black skin & painted facial features, paint imperfections, minor corrosion, ca. 1870, 12 1/2 x 16 1/2", 19 1/2" h., pr. **1,380**

Andirons, hand-wrought, miniature, gilded forward looped finial on a simple square shaft above curved front legs w/penny feet, American, early 19th c., 3 1/2" w., 5" h. **460**

Andirons, hand-wrought, miniature, knife blade-style, polyhedron finial on shaft, arched legs on penny feet, worn black paint, American, late 18th - early 19th c., 4" w., 6 3/4" h. **58**

Andirons, hand-wrought, modeled as an upright coiled serpent, the head w/open mouth & projecting tongue, S-form body ending in a coiled tail, bolted to a log support, found in New York state, surface rust, 19th c., 19 3/4" h. **5,463**

Andirons, hand-wrought, the tall shaft topped by a stylized goose head & beak above the serpentine neck continuing into the log bar & supported on boldly scrolled front strapwork legs, worn black paint, American, early 20th c., 18" h., pr. **1,880**

Architectural fragment, cast, large slightly curved plaque cast in bold relief w/a lion head, old weathered surface, American, late 19th c., w/stand, 1 x 11", 15" h. **1,725**

Airedale & Scottie Book End

Book ends, cast, a model of an Airedale & Scottie dog standing on a mound w/brushes & tree roots, bronzed finish, 4 1/2 x 5 1/4", pr. (ILLUS. of one).................. **130**

Cast-iron "The Thinker" Book End

Book ends, cast, bronze finish, image of Rodin's "The Thinker," marked w/style number 582, 2 x 4 1/4", 4 1/4" h., the pr. (ILLUS. of one) **85**

Cowboy & Bucking Bronco Book End

Book ends, cast, copper finish, flat rectangular base supporting upright featuring cowboy on bucking bronco, marked on front "OFW" and on reverse "Copyright A&C, 136," 2 x 4 1/4", 6" h., the pr. (ILLUS. of one) **195**

Cast-iron Book End with Galleon

Book ends, cast, gently arched square upright, cast in high-relief w/a galleon under full sail on a rolling sea, painted in blues, white, black, yellow & green, 5 x 5 1/2", pr. (ILLUS. of one) **55**

Cast-iron Owl Book End

Book ends, cast, gothic arch upright w/large relief cast spread-winged owl, original ivory paint w/wear, marked on back "Design Patented - 1155," 4 x 6 1/2", pr. (ILLUS. of one) **69**

Crouching Lion Book Ends

Book ends, cast, model of crouching lion on large rock, original gold paint, marked "COPR 1930 - Crouching Lion - 916" & "C" in triangle within circle, 5 1/2 x 6", pr. (ILLUS.).. **195**

Polychrome Cast-iron Book End

Book ends, cast, polychrome three-dimensional design of peasant girl at water fountain, w/leaf swags twining around edges of upright, 2 x 4", 5 1/2" h., the pr. (ILLUS. of one) **145**

Cast-iron Laughing Cat Book End

Book ends, cast, rounded square upright centered by cast model of laughing cat, overall shaded brown paint, marked "DAL," 1925, pr. (ILLUS. of one) **115**

Cast-iron Washington Book End

Book ends, cast, squared upright w/arched top, high-relief scene of George Washington on horseback w/troops, antiqued bronze finish, 5 1/2" h., pr. (ILLUS. of one) **115**

Book End with Longfellow Portrait

Book ends, flat gently arched back w/low-relief bust of Longfellow w/quill pen & inkwell, light rust on gold-painted finish, 3 5/8 x 4 1/2", pr. (ILLUS. of one)................... **60**

Cast-iron Parrot Bottle Opener

Bottle opener, cast, model of a stylized parrot on perch, original paint, 5" h. (ILLUS.) **95**
Calipers, hand-wrought, the handle in the form of a coiled snake continuing to a shaft w/four bifurcating riveted arms, w/stand, surface corrosion, possibly Boston Foundry, late 18th c., 12 3/4" w., 17" h. **2,875**

Eighteenth Century Candle Lantern

Candle lantern, hand-forged, w/tapered vents in conical top, applied strap handle, shaved horn panes instead of glass, French or English, ca. 1750, 7 x 9", 16" h. (ILLUS.) **700**

Iron Candle Lantern

Candle lantern, hand-forged, w/three glass panels, circular vents in conical top, ring-shaped strap handle, ca. 1820, 6 x 6 3/4", 13" h. (ILLUS.) **300-500**

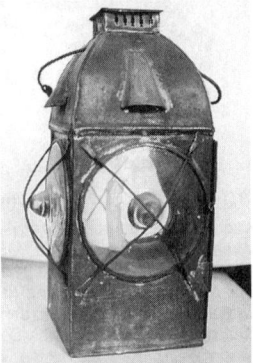

Candle or Whale Oil Lantern

Candle or whale oil lantern, hand-forged, w/tapering vents & pierced top, wire ring handle, bull's-eye glass panes, French, ca. 1710, 8 1/2 x 8 1/2", 13 1/2" h. (ILLUS.) **500-600**

Cast-iron Double Candleholder

Candleholder, cast, domed swag, ribbon & medallion decorated base, straight Greek-style shaft ending in flame decoration & supporting two curved candle branches w/swag designs, ribbons and medallions, ending in ribbed sockets w/flared rims atop drip pans, central support bisecting shaft and upcurving to meet each candle branch at midpoint, overall simulated verdigris patina, 15 1/2" h. (ILLUS.) **175**

Candlestand, wrought, floor-standing, high arched tripod base w/penny feet, scrolled cross bracket w/tension springs & two candle sockets, 61 1/4" h. (old pitted surface) **1,045**

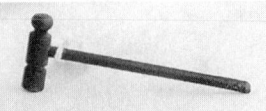

Cast-iron Candy Hammer

Candy hammer, cast, ball-peen, 3 3/4" l. (ILLUS.) **22**

Carriage fenders, cast, articulated horse hoof & ankle cast in the full round & backed by an L-shaped bracket & scrollwork, marked on sides w/maker's name & address, painted black, William Adams & Co., Philadelphia, late 19th c., 6 x 10", 25" h., pr. **2,585**

Crown Coffee Mill

Coffee mill, upright, Landers, Frary & Clark No. 11 Crown Coffee Mill, approx. 12" h. (ILLUS.) **325**

Cast-iron Advertising Dish/Ashtray

Dish/ashtray, cast, advertising-type, almond-shaped w/scalloped flanged rim, the back embossed "Enduro Enamel - Wincroft Stoveworks - Middletown, PA," interior coated in blue enamel, late 19th - early 20th c., 3 x 4" (ILLUS. of back) **145**

Door handle, hand-wrought, modeled as a snake, the head w/open mouth & teeth continuing to a curving body & coiled tail, w/stand, late 19th - early 20th c., surface corrosion, 12 1/4" l., 3 1/2" h. **1,150**

Figural Woodpecker Door Knocker

Door knocker, cast, figural, model of a red-bellied woodpecker hinged on a tree trunk, original worn paint, 2 1/2 x 3 3/4" (ILLUS.) **165**

Door lock, hand-wrought, the rectangular plate w/male & female silhouettes & a key w/quatrefoil terminal, w/stand, 19th c., minor surface corrosion, 8 1/2" w., 11" h. **633**

Cast-iron Ship Doorstop

Doorstop, cast, in the form of a polychrome three-masted ship w/billowing sails, on two feet, style number 205, 3 x 11", 11" h. (ILLUS.) **150**

Cast-iron Elephant Doorstop

Doorstop, cast, long narrow base holding figure of trumpeting elephant, style number indistinct, 2 1/4 by 11 1/4", 8 1/2" h. (ILLUS.) **250**

Doorstop, cast, model of a fat seated bear, open legs, painted brown, American, late 19th - early 20th c., 2 1/2 x 5 1/4", 4 1/2" h. **1,150**

Figural Airedale Doorstop

Doorstop, cast, model of a standing Airedale facing viewer, traces of original paint, 8 5/8" l., 8" h. (ILLUS.) **300**

Cast-iron Covered Wagon Doorstop

Doorstop, cast, pioneer couple driving covered wagon pulled by pair of oxen, worn original beige paint, marked w/style number 64, © and "LVL" (?), 2 x 10", 6 1/2" h. (ILLUS.) **145**

Down spout, cast, a shaped rectangular top w/pointed projection above a conforming frieze w/the wording "18 AD 68," over a tapering shaft, painted white, on a square base fitted w/a cylindrical attachment, American, dated 1868, 9 1/2 x 16", 17 1/2" h. **353**

Early Cast-iron Drawer Pull

Drawer pull, cast, long flat bar centered by an embossed face of a spaniel-type dog, worn black paint, late 19th - early 20th c., 4" l. (ILLUS.) **20**

Egg beater, cast, "Cyclone Pat. 6-25-1901 Reissue 8-26-1902," 11 1/2" **85**

Egg beater, cast, "Dover Egg Beater U.S.A.," 10 3/4" **40**

Egg beater, cast, "Holt's Patented Flared Dasher Egg Beater N.Y. U.S.A.," 10 1/2" **45**

Egg beater, cast, "Perfection Pat'd Feb. 22, 1898 Albany N.Y.," 10 1/4" **350**

R.P. Scott & Co. Eggbeater

Egg beater, cast, "R.P. Scott & Co. Newark N.J. Patented," 10 1/2" (ILLUS.) **1,250**
Flint striker, hand-wrought, silhouetted figure of a kneeling child on a scrolling sled, w/stand, late 18th - early 19th c., minor surface corrosion, found in Pennsylvania, 3 1/2" h. **1,265**

Patented Cast-iron & Steel Chopper

Food chopper, cast, iron loop handle w/four-section bell-shaped steel blade, handle marked "NRS & Co., Groton, NY - Patented May 2, 93 - No. 40," 5 1/2" l. (ILLUS.) **25**
Food chopper, hand-wrought, the rectangular blade pivoting on a female figural post above a shaped wood block base,

old red paint on wood, American, 19th c., paint wear at blade **489**

Unique Fraternal Order Emblem

Fraternal order emblem, cast, wall-type, for the Modern Woodmen of America, a large crossed ax & hammer joined by a ribbon & w/a center banner reading "MW of A," original red, white, gold & green paint, 7 3/4 x 12 1/4" (ILLUS.) **400**
Gate, cast, rectangular openwork form centering a War of 1812 cap surrounded by military trophies including crossed rifles, swords, bugle & shot bag marked "U.S.," & acorn leaves, flanked on each side by crossed darts & above & below by a band of circles, the top set w/stars flanked by spear points, repainted in green, red, black & white, American, late 19th c., 77" l., 45 1/4" h. **5,875**
Gate latch, sand-cast, model of a duck's head, the head forming the articulated handle, possibly California, late 19th c., w/stand, weathered surface, 3 3/4 x 7", 3 1/2" h. **230**
Gate weight, cast, modeled as a full sun face, loop handle at top, Massachusetts, late 18th c., w/stand, 9" d. **10,925**

Old Painted Harness Hook

Harness hook, cast, a long top hook w/up-turned tip above a short curved hook, old flaking white paint, late 19th - early 20th c., 7 1/2" l. (ILLUS.) **20**
Hitching post, cast, a realistic horse head finial cast in the round w/detailed curly mane, ears, eyes & nostrils, on a lobed capital over a tall fluted column footed by a lion heads & scrolls above a faceted base, modern sheet metal foot, American, late 19th c., 8 1/2 x 9", 48 3/4" h. **2,115**
Hitching post, cast, a ring finial above a tapering neck over a tall spiral-cast column w/a stylized leaf base band & plinth, new square foot, painted yellow, American, late 19th c., 11 3/4 x 12", 49" h. **1,058**

Hitching post, cast, a stylized horse head at the top w/pronounced ears & delineated mane above a side ring & a fluted column on a new square base, painted black, American, late 19th c., 27 1/2" h. **705**

Hitching post, cast, diminutive model of a horse head, long & small rings in the mouth, traces of black paint, Rochester, New York, ca. 1850, on stand, 4 1/2" w., 9 7/8" h. **1,840**

Hitching post, cast, model of a dog's head w/a large ring in its mouth, traces of black paint, w/stand, American, 19th c., minor surface rust, 11" w., 12"h. **4,025**

Hitching post, cast, model of a tall tree trunk w/molded bark, cast in the round w/stubby branches & a meandering berries vine above a grassy base, trunk painted brown, vine & grass painted green, American, 19th c., 35 3/4" h. **353**

Hitching post, cast, the top w/a realistic horse head w/detailed curly mane, ears, eyes, nostrils & mouth w/a ring above a lobed capital flanked by rings, over a fluted column w/lion heads & scrolls at the base, painted brown, modern square foot, American, late 19th c., 35 1/2" h. **2,233**

Hitching post, cast, the top w/an open trefoil finial above a flattened flaring shaft pierced w/quatrefoil & round openings, painted brown, American, late 19th c., modern base, 10 x 10", 39" h. **705**

Hitching post finial, cast, a stylized head of Napoleon cast in the full round, detailed hair & facial features, fringed epaulets on shoulders, a ring at the side of one shoulder, on a cylindrical attachment base, American, 19th c., 8" h. **4,465**

Hitching post finial, cast, model of a small horse head hinged on post cap so it nods, traces of black paint, patented in 1889 by W.H. Vaughn, Quincy, Illinois, no stand, losses, 7" w., 5" h. **316**

Hitching post finial, cast, modeled as a human hand w/closed fingers above a ruffled cuff, cast in the full round, a chain attached from side to side, on a modern base, American, late 19th c., overall 9 1/4" h. **3,760**

Hitching post finial, cast, stylized head of an African-American man holding a ring & chain in his mouth, 19th c., w/later stand, 5 1/2 x 6", 9 1/2" h. **2,300**

Hitching post finials, cast, model of a horse head w/articulated ears, eyes, mane & nostrils cast in the full round, mouth pierced & holding a bar w/a ring at each end, on a cylindrical base, on a modern rectangular foot, American, 19th c., overall 9 1/2" h., pr. **1,058**

Hitching post top, cast, model of a horse head w/loop at nose suspending a large ring, old weathered surface, American, 19th c., w/stand, 4 1/4 x 9 1/2", 11 1/2" h. **633**

Hitching posts, cast, a horse head w/articulated ears, mane, eyes & nostrils cast in the full round, pierced mouth w/iron ring above a cylindrical post, on a later square base, American, 19th c., 20 1/2" h., pr. **621**

Hitching posts, cast, the top cast as the head of an eagle w/detailed crown, eyes & beak above a feathered neck over a baluster-form shaft w/scrolled decorations above a ball & plinth base, traces of black paint, modern foot, American, mid-19th c., 46 1/2" h., pr. **4,465**

Hitching posts, cast, the top formed by a looped swan's head w/feathered & imbricated neck above a slender three-part ribbed shaft, painted black, modern square base, American, 19th c., 52 1/2" h., pr. **2,115**

Beehive-form Inkwell

Inkwell, cast, base w/flared scalloped rim holds beehive form w/stylized leaf decoration & hinged lid, marked "patent applied for," 2 1/2 x 4 1/4" (ILLUS.) **245**

Elaborate Cast-iron Double Inkwell

Inkwell, cast, elaborate double inkwell & pen rest decorated w/cherubs & pierced floral & scroll design, black finish may be repaint, 3 x 11 1/2 x 12 1/2" (ILLUS.) **265**

Jar lid reformer, cast, "The Eakin Mfg Co. Salem, Ohio," 7" **40**

Jar opener, cast, "Mfd by Hoffman Hinge & Fdry Co. Cleveland, O," 8" **30**

Knife sharpener, cast, "Dazey Sharpit, Dazey Churn & Mfg. Co. St. Louis, Mo.," 5 1/2" **25**

Cast-iron Elephant Match Holder

Match holder, cast, in the form of a walking elephant carrying box for matches on its back, folds of elephant's neck used for striking, black paint, 3 x 8", 5" h. (ILLUS.)... **75**

Victorian Shoe-form Match Holder

Match holder, cast, model of a high-topped Victorian lady's shoe raised on a rectangular base, worn original paint, late 19th c., 3 1/4 x 4 5/8", 5 1/2" h. (ILLUS.)................. **75**

Iron Crescent Stove Match Holder

Match holder, w/pierced silver-plate emblem w/"Crescent Stove - 1901," circular rimmed base, 2 x 3 1/4" (ILLUS.) **145**

Meat cleaver, hand-wrought, the blade in the form of a woman practicing calisthenics, her brass & wood extended leg form the handle, probably Northeastern United States, ca. 1880, w/stand, surface rust, minor nicks in blade, 12 3/4" l., 7" h. .. **1,840**

Meat cleaver, hand-wrought, the shaped blade w/an eagle's head at top corner, the wood & brass handle ending in a brass boot, 20th c., w/stand, minor surface corrosion, 11 1/2" l., 4 1/2" h. **431**

Meat rack, hanging type, five wrought iron three-pronged hooks w/large hanger at top, 14" d., 16" h... **385**

Iron Miner's Candlestick

Miner's candlestick, a.k.a. "sticking tommy," hand-forged, cylindrical holder for candle, w/two sharp prongs, one straight, one hooked, for fixing holder in mine wall, timber, hat, etc., ca. 1840, 1 3/4 x 2 3/4 x 7 1/2" (ILLUS.) **300**

Ornate Cast-iron Mirror Frame

Mirror frame, cast, table model, a large oval frame w/scrolls at the top swiveling between a wide U-form harp supported by the seated seminude woman, old gold finish, late 19th - early 20th c., marked w/style number 372, 14" h. (ILLUS.)............. **250**

Model of a cat head, cast, a large stylized head w/long whiskers, mounting holes in ears & nose, patinated, late 19th c., w/stand, 8 x 8" **1,495**

Model of a greyhound, cast, hollow body w/good detail & late black paint, 21" h., 50" l. (welded repairs to tail)........................ **1,430**

Model of a standing horse, hand-wrought, silhouetted sheet on a rectangular stand, old pitted surface, possibly New York state, 19th c., 9 1/2" l., 8 3/4" h. **978**

Model of an eagle, cast, small spread-winged bird perched on a rockwork base, old black paint w/white spots, American, late 19th c., 5 1/2 x 11", 3 1/2" h. **242**

Figural Cast-iron Paper Clamp

Paper clamp, cast, hanging-type, bold-relief bust of a smiling black man, old worn gold finish, marked on back w/style number 5247, 2 1/2 x 4" (ILLUS.) **125**

Cast-iron Scottie Paperweight

Paperweight, cast, figural, model of a seated Scottie dog, worn original paint, ca. 1930s, 3 1/4" h. (ILLUS.) **75**

Cast-iron Plant Holder or Lamp Arm

Plant holder or lamp arm, cast, Victorian, decorated w/tendrils & scrolls & stylized leaf motif, ca. 1880, 5 3/4 x 7 1/2 x 10 1/2" (ILLUS.) **150-200**

Cast-iron World War I Soldier Plaque

Plaque, cast, round w/relief cast scene of World War I soldier carrying German helmets & motto "And they thought we couldn't fight," 9" d. (ILLUS.) **195**

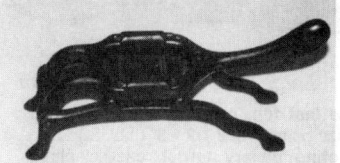

Patented Raisin Seeder

Raisin seeder, cast, four leg base, "Pat'd May 7, 95," 6" (ILLUS.) **500**
Raisin seeder, cast iron w/tin tray, "EZY Raisin Seeder, Pat May 21, 1895" **250**

Miniature Sausage Grinder

Sausage grinder, cast, miniature, marked "J.P. Co., NYC," 2 1/2 x 3 3/4" (ILLUS.) **35**

Cast-iron Shackles

Shackles, cast, original connecting chain, no key, 3 1/2" w., overall 16" l., pr. (ILLUS.) **185**

Old Iron Sheep Shears

Sheep shears, wrought, one-piece construction w/loop strap handle & long pointed blades, worn surface, 10 1/4" l. (ILLUS.) **20**

Cast-iron Shoe Last Top

Shoe last top, cast, w/original red paint, 1 3/4 x 5" (ILLUS.) **14**

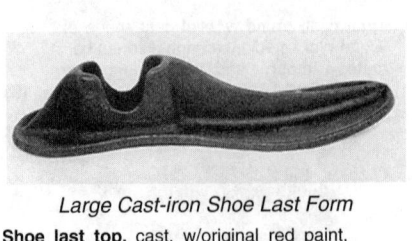

Large Cast-iron Shoe Last Form

Shoe last top, cast, w/original red paint, size number 3, 2 1/2 x 8" (ILLUS.) **12**

Shooting gallery target, cast elephant, white paint, rare large size, 9 1/2" l. (paint flaking).. **248**

Sign, painted sheet iron, in the shape of a large standing chicken, weathered putty-colored paint & faintly stenciled word "DINNERS," American, 23 1/2 x 28 3/4" **805**

Stable vents, cast, circular pierced form centering a relief-molded profile horse head above a torso on lattice ground enclosed by a roundel, one cast w/"C.G. Ellis - 1865," the other "J.C. Ellis - 1865," probably J.W. Fiske & Co., New York, New York, ca. 1865, 18" d., pr. **1,998**

Tobacco cutter, wood & hand-wrought iron, figural, the wooden handle joining a blade centered by a small silhouetted human head, pivoting on a post in the form of a full silhouetted human figure on a block of wood, 19th c., cracks in base block, surface rust on blade, base block 9 1/2 x 9 3/4", cutter overall 16" l., 6 1/2" h. **920**

Trade signs, cast, a standing figure of a Native American princess cast in the full round, articulated hair, facial features, fringed clothing & shoes, applied green-painted hair ornament & tobacco leaf held in right hand, on a rocky base, remnants of brown paint, American, late 19th c., 7 1/2 x 7 1/2", 25" h., pr. **11,163**

Strause Gas Iron Company Trivet

Trivet, cast, for gas iron, almond-shaped w/pierced center w/the design of an early iron, top edge reads "Double Point 'I Want U' Comfort Iron - Strause Gas Iron Co.," unpainted, early 20th c., 7 1/2" l. (ILLUS.).. **50**

Enterprise Sad Iron Trivet

Trivet, cast, for sad iron, pierced script "E" in the center, edges read "Enterprise M'f"g Co. Phil'a. U.S.A.," old black paint, 6 1/8" l. (ILLUS.)... **25**

W.H. Howell Sad Iron Trivet

Trivet, cast, for sad iron, pointed w/cast "H" in center, reads around edges "W.H. Howell Co. - Geneva, Ill.," old black paint, 6" l. (ILLUS.) **25**

Cleveland Foundry Company Trivet

Trivet, cast, for sad iron, pointed w/center pierced w/a star & sunburst, reads around the edge "The Cleveland Foundry Co.," old black paint, 6" l. (ILLUS.) **25**

Trivet, hand-wrought, modeled of a coiled snake, incised underside, on three short scroll legs, minor surface corrosion, found in Pennsylvania, 19th c., 4 3/4 x 10 1/2", 3 1/4" h. **978**

Wall plaques, cast, half-round model of a fruit-filled cornucopia, the horn painted bright red w/yellow trim, the fruits in red, green & black, American, early 20th c., 15" l., pr. **10,575**

Water trough, cast, rectangular, a high arched back splash plate w/the maker's name along the base & a small cast lion mask spout over a grilled overflow drain in the base, the main drain stopped w/a iron plug, the whole set on a bracket base, J.W. Fiske & Co., New York, New York, late 19th c., 24 x 35 1/2", 38" h. **1,293**

Mid-century Rooster Weathervane

Weathervane, stamped sheet iron, a rooster w/a fancy tail atop a long arrow over scrolls, plastic mount & egg-shaped sleeve above directionals, adjustable base, ca. 1950, 22 3/4" l., 26 3/4" h. (ILLUS.)... **400**

Windmill weight, cast, model of a large rooster, full round in Mogul form w/detailed orange-painted comb, eyes & wattle & white-painted beak, body & molded tail, on a rectangular base fitting over a later stepped stand, American, early 20th c., 19 1/2" w., 23" h. **8,813**

Early Iron Windmill Weight

Windmill weight, cast, model of a rooster w/arched grooved tail, worn original

white paint & red comb & wattle, ca. 1900, size without stand 18" w., 17" h. (ILLUS.) **2,400**

Windmill weight, cast, model of a rooster w/pointed comb, detailed eye, beak & wattle w/a rainbow-style arched tail above an integral rectangular base, on a later flaring cylindrical stand, painted red, American, 20th c., 16" w., 24 3/4" h. **5,640**

Windmill weight, cast, model of a seated squirrel, light brown paint, on original base, attributed to Elgin Wind Power & Pump Co., Elgin, Illinois, early 20th c., w/new black metal stand, 13 1/2 x 17 1/4" **3,220**

Windmill weight, cast, model of a small rooster w/detailed comb, eye, wattle & notched tail above an integral rectangular base, on a later stand, tail marked "Hummer - E184," American, 19th c., 3 1/4 x 10", 9 1/4" h. **1,998**

Windmill weight, cast, model of a stylized rooster head w/detailed comb, eyes, beak, wattle & sawtooth tail, tail marked "10 FT No 2," integral rectangular base, American, late 19th - early 20th c., 3 1/2 x 17", 15 1/2" h. **940**

Windmill weight, cast, model of a stylized rooster w/detailed comb, eyes, beak, wattle & sawtooth comb, on an integral rectangular base, late 19th - early 20th c., 3 1/2 x 17", 15 1/2" h. **1,410**

Lead

Cast-lead Paperweight

Paperweight, cast, figure of sleeping child curled up w/head resting on sleeping dog, made by Golden Novelty Manufacturing Co., 4 1/2" l. (ILLUS.) **45**

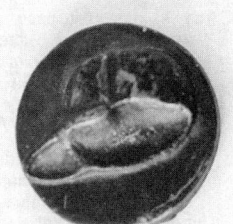
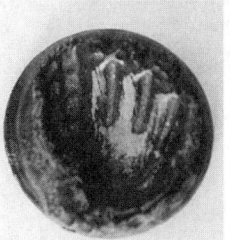

Baseball Cap & Glove Paperweights

Paperweights, cast, round, one cast w/a baseball cap, the other w/a baseball glove, worn black paint, ca. 1950, 3" d., pr. (ILLUS., bottom previous page) **80**

Miniature Cast Lead Statue

Statue, cast, miniature figure of a seated nude boy checking the bottom of one foot, 4 3/4" h. (ILLUS.) **35**

Charging Toy Soldier

Toy soldier, figure on flat base, holding rifle as though charging w/fixed bayonet, muzzle broken off, worn paint, 3" h. (ILLUS.) **20**

Lead Marching Toy Soldier

Toy soldier, figure on flat base, marching, w/rifle over shoulder, green helmet, marked "Made in USA," w/"M" in circle and style number "4578," 3 1/2" h. (ILLUS.) **24**

Lead Toy Soldier

Toy soldier, figure on flat base, standing at attention w/rifle at side, WWI-style helmet, worn paint, marked "Made in USA - 707," 3" h. (ILLUS.) **19**

Toy Soldier in Poncho

Toy soldier, flat base, marching figure wearing poncho & green helmet, rifle slung over shoulder, marked "USA - 523 - M," 2 3/4" h. (ILLUS.) **45**

Pewter

Basin, round w/upright sides, Thomas Badger, Boston, Massachusetts, 1737-1815, 9 1/4" d. (minor scratches) **1,380**

Candlesticks, typical ringed form, Henry Hopper, New York, New York, 1842-47, 12" h., pr. (minor surface imperfections) **633**

Chocolate Mold with Image of Diesel Engine

Chocolate mold, cast, hinged, incised design of a diesel train engine & tender, marked "E & Co. NY 1225," closed 7" l. (ILLUS. open)...................... 110

Dish, round shallow form, Thomas Danforth, Middletown, Connecticut, 1775-82, 13 1/4" d. (minor pitting, surface scratches)................................... 1,035

Dish, round w/deep sides, William Billings, Providence, Rhode Island, 1791-1806, 11 3/8" d. (scratches, minor pitting)........... 1,840

Flagon, cov., tall slightly tapering cylindrical body w/a round domed hinged cover, S-shaped spurred handle, eagle touch of Thomas D. Boardman, Hartford, Connecticut & Boardman & Co., New York, 1805-50, 11 1/4" h. (minor wear)............... 1,840

Plate, round w/flanged rim, "London" touch of John Skinner, Boston, Massachusetts, 1760-90, 8 1/2" d......................... 303

Plate, round w/flanged rim, Roswell Gleason, Dorchester, Massachusetts, 1822-71, 9 1/4" d. (some wear & dents)................. 275

Plates, set of eight, all have "London" touch marks, some are marked "Superfine," rims stamped "I.H.B.," 9 1/4" d., the set 935

Large Pewter Platter

Platter, oval Art Nouveau-style platter decorated w/raised images of a muskie chasing a smaller fish, w/crabs, sea horses, starfish and squid around rim, marked on back "Kayserzinn 4325," 11 1/2 x 23 3/4" (ILLUS.)............................. 170

Porringer, Gershom Jones, Providence, Rhode Island, 1744-1809, 5 1/2" d. (minor surface imperfections) 1,840

Porringer, pierced crown handle w/spline support on back, David Melville, Newport, Rhode Island, 1755-93, 4 1/4" d. (minor surface imperfections)..................... 1,495

Porringer, round w/pierced crown & scroll handle, Thomas D. & Sherman Boardman, Hartford, Connecticut, 1810-30, 5" d. (minor pitting & scratches, polished)...... 440

Porringer, round w/pierced floral scroll handle, Samuel Hamlin, Jr., Providence, Rhode Island, 1801-56, 5 3/8" d. (minor dents) 550

Porringer, round w/pierced floral scroll handle, Thomas D. & Sherman Boardman, Hartford, Connecticut, 1810-30, 5 1/4" d. (dent)................................... 660

Porringer, round w/pierced floral scroll handle, William Billings, Providence, Rhode Island, 1791-1806, 5 1/8" d. (minor pitting & scratches, polished) 550

Porringer, round w/pierced floral scroll handle, William Calder, Providence, Rhode Island, 1817-56, 5" d....................... 660

Porringer, round w/pierced geometric handle, Samuel E. Hamlin, Jr., Providence, Rhode Island, 1801-56, 4 1/8" d. (minor pitting, polished)............................ 495

Porringer, round w/pierced Old English-style handle, Thomas D. & Sherman Boardman, Hartford, Connecticut, 1810-30, 4" d. 715

Porringer, round w/pierced scroll & crown handle, touch mark "IG," New England, 4 1/4" d. (minor dent)............................... 330

Sugar bowl, cov., flattened ball-form decorated w/chased foliate decoration around the belly, S-scroll handles, Thomas D. Boardman, Hartford, Connecticut, 1805-50, 5 3/4" h. (possibly mismatched cover, interior pitting)................................. 374

Teapot, cov., lighthouse-form, tall tapering cylindrical body w/raised rings around the top & base & w/engraved shield-shaped panels surrounded by flowers on each side, domed hinged cover w/disk finial, pointed C-scroll black-painted wooden handle, swan's-neck spout, Eben Smith, Beverly, Massachusetts, 1813-56, 11 3/4" h. 468

Teapot, cov., pedestal base below the gently flaring cylindrical body w/a high waisted neck, domed cover w/wood finial, painted ornate scroll handle, swan's-neck spout, George Richardson, Sr., Boston, Massachusetts, & Cranston, Rhode Island, 1818-1828, 9 1/2" h. (handle repaint, minor cover repair)..................... 330

Teapot, cov., ring-turned round pedestal foot below a flaring cylindrical lower body & tall waisted upper body w/flaring rim, hinged stepped & domed cover w/disk finial, large pointed scroll black-enameled handle, swan's-neck spout, Rufus Durham, Westbrook, Maine, 1837-61, 12" h. (minor dent on base)........................... 468

Teapot, cov., round foot & short pedestal below the wide squatty bulbous body w/a wide shoulder tapering to a short flaring neck, hinged domed cover w/disk finial, re-enameled black metal C-scroll handle, swan's-neck spout, Daniel Curtis, Albany, New York,1822-40, 9" h. 440

Teapot, cov., round pedestal foot below the tall body w/a slightly flaring cylindrical lower section below a tall stepped & slightly waisted upper body w/flared rim, hinged domed cover w/finial, ornate black-painted C-scroll handle, swan's-neck spout, William Savage, Middletown, Connecticut, late 1830s, 10" h. (light overall pitting)... **440**

Teapot, cov., round stepped foot below the wide squatty bulbous body tapering to a short flaring neck, hinged domed cover w/wooden disk finial, pointed scrolled handle, swan's-neck spout, tooled line trim, Roswell Gleason, Dorchester, Massachusetts, 1822-71, 7 1/2" h. (light pitting).. **330**

Teapot, cov., short foot below the bulbous body w/a tall wide waisted neck & hinged domed cover, high C-scroll metal handle & swan's-neck spout, Josiah Danforth, Middletown, Connecticut, 1821-1843, 7" h. (minor dents)... **440**

Silver

American (Sterling & Coin)

Round Alvin Silver Bowl

Bowl, round, plain concentric sides, rim w/stylized leaf & scroll designs, marked "Alvin Sterling - 108," 5 5/8" d. (ILLUS.) **65**

Whiting Sterling Silver Bowl

Bowl, round, w/scalloped edge & raised design of flowers, leaves & scrolls, mark of the Whiting Mfg. Company & "Sterling - 5593," 925/1000 fine, 9" d. (ILLUS.) **395**

Bowl with Beaded Edge

Bowl, simple round, flat-bottomed bowl w/flaring sides w/beaded rim, engraved "WHS," marked on bottom "Sterling - AFRB - 5182," 7 3/4" d. (ILLUS.)..................... **85**

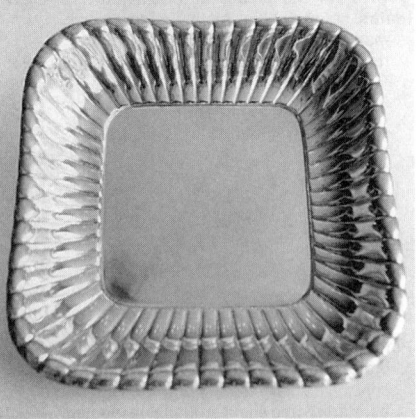

Square Reed & Barton Sterling Bowl

Bowl, square, flaring sides w/reeded design, Reed & Barton mark, style number "X301," 9 1/2" square (ILLUS.) **195**

Bowl, wide scrolling rim w/repoussé floral motifs, center monogram "DND," S. Kirk & Sons, early 20th c., 11 1/2" d. **364**

Compote, open, Martelé type w/fairy design, the wide shallow bowl w/shaped rim hammered w/chased fairies & poppies, on a slender flaring pedestal chased w/poppies & leaves, signed & dated on the base, Clemens Friedell, Pasadena, California, 1914, 10 1/2" d., 6 3/4" h. **9,775**

Sterling Silver Dish

Dish, flat bowl w/upraised rim consisting of pierced panels decorated w/scrolls & stylized leaves, Simpson, Hall, Miller & Co. mark & "Sterling - 660 - N.P.," 4 5/8" d. (ILLUS.)... **50**

Dish, round, a shallow dished center framed by a wide flattened rim ornately chased w/flowers & leaves, monogrammed in the center, S. Kirk & Son, Inc., early 20th c., 10" d., 1 1/4" h. **392**

Goblets, Patt. #1693, w/monogram "R," dated 1926, Gorham Mfg. Co., Providence, Rhode Island, 6 1/2" h., set of 12 ...... **952**

Ladle, scrolling leaf & floral design & monogram "JBH," Durgin Co., early 20th c., 12 1/2" l. **179**

Miniature Sterling Muffineer

Muffineer, miniature, baluster-form decorated w/stylized floral designs, marked "Sterling" w/indistinct company initials, 1 1/2" h. (ILLUS.).. **195**

Napkin Ring with Elephant Head

Napkin ring, arched band mounted w/the head of a trumpeting elephant, marked "Sterling," 2 1/4" l. (ILLUS.)............................... **55**

Porringer, coin, the round bombé body w/slightly domed center, the handle pierced w/geometric designs & engraved w/contemporary initials, the side of the body engraved w/a succession of later owners' initials, Johannis Nys, Philadelphia, ca. 1715-20, 5 1/8" d. **9,200**

Punch bowl, of bombé circular form, the hammered surface w/frosted finish, the handles formed as realistic horse heads, a bit below each, the sides applied in full-relief w/bunches of grapes & overlapping vines stemming from a tendril which encircles the short pedestal, stepped & molded foot, gilt interior, Dominick & Haff, New York, New York, retailed by Theodore B. Starr, 1882, overall length 21 3/4" **32,200**

Salver on foot, coin, circular shallow dish w/molded rim on a tall capstan foot w/molded base, the center of the top engraved w/contemporary initials, the back engraved w/scratch weight, marked three times, Johannis Nys, Philadelphia, ca. 1715-20, 5 1/16" d., 2 1/4" h. **60,250**

Soup tureen, cover, platter & ladle, Wave Edge patt., squatty lobed bombé form w/heavy loop handles, marked, Tiffany & Co., New York, New York, ca. 1885-95, tureen overall 17 1/2" l., the set **23,000**

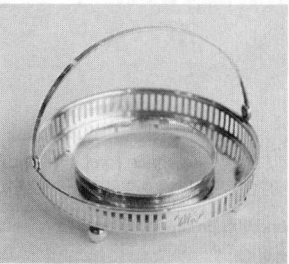

Sterling Sugar Cube Holder

Sugar cube holder, low pierced ring-form w/small ball feet & a thin swing handle, engraved initials on the rim, marked "925 Fine - Sterling" & a bird emblem, 5 1/4" d. (ILLUS.) **225**

Tankard, cov., plain slightly tapered cylindrical form w/molded rim & base band, flat domed cover w/shaped peak, lobate scroll thumb piece, the hinge decorated w/wrigglework, the scroll handle engraved w/early initials, shield terminal, John Coney, Boston, ca. 1690-1700, 6 1/4" h. **32,200**

Tankard, cov., tapered cylindrical form engraved w/arms in rococo cartouche above a molded girdle, stepped domed cover w/urn finial, scroll handle engraved w/early initials, the lower handle terminal applied w/a grotesque mask, marked on the body, William Simpkins, Boston, ca. 1750-60, 8 1/2" h. **6,325**

Tea & coffee service: cov. teapot, cov. coffeepot, cov. sugar bowl, creamer, waste bowl & kettle on lamp stand; each in

Classical Revival style of hexagonal vase form on pedestal bases, applied swags of flowers, beaded borders, matching elongated octagonal tray w/incurved sides, Redlich, New York, New York, ca. 1925, kettle on stand overall 13" h., the set **7,475**

Tea & coffee service: cov. teapot, cov. coffeepot, cov. sugar bowl, creamer, waste bowl & kettle on lamp stand; Aesthetic Movement style, each of tapered square form w/cast floral finials & branch-form ear handles w/shaped ivory heat stopper, each body w/overall embossed decoration of different flowers, on textured grounds, supported by four peg feet, w/inscriptions on the bottoms, Gorham Mfg. Co., Providence, Rhode Island, 1880-81, kettle overall 12 1/2" h., the set **12,650**

Sterling Silver Top

Toy top, w/sections denoting card hands, faceted spinning surface, probably ebony, made by Gorham & marked "Sterling 50P," 2 1/2" d. (ILLUS.) **125**

Tray, round, the gently flared rim w/a raised twig & grapevine border, the center decorated w/an engine-cut design & a center cartouche w/monogram, A.G. Schultz & Co., retailed by Sylvan Bros., ca. 1913, 14" d. **1,232**

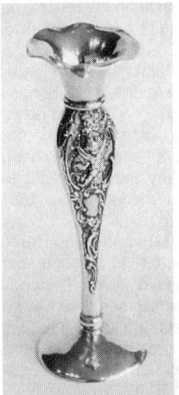

Small Sterling Bud Vase

Vase, bud-type, plain round foot below the slender swelled body chased w/cherubs & scrolls, 2 1/4" d., 6" h. (ILLUS.).................. **450**

Vases, 10" h., basket form w/loop handle & oval molded base, pierced leaf decoration, sterling liner, Tiffany & Co., ca. 1930, pr. **1,400**

English & Other

Miniature Book with Silver Covers

Book, sterling silver covers decorated w/a scrolling leafy vine & blossom & titled "A Christmas Carol," complete paper contents, worn English hallmarks, dated 1904, 3/8 x 1 1/8 x 2 1/8" (ILLUS.)................. **165**

Bowl, a blossom petal-form bowl w/a shaped rim, the sides chased & embossed w/panels of flowers, birds & carp on a textured ground, a plain roundel on one side, scrolling serpentine side handles, on a flaring round foot, China, Kaishu script marks, late 19th c., 13" l. **805**

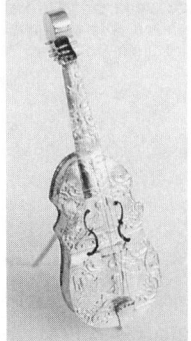

Silver Bass Fiddle Box

Box, cov., model of a bass fiddle, decorated w/cherubs & scrollwork, Europe, late 19th - early 20th c., 2 1/8 x 6 1/8" (ILLUS.) **795**

Small Round Silver Box

Box, cov., round w/flared base & rim, domed cover w/florette finial, Europe, late 19th - early 20th c., 1 1/2 x 1 1/2" (ILLUS.)... **125**

Sterling Victorian Butter Dish

Butter dish, cov., w/metal insert, domed cover heavily engraved w/scrollwork & the initial "H," maker's name & English hallmarks, late 19th c., 8 1/4" d., 5" h. (ILLUS.).. **1,695**

Silver Cart with Stork & Driver

Cart, figural two-wheeled cart w/a small figural boy driving, pulled by a large standing stork, worn hallmarks, Europe, late 19th c., 3" l., 2" h. (ILLUS.) **795**

Coffeepot, cov., Rococo style, tall pyriform on three curved legs w/pad feet headed by rocaille, the spirally-fluted body w/short spout & wood scroll handle, the high-domed hinged cover w/flower finial, engraved initials under base, struck w/French control marks for 1809-1819, Mons, Belgium, 1775, 11 1/2" h. **10,158**

Cup, deep rounded bowl w/embossed floral & prunus panels & a central shield cartouche, molded rim & cast dragon-form handles, knopped stem & domed foot w/embossed leaves, Hoaching, Canton, China, second half 19th c., 8 1/2" h. **2,415**

Ecuelle (shallow bowl), Louis XV Provincial-style, shallow round form w/two cast shell-form handles, one side engraved w/a coat-of-arms & supporters under a coronet, marked on base, Troyes, France, 1757-58, overall 12" l. **2,390**

Sterling Egg Server with Egg Cups

Egg server, an oval tray w/a low pierced gallery edge & a tall central scrolling loop handle fitted w/scroll spoon brackets, pierced scroll feet, fitted w/a set of six footed egg cups w/pierced sides, English hallmarks, late 19th - early 20th c., 6 1/2 x 8 1/2", 9" h., the set (ILLUS.) **2,495**

Inkstand, oval form on four shell-and-vine-clad feet, a border of shells & foliage, the stand set w/stiff-leaf frames enclosing two round silver-mounted cut glass ink bottles & a central rectangular cut-glass bottle w/domed silver cover w/bud finial, Paul Storr, London, England, 1817, 10 1/8" l. **4,780**

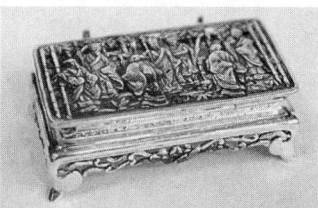

Silver Box-form Inkstand

Inkstand, rectangular low box on a scroll-trimmed base, the top cast in bold relief w/a band of Oriental figures, opens to three wells & a pen rest, Europe, late 19th - early 20th c., 3 1/2 x 5", 1 3/4" h. (ILLUS.) **295**

Unique Turtle Shell & Silver Box

Jewelry box, cov., model of a turtle, the lid formed by an actual turtle shell, the base w/head & legs in silver, artist-signed, Europe, late 19th - early 20th c., 5 1/4 x 7 1/2", 3 1/4" h. (ILLUS.).................... **495**

Silver Cross-end Knife Rest

Knife rest, pierced cross-form ends joined by a slender bar, stamped number, Europe, late 19th - early 20th c., 3 1/4" l. (ILLUS.)... **125**

Miniature Silver Crown

Model of a crown, miniature, pierced & engraved, marked w/a letter "M" under a crown & an indistinct animal mark, Europe, 1 1/2 x 2" (ILLUS.) **225**

Miniature Silver Slant-front Desk

Model of a desk, miniature, Rococo slant-front style, working drawers & fall-front, cabriole legs, indistinct hallmarks, Europe, late 19th - early 20th c., 2 1/8 x 2 1/4 x 3 1/8" (ILLUS.)........................ **695**

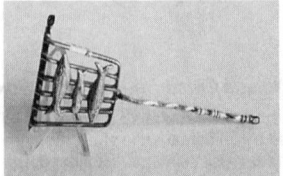

Miniature Fireplace Grill with Fish

Model of a fireplace grill, miniature, a square rack w/a slender twisted handle, complete w/tiny fish, impressed dagger mark, Europe, late 19th - early 20th c., 3 1/2" l. (ILLUS.)... **150**

Miniature Silver Floor Harp

Model of a harp, miniature, floor-model instrument fitted w/a tiny figure of an 18th c. man at the base & a small dog at the top, Europe, late 19th - early 20th c., 2 3/4" l., 4 1/4" h. (ILLUS.)............................... **195**

Miniature Silver Wirework Settee

Model of a settee, miniature settee w/pierced wirework resembling wicker, unmarked, probably Europe, early 20th c., 2 1/2" l. (ILLUS.) **195**

Miniature Sewing Rocker in Silver

Model of a sewing rocker, back w/thin crest rail & lower rail, square seat, Europe, late 19th - early 20th c., 1 3/4" h. (ILLUS.) **150**

Miniature Silver Sleigh

Model of a sleigh, miniature open cutter, probably Europe, early 20th c., 1 7/8" l. (ILLUS.).. **175**

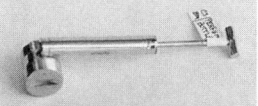

Pheasant-shaped Perfume Container

Perfume container, model of a pheasant, well-detailed, on an overall base w/a blue enamel band, removable head, Europe, late 19th - early 20th c., 5 7/8" l. (ILLUS.)...... **395**

Miniature Fly Sprayer Perfume Sprayer

Perfume dispenser, model of a miniature fly sprayer, Europe, late 19th - early 20th c., 3" l. (ILLUS.) **45**

Pig-shaped Silver Pincushion

Pincushion, model of a pig w/a cloth cushion in the top of the back, hallmarks for Birmingham, England, ca. 1905, 3 3/8" l. (ILLUS.) **395**

Plates, round w/flanged raised rim decorated w/a coat-of-arms, reeded border, mark of Carl Boianowski, St. Petersburg, Russia, 1835-1838, 8 5/8" d., set of 12 ..... **9,560**

Rare Server with Figure of Henry VIII

Serving spoon, figural handle, a detailed full-figure handle w/King Henry VIII of England, the figure above a blank cartouche over the English royal coat-of-arms & scrolls bordering the wide shovel-form bowl, marked "800," probably Europe, similar to one produced by the Gorham Mfg. Co. around 1901, 9 1/4" l. (ILLUS.)....... **525**

Silver Server with Cavalier Handle

Serving spoon, figural relief handle w/a standing cavalier blowing a horn, above pierced scrolls, chased scrolls in the large oval bowl, Europe, late 19th - early 20th c., 10 1/4" l. (ILLUS.) **550**

Chair-form Silver Pincushion

Pincushion, miniature model of a side chair, Victorian style balloon-back w/a pierced scroll & floral design, cloth cushion seat, scrolled apron & cabriole front legs, worn hallmarks, probably Birmingham, England, early 20th c., 2" h. (ILLUS.).................. **175**

Server with Frederick the Great Figure

Serving spoon, figural relief handle w/a standing figure of Frederick the Great of Prussia, royal emblems at base of handle, chased scrolls in the wide shovel-form bowl, Europe, early 20th c., 11" l. (ILLUS.)... **595**

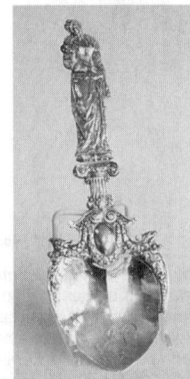

Mary, Queen of Scots on Silver Server

Serving spoon, figural relief handle w/a standing figure of Mary, Queen of Scots, engraved initials in the wreath & swag-trimmed wide shovel-form bowl, back marked "800," Europe, early 20th c., 10 1/2" l. (ILLUS.)... **645**

Silver Server with Napoleon Handle

Serving spoon, figural relief handle w/a standing figure of Napoleon I above his imperial emblem & his initial & swags in

the large shovel-form bowl, Europe, early 20th c., 10 1/2" l. (ILLUS.) **550**

Large Server with Lady on Handle

Serving spoon, figural relief handle w/a standing lady in Victorian dress, above a section of pierced entwined branches, chased musical instruments & sheet music in the wide oblong handle, marked "800," Europe, early 20th c., 11 1/4" l. (ILLUS.) **595**

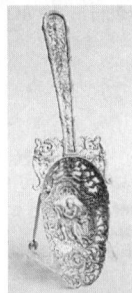

Ornate Pierced Serving Spoon

Serving spoon, the long oval bowl chased & pierced, a central figure of Moses & cherubs, a classical head below, the long flat handle w/pierced scrolls & masks & pierced griffins at the base, Europe, late 19th - early 20th c., 12" l. (ILLUS.)................ **750**

Sterling Silver Cat Shaker

Shaker, in the form of a cat sitting on its hind legs, screw closure in base, English hallmarks, early 20th c., 3" h. (ILLUS.) **195**

One of a Pair of Silver Shoe Buckles

Shoe buckles, rounded rectangular shape w/pierced decoration of stylized floral motifs, English, ca. 1790, 2 1/2 x 3", the pair (ILLUS. of one)... **112**

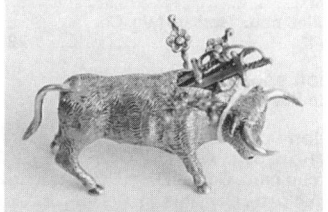

Bull-shaped Silver Skewer Set

Skewer set: full-figure model of a bull w/a slot in the back to hold the sword-shaped skewers, Europe, late 19th - early 20th c., 3 1/2" l., 2" h., the set (ILLUS.)....................... **260**

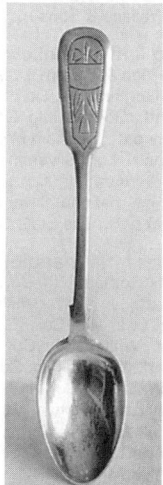

Russian Silver Spoon

Spoon, engraving on handle & back of bowl in geometric design, marked "AP - 1893 - 84" next to a crest, Russian, 5 1/4" l. (ILLUS.)... **125**
Stuffing spoon, simple handle w/crest, maker's mark "IF," London, England, 1807, 11 1/2" l.. **123**

English Silver Sugar Spoon

Sugar spoon, long, trowel-shaped bowl, handle flaring out at end, both engraved w/scrolls, indistinct hallmarks, 3 5/8" l. (ILLUS.) **195**

Russian Silver Sugar Spoon

Sugar spoon, scoop-shaped bowl, back engraved w/flowers, baluster-shape handle, Russian, 3 1/2" l. (ILLUS.)....................... **245**
Tea & coffee service: cov. teapot; cov. coffeepot, creamer, waste bowl, sugar tongs, tea caddy missing cover & kettle on lamp stand; each rounded & lobed body embossed w/iris, chrysanthemum, bamboo & cherry blossoms, openwork iris finials, in a fitted wood case, by Arthur & Bond, Yokohama, Japan, the oval tray w/a pebbled surface, the rim embossed w/chrysanthemums, by Samurai Shokar, Yokohama, Japan, early 20th c., the set **10,925**
Teapot, cov., inverted pear-form on an openwork rocaille foot, the body chased overall w/chinoiserie figures drinking tea, making music & playing w/a parrot against architecture & foliage, one side w/a vacant cartouche, the bird-head

spout cast w/scrolls, the foliate-clad handle w/ivory insulators, the hinged cover chased as a Chinese parasol & surmounted by a chinoiserie figure holding a parasol, Walter Morisse, London, England, 1859, 10 1/2" l., 8" h. **3,107**

Teapot & coffeepot, cov., each of lobed form on four scroll feet, leaf-clad scroll spout & handle w/ivory insulators, the hinged cover w/acorn finial, the coffeepot w/two engraved crests, each marked, Paul Storr, London, England, 1836-1837, teapot 10 3/4" l., coffeepot, 8 1/2" h., pr. **4,780**

Teapot & creamer, melon ribbed w/engraved scrollwork & cast & chased acanthus leaf feet & scrolled handles, cov. teapot w/ivory wafers & dove w/olive branch finial, both pieces have London hallmarks & were made by Edward, Edward Jr., John & William Barnard, the teapot in 1836, the creamer shortly after (date letter unclear, but has queen's head on it for Victoria), teapot 6 1/4" h", creamer 6 3/4" h. **633**

Oval Art Deco Silver Tray

Tray, long oval form decorated inside w/bands of leaftip & geometric Art Deco designs, probably Europe, early 20th c., 3 x 10 1/2" (ILLUS.) **85**

Tureen, cov., classical urn form, the domed cover w/urn finial, the molded rim w/beaded band, engraved decoration on the loop handles, the long oval base w/a beaded band, on a short oval pedestal base, engraved crests on cover & coats-of-arms on the body, John Schofield, London, England, 1785, 8 1/2 x 17 1/2", 12 1/2" h. **5,750**

Urn, cov., classical form, the body w/beaded & foliate bands above floral festoons, the tall pagoda-form cover w/cast & engraved bud finials, the cover w/bands of foliate & beaded decoration, loop handles w/molded acanthus terminals, on a slender pedestal w/circular base w/similar decoration, gilt interior, John Schofield, London, England, 1784, 16 1/2" h. **2,415**

Sterling (flatware)

Listed by item (individual pieces unless otherwise noted). All pieces are old and original.

Asparagus server

Olympian patt., Tiffany & Co., handle chased w/scene of Venus on her chariot w/putti riding dolphins trailing water leaves, the prongs w/chased fluting, engraved on reverse w/initials, 1878-91, 9 1/2" l. **920**

Baby forks
Marie Antoinette patt., Dominick & Haff...... **20-25**

Berry forks
Empire patt., Whiting Mfg. Co. **20-30**
Violet patt., R. Wallace & Sons **35-45**

Berry spoons
Chrysanthemum patt., Wm. B. Durgin Co., 9"... **275-375**
Colfax patt., Wm. B. Durgin Co., 8 3/4" **65-85**
Dauphin patt., Wm. B. Durgin Co. **475-575**
Egyptian patt., Whiting Mfg. Co. **250-350**
Honeysuckle patt., Whiting Mfg. Co. **175-225**
Ivory patt., Whiting Mfg. Co. **600-800**
Jefferson patt., Gorham Mfg. Co. **65-85**
Louis XIV patt., Towle Mfg. Co. **100-125**
Louis XV patt., Whiting Mfg. Co. **85-95**
Orange Blossom patt., Alvin Mfg. Co., 9"... **275-375**
Rustic patt., Towle Mfg. Co., gold-washed, 7 3/4".. **65-95**
Versailles patt., Gorham Mfg. Co., 8 3/4"... **225-275**

Bonbon spoons
Grande Baroque patt., R. Wallace & Sons.. **32-40**

Bouillon spoons
Bridal Rose patt., Alvin Mfg. Co. **35-45**
Buttercup patt., Gorham Mfg. Co. **20-25**
Etruscan patt., Gorham Mfg. Co. **18-25**
Georgian patt., Towle Mfg. Co. **35-45**
Lily patt., Whiting Mfg. Co. **40-55**
Louis XIV patt., Towle Mfg. Co. **18-25**
Madame Jumel patt., Gorham Mfg. Co. **15-20**
Marguerite patt., Gorham Mfg. Co. **20-25**
Mount Vernon patt., Lunt Silversmiths **15-20**
Versailles patt., Gorham Mfg. Co. **35-45**
Violet patt., R. Wallace & Sons **25-35**

Butter serving knives (hollow handle)
Francis I patt., Reed & Barton...................... **25-35**
Jac Rose patt., Gorham Mfg. Co. **20-25**
King Edward patt., Gorham Mfg. Co. **25-30**
Lily of the Valley patt., Gorham Mfg. Co. **20-25**
Mount Vernon patt., Lunt Silversmiths **20-25**
Nocturne patt., Gorham Mfg. Co. **15-20**
Pantheon patt., International Silver Co........ **25-35**
Rose (Baltimore) patt., The Steiff Co. **35-45**

Butter spreaders (flat handle)
Cambridge patt., Gorham Mfg. Co. **15-20**
English Shell patt., Lunt Silversmiths **12-14**
Georgian patt., Towle Mfg. Co. **36**
King Albert patt., Whiting Mfg. Co. **12-14**
King Edward patt., Whiting Mfg. Co............... **10**
Kings patt., R. Wallace & Sons **20**
Lily of the Valley patt., Gorham Mfg. Co. **12-14**
Louis XV patt., Whiting Mfg. Co. **23**
Madame Morris patt., Whiting Mfg. Co......... **12-14**
Majestic patt., Alvin Mfg. Co........................... **21**
Manchester patt., Manchester Mfg. Co. **18**
Mandarin patt., Whiting Mfg. Co. **12-14**
Marie Antoinette patt., Dominick & Haff............ **25**
Marlborough patt., Reed & Barton............... **16-18**
Melrose patt., Gorham Mfg. Co. **18-22**
Mount Vernon patt., Lunt Silversmiths **14-18**
Nocturne patt., Gorham Mfg. Co. **12-14**
Paul Revere patt., Towle Mfg. Co....................... **22**
Plymouth patt., Gorham Mfg. Co. **12-15**
Strasbourg patt., Gorham Mfg. Co.................... **22**

Violet patt., Whiting Mfg. Co. 25
William & Mary patt., Lunt Silversmiths **12-14**

Butter spreaders (hollow handle)
English Gadroon patt., Gorham Mfg. Co. **16-18**
Melbourne patt., Oneida Silversmiths **12-14**
Versailles patt., Gorham Mfg. Co. 18

Cake forks
Louis XIV patt., Towle Mfg. Co. 80

Cake knives
Louis XIV patt., Towle Mfg. Co. 75

Cake servers
Manchester patt., Manchester Mfg. Co. 31
Mandarin patt., Whiting Mfg. Co., silver
    plate blade 34

Cheese scoops
Cambridge patt., Gorham Mfg. Co. 45
Kensington patt., Gorham Mfg. Co. 125
Strasbourg patt., Gorham Mfg. Co. 120

Cheese servers
Grande Baroque patt., R. Wallace & Sons .. **25-30**

Chocolate muddlers
La Parisienne patt., Reed & Barton 135

Citrus spoons
Francis I patt., Reed & Barton **30-35**
Hampton Court patt., Reed & Barton, flut-
    ed **25-30**
Labours of Cupid patt., Dominick & Haff 75

Cocktail forks
Audubon patt., Tiffany & Co. 50
Chantilly patt., Gorham Mfg. Co. **14-18**
Grande Baroque patt., R. Wallace &
    Sons **25-30**
Marlborough patt., Reed & Barton **16-20**
Melrose patt., Gorham Mfg. Co. **20-25**
Old Newbury patt., Towle Mfg. Co. **18-22**
Paul Revere patt., Towle Mfg. Co. **16-20**
Raleigh patt., Alvin Mfg. Co. 17
Rose Point patt., R. Wallace & Sons **15-18**
Strasbourg patt., Gorham Mfg. Co. **18-22**
Versailles patt., Gorham Mfg. Co. 22

Cold meat forks
Etruscan patt., Gorham Mfg. Co. 55
Florentine patt., Alvin Mfg. Co. 140
Francis I patt., Reed & Barton **55-65**
French Antique patt., Reed & Barton,
    pierced 64
Grande Baroque patt., R. Wallace & Sons .. **60-68**
Hampton Court patt., Reed & Barton **55-60**
Madame Jumel patt., Whiting Mfg. Co. **42-50**
Manchester patt., Manchester Mfg. Co.,
    small 31
Marlborough patt., Reed & Barton 64
Orange Blossom patt., Alvin Mfg. Co. 185

Cracker scoops, pierced
Chrysanthemum patt., Wm. B. Durgin
    Co. **750-950**

Cream soup spoons
Camellia patt., Gorham Mfg. Co. **14-18**
Damask Rose patt., Oneida Mfg. Co. **16-20**
Francis I patt., Reed & Barton **30-35**

Grande Baroque patt., Wallace & Sons **28-32**
Lily of the Valley patt., Gorham Mfg. Co. **18-22**
Marlborough patt., Reed & Barton **25-30**
Nocturne patt., Gorham Mfg. Co. **12-16**
Old French patt., Gorham Mfg. Co. **28-32**

Cucumber servers
Fairfax patt., Wm. B. Durgin Co. 55
Lily patt., Whiting Mfg. Co. **375-425**
Morning Glory patt., Alvin Mfg. Co. 85
Paris patt., Gorham Mfg. Co. 165

Demitasse spoons
Arabesque patt., Whiting Mfg. Co. 24
Blossom patt., Georg Jensen, 1904-08,
    3 3/8", set of 12 .... **1,495**
Francis I patt., Reed & Barton **22-25**
Grande Baroque patt., Wallace & Sons 24
Hampton Court patt., Reed & Barton 18
Japanese patt., Tiffany & Co. 55
Lily patt., Whiting Mfg. Co. **25-30**
Louis XIV patt., Towle Mfg. Co. 15
Louis XV patt., Whiting Mfg. Co. **12-16**
Madame Jumel patt., Whiting Mfg. Co. **10-12**
Marlborough patt., Reed & Barton 21

Dessert forks
Audubon patt., Tiffany & Co. 80
Chantilly patt., Gorham Mfg. Co., in original
    case, set of 12 .... **350-375**

Dessert spoons
Francis I patt., Reed & Barton **55-65**
Frontenac patt., International Silver Co. **40-48**
King Edward patt., Whiting Mfg. Co. **35-45**
Louis XIV patt., Towle Mfg. Co. 52
Mignonette patt., Lunt Silversmiths 20
Old French patt., Gorham Mfg. Co. 36
Strawberry patt., Wm. B. Durgin Co. 40
Versailles patt., Gorham Mfg. Co. 55

Dinner forks
Angelo patt., Wood & Hughes 60
Bridal Rose patt., Alvin Mfg. Co. 38
Camellia patt., Gorham Mfg. Co. 20
Corinthian patt., Gorham Mfg. Co. 65
Damask Rose patt., Gorham Mfg. Co. 25
Etruscan patt., Gorham Mfg. Co. 38
Francis I patt., Reed & Barton **45-65**
King Edward patt., Gorham Mfg. Co. 35
Kings patt., R. Wallace & Sons 48
Lily of the Valley patt., Whiting Mfg. Co. 60
Louis XIV patt., Towle Mfg. Co. 35
Louis XV patt., Whiting Mfg. Co. **25-35**
Louis XV patt., Wood & Hughes 50
Madame Jumel patt., Gorham Mfg. Co. 32
Manchester patt., Manchester Mfg. Co. 24
Mandarin patt., Whiting Mfg. Co., silver
    plate blade 27
Marie Antoinette patt., Dominick & Haff 42
Marie Antoinette patt., Gorham Mfg. Co. 50
Melrose patt., Gorham Mfg. Co. **40-45**
Old Colonial patt., Towle Mfg. Co. **42-48**
Orange Blossom patt., Alvin Mfg. Co. 80
Paul Revere patt., Towle Mfg. Co. 45
Rose Point patt., R. Wallace & Sons 35
William & Mary patt., Lunt Silversmiths 20

Dinner knives
Buttercup patt., Gorham Mfg. Co. 49
Cambridge patt., Gorham Mfg. Co. 49

Damask Rose patt., Gorham Mfg. Co. 25
Etruscan patt., Gorham Mfg. Co. 36
Grand Duchess patt., Towle Mfg. Co. 34
Kings patt., R. Wallace & Sons 48
Louis XVI patt., Towle Mfg. Co. 38
Madame Jumel patt., Gorham Mfg. Co. 32
Majestic patt., Alvin Mfg. Co., silver plate
    blade 41
Marie Antoinette patt., Dominick & Haff 35
Old Colonial patt., Towle Mfg. Co. 32
Orange Blossom patt., Alvin Mfg. Co. 85
Rose Point patt., R. Wallace & Sons 35

Egg spoons
Japanese patt., Tiffany & Co., gold-washed
    bowl 75
Mayfair patt., Dominick & Haff 14

Fish forks
Old French patt., Gorham Mfg. Co. 55

Fish serving forks
Ivory patt., Whiting Mfg. Co. 475

Fish Serving sets (2-piece)
Luxembourg patt., Gorham Mfg. Co. 250
Undine patt., Wood & Hughes 495

Fruit knives
Grande Baroque patt., R. Wallace & Sons,
    hollow handle 41
Melrose patt., Gorham Mfg. Co. 28

Grapefruit spoons
Audubon patt., Tiffany & Co. 95

Gravy ladles
Angelo patt., Wood & Hughes 115
Cambridge patt., Gorham Mfg. Co. 42-48
Chantilly patt., Gorham Mfg. Co. 50-60
Chrysanthemum patt., Tiffany & Co. 395
Egyptian patt., Whiting Mfg. Co. 125
Francis I patt., Reed & Barton 60-70
Hampton Court patt., Reed & Barton 58
Italian patt., Tiffany & Co. 250
King Edward patt., Gorham Mfg. Co. 58
King Edward patt., Whiting Mfg. Co. 130
Louis XIV patt., Towle Mfg. Co. 48
Manchester patt., Manchester Mfg. Co. 31
Mount Vernon patt., Lunt Silversmiths 50
Nocturne patt., Gorham Mfg. Co. 55
Versailles patt., Gorham Mfg. Co. 145
Violet patt., R. Wallace & Sons 95

Gumbo spoons
Cambridge patt., Gorham Mfg. Co. 25-35
Manchester patt., Manchester Mfg. Co. 28
Mandarin patt., Whiting Mfg. Co. 24
Orange Blossom patt., Alvin Mfg. Co. 75-95

Ice cream forks
Louis XIV patt., Towle Mfg. Co. 40
Nocturne patt., Gorham Mfg. Co. 35
Violet patt., R. Wallace & Sons 45-65

Ice cream knives
Luxembourg patt., Gorham Mfg. Co. 225
Versailles patt., Gorham Mfg. Co. 250

Ice cream spoons
Lorraine patt., Alvin Mfg. Co. 35
Paul Revere patt., Towle Mfg. Co. 32
Peony patt., R. Wallace & Sons 38

Rose (Baltimore) patt., The Steiff Co. 28

Ice tongs
Florentine patt., Tiffany & Co. **450-550**

Iced tea spoons
Buttercup patt., Gorham Mfg. Co. 33
Chantilly patt., Gorham Mfg. Co. 22
Hampton Court patt., Reed & Barton 26
Louis XIV patt., Towle Mfg. Co. 24
Marie Antoinette patt., Dominick & Haff 28
Nocturne patt., Gorham Mfg. Co. 25
Rose patt., R. Wallace & Sons 30
Virginian patt., Gorham Mfg. Co., set of 5 138

Jelly servers
Francis I patt., Reed & Barton 30-35
Grande Baroque patt., R. Wallace & Sons.. 30-35
Lily of the Valley patt., Gorham Mfg. Co. 22-28

Lemon forks
Grande Baroque patt., R. Wallace & Sons 30
Hampton Court patt., Reed & Barton 25
King Edward patt., Gorham Mfg. Co. 18

Lettuce forks
Cottage patt., Gorham Mfg. Co. 55
Lily patt., Whiting Mfg. Co. 200-250
Renaissance patt., Dominick & Haff 175

Luncheon forks
Buttercup patt., Gorham Mfg. Co. 15
Camellia patt., Whiting Mfg. Co. 18
Chantilly patt., Gorham Mfg. Co. 18
Chrysanthemum patt., Wm. B. Durgin Co. 95
Etruscan patt., Whiting Mfg. Co. 18
Francis I patt., Reed & Barton 36
Hampton Court patt., Reed & Barton 30
King Edward patt., Whiting Mfg. Co. 24
Lily of the Valley patt., Gorham Mfg. Co. 26
Majestic patt., Alvin Mfg. Co. 28
Mandarin patt., Whiting Mfg. Co. 24
Melrose patt., Gorham Mfg. Co. 28
Mignonette patt., Lunt Silversmiths 18
Nuremburg patt., Alvin Mfg. Co. 45
Old Colonial patt., Towle Mfg. Co. 22
Orange Blossom patt., Alvin Mfg. Co. 55
Plymouth patt., Whiting Mfg. Co. 15
Rambler Rose patt., Reed & Barton 18
Rose Point patt., R. Wallace & Sons 32
Strawberry patt., Wm. B. Durgin Co. 45
Versailles patt., Gorham Mfg. Co. 30
Violet patt., R. Wallace & Sons 28
William & Mary patt., Lunt Silversmiths 18

Luncheon knives
Chantilly patt., Gorham Mfg. Co. 18
Etruscan patt., Whiting Mfg. Co. 16
Francis I patt., Reed & Barton, silver plate
    blade 27
Frontenac patt., International Silver Co. 40
Grande Baroque patt., R. Wallace & Sons,
    silver plate blade 31
Kings patt., R. Wallace & Sons 22
Lily of the Valley patt., Gorham Mfg. Co. 22
Majestic patt., Alvin Mfg. Co., silver plate
    blade 34
Mandarin patt., Whiting Mfg. Co., silver
    plate blade 23
Old Colonial patt., Towle Mfg. Co. 22
Parallel patt., Georg Jensen Silversmithy 65

Plymouth patt., Whiting Mfg. Co. 12
Rambler Rose patt., Reed & Barton................... 15
William & Mary patt., Lunt Silversmiths 15

Meat forks
Jac Rose patt., Gorham Mfg. Co. 55
Nocturne patt., Gorham Mfg. Co. 65

Mustard ladles
Dauphin patt., Wm. B. Durgin Co. 150-200
Versailles patt., Gorham Mfg. Co. 125-150

Nut picks
Audubon patt., Tiffany & Co. 150
Broomcorn patt., Tiffany & Co. 65
Grecian patt., Gorham Mfg. Co. 45
Grecian patt., Whiting Mfg. Co. 28

Nut spoons
Lily patt., Whiting Mfg. Co., round 175-225

Olive forks
Marguerite patt., Wood & Hughes 23

Olive spoons
Fairfax patt., Wm. B. Durgin Co. 20-25

Oyster ladles
Fairfax patt., Wm. B. Durgin Co. 175
Japanese patt., Tiffany & Co., 1871-80,
    10 3/4" 2,000-2,500

Pastry servers
Francis I patt., Reed & Barton, hollow han-
    dle 38
Hampton Court patt., Reed & Barton, hol-
    low handle 38
Louis XVI patt., Towle Mfg. Co. 85

Pickle forks
Cambridge patt., Gorham Mfg. Co. 30
Francis I patt., Reed & Barton 34
Grande Baroque patt., R. Wallace & Sons 27
Hampton Court patt., Reed & Barton. 25
Lily of the Valley patt., Gorham Mfg. Co. 24
Lily patt., Whiting Mfg. Co., long handle. 125
Louis XVI patt., Towle Mfg. Co. 30
Manchester patt., Manchester Mfg. Co. 17

Pie knife
Windham patt., Tiffany & Co., serrated 395

Punch ladles
Beacon patt., Manchester Silver Co. 150
Norfolk patt., Gorham Mfg. Co. 225

Salad forks
Broomcorn patt., Tiffany & Co. 115
Buttercup patt., Gorham Mfg. Co. 37
Camellia patt., Whiting Mfg. Co. 17
Chantilly patt., Gorham Mfg. Co. 25
Chrysanthemum patt., Tiffany & Co. 115-150
Damask Rose patt., Gorham Mfg. Co. 30
Essex patt., Wm. B. Durgin Co. 18
Etruscan patt., Gorham Mfg. Co. 24
Fontana patt., Towle Mfg. Co. 25
Francis I patt., Reed & Barton 30-35
Grand Duchesse patt., Towle Mfg. Co. 30
Louis XIV patt., Towle Mfg. Co. 36
Louis XV patt., Whiting Mfg. Co. 40
Marie Antoinette patt., Dominick & Haff. 32
Melbourne patt., Oneida Silversmiths 24

Pantheon patt., International Silver Co. 36
Richmond patt., Alvin Mfg. Co. 30
Rose (Baltimore) patt., The Steiff Co. 45-55
Rose Point patt., R. Wallace & Sons 34
Strawberry patt., Wm. B. Durgin Co. 75
Violet patt., R. Wallace & Sons 35-45
Windham patt., Tiffany & Co. 65

Salad serving forks
Bridal Rose patt., Alvin Mfg. Co., 9" 275-325
Francis I patt., Reed & Barton 125-150
Melrose patt., Gorham Mfg. Co. 100-125

Salad serving sets (2-piece)
Cambridge patt., Gorham Mfg. Co. 200-275
Canterbury patt., Towle Mfg. Co. 200-275
Francis I patt., Reed & Barton 250-325
Hampton Court patt., Reed & Barton,
    fluted 175-225
Japanese patt., Tiffany & Co., gold-washed
    bowls, 10" 2,500-3,000
Lily of the Valley patt., Gorham Mfg.
    Co. 175-225
Melrose patt., Gorham Mfg. Co. 200-250

Salad serving spoons
Bridal Rose patt., Alvin Mfg. Co. 275-325

Sauce ladles
Athenian patt., Whiting Mfg. Co. 35
Dresden patt., Whiting Mfg. Co. 65
Grande Baroque patt., R. Wallace &
    Sons 35-40
Hampton Court patt., R. Wallace & Sons 30-35
King Edward patt., Gorham Mfg. Co. 25-30
Lily of the Valley patt., Gorham Mfg. Co. 25-30
Louis XIV patt., Towle Mfg. Co. 45
Louis XV patt., Whiting Mfg. Co. 35-40
Radiant patt., Whiting Mfg. Co. 45
Rose (Baltimore) patt., The Steiff Co. 55
Washington patt., R. Wallace & Sons 30
Winthrop patt., Tiffany & Co. 175

Serving fork
Versailles patt., Gorham Mfg. Co., 7 7/8".. 225-275

Serving spoon
Bernadotte patt., Georg Jensen Silver-
    smithy, medium 250-325

Soup ladles
Empire patt., Whiting Mfg. Co., large 395
Honeysuckle patt., Whiting Mfg. Co. 265
Rosette patt., Gorham Mfg. Co. 138
Tomato Vine patt., Tiffany & Co., the han-
    dle chased w/tomatoes, vines & leaves in
    relief lapping over to the back, the oval
    bowl w/a wide scalloped rim,
    12 1/4" l. 1,300-1,600

Soup spoon
Old Colonial patt., Towle Mfg. Co. 25-35

Soup spoons, oval
Buttercup patt., Gorham Mfg. Co. 25
Georgian patt., Towle Mfg. Co. 28
Ivy patt., Whiting Mfg. Co. 35
Louis V patt., Whiting Mfg. Co. 25
Louis XV patt., Wood & Hughes 45
Manchester patt., Manchester Mfg. Co. 21
Marie Antoinette patt., Gorham Mfg. Co. 44

Old Colonial patt., Towle Mfg. Co. 28
Old French patt., Gorham Mfg. Co. 32
Rose patt., R. Wallace & Sons............................ 24
Strasbourg patt., Gorham Mfg. Co.................... 30
Violet patt., R. Wallace & Sons........................... 30

Steak carving forks
Mandarin patt., Whiting Mfg. Co......................... 30

Steak carving sets (2-piece)
Grande Baroque patt., R. Wallace & Sons 67

Strawberry fork
Louis XV patt., Whiting Mfg. Co. 25-30

Stuffing spoon
King George patt., Gorham Mfg. Co. 395

Sugar shells
Francis I patt., Reed & Barton 38
Hampton Court patt., Reed & Barton................. 26
Orange Blossom patt., Alvin Mfg. Co. 60

Sugar sifter
Virginia patt., Gorham Mfg. Co.......................... 295

Sugar spoons
Canterbury patt., Towle Mfg. Co......................... 38
Dauphin patt., Wm. B. Durgin Co....................... 85
Egyptian patt., Whiting Mfg. Co. 45
Fontainebleau patt., Gorham Mfg. Co. 40
Francis I patt., Reed & Barton 35-45
Georgian patt., Towle Mfg. Co. 38
Grande Baroque patt., R. Wallace & Sons .. 30-40
Honeysuckle patt., Whiting Mfg. Co.................. 55
King Edward patt., Gorham Mfg. Co. 28
Les Cinq Fleurs patt., Reed & Barton............... 26
Lion (Coeur de Lion) patt., Frank W. Smith
    Co., gold-washed 127
Marlborough patt., Reed & Barton 30
Nocturne patt., Gorham Mfg. Co. 25
Pantheon patt., International Silver Co. 35
Rose (Baltimore) patt., The Steiff Co. 35
Rose Point patt., R. Wallace & Sons.................. 20

Sugar tongs
Francis I patt., Reed & Barton 45-65
Lily patt., Whiting Mfg. Co., claw tips.......... 85-115
Louis XIV patt., Towle Mfg. Co. 45
Louis XV patt., Whiting Mfg. Co. 38
Madame Jumel patt., Whiting Mfg. Co............... 35
Medici patt., Gorham Mfg. Co........................... 150
Olympian patt., Tiffany & Co............................. 195

Table crumber
Lap-Over-Edge patt., Tiffany & Co., the
    handle bright-cut engraved w/bamboo
    branches & spider web, the shaped
    blade w/chased designs, 1880-91,
    12 3/4" l. 1,000-1,400

Tablespoons
Angelo patt., Wood & Hughes 65-85
Arabesque patt., Whiting Mfg. Co. 65-85
Buttercup patt., Gorham Mfg. Co. 50-65
Chantilly patt., Gorham Mfg. Co. 50-65
Francis I patt., Reed & Barton 55-65
Grande Baroque patt., R. Wallace & Sons,
    pierced 60-75
Hampton Court patt., Reed & Barton............ 50-60
Imperial Queen patt., Whiting Mfg. Co. 60-75
King Edward patt., Gorham Mfg. Co............. 45-55

Kings patt., R. Wallace & Sons.................... 35-45
Louis XV patt., Whiting Mfg. Co..................... 35-45
Madame Jumel patt., Whiting Mfg. Co. 35-45
Madame Royale patt., Wm. B. Durgin 50-58
Manchester patt., Manchester Mfg. Co. 25-35
Marie Antoinette patt., Dominick & Haff....... 45-55
Marlborough patt., Reed & Barton............... 48-55
Maryland patt., Alvin Mfg. Co. 25-30
Nocturne patt., Gorham Mfg. Co. 45-55
Old Colonial patt., Towle Mfg. Co. 45-55
Pantheon patt., International Silver Co. 45-55
Raleigh patt., Alvin Mfg. Co. 30-40
Strasbourg patt., Gorham Mfg. Co............... 50-65
Versailles patt., Gorham Mfg. Co. 55-70

Tea strainers
Repoussé patt., Samuel Kirk & Sons 250-300

Teaspoons
Buttercup patt., Gorham Mfg. Co. 14-18
Cambridge patt., Gorham Mfg. Co. 10-14
Camellia patt., Gorham Mfg. Co. 10-12
Chrysanthemum patt., Tiffany & Co............. 60-70
Damask Rose patt., Gorham Mfg. Co. 10-14
Eloquence patt., Lunt Silversmiths................ 15-20
English Gadroon patt., Gorham Mfg. Co..... 10-14
English Shell patt., Lunt Silversmiths........... 10-12
Etruscan patt., Gorham Mfg. Co. 12-14
Francis I patt., Reed & Barton 18-22
Grande Baroque patt., R. Wallace &
    Sons 18-20
King Edward patt., Whiting Mfg. Co. 14-18
King patt., Dominick & Haff............................ 14-18
Lily of the Valley patt., Whiting Mfg. Co. 20-25
Lily patt., Watson, Newell & Co..................... 18-22
Lily patt., Whiting Mfg. Co.............................. 20-25
Louis XIV patt., Towle Mfg. Co. 12-15
Louis XV patt., Whiting Mfg. Co..................... 10-13
Lucerne patt., R. Wallace & Sons................. 14-16
Madame Jumel patt., Whiting Mfg. Co. 10-13
Majestic patt., Alvin Mfg. Co. 15-18
Manchester patt., Manchester Mfg. Co. 10-12
Marguerite patt., Gorham Mfg. Co. 12-15
Marie Antoinette patt., Dominick & Haff....... 10-14
Marlborough patt., Reed & Barton............... 15-18
Marquise patt., Tiffany & Co.......................... 30-36
Maryland patt., Alvin Mfg. Co. 12-14
Mazarin patt., Dominick & Haff 12-16
Melbourne patt., Oneida Silversmiths........... 10-12
Melrose patt., Gorham Mfg. Co...................... 14-18
Michelangelo patt., Oneida Silversmiths...... 12-16
Mignonette patt., Lunt Silversmiths.............. 14-18
Mount Vernon patt., Lunt Silversmiths 10-14
Old Colonial patt., Towle Mfg. Co. 12-15
Old French patt., Gorham Mfg. Co................. 15-18
Pantheon patt., International Silver Co. 14-16
Plymouth patt., Gorham Mfg. Co. 10-12
Poppy patt., Gorham Mfg. Co......................... 20-25
Raleigh patt., Alvin Mfg. Co. 10-12
Rambler Rose patt., Reed & Barton 10-12
Renaissance (Bearded Man) patt., Domin-
    ick & Haff.. 26-32
Rose Point patt., R. Wallace & Sons 14-16
Tara patt., Reed & Barton............................... 14-16
Versailles patt., Gorham Mfg. Co. 20-25
Violet patt., R. Wallace & Sons 16-20
Violet patt., Whiting Mfg. Co.......................... 20-25
Wedgwood patt., International Silver Co. 12-14

Tomato servers
Chrysanthemum patt., Wm. B. Durgin Co....... 275

Francis I patt., Reed & Barton **75-85**
Hampton Court patt., Reed & Barton........... **55-65**
Louis XIV patt., Towle Mfg. Co................. **100-125**
Nocturne patt., Gorham Mfg. Co...................... **85**
Sir Christopher patt., R. Wallace & Sons **85-95**

Vegetable spoon
Grape patt., Dominick & Haff............................ **150**

Sets
Acanthus patt., dinner service: twelve each tablespoons, luncheon spoons, tea-spoons, coffee spoons, demitasse spoons, dinner forks, luncheon forks, fish forks, pastry forks, fish knives, dinner knives & luncheon knives, four cold cut forks, two each vegetable serving spoons, jelly spoons & salt spoons, one each large serving spoon, gravy ladle, serrated serving spoon, sugar spoon, meat fork, large salad serving spoon, large salad serving fork, small salad serving spoon, small salad serving fork, cake knife, tomato server, pastry server, small serrated knife & pierced server; knives & serving pieces w/stainless steel blades, tines or bowls, designed by Johan Rohde in 1917, Georg Jensen Silversmithy, Copenhagen, Denmark, various dates, 168 pcs. **8,500-10,500**
Acorn patt., dinner service: six luncheon forks, six pastry forks, eight teaspoons & eight luncheon knives w/stainless steel blades; Georg Jensen Silversmithy, Copenhagen, Denmark, post-1945, 26 pcs. **1,400-1,650**
Acorn patt., dinner service: twelve each dinner knives, dinner forks, luncheon knives, luncheon forks, fish knives, fish forks, pastry forks, cocktail forks, soup spoons, tablespoons, dessert spoons, iced tea spoons, teaspoons, coffee spoons, demitasse spoons, grapefruit spoons, fruit knives, fruit forks, steak knives, butter spreaders & lobster picks, three each serving forks & serving spoons, one each sauce ladle, sardine server, bottle opener, letter opener, pickle fork, pie slice, fish slice & jam spoon; Georg Jensen Silversmithy, Copenhagen, Denmark, 1921 & after, 272 pcs. **16,500-20,500**
Arcadia patt., dinner service: twelve each dinner knives, dinner forks, dessert spoons, luncheon forks & salad forks, eleven teaspoons & eight luncheon knives; Georg Jensen Silversmithy, Copenhagen, Denmark, post-1945, 79 pcs. **3,500-4,500**
Back Tipt patt., dinner service: eight each dinner knives, dessert knives, dinner forks, luncheon forks, salad forks, butter knives & soup spoons, ten teaspoons, two berry spoons & one each gravy ladle, lemon fork, cake server, cold meat fork, olive fork & seafood fork; Watson Company, Attleboro, Massachusetts, 74 pcs.... **1,092**
Bernadotte patt., dinner service: twelve each tablespoons, luncheon spoons, ice cream spoons, coffee spoons, demitasse

spoons, dinner forks, luncheon forks, salad forks, fish forks, fish knives, dinner knives, luncheon knives & butter knives, two each large servers, cold meat forks & fish servers, one each cake server, vegetable server, gravy ladle, meat fork, salad spoon, salad fork, cheese slice & cheese knife; some pieces w/stainless steel blades, tines or bowls, designed by Sigvard Bernadotte in 1930, Georg Jensen Silversmithy, Copenhagen, Denmark, post-1945, 170 pcs. **16,100**
Bittersweet patt., dinner service: eight each dinner forks, salad forks, cake forks, tablespoons, soup spoons, tea-spoons, dinner knives & butter knives, designed by Tias Eckhoff; Georg Jensen Silversmithy, Copenhagen, Denmark, 64 pcs. **5,750**
Brocade patt., dinner service: eight each salad forks, luncheon knives, luncheon forks, butter knives, teaspoons & iced tea spoons, four dessert spoons & one each sugar shell & master butter server; International Silver Co., Meriden, Connecticut, 54 pcs. **633**
Castilian patt., dinner service: twenty-four dinner knives, eighteen teaspoons, twelve each luncheon knives, cheese knives, soup spoons, butter knives, bouillon spoons, dinner knives, luncheon forks, salad forks, cocktail forks, grapefruit spoons, iced tea spoons & dessert forks, three serving forks; engraved w/monogram "NAY," Tiffany & Co., New York, New York, 20th c., 195 pcs............. **9,775**
Chateau Rose patt., dinner service: twelve each luncheon forks, soup spoons, salad forks, seafood forks, luncheon knives, teaspoons, 10 butter spreaders & a cake server; Alvin Corp., Providence, Rhode Island, ca. 1940, 83 pcs...................... **805**
Clinton patt., dinner service: thirty-six tea-spoons, twenty-four cocktail forks, eighteen each dinner forks, luncheon forks, salad forks, bouillon spoons, soup spoons, demitasse spoons, dinner knives, luncheon knives & butter spreaders plus a two-piece carving set & eight serving pieces; Tiffany & Co., New York, New York, 232 pcs...................... **9,775**
Cluny patt., dinner service: thirty-six tea-spoons, eighteen each dinner knives, luncheon knives, iced tea spoons, cocktail forks, salad forks, grapefruit spoons, dinner forks, butter spreaders, luncheon forks, soup spoons & dessert knives, twelve steak knives, seven tablespoons, six each sauce ladles, pairs of salad servers, dessert serving spoons, serving forks & fish knives, four each pie slices & paté slices, two cake combs & pair of ice tongs, basting spoon, crumb scoop & asparagus server; silver-gilt, some pieces monogrammed, Gorham Mfg. Co., Providence, Rhode Island, ca. 1890 & later, 297 pcs. **16,100**
Commonwealth patt., dinner service: eight each table forks, salad forks, cocktail forks, dessert forks, demitasse spoons,

dessert spoons, grapefruit spoons, soup spoons, butter spreaders, 9 1/2" knives & 8 3/4" knives, twelve five o'clock spoons, ten teaspoons, two-piece salad serving set, two-piece fish serving set & one each cold meat fork, large serving spoon, cake saw, cake server, gravy ladle, sugar spoon, sugar tongs, butter serving knife, lemon fork, jelly knife, cheese knife, jelly spoon, ice tongs & roast carving fork & knife; hand-wrought, Porter Blanchard, Calabasas, California, 129 pcs. **8,050**

Devon patt., dinner service: twelve each dinner forks, salad forks, cake forks, seafood forks, soup spoons, teaspoons, grapefruit spoons, demitasse spoons, dinner knives & luncheon knives, sixteen butter spreaders & six fruit knives; Reed & Barton, Taunton, Massachusetts, 142 pcs. **2,185**

Eloquence patt., dinner service: sixteen each salad forks, cocktail forks, iced beverage spoons, dessert spoons, cream soup spoons, luncheon knives, butter spreaders & steak knives, fifteen luncheon forks & teaspoons, thirteen demitasse spoons, twelve place spoons, three tablespoons, pierced tablespoons, butter serving knives & cake knives, two two-piece salad serving sets, buffet spoons, buffet forks, gravy ladles, sauce ladles, bonbon spoons, sugar spoons, jelly servers, olive forks & sugar tongs, one cheese serving knife; Lunt Silversmiths, Greenfield, Massachusetts, 218 pcs......... **4,312**

English Gadroon patt., dinner service: ten each luncheon forks, salad forks, luncheon knives & butter spreaders, eight cocktail forks, twenty-three teaspoons, six demitasse spoons, two tablespoons, one each cream soup spoon, gravy ladle & cake server; Gorham Mfg. Co., Providence, Rhode Island, 92 pcs...................... **1,265**

Federal Cotillion patt., dinner service: twelve each luncheon forks, salad forks, ice cream forks, luncheon knives & butter spreaders, sixteen teaspoons, eight demitasse spoons, two-piece steak carving set, one berry spoon, salad serving fork, tablespoon, gravy ladle, pierced flat server, cold meat fork, bonbon spoon, sugar tongs, cream ladle, sugar spoon, jelly server, butter serving knife, lemon fork, olive fork, cake server & cheese server; Frank Smith Silver Co., Gardner, Massachusetts, 110 pcs. **2,300**

Francis I patt., dinner service: eight each dinner knives, dinner forks, soup spoons, teaspoons, butter knives, luncheon forks & seafood forks, plus one each sugar spoon, salad serving set, gravy ladle & two serving spoons; Reed & Barton, Taunton, Massachusetts, 1907, 62 pcs................................. **2,000-2,500**

Francis I patt., dinner service: forty-two teaspoons, twenty-four each luncheon forks, salad forks, luncheon knives & butter spreaders (twelve w/silver blades), twenty bouillon spoons, twelve each dinner

knives, soup spoons, demitasse spoons, coffee spoons, dinner forks, cocktail forks, ice cream forks, eight grapefruit spoons plus fourteen serving pieces, w/two wood cases; Reed & Barton, Taunton, Massachusetts, 20th c., 276 pcs. **9,000-10,000**

Heiress patt., dinner service: twelve cocktail forks, butter spreaders, iced beverage spoons, soup spoons & luncheon knives, eighteen salad forks, nineteen luncheon forks, twenty-four teaspoons, two serving spoons & cold meat forks & one gravy ladle, butter serving knife & sugar spoon; Oneida Silversmiths, Sherrill, New York, in fitted wooden case, 128 pcs... **900-1,000**

Imperial Chrysanthemum patt., dinner service: twenty-four each table forks & dessert forks, twenty-one tablespoons, twelve each dessert forks, teaspoons, fruit spoons, demitasse spoons, fish forks, cocktail forks, fish knives & butter knives, four condiment spoons & one each fish server, fish slice, serving fork, punch ladle & lobster server plus twenty-four table knives & twelve dessert knives & fruit knives w/stainless steel blades; the terminals chased w/flower heads & leaves, also engraved w/a monogram, in fitted wooden case, 222 pcs. **6,500-8,000**

King Albert patt., dinner service: twelve each dinner knives, dinner forks, salad forks, ice cream forks, teaspoons, dessert spoons, cocktail forks & butter knives plus carving knife, meat fork, serving spoon, cheese knife, berry spoon & sugar castor spoon; Whiting Mfg. Co., Providence, Rhode Island, 102 pcs. **1,425**

King William patt., dinner service: eight each luncheon forks, salad forks, butter spreaders, dessert spoons, cream soup spoons & luncheon knives; monogrammed, Tiffany & Co., New York, New York, 1907-47, in fitted wooden case, 48 pcs.. **978**

Kings patt., dinner service: twelve each dinner forks, dinner knives, butter spreaders & dessert spoons, 24 each teaspoons & salad forks plus seven serving pieces; engraved monogram, Towle Silversmiths, Newburyport, Massachusetts, ca. 1904, 103 pcs. **1,265**

Lap-Over-Edge Etched patt., dinner service: twenty-four each teaspoons & luncheon forks, twelve each dinner knives, luncheon knives, butter spreaders, dinner forks, dessert spoons & dessert knives, ten tablespoons, one sauce ladle & butter knife; etched w/plants, animals & fish, some identified on the back, engraved w/name "Scoville" in script on back, Tiffany & Co., New York, New York, ca. 1885, 132 pcs. **20,700**

Louis XIII Richelieu patt., dinner service: twelve each dinner knives, dinner forks, luncheon knives, luncheon forks, tablespoons, dessert spoons, lobster forks, teaspoons, fish knives, fish forks, demitasse spoons, three butter knives, two serving forks & one each soup ladle, sauce ladle, slice, cake knife & cheese knife; monogrammed, w/rattail bowls, tri-fid ends & cannon-handled knives w/stainless steel blades, Puiforcat, Paris, France, 20th c., in three fitted trays stamped w/maker's name, 144 pcs. **28,750**

Mansion House patt., dinner service: twelve each dinner knives, butter knives, dinner forks, luncheon forks, soup spoons & teaspoons plus thirteen serving pieces; Heirloom, Oneida Silversmiths, Sherrill, New York, 85 pcs. **600-700**

Old English Feather Edge patt., dinner service: twelve each dinner knives, din-ner forks, salad forks, soup spoons, des-sert spoons & teaspoons, together w/twelve cheese knives w/bone handles; Garrard & Co., Ltd., London, England, 1962-63, 84 pcs.................................... **4,025**

Old English patt., dinner service: thirty-six each dinner knives & dinner forks, twen-ty-four each luncheon knives, luncheon forks & dessert spoons, twelve each fish knives, fish forks, dessert knives, dessert forks, tablespoons & teaspoons, four sauce ladles, pair of salad servers, pair of fish servers, one gravy spoon & four-piece carving set; in fitted oak cabinet w/five drawers & double doors, Francis Higgins, London, England, 1936, 229 pcs. **20,700**

Old French patt., dinner service: twelve each bread & butter plates, luncheon knives, dinner knives, fruit forks, lun-cheon forks, demitasse spoons, dessert forks, salad forks, iced tea spoons, egg spoons, citrus spoons, soup spoons, cream soup spoons, teaspoons & table-spoons, eleven each dinner forks & cock-tail forks, ten butter knives & two master butter knives; in mahogany case, Gorham Mfg. Co., Providence, Rhode Island, ca. 1915, 220 pcs............................ **4,675**

Old Newbury patt., dinner service: eight each luncheon forks, dessert spoons & dinner knives, seven luncheon forks & cocktail forks, six butter spreaders & tea-spoons & one each vegetable spoon, pastry server, cold meat fork & serving spoon; hand-wrought, Old Newbury Crafters, Newburyport, Massachusetts, 54 pcs... **1,265**

Pine Tree patt., dinner service: twelve each dinner forks, salad forks, cocktail forks, butter spreaders, teaspoons, bouillon spoons & dinner knives, two table-spoons, two-piece salad serving set, one gravy ladle & cake server; in fitted case, International Silver Co., Meriden, Con-necticut, 90 pcs..................................... **748**

Plymouth patt., dinner service: twelve each dinner forks, luncheon forks, salad forks w/gilt tines, cocktail forks, teaspoons, soup spoons, demitasse spoons w/gilt bowls, butter spreaders, dinner knives & luncheon knives, three tablespoons & one each cream ladle w/gilt bowl, olive spoon w/gilt bowl, pickle fork, butter serv-ing knife, salad serving fork w/gilt tines & cake server; monogrammed "H.W.B.,"

Gorham Mfg. Co., Providence, Rhode Is-land, 129 pcs. **920**

Repoussé patt., dinner service: eight each luncheon forks, salad forks, butter spreaders, teaspoons, coffee spoons & luncheon knives plus two serving spoons & ladles & one each serving fork, berry spoon, pickle fork, slice, sugar shell, but-ter knife, jelly slice & meat fork & knife; monogrammed, S. Kirk & Co., Baltimore, Maryland, 61 pcs................................ **2,875**

Romance of the Sea patt., dinner service: eight each dinner knives, butter knives, soup spoons, salad forks, dinner forks & teaspoons; in fitted wooden case, R. Wallace & Sons Mfg. Co., Wallingford, Connecticut, 48 pcs........................... **1,035**

Rose patt., dinner service: eight each lun-cheon forks, salad forks, butter spread-ers, bouillon spoons, demitasse spoons & luncheon knives, eleven small tea-spoons, seven teaspoons, three table-spoons, two-piece steak carving set & one jelly server, sugar spoon, butter pick, lemon fork & gravy ladle; in fitted case, monogrammed "C," Steiff Co., Baltimore, Maryland, 76 pcs.................................... **1,035**

Royal Danish patt., dinner service: twelve each luncheon forks, demitasse spoons, soup spoons & butter spreaders, ten ta-blespoons & dinner knives, nine dinner forks & teaspoons, eight cocktail forks & luncheon knives, seven salad forks, five dessert spoons, two large serving spoons & one salad serving fork, gravy ladle, large cold meat fork & pickle fork; International Silver Co., Meriden, Con-necticut, 120 pcs. **2,185**

Strasbourg patt., dinner service: eight each dinner knives, dinner forks, salad forks & butter knives, sixteen teaspoons, three serving spoons & one each ladle, berry spoon, slotted spoon & meat fork; gold-washed, in wooden cutlery box, Gorham Mfg. Co., Providence, Rhode Is-land, 55 pcs.. **1,330**

Suffolk patt., dinner service: twelve each dinner forks, salad forks, cocktail forks, teaspoons, soup spoons, grapefruit spoons w/gilt bowls, demitasse spoons, butter spreaders & dinner knives w/silver plate blades plus one each large serving spoon, pastry server, lettuce fork & sugar spoon; monogrammed "B," Alvin Corpo-ration, Providence, Rhode Island, 112 pcs.. **978**

Tapestry patt., dinner service: twelve each luncheon forks, dessert spoons, salad forks, luncheon knives, dessert knives, twenty-four teaspoons, plus nine serving pieces; Reed & Barton, Taunton, Massachusetts, ca. 1964, 93 pcs.............. **1,380**

Versailles patt., dinner service: twelve each dinner knives, luncheon knives, bouillon spoons, teaspoons, dinner forks, luncheon forks & ice cream spoons, elev-en each demitasse spoons & salad forks, eight butter knives, plus twelve serving pieces; Gorham Mfg. Co., Providence, Rhode Island, early 20th c., 126 pcs. **4,255**

Versailles patt., dinner service: twelve each salad forks, dinner forks, teaspoons, soup spoons, dinner knives & butter spreaders, ten small teaspoons & eight seafood forks; monogrammed, Gorham Mfg. Co., Providence, Rhode Island, 1888, 90 pcs. **2,300**

Winchester patt., dinner service: twelve each dinner forks, salad forks, teaspoons, cream soup spoons, dinner knives & butter spreaders, two tablespoons & one cold meat fork; in fitted wooden case, Shreve & Co., San Francisco, California, 75 pcs. **1,092**

Windsor patt., dinner service: eight each luncheon forks, teaspoons, demitasse spoons, luncheon knives, salad forks, soup spoons & butter spreaders, plus a meat fork & knife; monogrammed, Old Newbury Crafters, Inc., Newburyport, Massachusetts, retailed by Cartier, 58 pcs. (one handle separate from knife) **1,265**

Woodlily patt., dinner service: eight each luncheon forks, salad forks, butter spreaders, cream soup spoons & luncheon knives, sixteen teaspoons, two tablespoons & one gravy ladle & butter serving knife; in fitted wooden case, Frank Smith Silver Co., Gardner, Massachusetts, 60 pcs. **1,150**

Silver plate (hollowware)

Finely Woven Silver Plate Basket

Basket, wide shallow form composed of fine tightly woven silver wire w/blue glass beads around the rim & twisted wire loop handles, medallion in center bottom shows City Hall Square in Seattle, Washington, early 20th c., 6 1/4" d. plus handles (ILLUS.) **25**

International Silver Bowl

Bowl, slightly squared form w/low flaring sides w/wide plain panels alternating w/scroll-stamped corner panels, International Silver Co., No. 1048, 6 1/2" w. (ILLUS.) **25**

Bud Vase with Chickens on Base

Bud vase, a fancy Victorian silver plate holder w/a round base topped by a figural rooster & hen, a small upright ring supports the slender deep amethyst blown glass trumpet-form vase w/enameled flowers, overall 6 1/4" h. (ILLUS.) **445**

Rare Bud Vase with Stork Base

Bud vase, base w/ringed tapering platform supporting a figural crane w/its head down standing in front of a leafy tree supporting a lily-form blown cranberry glass vase, indistinct marks on the base, 19th c., overall 13 1/2" h. (ILLUS.) **1,295**

Rare Victorian Double Bud Vase

Bud vase, double-type, a domed base w/scroll tab feet, stamped w/ornate florals & issuing two ornate scrolling griffins, each holding a metal fitted w/a pale yellow blown glass vase w/a ruffled rim, base marked "H.L.& Co. - No. 4384," 19th c., 10 1/2" w., 9 3/4" h. (ILLUS.)......... **1,350**

Victorian Bud Vase with Girl on Base

Bud vase, figural base w/a round foot topped by a kneeling Victorian girl beside an upright stem w/long leaf brackets supporting the slender tapering shaded green to clear glass vase w/gilt enameling, base by Meriden, No. 66, overall 9 1/2" h. (ILLUS.).. **300**

Bud Vase with Unique Figural Base

Bud vase, ornate base w/small palmette feet on a rectangular platform supporting a pair of hippocampus issuing tall S-scroll supports ending in large flower heads & holding a tall slender trumpet-form green glass vase w/gold band trim, base by Reed & Barton, No. 2230, 19th c., overall 11 3/4" h. (ILLUS.) **695**

Bud Vase with Cherub Base

Bud vase, the base w/a round foot supporting a standing cherub in front of a pair of pierced flower & scroll uprights flanking a ring support for the clear trumpet-form blown glass vase, base w/Tufts mark & No. 1092, 19th c., overall 10 1/4" h. (ILLUS.) **595**

Silver Plate Candelabrum

Candelabra, three-light, the short central shaft cast w/blossoms & supporting a bulbous floral cast socket flanked by serpentine arms ending in matching sockets, round domed base w/wide cast blossom & scroll band, marked "Ballad Community," 9" w., 6 1/8" h., pr. (ILLUS. of one)... **170**

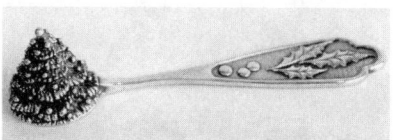

Christmas Tree Candle Snuffer

Candle snuffer, handle end decorated w/holly leaves & berries, snuffer is in the form of a decorated Christmas tree, 7 1/2" l. (ILLUS.)... **45**

Victorian Silver Plate Candlesticks

Candlesticks, square domed base, the shaft composed of two inverted bell-form sections centered by a knob, decorated overall w/panels of small rose sprigs, baluster-form socket w/wide rolled rim, Victorian, 12 3/8" h., pr. (ILLUS.) **195**

Columnar Silver Plate Candlesticks

Candlesticks, weighted, stepped, reeded, circular bases & flaring capitals on simple shaft, 9 1/2" h., the pr. (ILLUS.) **65**

Silver Plate Card Basket

Card basket, stepped circular base holder in form of dolphin, which supports round tray w/engraved floral decoration & scalloped rim, handle w/applied openwork floral decoration, 7 x 9 3/4" (ILLUS.) **959**

Fluted-rim Card Tray

Card tray, rectangular, footed, w/fluted rim and tray embossed w/design of oak leaves & acorns, w/applied bird perched atop two-pronged side handle curving over center of tray, marked on bottom "Jan. 31, 1893 - 1430," Pairpoint, 5 3/4 x 6 x 7" (ILLUS.) **395**

Silver Plate Cheese Ball Holder

Cheese ball holder, wide footed base decorated w/scrollwork curves up to flat circular holder w/three inward-curving prongs to hold cheese, applied handle w/scrollwork, made by Wilcox, style number 42, dated June 2, 1891, 4 1/2 x 6 3/4 x 10" (ILLUS.) **525**

Silver Plate Child's Cup

Child's cup, w/handle, slightly bulbous form embossed w/scene of little boy in hat playing a lute in wooded landscape w/rabbits & trees, made by Queen City Silver Co., Cincinnati, Ohio, 2 1/4 x 2 3/4 x 3 1/2" (ILLUS.).......................... **85**

Old Silver Plate Cigar Holder

Cigar holder, barrel-shaped w/ruffled rim, embossed floral band around the base, engraved w/a smoking cigar, Wilcox Silver mark on base, 2 3/4" d., 3" h. (ILLUS.) **25**

Covered Coffee Container with Spoon

Coffee container, cov., rolled foot, hand-hammered & pierced decoration above pierced letters spelling "COFFEE," blue glass liner, spoon attaches to holder, 3 7/8 x 5 1/2" (ILLUS.) **35**

Plated Coffeepot, Creamer & Sugar

Coffee service: cov. coffeepot, creamer & open sugar; Classical-style w/hammered surfaces decorated w/shields & garlands, stylized geometric handles, marked on bottom "Sheffield - made in USA" & other marks, style number 0618 on each, coffeepot 10" h., the set (ILLUS.) **245**

Coffee urn & warmer, cov., the tall ovoid lobed body w/a tall waisted neck w/flaring ruffled rim & inset domed cover, arched scroll handles from the rim to the shoulder, ornate spigot on the lower body, detailed cast leaf & flower design, raised on a matching scroll-trimmed base w/small burner raised on S-scroll legs, Reed & Barton, late 19th - early 20th c., overall 17" h., the set **275**

Coffeepot with Stand & Warmer

Coffeepot, cover, stand & warmer, domed rectangular stand w/warmer, decorated w/grape clusters, scrolls, flowers & leaves, 14 3/4" h., the set (ILLUS.) **425**

Apollo Silver Co. Collar Button Box

Collar button box, cov., round, footed, embossed decoration, lid decorated w/figure of prancing devil and "Where is my collar button?," Apollo Silver Co., 2 1/4 x 2 3/4" (ILLUS.) **185**

Late Victorian Decorated Compote

Compote, a wide round domed foot & short pedestal supporting a deep bowl w/a wide & deeply rolled & flared rim stamped w/ornate scrolls, swags & blossoms, Wilcox Silver mark, No. 819, last quarter 19th c., 9 1/2" d., 5 3/4"h. (ILLUS.) **125**

Victorian Silver Plate Cracker Jar

Cracker jar, cov., squatty bulbous body on tiny scroll feet, fitted low domed cover w/disk finial, twisted bail handle, engraved on the front w/"Crackers" enclosed by leafy flower sprigs, Rockford Silver Plate Co., No. 401, 6 1/4" d. (ILLUS.) **165**

Victorian Silver Plate Set

Creamer, cov. sugar & spooner, each w/a tapering cylindrical body bright-cut w/stylized flowers & leafy sprigs, flared mouth & angular handles, Meriden Britannia Co., No. 1800, ca. 1890, the set (ILLUS.)... **75**

Oval Dish with Stamped Grapes

Dish, long shallow oval form w/boldly stamped clusters of grapes & leaves, Homan Silverplate Co., No. 1685T, patented in 1903, 6 3/4 x 11" (ILLUS.)............... **295**

Pretty Dish with Grapevine Design

Dish, long shallow oval form w/the wide border stamped w/an ornate grapevine design, indistinct mark, late 19th - early 20th c., 8 x 12 1/4" (ILLUS.) **195**

Fancy Miniature Silver Plate Frame

Frame, table model, miniature, ornately stamped rococo scrolls around the sides w/roses at the top corners, Gorham mark & number 350, late 19th - early 20th c., 3 3/4 x 5" (ILLUS.) **95**

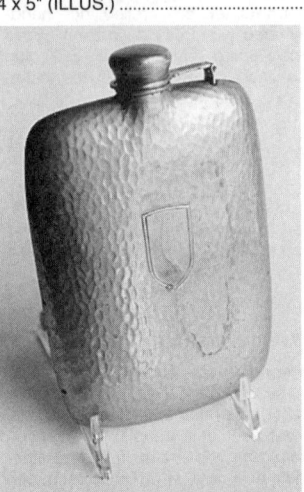

Old Silver Plate Hip Flask

Hip flask, flattened rectangular form w/rounded corners & hinged domed cap on spout, overall hammered finish w/engraved center shield, late 19th - early 20th c., 3 3/4 x 6" (ILLUS.) **65**

Elaborate Horse & Cart Napkin Ring

Napkin ring, in the form of a two-wheeled cart pulled by a prancing horse, ring sits atop cart & is engraved w/leaves & flowers, marked "Meriden," style number 213, 1 3/4 x 2 1/2 x 3 1/4" (ILLUS.)............... **750**

Serving Dish with Hammered Decor

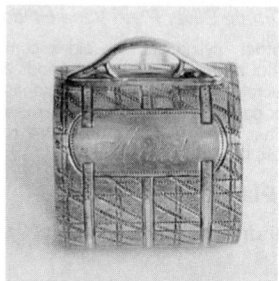

Valise Napkin Ring

Napkin ring, in the form of a valise complete w/strap handle and "Maud" engraved in rounded rectangular space on front, 1 3/4 x 2 x 2 1/4" (ILLUS.) **225**

Nut Dish with Squirrel

Nut dish, oval bowl in the form of sectioned petals creating scalloped rim, on triangular-shaped feet decorated w/flowers, applied figure of squirrel sits on branch curving over inside of bowl, marked on bottom w/indistinct style number, 6 1/2 x 8" (ILLUS.)... **225**

Victorian Salt Cellar with Sphinx

Salt cellar, a round dish perched atop three small figural sphinx feet, late 19th c., 3" d., 1 1/2" h. (ILLUS.) **40**

Modern Egg-shaped Shakers

Salt & pepper shakers, egg-shaped, rubber stoppers in base, 20th c., 3" h., pr. (ILLUS.) **10**

Serving dish, cov., flat-bottomed oval base w/wide flanged rim, flat-topped domed cover w/angled loop handles, hand-hammered surface, by Meriden, No. 2210, late 19th - early 20th c., 8 1/2 x 11" (ILLUS., top of page) **75**

Attractive Silver Plate Teapot

Teapot, cov., round foot below the wide squatty bulbous body tapering to a short flared neck w/a domed hinged cover, leafy scroll-trimmed spout & C-scroll handle, marked on bottom "Silver on Copper [crown] S [shield]," probably England, late 19th - early 20th c., 8" h. (ILLUS.) **100**

Victorian Silver Plate Humidor

Tobacco humidor, wide round foot below the wide squatty ringed body w/an applied band of flowers & scrolls, low domed cover fitted w/three long figural crossed pipes, Webster & Sons mark, No. 431, late 19th - early 20th c., 5 1/4" d., 4 5/8" h. (ILLUS.)................................ **85**

Hissing Cat Toothpick Holder

Toothpick holder, figural, form of a hissing cat w/raised tail stands next to cylinder-shaped holder decorated w/landscapes & flowers, marked on bottom "Tufts - 3411," 2 x 2 1/4 x 2 3/4" (ILLUS.) **350**

Bulldog Toothpick Holder

Toothpick holder, figural, growling bulldog sits next to holder w/fluted flaring rim, bottom marked "Derby Silverplate Co., - 2306," 2 1/8 x 2 3/4 x 3 1/2" (ILLUS.) **295**

Ornate Silver Plate Vase Holder

Vase holder, cylindrical, the sides composed of narrow pierced scroll bands & wide scroll & blossom-embossed bands, Wilcox company mark, No. 3377, missing glass liner, late 19th c., 2 3/4" d., 4 5/8" h. (ILLUS.) **33**

Silver Plate (Flatware)

Grosvenor (Oneida Community) - 1927

Detail of Grosvenor Pattern Flatware

Grosvenor Bonbon Spoon

Bonbon spoon (ILLUS.) **55**

Grosvenor Cheese Server

Cheese server (ILLUS.) **65**

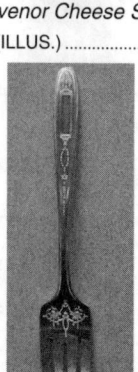

Grosvenor Salad Fork

Salad fork (ILLUS.) **20**

Japanese (Holmes Booth & Hayden) - 1879

Detail of Japanese Pattern Flatware

Japanese Berry Fork

Berry fork (ILLUS.) **32**

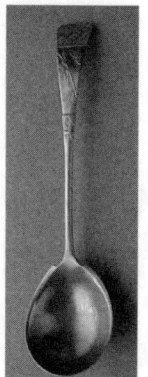

Japanese Gravy Ladle

Gravy ladle (ILLUS.) **40**

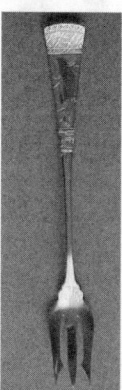

Japanese Oyster Fork

Oyster fork (ILLUS.) **25**

Japanese Seafood Fork

Seafood fork (ILLUS.) **25**

Newport (1847 Rogers Bros.) - 1879

Newport Cocktail Fork

Cocktail fork (ILLUS.) **42**

Detail of Newport Pattern Flatware

Newport Nut Pick

Nut pick (ILLUS.).. **20**

Newport Butter Serving Knife

Butter serving knife, master (ILLUS.)................. **25**

Newport Pie Fork

Pie fork (ILLUS.)... **40**

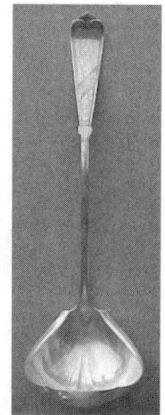

Newport Soup Ladle

Soup ladle (ILLUS.) **85**

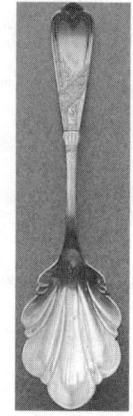

Newport Sugar Shell

Sugar shell (ILLUS.) **20**

Newport Sugar Tongs

Sugar tongs (ILLUS.) **45**

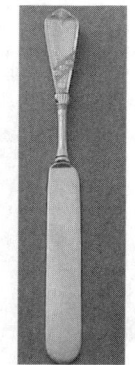

Newport Youth Knife

Youth knife (ILLUS.) **65**

Yale I (Wm. Rogers) - 1894

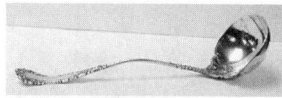

Large Silver Plate Ladle

Ladle, curved handle decorated w/flowers & scrollwork, 12 1/2" l. (ILLUS.) **78**

Spelter

Devil Ashtray

Ashtray, in the form of a spread-winged devil w/goatee, horns & bat ears, 1 3/4 x 5 x 5" (ILLUS.) **175**

Nodding-head Figure Ashtray

Ashtray, spelter & tin, base w/nodding-head figure of black boy standing smoking a cigar, original worn paint, made in Austria, 3 x 4 x 4 1/2" (ILLUS.)....................... **295**

Spelter Baby Shoe Bank

Bank, model of a baby shoe, copper finish, 2 x 5", 2 3/4" h. (ILLUS.) **14**

John Deere Tractor Bank

Bank, model of a John Deere tractor, issued by the Deere Credit Union, third edition, copper finish, 6" l., 3 1/4" h. (ILLUS.)............... **60**

Spelter "Despair" Book End

Book ends, bronzed finish, rounded arch upright, relief cast w/allegorical figure of "Despair," weighted base, 5 1/2 x 6 1/4", pr. (ILLUS. of one)... **69**

Musketeer Spelter Book End

Book ends, figure of a standing musketeer laughing & holding a broken sword, bronzed patina, marked "Artbronz - Copyright KB.W.," cracked surfaces, 8 1/2" h., pr. (ILLUS. of one) **60**

Frankart Scottie Book End

Book ends, model of a Scottie dog on a rectangular base w/backplate, bronzed finish, marked "Frankart Inc. Patent Applied for," 5 1/2" l., 3 3/4" h., pr. (ILLUS. of one)... **125**

Spelter Coffin Plate

Coffin plate, cartouche decorated w/engraved "At Rest," w/embossed flowers & leaves forming partial border, marked on back "CC Co. - 58," 4 x 8 1/2" (ILLUS.).......... **10**

Early Engraved Coffin Plate

Coffin plate, flat rectangular form w/scroll border, engraved "Our Loved One," 2 x 3 5/8" (ILLUS.)... **15**

Handled Commemorative Cup

Cup, three-handled, each handle in the form of a winged dragon, embossed on the side "October 3rd. 1899," silvered finish, 5" w., 4" h. (ILLUS.) **150**

Spelter Art Deco Holder with Woman

Dish holder, figural, a seated stylized Art Deco nude woman w/a dished tray in her lap & her arms outstretched, on a rectangular base, dark finish, 6" h. (ILLUS.)............ **145**

Figurine of Man Riding Elephant

Figurine, black man riding tusked elephant, w/original paint, 1 x 2 1/4 x 2 5/8" (ILLUS.).. **295**

Figurine of Hippo Swallowing Man

Figurine, hippo swallowing human, bottom half of which protrudes from hippo's mouth, w/applied swirls of water plants, original paint, 1 1/2 x 2 x 2 5/8" (ILLUS.) **395**

Figural Incense Burner

Incense burner, in the form of a Moor in cloak & turban sitting next to a lidded, handled woven basket w/holes in lid for incense, original paint in black, brown, red, blue & white, 3 1/4 x 4 1/8 x 5 1/2" (ILLUS.) **395**

Spelter Inkstand with Virgin Mary

Inkstand, footed oblong dish w/raised cov., inkwell & pen trough cast w/roses below a raised standing figure of the Virgin Mary, gold finish, 4 1/2 x 5", 4" h. (ILLUS.) **79**

Souvenir Inkstand

Inkstand, souvenir of Valley Forge, Pennsylvania, w/image of Washington's headquarters & "Washington Memorial Chapel" embossed on lid & base, pen rest in front, gold finish, 1 1/4 x 4 x 5 (ILLUS.) **95**

Inkwell with Seated Dog on Cover

Inkwell, cov., the hinged top w/a seated small spaniel-like dog drinking from a wine flask, atop a columnar base w/dolphins at each corner, worn gilt finish, 3 1/2" h. (ILLUS.) **95**

Cupid & Flowers on Jewelry Box

Jewelry box, cov., Art Nouveau style, flared undulating scroll & flower base, the flat cover w/a full-figure reclining Cupid holding an arrow, gold painted finish, lined in

fabric, early 20th c., 4 1/4 x 6 1/4", 4 1/2" h. (ILLUS.) **275**

Spelter Art Nouveau Jewelry Box

Jewelry box, cov., footed oval form boldly cast w/Art Nouveau-style roses, gold finish, lined in pink fabric, early 20th c., 4 x 6", 4 1/2" h. (ILLUS.) **75**

Jewelry box with Cupid on Cover

Jewelry box, cov., rectangular casket-form w/serpentine sides, the cover cast in relief w/a cupid & flowers, the base w/serpentine sides w/scrolls & peg feet, worn gold finish, marked on bottom "NB Rogers SP Co - 5," 3 x 4 1/2", 2 3/4" h. (ILLUS.) **50**

Spelter Heart-shaped Jewelry Box

Jewelry box, cov., stylized heart shape, the hinged cover trimmed w/scrolls around a central shield, further scrolls around base, worn silver finish, early 20th c., 3 x 3 3/8" (ILLUS.) **45**

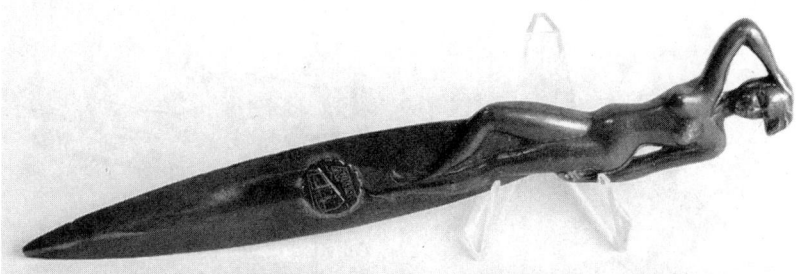

Advertising Letter Opener

base w/patent number 123112, 5 1/4" h.
(ILLUS.) **195**

Jewelry & Perfume Holder

Jewelry & perfume holder, oblong fabric-covered base w/pierced brass feet holds figure of girl holding a flower in one hand & a basket meant to hold jewelry in the other, flanked by two glass perfume bottles w/cut-glass stoppers that fit into indentations in base, 3 x 5 1/2 x 6 1/2"
(ILLUS.)... **595**

Letter opener, copper finish, handle in the figure of a nude woman w/arm raised behind head advertising the Minneapolis Auditorium, an image of which appears in circle on blade, marked "patent pending," 8 1/2" l. (ILLUS., top of page)........................... **65**

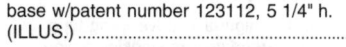

Typewriter Paperweight

Paperweight, commemorative, in the shape of a typewriter, marked at top "Underwood" and on reverse "Golden Jubilee Dinner, to Matthew S. Eglar, April 28, 1939," 1 3/8 x 2 3/4 x 2 3/4" (ILLUS.) **75**

Husky Dog Advertising Paperweight

Paperweight, copper finish, rectangular base holds figure of Husky dog standing w/head turned to side, side of base reads "Western Oil & Fuel Company" (which sold Husky Gas), 2 3/8 x 4 x 4 1/4"
(ILLUS.) **295**

Spelter Dog with Three Faces

Model of a dog, seated animal w/the head having three different faces, marked on

Bill Drite Figural Paperweight

Paperweight, figural advertising-type, standing bearded gnome smoking a pipe & holding a toolbox, marked on front of the square base "Bill Drite with Insulite," "Bill Drite" also on the sides of base, copper finish, 2 1/2" sq., 4" h. (ILLUS.).................. **85**

Black Uncle Sam Pencil Sharpener

Pencil sharpener, caricature of black man wearing Uncle Sam-type top hat & bow tie, original black, red, white & blue paint, made in Occupied Japan, 1/2 x 1 1/8 x 2" (ILLUS.).. **165**

Pistol Pencil Sharpener

Pencil sharpener, in the form of a pistol w/hinged tin top & original green paint, made in Germany, 1/2 x 1 3/4 x 2 5/8" (ILLUS.).. **75**

Greyhound Bus Salt & Pepper Shakers

Salt & pepper shakers, model of Greyhound bus, original rubber wheels, silver paint w/blue trim & cork stoppers, Japan, 2 3/4" l., pr. (ILLUS.).. **79**

Spelter Souvenir Shakers

Salt & pepper shakers, square tapering form, cast w/scenes & souvenir markings for Ft. Snelling, Minnesota, scroll trim, early 20th c., 2 3/8" h., pr. (ILLUS.)................. **20**

Spelter Sewing Case

Sewing case, rectangular, w/hinged lid, top w/rectangular miniature framed photo of the Mohawk Trail set in oval garland & bow border, 2 x 2 1/2" (ILLUS.) **75**

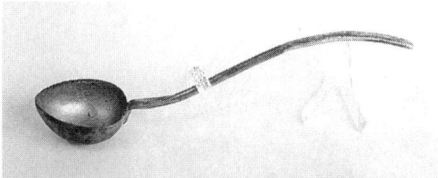

Advertising Snuff Scoop

Snuff scoop, advertising "Weyman's Copenhagen Snuff," bowl holds one ounce, long, curved applied handle, 10 1/2" l. (ILLUS.) **145**

Souvenir Thermometer

Thermometer, in the form of a dog standing in rustic doghouse, w/original paint in red, green, blue, yellow & white, souvenir of Lake Benton, Minnesota, 4 3/8" h. (ILLUS.) **225**

Frog & Snail Toothpick Holder

Toothpick holder, figural, in the shape of a frog pulling a snail shell w/a bee on the end, marked w/style number "3462," 2 x 2 1/2 x 4 1/2" (ILLUS.) **295**

Footed Spelter Vase

Vase, bulbous form tapering at neck & slightly flaring outward at lip, on three short feet, decorated w/figure of girl feeding carrots to rabbits, marked "Germany," 6 1/4" h. (ILLUS.) **195**

Figural Spelter Vase Holder

Vase holder, figural, weighted figure of a nude young girl bending backward w/arms outstretched to hold the missing vase, black finish, 8" h. (ILLUS.) **200**

Steel

Unusual Box with Scotties

Box, cov., cylindrical, w/three small figural Scottie dog feet & a standing Scottie finial on the cover, original worn pale green paint, marked on base w/number 3442, ca. 1930s, 3 1/2" d., 4 1/4" h. (ILLUS.) **175**

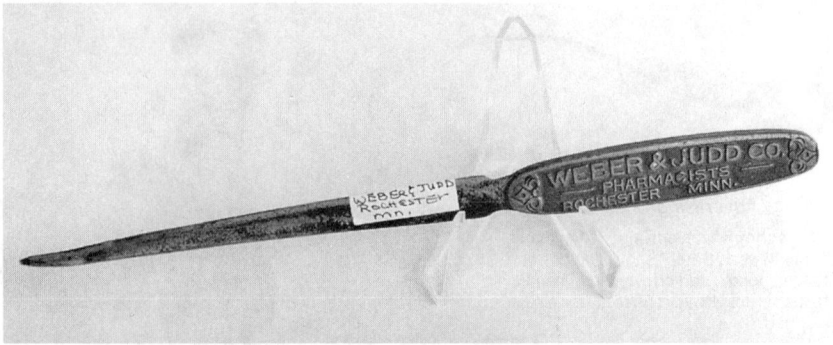

Advertising Letter Opener

Can opener, Sieger, 5 1/2" **15**

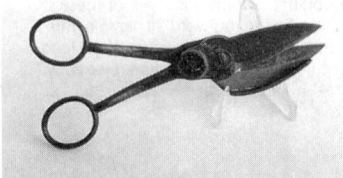

Steel Wick-trimming Snuffer

Candle snuffer, wick-trimming scissors w/old blackened surface & raised lip to catch wick trimmings, 6" l. (ILLUS.).................. **45**

Egg beater, "Ladd Beater July 7, 1908 Oct. 18, 1921," 11 1/2" **25**

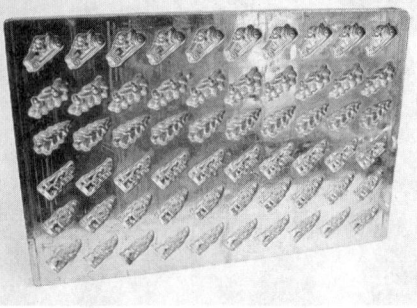

Christmas Chocolate Mold Sheet

Mold, chocolate, sheet w/Christmas shape molds, sheet measures 10 3/4 x 16 3/4" (ILLUS.) **295**

Pot scraper, advertising-type, marked "Case Tractors" **95**

Steel Key-wind Toy Truck

Toy, cast, keywind, pickup truck w/original box, made in U.S. Zone Germany, marked on bottom "Varianto Lasto 3042" & "patents applied for," Schuco, 1 1/2 x 1 3/4", 4 1/4" l. (ILLUS.) **250**

Stainless Steel Kraut Chopper

Kraut chopper, stainless, w/cast-iron handle, two blades, made by Acme & marked "patent pending," 1 3/8 x 5 1/4 x 5 1/2" (ILLUS.) **12**

Letter opener, w/brass handle embossed "Weber & Judd Co. - Pharmacists - Rochester Minn.," 7 1/4" l. (ILLUS., top of page) **35**

Mixer, stainless steel, "Japan Bicor Battery Power," 9" **15**

Heinz Toy Delivery Truck

Toy, stamped, Heinz delivery truck w/original worn paint, primarily white, green & red, rubber wheels, decorated w/Heinz pickle logo in center of circle that reads "Pure Food Products" around border & "57 Varieties" inside, signs on side of truck read "Baked Beans - Bottled Vinegars" & "Rice Flakes," top of cab has NRA eagle symbol in red, white & blue, marked on bottom "Metalcrafts Corporation - St. Louis," 4 x 5 1/2", 12" l. (ILLUS.).. **795**

Douglas Seven Seas Toy Airplane

Toy airplane, friction (when wheels are spun, the propellers revolve), in style of Douglas Seven Seas plane, red, white & blue, made in Japan, 17 1/4" l. (ILLUS.)........ **275**

Tin & Tole

American flag, tin, one-sided silhouetted waving flag w/red & white stripes & 20 white stars on blue, pierced overall w/holes for small electric light bulbs, early 20th c., 51 x 52" (imperfections) **4,600**
Candle lantern, tin, Paul Revere-style, cylindrical w/hinged door & conical top w/large ring handle, pierced overall w/starburst & other designs, old black paint, 19th c., overall 16 1/2" h. (ILLUS., below) **500**

Pierced Tin Paul Revere Lantern

Early Tin Candle Mold

Candle mold, tin, eight-tube, rectangular top & base plates, original worn black paint, 19th c., 3 1/2 x 6", 10 1/2" h. (ILLUS.)............. **160**

Old Tole Canister Set

Canister set, tole, rectangular low-sided tray w/overhead strap handle holding eight covered cylindrical canisters, original worn japanned surface, tray 5 3/8 x 8", 4 1/2" h., the set (ILLUS., bottom previous page) **95**

G.A.R. Souvenir Canteen

Canteen, tin, souvenir-type for the G.A.R., large inset copper medallion in the side w/picture of the U.S. Capitol & inscribed "Souvenir - Twenty-sixth Grand Annual - Encampment - Washington, D.C. - 1892," reverse medallion reads "We Drank From the Same Canteen - 1861-65," 4 3/8 x 5" (ILLUS.) **260**

Chandelier, tinned sheet metal & iron wire, 12-light, the wire stem headed by a hanging hook above four serpentine arms each ending in a four-leaf green-painted candle socket over four projecting wires w/ball termini above eight serpentine arms each ending in a similar yellow-painted candle socket, probably French, 19th c., 17 1/2" d., 15 1/2" h. **3,290**

Coffeepot, cov., tole, domed & hinged top above a flaring cylindrical body w/applied strap handle & arched spout, on a flaring round base, black ground painted w/red & green fruit & leaves & yellow trim, Pennsylvania, 19th c., 10 1/2" h. **4,465**

Cookie cutter, tin, early handmade heart in hand design, 3 x 4" **350**

Cookie cutter, tin, early handmade horse w/rider, spot-soldered, 5 x 6 1/2" **275**

Cookie cutter, tin, early handmade pig, spot-soldered, 3 x 4" **45**

Tin Fish Cookie Cutter

Cookie cutter, tin, model of fish, flat backplate w/large vent hole, 3 x 4" (ILLUS.) **14**

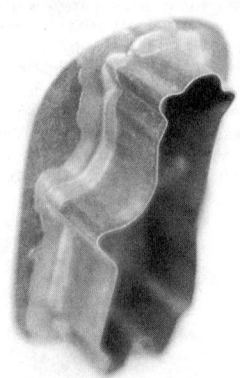

Tin Bear Cookie Cutter

Cookie cutter, tin, model of standing bear, flat backplate, 2 3/4 x 3 3/4" (ILLUS.) **14**

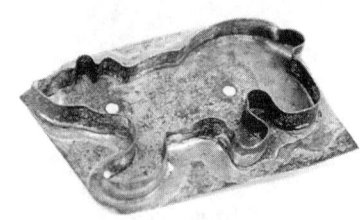

Tin Walking Bear Cookie Cutter

Cookie cutter, tin, model of walking bear w/flat backplate & vent holes, 2 1/4 x 3 1/4" (ILLUS.) **17**

Tin Cookie Cutters

Cookie cutter, tin, outline of bearded man in slouch hat, carrying a book, 9 3/4" l., minor rust & damage to hat (ILLUS. left) **935**

Deer Cookie Cutters

Cookie cutter, tin, outline of deer w/long ears or horn-like antlers, light rust, 7 5/8" l. (ILLUS. left)........................ **468**

Cookie cutter, tin, outline of man in round top hat & long coat, minor rust, 7 3/4" l. (ILLUS. right, w/other tin cookie cutters) **303**

Cookie cutter, tin, outline of reindeer w/impressive rack of antlers, strap handle, 6 7/8" l. (ILLUS. right, w/other deer cookie cutter)........................... **440**

Cookie cutter, tin, outline of Statue of Liberty, 9 5/8" l. (light rust) **2,475**

Cookie cutter, tin, outline of Teddy bear, strap handle, 5 1/4" l. (ILLUS. center, w/other tin cookie cutters)...................... **28**

Cookie cutter, tin, spread-winged eagle w/the head facing to one side, scallop-tipped tail, on a flat rectangular back w/pierced hole, 19th c., 6" h. (very light rust) **165**

Deed box, cov., tole, rectangular w/domed top w/applied wire bail handle, scrolled strap on front, the base decorated w/red, yellow & green painted floral decoration on a black ground w/yellow trim, Pennsylvania, 19th c., 4 x 8 1/4", 4 1/2" h. **1,998**

Document box, cov., tole, dome-top rectangular shape w/dark japanning w/yellow swags, front panel w/smoked white semicircle w/red & green flowers including tulip & yellow swags, tin hasp, brass bail handle, alligatored red & green, 3 5/8 x 8 1/2", 4 3/4" h. (wear)................. **215**

Document box, cov., tole, dome-top rectangular shape w/yellow vines & wavy line w/yellow, red & black floral front panel, tin hasp, brass bail handle, alligatored, 4 3/4 x 8 3/4", 5 1/2" h. (wear).................. **1,430**

Document box, cov., tole, original brown japanning w/yellow swag decoration on lid, white scallops on base w/red fruit & green leaves, 6 1/2 x 9 3/4", 7" h. (wear, brass handle is early replacement) **385**

Document box, cov., tole, original dark brown/black japanning w/yellow flourishes on sides, the front panel w/yellow swags & smoke decorated white band w/red flowers & olive brown leaves, wire bail handle, 5 x 9", 5" h. (lid & hasp are worn, no decoration left on lid, scratches) **220**

Document box, cov., tole, original light brown japanning w/yellow stripes & flourishes on lid, the front panel w/smoke decorated white band w/red & green flowers & yellow, green & red swags below, wire bail handle, 4 3/4 x 9", 5 1/2" h. (minor flaking, japanning is worn on lid & front)........ **248**

Doll head, tin, young girl w/center-parted hair, glass eyes, marked "Minerva" on front & "Germany" on back, original worn pink & tan paint, 3 3/4" h. (ILLUS., top of next column)...................... **95**

Down spout, tinned sheet metal, rectangular top above a double-tapering body, w/applied gold-painted stars & centering "1855" also painted gold, all on a black-painted ground w/shaped backing, on a later cylindrical fixture, American, 8 1/2 x 15", 20 1/2" h. **588**

Tin "Minerva" Doll Head

Egg beater, tin, base marked "Made In United States of America A&J," top marked "Full Vision Beater Set," 7 1/2" **40**

Egg beater, tin, Betty Taplin model w/red plastic cup, 6 oz., 6" l. **50**

Early Tin Flame Minder

Flame minder, tin, a flat-topped disk w/the narrow sides pierced w/diamond-shaped openings, the top stamped "Flame Minder [crown] Kitchen King," used to control heat intensity on a wood-burning kitchen range, 6 1/4" d., 1" h. (ILLUS.)........................ **10**

Old Tin Flour Scoop

Flour scoop, tin, deep rounded shovel end w/tubular handle, soldered construction, 9 1/2" l. (ILLUS.)................................ **15**

Graduated Set of Tin Measures

Tin Mammy Match Holder

Match holder, tin, hanging-type, backplate w/stamped image of a black Mammy against hammered background, leaning on two match containers w/hammered finish centered by striker section, overall gold paint, 4 3/4 x 5 1/2" (ILLUS.) **49**

Tin Owl Match Holder

Match holder, tin, hanging-type, stylized owl backplate w/pierced eyes, two half-round ridged match holders, black paint, 3 1/2 x 4 5/8" (ILLUS.) **29**

Measures, tin, pitcher-type, slightly tapering cylindrical body w/tapering flaring rim band, wide strap handle, each bearing the seal of the State of Minnesota Railroad and Warehouse Commission, tallest 6 5/8" h., graduated set of 3 (ILLUS., top of page) **125**

Model of a top hat, tin, full form w/applied, crimped & red, white & blue-painted tin cockade, black-painted hat band w/stylized tin buckle, weathered old painted surfaces, interior painted black w/opposing mounts, weathered old painted surfaces,   second   half   19th   c., 21 1/2 x 24 3/4", 19 1/2" h. **6,325**

Soccer Player Chocolate Mold

Mold, chocolate, boy soccer player w/crossed arms & w/foot resting on ball, 1 1/2 x 3 1/2", 7" h. (ILLUS.) **45**

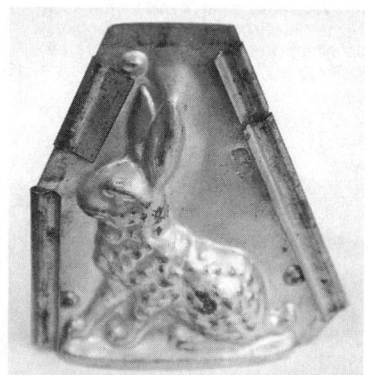

Tin Sitting Rabbit Chocolate Mold

Mold, chocolate, in the form of a sitting rabbit, 1 1/4 x 5 x 5 1/2" (ILLUS.) **95**

Toleware Domed Lid Storage Box

Storage box, cov., toleware, domed lid w/yellow scrolled foliate designs & turned wooden handle, the box w/red & white swags & yellow leaf embellishments on black field, America, early 19th c., 8 3/4 x 13 3/4", 9" h. (ILLUS.)......................... **764**

Tin Windup Walking Robot Toy

Toy, windup, tin, walking robot, eyes light up & clear plastic chest shows spinning gears, marked "KO Made in Japan," 11" h. (ILLUS.) **465**

Tin Frog Toy Clicker

Toy clicker, tin, stamped model of frog w/original green, yellow & red paint, marked "Life of the Party Products," 2 x 3" (ILLUS.) **13**

Tray, tole, rectangular w/rounded corners & cutout end handles, the rim in black & gold bronze bands, the center painted w/a walking tiger framed by a border of stenciled flowers & leaves in red, green & gold on a black ground, American, 19th c., 15 3/4 x 22" **3,290**

MID-CENTURY MODERN DESIGN

An area of increasing interest to collectors today is Mid-Century Modern Design. This broad field includes all sorts of objects first introduced immediately after World War II and continuing into the 1960s. Baby Boomers in particular recall with nostalgia the furniture, dishes, decorative accent pieces, appliances and kitchenwares that featured the hot new shapes, colors and materials widely sold in postwar America.

Some Mid-Century objects were the work of famous designers and can be expensive. However, there is still a plethora of everyday affordable wares that can provide a nostalgic touch to any home.

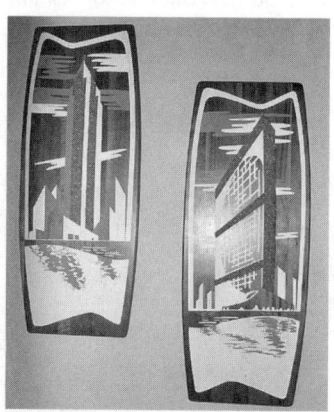

Skyscraper Designs in Silkscreen

Artwork, silkscreen & plastic on wood, oblong panels w/skyscraper designs, Belart, ca. 1950s, 29 1/2" h., pr. (ILLUS.).. **$30-50**

Art Pottery Ashtray

Ashtray, art pottery, square w/stylized geometric imprints, 8" sq. (ILLUS.) **30-45**

"Midas" Ashtray by Georges Briard

Ashtray, ceramic, oblong shape, "Midas" model by Georges Briard for Hyalyn Porcelain, ca. 1950s (ILLUS.) **35-45**

Gold Ceramic Swirl Design Ashtray

Ashtray, ceramic, rounded shape w/gold swirl design, Stangl, ca. 1950s, 8" d. (ILLUS.) **10-15**

Ceramic Chimney-style Ashtray

Ashtray, ceramic, white, ovoid form w/short chimney-style neck, on short feet, oblong opening in front for cigarettes/cigars, ca. 1950s, 6 x 7" (ILLUS.) **15-25**

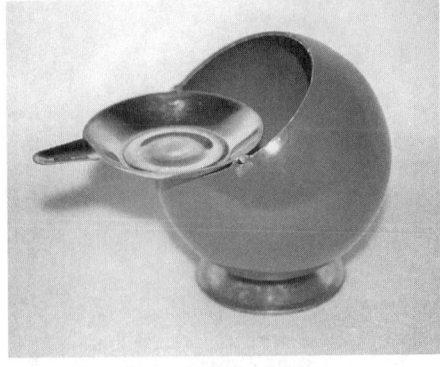

Chrome Globe Ashtray

Ashtray, chrome, red globe w/flip top, state souvenir on back, ca. 1950s, 3" h. (ILLUS.) **15-20**

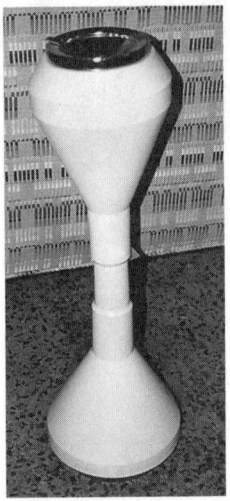

Standing Floor Model Ashtray

Ashtray, plastic stand w/metal ashtray insert, standing floor model, white, ca. 1970s, 21 1/2" h. (ILLUS.) **15-20**

Elliptical Abstract Pottery Ashtray

Ashtray, pottery, abstract shape, ca. 1960s, 10" l. (ILLUS.) **8-12**

"Mod" Metal Flowers Book Ends

Book ends, metal, simple form w/applied "mod" flowers, colors vary, ca. 1960s, 5" h., pr. (ILLUS.) **20-40**

Pink Glass Bowl in Abstract Form

Bowl, glass, pink, circular shape w/sides formed by rounded rectangular overlapping panels, Viking Glass, ca. 1950s, 6" d. (ILLUS.) **25-35**

Enamel on Metal Bowl

Bowl, metal, round, decorated w/black & aqua enamel in swirl pattern, ca. 1950s, 14" d. (ILLUS.) **20-35**

Bowl with Abstract Design

Bowl, pottery, abstract design on ovoid shape w/pedestal, Italy, ca. 1960s, 5 x 6" (ILLUS.) **25-35**

Salad Bowl by Red Wing

Bowl, salad, Red Wing, 12" d. (ILLUS.)......... **40-55**

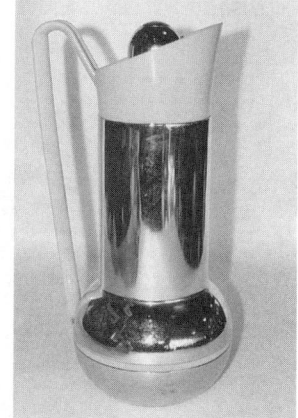

Chrome and Plastic Carafe

Carafe, chrome & plastic, chrome & yellow plastic, ca. 1960s, 12" h. (ILLUS.)............. **30-45**

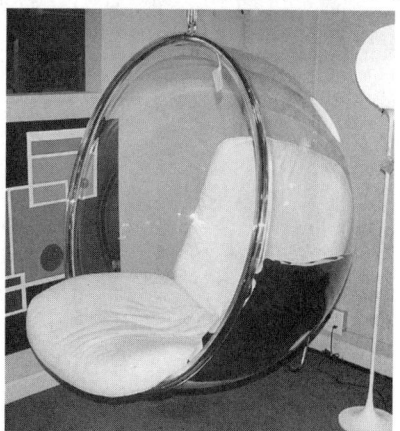

"Bubble" Chair by Eero Aarnio

Chair, clear plastic, "Bubble" model, half orb shape suspended from ceiling on chain, w/seat & back cushions inside, Eero Aarnio (ILLUS.).................................. **2,000-3,000**

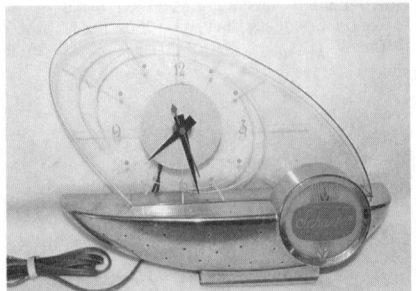

Schaefer Beer Advertising Clock

Clock, chrome & glass, advertising Schaefer Beer, elliptical glass face on boat-shaped chrome base, ca. 1950s, 12" h. (ILLUS.) **60-85**

Panasonic Clock Radio

Clock radio, plastic, white, sphere-shaped, Panasonic, ca. 1960s, 5 1/5" d. (ILLUS.).. **40-50**

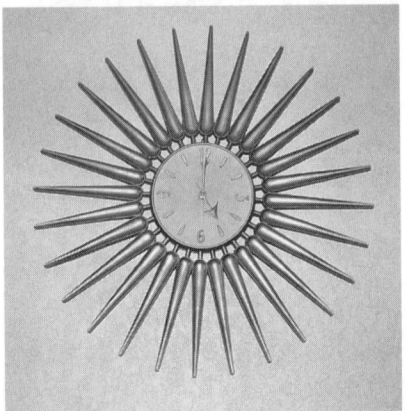

Sun Ray Starburst Design Clock

Clock, plastic, golden sun ray starburst design, Syroco, ca. 1960, 23" d. (ILLUS.) **35-50**

Stoneware Coffeepot and Teapot Set

Coffeepot and teapot, cov., stoneware, Danish Modern, white, ca. 1960, ea. (ILLUS.) **30-35**

"Mod" Clock with Moving Flower

Clock, yellow, black & white "mod" style w/flower that moves w/each tick, Spartus Corp., ca. 1969, 11 1/2" h. (ILLUS.)........... **50-75**

Color Wheel for Aluminum Tree

Color wheel, for aluminum Christmas tree, rotating plastic disk on white glittered base, ca. 1950s (ILLUS.) **45-65**

Taylorstone Cup and Saucer

Cup and saucer, "Cathay," Taylorstone, ca. 1950s (ILLUS.) **5-10**

Cups with Snack Tray

Cups and snack tray, gold & rust "mod" design, Rosenthal, Germany, ca. 1960s (ILLUS.) **20-25**

Dinette Set in the Tulip Style

Dinette set, metal, fiberglass & wood, "Tulip" style, ca. 1960s, the set (ILLUS.) **250-350**

Melmac Place Setting

Dinnerware, Melmac, pink & turquoise, Boontonware, ca. 1950s, place setting of

large & small plate, cup & saucer (ILLUS.) **8-12**

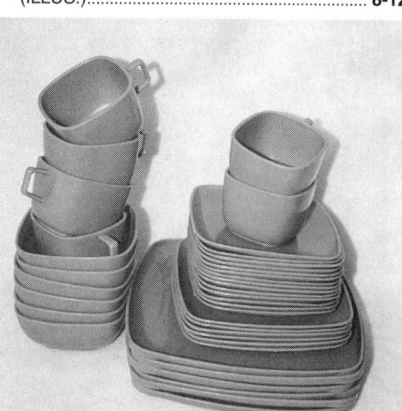

Tranquil Ware Service for Six

Dinnerware, plastic, Tranquil Ware, square shape, green, service for 6, Byrd Plastics, ca. 1960s, the set (ILLUS.) **20-30**

European Art Glass Dish

Dish, art glass, yellow & blue, European, ca. 1960s, 7" h. (ILLUS.) **25-35**

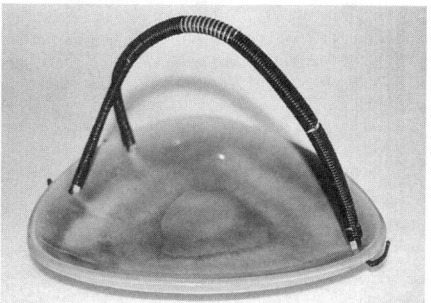

Napcoware Dish with Handle

Dish, handled, ceramic, turquoise, abstract design, Napcoware, ca. 1960s, 5 x 7 h. (ILLUS.).. **20-30**

Ice Bucket & Coasters

Ice Bucket & coasters, vinyl & plastic, op art-type design in wavy checks & stripes, Morgan Bucket Brigade, ca. 1960s, 9" h. (ILLUS.).. **40-60**

"Small Talk" Intercom System

Intercom, metal, box shape, "Small Talk" system, Masco, ca. 1950s, 4 x 9" l. (ILLUS.)... **15-20**

S-shaped Metal Frame Lamp

Lamp, metal, S-shaped metal frame w/two oval striped shades, ca. 1950s, 35 1/2" h. (ILLUS.) **200-250**

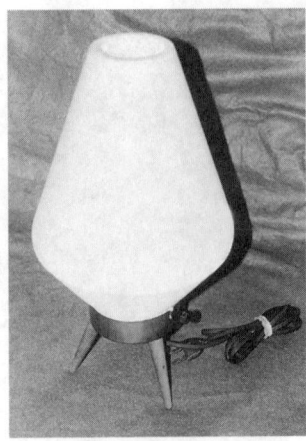

Wooden Tripod Base Lamp

Lamp, plastic and wood, ribbed plastic shade on wooden tripod base, ca. 1960s, 14" h. (ILLUS.)... **25-35**

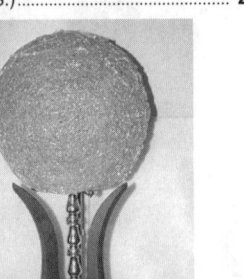

Abstract Wood and Metal Base Lamp

Lamp, plastic, wood, & metal, spaghetti glass (plastic) globe on abstract wood & metal base, ca. 1950s, 23 1/2" h. (ILLUS.) **40-65**

Ceramic Models of Birds

Models of birds, ceramic, Howard Pierce, set of three, 3" h., the set (ILLUS.) **45-75**

Oil Painting Signed "L. Marcos"

Painting, oil, stark, attenuated images of yellow horse & rider, signed "L. Marcos," ca. 1960s, 21 x 25" (ILLUS.)... **125-175**

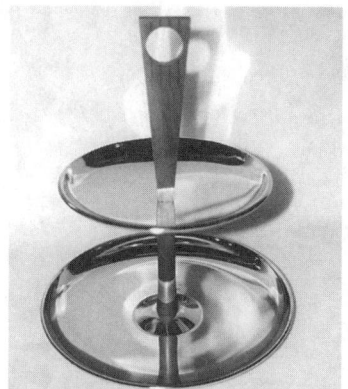

Chrome and Wood Tiered Party Tray

Party tray, chrome & wood, double-tiered, Denmark, ca. 1950s (ILLUS.)..................... **12-18**

Regal Ware Aluminum Pitcher

Pitcher, aluminum, red w/etched modern design, Bakelite handle, Regal Ware, ca. 1950s, 7 1/2" h. (ILLUS.) **15-25**

Ceramic Planter of Joined Globes

Planter, ceramic, three joined globes in graduated sizes, ca. 1950s, 11 1/2" l. (ILLUS.) **25-35**

Op Art Print

Print, divided into four panels, each w/red & green Op Art-style sun ray design, ca. 1960s-1970s, 18 x 24" (ILLUS.) **50-75**

Zenith Cylindrical Radio

Radio, cylindrical form w/speaker on top, AM/FM, Zenith, 1950s-1960s (ILLUS.) **40-60**

Radio Shaped as the Word "Radio"

Radio, plastic, white, shaped in joined block letters to read "Radio," the speaker in the letter "O," AM-FM, ca. 1960s-1970s, 3 x 10" l. (ILLUS.) **30-50**

Wood-inlaid Salt and Pepper Shakers

Salt & pepper shakers, wood w/wood inlaid decoration, ca. 1950s, 6" h., pr. (ILLUS.) **20-30**

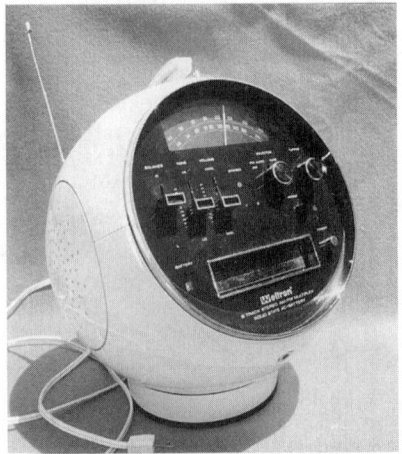

Radio/Eight-Track Tape Player

Radio/Eight-track tape player, plastic, sphere shape w/controls in panel at front, speakers on sides, handle, Weltron 2001 model, ca. 1970 (ILLUS.) **100-250**

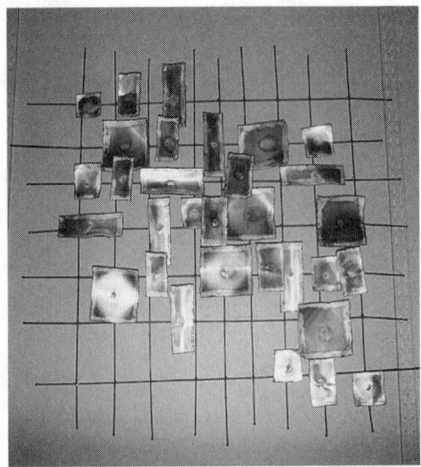

Abstract Wall Sculpture

Sculpture, metal, wall hanging, stylized geometric shapes randomly set on wire grid, unsigned, ca. 1960s, 30" sq. (ILLUS.) **100-175**

Pearlized Plastic Sunglasses

Op Art Pattern Record Case

Record case, plastic, Op Art pattern of wavy checks, w/handle, Platter-Pak, ca. 1960s, 8 x 8" (ILLUS.) **20-30**

Sunglasses, pearlized plastic w/gold flecks, cat's-eye shape, ca. 1950s (ILLUS.) **15-25**

Mod Flower Inlay Side Table

Table, molded plastic, "Tulip" style, round top w/"mod" flower inlay, unsigned, ca. 1960s, 20" (ILLUS.) **100-140**

Northern Telecom Touch-tone Phone

Telephone, plastic, round flat design, touch-tone model, Northern Telecom, ca. 1970s, 8 1/2" d. (ILLUS.) **20-35**

Rotary Dial Donut-Shaped Phone

Telephone, plastic, donut-shaped, w/rotary dial, Sculptura model by Western Electric, early 1970s (ILLUS.) **40-60**

Star-Lite Portable Television

Television, plastic, rectangular, Star-Lite portable model, ca. 1950s, 13" (ILLUS.) ... **50-65**

Classic Rotary Desk Phone

Telephone, plastic, red, desk type w/rotary dial, Bell System, Western Electric, ca., 1960s (ILLUS.) **15-30**

Predicta Table Top Television

Television, rounded rectangular table top Predicta model by Philco, 29" h. (ILLUS.)... **350-500**

Panasonic Orbitel TR-005 Television

Television, silvertone elliptical shape on tripod base, Orbitel TR-005 model, Panasonic, ca. 1971 (ILLUS.) **300-500**

Regal Ware Aluminum Tumblers

Tumblers, aluminum, variety of colors & styles, Regal Ware, ca. 1950s, 6" h., each (ILLUS.).. **2-4**

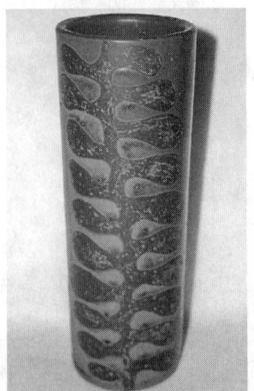

Vine Design Cylindrical Vase

Vase, ceramic, cylindrical shape w/stylized vine design, Asia, ca. 1960s, 10" h. (ILLUS.)... **25-35**

Tall Turquoise Floor Vase

Vase, glass, turquoise, tall floor vase w/ribbed body & drip top, ca. 1950-1960s, 26" h. (ILLUS.)................................. **35-60**

Black Line Pattern Milk Glass Vase

Vase, milk glass, ovoid shape w/black line design in random pattern, ca. 1950s, 5 1/2" h. (ILLUS.) **20-25**

Rust and Tan Pottery Vase

Vase, pottery, ovoid body w/cylindrical neck, rust & tan, unsigned, ca. 1950s-1960s, 9" h. (ILLUS.) **20-30**

Small Brown Studio Vase

Vase, studio-made, small brown pot w/rough speckled glaze, ca. 1960s, 6" h. (ILLUS.) **12-20**

MINIATURES (PAINTINGS)

Bust portrait of man, on ivory, oval shape, man w/brown hair & eyes wearing black coat w/neck scarf, brass frame has lens on back w/lock of hair & swatch of black cloth, 3" h. **$550**

Bust portrait of young woman, on ivory, figure in white wig, wearing pale blue dress & pink scarf w/gold pendant, initialed "K.Y.," black frame w/embossed copper liner, 4 5/8 x 5 5/8" **358**

Half length portrait of man, watercolor on paper, man w/curly black hair & wearing black frock coat, blue background, black cloth mat w/gilt frame, 4 3/4 x 5 7/8" **440**

Half length portrait of woman, watercolor on paper of woman wearing black dress w/puffy sleeves & elaborate hairdo w/ribbon & comb, old ink name on back "_ Porter," blue background, worn vintage eglomisé mat w/gilt frame, 4 3/4 x 5 7/8" (minor stains) **605**

Portrait of Brigadier General James Miller, pencil & watercolor on paper, in oval frame, unsigned, Peterboro, New Hampshire, late 18th/early 19th c., 4 3/4 x 5 3/4" **1,880**

Portrait of woman in burgundy wearing a lace bonnet, watercolor on ivory, in hinged red leather case w/ormolu mat, signed "G[eorge]. HARVEY," America, mid-19th c., 2 3/4 x 3 1/2" (leather loss on case) **705**

Portrait of young girl, watercolor on ivory, in brass & ebonized wood frame, unsigned, America, early 19th c., 4 x 5" **499**

MINIATURES (REPLICAS)

Blanket chest, pine, rectangular six-board chest w/semi-curved cutouts on ends w/bracket feet & shaped returns, original dark red over lighter red ground grained decoration, dark borders have narrow line detail that simulates banded inlay, 6 1/2 x 14 5/8", 7 7/8" h. (current brass hinges, in place for some time, replaced original wire hinges; hairlines in front feet) **$1,760**

Blanket chest, poplar, six-board chest by Bernard Harter, semi-curve cutouts on ends forming feet, dry green paint, 6 3/4 x 14 1/4", 9 1/4" h. **220**

Chest of drawers, Classical, mahogany, arched crest w/scrolled finials, small case on top w/two small drawers, three larger drawers at bottom, inset panels on either end, shaped pilasters w/turned rear & round front feet, wire nail construction, 7 x 13", 13 1/4" h. (small glued repairs) **550**

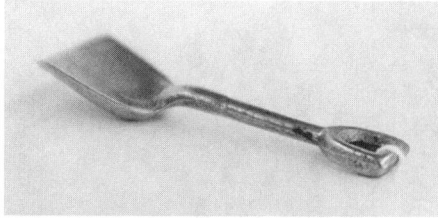

Miniature Cast-iron Coal Shovel

Coal shovel, cast iron, silvered finish, 3 1/2" l. (ILLUS.) **35**

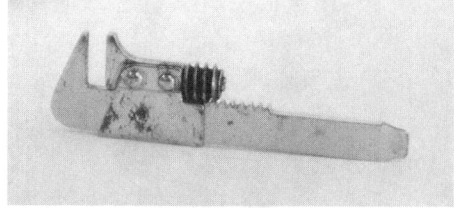

Miniature Wrench

Wrench, cast iron, silvered finish, marked "A.G. & J. Product," 3 1/4" l. (ILLUS.) **10**

MOLDS - CANDY, FOOD & MISCELLANEOUS

Also see METALS

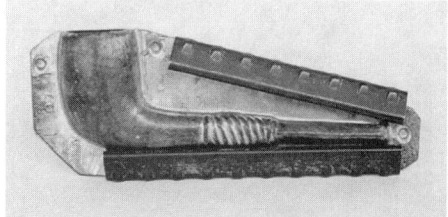

Pipe Tin Chocolate Mold

Chocolate, pipe, tin, two-piece, 2 1/2 x 6 1/2" (ILLUS.) **$35**

Running Rabbit Chocolate Mold

Chocolate, rabbit, tin, running animal, two-piece, 3 1/2 x 5" (ILLUS.)...................................... **49**

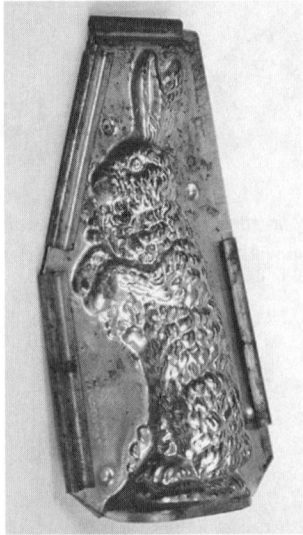

Seated Rabbit Chocolate Mold

Chocolate, rabbit, tin, seated on haunches, hinged, 5 x 8 1/2" (ILLUS.) **115**

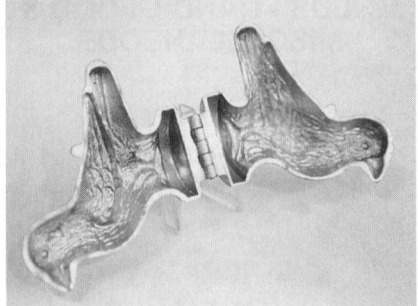

Standing Bird Ice Cream Mold

Ice cream, bird, pewter, standing, hinged, No. 172, closed 4 x 4 1/4" (ILLUS.)................. **85**

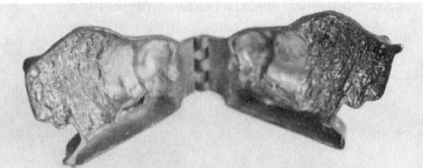

Standing Bison Ice Cream Mold

Ice cream, bison, pewter, standing animal, hinged, marked "413 E & Co. NY," closed 2 3/4 x 4 1/2" (ILLUS.)...................................... **150**

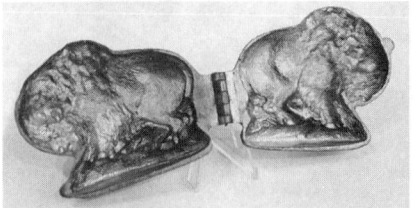

Bison with Lowered Head Mold

Ice cream, bison, pewter, standing animal w/head lowered, hinged, marked "E & Co. - 646," closed 3 1/2 x 5" (ILLUS.)........... **155**

Ice Cream Mold with Beethoven Bust

Ice cream, bust of Beethoven, pewter, hinged, marked "E & Co. - 1165," closed 3 1/4 x 4" (ILLUS.) **165**

Chinese Man Ice Cream Mold

Ice cream, Chinese man, pewter, hinged, marked "E & Co.," closed 2 1/4 x 5 1/2" (ILLUS.).. **165**

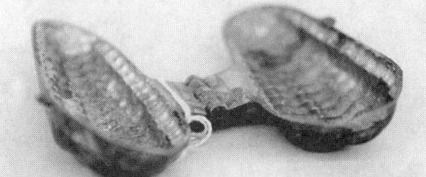

Corn Cob Ice Cream Mold

Ice cream, corn cob, pewter, hinged, closed 2 3/4 x 4 3/4" (ILLUS.)...................................... **69**

Flying Dove Ice Cream Mold

Ice cream, dove, pewter, flying bird, hinged, No. 677, closed 4 1/2 x 4 3/4" (ILLUS.) **195**

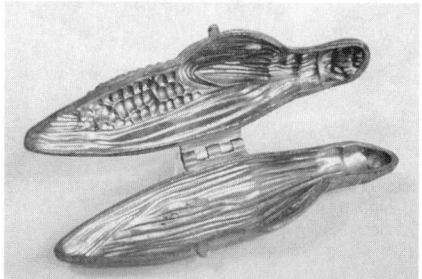

Ear of Corn Ice Cream Mold

Ice cream, ear of corn, pewter, hinged, No. 279, closed 3 x 7" (ILLUS.)............................. **175**

Early Auto Ice Cream Mold

Ice cream, early auto, pewter, No. 1021, closed 2 x 4" (ILLUS.) **215**

Irish Harp Ice Cream Mold

Ice cream, Irish harp, pewter, hinged, marked "S & Co. - 361," closed 4 x 4 1/2" (ILLUS.) **75**

Lily Ice Cream Mold

Ice cream, lily, pewter, hinged, marked "E & Co. - Patent Applied For - 319," closed 2 3/4 x 6 1/2" (ILLUS.).................................... **145**

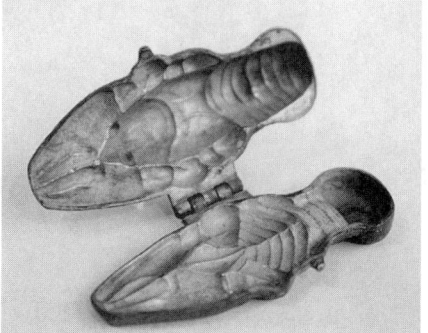

Lobster Ice Cream Mold

Ice cream, lobster, pewter, hinged, 3 x 5 1/2" (ILLUS.)... **175**

Milk Bottle Ice Cream Mold

Ice cream, milk bottle, pewter, hinged, closed 2 1/2 x 3 1/2" (ILLUS.) **75**

Patriotic Shield Ice Cream Mold

Ice cream, patriotic shield, pewter, decorated w/stars & stripes, hinged, No. 281, closed 4 x 4" (ILLUS.).. **65**

Potato-form Ice Cream Mold

Ice cream, potato, pewter, marked "E & Co." w/number, closed 3 x 3 1/2" (ILLUS.)............... **55**

Roman Boy Ice Cream Mold

Ice cream, Roman boy, pewter, hinged, closed 3 1/4 x 4 1/2" (ILLUS.) **225**

Rose Corsage Ice Cream Mold

Ice cream, rose corsage, pewter, hinged, No. 361, closed 3 x 3 1/4" (ILLUS.)................. **85**

Steam Locomotive Ice Cream Mold

Ice cream, steam locomotive, pewter, hinged, marked "E & Co. NY - 1047," closed 2 3/4 x 5 1/2" (ILLUS.) **325**

Stork with Baby Ice Cream Mold

Ice cream, stork with baby, pewter, hinged, marked "E & Co. NY - 1151," closed 5 x 5" (ILLUS.) **225**

Ice cream, sunflower, pewter, closed
3 1/4 x 4 1/4" 75

MOVIE MEMORABILIA
Costumes

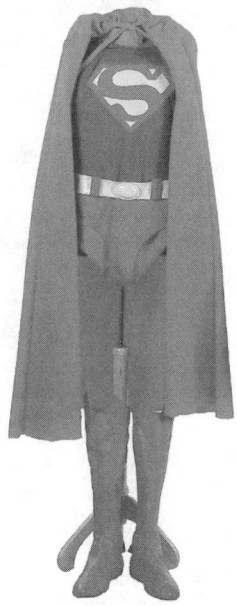

"Superman" Costume

Christopher Reeve, "Superman,"
1978/1980, Superman's blue tunic with
"S" inset at center chest, matching sky
blue leggings, bright red brief-style
shorts, bright red flowing cape w/"S" on
verso & autographed within in black
marker "Christopher Reeve," yellow vinyl
belt w/matching rounded buckle & red
leather knee-length boots, worn in "Superman" & "Superman II" (ILLUS.) **$56,400**

Jacket from "Speedway"

Elvis Presley, "Speedway," 1968, red wool
jacket w/two white stripes on left side
worn by character Steve Grayson,
speedway driver, hand-tailored w/red
satin lining & one exterior pocket on bottom right hem, no labels, numerous moth
holes (ILLUS.) **8,365**

Handbag from "Rear Window"

Grace Kelly, "Rear Window," 1954, Mark
Cross handbag carried by character Lisa
Carol Fremont, black leather rectangular
bag w/rust-colored leather lining, four inside pockets & mirror, the outside
w/brass clasp & four small brass feet,
handle is replacement, 9 1/2 x 13"
(ILLUS.) **5,019**

Handbags of M. Monroe Characters

Marilyn Monroe, "How to Marry a Million-
aire," 1953, cream cloth clutch-style
evening bag w/rhinestone clasp carried
by Monroe's character in the film, "Saks
Fifth Avenue" tag inside along with another tag w/inscription in black ink "1-6-3-
1667 M Monroe A-729" (ILLUS. left).......... **7,050**

Marilyn Monroe, vintage black evening bag decorated w/colorless bugle beads used by Monroe in early rehearsals of "Anna Christie" (ILLUS. right)................................. **4,700**

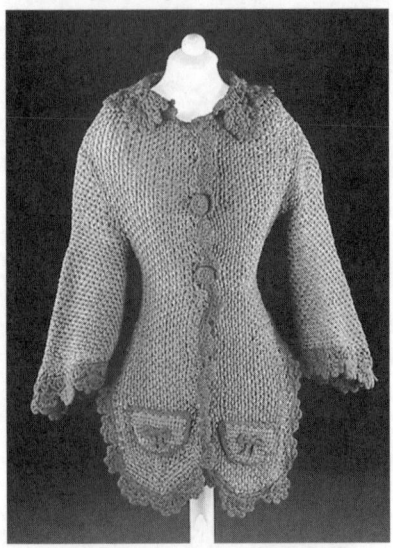

"Gone With the Wind" Sweater

Olivia de Havilland, "Gone With the Wind," 1939, wool sweater worn by character Melanie Hamilton Wilkes, hand-knitted to look like Civil War era item, natural w/dull orange trim, collar & two large buttons, three-quarter length flared sleeves, missing wardrobe labels (ILLUS.).................... **16,730**

Bonnet Worn in "The Heiress"

Olivia de Havilland, "The Heiress," 1949, tan silk bonnet worn by character Catherine Sloper, w/olive green piping, ruffles & bows, interior stamp reads "Paramount Pictures/Product of Paramount Pictures/Ladies Wardrobe," cloth label reads "Paramount" & handwritten "Olivia de Havilland" (ILLUS.) **777**

"Captain Marvel" Tunic

Tom Tyler (Captain Marvel), "The Adventures of Captain Marvel," 1940s, burgundy wool tunic w/bright gold lightning bolt across chest, double row of flat brass buttons & applied yellow-gold soutash gauntlets (ILLUS.)... **3,290**

Lobby Cards

"Casablanca" Lobby Card

"Casablanca," Warner Bros., 1942, full-color scene w/Ingrid Bergman flanked by Paul Henreid & Humphrey Bogart, 11 x 14" (ILLUS.)... **2,233**

"Casablanca," Warner Bros., 1942, title lobby card, full-color head shot of Ingrid Bergman & Humphrey Bogart cheek to cheek, names of three stars in bold deep aqua type across top, "Casablanca" in bright red-orange script at bottom, w/other info in smaller type below, 11 x 14"........ **4,113**

"Monkey Business" Lobby Card

"The Gold Rush" Lobby Card

"Gone With the Wind" Lobby Card

"Gold Rush, The," United Artists, 1925, tinted scene of Chaplin's character & another character w/their arms around each other, w/black & white image of Little Tramp character to the side, "Charlie Chaplin in 'The Gold Rush'" printed at bottom, framed, 11 x 14" (ILLUS.) **1,998**

"Gold Rush, The," United Artists, 1925, tinted scene of characters in cabin interior, w/black & white image of Little Tramp character to the side, "Charlie Chaplin in 'The Gold Rush'" printed at bottom, framed, 11 x 14" **1,058**

"Gone With the Wind," 1939, full-color depiction of all the main cast members, printed w/"Gone With the Wind" floral border, 11 x 14", set of 8............................. **4,183**

Gone With the Wind," 1939, full-color depiction of Vivien Leigh as Scarlett O'Hara, printed w/"Gone With the Wind" floral border, 11 x 14", from the set of 8 (ILLUS., to the right) **2,032**

""**Gone With the Wind,"** 1939, full-color portrait of Leslie Howard as Ashley Wilkes, on heavy stock w/"Gone With the Wind" floral border, hanging string taped to back, 18 x 19" **538**

"The Man Who Knew Too Much" Lobby Card

"Man Who Knew Too Much, The" Gaumont-British, 1934, full-color scene from the film, w/names of cast members printed along top border, a head shot of Peter Lorre in one bottom corner next to oval inset w/"The Man Who Knew Too Much" printed inside, production company logo in other bottom corner, only known copy, 11 x 14" (ILLUS.) **1,880**

"Monkey Business," Paramount, 1931, full-color depiction of four Marx Brothers standing in barrels marked "Kippered Herring," with "The Four Marx Brothers" printed at the top & "Monkey Business" at the bottom, 11 x 14", (ILLUS., top of previous page) **4,935**

"Monkey Business," Paramount, 1931, full-color depictions of various Marx Brothers w/other actors in scenes from the film, "The Four Marx Brothers" printed at the top & "Monkey Business" at the bottom of each, 11 x 14", set of three **1,763**

"Morocco" Lobby Card

"Morocco," Paramount, 1930, full-color depiction of Marlene Dietrich & Adolphe Menjou, 11 x 14" (ILLUS.) **2,233**

"Pardon Us," MGM, 1931, full-color scenes from the film, w/"Stan Laurel - Oliver Hardy" printed beneath scene & "Pardon Us" in red box at bottom, 11 x 14", set of four.. **1,410**

"Rear Window" Lobby Card

"Rear Window," Paramount, 1954, full-color depiction of James Stewart, Grace Kelly & Thelma Ritter, 11 x 14", seven cards from original set of eight (ILLUS. of one) **777**

"Shadow of a Doubt," Universal, 1943, full-color scenes from the film, w/"Shadow of a Doubt" & cast info prominently displayed on one, & "Shadow of a Doubt" & info in smaller box beneath graphics of Joseph Cotton w/oversized shadow in cutaway sections on the other seven, 11 x 14", set of eight **1,645**

"Son of Dracula," Universal, 1943, full-color scenes from the film, w/"Son of Dracula" & cast info on one, & "Son of Dracula" beneath graphics of bat & full moon in cutaway sections on the other seven, 11 x 14", set of eight **1,410**

"Sunset Boulevard," Paramount, 1950, full-color scenes from the film, w/"Sunset Boulevard" printed in image of knotted strip of film at bottom, 11 x 14", set of eight **1,763**

"Top Hat" Lobby Card

"Top Hat," RKO, 1935, Fred Astaire & Ginger Rogers shown dancing dwarfed by elaborate set in background, larger figures of them dancing in cutout section in lower left corner, title & movie info contained in drawing of black top hat in foreground, 11 x 14" (ILLUS.) **999**

Posters

"2001: A Space Odyssey," MGM, 1968, special set of 12 roadshow posters showing scenes from the film, 27 x 39" unfolded, the set **7,638**

"The 39 Steps" Poster

"39 Steps, The" Gaumont-British, 1935, three-sheet, monochromatic illustrations of disembodied heads of the two stars in greens, "The 39 Steps" in bright pink & white three-dimensional type, other info in pink at bottom, names of the stars in upper left corner, all on deep pink ground, linen-backed, 41 x 81" (ILLUS.) **7,050**

Advance Poster for "Alien"

"Alien," Twentieth Century-Fox, 1979, advance one-sheet, grey block w/wide black border filled w/"ALIEN" in block letters in white at top, then repeated in black, "a word of warning..." in white in upper border, a small silhouette in red of spacesuited figures near bottom, the lower section of the poster white w/cast & other info in grey type & "coming from Twentieth Century-Fox" in black at bottom (ILLUS.).. **100-150**

"An American in Paris," MGM, 1951, shows Gene Kelly in upper right corner & Kelly & Leslie Caron dancing in lower left corner, white background w/red & blue lettering, linen-backed, one-sheet, 27 x 41".. **1,058**

Poster for "Anatomy of a Murder"

"Anatomy of a Murder," Columbia, 1959, one-sheet, comprised of two solid blocks of color, the top one orange-gold w/a cutout block figure sprawled across center in black, on which "Anatomy of a Murder" is printed in the orange-gold of the back-

ground, the bottom block a melon color w/the names of the cast in black-outlined type, art by Saul Bass, 27 x 41" (ILLUS.) **1,410**

"Animal Crackers" Poster

"Animal Crackers," Paramount, 1930, three-sheet, lithograph depicts the heads of four Marx Brothers on springs popping out of green box, "'Cocoa nuttier' than ever! The Marx Brothers" printed at top, "in Animal Crackers" printed on the front of the box, w/other info printed in smaller type at bottom, linen-backed, only known poster from this film to exist, 41 x 81" (ILLUS.) **23,900**

"Attack of the 50 Ft. Woman," Allied Artists, 1958, one-sheet, full-color illustration of scantily clad woman towering over freeway & holding car in one hand, "Attack of the 50 Ft. Woman" in bolt type at top, on yellow-gold ground, linen-backed, 27 x 41".. **6,463**

"The Band Wagon" Poster

"Band Wagon, The," MGM, 1953, one-sheet, center illustration of Fred Astaire & Cyd Charisse in dramatic dancing pose, "Get Aboard - The Band Wagon" at top, "The Band Wagon" in black & various pastel shades curving around picture, other info in bright pink, lavender & black, 27 x 41" (ILLUS.)... **1,293**

"The Black Stallion Returns" Poster

"Black Stallion Returns, The," MGM/UA, 1984, one-sheet, color illustration of boy racing away from mounted pursuers on a black horse against a full moon, "They came by night to steal the magnificent stallion. Now, the boy will journey halfway around the world, brave any danger, take any risk. He had to save The Black" in white at upper left corner, the title & other info at bottom (ILLUS.) **15-25**

"Blondie for Victory" Poster

"Blondie for Victory," Columbia, 1942, insert, colorful yellow & red ground w/illustrations of Penny Singleton bandaging

youngsters at top, a screaming Arthur Lake lying prone at bottom w/five dogs climbing all over him, the title in deep blue across center, w/the downstroke of the "V" a flag motif of red & white stripes w/a star, the cast & other info directly beneath title (ILLUS.).. **40-65**

"The Blue Dahlia" Poster

"Blue Dahlia, The," Paramount, 1942, three-sheet, full-color illustrations of Alan Ladd & Veronica Lake against black ground under monochromatic disembodied head of William Bendix, w/names of stars in bold yellow type at top, the title of the film in shadowed type & the head of a dahlia, both in dusty blue, directly below the main illustration, the figure of a woman in black sitting on the "H" of the first word of the title, other info in black type on greyish green ground, linen-backed, 41 x 81" (ILLUS.).. **8,225**

Poster for "Cabin in the Sky"

"Cabin in the Sky," MGM, 1943, one-sheet, white ground w/"Cabin in the Sky" in yellow-shadowed bold orange type splashed across top above stylized illustration of two black figures dancing, the cast & other info in black type & script on bright yellow banners at the bottom, art by Al Hirschfeld, signed, linen-backed, 27 x 41" (ILLUS.) **11,750**

Czech Version of "Casablanca" Poster

"Casablanca," Warner Bros., 1942, full color head shot of Humphrey Bogart & Ingrid Bergman in center directly below "Humphrey Bogart - Ingrid Bergman - Paul Henreid" in bold type, black & white head shots of supporting players at right curving around center photo, "Casablanca" in bold red script directly below center picture, other info in smaller type, bottom of poster is solid yellow-gold w/"Casablanca" in bold blue script & other info in bold smaller blue type in Czech language, Czechoslovakian version, linen-backed, 12 x 35" (ILLUS.) **5,288**

"City Lights" Poster

"City Lights," United Artists, 1931, one-sheet, full-color drawing of Charlie Chaplin as boxer in derby hat standing in corner of boxing ring w/boxing gloved hands crossed at chest, two trainers looking on from outside the ring, "Charlie Chaplin" at top, "in 'City Lights' " in green stylized type at bottom, linen-backed, framed, 27 x 41" (ILLUS.) **26,290**

"Creature from the Black Lagoon"

"Creature from the Black Lagoon" (not 3-D version), Universal, 1954, one-sheet, full-color illustration of creature holding swimsuited screaming woman, a knife-wielding scuba diver approaching, the title in white at the top, three pictures of scenes from the film at the bottom directly under the names of the cast (ILLUS.) **2,500-4,000**

"Design for Living" Poster

"Design for Living," Paramount, 1933, half-sheet, full-length full-color illustration of three stars walking arm in arm at right under caption "Three hearts that beat as one" in orange script, to the left "Noel Coward's - Design for Living" followed by cast names, "Design for Living" in bold black type, the rest in orange, teal panels at far right & bottom, the bottom containing "an Ernst Lubitsch Production" in lighter type, unfolded, paper-backed, 22 x 28" (ILLUS.) **2,115**

Poster for "Dracula's Daughter"

"Dracula's Daughter," Universal, 1936, insert, illustrations of characters from the film in upper left corner & at bottom, w/monochromatic green head shot of red-eyed woman looming over the title in green type dripping yellow, "Look Out! She'll Get YOU!" in red type at top, other info in pale blue type centered under title (ILLUS.)..**2,500-4,000**

collage of characters & scenes from the film, w/"A Fistful of Dollars" in bold white lettering superimposed over picture, red type at top reads "In his own way he is, perhaps, the most dangerous man who ever lived!," other info in smaller type at the bottom, 27 x 41" (ILLUS.) **940**

"Flash Gordon" Poster

"Flash Gordon," Universal, 1936, one-sheet, color illustration of stars & action from the film, "Buster Crabbe - as - Flash Gordon" curving across center, "Buster Crabbe" in orange-bordered black type, "Flash Gordon" in orange-border white type, "Amazing Strange World Adventures!" in black at bottom, linen-backed, 27 x 41" (ILLUS.)....................................... **52,875**

"A Fistful of Dollars" Poster

"Fistful of Dollars, A," United Artists, 1967, one-sheet, monotone illustration of Clint Eastwood in serape & hat, holding gun against an illustrated background

"The Ghost of Frankenstein" Poster

"Ghost of Frankenstein, The," Universal, 1942, three-sheet, illustration of monster looming over castle & characters from the film, all on gloomy ground, "New Thrills as the Monster Stalks Again!" in white type at upper right corner, the title of the film in bold three-dimensional type slanted across center, cast & other info in cream-colored panel at bottom (ILLUS.).................................... **2,500-4,000**

reads "There NEVER was a woman like Gilda!" (the word "Gilda" in red), & to the right of the figure "Columbia Pictures presents - Rita Hayworth - as - Gilda - with - Glenn Ford" & other info in white, red & aqua type, linen-backed, 27 x 41" (ILLUS.) **8,365**

"Gilda" Poster

Poster for "Godzilla"

"Gilda," Columbia, 1946, one-sheet, at the left is a full-color picture of Rita Hayworth, head cocked, wearing strapless form-fitting aqua & lavender gown & holding wrap at side w/one hand, the other hand holding cigarette, from which smoke ascends to top of poster, white print at top

"Godzilla," Toho, 1954, one-sheet, illustration of fire-breathing Godzilla against background of scenes & characters from the film, Japanese writing, the title in bold red Japanese characters at left (ILLUS.) **2,500-5,000**

"Gone With the Wind" Half Sheet

"Gone With the Wind," 1939, half sheet, depicts Rhett & Scarlett in each other's arms w/Tara in the background, "Gone With the Wind" floral border, linen-backed, 22 x 28" (ILLUS., bottom previous page)... **4,541**

"Gone With the Wind," 1939, half sheet, text only, "Gone With the Wind" floral border, folded, 22 x 28"..................................... **1,195**

"House on Haunted Hill," Allied Artists, 1958, one-sheet, full-color illustration of skeleton holding woman by a noose around her neck, w/haunted house in background, Vincent Price w/candle & holding the head of a woman by her hair in foreground, "House on Haunted Hill" in gold type near bottom, 27 x 41".................. **1,293**

"Jailhouse Rock" Poster

"Jailhouse Rock," MGM, 1957, one-sheet, top half is color portrait of Elvis Presley from the neck up, bottom half shows dancing figure of Elvis & oversize guitar under "Elvis Presley at his greatest," "Jailhouse Rock" at the bottom, vivid red background w/white and yellow type, 27 x 41" (ILLUS.)... **2,390**

Jesse James," 20th Century-Fox, 1939, Style B one-sheet, illustrations of characters & scenes from the film cover top & left side, w/title in bold red type, names of stars in dark blue & black type & other info in smaller green type on the right, one of only two copies known to exist, 27 x 41 (ILLUS., top of next column) **10,575**

"Key Largo" Warner Bros., 1948, one-panel lithograph, monochromatic background illustration in greens of Edward G. Robinson holding gun, inset box w/illustrated head shot of Bogart holding Bacall,

the names of the stars in bold red type at the top, the title in white slanted type under picture inset, other info below that, art by Pierre Pigeot, France, linen-backed, 47 x 63"... **9,400**

Rare "Jesse James" Poster

"Little Women" Poster

"Little Women," RKO, 1933, one-sheet, full-color head portraits of four main characters, "Katharine Hepburn - in" at the top over "Louisa May Alcott's Little Women," cast & other info in smaller type in lower right corner along w/RKO logo, the words "Louisa May Alcott's" appears to be printed on the cover of a book that makes up the background, linen-backed, 27 x 41" (ILLUS.)... **3,055**

"Prince and the Showgirl, The" Warner Bros., 1957, one-sheet, stark black ground w/bright red text at top reading "There's only one Marilyn Monroe but there isn't one Marilyn Monroe picture that teases and tickles like Marilyn Monroe starring with Laurence Olivier in Warner Bros. 'The Prince and the Showgirl'" over full-color picture of Olivier embracing Monroe from the back & kissing her shoulder, Monroe in red gown w/plunging neckline & a medal prominently displayed on it, small white type to side of picture reading "Some countries have a medal for Everything," unbacked, 27 x 41".. **2,585**

"Rear Window," Paramount, 1954, dark side of building w/James Stewart & Grace Kelly looking out a window, linen-backed, style B half-sheet, 22 x 28".......... **2,820**

"Rebel Without a Cause" Poster

"Rebel Without a Cause," Warner Bros., 1955, one-sheet, right half is full-color full length picture of James Dean in jeans, T-shirt & jacket, the left half has full-color pictures of scenes from the film at top & bottom, the middle is filled w/"James Dean" in bold type over "The overnight sensation of 'East of Eden' becomes the star of the year" in smaller blue type followed by "Warner Bros. put all the force of the screen into a challenging drama of today's juvenile violence!" in larger blue type & "Rebel Without a Cause" in bold black type outlined in red, linen-backed, 27 x 41" (ILLUS.)... **3,290**

"Shall We Dance" Poster

"Shall We Dance," RKO, 1937, one-sheet, full-color drawing of Fred Astaire & Ginger Rogers dancing on roller-skates, "Fred Astaire - Ginger Rogers in Shall We Dance" in bright lime green, red & deep blue stylized type, other film info in smaller black, lime green & aqua type, RKO logo in one bottom corner, linen-backed, 27 x 41" (ILLUS.)............................ **7,170**

Large Poster for "Spellbound"

Poster for "The Thin Man"

"Spellbound," Selznick, 1945, 24-sheet, stark black background w/color depiction at left of Gregory Peck embracing Ingrid Bergman, a straight-edge razor clutched in his hand, white type at right reads "David O. Selznick - presents - Ingrid Bergman - Gregory Peck - in - Alfred Hitchcock's Spellbound" the word "Spellbound" in yellow & red stylized type, w/other info printed in smaller type at bottom, linen-backed, 9' x 20' (ILLUS., bottom previous page) **4,780**

"Thin Man, The" MGM, 1934, half-sheet, color picture of William Powell & Myrna Loy cheek to cheek at upper left, black & white pictures of supporting players at lower right, w/"William - Powell and - Myrna - Loy in" in stylized orange type followed by "'the - thin man'" in orange-shadowed black elongated type, all on yellow ground w/stylized green figure of hatted man in silhouette, 22 x 28" (ILLUS., top of page) **25,850**

"To Catch a Thief," Paramount, 1955, one-sheet, artwork featuring heads of Cary Grant & Grace Kelly ready to kiss against watery background at top, shadowy figure in foreground at bottom looking down at figures illuminated by light from high pillared doors, white box in upper right reads "Paramount presents - Cary - Grant - Grace - Kelly" in bold black type, "Alfred Hitchcock's - TO CATCH A THIEF" in bold white across center directly under picture of Grant & Kelly, 27 x 41" (ILLUS., to the right) **1,880**

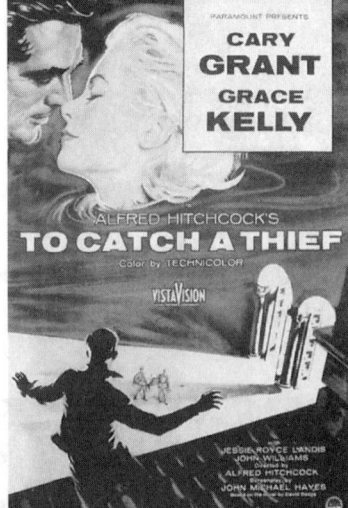

"To Catch a Thief" Poster

"Yellow Submarine," United Artists, 1968, three-sheet, illustrations of characters from the film in vibrant colors, "Nothing is real" in red at the top, w/red-rimmed black box in center containing a drawing of a yellow submarine & "The Beatles - Yellow Submarine" in orange-shadowed yellow type, linen-backed, 41 x 81" **2,115**

Miscellaneous

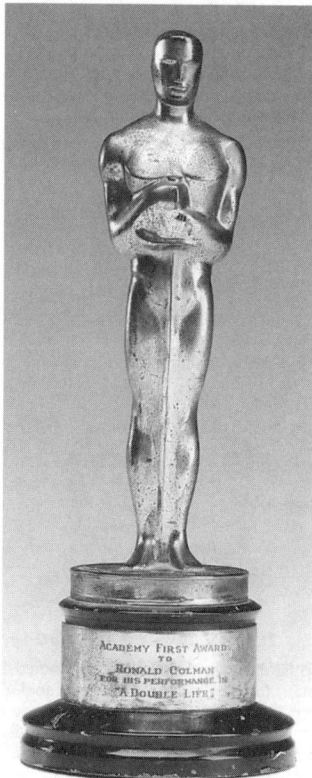

1947 Academy Award

Academy Award statuette, presented to Ronald Colman for "A Double Life," 1947, gold-plated "Oscar" stands on reel of film atop circular black lacquered base w/rectangular plaque reading "Academy First Award - to - Ronald Colman - For His Performance in - 'A Double Life'" & smaller brass plaque on back reading "Academy of - Motion Picture - Arts and Sciences - First Award - 1947," 13" h. (ILLUS.) **174,500**

Banner, display for "Speedy," dark blue skyline in silhouette against green ground, "Harold Lloyd" in red-bordered white type at left, "Speedy" in red at right, an illustration of Lloyd driving a caravan drawn by two hatted running horses in the center, a tan panel at bottom contains "a Paramount Release" & Paramount's logo, linen-backed, 1928, 36 x 118" (ILLUS., bottom of page) **4,113**

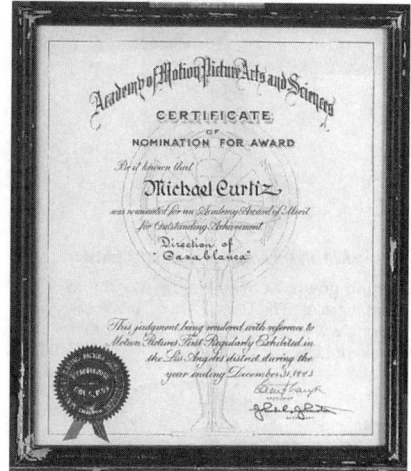

M. Curtiz Certificate of Nomination

Certificate of Nomination, presented to Michael Curtiz for "Outstanding Achievement for Direction of 'Casablanca'" by the Academy of Motion Picture Arts and Sciences (presented to Oscar nominees), 10 x 12" (ILLUS.)... **4,935**

Display Banner for "Speedy"

Marilyn Monroe Evening Gown

Evening gown, worn by Marilyn Monroe to premiere of "The Rose Tattoo," black silk crepe w/V-neck & spaghetti straps, small train (ILLUS.).. **28,200**

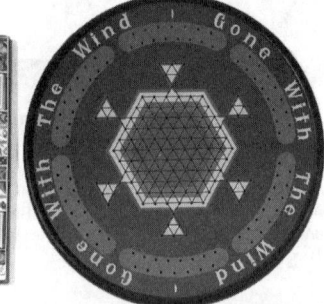

"Gone With the Wind" Board Game

Game, "Gone With the Wind," circular game board in green, red & yellow on brown, w/"Gone With the Wind" printed twice around circumference, includes instructions, dice, multicolored playing pegs & faux "Gone With the Wind" paper & coin money displaying images of Rhett & Scarlett, in original box, 1940, 21" d. (ILLUS.) **956**

1947 Golden Globe Award

Golden Globe award, presented to Ronald Colman for "A Double Life," 1947, gold-plated model of globe on circular black marble base w/rectangular brass plaque on front reading "To Ronald Colman - For His Outstanding Performance - In 'A Double Life' - 1947 - Hollywood Foreign Correspondents Association," comes w/letter to Colman announcing his win, 6" h. (ILLUS.) **9,560**

Humidor, sterling silver, rectangular molded shape, given to Ronald Colman by his wife, the lid engraved w/initials "R.C." & the names of all Colman's major films, hallmark on bottom reads "Gorham Sterling 301," 6 x 10", 2" h. (ILLUS., below) **6,573**

Sterling Silver Humidor

"King Kong" Jigsaw Puzzle

Jigsaw puzzle, "King Kong," RKO, 1933, framed puzzle of King Kong holding Fay Wray character in one hand & warding off Godzilla w/the other, "KING KONG" in yellow-shadowed red block type at bottom w/other info in smaller print, w/original mailing envelope, 10 1/2 x 21" (ILLUS.)... **2,350**

"The Ten Commandments" Prop

Movie prop, tablets of commandments from "The Ten Commandments," fiberglass &

other materials painted a rust color to resemble stone, w/early Canaanite-style script engraved on surface, one of six pairs made for film, 12 x 23" each, pr. (ILLUS.)... **11,750**

Movie script, "Some Like It Hot," 1959, mimeographed working script of Marilyn Monroe, w/"MMM" handwritten across top of cover & title page in red wax pencil, pages of script that include scenes w/Monroe's character, Sugar Kane, marked "Sugar" circled in red wax pencil, 122 pages, 9 x 12"..................................... **16,730**

J. Crawford as Mildred Pierce Mug

Mug, ceramic, in the image of Joan Crawford's head in caricature w/a leaning gold tone Oscar statuette forming the handle, to commemorate Crawford's Academy Award-winning performance in "Mildred Pierce," stamped on bottom "Hollywood Mugs by Barclay," 1946, only a few known to exist, minor repairs, 5" h. (ILLUS.) **470**

Title card, "Dark Victory," 1939, head of Bette Davis in profile against spread wings w/"Bette Davis" (w/picture of Oscar statuette between first & last names) below picture & "Dark Victory" at bottom, other film info printed in smaller type at the right of the image, 11 x 14" (ILLUS., below) **4,465**

"Dark Victory" Title Card

NAUTICAL ITEMS

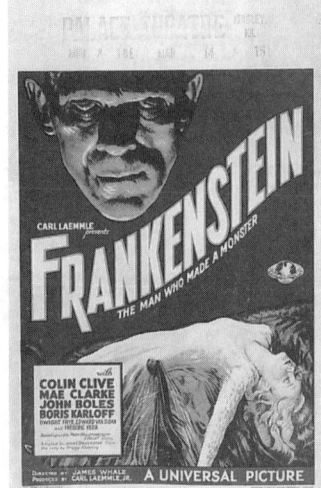

"Frankenstein" Window Card

Window card, "Frankenstein," Universal, 1931, illustrated w/disembodied face of the monster brooding over image of unconscious woman stretched out below, "FRANKENSTEIN" in orange-shadowed white block type curves across center w/"The Man Who Made a Monster" curving under it in smaller type, cast & other info in box in lower left corner, other info & Universal Pictures logo in white on dark blue ground, white space at top contains very faded print reading "PALACE THEATRE - Kinsley, KS. - Mon & Tue - Mar 14 & 15" 14 x 22" (ILLUS.)...................... **21,150**

The romantic lure of the sea, and of ships in general, has opened up a new area of collector interest. Nautical gear, especially items made of brass or with brass trim, is sought out for its decorative appeal. Virtually all items that can be associated with older ships, along with items used or made by sailors, are now considered collectible, for technological advances have rendered them obsolete. Listed below are but a few of the numerous nautical items sold in recent months.

Anchor, cast iron, ring at top mounted on later brackets, America, 56" w. x 107" h. (corrosion) **$823**

Anchor, iron, ring & chain mounted on later brackets, America, 54" w. x 106" h. (corrosion).. **823**

Billet head, wooden, carved in scrolled foliate design, painted black w/green & gilt highlights, 19th c., cracks, 7 1/2" w., 24" h. (ILLUS. center, w/other nautical items, bottom of page) **705**

Billet heads, wood, carved in scrolled foliate design, 19th c., weathered cracked surface, 27 1/2 x 5 1/2" & 23 x 7 1/4", pr. (ILLUS. second from right & second from left w/other nautical items) **4,994**

Blubber mincing knife, two-handled, w/original wooden scabbard, America, 19th c., 36" l. (partial loss to scabbard)........ **470**

Model of a whaling boat, painted wood & textile, the model w/full array of ropes, tools, spears, oars, hooks & flags, in a glass case w/a whale in the foreground, America, 20th c., 11 1/2 x 23 1/2", 20 1/4" h. **460**

Nautical Items

Various Ship Models

Model of five-masted ship "Gulf Swan," carved wood & metal implements, the hull painted red & black w/white & gilt trim, America, probably 20th c., small repairs, several breaks in rigging, 29" l., 22 1/4" h. (ILLUS. front right w/various ship models)... **353**

Model of ship "Constitution," wood, w/full rigging, life boats, cannon & copper-clad hull, painted black & white details, America, late 19th/early 20 c., some breaks, 33" l., 26" h. (ILLUS. front left w/various ship models).. **1,410**

Model of ship "Sea Serpent," finely detailed w/cabins, lifeboats, gear & carved & gilded serpent figurehead, mounted in mahogany & glass case, by George Ranes, ca. 1870, 7 1/2 h. x 36" l., case 15 1/4 h. x 42" l. **11,163**

Model of single-masted racing sloop, carved wood, sail & metal fittings, the hull painted green & white, light blue deck, includes wooden stand, America, early 20th c., breaks in rigging & on stand, lacking oars, 36" l., 45" h. (ILLUS. back right w/various ship models)........................ **2,703**

Model of sloop "Spray," wood, the hull painted white above red, blue deck, bentwood sails, wood & metal fittings, mounted on a water textured wood base, the base inscribed "CAPT. SLOCUM'S SLOOP 'SPRAY' IN WHICH HE SAILED AROUND THE WORLD APRIL 1895-JUNE 1898," America, late 19 - early 20 c., 30 " l., 32" h. w/base (break on mast) **529**

Model of three-masted clipper ship, carved wooden fittings, painted green & black w/white trim, mounted into mahogany framed display case, America, 20th c., 11 1/2 x 31 1/1", 21 1/2" h......................... **382**

Three Ship Models

Ship Builder's Half Model on Walnut Panel

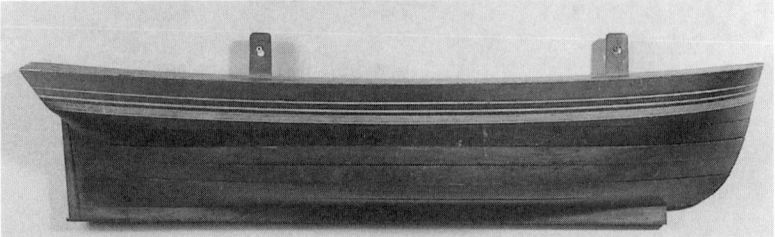

Ship Builder's Half Model with Gilt Trim

Ship Builder's Half Model on Pine Panel

Model of three-masted ship "Corsair," carved wood, ivory & metal implements & fittings, the hull painted green & black w/red, yellow & white details, mounted on wooden stand, America, late 19th c., some breaks, 31 1/2" l., 22 3/8" h. (ILLUS. right w/two other ship models, bottom previous page)...................................... 940

Model of three-masted ship "Ocean Monarch," carved wood, metal implements, sails, the hull painted black w/blue & gilt details, America, 19th c., some breaks in rigging, 111" l., 67" h. (ILLUS. center w/two other ship models) 4,994

Model of three-masted square-rigged ship, carved wood & metal fittings, hull painted black & white w/light blue details, on wooden stand, America, late 19th - early 20th c., some breaks in rigging, 31" l., 19 1/2" h. (ILLUS. left w/two other ship models)... 588

Model of two-masted fishing schooner, carved wood, w/sails & metal fittings, the hull painted two shades of green w/light blue details, America, 27" l., 23" h. (minor breaks) 353

Model of two-masted schooner, carved wood, sails, rigging & metal implements, the hull painted white w/green, red & black trim, mounted on wooden stand, America, probably early 20th c., 54" l.,

48 1/2" h. (ILLUS. center w/various ship models)... 1,293

Model of two-masted schooner, carved wood, w/sails & metal fittings, painted green, white & yellow, America, early 20th c., 37" l., 29 1/2" h. (several breaks in rigging)... 353

Model of two-masted schooner "Bluenose," carved wood, sails, rigging & metal implements, painted black w/white trim, America, second quarter 20th c., small repairs, few breaks in rigging, 39 1/2" h. (ILLUS. back left w/various ship models).. 646

Model of two-masted steamship "Lady Grey," carved wood, metal fittings, the hull painted white w/brown, red & yellow details, America, late 19th/early 20 c., 37" l., 22 1/4" h. (some breaks on fittings) 588

Seaman's chest, canted sides w/dovetailed construction, old rope handles, old green paint over an earlier blue, interior of lid retains original painting of sailing ship "Witchcraft built at Cheslea, 1852, William C. Rogers and Co. Boston" flying the American flag, picture of another ship in panel on the front, 17 1/2 x 44", 19" h. (age splits).. 1,980

Ship builder's half model, alternating laminated mahogany & other wood, mounted on walnut panel, America, 30" l. x 6" h. (ILLUS., top of page) 1,998

Ship builder's half model, natural finished pine w/black & gilt trim, America, loose stem post, 42" l. x 10 5/8" h. (ILLUS., second from top of previous page) **9,400**

Ship builder's half model, pine & other woods, mounted on pine panel, America, 37 1/2" l, 5" h. (ILLUS., third from top of previous page) **1,293**

Ship in a bottle, carved & painted diorama depicting a hillside coastal village w/a fishing trawler alongside having thread-like rigging w/attached bead pulleys, 19th c., 3 3/4" d., 11 1/2" l. (crack) **106**

Ship's bell, cast bronze, decorated w/raised linear bands, late 19th c., 14" d., 17" h. (ILLUS. far right w/other nautical items) **558**

Ship's bell, cast bronze, "J. WARNER & SONS LONDON 1855," weathered surface, 13" d., 13 1/2" h. (ILLUS. far left w/other nautical items) **1,175**

Ship's bell, cast bronze, verdigris surface, raised "1945" on shoulder, America, 1945, 14" d., 16" h. **441**

Ship's wheel, walnut, eight turned spokes & handles, 45" d. (one spoke has glued restoration) **275**

OFFICE EQUIPMENT

By the late 19th century business offices around the country were becoming increasingly mechanized as inventions such as the typewriter, adding machine, mimeograph and Dictaphone became more widely available. Miracles of efficiency when introduced, in today's computerized offices these machines would be cumbersome and archaic. Although difficult to display and store, many of these relics are becoming increasingly collectible today.

Calculator, "Thacker's Calculating Instrument," a version of a long cylindrical slide rule in mahogany & brass, the cylinder set between short uprights & a rectangular base & turned w/end knobs, w/original box labeled "Keuffel & Esser Co., New York," late 19th-early 20th c., 21 1/2" l. **$385**

World Globe Pencil Sharpener

Pencil sharpener, printed tin & cast spelter, model of a world globe printed in black, red, blue & white, held on the back of a

kneeling figure of Atlas w/a gold finish, sharpener hole in the back, Germany, 2 5/8" h. (ILLUS.) **14**

Telephone, wall-mounted, walnut case w/original finish, marked "Kellogg Co., Chicago, USA," 32" h. **358**

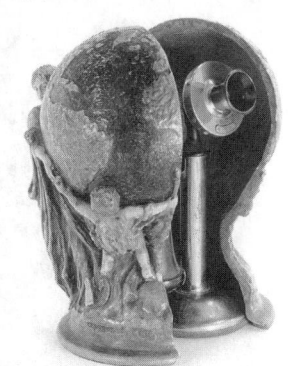

Unique Phone & Globe Cover

Telephone & cover, "Hide-a-Phone," a nickel-plated candlestick-style telephone housed in a hinged cast-metal cover modeled as a world globe supported by full-relief classical figures, globe painted in dark blue, white & reddish brown, ca. 1910, 2 pcs. (ILLUS.) **3,835**

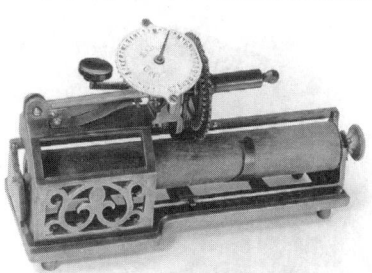

"Columbia Index No. 1" Typewriter

Typewriter, "Columbia Index No. 1," index-type, steel w/wooden roller, 1883, only produced six months, rarest American index-type typewriter (ILLUS.) **5,750**

Early Cipher Machine-Typewriter

"The Crown" Index-type Typewriter

Typewriter, index-type cipher machine & typewriter, "Discreet" model, 1899, on a rectangular wooden base (ILLUS.).......... **10,455**

Sholes Visible No. 4 Typewriter

Typewriter, "Sholes Visible No. 4," black steel frame, standard keyboard, 1901 (ILLUS.).. **7,318**

Typewriter, "The Crown," index-type, black steel & nickel plate on oak board base, Byron S. Brooks, New York, 1894 (ILLUS., top of page) **6,903**

PAPER COLLECTIBLES

Spencerian drawing, elaborate ink drawing of a dove w/a quill pen, feathers, fronds, flowers, a butterfly & banners, one reading "Father and Mother, 1909,"
frame w/worn gilt liner, 16 1/2 x 20 1/2" (stains, minor edge damage) **$248**

Spencerian drawing, figure of a horse, small calling card at the bottom w/gilt edge is signed "L. Pearce," in 19th c. paint decorated frame, 20 x 23 1/2" (minor fold lines, stains)....................................... **193**

Spencerian drawing, ink on paper drawing of a stag leaping over a quill pen, w/grains of wheat & banner reading "Drawn by L.M. Duvall, May 24, 1885," old patterned gilt frame, 15 1/2 x 18 1/8" (some foxing & wrinkles, frame has some edge damage) **303**

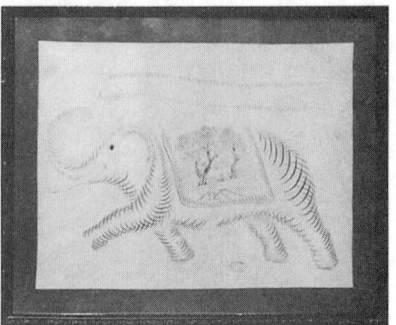

Spencerian Drawing of Elephant

Spencerian drawing, large drawing of charging circus elephant holding a flag in its trunk that stretches out to a ring on its tail, cloth covering on elephant depicts a scene of the Serengeti, red mat & black painted frame, stretcher back reads "Property of H.L. Holtzmuller," stains & white spots, 22 1/2 x 19 1/2" (ILLUS.).......... **660**

Spencerian Drawing of Leaping Stag

Spencerian drawing, leaping stag done in brown ink, the face & antlers in black ink w/unusual stippling technique, shadow box frame w/patterned gilt liner, stains & foxing, fold lines, few short tears, 26 1/2 x 32 1/2" (ILLUS.).................................. 330

Spencerian drawing, on laid paper, figure of sparrow w/a banner surrounded by leaves & feathers, finely grained frame in black on dark grey w/beaded liner, 10 3/4 x 13 3/4" (names on the banner have faded or been erased, light foxing, minor damage)... 132

gilt frame appears to be original, folded into fourths at one time & has a few small holes along those lines, 15 3/4 x 19 3/4" (ILLUS.) 715

Children's Greeting Cards

General

Beloved Belindy Greeting Card

Beloved Belindy, storybook and matching doll, 1972, card only (ILLUS.) **$10**

Spencerian Drawing of Flying Eagle

Spencerian drawing, ornate flying eagle w/banner signed "Flourished by James E. Wall, Piqua, Miami Co., Ohio," period

Betsy Clark Greeting Card

Betsy Clark, stand-up three-dimensional schoolhouse, 1970s, 6 x 14" (ILLUS.) **25**

Birthday, big-eyed little girl reading card, USA, 1941, 4 x 4".................................... **4**

Birthday, cowboy & cowgirl, flocked, Whitman, 1950s, 4 x 4" **10**

Birthday, cowboy, "To Brother," USA, 1940s, 6 x 6" **2**

Paper Doll Birthday Card

Birthday, "Cut-ups," paper doll card, no mark, 1930s, 4 x 5 1/2" (ILLUS.) **20**

Birthday, die-cut type, lamb, Hallmark, 1943, 3 x 5... **2**

Birthday, die-cut type, seal w/ball on nose, Hallmark, 3 x 3" **3**

Birthday, first birthday, bunny paper dolls, GB, USA, 1942 .... **20**

Birthday, flocked duck playing baseball, "For Nephew," Forget-Me-Not, 1944, 5 x 6" **9**

Birthday, folder-type, horse w/"I am a year older" pin, Forget-Me-Not, 1940s, 6 x 6.......... **20**

Birthday, folder-type, two miniature books inside, Barker, 1940s....................... **20**

Birthday Party Invitation

Birthday, invitation to party, Joan Walsh Anglund paper doll, Hallmark, 1973, 3 1/2 x 5" (ILLUS.) **7**

Stand-up Cat Birthday Card

Birthday, mechanical-type, stand-up cat holding card, Made in USA, 1940s, 6 1/2 x 10" (ILLUS.) **18**

Mechanical Birthday Card

Birthday, mechanical-type, television w/turning dial, Buzza, early 1950s, 5 1/2 x 6" (ILLUS.)... **15**

Strawberry Shortcake Birthday Card

Birthday, niece, Strawberry Shortcake dancing doll, American Greetings, 1970s, 15" l. (ILLUS.) **10**

Old King Cole Birthday Card

Birthday, Old King Cole song card, USA, 1949, 4 x 4" (ILLUS.) **8**
Birthday, old-time telephone, Hallmark, 1946, 6 x 6" **5**
Birthday, playable recording, authentic voice of Jiminy Cricket, Walt Disney, Buzza, 1960s, 6 x 6" **25**
Birthday, Popeye, Hallmark, 1929, 5 x 7" **18**

Queen of Hearts Story Card

Birthday, Queen of Hearts story card, American Greetings, late 1940s, 5 x 6" (ILLUS.) **12**
Birthday, Rupert Bear, British, 1980s.................. **9**

Stand-up Birthday Card

Birthday, stand-up type, duck carrying card, Made in USA, 1940s, 6 x 10 (ILLUS.).............. **18**

Hallmark Walking Doll Card

Birthday, walking doll, Hallmark, 1970s, 4 1/2 x 9" (ILLUS.)... **10**
Donald Duck, rocker-type, Rock-N-Play series, Hallmark, 1941 .... **15**

Get well, elephant w/rubber ball tail, USA, 1940s, 5 x 6 (ILLUS.).. **4**
Get well, folder-type, boy hanging on cliff, USA, 1948, 3 x 3 .... **2**
Get well, folder-type, crying puppy, no mark, 1950s, 4 x 4... **1**

Forget-Me-Not Get Well Card

Get well, folder-type, flocked pony, Forget-Me-Not, 1940s, 5 x 6" (ILLUS.).......................... **3**
Get well, folder-type, game inside, "Sorry You're Laid Low," J.S. Publishing Company, 1940s, 5 x 5.. **4**

Get Well Card

Get well, toy cards, USA, 1950s, 3 1/2 x 7, each (ILLUS.)... **2**
Lambkin, little boy shepherd & lambs on front, by Brownie, 1943, 4 x 4"............................ **2**

Little Red Riding Hood Greeting Card

Little Red Riding Hood, w/feather in bonnet, story inside, by Hallmark, 1947,
5 x 6" (ILLUS.) **25**

Holiday

Christmas, fold-out type, Santa w/arms full
of presents, Rust Craft, 1945, 4 x 5" **3**
Christmas, folder-type, baby reindeer
wearing bells around necks, USA, 1942,
5 x 5 .... **3**
Christmas, folder-type, dogs delivering
cards, National PTG Company, 1941,
4 x 4 .... **4**

A-meri-card Christmas Card

Christmas, folder-type, fuzzy Santa,
"Christmas Wish," A-meri-card, 1940s,
4 1/2 x 6 (ILLUS.) **4**
Christmas, folder-type, lamb jumping over
fence, Rust Craft, 1945, 3 x 5 .... **3**

Santa's Workshop Card

Christmas, folder-type, Santa's workshop
w/moveable Santa, Whitman, 1940s,
6 x 6 1/2" (ILLUS.) **12**
Christmas, folder-type, snowman sweep-
ing snow away, USA, 1939, 4 x 4" **2**

Whitman Christmas Card

Christmas, fuzzy Santa Claus, Whitman,
1940s, 4 x 6", each (ILLUS.) **4**

Fuzzy Santa Claus Card

"Twas the Night Before Christmas" Card

Clarabelle Cow Valentine Card

Easter Chicken Card

Easter Paper Doll Card

Halloween Care Bear Card

Halloween, Care Bears, American Greetings, 1987, opens to 18" h. (ILLUS.) 3

Halloween, die-cut type, fuzzy black cat, Hallmark, 1960s, 5 x 6" 5

Boy in Barrel Valentine Card

Valentine, boy in barrel, Campbell Kid look, 1930s, 4 x 7 (ILLUS.) 20

Valentine, chocolate soldier, Whitman, 1950s, 2 x 7" 1

Valentine, folder-type, boy building valentine box, Rust Craft, 1945, 3 x 4" 8

Scarecrow Halloween Card

Halloween, folder-type, scarecrow, Hallmark, 1970s, 3 x 5" (ILLUS.) 3

New Year, ringing jingle bells, folder, USA, 4 x 6", 1940s 4

St. Patrick's Day, O'Reilly, O'Neal and O'Rourke bears, folder, Hallmark, 1940s 2

Thanksgiving, die-cut type, flocked turkey, Hallmark, 1950s, 6 x 8" 10

Thanksgiving, die-cut type, Santa Maria w/put-together parts, Hallmark, 1960s, 8 x 12" 15

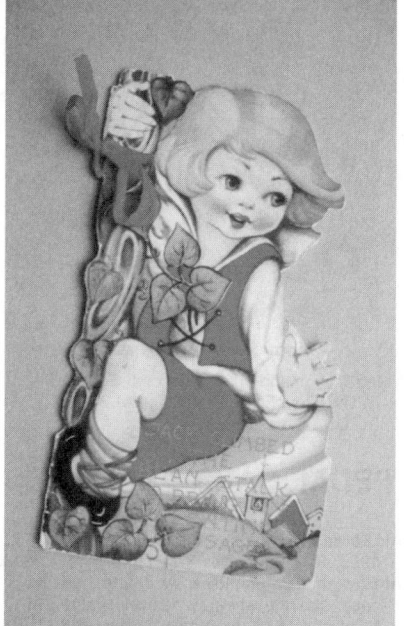

Jack & Beanstalk Valentine Card

Valentine, Jack & the Beanstalk, storybooktype tied w/ribbon, no mark, 1930s, 3 1/2 x 6 1/2" (ILLUS.) 12

Paper Doll Valentine Card

Valentine, paper doll, outfits in cellophane envelope, late 1920s-30s (ILLUS.)............... 30

Valentine, pop-out type, circus, USA, 1930s, 7 x 7... 3

Valentine, sailor boy w/oar, USA, 1944, 5 x 5" 8

Honeycomb Valentine Card

Valentine, stand-up honeycomb, panda fishing, Doubl-Glo, 1940s, 5 x 6 1/2" (ILLUS.).. 15

PEDAL CARS & VEHICLES

Air Force jeep, metal, chain drive, Garton, 1965, 40" l. (paint loss, surface rust).......... $385

Airflow, metal, turquoise w/chrome hubcaps, steering wheel, windshield frame, headlights & front bumper, Steelcraft, 1937, 41" l. 1,430

Airplane, three rubber wheels, engine w/propeller, red wings & tail w/white stripes, Steelcraft, 1930s, 38" l. 1,000

Airport Jet Service vehicle, three wheels, Murray, 1950s.. 700

American Graham Roadster, balloon rubber tires w/silver hubcaps, front bumper, air vents on each side of hood, headlights, fenders on front & back cover & protect tires, glass windshield w/side wings, blue body w/white fenders, 1938 2,200

Army pursuit plane, metal, steel spring-driven propeller turns when pedals are pumped, steering by single rear wheel, padded seat & seat sides, U.S. Army decals on wings, Murray, 1949-50, 45" l. 2,420

"Atomic Missile," three-wheeled body, w/windshield & controls in center of vehicle, "Motor Tone shift lever" & "Dyna chain drive" for maximum speed w/minimum effort, Murray, 1954, 25 x 45"............. 1,500

Austin J40 Roadster, fitted w/Dunlop 2 1/4 x 12 1/2" pneumatic tires, pressed steel wheels, upholstered seats, chromium bumpers, horn powered by two 4.5 volt batteries, dummy engine complete w/spark plugs, leads under bonnet, Austin Motor Company, England, late 1940s-50s, 22 x 27 1/2", 63" l. 400

Austin Pathfinder Special, resembles period race car, fitted w/Dunlop 2 1/4 x 12 1/2" pneumatic tires, pressed steel wheels, upholstered seats, chromium bumpers, horn powered by two 4.5 volt batteries, dummy engine complete w/spark plugs, leads under bonnet, made in various colors, late 1940s-50s, 26 1/2 x 27", 63" l. 500

Baby Bugatti, leather interior, spare wheel on side, manufactured in Italy in edition of 90, 1930s.. 30,000

BMC Special, metal, padded seat & insides, ca. 1940s, 40" l. (hood decal starting to peel, paint on wheels has some chips)... 1,650

Boat, Jolly Roger, metal, plastic outboard motor at back, plastic flag & light, seat pad, battery-operated, Murray, 1962, 38" l. 770

Cannonball Express locomotive, pressed steel painted red, pre-World War II style, w/cow catcher, Garton, 39" l. 300

Car, standard model w/no unique features, Murray, 1967, 15 x 33".................................... 200

Murray "Champion" Pedal Car

Champion curved-side car, "Champion - Jet Flow Drive" printed on side, w/chain drive, ball bearings & motor tone shift, Murray, 1940s (ILLUS.)................................. **300**

Champion straight-sided car, metal, chrome hubcaps, hood ornament & steering wheel, seat pad, Murray, 1949-50, 34" l.. **523**

Chrysler, metal, chrome hubcaps, steering wheel, windshield frame, airplane hood ornament, front & rear bumpers, padded seat & insides, 1941, 39" l. **1,650**

Chrysler, metal, chrome hubcaps, steering wheel, windshield, hood ornament & turn signal covers, Steelcraft, The Murray-Ohio Mfg. Co., 1941, 34" l. **1,760**

Comet, metal, chrome hubcaps, steering wheel, windshield frame, hood ornament, headlights & emblem, V12 Super Drive decal on back, padded seat, Murray, 37" l. **660**

Deusenberg racer, balloon tires, side exhaust pipes, bullhorn, metal front bumper, windshield, headlights & glass radiator cap hood decoration, Toledo Manufacturing, 1935 (ILLUS., to the right) **2,500**

Dick Tracy Ford, metal, chromed hubcaps, Dick Tracy decal on both sides, Garton, 35" l. **413**

Dodge, metal, chrome hubcaps, windshield, hood ornament, steering wheel & turn signal covers, Steelcraft, The Murray-Ohio Mfg. Co., 1939, 34" l. **2,200**

Dump truck, metal, Mack Bull Dog, International Motor Co., New York, decals on sides, Mack decal on front, Playboy trucking decals on bed sides, Steelcraft Mfg. Co., Murray, Ohio, 43 1/2" l. (one non-matching hubcap, no back gate)............ **825**

Deusenberg Pedal Car

Dump truck, replica of 5-ton Mack truck, adjustable pedals, steel springs, back section tilts to dump, realistic fenders, hood, radiator, seat, Steelcraft, 1930s, 25 x 64".. **2,200**

Field Ambulance, khaki colored, canvas cover w/cross in circle & "Field Ambulance" covers rear section, "USA Medical Corp" on doors, Garton, 1941, 15 x 33" **1,000**

Fire Chief car, red w/white striping on sides, bell in front, Murray, 1967, 15 x 33" **300**

Pedal Fire Engine

Fire engine, red w/white stripes on sides, handles at rear, steering wheel, storage compartment in back, maker unknown, possibly Murray, early 1960s (ILLUS.).......... **100**

Fire Patrol jeep, pressed metal & wood, w/windscreen & small compartment behind driver's seat, Steger, late 1940s............ **375**

Fire truck, hose reel in back of truck contains working fire hose, wooden ladders hang on each side of truck, headlights & taillights & spotlight work, clanging bell, bright red, American National, 1930s, rare, 64" l. **15,000**

Flat Face Speedway pace car, metal, Murray, 1960s, 34" l.. **550**

G-Man radio cruiser, metal, chrome hubcaps, windshield & hood ornament, plastic siren, padded seat, Murray, 35" l.............. **715**

Gas pump, made for pedal cars, City Gas, maker unknown, 1940s, 36" h........................ **150**

Good Humor Ice Cream truck, metal, three wheels, chain drive, bell, seat pad, back storage compartment opens, "Good Humor" on front below handle bars, Murray, 1955, 36" l. **880**

Hot rod, metal, chain drive, seat pad, Garton, ca. 1950s, 35" l. (slight scratching to back end).. **935**

Indy Speedster, "Gilmore Special #8" made for Gilmore Oil Company, which also operated a race track, leaping lion decorations on both sides, Gendron, 1931 .... **2,500**

"Kidillac" Deluxe, chain drive, battery-powered headlights & taillights, sold through Sears Roebuck & given away by dealers w/purchase of new Cadillac, Garton, 1954 (ILLUS., bottom of page)............... **350**

"Kidillac" Deluxe, metal, chromed headlight covers, hubcaps & door edges, rear-mounted spare, Garton, 1952, 45" l. (broken antenna).. **990**

"

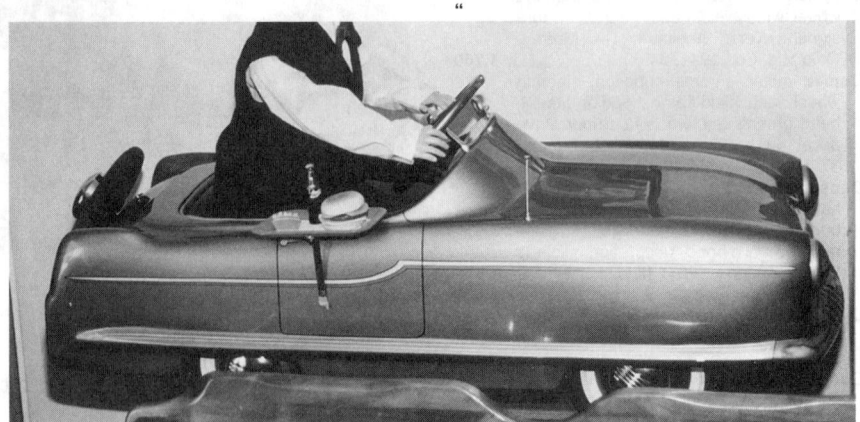

"Kidillac" Deluxe Pedal Car

Lotus Pedal Racing Car

Lotus racing car, modeled on the car driven by Grand Prix racer Jackie Stewart, deep green w/silvertone highlights, AMC, possible giveaway w/purchase of new Ford, 1960s (ILLUS.) 195

Mail truck, metal, GMC, back flap opens, AMF, 1959, 41" l. 880

Motor Scoot, Model KAR, Serial #5520, light yellow and red, three wheels, two in front, one in rear, working headlights, large enough to accommodate an adult, plans appeared in April 1939 issue of Popular Science Monthly 2,000

Oil truck, Red Crown Oil, BMC 1/6 scale model in red w/Red Crown logo in red, white & blue on doors, back deck w/box of miniature Red Crown oil cans, 1948 40

Oil truck, Sinclair Oil, BMC 1/6 scale model in company colors of green & white, w/Sinclair's dinosaur logo on doors, 1948 40

Oscar Mayer Wienermobile, plastic, bright orange, yellow & black, w/Oscar Mayer decals, 1970s, 21 1/2 x 45 1/2". 175

Packard Tandem, front & back seats allow driver plus passenger, windshield, 1930s, 25 x 64". 2,300

Planters Peanuts car, plastic, small wheels in front, larger ones in back, "Mr. Planters Peanut" on door & "Planters" on both sides, originally available for proof of purchase from 200 bags of Planters peanuts plus $50, rare, 1970s 250

Pontiac, metal, chrome hubcaps, front bumper & hood ornament, padded seat, Murray, 1949, 36" l. 715

Promotional car, modeled on Murray pickup truck, 691 manufactured for Coca-Cola & Raley Grocery Stores promotion of "Hot August Nights Car Show" in Reno, Nevada (each store received 5 to sell), hood features "Coca-Cola" & sides feature "Raley," 1990 400

Pumper fire engine, tin boiler, fuel compartment, two wooden ladders, siren on hood, bell on front, Toledo Manufacturing, 1930s, 60" l. 2,200

Pursuit plane, pressed steel, vinyl interior, pedal-driven propeller, two machine guns in front of cockpit, 1930s, 46" l. 3,000

Radar patrol car, three wheels, small aerial for radio communications behind seat, "Police" on front below handle bars, Murray, 1950s.. 700

"Royal Deluxe," metal, chrome windshield frame, hubcaps, hood ornament, w/rear mounted spare tire, Murray, ca. 1950s, 35" l. 770

"Sad Face" vehicle, "sad face" referring to look of front grille, three models made (dump truck, fire truck, station wagon) w/metal windshield, horn outside driver's side, Murray, 1951, each 500

"Skippy" DeSoto Pedal Car

"Skippy" DeSoto, named for comic character Skippy, originally red & cream w/red bumpers & wheels, taillights, Pioneer, 1930s, 38" l. (ILLUS. of yellow) 1,000

"Sky Rocket," three-wheeled body, w/windshield & controls in center of vehicle, "Motor Tone shift lever" & "Dyna chain drive" for maximum speed w/minimum effort, Murray, 1954, 25 x 45"............ 1,500

"Space Cruiser" Pedal Vehicle

"Space Cruiser," silver-grey three-wheeled aerodynamic body w/"Space Cruiser" printed on side, windshield & controls in center of vehicle, "Motor Tone shift lever" & "Dyna chain drive" for maximum speed w/minimum effort, Murray, 1954, 25 x 45" (ILLUS.).............................. **1,500**

Studebaker, rubber tires, working headlights, manufactured in a limited edition by Giodani, Bologna, Italy, 1950s, 45" l. **1,600**

"Supersonic Jet," three-wheeled body, w/windshield & controls in center of vehi-cle, "Motor Tone shift lever" & "Dyna chain drive" for maximum speed w/minimum effort, Murray, 1954, 25 x 45".............. **1,500**

Tin Lizzie, metal, original working plastic horn, seat pad, chromed headlamps, Garton Toy Co., ca. 1950s, 34" l. **715**

Tractor, molded plastic, three-wheel orange body, silver-grey grille & engine, black steering wheel, seat & wheels, Reliable Toys of Toronto, Ontario, Canada, 1960s, 17 1/5 x 24" (ILLUS., bottom of page) **50**

Pedal Tractor

Pedal Army Jeep Vehicle

Murray Pedal Tractor

Tractor, red & white, three wheels, Murray, 1950s (ILLUS.) **75**

U.S. Army jeep, khaki w/World War II military star in circle on side & "USA 82412" on side, no top, Garton, 1940s, 15 x 33" (ILLUS., top of page) **300**

Miscellaneous

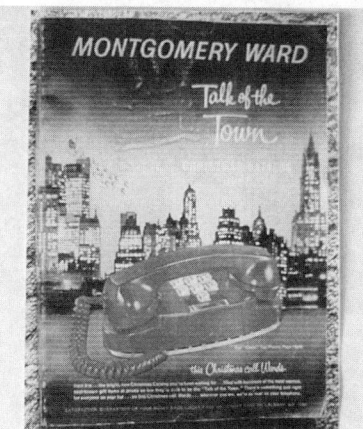

Christmas Catalog with Pedal Cars

Christmas catalog, Montgomery Ward, includes four pages of pedal cars, 1965 (ILLUS.) **100**

Published Illustrations

Magazine cover, Post magazine, features full-color drawing of boy in pedal car w/police officer standing over him, late 1930s (ILLUS. top) **45**

Promotional illustration, for Jones Motors, features full-color drawing of girl in pedal car in front of sign that says "E.P. Jones Jr. Cars For Sale" & boy walking by w/baseball bat, caption on illustration reads "Jones Motors," 1930s (ILLUS. bottom w/magazine cover) **45**

Sign, tin, replica of cover of 1926 Steelcraft catalog, "Juvenile Automobiles, Trucks, Tow Trucks, Scooters, Coaster Wagons," cover design features boy in his pedal car w/dog running alongside, part of Hallmark Cards Collection, 1990s, 10 x 14" 15

Sign, tin, replica of cover of 1943 Aviator Coloring Book, part of Hallmark Cards Collection, cover design features two children in leather helmets, goggles, aviator jumpsuits, one flying, the second ready to bail out, bombers in sky above, 1990s, 10 x 14" 20

PERFUME, SCENT & COLOGNE BOTTLES

Baccarat glass, clear bottle & stopper, apothecary shape w/disk stopper, label on front, in box decorated w/scenes of 1930s Paris, bottom signed "Baccarat," Baxx. #524, Molyneux Rue Royale, 4 3/8" $154

Baccarat glass, clear bottle & stopper, early decanter shape w/faceted stopper, Art Nouveau gold label on front of woman smelling a blossom, signed "Baccarat," w/paper label, colorful fabric box, Houbigant Le Parfum Idéal, Bacc. #10, 1907-23, 4 1/4" 77

Baccarat glass, clear bottle & stopper, pill form, empty, stopper molded w/sitting dog, brown patina, signed "Baccarat," D'Orsay Toujours Fidèle, Bacc. #162, 1912, 3 1/2" 246

Ceramic, figural perfume lamp, seated Oriental figure in lotus position holding a container for the perfume, maroon, yellow & gold, rewired, unmarked but probably German manufacture, 7 1/2" (hairline & repainted chip to top of hat) 176

Ceramic, figural scent bottle w/metal crown stopper, shape of happy Oriental figure w/gold gown, unmarked but of German manufacture, approx. 2" h. 77

Cut glass, clear bottle & stopper, bell-shaped, highly faceted & pleated, w/faceted ball stopper, unsigned, 5" h. 22

Cut overlay glass, blue cut to clear bottle & stopper amphora, cut w/windows, names & decoration enameled in gold, signed "Baccarat," blue velvet & silk box w/tassel, Bacc. #814, 1949, Christian Dior "Miss Dior," empty, 7" h. 1,320

Czechoslovakian glass, clear bottle & stopper, bottle cut w/feet & horizontal stepped facets, stopper cut w/vertical facets on one side & intaglio cut wreath of flowers on other, w/dauber, signed "Czechoslovakia" in circle, 6 1/2" h. 413

Czechoslovakian glass, clear bottle w/red crystal stopper, bottle cut w/diamond facets, molded stopper in form of cube standing on one point, dauber missing, unsigned, 4 3/8" l. 319

Lapis Lazuli Glass Bottle & Stopper

Czechoslovakian glass, lapis lazuli bottle & stopper, Ingrid, bottle molded w/large bird w/swirling feathers, stopper plumed bird, w/very long dauber, signed "Ingrid Czechoslovakia Cf. North #200" on one foot, very rare, 8 7/8" h. (ILLUS.)............... 2,200

Czechoslovakian glass, pink bottle & stopper, bottle cut w/facets & metal filigree, decorated w/pink stones, stopper spire shape & faceted diamond pattern, dauber missing, unsigned, 6 1/4" l. 440

Czechoslovakian glass, red translucent bottle w/clear stopper, bottle cut w/flower motif both sides, spire stopper w/dauber, bottom signed "Czechoslovakia" in oval, 5 1/8" h. 660

Czechoslovakian Vaseline Bottle

Czechoslovakian glass, vaseline bottle & stopper, stopper mounted w/faceted black glass finial & opalescent jewels, stopper w/white & black enameling, gold metal collar w/bow around neck, w/dauber, unsigned, 4 1/2" l. (ILLUS.).................... 1,650

Czechoslovakian Two-color Bottle

Czechoslovakian glass, yellow bottle w/clear stopper, bottle cut w/facets around bottom edge, stopper intaglio cut w/flowers & its edges scalloped, w/dauber, bottom signed "Czechoslovakia" in oval, 4 3/4" l. (ILLUS.) **231**

Lalique glass, frosted bottle & stopper, oblong, w/molded bands of overlapping leaves, subtle green patina, signed "R. Lalique," Maison Lalique Amélie, 3" l. **1,650**

Lalique glass, frosted & clear bottle & stopper, swirl design, bottom signed "Lalique France," Maison Lalique Samoa, 3 1/4" h. **154**

Metal Solid Perfume Compact

Metal, solid perfume compact, heart covered in lattice of pink stones, some perfume used, gold label on back, pink box, Schiaparelli Shocking, 1 1/2" l. (ILLUS.) **220**

Mold-blown glass, amethyst, ovoid body w/short cylindrical neck, sheared mouth & pontil base, diamond-daisy design, possibly Stiegel made at the American Flint Glass Manufactory, Manheim, Pennsylvania, 18th c., about 6" h. **3,300**

Molded & cut glass, green w/metal atomizer, bottle stem molded stork, wheel cut flowers on bottle well, new ball & tassel, signed "DeVilbiss," very rare, 6 5/8" h. **1,760**

Molded glass, clear bottle w/gold cap, wine bottle shape w/pedestal bottom, cap decorated w/rhinestones & a pearl, some perfume, bottom signed "Tilford," box decorated w/a peacock, w/outer box, 5 1/2" h. **121**

Molded glass, clear bottle w/white, red & silver label, gold metal form of nude male torch runner w/one foot atop the globe, Corinne Damier Dameo, 6 3/8" h. **413**

Molded glass, clear bottles w/metal caps, golf club-shaped, in red plaid golf caddy w/gold foil label attached to cords, Karoff Perfumes, each 5 15/16" h., set of three **231**

Molded glass, clear & frosted bottle & stopper molded as tulip bouquet, stopper bud shaped, amber patina, molded "Jaytho" vertically in front, "Made in France Utt #JT-1" on bottom, rare, Jay Thorpe & Co. Jaytho, 2 1/2" h. **605**

Molded glass, clear, miniature bottle & stopper, both w/flower form motif, label on shoulder of bottle, in circular box, bottom of bottle marked 1/4 oz., Corday "Miss Corday," near empty, almost 2" h. (box has perfume stain) **110**

Molded glass, clear w/black glass stopper, miniature, pretty red label on front, bottom signed "France" in the mold, red box imprinted w/gold, very early miniature, Bourjois "Ashes of Rose," empty, about 2" h. **220**

Molded glass, clear w/clear stopper in shape of woman's head & shoulders, name in gold enamel, some perfume, label on bottom of bottle & box, in light blue box, very difficult to find this tiny size in its box, Hattie Carnegie Perfume Carnegie 7, almost 2" h. **990**

Molded glass, clear w/clear stopper, shape of sword w/gold tip & gold cap, empty, black label around top, decorated w/orange & gold tassel, in cloth scabbard, Jean Desprez Escarmouche, almost 5" h. **110**

Molded glass, clear w/gold cap, scallops, label on front, bottom signed "Bourjois" in the mold, green & white box, ca. 1950s, Bourjois "Glamour," full, 2 1/2" h. **44**

Molded glass, clear w/metal atomizer attached, octagonal shape, molded as wine glass on long stem w/circular base, new atomizer ball, unsigned, 7 1/2" h. **165**

Molded glass, clear w/metal atomizer, ball-shaped, gold enameled, marked "A O Tillyer Crixité Lenses," original atomizer ball signed "DeVilbiss," possibly made for optometrists to clean lenses, very unusual, 5" h. **55**

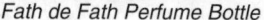

Fath de Fath Perfume Bottle

Molded glass, clear w/stopper, shape of eight-pointed star w/perfume, black flocked box, 1/2 oz. size, Jacques Faith "Fath de Fath," almost 2 1/2" h. (ILLUS.) **99**

Molded glass, clear, w/wood caps, figures of Mexicans, each dressed in colorful serape w/large colorful sombrero, empty, in original box, Karoff Castanettes set of Chypra, Xenia & Delicia, set of three 165

Molded glass, frosted bottle & stopper in the form of a woman in formal gown holding bouquet of flowers, empty, traces of brown patina, label on bottom, "Eisenberg 847-A," 3 1/2" h. 568

Molded glass, frosted bottle & stopper, model of a sitting cat, brown patina, unidentified, 3" h. 715

Molded glass, pink w/metal atomizer attachment, Industrial Modern style, original ball (hardened), bottom signed "DeVilbiss - Patent Pending," w/paper label, 2 1/2" h. 44

Pottery, perfume lamp, molded in two pieces as a ballerina, blue & violet w/painted face, air vents on the side of dancer's head, rewired, bottom signed very faintly "Fulper" in an impressed oval, 6" h. 440

Pressed glass, blue bottle, square shape w/gilded plastic top w/two intertwined snakes, front of cap signed "Niki de Saint Phalie," red & blue box w/outer box, 4 5/8" 209

Pressed glass, clear atomizer bottle w/brass attachment mounted on gold plated metal stand, Volupté, Art Deco motif, base signed "Volupté Patent Pending," 6" h. 231

Pressed glass, clear bottle pocket watch shape w/red label, unidentified, White Lilac, ca. 1898, 3 1/4" 55

Pressed glass, clear bottle & stopper, cylinder shape, colorful label, empty w/tiny bundle of scented wood inside, wooden box w/names burned into wood & decorated w/green & blue wool braid, exterior box marked "No. 377," Myrurgia Maderas de Oriente, 3 1/4" h. 66

Pressed glass, clear bottle & stopper, decanter shape, label on front, neck & side, ca. 1909-1915, A. Bourjois & Cle. Idéal Oeillet, rare, 4 1/2" h. 88

Pressed glass, clear bottle & stopper, decanter shape w/faceted stopper, unopened, label on front, original Art Nouveau box, L.T. Piver Floramye, ca. 1905....... 660

Pressed glass, clear bottle & stopper enameled in gold depicting a fountain, some perfume, gold label on bottom, Richard Hudnut Les Cascades, 2" h. 413

Pressed glass, clear w/figural stoppers in the form of firebirds, ribs interspersed w/square molded facets, unsigned, American manufacture, about 6 1/4" h. 33

Set of Clear Glass Perfume Bottles

Pressed glass, clear w/gold metal caps, labels on bottom of each bottle, mounted in corsage presentation of flowers, in round celluloid box, Matchabelli "Ave Maria, Duchess of York, Katherine the Great," about 1 1/3" h., set of three (ILLUS.)........... 385

Glass Perfume Atomizer

Pressed glass, clear w/metal atomizer attached, internally enameled perfume well in deep mauve, exterior decorated w/gold motifs, new ball & tassel, unsigned, 6 1/2" h. (ILLUS.) 110

Ben Hur Bottle and Box

Pressed glass, frosted bottle w/impressed flower & gold label, frosted stopper, empty, floral box w/gold label lined w/orange satin, Jergens Ben Hur, ca. early 1900s, 3 3/8" h. (ILLUS.) 143

Steuben glass, blue Aurene bottle & stopper, indentation on four sides, ruffled neck, ball stopper, unsigned, Atomic Cloud scent, very rare, 3 5/8"...................... 2,420

PHOTOGRAPHIC ITEMS

Albumen print, Abraham Lincoln, 1881 George B. Ayres print made from Alexander Hesler's 1860 sitting, sepia image of seated Lincoln from waist up looking off to side, 6 1/2 x 8 1/4" $991

Cabinet card, Sitting Bull, sepia image of seated figure holding pipe in oval cutout, caption beneath photo presents Sitting Bull's native name, "Tatonkaiyotonka," & a facsimile signature, one of a series of 24 historical images produced by Bailey, Dix & Mead, 1882 498

Hawaiian Royalty Cabinet Photos

Cabinet photo, Hideki Tojo, major general & prime minister of Japan believed to be the man who gave the order to bomb Pearl Harbor in 1941, black & white image of seated hatted figure in full dress uniform covered w/medals, signed in English characters "Hideki Tojo" near bottom of photo, on thick cardboard cabinet mount, photo 4 3/4 x 7 1/4" **1,150**

Cabinet photo, Thomas Edison, sepia tone, the silver gelatin photo shows Edison seated in study w/hands clasped, bottom margin of matte inscribed "To Holton H. Scott, Thos. A. Edison, April 3, 1915," in original mount, 6 1/2 x 8 1/2" **1,648**

Cabinet photos, separate photos of King David Kalakaua & Queen Kapiolani of Hawaii, sepia tone, signed in background on king's photo, in lower margin on queen's, J. Williams Studios, Honolulu, ca. 1880, each, 4 1/4 x 6 1/2", pr. (ILLUS., top of page)............................. **2,221**

Photo portrait, Susan B. Anthony, mid-tone bust portrait on cream paper labeled "Susan B. Anthony" under image, w/signature "K. Quinlan-1899," mounted behind glass in wooden frame, 18 3/4 x 23 3/4" overall (ILLUS., to the right)............................ **396**

Photograph, Albert Einstein, sepia tone, shows Einstein from knees up holding hat, umbrella & cigar before a crowd of people, signed in bottom margin "A. Einstein," 1920s, 2 1/2 x 4 1/4"........................ **2,657**

Photograph, Bela Lugosi, bust portrait in black & white of actor who portrayed Dracula on the screen in 1931, signed in blue ink "To Connie, Bela Lugosi" **2,581**

Photograph, Dr. Martin Luther King Jr. & Lyndon Johnson, black & white image of the two men shaking hands at press conference after the signing of the Civil Rights Act of 1964, signed in blue ballpoint at top center of image "Best Wishes, Martin Luther King, Jr.," matted & framed, photo 8 x 10" **2,657**

Susan B. Anthony Photo Portrait

Photograph, Franklin Delano Roosevelt, black & white bust portrait in profile, signed in black fountain pen in upper right "Franklin D. Roosevelt," matted & framed, photo 11 x 14" **1,938**

Photograph, General William Tecumseh Sherman, sepia bust portrait of general in uniform looking directly at camera, signed in lower border margin, "W.T. Sherman - General" in fountain pen, 1880s, 8 x 9 1/2" **2,132**

Signed Photo of Mercury Astronauts

Photograph, Mercury astronauts, black & white mat finish photo of America's seven original astronauts sitting at a table that holds a model of the Mercury capsule, inscribed at top "To Victor Phaneuf with Best Wishes - From The Mercury Astronauts," signed by each in lower margin, rare, ca. 1959, matted & framed, photo 8 x 10" (ILLUS.) **3,701**

Photograph, Supreme Court, black & white group photo of the nine Justices of the Supreme Court, signed by each in the lower margin in blue or black ink, Harris & Ewing, Washington, D.C., 1959, 10 7/8 x 13 7/8" **1,201**

Photograph, Warren G. Harding, sepia bust portrait, inscribed in bottom border "To Charles C. Pierce - With grateful greetings to a good friend and one of the best companions in the world. Sincerely, Warren G. Harding," matted & framed, Baker Art Gallery, 1920s, photo 6 3/4 x 8 3/4" **974**

Presentation photo, Pope Pius XI, black & white full-length image, ornately inscribed & signed beneath photo in Italian & Latin, 16 x 25" board w/mounted photo, handwritten dedication text by assistant, & huge signature in Pope's hand, all in wooden frame, 1930s............................ **1,761**

Tintype, bust of Confederate soldier, fitted in moulded case, ca. 1860s, 1" x 1 3/16" h. **303**

Tintype of Three Union Soldiers

Tintype, three Union soldiers in uniform and holding swords, the middle man is W.Q. Huybbel of Company 12, Kansas volunteers, others unknown, fitted in moulded case, ca. 1860s, 3 7/16 x 2 7/16" (ILLUS.) **728**

Tintype, three Victorian gentleman w/their pneumatic tire safety bicycles posed outside, late 19th c., 2 1/2 x 3 1/2" **44**

Tintype, two female textile mill workers posed w/shuttles, yarn, scissors, late-19th c., 2 1/2 x 3 1/4" **149**

Tintype, Union soldier from the hips up, in full uniform holding rifle, fitted in moulded case, ca. 1860s, 2 5/8 x 3 1/8"...................... **392**

Tintype, Union soldier, seated holding a rifle, w/arm resting on a table that also holds his hat, fitted in moulded case, ca. 1860s, 2 x 2 1/2" **280**

Civil War-era Tintype

Tintype, Union soldier seated in full uniform holding his sword, fitted in moulded case, ca. 1860s, 2 1/8 x 2 5/8" (ILLUS.)........ **392**

PICTURE CARDS, NON-SPORT

The catalog system of cards used for some of the cards listed here was developed by J.R. Burdick, who lived in Syracuse, New York, and whose collection is housed in books at the Metropolitan Museum in New York City.

"R" indicates cards that came in candy or gum packages after 1930. "T" indicates 20th century tobacco

cards, "N" 19th century tobacco cards, "D" cards that came with bakery items, and "E" candy cards prior to 1930. The number that appears after these letters is the number of the set.

America's Fighting Planes, Coca-Cola, color depictions of U.S. aircraft of World War II, 1943, set of 20 .... **$200**

America's Fighting Planes, Coca-Cola, color depictions of U.S. aircraft of World War II, 1944, set of 20 was 13 x 15", came w/hanger for hanging cards from ceiling, the set (original mailer envelope & wire hooks) **1,000**

"Anne Morgan" from Rails & Sails

"Anne Morgan," #146 from Topps Rails & Sails set (see separate entry), front features color illustration of New York Har-

bor tug boat, 1955, 2 5/8 x 3 3/4" (ILLUS.) **1,000**

Arcade Picture cards by Exhibit of Chicago, early space program, includes group shot of seven original astronauts, individual astronauts, the capsule, Atlas rocket, & various space probes from the 1950s, each (ILLUS. of four, bottom of page) **10**

Arcade Picture cards by Exhibit of Chicago, various sets w/sepia or black & white images of cowboy stars, movie stars, baseball players, radio stars & early television stars, distributed through arcade machines at various venues, 1940s-50s, each (more important stars have higher values) **15**

Atomic Doom card, #19 from Fight the Red Menace a.k.a. The Children's Crusade Against Communism set (see separate entry), Bowman, 1951, 2 1/2 x 3 1/8" **30**

Babe Ruth card, #41 from Topps Scoops set (see separate entry), "Babe Ruth Sets Record," commemorates his 60th home run, 1954-5, 2 1/16 x 2 15/16" **100**

Boxer Rebellion card, #74 from Topps Fighting Marines set (see separate entry), 1953, 2 1/16 x 2 5/16", rare **100**

Boxtop cards, Phoenix Candy Company, each box of candy featured a picture card of a comic strip character (Flash Gordon, Ming the Merciless, Dale Arden, et. al.), 1978, 8 boxes in set, each **35**

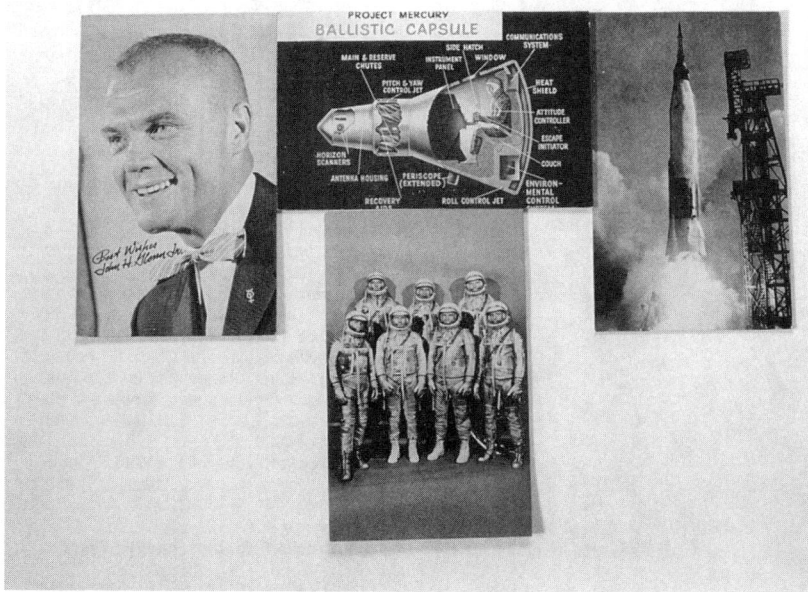

Arcade Space Program Cards

Topps Bubble Gum Wrapper

Bubble gum wrapper, Topps, yellow paper wrapper from card that came w/stick of Bazooka Bubble Gum shows character from "All New TV Series" based on movie Planet of the Apes, 1975 (ILLUS.)...................... **5**

Buck Rogers card, Comic Stars Inc. store giveaway, color portrait of Buck Rogers character, 1949, 2 1/4 x 3 1/2".......................... **60**

Buck Rogers portrait card, from Buck Rogers store giveaway set, 1936, 2 1/4 x 2 3/4".. **200**

Buck Rogers set, store giveaway, perforated strip cards w/characters & scenes from comic strip featured on front, "Buck Rogers" at bottom of each card, 1936, 2 1/4 x 2 3/4", set of 24, each......................... **125**

Captain Video Arcade Picture Card

Captain Video, from set by Arcade Picture Cards by Exhibit of Chicago (see separate entry) w/sepia image of star signed "Hal Hodge 'Cap Video'" (ILLUS.) **20**

Checklist card, #88 from Topps Civil War News set (see separate entry), 1962, 2 1/2 x 3 1/2".. **90**

Civil War Battle Scenes set, Duke, illustrations on front depict battle scenes, backs describe battle, list commanders and number of soldiers killed plus ad for tobacco company, 1888, 2 1/2 x 4 1/8" (N-99), each $20, set of 25 .... **1,000**

Civil War News set, Topps, issued for 100th Anniversary of start of Civil War, each features color depiction of famous event/action of the war, back has newspaper account of depiction on front, 1962, 2 1/2 x 3 1/2" (R-709-5), most individual cards $7, set of 88.............................. **700**

Confederate money, issued w/packs of cards from Civil War News set (see separate entry), 17 different notes in all, 1962, each $15, set of 17.............................. **300**

Arcade Cowboy Cards

Cowboy cards, from set by Arcade Picture Cards by Exhibit of Chicago (see separate entry), w/signed sepia or black & white images of various cowboy stars, each (ILLUS. of four).. **20**

Curly card, #1 of Three Stooges set by Fleer (see separate entry), 1959, 2 1/2 x 3 1/2".. **85**

Dare Devils set, National Chicle Company, cards featured scenes of firemen, policemen, government agents & others in action, 1933, 2 3/8 x 2 7/8" (R-39), each $30, set of 24.. **700**

Davy Crockett, King of the Wild Frontier set, Topps, green backs, 1956, 2 1/8 x 3 3/4" (R-712-B), each $8, set of cards 11A-80A.. **525**

Davy Crockett, King of the Wild Frontier set, Topps, orange backs, 1956, 2 1/8 x 3 3/4" (R-712-1A), each $7, set of cards 1-80 .... **325**

Defenders of America set, Popsicle Ice Cream, featured images of U.S. missiles & aircraft, distributed through ice cream truck vendors, 1959, each **10**

Famous Aviators Album

Disneyland set, Donruss, cards illustrated various characters & rides at Disneyland in California, backs contained pieces of puzzle (complete set had to be obtained to complete the puzzle), 1965, 2 1/2 x 3 1/2" (R 818-4), each $2, set of 66 .... **100**

Fighting Marines Card

Fighting Marines set, Topps, fronts feature color illustrations of U.S. Marine action, backs contain information on event pictured, 1953, 2 1/16 x 2 5/16" (R-709-1), individual cards #1-48, $6, individual cards #49-96, $8, set of 96 (ILLUS. of one) **800**

Flame D'Armour card, Comic Stars Inc. store giveaway, color portrait of character from Buck Rogers comic strip, 1949, 2 1/4 x 3 1/2" **50**

Eleanor Parker Card

Eleanor Parker card, maker unknown, color illustration of actress w/"Eleanor Parker" printed to side, 1950 (ILLUS.) **15**

Famous Aviators set, Heinz Foods, fronts feature color illustration of aviator, backs contain information on person pictured, 1930s, 1 7/8 x 3" (F277-4), set of 25 w/album (ILLUS. of open album, with spaces for individual cards to be glued w/information underneath, top of page) **100**

Fight the Red Menace a.k.a. The Children's Crusade Against Communism set, Bowman, fronts featured graphic images of Cold War events, backs carried short explanation of event on front, 1951, 2 1/2 x 3 1/8" (R701-12), most individual cards $15, set of 48 .... **850**

German Orders & Decorations

German Orders & Decorations set, given away in packages of German cigarettes, fronts feature color illustration of German medal or decoration, backs contain information on item pictured, 1940s, set of 50 w/album (ILLUS. of album cover showing individual cards)... **75**

Ghost City card, #23 from Fight the Red Menace a.k.a. The Children's Crusade Against Communism set (see separate entry), Bowman, 1951, 2 1/2 x 3 1/8"............. **90**

Green Hornet set, Donruss, cards featured scenes from TV show, backs had poster pieces & ads for the show, 1966, 2 1/2 x 3 1/2" (R718-8), each $7, #1 card $18, unopened full box of 36 5-cent packs $1,700, complete set of 44.................. **300**

Harbor Dredge from Rails & Sails

Harbor Dredge, #182 from Topps Rails & Sails set (see separate entry), front features color illustration of work barge, 1955, 2 5/8 x 3 3/4" (ILLUS.)............................ **10**

Hitler Border Tour card, #277 of Gum Inc.'s Horrors of War set, front features color illustration of event, backs contain story of event, 1938 .... **500**

Hitler Threatens Force card, #277 of Gum Inc.'s Horrors of War set, front features color illustration of event, backs contain story of event, 1938 .... **1,000**

Gloria Stuart Card

Hollywood Screen Star set, Shelby Candy Company of Shelby, Ohio, front features

color picture of star w/name of star & his/her next movie printed underneath, back contains fortune, wrapper includes two pieces of stage money to be cut out, 1930s, 2 3/8 x 3", set of 40 $1,100, each (ILLUS. of Gloria Stuart card) **20**

Hollywood Screen Star set, Shelby Gum Company, Shelby, Ohio, cards featured pictures of screen stars of the day w/bio on back w/card number, 1940s (R-68), most individual cards $30, set of 40........... **1,000**

Hopalong Cassidy Ways of the West Bread Labels, Bond Bread, each end label from loaf of bread featured Hoppy in action, front is color image, back is black & white, w/information, 1950, 2 x 3", set of 16, each **15**

Hopalong Cassidy Ways of the West wall poster, Bond Bread giveaway, meant to hold Hopalong Cassidy Ways of the West Bread Labels (see separate entry), 1950...... **100**

American Homes Looted in Hangchow

Horrors of War set, Gum Inc., fronts feature color illustrations of event, backs contain story of event, 1938 (R-69), most individual cards $25, set of 288 (ILLUS. of one) **10,000**

Howdy Doody set, Burry Cookies, cards featured characters from TV show, 1952, 2 1/8 x 2 7/8" (D44), each................................. **25**

Jaws 3-D Picture set, Topps, tie-in to 3-D movie, 1984, 2 1/2 x 3 1/2", each 10 cents, set of 44.. **6**

Jets, Rockets & Spacemen set, Bowman, fronts feature space scene & backs describe scene on front, 1951 (R710-13), card #1 $25, #2-#26 $8, #37-#72 $18, #73-#107 $15, #108 $25, set of 108.......... **1,600**

Ladies of the White House set, Consolidated, cards depict First Ladies, 1890s (N-353), each $10, set of 25 .... **450**

Larry card, #3 of Three Stooges set by Fleer (see separate entry), 1959, 2 1/2 x 3 1/2".. **45**

Lone Ranger Ed-U card set, fronts of cards featured scenes from new Lone Ranger TV show, cards came in panels of three cards, 40 panels in all, eight series of cards connected to four different story lines, 1950, 2 x 2 5/8" (W-536), each card $5, each panel $20, complete set of 40 panels of 3 attached cards $750, complete set of 120... **550**

Magazine Ad for Cigarettes & Cards

Lone Ranger premiums, Gum Inc., each features scene from Republic Studios serial of the day, copyright date of 1938 but not released until 1940 (R-83A), very rare, set of 5, #1 $900, #2-#5 $600 each, complete set of 5 .... **3,500**

Lone Ranger & Tonto insert card set, paper, found in Lone Ranger brand of ice cream cones, features black & white scene or figure on front, backs have coupon to send in for prize, 1939 (F-56), each $22, set of 13 .... **325**

Magazine ad, Better Homes & Gardens, for Player's Navy Cut Cigarettes, "Player's Please" appears on color illustration of ships & planes at sea w/British Navy flag in foreground, advertised both the cigarettes & the military-themed cards that came w/each pack, July 1941, 8 1/2 x 11 1/2" (ILLUS., top of page)............. **60**

Military card set, American Tobacco Company, w/color illustrations of historical military scenes, 1910, two sizes issued, 2 1/4 x 3 1/2" or 2 1/16 x 3 1/8" (T-50), each $10, set of 25 (ILLUS. of one)............. **250**

Unopened Military Uniforms Set

Military Uniforms set, each set contains five picture cards of military uniforms, 1960, 2 1/2 x 3 1/2" (ILLUS.)............................ **20**

Moe card, #2 of Three Stooges set by Fleer (see separate entry), 1959, 2 1/2 x 3 1/2" **60**

Battle of San Juan Hill, Military Set

Native American Chiefs Cards

Pier Angeli Card from Movie Star Set

New York World's Fair Card Set

Movie Star set, General Mills Cheerios, fronts feature color photo of movie star, backs contain short bio & info on upcoming movies, 1950s (F-272-20), set of 18, each (ILLUS. of one).. **15**

Native American Chiefs, Ganong Candy Company, color illustrations of various chiefs in native dress, chief's name & tribe printed below picture, given away w/candy, rare, 1910, each (ILLUS. of ten, top of page) **50**

New York World's Fair set, manufactured by Ed-U Cards, each card featured different color view of 1964 World's Fair, set of 24, $100, each (ILLUS. of sleeve)..................... **5**

Outer Limits set, Topps, cards feature color illustrations of the monsters that appeared on the TV show, back carried card number & "You Are in MY Power" (tag line of show), 1964, 2 1/2 x 3 1/2" (R713-2), each $8, set of 50 .... **600**

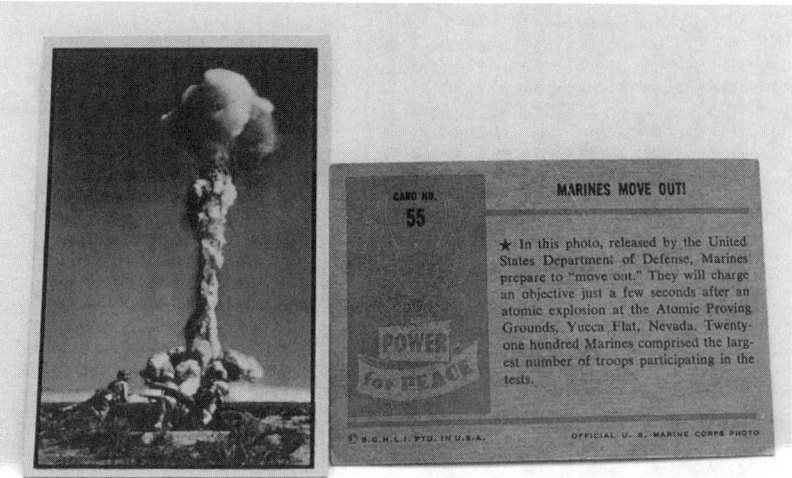

#55 of Power for Peace Series

Pirate Pictures set, Gum Inc., color illustrations of pirates, back w/explanatory text & card number, 1930s, 2 7/16 x 3 1/16" (R109), each $28, set of 72 .... **2,000**

Power for Peace set, Bowman, fronts feature color photo of U.S. military items, backs contain information on item pictured, 1954, 2 1/2 x 3 3/4" (R701-10), each card $3, set of 96 (ILLUS. of front & back of #55 in the series, Marines Move Out, top of page) **300**

Rails & Sails set, Topps, fronts feature color illustrations of locomotive or ship, backs contain information on item pictured & small sidebar on related topic, set included 130 cards w/locomotives & 70 w/ships, 1955, 2 5/8 x 3 3/4" (R714-17), each $10, set of 200 .... **1,300**

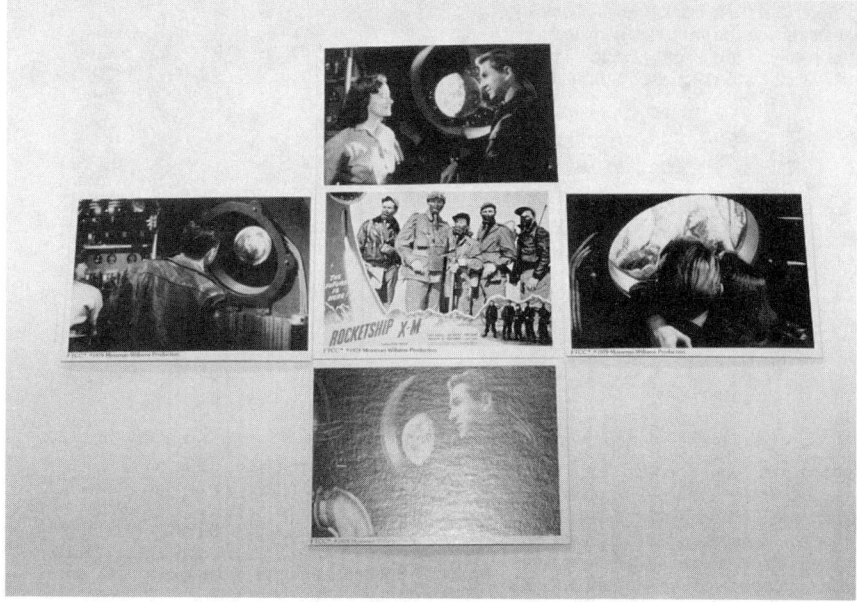

Rocket Ship X-M Cards

Rocketship X-M set, color & black & white images of scenes from early 1950s movie, 1979, set of 50 (ILLUS. of five) **30**

Unopened Pack of RCMP Cards

Royal Canadian Mounted Police card set, O-Pee-Chee Candy, unopened pack of picture cards featuring Royal Canadian Mounted Police, wrapper promises 8 cards & one stick of gum, in English & French, 1970, the pack (ILLUS.)...................... **12**

Scenes of World War I set, Goudey's World War Gum, black & white photos of battle scenes on front, card number & explanatory text on back, 1933, 2 3/8 x 2 7/8" (R174), each $10, set of 96...... **950**

Scoops Card of Peary at North Pole

Scoops set, Topps Chewing Gum, fronts feature color illustrations of newspaper "scoop" (of history-making event), backs contain newspaper story of event pictured, the masthead of the newspaper the story appeared in, & the card number, 1954-5, 2 1/16 x 2 15/16" (R714-19), most individual cards $4-8 (w/cards #1-78 less valuable than cards #79-156), set of 156 (ILLUS. of one) **1,600**

Card from Sergeant Preston Set

Sergeant Preston of the Yukon set, Quaker Oats, fronts feature color illustrations of Sergeant Preston in action sequence connected to radio & television series, backs contain information on action pictured, same cards released in 1950 & 1956, 2 1/4 x 3 1/2" (F-279-4 & 279-15), each $5, complete set (ILLUS. of one).......... **185**

Shirley Temple card, from Hollywood Screen Star set (see separate entry) by Shelby Gum Company, Shelby, Ohio, 1940s **60**

Card from Sky Birds Set

Sky Birds set, Goudey Gum, fronts feature color illustrations of aircraft in action, backs are blank, 1941, 2 5/16 x 2 13/16" (R-137), each $20, set of 24 (ILLUS. of one) **475**

Soldier premiums, American Mint Corporation, New York City, 2 9/16" figures of soldiers of various nations, front of container showed country of origin, set divided into Doughboys, Minutemen, Troopers & Yanks, each set came w/candy or

gum inside tube, rare, 1940, believed to
be 24 in set, each **150-250**

Card from Space Set

Space set, Topps, fronts feature color illustrations of men or events in space, backs
carry description of picture on front, blue-
backed cards also show card number inside satellite w/a rocket in the distance,
1958, 2 1/2 x 3 1/2" (R714-20), each $7,
set of 88 (ILLUS. of one) **500**
Spins & Needles set, Fleer, popular re-
cording artists of the day featured in
frame on front, back gives short bio in red
& blue on white & card number in crown
design, 1960, 2 1/2 x 3 1/2" (R730-3),
each $5, set of 80 .... **400**

Star Wars Card Packs

Star Wars card sets, Topps, 1977-83, each
unopened pack (ILLUS. of 7 packs) **10**

Box of Pac-Man Stickers & Rub-offs

Stickers & Rub-offs, Donruss, package of
Pac-Man stickers & rub-offs, 1980, full
box (ILLUS.) **25**

Unopened Box of Superman Cards

Superman cards, Topps, full box 36 unopened packs, box w/color image of
character from Superman The Movie,
1977 (ILLUS.) **60**
Superman set, distributed w/packs of gum,
illustrations on front depict Superman
rescuing people from various calamities,
back features explanatory text, 1941,
2 1/2 x 3 1/8" (R-145), card #2-#48 $25,
#49-#71 $100, #1 $60, #72 $150, set of
72 .... **4,400**

Tom Corbett Bread Labels

The Angry Man card, #1 from Topps Civil War News set (see separate entry), 1962, 2 1/2 x 3 1/2".. **40**

Three Stooges card #16, from color Fleer set, 1959, 2 1/2 x 3 1/2", rare **200**

Three Stooges card #63, from color Fleer set, 1959, 2 1/2 x 3 1/2", rare **200**

Three Stooges card #84, from color Fleer set, 1959, 2 1/2 x 3 1/2", rare **200**

Three Stooges set, Fleer, fronts feature black & white scenes from Three Stooges movies, each 5-cent pack contained five cards, 1965, 2 1/2 x 3 1/2", most individual cards $7, set of 66 .... **450**

Three Stooges set, Fleer, fronts feature color scenes from Three Stooges movies, each 5-cent pack contained five cards, 1959, 2 1/2 x 3 1/2" (R730-1), most individual cards $8, set of 96 .... **950**

Tom Corbett Bread Labels album, Fischer's Buttercup Bread, store giveaway to hold set of Tom Corbett Bread Labels (see separate entry), rare, unfilled **150**

Tom Corbett Bread Labels set, Fischer's Buttercup Bread, end seals of bread wrappers featured illustrations & "Tom Corbett - Space Cadet," in red, blue, yellow & black, 1952-3, each $15, set of 48 (ILLUS. of promotional material showing individual cards, top of page) **500**

Parachute Invasion, Uncle Sam Set

Uncle Sam set, Gum Inc., fronts feature color illustrations of military scene, backs contain brief description of front & company info, 1941 (R157/R158), each $30, set of 144 (ILLUS. of one) **4,000**

United States Presidents set, Bowman, fronts feature portrait & important event in president's life, back carries short history of man & presidency, 1952, 2 1/2 x 3 3/4" (R-701-17), each $5, set of 36 .... **200**

#47 of US Naval Victories Set

US Naval Victories set, Bowman, fronts feature color illustrations of Naval action, backs contain information on action pictured & Navy insignia, 1954, 2 1/2 x 3 3/4" (R701-16), each $9, set of 48 (ILLUS. of #47 from set, Merrimac & Monitor Battle) 400

Useful Birds of America Card

Useful Birds of America set, Church & Dwight, fronts feature color illustrations of birds, backs contain bird's name & information on it & ad, 1915, 2 x 3" (J5), set of 30 (ILLUS. of one) 100

Voyage to the Bottom of the Sea set, Donruss, black & white photos of scenes from TV show, back w/image of submarine Seaview (from the show) & "Watch Voyage to the Bottom of the Sea on your local ABC station," 1964 (R818-6), each $3, unopened pack $25, complete set of 66 200

Civil Airline Transport, Wings Set

Wings set, Topps, fronts feature color illustrations of aircraft, backs contain card number, a plane spotter section & short history w/technical info of aircraft pictured, "Wings" & two aircraft in blue or black, issued w/1-cent & 5-cent packs of chewing gum, 1953 (R707-4), set of 200, each w/wrapper (ILLUS. of one) 45

Wrapper, for Fight the Red Menace a.k.a. The Children's Crusade Against Communism set (see separate entry), Bowman, marked "Red Menace" w/red star, 1951 125

Wrapper, for Horrors of War set (see separate entry), Gum Inc., 1938 200

Wrapper, for Jets, Rockets & Spacemen cards (see separate entry), Bowman, w/picture of planet 125

Wrapper, for Pirate Pictures set (see separate entry) by Gum Inc., features pirate w/cutlass, 1930s, rare 300

Wrapper, for Scenes of World War I set (see separate entry), "World War Gum" & illustration of four advancing soldiers, 1933 200

Wrapper, for Sky Birds set (see separate entry), Goudey Gum, 1941 200

Wrapper, for Superman set (see separate entry), picture of Superman, bright red, yellow & blue, "Super Bubble Gum" & application to join Superman Club 350

Wrapper, from Civil War News set, Topps, shows soldier charging w/rifle & bayonet pointed, text reads "Extra Facsimile Confederate Money in Every Pack 5 Cents," 1962 50

Wrapper, from Voyage to the Bottom of the Sea set (see separate entry), Donruss, features image of submarine Seaview, "Voyage to the Bottom of the Sea" & price of 5 cents, 1964 45

PLANT WATERERS

Here's a collectible as popular and useful today as it was 50+ years ago. Plant waterers are the clever invention whose stored water supply seeps through a porous stem. Most are designed to feed plants up to seven days, keeping plants fed while the homeowner is away. Both decorative and functional, these often whimsical objects really have an identity problem. They're often confused, priced and sold as the expensive collectible pie birds. Now that the dish-sitting baby feeders have become so popular, plant waterers are also being incorrectly classified in this group. For the most part, plant waterers are still affordable but, as their popularity rises, it's only a matter of time before market prices start to climb.

Ceramic, bird w/open mouth, green & blue speckled, 3 1/2" h. $6-8

Ceramic, bird, white w/yellow beak, removable head, 5 1/8" h. 15-18

Ceramic, bumblebee, yellow & black, wearing blue tie & red shoes, sitting on lavender flower, 7" h. 8-12

Ceramic, butterfly, yellow, decorated w/pink flowers, 4 1/2" h. 8-12

Ceramic, cat, white, 4 3/4" h. 8-15

Ceramic, chick peeking out of egg shell, white & yellow, 4 1/2" h. 15-20

Ceramic, cowboy boot, brown, 5 3/8" h. 15-25

Ceramic, elf, green w/rust beard, 4 1/2" h. 15-20

Ceramic, fish, green, Shawnee, marked "USA," 5" h. **50-75**

Ceramic, flamingo, pink, 6" h. **20-30**

Ceramic, frog w/removable head, brown, 6 1/2" h. **15-22**

Ceramic, frog, yellow, in sitting position, 6 1/8" h. **6-10**

Ceramic, girl in blue dress, pink bow in hair, holding a pink flower, 5 1/4" h. **18-20**

Ceramic, pig, blue, 4 1/2" h. **35-45**

Ceramic, snail, light brown w/black eyes, 4 1/4" h. **8-15**

Ceramic, squirrel w/detachable head, brown, 4 1/2" h. **25-35**

Ceramic, tulip, blue & white Delft patt., 6" h. **18-25**

Ceramic, tulip, yellow, 4 1/4" h. **15-20**

Ceramic, turtle, green, 3 1/2" h. **6-10**

Ceramic, watering can, white w/yellow rose, 4 1/4" h. **10-18**

Ceramic, waterwheel house, green, marked "God Bless This House," 4" h. **10-15**

Ceramic, windmill, blue & white, flowers around base, 6" h. **15-20**

Ceramic, wishing well, brown, sticker marked "Enesco," 5" h. **18-25**

Ceramic, worm w/open mouth & bulging eyes, yellow, newer vintage, 6 1/2" l. **6-10**

Plastic, alligator, 4" h. **5-8**

Plastic, bird, blue, 4" h. **5-8**

Plastic, dog, white, 4" h. **5-8**

Plastic, elephant, pink, 4" h. **5-8**

POLITICAL & CAMPAIGN ITEMS

Campaign

Johnson/Humphrey Bracelet

Bracelet, 1964 campaign, brass-plated metal, seven-sided shape w/image of President Lyndon B. Johnson & Vice President Hubert H. Humphrey embossed in center, on link chain (ILLUS.).. **$25-30**

Jimmy Carter Keychain

Keychain, 1976 campaign, metal, round w/embossed image of Jimmy Carter on one side, "Into Our 3rd Century with Carter" on other, marked "Made in West Germany" (ILLUS.) **10-15**

"Nixon" Circle Pin

Pin, gold-plated metal, ribbed circle w/"NIXON" across center, pearl at top of circle, bow where pin attaches, 3/4" d. (ILLUS.)....... **6-8**

Landon-Knox Campaign Button

Pinback button, 1936 presidential campaign of Alf Landon & Frank Knox, round, black w/image of yellow elephant w/"GOP" in black on its side, block letters read "Landon" above & "Knox" below, on yellow felt backing shaped like a sunflower, signifying Kansas, Landon's state (ILLUS.)... **3**

Goldwater Campaign Button

Pinback button, 1964 campaign, metal, yellow w/image of Barry Goldwater in center & "GOLDWATER IN '64" in blue block letters around image, 5/8" d. (ILLUS.)................. **6-8**

"We Stand for Peace ..." Sheet Music

Sheet music, 1916 campaign, "We Stand for Peace While Others War," black & white, features photo of President Woodrow Wilson, 9 3/4 x 11 3/4" (ILLUS.).......... **25-30**

Framed Roosevelt Silk

Silk ribbon, image of Franklin D. Roosevelt, white background w/red & blue lettering & trim, marked "To Keep the Nation Firm, Give Him Another Term," framed, 5 3/4 x 7 3/4" (ILLUS.)................................. **15-20**

Non-Campaign

Washington Commemorative Biography

Book, "Pictorial Biography of the Father of Our Country - George Washington Bicentennial - 1732 - 1932," marked "1931 United States Pencil Co. Inc., New York, NY," 8 3/4 x 10 3/4" (ILLUS.) **30-35**
Bottle opener, metal, model of donkey, 2 3/8" h. **30-40**
Bottle opener, metal, model of elephant, 2 3/8" h. **30-40**

Lincoln Bronze

Bronze, profile of President Abraham Lincoln, 6" d. (ILLUS.)...................................... **30-40**

Framed Box Top w/Washington Portrait

Candy box top, color-lithographed metal w/image of President George Washington, border of gold leaves, marked "Pater, Patrie," black frame, 5 1/2" w., 7 1/2" l. (ILLUS.).. **40-50**

George Washington Bud Vase

Bud vase, ceramic, white w/gold trim, image of George Washington on front, floral decoration, 3" h. (ILLUS.) **10-15**

George Washington Dish

Dish, ceramic, rectangular, yellow w/gold rim, color image of George Washington in center, marked "Jon Roth, Made in Germany," early 20th c., 4 1/2 x 6" (ILLUS.) **15-18**

George & Martha Washington Buttons

Buttons, porcelain, oval, w/images of George & Martha Washington together & separately, 7/8 x 1", each (ILLUS of five).. **25-35**

George Washington Doily

Doily, crocheted image of George Washington flanked by flags, white, 23 1/2" w. x 18 1/4" l. (ILLUS.)................... **35-40**

Lyndon B. Johnson First Day Cover

First Day cover, features signature & photo of President Lyndon B. Johnson, postmarked "January 20, 1965," 10" w., 13" h. (ILLUS.) **20-30**

Flag, cloth, orange top & bottom stripes, w/blue stripe in middle, sepia image of George Washington w/"Washington" at top, "Bicentennial - 1732-1932" at bottom, 4" h. x 5 1/2" w. **12-15**

Lincoln Lithograph

Lithograph, image of President Abraham Lincoln, framed, late 19th c., 20 x 24" (ILLUS.) **450-500**

Model of hatchet, milk glass, head decorated w/cherries, handle reads "Washington's Birthday" in gilt, late 19th c., 6" l. .. **20-25**

George Washington Mug

Mug, ceramic, white w/brown transfer decoration of bust of George Washington in oval leaf border flanked by American flags, w/spread-winged eagle over all, "George Washington - 1776" under portrait, gold trim, marked "Manufactured by W.T. Copeland & Son, Solely for J.M. Shaw - Trademark Registered 1876," 3" h. (ILLUS.) **40**

George Washington Paperweight

Paperweight, bronze, disk w/image of George Washington in profile embossed in center, "George Washington President of the United States 1789" embossed around edge, 3 1/8" d. (ILLUS.) **25-30**

Harry Truman Paperweight

Paperweight, bronze, disk w/image of Harry S. Truman in profile embossed in center, "President of the United States" embossed around edge, 3 1/8" d. (ILLUS.).... **50-60**

Paperweight, square marble base holding metal disk w/embossed image of Franklin D. Roosevelt in profile, "President of the United States" embossed around edge, 4" sq. **50-60**

Pinback button, celluloid, round, w/image of George Washington in center surrounded by "George Washington Bicentennial Celebration, 1732-1932," in white, w/red, white & blue border, 1 1/2" d. **10-12**

Pitcher, ceramic, tapering cylindrical form with scalloped gilt top & D-form handle, white w/presidential eagle and image of Harry S. Truman, 6" h. **20-25**

Washington Anniversary Plaque

Plaque, cardboard, red, white & blue shield shape, w/"George Washington's 200th Anniversary - 1732 - 1932" above image of Washington, 6 1/2 x 7 3/8" (ILLUS.) **25-30**

Plate, ceramic, black & white image of President William McKinley below crossed flags & eagle, 6 7/8 d. **28-35**

Vernon Kilns Presidential Plate

Plate, ceramic, features sepia tone images of presidents Washington to Truman,

marked "A Presidential Gallery, Vernon Kilns U.S.A.," 10 1/2" d. (ILLUS.) **35-45**

George & Martha Washington Plate

Plate, ceramic, white w/open decoration around oval black & white image of George & Martha Washington in center, cut-out gold rim, marked "Germany Made," 4" d. (ILLUS.).................................. **12-15**

Garfield Commemorative Plate

Plate, pressed glass, commemorating President Garfield's death, reads "We Mourn Our Nation's Loss," clear, 10 1/2" d. (ILLUS.) **60-75**

James A. Garfield Plate

Plate, pressed glass, image of James A. Garfield embossed in center, rim decorated w/embossed stars, clear, ca. 1881, 8" d. (ILLUS.) **18-25**

Three Presidents Plate

Plate, pressed glass, oval, features image of Washington above "First in Peace," image of Lincoln above "Charity for All" & image of McKinley above "God Reigns," clear, 10 x 12 1/2" (ILLUS.) **100-125**

McKinley Memorial Plate

Plate, pressed glass, oval, McKinley memorial plate, full figure image of McKinley in center, reads "It Is God's Way, His Will Be Done - Born 1843 - Died 1901," clear, 8 x 10 3/4" (ILLUS.) **45-50**

Pressed Glass Washington Plate

Plate, pressed glass w/image of George Washington in center surrounded by border of stars & "1932," clear, 8" d. (ILLUS.) **18-20**

Woodrow Wilson Color Photo Print

Print, color photo print of President Woodrow Wilson signed by him, "Respectfully yours, Woodrow Wilson," matted & framed, 9 3/4 x 12 1/4" (ILLUS.) **25-30**

President Theodore Roosevelt Print

Print, photo of President Theodore Roosevelt, marked "One of the Greatest Americans of All Times," framed, 8 1/2 x 10" (ILLUS.) **30-40**

"A March to Eisenhower" Sheet Music

Sheet music, "A March to Eisenhower," features photo of President Dwight D. Eisenhower, marked "Souvenir of Inauguration, 1953," 7 3/4 x 12 3/4" (ILLUS.) .. **35-40**

Memorial Service Program

Program, for memorial service, black & white, reads "Held by the citizens of Attleboro held in honor of the late President William McKinley, Thursday, September the Nineteenth, Nineteen Hundred and One" (ILLUS.).. **20-25**

"America To Day" Sheet Music

Sheet music, "America To Day," features color illustration of Statue of Liberty w/flag, inset black & white bust photo of Wilson labeled "President Wilson," red block lettering reads "Don't Worry - Uncle Sam's All Right - Liberty's Still Standing in the Bay," 7 3/4 x 12 3/4" (ILLUS.) **35-40**

Sheet music, "Stars and Stripes Forever," features images of Presidents Wilson, Lincoln & Washington, 17 x 21"................. **40-50**

POP CULTURE COLLECTIBLES

Jazz Artists

Jazz is an American musical idiom that has gone through many stylistic changes throughout the 20th century. Because of this, it is hard to pin jazz down to one style. Jazz originated at the beginning of the 20th century. It developed out of different forms of black music, most notably spirituals, work songs and such. In the first decades it manifested itself in the form of Ragtime and Dixieland, with New Orleans being considered the epicenter of the style. By the 1920s, Jazz was most identified with any hot, rhythmic and up-tempo music (the 1920s ushered in the "Jazz Age"). By the 1930s and '40s, Jazz had moved into the white mainstream of popular music and was quickly assimilated with the "Swing" and "Big Band" sounds of the times.

Modern Jazz, as we know it today, was a product of the postwar decades. The brilliant jazz musicians of the times adopted a loose, freeform style to typify the new direction of jazz and to shift it away from the big band prewar sound. Though modern jazz was still mostly relegated to "Negro" musicians, beatniks and white intellectuals through the 1950s, the style continued to develop and gather new fans along the way. Jazz vocalists also appeared during this time (oddly enough, one of the only areas of jazz – a male-dominated art form – that featured women.) By the 1970s jazz had cross-pollinated with other musical styles (quite typical of the times) and produced jazz-rock, jazz-fusion and even jazz-flavored classical interpretations.

This price guide section deals primarily with Modern jazz from the postwar years of 1947-1969 (considered the Golden Age of Jazz) with a few prewar masters thrown in. Because of the vastness of the field, these listings do not represent the complete number of jazz artists of the times, but a sampling of the more popular ones. Jazz collectors tend to be primarily audiophiles, and recordings are of prime interest. Prices listed are for recordings in very good to better grade.

Some tips on Jazz collecting:• First pressings are the original release of the recording. Many Jazz recordings were re-released throughout years under the same catalog numbers. Collectors differentiate first from later pressings by label color, label word changes or other visual clues. Listings here are for 1st pressings unless otherwise indicated.• Since postwar Jazz was considered "underground" at the time, many recordings were made on small or obscure labels. These labels that focused on the cutting edge jazz artists are the most highly sought after – particularly Blue Note records.• Popular Jazz musicians liked to jam – play with other musicians. You will find numerous recordings of two musicians jamming as well as "jam sessions" with whole groups. Since Jazz is improvisational by nature, no two Jazz performances are the same – this makes each recording a unique performance!• Modern Jazz is/was extremely popular in Europe, and you will find European recordings as well as devout fans on both sides of the Atlantic.

Art Blakely recording, "A Night at Birdland," Blue Note 1522 .... **$10-25**
Art Blakely recording, LP, "A Night in Tunisia," Blue Note BLP4049, mono **30-75**
Art Blakely recording, LP, "Ugetsu," Riverside 9464, 1963 .... **10-25**
Art Tatum recording, 45 RPM, "Art Tatum," Camden CAE419 .... **5-10**

Art Tatum recording, LP, "The Art of War," Verve VSPS-33 .... **5-10**
Art Tatum recording, LP, "The Genius of Art Tatum #3," Verve MGV8038 .... **20-50**
Benny Goodman recording, LP, "The Essential Benny Goodman," Verve VG8582 .... **5-15**
Benny Goodman sheet music, "And The Angels Sing," from the Benny Goodman Story **5-10**

Billie Holiday Recording

Billie Holiday recording, 45 RPM EP, 4 songs, "Billie Holiday Sings," Clef Records EP 165 (ILLUS.) **10-15**
Billie Holiday recording, 78 RPM, "I Got The Right To Sing The Blues," Commodore #527 .... **4-8**
Billie Holiday recording, 78 RPM, "My Sweet Hunk O' Trash" w/Louis Armstrong, Decca 24785 .... **10-15**
Billie Holiday recording, EP, "Billie Holiday Sings," 10 songs, Columbia CL 6129, 10" **5-10**

Billie Holiday Recording

Billie Holiday recording, LP, "A Rare Live Recording of ...," Ric Records #2001, 1964 (ILLUS.) **10-25**
Billie Holiday recording, LP, "Lady in Satin," Columbia CS8048 .... **10-20**
Charlie Byrd recording, LP, "Aquarius," Columbia CS9841 .... **8-12**

Charlie Byrd Recording

Charlie Byrd recording, LP, "Byrd at the Gate," Riverside RM467, mono (ILLUS.).. **12-30**
Charlie Byrd recording, LP, "Byrdland," Columbia CL2592, mono **6-15**
Charlie Parker poster, shows "Bird" playing sax, 24" x 36" **5-10**

Charlie Parker recording, 78 RPM, "Dancing in the Dark," Mercury 11068 .... **10-25**

Charlie Parker recording, LP, "A Night at Carnegie Hall," Birdland LP425, 10" **150-300**

Charlie Parker recording, LP, "Big Band," Clef MGC609, mono **240-400**

Chet Baker book, "As Though I Had Wings," 1st edition, hardbound, 1997 .... **5-10**

Chet Baker Quartet recording, LP, Pacific Jazz PJLP3, 10" **100-200**

Chet Baker recording, LP, "Chet Baker in Paris," Bertelsmann 61133.D-1957 German **30-50**

Chet Baker recording, LP, "Hats Off - The Mariachi Brass," World Pacific ST1842, 1968 .... **6-15**

Chet Baker recording, LP, "In New York," Victor Riverside RLP12-281, mono **20-50**

Dave Brubeck Quartet recording, 45 RPM, "Alice in Wonderland," Fantasy 526, green vinyl **4-8**

Dave Brubeck Quartet recording, 45 RPM RP, 3 songs, Columbia B12511 .... **10-15**

Dave Brubeck Quartet recording, LP, "At Newport," Columbia CL932 .... **10-15**

Dave Brubeck Quartet recording, LP, "Time Out," Columbia CL 1397-7, mono .. **15-30**

Dave Brubeck Quartet sheet music, "Take Five," 1960 .... **3-6**

Dave Brubeck recording, reel-to-reel tape, "Jackpot," Columbia **4-8**

Dinah Washington arcade card, black & white portrait photo **3-6**

Dinah Washington recording, 45 RPM, "September in the Rain," Mercury 71876, picture sleeve **10-15**

Dinah Washington Recording

Dinah Washington recording, LP, "Dinah," Mercury EmArcy MG36065, mono (ILLUS.) **20-50**

Dinah Washington recording, LP, "Sings Fats Waller," Mercury EmArcy MG 36119 .... **20-50**

Dizzy Gillespie Recording

Dizzy Gillespie recording, LP, "Diz Big Band," Norgram 1090 (ILLUS.)................ **50-125**

Dizzy Gillespie recording, LP, "Dizzy Goes Hollywood," Phillips 600-123...... **8-20**

Dizzy Gillespie recording, LP, "Groovin High" w/Charlie Parker, Emos ES12017 .... **100-150**

Dizzy Gillespie recording, LP, "Portrait of Duke Ellington," Verve MGV8386, 1961 .... **25-60**

Django Reinhardt recording, 75 RPM, "The Continental/I'm Confessin'," Ultraphone AP1443....................................... **15-25**

Django Reinhardt Recording

Django Reinhardt recording, LP, French "Le Disque d' Or," Mode 9315, 1960s (ILLUS.) **10-20**

Django Reinhardt recording, LP, "Swing It Lightly," Columbia 31479 .... **10-20**

Django Reinhardt recording, LP, "Versatile Giant," Inner City Records, IC7004...... **10-20**

Duke Ellington recording, 45 RPM EP, 4 songs, French release RCA 75386 .... **15-20**

Duke Ellington recording, 45 RPM EP, 4 songs, Royale EP291 Red Vinyl, picture sleeve **5-10**

Duke Ellington recording, 78 RPM, 4 record set, Victor Records **10-20**

Duke Ellington recording, 78 RPM, "Jubilee Stomp/Black Beauty," Victor 21580 .... **15-25**

Duke Ellington recording, 78 RPM, "My Old Flame/Rockin' Chair," Mae West vocals, rare **10-15**

Duke Ellington recording, LP, "New World A'Coming," Decca DL710176 .... **10-20**

Duke Ellington recording, LP, "The Nutcracker Suite," Columbia CSP8341 .... **5-10**

Duke Ellington recording, Song Folio, "At The Piano," 17 songs, 1943 .... **4-8**

Ella Fitzgerald recording, 45 RPM, "Little Small Town Girl" w/Ink Spots, Decca 4580291... **4-8**

Ella Fitzgerald recording, 78 RPM, "Melancholy Me," Decca 29008........................... **5-10**

Ella Fitzgerald recording, "Ella Fitzgerald & Billie Holiday Newport," Verve MGV8234 .... **20-40**

Ella Fitzgerald recording, LP, "At The Opera House," Verve MGV8264, 1957.......... **10-15**

Ella Fitzgerald recording, reel-to-reel tape, "Ella," 10 songs, Reprise 6354 .... **4-8**

Ella Fitzgerald sheet music, "Into Each Life Some Rain Must Fall" w/Ink Spots **4-6**

Ella Fitzgerald trading card, portrait of El-
la, 1950s **5-10**
George Shearing Quintet recording, LP,
"Latin Escapade," Capitol T737 .... **5-15**
George Shearing Quintet recording, LP,
"Latin Lace," Capitol ST1082......................... **5-15**
George Shearing Quintet recording, LP,
"San Francisco Scene," Capitol Records.... **5-10**
George Shearing recording, 45 RPM EP,
w/Peggy Lee, Columbia EAP71219, pic-
ture sleeve.. **4-8**
George Shearing recording, LP, "Souve-
nirs," London LBP295, 10".......................... **10-25**
Gerry Mulligan Quartet recording, 78
RPM, "Lullaby of the Leaves," Pacific
Jazz 601, 1952 .... **5-10**
Gerry Mulligan Quartet recording, LP, re-
corded in Boston at Storyville, Pacific
1228.. **30-75**
Gerry Mulligan recording, LP, "and his
Ten-Tette," 8 songs, Capitol H439,
10".. **60-150**
Gerry Mulligan recording, LP, "Meets Ben
Webster," Verve V8343............................ **20-50**

Gerry Mulligan Recording

Gerry Mulligan recording, LP, "Meets Stan
Getz," Verve MGV8249 (ILLUS.)................ **10-20**
Glenn Miller postcard, portrait shot, 1940s....... **3-5**

Glenn Miller Recording

Glenn Miller recording, 45 RPM EP, 4
songs, RCA Victor EP148 (ILLUS.)................ **4-8**
Glenn Miller recording, LP, "Army Air
Force Band," 5 records, RCA LPT6702,
1955.. **60-150**
Glenn Miller recording, LP, "Selections
from the Glenn Miller Story," RCA
LPT3057, 10" **25-60**
Glenn Miller recording, "Unforgettable
Glenn Miller," 6 records, RCA RDA 64A,
Readers Digest...................................... **10-15**
Glenn Miller sheet music, "Chattanooga
Choo Choo," 1941.................................... **4-8**
John Coltrane recording, 45 RPM, "Mo-
ment's Notice Pts. 1 & 2," Blue Note
#1718 .... **10-20**

John Coltrane recording, LP, "Ballads,"
Impulse Records A-32................................ **15-30**

John Coltrane Recording

John Coltrane recording, LP, "Blue Train,"
Blue Note, 1957 (ILLUS.)........................... **20-30**
John Coltrane recording, LP, "Lush Life,"
Prestige 7188 .... **10-15**
Miles Davis poster, portrait shot, 24" x 26"..... **5-10**
Miles Davis recording, LP, "Birth of Cool,"
Capitol T762, mono **60-150**
Miles Davis recording, LP, "Kind of Blue,"
Columbia CL1355, mono............................ **10-25**
Miles Davis recording, LP, "Lee Konitz
w/Miles Davis," Prestige PRLP116,
10" **100-200**
Miles Davis recording, LP, "Live at the
Blackwater," Vol. 1, Columbia CL
1669 .... **12-30**
Miles Davis recording, LP, "Porgy and
Bess," Columbia CL1274, mono, 1959 .... **5-12**
Miles Davis recording, LP, "Sketches of
Spain," Columbia CS8271 .... **10-15**
Nina Simone recording, 45 RPM, "Love
Me or Leave Me," Bethlehem #11021 .... **4-8**
Nina Simone recording, LP, "Live At Carn-
egie Hall," Colpix SCP455.......................... **10-15**
Nina Simone recording, LP, "Nina Simone
Sings Ellington," Colpix CP425.................... **10-15**
Peggy Lee advertisement, Chesterfield
Cigarettes, portrait shot, 1953....................... **4-8**
Peggy Lee photograph, w/separate auto-
graph, matted, black & white, 11" x 14"..... **15-25**
Peggy Lee recording, 45 RPM, "Fever,"
Capitol F3998 .... **3-5**
Peggy Lee recording, LP, "Dream Street,"
Decca DL8411, mono **20-50**
Peggy Lee recording, LP, "Song of Inti-
mate Style," Decca DL5539, mono, 10".... **30-75**
Ray Charles concert program, 1960s **5-10**
Ray Charles recording, 78 RPM, "That's
Enough," Atlantic 2022, rare **10-20**
Ray Charles recording, LP, "At Newport,"
Atlantic 1289, 1958...................................... **5-12**

Ray Charles Recording

Ray Charles recording, LP, "Modern Sounds in Country/Western" Vol. 2, ABCS435 (ILLUS.)..................................... **5-10**
Sara Vaughn recording, 45 RPM EP, 4 songs, Bravo BR305, British picture sleeve **5-10**
Sara Vaughn recording, LP, "Golden Hits," Mercury MG 20645, mono, 1961 .... **10-20**
Sara Vaughn recording, LP, "Sara Vaughn Sings," Allegro Elite 4106, 10" **30-75**
Stan Getz recording, LP, "Volume 1," Prestige PRLP102, 1951, 10".................... **100-200**
Stan Getz recording, LP, "Volume 2," Prestige PRLP104, 1951, 10"..................... **100-200**
Stan Getz recording, reel-to-reel tape, "Getz Au Go Go," Verve............................. **5-10**
The Modern Jazz Quartet album, LP, "Patterns," United Artists Records, UAL 4072, mono, 1960 .... **10-25**
The Modern Jazz Quartet recording, LP, "Concorde," Prestige 7005, HiFi, 1955 ...... **30-75**

The Modern Jazz Quartet Recording

The Modern Jazz Quartet recording, LP, "Fontessa," Atlantic 1231 (ILLUS.) **10-20**
The Modern Jazz Quartet recording, LP, French release in "Haute Fidelite," 10" **5-10**
Thelonius Monk recording, LP, "Genius of Modern Music Vol.1," Blue Note BLP5002, 10" **300-500**
Thelonius Monk recording, LP, "Misterioso," Riverside RCP1133.............................. **15-40**
Thelonius Monk recording, LP, "Plays Duke Ellington," Riverside RLP12-201, mono **20-40**
Thelonius Monk recording, LP, "The Man I Love," Black Lion BL197 .... **4-8**

Women Singers - Pre-1950s

Female vocalists? Chanteuses? Divas? Whatever you may call them, women singers have been around almost as long as music, certainly as long as recorded music. In fact, when we think of famous singers, we almost always think of the women who have captured our hearts and souls with their voices.

Female singers made their appearance as stars in the world of opera in the 1800s. By the early 1900s, the music hall, musical "theater" and vaudeville provided other venues for female vocal talent. But with the arrival of recorded sound, the female "pop" singer emerged in all her glory. Jazz and popular recordings in the 1920s and '30s gave us the bluesy Bessie Smith and Ethel Waters while the "torch" singers like Ruth Ettlng and Helen Morgan held up the ballads and sentimental side. In the 1930s, Hollywood introduced singers like Judy Garland and Alice Faye. By the 1940s, big bands were adding female vocalists like Doris Day and Peggy Lee to "front" their songs. Many of these songbirds would go on to successful solo careers in the 1950s and beyond. Broadway musicals also arrived in the '40s, giving yet another arena for talented singers like Mary Martin and Ethel Merman.

The listings here are for pre-1950s memorabilia. Collectors and fans search not only for recordings by singers, but sheet music, autographs, photos, and other printed ephemera.

Alice Faye Photo

Alice Faye, photo, signed & inscribed, 5 x 7" (ILLUS.)... **$25-30**

Alice Faye Postcard

Alice Faye, postcard, color, shows Beverly Hills residence, ca. 1930s (ILLUS.)................ **4-8**
Alice Faye, publicity photo, ca. 1930s, 8 x 10" **5-10**

"You're A Sweetheart" Sheet Music

Alice Faye, sheet music, "You're A Sweetheart" from the film of the same name, copyright 1937, Robbins Music Corp. (ILLUS.) **5-10**

Andrews Sisters Album Set

Andrews Sisters, 78 rpm album set, 10 songs, Decca Records, the set (ILLUS.)... **10-25**

"Sabre Dance" Sheet Music

Andrews Sisters, sheet music, "Sabre Dance," copyright 1946, Leeds Music Corp. (ILLUS.).. **5-10**

Andrews Sisters, song folio, "Army, Navy & Marines," 60 songs, Leeds Music Corp., 1942.. **10-20**

Aunt Jemima (Tess Gardella), 78 rpm, #1304D, "Can't Help Lovin' Dat Man," Columbia Records, ca. 1929.................... **10-15**

Bessie Smith, 78 rpm, #2476, "St. Louis Blues/Reckless Blues," w/Louis Armstrong... **20-30**

Bessie Smith, 78 rpm, #2480, "Yellow Dog Blues/Trombone Cholly," Parlophone Records.. **10-20**

Bessie Smith, 78 rpm, "Cold in Hand Blues/You've Been a Good Old Wagon," Columbia Records.................................. **10-20**

Betty Hutton, sheet music, "Arthur Murray Taught Me Dancing in a Hurry," from the film The Fleet's In, copyright 1942, Famous Music Corp. **5-10**

Blossom Seeley, 78 rpm, #386D, "Yes Sir, That's My Baby," Columbia Records, ca. 1925... **5-10**

"Hawaiian Butterfly" Sheet Music

Blossom Seeley, sheet music, "Hawaiian Butterfly," copyright 1917, Leo Feist Inc. (ILLUS.)... **10-20**

The Boswell Sisters 78 rpm Record

Boswell Sisters, 78 rpm, #4495, "St. Louis Blues/Travelin' All Alone," Vocalion Label Corporation (ILLUS.) **4-8**

Boswell Sisters, 78 rpm, "Rock and Roll/The Object of My Affection," Columbia Records **5-10**

Deanna Durbin, book, "Deanna Durbin and the Feather of Flame," copyright 1941, Whitman Publishing Co................................ **5-10**

Deanna Durbin Magazine Cover

Deanna Durbin, magazine cover, Photoplay, May 1940, 102 pgs. (ILLUS.) **15-20**

Deanna Durbin, publicity photo, 4" x 6", signed & inscribed, "To Dennis Best Wishes".. **5-10**

Deanna Durbin Sheet Music

Deanna Durbin, sheet music, "Spring Will Be a Little Late This Year," copyright 1944, Saunders Publications, California (ILLUS.).. **5-10**

Deanna Durbin, song folio, "Deanna Durbin Sings," 11 songs, Leo Feist Inc., 1940.. **10-15**

Dinah Shore, 78 rpm, "Buttons and Bows/Daddy-O," Columbia Records, ca. 1950.. **4-6**

Dinah Shore, sheet music, "I'm Confessin'," copyright 1930, Bourne Music Publishing.................................... **10-12**

"Yes, My Darling Daughter" Music

Dinah Shore, sheet music, "Yes, My Darling Daughter," copyright 1940, Leo Feist Inc. (ILLUS.).................................. **5-10**

Dorothy Shay 10" Record

Dorothy Shay, 10" record, 8 songs by the "Park Avenue Hillbillie," Capitol Records (ILLUS.) **5-10**

Edith Piaf 10" Record

Edith Piaf, 10" record, Edith Piaf Sings, 8 songs, copyright 1950, Columbia Records (ILLUS.) **10-15**

Edith Piaf, programme, L'Etoile, 1947-48, 4 1/2" x 6".................................... **10-20**

Ethel Merman, 78 rpm, album set, 6 records with booklet, "Annie Get Your Gun," Decca Records................................. **10-20**

Ethel Merman Signed Magazine Photo

Ethel Merman, magazine photo, color, 8" x 12", signed (ILLUS.) **30-40**

Ethel Merman, program, The Playbill magazine, December 15, 1947, Broadway

production of "Annie Get Your Gun,"
6 1/2" x 9", 42 pgs.. **4-8**
Ethel Merman, sheet music, "Let's Be Bud-
dies," from Panama Hattie, copyright
1940, Chappell & Co. **5-10**
Ethel Waters, 78 rpm, #1837D, "Am I Blue,"
Columbia Records, ca. 1929 .... **10-20**
Ethel Waters, 78 rpm, #2183D, "What Did I
Do To Be So Black and Blue?," Columbia
Records, ca. 1930 .... **10-20**
Gay White, sheet music, "There's a Silver
Moon on the Golden Gate," copyright
1936, Irving Berlin Inc.................................. **5-10**
Ginny Simms, 1st edition, copyright 1943,
Cross Music Company, 52 pgs., 9" x
12"... **10-15**

"I Can't Get Started" Sheet Music

Ginny Simms, sheet music, "I Can't Get
Started," copyright 1935, Chappell & Co.
(ILLUS.)... **5-10**
Ginny Simms, sheet music, "With the Wind
and the Rain in Your Hair," copyright
1940, Paramount Music Corp. **5-10**

"Harry Holmes Ballads ... " Song Book

Ginny Simms, song book, "Harry Holmes
Ballads for Broadcasting - No. 1"
(ILLUS.).. **5-10**

"He's My Guy" Sheet Music

Helen Forrest, sheet music, "He's My Guy,"
copyright 1942, Leeds Music Co.
(ILLUS.) **5-10**
Helen O'Connell, magazine, Latest Hit
Songs, October-November 1943, photo
on cover .... **10 -2**

"Lili Marlene" Sheet Music

Hildegard, sheet music, "Lili Marlene,"
copyright 1943, Chappell & Co. (ILLUS.).. **10-15**
Irene Bordoni, sheet music, "Can't You
Hear Me Say I Love You," copyright
1928, J.W. Jenkins Sons **5-10**
Jeannette MacDonald (w/Nelson Eddy),
sheet music, "Italian Street Song," from
"Naughty Marietta," copyright 1931, M.
Witmark & Sons.. **5-10**
**Joan Davis (w/Jane Grazee & Judy Clar-
ke),** sheet music, "Shoo-Shoo Baby,"
from the film "Beautiful But Broke," copy-
right 1943, Leeds Music Corp....................... **5-10**

Judy Garland Life Magazine Cover

Judy Garland, magazine cover, Life Magazine, 12/11/44 (ILLUS.) **10-25**

Judy Garland, movie poster, one sheet linen, "The Harvey Girls," copyright 1946... **300-400**

Judy Garland, sheet music, "Nine Pins in the Sky," copyright 1938, Sun Music Publishing Co.. **10-20**

Judy Garland, song folio, "Judy Garland Sings," 15 songs, 1940, Leo Feist Inc. **10-20**

Kate Smith, 78 rpm, "God Bless America/The Star Spangled Banner," copyright 1939, Victor Records................................. **5-10**

Kate Smith, 78 rpm, "Moanin' Low/Waiting at the End of the Rainbow," Diva Records.. **10-12**

Kate Smith, magazine ad, color, for Jell-O, 1942, 9 1/4" x 12 1/2" **3-6**

Kate Smith's Favorite Recipes Booklet

Kate Smith, recipe booklet, "Kate Smith's Favorite Recipes," copyright 1940, Swans Down Flour & Calumet Baking Powder, 47 pgs. (ILLUS.)................................ **5-10**

"Last Time I Saw Paris" Sheet Music

Kate Smith, sheet music, "Last Time I Saw Paris," copyright 1940, Chappell & Sons (ILLUS.) **4-8**

Le Brun Sisters, sheet music, "The Starlit Hour," copyright 1939, Robbins Music Corp. **5-10**

Lee Morse, 78 rpm, #11592, "What A Girl/I Love You So," Perfect Records **10-20**

Lee Morse, 78 rpm, #11618, "A Little Love/Lonesome and Sorry," Perfect Records **10-20**

Margaret Whiting, magazine ad, "The Barry Wood Show," black & white, 1946........... **5-10**

Margaret Whiting, sheet music, "That's Where I Came In," copyright 1946 .... **4-8**

Marlene Dietrich Magazine Cover

Marlene Dietrich, magazine cover, Pelicula Magazine, 1932 (ILLUS.)............................ **10-20**

Marlene Dietrich, postcard, black & white, ca. 1930s, 4" x 6"................................. **4-8**

Mary Martin, 10" record, soundtrack to the musical "The Bandwagon," Columbia Records **5-10**

Mary Martin & Ethel Merman, 10" record, 4 recordings, from the Ford 50th Anniversary Television Show, Decca Records **10-15**

Mildred Bailey, sheet music, "Something Tells Me," copyright 1938, M. Witmark & Sons 5-10

Nancy Walker, sheet music, "Milkman Keep Those Bottles Quiet," from Broadway Rhythm, copyright 1944, Leo Feist Inc. 5-10

"I Want a Daddy to Cuddle Me"

Rae Samuels, sheet music, "I Want a Daddy to Cuddle Me," copyright 1927, J.W. Jenkins Sons Music Co. (ILLUS.).............. 10-15

Ruth Etting, 78 rpm, "If I Didn't Have You/Let Me Call You Sweetheart," Conqueror Records... 8-12

Ruth Etting, 78 rpm, "Love Me or Leave Me/I'm Bringing a Red Red Rose," Columbia D Disc Records.............................. 10-15

Ruth Etting, autograph, inscribed "To Howard - Every Good Wish"....................... 10-15

"Till To-Morrow" Sheet Music

Ruth Etting, sheet music, "Till To-Morrow," copyright 1932, Connelly, Robbins Music (ILLUS.)... 5-10

Sophie Tucker, 78 rpm, #23982, "My Yiddish Momme (sung in English)/My Yiddish Momme (sung in Yiddish)," Decca Personality Records.................................... 10-25

Sophie Tucker, 78 rpm, #29913, "I'm Doing What I'm Doing for Love/I'm Feathering a Nest," Victor Records 5-10

Sophie Tucker, promo advertisement, Billboard Magazine, copyright 1946 10-15

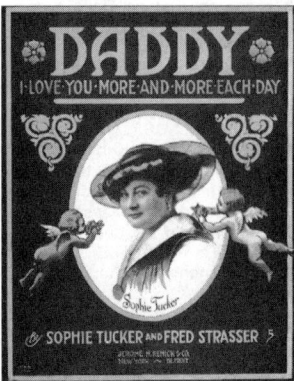

"Daddy I Love You ..." Sheet Music

Sophie Tucker, sheet music, "Daddy I Love You More and More Each Day," copyright 1914, Jerome H. Remich Co. (ILLUS.) 10-20

Sophie Tucker, sheet music, "My Heart Belongs to Daddy," copyright 1938, from the stage musical Leave it to Me, Chappell & Co. 5-10

Sophie Tucker, wax cylinder record, #10449, "Reuben Rag," Edison Molded Records 30-50

Vaughn De Leath, sheet music, "Cheerie-Beerie-Be," copyright 1927, Leo Feist Inc. 5-10

POSTERS

Also see: MAGIC COLLECTIBLES and MOVIE MEMORABILIA.

American League for Peace and Democracy, heavy cardstock, red & blue, images of man, woman & child walking hand in hand against outline of United States filled w/photomontage of masses of people, heading reads "90% of the People Want PEACE," "Join US" over inset w/"Protect and extend democratic rights for all sections of the American People. Keep the United States out of war and help to keep war out of the world," ca. 1938, 14 1/4 x 22".. $111

Debs/Seidel Jugate Campaign Poster

Campaign poster, Eugene Debs & Emil Seidel jugate poster w/"Socialist Party Candidates 1912" in red at top, "Working-men Vote Your Ticket - Unite at the Ballot Box" at bottom, bust images of the two candidates in oval garlands, 1912, 20 1/2 x 28 1/2" (ILLUS.)............................. **7,054**

Campaign poster, John F. Kennedy senatorial campaign, w/black & white photo of Kennedy in center circle, red top half w/"He has served ALL Massachusetts with Distinction!" in white, deep blue lower half w/"Re-elect U.S. Senator Kennedy," linen backed, 1956, 29 3/4 x 44 3/4"... **2,922**

Campaign poster, "Lyndon Johnson for United States Senator," w/8 x 10" black & white studio portrait photo of Johnson in center flanked by red, white & blue flag-like banners, red band at bottom, Allied Printing, Houston, Texas, 1948, 13 1/2 x 22" **805**

"Carter the Great," full color three-sheet poster featuring the turbaned magician gazing into a crystal ball, from which numerous imps, demons & playing cards seem to rise, "Carter the Great" at top, "The World's Weird Wonderful Wizard" at bottom, linen backed, ca. 1925, 41 x 77".. **1,730**

Civil defence, commissioned by city officials to notify Philadelphians of the impending danger of a Rebel attack in 1863, "Defence of the City of Philadelphia" in bold lettering at top, over illustrations of robed figures holding a scroll & a cornucopia & flanking images of scales, a plow & a ship at sea, the lower half w/text proclaiming the calling out of the home guard, 23 3/4 x 38"....................................... **3,058**

Japanese internment poster, "Instructions to All Persons of JAPANESE Ancestry Living in the Following Areas...," followed by instructions in black on white ground, dated May 3, 1942, at the onset of the internment of Japanese Americans during World War II, 14 x 22" **498**

Russian War Relief, multicolor image of soldier w/bandaged head wearing Russian helmet & aiming rifle, wasteland in background, heading reads "HELP RUSSIA," band under picture reads "HASTEN VICTORY," "Give to Russian War Relief, Inc." & address at bottom, illustrated by George Kanelous, World War II era, 14 x 22" (ILLUS.)... **341**

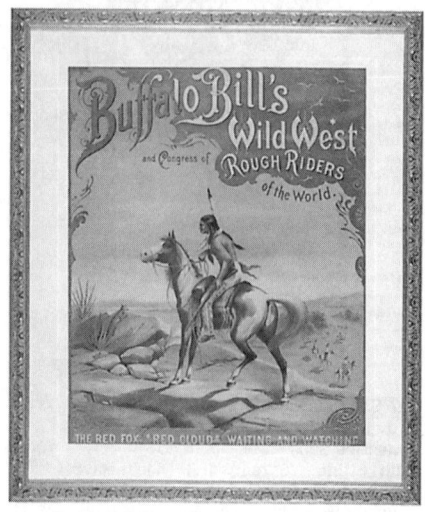

Buffalo Bill's Wild West show Poster

Wild West show, full color poster advertising "Buffalo Bill's Wild West and Congress of Rough Riders of the World" show, w/illustration of Indian scout on horseback over the caption "The Red Fox 'Red Cloud' Waiting and Watching," framed & matted, rare, ca. 1895, poster trimmed to 19 x 23" (ILLUS.)...................... **4,767**

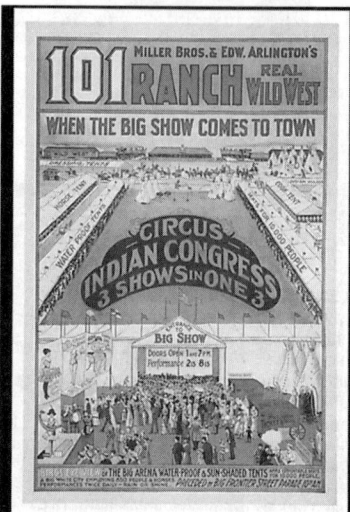

101 Ranch Wild West Show Poster

Russian War Relief Poster

Wild West show, full color poster advertising "Miller Bros. & Edw. Arlington's 101 Ranch Real Wild West" show, w/fully labeled layout of the showgrounds & "Circus - Indian Congress - 3 Shows in One" in center over illustration of people at the show, linen backed, early 20th c., 28 x 41" (ILLUS.) **1,761**

United War Work Campaign Poster

World War I, chromolithograph by Adolph Treidler depicts girl wearing brown uniform holding a biplane in one hand, a bomb in the other, in front of inverted "V," & the words "For every fighter a woman worker - United War Work Campaign - Care for Her through The YWCA," 30 x 40" (ILLUS.) **1,705**

World War I Bond Drive Poster

World War I, chromolithograph by Eugenie DeLand w/colorful patriotic scene w/Statue of Liberty & flag in the sky behind it, titled "Before Sunset, Buy a U.S. Government Bond of the 2nd Liberty Loan of 1917," tack holes & tears, 20 x 30" (ILLUS.) **440**

Air Service Recruitment Poster

World War I, chromolithograph by J. Paul Verreel, depicts a biplane & men in uniform w/"Join the Air Service and Serve in France" & "Do it now," additional piece added to the bottom in the period reads "Apply to Aviation Examining Board, Lakeside Hospital, Cleveland," 1917, minor wear, 25 x 42" (ILLUS.) **1,100**

War Bond Poster

World War I, chromolithograph depicting boy & girl holding an American flag and "Our Daddy is Fighting at the Front for You - Back him up - Buy a United States Gov't Bond of the 2nd Liberty Loan of 1917," margin tears, 20 x 30" (ILLUS.) **330**

World War I, chromolithograph, depicts a little girl w/fair hair wearing red bow & white dress holding a bond, underneath reads "My Daddy Bought Me a Government Bond of the Third Liberty Loan - Did Yours?" framed & matted, 28 1/4 x 38 3/4" (taped tears) **220**

World War I, chromolithograph, signed "Alfred Everitt Orr - 18," shows doughboy holding child & wife, "For Home and Country - Victory Liberty Loan" in red & black lettering, 20 x 30" (minor edge wear) **220**

World War I, chromolithograph, signed "Gil Spear," figure in military uniform watches over figure in undershirt & military helmet straining in effort, silhouette of soldier w/bayonet in background, top of poster reads "Workers," bottom reads "Lend Your Strength to the Red Triangle - Help the 'Y' Help the Fighters Fight - United War Work Campaign - November 11 to 18," "Y.M.C.A." appears over triangle, 20 x 27 1/4" (short margin tears) **110**

World War I, chromolithograph, signed "Leyendecker," shows Boy Scout on one knee holding sword in front of warrior w/shield & flag-like robe, reads "U.S.A. Bonds - Third Liberty Loan Campaign Boy Scouts of America" & "Weapons for Liberty" at bottom, 20 x 30" (tear at lower center & minor corner damage) **440**

RAILROADIANA

Assistant Conductor's cap, w/metal badge w/Pennsylvania Railroad emblem & title, 1950s **$125**

Badge, for American Electric Railway Association Convention, 1926 .... **20**

Railroad Bill of Lading

Bill of lading, from the Toronto-Hamilton-Buffalo Railway Company for transporting 10 bags of feed from the Caldwell Feed and Cereal Company to Kleepfer Coal Company, dated Oct. 17, 1917, 8 1/2 x 11" (ILLUS.) **20**

Calendar, advertising Missouri Pacific Lines, color litho image of steam passenger train, set of green metal date cards for days of week, 1940s, 13 x 19" **150**

Calendar, advertising Pennsylvania Railroad, w/illustrations by Grif Teller, 1950s **45**

Calendar, Great Northern Railroad "Indian" series, w/illustrations by Winold Ross, 1920s-30s, each **100**

Candy container, tin & white glass, in the form and size of a railroad lantern, held one ounce of candy, made in USA **18**

Card #714 from "Rails and Sails" Set

Card, from 200-card "Rails and Sails" set by Topps, fronts showed picture of train or ship, backs identified picture and gave general information on trains or ships, 1955, 2 5/8 x 3 3/4" (ILLUS.) **5**

Conductor's cap, w/metal badge w/Pennsylvania Railroad emblem & title, 1950s **135**

Dinner program, for National Railway Historical Society - Philadelphia Chapter dinner of April 6, 1957, Pennsylvania Railroad logo on front, red, black & gold, 6 x 9" **10**

Drumhead, University of Iowa drumhead features Santa Fe Railroad logo, from Iowa's 1959 trip to the Rose Bowl (sold in lot that included framed Rose Bowl tickets & program) **2,640**

Engineer's hat, generic, soft structure, black stripes, 1940s **15**

Flashlight, silvered metal, w/"P.R.R. Bright Star Domed," Pennsylvania Railroad, 1940s, 7 1/2" l **55**

Jigsaw puzzle, Twilight Express Train jigsaw puzzle, box depicting steaming locomotive pulling five cars, children waving at crew, finished puzzle about nine feet long, late 19th - early 20th century **150**

Lantern, fixed globe in pierced tin frame, Eastern Railroad, wire handle, globe engraved "E.R.R.," traces of black paint, America, 19th c., 11" h. (corrosion) **411**

Lantern, kerosene-type, w/handle & metal frame, company logo of New York Central Railroad, 1900 .... **45**

Lithograph, colored picture of newly constructed locomotive & tender "Calumet," labeled "Taunton Locomotive Manfg. Co., Taunton, Mass.," published by J.H. Bufford, ca. 1870, framed, 13 x 25" (some staining, other minor defects) **1,495**

Lithograph of Early Locomotive

Lithograph, hand-colored picture of locomotive & tender "New England," labeled "Taunton Locomotive Manfg. Co., Taunton, Mass.," published by J.H. Bufford, ca. 1870, framed, some staining & soiling, image 18 3/4 x 27 3/8" (ILLUS.).................. **1,840**

Life Magazine Ad for Pullman

Magazine ad, Life magazine full-page ad for Pullman features picture of a porter helping actor Herbert Marshall on w/his coat & the caption " 'It's the "Civilized" Way to Travel!' says Herbert Marshall" & the tag line "Go Pullman - Enjoy the Utmost in Travel Comfort," two inset pictures & more text, Nov. 11, 1940 issue (ILLUS.) **10**

fornia," w/black & white images of train & scenery & tag line "Southern Pacific The West's Greatest Transportation System," April 25, 1938 (ILLUS.)...................................... **20**

Color Ad for Southern Pacific

Magazine ad, Life magazine, full-page color ad for Southern Pacific, "How to see twice as much on your trip to the San Francisco World's Fair for little or no extra rail fare" w/graphic depictions of the Fair, a family planning their trip & various activities, clip-out coupon, Feb. 20, 1939 (ILLUS.) **30**

Magazine Ad for Canadian Pacific

Magazine Ad for Southern Pacific

Magazine ad, Life magazine, full-page ad for Southern Pacific, "How to see twice as much of the West on your trip to Cali-

Timken Ad

Magazine ad, Saturday Evening Post color ad for Canadian Pacific w/heading "Canada passes your train window" & featuring pictures of the train and views of Canadian Rockies & Lake Louise, May 2, 1953 issue, 13 1/2 x 5 1/2" (ILLUS.) **6**

Magazine ad, Saturday Evening Post, double-page spread features ad for Timken Tapered Roller Bearings, w/black & white pictures & text under heading "Wilderness railroad goes 'Roller Freight' to tap fabulous ore strike" & tag line "Watch the railroads Go ... on TIMKEN Tapered Roller Bearings," May 2, 1953 issue (ILLUS., top of page) **10**

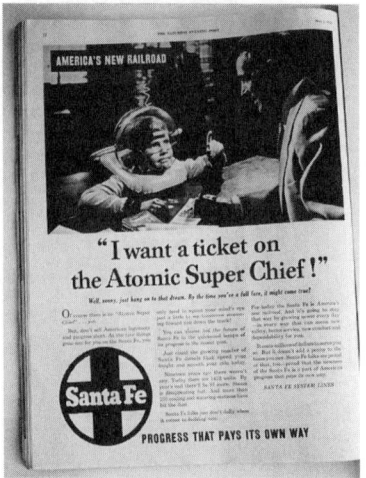

Ad from Saturday Evening Post

Magazine ad, Saturday Evening Post full-page ad for the Santa Fe, "America's New Railroad," w/a black & white picture of a boy in a space costume gesturing to a clerk over the caption "I want a ticket on the Atomic Super Chief!" & the clerk's reply "Well, sonny, just hang on to that dream. By the time you're a full fare, it might come true" & the tag line "Progress that pays its own way," May 2, 1953 issue (ILLUS.) **12**

Magazine feature, Life magazine, Jan. 16, 1939, double-page spread features story "Union Pacific's new turbine locomotive works like a ship," w/large black & white photos & graphic illustrations of the new locomotive (ILLUS., top of next page).. **10**

Matchbook, advertising The New York Central System, depicts scene of Art Deco-style streamlined train speeding down the tracks, reads "The Empire State Express," 1920s-30s **6**

Matchbook, advertising the New York Central System, depicts scene of steam locomotive traveling along the Hudson River from upstate New York to New York City, reads "Water Level Route," 1920s-30s **5**

Matchbook, advertising the New York Central System, picture of cowboy on rearing horse, cover reads "The New Southwestern Limited," 1920s-30s **5**

Matchbook, reads "The New Ohio State Limited," 1920s-30s... **5**

Life Magazine Feature Story

Dual Purpose Oil/Kerosene Can

Oil/kerosene can, metal, tapering cylindrical shape, dual purpose oil can could be filled w/kerosene & lit so flame would come out 5" l. spout for use in thawing frozen switches, 1920s, 8 1/2" h. (ILLUS.).. 30

Train Car Paperweight

Paperweight, spelter, in the form of a train car on rectangular base, w/"The First Vista Dome Car - 1945" embossed on the side in commemoration of the first Vista

Wheaties Giveaway

Railway guide, "1926 Official Guide to the Railroads," 1600+ pages of timetables, maps & historical information **250**

Sign, porcelain, round, Chicago Great Western Railroad bridge sign **800**

Chicago, Rock Island & Pacific Lock

Switch lock, cast brass, "Chicago, Rock Island & Pacific," marked w/initials & "Signal," 3 3/8" h. (ILLUS.)...................................... **39**

Rock Island Switch Lock

Switch lock, cast brass, "Rock Island Lines," also marked "Signal," 3 3/8" h. (ILLUS.) **39**

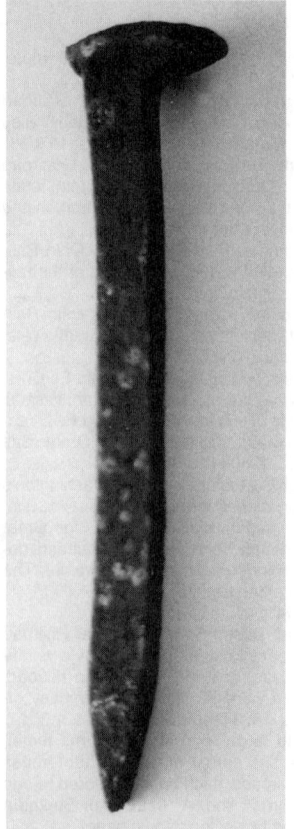

Railway Spike

Spike, heavy steel spike used in railways, 1930s, 3/4" w., 8" l. (ILLUS.) **8**

Canadian Pacific Timetable

Timetable, for Canadian Pacific, cover features color image of woman in Vista Dome car looking out window at mountains & lake, 1967, 9 1/4 x 4 1/4" (ILLUS.).. 10

World War II Train Timetable

Timetable, for New York Central, cover features color illustration of train against mountain backdrop & "ONE OF AMERICA'S RAILROADS - ALL UNITED FOR VICTORY - BUY UNITED STATES WAR BONDS AND STAMPS" in box, inside has information for traveling soldiers ("What Life is Like on a Troop Train," "Preparing for Taps," etc.), Dec. 5, 1943, 9 1/4 x 4 1/4" (ILLUS.) 25

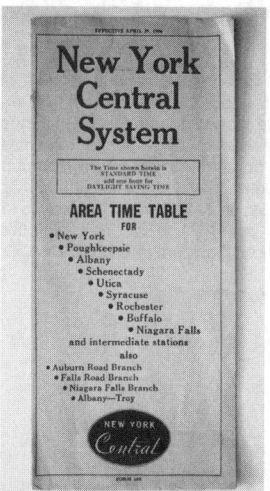

New York Central System Timetable

Timetable, for New York Central System, cover simply lists routes covered, 1956, 9 1/4 x 4 1/4" (ILLUS.)...................................... 8
Trade card, Reading Railroad, long rectangular form w/a multicolored panoramic

view of the 1876 Philadelphia Centennial Exhibition w/the Centennial Station of Philadelphia & the Reading Railroad in the foreground, timetable for Perekiomen Route on the back (some corner wear, light soiling) 44
Travel brochure, promotes travel to California, front features images of oranges & strawberries, 1949 5

RIBBON DOLLS

There was a time when a woman's success was measured in part by her skill with a needle. In addition to embroidery, making ribbon dolls or ribbon pictures was a popular pastime. Some of these items were completely homemade projects, from the actual design of the paper figure to all the lace, ribbon and trims that went into her ensemble. Others were purchased in kit form, complete with paper doll, ribbon supplies and the actual frame and glass. One could also purchase a paper pattern for a mere ten cents and add the necessary dress materials. Today collectors are particularly interested in ladies in unusual poses, pictured in a unique setting, or the hard-to-find male examples.

Girl, Dutch, beige dress w/large bow in back, white apron & cap w/lace trim & wooden clogs, carrying a red & yellow bouquet of flowers, 10 1/2" h. **$55-65**
Girl, in a green ribbon dress trimmed in lace & wearing a lace bonnet, holding a coordinating nosegay, 6" h................................ 35-55
Girl, in pink ribbon dress w/lace hem, large pink ribbon hat w/flower trim hiding face, holding a flower-encircled bouquet, 7" h. . 40-50
Girl, w/real long brown hair, pink & blue dress w/matching bonnet, 7 3/4" h............ 50-60
Lady, blonde bobbed hair, elongated neck, long-lashed eyes cast downward, yellow velvet dress trimmed in lace & ribbon, holding ribbon & lace bouquet 100-135
Lady, faceless, pink ribbon & white lace, trimmed w/pink & blue ribbon flowers, large pink ribbon hat, carrying a bouquet of ribbon flowers, 7" h. 50-65
Lady, made completely of green ribbon, trimmed in pink ruffled ribbon & decorated w/needlepoint designs & flowers, holding matching bouquet, 7 1/2" h. 45-65
Lady, on tiptoe, pink satin ribbon & lace dress, holding a string of ribbon flowers, 10" h... 65-85
Lady, rosy-cheeked, standing on toes, dressed in a light blue ribbon dress w/large lace collar & Colonial style hat, carrying an umbrella, 9 1/4" h. 60-75
Lady, w/blonde, curly bobbed hair, lace around the neck w/spread-out pink ribbon skirt, holding a multicolor bouquet, 12" h. 100-135
Lady, w/real light brown hair, wearing a pink ribbon layered dress, trimmed in pink lace, carrying a multicolor bouquet encircled in lace, 12 1/2" h. 45-65
Lady, w/red curls, square-topped hat, wearing a pale pink ribbon dress w/ecru lace trim & carrying a pastel ribbon flower bouquet, 11" h. 50-65
Lady, wearing a pale gold lace dress w/black velvet bows & chiffon cuffs & bodice, 18" h.. 40-60

Man, Colonial, green ribbon pantaloons & dark pink waistcoat w/ruffled ribbon cuffs & collar, 8 1/2" h. (companion to Colonial woman) **50-65**

Pattern, woman, black & white, ca. 1951 .... **3-6**

Set: boy & girl; the girl in red ribbon dress & hat w/lace & multicolored ribbon flower trim & green bow at neck, the boy in grey trousers & mauve shirt w/lace collar, holding multicolored ribbon flower bouquet w/ribbon streamers, each 3 1/2" h... **95-125**

Set: busts of Colonial man & woman; the man in top hat, lace cuffs & cravat, the blonde woman in bonnet, lace-trimmed bodice & black sash, pr. 4 3/4" h. **85-100**

Woman, blonde hair, black ribbon dress w/white ribbon petticoat, flaring skirt reveals legs, 9 1/4" h.................................. **75-100**

Woman, blonde hair piled high on head, wearing yellow ribbon dress, holding a multicolor ribbon bouquet in outstretched hand, 10" h..................................... **35-50**

Woman, Colonial, blonde, wearing a dark & light pink ribbon ruffled dress, sitting in a chair & working on a spinning wheel, 8 1/4" h....................... **75-85**

Woman, Colonial, blonde wearing pale blue velvet ribbon dress, lace petticoat showing on bottom, smelling a ribbon flower bouquet, 11 1/4" h. **65-85**

Woman, "Colonial Dame," white hair, pink ribbon dress w/lace trim, holding a red feather, Bucilla, ca. 1930s-40s, 8 3/4" h.... **75-95**

Woman, Colonial, dark pink ribbon dress & hat w/green ribbon sash & trim, holding multicolor ribbon bouquet, 8 1/2" h. (companion to Colonial man) **50-65**

Woman, Colonial, transparent yellow shell-like dress trimmed in marcasite beads & ribbon flowers, no hair, 9" h........................ **30-40**

Woman, flapper w/real hair, wearing sheer pajamas, reclining on a divan w/pillows, smoking a cigarette, 13"............................. **35-50**

Woman, in floral print dress w/pink ribbon bow at waist, large pink hat & carrying a painted bouquet, 12 3/8" h. **35-45**

Woman, in pale blue ribbon & ecru lace dress, lace pantaloons, wearing a bonnet, carrying a flower & lace bouquet w/pink ribbon streamers, 10 1/2" h. **40-55**

Woman, redhead wearing a ruffled yellow & gold ribbon dress, holding a garland of multicolored ribbon flowers in outstretched arms, 10" h. **65-85**

Woman, silk thread blonde in bright yellow ribbon dress w/gold threads, sash tied into large bow, lace pantaloons, holding a lace & velvet flower bouquet, 11 1/2" h. ... **60-75**

Woman, Southern belle w/beauty mark on cheek & three long curls of blonde hair, wearing a beige lace dress decorated w/ribbon flowers, large brimmed bonnet w/ribbon trim & bows, long black net gloves on hands, holding ribbon flower bouquet encircled by lace, 7 3/4" h. **45-50**

Woman, w/black hair wearing black & white ribbon dress w/ruffled cuffs & neck band, black hat w/blue feather in hat & hand, 9 1/2" h. **55-65**

Woman, w/red curls wearing a light green ribbon dress, carrying a lace bouquet, 11" h. **45-55**

Woman, wearing a peach-colored flared dress w/light green ribbon trim, holding finger up to her mouth, eyes downcast, 10" h................................... **65-85**

RUGS - HOOKED & OTHER

Hooked

Birds & Urn Hooked Rug

Birds & urn, rectangular, two blue & red birds face a black urn w/flowering tree on a white ground, surrounded by meandering black line & yellow border, olive green outer border w/pink & white diamonds, light green leaves, 23 x 35" (ILLUS.) **$468**

Calla lilies, white flowers w/grey leaves in a flower pot w/"8" on the front, pink floral border on black ground, 22 x 39" **132**

Cornucopia Hooked Rug

Cornucopia, wool, depicting two flower-filled blue-striped cornucopias surrounded by stylized flowers & red scrolls on mottled tan & brown ground, America, ca. 1880, 43 x 73" (ILLUS., bottom previous page) **4,113**

Cottage scene, rectangular, grey cottage w/black trim & red roof surrounded by bushes in shades of green, brown path & fence, blue sky w/flying birds, burgundy border is dated "1940," 26 x 48" **138**

Country village, w/train in the center, a church & houses on the green, horse-drawn carriages, people & farm animals, flowering trees & shrubs, blue & purple border, America, early 20th c., 35 x 75" (losses to center & border) **1,528**

Country winter scene, w/horse-drawn sleigh, red barn & pine trees on snowy ground, blue hills & sky in background, brown border, mounted on board, 28 x 35 1/2" **330**

Crowing Roosters Hooked Rug

Crowing roosters, rectangular, one grey & pink rooster & one pink & brown rooster, both w/red combs, face each other on a grey background in a white & green zigzag vine border of green & grey leaves w/a rosebud in each corner, framed, 33 x 44" (ILLUS.)....................................... **1,870**

Dog, large center panel contains image of spaniel lying on checked rug, center panel flanked by red roses, in olive green, grey, red, light green, tan & black, Edward Sands Frost pattern (small holes at edges) **633**

Hooked Rug with Spaniel

Dog, rectangular, image of spaniel in beige, brown & black lying on green, red & tan checked floor in large center tan & red oval, black ground w/small green leaves, Edward Sands Frost pattern, 26 1/2 x 43 1/2" (ILLUS.).............................. **578**

Floral, central oval & rectangular border of multicolored flowers on tan field surrounded by wide band of floral devices on navy field, w/inner & outer border of leaves & scrolls, overcast yarn edge,

America, early 20th c., 111 1/2 x 135" (damage) **764**

Floral, yarn hooked rug w/stylized floral pattern in central oval worked in shades of red, green, blue & tan on a black field surrounded by leafy border of grey & shaded red crescents on black, edged w/tan border, America, 20th c., 103 x 135" (edge wear) **705**

Floral runner, bright multicolor flowers w/yellow vines on brick red ground, violet, burgundy, grey & blue line borders on sides, 36 x 80" (restoration) **550**

Flowers, rectangular, depicting rosebuds & blossoms centered in a diamond-form grid, in shades of green, pink, brown & black, 19th c., 35 1/2 x 66 3/4" (imperfections) **690**

Foliate scrolls, rectangular, overall design of scrolled foliage in shades of blue, green, yellow, red & grey on a brown ground, America, 19th c., 33 x 62"............... **575**

Geometric, concentric rectangles in greys, pink, red & yellow, some black, 26 x 44" (some edge damage) **110**

Graphic runner, w/stepped block designs in green & tomato red w/multicolored "steps" on two sides, pink, brown & black borders, 31 1/2 x 69" **248**

Halloween Hooked Rug

Halloween, rectangular, orange jack-o'-lantern on rail fence flanked by black cats w/arched backs, a bat flying between tree branches lit by crescent moon, shaded maroon ground, black border, 38 3/4 x 46 1/2" (ILLUS.) **1,760**

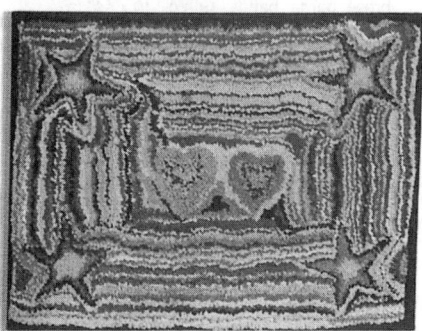

Hearts & Stars Hooked Rug

Pennsylvania Dutch-style Rug

Hearts & stars, centered w/two hearts, a star in each corner, multicolored striped field, mounted on cotton backing & stretched onto wooden frame, America, 19th c., minor edge losses, 30 3/4 x 40 1/8" (ILLUS., previous page) **2,115**

Horse & cat, in black & charcoal w/red eyes, burgundy ground, sawtooth designs on ends, initialed "E. 1943 H.," 23 x 36" **523**

Horses, five horses of various sizes in brown, blue & purple w/red mouths, sage green tree in background, ivory & tan striped ground w/tan border, on stretcher, 19 3/4 x 34 1/2" **825**

House, wool, house flanked by two trees, worked in shades of green, blue, red & brown on mottled blue & tan ground, mounted on wooden frame, America, 19th c., 16 1/2 x 26 1/2" **705**

Landscape, naive scene of a large tan red-roofed house w/pine trees in the background, a woman, cow, dog & pump in foreground, dark brown ground w/tan & brown border bands, 19th c., 40 x 44" (a few repairs) **10,350**

Leaf design, rectangular, large leaf medallion w/larger oak leaves around the borders in brown, blue, red, tan & black, on dark & light brown ground, 53 x 101" (small restorations & rebound edges) **330**

Oak leaves, wool, the center w/pattern of alternating oak leaves & quatrefoil motifs, scrolled leaf border, in shades of grey, green, red, tan, brown, pink & black, America, 19th c., 62" sq. (imperfections) .. **1,175**

Optical design, rectangular, unusual raised block designs in brown outlined in tan, shadows fading from light blue to navy, then black, 3-D effect, mounted on stretcher, 20 x 40" **330**

Oriental-design Hooked Rug

Oriental-style design, rectangular, resembling a prayer rug, central panel of geometric flowers & faux Arabic script in bright salmon, brick red, ivory, putty, brown & olive, w/dark purple/blue edging, stepped pyramid border, on stretcher, 37 1/2 x 60 1/2" (ILLUS.) **220**

Owl perched on tree branch, silhouetted by full moon, taupe colored owl on grey ground, green & black leaves on branches, blue & violet borders, 19 1/2 x 34 1/2" **358**

Pennsylvania Dutch design, bright colors of red, blue, yellow & green on grey ground, designs include a man & woman, roosters, hearts, pears, large flowers, grey center medallion w/early-style train & mountains, 20th c., 56 1/4 x 70" (ILLUS., top of page) **550**

Pinwheels, seven pinwheels, a large one at center, in muted colors of bluish grey, yellow, red, white & pink on brown ground, mounted on stretcher, 26 x 52" (edge wear, minor restoration) **385**

Hooked Rug with Rescue Scene

Rescue scene, depicting three figures & supply-laden sled pulled by seven dogs, worked in shades of brown, black, grey, green, blue & yellow, brown border, Grenfell Industries, Newfoundland, Labrador, 1900-25, staining, fading, 37 3/4 x 61 1/2" (ILLUS.) **1,410**

Rooster, rectangular, w/scene of rooster crowing at sun, w/house in background, earthtones, mounted on stretcher, American, early 20th c., 35 1/2 x 41 1/2" **35,250**

Sailing ship, square-rigged vessel on the high seas in olive green w/gold sails, pale blue skies, blue/green sea, two-tone gold border, 36 x 38" **220**

Star design, rectangular, ten-point star at center w/alternating colors of black, bluish brown, green & burgundy on medium blue ground, black scalloped border, mounted on stretcher, 23 3/4 x 40" **578**

Turkey Hooked Rug

Turkey, w/spread wings & fanned tail feathers, gold, yellow, tan, green & light blue on background of blues & grey resembling clouds, minor wear, 20 1/4 x 33" (ILLUS.) **1,320**

Other

Penny rug, elongated hexagonal shape, comprised of graduated stacks of three multicolor layers, red, black, blue, yellow, green & grey on pale yellow ground, 28 x 47 1/2" (one penny missing top layer) **330**

SCOTTISH TARTANWARE

Tartanware is a name we recognize today as describing plaid-covered souvenir items from Scotland. These tartan objects first appeared in the form of snuff boxes around the turn of the 19th century. About fifty years later many household and decorative tartanware items appeared throughout England and Scotland.

The principal company that produced tartanware was owned by the Smith brothers of Mauchline, Ayrshire in Scotland, who used sycamore wood to make their decorative goods. Known as Mauchlineware, these items were decorated with transfers, photographs and tartan paper. Many items were beautiful examples of applying tartan paper stamped in gold with the name of the Scottish family clan. Objects made include purely decorative cubes as well as sewing, desk and kitchen items and even jewelry and furniture.

The popularity of collecting tartanware has grown. Consequently, prices can be quite high, especially for the rare and unusual items.

Book with Tartanware Cover

Book, "Mementos of the Trasachs Loch Katrine, Loch Lomond" by Birket Foster, MDCCCLIV, Tartanware cover (ILLUS.) **$75**

Tartanware Book Mark

Book mark, flat knife shape (ILLUS.)................ **100**

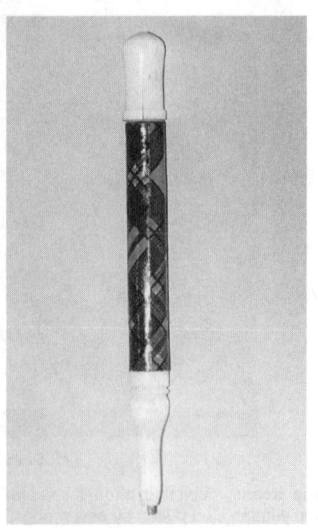

Tartanware Retractable Pencil

Pencil, lead, retractable, Tartanware barrel (ILLUS.) **100**

Match Holder

Match holder, cylindrical, "Go to bed" type (ILLUS.) **185**

Thread Holder Pincushion

Pincushion, footed cylindrical shape, black base, thread holder Tartanware body, blue top (ILLUS.)... **500**

Tartanware Paper Cutter

Paper cutter, flat, pointed rectangular shape (ILLUS.)... **100**

Pincushion with Tartanware Top

Pincushion, round, blue base w/Tartanware top (ILLUS.)... **225**

Tartanware Pincushion

Pincushion, round Tartanware box w/cloth
top (ILLUS.) **175**

Plaister with Tartanware Cover

Plaister, 1845, Tartanware cover (ILLUS.) **250**

SEWING ADJUNCTS

With sewing tools and accessories so popular, collectors in the United States, Canada and England actively search for these small antiques. The wide variety available gives buyers a good selection from which to choose - and allows for plenty of different price ranges too. Be cautious of reproductions - Victorian and Georgian style sterling thimbles and needle cases marked "Thailand" are found frequently, and new pewter thimble holders are sometimes sold as old. A good reference book on sewing tools and accessories is Gay Ann Rogers' An Illustrated History of Needlework Tools, which can be found in many bookstores. All items listed below are in good condition, with minor wear and no missing parts.

Bodkin, bone, America, 19th c. **$12**
Bodkin, brass ribbon threader, Prudential
Life Insurance, America **24**
Chatelaine, cut steel, three matching tools,
England, 19th c. **595**
Chatelaine, silver plate, ornate design
w/five matching tools, England, ca. 1880 .. **1,450**
Crochet hook, bone, w/turned end, America, 19th c. **12**
Crochet hooks, marked "Susan Bates," set
of four **35**
Darner, ebonized wood w/sterling silver
handle, America, ca. 1900 .... **65**
Darner, wood w/multicolor swirl marbleized
paint, America, 1930s **45**

Darner/needle case, wood, w/ornately
turned handle that unscrews to hold needles, original finish, England, 1870-
1880s **165**
Emery, in the form of a strawberry, Shaker,
America, 1920s **125**
Emery, in the form of a strawberry, velvet
w/h.p. seeds, America, 19th c., 1 1/2" l. **175**
Emery, in the form of a strawberry, w/overall
bead decoration & bead fringe,
America, ca. 1900 .... **145**
Emery, in the form of a strawberry w/sterling
silver top, America, 20th c. **135**
Emery, souvenir of New Hampshire,
Mauchline, 1880s **145**
Glove darner, wood w/marbleized colors,
America, 1930s **45**
Glove darner/needle case, sterling silver,
w/floral repoussé, rare, America, 1880s **195**
Hem marker, sterling silver, decorated
w/Art Nouveau-style image of woman's
face, unmarked, America, 1910s **195**
Knitting needle guards, ivory, in the form
of riding boots, England, ca. 1850 .... **275**
Knitting needle guards, sterling silver, in
the form of boots, Europe, ca. 1870 .... **215**
Knitting needles, red, white & blue, America, 1940s **25**
Knitting needles, steel, small heads, America, 19th c. **24**
Knitting needles, wood, America, 19th c. **15**
Knitting sheath, wood, w/hand-carved initials & crosshatch design, England, early
19th c. **345**
Nanny brooch, brass w/goldstone setting,
England **195**
Needle book, leather cover w/flannel interior leaves, America, ca. 1900 .... **20**
Needle case, beadwork, England, ca. 1840 ..... **185**
Needle case, bone, in the form of an umbrella w/Stanhope, England, ca. 1870 .... **175**
Needle case, brass, in the form of a butterfly w/antennae intact, Avery, England,
19th c. **1,400**
Needle case, brass, quadruple casket form,
Avery, England, late 1800s **195**
Needle case, ivory, figural pea pod,
England, ca. 1830 .... **200**
Needle case, metal, mitrailleuse style,
green finish, promotional, England, ca.
1900 .... **55**
Needle case, sterling silver repoussé, England, 19th c. **125**
Needle case, turned wood, America, ca.
1860s **55**
Needle holder, brass, in the form of a mitrailleuse, red finish, England, ca. 1900 .... **45**
Needle holder, wood barrel form w/top that
rotates for different needle sizes,
Germany, ca. 1900 .... **80**
Pin disk, carved ivory, Dieppe work,
France, 1820 .... **150**
Pin disk, glass, decorated w/h.p. butterflies,
rare, England, 1860s **165**
Pin disk, in the shape of a heart, w/seaweed design, Mauchline, Scotland **195**
Pincushion, brass, in the form of a chair,
England, 1880s **135**

Pincushion, in the form of an apple, Occupied Japan, 1940s 35

Pincushion, pierced bone & silk, in the shape of bellows, w/original green silk, England, 1840s 225

Pincushion, round w/hand painted face, America, 1920s 50

Pincushion, vegetable ivory, in the form of a basket w/handle, England, 1880s 95

Pincushion, vegetable ivory, in the form of a man's head w/h.p. face, rare 175

Pincushion, velvet, in the shape of a carrot, America, ca. 1900, 7" 95

Pincushion, velvet, in the shape of a quarter moon, uncommon, America, 19th c., 12" 185

Pincushion/waxer, vegetable ivory, England, 1860s 95

Scissors, steel, heart-shaped handles, England, 1850s 60

Scissors, steel, in the form of a stork, Germany, ca. 1900 46

Scissors, steel, w/ornate engraving & "Toledo," Spain, 20th c. 60

Scissors, sterling silver, simple beaded design, America, ca. 1910 65

Scissors, sterling silver, w/floral Art Nouveau handle, America, 1910s 145

Scissors set, steel, three in leather case, England, late 19th c., the set 165

Shaker Sewing Basket

Sewing basket, maple, four Gothic or swallowtail fingers w/copper tacks & a bentwood swing handle w/brass pins, the interior lined w/burgundy silk over padding attached to sides w/red silk ribbons, contains matching silk pincushion & resin strawberry plus a woven splint needle case, Shaker, attributed to Canterbury, New Hampshire, silk worn, handle w/well-done repair, 6 1/4 x 9 1/4", 3 1/2" h. plus handle (ILLUS.) 1,100

Sewing bird, brass, w/single pincushion, England, wing's edge dated 1853 350

Sewing bird, brass, w/two pincushions, America, wing edge dated 1853 325

Sewing box, Chinese Export lacquered rectangular shape, the exterior chinoiserie decorated w/scenic panels surrounded by mosaic patterns & Greek key border, w/brass bail handles on each end, the interior w/mirrored lid & fitted compartments containing various sewing implements above a single fitted drawer, 19th c., 11 1/2 x 17 1/4", 5 3/4" h. (minor wear & crackling) 470

Sewing clamp, carved ivory w/butterflies, birds & floral design, China, 1840s 140

Sewing clamp, cast iron, America, 19th c. 115

Sewing clamp, wood, simple design w/pincushion top, America, 1860s 125

Sewing kit, brass, egg-shaped, w/overall pattern, contains thread holder & thimble, 1930s 65

Sewing kit, "Compliments of the Butcher's and Meat Cutters Union Local #506," contains two buttons, needle, thread & small patches of cloth, 1930s 10

Sewing kit, leather book-form decorated w/floral design on top, brass thimble, ca. 1900 110

Sewing kit, leather book-form decorated w/images of children, England, 1870s 150

Sewing kit, metal, egg-shaped, w/marbleized paint exterior, thread & thimble inside, 1920s 48

Tambour hook, mother-of-pearl, complete w/multiple hooks, England, 1820 275

Tape measure, brass, in the form of a pig w/windup tail, England, ca. 1870 165

Tape measure, celluloid, in the form of a black cat, Germany 295

Tape measure, celluloid, in the form of an Indian boy w/hatchet 110

Tape measure, plastic, in the form of a pig, Japan, 1950s 45

Tape measure, Tunbridgeware, England, ca. 1840 240

Tape measure, vegetable ivory, barrel form, manual wind, England, 1860s 120

Tatting shuttle, Bakelite, red swirl design, America, 1930s 30

Tatting shuttle, mother-of-pearl, England, ca. 1860s 95

Tatting shuttle, tortoiseshell, England, ca. 1870 125

Thimble, brass, Prudential Insurance promotion, America, 20th c. 12

Thimble, gold-plated, simple design 85

Thimble, sterling silver, octagonal shape decorated w/floral engraving, Simons, ca. 1890 45

Thimble, sterling silver, Salem witch 375

Thimble, sterling silver, "Stitch in Time Saves Nine" 395

Thimble, sterling silver w/gold-plated band, swirling leaf design, unmarked, 19th c. 55

Thimble, sterling silver, w/heavy repoussé band of dogwood florals, unmarked 95

Thimble holder, cov., sweet grass basket, America, early-20th c. 30

Thimble holder, glass, in the form of a shoe, "Button & Daisy" patt., clear, America, 20th c. 75

Thimble holder, sterling silver, ornate loop design, America, 1880s 350

Thimble holder, walnut burl, in the shape of an acorn, America, 1860s 95

Thread winder, bone, snowflake form, England, 19th c. 38

SHEET MUSIC

Patriotic

Patriotism is currently at a high level in America, making sheet music with patriotic themes a popular collectible. Some collectors specialize and search only for those sheets with specific reference to the United States of America. Others add in the categories of Dixie, Wars and Presidents. Also included can be those sheets that feature government buildings. It is a large category with covers that are often full of colors, many of them red, white and blue. Be aware that these are dealer, shop and auction prices. When found at an estate or garage sale, costs may be less.

"**A Toast to the Flag,**" by Daly & Ortman,
1937.. $8
"**A-M-E-R-I-C-A Means I Love You My
Yankee Land,**" by Frost, 1917, WWII 10
"**After the Was Is Over,**" by Pourmon,
Sterling & Woodruff, 1918, cover artist
Starmer 15
"**All Aboard for Dixie Land,**" by Yellen &
Cobb, 1913, cover artist Starmer...................... 7
"**America Forever March Song,**" by E.T.
Paull, 1917, cover artist E.T. Paull 30
"**America I Love You,**" by Leslie & Gottler,
1915, cover artist Barbelle 18
"**America, Make the World Safe for De-
mocracy,**" 1918, by Vivo & Levy, cover
artist Pfeiffer.. 12

"Anchors Aweigh" Sheet Music

"**Anchors Aweigh, Song of the Navy,**" by
Zimmermann, WWII (ILLUS.).............................. 5

"Any Bonds Today?" Sheet Music

"**Any Bonds Today?**" by Berlin, 1941,
theme song of the National Defense Sav-
ings Program (ILLUS.) 25

"Are You From Dixie?" Sheet Music

"**Are You From Dixie?**" by Yellen, 1915,
cover artist Starmer (ILLUS.) 20
"**Ballad for Americans,**" by Latoche &
Robinson, 1918 7
"**Beginning of the U.S.A.,**" by Costello &
Vanderveer, 1916 8

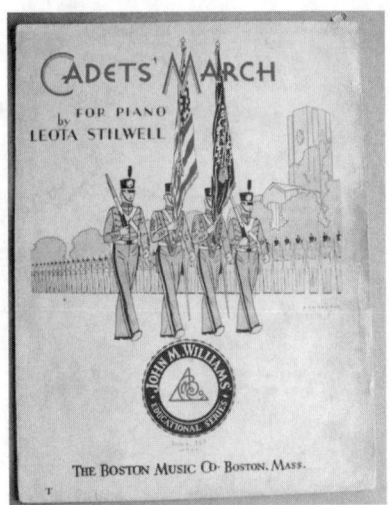

"Cadet's March" Sheet Music

"Cadet's March," by Stilwell, 1932 (ILLUS.).......... **4**

"Don't Forget the Salvation Army" Sheet Music

"Don't Forget the Salvation Army (My Doughnut Girl)," by Brown, Frisch & Leffingwell, cover artist E.E., 1919 (ILLUS.) **30**

"Capitol City March" Sheet Music

"Capitol City March," by Lincoln, features U.S. Capitol Building, 1911 (ILLUS.)............... **20**

"Columbia March," by Lewis (all royalty earnings to provide during WWI), 1917 .... **25**

"Dear Old Stars and Stripes," by Reynolds, 1905.. **12**

"Dear Old Stars and Stripes Good-bye," by Briggs & Wilson, 1902.................................. **20**

"Father of the Land We Love" Sheet Music

"Father of the Land We Love," by Cohan, cover artist Flagg, 1931 (ILLUS.) **50**

"Fighting Navy of the Good Old U.S.A.," by Shannon & Vandersloot, cover artist Starmer, 1918... **18**

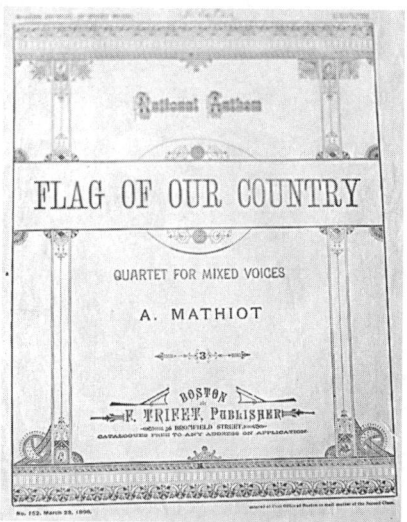

"Flag of Our Country" Sheet Music

"Good-Bye France" Sheet Music

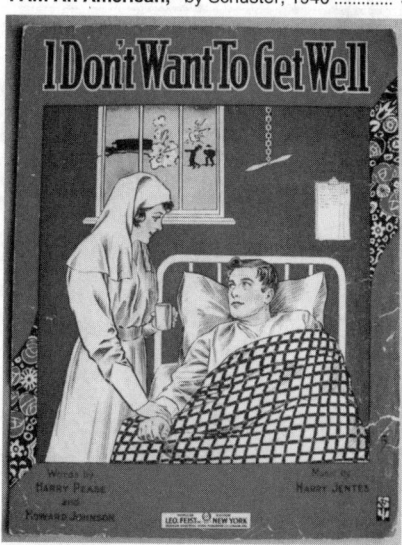

"I Don't Want to Get Well" Sheet Music

"I Know Now" Sheet Music from "The Singing Marine"

"Patriotic Compositions (The Blue and the Gray)" Sheet Music

"Johnny's In Town" Sheet Music

"Pledge of Allegiance to the Flag" Sheet Music

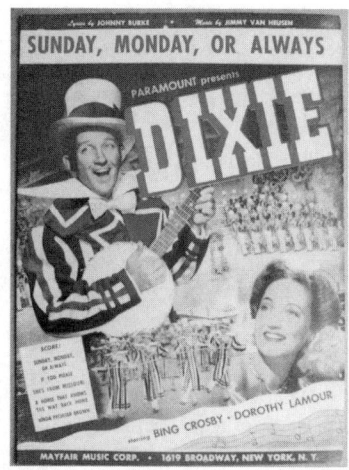

"Sunday, Monday, or Always" Sheet Music

"The Marines' Hymn" Sheet Music

"The Navy Took Them Over and the Navy Will Bring Them Back" Sheet Music

"The Girls of America March" Sheet Music

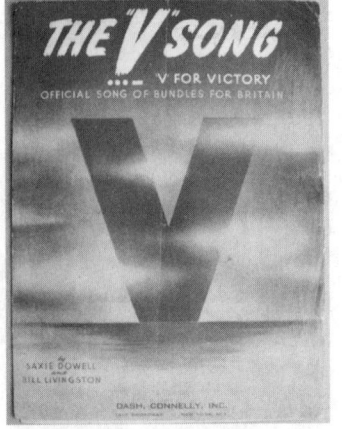

"The 'V' Song" Song Sheet

"We'll Win the Victory" Sheet Music

"Where Do We Go From Here" Sheet Music

"You're A Grand Old Flag" Sheet Music

SIGNS & SIGNBOARDS

Framed Pabst Blue Ribbon Beer Sign

Beer, "Pabst Blue Ribbon Beer," rectangular color lithograph scene of two bottles
w/blue ribbons tied around the necks, a
filled glass & a plate of oysters, signed
wood frame, ca. 1920s, Pabst Brewing
Company, Milwaukee, Wisconsin,
22 x 25 1/2" (ILLUS.) **$225-300**

Ziegler's Beer Sign

Beer, "Ziegler's Beer," rectangular tin
w/cardboard back, black w/bottle on
right, white & white outlined w/red lettering reading "Drink Ziegler's Beer - Beaver
Dam,   Wisconsin," ca.   1920s,
8 1/4 x 11 1/2" (ILLUS.) **175-225**

Cook's Beer & Ale Sign

Beer & ale, "Cook's Beer and Ale," tin, oval
blue center w/hand holding a bottle of beer
& a bottle of ale, self-framed brown border
marked at the top "Cook's Goldblume" & at
the bottom "Beer and Ale," F.W. Cook
Company, Evansville, Indiana, ca. 1920,
14 x 17 1/2" (ILLUS.) **175-225**

White Rock Lithia Water Sign

Beverage, "White Rock Lithia Water," oval tin, embossed self-edge tin w/beautiful lithograph scene of fairy kneeling on rock at water's edge, by Chas. W. Shonk Co., wear on self-edge, minor scratches & dings, 16 1/2 x 19 3/4" (ILLUS.).................. **1,210**

Boat, "Starcraft Boats," rectangular embossed tin, yellow, blue & red, image of boat on water, blue & red letters read "Starcraft - Metal Boats of Distinction - Authorized Dealer," 17 3/8 x 23 3/8" (grainy paint, flecks & wear) **121**

"Boots and Shoes Repaired" Sign

Boot & shoe repair, wood, rectangular, old painted surface w/black & red lettering reading "Boots and Shoes Repaired," signed "Gray," molded black frame, America, 19th c., 18 x 31 3/4" (ILLUS.) **1,293**

Lyre-frame Bootmaker's Sign

Bootmaker, trade-type, zinc, molded in the form of a boot within a lyre-shaped frame, the boot painted red, the frame painted mustard, iron wall bracket, America, 19th c., 37 3/4 x 38" (ILLUS.).............................. **3,525**

Baum's Polish Sign

Car polish, "Baum's Polish," rectangular, die-cut cardboard, yellow w/image of early red auto w/woman at wheel, red & black letters reading "Baum's Wonderful Polish - Shines Like Magic - Never Injures - Will Not Scratch the Finest Surfaces," cutouts at center to display a product bottle, 9 1/4 x 10 3/8" (ILLUS.)........................ **187**

Car radio, "Motorola Car Radio," rectangular tin, double-sided, both sides white & blue w/red & white letters reading "Motorola - Car Radio - Installation Station," 20 x 28" (nicks, scratches & soiling) **110**

"Cattle Crossing," tin, rectangular, black painted cattle & stenciled lettering reading "Cattle Crossing," black wood frame, America, late 19th - early 20th c., weathered surface, 20 x 25 3/4" (ILLUS. bottom row left w/various signs, below) **646**

Various Signs

Nabisco Building Logo Sign

Cereal, "Nabisco," die-cut porcelain architectural building sign w/reverse lip, company logo, red & white, removed from a
corporate building, bends & chips at "antenna," 33 1/4 x 48", unusual & scarce
item (ILLUS.) **385**

Kis-Me Gum Sign

Chewing gum, "Kis-Me Chewing Gum,"
die-cut cardboard in wood frame, scene
of two young girls under a yellow umbrella, one dressed in long blue dress, the
other in pink, marked at bottom "'Kis-Me'
- Kis-Me Gum Co., Louisville, KY," ca.
1900, 11 x 13" (ILLUS.) **550-700**

Wrigley's Gum Trolley Sign

Chewing gum, "Wrigley's Gum," rectangular cardboard, trolley-type, yellow
w/"Help Yourself! - Wrigley's" in black &
red letters & "Good For You" in white letters on green arrow pointing to product
displays, "On Every Dealer's Counter" in
yellow letters at bottom, wood frame, ca.
1927, 12 1/4 x 22" (ILLUS.) **750-850**

La Venga Cigars Sign

Cigars, "La Venga Cigars," rectangular, re-
verse-painting on glass, black w/logo in
center flanked by embossed brass
scrolls, "La Venga" above & "Havana Cigars - Celestino Vega & Co. Tampa, Fla."
below, wood frame, ca. 1910,
20 1/2 x 26 1/2" (ILLUS.) **235-300**

Optimo Cigars Sign

Cigars, "Optimo Cigars," rectangular tin
w/center oval depicting bust of man
w/mustache & wearing hat, tie & coat
w/colorful tropical scene in background,
reads "Optimo - Mild - Aromatic - Sweet,"
wood frame, ca. 1910, 23 x 27"
(ILLUS.) **475-550**

San Felice Cigars Sign

Cigars, "San Felice Cigars," rectangular, embossed tin, yellow w/center black circle w/box of cigars, black & red lettering reads "San Felice Cigars - 'For Gentlemen of Good Taste'" & "5¢" on each side, wear & scratches, 11 1/2 x 17 1/2" (ILLUS.)... 182

White Label Cigars Sign

Cigars, "White Label Cigars," rectangular embossed colored tin w/suspension chain, image of open box of cigars next to "Smoke The White Label 5¢ Cigars - The Favorite Everywhere," 10 x 13 1/2" (ILLUS.) 288

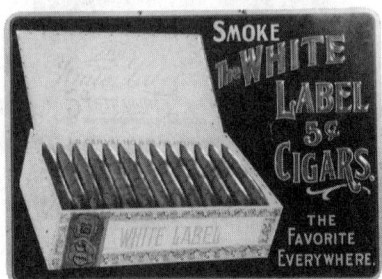

White Label Cigars Sign, Ca. 1900

Cigars, "White Label Cigars," rectangular tin, black w/lithographed image of white box containing cigars on the left, right side marked in yellow "Smoke - The Favorite Everywhere," green embossed letters outlined in yellow read "The White Label 5¢ Cigars," litho by Sentenne & Green, New York, ca. 1900, 9 1/2 x 14" (ILLUS.) 185-250

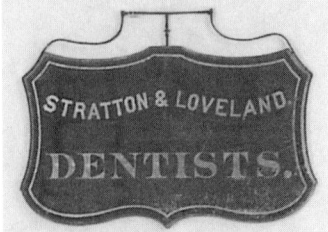

Dentist Trade Sign

Dentist, trade-type, wood & iron, "STRATTON & LOVELAND, DENTISTS" in gilt lettering against a brown ground on double-sided shield-shaped sign w/iron frame, America, 19th c., 23 x 33" (ILLUS.)...... 558

Dry Goods Sign

Dry goods, trade-type, wood, black painted panels w/white lettering reading "McBURNEY'S FOR DRY GOODS CARPETS AND CLOAKS TIPTON IOWA," America, early 19th c., 36 x 48" (ILLUS.)...... 588

Exterminator, trade-type, "Rose Exterminator Co.," oval, die-cut porcelain, white w/owl logo bottom center & red & blue letters reading "Rose - Exterminator Co. - Since 1860 - Wise Protection," 11 1/4 x 18 3/4" 149

Colt Firearms Sign

Firearms, "Colt Firearms," rectangular, lithograph of smiling girl wearing Western hat, brown skirt & belt, white blouse w/striped brown neckerchief, ammunition belt around hips & holding pistol, ca. 1900, wood frame, this version without Colt imprint cost 25¢, 39 1/2 x 37" (ILLUS.) 1,800-2,500

Ceresota Flour Die-cut Sign

![Footwear sign]

"Footwear" Sign

Flour, "Ceresota Flour," die-cut cardboard in wood frame, small boy wearing boots & large hat sitting on stool & slicing a loaf of bread, flour sack behind him, marked "Ceresota Flour - Prize Bread Flour of Minnesota," by Edward Deutsch & Co., Chicago, Illinois, ca. 1900, 13 x 17 1/2" (ILLUS.).. **1,300-1,600**

Footwear, trade-type, wood, rectangular, w/carved & gilded letters reading "FOOT-WEAR" on black painted ground, Chattanooga, Tennessee, 6 1/4 x 70 1/4" (ILLUS., top of page) **646**

Standard Gasoline Mickey Mouse Sign

Gasoline, "Standard Gasoline," rectangular cardboard, coated cardboard, Disney theme showing Mickey Mouse on skis, his muffler marked "Unsurpassed," minor edge & field wear w/a few creases, 14 x 17" (ILLUS.).. **1,100**

Gasoline, "White Rose Motor Gasoline," rectangular, lithographed tin, green & black, rose blossom & bud shown in upper right corner, reads "White Rose Motor Gasoline and National Carbonless Motor Oil," 9 3/4 x 13 3/4" (edge wear, soiling & wrinkles) **743**

Gunmaker, trade-type, pine, carved in the form of a percussion musket w/oversized hammer, buttstock is laminated wood w/round nails added, 118" l. (pine refinished, trigger guard partially missing) **385**

Hall's Hair Renewer Sign

Hair renewer, "Hall's Hair Renewer," rectangular chromolithographic depicting a Victorian couple, the man holding a hand mirror, the woman w/calf-length hair handing him a bottle, w/"Use Hall's Vegetable Sicilian Hair Renewer - And your thin GRAY LOCKS will thicken up and be restored to their YOUTHFUL COLOR AND BEAUTY," & "R.P. Hall & Co. Proprietors – Nashua, N.H.," 16 1/2 x 22 1/2" (ILLUS.) **316**

![Van Camp Hardware Sign]

Van Camp Hardware Sign

Hardware, "Van Camp Hardware," round die-cut tin, flange-type, blue & white w/center image of windmill under large red letters reading "Van Camp - Trade Mark" & white letters around border reading "Highest Grade - Van Camp Hardware & Iron Co. Indianapolis, Ind." & blue letters on flange reading "Goods Bearing This Trade-Mark Are Of The Highest Quality," litho by New York Metal Sign Works, New York, ca. 1890, 13 1/2 x 18" (ILLUS.) **650-750**

"HENRY," tin, in the shape of a conical hat w/wide brim, painted in red w/black band, the front inscribed "HENRY" in gilt, wall bracket included, America, 19th c., wear to paint, scratches, 25" d., 22 1/2" h. (ILLUS. bottom row center w/various signs) **4,406**

Foster Hose Supporters Sign

Hose supporters, "Foster Hose Supporters," rectangular, porcelain over cardboard, image of corset & hose supporters & woman wearing red skirt & green blouse, reads "The Foster Hose Supporters - 'The Name is on the buckles,'" litho by F.F. Pulver Co., Rochester, New York, ca. 1890, 9 x 17" (ILLUS.) **900-1,300**

House painting, oval, brown lettering spelling "C.D. HAVENS HOUSE PAINTING" on blue ground, black frame, America, 19th c., weathered paint, loss & cracks on frame, 20 1/2 x 31" (ILLUS. middle row left w/various signs).................................. **764**

Invincible Motor Insurance Sign

Insurance, "Invincible Motor Insurance," rectangular, lithographed tin, green w/image of battleship & touring car, marked "Invincible - Motor Insurance by Instalments - Invincible Policies Limited," British origin, minor edge wear, 9 1/2 x 20" (ILLUS.)... **242**

Traders Insurance Company Sign

Insurance, "Traders Insurance Company," rectangular tin, lithograph by Charles Shonk, black w/gold lettering reading "The Traders Insurance Co. Chicago," wood frame, ca. 1910, 17 x 23" (ILLUS.) **325-425**

Jeweler, trade-type, painted tin & cast iron, double-sided, a central tin black & white painted watch dial mounted in a decorated cast-iron frame flanked by facing images of Father Time & inscribed "Jewelry, Watches and Clocks" w/gold paint, silver & black-painted surfaces, late 19th c., 24" w., 29 1/2" h. (imperfections) **2,185**

Mission Orange Juice Sign

Juice, "Mission Orange Juice," rectangular tin, black w/yellow sun & sunrays, embossed red letters outlined in white &

white letters reading "Drink Mission Orange - It's Real Juice," wood frame, ca. 1920s, 13 x 31" (ILLUS.)........................ **125-175**

Pearl Oil Kerosene Sign

Kerosene, "Pearl Oil Kerosene," rectangular cardboard, string-hung, center w/kerosene can, label reads "Pearl Oil Kerosene for Oil Heaters, Cook Stoves & Lamps," household images at bottom, also marked "We Sell Heat and Light - Refined by Standard Oil Company California," minor soiling & warping & wear, 10 3/8 x 14" (ILLUS.) **303**

Sign for Franklin Inn

Lodgings, wood, "Franklin Inn," two-sided polychrome sign depicting a stylized portrait of Benjamin Franklin in oval, w/painted lettering reading "FRANKLIN INN" & "J.H. WINGERT," applied molded frame, wrought iron hardware, America, 19th c., 34 x 62" (ILLUS.)...................................... **5,875**

Milk, wood, rectangular two-sided sign w/blue asphaltum ground w/white & light blue border & white lettering reading "PURE MILK FOR BABIES MILK STA-TION of the Visiting Nurse Asso.," black frame, America, early-20th c., minor paint losses to frame, 12 x 18" (ILLUS. top row right w/various signs)........................ **940**

Monogram Motor Oil Sign

Motor oil, "Monogram Motor Oil," rectangular cardboard w/wood lathe board backing, depicts a long line of soldiers in grey & white uniforms w/large black hats, the lineup disappearing into the distance, white top w/red letters reading "Monogram Motor Oil," the lower section shaded yellow, green & gold w/black letters reading "Stands Up!," glossy slick finish, crazing & cracking to finish, scattered nail holes at borders, 11 1/4 x 35 1/2" (ILLUS.).. **248**

Motor oil, "Pennfield Motor Oil," rectangular, embossed tin, image of oil derrick & red letters on yellow read "Pennfield" w/yellow lettering on black reading "Motor Oils - Finest from Pennsylvania Fields," 13 3/4 x 19 5/8" (discoloration at left side, few small wrinkles & scratches) **330**

Rajah Motor Oil Sign

Motor oil, "Rajah Motor Oil," die-cut tin, top w/head of man wearing turban & marked "100% Pure Pennsylvania," the rectangular base w/rounded bottom reads "Double Mileage - Rajah Motor Oil - A Penn-O-Tex Product," yellow & blue, three mount holes at center, scratches & wear, small minor bend at top left edge, 10 x 28" (ILLUS.).. **468**

Motor oil, "Richlube Motor Oil," rectangular tin, double-sided rack-type, red w/yellow & white letters reading "Richlube - All-

Weather Motor Oil - 30¢ Per Quart - 100% Pure Pennsylvania," date coded 7-38, 12 x 16" (minor edge wear, light surface scratches).. **523**

Optician, trade-type, lithographed metal & neon, a small rectangular black metal frame around a printed colored pair of eyes framed by neon spectacles, early 20th c., 28 1/2" l., 11 1/8" h. **805**

Optician, trade-type, wood & glass, in the shape of eyeglasses, eyes painted on board w/carved wood gilt eyeglass frames, glass panel lenses, America, 19th c., 13 1/2 x 39" (ILLUS. top row left w/various signs)..................................... **4,113**

Plumber, trade-type, wood, w/gilt lettering reading "R.L. SPEIRS & CO. PLUMB-ERS STEAM & GAS FITTERS," on sand textured black painted ground, America, late 19th c., 32 x 37" (ILLUS. middle row right w/various signs)............................... **558**

Saddle shop, trade-type, gilded zinc molded in the form of a horse's head, America, 19th c., 12 x 15" (ILLUS. bottom row right w/various signs)................................... **4,113**

Walsh Shoe Repair Sign

Shoe repair, trade-type, plywood cut in the shape of a figure w/hammer & awl repairing a shoe, rectangular base w/black painted cutout lettering reading "WALSH SHOE REPAIR SYSTEM" on gold-painted ground, America, second quarter 20th c., 34 x 38" (ILLUS.) **353**

Sign for "Shoe Repairing"

Shoe repair, trade-type, tin, rectangular, drawing of a man's shoe in center, black & white lettering reading "SHOE RE-PAIRING," painted red ground, molded black wooden frame, America, early 20th c., scratches & frame loss, 17 1/4 x 18" (ILLUS.) **999**

Arch-top Shoe Repair Sign

Shoe repair, trade-type, wood, rectangular w/arched top & columns at sides, painted black w/gilt lettering reading "SHOE RE-PAIRS DONE ON PREMISES" in center panel, "DONE TO TIME" & "SEND US YOUR NEXT" on side columns, gilt high-lights, America, 19th c., 22 x 79 1/2" (ILLUS.).. **823**

Red Goose Shoes Sign

Shoes, "Red Goose Shoes," rectangular paper, red goose holding black high-top shoe by the laces in its beak, reads "Red Goose Shoes - The All Leather Shoe For Boys and Girls - 'They're Half the Fun of Having Feet,'" green, yellow, red & black, ca. 1910, Friedman-Shelby Shoes, 8 x 18" (ILLUS.)........................... **275-325**

Red Goose Shoes Sign with Crying Boy

Shoes, "Red Goose Shoes," rectangular paper, scene of mother examining shoe of crying boy, reads "Don't blame the Boy - Buy him All-Leather Shoes - Red Goose Shoes for Boys for Girls - The Friedman-Shelby 'All-Leather Shoe,'" yellow, red & green, ca. 1910, Friedman-Shelby Shoes, 8 x 18" (ILLUS.)........................... **275-325**

Shoes, "Star Brand Shoes," round, reverse-painted on convex glass, white back-ground w/red & yellow letters reading "Star Brand - Shoes - Are Better," wood frame, ca. 1920s, 22" d. (ILLUS.) **450-600**

Sign maker, trade-type, wood, in the shape of an artist's palette w/three brushes, gilt lettering spelling "COMMERCIAL NEON ELECTRIC" in gilt w/gilt border against brown ground, America, early-20th c., 24 x 38 1/2" (ILLUS. middle row center w/various signs)... **353**

Andrew Jergens & Co. Soap Sign

Soap, "Andrew Jergens Toilet Soap," rect-angular, die-cut cardboard in wood frame, depicts two young girls in long dresses w/a large white & brown dog, marked at lower left corner "Andrew Jer-gens & Co. Fine Toilet Soaps - Always Pure," ca. 1880, rare, 20 x 22 1/2" (ILLUS.) **1,500-1,800**

Smile Orange Beverage Sign

Soft drink, "Drink Smile," die-cut tin, dou-ble-sided flange-type, round, black & or-ange w/logo at bottom, both sides w/same display, minor scratches, 10 x 12 3/8" (ILLUS.)....................................... **385**

Star Brand Shoes Sign

Green Spot Orange-Ade Sign

Soft drink, "Green Spot Orange-Ade," rect-angular cardboard, young woman re-moving a bottle from ice-filled cooler, reads "Thirsty?," cooler marked "Ice Cold - Green Spot - Orange-Ade 5¢," ca. 1920s, 23 x 33" (ILLUS.).......................... **125-175**

Howel's Root Beer Figural Sign

Soft drink, "Howel's Root Beer," embossed die-cut tin bottle shape, minor soiling & wear, 8 3/8 x 29 1/2" (ILLUS.)........................ **413**

Hires Root Beer Sign

Soft drink, "Hires Root Beer," rectangular tin, flange-type, green w/yellow & black lettering reading "Hires - Made with Roots - Barks - Herbs - So Refreshing," ca. 1940s, 12 x 14" (ILLUS.) **225-300**

Kist Beverage Die-cut Sign

Soft drink, "Kist," die-cut cardboard dimen-sional easel-back display, young woman in low-cut black top w/bottle & glass, background of large pink flowers & leaves, reading "Get Kist here - Orange and Other Flavors," edge wear, 5 x 9 x 12" (ILLUS.) **237**

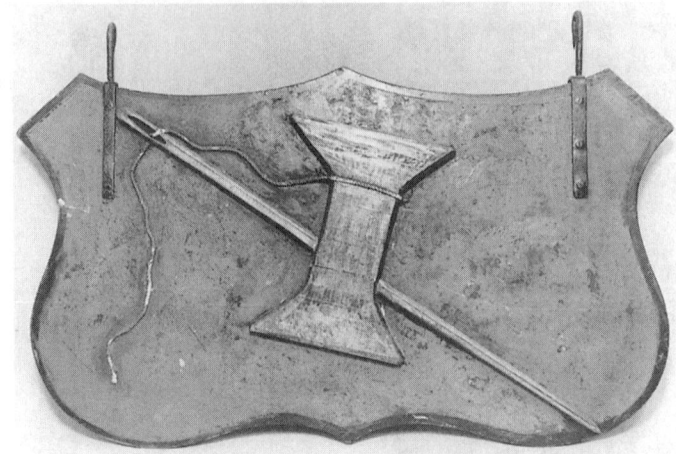

Tailor/Seamstress Trade Sign

Lime Cola Sign

Soft drink, "Lime Cola," round, celluloid over cardboard, string-hung, tan w/bottle in center & reading "Drink - Lime Cola - Trade-Mark Registered," 9" d. (ILLUS.)........ **413**

Nehi Sign

Soft drink, "Nehi," rectangular cardboard w/easel back, outdoor scene of two boys running, reads "Hey Gang! Mom's Treat-

ing Us to Nehi - in Your Favorite Flavor," ca. 1930, 26 x 39" (ILLUS.).................... **550-750**

Orange-Julep Sign

Soft drink, "Orange-Julep," rectangular paper, black w/yellow lettering outlined in red, "Drink - In Bottles - At Fountains - How's Orange-Julep - The Perfection of Orange Drinks," wood frame, ca. 1915, 12 x 30 1/2" (ILLUS.)............................... **125-175**

Peninsular Stoves Flange-type Sign

Stove, "'Peninsular Stoves,'" rectangular, flange-type, porcelain on tin, black, white & red, marked on ribbon at top "A Guarantee Bond - With Every Stove" & "'Pen-

insular' - Furnaces - Stoves and Ranges"
w/"Warranted - The Best," ca. 1890,
15 1/2 x 23 1/2" (ILLUS.).................. **1,800-2,500**
Tailor/Seamstress, trade-type, wood, two-
sided oblong shield shape w/applied
spool & threaded needle on one side &
scissors on the other, old gold, black,
red-brown & green paint w/evidence of
other colors underneath, two wrought-
iron hooks on top for hanging, 31 x 48"
(ILLUS., top of previous page) **2,420**

Mennen's Talcum Powder Sign

Talcum powder, "Mennen's Talcum Powder," rectangular, die-cut cardboard in
wood frame, depicts young child writing
in a book w/a quill pen, the page w/black
letters reading "Mennen's Borated Talcum Toilet Powder - For Infants and
Adults - It Cures: Prickly Heat, Nettle
Rash, Chafing, Measles, Eczema,
Sweaty Feet, Pimples, Etc. - Delightful
After Shaving - 25¢ Per Box" & at bottom
"Mennen's Sure Corn Killer," ca. 1880,
rare, 19 1/2 x 22 1/2" (ILLUS.) **1,500-1,800**
Tires, "Corduroy Tires," rectangular, embossed self-framed tin, red & black
w/white letters reading "Replace With
Corduroy - Factory Fresh Tires - Extra
Quality Since 1919," 15 1/4 x 60" (soil-
ing, scratches & wear, minor denting at
edges) **413**

Savage Tires Sign

Tires, "Savage Tires," oil board tullograph,
depicts "Little Heap" leaving a roadside
sign & offering a peace pipe to a motorist
w/poem about the little Indian & the quality of Savage Tires at bottom, framed,
surface wear, 23 x 30" (ILLUS.).................. **1,760**

Bagley's Smoking Tobacco Sign

Tobacco, "Bagley's Smoking Tobacco," figural wood covered w/paper, window motion display-type w/arms that move, figure of a man wearing long red trousers,
long-tailed grey jacket, yellow vest & red
bow tie, the black top hat marked "Bagley's Long Tom Smokin Tobacco," ca.
1890, 36" h. (ILLUS.)....................... **1,100-1,500**
Tobacco, "Bull Durham Tobacco," color
lithograph, shows bullfight scene in arena w/spectators in stands and banner
w/"A Royal Victor - Bull Durham," in original   veneer   frame   w/label,
33 1/2 x 51 1/2" (stains & veneer dam-
age at one end) **385**

M. Hommel Wines Sign

Wine, "M. Hommel Wines," rectangular,
lithograph w/center scene of vineyard below medals & bunches of grapes flanked
by wine bottles, top marked "M. Hommel -

Highest Awards Over All American Champagnes - At World's Columbian Exposition - 1893," the bottom marked "Sandusky, Ohio - U.S.A.," wood frame, litho by Wittemann Litho Co., New York, ca. 1910, 28 x 34 1/2" (ILLUS.) **225-300**

SILHOUETTES

These cut-out paper portraits in profile were named after Etienne de Silhouette, Louis XV's unpopular minister of finance and an amateur profile cutter. As originally applied, the term was synonymous with cheapness, or anything reduced to its simplest state. These substitutes for the more expensive oil painting or miniatures were popular from about 1770 until 1850 when daguerreotype images replaced the vogue. Silhouettes may be either hollow-cut, with the head cut away leaving the white paper frame for mounting against a dark background, or the profile itself may be cut from black paper and pasted to a light background.

Bust of boy, hollow-cut portrait of boy w/high collar, black cloth background, black oval frame w/brass liner, 4 1/2 x 5" (minor water stains, wear to frame)............ **$165**

Bust of girl, black ink portrait of girl in profile w/long, curly hair & ruffled collar, black oval frame, back w/collection labels & inked note "No label but undoubtedly by S. Houghton", 4 5/8 x 5 3/8" **248**

Bust of man, black ink profile of man w/pigtail & ruffled collar, hair, ribbon & collar done in grey wash, embossed oval frame w/convex lens, 4 x 4 1/2" **303**

Bust of man, grey ink profile of middle-aged man wearing white neck scarf, backing paper has stenciled label reading "Herve Artist, 172 Oxford St.," black composition frame w/brass liner & acorn & oak leaf hanger, 4 1/4 x 5 1/8" **110**

Bust of man, hollow-cut portrait in profile of a man w/inked hair & collars, black painted frame w/printed paper mat & brass liner, 7 x 7 3/4"............................... **330**

Bust of man, hollow-cut portrait of man in profile, w/embossed "Museum" (Peale) stamp, mahogany veneer frame, 5 5/8 x 6 5/8" (frame has wear & split but old glass) **440**

Bust of man, hollow-cut portrait of man in profile, w/partial embossed "Peales Museum" label w/eagle, traces of ghost image of another silhouette, black painted frame w/gilt beading, 4 x 5" (small water stain, wear to frame)............................... **165**

Bust of man, hollow-cut portrait of man in profile wearing scarf & ruffled shirt, penciled hair & chalk details, black frame w/gilt liner, 4 3/4 x 5 1/2" **275**

Bust of man, hollow-cut profile of man wearing frock coat & ruffled shirt, details painted in gold on painted black background, hair painted in black, beveled frame, 5 7/8 x 6 1/2" (stains) **165**

Bust of man, identified on later paper label as "Dr. Oliver Hubbard, Salem, Mass. - born 1772," reverse-painted on glass in black w/eglomisé mat, black & gilt frame, 4 1/2 x 5 1/4" **303**

Bust of woman, black ink on paper of young woman in profile w/hair held up w/comb & wearing gold bead necklace, papier-mâché frame w/black paint & brass liner & acorn hanger, 3 3/4 x 4 5/8" (water stain) **110**

Bust of woman, black ink w/bonnet, hair & collar in white ink, old gilt frame, 3 3/4 x 4 3/4" (minor paper darkening w/traces of silver foil) **605**

Bust of woman, black paper cutout of woman wearing ruffled bonnet, papier-mâché frame w/black paint & brass acorn hanger, 5 x 6 5/8" (wear, brass liner is replaced)............................... **138**

Bust of woman, cutout of middle-aged woman wearing bonnet & shawl facing left, in oval opening, black w/gold ink detail, embossed gold-colored metal liner w/repainted black frame, 4 1/2" w., 5 1/4" h. **220**

Bust of woman, cutout portrait of the wife or mother of Thomas Seabert, penciled label on back, detail in gold ink, beveled mahogany veneer frame, 5 1/8 x 5 5/8" **413**

Bust of woman, elaborately braided & sausage-curled hair, white lace collar, black ink accented w/gold, gutta-percha floral case w/brass liner, 2 1/2 x 3 7/8" **165**

Bust of woman, hollow-cut portrait of woman w/hair comb, her dress w/a high lace collar & blue ribbon done in watercolor, glued down to black paper, late mat w/early gilt frame, 4 5/8 x 6 1/4" (wear)........ **358**

Bust of woman, hollow-cut profile of woman w/ruff collar & hair up in a bun, faded black cloth ground, round copper frame w/silvered rim glass, 3 3/4" d. **165**

Bust of young woman, hollow-cut portrait of woman in profile, w/embossed "Museum" (Peale) stamp, a few impressed outlines, gilt frame, 4 1/8 x 5 1/2" (frame has some gold repaint) **220**

Bust of young woman, hollow-cut silhouette of young woman w/upturned nose & w/her hair in a bun, inked date "Jan. 29, 1808," paper backing, worn black frame w/gilt liner, 5 1/2 x 6 1/2" h. **358**

Busts of man & woman, hollow-cut portraits of man in profile w/black ink detail to hair & clothes, woman wears tortoiseshell comb, in separate pine frames w/embossed brass coverings, 4 1/2 x 5 1/4", pr.............................. **990**

Busts of man & woman, inked portraits in profile of husband & wife, in separate refinished pine frames, 6 x 7", pr. **440**

Busts of man & woman, portraits in profile of husband w/wavy hair & wife w/ringlets, w/both cutout & embossed details, in oval black painted frames w/worn gilt liners, 4 1/4 x 5 1/4", pr. (one w/repaired edge) **165**

Busts of man & woman, two facing profile portraits by the same hand combined in one frame, both w/embossed "Peales Museum" labels w/eagles, mahogany beveled frame, 7 x 10 1/4"............................... **440**

Family group, cutout figures in profile of mother, father & four children of various sizes, partial penciled background & a few inked details, frame w/old black & worn gilt liner, 6 1/4 x 8 1/4" (ink details may have been enhanced later) **660**

Family Group Silhouette

Family group, mother, daughter w/doll & two sons, one w/horse pull toy, one w/cap, all done in black ink detailed in gold, 12 3/4 x 18 5/8", in bird's-eye frame w/gold repainted liner 16 1/4 x 22 1/8", smudges, stains, surface wear, edge damage to frame (ILLUS.) **1,980**

Detail of a Hutton Silhouette

Family group, nine full-length silhouettes of members of the Hutton family (& servant) of Birmingham, individual descriptions handwritten in ink both on backs of silhouettes & below them on pages, two pages w/images on both sides, by Edouart, probably from one of his copy folios, stains, foxing, minor edge damage, 10 1/4 x 14" (ILLUS. detail of one page) **825**

Full-length figure of cadet, portrait in profile of young cadet in uniform holding cap & dagger, black ink w/gold inked features, framed (minor fading to eglomisé mat) **880**

Full-length figure of child, cutout portrait of child in profile wearing long dress &

pantaloons, glued on laid paper, gilt frame, 7 1/4 x 8 3/4" (some foxing) **825**

Full-length figure of "Hon. Oliver Hatcher," cutout portrait of hatted figure in profile holding cane, handpainted background in ink wash on laid paper, signed "Aug. Edouart - fecit 1840," gilt frame, 12 1/4 x 15 1/2" **990**

Full-length figure of man holding cane, cutout figure probably from portfolio, identified on back as "Geo. Frederick Muntz Birmingham 23d. Jany. 1838," paper watermark "Weatherley 1835," cane & arm separate, matted w/contemporary wood frame, 13 3/4 x 16" **220**

Full-length figure of man in profile, cutout figure w/lithograph background of a balcony, signed in ink "Aug. Edouart, fecit 1846 Saratoga," bird's-eye maple veneer frame, 8 1/2 x 12" **1,650**

Full-length figure of "Rebecca Smith Stamsbury," (?) profile of woman carrying bouquet of flowers, handpainted background in ink wash on laid paper, signed "Aug. Edouart - fecit 1841," beveled mahogany veneer frame w/gilt liner, 11 1/4 x 14 1/4" (light foxing) **770**

Full-length figure of woman, profile portrait of woman wearing lace bonnet & collar, shawl & full-skirted dress, holding a book & bouquet of flowers, black ink w/details & features in white & gold, beveled frame w/alligatored varnish & gilt liner, 10 3/4 x 13" (minor wear to liner) **770**

Watercolor-decorated Silhouette

Full-length figure of young girl, profile of girl playing w/yellow ball & cup, face & arm are in black, while green dress & shoes, dark blue sash, white pantaloons & yellow ball & cup are in watercolor, 4 1/4 x 6 3/4, matted w/gilt frame 6 1/4 x 8 1/8", some foxing & stains, wear to frame (ILLUS.) **3,630**

SNOWDOMES

Although some snowglobes were produced in the late 19th and early 20th centuries, since the 1930s domes have been manufactured as advertising pieces or as point-of-sale giveaways for certain companies. These companies have included Coca-Cola, IBM and Goodyear. Prices for these can vary from $15 to $60, depending on the material used and the company brand.

Airplane, shows airplane in a dive, w/decal on front w/"Cochran Airfield," 1940s, rare w/decal **$110**

Art Deco woman, figure of nude woman, on dark ceramic base, Germany, 1920s, rare 130

Black Watch Bagpiper Snowdome

Black Watch bagpiper, bottle-shaped dome, holding 5" h. painted metal figure of kilted bagpiper manufactured by Caledonian Hand-Crafts of Edinburgh, Scotland, souvenir of Scotland, 1960s (ILLUS.).. 20

Musical Christmas Snowdome

Christmas, musical, round base w/cylindrical dome, winding the base causes music to play & base to rotate, w/snow swirling onto decorated Christmas tree inside & figures moving around base, Hong Kong, 1970s (ILLUS.)..................................... 50

Civil War commemorative, in honor of 100th Anniversary of the war, various scenes of combat w/Union or Confederate flags, on plastic base of various colors, some w/identifying decals, 1960s............. 18

Cowgirl, figure of hatted cowgirl, dark base, Atlas Crystal Works, 1940s 60

Davy Crockett, made by Driss Company of Chicago, Illinois, decal on base features Davy Crockett in profile, 1950s...................... 65

Eisenhower (Dwight), bust of Eisenhower as general, decal on front reads "General Dwight D. Eisenhower - Commander in Chief of Allied Invasion Forces. Atlas Crystal Works - Covington, Tennessee," 1940s 80

Empire State Building, on black Bakelite base that doubles as ashtray, 1940s.............. 50

Empire State Building, souvenir of New York City, dark ceramic base (generic globes were manufactured & decal could be added by each souvenir shop), 1940s 60

Fisherman, figure of man standing in boat w/fish at end of his line jumping through water, heavy dark base, sold as souvenir of various fishing/tourist sites in Ontario, 1940s 55

Hoover Dam, plastic dome w/scene of dam, white base w/plate reading "Hoover Dam," 1970s 12

Liberty Bell, souvenir of Philadelphia, identifying decal on front, 1940s 85

Lincoln (Abraham), bust of Lincoln in white, "Abraham Lincoln" on tag in front, 1940s 200

Lone Ranger, figure of Lone Ranger on green Bakelite base w/decal reading "The Lone Ranger - the Last Roundup," 1940s 55

MacArthur (Douglas), bust of MacArthur in white, tag on front reads "General Douglas MacArthur - America's Hero," 1940s 110

Marine Corps Training Base at Parris Island, shows uniformed World War II Marine saluting, on dark base w/decal showing location, rare, 1940s.................................. 100

Mountain Choir Snowdome

Mountain choir, plastic white oval base, globe showing choir singing is held in frame molded to resemble Alpine village, 1970s, 3 3/4" l. (ILLUS.)................................... 7

Mt. Vernon, Virginia home of George Washington is depicted on printed insert inside globe, identifying decal on front, 1940s 50

Natural Bridge of Virginia, heavy base w/identifying decal, offered in 3D or w/flat postcard-type insert, 1940s............................ 50

Nautilus, "Nautilus - The First Atomic Submarine," globe sits on red base & contains model of the Nautilus, America's first nuclear submarine, amid stylized seaweed, 1950s.. 120

New Orleans, souvenir of the city w/scene of African-American boy eating watermelon, identifying decal on ceramic base, marked "Atlas Crystal Works, Covington, Tennessee," 1940s.............................. 90

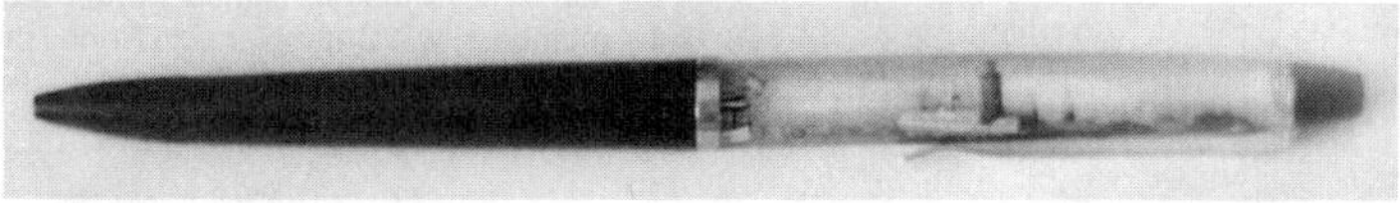

Pen with Scene of Stockholm

New York World's Fair, 1939-40, contains white bisque model of World's Fair Administration Building, on dark ceramic base, rare **100**

New York World's Fair, 1939-40, enclosed are symbols of the Fair, the Trylon & Perisphere, on brown ceramic base, $65 if World's Fair decal missing from front, w/decal **80**

Niagara Falls Snowdome

Niagara Falls, round, w/paper insert of the Falls, globe sits on dark ceramic base, Germany, 1920s (ILLUS.) **95**

Old Man of the Mountain, souvenir of New Hampshire, dark base w/decal on front reading "Old Man of the Mountain of the White Mountains of New Hampshire," 1940s **50**

Pen, ball-point type, case of pen shows scene of the islands of the city of Stockholm, Sweden, where a ship appears to sail from one end of the harbor to the other, 1989 (ILLUS., top of page) **4**

Popeye, figures of Popeye, Olive Oyl, Swee' Pea & Wimpy seated in rowboat, plastic base, marked "King Features Syndicate," 1950s **45**

RCA Building at Radio City, souvenir of New York City, dark ceramic base (generic globes were manufactured & decal could be added by each souvenir shop), 1940s **60**

Sailor, generic globe w/figure of saluting sailor, decal w/location would be added to make into souvenir of different naval bases, 1940s **50**

Sailor hugging woman, figure of standing sailor hugging seated woman, both looking out at viewer, dark Bakelite base, type sold at bases & shops **35**

Sailor w/woman, generic globe of figure of sailor w/arm around woman's shoulder, decal w/location would be added to make into souvenir of different naval bases, 1940s **45**

Santa Claus Snowdome

Santa carrying toys, plastic white oval base, winter scene of Santa Claus walking past a farmhouse w/a bag of toys, three pine trees in background, red ground, 1970s, 3 3/4" l. (ILLUS.) **7**

Snowdome with Santa Riding Rocket

Santa on rocket, plastic white oval base, dome w/blue ground shows figure of Santa Claus carrying bag of toys & waving while riding a rocket over five snow-covered pine trees, Hong Kong, late 1960s, 3 1/2" l. (ILLUS.) **10**

Skyline Drive, depicts mountain scenery along Skyline highway of Virginia, on heavy base (sold at tourist sites along the route, some w/identifying decals) **50**

Snow Baby, on Bakelite base that doubles as ashtray, Germany, 1920s-30s **85**

Soldier, uniformed World War II soldier saluting, Fort Leonard Wood, dark base, 1940s **65**

Soldier w/woman, generic globe of figure of soldier w/arm around woman's shoulder, decal w/location could be added to make into souvenir of different army bases, 1940s **55**

South Dakota, scene of buffalo standing amid pine trees w/mountains in background, white plastic base w/"South Dakota," 1970s **10**

Statue of Liberty Snowdome

Statue of Liberty, plastic, square base holds rectangular dome containing scene of a ship sailing into New York Harbor w/skyscrapers in the background, a green model of the Statue of Liberty stands atop dome, Hong Kong, 1981 (ILLUS.) **7**

Statue of Liberty, statue encased in globe, "New York" on base, manufactured by Atlas, U.S.A., 1940s **50**

Trigger, souvenir of Roy Rogers & Dale Evans Museum in California, shows Rogers' Palomino horse in barn, plastic, 1960s **20**

WAC saluting, figure of uniformed Army WAC on dark ceramic or Bakelite base (generic globes were manufactured by Atlas that contained figures of women of various branches of the military, to which a decal could be added that identified a particular base or station), 1940s **80**

WAVE saluting, w/decal reading "Naval Air Tech. School" generic globe manufactured by Atlas, 1940s **90**

Williamsburg, model of building identified by decal on Bakelite base as Capital Building at Williamsburg, Virginia, 1940s **95**

SPORTS MEMORABILIA
Also see BASEBALL MEMORABILIA

Basketball

Award, Russ Critchfield 1968-69 Oakland Oaks ABA Champions award, wood & metal, walnut rectangular plaque mounted w/a silver wreath around a design of players above an inscribed rectangular plaque, overall 6 x 9" **$731**

Basketball, 1947-48 Baltimore Bullets World Champion team-signed ball, Wil-

son Official model, signed by ten team members, w/a Championship Series program dated April 13, 1948, 2 pcs. **3,780**

Chicago Bulls Team-signed Ball

Basketball, 1995-96 Chicago Bulls World Champion team-signed ball, signed by 15 team members, official Spalding model (ILLUS.) **2,132**

Jersey, 1974-75 Willie Sojourner New York Nets ABA home game-worn jersey, white w/lettering & number 40 in red, red & blue stripes down side w/white stars, Rawlings, size 44 .... **991**

Jersey, Dennis Rodman 1996 Chicago Bulls game-worn home jersey, white w/red letters & numbers & red & white trim, Champion label, size 46 .... **1,321**

Jersey, Harlem Globetrotters late 1960s model, dark blue w/gold & red & white lettering & red & white stars, game-used, Wilson label, size 44 .... **914**

Jersey, Michael Jordan 1989-90 Chicago Bulls game-worn road jersey, dark red w/black & white letters & numbers, narrow red trim bands, MacGregor Sand-Knit label, size 44 .... **7,225**

Jersey, Pete Maravich 1972-74 Atlanta Hawks game-worn road jersey, dark red w/gilt-trimmed white letters & numbers, w/three-page description from authenticator **21,847**

Scarce Walt Frazier Road Jersey

Jersey, Walt Frazier ca. 1975 New York Knicks game-worn road jersey, dark blue w/red & white letters & numbers & name in white on the back, Gerry Cosby Athletic label, size 40 (ILLUS. of front & back) ... **6,412**

Early Wilt Chamberlain Jersey

Jersey, Wilt Chamberlain 1967-68 Philadelphia 76ers game-worn road jersey, dark blue w/red & white letters & numbers, Wilson label, from Chamberlain's last season in Philadelphia (ILLUS.) **21,847**

Shoes, Michael Jordan 1996-97 autographed game-worn shoes, white & red Nike hightops, the pair................................. **2,922**

1957 Bill Russell Rookie Card

Trading card, 1957 Topps #77 Bill Russell rookie card, near mint (ILLUS.).................. **3,939**

Trading card, 1969-70 Topps #25 Lew Alcindor rookie card, mint................................... **991**

Trading card, 1970-71 Topps #123 Pete Maravich autographed rookie card, excellent to mint.. **1,298**

Michael Jordan 1986 Rookie Card

Trading card, 1986 Fleer #57 Michael Jordan rookie card, gem mint condition (ILLUS.) **6,412**

Trading card pack, 1986-87 Fleer pack, perfect & unopened, includes 12 cards, 1 sticker & 1 stick of gum, red, white & blue label w/brown basketball, the pack **1,624**

Trading cards, 1948 Bowman complete set, graded cards in Excellent or better condition, set of 72....................................... **1,995**

Trading cards, 1969-70 Topps complete set, includes Chamberlain, Alcindor, Robertson & more, set of 99 .... **12,368**

Uniform, 1955 Tom Gola East-West Game game-worn autographed uniform, black jersey w/white lettering & number, matching shorts w/white bands & silver buckled black belt, made by Thorp Sporting Goods of New York, signed by Gola on a number on the jersey, the set............. **1,201**

Boxing

Rare Jake Kilrain Bandana

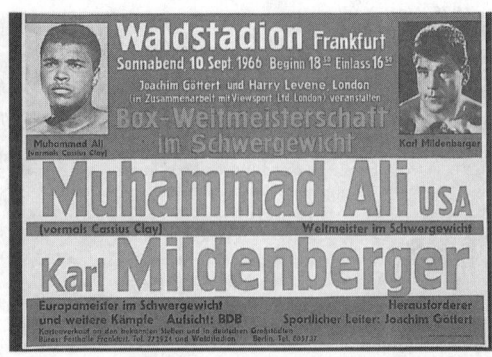

Rare Ali vs. Mildenberger Poster

Bandana, commemorative, color-printed silk, 1887 Jake Kilrain Heavyweight Championship, white ground w/red, white & blue square around a design of an American & Irish shield at top & crossed American & Irish flags at the bottom, black & white half-length image of bare-chested Kilrain in the center above wording "Jake Kilrain, - Champion Pugilist of America...," near mint, 32" sq. (ILLUS., previous page) **2,881**

Bandana, John L. Sullivan commemorative, white silk w/green band around large black & white half-length portrait of Sullivan, Irish & American symbols in each corner, ca. 1890, 25 1/2 x 31" **1,063**

Books, titled "Boxiana," five hard-bound volumes covering the origins & evolution of pugilism in the 18th & early 19th c., many etched full-page illustrations, England, mid-19th c., total of some 550 gilt-edged pages, 5 3/4 x 8", the set **805**

Boxing gloves, Rocky Marciano-endorsed gloves, produced by Benlee Sporting Goods Company, w/original red, white & blue cardboard box photo of Marciano, two pairs w/original insert foldover & box, 1950s, the set **513**

Poster, German, Ali vs. Mildenberger fight on September 10, 1966, printed in red, white & blue w/a photo of each fighter in the upper corners, minor faults, 23 1/4 x 33" (ILLUS., top of page) **1,814**

Sweater, Sugar Ray Robinson, periwinkle blue fight-used cardigan style w/white felt letters, Everlast label, w/letter of authenticity from Robinson's son (ILLUS.) **1,995**

Rare Sullivan vs. Corbett Ticket

Ticket, 1892 full ticket to Sullivan vs. Corbett, engraved in black & white w/elaborate text, original $15 ticket price, held September 7, 1892 (ILLUS.) **2,922**

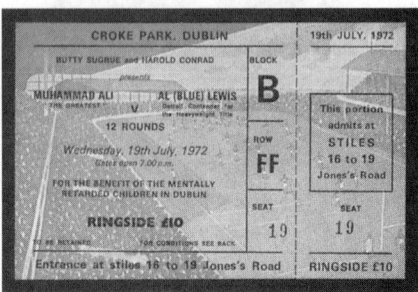

1972 Ali vs. Al Lewis Ticket

Ticket, 1972 Ali vs. Al "Blue" Lewis full ticket for fight in Dublin, Ireland, pink & red background w/black wording (ILLUS.) **1,091**

Sugar Ray Robinson Sweater

Rare Turkey Red Boxing Cards

Trade cards, 1911 T9 Turkey Red Cabinets complete set, printed in full color, includes James Jeffries, Sam Langord, Jack Johnson & more, all excellent to mint, set of 26 (ILLUS. of part) **12,788**

Trading cards, 1948 Leaf complete set, includes Dempsey, Johnson, Lewis, Sullivan, LaMotta & more, middle to high grades, set of 49 .... **1,201**

Football

Banner, 1897 Yale University, two black silk panels sewn together, gold fringe along three edges, silk-screened gilt lettering reading "Yale University Foot Ball Ass'n 1897 - Cambridge. Nov. 13th Yale 0 - Harvard 0 - New Haven. Nov. 20th - Yale 6 - Princeton 0 - G.L. Cadwalader. C.," fold lines w/some separations, minimal fraying, small tear on one edge, 23 3/4 x 28" (ILLUS., below) **2,094**

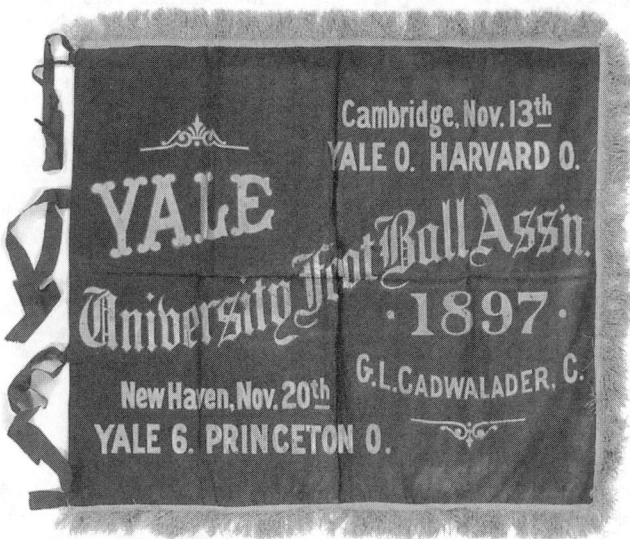

Early Yale Football Silk Banner

Paul Hornung Record Game Ball

Knute Rockne Signed Book

Book, "The Four Winners" by Knute Rockne, 1925 first edition signed by Rockne, orange hard cover w/black wording & images, 251 pp., very good condition (ILLUS.) **2,381**

Chicago Cardinals 1947 Gold Charm

Charm, 1947 Chicago Cardinals NFL Championship charm, figural gold football embossed "Chicago Cardinals 1947 World Champions," 33 grams, near mint (ILLUS. actual size)..................................... **1,022**

Football, 1971 Dallas Cowboys World Champions team-signed ball, white w/black logo & wording, signed w/44 blue or black ink signatures including Staubach, Adderley, Pugh, Hayes & more, w/letter of authenticity **1,572**

Football, Paul Hornung's 1961 Green Bay Packers team-signed record breaking ballgame ball, Wilson Official model stamped "The Duke" & inscribed in white "Packers 45 - Colts 7 - Oct. 8, 1961," 41 bold black signatures including Lombardi, Starr & more (ILLUS., top of page)..... **11,364**

Football, Wilson Official NFL Bert Bell model ball, 1950s (very minor wear & soiling)... **665**

Game, board-type, "Vince Lombardi's Game," white box w/color image of Lombardi, black & red wording, subtitled "This is the most realistic Pro Football game ever developed!," 1973, new-old stock......... **335**

Helmet, 1948 D&M picture-signature Frank Leahy model helmet, blue & white leather w/Leahy decal on forehead, complete w/brochure, mint in box, box 8 1/2 x 8 3/4", 9" h. **1,180**

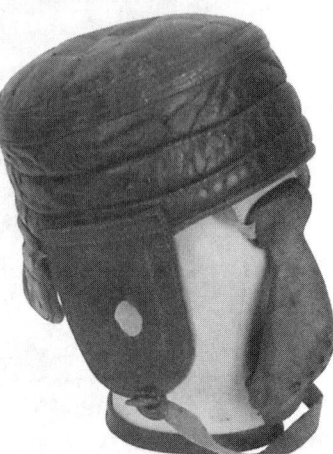

Early Leather Football Helmet

Helmet, all-leather flattop style w/nose guard, fully intact padded lining, soft & supple, marked "Morrill's - Patent - Nose Mask," early 1900s" (ILLUS.) **1,360**

Johnny Unitas Signed Helmet

Helmet, Johnny Unitas 1960s Baltimore Colts autographed game-used helmet, white w/blue bands & numbers, black Sharpie inscription on the top (ILLUS.).... **41,515**

Helmet, Wilson 1930s pro model, two-tone leather w/white top & brown borders & flags, size 7 3/8, near mint............................. **411**

Jacket, Dallas Cowboys warm-up style, heavy blue w/white letters & numbers, leather trim, size 46, late 1960s, near mint.. **818**

Jersey, Bob Lilly autographed 1972 Pro Bowl game-worn jersey, dark blue w/silver & white letters & numbers, red & white bands around sleeves, signed in blue Sharpie on one of the numbers, Rawlings, size 54, w/letter of authenticity from Lilly **3,780**

Jersey, Dan Marino 1994 Miami Dolphins autographed game-worn jersey, green w/orange-outlined white letters & numbers, signed on a back number, Wilson, size 50, w/letter of authenticity.................. **2,990**

Gene Lipscomb Game-worn Jersey

Jersey, Gene "Big Daddy" Lipscomb Baltimore Colts game-worn jersey, white w/blue numbers & shoulder stripes, w/letter of authenticity, late 1950s (ILLUS.)....... **5,244**

Photograph, 1919 Notre Dame team photo w/George Gipp, sepia-toned w/players arranged in three rows, titled at the bottom "Western Champions," near mint, 9 1/2 x 13 3/4"... **1,600**

Photograph, black & white autographed picture of Brian Piccolo, live action pose, signed in blue ink, near mint, 8 x 10"......... **1,321**

Program, 1907 University of Michigan, white cover w/colored sketch of a standing Michigan player, black print reads "Pennsylvania vs Michigan - Ferry Field - Ann Arbor - Nov. 16, 1907," includes fight songs, team photos, individual photos, campus photos & advertisements (some discoloration along bottom of cover, short tear in top left corner) **1,180**

Program, 1920 Notre Dame vs. Northwestern, white cover w/deep purple wording & football scene in center, game played November 20, 1920, last game played by George Gipp, 20 pp., 6 x 9" (staining along right cover)... **2,839**

Ring, 1972 Miami Dolphins Super Bowl employee ring, gold, diamonds & black enamel, w/letter of authenticity................... **5,970**

Sign, 1958 Baltimore Colts World Champions easel-back cardboard display sign w/advertising for National Bohemian Beer along the bottom edge, large red panel w/color photo of the whole team, grey border, 19 x 28" **665**

Early Detroit Lions Wool Sweater

Sweater, Detroit Lions heavy wool sideline-type, dark blue cardigan style w/zipper, grey trim & yellow, blue & grey team logo on front, Lamb Knit label, 1930s (ILLUS.) **2,839**

Ticket, Super Bowl IV - January 11, 1970 full ticket, white w/red, blue & black wording, excellent condition.................................... **900**

Tie bar, 1948 Cleveland Browns World Champions commemorative, 10k gold, pierced large letters spell "Browns" & centered by a model of a football engraved "Cleveland 1948 World Champions," 2 3/4" l. **4,575**

Rare Knute Rockne Trading Card

Trading card, 1935 National Chicle #9 Knute Rockne, near mint (ILLUS.) **4,478**

Trading card, 1952 Bowman large #1 Norm Van Brocklin card, color image, near mint **2,581**

1961 Fleer #11 Jim Brown Card

Trading card, 1961 Fleer #11 Jim Brown, mint condition (ILLUS.) **1,107**

Walter Payton Topps Rookie Card

Trading card, 1978 Topps #148 Walter Payton rookie card, color photo of Payton, gem mint (ILLUS.) **4,767**

Trading cards, 1962 Post Cereal complete set, color photos, all high grades, set of 200 .... **1,761**

Trading cards, 1963 Fleer complete set, color photos of players, all near mint to mint, set of 89 .... **6,981**

Don Joyce Championship Watch

Wristwatch, Don Joyce 1959 Baltimore Colts World Champions Rolex model, presented to Joyce, bright gold case, Colts' logo in blue on the dial, near mint (ILLUS.) **5,244**

Yearbook, 1941 Chicago Bears world champions autographed yearbook, red & white cover w/pictures of players, pictures & biographies of 38 team members, each photo signed by the person, excellent condition **974**

STATUARY - BRONZE, MARBLE & OTHER

Bronze

Bousquet (possibly Robert Bousquet), model of a trumpeting stag on chiseled stone base engraved "Bousquet," 15" l., 18" h. **$550**

Bronze Pack Mule

Cain, Auguste Nicolas, figure of pack mule standing on oval stepped base, brown patina, signed & titled on base, France, 19th c., 5 7/8" h. (ILLUS.) **2,688**

Cavelier Bronze of Seated Woman

Cavelier, A.J. (Pierre-Jules), copper clad bronze figure of a woman in classic dress sitting in a chair w/head hanging to side, w/large cat resting underneath, marked name of founder, "F. Barbedienne" & includes special quality seal of "Reduction Mecanique, A. Collas Brevette," 15" h. (ILLUS.) **1,300**

Daillion, Horace, figure of a nearly nude winged classical male alighting on one foot, his arms up & away from body, brown patina, late 19th - early 20th c., 49" h. **6,600**

Dumaige, Étienne Henri, figures of French soldiers, one a standing soldier leaning on his rifle & lighting his pipe titled "Apres Le Combat - Grenadier de 1792 - par Dumaige MC," the second a standing soldier w/a drum titled "Avant Le Combat - Volontare de 1792 par Dumaige MC," both signed by artist, dark brown patina, France, late 19th c., each 28" h., pr. **4,800**

Bronze Sculpture on Marble Base

Figure group, bronze doré figure of a monkey on a stone floor near tap & wash tub & pail, holding a cat down on a braided circular rug as if to wash the cat, mounted on marble base, unmarked, ca. 1920s-1930s, 5" d. (ILLUS.) **375**

Fremiet Bronze of Joan of Arc

Fremiet, Emmanuel, rectangular base holds figure of Joan of Arc in armor riding horse & holding pennant in one hand (ILLUS.) **7,840**

Gladiator, after the antique, seated figure in full armor & holding a heavy rod across his lap, brown patina, 19th c., on a square marble base, now mounted as a lamp, 28 1/2" h. **5,700**

Japanese Bronze of Woman & Cow

Japanese, woman seated on a cow w/a large woven basket on her back, narrow rectangular base, late 19th - early 20th c., 4 x 6 1/2", 6 1/2" h. (ILLUS.).............................. **275**

Leonard Bronze of Woman

Leonard, A. (Agathon), figure of woman in flowing gown w/right arm upraised, the other reaching behind to upraised left foot as if to adjust sandal, base of upraised foot inscribed "A Gift from J.A. Coles MD, L.L., D.," Paris Founders seal "Susse Freres Editeurs, de Paris," 20 7/8" h. (ILLUS.) **5,000**

Bronze Stag

Lugerth, Ferdinand, figure of roaring stag on rectangular base, greenish black patina, signed on base "Ferd Lugerth, FR," late 19th - early 20th c., 13" h. (ILLUS.) **952**

Moreau, Mathurin, figure of a dancing classical maiden wearing a shear gown, her arms above her head w/a lyre in one hand, gilt finish, raised on a round swivel base, France, late 19th c., 23" h. **7,200**

Plé (Henri Honoré), figure group of a standing Native American warrior in full regalia w/a Native American woman crouching beside him, on a rectangular brown base, stamped signature, dark brown patina, France, late 19th - early 20th c., 44" h. .. **18,000**

Signoret, Lucie Ledieu, figure of a young classical maiden, seated on a stump wearing a short tunic, holding a blossom to her nose, brown patina, late 19th c., 26" h. **7,200**

Marble

Marble Mother & Child Group

Bronelleschi, E., half-length figure group of a young mother w/thick curly hair hugging a young girl who has her arms around her mother's neck, late 19th - early 20th c., w/marble pedestal, sculpture 25" h. (ILLUS.).. **9,600**

Figure of a cherub, nearly nude standing figure w/a finger to its mouth, the other hand extended w/palm out, on a low socle base, late 19th - early 20th c., 32" h..... **4,800**

Figure of a young male painter, standing wearing Renaissance clothing & holding a palette in one hand, late 19th c., raised on a modern ebonized wood pedestal, sculpture 62" h. **20,300**

Figure of Diana the Huntress, standing nude carrying a bow & arrow, set on a gilt-bronze round base, late 19th c., 34 1/2" h. (restorations).............................. **7,200**

Powers, Hiram, based on his work "The Greek Slave," nude classical female w/chains at wrists, standing & leaning on a draped short column, 19th c., 36" h. (restorations, losses) **2,400**

Art Nouveau Maiden in Marble

Romanelli, Tlli, nude Art Nouveau maiden w/long flowing hair emerging amid &

above flowering vines & rockwork, signed "Tlli Romanelli Firenze," Italy, on a short paneled plinth & a tall separate pedestal, late 19th c., sculpture 46" h. (ILLUS.).. **10,200**

Other

Spelter, Art Nouveau-style bust of young woman w/long hair & Dutch-style cap w/feather, bronze finish, cast signature of "Ant. Nelson," 19 1/2" h. **385**

Spelter, cast figures of "Industry" & "Art" w/bronzed finish, "Industry" depicts a blacksmith w/hammer & tongs next to an anvil, 25" h., "Art" shows an artist sculpting a figure of a woman, 25 1/2" h., both on black enameled bases (minor surface wear, split at elbow of "Industry"), pr............. **495**

Terra Cotta Blackamoor Busts

Terra cotta, bust of male & female blackamoors, wearing elaborate colorful striped head scarfs & shawls, smiling, well-detailed features, on tapering rectangular plinths w/names inscribed on front panels, late 19th c., each 24" h., pr. (ILLUS.).. **4,800**

STEIFF TOYS & DOLLS

From a felt pincushion in the shape of an elephant, a world-famous toy company emerged. Margarete Steiff (1847-1909), a polio victim as a child and confined to a wheelchair, planned a career as a seamstress and opened a shop in the family home. Her plans were dramatically changed, however, when she made the first stuffed elephant in 1880. By 1886 she was producing stuffed felt monkeys, donkeys, horses and other animal forms. In 1893 an agent sold her toys at the Leipzig Fair. This venture was so successful that a catalog was printed and a salesman hired. Magarete's nephews and nieces became involved in the business, assisting in its management and the design of new items.

Through the years, the Steiff Company has produced a varied line including felt or plush animals, Teddy Bears, gnomes, elves, felt dolls with celluloid heads, Kewpie dolls and even radiator caps with animals or dolls attached as decoration. Descendants of the original family members continue to be active in the management of the company, still adhering to Margarete's motto, "For our children, the best is just good enough."

Teddy bear, blonde mohair, glass eyes, embroidered nose, mouth & claws, ex-celsior-stuffed fully jointed body, script ear button, mid-20th c., 30" (felt feet pads w/moth holes, break at sides) **$1,955**

Teddy bear, blonde mohair, glass eyes, embroidered nose & mouth, no-pad style, wearing a pink print dress w/pink checked collar, yellow knit overalls, green corduroy jacket, red scarf, black felt hat & bell around the neck, ca. 1930, 5 1/2".. **345**

Teddy bear, golden mohair, embroidered nose & claws, black shoe button eyes, squeaker, fully jointed body, excelsior stuffing, ear button, original felt pads, ca. 1905, 14" (mouth embroidery missing, thin small fabric tear on right front arm joint, very minor fur loss, overall soil)......... **1,955**

Teddy bear, light apricot, shoe button eyes, embroidered nose, mouth & claws, fully jointed body w/excelsior stuffing, felt pads, ear button, ca. 1905, 12 1/2" (fur loss, slight moth damage on pads) **1,610**

Teddy bear, light brown mohair, shoe button eyes, jointed arms & legs, swivel head, ca. 1910, 14"... **450**

Teddy bear, light golden mohair, black shoe button eyes, center seam, black embroidered nose, mouth & claws, fully jointed body, felt pads, underscored ear button, ca. 1905, 17" (holes in paw pads) .. **4,888**

Teddy bear, miniature, blonde mohair, rattle-type, black shoe button eyes, embroidered nose & mouth, fully jointed body, working rattle, excelsior stuffing, no-pad style, no ear button, ca. 1910, 5" (overall wear, stains & rip on arm)............................. **403**

Teddy bear, miniature, honey blonde mohair, black bead eyes, embroidered nose & mouth, fully jointed body, padless style, ca. 1950s, 3 1/2"..................................... **98**

Teddy bear, "Zotty," long curly beige mohair, apricot chest, fully jointed body, glass eyes, airbrushed mouth, embroidered nose, peach felt pads, 1950s-60s, 21" **173**

Teddy bear, silver "Steiff" button in left ear, caramel mohair plush swivel head, brown glass eyes, brown floss nose & mouth, five-piece body w/non-working squeaker in tummy, gold felt pads on paws & feet, four brown floss claws on each, 11" **230**

STEINS

Devil Head Character Stein

Character, porcelain, Devil head, grotesque leering expression, by E. Bohne Sohne, 1/4 liter (ILLUS.)............................... **$633**

Dutch Girl Character Stein

Character, porcelain, Dutch Girl, full-figure of a young Dutch girl wearing white cap, orange blouse & tan skirt, shoulders & head form cover, designed by Schierholtz, Musterschutz mark, 1/2 liter (ILLUS.).. **2,645**

Indian Chief Head Character Stein

Character, porcelain, Indian Chief head, smiling face in color w/black & white headdress, by E. Bohne Sohne, 1/2 liter (ILLUS.)... **460**

Character, porcelain, Skull & Devil, double-sided, one face on each half, unmarked E. Bohne Sohne, 1/4 liter............................... **776**

Faience, cylindrical body decorated in color w/a continuous scene of a milkmaid & two cows w/ruins in the background, pewter base band & low domed cover w/ball thumb lift, Nurnberg mark, mid-18th c., 9" h., 1 1/4 liter (two small chips on upper interior rim, a few minor hairlines)... **4,830**

Handpainted Faience Stein

Faience, cylindrical ceramic body in white h.p. in magenta w/a long-billed exotic bird & flowers on rockwork design, stepped flaring pewter band foot & flattened domed pewter lid w/large ball thumb lift, vertical handle strap, probably Thuringia, mid-19th c., 1 1/4 liters (ILLUS.).. **1,208**

Mettlach, No. 777 (2140), PUG (printed-under-glaze), color scene of dragoons on horseback, domed pewter lid, 1/2 liter.......... **834**

Mettlach, No. 967 (2184), PUG, color scene of gnomes drinking, signed by Schlitt, inlaid pewter lid, 1/3 liter **304**

Mettlach, No. 1526, h.p. w/wide color scene of a lady & gentleman in 18th c. costume dancing w/a rectangular vertical panel w/inscription & bottom row of red hearts behind them, design by F. Ringer, low domed pewter lid, 1/2 liter **403**

Mettlach, No. 1526, PUG, black on cream scene of fox & bird, figural horn on pewter lid, 1/2 liter.. **546**

Mettlach, No. 1566, etched scene of a man on a high-wheeled bicycle, signed by Gorig, inlaid lid, 1/2 liter **834**

Mettlach, No. 1570, mosaic, a wide center band of horizontal blue leaves & brown vine against white, bands of sawtooth design in dark blue & brown above & below, inlaid pewter lid, 1/2 liter **489**

Mettlach, No. 1724, etched scene of a standing fireman within front panel, figural fireman's hat on inlaid lid, figural fireman thumb lift, 1/2 liter.................................. **1,323**

Mettlach, No. 1733, etched scene of a jockey riding a leaping horse in arched front panel, figural jockey cap on inlaid lid, 1/2 liter.. **1,150**

Mettlach, No. 1742, etched reserve w/scene of the city of Gottingen, inlaid lid, 1/2 liter **633**

Mettlach, No. 2001 B, Book stein, etched & h.p., shows bindings of books on medicine, inlaid lid, 1/2 liter **446**

Mettlach, No. 2028, etched scene of men drinking in tavern, inlaid lid, 1/2 liter **546**

Mettlach, No. 2050, Slipper stein, etched wide band w/stylized color figures of a Victorian man facing a Victorian woman, a wide inscribed band around the bottom, inlaid lid w/figural slipper, 1/2 liter **1,323**

Mettlach, No. 2089, etched wide scene of an angel serving dinner & beer to a seated gentleman, inlaid lid, 1/2 liter **863**

Mettlach Card Stein

Mettlach, No. 2093, Card stein, bulbous body, etched w/four panels each w/a playing card in color, pewter base band & inlaid lid, 1/2 liter (ILLUS.) **633**

Cavaliers in Tavern Mettlach Stein

Mettlach, No. 2231, etched scene in wide band showing Cavaliers drinking in a tavern, inlaid lid, 1/2 liter (ILLUS.) **575**

Mettlach, No. 2277, etched scene of the city of Nurnberg, inlaid lid, 1/2 liter **575**

Mettlach, No. 2394, etched arched panels w/scenes from Siegfried's youth, inlaid lid, 1/2 liter **690**

Mettlach, No. 2401, etched wide color scene of Tannhauser in the Venusberg, 1/2 liter **719**

Mettlach, No. 2479, cameo, Hildebrand stein, three arched panels w/white relief

scenes against pale blue, brown ground, lid inset w/castle turret, 1/4 liter **334**

Mettlach, No. 2524, Die Kannenburg stein, etched scene of a knight in armor in a castle holding up a stein, pewter turret-form lid, 4 1/4 liters (fine repair line around base) **1,495**

Mettlach, No. 2808, etched scene of a barmaid bowling w/men looking on, inlaid lid, 1/2 liter **633**

Mettlach, No. 2829, relief decorated, continuous molded design of the Town of Rodenstein, bands of buildings in white & brown between bands of greenery w/inscriptions, inlaid lid w/figural buildings, 1/2 liter **1,955**

Etched Art Nouveau Leaf Stein

Mettlach, No. 2935, etched Art Nouveau design, large white panels w/green three-leaf sprigs, cobalt blue bands & tan stylized wheat stripes, inlaid lid, 1/2 liter (ILLUS.) **518**

Mettlach, No. 2951, cameo, Prussian eagle emblem in white against a dark green ground, low domed pewter lid, 1/2 liter **575**

Tapestry Postman Mettlach Stein

Mettlach, No. 3085, tapestry-type, large color scene of an elderly postman seated & drinking from stein, low domed pewter lid, 1 liter (ILLUS.) **805**

Mettlach, No. 3093, etched scene of a large hairy brown troll w/long horns holding a large bottle & seated cross-legged on a barrel, signed by Schlitt, inlaid lid, 1/2 liter.. **1,438**

Capo-di-Monte-type Stein

Porcelain, Capo-di-Monte-type, narrow flaring base band w/pink lappet band, tall cylindrical body molded in relief w/a colorful scene of classical figures bathing & cavorting in water, inset low domed porcelain lid w/full-figure putto finial, crown & "N" mark, late 19th c., 3/4 liter (ILLUS.) **690**

Porcelain, Capo-di-Monte-type, wide rounded base band below the cylindrical body molded in relief w/a Roman cavalry battle scene in color, low domed inset porcelain lid w/figural helmet finial, crown & "N" mark, late 19th c., 1/2 liter **546**

Porcelain, color photograph of middle class gentleman within a gold border against a deep red ground, inlaid lid, lithophane in bottom, 1/2 liter **431**

Porcelain Stein with Rugby Scene

Porcelain, cylindrical, w/molded base band, h.p. dark blue landscape scene of rugby players, inlaid pewter lid marked "Yale University," base marked "Delft by Swaine & Co.," lithophane in bottom, 1/2 liter (ILLUS.) **776**

Porcelain, occupational, baker, wide center band transfer-printed in color w/the crest of the baker's guild centered by a pretzel, relief-molded pewter lid w/pretzel, lithophane in the bottom, 1/2 liter **460**

Porcelain, occupational, beer wagon driver, wide center band w/a transfer-printed color scene of a large horse-drawn beer wagon, inscriptions around the rim & base bands, stepped, domed pewter lid, lithophane in bottom, 1/2 liter **460**

Porcelain, political Socialist design, wide transfer-printed color center band featuring an allegorical figure of a classical woman w/banners & flags, inscriptions around the rim & base bands, includes owner's name & roster of members, domed pewter lid, 1/2 liter **719**

HR No. 425 Pottery Stein

Pottery, cylindrical, w/flaring foot, etched scene of barmaid & drinkers framed by scrolling leaves, high domed pewter lid & thumb rest, Hauber & Reuther No. 425, 1/2 liter (ILLUS.) **374**

Pottery, tall, slender & slightly tapering cylindrical form decorated in Delft blue w/large bust portrait of a knight in armor surrounded by delicate flowering vines & a crest, hinged domed pewter lid, Royal Bonn mark, No. 6324, 2 liter **299**

Delft-style Pottery Stein

Pottery, tall, slender & slightly tapering cylindrical form decorated in Delft blue w/large bust portrait of a knight in armor facing right & surrounded by delicate flowering vines & a crest, hinged domed pewter lid, Royal Bonn mark, No. 4570/4, minor tear in lid, 4 liter (ILLUS.) **460**

Rare Pottery Golfer Stein

Pottery, tall, slightly tapering cylindrical form w/flared base band, etched w/a large scene of a male golfer in brown swinging his club, green grass & grey sky, stepped & domed pewter lid, marked "M.W.G.," very rare, 1/2 liter (ILLUS.)........ **2,645**

Regimental, porcelain, a wide color band w/a standing figure of a soldier & a large

white & blue flag & red shield below a stag head coat-of-arms, inscriptions around top & base bands, two color side scenes, roster list, name of owner, domed pewter lid w/seated soldier finial, Marburg, 1903-05, 12 1/4" h., 1/2 liter........ **2,070**

Regimental, porcelain, wide center band in color showing soldiers on horseback above a small oval portrait, four side scenes, roster & name of owner, Straubing, 1908-1911, domed pewter lid w/screw-off finial of horse & rider, lithophane in bottom, 12 1/2" h., 1/2 liter (faint lines in lithophane)... **518**

Regimental Stein for New Ulm

Regimental, porcelain, wide color band centered by a large red "1" in a white rectangle above a crest, two color side scenes, inscribed bands w/roster & name of owner, pewter lid w/pointed top & figural lion thumb lift, Neu Ulm, 1903-05, 9 1/4" h., 1/2 liter (ILLUS.) **719**

Regimental Stein for Beeskow

Regimental, porcelain, wide color band w/a cluster of oval emblems below vignettes of soldiers in action, four side scenes, printed bands w/roster & name of owner, tall rounded pewter screw-fuse lid, Beeskow, 1907-09, rare unit, 10" h., 1/2 liter (ILLUS.) **863**

Regimental, porcelain, wide color band w/a large round center vignette of a hunter & stag flanked on one side by a waving soldier, a badge above, two side scenes, roster list & name of owner, domed pewter lid w/figural helmet finial & eagle thumb lift, Potsdam, 1904-06, repaired tear in rear of lid, 9 1/2" h., 1/2 liter **1,898**

Regimental, porcelain, wide color center band decorated w/figures of soldiers around a central oval portrait reserve, roster list, inscription for Stuttgart regiment, 1905-07 & name of owner, high domed pewter lid w/figure of seated classical female warrior, 12" h., 1/2 liter **546**

Regimental, porcelain, wide color center band w/a vignette of a city above two bust portraits in ovals flanked by figure of a soldier & the unit number, four side scenes, roster & name of owner, Regensburg, 1911-1913, lithophane in bottom, domed pewter lid w/figural finial of standing soldier, 12 1/3" h., 1/2 liter (faint line in lithophane) **345**

Regimental, porcelain, wide color center band w/scene of soldier on horseback above other figures, four side scenes, inscription & name of owner, Nurnberg, 1909-1912, domed pewter lid w/figural soldier on horseback finial & lion thumb lift, 12 1/4" h., 1/2 liter **834**

Regimental, porcelain, wide color transfer-printed band centered by a crowned shield w/a red cross flanked by standing soldiers, medical side scenes, high domed cover w/wreath thumb lift, Dillingen, 1909-1911, name of owner in bottom band, 9 7/8" h., 1/2 liter **2,415**

Rare Regimental Stein

Regimental, porcelain, wide flared base band below cylindrical sides, wide color center band w/a crown over a blue shield w/"170" in red, flanked by standing figures of soldiers, two side scenes, roster list & name of owner, small color vignettes around base band, domed pewter lid w/large figural griffin thumb lift, Offenburg, 1904-1906, very rare body form, 12 1/4" h., 1/2 liter (ILLUS.) **1,783**

Regimental, pottery, a wide slightly flaring base band molded w/leafy vines & scrolls trimmed in dark green centered by a shield w/monogram, two narrow body bands flank the wide color scene of the Kaiser mounted on horseback in front of large building, inscription around top rim, domed pewter lid w/figural Kaiser on horseback finial, two side scenes, 12-man roster & name of owner, figural eagle thumb lift, Potsdam, 1910-13, very rare units, 14" h., 1/2 liter............................. **5,750**

Art Nouveau-style Stoneware Stein

Stoneware, Art Nouveau-style, spherical form w/flattened bottom, bands of incised small diamond & fan designs over a scalloped base band, all highlighted in cobalt blue, flattened hinged pewter lid, by R. Merkelbach, design by R. Riemerschmid, No. 1728, 1/2 liter (ILLUS.)............................. **633**

Stoneware, cylindrical body, grey incised & trimmed in cobalt blue w/a round reserve w/the Munich Child above "XVI Bundestag - Munchen - 1899," pewter lid w/bronze inlay reading "Deutsches Rad Fahrer Bund," 1 liter....................................... **403**

Stoneware, cylindrical, decorated on the front w/a colorful coat-of-arms under plumes, all against a speckled brown ground, slightly domed hinged pewter lid, by R. Merkelbach, designed by L. Hohlwein, No. 2176, ca. 1910, 1/2 liter.............. **1,783**

Stoneware, cylindrical, transfer-printed color scene on front of young German maiden holding flowers & reaching out to a facing young man holding his hat out, signed by F. Ringer, flat-topped relief-molded hinged pewter lid, HB, 1903, 1 liter... **489**

Stoneware, cylindrical, transfer-printed & enameled in color w/the tall figure of an Art Nouveau maiden in a green robe standing in front of a large standing lion, banner with "Gruss aus Munchen" near top, relief-molded pewter lid w/Munich Child, 1 liter **242**

Early Westerwald Stoneware Stein

Stoneware, footed spherical body tapering to a cylindrical neck w/flat rim, incised w/starburst design w/large round rays alternating w/smaller petals, all trimmed in cobalt blue, applied central medallion w/cobalt blue relief initials "GR," purple band trim, Westerwald, mid-18th c., small upper rim chip, 2 liters (ILLUS.) **776**

Stoneware, plain spherical body molded on the side w/a stylized floret & vine in cobalt blue, raised on three cobalt blue peg feet, hinged pewter lid, by R. Merkelbach, design by R. Riemerschmid, No. 1757, 1/2 liter **863**

Large Stoneware Stein with Crest

Stoneware, tall wide cylindrical tan body, the wide center band molded in relief in the middle w/a family crest surrounded by small white relief shell-like devices,

many w/cobalt blue trim, all between thin cobalt blue bands, pewter foot ring & low domed pewter cover w/large knob thumb lift, repaired tear in rear of lid, Altenburg, 1 1/2 liter (ILLUS.) **2,415**

Stoneware, Third Reich era, engraved color scene of city titled "Regensburg," hinged pewter lid w/impressed eagle & swastika, engraved inscription around base, 1/2 liter **546**

Wood, wide cylindrical wooden body w/low scroll-carved tab feet, hinged lid w/intricately carved center circle, thick wooden handle, Norway, early 19th c., 1 1/2 liters .. **1,208**

TEA PREMIUMS & FIGURES

For many years the main premiums in tea in the United States, the United Kingdom and Canada have been Wade figures or various picture card sets or the opportunity to order an album for 25 cents. Many of the sets were similar (except that Canada had a requirement that text on the cards be in both English and French). The same sets were at times issued in the United States with a slight variation in color. Brooke Bond continued to issue premiums until about 2000. Other companies offering premiums included Red Rose, Lipton, and Blue Ribbon.

Note that Brooke Bond Tea also owned Red Rose Tea and Blue Ribbon Coffee. Many of the card sets and albums were available in the United States but were a different color and in English only. The Wade figures were only available in Canada in Red Rose Tea boxes.

Album, for Brooke Bond Tea premium cards in Animals of North America series, 1962, without cards **$5**

Brooke Bond Tea's Armadillo Card

Card, #11 "Armadillo" from Brooke Bond Tea's "Animals and Their Young" series of 48, 1972, each (ILLUS.) .... **25¢**

"Exploring the Ocean" Card

Card, #3 "The Challenger Voyage" from Brooke Bond Tea's "Exploring the Ocean" series of 48, 1971, each (ILLUS.) .... **25¢**

"The Arctic" Series Card

Card, #30 "Polar Bear" from Brooke Bond Tea's "The Arctic" series of 48, 1973, each (ILLUS.)... **25¢**

"Underground Log Cabin" Card

Card, #34 "Underground Log Cabin" from Brooke Bond Tea's "Indians of Canada" series of 48, 1973, each (ILLUS.)................. **25¢**

"Birds of North America" Card

Card, #47 "Long Eared Owl" from Brooke Bond Tea's "Birds of North America" series of 48, 1962, each (ILLUS.)...................... **25¢**

Card, "Indians of Canada" Series

Card, #6 "Algonkian Portage" from Brooke Bond Tea's "Indians of Canada" series of 48, 1973, each (ILLUS.)................................. **25¢**

Card, Blue Ribbon Tea premium, #51 of Professional Canadian Football League players series, John Bright of Calgary Stampeders, 1954, 2 1/2 x 4"......................... **300**

Card, Blue Ribbon Tea premium, #64 of Professional Canadian Football League players series, Alex Webster of Montreal Alouettes, 1954, 2 1/2 x 4" **100**

Card, Blue Ribbon Tea premium, #7 of Professional Canadian Football League players series, Bud Grant of Winnipeg Blue Bombers, 1954, 2 1/2 x 4" **250**

Card set, Blue Ribbon Tea premium, Professional Canadian Football League players, color picture of player on front w/white border, back is black w/bilingual information (number, position, short bio), printed by Canadian Colorgraphics of Toronto, Ontario, 1954, 2 1/2 x 4", set of 80.. **7,000**

Brooke Bond Album No. 12

Card set, Brooke Bond Album No. 12 on "The Space Age," 48 cards in set traced history of space missions & info on solar system, 1969, 5 x 7 1/2", complete set w/album (ILLUS. of album)............................... **10**

Card set, Brooke Bond Tea premium, "African Animals" series, 1964, set of 48............... **12**

Card set, Brooke Bond Tea premium, "Animals of North America" series, color picture of animal on front, info on back, black backs, 1960s, set of 48........... **15**

Card set, Brooke Bond Tea premium, "Animals of North America" series, color picture of animal on front, info on back, blue backs, 1960s, set of 48 .... **15**

Card set, Brooke Bond Tea premium, "Birds of North America" series, color picture of bird on front, info on back, 1962, set of 48 .... **15**

Card set, Brooke Bond Tea premium, "British Birds" series, 1954, set of 50 .... **25**

Card set, Brooke Bond Tea premium, "Butterflies of North America" series, color picture of butterfly on front, info on back, 1965, set of 48.. **18**

Card set, Brooke Bond Tea premium, "Canadian and American Song Birds" series, color picture of bird on front, info on back, 1966, set of 48.. **20**

Card set, Brooke Bond Tea premium, "Dinosaurs" series, color picture of dinosaur on front, info on back, 1963, set of 48 .... **15**

Card set, Brooke Bond Tea premium, "Song Birds of North America" series, color picture of bird on front, info on back, 1959, 2 3/4 x 1 1/2", set of 48 .... **12**

Card set, Brooke Bond Tea premium, "The History of Clothes" series, 1967, set of 50 .... **20**

Card set, Brooke Bond Tea premium, "Transportation Through the Ages" series, 1967, set of 48 .... **12**

Card set, Brooke Bond Tea premium, "Trees in Britain" series, 1966, set of 50 .... **25**

Card set, Brooke Bond Tea premium, "Tropical Birds" series, color picture of bird on front, info on back, 1964, set of 48........ **12**

Card set, Brooke Bond Tea premium, "Wild Flowers of North America" series, color picture of flower on front, info on back, 1961, set of 48.. **15**

Figure of Bo Peep, from Red Rose Tea's "Nursery Rhyme" set, porcelain, Wade, England, 1960s... **6**

Red Rose Tea's Gingerbread Man

Figure of gingerbread man, #56 from Red Rose Tea's "Nursery Rhyme" set, porcelain, Wade, England, 1960s, rare (ILLUS.).. **100**

Figure of Jacques Cartier, #2 (of set of 40) in Lipton's "Famous Explorers" series, Louis Marx Toy Company, New York City, 1960s, 3" h., w/card **12**

Jean Talbin from Lipton Tea Series

Figure of Jean Talbin, man dressed in 17th-c. garb posed w/one hand on hip, square base, #19 (of set of 40) in Lipton's "Famous Explorers" series, Louis Marx Toy Company, New York City, 1960s, 3" h., $20 with accompanying card, without card (ILLUS.).. **10**

Figure of John Cabot, #1 (of set of 40) in Lipton's "Famous Explorers" series, Lou-

is Marx Toy Company, New York City, 1960s, 3" h., w/card.. **12**

Red Rose Tea's African Figure

Figure of man, African figure in robe, part of Red Rose Tea's promotional series on people of the world, 1960s, 3" h. (ILLUS.) **5**

The Old Woman Who Lived in a Shoe

Figure of Old Woman Who Lived in a Shoe, #40 from Red Rose Tea's "Nursery Rhyme" set, figure of woman stands next to shoe, 1960s (ILLUS.) **7**

Pierre Radisson from Lipton Series

Figure of Pierre Radisson, man dressed in buckskin & carrying kit on back, square base, #10 (of set of 40) in Lipton's "Famous Explorers" series, Louis Marx Toy Company, New York City, 1960s, 3" h. without card (ILLUS.)...................................... **11**

Figure of Puss 'n Boots, from Red Rose Tea's "Nursery Rhyme" set, porcelain, Wade, England, 1960s...................................... **9**

Figure of Samuel De Champlain, #3 (of set of 40) in Lipton's "Famous Explorers" series, Louis Marx Toy Company, New York City, 1960s, 3" h., w/card......................... **12**

Figure of Tom, Tom, the Piper's Son, from Red Rose Tea's "Nursery Rhyme" set, porcelain, Wade, England, 1960s **6**

Red Rose Tea's Jack & Jill

Figures of Jack & Jill, #39 & 41 from Red Rose Tea's "Nursery Rhyme" set, 1960s, each (ILLUS.).. 5

Figures of The Three Bears, from Red Rose Tea's "Nursery Rhyme" set, porcelain, Wade, England, 1960s.............................. 16

Model of bear cub, from Red Rose Tea's animal set, porcelain, Wade, England, 1960s... 4

Red Rose Tea's Bushbaby

Model of bushbaby, porcelain, #19 in Red Rose Tea's animal set, Wade, England, 1960s (ILLUS.)... 2

Model of butterfly, from Red Rose Tea's animal set, porcelain, Wade, England, 1960s... 6

Model of giraffe, from Red Rose Tea's animal set, porcelain, Wade, England, 1960s... 5

Red Rose Tea's Pelican

Model of pelican, from Red Rose Tea's animal set, porcelain, Wade, England, 1960s (ILLUS.)... 3

Model of sea lion, from Red Rose Tea's animal set, porcelain, Wade, England, 1960s... 2

Red Rose Tea Promotional Packaging & Teapot Figurines

Packaging, for Red Rose Tea, promoting its collectible teapot figurines, shows box of tea on front w/"FREE INSIDE" in banner & "Collect All 8 Roseville Teapot Figurines" above picture of one of the figurines, 1996, 6 x 7 1/2" (ILLUS. w/two figurines)... 5

Plush toy, Cyril the Cyclist Chimp, Brooke Bond PG Tip Tea store premium, dressed in green & red striped outfit & sunglasses, rare, 1970s, 20" h. 150

Promotional Piece for Red Rose Tea

Promotional teapot figurine, in the form of a bright red jack-in-the-box w/joker popping out the top holding yellow banner that reads "FREE INSIDE" in green, front of box shows picture of a box of Red Rose tea & one of the giveaway items & "From the RED ROSE Toy Chest - Collect All 8 Toy Teapot Figurines," 1997, 6 x 7 1/2" (ILLUS.) 5

Promotional teapot figurine, Red Rose giveaway item, in the form of a barber shop, 1996 (ILLUS. right w/packaging) 3

Promotional teapot figurine, Red Rose giveaway item, in the form of a dessert shop, 1996 (ILLUS. left w/packaging)............... 3

Model of Stove Teapot

Promotional teapot figurine, Red Rose giveaway item, in the form of a grey stove w/pots on top, black oven door w/window showing chicken or turkey cooking inside, 1996 (ILLUS.)... 3

Model of Restaurant Counter Teapot

Promotional teapot figurine, Red Rose giveaway item, in the form of a pink restaurant counter w/containers on top, drawers painted on side, 1996 (ILLUS.)............ **3**

Model of Teddy Bear Teapot

Promotional teapot figurine, Red Rose giveaway item, model of brown Teddy bear w/red bow tie forms body, blue handle & spout, 1997, double the value for items in original plastic pouch (ILLUS.) **2**

Model of Jack-in-the-Box Teapot

Promotional teapot figurine, Red Rose giveaway item, rectangular yellow body w/purple & green design on sides, purple spout & handle, lid in the form of a jack-in-the-box figure, 1997, double the value for items in original plastic pouch (ILLUS.).. **1**

Sign, tin, Red Rose Tea advertisement, "Red Rose Tea - is Good Tea," 1950s, 17 x 24"... **85**

Store advertisement, "There is a picture card in every packet of Brooke Bond Tea also in Crown Cup Instant Coffee - 2 oz.=2 cards, 4 oz.=3 cards, 8 oz.=4 cards," United Kingdom, 1950s......................... **40**

Teapot, cov., w/inner basket for loose tea & insulated aluminum cozy that fits around pot, yellow, Lipton premium, Hall, 1940s, 6 1/2" h., 9 1/2" l. **40**

TEDDY BEAR COLLECTIBLES

Advertisement

Advertising, Cream of Wheat, children w/doll & Teddy "Saying Grace," 1917 (ILLUS.) **$25**

Advertising, Papa bear, cut-&-stuff doll, offered by Kellogg Company, 1925, 15"............ **35**

Baby cup, silver plated, marked "Forbes Silver," ca. 1915, 3" h. **100**

Cast-iron Bank

Bank, cast iron, Teddy bear bank, no markings, 6 1/2" h. (ILLUS.)...................................... **25**

Bear, excelsior-stuffed cinnamon mohair swivel-head bear w/brown glass eyes, shaved mohair muzzle w/black floss nose, open red felt mouth, applied ears, five-piece body jointed at shoulders & hips, felt pads on paws, two black floss claws on front paws (but none on back paws), unmarked, 22" (excelsior visible on left paw & where red felt of lower lip is worn through, left ear reattached, pads on paws re-covered, some thinning mohair) **155**

Book, cutout bear shape, "Moving Picture Teddies," R.H. Graham, 1907 .... **55**

"Little Johnny and The Teddy Bears"

Book, "Little Johnny and the Teddy Bears," J.R. Bray, Reilly & Britton, 1907 (ILLUS.)... **130**

Book, "Mother Goose's Teddy Bears," Frederick L. Cavally, color illus., not dated **325**

Book, "The Roosevelt Bears Abroad," Seymour Eaton, illustrated, 1906 .... **100**

Gabriel Teddy Bear Book

Book, "The Teddy Bear That Prowled At Night," Samuel Gabriel, 1924 (ILLUS.)............ **45**

"Three Little Cotton Tails ..." Book

Book, "Three Little Cotton Tails and Uncle Teddy Bear," Donahue, 1922 (ILLUS.)........... **50**

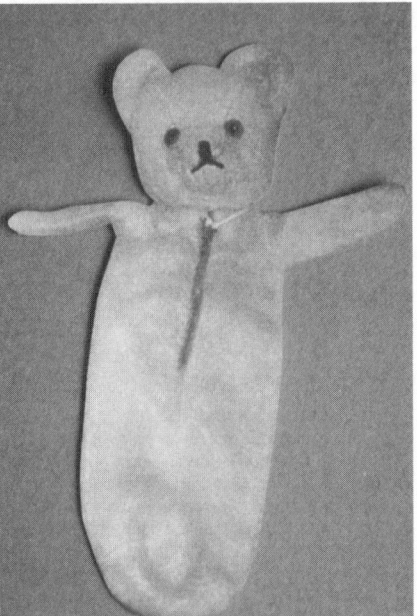

Bear Head Bottle Holder

Bottle holder, straw-stuffed bear head w/glass eyes (ILLUS.) **55**

Calendar, w/Teddy bears, for 1927 .... **25**

Card game, "Three Bears," Milton Bradley, ca. 1920.. **40**

Chocolate service, child's, lithographed tin, Teddies on tray, cups & pot..................... **125**

Cookie tin, printed w/picture of little boy holding Teddy bear, marked "Edward Sharpe," ca. 1940... **45**

Child's Handkerchief

Handkerchief, child's, featuring four bears, 1950s (ILLUS.)... **15**

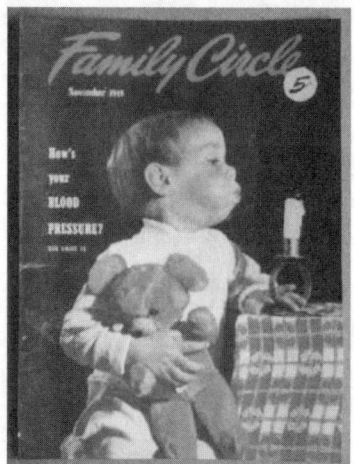

Family Circle Magazine Illustration

Illustration, Family Circle Magazine, little boy holding bear, November 1949 (ILLUS.).. **6**

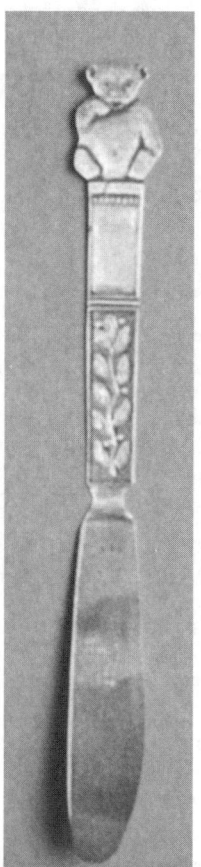

Child's Knife

Knife, child's, marked "Sweden," 6" l. (ILLUS.).. **35**

Paper doll set, "The Animated Goldilocks Doll with the Three Bears," Milton Bradley **20**

Paper doll set, "The Three Bears Home," McLoughlin Brothers, 1933 .... **45**

Photograph, child holding Teddy bear, complete in frame, 1906 .... **60**

British Picture Postcard

Postcard, British deckle edge picture postcard by Beagles, no date (ILLUS., bottom previous page) **15**

Postcard with Shirley Temple

Postcard, Shirley Temple taking picture of Teddy bear, 1930s (ILLUS.) **18**
Postcard, signed Ellen Clapsaddle, International Art Publishing Co., Teddy bear in Santa's pack, 1907 .... **18**

Postcard, signed John Winsch, Santa holding Teddy bear, 1913 .... **40**
Pull toy, Drummer Bear, Fisher-Price No. 102, 1932 .... **700**
Pull toy, Teddy Bear Parade, Fisher-Price No. 195, 1938 .... **600**
Pull toy, Teddy Tooter, Fisher-Price No. 150, 1940 .... **400**
Pull toy, Teddy Xylophone, Fisher-Price No. 752, 1948 .... **350**

Fisher-Price Teddy Bear

Pull toy, Tiny Teddy Xylophone, Fisher-Price No. 636, 1958 (ILLUS.) **100**
Puzzle, block-type, "The Three Bears," 1950s (ILLUS., below) **20**

Block Puzzle

Handmade Quilt

Quilt, handmade, Teddy bear blocks, will fit double bed, ca. 1950s (ILLUS.) **75**
Sand pail, lithographed tin, Roosevelt riding Teddy bear, Butler Brothers, 1908 .... **400**

Sheet Music

Sheet music, "Teddy Bear's Lullaby," Chandler Held Music Company, 1907 (ILLUS.) **25**
Teddy bear, 75th Anniversary, boxed, Ideal, 1978 (ILLUS., to the right) **50**
Teddy bear, black mohair, brown glass eyes, reembroidered nose & mouth, fully jointed body, velveteen pads, American-made, ca. 1920, 24" (pad wear) **1,610**
Teddy bear, brown-tipped blonde long mohair, brown glass eyes, embroidered nose, mouth & claws, shaved muzzle &

inner ears, crier, fully jointed body, felt pads, American-made, mid-20th c., 21" **173**

Boxed Teddy Bear

Teddy bear, "Cheeky" by Merrythought, jointed limbs, swivel head, 12" h. **70**
Teddy bear, circus bear, gold mohair over papier-mâché, leather muzzle & chain, wind-up mechanism moves head from side to side, right leg raises & waves, early 1900s, 5 1/2" **200**
Teddy bear, golden yellow mohair plush, embroidered mouth, brown twill nose, fully jointed body w/excelsior stuffing, felt pads, probably American, ca. 1920, 16" (one eye pitted, light fur loss, felt pads damaged) **259**

Knickerbocker Teddy Bear

Teddy bear, jointed arms & legs, swivel head, Knickerbocker, 16" (ILLUS.).................. **45**

Panda Teddy Bear

Teddy bear, one-piece panda, straw stuffed, 1940s, worn (ILLUS.) **20**

One-piece Teddy Bear

Teddy bear, one-piece, vinyl snout, 1950s, 13" (ILLUS.) **25**

Japanese-made Teddy Bear

Teddy bear, panda, straw-stuffed, Japan, 1940s, 5" h. (ILLUS.)... **15**

Schuco Yes/No Miniature Bear

Teddy bear, Schuco Yes/No miniature, brown fur, 3 1/2" h. (ILLUS.)........................... **385**

Early Ideal Teddy Bear

Teddy bear, shoe button eyes, excelsior stuffed, jointed arms & legs, swivel head, Ideal, ca. 1910, 14", worn condition (ILLUS.).. 250

Teddy bear, white mohair, shoe button eyes, jointed arms & legs, swivel head, unknown maker, ca. 1930............................... 95

Teddy Bear Squeaky Toy

Toy, squeaker-type, vinyl bear, no maker mark, 7" h. (ILLUS.) 50

Toy, Teddy bear ABC blocks, 1907, the set...... 150

Valentine, bear w/jointed legs & arms, verse on back, Raphael Tuck, ca. 1909, 12".. 50

Valentine, fuzzy bear, 1948, 12" 8

Other Bear Collectibles

Advertisement, Magic Yeast, "Bear in Mind," die-cut cardboard of a sitting polar bear 20

Advertisement, "The Big Bear Cigar," cigar box liner, shows bruin holding large cigar in forest setting, Schmidt & Co., 1903 20

Battery-operated Bank

Bank, battery-operated, tin, fishing bears, 1940s (ILLUS.).. 65

Bank, mechanical-type, cast iron, Teddy Roosevelt shoots coin into tree trunk & bear's head appears out of trunk, 1907, 10" 200

Bear Book

Book, "O-U-Bear," E.M. Leaven, Inc., 1919 (ILLUS.) 27

Book, Prudential Book, cover art w/two bears having tea party, 1910............................ 35

Book, "The True Story of Smokey the Bear," Big Golden Book, 1950s 15

Smokey the Bear Comic Book

Comic book, "The True Story of Smokey Bear," Forestry Department (ILLUS.)................ 8

Bear Egg Cup

Egg cup, ceramic, cream w/emerald green trim, 1920s, 1 3/4" h. (ILLUS.)............................ 30

Fan, cardboard, handheld, scene of Smokey by campfire, 1950s 18

Figurines, china, bears in various poses, made in Germany, early 1900s, each.............. 75

Judge Magazine Illustration

Illustration, Judge Magazine, full page, full color, 1907 (ILLUS.)... 22

Inkwell, silver-colored metal, no maker or date, head hinged, glass inkwell insert.......... 130

Paper Doll

Paper doll, advertising for Behr-Manning company, Barney, ca. 1930 (ILLUS.)............... 22

Perfume bottle, model of a bear, mohair, head removes to show glass bottle, early 1900s, 3 3/4" h.. 200

Toy, Pantin paper toy, Raphael Tuck & Sons, ca. 1909, 12".. 125

Toy, squeaker-type, bear, vinyl w/swivel head w/cloth ears & moving eyes, Edward Mobley, 10" h.. 80

Toy, squeaker-type, bear w/red cap, Arrow Rubber, 8" h... 40

TELEVISION SETS

Admiral Bakelite TV

Admiral, Model 19A1, Bakelite 7" tabletop, late 1940s (ILLUS.)..................................... $150

Admiral, Model 20T1, 14" Bakelite console, ca. 1950.. 75

Admiral, Model 20X122, 10" Bakelite console.. 250

Andrea, Model KTE-5, kit TV w/5" CRT, 1938.. 3,500

Andrea, Model T-VJ12, console, 12" picture tube, late 1940s... 85

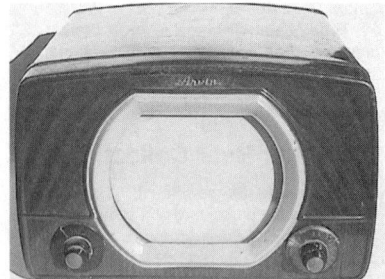

Arvin Portable TV

Arvin, Model 4080T, 8" metal portable, ca. 1950 (ILLUS.) 175

CBS Columbia, Model 205C1, color TV w/19" round CRT, 1955.................................... 550

CBS Columbia, Model 22C05, black & white console w/21" picture tube, 1955........... 55

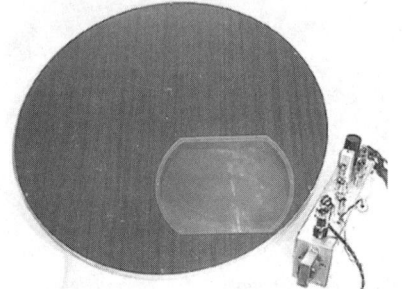

Col-R-Tel Color Wheel Attachment

Col-R-Tel, color wheel attachment, produces color image on black & white TV (ILLUS.)... 550

DuMont TV

DuMont, Chatham Model RA-103, dog house-shaped 12" TV, ca. 1947 (ILLUS.)...... 400
DuMont, Model RA-103-D3, square 12" tabletop, ca. 1949................................ 65

DuMont Tabletop TV

DuMont, Model RA-105, large square tabletop, ca. 1949 (ILLUS.)................................ 75
DuMont, Model RA-113, interestingly styled console TV, late 1940s............................ 125
DuMont, Model RA-160, large-screen TV w/FM radio, 1950s............................ 75

Emerson Pop-up Console TV

Emerson, Model 508, pop-up wooden 16" console (ILLUS.) **350**
Emerson, Model 639, 7" portable, ca. 1948 ..... **150**
Emerson, Model 663, 14" wooden tabletop, ca. mid-1950s.................................... **45**

Garod Tabletop TV

Garod, Model 10TZ, tall wooden tabletop, unusual style, screen above knobs (ILLUS.) **450**
General Electric, Model 10T1, unusual 10" Bakelite tabletop.. **300**
General Electric, Model 14T, painted metal portable, 1950s.. **65**
General Electric, Model 803, 10" tabletop w/speaker above screen, unusual, 1947....... **375**
General Electric, Model 807, 10" tabletop w/glass front plate, tall.. **85**

General Electric Tabletop TV

General Electric, Model 810, wide wooden tabletop, 1948 (ILLUS.).................................... **100**
Jenkins, Model 100, scanning disc TV, complete, 1932... **3,500**
JVC, Model 3100R Video Capsule, pyramid-shaped set, 1970s.................................... **350**
JVC, Model 3240 Video Sphere, ball-shaped set, ca. 1970 .... **200**

Meissner Kit Television

Meissner, Model 10-1153, metal kit television, 1938 (ILLUS.) **2,500**
Motorola, Model 17T5, 17" Bakelite tabletop, ca. 1950 .... **50**
Motorola, Model 19P1 "Astronaut," large transistor portable, ca. 1954 .... **175**
Motorola, Model VT-105, unusual 10" wooden tabletop, ca. 1948 .... **250**
Motorola, Model VT-71, 7" wooden tabletop, 1947 .... **150**

Panasonic "Flying Saucer" TV

Panasonic, "Flying Saucer" model, ca. 1971 (ILLUS.) **375**
Philco, Model 48-1001, 10" tabletop, ca. 1948 .... **150**
Philco, Model 48-700, wide wooden 7" tabletop **250**

Philco Tabletop TV

Philco, Model 50-702, wooden 7" tabletop (ILLUS.) **250**
Philco, Predicta console, Barber Pole, mahogany **550**
Philco, Predicta table top, metal, working **350**
Philco, Predicta Tandem two-piece (as found) **400**
Philco, Safara Model H2010, first transistor TV, working **175**
RCA, Model 17PD series, large metal portable, ca. mid-1950s **65**
RCA, Model 21-CT-55, color TV w/21" CRT, 1955 .... **275**

RCA Console TV

RCA, Model 21T, blond 21" console, ca. 1953 (ILLUS.) **75**

RCA Wooden TV

RCA, Model 630-TS, 10" mass-produced wooden set, ca. 1946 (ILLUS.) **175**
RCA, Model 8-TS-30, 10" tabletop, ca. 1948...... **125**
RCA, Model 9PC41, buffet-shaped projection set, 1949 .... **250**

Scott, Model 6T11, tabletop projection set, ca. 1949 (ILLUS.) **450**

First Imported Transistor TV

Sony, Model 8-301W, first imported transistor TV, w/metal case (ILLUS.)........................ **250**

Early RCA Color TV

RCA, Model CT-100, first mass-produced color TV, 15" screen, not working (ILLUS.)... **1,000**
RCA, Model T120, metal 12" tabletop **125**
RCA, Model TRK-120, console w/mirror in lid, 1940 .... **4,000**

Transvision Kit TV

Transvision, 7" kit TV in unusual cabinet (ILLUS.) **250**
Westinghouse, Model TRK-12, console w/12" mirror in lid (ILLUS., top of next page)... **4,500**
Zenith, Model 24G20, tabletop port-hole style w/button below screen **250**
Zenith, Model 28T96, 16" port-hole model w/brass around screen..................................... **150**

Scott Tabletop Projection TV Set

Westinghouse Console TV

Zenith, Model T-2294, 27" rectangular screen radio/TV/phone set.................................. 65

TEXTILES

Coverlets

Jacquard, double-weave, one-piece, burgundy, medium blue, green & white in floral medallions w/double vining tulip borders, dated "1824" along border, 66 x 90"... **$275**

Jacquard, double-weave, two-piece, bands of navy blue, tomato red & burgundy w/natural in floral & star medallions w/borders of stars & birds w/urns & buildings, flower corner block for Sarah (1822-1914) & Henry LaTourette, Fountain County, Indiana, "Year 1850," 72 x 86" (edge damage & bleach spots)...................... **743**

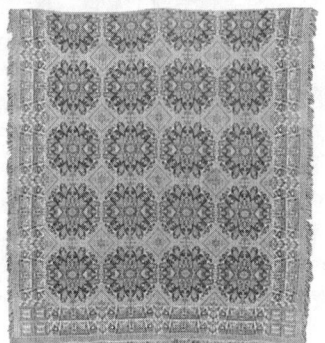

Intricate Jacquard Coverlet

Jacquard, double-weave, two-piece, crisscross bands of tomato red, navy blue & teal blue w/natural in intricate design of floral medallions, diamonds & foliage, double border w/birds, oak leaves & elaborate building w/double towers, corner blocks have four frames w/"1859" inside, stains, top edge bound in plaid cloth, 76 x 84" (ILLUS.)... **633**

Jacquard, double-weave, two-piece, in dark blue & natural, elaborate urns of fruit & birds feeding their young, Christian & Heathen border, no corner blocks, attached tag attributes piece to Jefferson County, Ohio, 66 x 76" (some fringe loss & one end is turned over & stitched)............. **935**

Jacquard, double-weave, two-piece, navy blue & natural geometric design w/pine tree border, 78 x 90 .... **275**

Jacquard, double-weave, two-piece, navy blue & natural in floral medallions w/border of acanthus leaves & baskets of flowers, 72 x 86" (staining) **440**

Jacquard, double-weave, two-piece, navy blue, tomato red, mustard & natural in medallions w/roses & thistles, double borders of roses & leaves, four-part corner blocks w/leaves, 75 x 84" (minor wear, fringe loss, some bleeding)................. **660**

Jacquard, one-piece, single-weave, in colors of tomato red, navy blue & green on natural ground, unusual double border w/woodpeckers on stumps separated by flowering plants & dates at the lower corners, 25 large stars, each surrounded by floral wreath & smaller stars, dated "1858," 75 x 92" (minor moth damage & stains) **880**

Jacquard, single-weave, one-piece, red on white, star medallion at center surrounded by a rose wreath & eagles in each corner, signed in corner block "Made By J.D. Wieand Allentown, 1868," vintage side borders w/tulip, rose & urn end borders, 80 x 86" (minor stains) **413**

Jacquard, summer/winter, two-piece, blue, star & heart pattern w/bird & flowering tree border, signed "MADE BY D L MYERS BETHEL TOWNSHIP FOR CATHARIN FLICK 1844," Pennsylvania, 67 x 98" (minor seam separation) **294**

Jacquard, summer/winter, two-piece, dyed blue warp & red weft, floral medallions w/hearts, border w/grapevines & vining flowers, tulips, corner block w/"Middletown Fred K. County Maryland," 84 x 87" (one end turned down, some fringe loss, minor stain, few small holes)........................... **275**

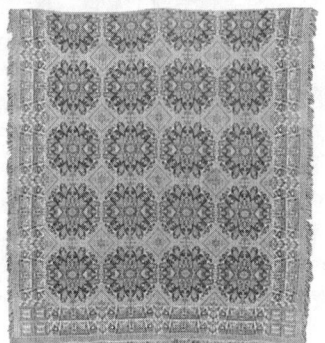

Signed Jacquard Coverlet

Jacquard, summer/winter, two-piece, navy blue, tomato red & olive green w/natural in design w/rose & sun medallions, unusual garland swag border w/tassels & Maltese crosses, corner blocks signed "Peter Lorenz 1842," minor fringe loss, 76 x 86" (ILLUS.) **770**

Jacquard, summer/winter, two-piece, tomato red, navy blue & olive bands w/natural in fruit & floral medallions, corner blocks dated 1855, 76 x 88" (fringe loss & seam needs resewing) **220**

Jacquard, two-piece Biederwand in green, navy blue, tomato red & white w/circular & rose medallions w/borders of double-headed eagles, foliage swags, tassels & Maltese crosses, corner block w/"Peter Lorenz 1841," 78 x 85" **1,320**

Jacquard, two-piece, large oval star & vintage medallion at center flanked by two large baskets, signed across bottom "Made By Peter Siebert, Easton, Pennsyl.," harp & scrolled foliage borders, green, navy blue & red on natural ground, 88 x 94" **633**

Jacquard, two-piece, meandering grapevines w/grapes arranged in a geometric design of navy blue, green & red on white, signed by weaver in corner blocks "F.E. Hesse, Weaver, Logan, Ohio, 1860," 70 x 91 1/2" (edge wear) **440**

Flags

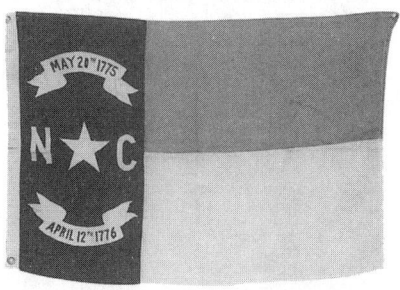

North Carolina Flag

North Carolina, blue, red & white panels, two horizontal, the vertical panel w/yellow banners reading "May 20th 1775" & "April 12th 1776," w/"N [star] C" in between banners, minor holes, 25 x 36" (ILLUS.) **83**

Texas, blue, red & white w/large star, 51 1/2 x 73" (stains) **83**

Linens & Needlework

Family record, a small central square headed "Family Record" followed by "Mr. Samuel Hildreth Born Oct 9 1794" & "Miss Mary Morgan Born Sept 30 1796, Married Dec 16 1819" above vital records of their seven children, followed by inscription "Thirza J Hildreth Lynn 1836 Aged 12 Years," all in sawtooth border, surrounded by solidly stitched vining foli-

ate design, in period frame, 20 1/8 x 22" (ILLUS., below) **3,819**

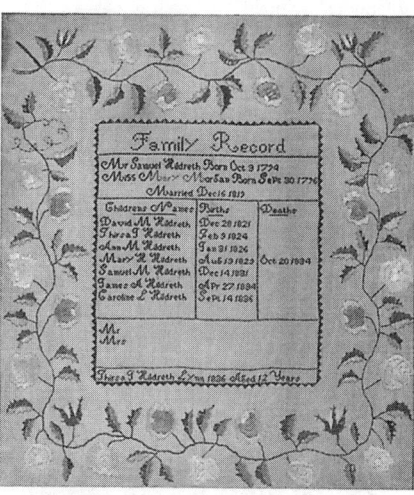

Hildreth Family Needlework Record

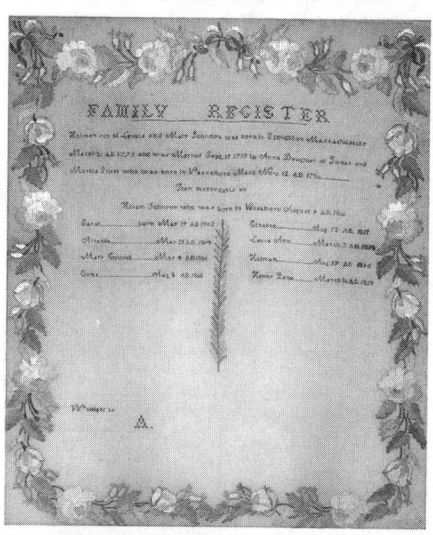

Johnson Family Needlework Register

Family register, center headed "Family Register" followed by "Holman son of Lewis and Mary Johnson was born in Stoughton Massachusetts March 21 AD 1775 and was married Sept. 12 1799 to Anna Daughter of Jonas and Martha Priest who was born in Vassalboro Mass Nov. 12 AD 1780," followed by vital records of their nine children, followed by "wrought by ...A," a leafy branch in the middle & solidly stitched flowering border in shades of blue, green & pink, ca. 1820, toning, fading, minor staining at margins, 22 1/2 x 26", (ILLUS.) **441**

Needlework Pictures

Allegorical scene, "The Death of Sylvia's Stag," solidly stitched silk threads on silk ground, watercolor features & distant landscape, embroidered verse worked beneath picture, titled & signed "Wrought at Mrs. Saunders and Miss Beach's Academy," Dorchester, Massachusetts, note on back identifies the needleworker, early 19th c., 24 1/4 x 25 1/4"................. **14,950**

"Caroline" Needlework Picture

"Caroline, the Heroine of Litchfield," square, w/round center panel depicting young woman seated in pastoral setting under willow trees, a book in her lap & a dog by her side, stitched in silk & chenille threads of greens, golds, brown & blue w/watercolor features & background, églomisé mat, period frame, possibly Litchfield Female Academy, Litchfield, Connecticut, ca. 1800, repairs, 17 1/2 x 18" (ILLUS.) **940**

Needlework Picture of Mt. Vernon

Landscape, silk needlework & watercolor depiction of Mount Vernon, the stitched view of the estate w/General Washington standing on the porch overlooking the hand-painted Potomac River w/sailing vessels, pink & blue sky in background, the foreground w/two women & groom w/hand-painted features, a horse & colt, flowers & tall grass, trees & shrubs, framed, America, early 19th c., 20 x 24 1/2" (ILLUS.) **9,988**

Spicer Memorial Needlework Picture

Memorial picture, silk needlework & watercolor depiction of large monument w/tablet inscribed "Mrs. Fanny Spicer Ob't. Aug 18th 1795, AE 20 Mrs. Mary Thayer Ob't. Sept. - 1806, AE 36 Mrs. Sarah Clark Ob't. Oct. 12 1810, AE 24," the monument surrounded by grieving figures in mourning clothes, the figures, landscape & sky painted in watercolor and gouache, the monument, foliate tree & shrubbery solidly stitched in silk & chenille threads on a silk ground, in églomisé mat & period frame, America, early 19th c., splits to silk inscriptions, some paint separation on the glass, losses to mat & frame (ILLUS.) **4,700**

Needlework Memorial Picture

Memorial picture, silk needlework & watercolor depiction of two painted urn-topped monuments beneath willow tree, inscribed "Sacred to the Memory of Mrs. Hannah Richardson who died May 31st 1820 Aged 36," the other "Sacred to the memory of John Gilson who died April 21st 1816 Ae 7 wks.," two painted gravestones in foreground, another tree & small church, hills & blue sky in background, gilt & églomisé mat frame, ca. 1820, 24 x 24 1/4" (ILLUS.)......................... **4,700**

Minstrel Needlework Picture

Minstrel couple, figures of man & woman in painted black face, the man dressed in military uniform & holding sword, the woman in period dress & bonnet holding handkerchief, amid whimsical landscape of flowers, birds & butterflies above romantic verse, the solidly stitched figures in silk threads of pinks, greens, pale blue & brown on linen ground, signed lower right "J. Adams June 1836," New Orleans, Louisiana, 16 1/4 x 19 3/4" (ILLUS.)... **12,925**

Mourning picture, solidly stitched silk thread & watercolor on a silk ground, showing a monument of lithographed silk ribbons w/inscription dated 1856, flanked by family members whose faces are photographic images, mounted in a mirrored shadowbox frame, inscribed by maker & dated 1866, Milwaukee, Wisconsin, 29 1/2 x 33 1/2" (minor imperfections to mirrored panels) **16,100**

Quilts

Appliqué, central star surrounded by American eagles in corners, calicos in light pink, pale yellow, peach & green, hand-stitched, attributed to Pennsylvania, minor fading & edge wear, 81 x 87" (ILLUS., below).. **660**

Appliqué Quilt with Star & Eagles

Appliqué Quilt with Tulip Border

Appliqué, floral medallions in red, orange & printed pink w/radiating green calico leaves & additional red & orange flowers, vining bud border, handstitched small princess feather medallions & concentric outlines, 75 x 88" (stains & wear) **798**

Appliqué, four-petal flowers in light pink w/green & pink buds & draped swags in darker pink, handstitched w/diamond & sunflower quilting, pink binding, 76 x 92" (light stains) **193**

Appliqué, holly & flower medallions in plain red w/green, pink & yellow calico, vining tulip border in red & green, handstitched w/diamonds & oak leaves, stains, 81" sq. (ILLUS., top of page) **550**

Appliqué, nine floral medallions in red calico & green w/princess feather quilting, red calico edging, handstitched w/embroidered initials "CS," 79" sq. (minor wear, faded spot).............................. **413**

Appliqué, nine red, white & yellow flower medallions w/green foliage on a white diamond quilted ground, green zigzag borders, attached note states that quilt was "Made by Mary Magdaline Recher, 1850," & gives her birth & death dates, 87 x 87" **1,210**

Baskets Appliqué Quilt

Appliqué, twelve flower baskets & double sawtooth borders in tan & red on white, handsewn w/princess feather medallion quilting, intact pencil marks, stains, 72 x 90" (ILLUS.).. **523**

Appliqué Rose of Sharon patt., , cotton, worked in red, green, pink & yellow calico fabrics on white ground & backing w/red binding, quilted in conforming floral patt., pieced scalloped border, probably Pennsylvania, ca. 1840, 88 x 90" **1,528**

Appliqued Calamanco-type, panels of glazed indigo & dark olive green worsted fabric quilted in scrolling feather & grapevine patterns, backed w/brown woven tabby fabric, New England, ca. 1800, 82 x 83"... **2,115**

Appliquéd Carolina Lily patt., red & green prints on white quilted ground, each plant divided by a diamond block w/large quilted flowers, meandering line borders w/small tulips, no batting, 56 x 57" (minor stains w/areas of pencil marks remaining)... **605**

Appliquéd Eagle patt., composed of red, green & gold eagles in bordered nine-block patt. on white ground, quilted in conforming eagle & geometric patt., Missouri, early 20th c., 77 x 83"...................... **2,350**

Appliquéd Friendship quilt, twenty panels w/flowers or trees in various red, green, pink & yellow calicos, red, green & yellow vining flower border w/fishscale quilting, handstitched w/meandering princess feathering between the panels, all panels

but one have inked signatures, some w/place names, dates & an occasional verse, most from Ohio, most dates from 1854/1855, 77 x 90" (some ink fading, minor stains, one panel has small stitched repair)... **2,860**

Crib quilt, Pieced Hills of Vermont patt., red calico w/white & blue printed flowers & white, hanstitched, 42 x 57" (stains)............. **523**

Pieced Aunt Eliza's Star variation patt., in strong colors of red, yellow & white calico on vivid blue calico, handstitched w/wavy lines & diamonds, Lebanon County, Pennsylvania, 78" sq. (minor stains)............. **385**

Pieced Bear Paw, in light red calico on white quilted blocks divided by blue & white lines, small bright red blocks where lines intersect, 86 x 87" (stains)..................... **358**

Pieced Birds in Flight patt., on red calico, dark multicolored triangles alternating w/lighter triangles inside 6 1/8" blocks, 65 x 72" (small stains).................................... **468**

Pieced Broken Star patt., medium rainbow colors, handstitched w/princess feather medallions & original pencil lines, blue edging, 75" sq. (ILLUS., bottom of page)...... **743**

Broken Star Quilt

Amish Quilt with Center Diamond

Pieced Center Diamond patt., red central diamond on dark green ground, surrounded by mint green border & wide black outer border, the mint green corner blocks w/handquilted tulips, the center diamond w/quilted star & feather medallion, Amish, 20th c., 86" sq. (ILLUS.) 715

Patriotic Civil War Quilt

Pieced Civil War patriotic, cotton, blue center w/three panels, the upper w/the American eagle pieced in yellow & brown, holding in its beak a red banner inscribed "THE UNION FOREVER," the middle panel a blue field dotted w/34 white stars arranged in the Great Star patt., the bottom panel a white field containing the symbolic broken chain & pieced letters "END OF THE WAR," the panels all quilted w/stars & ships, the center panels flanked by 13 red & white stripes quilted alternately w/guns & swords, all backed w/white cotton & edged in blue, New York, ca. 1861, 79 x 84 1/2" (ILLUS.) **21,150**

Pieced Diamond & Medallions patt. composed of colored blocks on white w/prin-

cess feather quilting, wedding-type, Pennsylvania, 68" sq. (minor stains) 413

Pieced Diamond Nine Patch & Block patt., cotton, pink, green, red, blue & brown w/alternating yellow blocks & brown border, backed w/brown & white printed striped fabric, quilted in diagonal lines design, Pennsylvania, ca. 1840, 90 x 92" (staining & wear on back) 353

Pieced Double Irish Chain patt., composed of red & white blocks, hand-stitched, 76 x 82" (stains) 413

Pieced Flower Baskets patt., chinz, flower baskets in pastel green & two shades of pink w/triple border in same colors, on white ground, hand-stitched w/princess feather medallions w/diamond centers, 78 x 91" (minor stains) 440

Pieced Irish Chain patt., composed of green & brick red calico on white ground w/finely quilted cross hatching, 79 x 81" (minor stains) 605

Pieced Log Cabin w/straight furrow patt., colorful gingham & prints w/red centers, 68 x 82" 495

Pieced Lone Star patt., bold design w/smaller stars in each corner in red, orange, greenish brown & sage green on bright yellow calico ground, hand-stitched, Pennsylvania, 86" sq. (stains, orange has bled through to back).................. 330

Pieced Lone Star patt., composed of red, golden yellow & olive blocks on white, hand-titched w/floral & leaf quilting, 74" sq. 248

Pieced Moon & Stars patt., woven wool, composed of49 full & three-quarter circles composed of four pie-shaped wedges in shades of rust & green, tan twill binding & woven wool backing, America, 19th c., 83 x 96" (fading, stains, small holes) 764

Pieced Nine Patch patt., composed of green & pale orange calico blocks, brown backing w/floral print designs, Amish, Harrisburg, Pennsylvania area, 74 x 83"...... 523

Pieced Nine Patch patt., composed of postage stamp squares in blue & brown calico on white, alternating w/brown floral print, floral print border in light browns & greens, hand-stitched in various quilted designs in brown & white thread, one block is initialed, Pennsylvania, 68 x 84" (stains) 495

Pieced Ocean Waves patt., composed of connected octagonal rings of pink calico & floral print light blue triangles on green calico ground w/pink stripe & brown calico border, hand-stitched, 82 x 86" 275

Pieced Octagonal Medallions patt., composed of pink, red & navy blue calico on white, handsewn w/machine-sewn blue binding, princess feather medallion quilting, 67 x 86" (stains)....................................... 633

Pieced Odd Fellows Patch patt., composed of green & pale orange calico blocks, hand-stitched w/princess feather quilting, 76 x 90" (light stains) 495

Amish Sawtooth Diamond Quilt

Pieced Pine Tree patt., composed of various plain & printed fabrics including blues, greens, pink, yellow, purple & red, three-part border in dark green, lavender & yellow calico, handstitched w/quilting of leaves & princess feather medallions, original pencil lines remain, 66 x 76" (light stains) **385**

Pieced Pineapple (Log Cabin variation) patt., composed of cotton calico blocks, two yellow, one green, one pink, backed w/brown figured print & bound w/green, w/border of four bands, Mennonite, Washington, Pennsylvania, ca. 1880, 84 x 96" **1,175**

Pieced Pineapple patt., composed oftomato red & navy blue wool blocks, handstitched w/brown thread, tan cloth backing, Amish, 66" sq. (small hole, two pieces of blue are mismatched) **935**

Pieced Pineapple variant patt., composed of pink & yellow calico blocks w/red center on green calico ground, navy blue calico backing, 69 x 80" **330**

Pieced Postage Stamp patt., composed of concentric diamonds w/sawtooth border, bands of plain color & printed fabrics in between, hand-stitched w/lavender backing, 78 x 98" **1,045**

Pieced Rainbow Stripes patt., handstitched w/alternating quilting patterns, pencil & chalk lines remain, diagonal border, Amish, 20th c., 78 x 83" (ILLUS., to the right) **468**

Amish Quilt with Rainbow Stripes

Pieced Sawtooth Diamond patt., composed of red sawtooth diamond blocks & border on ivory ground, wide purple border & black binding, hand-stitched in red thread w/quilted princess feather meandering, grapevines & diamonds, Amish, 20th c., 102" sq. (ILLUS., top of page) **468**

Pieced Squares & Diamond Chain patt., composed of red on white blocks w/red edging, handsewn w/quilted spoked wheels & wavy lines, 66 x 82" **743**

Pieced Star of Bethlehem patt., a central radiating star w/smaller stars worked on a white field, a diamond border surrounded by a second border of printed chintz in a floral pattern, mid-19th c., 114 1/2 x 115" (some staining on reverse) **2,070**

Pieced Sunburst patt., composed of double pink calico blocks on white, hand-quilted w/wide white border & interlocking looped lines, pink edging, Pennsylvania, 74" sq. **495**

Pieced Trapunto Quilt

Pieced trapunto, softly faded blue calico star medallions & diamond band borders on white, handsewn w/trapunto roses between the medallions & borders, minor edge wear, small pieced corner repairs, stains, 76 x 90" (ILLUS.) **2,475**

Amish Trip Around the World Quilt

Pieced Trip Around the World patt., composed of blocks indark shades of blue, brown, green, purple, grey & pink w/hunter green border, brown corner blocks & black binding, hand-stitched w/floral quilting, embroidered initials "MS," Amish, 20th c., some fabric separation, 82 x 84" (ILLUS.) **935**

Pieced Trip Around the World Quilt

Pieced Trip Around the World patt., vibrant polychrome colors in solid & calico, four borders are orange, black, slate & red, handstitched w/printed paisley backing, minor staining & fading, 82 x 85" (ILLUS.) **825**

Samplers

"Christiana G. Robb" Sampler

Alphabets, dark & light brown w/light blue floss on natural, signed "Christiana G. Robb, Oct. 27, 1845," brown & green foliage border, in curly maple frame w/broad stripe & old finish, corner chip, 20 x 21" (ILLUS.) **715**

Alphabets, multicolored floss on tan linen ground w/"Done By Me Aged 13, 1794, M. Gray" & "H. Common" w/crown, framed, 11 1/2 x 13 1/3" (fabric stitched around the backing board so some of the borders are hidden behind frame) **495**

Alphabets, worked in black, blue & red threads, inscribed "Jane Collins born July the 26 1822 aged 10 years," 7 1/4 x 16 1/2" (thread losses, scattered staining, toning & fading) **470**

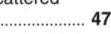

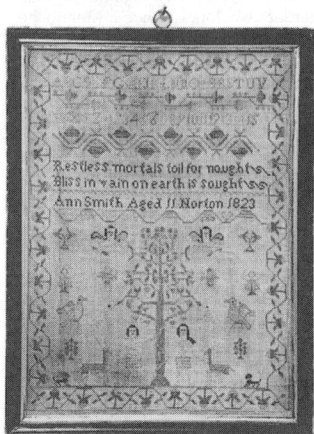

Alphabet Sampler with Adam & Eve

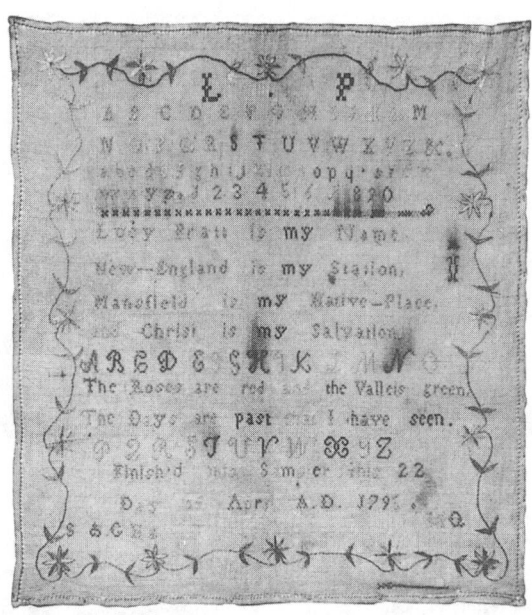

New England Sampler

Alphabets & Adam & Eve, shades of mostly pink silk thread w/green, brown, black & some soft orange on linen, w/verse, strawberries, birds, & Adam & Eve near the apple tree w/deer & dogs, "Ann Smith Aged 11 Norton 1823," black painted frame w/gilt liner, stains, 14 1/2 x 19" (ILLUS.) **935**

Alphabets & animals, stylized floral upper border above two alphabet panels over a panel of flowering shrubs & birds, worked in black, green & pink silk threads, inscribed "Lydia Wood's sampler Anno Domini 1799," unframed, America, 10 1/2 x 15 1/4" (fading, toning).................... **705**

Alphabets & family register, cross-stitch & satin stitch in silk thread on linen in shades of blue, salmon, green & brown w/vining strawberry border & two urns of flowers in blues, green, ivory, salmon & yellow, signed "Helen M. Miller Age 20," & dated January 19, 1850, in gilt frame, 17 1/2 x 19" without frame **990**

Alphabets & figures, alternating rows of large & small vines & flowers in burgundy, tan, green, black & blue on white, images of girl w/cat or dog on leash, a bird & monkey, dated "1850" & initialed "O.B.," framed, 13 x 14 1/4" (wear, later date is an addition, reduced in size along left margin, small restorations, staining)....... **440**

Alphabets & landscape, five alphabet panels above scene w/Federal-style buildings, trees, a bird & inspirational verse, inscribed "Mary Jane Flint aged 11 years April 19 1850," fading, staining & toning, 19 1/2 x 22 1/2" (ILLUS., at right) **1,175**

Alphabet Sampler

Alphabets & numerals, cross-stitch alphabets & numbers in sage green, brown & slate blue thread on linen ground, stitched by "Christinah Haner, Her example made in the year AD 1813," framed, 16 1/2 x 18 1/2" (minor stains, edge wear) **495**

Alphabets & pious verse, basket of flowers over alphabet panels above pious verse, surrounded by floral decorated banner, worked in shades of red, blue, green, yellow & blue threads, inscribed "Frances Croll 1810," framed, England or America, 12 3/4 x 16 3/8" **823**

Adam & Eve Sampler

Alphabets & pious verse, cross-stitch alphabets, numbers & verse quoted from "Judge Hale," all in black thread on linen ground, done by "Sarah Selfe Ackworth School 6th mo. 1784," handwritten note on back gives brief history of Ackworth School in England, in old gilt frame, 16 x 18 1/2" (rebacked on linen w/small holes & repairs, frame has minor edge damage & touchup)..................................... **1,540**

Alphabets & pious verse, linen w/silk thread in shades of soft green, tan & ivory & darker shades of blue, pink & brown, vining starflower border w/verse, alphabets, man in a hat & "Lucy Pratt is my Name, New-England is my Station, Mansfield is my Native-Place...," finished April 22, 1795, carved maple frame, dark browns have run some, 25 1/4 x 28 1/2" (ILLUS., top of previous page) **1,100**

Lord's Prayer, linen w/tiny precise stitches in silk thread in shades of green, ivory, gold, blue & dark pink w/the Lord's Prayer, urns of flowers, strawberries, acorns & "Ann Wilks fecit June 7th 1791," plain wood frame, 14 x 18 3/4" (few small holes) **495**

Miniature alphabets, three alphabets, trees & various devices & "Abigail A Jenney," w/upper & lower borders, worked in silk threads on linen ground in shades of green, yellow & brown, Plainfield, New Hampshire, ca. 1808, 3 3/4 x 4 3/4" without frame.. **2,585**

Pious verse & Adam & Eve, small center panel w/verse, floral symbols enclosed in a panel above Adam, Eve, the tree & entwined serpent, flanked by various religious, animal & floral devices, surrounded by stylized floral border, on grey/blue ground, framed, England, 1805, 15 x 29" (ILLUS., top of page) **1,880**

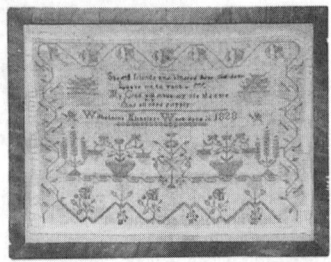

"Wilhelmina Nicholas" Sampler

Pious verse & baskets, green & brown floss on natural, w/verse, four baskets of fruit & flowers, meandering floral vine border, & "Wilhelmina Nicholas Work done in 1828," cloth tape edge binding, mahogany veneer frame, small holes & minor stains, the word "My" added later to verse, 15 3/4 x 20 3/4" (ILLUS.) **550**

"Rose of Sharon" Verse Sampler

Pious verse & landscape, linen w/satin, chain & tiny cross-stitch in blue, pink, ivory, yellow, brown & green silk thread depicting birds, butterflies, trees & angels w/the verse "The Rose of Sharon" & "Ann Broadbent, hir [sic] work done in the year of our Lord 1814 aged 12 yrs," all in multicolored strawberry border, in faux tortoiseshell shadow box frame w/gold repaint, minor thread loss & stain, 16 x 19" (ILLUS.) **1,320**

Verse Sampler by "Sarah Davey"

Pious verse & landscape, linen w/satin & cross-stitch in soft shades of green, ivory, gold & pink depicting urns of tulips & other flowers, birds, a two-story house w/fruit trees, strawberry border, verse & "Sarah Davey 179_," some stains, 23 1/2 x 26 1/2" (ILLUS.) **770**

Verse Sampler

Pious verse & landscape, linen w/tiny precise stitches in shades of green, ivory, pale gold, brown & dark blue silk thread depicting trees, flowers, vining border & a man & woman w/dog & bird on either side of an urn, verse in center & "Done by Jane Weekes at E. Mardon's School Aged 11 years. November 15th," nailed to stretcher & framed, 10 1/2 x 14" (ILLUS.) **1,210**

"On Virtue" Verse Sampler

Pious verse & landscape, natural linen w/green, red, brown, tan, silver & blue floss depicting six birds within trees or vines surrounding two flowering plants in urns, "On Virtue" verse at top surrounded by thin green border, two crowns, floral zigzag border, fanciful flower in urn, baskets & central bouquet, in 20th c. curly maple frame, small moth holes, 17 1/4 x 19 1/4" (ILLUS.) **990**

Sampler with Inspirational Verse

Pious verse & landscape, the verse above depiction of attached buildings, trees, vines & floral & animal devices, all surrounded by stylized floral border, inscribed "Isabella Lunds Work Aged 16 AD 1840," fading & toning, 26 3/4 x 32 1/4" (ILLUS.) **2,468**

Pious verse & landscape, the verse flanked by stylized vases of flowers & upper borders above birds on branches & a landscape w/thatched roof cottages, inscribed "SALLY CLARK AGED 8 YEARS 1801," framed, America or England, 1801, 17 x 21 (fading) **881**

TOOTHPICK HOLDERS

Reference numbers listed after the holders refer to the late William Heacock's books, Encyclopedia of Victorian Colored Pattern Glass, Book 1 *(1974) or* 1000 Toothpick Holders *(Antique Publications, 1977) and* Toothpick Holders: China, Glass and Metal, *prepared by members of the National Toothpick Holder Collector's Society (Antique Publication, 1992).*

China, Glass, Metal

There was a time when cleaning one's teeth at the table after enjoying a meal was considered to be quite proper. In fact, a toothpick holder was often included as part of the table service. Later it was considered permissible only if one hid the procedure discretely behind a napkin.

In the late Victorian era decorative items were all the rage. It was because of that love of novelty that toothpick holders were made in nearly every conceivable material - Art glass to pot metal. Fortunately, the advent of pressed glass made it possible for even those of modest means to have a beautiful toothpick holder on their well-laid table.

Today's collector needs to be well informed to make wise decisions when buying toothpick holders since there are many new and reproduced toothpick holders on the market. Those items in the listing below that have been reproduced in recent years are marked with an asterisk (*).

Art glass

Amberina, Diamond Quilted patt., tri-corner... **$325**
Blown, vaseline threading over cranberry, trumpet shape, polished pontil **60**

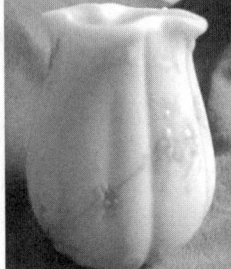

Burmese Toothpick Holder

Burmese, satin finish, footed lobe shape w/decoration (ILLUS.)...................................... **475**
Burmese, satin finish, square top, w/Queen's decoration...................................... **625**
Cranberry, Venecia patt., slightly ovoid form w/short flared rim.. **60**
Green Opaque, mottling around top, Mt. Washington **1,100**
Pink cased, Shell & Seaweed patt., ovoid form, Consolidated Lamp & Glass Co. **110**
Pomona, tri-corner... **350**
Spider Web, lusterless white w/decoration, Mt. Washington... **225**

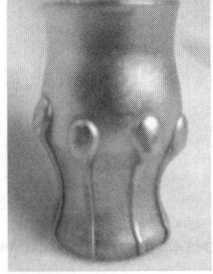

Tiffany Lily Pad Toothpick Holder

Tiffany, Lily Pad design, gold iridescent, signed (ILLUS.) **350**
Tiny Fingers, lusterless white w/decoration **900**

China

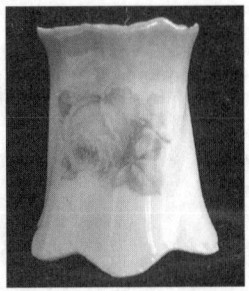

Austria Toothpick Holder

Austria, swirled mold, pink rose, grey lustre near top (ILLUS.)...................................... **35**
Bisque, boy on knees pulling T-shirt over head **75**
Elfinware, floral w/basketweave, Germany......... **35**
Germany, marked "D" crossed pipes, boats **45**
Germany, swirled mold, floral.............................. **35**
Japanese, Geisha Girl, h.p. **28**

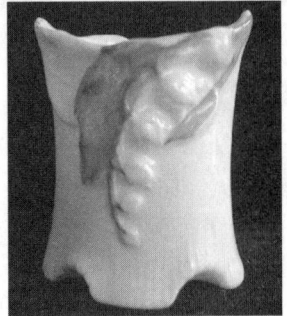

Lily of the Valley Toothpick Holder

Lily of the Valley, embossed & h.p., un-marked (ILLUS.).. **28**

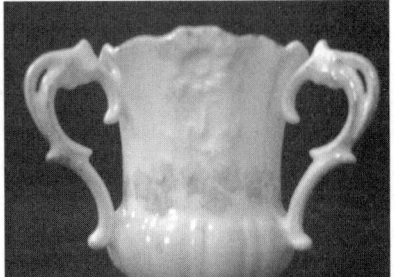

R.S. Prussia Toothpick Holder

R.S. Prussia, Ivy Vine, three-handled (ILLUS.) **165**
Royal Bayreuth, Rose Tapestry........................ **425**
Royal Bayreuth, Sun Bonnet Babies iron-ing.. **450**

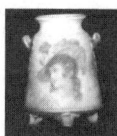

Royal Bayreuth Toothpick Holder

Royal Bayreuth, " tapestry"-type, w/female
portrait, four small feet, two small han-
dles (ILLUS.) **425**
Royal Satsuma, h.p., lots of gold **65**

Glass Figurals

Blue Alligator Toothpick Holder

Alligator, blue (ILLUS.) **325**
Butterfly, milk glass **75**
Chick with cracked eggshell,* clear **45**
Drawers, clear, Findlay, Ohio **100**
Fleur-de-Lis (a.k.a. Royal Lily), clear **25**
Monkey w/top hat, milk glass **175**

"Preparedness" Toothpick Holder

Preparedness, crossed flags & sabers be-
neath "PREPAREDNESS" on front, sol-
dier & sailor on either side, clear
(ILLUS.) **200**
Saddle over barrel,* clear **45**
Tight corset, decorated milk glass **110**
Turkey, pressed amber glass **28**

Glass - Pattern
Acorn, black opaque w/decoration **145**

Arched Ovals Toothpick Holder

Arched Ovals, clear (ILLUS.) **25**
Atlanta, clear, Fostoria **50**

Bead and Scroll Toothpick Holder

Bead and Scroll, clear (ILLUS.) **45**
Beaded Grape, a.k.a. California, green,
U.S. Glass **65**

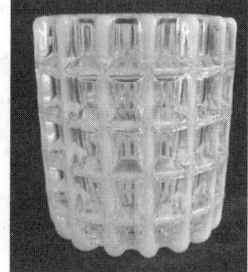

Beatty Waffle Toothpick Holder

Beatty Waffle, opalescent (ILLUS.) **55**
Box-in-Box, emerald green w/gold, River-
side **90**
Button Arches, ruby-stained **30**

Champion Toothpick Holder

Champion, emerald green, McKee (ILLUS.)........ 65
Colorado, blue w/gold, U.S. Glass 75
Colorado, green w/gold, U.S. Glass................... 50
Cornell, green, Tarentum..................................... 65
Croesus, amethyst w/gold, Riverside (beware of recent reproductions) 90
Diamond Ridge, clear, Duncan 60
Geneva, Custard w/decoration, Northwood....... 165
Grated Diamond and Sunburst, clear, Duncan... 40
Heart Band, ruby-stained...................................... 28
Idyll, blue opalescent, Jefferson......................... 300
Idyll, clear, Jefferson... 75
Imperial #3, a.k.a. Bow Tie, clear (beware of recent reproductions) 40
Iris with Meander, blue opalescent, Jefferson... 155

King's Crown, a.k.a. XLCR, clear (ILLUS.)........ 20
Ladder with Diamonds, clear, Duncan.............. 45
Nestor, amethyst w/decoration, Northwood....... 85
New Hampshire, clear w/gold, U.S. Glass 40
Pennsylvania, clear w/gold 40
Prize (The), clear, National 55

The Prize Toothpick Holder in Ruby

Prize (The), ruby-stained, National (ILLUS.) 145
Reeding, clear... 40
Reverse Swirl, white opalescent, Albany........... 95
Ribbed Base, milk glass w/decoration................ 30
Rising Sun, clear w/gold, U.S. Glass................. 45

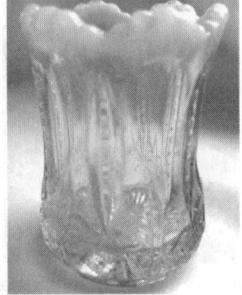

Iris with Meander Toothpick Holder

Iris with Meander, green opalescent, Jefferson (ILLUS.) 95
Iris with Meander, white opalescent, Jefferson 65

Rising Sun Toothpick Holder

Rising Sun, clear w/rose stain, U.S. Glass (ILLUS.) 55
Rosby, clear, Fostoria... 50
Royal, ruby-stained, Co-operative 35
Royal Ivy, rubina, Northwood............................... 95
Royal Oak, rubina, satin finish, Northwood....... 145

Rare Jefferson #254 Toothpick Holder

Jefferson #254, clear, rare (ILLUS.) 95

King's Crown Toothpick Holder

Scalloped Skirt Toothpick Holder

Scalloped Skirt, green w/enamel decoration, Jefferson (ILLUS.)...................................... 70

Scroll with Acanthus, dark purple slag, Northwood 220
Serrated Ribs and Panels, ruby-stained 95
Serrated Spearpoint, clear.................................... 45
Shamrock, ruby-stained 65
Stippled Fans, clear.. 30
Sunk Daisy, clear w/gold, Co-operative 45
Texas, clear w/gold.. 45
Tuxedo, clear, Fostoria... 65
Victoria, amber-stained, Riverside 365
Wheeling Block, clear, pedestal base, Cambridge... 60
Winged Scroll, Ivorina verde w/gold, Heisey... 220
X-Ray, amethyst, Riverside................................. 165
X-Ray, green w/gold, Riverside 65

Metal

Adelphia, quadruple plate, vertical ribs, tiny beading around top, four small feet................. 50
Derby Silver, leaf & beetle design, ruffled top, 2 1/8" h... 50
Meridan, silver plate, umbrella on small openwork design, eight-point base, 6" h. 65
Pairpoint, quadruple plate, birds w/long beaks form two handles, ball feet.................... 60
Queen City Silver, silver plate, Billiken, Billiken stamp on base...................................... 95
Queen City Silver, silver plate, four floral feet, openwork on top third of body, eight points around top... 65
Tufts, silver plate, plain body, scrolled rim, "Try our [picture of pickaxe]"............................. 40
Webster & Son, silver plate, four ornate feet, two ornate handles, floral pattern on lower body, tiny beading on top rim 55
Webster & Son, silver plate, square, two ornate handles, floral & scroll design top & bottom 75

TOYS

Aerial fire wagon, cast iron, Wilkins, oversized, dashing three-horse team of one white & two black horses drawing a hose tower w/nozzle which swings up to a height of 35", w/original driver & rubber squeeze bulb used to pump water, w/two brass & blue lanterns, believed to be the largest cast-iron toy ever produced in the 19th century, ca. 1895, 43 1/2" l. (paint chipping on green paint, some staining & paint loss on white horse, paint loss on driver) **$4,800**

Balancing Teeter-Totter

Balancing toy, cast iron, unusual, woven basket on one end & girl w/basket on the other, balancing boy in center, placing penny or piece of candy in either causes teeter-totter to rock back & forth, mounted on fancy base, possibly by J. & E. Stevens, ca. 1885, 10" l. (ILLUS.)............ **13,200**
Barouche, cast iron, two yellow horses trimmed in gold w/brick red hitch pulling malleable iron open carriage finished in black w/gold & red accents, interior of coach features gold painted button-tufted seats & gold simulated carpet on the floors, comes w/original driver, Pratt & Letchworth, ca. 1895, 17" l. (undercarriage sealed w/protective finish).............. **11,400**
Bell toy, cast iron, cat & boy, grassy green platform housing seated boy pulling tail of surprised cat as bell rings, N.N. Hill Brass Co., ca. 1900, 6" l. (wear on boy & bell finish)... **4,200**

Wheeled Bell Toy

Bell toy, cast iron, chime w/soldiers, tin dome housing clockwork mechanism fitted w/standing soldier bearing flag, w/two soldiers w/rifles at shoulder arms behind two fancy wheels centering a nickel-plated chime, when wound soldiers march forward, the flag waves & chimes sound, working, Althof, Bergmann patent, ca. 1875, old overpainting on coats & sides of mechanism, 9" l. (ILLUS.) **41,000**
Bell toy, cast iron, Cinderella's chariot, swirling grey chariot w/gold highlights fitted w/chime, drawn by single horse, embossed on blanket "Cinderella's Chariot," when pulled bell rings, J. & E. Stevens, ca. 1890, 9" l. (paint wear throughout)... **480**
Bell toy, cast iron, dog & cat, green grassy base fitted w/elaborately cast doghouse & shrinking cat, when pulled dog charges from his house to threaten kitty, Gong Bell Mfg., ca. 1903, 8 1/2" l. (paint wear

underneath dog's paws, substantial paint loss to dog, missing bell)............................ **1,200**

Bell toy, cast iron, drummer boy, light blue curvilinear base elaborately cast w/raised rose, leaf & vine, "The Drummer Boy" in raised letters, standing drummer boy figure in black Shako w/gold braiding, red jacket w/epaulets, gold striped blue pants, articulated arms, base drumsticks, carries nickle-plated chime, triangular front of toy mounted w/eagle, when rolled forward boy beats a tune on ringing chimes, possibly by J. & E. Stevens, ca. 1885, colors are extremely bright & strong, small crack on rim of base, 10 1/2" l. **24,900**

Bell toy, cast iron, elaborately cast little girl clutching her doll, covered by a cutter blanket on a green sleigh marked "Daisy," w/horse head over two horse head medallions, raised on four wheels fitted w/chimes that play when drawn along, Gong Bell Mfg., ca. 1903, 8 1/2" l. (small spots of paint chipping) **2,700**

Evening News Baby Quieter Bell Toy

Bell toy, cast iron, father reclining on couch, balancing baby on one leg & reading newspaper w/title "Evening News" & announcing "Baby Quieter," raised on three-star copper wash wheels, when pulled father bounces baby up & down as bell rings, J. & E. Stevens, ca. 1893, near mint, bare spot on baby looks unpainted rather than worn (ILLUS.) **13,200**

Elephant Bell Toy

Bell toy, cast iron, grey elephant w/articulated trunk suspending a bell & standing on a grassy base on four wheels, when rolled elephant raises & lowers trunk ringing the bell, N.N. Hill Brass Co., ca. 1905, elephant sealed w/protective coat, 7" l. (ILLUS.).. **2,280**

Horse & Rider Bell Toy

Bell toy, cast iron, horse & rider, tin h.p., butter-yellow horse w/blue blanket, w/rider dressed in red w/cap & riding boots, horse fitted w/bell on pole w/three clappers, green base fitted w/heart cast wheels, small ones at back & larger ones in front, when pulled toy creates appearance of horse galloping as bells sound, attributed to Althof, Bergmann, America, ca. 1875, paint loss on green base, 9" l. (ILLUS.)....................................... **6,000**

Landing of Columbus Bell Toy

Bell toy, cast iron, Landing of Columbus, fancy golden boat on wheels suspending bell, holds oarsmen trimmed in silver, separate standing Columbus figure, when pulled the bell rings, Gong Bell Mfg., ca. 1908, minor rubbing, base repaired on Columbus (ILLUS.) **360**

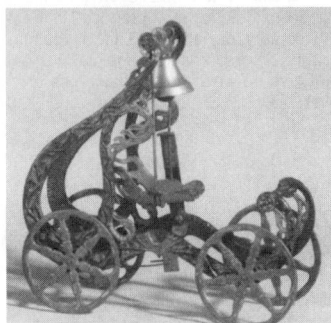

Swing Bell Toy

Bell toy, cast iron, large & elaborate, richly embellished carriage finished in blue w/gold accents, suspending bell over pierced seat raised on four wheels, when pulled seat swings back & forth as bell rings, ca. 1890, repair on frame at top of support, some paint rubbing, missing doll, 9" h., 9 1/2" l. (ILLUS.) **1,800**

Bell toy, cast iron, man w/alligator, silver base w/green highlights fitted w/alligator w/articulated jaw & suspicious grin, man holding bell, when pulled man leans forward warding off advancing snapping alligator as bell rings, raised on two large & two small wheels, Gong Bell Mfg., ca. 1903, 8 1/2" l. (spots of light paint wear & chipping) **4,200**

Bell toy, cast iron, men sawing watermelon, grassy green base centering a pile of watermelons, man on each side w/two-man saw, when pulled the saw moves back & forth on watermelon as bell rings, Gong Bell Mfg., ca. 1900, 9" l. (minor paint rubs, missing rod that goes through melon) **5,400**

Bell toy, cast iron, monkey & coconut, originally cataloged as Monkey Mobile Bell Toy, featuring monkey on wheeled log fitted w/bell, when pulled monkey raises & lowers its arm striking log w/coconut as bell rings, N.N. Hill Brass Co., ca. 1905, 6" l. (minor paint chips, finish wear to bell).. **1,560**

Bell toy, cast iron, monkey velocipede, finely cast japanned monkey in jacket & cap w/articulated legs, riding tricycle w/copper finish wheels & black frame, as tricycle moves forward the monkey's legs pump up & down in a pedaling motion & a gold bell on back of cycle rings, J. & E. Stevens, ca. 1885, one tiny casting fault or hairline crack on rim of front wheel, slight chipping to red paint on hat, 8" l. **4,800**

Bell toy, cast iron, New Improved Fish model, fish w/upturned tail & clown rider holding a bell, mounted on one small & two larger wheels, as fish swims forward opening mouth clown rises to ring bell, as fish closes mouth clown returns to seated position, ca. 1890, 5" l. (moderate to substantial paint wear) **2,400**

Bell toy, cast iron, pig in cart w/clown driver, small cart fitted w/bell beneath driver in peaked cap pulled by racing pig, Gong Bell Mfg., ca. 1905, 6 1/2" l. (paint thin & worn) **480**

Bell toy, cast iron, pony & carriage, small cart fitted w/boy seated over single bell pulled by white horse, Gong Bell Mfg., ca. 1905, 6 1/2" l. (paint thin & worn) **480**

Bell toy, cast iron, prancing horses on platform, yellow shaped base fitted w/two prancing horses flanking a bell, w/clapper connected to rear axle, when toy is moved clappers strike the bell, ca. 1895, 6 1/2" l. (moderate paint wear on platform, clapper mechanism replaced, toy was probably originally fitted w/a clown) ... **1,320**

Bell toy, cast iron, Rastus & his mother, woman in green, yellow, blue & red on one end & boy dressed in yellow & red on

other, connected by chain suspending bell, when pulled bell rings, on shaped base embossed "No. 59," Gong Bell Mfg., ca. 1900, 7 1/2" l. (finish on bell worn) **5,700**

Bell toy, cast iron, tin figure in walking pose, connected to simple mechanism on wheeled base & brass bell on S-curved wire supports, drawn by tan horse on single wheel, when rolled forward boy moves back & forth, as if walking, while ringing bell, platform fancy cast pierced iron, Merriam Mfg. American Tin, ca. 1875, 15" l. (scuffs on boy's coat) **42,150**

Bell toy, cast iron, Two Billys, one white goat & one black goat centering a bell, split base to straddle the axles, when pulled the goats alternately ram the bell w/their heads, raised on heart cast wheels, Gong Bell Mfg., embossed "No. 51. Billys," ca. 1903, 7 1/2" (moderate finish wear throughout)... **1,800**

Bell toy, cast iron, two nursery rhyme figures at opposite ends, centering bell hung in well house embossed on side "Ding Dong Bell Pussy's Not in the Well," cat in arms of one figure, Gong Bell Mfg., 7" l. **5,700**

Uncle Sam & John Bull Bell Toy

Bell toy, cast iron, Uncle Sam & John Bull, two figures representing U.S. & Great Britain standing before bell centering a star-embossed clapper mounted on curvilinear fancy cast base painted deep blue, mounted on four wheels, when pulled clapper that straddles the axle hits one bell, then the other, N.N. Hill Brass Co., ca. 1900, minor paint chipping on figures, slight retouch on one figure, bells lightly corroded & buffed (ILLUS.).............. **5,100**

Bell toy, cast iron, washerwoman & child, shaped base embossed w/stars at front & back, fitted w/washtub & stool w/seated child watching his mother toiling at washtub, when pulled she rocks back & forth scrubbing vigorously as the bell rings, Ives, ca. 1885, 7 1/2" l. (substantial paint loss on woman's face, fabric is replaced) .. **8,400**

Bell toy, cast iron, white circus cage wagon fitted w/bell on back w/semi-round driver & seat mounted on front, interior features revolving bear & kangaroo, lion & four cubs, raised on shaped spoked wheels drawn by two japanned horses, Kyser & Rex, ca. 1890, 12 1/2" l. (mechanism appears to be missing parts & is therefore presently inoperable).................................... **5,100**

Four-seat Carriage

Large Royal Circus Band Wagon

Bell toy, cast iron, "Whoa Dar Caesar," platform embossed on each side "Whoa Dar Caesar," fitted w/bell & rider on mule, japanned finish, when pulled mule bucks up into air landing on lever which rings bell, N.N. Hill Brass Co., ca. 1905, 5 1/2" l. **2,700**

Bell toy, cast iron, Wild Mule Jack, grassy base embossed "Wild Mule Jack" having bolting white mule w/Jack clutching its neck, when pulled the mule's tail swings up & down ringing the bell, Gong Bell Mfg., ca. 1903, 8" l. (repaired crack on base) **840**

Buggy, cast iron, early, drawn by single white horse, black buggy w/red wheels & button-tufted seats, fitted w/rare early figure of a mustached man in top hat, Wilkins, 11" l. (possible old repair on interior corner of buggy) **1,680**

Cabriolet, cast iron, black carriage w/orange interior featuring open open windows on each side, raised on yellow wheels drawn by single black horse w/silver mane & tail & gold accents, comes w/original driver & woman passenger, Kenton Hardware, ca. 1905, 15 1/2" l. (slight touchup on corner of roof of cab, small wheel under horse's hoof replaced, substantial paint loss on woman, coupling pin & axles replaced).......................... **4,500**

Carriage, cast iron, two teams of white & black horses drawing a grey carriage framed in gold w/yellow accents raised on red spoked wheels & carrier, four button-tufted seats come w/six original passengers, modeled after carriages used by hotels & resorts to transport guests in style, Hubley, ca. 1906, slight chipping on white horses & carriage, figures have some paint chipping, two figures missing, front seat has small nick on support tab, 27" l. (ILLUS., top of page) **20,300**

Circus band wagon, cast iron & pressed-steel body, Royal Circus open carriage adorned w/raised relief decoration depicting child w/horn on both sides & eagle w/federal flag on back, original driver & eight bandsmen in pale blue, Hubley, ca. 1922, some paint wear, moderate paint loss to driver, bandsmen were repainted some time ago & have mellow textured patina, 30" l. (ILLUS., second from top) **5,100**

Circus band wagon, cast iron & pressed-steel body, Royal Circus open carriage w/raised relief decorations of scrolling vines & eagle, w/original driver in blue & eight bandsmen in black drawn by double red hitch & four prancing grey horses trimmed in gold, Hubley, ca. 1922, 23" l. ... **7,200**

Circus cage wagon, cast iron & steel Royal Circus rear gate version mounted on yellow wheels & carrier, w/two original brown bears & driver pulled by two brown plumed horses, Hubley, ca. 1920, 16" l. (minor paint chipping to steel surfaces)...... **3,300**

Circus calliope wagon, cast iron & steel Royal Circus van body, decorated w/raised relief images of angels blowing horns, raised relief images of organ pipes encompassing top of steam boiler, fitted w/bell-ringing mechanism mounted on gold & red starburst wheels, pulled by two black plumed horses, comes w/original driver & passenger, Hubley, ca. 1922, 16" l. (substantial paint loss to roof & steel surfaces) **3,000**

Circus chariot, cast iron, three-horse red chariot w/lion & musicians in raised relief trimmed in gold on fancy cast wheels, drawn by team of three black horses, w/standing woman figure, Hubley, ca. 1890, 10 1/2" l. (some paint loss, woman figure is a replacement) **960**

Circus farmer van, cast iron & pressed-steel Royal Circus van featuring rhino in raised relief, incorporates mechanism that causes farmer's head to emerge from top of van when pushed forward, turn 180 degrees, return & drop back into place, mounted on red & gold starburst wheels w/red carrier pulled by two black plumed horses trimmed in gold, w/original driver, Hubley, ca. 1920 (minor chipping, gate may be old replacement) **9,000**

Circus giraffe cage wagon, cast iron & pressed steel, Royal Circus model, cage designed in two levels, top level features two movable retainers on roof which hold large giraffe in place, standing baby giraffe on second level, cage painted red, rides on yellow wheels & is pulled by two black plumed horses, w/original driver, Hubley, ca. 1920, some minor paint chipping, 16" l. **9,000**

Circus lion cage wagon, cast iron & pressed steel, Royal Circus rear gate version, red cage wagon mounted on yellow wheels w/yellow carrier, w/two original lions & original driver, drawn by two brown plumed horses trimmed in gold & red, Hubley, ca. 1920, 10 1/2" l. **4,500**

Circus polar bear cage wagon, cast iron & pressed steel, Royal Circus rear gate version, green cage wagon mounted on yellow carrier w/yellow wheels, drawn by two black plumed horses trimmed in gold & red, w/original driver & two original polar bears, Hubley, ca. 1920, 16" l. (one marquee is a rough casting, polar bears & roof have paint chipping) **1,680**

Circus rhino cage wagon, cast iron & pressed steel, Royal Circus rear gate version, red cage wagon in red w/gold accents, mounted on yellow carrier & spoked wheels, drawn by two black horses, comes w/two original rhinos & driver, Hubley, ca. 1920, 16" l. (moderate paint chipping on rhino & driver, one plume missing) **2,400**

Circus rhino van, cast iron & pressed steel Royal Circus red van having raised image of rhino in gold on both sides, mounted on yellow wheels w/yellow carrier pulled by two black horses, w/original driver, Hubley, ca. 1920, 16" l. **3,600**

Circus tiger cage wagon, cast iron & pressed steel, side gate Royal Circus version, green cage wagon trimmed in

gold containing two original tigers, mounted on yellow wheels & carrier drawn by two brown horses accented in red & gold, w/original driver, Hubley, ca. 1920, 16" l. (minor paint chipping to driver) **3,900**

Clown cart, cast iron, small green cart fitted w/seated clown driver dressed in yellow w/red conical hat, articulated arm, clown fans himself as cart is pulled, Gong Bell Mfg., ca. 1903, 7" l. (wear to finish on face & hat, substantial paint loss to horse) **960**

Coal wagon, cast iron, painted red, marked "Coal" in silver raised letters on each side, mounted on yellow wheels w/black piping, drawn by silver horse trimmed in black & red, comes w/mismatched Arcade driver, Harris, ca. 1903, 15" l. (minor paint chipping throughout & some spots of natural darkening to finish) **2,700**

Coal wagon, cast iron, red wagon adorned w/"Coal" in raised letters on each side, fitted w/tipping or dumping mechanism, comes w/original driver & copper finish shovel, drawn by superbly cast donkey in striking pose & meticulously detailed coat, Ives, ca. 1890, 14" l. (paint scrapes on wagon, figure has moderate paint loss) **1,680**

Coal wagon w/chute, cast iron, green wagon trimmed in gold featuring tapered sides w/raised baton & "Coal" on each side, red spoked wheels & chassis drawn by one white & one black horse, w/original tinplate coal chute, chute door, painted & japanned driver, Dent, ca. 1910, 16" l. (minor paint chipping on chute) **4,500**

Dump truck, cast iron, Mack-type, C-ab finished in bright red w/black roof, w/separate original steering wheel & driver, bed fitted w/dump mechanism & hinged tailgate, finished in light blue w/gold accents, Dent, ca. 1923, 15" l. (paint chips) **10,800**

New York-Philadelphia Express Truck

Express truck, cast iron, w/factory sample tag, finely cast enclosed bed, each side incorporating grillwork panels & cast-in door marked "Junior Supply Co." flanked by "New York & Philadelphia," w/opening back doors having matching grillwork, on red chassis raised on silver tires w/yellow rims & gold piping, fitted w/an original driver & steering wheel, w/circular tag reading "The Dent Hardware Co. Sample, Fullerton, Pa No." & written in ink

"1282 Blue," opposite side written in ink "Jr. Supply Co. Truck," Dent, ca. 1923, 15 1/2" l. (ILLUS.)...................................... **13,200**

Express wagon, cast iron, h.p., finished in red, sides of wagon are marked in gold "Express" & framed in elaborate stenciling, raised on crisply bronzed cast-iron wheels, drawn by two white horses, American Tin, attributed to Merriam Mfg., ca. 1880, 20" l. (solder repair to replace hitching loops under wagon)............. **9,600**

Express wagon, cast iron, two butterscotch Percheron horses trimmed in cream yellow, pulling red cast-iron wagon w/movable tailgate, yellow spoked wheels, w/original seated driver on top & three wooden accessories, Pratt & Letchworth, ca. 1888, 17" l. (paint loss inside wagon & on seat & minor chipping on yellow wheels, horses possibly overpainted, coupling attachment on wagon replaced).. **2,700**

Farm set, cast metal, Britains, Set No. 125F, Farm Animals, Farm Series, w/standing cows, sitting calves, sheep & dog, issued 1947-54, original box w/color-illustrated lid, set of 7 (chips, some fraying on box lid)... **90**

Combination Hose Reel & Ladder Wagon

Fire hose reel & ladder combination wagon, cast iron, green wagon is trimmed w/gold & marked on each side in raised letters "Combination," fitted w/blue & gold hose reel & two yellow ladders, drawn by a three-horse team comprising a dashing white horse flanked by black horses, comes w/original driver, Dent, ca. 1910, near mint condition, except for minor chipping to wheels, ladders & whiffle tree, 21" (ILLUS.)... **9,600**

Fire Ladder Wagon

Fire ladder wagon, cast iron, drawn by one black & one butterscotch horse, elegant lines detailed w/delicate casting including geometric pattern, tool box behind driver's seat, circle & stylized leaf decoration framing truck bed, thin spoked wheels

w/ringing bell mechanism, comes w/fireman driver & tillerman w/steering wheel at back as well as a red wooden ladder, Pratt & Letchworth, ca. 1885, minor paint chipping on green finish, worn in places on black horse, one helmet has old repair under brim, 23" l. (ILLUS.)........................... **1,800**

Fire patrol wagon, cast iron, comprising two brown horses pulling black & gold wagon marked in gold on each side "Patrol," fitted w/nickel-plated railing, comes w/original driver & two seated firemen, Ideal, ca. 1895, 21 1/2" l. (some paint chipping)......... **2,040**

Fire pumper wagon, cast iron, attributed to James Fallows, two white horses drawing tin pumper having orange/red boiler w/stylized stencil design, connected to cylindrical tank fitted w/seat & driver, mechanism works, American Tin Clockwork, ca. 1875, 14" l. (solder repair, one horse is loose, wear on driver)............. **4,200**

Fire Pumper

Fire pumper wagon, cast iron, black w/gold accents on red wheels & undercarriage, drawn by one white & one japanned horse, comes w/two figures, Ives, ca. 1895, figures & eagle finial are replaced, 16 1/2" l. (ILLUS.).. **2,700**

Fire pumper wagon, cast iron, drawn by the earliest, larger P. & L. horses, one black, one white, wagon fitted w/nickel-plated boiler & features fancy scalloping on seat above star motif, comes w/original fireman driver & later fireman standing at boiler door, Pratt & Letchworth, ca. 1885, 17 1/2" l. (spots of light corrosion on boiler, moderate paint chipping & wear throughout).. **2,700**

Fire pumper wagon, cast iron, nickel-plated boiler w/copper finish steam chamber, sits on red spoked wheels & is drawn by two charging black horses, comes w/original Pratt & Letchworth figure, Welker & Crosby, ca. 1885, 17 3/4" l. (small pinhole on steam chamber, some paint chipping, some paint loss and wear)........................... **5,100**

Fire pumper wagon, cast iron, one butterscotch & two cream horses, drawing red wagon fitted w/nickel-plated boiler & steam chamber, w/original driver & standing fireman at back of boiler, Kenton Hardware, ca. 1905, 21" l. (minor paint chipping, hoses are missing, figures have some paint wear)......................... **4,500**

Wilkins Fire Pumper Wagon

Flying Artillery with Caisson

Fire pumper wagon, cast iron, oversized, black carriage framed in green & gold, fitted w/nickel-plated boiler & rubber squeeze bulb used to pump water, comes w/two of the largest original figures ever made, on red spoked wheels drawn by a three-horse team comprising two black horses flanking one white, Wilkins, ca. 1888, bell is worn but original, some paint chipping, old adhesive repair under brim of fireman's helmet, squeeze bulb a bit sticky but may be original, 25" l. (ILLUS., top of page) **10,200**

Fire pumper wagon, cast iron, oversized, one japanned & one white horse, drawing black pumper w/gold trim on red spoked wheels, w/original driver, fireman standing at boiler door & eagle finial, Ives, ca. 1890, 23 1/2" l. (old repair on boiler behind wheel, overpaint on wheels, undercarriage & white horse, eagle finial original but has slight solder repair on shaft) ... **3,900**

Flying artillery w/caisson, cast iron, two teams of various color horses, two are mounted w/soldiers resplendent in full dress uniforms including plumed helmets, hard blue jackets, red striped light blue pants, drawing a lumber wagon finished in dark green w/red piping & accents, fitted w/hinged ammunition seat w/two articulated cross-armed soldiers drawing a caisson finished in matching dark green w/raised decoration in red & a black cannon, patented in 1883 & again in November 1885, Pratt &

Letchworth, ca. 1895, 33" l. (ILLUS., second from top) **65,150**

Hook & ladder wagon, cast iron, oversized, drawn by two-horse team, one white & one japanned, wagon features elaborate scroll & oval sides, front seat w/driver & footrest intact & driver at steering wheel at back, comes w/several pieces of fire fighting apparatus comprising two yellow & one red cast-iron ladders, two replaced buckets & a fire ace, Ives, ca. 1890, 34" l. **7,200**

Horse Cart

Horse cart, cast iron, Victor No. 33, articulated, small deep red cart stamped "Victor" in gold on both sides & "No. 33" on back, interior of cart is light blue, pulled by black horse trimmed in yellow w/articulated legs that move back & forth when toy is drawn forward, Ives, ca. 1890, 9 1/2" (ILLUS.) **2,040**

Hose reel wagon, cast iron, oversized, wagon finished in black fitted w/starburst reel highlighted in gold, pulled by one grey & one black horse, comes w/original driver & fireman standing on top of toolbox, Ives, ca. 1912, 24" l. (some restoration, including replaced front axle & possible repair to back end) **5,700**

Hose reel wagon, cast iron, pulled by black horse, hose reel consists of a black body w/gold trim, starburst reel, two lanterns, driver in red w/black & cream helmet, articulated arms, Welker & Crosby, ca. 1885, 14" l. (paint chipping to the red wheels & blue seat)..................................... **3,000**

Hose reel wagon, cast iron, two running horses mounted on three wheels drawing light blue wagon fitted w/red hose reel decorated in swirling pattern accented in gold, riding on four yellow spoked wheels w/two near mint Dent figures, Ideal, ca. 1895, 23 1/2" l. (paint chipping & rubs, figures mismatched to toy).......................... **4,500**

Hose reel wagon, cast iron, w/single white horse w/red harness & wheels fitted w/bell, drawing green wagon w/distinctive P. & L. fireman driver, painted green & red, reel decorated w/sharp heart design, Pratt & Letchworth, ca. 1885, 14 1/2" l. (paint chipping on wheels, seat & footers, old adhesive repair under fireman's helmet, hose is missing).................. **2,700**

Hygeia Ice Wagon

Ice wagon, cast iron, complete back end, w/front shaft finished in red, two front wheels & grey wagon embossed in gold "Hygeia Ice," comes w/driver & boy on ice drop-off step, missing two horses, Ives, ca. 1895, paint chipping to driver's area, driver is a rare Ives figure, but not original to the piece, 20" l. (ILLUS.)............ **4,200**

Ice wagon, cast iron, orange enclosed wagon is marked "Polar Ice" in raised letters on each side, mounted on red spoked wheels & drawn by a sturdy black horse trimmed in silver, comes w/mismatched driver, Kenton Hardware, ca. 1905, 13 1/4" (paint loss on the roof of the wagon)... **1,800**

Ice wagon, cast iron, two-horse team finished in black & gold pulls an enclosed green wagon w/raised baton & "Ice" trimmed in gold on each side, mounted on red wheels w/mismatched original Arcade driver, Hubley, ca. 1910, 15" l. (moderate paint chipping, substantial paint loss to figure)..................................... **1,800**

Aurora Blackbeard Kit

Model kit, Blackbeard, 1/10.5 scale, painted by Evan Stuart, Aurora, 1965 (ILLUS.) **75-200**

Aurora Blue Knight of Milan — 1520 Kit

Model kit, Blue Knight of Milan — 1520, reissue, Aurora, 1963, 9" h. (ILLUS.) **20-50**

Hawk Bopped Out Steel Pluckers ... Kit

Model kit, Bopped Out Steel Pluckers
Havin' a Bash, Hawk, Frantics, designed
by Reuben Klamer, 1965 (ILLUS.) **40-80**

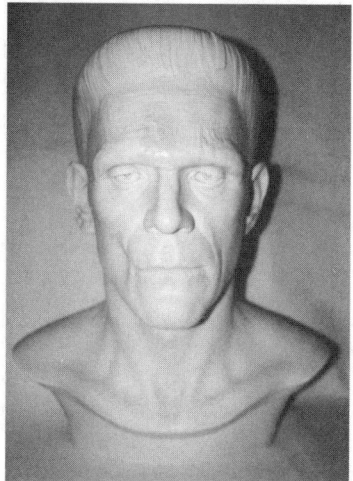

Ciné Art Frankenstein Bust

Model kit, Boris Karloff likeness, by Miles
Teves, life-size, resin & vinyl kit, J, Ciné
Art, Tsukuda, apan, 1990s (ILLUS.) **595-650**
Model kit, Brachiosaurus diorama, Tamiya,
plastic kit, Japan, 1994 .... **70-90**
Model kit, Brontosaurus, Pyro reissue,
Lindberg, plastic kit, 1979 .... **10-18**
Model kit, Brontosaurus, reissue of Airfix,
MPC, plastic kit, 1982 .... **10-20**
Model kit, Brontosaurus skeleton, Palmer,
plastic kit, late 1950s, 13" h. **20-40**

Revell Brother Rat Fink Kit

Model kit, Brother Rat Fink, painted by
Evan Stuart, Revell, plastic kit, Custom
Monsters Series, designed by Ed "Big
Daddy" Roth, 1963 (ILLUS.) **40-90**
Model kit, Busby the Tasselated Afghan
Yak, Revell, plastic kit, Dr. Seuss Series,
1959 .... **100-250**

Aurora Cave Bear Kit

Model kit, Cave Bear, No. 738, 1/13 scale,
dark brown, Aurora, 1971 (ILLUS.) **40-50**
Model kit, Cave (The), No. 732, 1/13 scale,
grey, Aurora, 1971 .... **40-50**

Chamber of Horrors, Le Guillotine Kit

Model kit, Chamber of Horrors, Le Guillo-
tine, Aurora, 1964 (ILLUS.) **125-450**
Model kit, Chasmosaurus with baby diora-
ma, plastic kit, Tamiya, Japan, 1994 .... **25-35**

Airfix Corythosaurus Kit

Model kit, Corythosaurus, Airfix, plastic kit, Britain - France, 1979 (ILLUS.) **30-40**

Aurora Cougar Kit

Model kit, cougar, 1/8 scale, Aurora, 1962 (ILLUS.).. **25-65**
Model kit, Daddy the Way-out Suburbanite, Hawk, Weird-ohs, designed by Bill Campbell, 1963 .... **40-90**
Model kit, Davey the Way-out Cyclist, Hawk, Weird-ohs, designed by Bill Campbell, 1963 .... **40-90**
Model kit, Dead Elvis, "Tiny Terrors," zombie in Elvis jumpsuit, Mad Lab, resin kit sculpted by Michael Parks, 1990s-present.. **15-30**

Aurora Dempsey vs Firpo Kit

Model kit, Dempsey vs Firpo, Great Moments in Sport series, 1/14 scale, Aurora, 1965 (ILLUS.) **45-110**
Model kit, Digger the Way-out Dragster, Hawk, Weird-ohs, designed by Bill Campbell, 1963 .... **40 -0**
Model kit, Dimetrodon, 1/10 scale, Pyro, plastic kit, late 1950s - late 1960s **20-40**
Model kit, Dimetrodon, 1/13 scale, Monogram (re-issues from Aurora's Prehistoric Scenes line), 1979 & 1987 .... **15-25**
Model kit, Dimetrodon, Pyro reissue, 8 1/4" l., Lindberg, plastic kit, 1979 .... **10-18**
Model kit, dinosaurs, 1/13 scale, reissues from Aurora Prehistoric Scenes, Revell/Monogram, plastic kit, 1992-93, each... **12-30**

Revell Drag Nut Kit

Model kit, Drag Nut, Revell, plastic kit, Custom Monsters Series, designed by Ed "Big Daddy" Roth, 1963 (ILLUS.) **45-150**
Model kit, Elasmosaurus, 1/30 scale, Horizon, vinyl kit, 1980s-90s............................ **35-45**
Model kit, Endsville Eddy, Hawk, Weird-ohs, designed by Bill Campbell, 1963 .... **30-75**
Model kit, Evel Knievel's Sky Cycle, Addar, plastic kit, 1974... **30-75**

Revell Knight Rider Chopper Trike Kit

Model kit, Evil Iron, Knight Rider Chopper
Trike, Revell, plastic kit, 1976, 14" l.
(ILLUS.)... **15-40**

Mad Lab Famous Monsters Cover Card

Model kit, Famous Monsters cover card,
Curse of the Werewolf, painted by Joe
Fex, Mad Lab, resin kit sculpted by
Michael Parks, 1990s-present, 4 1/2" h.
(ILLUS.)... **10-25**
Model kit, Fat Max, Lindberg, plastic kit,
Lindy Loonys, "The Hep Model in the
'Square' Box," 1965 .... **35-80**
Model kit, Fink-Eliminator, Revell, plastic
kit, Custom Monsters Series, designed
by Ed "Big Daddy" Roth, 1965 .... **50-200**
Model kit, Flying Reptile, No. 734, 1/13
scale, orange, Aurora, 1971 .... **50-75**
Model kit, Forgotten Prisoner of Castel-
Mare (The), Frightening Lightning, glow
version, Aurora, 1969 .... **150-350**

Prisoner of Castel-Mare, Glow Version

Model kit, Forgotten Prisoner of Castel-
Mare (The), glow version, Aurora, 1972
(ILLUS.) **100-300**

Forgotten Prisoner of Castel-Mare Kit

Model kit, Forgotten Prisoner of Castel-
Mare (The), painted by Evan Stuart, Au-
rora, 1966 (ILLUS.).................................... **150-400**
Model kit, Francis the Foul, Hawk, Weird-
ohs, designed by Bill Campbell, 1963 .... **30-75**
Model kit, Frantic Banana Punishing the
Skins, Hawk, Frantics, designed by Re-
uben Klamer, 1965 .... **40-80**

Hawk Freddy Flameout Kit

Model kit, Freddy Flameout, Hawk, Weird-
ohs, designed by Bill Campbell, 1963
(ILLUS.) **30-75**
Model kit, Freddy Kreuger, 1/6 scale, reis-
sue of Kaiyodo mold, Screamin' Produc-
tions, large vinyl kit, 1980s-90s.................. **45-65**
Model kit, Giant Bird, No. 739, 1/13 scale,
blue-silver, Aurora, 1971............................ **40-50**

Lindberg Glo-Monster Fiend Kit

Model kit, Glo-Monster Fiend, reissue of 1964 "Glob," Lindberg, plastic kit, 1971 (ILLUS.).. **25-45**

Polar Lights Go Cart Kit

Model kit, Go Cart (The), Polar Lights, Aurora reissue of Godzilla's Go Cart, box art modified, 1999 (ILLUS.) **15-25**

Lindberg Goofy Klock Kit

Model kit, Goofy Klock, motorized, Lindberg, plastic kit, 1965 (ILLUS.)................. **70-140**

Mad Lab Gorgo Kit

Model kit, Gorgo, "Tiny Terrors," Mad Lab, resin kit sculpted by Michael Parks, 1990s-present, 4" h. (ILLUS.) **15-35**

Gowdy the Dowdy Grackle Kit

Model kit, Gowdy the Dowdy Grackle, plastic wrap intact, Revell, plastic kit, Dr. Seuss Series, 1958, 7 1/8 x 10 1/2" (ILLUS.) **100-300**
Model kit, Grickily the Gractus, Revell, plastic kit, Dr. Seuss Series, 1959................ **100-250**

Fundimensions Ape Man Glo Head Kit

Model kit, Haunted Glo-Head, Ape Man, undecorated (decorated version shown w/Mummy on Glo-Head box), Fundimensions, 1975 (ILLUS.).................................... **20-45**

Fundimensions Haunted Glo-Head Boxes

Model kit, Haunted Glo-Head, Mummy, one
of four versions, Fundimensions, 1975
(ILLUS. of box).. **20-45**
Model kit, Haunted Glo-Head, Vampire, one
of four versions, Fundimensions, 1975
(ILLUS. w/Mummy on Glo-Head box) **20-45**
Model kit, Haunted Glo-Head, Werewolf,
one of four versions, Fundimensions,
1975 (ILLUS. w/Mummy on Glo-Head
box)... **20-45**
Model kit, Henry VIII, Airfix, plastic kit, Brit-
ain/France, 1973 .... **5-10**

Hawk Hodad Makin' the Scene

Model kit, Hodad Makin' the Scene with a
Six-Pack, Hawk, Silly Surfers, 1964
(ILLUS.)... **35-75**
Model kit, Horned Dinosaur,
Triceratops, 1/40 scale, Pyro, plastic kit,
late 1950s-late 1960s **20-40**
Model kit, Horton the Elephant, Revell,
plastic kit, Dr. Seuss Series, 1960.......... **300-500**
Model kit, Hot Dogger and Surf Bunny
Riding Tandem, Hawk, Silly Surfers,
1964.. **40-80**
Model kit, Hot Dogger Hangin' Ten, Hawk,
Silly Surfers, 1964 .... **30-60**

Model kit, Huey's Hut Rod, Hawk, Weird-
ohs, designed by Bill Campbell, 1963 .... **25-60**
Model kit, Human Heart, life-size, Pyro,
plastic kit, 1960s... **15-35**
Model kit, Hunting Velociraptor, sculpted by
Darga, Horizon, vinyl kit, 1980s-90s,
30" l. **65-75**

Horizon Invisible Man Kit

Model kit, Invisible Man, w/optional poses,
Sci-Fi Art Kits, painted by Joe Fex, Hori-
zon, vinyl kit, 1988 (ILLUS.) **25-40**
Model kit, James Bond's Aston Martin DB-5,
Airfix, plastic kit, Britain - France, 1965..... **75-200**
Model kit, Jason, from Friday the 13th mov-
ie series, w/removable mask, 1/4 scale,
Screamin' Productions, large vinyl kit,
1988, 18" h.. **50-85**
Model kit, Jaws, based on Spielberg's
shark film, Addar, plastic kit, 1975 .... **40-100**
Model kit, Jungle Swamp, No. 740, 1/13
scale, orange & green, Aurora, 1971........ **50-75**
Model kit, Jurassic Park, Brachiosaurus,
1/19 scale, Horizon, vinyl kit, 1980s-90s **100-135**
Model kit, Jurassic Park, Hadrosaurus
(Corythosaurus), Lindberg, plastic kit,
1993 .... **10-15**
Model kit, Jurassic Park, Lost World Tyran-
nosaurus Rex, 1/25 scale, Revell/Mono-
gram, plastic kit, 1997 .... **10-15**
Model kit, Jurassic Park, Lost World vehi-
cle, Hunter's Humvee Snagger, snap-together, Revell/Monogram, plastic kit,
1997 .... **7-10**
Model kit, Jurassic Park, Lost World vehi-
cle, Mercedes-Benz, snap-together,
Revell/Monogram, plastic kit, 1997 .... **7-10**

Lost World Velociraptors Kit

Model kit, Jurassic Park, Lost World Velociraptors, 1/25 scale, snap-together, Revell/Monogram, plastic kit, 1997 (ILLUS.).................................... **10-15**

Model kit, Jurassic Park, Spitter (Dilophosaurus), Horizon, vinyl kit, 1990s............. **80-110**

Model kit, Jurassic Park, Spitter, Lindberg, plastic kit, 1993.. **15-22**

Model kit, Jurassic Park, Stegosaurus, Lindberg, plastic kit, 1993...................... **10-15**

Model kit, Jurassic Park, Tyrannosaurus, Horizon, vinyl kit, 1990s......................... **100-135**

Model kit, Jurassic Park, Tyrannosaurus, Lindberg, plastic kit, 1993........................ **20-25**

Model kit, Jurassic Park, Tyrannosaurus Rex, 1/24 scale PVC kit, Tsukuda, Japan, 1980s-present................................... **80-120**

Model kit, Jurassic Park, Velociraptor, Horizon, vinyl kit, 1990s.................................... **80-110**

Lindberg Velociraptor Kit

Model kit, Jurassic Park, Velociraptor, Lindberg, plastic kit, 1993 (ILLUS.)................... **15-22**

Model kit, Killer McBash, Hawk, Weird-ohs, designed by Bill Campbell, 1963............. **60-140**

Model kit, Leaky Boat Louie, Hawk, Weirdohs, designed by Bill Campbell, 1963...... **50-120**

Model kit, life-size Hatchling T-Rex, sculpted by Darga, Horizon, vinyl kit, 1980s-90s... **55-70**

Mad Lab Little Red & Big Bad Wolf Kit

Model kit, Little Red & the Big Bad Wolf (werewolf), 1/6 scale, Mad Lab, resin kit sculpted by Michael Parks, 1990s-present (ILLUS.)..................................... **120-165**

Model kit, Mesozoic Creatures, six different models, plastic kit, Tamiya, Japan, 1994, each... **15-25**

Horizon Mole People Kit

Model kit, Mole People, Sci-Fi Art Kits, Horizon, vinyl kit, 1988 (ILLUS.).................... **25-40**

Revell Norval the Bashful Blinket Kit

Model kit, Norval the Bashful Blinket, Revell, plastic kit, Dr. Seuss Series, 1959 (ILLUS.)... **100-250**

Model kit, Outlaw with Robbin' Hood Fink, Revell, plastic kit, Custom Monsters Series, designed by Ed "Big Daddy" Roth, 1965... **200-500**

Model kit, Parasaurolophys and Nystosaur diorama, plastic kit, Tamiya, Japan, 1994. **25-35**

Model kit, Passenger Rocket, 1/192 scale, Willy Ley on box art, Monogram (most reissued Aurora), 1950s............................. **75-225**

Model kit, Phantom and the Voodoo Witch Doctor, 1/8 scale, Revell, plastic kits, 1965... **125-350**

Model kit, Pinhead Cenobite, from Hellraiser, 1/4 scale, Screamin' Productions, large vinyl kit, 1989...................... **75-100**

Pinhead Cenobite Kit

Model kit, Pinhead Cenobite, from Hellraiser, w/altar of souls, 1/4 scale, Screamin' Productions, large vinyl kit, 1993 (ILLUS.).. **75-100**

Pyro Plated Dinosaur Kit

Model kit, Plated Dinosaur, Stegosaurus, 1/32 scale, Pyro, plastic kit, late 1950s - late 1960s (ILLUS.)..................................... **20-40**

Aurora Porthos Kit

Model kit, Porthos, of "The Three Musketeers," 1/8 scale, Aurora, 1958 (ILLUS.)... **25-75**

Model kit, Predator, 1/8 scale, limited edition of 1,000, Dark Horse, cold-cast porcelain kit... **125-175**

Halcyon Predator 2 Creature Kit

Model kit, Predator 2 Creature, Movie Classic series, plastic, painted by Joe Fex, Halcyon, 1990s (ILLUS.)............................. **30-45**
Model kit, Predator, soft vinyl, Billiken, 1991, 12".. **35-75**
Model kit, Prehistoric Dinosaurs, Addar, plastic kit, Super Scenes series, 1976...... **40-50**

Revell Roscoe the Many-footed Lion Kit

Model kit, Roscoe the Many-footed Lion, Revell, plastic kit, Dr. Seuss Series, 1959 (ILLUS.) **100-250**
Model kit, S-Files, Flukeman, Dark Horse, cold-cast porcelain kit, 1990s................. **100-150**

Aurora Saber Tooth Tiger Kit

Model kit, Saber Tooth Tiger, No. 733, 1/13 scale, yellow, painted by Evan Stuart, Aurora, 1971 (ILLUS.) 30-40

Model kit, Sail Back Reptile (Dimetrodon), No.745, 1/13 scale, copper & green, Aurora, 1971 50-75

Model kit, Satan's Crate, Lindberg, plastic kit, Lindy Loonys, "The Hep Model in the 'Square' Box," 1965 35-80

Model kit, Scuttle Bucket, Lindberg, plastic kit, Lindy Loonys, "The Hep Model in the 'Square' Box," 1965 35-80

Model kit, Scuz-Fink, Revell, plastic kit, Custom Monsters Series, designed by Ed "Big Daddy" Roth, 1964 165-300

Model kit, Silver Knight of Augsburg - 1560, Aurora, 1956, 9" h. 20-50

Model kit, Sling Rave Curvette, Hawk, Weird-ohs, designed by Bill Campbell, 1964 15-40

Model kit, Spiked Dinosaur, No. 742, 1/13 scale, tan & green, Aurora, 1971 70-85

Model kit, Stegosaurus, 1/30 scale, Horizon, vinyl kit, 1980s-90s 35-45

Model kit, Stegosaurus, Airfix, plastic kit, Britain/France,1979 25-35

Model kit, Stegosaurus, Pyro reissue, Lindberg, plastic kit, 1979 10-18

Model kit, Styracosauarus, Monogram (reissues from Aurora's Prehistoric Scenes line), 1987 30-40

Model kit, Super Fink, Revell, plastic kit, Custom Monsters Series, designed by Ed "Big Daddy" Roth, 1964 150-350

Model kit, Superhero series, Marx, paintable plastic figures, 1960s-70s, each 4-9

Model kit, Surfink, Revell, plastic kit, Custom Monsters Series, designed by Ed "Big Daddy" Roth, 1965 55-165

Aurora Three-Horned Dinosaur Kit

Model kit, Three-Horned Dinosaur (Triceratops), No. 741, 1/13 scale, silver, Aurora, 1971 (ILLUS.) 70-85

Model kit, Thunder Lizard, Brontosaurus, 1/72 scale, Pyro, plastic kit, late 1950s - late 1960s, 11" h. 20-40

Model kit, Tingo the Noodle Stroodle, Revell, plastic kit, Dr. Seuss Series, 1958 100-250

Titanic Kit

Model kit, Titanic, 1/570 scale, Revell, plastic kit, 1976, 18 1/2" l. (ILLUS.) 400-475

Hawk Totally Fab Kit

Model kit, Totally Fab, Hawk, Frantics, designed by Reuben Klamer, 1965 (ILLUS.) . 40-80

Model kit, Triceratops, Monogram (re-issues from Aurora's Prehistoric Scenes line), 1987 30-40

Model kit, Triceratops with Velociraptor diorama, plastic kit, Tamiya, Japan, 1994.... 35-45

Model kit, Tyrannosaurus, Pyro reissue, Lindberg, plastic kit, 1979 10-18

Aurora Tar Pit Kit

Model kit, Tar Pit, No. 735, 1/13 scale, orange, Aurora, 1971 (ILLUS.) 40-50

Model kit, Tyrannosaurus, reissue of Airfix, MPC, plastic kit, 1982, 14" h. **10-20**

Monogram Tyrannosaurus Rex

Model kit, Tyrannosaurus Rex, 1/13 scale, Monogram (re-issues from Aurora's Pre-historic Scenes line),1979 & 1987 (ILLUS.).. **40-55**

Horizon Tyrannosaurus Rex Kit

Model kit, Tyrannosaurus Rex, 1/30 scale, Horizon, vinyl kit, 1980s-90s (ILLUS.) **40-60**

Airfix Tyrannosaurus Rex Kit

Model kit, Tyrannosaurus Rex, Airfix, plastic kit, Britain/France, 1976, 14" h. (ILLUS.) **25-35**

Model kit, Tyrannosaurus Rex, No. 746, 1/13 scale, red w/glow parts, Aurora, 1971, 35" l. **150-200**

Model kit, Tyrannosaurus Rex with figure diorama, plastic kit, Tamiya, Japan, 1994.. **40-50**

Model kit, Tyrant King, Tyrannosaurus, 1/48 scale, Pyro, plastic kit, late 1950s - late 1960s, 10" h... **20-40**

Model kit, UFO, classic saucer w/little green alien inside, Lindberg, plastic kit, 1956 ... **125-175**

Model kit, UFO, reissue of 1956 kit, glows in the dark, Lindberg, plastic kit, 1972...... **40-65**

Marx Universal Monster Figure

Model kit, Universal Monster series, Marx, paintable plastic figures, 1960s-70s, about 5" h., each (ILLUS. of one)................. **5-10**

Model kit, Visible Woman, w/optional womb & fetus, Revell, plastic kit, 1950s - present, frequently reissued.......................... **8-20**

Model kit, Wade A. Minit, Hawk, Weird-ohs, designed by Bill Campbell, 1964 .... **20-50**

Hawk Weird-ohs Glow Kit

Model kit, Weird-ohs, Glows in the Dark versions, Hawk, Weird-ohs, designed by Bill Campbell, 1969-70, each (ILLUS. of Endsville Eddie).. **25-65**

Aurora White-tailed Deer Kit

Model kit, white-tailed deer, 1/8 scale, Aurora, 1962 (ILLUS.) **25-50**

Aurora Whoozis? Kit

Model kit, Whoozis?, "So What if I Ain't Smart — I'M LOVELY," Aurora, 1968 (ILLUS.)... **25-75**

Aurora Willie Mays Kit

Model kit, Willie Mays, Great Moments in Sport series, 1/10 scale, painted by Evan Stuart, Aurora, 1965 (ILLUS.) **100-200**

Model kit, Witch, glow version, Aurora, 1972.. **100-250**

Aurora Witch Kit

Model kit, Witch, painted by Evan Stuart, Aurora, 1965 (ILLUS.)............................ **150-400**

Model kit, Woodie on a Surfari, Hawk, Silly Surfers, 1964 .... **35-75**

Model kit, Woolly Mammoth, 1/13 scale, Monogram (re-issues from Aurora's Prehistoric Scenes line), 1979 & 1987............ **30-40**

Arcade Cast-iron Motorcycle Cop

Motorcycle policeman, cast iron, original dark blue paint, vulcanized rubber wheels, Arcade, ca. 1930s, 6" l. (ILLUS.) **425**

Marx Windup Police Motorcycle

Motorcycle policeman, steel, windup-type, w/working siren, by Marx, paint wear, 8 1/2" l. (ILLUS.).. **325**

Omnibus

Omnibus, tin, h.p., wagon roof finished in blue w/yellow ornamentation enclosed by shaped border embossed in swirling pattern above three windows festooned w/painted drapery swags, sides adorned w/floral motif framed by curling vines, coach fitted w/back steps w/embossed horse head sides & embossed roof above entrance to yellow interior fitted w/two bench seats, driver sits atop roof w/curvilinear footrest w/leaf & vine supports, drawn by two golden-maned white horses w/black & red accents, finished in a broad spectrum of bright colors, imaginative embossing & fanciful cutouts, Francis, Field & Francis American Tin, ca. 1860, 21" l. (ILLUS.)..................... **43,300**

Open dray, cas iron, stake-sided wagon finished in blue w/gold tips on stakes & red spoked wheels, drawn by single white horse trimmed in red & black, comes w/original driver & two wooden barrels, Harris, ca. 1905, 15" l. (one small rough spot underneath bed, minor paint chips, driver has moderate paint wear) **1,800**

Oxen tip cart, cast iron, simple black cart trimmed in red w/tipping bed fitted w/removable gates at front & rear, drawn by two burly brown oxen, Welker & Crosby, ca. 1882, 11" l. (paint loss at rear of interior bed, oxen have moderate paint loss) **2,700**

Pull toy, cast iron, boy whipping donkey, boy holds whip & has an articulated arm which raises & lowers as donkey is pulled forward, J. & E. Stevens, ca. 1895, 9" l. **1,440**

Chirping Chick

Pull toy, cast iron, chirping chick, listed in 1881 catalog as "The Lost Chicken," white chick w/articulated tail & beak standing atop cylinder adorned w/holly leaves, mounted on two large wheels & small wheel up front, when pulled the chick flaps its tail feathers & opens its mouth emitting a clicking sound provided by concealed mechanism, ca. 1890, eyes replaced, slight damage to mechanism casing, 5" l. (ILLUS.) **3,600**

Pull toy, cast iron, crawling monkey, w/original hat, dress & matching pantaloons, on all fours in crawling position, rubber band mechanism, in operation the monkey appears to crawl forward, retains one of the original elastic bands on one hand, Ives, ca. 1893, 5 1/2" l. (one ink spot stain, one tear & some browning & fraying to lace trim) **1,440**

Dog w/Rider Platform Toy

Pull toy, cast iron, dog w/rider platform, brown dog w/jockey in red & yellow habit riding on its back, mounted on shaped green base w/four small cast wheels, American Tin, attributed to James Fallows, ca. 1880, one tear on base, one tear on dog, scrapes on base & one leg of jockey, 9 1/2" (ILLUS.) **1,920**

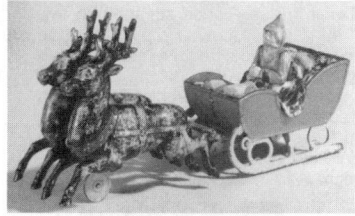

Monkeys on a Stick

Pull toy, cast iron, monkeys on a stick, two monkeys w/articulated limbs on a stick, when pulled forward the monkeys arch their backs as if climbing, base is decorated w/cutout star & circle design & the toy rides on two enormous red wheels, J. & E. Stevens, ca. 1885, 11" l. (ILLUS.) **5,400**

Pull toy, cast iron, two bicycles joined side-by-side w/sprocket & chain mechanism, each cycle features cast-iron messenger in blue hat & jacket, when pulled forward they appear to pedal cycle w/articulated pressed-steel legs on Wilkins cast-iron star wheels, Wilkins, ca. 1890, 6" l. (paint loss on legs & wheels) **11,400**

Santa Sleigh

Santa sleigh, cast iron, red sleigh framed in gold trim, seated Santa w/articulated arms is bundled up in dark blue blanket sprinkled w/snow, seated before stack of presents in multitude of colors, shapes & sizes, raised on yellow runners pulled by two deeply japanned dashing reindeer dappled in snow, Kyser & Rex, ca. 1885, minor scrape on runners & hitch, 13" l. (ILLUS.) **15,600**

Santa sleigh, cast iron, two large reindeer w/full racks finished in brown w/black & gold accents pulling a richly cast sleigh finished in green & highlighted in gold, w/button-tufted seat having original Santa figure w/articulated arms, Hubley, ca.

1905, 15 1/2" l. (minor chipping on reindeer & Santa, paint loss on seat) **6,600**

Sled, child-sized, painted wood, turned wood handle on platform w/blue-painted shaped seat w/linear yellow trim, curved wood & iron runners, stenciled manufacturer's label "Paris Mfg. Co. South Paris, ME USA," late 19th - early 20th c., 16 3/4 x 46", 37 3/4" h. **1,840**

Sleigh, cast iron, drawn by nickel-plated horse, blue sleigh is outlined in raised gold trim & fitted w/integrated red runners, w/original woman driver, Dent, ca. 1905, 15 1/2" l. (buffed, very light browning, paint chipping on carriage, paint loss on figure)..................... **2,700**

Sleigh, cast iron, two-horse sleigh, one black & one nickel-plated horse pulling fancy cast sleigh finished in green w/gold highlights & button-tufted seats, comes w/Pratt & Letchworth woman figure, Hubley, ca. 1905, 15" l. (browning to plated horse, minor rubs & wear, figure mismatched to toy)........................... **2,160**

Squeeze toy, Andy Panda, vinyl, "Vinfloat Products" stamped on toy, 7" **45**

Squeeze toy, baby, rubber, w/arms stretched to sides, Rempel Enterprises, 1950s, 7" h. **100**

Squeeze toy, Bambi look-a-like, rubber, marked "Comlex Creations Made in England," 6" **25**

Squeeze toy, car, early vinyl, w/a face, no mark, 1940s, 3"..................... **50**

Squeeze toy, cat, rubber, molded red ribbon around neck, open smiling mouth, Rempel Enterprises, early 1950s, 12" **50-60**

Squeeze toy, Charlie Chaplin, thin early rubber, no mark, 8" **200-300**

Squeeze toy, cow, rubber, Rempel, 6" h., 1950s.................. **100**

Squeeze toy, Disney characters, rubber, small, 1949, 3" h., each................... **40**

Squeeze toy, dog, rubber, looks like "Tramp," Blue Ribbon stamped on toy, 7" h. **30-40**

Squeeze toy, dog, rubber, spotted coat, Rempel, 1950s, 8".......................... **100**

Squeeze toy, dolls, advertised as being made of plastic vinylite, jointed, names such as "Cappy" & "Robin," molded clothes, by Irwin, late 1940s-early 1950s, each.................. **90**

Squeeze toy, Donald Duck, rubber, early style, unmarked, 6" h. (ILLUS.)........................ **85**

Late Style Donald Duck

Squeeze toy, Donald Duck, vinyl, late style, Shelcore, 1986 (ILLUS.) **20-25**

Squeeze toy, elephant, vinyl, "Alan Jay" stamped on toy, 6" h.................................. **20-25**

Elephant with "Blanket Like Ears"

Squeeze toy, elephant, vinyl, w/"blanket like ears," sleeping eyes & turning head, Edward Mobley Company & Patent Pending marks, dated 1962, 10" h. (ILLUS.)................ **100**

Squeeze toy, frog, rubber, marked "McConnell," 4" h. **18-22**

Squeeze toy, giraffe, rubber, Rempel Enterprises, 1950s, 7 1/2"................................. **70-80**

Early Style Donald Duck

Girl in Sun Dress

Squeeze toy, girl in sun dress, rubber, "Sun
Rubber" & "Ruth Newton" stamped on
toy, 8" h. (ILLUS.).. 50-60
Squeeze toy, girl, vinyl, dressed in molded
yellow dress w/molded yellow flowers in
her hair, Edward Mobley, 1950s, 7"........... 70-80
Squeeze toy, girl, vinyl, w/puppy dog at feet
& holding a rag doll, "JL Prescott Co."
stamped on toy, late 1950s-early 1960s ... 30-40

Goofy Look-a-Like in Santa Costume

Squeeze toy, Goofy look-a-like, thin rubber,
dressed in Santa outfit, 1940s, 6"
(ILLUS.)... 25
Squeeze toy, Indian, rubber, w/molded
clothes & feather, marked "Made in Ger-
many," 1950s, 8" h...................................... 50-55
Squeeze toy, Kewpie doll, vinyl, red or blue,
Cameo, 1963, 7".. 80-100
Squeeze toy, kitten in shoe, rubber, Rem-
pel, 1950s, 5" h.. 70-80

Kitten with Bow Around Neck

Squeeze toy, kitten, rubber, w/molded red
or blue bow around neck, Sun Rubber, 4"
(ILLUS.)... 20-25

Lamb with Neck Ribbon

Squeeze toy, lamb, hard rubber, w/molded
blue neck ribbon, marked "Edward Mob-
ley, 1955," 5 1/2" (ILLUS.)........................ 40-50

Lamb Turning Head

Squeeze toy, lamb, rubber, pink & white,
turning head, Sun Rubber Co., early
1960s, 12" h. (ILLUS.)................................ 30-40
Squeeze toy, mice, thin rubber, usually no
mark, 1940/50s, 2"-4"................................ 10-20
Squeeze toy, Mickey look-a-like, rubber, no
mark, 1950s, 8" h....................................... 30
Squeeze toy, Mickey & Minnie Mouse dolls,
vinyl, wearing removable cotton clothes,
marked "Disney," 1950s, 8" h., pr. if in
original clothes.. 300

Peanuts Characters

Squeeze toy, Peanuts characters, vinyl, marked "United Features Syndicate," 1960s, 4", each (ILLUS.) **10-20**
Squeeze toy, peasant girl, vinyl, marked "Made in Japan," late 1940s, 5" **15-25**
Squeeze toy, Peter Pan, vinyl, stamped "Disney," 1950s, 10" h. **50-60**
Squeeze toy, Popeye, vinyl, marked "Cameo," 1950s, 13" **275**
Squeeze toy, Porky Pig look-a-like, vinyl, in red hat & coat, no marks, 6" h **40-45**

Rocking Horse

Squeeze toy, rocking horse, rubber, marked "IWAI Industrial Co., Ltd. - Made in Japan," 7 1/2" h. (ILLUS.) **65**
Squeeze toy, Santa, rubber, Rempel Enterprises, 1950s, 11"... **85**
Squeeze toy, Santa, vinyl, "Stahlwood Toy" stamped on toy, 1950s, 5" **35**
Squeeze toy, stork, rubber, Rempel, 1957, 8"... **150**
Squeeze toy, stuffed toy animals w/vinyl faces, various animals w/squeakers, tag reads "Made in Japan, 1940s," 10", each........ **35**
Squeeze toy, Tom, the cat, green vinyl, of "Tom and Jerry," "Joy" stamped on toy, early 1960s, 6" **25**

Dent Mack Stake Truck

Stake truck, cast iron, Mack-type, w/factory sample tag, red C-ab fitted w/separate original steering wheel & driver w/separately cast stakes w/chain enclosing the light blue bed, comes w/original tag marked "The Dent Hardware Co. Sample, Fullerton, PA No.," & written in ink "277 Blue," opposite side also written in ink "Stake Truck," Dent, ca. 1923, 15 1/2" l. (ILLUS.)...................................... **10,200**

Jean De Noyers Soldier

Toy soldier, Greenhill, Jean De Noyers, Sieur De Rimaucourt, position G-3, kneeling, sword in left hand in token of surrender, engraved under base "Greenhill/England" (ILLUS.) **375**
Toy soldier, Grey Iron, cast-metal, Foreign Legion soldier in blue uniform, 1930s........ **20-45**
Toy soldier, Grey Iron, cast-metal, wounded sitting soldier, 1930s **40-65**
Toy soldier, Manoil, cast-metal, soldier throwing hand grenade, 1950s, 2 3/4" h. ... **13-18**
Toy soldier, Manoil, cast-metal, soldier w/pistol, 1950s, 2 3/4" h............................ **13-18**
Toy soldier, Marx, plastic, German soldier throwing grenade, 1963, 6" h....................... **6-8**

Marx Roman Soldier

Toy soldier, Marx, plastic, Roman soldier, from "Warriors of the World" series, 1960s, 2 3/8" h., each in box (ILLUS.)......... **8-15**
Toy soldier, Mignot, French Napoleonic Grenadier A Cheval/mounted Grenadier, 1810, in blue & white uniform & plumed bearskin, horse w/detachable saddle trappings, large size/75mm, original box (a few chips, fraying box, small creases) **110**

Toy soldier, Miller (J.H.) of Chicago, composition, General MacArthur, 1952, 5" h. .. **35-75**

Toy soldier, Miller (J.H.) of Chicago, composition, machine gunner in prone position, 1952, 5" l. **15-25**

Toy soldier, Playwood Plastics, flag bearer, 1940s.. **6-8**

Toy soldier, Playwood Plastics, soldier w/machine gun, 1940s **6-8**

Toy soldier, Tommy Toy, cast-metal, officer w/gas mask, 1930s **125-225**

The Devonshire Regiment

Toy soldiers, Britains, Set No. 110, The Devonshire Regiment, marching at the slope in Boer War-period khaki service uniforms & pith helmets, marked "Deposé" under bases, ca. 1930, original Whisstock box, set of 8, chips, fraying on box lid (ILLUS.).................................... **475**

Toy soldiers, Britains, Set No. 125, The Royal Horse Artillery, Early "B" Series, small scale, mounted at the gallop in review order w/six-horse team, limber, gun, outriders & officer, dated 1904, rare, set of 12 (one outrider missing, chips, wear on cannon, one outrider's busby plume missing, some retouching to one horse's legs).. **300**

Toy soldiers, Britains, Set No. 1284, The Royal Marines Marching & Running at the Trail, comprising seven marines marching at the slope w/officer & seven marines running at the trail w/officer, original box, set of 16 (some chips, one marching man missing bayonet, stains on box lid, glue repairs to box, tie-in card not original).. **160**

Toy soldiers, Britains, Set No. 138, French Army Cuirassiers, comprising three troopers & two officers, original Britains postwar box, set of 5 (not a complete set, tie-in card not original).................................. **90**

Toy soldiers, Britains, Set No. 142, French Army Zouaves, charging in review order w/mounted officer, original box, set of 7 (chips, mainly on ankles of charging men, tie-in card not original)................................. **160**

Toy soldiers, Britains, Set No. 1425, Abyssinian Tribesmen, marching in native robes w/rifles, original box, set of 8 (slight paint dulling, one figure slightly mismatched, tie-in card not original) **80**

Toy soldiers, Britains, Set No. 147, Zulu Warriors, charging w/spears & knobkerries, original box, set of 8 (some chips, tie-in card not original)................................ **170**

Toy soldiers, Britains, Set No. 160, Territorial Infantry, marching at the trail in khaki service dress & peak caps, w/officer, ca. 1930, original Whisstock box, set of 8, (some chips).. **325**

Toy soldiers, Britains, Set No. 1603, Irish Free State Infantry, prewar version, marching at the slope in service dress & peak caps, w/officer, ca. 1940, original "Armies of the World" box, set of 8 (chips in several bases, dirt stains on box lid) **550**

Royal Air Force

Toy soldiers, Britains, Set No. 2011, Royal Air Force, w/display box, comprising standing & walking pilots, firefighters in asbestos uniforms, flight sergeants, aircraftsmen & officer holding document in blue service uniforms, motorcycle dispatch rider, & Royal Air Force detachment marching w/slung arms, Bren gunner & officer, rare, in reproduction box, set of 22, a few chips (ILLUS.)..................... **750**

Toy soldiers, Britains, Set No. 2027, Red Army Guards Infantry, marching w/slung arms in winter parade uniforms, w/officer holding sword, original box lid & reproduction box tray, set of 8 (a few chips noticeable on one base).................................. **100**

Toy soldiers, Britains, Set No. 2035, Swedish Life Guard/Svea Livgarde, marching at the slope in review order w/officer, original box, set of 8 (box has small tears, fraying).. **110**

Toy soldiers, Britains, Set No. 205, The Coldstream Guards at Present Arms, w/officer holding sword at the salute, correct feet at present arms version, issued only 1937-1941, ca. 1940, original Whisstock box, set of 8 (a few chips, stains on box lid).. **250**

Toy soldiers, Britains, Set No. 2089, Gloucestershire Regiment, marching at the slope in Number One Dress, w/officer holding sword at the carry, issued only 1954-59, original box, set of 8 (some chips, some fraying on box lid) **250**

Pipes & Drums of the Irish Guards

Toy soldiers, Britains, Set No. 2096, Pipes & Drums of the Irish Guards, comprised of six pipers in green tunics & caubeen caps & brown kilts, bass & side drummers, cymbalist & drum major in Guards uniforms, metal drum version issued only 1954-56, original box, set of 12, a few chips, fraying on box lid (ILLUS.)................... **550**

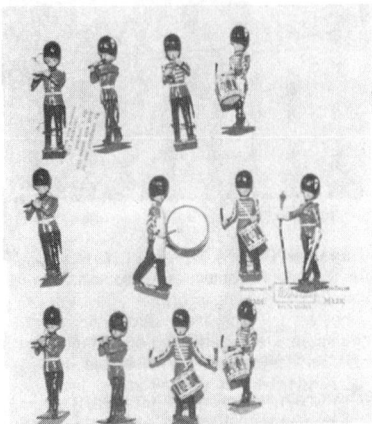

Drums & Fifes of the Welch Guards

Toy soldiers, Britains, Set No. 2108, Drums & Fifes of the Welch Guards, marching in review order w/five fifers, three side drummers, tenor drummer, bass drummer, cymbalist & drum major, issued only 1956-1960, plastic drums, ca. 1960, original box, rare, chips, drum decals are replacements, set of 12 (ILLUS.) **700**

Toy soldiers, Britains, Set No. 212, The Royal Scots, marching at the slope in review order w/piper, original box, set of 5 (dirt stains on box lid, tie-in card not original)... **110**

South African Mounted Infantry

Toy soldiers, Britains, Set No. 38, South African Mounted Infantry, mounted at the gallop w/rifles & officer holding pistol, ca. 1920, in earlier printer's box, marked "Dr. Jameson and the African Mounted Infantry," rare, set of 5, some chips, small tears in box lid & fraying (ILLUS.).............. **1,300**

Toy soldiers, Britains, Set No. 47, Skinner's Horse, mounted at the gallop in review order w/trumpeter, original box, set of 5 (some chips noticeable on legs of three horses, glue repairs to tears in box lid & tray)... **100**

Toy soldiers, Britains, Set No. 76, The Middlesex Regiment/Duke of Cambridge's Own, marching at the slope in review order w/officer, ca. 1945, original Whisstock box, set of 8 .... **140**

Toy soldiers, Britains, Set No. 77, The Gordon Highlanders, marching at the slope in review order w/piper, original box, set of 6 (one feather missing from piper's Glengarry cap).. **130**

Spanish Infantry

Toy soldiers, Britains, Set No. 92, Spanish Infantry, marching at the slope in review order, ca. 1935 set, original "Types of the Spanish Army" printer's box, set of 8, a few chips, some fraying & small crease on box lid (ILLUS.)............................. **425**

Toy soldiers, Built Rite, cardboard, soldiers, 1930s, each.. **10-20**

Toy soldiers, Ducal, Set No. 176, Regimental Band of the Black Watch, 1905, marching in review order w/full instrumentation & drum major, original box, set of 12 (a few chips).. **170**

British Military Units

Toy soldiers, Greenwood & Ball & Graham Farish, British Military Units, comprised of officers of the Cameron Highlanders, 16th Lancers, Royal Horse Artillery, Argyll & Sutherland Highlanders, Greenwood & Ball; two boxed figures of the Garter King of Arms, 1953 Coronation, Royal Artillery officer, 1835, Graham Farish, set of 6 (ILLUS.).. **475**

Boy Scouts

Toy soldiers, Mignot, Boy Scouts, marching w/poles, w/scout bugler, original box, set of 12, a few chips, end label missing on box (ILLUS.) 325

Toy soldiers, Mignot, French Alpine Chasseurs, 1890-1914, in action in summer white uniforms, standing, kneeling, lying firing & charging w/officer firing pistol, original box, set of 12 275

Toy soldiers, Mignot, French Army Bicycle Dispatch Riders, 1915, standing w/bikes in horizon blue uniforms & steel helmets, original box, set of 6 (a few chips)................. 150

Toy soldiers, Mignot, French Army Hay Wagon, 1914, comprised of four-horse team, two drivers w/whips in horizon blue uniforms & hay wagon, original box, set of 5 (some chips, connecting rod between rear team of horses detached & slight damage to hay racks)............................ 225

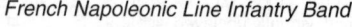

Horse-Drawn Field Artillery Caisson

Toy soldiers, Mignot, French Army World War I Horse-Drawn Field Artillery Caisson, 1915, comprised of four-horse team, two drivers w/whips in horizon blue uniforms, limber & ammunition caisson, ca. 1980, original box, set of 6, tape on box lid (ILLUS.) 325

Toy soldiers, Mignot, French Colonial Infantry, 1890-1914, assaulting w/fixed bayonets in blue & white uniforms & pith helmets, w/officer & standard bearer, original box, set of 12 190

Toy soldiers, Mignot, French Foreign Legion, 1930, in action, standing, kneeling, lying firing & charging, in khaki service uniforms & white kepis, original box, set of 12... 190

Toy soldiers, Mignot, French Marine Fusiliers, 1900-14, marching at the slope in winter blue uniforms & sailor caps, w/officer, drummer & standard bearer, original box, set of 12.. 250

French Napoleonic Line Infantry Band

Toy soldiers, Mignot, French Napoleonic Line Infantry Band, 1812, marching in

blue & white uniforms faced in red, w/full instrumentation, including serpentine, long drum, "Jingling Johnny" & band director, original box, set of 12 (ILLUS.).......... 375

Toy soldiers, Mignot, Royal Guard of Monaco/Carabiniers, marching at the slope in winter blue uniforms w/officer & standard bearer, original set in original window box, set of 4... 90

Toy soldiers, Mignot, Russian Cossacks, 1910-14, charging w/lances in red & blue uniforms, w/bugler & standard bearer, original box, set of 5 (some chips, water stains & fraying on box) 275

Toy soldiers, Mignot, Set No. B8, French Sailors/Naval Landing Party, 1900, marching w/rifles at the trail in summer white uniforms, w/officer holding sword, original box, set of 8 60

Toy soldiers, Mignot, U.S. Cavalry, 1917, mounted w/sabers in khaki service dress & steel helmets, w/trumpeter & standard bearer, original box, set of 5........................... 225

Toy soldiers, Mignot, U.S. Infantry, 1917-18, marching at the slope in khaki service uniforms, fall packs & steel helmets, w/officer, drummer & standard bearer, original box, set of 12... 250

Napoleonic 67th Infantry Regiment

Toy soldiers, Mignot-Lucotte, Band of the French Napoleonic 67th Infantry Regiment of the Line, 1810, limited edition, marching in yellow & white uniforms faced in blue & plumed shakos w/"LC" flanking Imperial Bee emblem on bases, w/full instrumentation, including glockenspiel, serpentine & "Jingling Johnny," & drum major & band director, original box, set of 16 (ILLUS.)...................................... 1,000

Toy soldiers, Minot of France, World War I French Infantry set, in blue uniforms, 1970, the set 20-50

Reliable Fighting Commandos

Floor Train

Toy soldiers, Reliable of Canada, plastic, "Canada's Fighting Commandos," World War II-style soldiers, boxed set (ILLUS.).. **100-150**

Toy soldiers, Sonsco, Japan, soldiers marked "Made in Occupied Japan," 1947, each.. **25-100**

Train set, cast iron, floor-type, 2-2-0 steam locomotive finished in black w/red & gold accents, marked on cab in raised letters "Big 6," together w/red tender & three red gondolas w/green beds marked "U.P.R.R.," comes w/three recast figures, w/engraved copper on woodblock for printing an image of the Big 6 train set, J. & E. Stevens, ca. 1895, 28" l. (moderate paint loss to tender) **1,200**

Train set, cast iron, floor-type, 4-4-0 steam locomotive w/original bell, w/eight-wheel tender, embossed "1890," brown car embossed in gold "Limited Vestibule Express" & matching brown baggage car w/embossed stars and "Union Line" in gold, on eight wheels, together w/lithographed tinplate clock marked "Next Train Leaves," w/John V. Farwell company catalog which illustrates similar train set as New Iron Cannon-ball train, Ives, ca. 1890, 52" (minor paint loss, baggage missing one door, minor touchups of red accents on locomotive, some wear to catalog) **3,600**

Train set, cast iron, floor-type, iron & steel, 4-4-0 steam locomotive finished in black w/870 pressed steel tender & two red pressed steel gondolas, w/original engineer figure, Pratt & Letchworth, ca. 1885, 32" l. (scrapes & scratches)............................ **720**

Train set, cast iron, floor-type, large, one of Kenton's top-of-the-line trains, 4-0-4 locomotive finished in black w/red accents & gold piping fitted w/handsome cowcatcher, cab marked "999," tender marked "Empire State Express," comes w/New York Central & Hudson River baggage car & Chicago passenger car both finished in red & blue, Kenton Hardware, ca. 1910, 50" l. (minor paint chipping, tender has small areas of paint loss).. **4,200**

Train set, cast iron, floor-type, simple but early train set, steam engine finished in black & red & fitted w/original engineer standing on rear of cab, w/three gondolas & caboose in red, distinction of being one of first trains in cast iron, Carpenter, ca. 1885, 24" l. (moderate paint chipping throughout)... **720**

Train set, cast iron, floor-type, steam locomotive embossed "Ptd. June 8, 80," the black 2-2-0 fitted w/brass & wood smoking mechanism provides compressed air w/each wheel rotation, puffing smoke from lit cigarette in smokestack, originally sold individually without tender, toy comes with a Carpenter tender, C.P.R.R. passenger car, w/one original & one replaced removable brakeman, Carpenter, ca. 1890, substantial paint loss on loco & tender, small chip on corner of tender, 20" l. (ILLUS., top of page)... **960**

Transfer wagon, cast iron, green wagon trimmed in gold & marked in raised letters "Transfer," mounted on red spoked wheels & chassis, drawn by three-horse team comprising a grey flanked by two caramel steeds, comes w/original rotund driver, japanned finish & painted features, three wooden barrels, Dent, ca. 1910, 19" l. **5,400**

One-horse Trolley

Trolley, cast iron, one-horse model, finished in red & stenciled "Broadway Car Lines 75" on each side w/two later figures drawn by black horse, Wilkins, ca. 1895, 18" l. (ILLUS.)...................................... **3,900**

Truck, cast iron, American Oil Co. Macktype, C- cab houses original separate driver w/steering wheel, finished in red w/blue tank accented in gold & embossed "American Oil Co.," raised on silver wheels w/yellow spokes, comes w/tag marked "The Dent Hardware Co. Fullerton, PA Sample," & "1278 blue" in ink after No., verso is marked "American Oil Co. Truck," ca. 1923, 15 1/2" l. (near mint, virtually unplayed with condition)... **16,800**

Junior Oil Tank Truck

Truck, pressed steel oil tanker, open cab w/driver, oblong tank marked "Junior Oil Tank," worn & slightly rusted red, yellow, blue & white paint, red metal wheels, 8" l. (ILLUS.).. **125**

Wyandotte Steel Stock Truck

Truck, pressed steel stock truck w/open bed w/slatted sides in red, green cab, battery-powered headlights, black rubber tires, Wyandotte, some paint wear, 10" l. (ILLUS.).. **155**

Tootsie Toy Delivery Van

Van, cast spelter closed delivery van, original worn green paint, black rubber tires, marked inside "Tootsie Toy Chicago - Made in USA," 3" l. (ILLUS.)............................... **15**

TRADE CATALOGS

1938 Pontiac Dealer Catalog

Automobile, "1938 Pontiac - New Silver Streak - Sixes & Eights," dealer version w/22 color pages, color image of standing American Indian on the cover w/a red ground & white & gold lettering, unused, 8 1/2 x 11" (ILLUS.) **$55**

1938 DeSoto Auto Catalog

Automobile, "DeSoto - America's Smartest Low-priced Car," 1938 dealer catalog, cover w/dark blue ground & large image on the front of a deep orange car, light blue & gold wording, 20 color pages, 9 x 11 1/2" (ILLUS.) **55**

1938 Hudson Auto Catalog

Automobile, "Meet Hudson for 1938 - Hudson Terraplane - Hudson Six - Hudson Eight," yellow & blue wording, color scene w/a red, green & yellow auto, 16 color pages, 6 x 11" (ILLUS.)......................... **44**

1938 Oldsmobile Sale Catalog

Automobile, "Oldsmobile Six and Eight," color cover showing two large stylized autos in red & blue, 28 pages showing all models, 1938, 8 1/2 x 11" (ILLUS.)................. **55**
Bicycle, "Stover Bicycle Mfg. Co., Freeport, Ill.," color cover design of elves riding a bicycle down a moonlit lane, ca. 1891, possibly ex-library, binder holes at edge........ **94**

Colorful Colt Firearms Catalog

Firearms, "Colt," bright red ground w/the name in black & gold, decorated w/a naturally colored hand holding a Colt revolver, all models included, ca. 1950s, 28 pp., 7 1/4 x 10" (ILLUS.)................................... 55

Miniature Savage Arms 1935 Catalog

Firearms, "Savage Arms," catalog No. 35 miniature size w/the cover picturing a color head portrait of a screaming Native American chief holding up a rifle, 28 pages illustrating all their various firearms, 1935 (ILLUS.)................................... 203

Ithaca Guns Trade Catalog

Guns, "Ithaca Guns," color-printed cover showing part of a rifle w/flying ducks in the background, fully illustrated, 1936, No. 54, 22 pp., 8 1/2 x 11" (ILLUS.).............. 154

Lionel Trains, 1937 edition, features Locomotive 5344 surrounded by drawings of train engines & coal cars on front cover 150

Lionel Trains, 1949 edition, mother, father, son & daughter featured on front cover w/steam locomotives & the Santa Fe diesel w/accessories 100

Lionel Trains, 1957 edition, front cover features Lionel trains coming at you 50

Lionel Trains, 1959 edition, back cover features "Missile Age" equipment 50

Lionel Trains, 1959 edition, front cover features locomotive for Civil War period on bottom w/engine firing missiles above 50

Lionel Trains, 1975 edition, celebrating 75th Anniversary of Lionel "O" 40

Lionel Trains, 1987 edition, featuring handcars & two engines on cover 15

Rifles, "Savage Rifles," No. 15, rectangular printed in color w/a head portrait of a screaming Native American chief holding up a rifle, 1905, 48 pp., 5 1/2 x 9".................. 215

TRAMP ART

Tramp art flourished in the United States from about 1875 into the 1930s. These chip-carved woodenwares, mostly in the form of boxes or other useful items, were made mainly from old cigar boxes although fruit and vegetable crates were also used. The wood is predominately edge-carved and subsequently layered to create a unique effect. Completed items were given an overall stained finish which was sometimes further enhanced with painted highlights. Though there seems to be no written record of the artists, many of whom were itinerants, there is a growing interest in collecting this ware.

Birdcage, two tiers w/cupola, doors decorated w/carved starbursts, peak decorated w/carved birds, white w/red & green accents, two drawers for cleaning, 8 3/4 x 14 1/2", 29 3/4" h. (edge damage) $1,430

Birdhouse, dark varnished finish, three mesh-covered windows & two openings, door on one end, w/articulated figure of Native American, hatchet in one hand, knife in the other, standing next to two hands w/first fingers raised, 20" l., 19" h. (edge damage)...................................... 1,430

Box, cov., rectangular shape, w/stepped rectangular & square designs, lid w/center panel decoration of carved hearts & teardrops, canted feet, walnut & maple colored varnish, 7 x 10 1/2", 7" h. 165

Large Tramp Art Frame

Frame, rectangular, molded edge w/two interior bands of diamond designs, molded liner, warm brown finish, fitted w/mirror, 25" w., 29" h. (ILLUS.).................................... 770

Frame, rectangular, stepped designs, w/hearts in corners, dark varnished finish, fitted w/mirror, 19 1/2" w., 24" h. (ILLUS., top next page)................................ 440

Jewelry box, cov., stepped rectangular design, canted feet, divided interior, brown varnish, 7 1/4 x 10", 5 1/2" h. (minor wear) 303

Tramp Art Frame with Hearts

Mirror, three-part dresser-top type, w/arched panels, each holding rectangular mirror w/smaller square mirror in arch, frame decorated w/carved hearts, diamonds & rosettes, chip carved base, multicolor varnishes, light to dark, 15 1/2" w., 12" h. **275**

Sewing box, cov., stepped design w/opaque white ball finials & feet, heart pincushion on lid, center panel w/"Felicie," interior lined w/purple velvet, brown varnish, 10 x 13", 6 1/2" h. (minor damage/wear)... **330**

Window planter, arched gateway flanked by gabled trellises, picket fencing, old creamy white paint, 6 1/2 x 20", 16 1/2" h. (paint wear, minor damage) **138**

TRAYS - SERVING & CHANGE

Robert Burns Cigar Change Tray

Change, "Robert Burns Cigars," metal, round, bust portrait of man in center, bor-

der w/"Robert Burns - Cigars," ca. 1910, 4" d. (ILLUS.) **$75-125**

Rock Island Buggy Co. Change Tray

Change, "Rock Island Buggy Co.," metal, rectangular, ornate scrolled, pleated & scalloped border centering scene of buildings & trees, marked in upper left corner "Compliments of Rock Island Buggy Co., Rock Island, ILL," souvenir of St. Louis World's Fair, ca. 1904, 3 1/4 x 5" (ILLUS.) **125-175**

Rockford Watches Change Tray

Change, "Rockford High-Grade Watches," tin, rectangular w/flared sides & crimped corners, center color scene of seated pretty young maiden w/flowers, some wear, early 20th c., 3 x 4 5/8" (ILLUS.)............ **45**

Rockford Watch Co. Change Tray

Change, "Rockford Watches," lithographed metal, rectangular, white, green & pink geometric design border centering an outdoor scene of a young woman in a long green gown sitting on a bench before a tree, at the top "Rockford High Grade Watches" & "For Sale at Dan S. Jones - Independence, IA," litho by H.D. Beach Co., Coshocton, Ohio, ca. 1900, 3 1/4 x 5" (ILLUS.).................................... 125-175

Blatz Old Heidelberg Brew Serving Tray

Serving, "Blatz Old Heidelberg Brew," lithographed tin, rectangular w/rounded corners, center w/color scene of a bottle & glass of beer w/a dish of food against a black ground, wording in white & blue w/a red band, slight wear, 10 1/2 x 13" (ILLUS.) 66

S&H Stamps Change Tray

Change, "S&H Green Trading Stamps," metal, round, w/chromolithographic image of woman in profile wearing off-the-shoulder dress, pearl-like choker & holding feather fan in center, raised border features company name & images of trading stamps, 1907, 4 1/4" d. (ILLUS.).. 104

Change, "Woodland Whiskey," metal, round, a colorful design w/a red central panel w/gold wording & a full-length color portrait of a pretty late Victorian woman dressed in blue, green side panels w/color images of the product, 4 1/4" d. (edge scrapes & dings).. 358

Braumeister Beer Tray

Serving, Braumeister Beer, Independent Milwaukee, Milwaukee, Wisconsin, metal, 1950s, some very light scratches, 12" d. (ILLUS.)... 50

Barmann Beer Tray

Serving, Barmann Beer, P. Barmann Brewing Co., Kingston, New York, metal, round, 1930s, some spotting overall, mostly on rim, a few dings, 12" d. (ILLUS.)... 100

Congress Beer Tray

Serving, Congress Beer, Haberle Brewing Co., Syracuse, New York, metal, round, 1930s, many chips & scratches overall, pair of dings, 12" d. (ILLUS.)............................ 96

round, 1930s, scratches overall, rim
chips, 12" d. (ILLUS.) **328**

Congress Beer Tray

Serving, Congress Beer, Haberle-Congress, Syracuse, New York, metal round, 1930s, several nicks overall, 13" d. (ILLUS.) **181**

Dutch Club Tray

Serving, Dutch Club, Pittsburgh Brewing Co., Pittsburgh, Pennsylvania, metal, round, 1940s, very minor nicks or scratches, 12" d. (ILLUS.) **110**

Dawson's Ale & Beer Tray

Serving, Dawson's Ale & Beer, Dawson Brewing Co., New Bedford, Massachusetts, metal, round, 1930s, a few chips & scratches, 12" d. (ILLUS.) **76**

Edelbrew Brewery Tray

Serving, Edelbrew Brewery, Brooklyn, New York, metal, round, 1940s, very tiny ding at 7 o'clock, 12" d. (ILLUS.) **55**

Derby Cream Ale Tray

Serving, Derby Cream Ale, National Brewing Co., Syracuse, New York, metal,

Eichler Beer Tray

Serving, Eichler Beer, Eichler Brewing Co., New York, New York, metal, round, pre-

Prohibition, some chips on rim, spider web cracking overall (ILLUS.) **116**

Esslinger's Ale Tray

Serving, Esslinger's Ale, Esslinger Brewing Co., Philadelphia, Pennsylvania, metal, round, 1940s, back w/minor spotting, 12" d. (ILLUS.) **81**

George Ehrets Extra Tray

Serving, George Ehrets Extra, Ehrets Brewing Co., New York, New York, metal, round, 1910s, overall wear, lots of small chips in rim, 12" d. (ILLUS.) **46**

Good Old German Lager Tray

Serving, Good Old German Lager, Independent Brewing Co., brewery location unknown, metal, round, 1930s, minor scratching, 12" d. (ILLUS.) **160**

Horse Head Beer & Ale Tray

Serving, Horse Head Beer & Ale, Lang Brewery, Buffalo, New York, metal, round, 1940s, Champion Don Juan picture, minor rim chips, 12" d. (ILLUS.) **162**

Loewer's Gambrinus Beer & Ale Tray

Serving, Loewer's Gambrinus Beer & Ale, Loewer's Brewing Co., New York, New York, metal, round, 1930s, some small rim chips, crackled overall, 12" d. (ILLUS.) **125**
Serving, mahogany dish-top style, round w/molded edge, brass handles, America, early 19th c., 18" d. (cracks, patch)............... **499**

Monarch Tray

Serving, Monarch, Eagle Brewing Co., Utica, New York, metal, round, pre-Prohibition, a few chips, 12" d. (ILLUS.) **257**

North Western Beer Tray

Serving, North Western, lithographed metal, round, shows scene of Native American riding a buffalo & carrying a banner aloft reading "North Western" flanked by North Western logo, border marked "Zacherl - Bohemian - Malt Tonic - Pale Export" alternating w/bottles on sheaves of hops (ILLUS.) **6,050**

Old Timers Lager Tray

Serving, Old Timers Lager, West Bend Lithia, West Bend, Wisconsin, metal, round, 1940s, several scratches overall, 12" d. (ILLUS.) **55**

Pickwick Ale Tray

Serving, Pickwick Ale, Haffenreffer & Co., Boston, Massachusetts, metal, round,

1930s, spotting & scratches overall, 12" d. (ILLUS.) **30**

Ruhstaller's Gilt Edge Lager Tray

Serving, Ruhstaller's Brewing Co., Sacramento, California, lager-style, metal, round, pre-Prohibition, rim chipped, minor spotting & scratches, 12" d. (ILLUS.)...... **101**

Colorful Seipp's Extra Pale Beer Tray

Serving, Seipp's Extra Pale Beer, C. Seipp Brewing Co., Chicago, Illinois, metal, round, pre-Prohibition, nicked & spotted overall, 12" d. (ILLUS.) **196**

Sunrise Beer Tray

Serving, Sunrise Beer, Sunrise Brewing Co., Cleveland, Ohio, metal, round, 1930s, a few minor scratches & chips, 12" d. (ILLUS.) **182**

Theo. Gier Co. Sign

Serving, Theo. Gier Co., lithographed tin, round, center scene of people seated at a table drinking wine, vineyard scene in background, red border w/"Theo. Gier Co. Oakland, Cal. - Vineyards - Napa & Livermore" (ILLUS.) **1,293**

Serving Tray with Nautical Scene

Serving, tin, rectangular, cutout handles, center panel w/depiction of three-masted ship "Red Jacket" at sea surrounded by ice floes, on black ground, gilt border decoration, 19th c., dent & minor wear, 20 3/8 x 28" (ILLUS.) **2,938**

Trommer's Malt Beers Tray

Serving, Trommer's Malt Beers, Trommer Brewing Co., Brooklyn, New York, metal, round, 1930s, NRA logo on rim, repaired hole in center & some scratches, 12" d. (ILLUS.) **135**

Wehle Ale & Beer Tray

Serving, Wehle Ale & Beer, Wehle Brewing Co., New Haven, Connecticut, metal, round, 1930s, minor rim chips, 12" d. (ILLUS.) **117**

TRUMP INDICATORS

A trump indicator is a device that was placed on the table during card games such as Whist and its successor, Bridge. They were to remind the players what the trump suit was. The earlier trump indicators from the 19th century, used in the game of Whist, had only the four suits of hearts, spades, diamonds and clubs. Later, in the game of Bridge, "No Trump" was added.

These gadgets are difficult to find and appear in many forms: people, animals, buildings, useful objects, etc. Some are made of beautiful porcelain while others are crudely made from metal and wood. The ones made from celluloid can be dated from the first half of the 20th century. One thing trump indicators all have in common is their movable pointer or spinner displaying what card suit is trump.

As with so many items from the past, their usefulness has become outdated. In the modern game of Bridge, a player would probably be reminded "If you can't remember what the trump is, you shouldn't be playing Bridge." But, as gaming collectibles increase in popularity, the desirability of trump indicators will continue to score high.

Pig Trump Indicator

Brass, pig holds frame w/flip suit cards
(ILLUS.)... **$300**

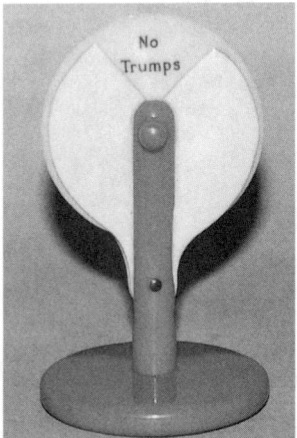

Celluloid Trump Indicator

Celluloid, round disk on stand, turn ring
shows suit (ILLUS.)... **95**

Asian Woman Trump Indicator

Metal, Asian woman w/fan beside large circular turn ring that shows suit (ILLUS.) **400**

Donkey by Wall Indicator

Metal, donkey by wall w/suits marked in circles, head points to suit (ILLUS.).................... **400**

Figural Man Indicator

Metal, figural man on round stepped base,
post holds flip suit cards (ILLUS.).................. **350**

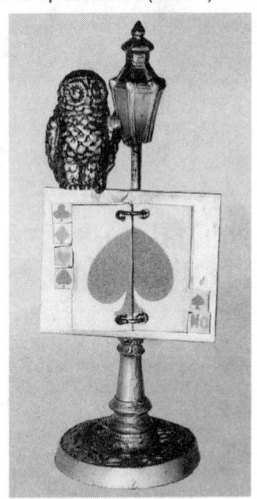

Owl & Lamppost Indicator

Metal, owl on lamppost, flip suit cards at
center (ILLUS.) **200**

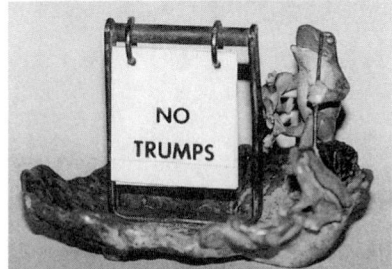

Frogs on Lily Pad Indicator

Metal, two frogs on lily pad, metal frames for suit flip cards (ILLUS.) **500**

Clover-shaped Dish Indicator

Silver plated, three-leaf clover dish, suit indicator in center (ILLUS.) **250**

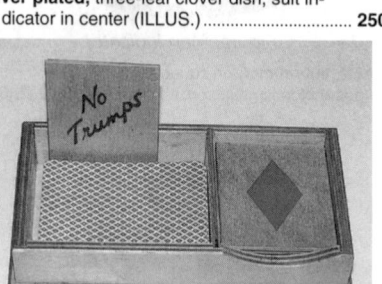

Wooden Card Box & Suit Indicators

Wooden, card box, divided w/wooden suit pieces stored in one compartment (ILLUS.) **75**

Card Box with Pig Indicator

Wooden, card box w/metal pig pointing to suits (ILLUS.) **125**

Card Holder with Cat Indicator

Wooden, card holder w/figural black cat on front, paws point to suits (ILLUS.) **150**

Black Cat Indicator

Wooden, cat, black w/long tail that marks suit (ILLUS.) **200**

Wooden Figural Indicator

Wooden, figural man (English character?) holds suit card in hand (ILLUS.) **300**

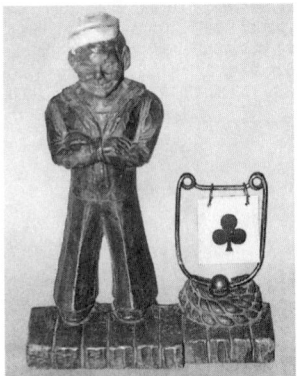

Sailor Trump Indicator

Wooden, sailor on planks, standing beside coiled rope that holds metal frame w/flip suit cards (ILLUS.) 350

VENDING & GAMBLING DEVICES

Sherbits Candy Vending Machine

Candy vendor, metal, shallow upright rectangular wall-mounted style, the front in red, white & blue, reads "Sherbits - delicious candy," Jennings and Co., Chicago, w/key, ca. 1950s-60s, slight paint touch-up, some scratching, 7 x 15", 25 1/4" h. (ILLUS.) **$61**

Jennings "Little Duke" Slot Machine

Gambling, Jennings "Little Duke" countertop slot machine, cast-metal front w/red, yellow & black enamel trim, wood sides & back, 1-cent play, some overall wear, no key, nail added in back, ca. 1930s, 11 x 16", 22" h. (ILLUS.) **1,650**

Gaming Wheel

Gaming wheel, wooden, round, center w/flower cutout, surrounded by panels w/various three-number combinations on them, mounted on wooden stand, original paint, 32 1/2" d., 22" h., American, late 19th - early 20th c., some paint loss (ILLUS.) 173

Gum vendor, stainless steel & glass, tall upright rectangular steel case w/six columns across the front, push-in black selection buttons across the bottom front, Mills Automatic Merchandising Corp., New York, ca. 1936, key present, 5 x 9 3/4", 16 1/4" h. (some surface scratching)....................................... 66

Gumball vendor, aluminum & glass, a black metal cap above a clear spherical glass globe on a cylindrical green-painted metal base w/nickel flag, Columbus Model 46, post-World War II, keys present, 7 3/4" d., 13 1/2" h. (paint wear & soiling, lever for reaching product missing)....................................... 97

Columbus Model M or MG Machine

Gumball vendor, cast iron & glass, a black cast-iron cap above the clear octagonal glass globe w/a 1¢ decal, red & black iron cylindrical base, Columbus Model M or MG, ca. 1930s-40s, w/key, some soiling, paint chips & repaint (ILLUS.) 264

Gumball vendor, cast iron & glass, a flat rounded stepped metal top on the clear cylindrical glass globe w/yellow, blue & red decal, squared cast-iron base, National 5¢ model, ca. 1940s-50s, 12" h. (missing key, some scuffs & soiling) 60

Gumball vendor, cast iron & glass, metal cap on clear glass globe above red cast-iron pedestal base, Columbus Model A, ca. 1920s, 8 1/4" d., 16 1/2" h. (flap missing, rust to interior, some soiling) 187

Master 1¢ Gumball Vendor

Gumball vendor, metal, porcelain & glass, tall upright square case w/flat black top overhanging case w/glass windows on three sides, red sides & ornate cast metal mechanism on lower front, square black base, Master company patented model, ca. 1925, keys missing, some edge chipping & slight wear, 8" sq., 16" h. (ILLUS.)... 185

YuChu Gumball Machine

Gumball vendor, "YuChu Ball Gum" on worn paper label, glass & cast iron, large upright squared glass top on a flaring round base on four small projecting round legs, ca. 1920s, 13 1/8" h. (ILLUS.)................ 176

Rosebud Matches Vending Machine

Match vendor, "Rosebud Matches" by Northwestern, metal wall or countertop model in dark green w/red & yellow details, original key, 13 1/2" h. (ILLUS.) 578

Nut vendor, Sun Nut machine, cast aluminum & glass, square upright form w/black metal stepped top above glass sides & plain aluminum corner brackets, deep square flaring black base, w/key, mid-20th c., 7 3/4 x 9 3/4", 13 3/4" h. (some soiling)... 44

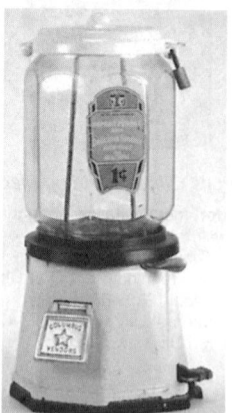

Columbus Model 21 Peanut Vendor

Peanut vendor, metal & glass, white metal cap on octagonal clear glass globe w/large blue, red, yellow, white & black decal, tall slightly flaring paneled white-enameled base w/nickel-plated flap, Columbus Model 21, ca. 1934, no keys, repainted, slight scratching, 6 1/2" d., 13 1/4" h. (ILLUS.) 231

Peanut vendor, porcelain & glass, green porcelain-coated metal round cap on tall bulbous cylindrical clear glass globe w/worn & faded decal above flaring paneled green porcelain base w/black flap, Northwestern Model 33, ca. 1933, 8 1/4" d., 15 1/2" h. (chip on lid, crack in globe, some scratches & wear to base) **121**

Advance Big Mouth Peanut Vendor

Peanut vendor, steel & glass, round metal cap on clear round glass globe w/1¢ decal, tall slightly tapering red & black metal base w/nickel-plated brass front mechanism & opening, Advance Machine Company "Big Mouth" model, ca. 1925, some minor overall wear & surface rust on knob (ILLUS.).. **101**

Postage stamp vendor, metal & glass, countertop double-style, upright rectangular black metal case w/two white porcelain plaques w/stamp prices in black above small glass windows, crank handle below windows & above dispensing slot, Schermack Sanitary Stamp Selling Machine, Detroit, ca. 1920s-30s, 7 1/2 x 11 1/2", 13 1/4" h. (paint chipping & wear, rust spotting, top glass pane w/chip in corner, key missing) **83**

Patriotic Stamp Vending Machine

Postage stamp vendor, porcelain, tall narrow rectangular wall-mounted style, the front w/a dark blue border w/white stars & wording around a white center panel

w/wording in red & dark blue & two small windows above a bust image of Uncle Sam over the bottom slot, Victory model by The Field Company, Los Angeles, California, ca. 1950s, no key, some edge chipping, 4 1/4 x 8", 20 1/4" h. (ILLUS.) **83**

Postage stamp vendor, steel, narrow upright metal case w/rounded top corners & side crank handles, white w/thin red bands around the bottom, gold-colored center panel w/coins decorated w/a red sketch of the U.S. Capitol & stars & black lettering reading "U.S. Postage Stamps," w/key, Northwestern Corporation, Morris, Illinois, ca. 1930s-40s, 8 1/4 x 8 3/4", 14 3/8" h. (some soiling & scratching) **39**

Roulette Wheel

Roulette wheel, ten glass panels, each featuring a jockey on a running horse against a background of green fields & blue sky, ornate leaf border, the center w/a fitted nickel-plated 12-point star w/four reverse-painted mirrored panels w/stylized fleur-de-lis, comes w/stand, H.C. Evans & Co., early 1900s, some spindles missing, paint loss, 60" d. (ILLUS.) **3,737**

Albert Pick Co. Trade Stimulator

Trade stimulator, a golden oak framework w/a large round molded frame around a spinning dial raised on scroll brackets above a rectangular glass-sided compartment on a molded rectangular base, Albert Pick Co., Chicago, patented in 1895, back door a replacement, Plexiglas in windows, 5 1/2 x 14", 22" h. (ILLUS.).. **688**

Cigar Trade Stimulator

Trade stimulator, "Nickel Drop" cigar trade stimulator, oak cabinet w/bead & carved trim, mirrored back, diamond-shaped top piece features center dial & reads "Try our choice cigars - We handle the best," rectangular base reads "You always get one - and sometimes more," Drobisch

Bros., 1897, 6 1/2 x 14 1/2", 19 1/2" h. (ILLUS.)... **2,200**

Gum Trade Stimulator

Trade stimulator, "The Official Sweepstakes" gum vendor, rectangular, top glassed panel w/various-colored horses & riders racing around a bright yellow disk, the front w/glass panel showing gumballs inside, Rock-ola (ILLUS.)............ **2,100**

WEATHERVANES

Arrow, copper, sphere finial on old gilded surface, America, 19th c., 31" l., 17" h. **$588**

Arrow, copper, spire & belted ball finial on vane w/verdigris surface, no stand, America, 19th c., 60" l., 29" h. (several bullet holes)... **940**

Arrow, gilt copper, ball finial w/weathered gilt surface, no stand, America, 19th c., 36" l., 16" h.. **353**

Arrow, iron & copper, spire & sphere finial on vane w/iron arrow & corrugated copper tail, weathered gilt surface, America, 19th c., 25 1/2" l., 17" h. (sphere loose, minor dents)... **558**

Sheet Copper Banner Weathervane

Banner, pierced scrolled sheet copper, old surface w/traces of gilt, no stand, America, mid-19th c., 71 1/2" l., 17 3/4" h. (ILLUS.).. **2,703**

Five Weathervanes

Banner, sheet iron, iron ball finial on shaft above banner w/heart & oval cutouts, weathered black paint, w/stand, America, 19th c., 15 3/4" l., 37" h. (ILLUS. back left w/four other weathervanes, above) **1,645**

Cat, sheet iron, silhouetted figure of a prancing cat, painted black, w/stand, America, 19th c. (wear, corrosion) **4,025**

Dolphin, copper, leaping pose above scrolled copper wire directionals, no stand, America, late-20th c., 34 1/2" l., 22 1/2" h. **441**

Double-masted schooner, metal, weathered red & mustard paint, no stand, America, probably 20th c., 33 1/2" l., 38 1/4" h. (imperfections) **264**

Eagle, gilt copper bird w/outstretched wings perched on belted sphere over arrow directional, old gilt over verdigris surface, no stand, America, 19th c., 14 3/4 x 15 1/2", 9 1/8" h. **1,058**

Eagle, molded gilt copper bird perched on belted ball w/arrow directional, w/stand, America, 19th c., 24" l., 25 5/8" h. (regilded) **441**

Fisherman in rowboat, copper & brass, interior impressed "9 . 95 H. J. WHITE 36," America, late 20th c., 28 1/2" l., 18" h. **323**

Various Weathervanes

Horse Weathervanes

Gamecock, molded copper w/embossed sheet copper tail, weathered gilt surface, no stand, America, 19th c., repair on neck, bullet hole on breast, 17 1/2" l., 18 1/2" h. (ILLUS. lower left w/various weathervanes, bottom previous page)....... **4,994**

Horse, copper flattened full body running form w/verdigris surface & traces of gilt, raised on cast-iron directionals, copper sphere & pyramidal roof mount, America, repair to knee, 37 1/2" l., 63" h. (ILLUS. center w/four other weathervanes, top previous page)... **7,050**

Horse, copper, running form w/flying mane & tail, verdigris surface w/traces of gilt, no stand, America, 19th c., 27 1/4" l., 15" h. (minor imperfections)................................... **1,495**

Horse, copper & zinc full body running form, weathered silvered paint w/traces of old gilt, no stand, America, 19th c., repaired bullet holes, 32 1/2" l., 18 1/2" h. (ILLUS. center w/other horse weathervanes, top of page)......... **2,468**

Horse, gilded copper full body running form, zinc head, w/stand, America, 19th c., repair to tail, seam separations, 30" l., 20" h. (ILLUS. front right w/four other weathervanes, top previous page)............ **2,703**

Horse, gilt copper full body running form w/zinc head, no stand, America, late 19th c., later gilt, replaced rod, 31 1/8" l., 20 5/8" h. (ILLUS. front left w/four other weathervanes, top previous page)............. **1,175**

Horse, gilt copper & zinc "Ethan Allen" running form, weathered gilded surface, w/stand, America, 19th c., 25 1/2" l., 16 3/4" h. (restoration) **2,585**

Two Horse Weathervanes

Horse, molded copper & cast zinc running form, verdigris surface, no stand, attributed to A.L. Jewell & Co., Waltham, Massachusetts, 1850-67, seam separation, 29" l., 14" h. (ILLUS. bottom) **4,700**

Horse, molded copper full body running form, verdigris surface, traces of gilt, no stand, America, 19th c., hole, 29 5/8" l., 17" h. (ILLUS. upper left w/various weathervanes, bottom previous page) **3,408**

Various Animal Weathervanes

Horse, molded copper prancing form, weathered gilt surface w/vestiges of sizing, w/stand, America, 19th c., 34" l., 25 1/2" h. (ILLUS. upper right w/various weathervanes, bottom page 1155)............ **4,113**

Horse, molded copper, running form, gold painted surface, no stand, America, 19th c., 32" l., 17 1/2" h. (repaired bullet holes, seam separations)...................................... **1,410**

Horse, molded copper running form, old later gold painted surface, no stand, 19th c., 32" l., 18" h. (repaired bullet hole)............. **1,410**

Horse, molded copper running form, old later painted surface impressed "A.J. Harris & Co." on one side, no stand, late-19th c., seam separations, 32 1/2" l., 22" h. (ILLUS. right w/other horse weathervanes, on previous page)............................. **2,350**

Horse, molded zinc head & torso, copper body, tail & legs, old surface, no stand, attributed to J. Howard & Co., West Bridgewater, Massachusetts, 25" l., 19" h. (ILLUS. second from left w/various animal weathervanes, top of page)......... **12,925**

Horse, painted copper flattened full body running form, older darkened putty painted surface w/traces of gilt, no stand, America, late 19th c., 32" l., 17" h. (bullet hole repairs)... **1,410**

Horse, zinc torso, copper ears, legs, body, corrugated copper tail, old surface w/vestiges of gilt, no stand, attributed to J. Howard & Co., West Bridgewater, Massachusetts, third quarter 19th c., 24" l., 18 1/2" h. (ILLUS. left w/other horse weathervanes, top previous page)............. **7,638**

Horse & jockey, copper, old yellow sizing surface, no stand, America, late-19th c., 31 1/2" l., 22 3/4" h. (ILLUS. center w/various animal weathervanes, above).... **9,400**

Horse & rider, copper, sheet copper straight-back rider wearing a top hat & waistcoat riding on a flattened full-body trotting horse, verdigris surface, w/stand, attributed to A.L. Jewell & Co., Waltham, Massachusetts, 19th c., 27 1/2" l., 28 1/4" h. **19,550**

Horse & rider, molded sheet iron hollow body, original mustard painted surface, America, early 19th c., 36" l., 28 3/4" h. (ILLUS. top w/Jewell horse weathervane, on previous page)................ **6,463**

Horse-drawn Fire Wagon Vane

Horse-drawn fire wagon, painted copper w/iron supports on underside, steam fire engine pulled by two horses, carrying helmeted driver, in red, black & gold paint, includes stand, probably L.W. Cushing & Sons, Waltham, Massachusetts, late 19th c., 40" l., 29 1/4" h. w/stand (ILLUS.)... **15,275**

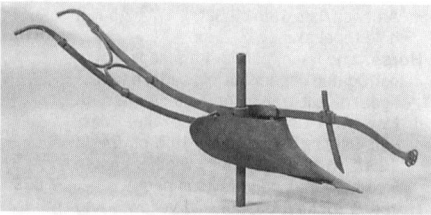

Plow Weathervane

Plow, iron & bronze, old surface, no stand (might be trade sign), America, 19th c., 38 1/4" l., 13 1/2" h. (ILLUS.)...................... **3,408**

Pointing finger, iron & wood, two wood finials on iron shaft, sheet metal vane formed by hand w/pointing finger on one end & starburst on other end, no stand, America, 19th c., 23" l., 35 1/4" h. (ILLUS. back right w/four other weathervanes, top of page 1155) **2,233**

Quill pen, iron & copper, spire & sphere finial w/weathered regilded surface, attributed to L.W. Cushing & Sons, Waltham, Massachusetts, late 19th c., repaired, 36 1/2" l., 23 1/2" h. (ILLUS. center w/various weathervanes, botom page 1155) **2,468**

Rooster, sheet copper, old verdigris surface, traces of gilt, no stand, America, early 19th c., 42" l., 26 1/2" h. (ILLUS. second from right w/various animal weathervanes, on previous page) **5,581**

Stag, molded copper full body leaping form, regilded old surface, including stand, attributed to A.J. Harris & Son, Waltham, Massachusetts, 1868-1882, 55 1/2" l., 41 5/8" h. (ILLUS. far right w/various animal weathervanes, on previous page).... **12,925**

Stag, molded copper leaping form, w/old regilded surface, on wooden stand, America, 19th c., 21 1/2" l., 17 3/4" h. (ILLUS. lower right w/various weathervanes, bottom of page 1155) **5,288**

Steer, zinc head on molded hollow copper body, old painted surface w/traces of gilt, no stand, America, 19th c., 29 3/8" l., 20" h. (ILLUS. far left w/various animal weathervanes, on previous page) **6,463**

Woman with Telescope Vane/Finial

Woman looking through telescope, wearing nautical-style outfit, including yellow & white striped dress w/red double-breasted coat, black billed hat & blue scarf, old repaint w/surface rust beneath, might be finial, 32 1/4" h. (ILLUS.) **523**

WOOD SCULPTURES

American folk sculpture is an important part of the American art scene today. Skilled wood carvers turned out ships' figureheads, cigar store figures, plaques and carousel animals of stylized beauty and great appeal. The wooden shipbuilding industry, which had originally nourished this folk art, declined after the Civil War, and the talented carvers then turned to producing figures for tobacconists' shops, carousel animals and show figures for circuses. These figures and other early ornamental carvings that have survived the elements and years are eagerly sought.

Mermaid Brackets

Brackets, polychrome carved figures of mermaids w/gilded bifurcated scrolled tails, America, 19th c., 19 3/4" h., pr. (ILLUS.).. **$4,230**

Bust of woman, w/carved facial features, ears & hairstyle, raised on stepped base w/dentil carving & stamped decoration, old surface, America, early 20th c., 8 1/4" h.. **646**

Cigar Store Indian Maiden

Cigar store Indian maiden, carved polychrome standing figure of woman wearing feather headdress, earrings, necklace & native costume, holding banded

bunch of cigars in one hand, America, 3rd quarter 19th c., 71 3/8" h. (ILLUS.) ... **36,425**

Cigar Store Turk

Cigar store Turk, carved polychrome standing figure wearing turban & exotic clothing, holding knife in one hand, pouch in the other, America, ca. 1830, 62 1/2" h. (ILLUS.) **23,500**

Circus wagon panel, carved & painted in high-relief w/a lion, old brown over white & green-painted surface, ca. 1875, 30 x 74 1/2" (imperfections) **2,300**

Dancing figure, carved black folk art articulated figure wearing blue suit, red hat & black boots, attached to wire rod & turned pole supported on two movable paddles, America, early-20th c., 8 3/4" h. (incomplete) **382**

Pilot House Giltwood Eagle

Eagle, carved giltwood, ship pilot house-type, in the form of an eagle w/spread wings as if about to take flight, perched on carved rockery, America, ca. 1875, old regilding, minor wear, 26 x 31", 25" h. (ILLUS.) **2,468**

Eagle, carved & painted, ship pilot house-type, bird w/outstretched wings alighting on a domed rock, brown, black, white, yellow & red paint, old repainted surface, 19th c., 31 x 40", 33 3/4" h. (minor losses).................... **1,725**

Figure of woman, carved burlwood folk art-style woman w/carved facial features & hair style in a bun, ruffled collar, old dark stained surface, America, late 19th - early 20th c., 4 3/4" h. **411**

Head of a woman, folk art-style carved in soft wood w/dark brown stain, figure has long wavy hair & two old, uneven holes in its ears, unsigned, early 20th c., 9 1/4" h. (minor surface wear, some scorching).......... **110**

House, rustic twig folk art-style two-story house w/center chimney, arched & bay windows, set on rustic twig & green shingle decorated platform, natural finish w/green highlights, America, late 19 - early 20th c., 11 1/4 x 15", 19 1/2" h. **411**

Fine Carved Public Building Model

Public building, carved & painted multi-story structure w/a dome on tiered round colonnaded roof cupola centered on the flat roof, classical facade w/two tiers of columns surrounding the sides & flanking window openings & doors, pedimented portico over front door, old brown & white paint, early 20th c., imperfections, 39 x 40", 56" h. (ILLUS.) **5,175**

Whirligig, cutout figure of witch w/rotating sheet iron paddle arms/broom, weathered off-white paint w/brown trim, w/stand, America, probably early 20th c., 17" l., 22" h. **4,406**

Whirligig, figure of man w/arms forming cranking blades, polychrome paint & stenciled business name "Boswell Bros., Groceries and Dry Goods," 20th c. (imperfections).. **575**

Whirligig, figure of mustachioed man wearing a black top hat & jacket, red trousers, w/rotating paddle arms, on a wood plinth, late 19th c., 14 5/8" h. (imperfections) **2,070**

Whirligig, figure of soldier, painted black, grey & white, on wooden stand, 13" h. **353**

Whirligig, model of windmill & figures, carved & painted wood & wrought iron, four flat-ended wrought-iron blades power an elaborate pulley system animating carved wooden figures of a press operator, carpenter & blacksmith on the platform below, weathered original paint,

America, early 20th c., 12 x 32 1/2", 47" h.. **2,760**

Whirligig, model of windmill, painted wood w/sheet metal blades & armature activated by a crank operated by two carved & articulated figures of men at the base of the tower, painted grey w/blue & black trim, 20th c., 31" w., 56" h. (minor wear).... **2,760**

Whirligig, primitive, covered open-sided platform w/figure of man pumping water on one end & woman at wash tub on the other, small dog between them, a woodpecker on top, old worn white, blue, red, black & green paint, 28 1/2" w., 26" h. (missing propeller) **330**

WOODENWARES

The patina and mellow coloring, along with the lightness and smoothness that come only with age and wear, attract collectors to old woodenwares. The earliest forms were the simplest, and the shapes of items whittled out in the late 19th century varied little in form from those turned out in the American colonies two centuries earlier. A burl is a growth, or wart, on some trees in which the grain of the wood is twisted and turned in a manner that strengthens the fibers and causes a beautiful pattern to be formed. Treenware is simply a term for utilitarian items made from "treen," another word for wood. While maple was the primary wood used for these items, they are also abundant in pine, ash, oak, walnut and other woods. "Lignum Vitae" is a species of wood from the West Indies that can always be identified by the contrasting colors of dark heartwood and light sapwood and by its heavy weight, which caused it to sink in water.

Basket, carved freeform burl construction, America, 19th c., 10 3/4" l., 5 3/4" h. **$1,116**

Bible cover, chip carved hollow shape w/intricately detailed chip carved designs of a cross w/a heart on one side & a medallion w/a Maltese cross & heart on the other, the spine w/several designs & initials "EKD," carved strap w/hinges, 1 3/4 x 4 x 5 1/2" (age split in spine)............. **633**

Bowl, burl thinly turned w/slightly raised foot & broad band around rim, natural dry finish, 13 1/2" d., 4 1/4" h. **1,045**

Bowl, burl w/old dark patina, two incised lines around exterior, old handwritten note on base reads "Christina MaBee born 1837, Fed kittens from this dish...She was my great-grandmother. J.A. 1929," 5 1/8" d., 1 1/2" h. **1,375**

Bowl, burl w/tight figure & overall pleasant brown stain, 10 1/2" d., 3 1/4" h. (wear, short age split)... **880**

Bowl, maple, turned foot w/slightly raised rim, old red paint, interior w/scrubbed surface, 19" d., 6" h. **880**

Large Pine Bowl

Bowl, pine w/dark varnished finish, slightly turned foot & raised rim, areas of putty fill in small holes, 25 3/4" d., 9" h. (ILLUS.) **550**

Bowl, thinly turned ash burl, a raised handle on the rim on either side, mellow brown surface inside & out, 14 1/4" d., 4 3/4" h. .. **3,300**

Bowl, turned maple w/raised rim, small hole near rim for hanging, old natural finish, 16" d., 4 1/2" h. **55**

Bowl, turned & painted salmon color, America, 19th c., 15 5/8" d., 4 1/2" h. **1,528**

Bowl, turned rim w/an area of hand planing & a worn dip in rim, interior has old dark patina, outside has original red stain, 20 x 21 1/2", 6 1/2" h. **1,155**

Bowl, turned rim, worn blue paint on exterior, interior w/old dark patina, attributed to Vermont, 17 3/4 x 19", 6" h. **660**

Bowl, turned, w/thick rim, exterior w/layers of red paint, interior w/worn surface from use, 18 1/2" d., 6" h. (flaking) **523**

Bucket, cov., oak staves w/iron bands, old decoration similar to Lehnware, vertical stripes in shades of red & dark salmon w/floral vines in yellow, white, green & red on the bands & lid, 7" d., 9 1/2" h. (ground spot on rim of lid) **935**

Bucket, hanging-type, cylindrical stave construction wrapped w/five narrow lappet bands, one stave extended up past rim to form handle w/hanging hole, worn yellow paint, New England, early 19th c., 9 1/4" d., 8" h. plus handle **690**

Bucket, wooden staves w/tin bands, wire bail handle w/wood grip, original dark red alligatored paint, 6 7/8" d., 6" h. **248**

Butter churn, w/four interlocking staves w/wrought-steel hardware on removable lid, serpentine crank w/wooden handle retains original dasher on inside, on sawbuck base pegged on either side of center support, in old red paint, 35" h. (edge chips & touchup on base, one leg has nailed split) **110**

Bird's-eye Maple Butter Paddle

Butter paddle, bird's-eye maple, simply carved hook handle, 10" l. (ILLUS.) **165**

Canteen, painted, stave construction w/two single finger lappets, red paint, initialed "D.M.," traces of a leather carrying strap, New England, early 19th c., 10 1/2" d., 6 1/4" h. (minor imperfections) **316**

Cookie board, ash, rectangular, w/deeply carved & very detailed image of snail on a leaf, 3 1/8 x 4 3/8" **578**

Cookie board, carved heart shape w/inner vine & two intertwined flowers, beveled corners, scrubbed finish, 7 1/4 x 9" (age cracks) **413**

Cookie board, walnut, full length carving of a man wearing a striped vest, leggings, frock coat, ribbed stockings & conical hat w/turned-up brim, found in North Carolina, 5 1/2 x 15 1/4" (minor wear) **165**

Cookie board, walnut, thick carved full length image of a man wearing feather cap, floral embroidered frock coat & stockings carrying baby in a reeded pack on his back, 10 x 26 1/2" **303**

Firkin, cov., staved container painted red & inscribed in white "CASSIA," w/green lapped bands, swing handle fastened w/pegs, America, mid-19th c., 12" d., 12 1/2" h. **529**

Firkin, stave construction w/four wooden bands, painted red, hand-forged iron bail handle & wooden stopper, America, early 19th c., 7" h. **264**

Flax wheel, various hardwoods, bold turnings & tree branch distaff, 32" h. (some edge damage) **275**

Funnel, stave construction, slightly tapered sides w/two wooden staves & tapered spout on bottom, original green paint, cut nails, attributed to the Shakers, 9" d., 7 1/2" h. (edge wear, rim chips) **330**

Noggin, straight sides w/slightly flared spout & cutout handle, 6 3/4" h. (edge chips on spout) **83**

Curly Maple Oven Peel

Oven peel, curly maple, all one piece w/short substantial handle, old refinishing, age splits, chip on underside, wear, 15" d., 27" l. (ILLUS.) **550**

Pail, painted pine, stave construction w/iron hoop, wire bail handle, green block-painted decoration depicting birds, a horse, a dog, a stag, stars & foliage, 19th c., 5 5/8" h. (rim chips) **1,035**

Primitive Maple Pitcher

Pitcher, curly maple, primitive style, one-piece handle, nose-shaped finger rest under spout, old rim damage, 6 1/2" h. (ILLUS.) **770**

Pump cover, poplar w/old red & white scroll decoration painted on green ground, cast-iron spout & bands, signed "Consolidated Pump Co., Toledo, O.," 74" h. (evidence of earlier salmon paint underneath, top cap & finial are replacements)...... **275**

Rolling pin, curly maple, w/deep ridges, 19" l. **275**

Sugar bowl, cov., turned & painted, slightly swelled short cylindrical form w/molded base & rim band, low domed cover w/button finial, mustard yellow w/brown graining, New England, mid-19th c., 5 1/4" d., 5" h. (minor paint wear) **1,840**

Sugar bucket, cov., stave construction, tapered sides, arched swing handle, partial original label remaining beneath old blue paint, steel tacks, 14" h. w/handle (edge chips on lid & one stave partially missing)...... **413**

Sugar bucket, cov., stave construction, tapered sides, bale handle, grey over earlier green paint, 11 1/4" h. w/handle (minor chips on lower edge of lid) **330**

Sugar bucket, cov., stave construction w/three single-finger wooden bands, bentwood handle, old slate grey paint, 9 1/4" d., 9 3/4" h. (handle & lid worn) **523**

Sugar bucket, cov., stave construction w/two wooden bands w/copper tacks, wire bail handle w/turned wooden grip, layers of old medium blue paint, 6 1/2" d., 6 3/4" h. (wear, split on lid) **468**

Swift, tabletop-type, maple & other hard woods w/red stain, expandable ribs are tied top & bottom w/rosehead nails in the centers, post has cup finial & holes to adjust ribs (no peg), "X" base has chamfered edges w/turned peg feet, 30 1/2" h. (top & bottom rings split & repaired w/glue or wire, top loose & slides down post, one peg foot replaced)........................... **193**

Swift, tabletop-type, maple & other hardwoods, natural varnish finish, bottom sliding ring w/brass peg to adjust height & diameter, tabletop clamp, 23 1/2" h. (several ribs not tied at top)................................... **55**

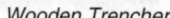

Wooden Trencher

Trencher, planed sides, exterior w/layers of old blue paint, the interior w/good patina & general wear from use, drilled hole for hanging, 12 1/4 x 21 1/2", 5 1/2" h. (ILLUS.) **440**

WRITING ACCESSORIES

Early writing accessories are popular collectibles and offer a wide variety to select from. A collection may be formed around any one segment —pens, letter openers, lap desks, inkwells, etc.—or the collection may revolve around choice specimens of all types. Material, design and age usually determine the value. Pen collectors like the large fountain pens developed in the 1920s but also look for pens and mechanical pencils that are solid gold or gold-plated. Also see: BOTTLES & FLASKS

Inkwells & Stands

Figural Dog Inkwell

Brass well, orb inkwell fitted w/glass liner, raised on three silver seated hound figures joined by chains at collars, set w/marcasite eyes on round socle base, France, late 19th c., 4 1/4" d., 4 5/8" h. (ILLUS.) **$374**

Bronze stand, an oblong pen tray ends in a horse head within horseshoe decoration on one side & a square cov. inkwell w/glass liner on the other, Austria, early 20th c., 12 3/8" l. **288**

Enameled Silver Captain's Inkwell

Enameled silver well, circular captain's inkwell, the lid w/an enameled fishing boat, the well above a circular dish w/raised lip, enameled anchor to one side, weighted, A. & J. Zimmerman, Ltd., Birmingham, England, 1909, 8" d. (ILLUS.).. 575

Gilt-metal stand, Art Nouveau, stylized shell form base raised on four flattened ball feet, chased & embossed w/a bird on a branch on stippled ground, stylized shell-form inkwell w/removable liner, two scrolled pen supports, early 20th c., 12" l...... 144

Green Glass Inkwell

Glass well, dark green, cylindrical base w/overall embossed design flaring out at top, hinged cut-glass top, metal rims where base & top meet, 3 3/4" h. (ILLUS.) 295

Amber Glass Inkwell

Glass well, deep amber glass, square base holds footed metal neck w/hinged top of heavy amber glass w/bubbles, 3 1/4" h. (ILLUS.).. 275

Glass well, emerald green, silver hinged lid, metal plate (slightly clouded)........................... 95

Glass well, figural, a log cabin, w/hinge-back roof to expose white glass cup, rustic look, 3 x 4 1/2" 85

Ribbed Glass Inkwell

Glass well, green footed base w/embossed ribs resembling bamboo, gently flared at base, w/more pronounced flare at neck w/scalloped rim, hinged ball top, metal rims where top & base meet, 4 3/4" h. (ILLUS.) 295

Glass well, cranberry w/gold striping & floral decoration, 3" h................................. 80

Glass well, clear cube w/lift-off lid, type made by Imperial Glass Co., 3"..................... 60

Glass well, cube w/crosshatched lift-off lid, 3".. 75

Glass well, square, cobalt, metal ink cup, ca. 1930s, 3 1/2 x 3 1/2" 145

Glass well, clear, in the form of an apple, w/removable lid, probably 1925-30, 3 7/8" d. 125

Iron well, grapevine w/leaves decoration, painted flat black, highly detailed leaves cradling round crystal ink cup w/hinged black lid, marked "J. Bosse, Freres," ca. 1890, 7" w. at widest part, 13" l................. 1,200

Marble & bronze stand, model of a dog in bronze on black marble stand, ink cup in ramps 75

Doulton Stoneware Inkstand

Silver-mounted stoneware stand, tapered cylindrical form w/molded floral sprays, blue, ochre & brown glazes, silver hallmarked London, stoneware by Doulton Lambeth, 1901, 3" h. (ILLUS.) 201

Lap Desks & Writing Boxes

Bird's-eye Maple Lap Desk

Bird's-eye maple veneer, rectangular w/hinged lid, the interior fitted w/felted writing surface above storage, pen & ink compartments, lower drawer at one end w/a brass bail handle, America, late 19th c., cracks in lid, 10 3/4 x 21 1/4", 8" h. (ILLUS.) 978

Carved & inlaid wood, cov., rectangular box w/sliding lid & lollipop handle, scribed & decorated w/heart, stars, diamonds & circles in ivory, dark & light wood inlays w/tiny steel brads, initialed "FTG 1839," Portsmouth, New Hampshire, 1 3/8 x 9", 1 1/2" h. (two pieces of inlay missing) 1,116

INDEX